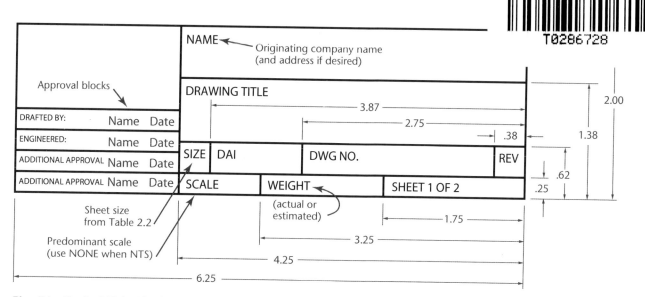

Fig. IV   Typical Title Block

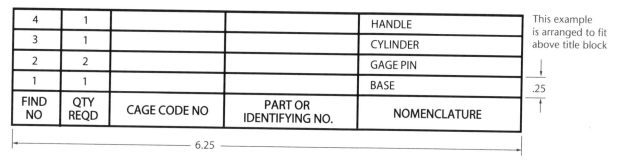

FIND NO	QTY REQD	CAGE CODE NO	PART OR IDENTIFYING NO.	NOMENCLATURE
4	1			HANDLE
3	1			CYLINDER
2	2			GAGE PIN
1	1			BASE

This example is arranged to fit above title block

Fig. V   Typical Parts List or Materials List

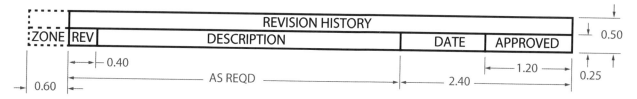

Fig. VI   Typical Revision History Block

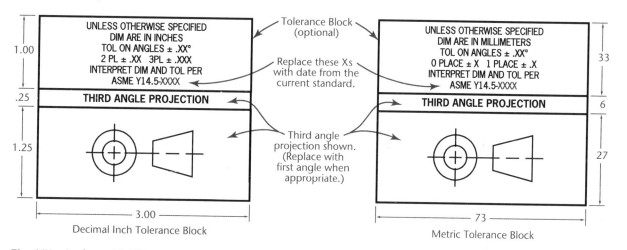

Decimal Inch Tolerance Block

Metric Tolerance Block

Fig. VII   Inch and Millimeter Tolerance Block Examples. *Note that both show third angle projection. Use the symbol for first angle projection when appropriate.*

SIXTEENTH EDITION

TECHNICAL DRAWING WITH ENGINEERING GRAPHICS

FREDERICK E. GIESECKE

Late Professor Emeritus of Drawing
Texas A&M University

SHAWNA LOCKHART

Formerly Adjunct Professor, Engineering Graphics
Department of Industrial and Mechanical Engineering
Montana State University

MARLA GOODMAN

CINDY M. JOHNSON

Pearson

Editor in Chief: Mark Taub
Acquisitions Editor: Anshul Sharma
Project Manager: Tracey Croom
Managing Editor: Sandra Schroeder
Operations Specialist: Deidra Skahill
Cover Designer: Chuti Prasertsith
Cover Image: FotoStocker/Shutterstock
Full-Service Project Management: Publishing Services
Composition: Publishing Services

Credits and acknowledgments borrowed from other sources and reproduced, with permission, in this textbook appear on the appropriate page within the text. Credits for artwork from *Engineering Design Communication, Second Edition*, by Lockhart and Johnson, appear on page C-1. Unless otherwise stated, all artwork has been provided by the authors.

SolidWorks® is a registered trademark of Dassault Systèmes SolidWorks Corporation.

Certain images and materials contained in this text were reproduced with permission of Autodesk, Inc. © 2022. All rights reserved. Autodesk, AutoCAD, Autodesk Inventor, Civil 3D, DWG, and the DWG logo are registered trademarks of Autodesk, Inc., in the U.S.A. and certain other countries.

PTC, Creo, and Windchill are trademarks or registered trademarks of PTC Inc. or its subsidiaries in the United States and in other countries.

Library of Congress Control Number: 2022950831

1 2023

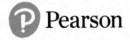 pearson.com

ISBN 10: 0-13-806572-1
ISBN 13: 978-0-13-806572-0

SIXTEENTH EDITION

TECHNICAL DRAWING WITH ENGINEERING GRAPHICS

ABOUT THIS BOOK

The sixteenth edition of Giesecke's *Technical Drawing with Engineering Graphics* is a comprehensive introduction and detailed reference for creating 3D models and 2D documentation drawings.

Continuing its reputation as a trusted reference, this edition is updated to convey recent standards for documenting 2D drawings and 3D CAD models. It provides excellent integration of its hallmark illustrations with text and contemporary examples, and consistent navigational features make it easy to find important information.

This edition illustrates the application of both 3D and 2D modeling and technical drawing skills to real-world work practice and integrates drawing and CAD skills in a variety of disciplines. Reviewers advised us on how to make *Technical Drawing with Engineering Graphics* a superb guide and resource for today's students.

Updated Content

- Coverage of 3D design and modeling techniques
- Updated for current ASME standards, particularly for GD&T and surface finish symbology
- Updated examples of rapid prototyping and direct printing
- Updated software examples
- Thoroughly checked for accuracy
- Web chapters available for axonometric projection and perspective drawing

Teaching/Learning Features

Visually oriented students and busy professionals will quickly locate content by navigating these consistent chapter features.

- *Splash Spread* An attention-getting chapter opener interests readers and provides context for chapter content.
- *References and Web Links* Applicable references to standards and links to handy websites are at the beginning of each chapter.
- *Foundations Section* An introductory section, set off by a topic heading tab at the top of the page for easy navigation, covers the topic's usage and importance, visualization tips, and theory related to the drawing techniques.

- *Detail Section* This is the "brass tacks" part of the book, where detailed explanations of drawing and modeling techniques, variations, and examples are organized into quick-read sections, each numbered for quick reference in the detailed table of contents.
- *CAD at Work* This breakout page includes tips related to using the 2D or 3D CAD model to generate drawings.
- *Industry Case* 3D modeling practitioners share their best practices for modeling and documenting design.
- *Portfolio* Examples of finished drawings wrap up the chapter by showing real-world application of topics presented.
- *Key Words* Set in bold italics on first reference, key words are summarized at the end of the chapter.
- *Chapter Summary*
- *Review Questions*
- *Chapter Exercises* The excellent Giesecke problem sets feature updated exercises, including plastic and sheet metal parts, modeling exercises, assembly drawings from CAD models, and sketching problems.

The following features were designed to provide easy navigation and quick reference for students and professionals who look to Giesecke both as a helpfully-organized teaching text and a lasting reference.

CHAPTER OPENER

Topics that you can expect to learn about in this chapter are listed here.

A large illustration and an interesting overview give you a real-world context for what this chapter is about.

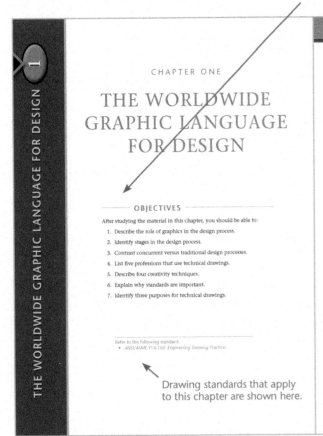

CHAPTER ONE

THE WORLDWIDE GRAPHIC LANGUAGE FOR DESIGN

THE WORLDWIDE GRAPHIC LANGUAGE FOR DESIGN

1

THE WORLDWIDE GRAPHIC LANGUAGE FOR DESIGN   3

OBJECTIVES

After studying the material in this chapter, you should be able to:

1. Describe the role of graphics in the design process.
2. Identify stages in the design process.
3. Contrast concurrent versus traditional design processes.
4. List five professions that use technical drawings.
5. Describe four creativity techniques.
6. Explain why standards are important.
7. Identify three purposes for technical drawings.

Refer to the following standard:
• ANSI/ASME Y14.100 Engineering Drawing Practices

Drawing standards that apply to this chapter are shown here.

Conceptual Sketches. Exploring many design options through quick sketches is one method that Lunar, recently named one of the top 10 award-winning American product design firms by BusinessWeek magazine, uses to create beautiful products and successful brands. (Images courtesy of LUNAR.)

OVERVIEW

Regardless of the language they speak, people all over the world use technical drawings to communicate their ideas. Graphic representation is a basic, natural form of communication that isn't tied to a particular time or place. It is, in a sense, a universal language.

Accomplishing ideas, from the simplest to the most elaborate, requires teamwork. A new product, machine, structure, or system may exist in the mind of the engineer or designer, but before it can become a reality, the idea must be communicated to many different people. The ability to communicate design concepts quickly and accurately through technical drawings is key to meeting project budgets and time constraints. Effective graphic communication is also an advantage in the global marketplace, where team members may not always share a common language.

Like carpenters who learn to use the tools of their trade, engineers, architects, drafters, designers, manufacturers, and technicians learn the tools of technical drawing. They learn specific methods to represent ideas, designs, and specifications in a consistent way that others can understand. Being an effective graphic communicator ensures that the product, system, or structure that you envision is produced as you specified.

"SPOTLIGHT" SECTIONS

These sections add background information for key topics.

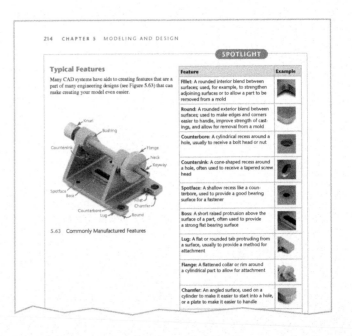

214   CHAPTER 5   MODELING AND DESIGN

SPOTLIGHT

Typical Features

Many CAD systems have aids to creating features that are a part of many engineering designs (see Figure 5.63) that can make creating your model even easier.

5.63   Commonly Manufactured Features

Feature	Example
Fillet: A rounded interior blend between surfaces; used, for example, to strengthen adjoining surfaces or to allow a part to be removed from a mold	
Round: A rounded exterior blend between surfaces; used to make edges and corners easier to handle, improve strength of castings, and allow for removal from a mold	
Counterbore: A cylindrical recess around a hole, usually to receive a bolt head or nut	
Countersink: A cone-shaped recess around a hole, often used to receive a tapered screw head	
Spotface: A shallow recess like a counterbore, used to provide a good bearing surface for a fastener	
Boss: A short raised protrusion above the surface of a part, often used to provide a strong flat bearing surface	
Lug: A flat or rounded tab protruding from a surface, usually to provide a method for attachment	
Flange: A flattened collar or rim around a cylindrical part to allow for attachment	
Chamfer: An angled surface, used on a cylinder to make it easier to start into a hole, or a plate to make it easier to handle	

"FOUNDATIONS" SECTION

This introductory section covers the chapter topic's usage and importance, visualization tips, and theory related to the drawing and modeling techniques.

Color at the top of the page makes it easy to flip to the "Foundations" section.

"DETAIL" SECTION

This is the "brass tacks" of the book, where detailed techniques, variations, and examples are organized into quick-read sections, numbered for easy reference.

Content is broken into individual, numbered sections.

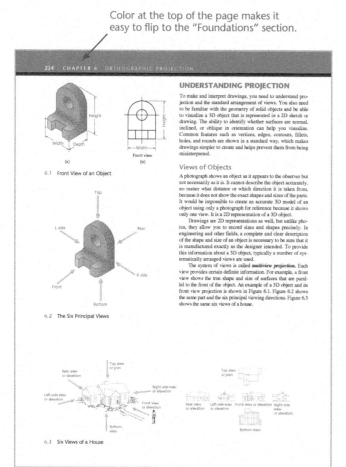

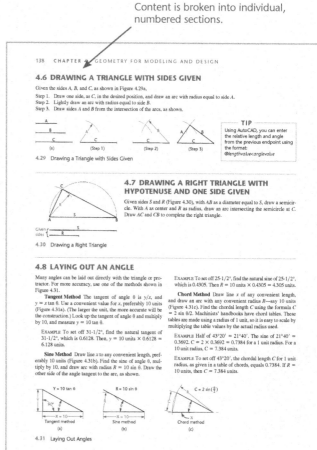

"STEP BY STEP" ACTIVITIES

Complicated processes are shown as step-by-step activities with each illustration right next to the text that explains it.

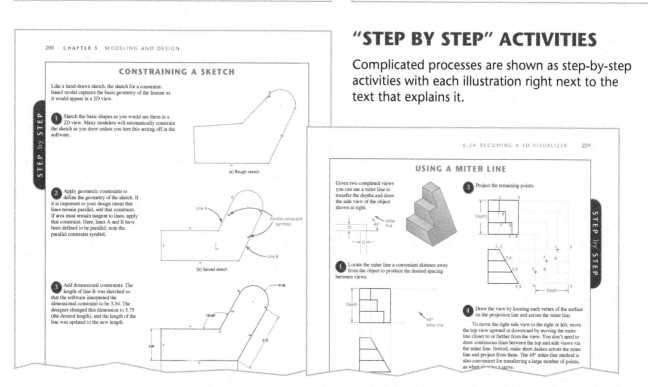

"CAD AT WORK"

CAD at Work sections break out examples related to using the 2D or 3D CAD model to generate drawings.

"INDUSTRY CASE"

Several industry practitioners share their approaches to modeling and documenting design.

INDUSTRY CASE

THE GEOMETRY OF 3D MODELING: USE THE SYMMETRY

Strategix ID used magnets to create a clean, quiet, zero main-tenance brake for the exercise bike it designed for Park City Entertainment. When copper rings on the bike's iron flywheel spin past four rare-earth magnets, they create current in circu-lar flow (an eddy current) that sets up a magnetic field.

This opposing magnetic field dissipates power and slows the wheel. Moving the magnets onto and off the copper rings varies the amount of resistance delivered. When Marty Albini, Senior Mechanical Engineer, modeled the plastic magnet car-rier for the brake, he started with the magnets and their behav-ior as the carrier moved them onto and off the copper rings (see Figure 4.84). "There is no one way to think about modeling a part," Albini said. "The key is to design for the use of the part and the process that will be used to manufacture it." To make the magnet carrier symmetrical, Albini started by modeling half of it.

The magnet carrier was designed as a part in the larger flywheel assembly, parts of which were already completed.

Each pair of magnets was attached to a backing bar that kept them a fixed distance apart. To begin, Albini started with the geometry he was sure of: the diameter of the magnets, the space between them, and the geometry of the conductor ring. He sketched an arc sized to form a pocket around one of the magnets so that its center point would be located on the center-line of the conductor ring (see Figure 4.85). He then sketched another similar arc but with its center point positioned to match the distance between the centers of the two magnets. He con-nected the two arcs with parallel lines to complete the sketch of the inside of the carrier. This outline was offset to the out-side by the thickness of the wall of the holder. (Because this is an injection-molded plastic part, a uniform wall thickness was used throughout.) One final constraint was added to position

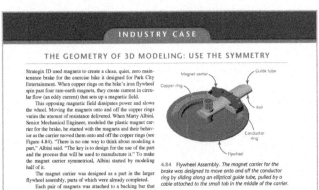

4.84 Flywheel Assembly. *The magnet carrier for the brake was designed to move onto and off the conductor ring by sliding along an elliptical guide tube, pulled by a cable attached to the small tab in the middle of the carrier.*

the carrier against the rail on the elliptical tube along which it would slide: the outside of the inner arc is tangent to this rail. With the sketch geometry fully defined, Albini extruded the sketch up to the top of the guide tube and down to the running clearance from the copper ring.

To add a lid to the holder, Albini used the SolidWorks **Offset** command to trace the outline of the holder. First, he clicked on the top of the holder to make its surface the active sketch plane. This is equivalent to changing the user coordinate system in other packages: it signals to SolidWorks that points picked from the screen lie on this plane. He then selected the

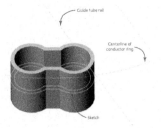

4.85 Extruding the Carrier. *The magnet carrier was extruded up and down from the sketch, shown here as an outline in the middle of the extruded part. Notice that the sketch is tangent to the guide tube rail, and the centers of the arcs in the sketch are located on the centerline of the conductor ring.*

CAD at WORK

MODEL SPACE AND PAPER SPACE IN AUTOCAD

Using CAD, you can make an accurate model of the device or structure. To do this, you create the object at the actual size that it exists in the real world, using whatever system of measurement that you would use when constructing it.

On paper it is a different matter. You would have to have some really large sheets to print your building full size. AutoCAD software uses the concept of two "spaces," model space and paper space, to describe how to transform the full-size CAD model to proportionate views that fit your sheet of paper.

Understanding scale as it relates to paper drawings or as it relates to creat-ing layouts from a CAD drawing is an important concept for technical drawing because the ultimate goal is for draw-ings to be interpreted and used in the real world. Therefore, they must be easy to print and read.

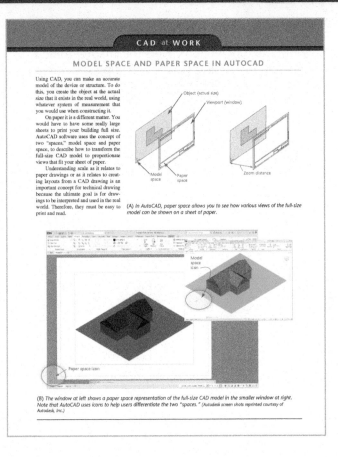

(A) *In AutoCAD, paper space allows you to see how various views of the full-size model can be shown on a sheet of paper.*

(B) *The window at left shows a paper space representation of the full-size CAD model in the smaller window at right. Note that AutoCAD uses icons to help users differentiate the two "spaces." (Autodesk screen shots reprinted courtesy of Autodesk, Inc.)*

"PORTFOLIO"

These pages offer examples of finished drawings showing real-world application of topics presented.

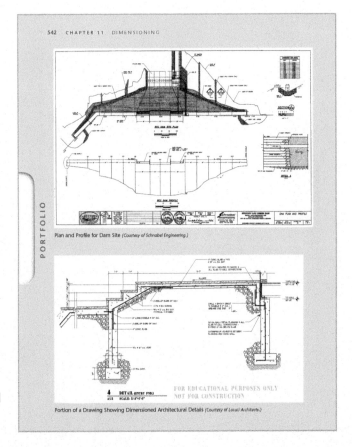

542   CHAPTER 11   DIMENSIONING

Plan and Profile for Dam Site *(Courtesy of Schnabel Engineering.)*

Portion of a Drawing Showing Dimensioned Architectural Details *(Courtesy of Local Architects.)*

PORTFOLIO

SOLID MODEL VISUALIZATION ART

Solid models bring views to life on the page to help you visualize the drawing.

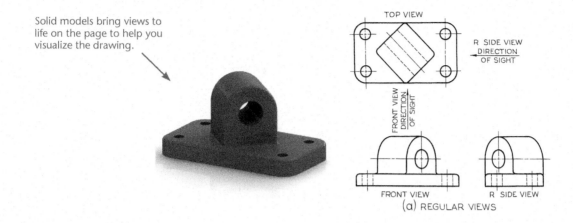

ILLUSTRATIONS

Colored callouts differentiate explanatory text from annotations in technical drawings. Consistent use of color helps differentiate the meaning of projection lines, fold lines, and other drawing elements. A color key is provided for easy reference.

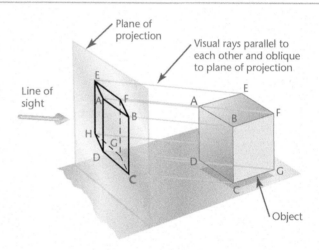

Color Key for Instructional Art

Item	In instructional art	In a technical drawing
Callout arrow	⟶	*
Dimension line	⟷	⟷ a thin (0.3mm) black line
Projection line	————	———— a lightly sketched line
Folding line	– – – –	— — — used in descriptive geometry
Picture plane on edge	————	*
Plane of projection	▨	*
Cutting plane on edge	— – – — – – —	↑ – – – ↑ (see Chapter 6)
Cutting plane	▨	*
Reference plane on edge	————	— – – — used in descriptive geometry
Reference plane	▨	*
Viewing direction arrow	⟹	↑ – – – ↑
Horizon + ground line	————	————
Rotation arrow	⤸	30° ⤸

* Not a typical feature of technical drawings. (Shown in this book for instructional purposes.)

CHAPTER REVIEW

Each chapter ends with Key Words, a Chapter Summary, and Review Questions.

Review and exercises are tabbed to make them easy to find. The color stripe corresponds to the alternating chapter color.

CHAPTER EXERCISES

The Giesecke problem sets feature updated exercises including plastic and sheet metal parts, constraint-based modeling, sketching problems, and reverse engineering projects.

Exercises for two reverse engineering projects are keyed to the chapter they best accompany.

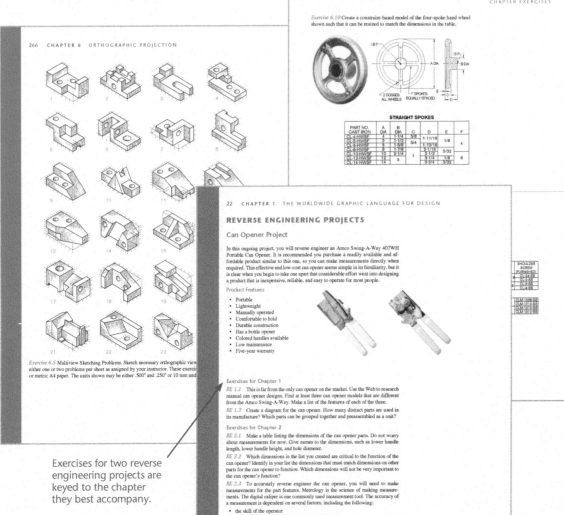

PREFACE

For many decades, *Technical Drawing with Engineering Graphics* has been recognized as an authority on the theories and techniques of graphics communication. Generations of instructors and students have used and retained this book as a professional reference. The long-standing success of *Technical Drawing with Engineering Graphics* can be attributed to its clear and engaging explanation of principles, and to its drawings, which are unsurpassed in detail and accuracy.

Although not a departure from its original authoritative nature and hallmark features, the book is thoroughly revised and updated to the latest technologies and practices in the field. With the addition of topics related to the role of the 3D CAD database in design and documentation, this sixteenth edition of *Technical Drawing with Engineering Graphics* will prepare students to enter the marketplace of the twenty-first century and continue to serve as a lasting reference.

Shawna Lockhart, contributing author since the ninth edition, first used Giesecke's *Technical Drawing* when teaching engineering graphics at Montana State University. Throughout her 15 years as an award-winning professor, she selected this text because, in her words, "It was the most thorough and well-presented text with the best graphic references and exercises on the market."

The quality of the illustrations and drawing examples was established by the original author, Frederick E. Giesecke, who created the majority of the illustrations in the first edition of *Technical Drawing*, published in 1933.

Giesecke, founder of the first formal architectural education program in Texas at what is today Texas A&M University, has been described as "a wunderkind of the first magnitude." He joined the A&M faculty at the age of 17, after graduating in 1886 with a B.S. in Mechanical Engineering, and by the age of 19, was appointed head of A&M's Department of Mechanical Drawing. Having studied architectural drawing and design at Cornell University and the Massachusetts Institute of Technology, Giesecke also served as head of the Department of Architecture and the official college architect at Texas A&M, designing many campus buildings that are still standing today.

A long-time admirer of Giesecke's legacy, Lockhart was honored to carry on the commitment to clear, engaging, thorough, and well-organized presentation that began with the original author.

Lockhart is known as an early adopter and authority on CAD technologies. She is an instructor noted for outstanding dedication to students and for encouraging a broad spectrum of individuals, particularly women and minorities, to follow careers in engineering-related fields. Lockhart now works full time to ensure that the Giesecke graphics series continually applies to an evolving variety of technical disciplines.

ONLINE RESOURCES

An Instructor's Manual (9780138065676) and Lecture Slides in PowerPoint format (9780138104405) are available on the companion site for this book at https://www.pearson.com/en-us/subject-catalog/p/technical-drawing-with-engineering-graphics/P200000009880.

Web chapters on axonometric projection and perspective drawing may be downloaded from www.peachpit.com. To access and download the bonus chapters:

1. Visit www.peachpit.com/techdrawing16e.
2. Log in with your Peachpit account, or if you don't have one, create an account.
3. Register using this book's ISBN, 9780138065720, then click the Access Bonus Content link next to this book on your account's Registered Products page.

ACKNOWLEDGMENTS

Sincere thanks to all the individuals and companies who shared their expertise through drawings and advice with the readers of this book:

Robert A. Ackein, Marty Albini, Jacob Baron-Taltre, Albert Brown, Jr., Will Callahan, Ryan Cargo, Jason Cohn, David and Caroline Collett, André Cotan, David Demchenkov, Tim Devries, Jost Diedrichs, Steve Elpel, Joe Evers, Carl Fehres, Mark Gerisch, Joe Graney, Leo Greene, Tom Jungst, Scott Keller, Robert Kincaid, Brandon Larocque, Matt McCune, Stan McLean, Laine McNeil, Rob Mesaros, Cliff Moore, Jeremy Olson, Andrea Orr, Kelly Pavlik, Jeffrey Pentecost, Mark Perkins, David Pinchefsky, Robert Rath, Jake Reis, Erik Renna, Steve Sanford, Chad Schipman, Scott Schwartzenberger, Timothy Seaman, Mark Soares, Ben Staal, Bryan Strobel, Lee Sutherland, Kent Swendseid, Bill Townsend, Michael T. Wheelock, Alex Wilson, Douglas Wintin, Brandon Wold, Rick Zaik, and Jeff Zerr.

We gratefully acknowledge the reviewers' many contributions to the development of *Technical Drawing with Engineering Graphics:*

Tarek Abdel-Salam, *East Carolina University*
Robert A. Ackein, *Bates Technical College*
Fred Brasfield, *Tarrant Community College*
Charles Richard Cole, *Southern Polytechnic State University*
Robert Conn, *Illinois Eastern Community Colleges—Wabash Valley College*
Steven L. Dulmes, *College of Lake County*
Jeff Levy, *New River Community College*
J.D. Mather, *Pennsylvania College of Technology*
Saeid Motavalli, *California State University East Bay*
Mostafa A. Tossi, *Pennsylvania State Worthington Scranton*
Michael T. Wheelock, *Idaho State University*
Paige Wyatt, *Columbia Basin College*

A very special thanks to Robert Conn and J.D. Mather for their constructive comments and suggestions.

PEARSON'S COMMITMENT TO DIVERSITY, EQUITY, AND INCLUSION

Pearson is dedicated to creating bias-free content that reflects the diversity of all learners. We embrace the many dimensions of diversity, including but not limited to race, ethnicity, gender, socioeconomic status, ability, age, sexual orientation, and religious or political beliefs.

Education is a powerful force for equity and change in our world. It has the potential to deliver opportunities that improve lives and enable economic mobility. As we work with authors to create content for every product and service, we acknowledge our responsibility to demonstrate inclusivity and incorporate diverse scholarship so that everyone can achieve their potential through learning. As the world's leading learning company, we have a duty to help drive change and live up to our purpose to help more people create a better life for themselves and to create a better world.

Our ambition is to purposefully contribute to a world where:

- Everyone has an equitable and lifelong opportunity to succeed through learning.
- Our educational products and services are inclusive and represent the rich diversity of learners.
- Our educational content accurately reflects the histories and experiences of the learners we serve.
- Our educational content prompts deeper discussions with learners and motivates them to expand their own learning (and worldview).

While we work hard to present unbiased content, we want to hear from you about any concerns or needs with this Pearson product so that we can investigate and address them.

Please contact us with concerns about any potential bias at https://www.pearson.com/report-bias.html.

CONTENTS

CHAPTER EIGHT
SECTION VIEWS 326

CHAPTER NINE
AUXILIARY VIEWS 362

CHAPTER TEN

MODELING FOR MANUFACTURE AND ASSEMBLY   414

DESIGN FOR MANUFACTURE, ASSEMBLY,
DISASSEMBLY, AND SERVICE   416

CHAPTER FOURTEEN
WORKING DRAWINGS 636

CHAPTER FIFTEEN
DRAWING CONTROL AND DATA MANAGEMENT 710

SIXTEENTH EDITION

TECHNICAL DRAWING WITH ENGINEERING GRAPHICS

CHAPTER ONE

THE WORLDWIDE GRAPHIC LANGUAGE FOR DESIGN

OBJECTIVES

After studying the material in this chapter, you should be able to:

1. Describe the role of graphics in the design process.

2. Identify stages in the design process.

3. Contrast concurrent versus traditional design processes.

4. List five professions that use technical drawings.

5. Describe four creativity techniques.

6. Explain why standards are important.

7. Identify three purposes for technical drawings.

Refer to the following standard:
- *ANSI/ASME Y14.100 Engineering Drawing Practices*

Conceptual Sketches. *Exploring many design options through quick sketches is one method that Lunar, recently named one of the top 10 award-winning American product design firms by* BusinessWeek *magazine, uses to create beautiful products and successful brands.* (Images courtesy of LUNAR.)

OVERVIEW

Regardless of the language they speak, people all over the world use technical drawings to communicate their ideas. Graphic representation is a basic, natural form of communication that isn't tied to a particular time or place. It is, in a sense, a universal language.

Accomplishing ideas, from the simplest to the most elaborate, requires teamwork. A new product, machine, structure, or system may exist in the mind of the engineer or designer, but before it can become a reality, the idea must be communicated to many different people. The ability to communicate design concepts quickly and accurately through technical drawings is key to meeting project budgets and time constraints. Effective graphic communication is also an advantage in the global marketplace, where team members may not always share a common language.

Like carpenters who learn to use the tools of their trade, engineers, architects, drafters, designers, manufacturers, and technicians learn the tools of technical drawing. They learn specific methods to represent ideas, designs, and specifications in a consistent way that others can understand. Being an effective graphic communicator ensures that the product, system, or structure that you envision is produced as you specified.

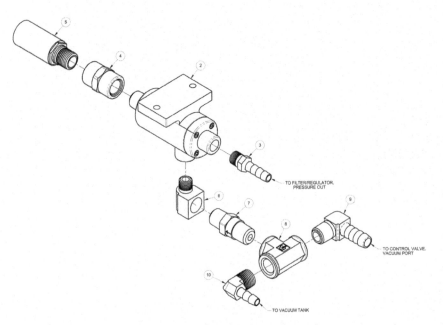

1.1   Computation Sketch Detail *(Courtesy of Jeffrey J. Zerr.)*

1.2   Excerpt from an Assembly Drawing *(Courtesy of Woods Power-Grip Co., Inc.)*

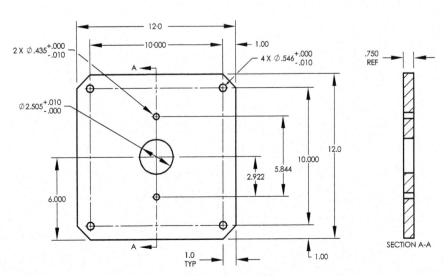

1.3   A Part Drawing *(Courtesy of Dynojet Research, Inc.)*

UNDERSTANDING THE ROLE OF TECHNICAL DRAWINGS

Drawings and specifications control the many details of product manufacture, assembly, and maintenance. Both ease in freehand sketching and the ability to use computers to produce CAD models and technical drawings are valued skills in the global marketplace. Conveying information graphically requires knowledge of the standards that allow drawings to concisely communicate designs around the world.

Technical drawings can take many forms: idea or concept sketches (such as the sketches on the previous page), computation sketches, design sketches, layout drawings, part drawings, working or construction drawings, electrical drawings, installation drawings, and assembly drawings are all examples. Sketches, 2D CAD drawings, and 3D CAD models are all forms of technical drawing. Some of these types of technical drawings are shown in Figures 1.1 through 1.3. Each of these types of drawings and others have a place in the process of designing and building a product, system, or structure. In general, technical drawings serve one of three purposes:

- *Visualization*
- *Communication*
- *Documentation*

A wide variety of professions use technical drawings to communicate and document designs. Some examples are civil engineering, mechanical engineering, electrical engineering, architecture, bio-resource engineering, landscape design, landscape architecture, industrial design, construction engineering, construction technology, pattern making, project management, fabrication, and manufacturing. There are many others.

Whether you are designing a bridge, installing underground power lines in a subdivision, or designing a plastic housing for a new toaster, understanding and using technical drawing is a key skill you will need.

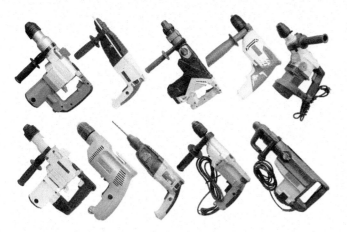

1.4 *These drills all perform similar functions, but a consumer's choice of one over another may depend on the product's styling and aesthetics as well as function.* (©Shutterstock/Vereshchagin Dmitry.)

1.5 *Project engineers in hard hats examine a blueprint.* (Goodluz/Shutterstock.)

The Design Process

The organized and orderly approach to solving problems is known as the ***design process.*** The engineering design process addresses society's needs, desires, and problems by applying scientific principles, experience, and creativity.

Different types of technical drawings have a specific function in the engineering design process. For example, freehand sketches capture and document the ideation process. Later in the process, CAD models and drawings capture the design and specify the details necessary for manufacture.

The design process for any product requires a clear understanding of the functions and the performance expected of that product. The construction project shown in Figure 1.5 is very different from the styling and functional requirements of the products shown in Figure 1.4, but the stages in the design process are similar for both.

It has been estimated that 70% to 80% of the cost of product development and manufacture is determined during the initial design stages. Although many industrial groups may identify them in their own way, one procedure for designing a new or improved product follows the stages shown in Figure 1.6:

1. ***Problem identification***: First, a clear statement of the need for and objectives for the design must be written.
2. ***Ideation***: Technical sketches are often used to convey concepts to multidisciplinary teams.
3. ***Refinement/analysis***: Designs may be rethought, based on engineering analysis. CAD models and sketches are useful during the analysis and compromise stage. Accurate 2D or 3D CAD models and drawings are created to refine the design.
4. ***Implementation/documentation***: The production and/or working drawings that provide the details of manufacture and assembly are finalized and approved.

Ideally, the design moves through these stages, but as new information becomes available, it may be necessary to return to

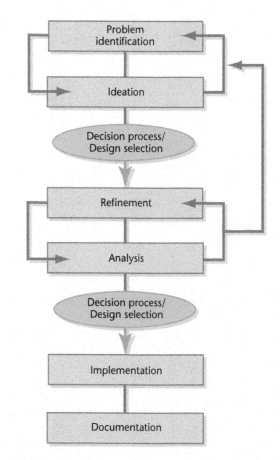

1.6 The Stages of the Design Process

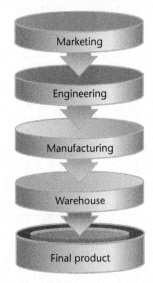

(a) Sequential Process

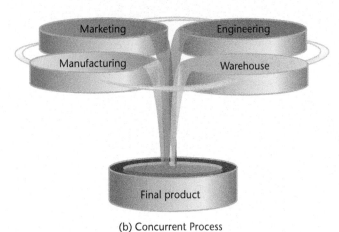

(b) Concurrent Process

1.7 A Model of the Concurrent Design Process

1.8 The Life Cycle of a Product

a previous stage and repeat the process. For example, based on engineering analysis, the familiar phrase "back to the drawing board" might come into play at the refinement/analysis stage.

Concurrent Engineering

Traditionally, design and manufacturing activities have taken place in sequential order rather than concurrently (simultaneously). Designers would spend considerable effort and time analyzing components and preparing detailed part drawings, and then forward them to other departments. For example, the materials department would use the drawing to identify the particular alloys and source vendors to use. The manufacturing department would then identify the processes needed for efficient production. This step-by-step approach seems logical, but in practice it has been found to be wasteful.

For example, if a manufacturing engineer wanted to taper the flange on a part to make it easier to cast in metal, or to choose a different alloy, the design analysis stage would have to be repeated to ensure that the product would still function effectively. These iterations, illustrated in Figure 1.7a, may be necessary, but they waste resources, and more importantly, time. Time is important because early product introduction makes possible a greater market percentage (and hence greater profits) and a longer life before the product becomes obsolete (clearly a concern with products such as consumer electronics).

Concurrent engineering is a systematic approach that integrates the design and manufacture of products with the goal of optimizing all elements involved in the life cycle of the product. Figure 1.7b illustrates the concurrent design process.

Life cycle design means that all aspects of a product (such as design, development, production, distribution, use, and its ultimate disposal and recycling) are considered simultaneously. Figure 1.8 depicts the life cycle of a product from conception to disposal.

The basic goals of concurrent engineering are to minimize product design and engineering changes and to reduce the time and cost involved in taking a product from concept through production and ultimately to the marketplace. In concurrent engineering, all disciplines are involved in the early design stages, so that natural iterations result in less wasted effort and lost time.

Communication between and within disciplines is especially important in a concurrent design process. Effective interaction among engineering, marketing, and service functions, as well as among engineering subdisciplines, is recognized as crucial to this type of process. Cross-disciplinary communication also helps provide a fertile environment for innovative approaches that can lead to savings in material and production costs.

Computer-Aided Design and Product Development

For both large and small companies, product design often involves preparing analytical and physical models of the product that can be used to study factors such as forces, stresses, deflections, and optimal part shape. The necessity for these

A Mechanical Engineer Working with CAD (Gorodenkoff/ Shutterstock.)

types of models depends on how complex the product is. Today, the process of constructing and studying analytical models is simplified by using *computer-aided design* (CAD), *computer-aided engineering* (CAE), and *computer-aided manufacturing* (CAM) techniques. These systems allow rapid design analysis for simple objects as well as complex structures.

CAD allows for a range of activities, from modeling 2D and 3D geometry to creating drawings that document the design for manufacturing and legal considerations.

CAM provides computerized control for manufacturing processes. Examples include using a computer interface to control a lathe, or generating the path for milling machine tools directly from the CAD model. In more sophisticated systems, CAM can be used in materials handling, assembly, and inspection.

CAE allows users to simulate and analyze structures that will be subject to various temperatures, static loads, or fluctuating loads. Kinematic analysis studies moving parts. Some of these functions are integrated with CAD software, and other packages import data from a CAD system. Using these tools, engineers can simulate, analyze, and test designs efficiently, accurately, and quickly.

Designing Quality into Products

Companies use a number of systematic ways to try to design "quality" into their products as well as to measure performance and make decisions based on data. Designers may feel that their creative approach to problem solving is stifled when these systems are poorly implemented in the workplace; but when these systems are well implemented, organizations can show quality improvement.

DFSS *Design for Six Sigma* is an approach that uses engineering and statistical tools to design products in a way that predicts and minimizes customer and manufacturing problems.

Six Sigma is a process originated at Motorola to improve quality by reducing or eliminating defects.

DMAIC *Define, Measure, Analyze, Improve, and Control* are steps defined in a continuous improvement process that attempts to define and ensure critical to function (CTF) characteristics.

QFD *Quality Function Deployment* is a tool for decision making that helps companies focus on a customer-driven approach and set of product characteristics.

The Digital Database

Computer use continues to change the way products are produced. All the information to manage, design, analyze, simulate, package, market, and manufacture a product can be shared with a diverse (and perhaps geographically distant) group of users through a single complex digital database.

Product data management (PDM) systems or *enterprise data management* (EDM) systems electronically store the various types of data associated with designing and manufacturing a product. An effective PDM system allows all the product data to be quickly stored, retrieved, displayed, printed, managed, and transferred to anywhere in the organization. This allows for designs to be optimized or directly modified at any time. Costs, product revisions, and *engineering change orders* (ECOs) can be analyzed, tracked, and implemented quickly. Managing enterprise data requires commitment and planning, but companies who implement PDM effectively can capture product data once and utilize it many ways to achieve a competitive advantage (Figure 1.9).

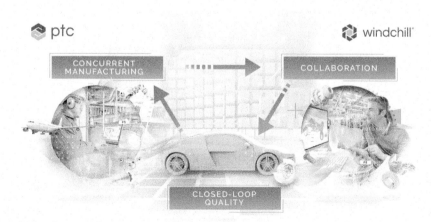

1.9 Product Data Management. *PTC's Windchill is an enterprise-wide product data management system designed to be extended to serve data over the internal network (or intranet). Data from the database are provided to external users via a secure, password-protected site (to share nonpublic information with suppliers and other partners in remote locations). (Image courtesy of PTC, Inc. All rights reserved.)*

1.1 GRAPHICS TOOLS IN ACTION

Designers and engineers use graphics for visualization, communication, and documentation throughout the design process. A case study from Santa Cruz Bicycles will illustrate the tools used in the redesign of its V10 model, a downhill racing mountain bike, shown in Figure 1.10.

Design Phase: Problem Identification

The impetus for the V10, as for most racing bikes, was higher performance. In 2000, Santa Cruz Bicycles (SCB) purchased three patents for suspension systems that had never been developed. Most bikes have suspension on the front wheel; these patents showed how rear suspension could be manipulated to improve performance and control.

The bicycle's suspension has two roles: absorbing bumps and translating the pulsing motion coming from the human pedaler into forward movement. The balance between how far the wheel can move up and down and maximal forward motion determines bike performance.

The first V10 was ridden in 2002. Its rear suspension allowed the wheel to travel vertically 10 inches. At that time, 8–8.5 inches of travel was common among competitors.

When SCB set out to update the V10 design, better performance was a key criterion. The design team included the product manager (who interfaced with marketing), two design engineers, and racers who rode the V10. The team members had plenty of information for defining the problem: they were familiar

1.10   *The V10 is a generation of downhill racing bikes first sold in 2002 and continually improved based on race team results and rider feedback. The 3D model of the new design is shown here. (Courtesy of Santa Cruz Bicycles.)*

with the design drawings, performance specifications, and manufacturing costs of the V10 already being produced. Racing teams provided feedback about how the current design handled and where they envisioned improvement. Racers and engineers viewed race videos to see how the bike performed on courses with more or less rugged terrain. Marketing provided information about competitors' bikes and how the V10 measured up against them.

At the problem identification stage, the team worked to enlarge the criteria for judging the solution. The team identified three primary goals for the redesign:

- Get maximum forward movement from a suspension that also absorbs bumps.
- Improve the handling to give the rider better control.
- Minimize the weight to make a lighter bike.

SPOTLIGHT

Santa Cruz Bicycles

The team at Santa Cruz Bicycles believes that to build a good bike, you have to first really love riding bikes. They all ride daily—from the owner to the engineers to the salespeople. This creates a very strong relationship between the design team and their customers—each model is constantly being refined and improved based on feedback from riders who want to—and do—win races with a Santa Cruz bike. Their engineers are proficient 3D modelers who use the many features of Pro/ENGINEER to visualize, analyze, and test designs before they are built. More important, the 3D model supports the continual improvement that is built into the Santa Cruz culture. They can quickly modify parts, see how the new part affects the movement of the bike, assess the stresses on the new part, and send it to be prototyped for the ultimate test: riding on unpredictable terrain.

1.11 *The V10's rear wheel attaches to a triangular swingarm that connects to the front part of the frame with a pivot. This allows the rear wheel to travel up and down. (Courtesy of Santa Cruz Bicycles.)*

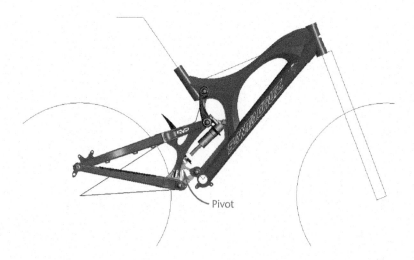

Pivot

Design Phase: Ideation

The design team focused first on the geometry of how the parts of the bike are arranged. Unlike the frame of a conventional bicycle, the V10's frame is in two parts. The back wheel connects to a triangular "swingarm" that attaches to the front frame with a pivot (see Figure 1.11). The length of the parts, the angles between them, and their movement determine how the bike handles. In the ideation phase, the team captured and evaluated different combinations of handlebar placements, seat, crank, pivots to the wheels and shock absorbers, and more. How much the shock absorbers allow the wheel to travel vertically, the pivot locations, and link sizes all affect how the bike will perform.

At the ideation stage, being able to draw a readable free-hand sketch is vital to "selling" your idea to your design team colleagues. This stage is called *universal possibilities* because the group seeks to consider every possible solution and not limit the design by preconceived notions of what will be best.

For each subsystem of the bike, the team generated and evaluated many concepts. For example, they brainstormed all the ways a pivot assembly might be made. They also employed a kind of "contest" to spur creativity and generate options. One engineer would be given 1.5 days to come up with a combination of parts and materials to make a subsystem, such as a link mechanism. Then, the design tasks would be shuffled and a different engineer would have 1.5 days to define an alternative approach to the link mechanism. Using a whiteboard, the team would then list the pros and cons of each subsystem design.

Design Phase: Decision Process/Design Selection

The design selection process varies by company and by the design challenge. It may be informal and conducted by a single individual, or it may be a highly formal process in which different teams compete for development dollars for new products. In all cases, design selection narrows the field of options for the final design.

SCB's team needed to evaluate how the parts would *move*. They created 3D skeleton models in CAD. A skeleton model is a simplified representation of the centerlines and other shapes that capture the design geometry. These skeleton models are useful for kinematic analysis (Figure 1.12).

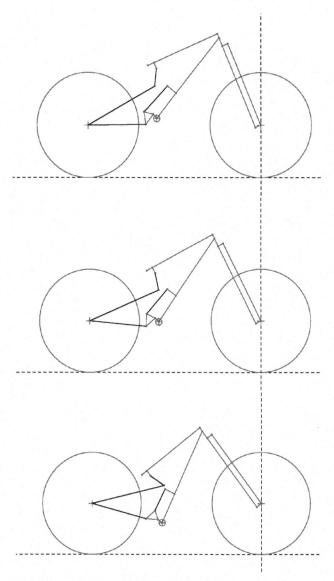

1.12 *Skeleton models were used for kinematic analysis of different combinations of the swingarm geometry. The model shows how much the swingarm can pivot. (Courtesy of Santa Cruz Bicycles.)*

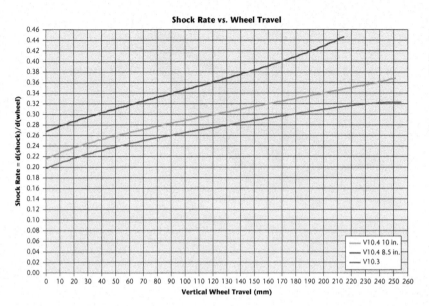

1.13 *This graph compares the measure of rear-wheel travel produced from the skeleton model during ideation. (Courtesy of Santa Cruz Bicycles.)*

Data generated from each model showed the behavior of the suspension and how the bike handled. Data from the kinematic analysis were captured in a spreadsheet and used to compare the various arrangements of lengths and angles in the designs (Figure 1.13).

Even at this early stage, drawings and models can be used to elicit customer feedback. If the user interface is important to a product, a 3D model or a computer simulation provides a way to get early user feedback. These models may be shown to customers informally, or more formally through focus groups.

At SCB, promising combinations were translated into simple prototypes that could be used to verify the concept. Called "mules," these proto-bicycles were fabricated so that a human rider could evaluate the handling (see Figure 1.14).

For a new product, the design team generally prepares a product proposal to show the management group approving new products. Drawings or sketches are used to communicate key features of the device. Rendered models or ***prototypes*** convey options for the final look. The proposal may include a product plan, sales estimates, and cost figures for developing the product. It estimates the profit to be generated by the product and describes how it will meet the criteria for a new product, such as helping to achieve company goals or promising the best return on investment. The ability of the design team to communicate effectively through drawings, spreadsheets, written communication, and oral presentation all play a role in the product's acceptance for development.

The preliminary design selection group for the V10 consisted of design engineers, manufacturing engineers, and the product manager. (At some companies, the team might also include members from finance or executive management.)

Function was the primary criterion for this review of the V10's redesign. Spreadsheets with data from the skeleton models, graphs comparing different options, and measurements from the prototypes were used to make the selection. Feedback from the riders who rode the "mules" was an important part of the process as well.

1.14 *This prototype "mule" for the V10 can be ridden and evaluated by a human rider. (Courtesy of Santa Cruz Bicycles.)*

Design Phase: Refinement

When a product is approved for further development, the team moves into the refinement and analysis phases of the project. Because these two phases form another "loop" in the design process, they are often combined into a single stage called the ***development phase***.

During the refinement stage, the product concept is solidified into an accurate plan for making the product. Different options are evaluated in terms of how much they will cost, how long they will take to make, how well they satisfy the customer's requirements, how durable they will be, how difficult they are to assemble and service, how environmentally sustainable the design is, and so forth. At this stage members may join the design team to provide expertise in these different areas.

At Santa Cruz Bicycles, the team had chosen a functional design and was now ready to begin defining the part features, styling, and materials for the bike. During refinement, the design is updated as more information is determined about the designed components and their manufacturing processes (see Figure 1.15).

At this point, time and money are invested in creating a model to represent the product accurately. At Santa Cruz, two or three combinations of features were modeled in 3D and used to analyze and test the design further.

The following were criteria at this point:

Weight: How much will a component or choice of material add to the weight of the bike?

Strength: Can the material used to make the part stand up to the stresses generated during a bike race?

Cost: Is a lower-cost option available? Or is the cost justified because of what it adds to performance?

Optimization: Does the choice result in fewer parts to make or better clearance between parts?

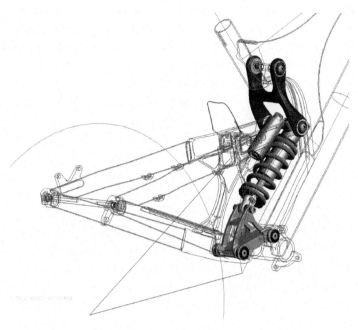

1.15   *This subassembly is a combination of features that were evaluated during refinement. (Courtesy of Santa Cruz Bicycles.)*

The team used an informal concept/criteria matrix to evaluate the options against multiple criteria. For example, manufacturing the frame using carbon fiber instead of aluminum would affect the cost but would decrease the weight of the bike by 15%–17%. The matrix can tally the pluses and minuses of various options to aid in comparing them.

At Santa Cruz, bicycles are modeled in Pro/ENGINEER, a parametric solid modeling package. Parametric or ***constraint-based modeling*** captures *relationships* between part features and the sizes of the features. These relationships capture the ***design intent*** for the part. They define features in terms of characteristics that must be preserved when the part changes. For example, the key design criteria for a pair of holes for mounting a bracket might be that each be the same distance from the center of the part. Defining the location of the holes to be half the width of the bracket from its midline ensures that when the bracket gets wider, the holes will move accordingly. Similarly, when a part is defined in terms of its relationship to another part, changes in that part will cause any related parts to be updated automatically (see Figure 1.16). This flexibility makes it easy to test many different versions of a design—and is ideal for continually refining and improving racing bikes like the V10.

Design Phase: Analysis

The analysis phase tests the design and feeds back information to refine the design further, forming the second key iteration or "loop" in the design process. Crucial here are the performance criteria that the design must meet.

For the V10, the assembled solid model could be tested like a real bike. By specifying the material for each part, the team assessed the total weight of the bike as designed. Stress analysis (finite element analysis) predicted where parts or the frame might be likely to break (see Figure 1.17). The model was also used to evaluate the bike's fit for riders of different sizes. Human factors software provides a database of different body types and sizes for this purpose. The team can simulate what an Asian female in the 50th percentile for height and weight sees while riding, what she can reach, and the location of her center of mass. The same can be done for a white male in the 50th percentile (see Figure 1.18).

1.16   *The rib shown here in red is constrained to be 10 mm back of and 12 mm down from the pivot point. If the pivot location is changed, the rib will be updated to preserve the relationship defined by the constraints. (Courtesy of Santa Cruz Bicycles.)*

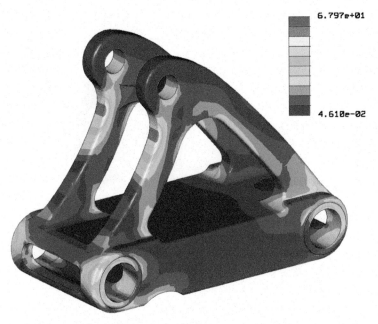

6.797e+01

4.610e-02

1.17   *Finite element analysis can be performed within the solid modeling software, or the model can be imported into a separate analysis package.* (Courtesy of Santa Cruz Bicycles.)

1.18   *"Mannequins" of various shapes and sizes can be added to the solid model to assess ergonomic factors.* (Courtesy of Santa Cruz Bicycles.)

At this point, the model can also be used for manufacturing analysis. At Santa Cruz, manufacturing engineers identify aspects of the design that will be hard to manufacture: a part shape that will require special tooling or be difficult to weld, or parts that must be made to a high degree of precision (tolerance).

Tools that work within the solid modeling packages are available for much of the analysis. Analysis for moving parts, such as the rear wheel suspension, can be done in Pro/ENGINEER (and other modelers) and tested under a wide range of physical conditions—even zero gravity! Human factors and stress testing are two more examples of analysis that can be done in the 3D modeler. For more advanced or specialized testing, a wide range of software can import the 3D model data.

Whether the analysis software recommends a change or simply reports results, it is up to the design engineer to interpret the tests and take steps to refine and test the design further until the desired results are achieved.

Design Phase: Decision Process/Design Selection

Once a design is ready to manufacture, another design review may be required. At each stage of the design process, more is invested in the design, and design changes become more costly. At the ideation stage, many ideas are investigated at relatively low cost. In the refinement stage, more time and money are devoted to building and testing models, and the cost of making major design changes increases. After the second design review, companies commission molds and tooling, purchase materials, and commit other resources to manufacturing the product. After this point, major design changes become very costly and can threaten a product's success. The second selection process, often called *critical design review*, is a filter that allows only the products with the greatest chance of success to proceed.

The selection team and review process may be very similar to the one that precedes refinement, or it may involve a completely different set of criteria. Understanding the review criteria helps you make an effective presentation and also helps you make better design decisions in the context of your company's goals.

For the V10, more stakeholders evaluated the design at this point. Representatives from marketing, sales, and graphic design were added to the team, and the aesthetics of the design were considered (see Figure 1.19). How will the logo fit onto

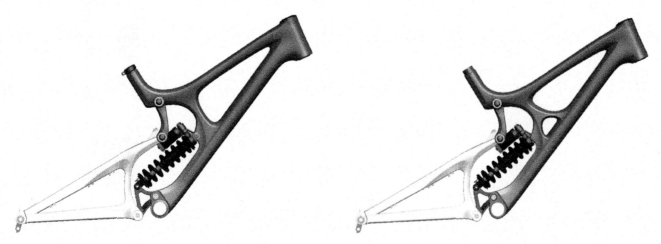

1.19 *Multiple options for the look of the frame triangle were considered in the final design review. (Courtesy of Santa Cruz Bicycles.)*

the bike as designed? Which look is more marketable? Should a straight or a curved tube be used for the swingarm? What are the implications of the manufacturing cost for the bike's sales potential?

Design Phase: Implementation

During the implementation phase, the design is communicated to those responsible for manufacturing, assembling, and distributing the product. Up to this point, drawings and models served a variety of purposes. In the implementation phase, they become contracts with suppliers. The model and the accompanying drawings (if any) must clearly specify what constitutes an acceptable part.

As in refinement, the 3D solid model serves as the information database. Dimensioned multiview drawings may be generated directly from the solid model. Increasingly often, manufacturing processes are directed from the model itself, with no need for an intermediate drawing. In these cases, tolerances may be noted in the model, or critical dimensions and tolerances marked on a drawing may be sufficient.

Tooling for a bicycle's design can cost as much as $120,000, so care is taken to be sure that the tools are correct. SCB uses a detailed checklist to ensure that they are ready to have the tools made for manufacturing the bicycle. Because the 3D model is used to communicate the design to the toolmakers, it is sent to them for review and analysis before the final design is documented.

Sample parts are requested so that the physical parts can be measured against the model and tested to see how they fit together. Mechanical testing, ride testing, and destructive testing are done on the sample parts while there is still time to make a change to alleviate problems (see Figure 1.20). Once engineering is satisfied with parts as manufactured, the models for the design are approved.

Although the design has been finalized, there still may be changes during the implementation phase (as well as later when the product is in production). With rapid prototyping and design simulations using the solid model, it is easier and more cost effective to anticipate these issues in the refinement stage, but it is not uncommon for fine-tuning to occur during implementation. Unavailable parts or materials can force a substitution, a supplier may recommend a cheaper alternative, standard parts may be substituted for newly designed ones, or unanticipated problems may crop up during assembly. Sustainability issues can affect a design throughout the lifetime of the product.

Assembly drawings may be generated to document the parts included in an assembly and to illustrate how they fit together. The parts list, or bill of materials, is an important facet of inventory planning and assembly. Parts from the solid model may be catalogued in a company-wide parts database. Parts in the database can be reused or shared by other products, and standard parts inventories can be tracked and monitored.

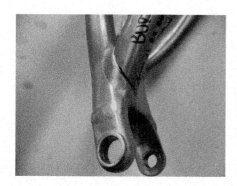

1.20 *This sample part for the swingarm failed during testing. (Courtesy of Santa Cruz Bicycles.)*

Design Phase: Documentation

The documentation phase of the design process captures the final design and freezes it. Each company has its own procedures for managing models and controlling changes to the model database, but it must create permanent records for archival purposes, patent applications, and other legal uses (see Figure 1.21).

At Santa Cruz Bicycles, the 3D model is archived at each stage of the process. The model is sufficiently documented so that no 2D drawings are needed. Occasionally, a 2D drawing generated from the model is used to call a toolmaker's attention to a key dimension or tolerance.

Sometimes, after a model is sent to the manufacturer, dimensioned drawings are prepared to document the final product as manufactured and assembled. Measurements are taken from the actual parts, and the solid model is modified to match them, then dimensioned drawings from the final model are stored in the archive. (This is the reverse of the traditional model, in which the documentation drawings are prepared first to transmit the design to manufacturing.)

The 3D design database (solid model) may be archived as the permanent record. Fully dimensioned engineering drawings also may be used to provide a permanent record of the design at some point. Companies that use the model for documentation have well-defined procedures for archiving the final model. Because files stored in

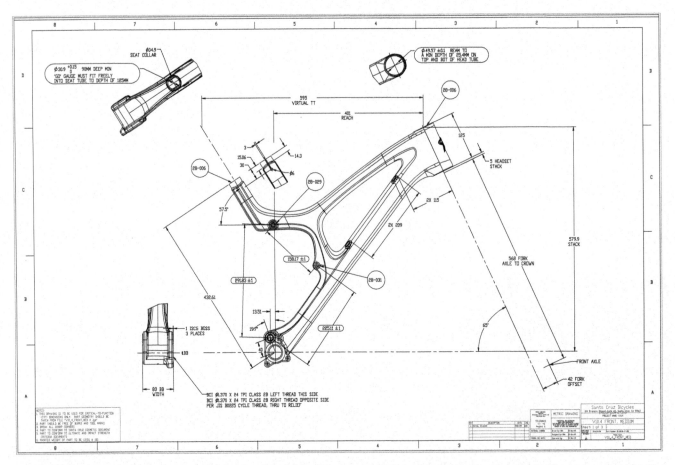

1.21   *This drawing generated from the solid model includes notes that call attention to the fit with other parts that the V10's frame must achieve. (Courtesy of Santa Cruz Bicycles.)*

electronic format can be altered so that they no longer represent the actual product design, companies must control access to the information in the solid model—or capture it in another medium—to create a permanent record. Once a model has been archived, only authorized personnel may make changes to it.

The solid model can also be used to generate a wide range of graphics used to document a product or process. Views of the model are imported into step-by-step illustrated guides for assembly line personnel (Figure 1.22), and the same guides are sent to service personnel who need to disassemble and reassemble the products after sale.

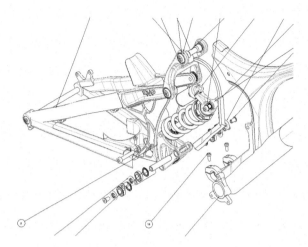

1.22 *Exploded views such as this one can be used to illustrate assembly or service manuals for the V10. (Courtesy of Santa Cruz Bicycles.)*

1.2 RAPID PROTOTYPING

While refining design ideas, the design team often works concurrently with manufacturing to determine the best ways to make and assemble the necessary parts. After several cycles of refining, analyzing, and synthesizing the best ideas, *rapid prototyping* systems allow designers to generate parts quickly, directly from 3D models, for mockup and testing. For example, they can check usability for humans or explore customer reactions in consumer focus groups by showing them facsimile products created using rapid prototyping. 3D design data can be formatted for use by rapid prototyping equipment. Figure 1.23 shows the prototyped part emerging from the unfused material of the rapid prototyper, which can "print" a color part like the one shown in about four hours. You will learn more about rapid prototyping in Chapter 10.

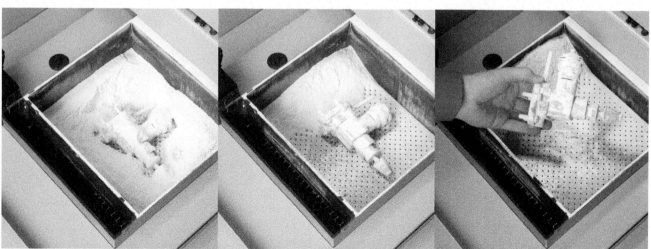

1.23 Rapid Prototyping. *The ZPrinter 450 "printed" the colored part shown in about four hours. (Courtesy of 3D Systems.)*

1.3 DRAFTING STANDARDS

There are **standards** that support a uniform, effective graphic language for use in industry, manufacturing, engineering, and science. Technical drawing texts like this book can help you learn them. In the United States, providing these standards has been the work of the American National Standards Institute (ANSI) with the American Society for Engineering Education (ASEE), the Society of Automotive Engineers (SAE), and the American Society of Mechanical Engineers (ASME).

Participants in these organizations help develop the *American National Standard Drafting Manual—Y14*, which is composed of a number of separate sections that are published as approved standards as they are completed (see Appendix 1).

These standards are frequently updated to communicate information so that it meets the needs of modern industry and engineering practice. They are considered the most authoritative guide to uniform drafting practices in the United States today.

International standards, often defined by the International Organization for Standardization (ISO), and the ASME or ANSI standards for drawing practices are similar in many respects. The greatest differences are in the preferred method of projection: first-angle versus third-angle projection, and in the units of measurement in dimensioning. Third-angle projection is the projection method that you will be learning in this text. Where practical, information for both U.S. and international drawings will be presented.

1.4 CREATIVITY TECHNIQUES

Some people are naturally gifted at design and drawing, but all persons can improve their design ability if they learn to use the proper tools and techniques. It is similar to learning to play a musical instrument; it comes more naturally to some people than to others, but all can learn to play if they practice.

How do you develop new ideas? Here are some proven techniques you can practice.

Examine Manufactured Products

It is common for design engineers to dismantle manufactured products, evaluate them, and study how their parts are designed to work together. As you use and examine manufactured products, ask yourself, How could they be improved? What would you do differently? How could you expand/change the design to guarantee better performance? What could you do to expand the life of the product? How could you make it more efficient, more cost-effective, and so forth?

Reverse engineering is a term that refers to designing products based on existing designs, usually through measurement and deconstruction of an existing product. A **coordinate measuring machine** (CMM) aids in speeding the time to reverse engineer some products. A CMM measures the object using a probe or laser and stores the pertinent geometric information into a database where it can be manipulated using CAD.

Functional decomposition is a term for determining the subfunctions involved

A Drill Housing Cut in Half to Expose Interior Part Functions *(bit mechanic/ Shutterstock.)*

in a design and then using those functions to reconstruct a similar product.

Study the Natural World

Noting how other creatures and organisms function and interact with their surroundings can provide a wealth of information and creativity. Such things as beehives and spiderwebs are masterpieces of structural design that have inspired human designers for centuries. A hummingbird's wings are aerodynamic wonders. There is much to be learned by studying natural forms and expanding on their designs, as Leonardo da Vinci did with his flying machine (Figure 1.24).

Watch the Web

Excellent resources for engineering and design are available on the World Wide Web. Reading technology blogs and news feeds and visiting engineering sites is a way to stay current and keep in touch with peers. The following websites are useful for engineering design:

- www.uspto.gov (U.S. Patent Office online search site)
- www.practicalmachinist.com
- www.engineeringtoolbox.com
- www.engnetglobal.com
- www.efunda.com
- www.thomasnet.com
- www.mcmaster.com
- www.howstuffworks.com

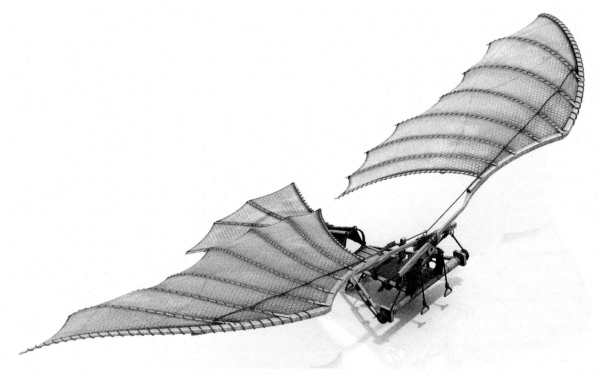

1.24 3D Model of the Ornithopter, a Flapping-Winged Flying Machine Conceived by Leonardo da Vinci *(Leo Blanchette/Shutterstock.)*

Research Patent Drawings

Patents can be a great source of ideas. A patent is issued by the U.S. government and grants the holder the "right to exclude others from making, using, or selling" a specific product for a specific time period. The patent process was first developed as a way to promote the disclosure of technical advances. You can research the current state of design for your product idea at the U.S. Patent and Trademark Office's searchable website (www.uspto.gov). The U.S. Patent and Trademark Office has strict regulations as to how designs are presented in *patent drawings* to ensure that the drawings are easy to reproduce (Figure 1.25).

Design Groups

To bring complex products and systems to market, most individuals end up working in a team environment. Teams combine the expertise of individuals familiar with materials, production processes, marketing, finance, and so on, so most projects become a team effort long before a product is produced and marketed. In addition to supplying the varied expertise that it takes to bring an idea from concept to manufacture, interaction between people of varied talents plays an important role in the creative design process. The ability to create and understand technical drawings helps group members contribute to and benefit from team communication.

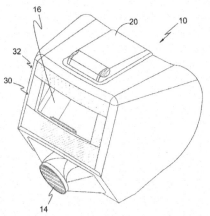

1.25 Patent Drawing for a Healthier Helmet

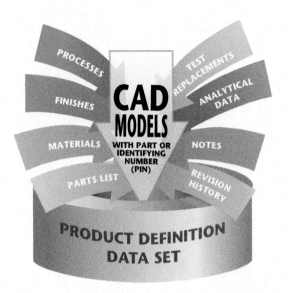

1.26   Possible Contents of a 3D Data Set

1.5 PRODUCT DEFINITION

As stated before, technical graphics play three important roles: visualization, communication, and documentation. Drawings and CAD models are an important part of product definition. **Product definition** refers to the collection of digital or hard copy documents that specify the physical and functional requirements for a product. These can range from a 3D CAD model that specifies manufacturing requirements within the CAD file to a dimensioned paper sketch.

Many companies prefer storing information in a digital format because the storage cost is comparatively low and the data can be easily searched, retrieved, and utilized by many individuals. Figure 1.26 represents the range of contents in a product definition data set. A thorough understanding of the graphic language, from hand sketches to complex 3D models, is necessary to be a player in the competitive world marketplace.

1.6 SHOWING THE DESIGN PROCESS IN A PORTFOLIO

A portfolio is a representative sample of work that helps communicate your skills and talents, usually to a prospective employer or client. Many companies and individuals post portfolios on the Web to promote their capabilities and accomplishments. Larger companies tend to show more models and completed projects because working drawings may be proprietary information. Individuals, particularly recent students, may focus more on showing correct drawing practices and creative problem-solving skills.

Whether you are a consulting engineer, an architect, an industrial designer, or a draftsman, showing samples of your work offers an advantage over just talking about it. Drawings are proof that you not only have good ideas but also have the skill to communicate clearly and accurately throughout the stages of a project, from concept to completion.

If you are seeking an entry-level job, don't worry if your portfolio looks like an entry-level portfolio. Clean, correct student work is a good indication of your potential. Don't try to cover a lack of well-drawn examples with a more expensive portfolio case, or decorative presentation. Instead, spend that energy completing a project that shows your ability.

A portfolio is an opportunity to tell concise success stories. For example, you may want to show four to six projects, including the design brief (or assigned problem), sketches, development drawings, and final presentation (including working drawings, renderings, and physical or 3D models) for each. Your portfolio samples make great talking points in an interview, so take advantage of the chance to show how you tackled challenges such as cutting costs, improving function, or solving problems that arose along the way.

Some more tips for creating a successful portfolio are:

1. Less is more. Others will assume that your portfolio is your best work, so a few good examples are better than a million mediocre examples. Four to six projects are usually plenty.

2. Show correct drawing practices. Especially if you are seeking a drafting position, but even if your strength is creativity, be sure that lineweights, dimensioning, notes, and other parts of the drawing conform to technical drawing standards.

3. Keep several versions of your current portfolio, including hard copy, digital, and Web presence. Use widely accessible formats (such as PDF or PowerPoint) to make your digital portfolio easy to access. Including your Web address in correspondence allows people to view your work or refer to your samples at their convenience.

4. Never rely entirely on electronic equipment. Even if you have a great digital presentation, bring a portfolio of printed samples. Drawings should be clean and legible. Depending on your discipline, you may want a larger or smaller portfolio case, keeping in mind how convenient it is to transport and view. You may fold large drawings to fit, as long as they are easy to take out and look at.

5. Save good examples as you create them. It is easy to forget what you did last year, or four years ago. Keep copies (both digital and paper) of your best work in a file for portfolio samples and remember to save some development sketches from successful projects, too.

6. Depending on your career goals, let your portfolio reflect the area you want to explore. If you are seeking a creative position and you have related skills (such as artistic drawing or photography) you may want to include appropriate examples. If you are mainly interested in a drafting position, you may want to include more working drawings and models.

Throughout this book, the Portfolio sections give you some exposure to real-world drawings that apply to chapter topics. However, the Portfolio section in this chapter shows how an industrial design student successfully communicated the design process through a well-conceived portfolio page.

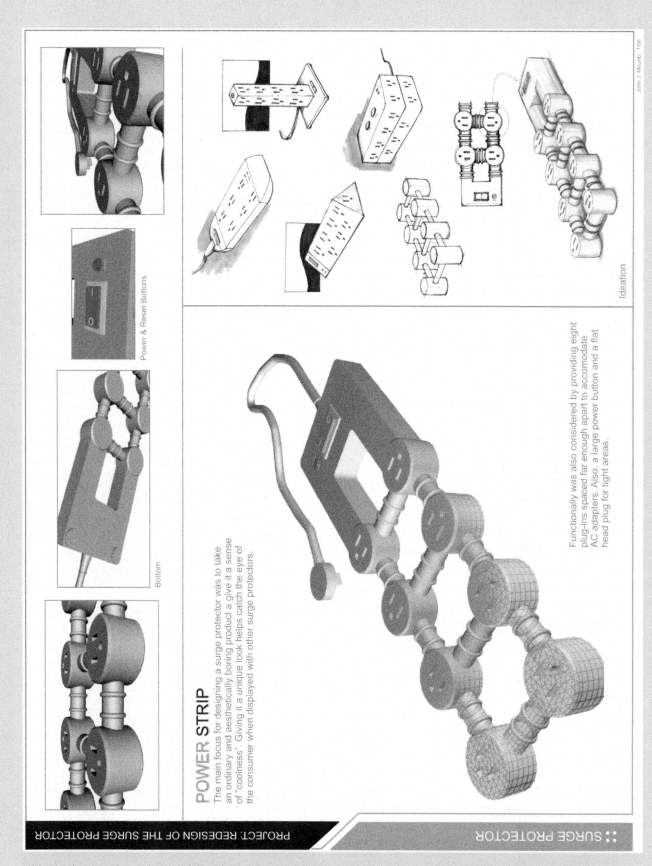

This single page from the portfolio of John Mountz begins with the design brief and rationale for the design. It includes initial concepts, more refined sketches, a solid model, and details. Mountz showed the final presentation drawing on an additional portfolio page. At the time, he was a student of industrial designer Doug Wintin, then Chair of the School of Design at ITT Technical Institute. (Courtesy of John Mountz.)

KEY WORDS

Communication

Concurrent Engineering

Computer-Aided Design

Computer-Aided Engineering

Computer-Aided Manufacturing

Constraint-Based Modeling

Coordinate Measuring Machine

Define, Measure, Analyze, Improve, Control (DMAIC)

Design for Six Sigma (DFSS)

Design Intent

Design Process

Development Phase

Documentation

Engineering Change Orders

Enterprise Data Management

Functional Decomposition

Ideation

Implementation/Documentation Phase

Life Cycle Design

Parametric Modeling

Patent Drawings

Product Data Management

Product Definition

Prototype

Quality Function Deployment (QFD)

Rapid Prototyping

Refinement/Analysis Phase

Reverse Engineering

Six Sigma

Standards

Universal Possibilities

Visualization

CHAPTER SUMMARY

• The graphic language is the universal language used to design, develop, and construct products and systems throughout the world.
• The design process combines ideas, scientific principles, resources, and existing products into a solution for a problem. It consists of five specific stages.
• Every technical drawing is based on standards that prescribe what each symbol, line, and arc means.
• The members of a engineering design project team must be able to communicate among themselves and with the rest of the project team to contribute to the team's success.
• The basic principles for communicating information using technical drawings are the same whether drawings are created by hand or using CAD.
• Successful companies hire skilled people who can add value to their team. A thorough understanding of the graphic language is an essential skill that employers value.

REVIEW QUESTIONS

1. When is sketching used as graphic communication?
2. Why are standards so important for members of the engineering design team?
3. What is the design process?
4. What are the five phases of the design process?
5. Describe the difference between concurrent and traditional design process models.
6. What does PDM or EDM stand for? What are some advantages of PDM?
7. When are rapid prototypes useful?
8. List three ways a CAD database can be used.
9. List five techniques you can use to enhance creativity.

CHAPTER EXERCISES

If necessary, refer to the appropriate section of the chapter to check your answers.

Exercise 1.1 Define the following terms as they apply to the design process: needs statement, concept, compromise solutions, prototype, layout sketch.

Exercise 1.2 Sketch a flowchart that depicts the design process as you understand it.

Exercise 1.3 The hypothetical "Flies R Us" fishing tackle company has contracted your services to restructure their design process and increase profitability. Read the job descriptions accompanying the "Flies R Us" design flowchart and decide at what stages of the design process each team member should be involved. Sketch out a flowchart that illustrates the new reporting relationships for these individuals or groups.

Exercise 1.4 Using the "Flies R Us" flowchart as a guide, answer the following:

- What sort of information does Randy Edwards need before he can source raw goods for the manufacture of a new product?
- At what point should Todd Benson be involved in the design process, and why?
- What might happen if Samir Raol was out of the communication loop?
- Would Annette Stone be likely to see a prototype?
- Which team members do you think Monte VanDyke has on the speed-dial function of his office phone?

James Washington
Company President

In charge of $24 million fly fishing accessory manufacturing company; makes ultimate company-wide decisions based on advice from management team members

Amy Rutledge
Controller

In charge of company finances

Randy Edwards
Purchasing Agent

Sources pricing of raw goods and maintains accounts with vendors

Helen Ramirez
Product Manager

In charge of steering a line of high-tech fishing reels; attends trade shows; monitors technological advances, activity of competitors, and customer requests

Annette Stone
Sales Manager

In charge of a commissioned sales force of 120 representatives; maintains accounts with major distributors

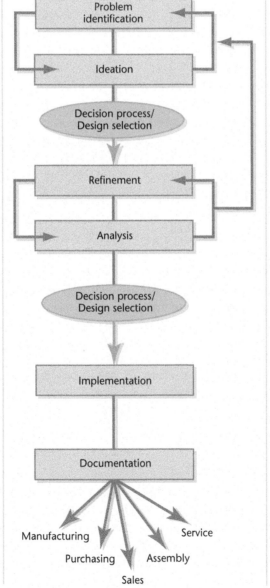

Todd Benson
Production Manager

In charge of mass producing goods; oversees production machinery, facilities, and personnel; performs production cost analysis

Sarah Nordsen
Manufacturing Engineer

Uses specialized knowledge of manufacturing processes and materials to ensure manufacturability of products; determines fits between parts; designs tooling and production processes

Monte VanDyke
Design Engineer

Supervises a crew of six design engineers in developing and testing new products

Joe Chang
Composite Specialist

Develops specialized materials on a contract basis for use in specific products

Samir Raol
Customer Service Manager

Takes orders directly from retailers and determines delivery dates based on product availability

Flies R Us Job Descriptions

REVERSE ENGINEERING PROJECTS

Can Opener Project

In this ongoing project, you will reverse engineer an Amco Swing-A-Way 407WH Portable Can Opener. It is recommended you purchase a readily available and affordable product similar to this one, so you can make measurements directly when required. This effective and low-cost can opener seems simple in its familiarity, but it is clear when you begin to take one apart that considerable effort went into designing a product that is inexpensive, reliable, and easy to operate for most people.

Product Features

- Portable
- Lightweight
- Manually operated
- Comfortable to hold
- Durable construction
- Has a bottle opener
- Colored handles available
- Low maintenance
- Five-year warranty

Exercises for Chapter 1

RE 1.1   This is far from the only can opener on the market. Use the Web to research manual can opener designs. Find at least three can opener models that are different from the Amco Swing-A-Way. Make a list of the features of each of the three.

RE 1.2   Create a diagram for the can opener. How many distinct parts are used in its manufacture? Which parts can be grouped together and preassembled as a unit?

Exercises for Chapter 2

RE 2.1   Make a table listing the dimensions of the can opener parts. Do not worry about measurements for now. Give names to the dimensions, such as lower handle length, lower handle height, and hole diameter.

RE 2.2   Which dimensions in the list you created are critical to the function of the can opener? Identify in your list the dimensions that must match dimensions on other parts for the can opener to function. Which dimensions will not be very important to the can opener's function?

RE 2.3   To accurately reverse engineer the can opener, you will need to make measurements for the part features. Metrology is the science of making measurements. The digital caliper is one commonly used measurement tool. The accuracy of a measurement is dependent on several factors, including the following:

- the skill of the operator
- the temperature at which the measurements are taken
- how stationary the part is while being measured
- the accuracy of the measurement device

Measure the critical dimensions of the lower handle part. Make each measurement five times. Calculate the mean and standard deviation for each set of measurements. Determine what value you will use when modeling that dimension. Label the values on the sketch you drew for the lower handle.

RE 2.4   What factors influence the accuracy of the value you chose for the dimension?

Exercises for Chapter 3

RE 3.1   Sketch a concept for an innovative can opener design.

RE 3.2   Sketch a pictorial drawing of the can opener part assigned by your instructor, such as the one shown here for the upper handle.

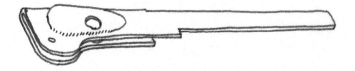

Exercises for Chapter 4

RE 4.1   Sketch and model a 3D wireframe drawing showing the main centerlines of the can opener parts. Use your 3D modeling software to create a single 3D sketch that shows the centerlines of each main part of the can opener, similar to that shown. Draw the 3D sketch lines only. You will model the can opener parts later.

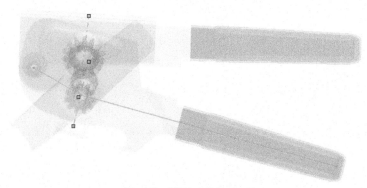

Draw the 3D sketch lines only.
You will model the can opener parts later.

Exercises for Chapter 5

Begin modeling the can opener's parts, with emphasis on the dimensional and geometric constraints that are appropriate.

RE 5.1   Model the pin, rivet, and bushing for the can opener using your 3D modeling software.

RE 5.2   Create constraint-based part models of the top handle, bottom handle, cutter, knob, and gears (see next page). Consider part fit, and make your model so that the major dimensions can flexibly change. Review the dimension names you assigned for the lower handle, and revise them if needed. Assign dimension names to these parts wherever it makes sense for the can opener assembly.

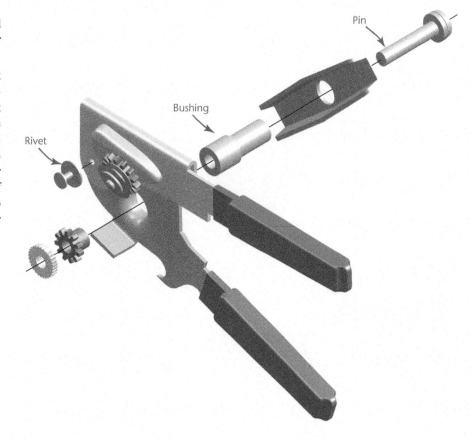

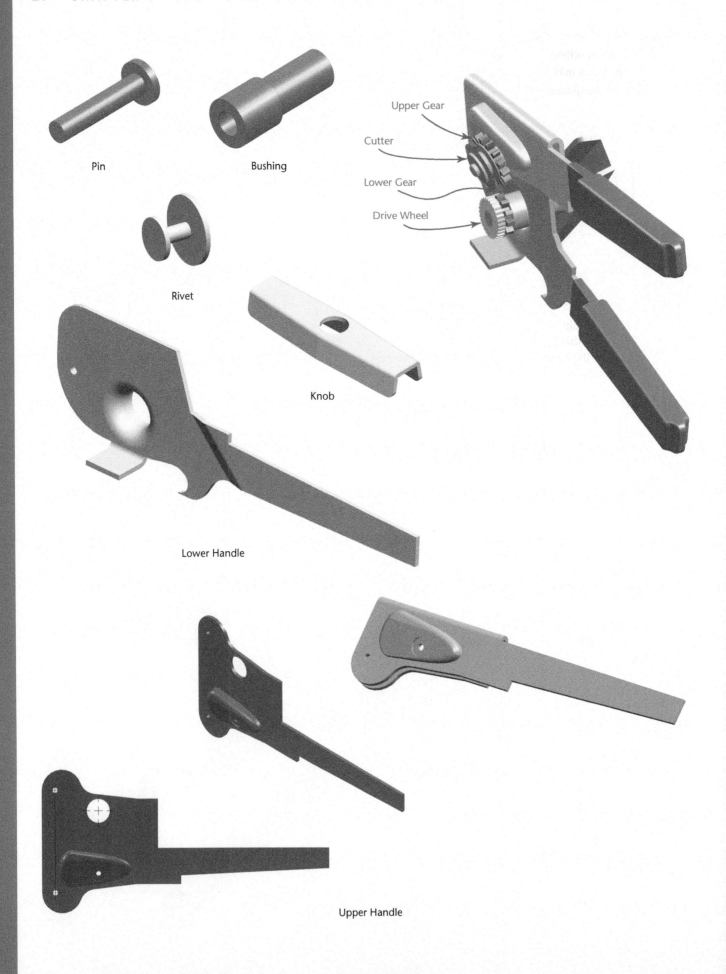

Pin

Bushing

Upper Gear

Cutter

Lower Gear

Drive Wheel

Rivet

Knob

Lower Handle

Upper Handle

Exercises for Chapter 6

RE 6.1 Create an orthographic view sketch of the lower handle for the can opener similar to that shown here for the upper handle.

RE 6.2 Name the dimensions. Add dimensions to your orthographic sketch of the handle.

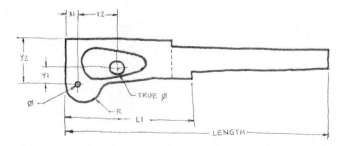

Exercises for Chapter 7

RE 7.1 Create a multiview part drawing for the upper handle. The upper handle is a sheet metal part that is bent to form its shape. Consider this manufacturing process as you create the dimensioned drawing. An example drawing is shown below with dimensions added. Complete Chapter 11 before adding the dimensions to your drawing.

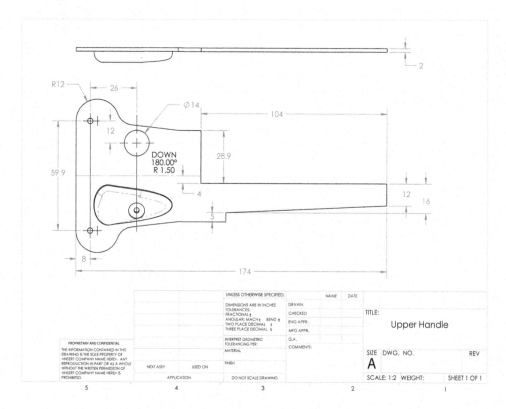

Exercises for Chapter 8

RE 8.1 Create an orthographic drawing for the bushing part. Show the front view in section.

Exercises for Chapter 10

RE 10.1   Use the parts you created to create an assembly of the can opener.

RE 10.2   Use the capabilities of your software to animate the motion of the can opener. What is the minimum distance between the cutting wheel and the lower gear?

RE 10.3   Assign appropriate materials to each of the parts and determine the weight of the can opener from your assembly model. Weigh the actual can opener and compare the two. Are they close?

RE 10.4   Next, determine the center of gravity (COG) for the can opener assembly. Do you think the can opener will feel balanced when you are operating it based on the location of its center of gravity?

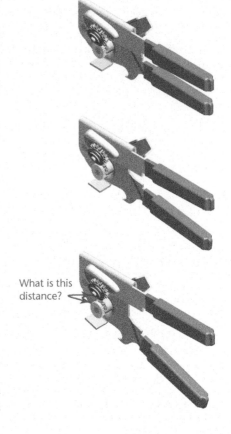

RE 10.5   Change the handle parts to make a new pistol-grip design. Analyze the part again to determine the mass properties and COG.

RE 10.6   Experiment with different options by making changes to your can opener parts and updating the assembly. List two options for changing the design if you are required to reduce the overall weight by 20%.

What is this distance?

RE 10.7   Create an assembly drawing for your can opener, similar to the one shown. Use an exploded view and a fully assembled view. Add balloon numbers and a parts list.

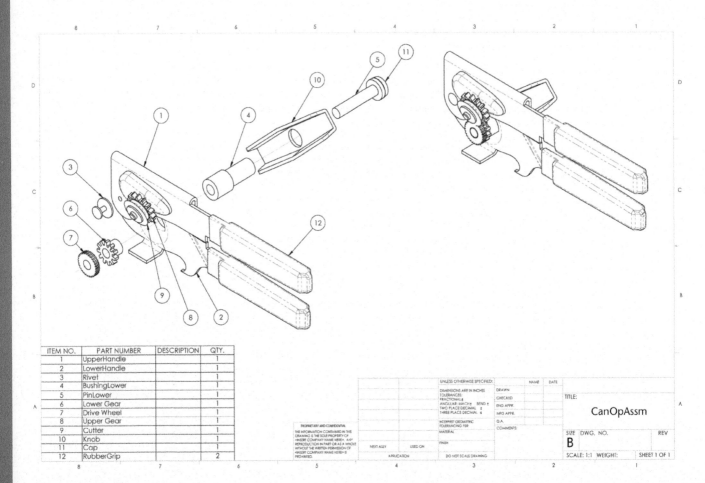

ITEM NO.	PART NUMBER	DESCRIPTION	QTY.
1	UpperHandle		1
2	LowerHandle		1
3	Rivet		1
4	BushingLower		1
5	PinLower		1
6	Lower Gear		1
7	Drive Wheel		1
8	Upper Gear		1
9	Cutter		1
10	Knob		1
11	Cap		1
12	RubberGrip		2

TITLE:

CanOpAssm

SIZE DWG. NO.   REV
B

SCALE: 1:1 WEIGHT: SHEET 1 OF 1

Exercises for Chapter 11

RE 11.1   Add dimensions to the multiview orthographic part drawings you created earlier.

Exercises for Chapter 12

RE 12.1   Assign tolerances to the part model of the lower handle of your can opener. Then, add tolerances to your drawing of the lower handle part. Your drawing should look similar to the example below.

RE 12.2   What parts of the can opener have fits that are critical to the can opener function? This can opener sells for around $5.00. Consider and describe some of the effects on the price of the can opener if highly-precise fits are required.

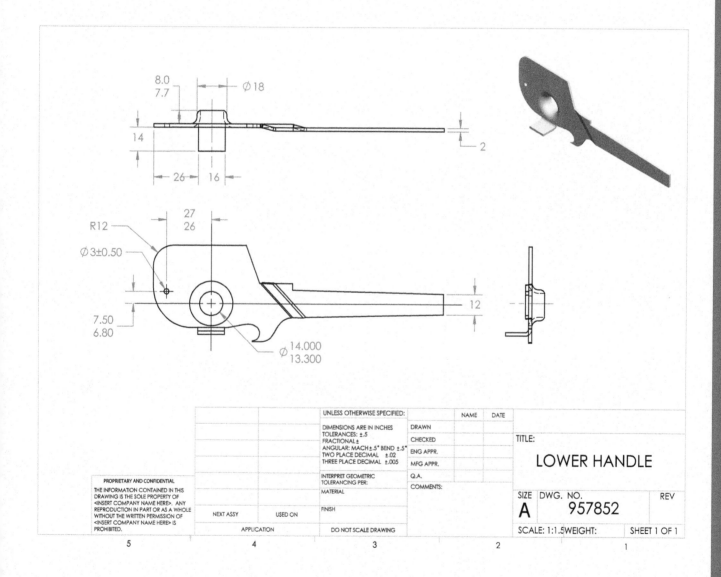

UNLESS OTHERWISE SPECIFIED:		NAME	DATE			
DIMENSIONS ARE IN INCHES TOLERANCES: ±.5	DRAWN					
FRACTIONAL ±	CHECKED			TITLE:		
ANGULAR: MACH±.5° BEND ±.5° TWO PLACE DECIMAL ±.02 THREE PLACE DECIMAL ±.005	ENG APPR.					
	MFG APPR.			**LOWER HANDLE**		
INTERPRET GEOMETRIC TOLERANCING PER:	Q.A.					
MATERIAL	COMMENTS:			SIZE	DWG. NO.	REV
FINISH				**A**	957852	
DO NOT SCALE DRAWING				SCALE: 1:1.5 WEIGHT:		SHEET 1 OF 1

PROPRIETARY AND CONFIDENTIAL

THE INFORMATION CONTAINED IN THIS DRAWING IS THE SOLE PROPERTY OF <INSERT COMPANY NAME HERE>. ANY REPRODUCTION IN PART OR AS A WHOLE WITHOUT THE WRITTEN PERMISSION OF <INSERT COMPANY NAME HERE> IS PROHIBITED.

NEXT ASSY   USED ON

APPLICATION

Locking Pliers Project

RE Locking Pliers 1.   Use stages similar to those for the can opener to create sketches, models, and drawings for the locking pliers shown below.

RE Locking Pliers 2.   Create solid models for the locking pliers parts (shown on the next page). Use dial calipers, a micrometer, or machinist scales to make measurements from your pliers. Consider the mating features and alignment that make the locking plier mechanism function. If assigned, make an assembly skeleton as represented below and assemble your completed parts onto it.

RE Locking Pliers 3.   Ensure your parts will fit and function in the assembly. Perform a fit study on the completed assembly to identify any interference issues in your model.

RE Locking Pliers 4.   Make part drawings as assigned by your instructor.

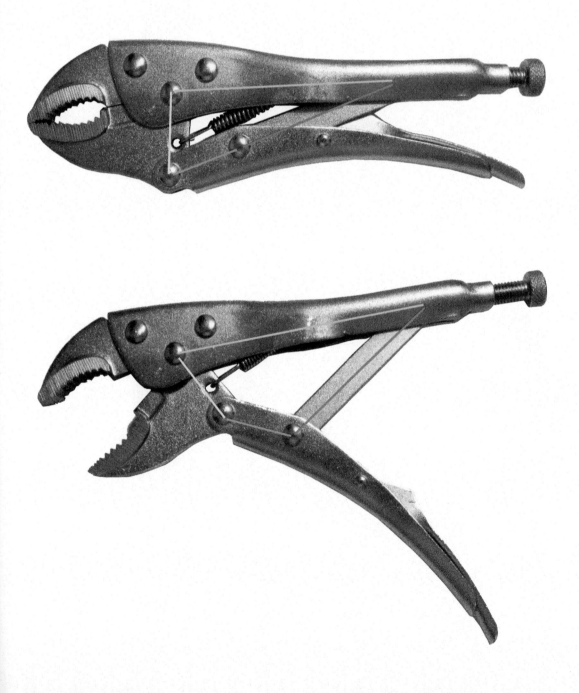

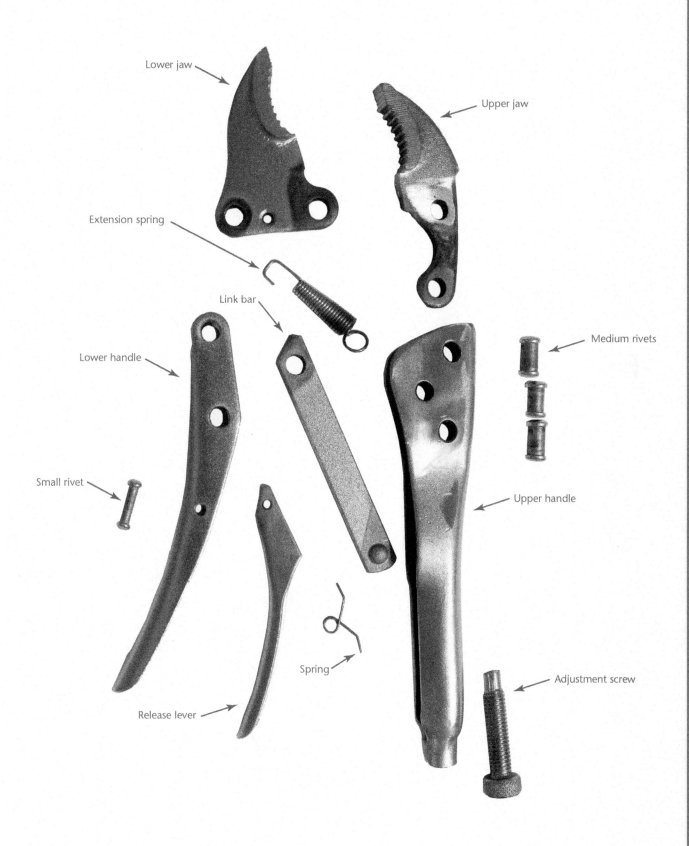

Lower jaw

Upper jaw

Extension spring

Link bar

Medium rivets

Lower handle

Small rivet

Upper handle

Spring

Adjustment screw

Release lever

CHAPTER TWO

LAYOUTS AND LETTERING

OBJECTIVES

After studying the material in this chapter, you should be able to:

1. Identify six types of technical drawings based on the projection system they use.

2. Identify the line patterns used in technical drawings and describe how they are used.

3. Identify standard drawing media and sheet sizes.

4. Label drawing scale information.

5. Add lettering to a sketch.

6. Fill in a standard title block with the appropriate information.

7. Lay out a drawing sheet.

Refer to the following standards:
- *ANSI/ASME Y14.100 Engineering Drawing Practices*
- *ANSI/ASME Y14.2 Line Conventions and Lettering*
- *ANSI/ASME Y14.1 Drawing Sheet Size and Format*

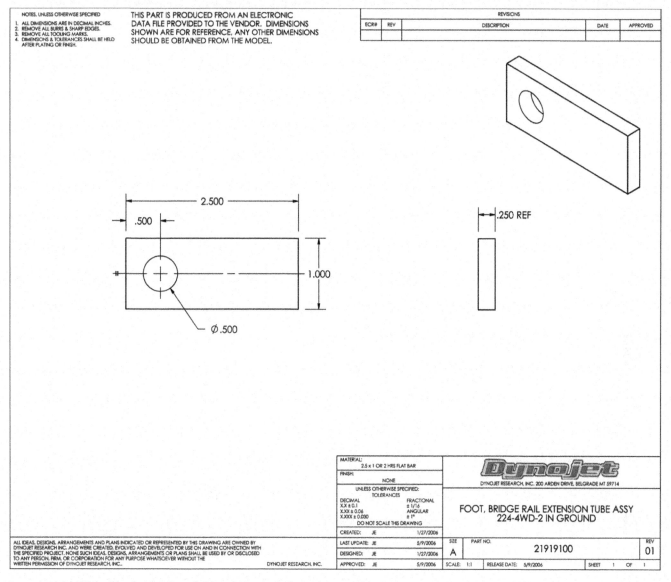

Layout with Title Block of a Small Part at Scale 1:1 *(Courtesy Dynojet Research, Inc.)*

OVERVIEW

Two-dimensional technical drawings, whether they are sketched by hand, drawn using instruments, drawn using a CAD program, or generated from 3D solid models, follow certain rules so that they can be correctly interpreted. Unlike artistic drawings, which communicate self-expression and emotional content, technical drawings communicate size, shape, and feature information about a product, system, or device. To clearly describe this information, technical drawings adhere closely to formal standards.

These formal standards include systems of projection for developing and understanding drawing views. They also include an "alphabet of lines," in which each line of the drawing represents certain information. Lettering is also standardized, to make drawings quick to create and easy to read and reproduce. Standard sheet sizes for drawings include a title block that provides important information such as the drawing name, company information, scale, revision numbers, and approvals for release of the drawing.

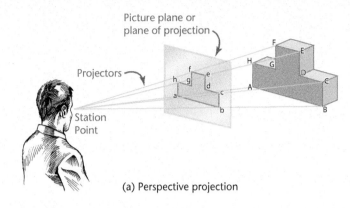

Picture plane or plane of projection

Projectors

Station Point

(a) Perspective projection

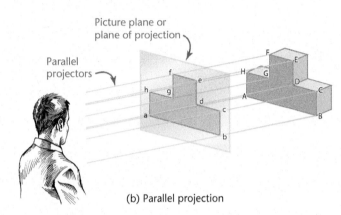

Picture plane or plane of projection

Parallel projectors

(b) Parallel projection

2.1   The Concept of Projection

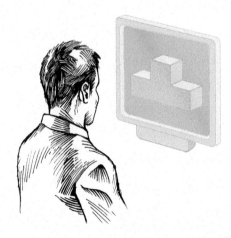

2.2   A View of a 3D Object "Projected" onto a Computer Monitor

UNDERSTANDING PROJECTION

Behind every 2D drawing of an object is a space relationship involving the object and three "imagined" things:

1. The observer's eye, or *station point*
2. The *plane of projection*
3. The *projectors* (also called *visual rays* or *lines of sight*)

Figure 2.1 shows two drawings of a shape projected onto a plane as viewed by an observer, whose eye represents the station point. The lines projecting from the corners (or vertices) of the object are the imagined lines, called projectors.

To understand projection, imagine that the drawing is produced by points, called *piercing points,* where the projectors would pierce the projection plane. The drawing may be a two-dimensional representation on a sheet of paper, or it may be a two-dimensional representation shown on your computer screen, as shown in Figure 2.2, but the basic principles are the same. One reason 2D projection skills remain relevant, even with the advent of 3D modeling, is that computer monitors still display a 2D view on their flat screens.

Types of Projection

There are two main types of projection: perspective and parallel. These are broken down into subtypes, as shown in Figure 2.3.

In *perspective projections,* the projectors come together at the station point to form a cone, as in Figure 2.1a. Perspective drawings represent objects as we see them or as they would appear in a photograph.

In *parallel projections,* the projectors are parallel, as shown in Figure 2.1b.

Orthographic projections are one type of parallel projection. In orthographic (meaning right-angle) projections, the parallel projectors are perpendicular to the plane of projection. Because orthographic projections show objects in a way that their features can be represented at true size or scaled at a proportion of true size, they are especially useful in specifying the dimensions needed in technical applications.

If the projectors are parallel to each other, but are at an angle *other than 90°* to the plane of projection, the result is called an *oblique projection.*

Technical drawings of 3D objects usually use one of four standard types of projection, shown in Figure 2.3:

- Multiview
- Axonometric (includes isometric)
- Oblique
- Perspective

Multiview projection shows one or more necessary views. Either of two systems is used to arrange the views in a multiview drawing: third-angle or first-angle. You will learn about multiview projection in Chapter 6.

Axonometric, oblique, and perspective sketches are methods of showing the object pictorially in a single view. They will be discussed in Chapter 3.

The main types of projection are listed in Table 2.1.

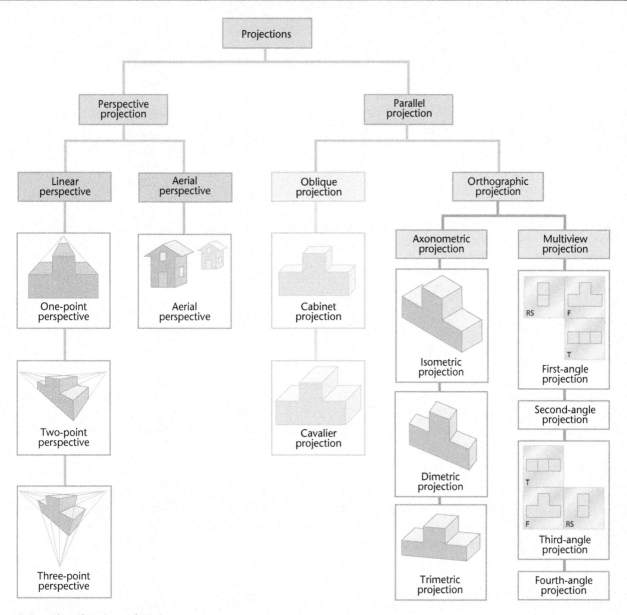

2.3 Classification of Projections

Table 2.1 Classification by Projectors

Class of Projection	Distance from Observer to Plane of Projection	Direction of Projectors
Perspective	Finite	Radiating from station point
Parallel	Infinite	Parallel to each other
Oblique	Infinite	Parallel to each other and oblique to plane of projection
Orthographic	Infinite	Perpendicular to plane of projection
Axonometric	Infinite	Perpendicular to plane of projection
Multiview	Infinite	Perpendicular to plane of projection

Drawing Vocabulary

Drawing lines, lettering, measurement systems, scale, sheet sizes, and title blocks are presented in this chapter.

Drawing Lines Projected drawing views use specific line patterns to represent object features. For example, when showing a 3D object, some lines represent the edges of surfaces that are hidden from that viewing direction. These hidden lines have a dashed line pattern to help the reader understand the drawing. Another type of line indicates the location of the center of a symmetrical feature, such as a hole. Familiarity with the types of lines used in technical drawings helps you read drawings and create drawings that others can easily understand.

Lettering The shapes of letters that are easy to read and write are described as part of drawing standards. Often, freehand sketching is used early in the design process to present ideas. Showing notes and information legibly helps present your ideas to others clearly. Good lettering often makes or breaks a sketch.

Measurement Systems Two measurement systems are used for technical drawings: the metric system and U.S. customary units. It is important to be familiar with both measurement systems to create and read drawings that are used worldwide.

Scale Obviously, a large item (a house or bridge for example) cannot be shown full size on a paper sheet. To clearly convey important information about particularly large or small objects, you need to select an appropriate sheet size and show drawings to scale (proportionately smaller or larger than the actual size). Standard lettering sizes for drawings depend on the sheet size.

Title Blocks Company information, the drawing scale, sheet size, and other information is included in a standard title block located in the lower right corner of the drawing to make it easy to locate these important details on every drawing layout.

2.1 ALPHABET OF LINES

The meaning of each line on a technical drawing is indicated by its width (thick or thin) and its particular line style. The person who reads the drawing will depend on these line styles to know if a line is visible or hidden, if it represents a center axis, or if it conveys dimension information.

To make your drawings easy to read, make the contrast between thick and thin lines distinct. *Thick lines* (0.6 mm) should be twice the width of *thin lines* (0.3 mm), as shown in Figure 2.4. The line gage in Figure 2.5 shows various widths.

Figure 2.6 shows freehand line technique. You may find it helpful to use 1/8″ graph paper at first to get a feel for the length of dashes used in hidden lines and centerlines. Soon you will be able to estimate the lengths by eye.

Figure 2.7 illustrates line styles for technical drawings. All lines (except construction lines) must be sharp and dark. For visible, cutting-plane, and short-break lines use thick lines. Thin drawing lines should be just as sharp and black, but only half the thickness of thick lines. Construction lines and lettering guidelines should be thin and light so that they can barely be seen at arm's length and need not be erased. All lines should be uniform in width and darkness. Ideal lengths of the dashes used to form the line patterns are also shown in Figure 2.7.

Thick (0.60 mm)

Thin (0.30 mm)

2.4   Thick and Thin Drawing Lines

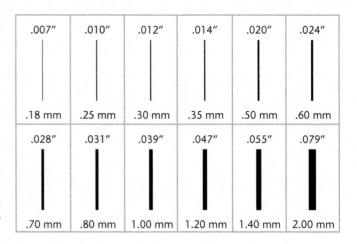

.007″	.010″	.012″	.014″	.020″	.024″
.18 mm	.25 mm	.30 mm	.35 mm	.50 mm	.60 mm
.028″	.031″	.039″	.047″	.055″	.079″
.70 mm	.80 mm	1.00 mm	1.20 mm	1.40 mm	2.00 mm

2.5   Line Gage

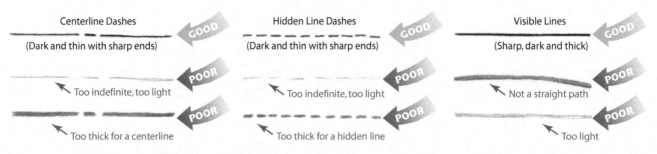

Centerline Dashes
(Dark and thin with sharp ends)   GOOD

Hidden Line Dashes
(Dark and thin with sharp ends)   GOOD

Visible Lines
(Sharp, dark and thick)   GOOD

POOR   Too indefinite, too light

POOR   Too indefinite, too light

POOR   Not a straight path

POOR   Too thick for a centerline

POOR   Too thick for a hidden line

POOR   Too light

2.6   Good and Poor Freehand Line Technique

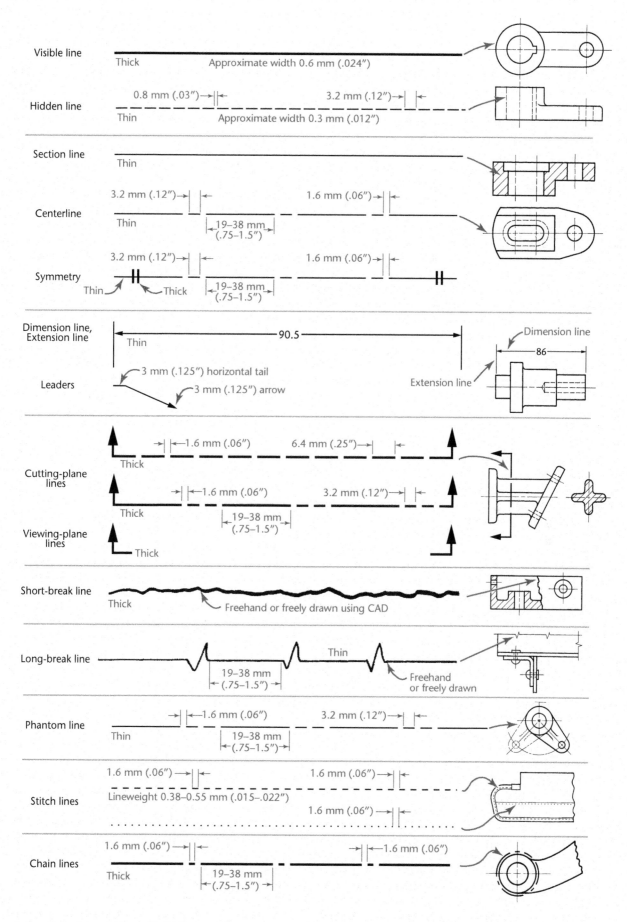

2.7 Alphabet of Lines (Full Size)

2.2 FREEHAND LINES

The main difference between an instrument or CAD drawing and a freehand sketch is in the appearance of the lines. A good *freehand line* is not expected to be precisely straight or exactly uniform, as is a CAD or instrument-drawn line. Freehand lines show freedom and variety. Freehand *construction lines* are very light, rough lines. All other lines should be dark and clean.

2.3 MEASUREMENT SYSTEMS

When you create a technical drawing, the item you show will be manufactured or constructed using a particular system of measurement, which you indicate on the drawing. The metric system is the world standard used for measuring lengths.

U.S. Customary Units

U.S. customary units based on inch-foot and yard measurements (where there are 3 feet to the yard, and 12 inches to the foot; a yard equals exactly 0.9144 meter) continue to be used in the United States. Drawings may use either measurement system and still follow ANSI/ASME drawing standards as long as the system of measurement is stated clearly on the drawing. Figures 2.8 and 2.9 show the same part dimensioned with the two different measurement systems.

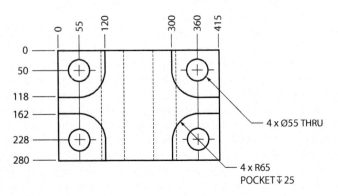

2.8   A Drawing Dimensioned Using Metric Units

The Metric System

Today's metric system is the International System of Units, commonly referred to as SI (from the French name, le Système International d'Unités). It was established in 1960 by international agreement and is now the international standard of measurement, with all countries in the world adopting it, although some continue using traditional U.S. units to a greater or lesser degree.

The meter was established by the French in 1791 as the length of one ten-millionth of the distance from the Earth's equator to the pole along the meridian that, coincidentally, passes through Paris. Since then the definition has been updated to be the distance that light travels in a vacuum in 1/299,792,458 of a second. A meter equals 39.37 inches or approximately 1.1 yards.

The metric system for linear measurement is a decimal system similar to the U.S. system of counting money. For example,

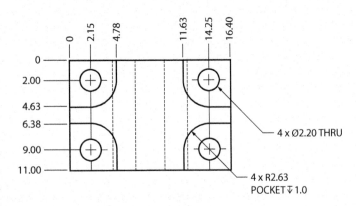

2.9   A Drawing Dimensioned Using U.S. Customary Units

1 mm	=	1 millimeter (1/1000 of a meter)
1 cm	=	1 centimeter (1/100 of a meter)
	=	10 mm
1 dm	=	1 decimeter (1/10 of a meter)
	=	10 cm = 100 mm
1 m	=	1 meter
	=	100 cm = 1000 mm
1 km	=	1 kilometer = 1000 m
	=	100,000 cm = 1,000,000 mm

The primary unit of measurement for engineering drawings and design in the mechanical industries is the millimeter (mm). Secondary units of measure are the meter (m) and the kilometer (km). The centimeter (cm) and the decimeter (dm) are rarely used on drawings.

Some industries have used a dual dimensioning system of millimeters and inches on drawings. However, this practice can

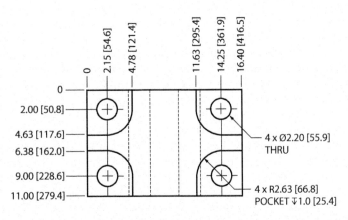

2.10   A Dual-Dimensioned Drawing Using U.S. Customary Units as the Primary Units

be confusing because the sizes displayed in the two systems may contain rounding errors. If two systems are shown, the primary units are used for all manufacturing measurements, and the secondary system units (shown in parentheses or brackets) are for general information purposes only. Figure 2.10 shows a drawing using dual dimensioning. Most large manufacturers use all metric dimensions on the drawing for ease and consistency.

Dimensions that are given in U.S. customary units (inches and feet, either decimal or fractional) can be converted easily to metric values. In standard practice, the ratio 1 in. = 25.4 mm is used. Decimal-equivalents tables can be found inside the back cover, and conversion tables are also given in Appendix 30. Many handy unit conversion sites are also available on the Web at sites such as www.onlineconversion.com.

2.4 DRAWING SCALE

Unlike a computer drawing (where an object is drawn actual size so that the information stored in the computer file is accurate), a printed or paper drawing may represent the object at its actual size (full size) or may be larger or smaller than the object, depending on the size of sheet used. *Drawing scale* is the reduction or enlargement of the drawn object relative to the real object (Figure 2.11).

Scale is stated as a ratio of the number of drawing units to the number of actual units. For example, a machine part may be shown on a sheet at half its actual size, a scale of 1:2; a building may be drawn 1/48 of its size, a scale of 1:48 (or in U.S. customary units, 1/4″ = 1′); a map may be drawn 1/1200 actual size, a scale of 1″ = 100′ or 1:1200; or a printed circuit board may be drawn four times its size, a scale of 4:1.

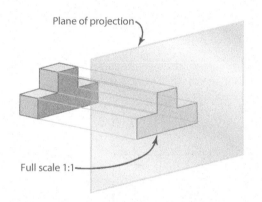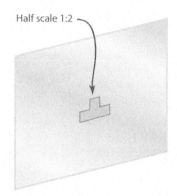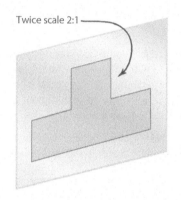

2.11   Reduced and Enlarged Scale. *Many drawings must be shown at reduced scale for the object to fit on the paper.*

2.5 SPECIFYING THE SCALE ON A DRAWING

There are several acceptable methods of noting scale on the drawing, but all of them show the relationship of the size of the object as drawn to the size of the actual object. For a part that is shown on the paper at half its actual size, the scale is listed in one of these three ways:

SCALE: 1:2
SCALE: 1/2
SCALE: .5

For machine drawings, the scale indicates the ratio of the size of the drawn object to its actual size, regardless of the unit of measurement used. Expansion or enlargement scales are given as 2:1, 4:1; 5:1, 10:1, and so on. Figure 2.11 illustrates how the actual object relates to a drawing at half size and how that might be noted in the title block of the drawing. Figure 2.12 shows the scale for a 1 to 24 reduction noted in a title block.

Architectural drawings in the United States typically list the scale based on the number of fractions of an inch on the drawing that represent one foot on the actual object. For example, SCALE: 1/8″ = 1′.

The various scale calibrations available on the metric scale and the engineers' scale provide almost unlimited scale

ratios. Preferred metric scale ratios are 1:1; 1:2; 1:5, 1:10, 1:20, 1:50, 1:100, and 1:200.

Map scales are indicated in terms of proportions such as Scale 1:62500, fractions such as Scale 1/62500, or graphically, such as: 400 0 400 800 Ft

2.12   *List the predominant drawing scale in the title block. (Courtesy of Dynojet Research, Inc.)*

USING A MEASURING SCALE TO LAY OUT A ONE-FIFTIETH SIZE METRIC DRAWING

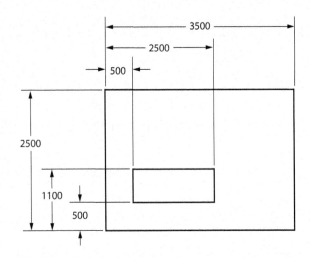

4 Check the length of your scaled line by calculating how many millimeters the length should be, then measuring the line you have drawn with a full-scale metric scale. In this case the 3500-mm length should be 70 mm when shown at 1:50 scale.

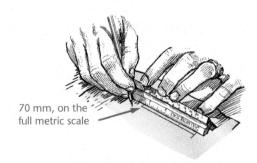

70 mm, on the full metric scale

1 Determine the full-size measurements of the object you will draw. This example will lay out a 3500 × 2500-mm flat plate with a rectangular slot in it. A picture of the part to be drawn with dimensions representing its actual size is shown above.

2 Many measuring scales are available that use standard drawing scales, like this 1:50 ratio metric one.

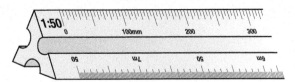

5 Continue to lay out the remaining lengths. Even slight errors in measurements when using a scale may accumulate to produce a significant error, so work carefully.

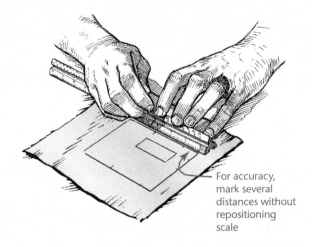

For accuracy, mark several distances without repositioning scale

3 Starting from the 0 end of the 1:50 scale, use a sharp pencil to make a thin, light, short line to mark off the length of the 3500-mm line. To make accurate measurements, be sure to place the scale edge parallel to the line you are measuring on the drawing, and make your dashes at right angles to the scale, at the correct graduation mark, as shown.

To avoid cumulative errors, instead of setting off distances individually by moving the scale to a new position each time, position the scale once and mark all of the distances by adding each successive measurement to the preceding one.

This is useful in dimensioning drawings, too. Keep in mind that providing dimensions from one end to each successive location (say, in the case of building a wall) makes it easier for the worker to lay it out quickly and accurately.

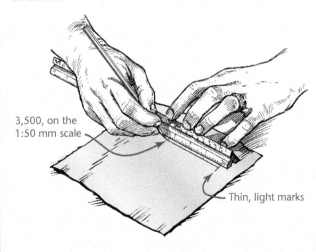

3,500, on the 1:50 mm scale

Thin, light marks

For more about the use of measuring scales, see Appendix 51.

MEASURING WITH WITH AN ARCHITECTS' SCALE

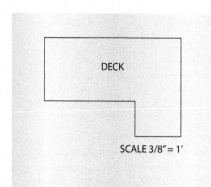

DECK

SCALE 3/8" = 1'

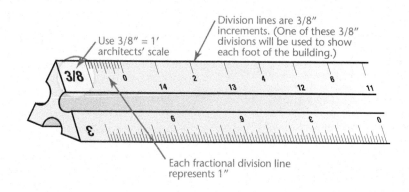

Use 3/8" = 1'
architects' scale

Division lines are 3/8"
increments. (One of these 3/8"
divisions will be used to show
each foot of the building.)

Each fractional division line
represents 1"

STEP by STEP

1 To make measurements with an architects' scale, first determine which scale to use by reading the scale noted in the title block or noted below the view. In the example above, 3/8 inch = 1 foot.

2 Position the scale so that the 0 value is aligned with the left end of the line being measured and note the division mark nearest to the line's right end (in this case, 2).

3 Slide the scale to the right so that the closest whole division you noted in Step 2 lines up with the right end of the line you are measuring.

A fractional portion of the line you are measuring now extends on the left, past the scale's 0 mark.

Counting toward the left, note how many fractional division marks are between zero and the left end of the line. (In this example, there are two.)

Add the fractional value to the whole value that you noted in Step 2. In this example, you noted two whole division lines, plus two fractional division lines, so the length of the line is 2'–2" at actual size.

On architects' scales, there are 12 fractional divisions because there are 12 inches per foot.

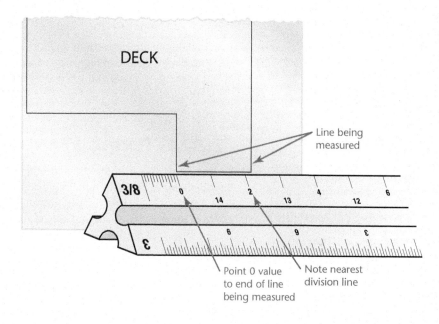

DECK

Line being
measured

Point 0 value
to end of line
being measured

Note nearest
division line

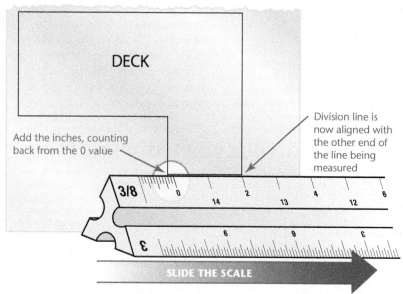

DECK

Add the inches, counting
back from the 0 value

Division line is
now aligned with
the other end of
the line being
measured

SLIDE THE SCALE

For more about the use of measuring scales, see Appendix 51.

A B C D E F G H
a b c d e f g h

Sans serif lettering has no serifs,
or spurs, at the ends of the strokes

A B C D E F G H
a b c d e f g h

Serif letters have serifs and are accented
by thick and thin lineweights

A B C D E F G H
a b c d e f g h

Roman refers to the upright form of letters,
but it was used to mean letters with serifs

A B C D E F G H
a b c d e f g h

Italic letters are slanted,
whether serif or sans serif

2.13   Distinctions Among Letter Forms

AUTOCAD TXT FONT
ROMAN SIMPLEX
ROMAN DUPLEX
BASKERVILLE
TIMES NEW ROMAN
PLAYBILL
ARIAL
LETTER GOTHIC

2.14   Examples of Lettering Using CAD

2.6 LETTERING

Lettered text is often necessary to completely describe an object or to provide detailed specifications. Lettering should be legible, be easy to create, and use styles acceptable for traditional drawing and CAD drawing.

Engineering drawings use single-stroke sans serif letters because they are highly legible and quick to draw. (*Sans serif* means without serifs, or spurs.) The sans serif letters used for drawings are also referred to as Gothic. (Serif letters are sometimes called Roman, but today that term is commonly used for the upright form of the letters.) A *font* is the name for a set of letters with the same style. Figure 2.13 shows the distinctions among **Roman**, *italic*, **serif**, and **sans serif** fonts.

Lettering is a standard feature available in computer graphics programs. With CAD software, you can add titles, notes, and dimensioning information to a drawing. Several fonts and a variety of sizes may be selected. When modifications are required, it is easy to make lettering changes on the drawing by editing existing text.

Freehand lettering ability has little relationship to writing ability. You can learn to letter neatly even if you have terrible handwriting. There are three necessary aspects of learning to letter:

- Knowing the proportions and forms of the letters (to make good letters, you need to have a clear mental image of their correct shape)
- Spacing of letters and words for legibility
- Practice

2.7 LETTERING STANDARDS

Most hand-drawn notes use lettering about 3 mm (1/8″) high. Light horizontal *guidelines* are useful for producing consistent letter heights. CAD notes are set using the keyboard and sized to be in the range of 3 mm (1/8″) tall according to the plotted size of the drawing. Lettering heights vary with the size of the sheet and the intended use of the drawing.

CAD drawings typically use a Gothic (sans serif) lettering style but often use a Roman (serif) style for titles. When adding lettering to a CAD drawing, a good rule of thumb is not to use more than two fonts within the same drawing. See Figure 2.14 for a sample of the fonts available using CAD. You may want to use one font for the titles and a different font for notes and other text. Keep in mind that if you open a drawing created with software such as AutoCAD, you must have the fonts available that were used in the drawing, otherwise the software will have to substitute different fonts. This can be a problem because the horizontal spacing may be different and the text will no longer fit correctly. It may be tempting to use many different fonts in a drawing because of the wide variety available, but this tends to look distracting on the drawing. Drawings that use too many lettering styles and sizes have been jokingly referred to as having a "ransom note" lettering style.

2.8 USING GUIDELINES FOR HAND LETTERING

Use extremely light horizontal *guidelines* to keep letter height uniform, as shown in Figure 2.15. Capital letters are commonly made 3 mm (1/8″) high, with the space between rows of lettering being from three-fifths to full height of the letters. Do not use vertical guidelines to space the distance from one letter to the next within a word or sentence. This should be done by eye while lettering. If necessary, use a vertical guideline at the beginning of a column of hand-lettered text to help you line up the left edges of the following rows. Beginners can also use randomly spaced vertical guidelines to practice maintaining the correct slant.

Vertical guidelines drawn at random

LETTERING IS EASIER
IF YOU REMEMBER TO
USE GUIDELINES

Space between lines usually from 3/5 to total height of letters

2.15   Using Guidelines

2.9 VERTICAL AND INCLINED LETTERS AND NUMERALS

The proportions of *vertical* capital letters and numbers are shown in Figure 2.16. The letter shapes are probably a little wider than your usual writing. Hand lettering and text added to engineering drawings is typically upper case. Lowercase letters are rarely used except for large volumes of notes or when there is some other particular need for it. Lowercase letters are shown in Figure 2.17. The lower part of the letter (or descender) is usually two thirds the height of the capital letter.

Inclined (italic) capital letters and numerals are shown in Figure 2.18. They are similar to vertical lettering, except the slope is about 68° from the horizontal. Although you may practice hand lettering slanted at approximately this angle, it is important in CAD drawings to always set the amount of incline for the letters at the same value within a drawing so that the lettering is consistent. Inclined lowercase letters, shown in Figure 2.19, are rarely used.

Keep in mind that only one style of lettering or font, either vertical or inclined, should be used throughout a drawing.

2.16 Vertical Capital Letters and Numerals

Straight-line letters

Letter I has short bars

W is only letter over 6 units wide. Letters in "TOM Q. VAXY" are 6 units wide—all others are 5, except I and W

Curved-line letters

The letters O, Q, C, G and D are based on a true circle. The lower portion of the J and U is elliptical

Curved-line letters and numerals

The 8 is composed of two ellipses. The 3, S, and 2 are based on the 8

Curved-line letters and numerals

Number 1 is a straight line. The 0, 6, and 9 are elliptical

2.17 Vertical Lowercase Letters

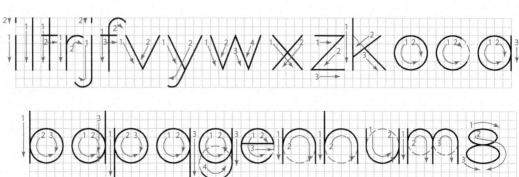

2.18   Inclined Capital Letters and Numerals

Straight-line letters

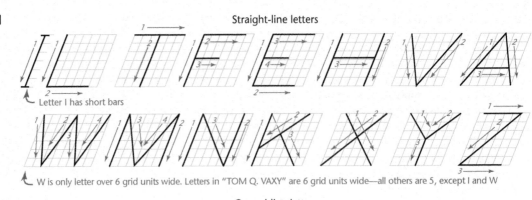

Letter I has short bars

W is only letter over 6 grid units wide. Letters in "TOM Q. VAXY" are 6 grid units wide—all others are 5, except I and W

Curved-line letters

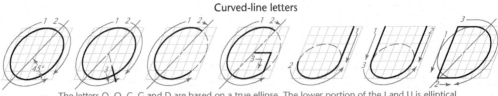

The letters O, Q, C, G and D are based on a true ellipse. The lower portion of the J and U is elliptical

Curved-line letters and numerals

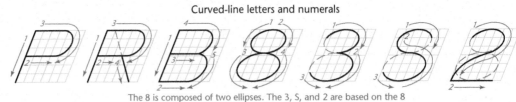

The 8 is composed of two ellipses. The 3, S, and 2 are based on the 8

Curved-line letters and numerals

Number 1 is a straight line. The 0, 6, and 9 are elliptical

2.19   Inclined Lowercase Letters

TIP

For Even Freehand Letters

- Use 1/8" gridded paper for drawing to make lettering easy.
- Use a scale and set off a series of spaces, making both the letters and the spaces between lines of letters 1/8" high.
- Use a guideline template like the Berol Rapidesign 925 shown in Figure 2.20.
- For whole numbers and fractions, draw five equally spaced guidelines.

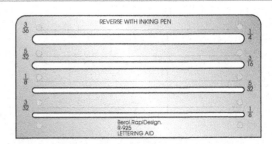

2.20   *The Berol Rapidesign 925 template is used to create guidelines quickly for lettering.*

2.10 FRACTIONS

Fractions are shown twice the height of the corresponding whole numbers. Make the numerator and the denominator each about three-fourths as high as the whole number to allow enough space between them and the fraction bar. For dimensioning, the most commonly used height for whole numbers is 3 mm (1/8″), and for fractions 6 mm (1/4″), as shown in Figure 2.21.

- Never let numerals touch the fraction bar.
- Center the denominator under the numerator.
- Avoid using an inclined fraction bar, except when lettering in a narrow space, as in a parts list.
- Make the fraction bar slightly longer than the widest part of the fraction.

Dimensioning in fractions is still used in the US, but even there it is less and less common. Calculating with fractions often takes manufacturing workers extra time and errors are common. Much of the numerically-controlled manufacturing for cabinets and countertops uses millimeters as the default units, even in the United States.

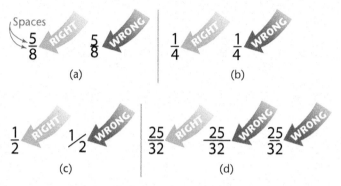

2.21   Common Errors in Lettering Fractions

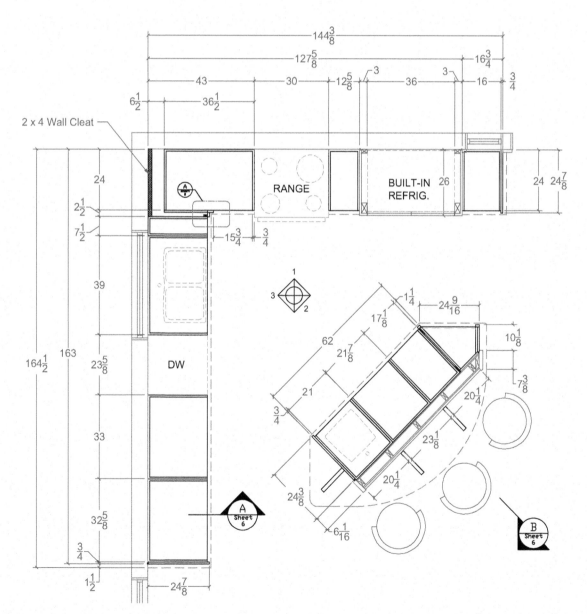

2.22   Custom Cabinetry Dimensioned in Fractional Inches *(Courtesy of Centermark Industries, Inc.)*

2.11 SPACING OF LETTERS AND WORDS

Spacing between Letters

Uniform spacing between letters is done by eye. Contrary to what might seem logical, putting equal distances from letter to letter causes them to appear unequally spaced. The background areas between letters, not the distances between them, should be approximately equal to get results that appear balanced. Figure 2.23 illustrates how using equal spacing from one letter to the next does not actually appear equal. Space your lettering so that background areas appear equal, like the example shown in the bottom half of the figure.

Some combinations, such as LT and VA, may have to be slightly closer than other letters to look correctly spaced. In some cases, the width of a letter may be decreased slightly. For example, the lower stroke of the L may be shortened when followed by A. In typesetting, pairs of letters that need to be spaced more closely to appear correctly are called ***kerned pairs.***

Spacing between Words

Space letters closely within words to make each word a compact unit, but space words well enough apart to clearly separate them from adjacent words. For both uppercase and lowercase lettering, make spaces between words approximately equal to a capital O.

Spacing between Rows

Be sure to leave space between rows of lettering, usually equal to the letter height. Rows spaced too closely are hard to read. Rows spaced too far apart do not appear to be related.

LATHING

literate

If equal spacing is used from one letter to another, spacing does not actually appear equal, as in this example

LATHING

literate

Space your lettering so that background areas appear equal, as in this example

2.23 Visually Balancing Letter Spacing

— TIP —

Creating Letters that Appear Stable

Certain letters and numerals appear top-heavy when they are drawn with equal upper and lower portions as in the example below.

To correct this, reduce the size of the upper portion to give a balanced appearance, as in the example below.

If you put the central horizontal strokes of the letters B, E, F, and H at midheight, they will appear to be below center.

To overcome this optical illusion, draw the strokes for B, E, F, and H slightly above the center as you letter, keeping letters uniform, as in the second example below.

CGBEKSXZ

CGBEKSXZ

The same practice applies to numerals. In the illustrations below, the example at left looks top-heavy. Note how the example at right looks more balanced.

3852   3852

A good example of uniform lettering — RELATIVELY

These examples show what not to do

Nonuniform style — Relatively

Nonuniform letter height — RELATIVELY / RELATIVELY

Nonuniform angle — RELATIVELY / *RELATIVELY*

Nonuniform stroke thickness — RELATIVELY / RELATIVELY

Nonuniform letter spacing — RELATIVELY

Nonuniform word spacing — NOW IS THE TIME FOR EVERY GOOD PERSON TO COME TO THE AID OF HIS OR HER COUNTRY

2.12 LETTERING FOR TITLES

In most cases, the title and related information are lettered in title boxes or title strips as shown in Figure 2.24. The main drawing title is usually centered in a rectangular space, which is easy to do using CAD.

In any kind of title, give the most important words prominence by making the lettering larger, heavier, or both. Other data, such as scale and date, can be smaller. One technique for centering words in the title block when hand lettering is to roughly letter the words on a scrap of paper, slide it in the available space, and make a light mark to indicate where to begin lettering the title (Figure 2.25).

Figure 2.26 shows examples of freehand lettering at actual size.

TOOL GRINDING MACHINE
TOOL REST SLIDE
SCALE : FULL SIZE
AMERICAN MACHINE COMPANY
NEW YORK CITY

DRAWN BY ____ CHECKED BY ____

2.24   Balanced Machine-Drawing Title

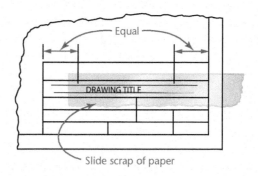

2.25   Centering Title in Title Box

THE IMPORTANCE OF GOOD LETTERING CANNOT BE
OVEREMPHASIZED. THE LETTERING CAN MAKE OR
BREAK AN OTHERWISE GOOD DRAWING.

PENCIL LETTERING SHOULD BE DONE WITH A FAIRLY
SOFT SHARP PENCIL AND SHOULD BE CLEAN-CUT
AND DARK. ACCENT THE ENDS OF THE STROKES.

2.26   Pencil Lettering (Full Size)

--- TIP ---

Lettering with a Pencil

- Because practically all pencil lettering will be reproduced, the letters should be dense black, not gray or blurred. Use a sharp, soft pencil, such as an F, H, or HB to make lettering dark and sharp.
- If you like using wooden pencils, sharpen them to a needle point, then dull the point very slightly.
- Don't worry about making the exact letter strokes unless you find it difficult to make the letters look right, but do use them as a reference if you are having trouble drawing uniform, symmetrical letters.
- Use extremely light, 1/8" (3 mm) horizontal guidelines to regulate the height of letters. A few light vertical or inclined lines randomly placed help you visually keep the letters uniformly vertical or inclined.

- Draw vertical strokes downward with a finger movement.
- Draw horizontal strokes from left to right with a wrist movement and without turning the paper.
- Draw curved strokes and inclined strokes with a downward motion.

Left-handers: Traditional lettering strokes were designed for right-handed people. Experiment with each letter to develop a system of strokes that works best for you.

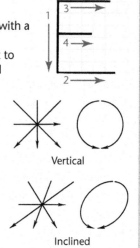

Vertical

Inclined

2.13 DRAWING PENCILS

High-quality drawing pencils help produce good-quality technical sketches and drawings. Use light lines for construction lines, lettering guidelines, and precise layout work. Use dark, dense black lines for the final lines, lettering, and arrowheads. Drawings are often reproduced, and the lines need to be dark for the copies to turn out well.

Drawing pencils are made of graphite with a polymer binder or clay binder. They are divided into 18 grades from 9H (the hardest) to 7B (the softest) as shown in Figure 2.27. Specially formulated leads of carbon black particles in a polymer binder are also available in several grades for use on polyester film (Mylar).

Hard leads are used where accuracy is required, such as on graphical computations and charts and diagrams. For other uses, their lines are apt to be too light.

Medium leads are used for general-purpose technical drawing, such as sketching, lettering, arrowheads, and other freehand work on mechanical drawings.

Soft leads are not useful in technical drawing. They make smudged, rough lines that are hard to erase, and the lead dulls quickly. These grades are generally used for artistic drawing.

Which grade of pencil works best for you depends on your hand pressure, the humidity, and the type of paper you are using, among other things. For light lines, use a hard lead in the range of 4H to 6H. For dark lines, use a softer lead in the range of 2H to B.

Mechanical pencils are available with 0.3-, 0.5-, 0.7-, or 0.9-mm-diameter drafting leads in several grades (Figure 2.28). Their thin leads produce uniform-width lines without sharpening. The .5-mm lead is a good general size, or you can use a .7-mm lead for thick lines and .3 mm for thin lines.

9H 8H 7H 6H 5H 4H   3H 2H H F HB B   2B 3B 4B 5B 6B 7B

Hard
The hard leads in this group (left) are used where extreme accuracy is required, as on graphical computations and charts and diagrams. The softer leads in this group (right) are sometimes used for line work on engineering drawings, but their use is limited because the lines are apt to be too light.

Medium
These grades are for general-purpose work in technical drawing. The softer grades (right) are used for technical sketching, lettering, arrowheads, and other freehand work on mechanical drawings. The harder leads (left) are used for line work on machine drawings and architectural drawings. The H and 2H leads are widely used on pencil tracings for reproduction.

Soft
These leads are too soft to be useful in mechanical drafting. They tend to produce smudged, rough lines that are hard to erase, and the lead must be sharpened continually. These grades are used for artwork of various kinds, and for full-size details in architectural drawing.

2.27   Lead Grade Chart

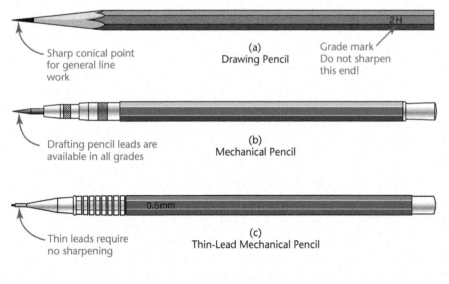

Sharp conical point for general line work

(a)
Drawing Pencil

Grade mark
Do not sharpen this end!

Drafting pencil leads are available in all grades

(b)
Mechanical Pencil

Thin leads require no sharpening

(c)
Thin-Lead Mechanical Pencil

2.28   Drawing Pencils

--- TIP ---

You might be surprised how much your drawings benefit from finding a style of pencil that suits your use. Soft pencils, such as HB or F, are mainly used in freehand sketching. Choose a pencil that:

- Is soft enough to produce clear black lines, but hard enough not to smudge too easily.
- Is not so soft that the point breaks easily.
- Feels comfortable in your hand.
- Grips the lead without slipping.

Be aware that some lead holders require special sharpeners.

You can sometimes tell the difference in hardness of a mechanical pencil lead just by looking at it. Smaller-diameter leads are used for the harder grades, and larger-diameter leads are used to give more strength to the softer grades.

Plain wooden pencils work great. They are inexpensive, and it is easy to produce thick or thin lines by varying the amount that you sharpen them. An old trick to keep the lead sharp longer is to turn the pencil frequently as you work to wear it down evenly.

Gum erasers and nylon erasers work well to pick up smudges without leaving much eraser dust.

Nylon eraser strips that come in refillable holders like mechanical pencils can be convenient for areas that require some precision. A trick for erasing fine details is to sharpen the end of the eraser strip in a small handheld pencil sharpener.

2.14 TEMPLATES

Templates are available for a great variety of specialized needs (Figure 2.29). Templates may be found for drawing almost any ordinary drafting symbol or repetitive feature.

2.15 CAD TOOLS

Most people who create technical drawings use CAD. Advantages include accuracy, speed, and the ability to present spatial and visual information in a variety of ways.

However, these advantages do not eliminate the need for drawings to be easily and accurately interpreted. CAD drawings use the same general concepts and follow the same drafting standards as drawings created by hand.

Most CAD drawings are plotted on standard sheet sizes and to similar scales as hand drawings. Both CAD and hand drawings should contrast thick lines for objects with thin lines for hidden, center, and dimension lines to make the printed drawing easy to read.

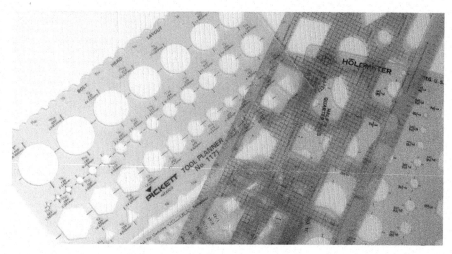

2.29 Drawing Templates

CAD drawings should use correct line patterns. Likewise, lettering on CAD drawings should follow these same general guidelines as for hand drawings.

One benefit of CAD is the ability to draw perfectly straight uniform lines and other geometric elements. Another is the ability to quickly represent the various styles of lines (Figure 2.30). Making changes to a CAD drawing takes about a tenth the time that it takes

to edit a drawing by hand. Using CAD, you can quickly plot drawings to different scales.

Keeping CAD drawing files organized, backing up data regularly, and following conventions for naming files so that you can find them again are important considerations. Even skilled CAD users use freehand sketching, to quickly get ideas down on paper and to show their ideas on a whiteboard.

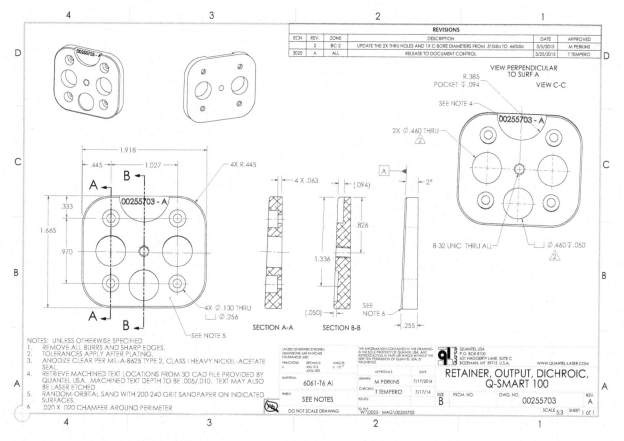

2.30 A Drawing Created Using CAD (Courtesy of Mark Perkins.)

MODEL SPACE AND PAPER SPACE IN AUTOCAD

Using CAD, you can make an accurate model of the device or structure. To do this, you create the object at the actual size that it exists in the real world, using whatever system of measurement that you would use when constructing it.

On paper it is a different matter. You would have to have some really large sheets to print your building full size. AutoCAD software uses the concept of two "spaces," model space and paper space, to describe how to transform the full-size CAD model to proportionate views that fit your sheet of paper.

Understanding scale as it relates to paper drawings or as it relates to creating layouts from a CAD drawing is an important concept for technical drawing because the ultimate goal is for drawings to be interpreted and used in the real world. Therefore, they must be easy to print and read.

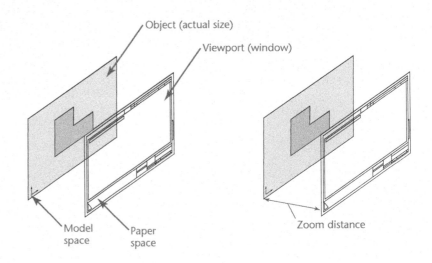

(A) In AutoCAD, paper space allows you to see how various views of the full-size model can be shown on a sheet of paper.

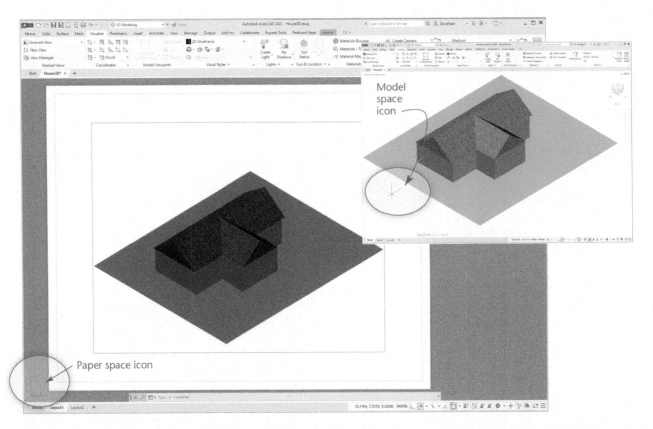

(B) The window at left shows a paper space representation of the full-size CAD model in the smaller window at top right. Note that AutoCAD uses icons to help users differentiate the two "spaces." (Autodesk screen shots reprinted courtesy of Autodesk, Inc.)

2.16 SKETCHING AND DRAWING MEDIA

Many choices of *media* (paper and other) are available for particular sketching or drawing purposes. Whether you are sketching or are plotting a drawing from a CAD workstation, choose the type of sheet and size that suits your needs.

Small notebooks or sketch pads are useful when working at a site or when it is necessary to quickly record information. Many companies require bound notebooks of graph paper for recording engineering design notes so they are preserved for patent and documentation purposes. Graph paper can be helpful in making neat sketches like the one in Figure 2.31. Paper with 4, 5, 8, or 10 squares per inch is convenient for maintaining proportions.

A sketch pad of plain paper with a master grid sheet showing through underneath works well as a substitute for grid paper. You can create your own master grid sheets using CAD. Specially ruled isometric paper is available for isometric sketching, or you can use CAD to create masters.

The best drawing papers have up to 100% pure rag stock. Their strong fibers hold up well to erasing and folding, and they will not discolor or grow brittle with age. Good drafting paper should have a fine grain (or tooth) to pick up the graphite and produce clean, dense black lines. Paper that is too rough produces ragged, grainy lines, is harder to erase, and wears down pencils quickly. Look for paper that has a hard surface that will not groove too easily under pencil pressure.

Polyester film is a high-quality drafting material available in rolls and standard sized sheets. It is made by bonding a matte surface to one or both sides of a clear polyester sheet. Its transparency and printing qualities are good and it provides an

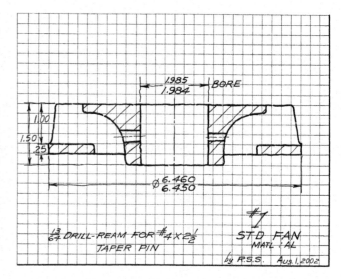

2.31   Sketch on Graph Paper

excellent matte drawing surface for pencil or ink. It is easy to erase without leaving ghost marks, and it has high dimensional stability. Its resistance to cracking, bending, and tearing makes it very durable. Many companies still plot their drawings in ink on polyester film for long-term storage and reproduction.

Even large coated sheets of aluminum (which provides a good dimensional stability) have been used in the aircraft and auto industry for full-scale layouts that were scribed into the coating with a steel point rather than a pencil.

2.17 STANDARD SHEETS

There are ANSI/ASME standards for international and U.S. *sheet sizes.* Table 2.2 describes the height and width of these standard sheets, the letters used to refer to them, and their margins and zones. Note that drawing sheet size is given as height × width. Most standard sheets use what is called a "landscape" orientation.

The use of the basic sheet size, 8.5″ × 11.0″ or 210 mm × 297 mm, and its multiples permits filing folded prints in standard files with or without correspondence. These sizes can be cut from standard rolls of media.

Table 2.2 Sheet Sizes

Nearest International Size (mm)	International Number of Zones	International Margin	Standard U.S. Size (in.)	U.S. Number of Zones (width)	U.S. Margin (in.)
A4 210 × 297	6	10	A* 8.5 × 11.0	2 (optional)	.50
A3 297 × 420	6	10	B 11.0 × 17.0	2 (optional)	.50
A2 420 × 594	8	10	C 17.0 × 22.0	4	.50
A1 594 × 841	12	20	D 22.0 × 34.0	4	.50
A0 841 × 1189	16	20	E 34.0 × 44.0	8	.50

* May also be used as a vertical sheet size at 11″ tall by 8.5″ wide.

2.18 STANDARD LAYOUT ELEMENTS

Margins and Borders

Each layout begins with a border drawn inside the sheet margin. Drawings in the U.S. use a .50″ margin. Refer to Table 2.2 for international sheet sizes and margins. Some companies use slightly larger sheets to allow drawings to be bound into a set. This extra allowance should be added on to the standard sheet size so that the drawing border meets the size standards (see Figure 2.32). Figure 2.33 shows the alternative orientation of an A size drawing.

Zones

You have probably seen *zone numbers* on maps, where the margin is subdivided by letters along one side and by numbers along the other. These are also used along the outer edges of technical drawings so that you can refer to items by the area on the sheet where they are located. This is particularly useful when a client calls with a question. You can use zone numbers to make sure you are talking about the same item. Zone numbers are also useful for locating revisions. You should provide zone numbers on all sheets larger than size B.

Typical Letter Sizes

Most lettering on drawings should be at least 3 mm or .12″ (about 1/8″) tall. Lettering is typically sized as follows:

> Drawing Title, Drawing Size
>   6 mm (.24″)
> DAI
>   6 mm (.24″)
> Drawing Number, Revision Letter
>   6 mm (.24″)
> Section and View Letters
>   6 mm (.24″)
> Zone Letters and Numbers
>   6 mm (.24″)
> Drawing Block Headings
>   2.5 mm (.10″)
> All Others
>   3 mm (.12″)

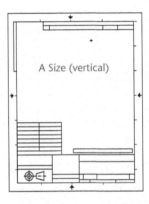

2.33 Vertical Orientation of A Size

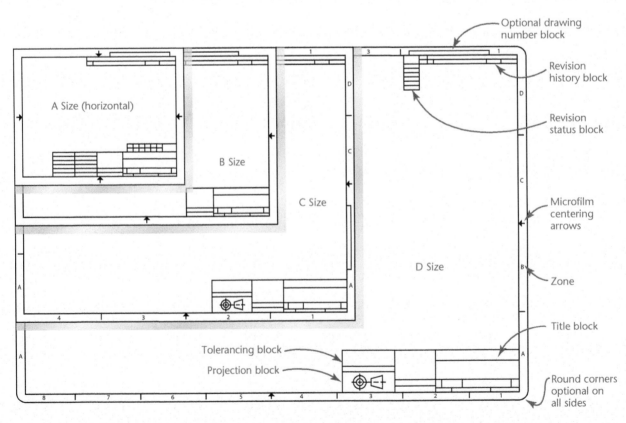

2.32 Typical Sheet Sizes and Borders (*See Table 2.2 for E-size and international standard sizes.*)

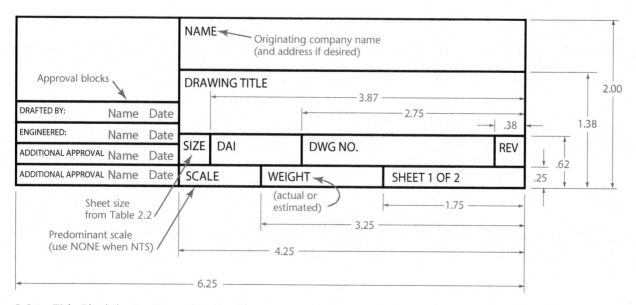

2.34 Title Block for A-, B-, and C-Size Sheets

Title Block

The title block is located in the lower right corner of the format. Refer to Figure 2.34 for dimensions for a typical title block for A-, B-, and C-size sheets.* Standard areas in the title block provide the following information.

Name Show the name of the originating company or business (and address if desired).

Drawing Title Briefly describe the item using a singular noun or noun phrase and modifiers if necessary to distinguish it from similar items. Do not use the terms "for" or "or" in the title. For example, "Dust Cap" would be preferred over "Cap or Cover for Dust Protection," which is too wordy.

Drawing Number Give each drawing a unique number, using the company's numbering system.

Sheet Revision Block Track the drawing version using the number of the revision. The original release of the drawing typically shows revision 0.

Approval Block List the name(s) of the person(s) approving the drawing and the date it was approved. Additional areas of this block can be used for various design activities, if separate approval is required. For example, a company may use separate areas for structural design or manufacturing engineering approvals (Figure 2.35). Specify the dates numerically using a year-month-day format. For example, June 10, 1989, would be any of the following 1989-06-10, 19890610, or 1989/06/10. This is particularly helpful as items are easily sorted into date order by computer algorithms. It also avoids the ambiguity caused by some countries showing month before day, and others using the day, month, year format.

Scale List the predominant scale for the drawing. Drawings may include details at other scales, which should be noted below the detail. If the drawing is not made to a particular scale, note NONE in the scale area.

Drawing Size List the sheet size used for the drawing. This helps track the original size when the drawing is reproduced at a smaller size.

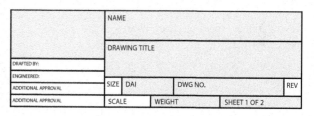

2.35 Approval Block, Scale, Revision, and Drawing Size

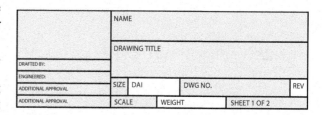

2.36 DAI and Weight May Be Listed

Sheet Number List the number of the sheet in the set, using whole numbers starting at 1. A format that lists this sheet out of the total number helps keep track of the entire set, for example, 1 OF 2.

DAI List the Design Activity Identification in this area when it is required. This block may be left blank or the block removed if it is not needed. Examples of DAI include: design activity name, activity name and address, and Commercial and Government Entity (CAGE) codes if applicable. CAGE codes are numbers assigned to entities that manufacture items for the government, based on the DAI.

Weight List the actual or estimated weight of the part if required (Figure 2.36).

*For more formats, title blocks, revision blocks, and materials blocks, see inside the front cover of this book.

2.19 LAYOUTS

A particular size sheet with a drawing border is called a *layout.* Using a CAD system, you may often be able to select from standard layouts or templates that set the sheet size limits, the border, and even the title block as the starting point for your drawing. Regardless of whether you draw by hand or use CAD or 3D modeling methods, you need to plan your sheet so that the information will fit and show clearly.

When you are sketching, your layout may be a simple border and title strip along the bottom of the sheet (or you may be using preprinted tablets that have space to record the sketch title, date, and other pertinent data).

When creating a 2D CAD drawing, you may use a drawing template showing the sheet and border and title block, perhaps using different templates or even software interface settings for different types of drawings, such as mechanical/manufacturing, architectural, or civil.

When creating a 2D drawing from a 3D solid model, you may use a layout space that contains different viewports that allow you to show different views of the same 3D model with a border and title block.

2.20 PLANNING YOUR DRAWING OR SKETCH

When laying out a drawing sheet, you will need to consider:

- the size and scale of the object you will show;
- the sheet size;
- the measurement system (units) for the drawing; and
- the space necessary for standard notes and title block.

The object you are drawing is the "star" of the sketch. Keep the object near the center of the sheet. It should be boldly drawn, using thick visible lines. Make it large enough to fill most of the sheet and so that details show clearly (Figure 2.37).

Show Details Clearly

Show small objects larger than their actual size to represent the details clearly. If the details are too small, switch to a larger sheet size and use a larger scale.

You can also add details at a larger scale if necessary to show features that are smaller than the typical features of the drawing. If you add details at a different scale, label the view, for example, DETAIL A, and note the scale for the detail below it.

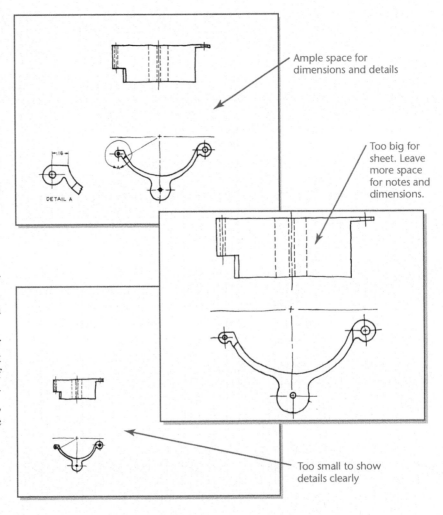

Ample space for dimensions and details

Too big for sheet. Leave more space for notes and dimensions.

Too small to show details clearly

2.37 *Show details clearly by selecting the appropriate scale and sheet size.*

SHEET LAYOUT

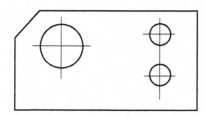

Given drawing

1 To draw the part shown in the given figure, select the sheet size, keeping in mind the size of the objects. Show the part large enough to represent features clearly. Use larger sheets for larger or more detailed objects. (8.5″ × 11″ will be large enough for the part shown.) Add the border and title block to the sheet using the margin sizes specified in the standards. Refer to Table 2.2.

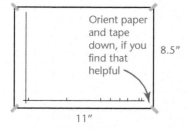

Orient paper and tape down, if you find that helpful

8.5″

11″

2 Determine the units for the drawing. Will it be metric or U.S. Customary (inches, feet and inches)? What system will be used to construct, manufacture, and inspect the actual object? Use that system of measurement for the drawing. This part is in inches.

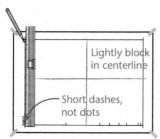

Lightly block in centerline

Short dashes, not dots

Before you begin drawing, determine the scale at which the object will best fit on the sheet.

First, figure the available space within the drawing border. For example, the horizontal 8.5″ × 11″ sheet with a .5″ margin leaves 7.5″ × 10″. If you subtract space for a .375″ title strip across the bottom, it leaves 7.125″ × 10″ for the drawing.

Now, consider the size of the object. Will it fit on the sheet at full size? Half size? Do you need to enlarge it to show small features larger than actual size? The 12″ gasket shown in the example will fit well at half size on the 8.5″ × 11″ sheet and still show the details clearly. Use typical scales when possible. Refer to Section 2.5.

Approximately center the object on the sheet. To do this, subtract the size of the scaled drawing from the available sheet space and use half of the difference on each side of the object.

3 One quick technique is to find the center of the available space and lay out the drawing on each side of that centerline. Using CAD, you can easily move the drawing to the center of the sheet visually.

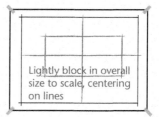

Lightly block in overall size to scale, centering on lines

Sketches do not have to be perfectly centered, but plan ahead so the drawing isn't crammed in one corner of the sheet. Let your drawing be the "star" of the page. Remember to leave enough space around your drawing for notes and dimensions. If you don't, you will run out of room and your layout will look crowded.

4 Lightly add details of the drawing.

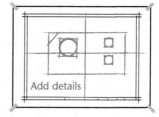

Add details

5 Darken final drawing lines.

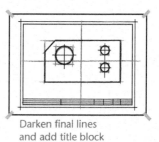

Darken final lines and add title block

TIP
Scale When Using CAD

Keep in mind that when using CAD you will create the object the size that it actually exists in real life. On the plotted sheet, when showing the drawing to scale, it is easy to try a few different scales and see which fits. You can always change the scale later if needed.

STEP by STEP

SCALING ANNOTATIONS AUTOMATICALLY USING AUTOCAD

You might think that displaying text in a CAD drawing is one of the easiest things to do. You can quickly type in the text you want to display and select the font, height, slant, and rotation angle. That part is easy, but annotations are useless if nobody can read them.

When you create drawings that will be plotted on different sized sheets or at different scales, sizing the text can require a lot of planning. Take the architectural plan drawing shown in Figure A for example. When plotted to scale 1/2″ = 1′, the text showing dimensions is clearly visible. But when shown at one tenth of that size, scale 1/2″ = 10′, that same text becomes illegible.

The ability to reuse the same CAD data at different scales without having to recreate the drawing is one of its big advantages over pen and paper drawings. Yet, cumbersome workarounds were once necessary to make legible text at different scales. One workaround was to have several different sizes of the same text, which the user would turn on or off depending on what drawing scale was used.

Now, AutoCAD software provides a feature called annotation scaling. Here is how it works: Drawing objects that are commonly used to annotate drawings (provide text information) can have their annotation property turned on. This allows you to create one annotative object that displays at different sizes, based on scale properties.

In the AutoCAD software, object types that can have annotative object properties include text, mtext, dimensions, hatches, tolerances, multileaders, leaders, blocks, and attributes.

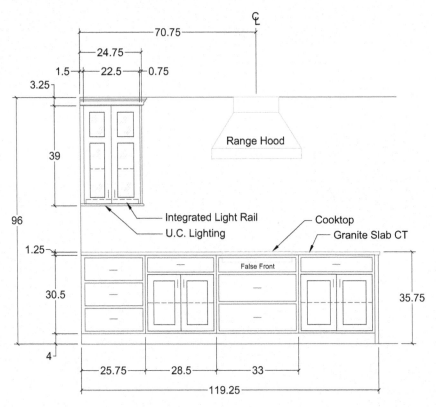

(A) *When plotted to a scale of 1/2″ = 1′ on an 11″ × 8.5″ sheet, the text showing the dimensions is clearly visible. (Courtesy of Centermark Industries, Inc.)*

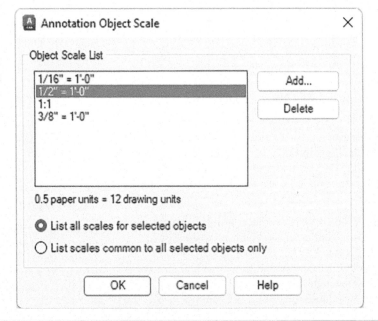

(B) *The annotation scaling feature of AutoCAD software allows annotative text to be made legible at various scales. (Autodesk screen shots reprinted courtesy of Autodesk, Inc.)*

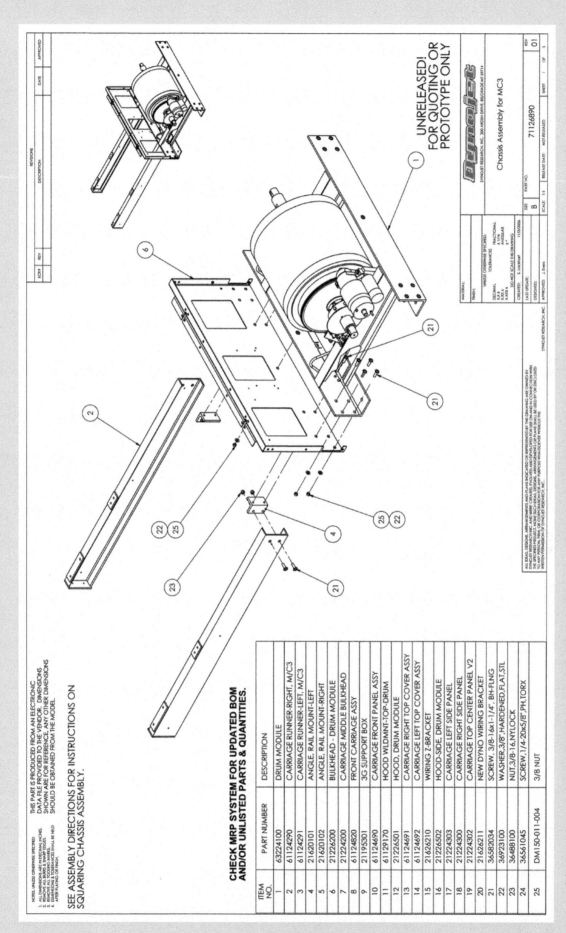

Assembly Drawing. An assembly drawing showing a revision block and a standard title block. (Courtesy of Dynojet Research, Inc.)

PORTFOLIO

MODEL UNLESS OTHERWISE SPECIFIED:

1. ALL DIMENSIONS ARE IN DECIMAL INCHES.
2. REMOVE ALL BURRS & SHARP EDGES.
3. REMOVE ALL TOOLING MARKS.
4. DIMENSIONS & TOLERANCES SHALL BE HELD AFTER PLATING OR FINISH.

THIS PART IS PRODUCED FROM AN ELECTRONIC DATA FILE PROVIDED TO THE VENDOR. DIMENSIONS SHOWN ARE FOR REFERENCE. ANY OTHER DIMENSIONS SHOULD BE OBTAINED FROM THE MODEL.

SEE ASSEMBLY DIRECTIONS FOR INSTRUCTIONS ON SQUARING CHASSIS ASSEMBLY.

CHECK MRP SYSTEM FOR UPDATED BOM AND/OR UNLISTED PARTS & QUANTITIES.

ITEM NO.	PART NUMBER	DESCRIPTION
1	63224100	DRUM MODULE
2	61124290	CARRIAGE RUNNER-RIGHT, M/C3
3	61124291	CARRIAGE RUNNER-LEFT, M/C3
4	21620101	ANGLE, RAIL MOUNT-LEFT
5	21620102	ANGLE, RAIL MOUNT-RIGHT
6	21226200	BULKHEAD - DRUM MODULE
7	21224200	CARRIAGE MIDDLE BULKHEAD
8	61124820	FRONT CARRIAGE ASSY
9	21195301	3G SUPPORT BOX
10	61124690	CARRIAGE FRONT PANEL ASSY
11	61129170	HOOD WLDMNT-TOP-DRUM
12	21226501	HOOD, DRUM MODULE
13	61124691	CARRIAGE RIGHT TOP COVER ASSY
14	61124692	CARRIAGE LEFT TOP COVER ASSY
15	21626210	WIRING Z-BRACKET
16	21226502	HOOD-SIDE, DRUM MODULE
17	21224303	CARRIAGE LEFT SIDE PANEL
18	21224300	CARRIAGE RIGHT SIDE PANEL
19	21224302	CARRIAGE TOP CENTER PANEL V2
20	21626211	NEW DYNO WIRING BRACKET
21	36582034	SCREW, 3/8-16x1-1/4", BH-FLNG
22	36923100	WASHER,3/8",HARDENED,FLAT,STL
23	36488100	NUT,3/8-16,NYLOCK
24	36561045	SCREW,1/4-20x5/8",PH,TORX
25	DM150-011-004	3/8 NUT

REVISIONS

ECR#	REV	DESCRIPTION	DATE	APPROVED

UNRELEASED!
FOR QUOTING OR
PROTOTYPE ONLY

Dynojet

DYNOJET RESEARCH, INC. 200 ARDEN DRIVE, BELGRADE MT 59714

Chassis Assembly for MC3

MATERIAL:		
FINISH:		

UNLESS OTHERWISE SPECIFIED
TOLERANCES
DECIMAL   FRACTIONAL
X.X ±   ± 1/16
X.XX ±   ANGULAR
X.XXX ±   ±

DO NOT SCALE THIS DRAWING.

CREATED: S. Lockhart   11/20/2006

SIZE B	PART NO. 71126890	REV 01
SCALE: 1:4		SHEET 1 OF 3

LAST UPDATE:
DESIGNED:
RELEASE DATE: NOT RELEASED
APPROVED: J. Evers

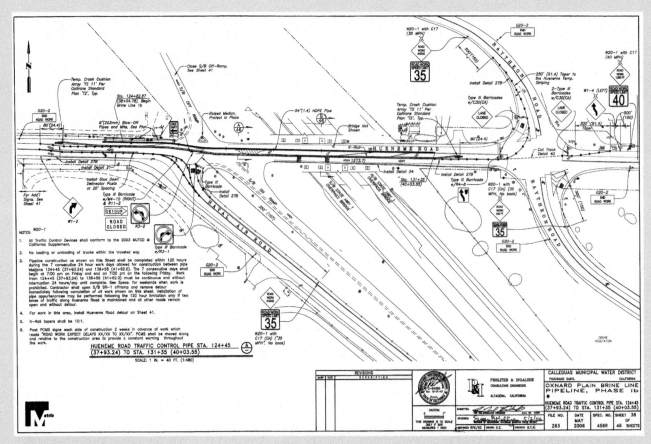

A Civil Drawing. *The drawing shows approval blocks and engineers' stamp. (Courtesy of Perliter and Ingalsbe Consulting Engineers and Calleguas Municipal Water District.)*

PORTFOLIO

WINDOW SCHEDULE					
MK	MANUFACTURER / LINE	TYPE	UNIT SIZE / MODEL #	R.O.	NOTES
A	PITTSBURG CORNING "LIGHTWISE"	GLASS BLOCK	32X80	33 3/16" X 79 7/8"	8X8 GLASS BLOCK PANEL W/ WHITE VINYL FRAME PATTERN TO BE DETERMINED
B1	SUMMIT VINYL	AWNING	24X24	24" X 24"	PROVIDE AUTOMATIC OPENERS FOR CLERESTORY WINDOWS
B2	SUMMIT VINYL	PICTURE	24X24	24" X 24"	
C	PITTSBURG CORNING "LIGHTWISE"	GLASS BLOCK	24X24	25 3/8" X 25 3/8"	8X8 GLASS BLOCK PANEL W/ WHITE VINYL FRAME PATTERN TO BE DETERMINED
D	KOLBE & KOLBE "TILT N TU..."	SPECIALTY	48X64	48 1/2" X 54 1/2"	WOOD/ CLAD EXTERIOR
E	SUMMIT VINYL				
F	PITTSBURG "LIGHTWISE"				
	PITTSBURG "LIGHTWISE"				

DOOR SCHEDULE							
MK	SIZE	DOOR TYPE	MANUFACTURER / LINE	STYLE	MATERIAL	SPECIAL HARDWARE	NOTE
1	10070	OVERHEAD DOOR		FLUSH PANEL		AUTOMATIC OPENER	(4) WINDOWS IN UPPER PANEL
2	3068	EXTERIOR DOOR	SOUTHWEST DOOR/ CLASSIC	18 LITE	ALDER		FINISH & TEXTURE TO BE DETERM...
3	6080	EXTERIOR DOUBLE FRENCH DOORS	WEATHERSHIELD / PROSHIELD	SINGLE PANE	VINYL		WHITE FRAME, TEMPERED GLASS
4	5068	EXTERIOR DOUBLE FRENCH DOORS	WEATHERSHIELD / PROSHIELD	SINGLE PANE	VINYL		WHITE FRAME, TEMPERED GLASS
5	2668	INTERIOR DOOR		SINGLE PANE			TEMPERED GLASS
6	2468	POCKET DOOR		FLUSH HOLLOW CORE	WOOD		FINISH TO BE DETERMINED
7	2468	POCKET DOOR		FLUSH HOLLOW CORE	WOOD		FINISH TO BE DETERMINED

Window and door schedules are used in architectural drawings to specify the type of window or door, rough opening size, manufacturer, and other information. (Courtesy of Frog Rock Design, LLP.)

KEY WORDS

Approval Block
Architects' Scale
Construction Lines
Decimal Inch
Decimal-Inch Scale
Drawing Lines
Drawing Number
Drawing Scale
Drawing Size
Drawing Title
Engineers' Scale
Font
Freehand Line
Guidelines
Inclined
Italic
Kerned Pairs
Layout
Lettering
Measurement Systems
Mechanical Engineers' Scale
Media
Multiview Projection
Name
Oblique Projection
Orthographic Projections
Parallel Projections
Perspective Projections
Piercing Points
Plane of Projection
Projectors
Roman
Sans Serif
Scale
Scales
Serif
Sheet Number
Sheet Revision Block
Sheet Sizes
Station Point
Thick Lines
Thin Lines
Title Blocks
Vertical
Weight
Zone Numbers

CHAPTER SUMMARY

Now that you have completed this chapter you should be able to:

- Understand the basic principles of projection used in drawings.
- Demonstrate the lineweights (thickness) and types (dashed or solid) of lines used in the alphabet of lines that specify meaning in technical drawings.
- List the two main systems of measurement used on drawings.
- Use different types of scales to make measurements.
- Note the scale for a drawing in the title block. Paper drawings are scaled before they are drawn. CAD drawings are scaled when they are to be printed.
- List the advantages of several different drawing media and the qualities that distinguish them.
- Add legible and quick notes and dimensions to sketches using uppercase letters drawn by hand.
- Lay out a sheet and fill in the information in the title block using standard letter shapes.

REVIEW QUESTIONS

1. Draw the alphabet of lines and label each line.
2. What are the main advantages of polyester film as a drawing media?
3. What are the four standard types of projection?
4. Which drawing lines are thick? Which are thin? Which are very light and should not reproduce when copied?
5. What font provides the shape of standard engineering lettering?
6. Describe the characteristics of good freehand lettering.
7. Why should guidelines be used for lettering?
8. List the standard items found in a title block.

CHAPTER EXERCISES

Drawing Exercises

Practice your skills for making measurements, laying out drawing sheets, and forming neat standard lettering with these drawing exercises.

These problems are designed to fit easily on a sheet. (See the inside front cover of this book). Draw all construction lines lightly, using a hard lead (4H to 6H), and all required lines dense black with a softer lead (F to H). Draw your construction lines lightly so that they do not need to be erased.

In Exercises 2.1–2.3 you will practice measuring, and in Exercises 2.4–2.6 you will practice drawing layouts.

Exercise 2.1 Measure the lines shown above and list their lengths using millimeters. List the inch measurements for each in square brackets [ ] to the right of the millimeter measurement.

Exercise 2.2 Measure the lines shown above and draw them at Scale 1:2, Scale 2:1, and list their scales below them using the form Scale: X:X.

Exercise 2.3 Measure the overall interior dimensions of your room. Letter the measured length neatly in the first column as shown in the example. In the second column list how long you would draw that line at a scale of $1/4'' = 1'$, third column at $3/8'' = 1'$, fourth column at $1''= 1'$, fifth column at 1:100 metric scale (10 mm = 1 meter).

Measurement	1/4″ = 1′	3/8″ = 1′	1″ =1′	1:100 Metric
10′-6″	2.625″	3.9375″	10.5″	32mm

Exercise 2.4 Create the layout for an 8.5″ × 11″ sheet as shown at right.

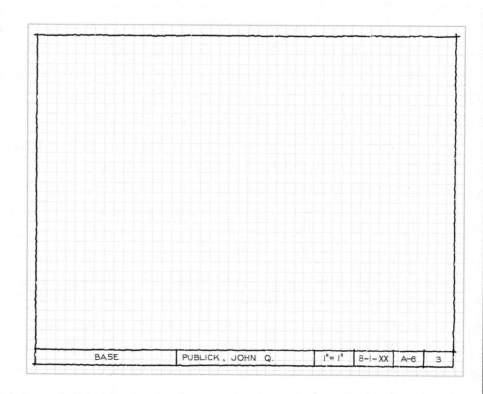

Exercise 2.5 Create the layout for the 210 mm × 297 mm sheet shown at right.

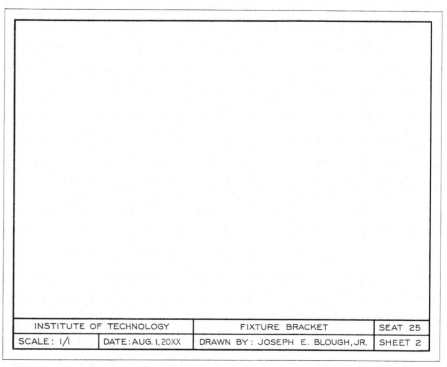

Exercise 2.6 Design a title block and layout for a C-size sheet. Create a name and logo for your company. Use an attractive but legible font for the titles on your layout. If assigned, design a special north arrow to be used on your drawings.

Lettering Exercises

Layouts for lettering problems are given in Exercises 2.7–2.11. Draw complete horizontal and vertical or inclined guidelines very lightly. Draw the vertical or inclined guidelines through the full height of the lettered area of the sheet. For practice in ink lettering, the last two lines and the title strip on each sheet may be lettered in ink, if assigned by the instructor. Omit all dimensions.

Exercise 2.7 Letter the words to your favorite song, joke, or inspirational quote of 50 words or more. Use 1/8″ tall UPPERCASE engineering lettering. Center the words near the middle of the sheet. Make sure to leave a row of space between each row of lettering. Make sure that the subject you choose is professional and appropriate.

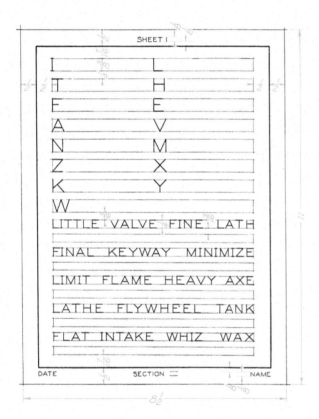

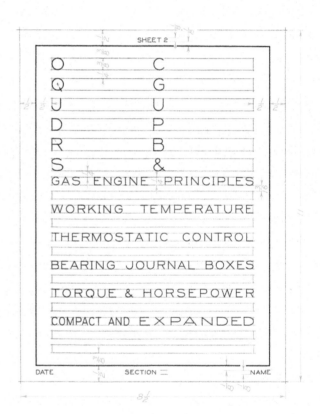

Exercise 2.8 Lay out sheet as shown. Add vertical or inclined guidelines and fill in vertical or inclined capital letters as assigned. For decimal-inch and millimeter equivalents of given dimensions, see the inside back cover.

Exercise 2.9 Lay out sheet as shown. Add vertical or inclined guidelines and fill in vertical or inclined capital letters as assigned. For decimal-inch and millimeter equivalents of given dimensions, see the inside back cover.

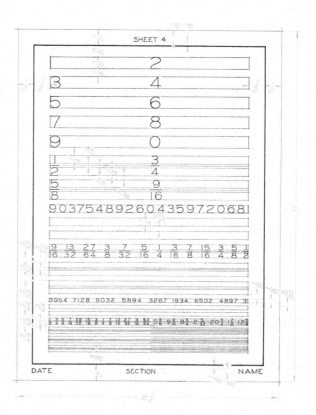

Exercise 2.10 Lay out sheet as shown. Add vertical or inclined guidelines and fill in vertical or inclined lowercase letters as assigned. For decimal-inch and millimeter equivalents of given dimensions, see the inside back cover.

Exercise 2.11 Lay out sheet as shown. Add vertical or inclined guidelines and fill in vertical or inclined numerals and fractions as assigned. For decimal-inch and millimeter equivalents of given dimensions, see the inside back cover.

CHAPTER THREE

VISUALIZATION AND SKETCHING

OBJECTIVES

After studying the material in this chapter, you should be able to:

1. Define the terms vertex, edge, plane, surface, and solid.

2. Identify four types of surfaces.

3. Identify five regular solids.

4. Draw points, lines, angled lines, arcs, circles, and ellipses.

5. Apply techniques that aid in creating legible well-proportioned freehand sketches.

6. Apply techniques to draw irregular curves.

7. Create a single-view sketch.

8. Create an oblique sketch.

9. Create perspective sketches.

10. Create an isometric sketch of an object.

Refer to the following standard:
- *ANSI/ASME Y14.3 Orthographic and Pictorial Views*

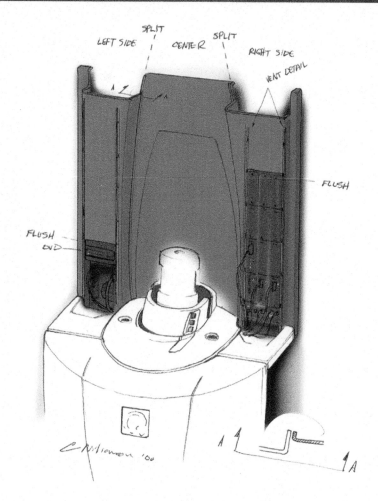

SPLIT
LEFT SIDE   CENTER   SPLIT
RIGHT SIDE
VENT DETAIL
FLUSH
FLUSH
DVD
A

Shaded Sketch Showing Details of Wire Placement *(Courtesy of Quantum Design.)*

OVERVIEW

The ability to envision objects in three dimensions is one of the most important skills for scientists, designers, engineers, and technicians. Learning to visualize objects in space, to imagine constructively, is something you can learn by studying technical drawing. People who are extraordinarily creative often possess outstanding ability to visualize, but with practice anyone can improve his or her ability.

In addition to its role in developing spatial thinking skills, sketching is a valuable tool that allows you to communicate your ideas quickly and accurately. During the development stage of an idea, a picture is often worth a thousand words.

Sketching is also an efficient way to plan your drawing and record notes needed to create a complex object. When you sketch basic ideas ahead of time, you can often complete a final CAD drawing sooner and with fewer errors. Using good technique makes sketching faster, easier, and more legible.

Complex Surface Models Created Using 3D CAD *(Courtesy of Professor Richard Palais, University of California, Irvine, and Luc Benard.)*

UNDERSTANDING SOLID OBJECTS

Sketches and drawings are used to communicate or record ideas about the shape of 3D objects. Before starting to sketch, it helps to develop a vocabulary for understanding and discussing 3D shapes.

Three-dimensional figures are referred to as *solids.* Solids are bounded by the *surfaces* that contain them. These surfaces can be one of the following four types:

- *Planar*
- *Single curved*
- *Double curved*
- *Warped*

Regardless of how complex a solid may be, it is composed of combinations of these basic types of surfaces. Figure 3.1 shows examples of the four basic types of surfaces.

Types of Solids

Polyhedra

Solids that are bounded by plane surfaces are called *polyhedra* (Figures 3.2–3.4). These planar surfaces are also referred to as *faces* of the object. A polygon is a planar area that is enclosed by straight lines.

Regular Polyhedra

If the faces of a solid are equal regular polygons, it is called a *regular polyhedron.* There are five regular polyhedra: the tetrahedron, hexahedron, octahedron, dodecahedron, and icosahedron (Figure 3.2).

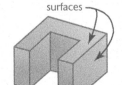

Planar surfaces

(a)

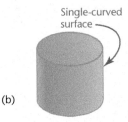

Single-curved surface

(b)

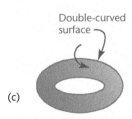

Double-curved surface

(c)

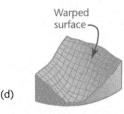

Warped surface

(d)

3.1   Types of Surfaces

Tetrahedron
(4 triangles)

Hexahedron
(cube)

Octahedron
(8 triangles)

Dodecahedron
(12 pentagons)

Icosahedron
(20 triangles)

3.2   Regular Polyhedra

Prisms

A *prism* has two bases, which are parallel equal polygons, and three or more additional faces, which are parallelograms (Figure 3.3). A triangular prism has triangular bases, a rectangular prism has rectangular bases, and so on. (If a prism's bases happen to be parallelograms, the prism is a called a parallelepiped, a word rarely heard in everyday conversation.)

A right prism has faces and lateral (side) edges that are perpendicular to the bases; an oblique prism has faces and lateral edges that are angled to the bases. If one end is cut off to form an end that is not parallel to the bases, the prism is said to be truncated (a word that simply means "shortened by having a part cut off").

Pyramids

A *pyramid* has a polygon for a base and triangular lateral faces that intersect at a common point called the vertex (Figure 3.4). The line from the center of the base to the vertex is called the axis. If the axis is perpendicular to the base, the pyramid is called a right pyramid; otherwise, it is an oblique pyramid. A triangular pyramid has a triangular base, a square pyramid has a square base, and so on. If a portion near the vertex has been cut off, the pyramid is truncated; if the face formed by truncation is parallel to the base, the shape is referred to as a *frustum*.

Cylinders

A *cylinder* has a single-curved exterior surface (Figure 3.5). You can think of a cylinder as being formed by taking a straight line and moving it in a circular path to enclose a volume. Each position of this imaginary straight line in its path around the axis is called an *element* of the cylinder.

Cones

A *cone* has a single-curved exterior surface (Figure 3.6). You can think of it as being formed by moving one end of a straight line around a circle while keeping the other end fixed at a point, the vertex of the cone. An element of the cone is any position of this imaginary straight line.

Spheres

A *sphere* has a double-curved exterior surface (Figure 3.7). You can think of it as being formed by revolving a circle about one of its diameters, somewhat like spinning a coin. The poles of the sphere are the points at the top and bottom of the sphere that would not move while it was spinning. The axis of the sphere is the term for the line between its poles.

Tori

A *torus* is shaped like a doughnut (Figure 3.8). Its boundary surface is double curved. You can think of it as being formed by revolving a circle (or other closed curve) around an axis that is positioned away from (outside) the curve.

Ellipsoids

An oblate or prolate *ellipsoid* is shaped like an egg (Figure 3.9). You can think of it as being formed by revolving an ellipse about its minor or major axis, respectively.

Right
square

Right
rectangular

Oblique
rectangular

Right
triangular

Right
pentagonal

Oblique
hexagonal

3.3   Right Prisms and Oblique Prisms

Right
rectangular

Right square
(truncated)

Oblique
pentagonal

3.4   Pyramids

Right
circular

Oblique
circular

3.5   Cylinder and Oblique Cylinder

Right
circular

Oblique circular
(frustum)

Oblique circular
(truncated)

3.6   Cones

Sphere

Torus

3.7   Sphere   **3.8   Torus**

Oblate
Ellipsoid

Prolate
Ellipsoid

3.9   Ellipsoids

UNDERSTANDING SKETCHING TECHNIQUES

Analyzing Complex Objects

The ability to break down complex shapes into simpler geometric primitives is an essential skill for sketching and modeling objects.

Before you begin to draw the outline of an object, consider its overall shape and the relationships between its parts. Construction lines can help you preserve the overall dimensions of the object as you sketch.

Bear in mind that you should be thinking in terms of basic shapes whether you are sketching by hand or using a CAD program. Because basic curves and straight lines are the basis of many of the objects that people create, practice in creating the basic elements of a drawing will help you sketch with ease.

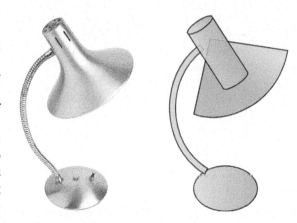

3.10   Identifying Essential Shapes

3.11   *The essential shapes of the corkscrew in the photo are sketched at right.*

3.12   Using Construction Lines

Essential Shapes

Look for the essential shapes of objects. If you were to make a clay model of an object, what basic shape would you start with? A ball? A box?

Try squinting your eyes and looking at familiar objects. Do you see their shape as a rectangle? A circle? What other basic shapes do you notice when you look at objects this way?

Think about breaking down more complex objects into their simpler geometric shapes as shown in Figure 3.10. You can block in these shapes using construction lines to show their relationships to one another. Then, add details, continuing to pay attention to the spatial relationships between them.

Construction Lines

Artists often begin a sketch by blocking in light guidelines to help them preserve basic shapes and proportions. In technical drawing these are called ***construction lines*** (Figure 3.12).

It is often helpful to begin a sketch by describing the object's main shapes with construction lines, taking some care to accurately represent the relative size and placement of features.

Use the basic shapes as a guide to place key features, then use those main features as a "reference map" to place smaller details. For example, the sixth fret line is about halfway up the rectangular guitar neck.

Throughout this chapter you will use light construction lines to draw circles, arcs, and ellipses. Section 3.4 discusses the process of estimating and maintaining the proportions of an object in further detail.

Contours and Negative Space

The **contours** of an object are the main outlines that separate it from the surrounding space. One way to think about the contours of objects is to look at the contrast between the positive and negative space. Positive space is the space occupied by the object. **Negative space** is the unoccupied space around it.

In Figure 3.13 the space occupied by the contour of a pair of scissors is shown. Note how you can identify specific shapes by looking at the negative space. The individual shapes that make up the negative space are shown in different colors to make them easier for you to see. Some people sketch more accurately when they try to draw the negative space that surrounds the object.

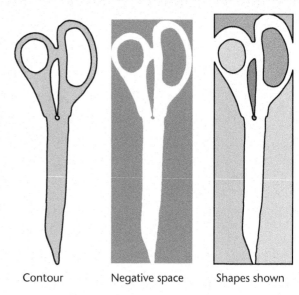

Contour   Negative space   Shapes shown

3.13   Negative Space

Practice Drawing Contours

Try sketching the negative spaces that define the shape of a chair. Look at each space as an individual shape. What is the shape of the space between the legs? What is the shape of the space between the rungs and the seat?

Make a sketch of a chair, paying careful attention to sketching the negative spaces of the chair as they really appear. The positive and negative spaces should add up to define the chair.

If you have difficulty, make corrections to your sketch by defining the positive shapes and then check to see if the negative shapes match.

An 8.5″ × 11″ sheet of Plexiglas® (available at most glass stores) is an excellent tool for developing sketching ability. Using a dry-erase marker, hold the Plexiglas up in front of an object and trace the object's contours on the Plexiglas. If you don't move, the outline should match the object's outline exactly. Lower the Plexiglas and look at the orientation of the lines. Are they what you expected?

Try looking at the object and drawing the sketch with the Plexiglas lying on your desktop or knees. Then, raise it and see if your drawing matches the object.

To develop sketching ability, try drawing everyday objects like your toaster, printer, or lamp, as well as exterior and interior views of buildings and equipment.

First try   Examine negative shapes   Note differences   More accurate proportions

3.14   Rubber Stamp   **3.15**   Hatching   **3.16**   Stippling

Viewpoint

As you sketch objects, keep in mind that you want to maintain a consistent *viewpoint,* as a camera does. This is easier when you are sketching a picture from a book, because you can't move around the object. When you move, you see a different view of the object depending on where you stand.

Sometimes people have difficulty sketching because they want to show parts of the object that cannot really be seen from a single viewpoint. For example, knowing that the handle of the rubber stamp in Figure 3.14 appears circular from the top, you may be tempted to show it as round, even though it may appear elliptical from your viewpoint.

When you are sketching an object pictorially, temporarily set aside your knowledge of the shapes the object is actually made of and carefully examine the shapes you see from a single, static viewpoint. In this type of sketching, instead of trying to envision the object as it is, try only to see it as it looks.

Shading

Adding *shading* to your sketch can give it a more realistic appearance because it represents the way the actual object would reflect light. Shading doesn't mean "coloring in." You may want to shade only the most prominently shadowed areas. First, identify the darkest and lightest areas on an object. If you want, you can shade various middle tones, placed exactly as they look on the object.

In some ways, shading is like doing a drawing within a drawing, because it is a matter of identifying shapes. When you are shading, instead of identifying the shapes of the object's contours, you are identifying the shape and relative darkness of the shadows.

Hatching lines, shown in Figure 3.15, and stippling, shown in Figure 3.16, are commonly used methods to add shading because they are easier to reproduce with a photocopier than continuous-tone pencil shading. In the illustration, you can see that shadowed areas are darkened simply by adding more hatching lines or stippling dots.

It is not uncommon for people to draw outlines by hand and add digital shaded fills to a scan of the outline. Another way to make a subject the clear focal point of a drawing is to stylize the shadows. Industrial designers often use markers to add a stylized shadow to their sketches. You can use a straight

edge to protect the original sketch from the marker and quickly sketch the shadow (Figure 3.17).

Regardless of how you apply shading, darken the outline to define the shape clearly and boldly. Remember that when you are communicating by using a sketch, its subject should be clear. To make the subject—in this case, a rubber stamp—clear, make it stand out with thick bold contour lines.

3.17   Marker Shading in a Concept Sketch *(Courtesy of Douglas Wintin.)*

Edges and Vertices

Edges

An *edge* of a solid is formed where two surfaces intersect. Edges are represented in drawings by visible or hidden lines (Figure 3.18).

Vertices

A *vertex* (plural, vertices) of a solid is formed where three or more surfaces intersect. The end of an edge is a vertex. These vertices or "points" are very useful in defining the locations of the solid object feature that you will sketch (Figure 3.18).

Points and Lines

A *point* is used to represent a location in space but has no width, height, or depth (Figure 3.19). A point in a drawing is represented by the intersection of two lines (Figure 3.19a), by a short crossbar on a line (Figure 3.19b), or by a small cross (Figure 3.19c). Do not represent points by simple dots on the paper. This makes the drawing look "blobby" and is not as accurate.

A *line* is used in drawings to represent the edge of a solid object. A straight line is the shortest distance between two points and is commonly referred to simply as a "line." If the line is indefinite in extent, in a drawing the length is a matter of convenience, and the endpoints are not marked (Figure 3.20a). If the endpoints of the line are significant, they are marked by small drawn crossbars (Figure 3.20b). Other common terms are illustrated in Figures 3.20c to i. Either straight lines or curved lines are parallel if the shortest distance between them remains

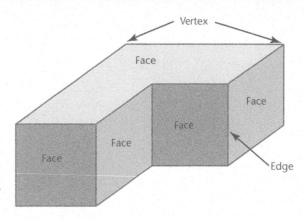

3.18   Edges and Vertices of a Solid

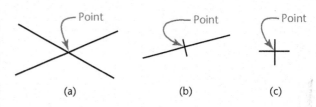

3.19   Showing Points

constant. The common symbol for parallel lines is ‖, and for perpendicular lines it is ⊥. Two perpendicular lines may be marked with a "box" as shown in Figure 3.20g. Such symbols may be used on sketches, but not on production drawings.

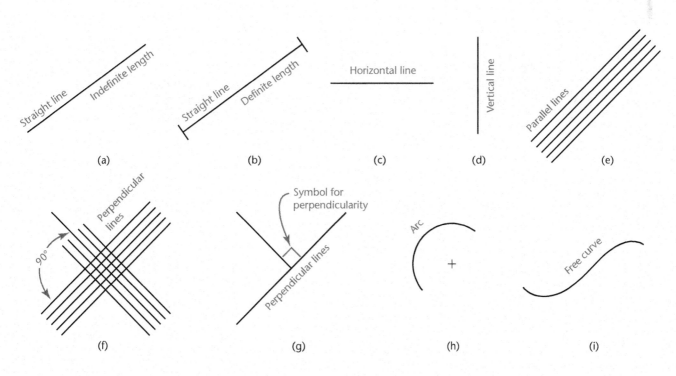

3.20   Showing Lines

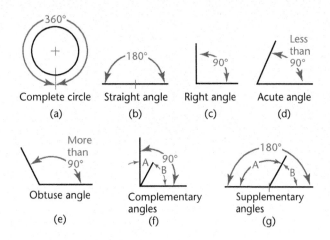

3.21   Showing Angles

Angles

An *angle* is formed by two intersecting lines. A common symbol for angle is ∠.

There are 360 degrees (360°) in a full circle, as shown in Figure 3.21a. A degree is divided into 60 minutes (60′), and a minute is divided into 60 seconds (60″). The angle value 37°26′10″ is read 37 degrees, 26 minutes, and 10 seconds. When minutes alone are indicated, the number of minutes should be preceded by 0°, as in 0°20′. If the minutes value were listed alone without showing the zero value, it might be mistaken for a distance measurement. For example, 20 minutes, 10 seconds written as 20′10″ might be mistaken for 20 feet 10 inches.

The different kinds of angles are illustrated in Figure 3.21. Two angles are complementary if they total 90° (Figure 3.21f) and are supplementary if they total 180° (Figure 3.21g).

In sketching, most angles can be estimated. Use a protractor if necessary when drawing odd angles.

Drawings and Sketches

The following are important skills to keep in mind for sketches and drawings:

1. Accuracy. No drawing is useful unless it shows the information correctly.
2. Speed. Time is money in industry. Work smarter and learn to use techniques to speed up your sketching and CAD drawings while still producing neat accurate results.
3. Legibility. A drawing is a means of communicating with others, so it must be clear and legible. Give attention to details. Things that may seem picky and small as you are drawing may be significant and save money or even lives when the product is built.
4. Neatness. If a drawing is to be accurate and legible, it must also be clean.

ACCURACY COUNTS

Accuracy and legibility in drawings is serious business, as is demonstrated in this article from New Scientist *magazine about the September 2004 Genesis dizzy probe crash.*
(Photo courtesy of NASA.)

Dizzy Probe Crash

You would think that by now, NASA should be able to tell up from down. Not so in the case of their Genesis space capsule, which crashed into the desert in Utah instead of parachuting gently down so that helicopter stunt pilots could pluck it to safety.

Since its launch in August 2001, the capsule had been collecting precious particles from the solar wind that would have told us something about the composition of the solar system.

But after reentering Earth's atmosphere on September 8, 2004, Genesis plunged into the ground, and much of its payload was lost.

On October 15, investigators released their preliminary conclusions, blaming the crash on "a design error that involves the orientation of gravity-switch devices." Huh?

The four small cylindrical switches were designed to sense the reentry and trigger the parachute. But they were drawn upside down in Lockheed Martin's technical drawings, so they were installed upside down—although NASA's Michael Ryschkewitsch, who led the investigation, is reluctant to use those exact words. The switches never detected the reentry. Similar devices are installed on another sample-collecting mission called Stardust. Ryschkewitsch believes these were installed the right way up.

(Courtesy of New Scientist *magazine.)*

Freehand Sketching

Freehand sketches are a helpful way to organize your thoughts and record ideas. They provide a quick, low-cost way to explore various solutions to design problems so that the best choices can be made. Investing too much time in creating a detailed layout before exploring your options through sketches can be costly.

The degree of precision needed in a given sketch depends on its use. Quick sketches to supplement verbal descriptions may be rough and incomplete. Sketches can be used to convey important and precise information when they are clearly drawn and annotated.

Freehand sketching requires only pencil, paper, and eraser. Mastering the techniques in this chapter for showing quick single-view, oblique, perspective, and isometric drawings using good freehand line technique will give you a valuable tool for communicating your ideas.

The term *freehand sketch* does not mean a sloppy drawing. As shown in Figure 3.22, a freehand sketch shows attention to proportion, clarity, and correct line widths. Figure 3.23 shows an as-built drawing with corrected items sketched on the printed CAD drawing.

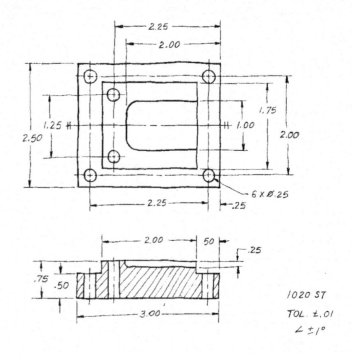

3.22 Sketch on Graph Paper. *Sketches are also used to clarify information about changes in design or to provide information on repairing existing equipment.*

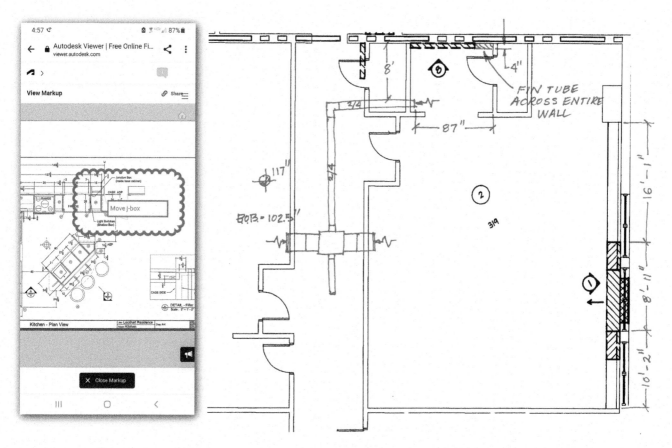

3.23 An As-Built Drawing with Corrected Items Sketched on the Printed CAD Drawing. *Computers and even cell-phones can run apps allowing you to mark up drawings, as shown in inset at left. (Autodesk screen shots reprinted courtesy of Autodesk, Inc.)*

3.1 TECHNIQUE OF LINES

The chief difference between a drawing and a freehand sketch lies in the character or technique of the lines. A good freehand line is not expected to be as rigidly straight or exactly uniform. A good freehand line shows freedom and variety, whereas a line drawn using CAD or instruments should be exact. Still, it is important to distinguish between line patterns to make your drawing legible.

The *line patterns* in Figure 3.24 are examples of good freehand quality. Figure 3.25 shows examples of good and poor technique.

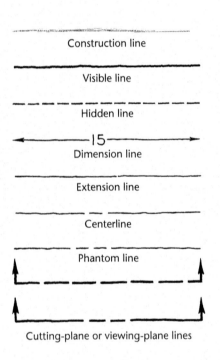

3.24   Freehand Alphabet of Lines (Full Size)

Lineweights

- Make dimension, extension, and centerlines thin, sharp, and black.
- Make hidden lines medium and black.
- Make visible and cutting-plane lines thick and black.
- Make construction lines thick and light.

TIP

Even in freehand drawings, thick lines should be twice the width of thin lines.

Thicknesses do not have to be exact, but there should be an obvious difference between thick and thin lines.

Because visible lines and cutting-plane lines are the two thick line patterns, other lines should be distinctly thinner in comparison.

To draw thick and thin lines freehand, you might like to keep two pencils handy, one that is razor sharp for thin lines and another that is dulled, to create thicker lines.

As the sharp point becomes dulled, switch it with the dull pencil, and sharpen the other, so that there is always one sharp and one dulled point ready to use.

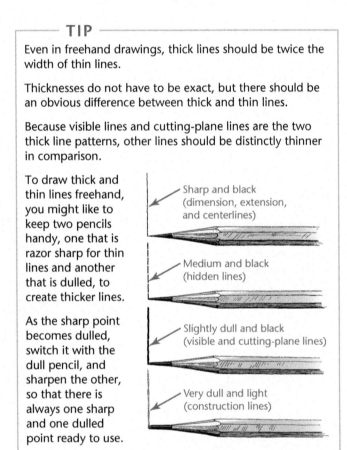

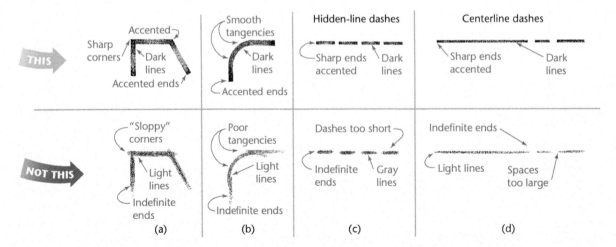

3.25   Technique of Lines (Enlarged)

3.2 SKETCHING STRAIGHT LINES

Most of the lines in an average sketch are straight lines. With practice, your straight lines will naturally improve, but these basics may help you improve quickly.

- Hold your pencil naturally, about 1" back from the point, and approximately at a right angle to the line to be drawn.
- Draw horizontal lines from left to right with a free and easy wrist and arm movement.
- Draw vertical lines downward with a wrist and arm movement.
- Draw curved lines using finger and wrist movements.

Blocking in a Freehand Drawing

Over the years, freehand sketchers have developed all sorts of tricks to improve speed and accuracy. Methods for finding midpoints or quickly blocking in straight vertical and horizontal lines are just a few secrets of the technical sketching craft that can come in handy, even today. When a great idea hits, or you need to sketch quickly at a meeting or on a job site, you might not have access to a CAD system, or even a ruler.

TIPS

Drawing Long Freehand Lines

For long freehand lines, make light end marks and lightly sweep your pencil between them, keeping your eye on the mark toward which you are moving. When you are satisfied with the accuracy of your strokes, apply more pressure to make a dark line.

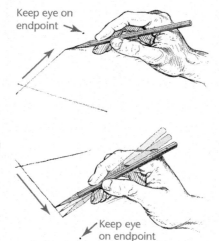

Keep eye on endpoint →

↙ Keep eye on endpoint

Blocking in a Border Freehand

Hold your hand and pencil rigidly and glide your fingertips along the edge of the paper to maintain a uniform border.

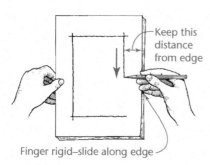

← Keep this distance from edge

Finger rigid–slide along edge

Blocking in a Border Using a Strip of Paper

Mark the distance on the edge of a card or a strip of paper and use it like a ruler to mark at intervals, then draw a final line through the points.

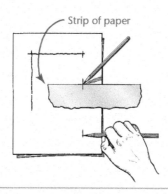

Strip of paper

If your line looks like this, you may be gripping your pencil too tightly or trying too hard to imitate mechanical lines.

Slight wiggles are OK as long as the line continues on a straight path.

Occasional very slight gaps are fine and make it easier to draw straight.

Finding a Midpoint Freehand

Use your thumb on your pencil to guess half the distance. Try this distance on the other half. Continue adjusting until you locate the center, then mark it.

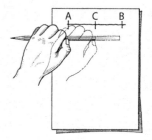

Folding a Paper to Find a Midpoint

Mark the total distance on the edge of a strip of paper, then fold the paper to locate its center at the crease. You can fold one half to find quarter points, and so on.

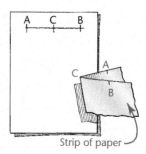

Strip of paper

DIVIDING LINES INTO EQUAL OR PROPORTIONAL PARTS

Proportional Parts

To divide the given line shown into proportions of (for example) 2, 3, and 4 units:

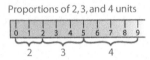

Proportions of 2, 3, and 4 units

1 Draw a vertical construction line at one end of the line you are dividing.

Sketch vertical line from end

2 Set the zero point of your scale at the other end of the line.

3 Swing the scale so the desired unit falls on the vertical line. In this case it will be the 9th unit, because 2 + 3 + 4 = 9.

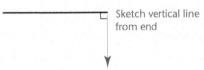

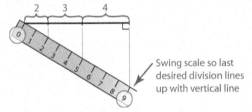

Swing scale so last desired division lines up with vertical line

4 Draw vertical lines upward from the corresponding scale divisions and mark tiny crossbars on the line as shown.

Equal Parts

If you use uniform divisions for the steps above (every third division, for instance) you will get equal parts. Examples of practical applications for dividing lines equally are shown below.

Calculated Proportions

To divide a line into proportions equal to the square of 1, 2, 3, and 4 (1, 4, 9, and 16), find 16 divisions on your scale.

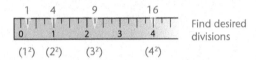

Find desired divisions

(1^2) (2^2) (3^2) (4^2)

1 Set the zero point of your scale at the end of the line and draw a light construction line at any convenient angle from one end of the line you are dividing to the appropriate division on the scale. In this case the 4 mark is 16 equal divisions from the 0.

2 Draw construction lines parallel to the end line through each proportionate scale division.

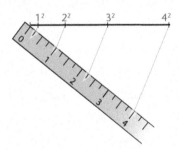

--- TIP ---

Exaggerating Closely Spaced Parallel Lines

Sometimes it is helpful to exaggerate the distance between closely spaced parallel lines so there is no fill-in when the drawing is reproduced.

Usually this is done to a maximum of 3 mm or .120". When using CAD it is better to draw the features the actual size and include a detail showing the actual spacing.

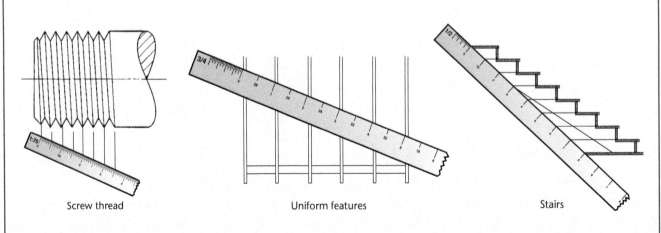

Screw thread   Uniform features   Stairs

3.26 *Many objects have rounded features that circles, arcs, and ellipses are used to represent. (Dennis MacDonald/ Alamy Stock Photo.)*

3.3 SKETCHING CIRCLES, ARCS, AND ELLIPSES

Circles

Small circles can be sketched using one or two strokes, without blocking in any construction lines. Circle templates also make it easy to sketch circles of various sizes.

For better looking freehand sketched circles of larger sizes, try the construction methods shown here. Figure 3.26 shows an object with rounded features to sketch using circles, arcs, and ellipses.

TIP

The Freehand Compass

Using your hand like a compass, you can create circles and arcs with surprising accuracy after a few minutes of practice.

1. Place the tip of your little finger or the knuckle joint of your little finger at the center.

2. "Feed" the pencil out to the radius you want as you would do with a compass.

3. Hold this position rigidly and rotate the paper with your free hand.

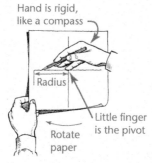

Hand is rigid, like a compass

Radius

Little finger is the pivot

Rotate paper

METHODS FOR SKETCHING CIRCLES

Enclosing Square Method

1 Lightly sketch an enclosing square and mark the midpoint of each side.

2 Lightly draw in arcs to connect the midpoints.

3 Darken the final circle.

Centerline Method

1 Sketch the two centerlines of the circle.

2 Add light 45° radial lines and sketch light arcs across them at an estimated radius distance from the center.

3 Darken the final circle.

Paper Method

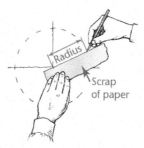 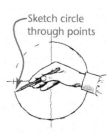

Radius

Scrap of paper

Sketch circle through points

1 Mark the estimated radius on the edge of a card or scrap of paper and set off from the center as many points as desired.

2 Sketch the final circle through these points.

STEP by STEP

METHODS FOR SKETCHING ARCS

Radius Method

1 Locate the center of the arc and lightly block in perpendicular lines. Mark off the radius distance along the lines.

2 Draw a 45° line through the center point and mark off the radius distance along it.

3 Lightly sketch in the arc as shown. Darken the final arc.

Trammel Method

1 Locate the center of the arc and lightly block in perpendicular lines. Mark off the radius distance along the lines.

2 Mark the radius distance on a strip of paper and use it as a trammel.

3 Lightly sketch in the arc, then darken the final arc.

Trammel

Tangent Method

Use these steps to draw arcs sketched to points of tangency.

1 Locate the center of the arc and sketch in the lines to which the arc is tangent.

2 Draw perpendiculars from the center to the tangent lines.

3 Draw in the arc tangent to the lines ending at the perpendicular lines.

4 Darken in the arc and then darken the lines from the points of tangency.

METHODS FOR SKETCHING ELLIPSES

Freehand Method

1 Rest your weight on your upper forearm and move the pencil rapidly above the paper in an elliptical path.

2 Lower the pencil to draw very light ellipses.

3 Darken the final ellipse.

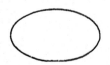

Rectangle Method

1 Lightly sketch an enclosing rectangle.

2 Mark the midpoint of each side and sketch light tangent arcs.

3 Darken in the final ellipse.

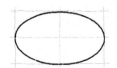

Axes Method

1 Lightly sketch in the major and minor axes of the ellipse.

2 Mark the distance along the axes and lightly block in the ellipse.

3 Darken the final ellipse.

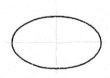

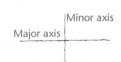

Trammel Method

1 To sketch accurate ellipses, you can make a trammel.

2 Mark half the desired length of the minor axis on the edge of a strip of paper (A-B). Using the same starting point, mark half the length of the major axis (A-C). (The measurements will overlap.)

3 Line up the last two trammel points (B and C) on the axes and mark a small dot at the location of the first point (A).

4 Move the trammel to different positions, keeping B and C on the axes, and mark more points at A. Sketch the final ellipse through the points.

Minor axis
Major axis

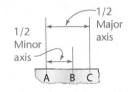

1/2 Minor axis
1/2 Major axis

A B C

Line up with axes

Mark

A B C

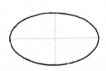

Sketching Arcs

Sketching arcs is similar to sketching circles. In general, it is easier to hold your pencil on the inside of the curve. Look closely at the actual geometric constructions and carefully approximate points of tangency so that the arc touches a line or other entity at the right point.

3.27   A Circle Seen as an Ellipse

Sketching Ellipses

If a circle is tipped away from your view, it appears as an ellipse. Figure 3.27 shows a coin viewed so that it appears as an ellipse. You can learn to sketch small ellipses with a free arm movement similar to the way you sketch circles, or you can use ellipse templates to help you easily sketch ellipses. These templates are usually grouped according to the amount a circular shape would be rotated to form the ellipse. They provide a number of sizes of ellipses on each template but usually include only one or two typical rotations.

3.4 MAINTAINING PROPORTIONS

Sketches are not usually made to a specific scale, although it can be handy to do so at times. The size of the sketch depends on its complexity and the size of the paper available. The most important rule in freehand sketching is to keep the sketch in *proportion,* which means to accurately represent the size and position of each part in relation to the whole. No matter how brilliant the technique or how well drawn the details, if the proportions are off, the sketch will not look right.

To maintain proportions, first determine the relative proportions of height to width and lightly block them in. You can mark a unit on the edge of a strip of paper or use your pencil (as in Figure 3.28) to gauge how many units wide and high the object is. Grid paper can help you maintain proportions by providing a ready-made scale (by counting squares). As you block in the medium-size areas, and later as you add small details, compare each new distance with those already established.

3.28   Estimating Dimensions

MAINTAINING PROPORTIONS IN A SKETCH

1 If you are working from a given picture, such as this utility cabinet, first establish the relative width compared to the height. One way is to use the pencil as a measuring stick. In this case, the height is about 1-3/4 times the width.

Difference between height and width

2 Sketch the enclosing rectangle in the correct proportion. This sketch is to be slightly larger than the given picture.

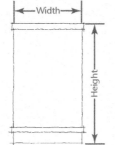
Width / Height

3 Divide the available drawer space into three parts with the pencil by trial. Hold your pencil about where you think one third will be and then try that measurement. If it is too short or long, adjust the measurement and try again. Sketch light diagonals to locate centers of the drawers and block in drawer handles. Sketch all remaining details.

4 Darken all final lines, making them clean, thick, and black.

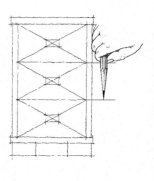

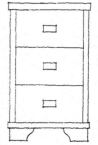

STEP by STEP

STEP by STEP

HOW TO BLOCK IN AN IRREGULAR OBJECT

1 Capture the main proportions with simple lines.

2 Block in the general sizes and direction of flow of curved shapes.

3 Lightly block in additional details.

4 Darken the lines of the completed sketch.

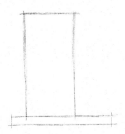
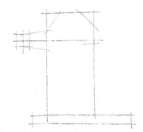
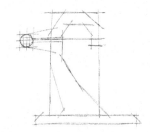

STEP by STEP

GEOMETRIC METHODS FOR SKETCHING PLANE FIGURES

Sketching a Polygon by the Triangle Method

1 Divide the polygon into triangles as shown. Use the triangles as a visual aid to sketch the shape.

Sketching a Polygon by the Rectangle Method

1 Imagine a rectangle drawn around the polygon as shown.

2 Sketch the rectangle and then locate the vertices of the polygon (points a, b, c, and so on) along the sides of the rectangle.

3 Join the points to complete the shape.

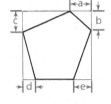

Visual Aids for Sketching Irregular Figures

1 Visualize shapes made up of rectangular and circular forms by enclosing those features in rectangles.

2 Determine where the centers of arcs and circles are located relative to the rectangles as shown.

3 Sketch the features inside the rectangular shapes you have lightly blocked in and darken the final lines.

Creating Irregular Shapes by Offset Measurements

1 Enclose the shape in a rectangle.

2 Use the sides of the rectangle as a reference to make measurements that locate points along the curve.

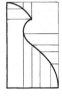

Enlarging Shapes Using a Grid of Squares

1 Complex curved shapes can be copied, enlarged, or reduced by hand, if necessary.

2 Draw or overlay a grid of squares on the original drawing.

3 To enlarge, draw the containing rectangle and grid of squares at the desired percentage and transfer the lines of the shape through the corresponding points in the new set of squares.

3.5 ONE-VIEW DRAWINGS

Frequently, a single view supplemented by notes and dimensions is enough information to describe the shape of a relatively simple object.

In Figure 3.29, one view of the shim plus a note indicating the thickness as 0.25 mm is sufficient.

Nearly all shafts, bolts, screws, and similar parts should be represented by single views in this way.

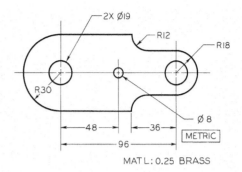

3.29 One-View Drawing of a Shim

SKETCHING A SINGLE-VIEW DRAWING

Follow the steps to sketch the single-view drawing of the shim shown in Figure 3.29.

1 Lightly sketch the centerlines for the overall width and height of the part. Estimate overall proportions by eye, or if you know the dimensions, use a measuring scale to sketch accurately sized views. Space the enclosing rectangle equally from the margins of the sheet.

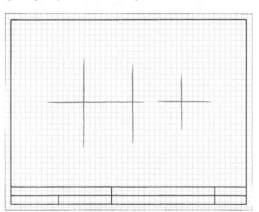

2 Block in all details lightly, keeping the drawing proportions in mind. Use techniques introduced in this chapter to help you.

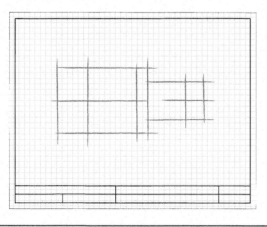

3 Locate the centers of circles and arcs. Block in where they will fit using rectangles. Then, sketch all arcs and circles lightly.

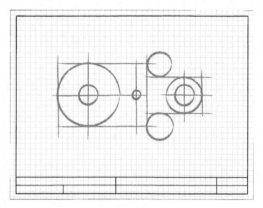

4 Darken your final lines.

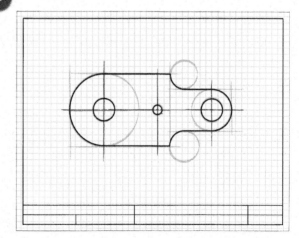

5 Add annotations to the drawing using neat lettering. Fill in the title block or title strip. Note the scale for the sketch if applicable. If not, letter NONE in the Scale area of the title block.

STEP by STEP

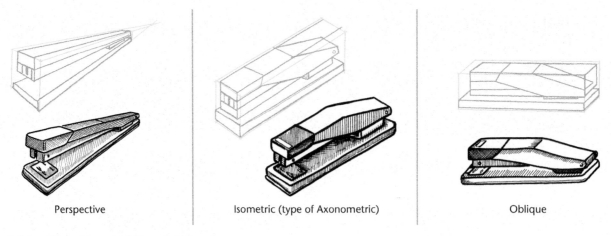

| Perspective | Isometric (type of Axonometric) | Oblique |

3.30 Three Types of Pictorial Sketches

3.6 PICTORIAL SKETCHING

A *pictorial sketch* represents a 3D object on a 2D sheet of paper by orienting the object so you can see its width, height, and depth in a single view.

Pictorial sketches are used frequently during the ideation phase of engineering design to record ideas quickly and communicate them to others. Their similarity to how the object is viewed in the real world makes them useful for communicating engineering designs to nonengineers. Later in the design process, pictorial drawings are often used to show how parts fit together in an assembly and, in part catalogs and manuals, to make it easy to identify the objects.

This chapter examines three common methods used to sketch pictorials: isometric sketching, which is a subtype of the general category of axonometric projection, oblique sketching, and perspective sketching. Figure 3.30 shows perspective, isometric, and oblique sketches of a stapler. Figure 3.31 shows pictorial sketches for backpack concepts.

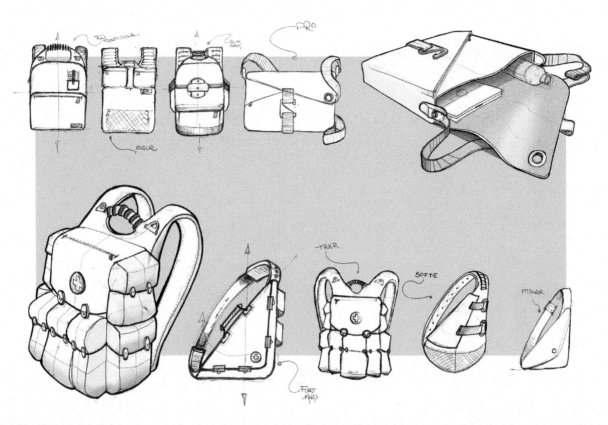

3.31 *Pictorial sketching is used frequently to convey preliminary design ideas, as in these backpack concept sketches. (Courtesy of André Cotan.)*

Each of the pictorial methods differs in the way points on the object are located on the 2D viewing plane (the piece of paper).

A perspective sketch presents the most realistic looking view. It shows the object much as it would appear in a photograph—portions of the object that are farther from the viewer appear smaller, and lines recede into the distance.

An axonometric sketch is drawn so that lines do not recede into the distance but remain parallel. This makes isometric views easy to sketch but takes away somewhat from the realistic appearance.

An oblique sketch shows the front surface of the object looking straight on and is easy to create, but it presents the least realistic representation because the depth of the object appears to be out of proportion.

Various types of pictorial drawings are used extensively in catalogs, sales literature, and technical work. They are often used in patent drawings; in piping diagrams; in machine, structural, architectural design, and in furniture design; and for ide-ation sketching. The sketches for a wooden shelf in Figure 3.32 are examples of axonometric, orthographic, and perspective sketches.

In axonometric and oblique drawings, distant features are not shown proportionately smaller, the way they appear in a photograph or to our vision. Edges that are parallel on the object always appear parallel in an axonometric view. The most common axonometric projection is isometric, which means "equal measure." When a cube is drawn in isometric, the axes are equally spaced (120° apart). Though not as realistic as perspective drawings, isometric drawings are much easier to draw. CAD software often displays the results of 3D models on the screen as isometric projections. Some CAD software allows you to choose between isometric, axonometric views (see Figure 3.35 for examples), or perspective representation of your 3D models on the 2D computer screen. In sketching, dimetric and trimetric sometimes produce a better view than isometric but take longer to draw and are therefore used less frequently.

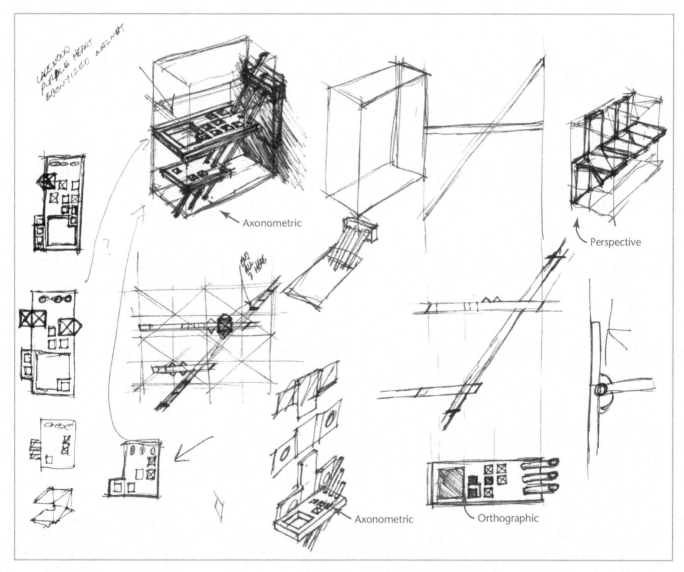

3.32 Sketches for a Wooden Shelf Using Axonometric, Orthographic, and Perspective Drawing Techniques. *The axonometric projections in this sketch are drawn in isometric. (Courtesy of Douglas Wintin.)*

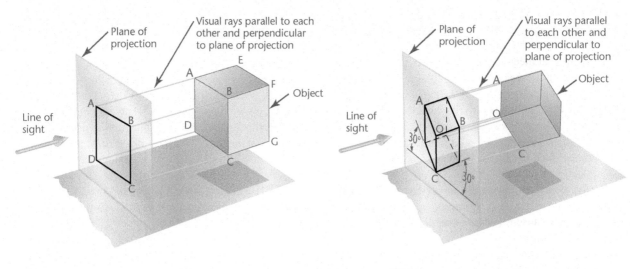

(a) Multiview projection

(b) Axonometric projection (isometric shown)

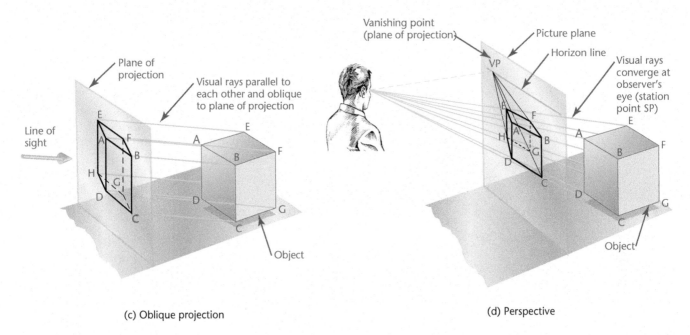

(c) Oblique projection

(d) Perspective

3.33 Four Types of Projection

3.7 PROJECTION METHODS

The four principal types of projection are shown in Figure 3.33. All except the regular multiview projection (Figure 3.33a) are pictorial types, because they show several sides of the object in a single view. In both *multiview projection* and *axonometric projection,* the visual rays are parallel to each other and perpendicular to the plane of projection. Both are types of *orthographic projection* (Figures 3.33a and 3.33b).

In *oblique projection* (Figure 3.33c), the visual rays are parallel to each other but at an angle other than 90° to the plane of projection.

In perspective (Figure 3.33d), the visual rays extend from the observer's eye, or station point (SP), to all points of the object to form a "cone of rays," so that the portions of the object that are farther away from the observer appear smaller than the closer portions of the object.

3.8 AXONOMETRIC PROJECTION

The feature that distinguishes axonometric projection from multiview projection is the inclined position of the object with respect to the planes of projection. When a surface or edge of the object is not parallel to the plane of projection, it appears foreshortened. When an angle is not parallel to the plane of projection, it appears either smaller or larger than the true angle.

To create an axonometric view, the object is tipped to the planes of projection so that principal faces, such as the top, side, and front, show in a single view. This produces a pictorial drawing that is easy to visualize, but because the principal edges and surfaces of the object are inclined to the plane of projection, the lengths of the lines are foreshortened. The angles between surfaces and edges appear either larger or smaller than the true angle. There are an infinite variety of ways that the object may be oriented with respect to the plane of projection.

The degree of *foreshortening* of any line depends on its angle to the plane of projection. The greater the angle, the greater the foreshortening. Once the degree of foreshortening is determined for each of the three edges of the cube that meet at one corner, scales can be easily constructed for measuring along these edges or any other edges parallel to them (Figure 3.34).

Use the three edges of the cube that meet at the corner nearest your view as the axonometric axes. Figure 3.35 shows three axonometric projections.

Isometric projection (Figure 3.35a) has equal foreshortening along each of the three axis directions.

Dimetric projection (Figure 3.35b) has equal foreshortening along two axis directions and a different amount of foreshortening along the third axis. This is because it is not tipped an equal amount to all the principal planes of projection.

Trimetric projection (Figure 3.35c) has different foreshortening along all three axis directions. This view is produced by an object that is unequally tipped to all the planes of projection.

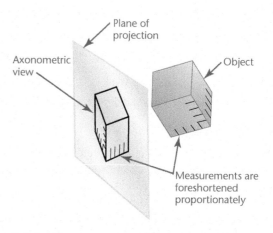

3.34   *Measurements are foreshortened proportionately based on the amount of incline.*

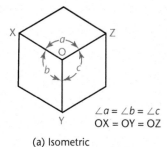

$\angle a = \angle b = \angle c$
OX = OY = OZ

(a) Isometric

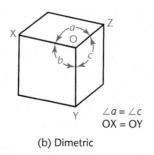

$\angle a = \angle c$
OX = OY

(b) Dimetric

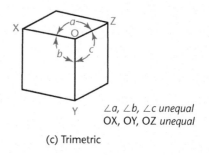

$\angle a$, $\angle b$, $\angle c$ *unequal*
OX, OY, OZ *unequal*

(c) Trimetric

3.35   Axonometric Projections

Axonometric Projections and 3D Models

When you create a 3D CAD model, the object is stored so that vertices, surfaces, and solids are all defined relative to a 3D coordinate system. You can rotate your view of the object to produce a view from any direction. However, your computer screen is a flat surface, like a sheet of paper. The CAD software uses similar projection to produce the view transformations, creating the 2D view of the object on your computer screen.

Most 3D CAD software provides a variety of preset isometric viewing directions to make it easy for you to manipulate the view. Some CAD software also allows for easy perspective viewing on screen.

After rotating the object you may want to return to a preset typical axonometric view like one of the examples shown in Figure 3.36.

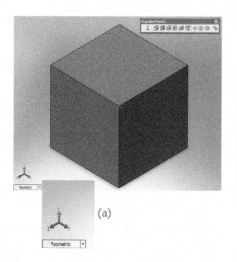

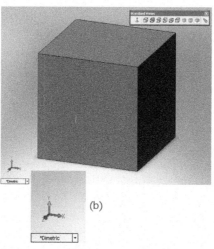

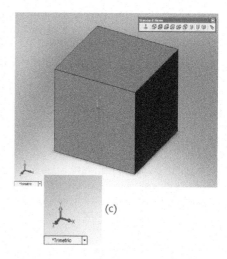

3.36   (a) Isometric View of a 1″ Cube Shown in SolidWorks; (b) Dimetric View; (c) Trimetric View
(Images courtesy of ©2016 Dassault Systèmes SolidWorks Corporation.)

3.9 ISOMETRIC PROJECTION

In an isometric projection, all angles between the axonometric axes are equal. To produce an isometric projection, you orient the object so that its principal edges (or axes) make equal angles with the plane of projection and are therefore foreshortened equally. Oriented this way, the edges of a cube are projected so that they all measure the same and make equal angles (of 120°) with each other, as shown in Figure 3.37.

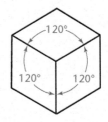

3.37   Isometric Projection

Isometric Axes

The projections of the edges of a cube make angles of 120° with each other. You can use these as the isometric axes from which to make measurements. Any line parallel to one of these is called an isometric line. The angles in the isometric projection of the cube are either 120° or 60°, and all are projections of 90° angles. In an isometric projection of a cube, the faces of the cube, and any planes parallel to them, are called isometric planes. See Figure 3.38.

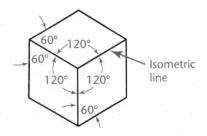

3.38   Isometric Axes

Nonisometric Lines

Lines of an isometric drawing that are not parallel to the isometric axes are called nonisometric lines (Figure 3.39). Only lines of an object that are drawn parallel to the isometric axes are equally foreshortened. Nonisometric lines are drawn at other angles and are not equally foreshortened. Therefore the lengths of features along nonisometric lines cannot be measured directly with a scale.

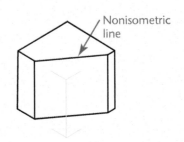

3.39   Nonisometric Edges

Isometric Scales

An isometric scale can be used to draw correct isometric projections. All distances in this scale are 2/3 × true size, or approximately 80% of true size. Figure 3.40a shows an isometric scale. More commonly, an isometric sketch or drawing is created using a standard scale, as in Figure 3.40b, disregarding the foreshortening that the tipped surfaces would produce in a true projection. Figure 3.40c shows an isometric view of a 10″ cube modeled in 3D. When measured parallel to the view, the length appears to be 8.1650 due to the foreshortening (near 80% of the actual size).

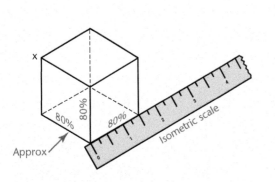

(a) Isometric projection

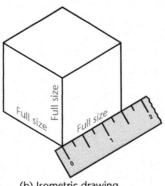

(b) Isometric drawing

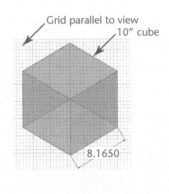

(c) CAD model in isometric view

3.40   Isometric and Ordinary Scales

TIP

Making an Isometric Scale

You can make an isometric scale from a strip of paper or cardboard by placing an ordinary scale at 45° to a horizontal line and the paper (isometric) scale at 30° to the horizontal line. To mark the increments on the isometric scale, draw straight lines (perpendicular to the horizontal line) from the division lines on the ordinary scale.

Alternatively, you can approximate an isometric scale. Scaled measurements of 9″ = 1′–0, or three-quarter-size scale (or metric equivalent) can be used as an approximation.

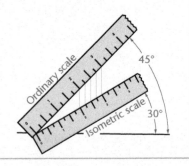

3.10 ISOMETRIC DRAWINGS

When you make a drawing using foreshortened measurements, or when the object is actually projected on a plane of projection, it is called an isometric projection (Figure 3.40a). When you make a drawing using the full-length measurements of the actual object, it is an isometric sketch or *isometric drawing* (Figure 3.40b) to indicate that it lacks foreshortening.

The isometric drawing is about 25% larger than the isometric projection, but the pictorial value is obviously the same in both. Because isometric sketches are quicker (because you can use the actual measurements), they are much more commonly drawn.

Positions of the Isometric Axes

The first step in making an isometric drawing is to decide along which axis direction to show the height, width, and depth, respectively. Figure 3.41 shows four different orientations that you might start with to create an isometric drawing of the block shown. Each is an isometric drawing of the same block, but with a different corner facing your view. These are only a few of many possible orientations.

You may orient the axes in any desired position, but the angle between them must remain 120°. In selecting an orientation for the axes, choose the position from which the object is usually viewed, or determine the position that best describes the shape of the object, or better yet, both.

If the object is a long part, it will look best with the long axis oriented horizontally.

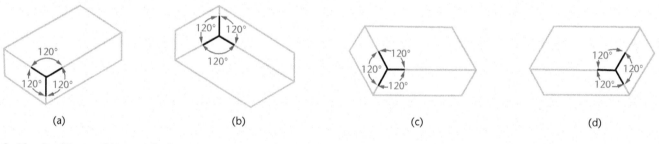

(a)　　　　(b)　　　　(c)　　　　(d)

3.41　Positions of Isometric Axes

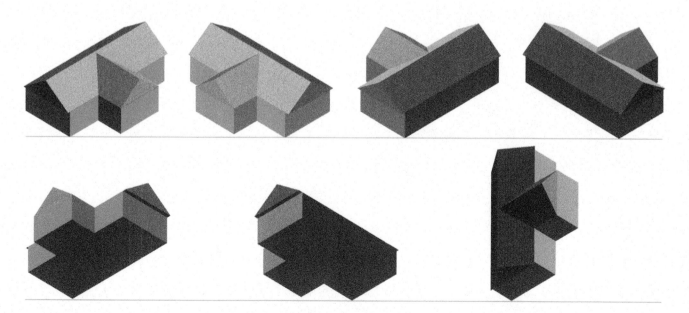

3.42　Isometric Options. *These views of a simple model of a house are all isometric, but some show the features better than others.*

3.11 MAKING AN ISOMETRIC DRAWING

Rectangular objects are easy to draw using ***box construction,*** which consists of imagining the object enclosed in a rectangular box whose sides coincide with the main faces of the object. For example, imagine the object shown in the two views in the Step by Step feature at right enclosed in a construction box, then locate the features along the edges of the box as shown.

The Step by Step feature on the next page shows how to construct an isometric drawing of an object composed of all "normal" surfaces. ***Normal*** is used technically to mean "at right angles." A normal surface is any surface that is parallel to the sides of the box. Notice that all measurements are made parallel to the main edges of the enclosing box—that is, parallel to the isometric axes. No measurement along a nonisometric line can be measured directly with the scale, as these lines are not foreshortened equally to the normal lines. Start at any one of the corners of the bounding box and draw along the isometric axis directions.

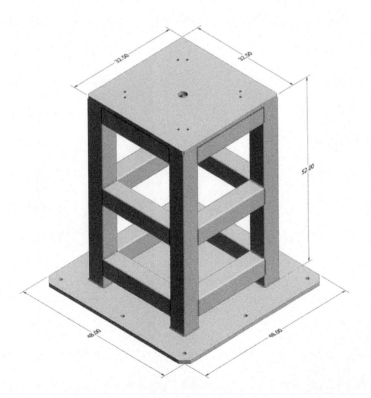

BOX CONSTRUCTION

Follow these steps to create an isometric sketch of a rectangular object.

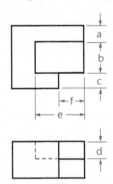

1 Lightly draw the overall dimensions of the box.

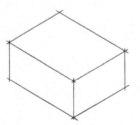

2 Draw the irregular features relative to the sides of the box.

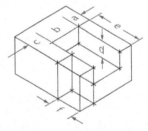

3 Darken the final lines.

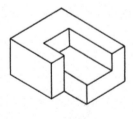

3.43 *Isometric drawings are not typically dimensioned. When they are, the dimensions should appear in the same plane as the isometric axes and read from the bottom of the sheet or aligned in the isometric planes.*
(Courtesy of Brandon Wold.)

DRAWING NORMAL SURFACES IN ISOMETRIC

Follow these steps to create an isometric drawing of the object shown below, which has normal surfaces only.

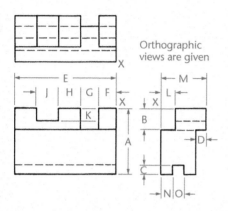

Orthographic views are given

3 Lightly block in any remaining portions to be removed through the whole block.

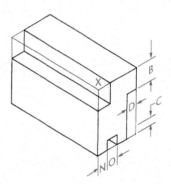

1 Select axes along which to block in height, width, and depth dimentions.

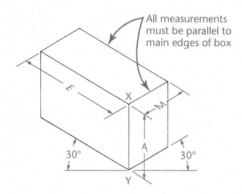

All measurements must be parallel to main edges of box

4 Lightly block in features to be removed fom the remaining shape along isometric axes.

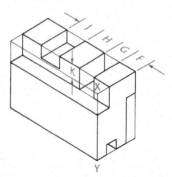

2 Locate main areas to be removed from the overall block. Lightly sketch along isometric axes to define portion to be removed.

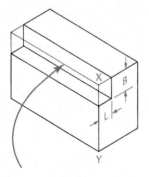

5 Darken final lines.

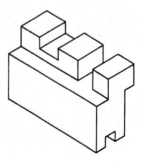

3.12 OFFSET LOCATION MEASUREMENTS

Use the method shown in Figures 3.44a and b to locate points with respect to each other. First, draw the main enclosing block, then draw the offset lines (CA and BA) full size in the isometric drawing to locate corner A of the small block or rectangular recess. These measurements are called *offset measurements*. Because they are parallel to edges of the main block in the multiview drawings, they will be parallel to the same edges in the isometric drawings (using the rule of parallelism).

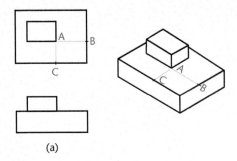

(a)

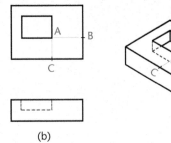

(b)

3.44 Offset Location Measurements

STEP by STEP

DRAWING NONISOMETRIC LINES

How to Draw Nonisometric Lines

The inclined lines BA and CA are shown true length in the top view (54 mm), but they are not true length in the isometric view. To draw these lines in the isometric drawing, use a construction box and offset measurements.

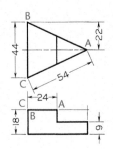

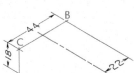

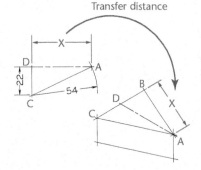

Transfer distance

1 Directly measure dimensions that are along isometric lines (in this case, 44 mm, 18 mm, and 22 mm).

2 Because the 54 mm dimension is not along an isometric axis, it cannot be used to locate point A.

Use trigonometry or draw a line parallel to the isometric axis to determine the distance to point A.

Because this dimension is parallel to an isometric axis, it can be transferred to the isometric.

3 The dimensions 24 mm and 9 mm are parallel to isometric lines and can be measured directly.

TIP

To convince yourself that nonisometric lines will not be true length in the isometric drawing, use a scrap of paper and mark the distance BA (Step 2) and then compare it with BA on the given top view. Do the same for line CA. You will see that BA is shorter and CA is longer in the isometric than the corresponding lines in the given views.

DRAWING OBLIQUE SURFACES IN ISOMETRIC

1 Find the intersections of the oblique surfaces with the isometric planes. Note that for this example, the oblique plane contains points A, B, and C.

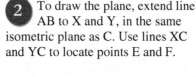

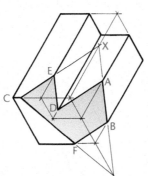

2 To draw the plane, extend line AB to X and Y, in the same isometric plane as C. Use lines XC and YC to locate points E and F.

3 Draw AD and ED using the rule, "Parallel edges on a part will appear parallel in any axonometric view." Because the inclined surface is planar and the surfaces it intersects are parallel to each other, the edges that lie in those planes will also be parallel.

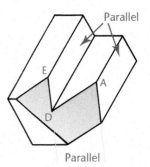

STEP by STEP

Isometric Drawings of Inclined Surfaces

Figure 3.45 shows how to construct an isometric drawing of an object that has some inclined surfaces and oblique edges. Notice that inclined surfaces are located by offset or coordinate measurements along the isometric lines. For example, dimensions E and F are measured to locate the inclined surface M, and dimensions A and B are used to locate surface N.

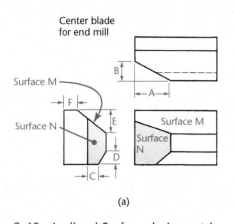

(a)

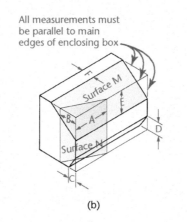

(b)

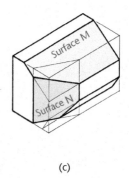

(c)

3.45 Inclined Surfaces in Isometric

3.13 HIDDEN LINES AND CENTERLINES

Hidden lines in a drawing represent the edges where surfaces meet but are not directly visible. Hidden lines are omitted from pictorial drawings unless they are needed to make the drawing clear. Figure 3.46 shows a case in which hidden lines are needed because a projecting part cannot be clearly shown without them. Sometimes it is better to include an isometric view from another direction than to try to show hidden features with hidden lines. You will learn more about hidden lines in Chapter 6.

Draw centerlines locating the center of a hole only if they are needed to indicate symmetry or for dimensioning. In general, use centerlines sparingly in isometric drawings. If in doubt, leave them out, as too many centerlines will look confusing.

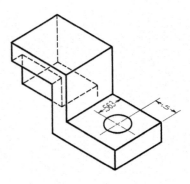

3.46 Using Hidden Lines

3.14 ANGLES IN ISOMETRIC

Angles project true size only when the plane containing the angle is parallel to the plane of projection. An angle may project to appear larger or smaller than the true angle depending on its position.

Because the various surfaces of the object are usually inclined to the front plane of projection, they generally will not be projected true size in an isometric drawing.

STEP by STEP

HOW TO DRAW ANGLES IN ISOMETRIC

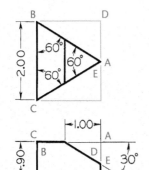

The multiview drawing at left shows three 60° angles. None of the three angles will be 60° in the isometric drawing.

3 Transfer dimension X to the isometric to complete the enclosing box. Find dimension Y by a similar method and then transfer it to the isometric.

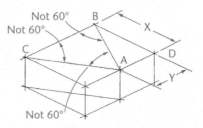

1 Lightly draw an enclosing box using the given dimensions, except for dimension X, which is not given.

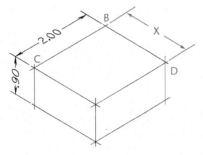

2 To find dimension X, draw triangle BDA from the top view full size, as shown.

4 Complete the isometric by locating point E by using dimension K, as shown. A regular protractor cannot be used to measure angles in isometric drawings. Convert angular measurements to linear measurements along isometric axis lines.

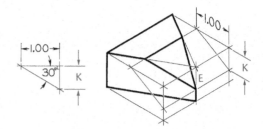

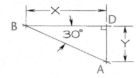

TIP

Checking Isometric Angles

To convince yourself that none of the angles will be 60°, measure each angle in the isometric in the figure above with a protractor or scrap of paper and note the angle compared with the true 60°. None of the angles shown are the same in the isometric drawing. Two are smaller and one is larger than 60°.

Estimating 30° Angles

If you are sketching on graph paper and estimating angles, an angle of 30° is roughly a rise of 1 to a run of 2.

3.15 IRREGULAR OBJECTS

You can use the construction box method to draw objects that are not rectangular (Figure 3.47). Locate the points of the triangular base by offsetting a and b along the edges of the bottom of the construction box. Locate the vertex by offsetting lines OA and OB using the top of the construction box.

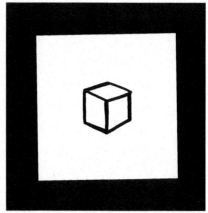
TIP

It is not always necessary to draw the complete construction box as shown in Figure 3.47b. If only the bottom of the box is drawn, the triangular base can be constructed as before. The orthographic projection of the vertex O' on the base can be drawn using offsets O'A and O'B, as shown, and then the vertical line O'O can be drawn, using measurement C.

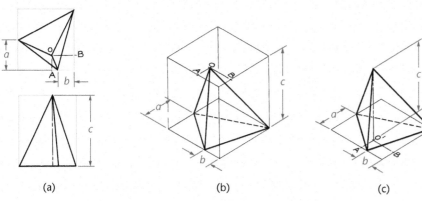

(a)   (b)   (c)

3.47   Irregular Object in Isometric

3.16 CURVES IN ISOMETRIC

You can draw curves in isometric using a series of offset measurements similar to those discussed in Section 3.12. Select any desired number of points at random along the curve in the given top view, such as points A, B, and C in Figure 3.48. Choose enough points to accurately locate the path of the curve (the more points, the greater the accuracy). Draw offset grid lines from each point parallel to the isometric axes and use them to locate each point in the isometric drawing as in the example shown in Figure 3.48.

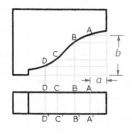

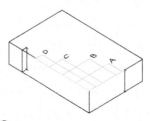

① Use offset measurements *a* and *b* in the isometric to locate point A on the curve.

② Locate points B, C, and D, and so on.

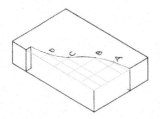

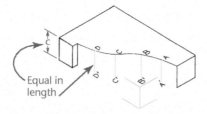

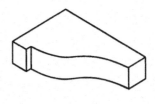

③ Sketch a smooth light freehand curve through the points.

④ Draw a line vertically from point A to locate point A', and so on, making all equal to the height of block (c), then draw a light curve through the points.

⑤ Darken the final lines.

3.48   Curves in Isometric

3.17 TRUE ELLIPSES IN ISOMETRIC

If a circle lies in a plane that is not parallel to the plane of projection, the circle projects as an ellipse. The ellipse can be constructed using offset measurements.

STEP by STEP

DRAWING AN ISOMETRIC ELLIPSE BY OFFSET MEASUREMENTS

Random-Line Method

1 Draw parallel lines spaced at random across the circle.

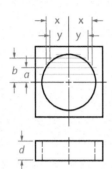

2 Transfer these lines to the isometric drawing. Where the hole exits the bottom of the block, locate points by measuring down a distance equal to the height *d* of the block from each of the upper points. Draw the ellipse, part of which will be hidden, through these points. Darken the final drawing lines.

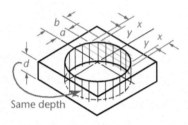

Same depth

Eight-Point Method

1 Enclose the given circle in a square, and draw diagonals. Draw another square through the points of intersection of the diagonals and the circle as shown.

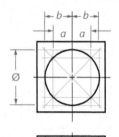

2 Draw this same construction in the isometric, transferring distances *a* and *b*. (If more points are desired, add random parallel lines, as above.) The centerlines in the isometric are the conjugate diameters of the ellipse. The 45° diagonals coincide with the major and minor axes of the ellipse. The minor axis is equal in length to the sides of the inscribed square.

When more accuracy is required, divide the circle into 12 equal parts, as shown.

12-point method

Nonisometric Lines

If a curve lies in a nonisometric plane, not all offset measurements can be applied directly. The elliptical face shown in the auxiliary view lies in an inclined nonisometric plane.

1 Draw lines in the orthographic view to locate points.

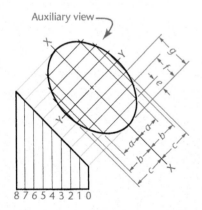

Auxiliary view

8 7 6 5 4 3 2 1 0

2 Enclose the cylinder in a construction box and draw the box in the isometric drawing. Draw the base using offset measurements, and construct the inclined ellipse by locating points and drawing the final curve through them.

Measure distances parallel to an isometric axis (*a*, *b*, etc.) in the isometric drawing on each side of the centerline X–X. Project those not parallel to any isometric axis (*e*, *f*, etc.) to the front view and down to the base, then measure along the lower edge of the construction box, as shown.

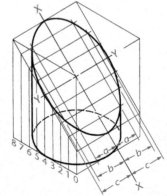

3 Darken final lines.

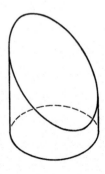

3.18 ORIENTING ELLIPSES IN ISOMETRIC DRAWINGS

Figure 3.49 shows four-center ellipses constructed on the three visible faces of a cube. Note that all the diagonals are horizontal or at 60° with horizontal. Realizing this makes it easier to draw the shapes.

Approximate ellipses such as these, constructed from four arcs, are accurate enough for most isometric drawings. The four-center method can be used only for ellipses in isometric planes. Earlier versions of CAD software, such as AutoCAD Release 10, used this method to create the approximate elliptical shapes available in the software. Current releases use an accurate ellipse.

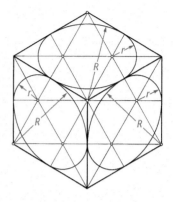

3.49 Four-Center Ellipses

DRAWING A FOUR-CENTER ELLIPSE

1 Draw or imagine a square enclosing the circle in the multiview drawing. Draw the isometric view of the square (an equilateral parallelogram with sides equal to the diameter of the circle).

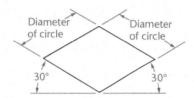

2 Mark the midpoint of each line and draw a perpendicular line from each.

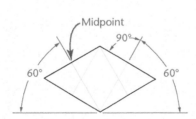

— **TIP** —

Here is a useful rule. The major axis of the ellipse is always at right angles to the centerline of the cylinder, and the minor axis is at right angles to the major axis and coincides with the centerline.

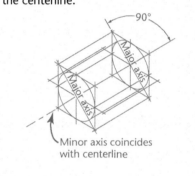

3 Draw the two large arcs, with radius *R*, from the intersections of the perpendiculars in the two closest corners of the parallelogram.

4 Draw the two small arcs, with radius *r*, from the intersections of the perpendiculars within the parallelogram, to complete the ellipse.

— **TIP** —

As a check on the accurate location of these centers, you can draw a long diagonal of the parallelogram as shown in Step 4. The midpoints of the sides of the parallelogram are points of tangency for the four arcs.

More Accurate Ellipses

The four-center ellipse deviates considerably from a true ellipse. As shown in Figure 3.50a, a four-center ellipse is somewhat shorter and "fatter" than a true ellipse. When the four-center ellipse is not accurate enough, you can use a closer approximation called the Orth four-center ellipse to produce a more accurate drawing.

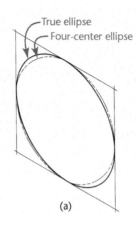
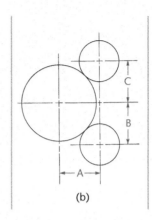
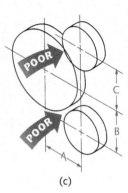

(a)   (b)   (c)

3.50   Inaccuracy of the Four-Center Ellipse

DRAWING AN ORTH FOUR-CENTER ELLIPSE

STEP by STEP

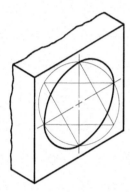

To create a more accurate approximate ellipse using the Orth method, follow the steps for these methods. The centerline method is convenient when starting from a hole or cylinder.

Centerline Method

1 Draw the isometric centerlines. From the center, draw a construction circle equal to the actual diameter of the hole or cylinder. The circle will intersect the centerlines at four points, A, B, C, and D.

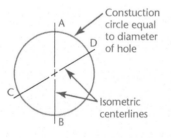

2 From the two intersection points on one centerline, draw perpendiculars to the other centerline. Then draw perpendiculars from the two intersection points on the other centerline to the first centerline.

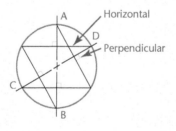

3 With the intersections of the perpendiculars as centers, draw two small arcs and two large arcs.

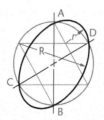

Enclosing-Rectangle Method

1 Locate center of circle and block in enclosing isometric rectangle.

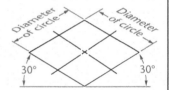

2 Use the midpoint of the isometric rectangle (the distance from A to B) to locate the foci on the major axis.

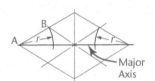

3 Draw lines at 60° from horizontal through the foci (points C and D) to locate the center of the large arc R.

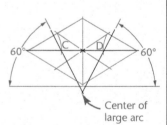

4 Draw the two large arcs R tangent to the isometric rectangle. Draw two small arcs r, using foci points C and D as centers, to complete the approximate ellipse.

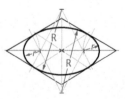

Note that these steps are exactly the same as for the regular four-center ellipse, except for the use of the isometric centerlines instead of the enclosing parallelogram. (When sketching, it works fine to just draw the enclosing rectangle and sketch the arcs tangent to its sides.)

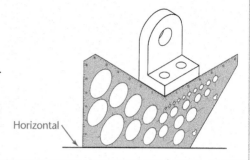
3.19 DRAWING ISOMETRIC CYLINDERS

A typical drawing with cylindrical shapes is shown in Figure 3.51. Note that the centers of the larger ellipse cannot be used for the smaller ellipse, though the ellipses represent concentric circles. Each ellipse has its own parallelogram and its own centers. Notice that the centers of the lower large ellipse are drawn by projecting the centers of the upper large ellipse down a distance equal to the height of the cylinder.

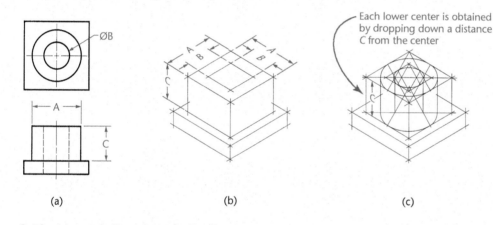

Each lower center is obtained by dropping down a distance C from the center

ØB

(a)　　　　(b)　　　　(c)　　　　(d)

3.51 Isometric Drawing of a Bearing

3.20 SCREW THREADS IN ISOMETRIC

Parallel partial ellipses equally spaced at the symbolic thread pitch are used to represent only the crests of a screw thread in isometric (Figure 3.52). The ellipses may be sketched, drawn by the four-center method, or created using an ellipse template.

3.52 Screw Threads in Isometric

3.21 ARCS IN ISOMETRIC

The four-center ellipse construction can be used to sketch or draw circular arcs in isometric. Figure 3.53a shows the complete construction. It is not necessary to draw the complete constructions for arcs, as shown in Figures 3.53b and c. Measure the radius R from the construction corner, then at each point, draw perpendiculars to the lines. Their intersection is the center of the arc. Note that the R distances are equal in Figures 3.53b and c, but that the actual radii used are quite different.

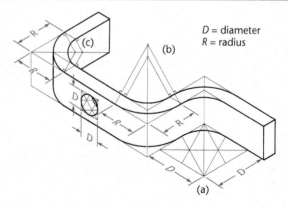

D = diameter
R = radius

3.53 Arcs in Isometric

3.22 SPHERES IN ISOMETRIC

The isometric drawing of any curved surface can be constructed from all lines that can be drawn on that surface. For spheres, select the great circles (circles cut by any plane through the center) as the lines on the surface. Because all great circles, except those that are perpendicular or parallel to the plane of projection, are shown as ellipses having equal major axes, they enclose a circle whose diameter is the major axis of the ellipse.

Figure 3.54 shows two given views of a sphere enclosed in a construction cube. Next, an isometric of a great circle is

drawn in a plane parallel to one face of the cube. There is no need to draw the ellipse, since only the points on the diagonal located by measurements *a* are needed to establish the ends of the major axis and thus to determine the radius of the sphere.

In the resulting isometric drawing, the diameter of the circle is $\sqrt{2/3}$ times the actual diameter of the sphere. The isometric projection is simply a circle whose diameter is equal to the true diameter of the sphere.

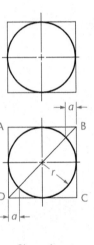

Given views

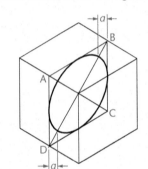

Determining the radius

1 Draw the the isometric of a great circle parallel to one face of the cube, then determine the radius of the sphere by locating points on the diagonal using measurement *a* to establish the ends of the major axis.

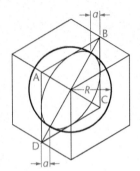

Isometric drawing

2 The diameter of the circle in the isometric drawing is $\sqrt{2/3} \times$ the diameter of the sphere.

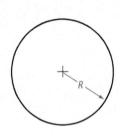

Isometric projection

3 The diameter of the circle in the isometric projection is equal to the true diameter of the sphere.

3.54   Isometric of a Sphere

STEP by STEP

ISOMETRIC SKETCHING FROM AN OBJECT

Positioning the Object

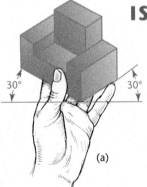

(a)

To make an isometric sketch from an actual object, first hold the object in your hand and tilt it toward you, as shown in the illustration. In this position the front corner will appear vertical. The two receding bottom edges and those edges parallel to them should appear to be at about 30° with horizontal. The steps for sketching the object follow.

1 Sketch the enclosing box lightly, making AB vertical and AC and AD approximately 30° with horizontal. These three lines are the isometric axes. Make AB, AC, and AD approximately proportional in length to the actual corresponding edges on the object. Sketch the remaining lines parallel to these three lines.

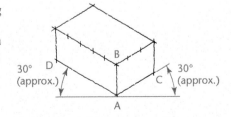

2 Block in the recess and the projecting block.

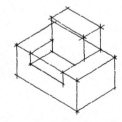

3 Darken all final lines.

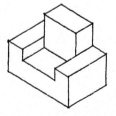

ISOMETRIC SKETCHES USING AUTOCAD SOFTWARE

Need a quick isometric sketch? AutoCAD software has special drafting settings for creating an isometric style grid.

Figure A shows the Drafting Settings dialog box in Auto-CAD. When you check the button for Isometric snap, the software calculates the spacing needed for an isometric grid. You can use it to make quick pictorial sketches like the example shown in Figure B. Piping diagrams are often done this way, although they can also be created using 3D tools.

Even though the drawing in Figure B looks 3D, it is really drawn in a flat 2D plane. You can observe this if you change the viewpoint so you are no longer looking straight onto the view.

(A) Selecting Isometric Snap in the AutoCAD Drafting Settings Dialog Box *(Autodesk screen shots reprinted courtesy of Autodesk, Inc.)*

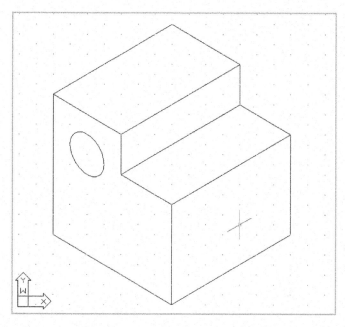

(B) A Pictorial Sketch Created from a Flat Drawing Using Isometric Snap

The **Ellipse** command in AutoCAD has a special Isocircle option that makes drawing isometric ellipses easy. The isocircles are oriented in different directions depending on the angle of the snap cursor. Figure C shows isocircles and snap cursors for the three different orientations. In the software, you press **<Ctrl>** and **E** simultaneously to toggle the cursor appearance.

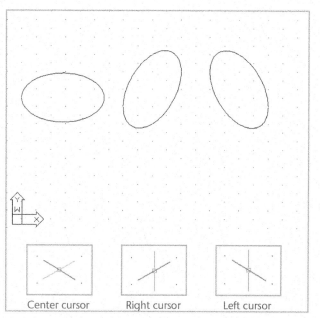

(C) Variously Oriented Isometric Circles and the Corresponding Snap Cursors Used to Create Them

3.23 OBLIQUE SKETCHES

Oblique drawing is an easy method for creating quick pictorials (Figure 3.55). In most oblique sketches, circles and angles parallel to the projection plane are true size and shape and are therefore easy to construct. Although circular shapes are easy to sketch in the front oblique plane, they would appear elliptical in the top or sides. Oblique views are primarily a sketching technique used when the majority of circular shapes appear in the front view or when the object can be rotated to position circles in the front view.

CAD is not typically used to create oblique views because better-appearing isometric or perspective drawings can be created easily from 3D CAD models.

Appearance of Oblique Drawings

Three things affect the appearance of your oblique sketch:

1. The surface of the object you choose to show parallel to the projection plane
2. The angle and orientation you choose for the receding lines that depict the object's depth
3. The scale you choose for the receding lines depicting the object's depth (Figure 3.56)

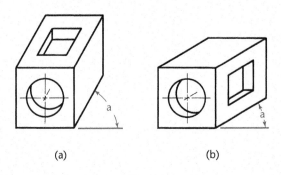

(a)   (b)

3.56   Angle of Receding Axis

Meat Cereals. *Oblique sketching shows the front surface parallel to the view, making these meat cereal boxes easy to draw. (Courtesy of Randall Munroe.)*

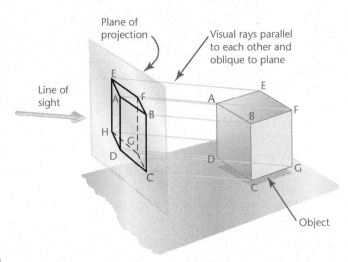

3.55   Oblique Projection Theory

Choosing the Front Surface

Think about which surface of the object would be the best one to think of as parallel to the plane of projection. For example, a cube has six different surfaces. As you are creating your sketch, any of those six surfaces could be oriented as the "front" of the part. Of course, with a cube it wouldn't matter which one you chose. But a cube with a hole through it will make a much better oblique sketch when the round hole is oriented parallel to the projection plane.

Angle of Receding Lines

An angle of 45° is often chosen for the angle of the receding lines because it makes oblique sketches quick and easy. You can use graph paper and draw the angled lines through the diagonals of the grid boxes. An angle of 30° is also a popular choice. It can look more realistic at times. Any angle can be used, but 45° is typical. As shown in Figure 3.57, you can produce different oblique drawings by choosing different directions for the receding lines.

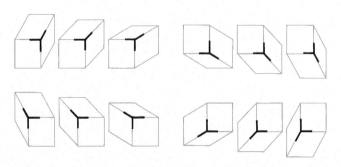

3.57   Variation in Direction of Receding Axis

Cavalier projection

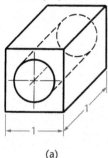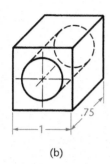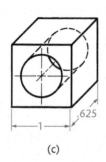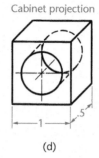

Cabinet projection

(a)   (b)   (c)   (d)   (e)

3.58 Foreshortening of Receding Lines

3.24 LENGTH OF RECEDING LINES

Theoretically, *oblique projectors* can be at any angle to the plane of projection other than perpendicular or parallel. The difference in the angle you choose causes *receding lines* of oblique drawings to vary in angle and in length from near zero to near infinity. However, many of those choices would not produce very useful drawings. Figure 3.58 shows a variety of oblique drawings with different lengths for the receding lines.

Because we see objects in perspective (where receding parallel lines appear to converge) oblique projections look unnatural to us. The longer the object in the receding direction, the more unnatural the object appears. For example, the object shown in Figure 3.58a is an isometric drawing of a cube in which the receding lines are shown full length. They appear to be too long and they appear to widen toward the rear of the block. Figure 3.59b shows how unnatural the familiar pictorial image of railroad tracks leading off into the distance would look if drawn in an oblique projection. To give a more natural appearance, show long objects with the long axis parallel to the view, as shown in Figure 3.60.

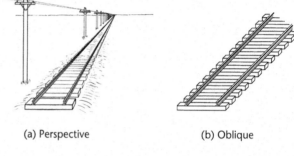
(a) Perspective   (b) Oblique

3.59 Unnatural Appearance of Oblique Drawing

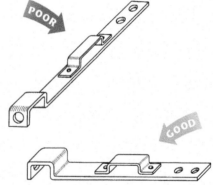

3.60 Long Axis Parallel to Plane of Projection

Cavalier Projection

When the receding lines are true length—(the projectors make an angle of 45° with the plane of projection)—the oblique drawing is called a *cavalier projection* (Figure 3.58a). Cavalier projections originated in the drawing of medieval fortifications and were made on horizontal planes of projection. On these fortifications the central portion was higher than the rest, so it was called cavalier because of its dominating and commanding position.

Cabinet Projection

When the receding lines are drawn to half size (Figure 3.58d), the drawing is known as a *cabinet projection*. This term is attributed to the early use of this type of oblique drawing in the furniture industries. Figure 3.61 shows a file drawer drawn in cavalier and cabinet projections.

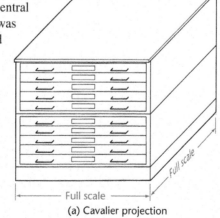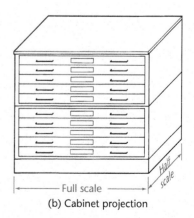
(a) Cavalier projection   (b) Cabinet projection

3.61 Comparison of (a) Cavalier and (b) Cabinet Projections

3.25 CHOICE OF POSITION IN OBLIQUE DRAWINGS

Orient the view so that important shapes are parallel to the viewing plane, as shown in Figure 3.62. In Figures 3.62a and c, the circles and circular arcs are shown in their true shapes and are easy to draw. In Figures 3.62b and d they are not shown in true shape and must be plotted as free curves or ellipses.

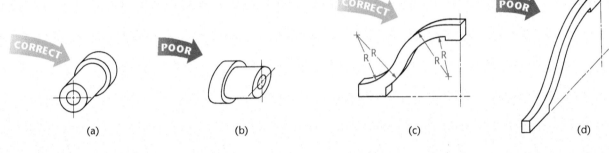

(a)   (b)   (c)   (d)

3.62   Essential Contours Parallel to Plane of Projection

3.26 ELLIPSES FOR OBLIQUE DRAWINGS

Circular shapes that are parallel to the front plane of projection appear as circles in oblique view. In isometric views they appear elliptical. Figure 3.63 shows a comparison of a cylinder drawn in isometric and oblique views.

It is not always possible to orient the view of an object so that all its rounded shapes are parallel to the plane of projection. For example, the object shown in Figure 3.64a has two sets of circular contours in different planes. Both cannot be simultaneously placed parallel to the plane of projection, so in the oblique projection, one of them must be viewed as an ellipse.

If you are sketching, you can just block in the enclosing rectangle and sketch the ellipse tangent to its sides. Using CAD, you can draw the ellipse by specifying its center and major and minor axes. In circumstances where a CAD system is not available, if you need an accurate ellipse, you can draw it by hand using a four-center arc approximation.

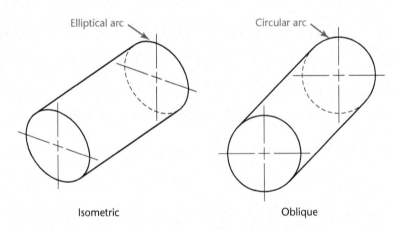

Elliptical arc   Circular arc

Isometric   Oblique

3.63   Oblique and Isometric Projections for a Cylinder

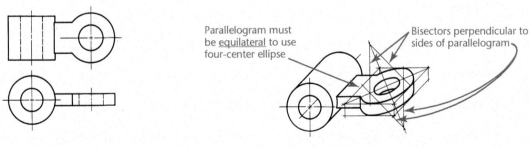

(a) Object with circles in different planes

Parallelogram must be _equilateral_ to use four-center ellipse

Bisectors perpendicular to sides of parallelogram

(b) Use of four-center ellipse

3.64   Circles and Arcs Not Parallel to Plane of Projection

3.27 ANGLES IN OBLIQUE PROJECTION

When an angle that is specified in degrees lies in a receding plane, convert the angle into linear measurements to draw the angle in an oblique drawing. Figure 3.65a shows a drawing with an angle of 30° specified.

To draw the angle in the oblique drawing, you will need to know distance X. The distance from point A to point B is given as 32 mm. This can be measured directly in the cavalier drawing (Figure 3.65b). Find distance X by drawing the right triangle ABC (Figure 3.65c) using the dimensions given, which is quick and easy using CAD.

You can also use a mathematical solution to find the length of the side: The length of the opposite side equals the tangent of the angle times the length of the adjacent side. In this case, the length of the opposite side, X, is about 18.5 mm. Draw the angle in the cavalier drawing using the found distance.

Remember that all receding dimensions must be reduced to match the scale of the receding axis. In the cabinet drawing in Figure 3.65c, the distance BC must be half the side BC of the right triangle in Figure 3.65c.

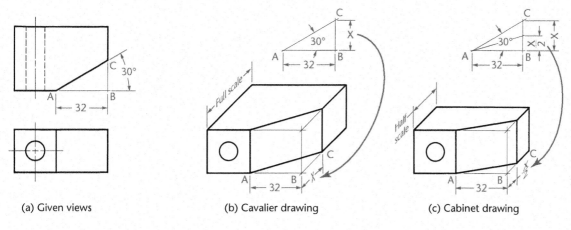

| (a) Given views | (b) Cavalier drawing | (c) Cabinet drawing |

3.65 Angles In Oblique Projection

USING BOX CONSTRUCTION TO CREATE AN OBLIQUE DRAWING

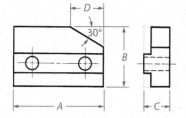

Follow these steps to draw a cavalier drawing of the rectangular object shown in the two orthographic views.

1 Lightly block in the overall width (*A*) and height (*B*) to form the enclosing rectangle for the front surface. Select an angle for the receding axis (OZ) and draw the depth (*C*) along it.

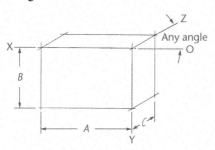

2 Lightly block in the details of the front surface shape including the two holes, which will appear round. Add the details of the right-side surface shape. Extend lines along the receding axis connecting the edges to form the remaining surface edges.

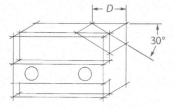

3 Darken the final lines.

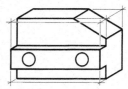

USING SKELETON CONSTRUCTION IN OBLIQUE DRAWING

STEP by STEP

Oblique drawings are especially useful for showing objects that have cylindrical shapes built on axes or centerlines. Follow these steps to construct an oblique drawing of the part shown using projected centerlines.

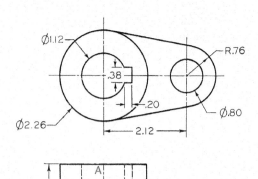

1. Position the object in the drawing so that the circles shown in the given top view are parallel to the plane of projection. The circles will show true shape in the oblique view. Draw the circular shape in the front plane of the oblique view and extend the center axis along the receding axis of the oblique drawing.

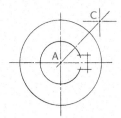

2. Add the centerline skeleton as shown.

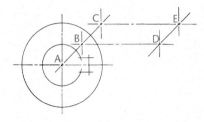

3. Build the drawing from the location of these centerlines.

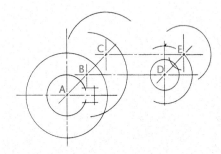

4. Construct all important points of tangency.

Important: Determine all points of tangency

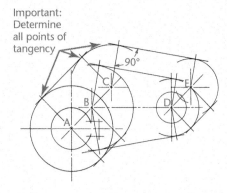

5. Darken the final cavalier drawing.

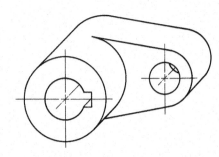

3.28 SKETCHING ASSEMBLIES

Assembly drawings are used to show how parts fit together. Because they do not need to provide all the information to make individual parts, isometric sketches or drawings are often used that show only the exterior view of the assembled parts. You can use assembly sketches as you design to identify areas that must fit together or have common dimensions, or to maintain critical distances to ensure that the device will function as expected. Figure 3.66 shows an isometric sketch of an assembly.

Sketched assembly drawings are useful in documenting your ideas in a rougher state. An exploded isometric assembly drawing shows the individual parts moved apart from one another along the isometric axis line directions. A centerline pattern is used to show how the parts relate and fit together.

When creating an exploded assembly sketch, keep the parts lined up with the other parts where they assemble. If possible, move any single parts along only one axis direction. In Figure 3.67, all exploded parts are moved along only one axis direction. Notice the centerline pattern showing how the parts align. If you must move a part in two different directions so that it can be seen clearly, add a centerline showing how the part must move to get to its proper location in the assembly. In Figure 3.68, parts have been moved in two axis directions. You can see the jog in the centerline indicating how the part has been moved.

Finished assembly drawings that will be given to manufacturing workers to show them how to produce a device also contain a parts list that identifies each part in the assembly, the quantity necessary, the material of each part, and a number identifying which item it is on the drawing. A parts list can also be included on a sketched assembly drawing. Sometimes it is helpful to give a quick assembly sketch to manufacturing along with part drawings, especially if they are parts you need to have manufactured quickly from a sketch. Seeing how the parts fit together in assembly will help the manufacturer understand the entire device and identify potential problems.

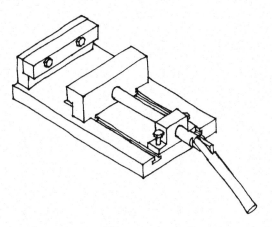

3.66 Isometric Assembly Sketch

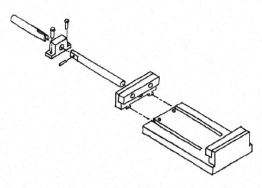

3.67 Exploded Isometric Assembly Sketch. *Centerlines have been added to show where parts line up in the assembly.*

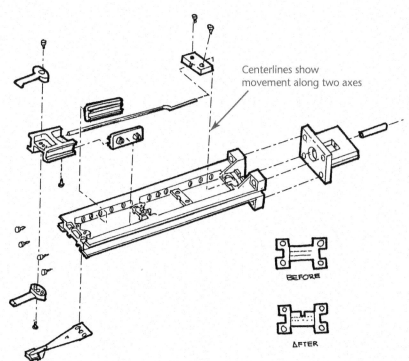

Centerlines show movement along two axes

BEFORE

AFTER

3.68 Isometric Assembly Sketch. *Some parts have been exploded in two directions so they do not overlap other parts in the assembly. The centerlines indicate the path the part must follow to assemble correctly.* (Courtesy of Albert W. Brown, Jr.)

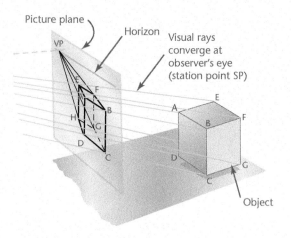

3.69   Perspective Drawing Theory

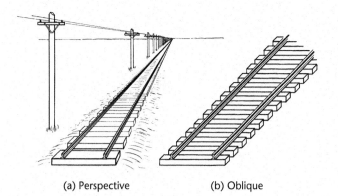

(a) Perspective   (b) Oblique

3.70   Perspective vs. Oblique. *Perspective drawings appear more natural than oblique drawings.*

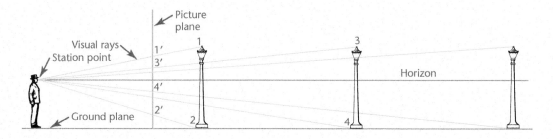

3.71   Looking through the Picture Plane

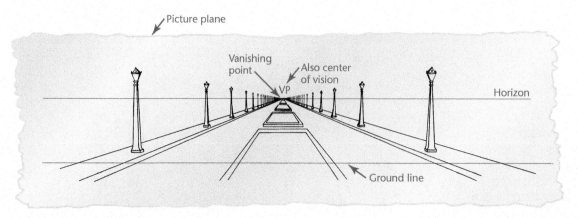

3.72   A Perspective

3.29 SKETCHING PERSPECTIVES

Perspective pictorials most closely approximate the view produced by the human eye. Perspective views are the type of drawing most like a photograph. Examples of a perspective drawing can be seen in Figures 3.69, 3.70a, and 3.72. Although complex perspective views are time consuming to sketch, they are easy to create from 3D CAD models.

Unlike parallel types of projection, perspective projectors converge. The point at which the projectors converge is called the ***vanishing point.*** This is clearly seen in Figure 3.70a.

The first rule of perspective is that all parallel lines that are not parallel to the picture plane vanish at a single vanishing point, and if these lines are parallel to the ground, the vanishing point will be on the horizon. Parallel lines that are also parallel to the picture plane remain parallel and do not converge toward a vanishing point (Figures 3.71 and 3.72).

When the vanishing point is placed above the view of the object in the picture plane, the result is a bird's-eye view, looking down onto the object. When the vanishing point is placed below the view of the object, the result is a worm's-eye view looking up at the object from below (see Figure 3.74 on page 107).

There are three types of perspective: one-point, two-point, and three-point perspective, depending on the number of vanishing points used.

The Three Types of Perspective

Perspective drawings are classified according to the number of vanishing points required, which in turn depends on the position of the object with respect to the picture plane.

If the object sits with one face parallel to the plane of projection, only one vanishing point is required. The result is a *one-point perspective,* or *parallel perspective*.

If the object sits at an angle with the picture plane but with vertical edges parallel to the picture plane, two vanishing points are required, and the result is a *two-point perspective,* or an *angular perspective*. This is the most common type of perspective drawing.

If the object sits so that no system of parallel edges is parallel to the picture plane, three vanishing points are necessary, and the result is a *three-point perspective*.

One-Point Perspective

To sketch a one-point perspective view, orient the object so that a principal face is parallel to the picture plane. If desired, this face can be placed in the picture plane. The other principal face is perpendicular to the picture plane, and its lines will converge toward a single vanishing point.

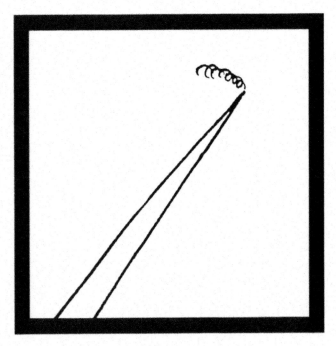

8:12 Train as Seen by 8:12 1/2 Commuter
(Excerpted from The Ultimate Droodles Compendium by Roger Price ©2019 by Tallfellow Press. Used by permission. All rights reserved.)

ONE-POINT PERSPECTIVE

To sketch the bearing in one-point perspective—that is, with one vanishing point—follow the steps illustrated below.

1 Sketch the true front face of the object, just as in oblique sketching. Select the vanishing point for the receding lines. In many cases it is desirable to place the vanishing point above and to the right of the picture, as shown, although it can be placed anywhere in the sketch. However, if the vanishing point is placed too close to the center, the lines will converge too sharply and the picture will be distorted.

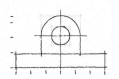

2 Sketch the receding lines toward the vanishing point.

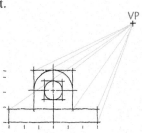

3 Estimate the depth to look good and sketch in the back portion of the object. Note that the back circle and arc will be slightly smaller than the front circle and arc.

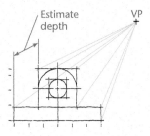

4 Darken all final lines. Note the similarity between the perspective sketch and the oblique sketch earlier in the chapter.

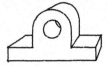

Two-Point Perspective

Two-point perspective is more true to life than one-point perspective. To sketch a two-point perspective, orient the object so that principal edges are vertical and therefore have no vanishing point; edges in the other two directions have vanishing points. Two-point perspective is especially good for representing buildings and large civil structures, such as dams or bridges.

STEP by STEP

TWO-POINT PERSPECTIVE

To sketch a desk using two vanishing points, follow these steps.

1 Sketch the front corner of the desk at true height. Locate two vanishing points (VPL and VPR) on a horizon line (at eye level). Distance CA may vary—the greater it is, the higher the eye level will be and the more we will be looking down on top of the object. A rule of thumb is to make C–VPL one third to one fourth of C–VPR.

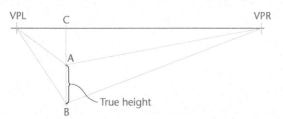

2 Estimate depth and width, and sketch the enclosing box.

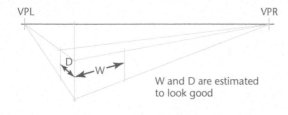

W and D are estimated to look good

3 Block in all details. Note that all parallel lines converge toward the same vanishing point.

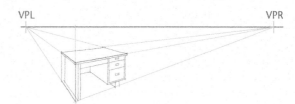

4 Darken all final lines. Make the outlines thicker and the inside lines thinner, especially where they are close together.

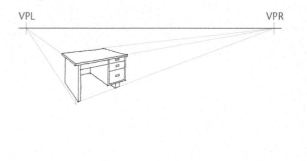

Three-Point Perspective

In **three-point perspective,** the object is placed so that none of its principal edges is parallel to the picture plane. Each of the three sets of parallel edges has a separate vanishing point. See Figure 3.73.

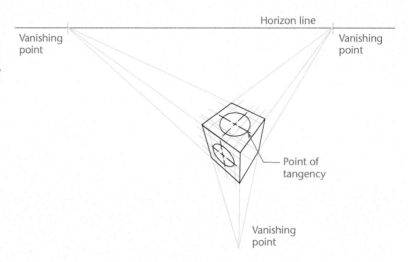

3.73 Three-Point Perspective

Bird's-Eye View versus Worm's-Eye View

The appearance of a perspective sketch depends on your viewpoint in relation to the object. Select some reachable object in the room and move so that you are looking at it from above and really notice its shape. Now gradually move so that you are looking at it from below. Notice how the change of viewpoint changes the appearance of its surfaces—which ones are visible and their relative size.

The *horizon line* in a perspective sketch is a horizontal line that represents the eye level of the observer. Locating the sketched object below the horizon line produces a view from above (or a bird's-eye view). Locating the sketched object above the horizon line produces a view from below (or a worm's-eye view). Figure 3.74 illustrates the horizon line in a drawing and the effect of placing the object above or below the horizon line.

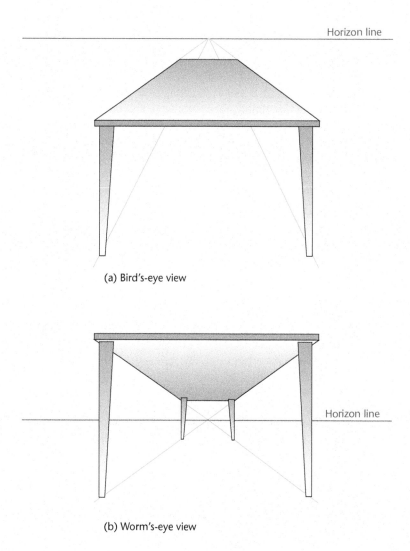

Horizon line

(a) Bird's-eye view

Horizon line

(b) Worm's-eye view

3.74 (a) Object below the Horizon Line; (b) Object above the Horizon Line

---

3.30 CURVES AND CIRCLES IN PERSPECTIVE

If a circle is parallel to the picture plane, its perspective view is a circle. If the circle is inclined to the picture plane, its perspective drawing may be any one of the conic sections in which the base of the cone is the given circle, the vertex is the station point, and the cutting plane is the picture plane (see Figure 3.71). The centerline of the cone of rays is usually approximately perpendicular to the picture plane, so the perspective will usually be an ellipse.

An ellipse may be drawn using a method of blocking in its center and a box tangent to the ellipse as shown in Figure 3.75. Also shown is a convenient method for determining the perspective of any planar curve.

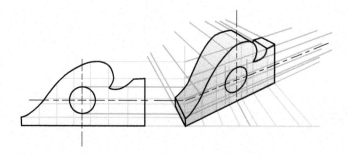

3.75 Blocking in Curves in Two-Point Perspective

3.31 SHADING

Shading can make it easier to visualize pictorial drawings, such as display drawings, patent drawings, and catalog drawings. Ordinary multiview and assembly drawings are not shaded. The shading should be simple, reproduce well, and produce a clear picture. Some of the common types of shading are shown in Figure 3.76. Two methods of shading fillets and rounds are shown in Figures 3.76c and d. Shading produced with dots is shown in Figure 3.76e, and pencil tone shading is shown in Figure 3.76f. Pencil tone shading used in pictorial drawings on tracing paper reproduces well only when making blueprints, not when using a copier.

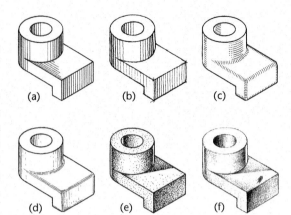

(a) (b) (c) (d) (e) (f)

3.76   Methods of Shading

3.32 COMPUTER GRAPHICS

Pictorial drawings of all types can be created using 3D CAD (Figures 3.77 and 3.78). To create pictorials using 2D CAD, use projection techniques similar to those presented in this chapter. The advantage of 3D CAD is that once you make a 3D model of a part or assembly, you can change the viewing direction at any time for orthographic, isometric, or perspective views. You can also apply different materials to the drawing objects and shade them to produce a high degree of realism in the pictorial view.

ITEM NO.	PART NAME	QTY.
1	Outer Tube	1
2	End	1
3	Top	1
4	Inner Tube	1
5	Heat exchanger	1
6	Assem Sampler	1
7	Fan	1
8	Sample Bottom	1
9	HX Mounting Plate	1
10	Cooling Hose	1
11	Door	1

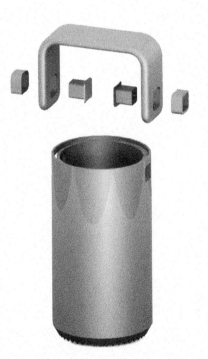

3.77   Shaded Dimetric Pictorial View from a 3D Model *(Courtesy of Robert Kincaid.)*

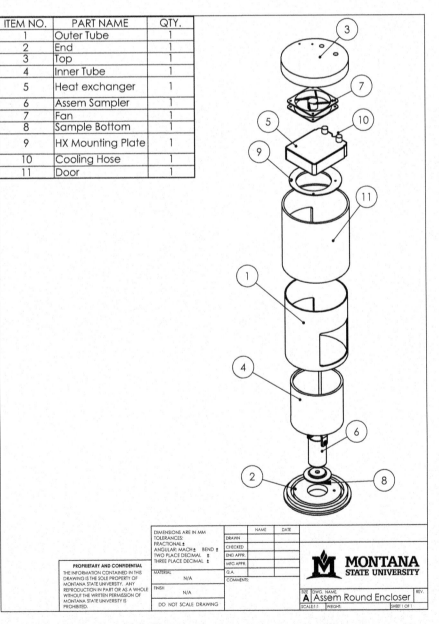

3.78   Isometric Assembly Drawing *(Courtesy of Robert Kincaid.)*

3.33 DRAWING ON DRAWING

Because CAD helps people produce accurate drawings that are easy to alter, store, and repurpose, computer automation has made the painstaking aspects of hand-rendering technical drawings nearly obsolete. Still, the ability to sketch with clarity is an immediate and universal way to record and communicate ideas.

The ability to think of complex objects in terms of their basic solid components and to identify relationships between various surfaces, edges, and vertices is basic to creating both hand-drawn (Figure 3.79) and computer-generated technical drawings. By understanding how to represent objects accurately, you can communicate efficiently as part of a team and increase your constructive visualization ability, or your ability to "think around corners."

"... I want to be able to draw any kind of line I want."

Jacob Baron-Taltre works as a product designer for a midsize furniture manufacturer in the Seattle region. He sketches nearly every day at work.

"Sometimes the sketches are very loose ... just tools for me to work out some detail that I am designing. Other times they are more elaborate and crisp because they will likely be part of a conversation or presentation."

A computer is not the first tool he reaches for when beginning a project. "Scribbling notes or quick sketches on paper is the fastest way to document the most ideas in the least time. Later, I'll develop some of those ideas more fully by hand and only then begin to use the computer to document the concepts as 2D or 3D CAD work. If I can't draw an idea by hand, I won't likely have more success (if any) using CAD."

Baron-Taltre said he sketches to explore various forms, sizes, and materials. "CAD is more precise and that precision can be somewhat limiting. When I want to draw a line I want to be able to draw any kind of line I want. In CAD, I have to use a specific tool for each line type."

"CAD is a great way to communicate finished thoughts and explore precise relationships. It's also great for quickly building accurate environments and models that can be rotated and examined. You can share these files and edit without having to redraw. Drawing by hand is faster for depicting specific ideas and can be used to communicate with someone in front of you. Plus, you can add detail to key areas of the drawing and leave out detail in areas needed only for context."

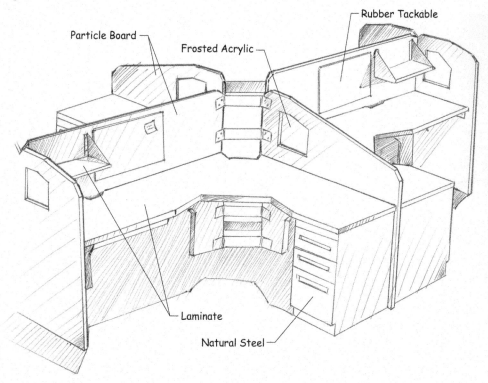

3.79 Hand Sketch Conveying Custom Workstation Furniture Concept *(Courtesy of Jacob A. Baron-Taltre.)*

SKETCHING AND PARAMETRIC MODELING

The Design Process

The parametric modeling process in many ways mirrors the design process. Parametric CAD software lets you specify geometry, dimensions, and other essential parameters that control the model. To get the rough ideas down, the designer starts by making hand sketches. Then as the ideas are refined, more accurate drawings are created either with instruments or using CAD. Necessary analysis is performed and, in response, the design may change. The drawings are revised as needed to meet the new requirements. Eventually the drawings are approved so that the parts may be manufactured.

Rough Sketches

Using parametric modeling software, the designer first roughly sketches the basic shapes on the computer screen as though sketching freehand. These sketches do not need to have perfectly straight lines or accurate corners. The software interprets the sketch much as you would interpret a rough sketch given to you by a colleague. If the lines are nearly horizontal or vertical, the software assumes that you meant them to be so. If the line appears to be perpendicular, the software assumes that it is.

Constraining the Sketch

Using a parametric CAD system, you next refine the two-dimensional sketch by adding geometric constraints, which tell how to interpret the sketch, and by adding parametric dimensions, which control the size of sketch geometry. Once the sketch is refined, you can create it as a 3D feature to which other features can be added. As the design changes, you can change the dimensions and constraints that control the sketch geometry, and the parametric model will be updated to reflect the new design.

When you are creating sketches by hand or for parametric modeling, think about the implications of the geometry you are drawing. Does the sketch imply that lines are perpendicular? Are the arcs that you have drawn intended to be tangent or intersecting? When you create a parametric model, the software applies rules to constrain the geometry, based on your sketch. You can remove, change, or add new constraints, but to use the software effectively you need to accurately depict the geometry you want formed.

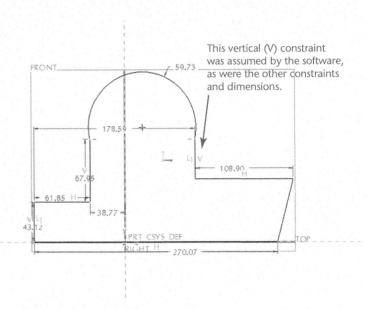

This vertical (V) constraint was assumed by the software, as were the other constraints and dimensions.

A Rough Sketch in Pro/ENGINEER Sketcher

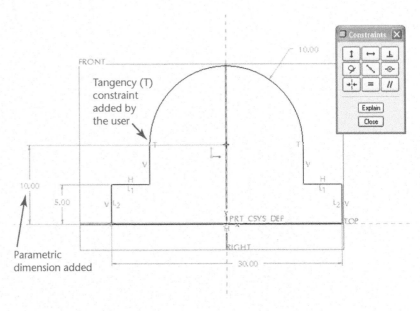

Tangency (T) constraint added by the user

Parametric dimension added

A Constrained Sketch

PERSPECTIVE VIEWS IN AUTOCAD

AutoCAD software provides options for parallel and perspective viewing. You can use the menu for the ViewCube to quickly select Parallel or Perspective viewing options (Figure A). The defaults for perspective viewing determine the basic appearance when you select the perpective view types. Notice that the grid squares in the figure appear larger closer to the view and smaller when they are farther away. When parallel projection is selected, the grid lines remain parallel.

An interactive command, **Dview** (dynamic viewing), lets you show 3D models and drawings in perspective (or parallel view) and interactively change the viewing options. Dview uses a camera and target analogy to create perspective views. Using the Camera option, you select a camera position (similar to the station point) with respect to the target point at which the camera is aimed. The Dview Distance option lets you change the distance between the camera and the object and calculate a new view. The Off option of the command turns perspective viewing off to return to a parallel view.

Specifying a distance that is too close can fill up the entire view with the object, in the same way that a close-up shot with a camera does.

The Zoom option of the Dview command acts like a normal zoom command when perspective viewing is off. When perspective viewing is on, you can zoom dynamically by moving the slider bar shown in Figure B to adjust the camera lens

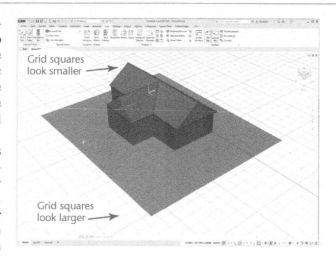

(A) A Perspective View Created Using the DView Command in AutoCAD *(Autodesk screen shots reprinted courtesy of Autodesk, Inc.)*

to change the field of view. The default is to show the view similar to what you would see through a camera with a 50 mm lens. During the Zoom option, moving the slider is similar to choosing the focal length for a camera lens, which changes the relative perspective appearance (Figure B). Shorter focal lengths exaggerate the perspective effect of closer features.

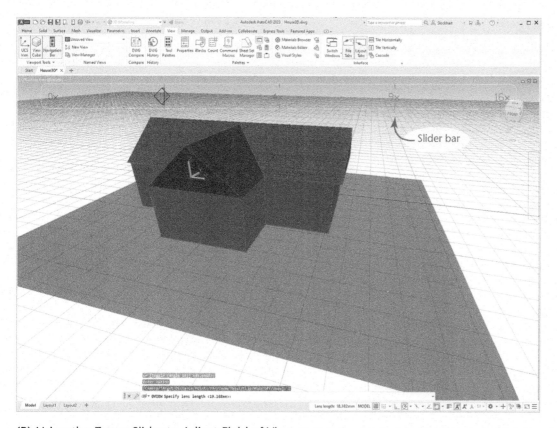

(B) Using the Zoom Slider to Adjust Field of View *(Autodesk screen shots reprinted courtesy of Autodesk, Inc.)*

SKETCHING FOR IDEATION: A CROSSACTION BREAKTHROUGH

When Oral-B hired LUNAR to create an innovative approach to brushing (and a new flagship product), they had no preconceived notions of what that would mean. But they knew that they wanted a brush that was ergonomically superior to the traditional "flat stick" design, and they wanted the brush to improve brushing effectiveness. The development of the Oral-B CrossAction Toothbrush is an example of the power of ideation in product design.

Jeff Salazar, lead designer for the project, started first not with sketches but with extensive research into the kinesiology of brushing teeth. A research firm had been hired to do a study of how people hold their toothbrushes as they brush. They found that there are five basic grips. Each person might use more than one depending on the part of the mouth to be brushed. Two or three grips were the ones used by most people.

As the kinesiology study was underway, the design team at LUNAR undertook their own study of brushing. Given that the design constraints were focused almost totally on ergonomics, they studied how people brush. They engaged team members and others and watched them brush. They used models of teeth to investigate brushing. They bought "flat stick" toothbrushes, heated them so they could be bent at different angles,

and had a variety of people report back on their brushing experience with handles of different shapes. People of various sizes and backgrounds, male and female, were asked to brush with the angled handles. This helped them understand the extremes of the angles forward and back that the handle could form.

They also studied the competition. A competitor had come out with what it promised was a superior toothbrush—one that was "bent like a dental instrument." After trying the toothbrush, however, the team concluded that the shape was only superior if someone else (e.g., the dental hygienist) was brushing your teeth. This key insight helped them focus the next stage of ideation on shapes with potential.

After discussing their results, the team selected five to six angle configurations for further study. The ergonomic results of the team's efforts were an instinct that people wanted a toothbrush that would "fill the hand" more than the thin stick. But where should the brush

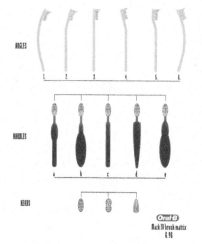

3.80 The Matrix Used to Drive Concept Generation

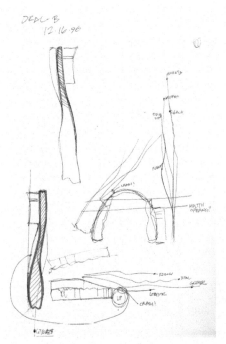
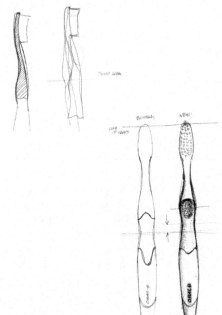
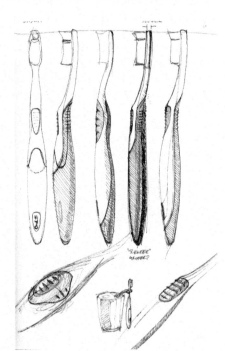

3.81 Sketches and Notes on the Concept as It Was Developed

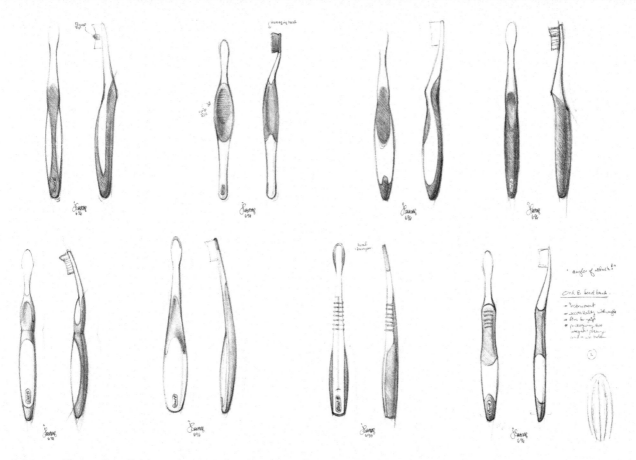

3.82   Full-Size Sketches Used to Create the Foam "3D Sketches"

be thicker? The team created a matrix that paired each of the angle configurations with the range of options for the handles' thickness (Figure 3.80). Then, Jeff began sketching all the various combinations (see Figure 3.81).

After about a week of generating pencil sketches, Jeff decided he needed to "sketch" in 3D. Starting with a full-size sketch (Figure 3.82), he used a band saw to cut the shape of the sketch in foam, then shaped the foam into a model that he and others could hold and evaluate for various grips (Figure 3.83). Those that didn't work for one grip or another were eliminated. The LUNAR team and their counterparts at Oral-B reviewed the various options and selected four for further development.

At this point, the team created 3D models of the four candidates. Oral-B had prototypes made from the CAD models for the handles (Figure 3.84), added bristles, and embarked on consumer research that would drive the next stage of refinement. Consumers were asked to brush for one month, then attend a focus group to report on their experience. LUNAR Design was present to hear consumer reactions.

What they found was that consumers loved the fatter handle. Its shape in the hand gave them more control when moving the brush to different parts of their mouth. The form provided optimal ergonomics for each of the five common grips. The faceted surface on the handle gave users a tactile clue as to

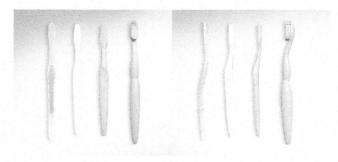

3.83   Foam Models Used as 3D Sketches

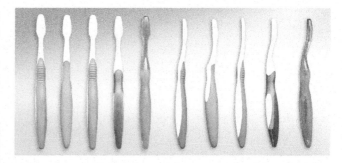

3.84   Prototypes Generated from the 3D Model

where to place their fingers when gripping. The rubberlike material used for the facets was located where users exerted the most finger pressure—and it made it easier to hold the brush when wet. The very positive response indicated that the ergonomic handle could make a significant difference in brushing that consumers would appreciate. People reported that they loved their toothbrush now!

At the same time, Jeff and the LUNAR and Oral-B teams had to listen and interpret what they heard. Focus groups are a wealth of different reactions, and it is up to the team to determine what is relevant and what is peripheral. For example, one reaction was that the fatter handle did not fit in the standard toothbrush holder. The team had to assess whether this was an issue that would hamper acceptance of the toothbrush or whether the improved brushing experience would outweigh its importance to the customer.

The refinement of the design proceeded through two more prototypes (and additional ideation around packaging; see Figure 3.85) before the final Oral-B CrossAction was launched. The intensity of the ideation stage—and the many techniques used to generate and evaluate design ideas—were critical to the team's success in achieving this breakthrough in brushing.

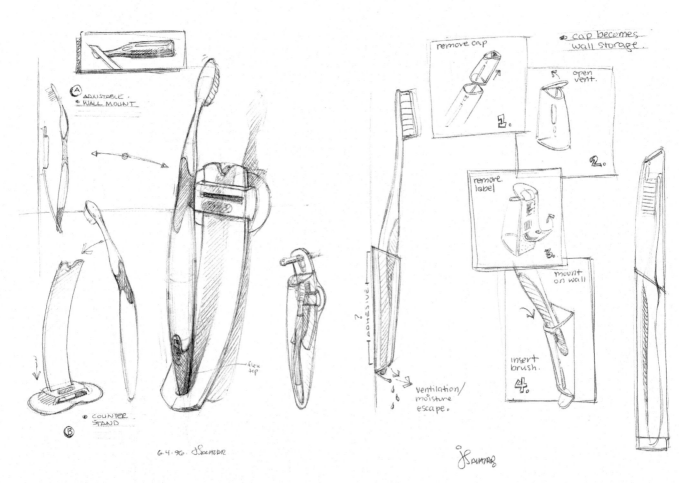

3.85 Ideation Sketches for CrossAction Packaging

(All images courtesy of LUNAR.)

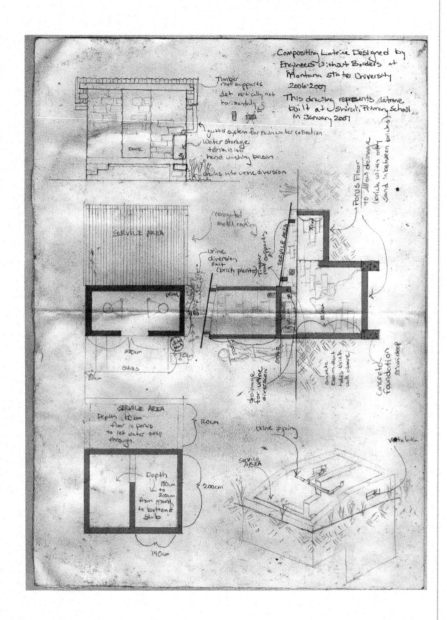

Sketch for a Composting Latrine. *The student chapter of Engineers Without Borders at Montana State University is collaborating with 57 schools in the Khwisero Division of southwestern Kenya to provide sustainable sanitary improvements including wells and composting latrines. (Sketch courtesy of Andrea Orr, Engineers Without Borders, MSU.)*

Andrea Orr was a student in environment design at Montana State University and a co-fundraiser and co-project designer in the MSU chapter of Engineers Without Borders.

She created the sketch above during the building of a composting latrine that she and Chris Allen designed for a school in the Khwisero Division of southwestern Kenya. The sketch showed instructors and local government officials how the latrine would work.

Though they had done multiple sketches ahead of time, she and Allen did this sketch to clarify their ideas into one concept.

Orr did the sketch outdoors, sitting next to the school building. There was no computer available, because at the remote location, electricity was rarely available. She also did a drawing explaining how to use and maintain the latrine, which was posted inside the finished structure.

Orr said that when she is not working in the field, she still sketches by hand before transferring to CAD.

"There's little bit of vagueness in a hand-drawn sketch that keeps it open to creativity," said Orr.

"If you show a sketch to someone they are more likely to offer input and ideas than if it looks like a finished CAD rendering. That's one of the reasons I don't work in CAD until quite a few revisions into the project."

KEY WORDS

Angle
Angular Perspective
Axonometric Projection
Box Construction
Cabinet Projection
Cavalier Projection
Cone
Construction Lines
Contours
Cylinder
Dimetric Projection
Double-Curved
Edge
Ellipsoid
Foreshortening
Freehand Sketch
Hatching
Horizon Line
Isometric Axes
Isometric Drawing
Isometric Projection
Isometric Scale
Isometric Sketch
Line
Line Patterns
Multiview Projection
Negative Space
Nonisometric Lines
Normal
Oblique Drawing
Oblique Projection
Oblique Projectors

Offset Measurements
One-Point Perspective
Orthographic Projections
Perspective
Pictorial Sketch
Planar
Point
Polyhedra
Prism
Proportion
Pyramid
Receding Lines
Regular Polyhedron
Shading
Single-Curved
Solids
Sphere
Stippling
Surfaces
Three-Point Perspective
Torus
Trimetric Projection
Two-Point Perspective
Vanishing Point
Vertex
Viewpoint
Warped

CHAPTER SUMMARY

- Sketching is a quick way of visualizing and solving a drawing problem. It is an effective way of communicating with all members of the design team.
- Three-dimensional figures are bounded by surfaces that are either planar, single-curved, double-curved, or warped.
- Prisms, pyramids, cylinders, cones, tori, and ellipsoids are common shapes in engineering drawings. There are also five regular polyhedra: the tetrahedron, hexahedron, octahedron, dodecahedron, and icosahedron.
- There are special techniques for sketching lines, circles, and arcs. These techniques should be practiced so they become second nature.
- Using a grid makes sketching in proportion an easy task.
- Circles can be sketched by constructing a square and locating the four tangent points where the circle touches the square.
- A sketched line does not need to look like a CAD or mechanical line. The main distinction between CAD and instrumental drawing and freehand sketching is the character or technique of the line work.
- Freehand sketches are made to proportion, but not necessarily to a particular scale.
- Sketching is one of the most important skills for accurately recording ideas.
- Isometric, oblique, and perspective are three methods used to create pictorial sketches.

REVIEW QUESTIONS

1. What are the advantages of using grid paper for sketching?
2. What is the correct technique for sketching a circle or arc?
3. Sketch the alphabet of lines. Which lines are thick? Which are thin? Which are very light and will not reproduce when copied?
4. What type of pictorial drawing can easily be drawn on square grid paper?
5. What is the advantage of sketching an object first before drawing it using CAD?
6. What is the difference between proportion and scale?

SKETCHING EXERCISES

Exercise 3.1 Sketch the objects shown using isometric, oblique, and one- or two-point perspective.

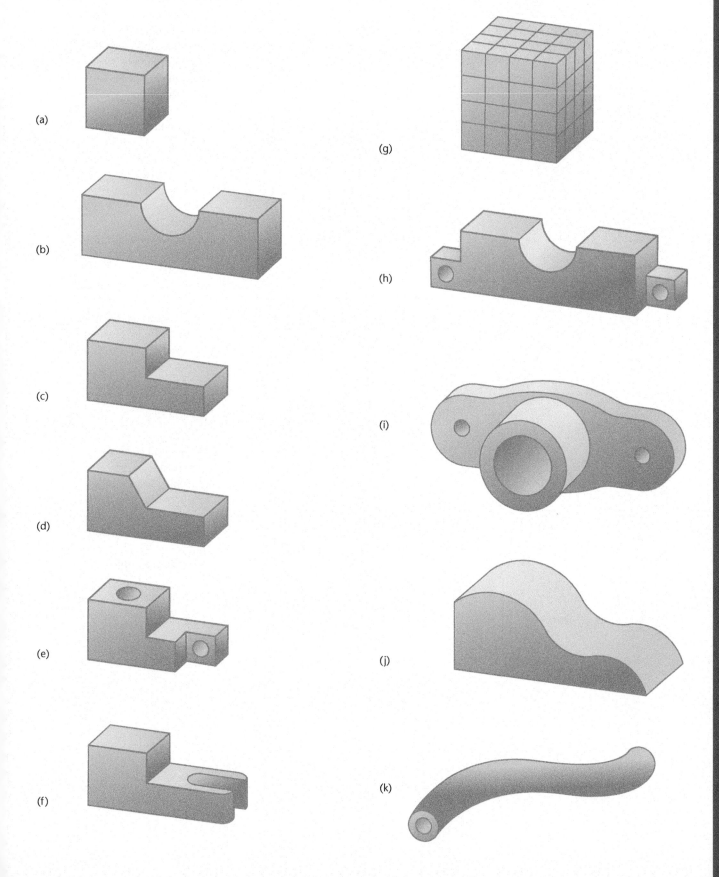

(a)

(b)

(c)

(d)

(e)

(f)

(g)

(h)

(i)

(j)

(k)

Exercise 3.2 Quick Sketch.

1. Practice the sketching skills and techniques you have learned for construction lines and ellipses. Set a timer for 10 minutes and make quick sketches of these nine different containers.
2. Select one container and create isometric, oblique, and perspective drawings.
3. Design a new piece of drinkware, using your sketching skills.
4. Select one container. Draw an enclosing box and shade in the negative space so that the contour of the container remains white.

a. *(Copyright Vitaly Korovin/Shutterstock.)*

b. *(Copyright Odua Images/Shutterstock.)*

c. *(Copyright Olga Popova/Shutterstock.)*

d. *(Copyright tanuha2001/Shutterstock.)*

e. *(Copyright Africa Studio/Shutterstock.)*

f. *(Copyright Everything/Shutterstock.)*

g. *(Copyright S-Photo/Shutterstock.)*

h. *(Copyright loskutnikov/Shutterstock.)*

i. *(Copyright PERLA BERANT WILDER/Shutterstock.)*

Exercise 3.3 Quick Sketch. Practice the sketching skills and techniques you have learned for construction lines and ellipses. Set a timer for 10 minutes and make quick sketches of these six different chairs.

a. *(Copyright violetblue/Shutterstock.)*

b. *(Copyright Yeamake/Shutterstock.)*

c. *(Copyright Atiketta Sangasaeng/ Shutterstock.)*

d. *(Copyright Ljupco Smokovski/ Shutterstock.)*

e. *(Copyright Aleksandr Kurganov/ Shutterstock.)*

f. *(Copyright Photobac/Shutterstock.)*

Exercise 3.4 Quick Sketch. Practice the sketching skills and techniques you have learned for construction lines and ellipses. Set a timer for 10 minutes and make quick sketches of these tools.

a. *(Copyright WilleeCole Photography/ Shutterstock.)*

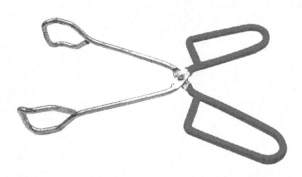

b. *(Copyright aodaodaodaod/Shutterstock.)*

c. *(Copyright Planner/Shutterstock.)*

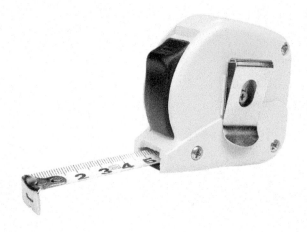

d. *(Copyright Seregam/Shutterstock.)*

e. *(Copyright Ingvar Bjork/Shutterstock.)*

f. *(Copyright Yanas/Shutterstock.)*

Exercise 3.5 Sketching. Practice the sketching skills and techniques you have learned for construction lines and ellipses. Set a timer for 10 minutes and make quick sketches of these items.

a. *(Copyright Mile Atanasov/Shutterstock.)*

b. *(Copyright Mile Atanasov/Shutterstock.)*

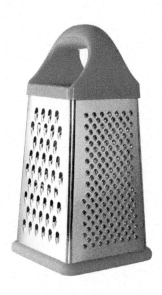

c. *(Copyright Olga Kovalenko/ Shutterstock.)*

d. *(Copyright Berents/Shutterstock.)*

e. *(Copyright Jiggo_thekop/Shutterstock.)*

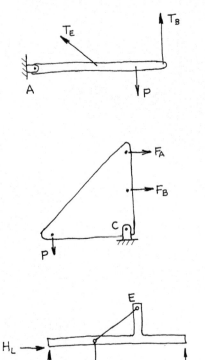

Exercise 3.6 Parking Meter. Create an oblique pictorial sketch of the parking meter shown here. Use construction lines to keep the features in proportion.

Exercise 3.7 Free-Body-Diagram Sketches. Sketch the free body diagrams as shown.

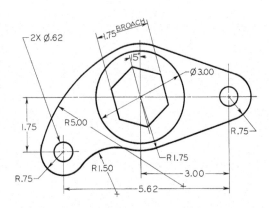

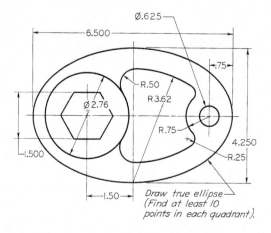

Exercise 3.8 Rocker Arm. Create a freehand sketch. Use the dimensions to help in estimating proportions. Leave the dimensions off your sketch unless directed otherwise by your instructor.

Exercise 3.9 Special Cam. Create a freehand sketch. Use the dimensions to help in estimating proportions. Leave the dimensions off your sketch unless directed otherwise by your instructor.

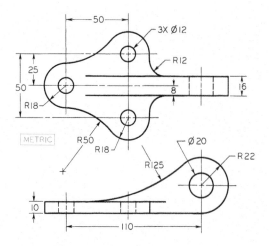

Exercise 3.10 Boiler Stay. Create a freehand sketch. Use the dimensions to help in estimating proportions. Leave the dimensions off your sketch unless directed otherwise by your instructor.

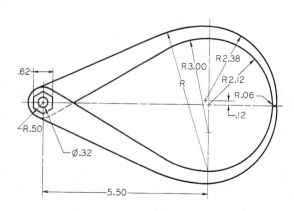

Exercise 3.11 Outside Caliper. Create a freehand sketch. Use the dimensions to help in estimating proportions. Leave the dimensions off your sketch unless directed otherwise by your instructor.

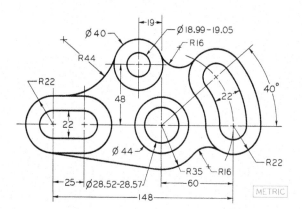

Exercise 3.12 Gear Arm. Create a freehand sketch. Use the dimensions to help in estimating proportions. Leave the dimensions off your sketch unless directed otherwise by your instructor.

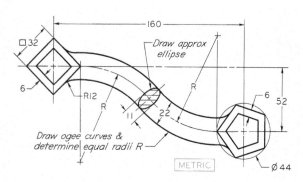

Exercise 3.13 Special S-Wrench. Create a freehand sketch. Use the dimensions to help in estimating proportions. Leave the dimensions off your sketch unless directed otherwise by your instructor.

CHAPTER FOUR

GEOMETRY FOR MODELING AND DESIGN

OBJECTIVES

After studying the material in this chapter, you should be able to:

1. Identify and specify basic geometric elements and primitive shapes.

2. Select a 2D profile that best describes the shape of an object.

3. Identify mirrored shapes and sketch their lines of symmetry.

4. Identify shapes that can be formed by extrusion and sketch their cross sections.

5. Identify shapes that can be formed by revolution techniques and sketch their profiles.

6. Define Boolean operations.

7. Specify the Boolean operations to combine primitive shapes into a complex shape.

8. Work with Cartesian coordinates and user coordinate systems in a CAD system.

9. Identify the transformations common to CAD systems.

Additional geometric constructions are located in Appendix 52.

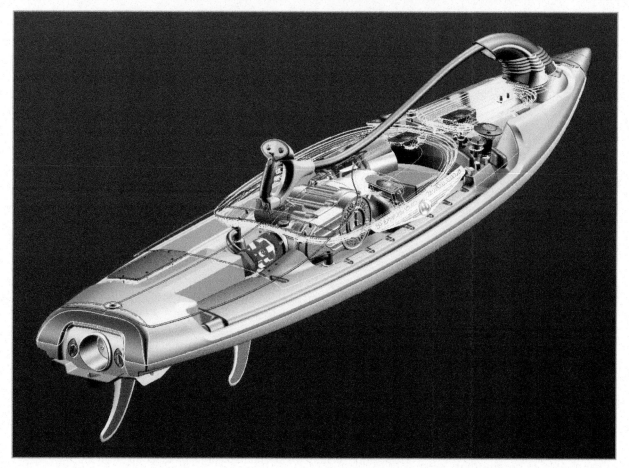

Many different geometric shapes were used to model this jetboard. The wireframe view of the top cover reveals several regular geometric shapes used to model the interior components. The graceful lines of the outer hull are defined by the irregular curves used to model it. (Courtesy of Leo Greene, www.e-Cognition.net.)

OVERVIEW

Engineering drawings combine basic geometric shapes and relationships to define complex objects. 2D drawings are composed of simple entities such as points, lines, arcs, and circles, as well as more complex entities such as ellipses and curves. Reviewing the basic geometry of these elements helps you define and combine these elements in your drawings and CAD models.

Accurate construction is critical to creating useful drawings. Lines drawn using a CAD system are highly accurate definitions—much greater than you can see on a computer monitor. Good manual drawing technique can typically produce a drawing accurate to about 1/40th of the drawing scale. For example, a hand-drawn survey created at 1″ = 400′ might be accurate to a range of plus or minus 10′. The internal precision of drawings created using CAD systems is limited by the 64 bits (base-2 places) typically used to represent decimal numbers in a CAD system. This produces a theoretical accuracy of around 1 in 10 quadrillion (10^{16}). If you drew two beams, each three times the distance from the Sun to Pluto, and made one of the beams just 1 mm longer than the other one, a CAD system could still accurately represent the difference between the two beams. Wow! That's a lot better than the 1 in 40 accuracy of a manual drawing. However, CAD drawings are accurate only if the drawing geometry is defined accurately when the drawing is created.

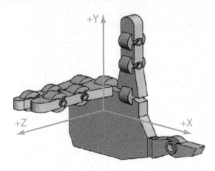

4.1   Right-Hand Rule

4.2   The Z-Axis. *In systems that use the right-hand rule, the positive Z-axis points toward you when the face of the monitor is parallel to the X-Y plane.*

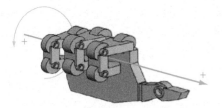

4.3   Axis of Rotation. *The curl of the fingers indicates the positive direction along the axis of rotation.*

COORDINATES FOR 3D CAD MODELING

2D and 3D CAD drawing entities are stored in relationship to a Cartesian coordinate system. No matter what CAD software system you will be using, it is helpful to understand some basic similarities of coordinate systems.

Most CAD systems use the ***right-hand rule*** for coordinate systems; if you point the thumb of your right hand in the positive direction for the X-axis and your index finger in the positive direction for the Y-axis, your remaining fingers will curl in the positive direction for the Z-axis (shown in Figure 4.1). When the face of your monitor is the X-Y plane, the Z-axis is pointing toward you (see Figure 4.2).

The right-hand rule is also used to determine the direction of rotation. For rotation using the right-hand rule, point your thumb in the positive direction along the axis of rotation. Your fingers will curl in the positive direction for the rotation, as shown in Figure 4.3.

Though rare, some CAD systems use a left-hand rule. In this case, the curl of the fingers on your left hand gives you the positive direction for the Z-axis. In this case, when the face of your computer monitor is the X-Y plane, the positive direction for the Z-axis extends into your computer monitor, not toward you.

A 2D CAD system uses only the X- and Y-coordinates of the Cartesian coordinate system. 3D CAD systems use X, Y, and Z. To represent 2D in a 3D CAD system, the view is straight down the Z-axis. Figure 4.4 shows a drawing created using only the X- and Y- values, leaving the Z-coordinates set to 0, to produce a 2D drawing.

Recall that each orthographic view shows only two of the three coordinate directions because the view is straight down one axis. 2D CAD drawings are the same: They show only the X- and Y-coordinates because you are looking straight down the Z-axis.

When the X-Y plane is aligned with the screen in a CAD system, the Z-axis is oriented horizontally. In machining and many other applications, the Z-axis is considered to be the vertical axis. In all cases, the coordinate axes are mutually perpendicular and oriented according to the right-hand or left-hand rule. Because the view can be rotated to be straight down any axis or any other direction, understanding how to use coordinates in the model is more important than visualizing the direction of the default axes and planes.

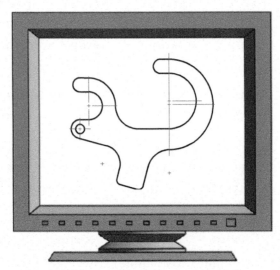

4.4   2D CAD Drawing. *This drawing was created on the X-Y plane in the CAD system. It appears true shape because the viewing direction is perpendicular to the X-Y plane—straight down the Z-axis.*

The vertices of the 3D shape shown in Figure 4.5 are identified by their X-, Y-, and Z-coordinates. Often, it is useful when modeling parts to locate the origin of the coordinate system at the lower left of the part, as shown in Figure 4.5. This location for the (0,0,0) point on a part is useful when the part is being machined, as it then makes all coordinates on the part positive (Figure 4.6). Some older numerically-controlled machinery will not interpret a file correctly if it has negative lengths or coordinates. CAD models are often exported to other systems for manufacturing parts, so try to create them in a common and useful way.

Specifying Location

Even though the model is ultimately stored in a single Cartesian coordinate system, you may usually specify the location of features using other location methods as well. The most typical of these are relative, polar, cylindrical, and spherical coordinates. These coordinate formats are useful for specifying locations to define your CAD drawing geometry.

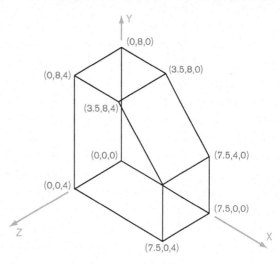

4.5   3D Coordinates for Vertices

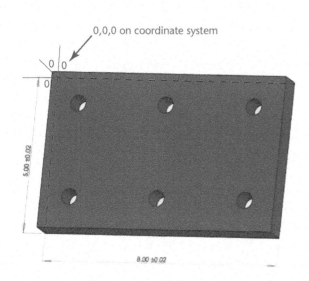

4.6   This CAD model for a plate with 6 holes has its origin (0,0,0) at the back left of the part when it is set up for numerically-controlled machining. (Courtesy of Matt McCune, Autopilot, Inc.)

4.7   The part is clamped in place during machining. The back left corner of the part is the 0,0,0 location during the machining process. (Courtesy of Matt McCune, Autopilot, Inc.)

The First Coordinate System

René Descartes (1596–1650) was the French philosopher and mathematician for whom the Cartesian coordinate system is named. Descartes linked algebra and geometry to classify curves by the equations that describe them. His coordinate system remains the most commonly used coordinate system today for identifying points. A 2D coordinate system consists of a pair of lines, called the X- and Y-axes, drawn on a plane so that they intersect at right angles. The point of intersection is called the *origin*. A 3D coordinate system adds a third axis, referred to as the Z-axis, that is perpendicular to the two other axes. Each point in space can be described by numbers, called coordinates, that represent its distance from this set of axes. The Cartesian coordinate system made it possible to represent geometric entities by numerical and algebraic expressions. For example, a straight line is represented by a linear equation in the form $ax + by + c = 0$, where the x- and y-variables represent the X- and Y-coordinates for each point on the line. Descartes' work laid the foundation for the problem-solving methods of analytic geometry and was the first significant advance in geometry since those of the ancient Greeks.

4.8 *Absolute coordinates define a location in terms of distance from the origin (0,0,0), shown here as a star. These directions are useful because they do not change unless the origin changes.*

4.9 *Relative coordinates describe the location in terms of distance from a starting point. Relative coordinates to the same location differ according to the starting location.*

4.10 *Polar coordinates describe the location using an angle and distance from the origin (absolute) or starting point (relative).*

Absolute Coordinates

Absolute coordinates are used to store the locations of points in a CAD database. These coordinates specify location in terms of distance from the origin in each of the three axis directions of the Cartesian coordinate system.

Think of giving someone directions to your house (or to a house in an area where the streets are laid out in rectangular blocks). One way to describe how to get to your house would be to tell the person how many blocks over and how many blocks up it is from two main streets (and how many floors up in the building, for 3D). The two main streets are like the X- and Y-axes of the Cartesian coordinate system, with the intersection as the origin. Figure 4.8 shows how you might locate a house with this type of absolute coordinate system.

Relative Coordinates

Instead of having to specify each location from the origin, you can use ***relative coordinates*** to specify a location by giving the number of units from a previous location. In other words, the location is defined relative to your previous location.

To understand relative coordinates, think about giving someone directions from his or her current position, not from two main streets. Figure 4.9 shows the same map again, but this time with the location of the house relative to the location of the person receiving directions.

Polar Coordinates

Polar coordinates are used to locate an object by giving an angle (from the X-axis) and a distance. Polar coordinates can either be absolute, giving the angle and distance from the origin, or relative, giving the angle and distance from the current location.

Picture the same situation of having to give directions. You could tell the person to walk at a specified angle from the crossing of the two main streets, and how far to walk. Figure 4.10 shows the angle and direction for the shortcut across the empty lot using absolute polar coordinates. You could also give directions as an angle and distance relative to a starting point.

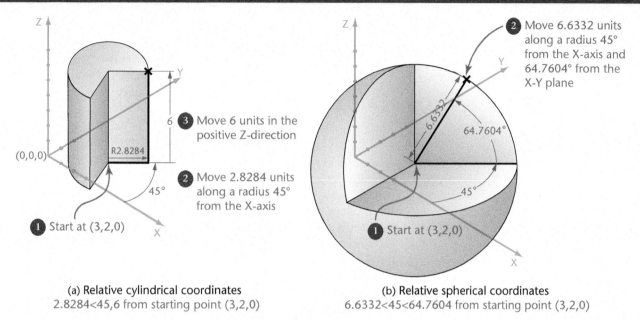

(a) Relative cylindrical coordinates
2.8284<45,6 from starting point (3,2,0)

(b) Relative spherical coordinates
6.6332<45<64.7604 from starting point (3,2,0)

4.11   Relative Cylindrical and Spherical Coordinates. *The target points in (a) and (b) are described by relative coordinates from the starting point (3,2,0). Although the paths to the point differ, the resulting endpoint is the same.*

Cylindrical and Spherical Coordinates

Cylindrical and spherical coordinates are similar to polar coordinates except that a 3D location is specified instead of one on a single flat plane (such as a map).

Cylindrical coordinates specify a 3D location based on a radius, angle, and distance (usually in the Z-axis direction). This gives a location as though it were on the edge of a cylinder. The radius tells how far the point is from the center (or origin); the angle is the angle from the X-axis along which the point is located; and the distance provides the height where the point is located on the cylinder. Cylindrical coordinates are similar to polar coordinates, but they add distance in the Z-direction. Figure 4.11a depicts relative cylindrical coordinates used to specify a location, where the starting point serves as the center of the cylinder.

Spherical coordinates specify a 3D location by the radius, an angle from the X-axis, and the angle from the X-Y plane. These coordinates locate a point on a sphere, where the origin of the coordinate system is at the center of the sphere. The radius gives the size of the sphere; the angle from the X-axis locates a place on the equator. The second angle gives the location from the plane of the equator to a point on the sphere in line with the location specified on the equator. Figure 4.11b depicts relative spherical coordinates, where the starting point serves as the center of the sphere.

Even though you may use these different systems to enter information into your 3D drawings, the end result is stored using one set of Cartesian coordinates.

Using Existing Geometry to Specify Location

Most CAD packages offer a means of specifying location by specifying the relationship of a point to existing objects in the model or drawing. For example, AutoCAD's "object snap" feature lets you enter a location by "snapping" to the endpoint of a line, the center of a circle, the intersection of two lines, and so on (Figure 4.12). Using existing geometry to locate new entities is faster than entering coordinates. This feature also

4.12 *Object snaps are aids for selecting locations on existing CAD drawing geometry. (Autodesk screen shots reprinted courtesy of Autodesk, Inc.)*

allows you to capture geometric relationships between objects without calculating the exact location of a point. For example, you can snap to the midpoint of a line or the nearest point of tangency on a circle. The software calculates the exact location.

GEOMETRIC ENTITIES

Points

Points are geometric constructs. Points are considered to have no width, height, or depth. They are used to indicate locations in space. In CAD drawings, a point is located by its coordinates and usually shown with some sort of marker like a cross, circle, or other representation. Many CAD systems allow you to choose the style and size of the mark that is used to represent points.

Most CAD systems offer three ways to specify a point:

- Type in the coordinates (of any kind) for the point (see Figure 4.13).
- Pick a point from the screen with a pointing device (mouse or tablet).
- Specify the location of a point by its relationship to existing geometry (e.g., an endpoint of a line, an intersection of two lines, or a center point).

Picking a point from the screen is a quick way to enter points when the exact location is not important, but the accuracy of the CAD database makes it impossible to enter a location accurately in this way.

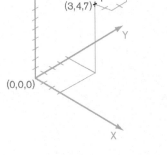

4.13   Specifying Points. *Point 1 was added to the drawing by typing the absolute coordinates 3,4,7. Point 2 was added relative to Point 1 with the relative coordinates @2,2,2.*

Lines

A straight line is defined as the shortest distance between two points. Geometrically, a line has length but no other dimension such as width or thickness. Lines are used in drawings to represent the edge view of a surface, the limiting element of a contoured surface, or the edge formed where two surfaces on an object join. In a CAD database, lines are typically stored by the coordinates of their endpoints.

For the lines shown in Figure 4.14, the table below shows how you can specify the second endpoint for a particular type of coordinate entry. (For either or both endpoints, you can also snap to existing geometry without entering any coordinates.)

The @ sign in AutoCAD indicates relative →

	(a) Second Endpoint for 2D Line	(b) Second Endpoint for 3D Line
Absolute	6,6	5,4,6
Relative	@3,4	@2,2,6
Relative polar	@5<53.13	n/a
Relative cylindrical	n/a	@2.8284<45,6
Relative spherical	n/a	@6.6332<45<64.7606

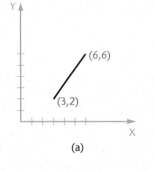

(a)

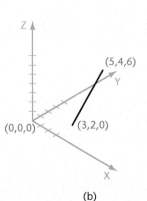

(b)

4.14   Specifying Lines. *(a) This 2D line was drawn from endpoint (3,2) to (6,6). (b) This 3D line was drawn from endpoint (3,2,0) to (5,4,6).*

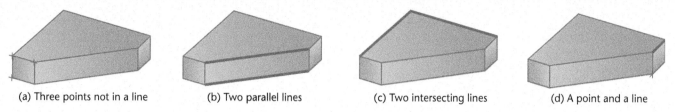

(a) Three points not in a line   (b) Two parallel lines   (c) Two intersecting lines   (d) A point and a line

4.15 Defining a Plane. *The highlighted entities in each image define a plane.*

Planes

Planes are defined by any of the following (see Figure 4.15):

- Three points not lying in a straight line
- Two parallel lines
- Two intersecting lines
- A point and a line

The last three ways to define a plane are all special cases of the more general case—three points not in a straight line. Knowing what can determine a plane can help you understand the geometry of solid objects and use the geometry as you model in CAD.

For example, a face on an object is a plane that extends between the vertices and edges of the surface. Most CAD programs allow you to align new entities with an existing plane. You can use any face on the object—whether it is normal, inclined, or oblique—to define a plane for aligning a new entity.

Defining planes on the object or in 3D space is an important skill for working in 3D CAD. The software provides tools for defining new planes (see Figure 4.16). The options for these tools are based on the geometry of planes, as defined in the preceding list. Typical choices allow the use of any three points not in a line, two parallel lines, two intersecting lines, a point and a line, or being parallel to, perpendicular to, or at an angle from an existing plane.

A plane may serve as a coordinate-system orientation that shows a surface true shape. You will learn more about orienting work planes to take advantage of the object's geometry later in this chapter.

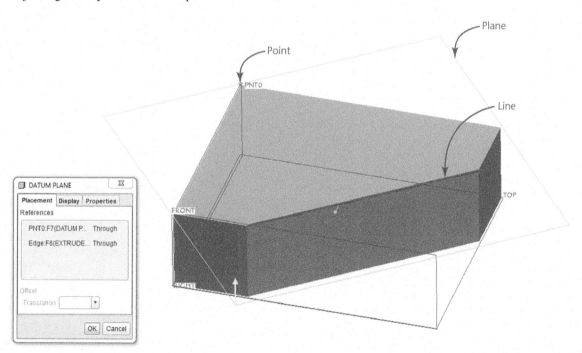

4.16 Defining a Plane in CAD. *A point and a line (the edge between two surfaces in this case) were used to define a plane in this Pro/ENGINEER model.*

Circles

A circle is a set of points that are equidistant from a center point. The distance from the center to one of the points is the radius (see Figure 4.17). The distance across the center to any two points on opposite sides is the diameter. The circumference of a circle contains 360° of arc. In a CAD file, a circle is often stored as a center point and a radius.

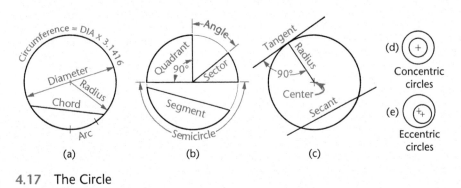

4.17   The Circle

(a)   (b)   (c)   (d) Concentric circles   (e) Eccentric circles

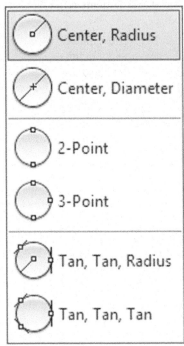

Center, Radius

Center, Diameter

2-Point

3-Point

Tan, Tan, Radius

Tan, Tan, Tan

4.18   AutoCAD Circle Construction Options *(Autodesk screen shots reprinted courtesy of Autodesk, Inc.)*

SPOTLIGHT

Formulas for Circles and Arcs

r = radius
C = circumference
π = pi $\cong$ 3.14159
a = arc length
A = area
L = chord length
θ (theta) = included angle
rad (radian) = the included angle of an arc length such that the arc length is equal to the radius

$C = 2\pi r$, the curved distance around a circle
$A = \pi r^2$, the area of a circle
$a = 2\pi r \times \theta/360$, so the arc length = $0.01745r\theta$ when you know its radius, r, and the included angle, θ, in degrees
$a = r \times \theta$ (when the included angle is measured in radians)

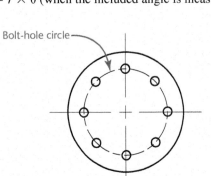

Bolt-Hole Circle Chord Lengths

To determine the distance between centers for equally spaced holes on a bolt-hole circle:

n = 180/number of holes in pattern
L = sin n × bolt-hole circle diameter

EXAMPLE: 8-hole pattern on a 10.00-diameter circle:

180/8 = 22.5
sin of 22.5 is .383
.383 × 10 = 3.83 (chord length)

For more useful formulas, see Appendix 3.

Most CAD systems allow you to define a circle by specifying any one of the following:

- The center and a diameter
- The center and a radius
- Two points on the diameter
- Three points on the circle
- A radius and two entities to which the circle is tangent
- Three entities to which the circle is tangent

These methods are illustrated in Figure 4.19.

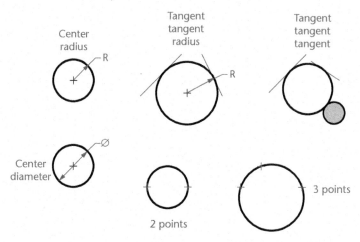

4.19   Ways to Define a Circle

Arcs

An arc is a portion of a circle. An arc can be defined by specifying any one of the following (see Figure 4.20):

- A center, radius, and angle measure (sometimes called the *included angle* or *delta angle*)
- A center, radius, and chord length
- A center, radius, and arc length
- The endpoints and a radius
- The endpoints and a chord length
- The endpoints and arc length
- The endpoints and one other point on the arc (3 points)

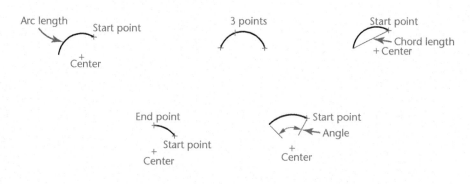

4.20   Defining Arcs. *Arcs can be defined many different ways. Like circles, arcs may be located from a center point or an endpoint, making it easy to locate them relative to other entities in the model.*

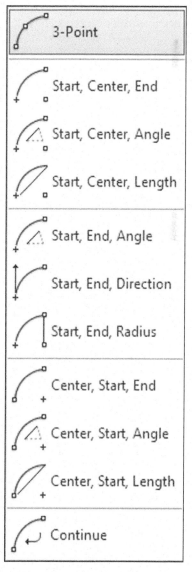

4.21   AutoCAD Arc Construction Options *(Autodesk screen shots reprinted courtesy of Autodesk, Inc.)*

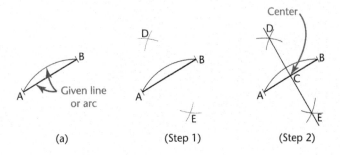

(a)   (Step 1)   (Step 2)

4.22   Bisecting a Line or a Circular Arc

4.1 MANUALLY BISECTING A LINE OR CIRCULAR ARC

Figure 4.22a shows the given line or arc *AB* to be bisected.

Step 1.   From *A* and *B* draw equal arcs with their centers at the endpoints and a with radius greater than half *AB*.

Step 2.   Join intersections *D* and *E* with a straight line to locate center *C*.

TIP

Accurate Geometry with AutoCAD

Using object snaps (Figure A) to locate drawing geometry, such as the midpoint of the arc shown in Figure B, is a quick and easy way to draw a line bisecting an arc or another line.

(A) *The AutoCAD Drafting Settings dialog box can be used to turn on objects snaps, a method of selecting locations on drawing geometry. (Autodesk screen shots reprinted courtesy of Autodesk Inc.)*

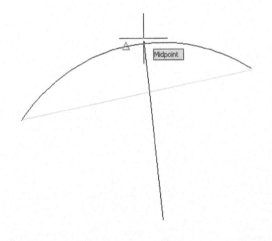

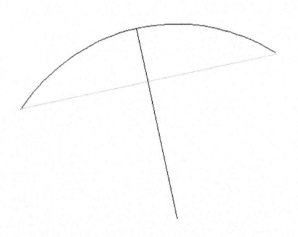

(B) Bisecting a Line or a Circular Arc Using AutoCAD's Midpoint Object Snap

4.2 DRAWING TANGENTS TO TWO CIRCLES

When drawing entities tangent to a circle, there are two locations that satisfy the condition of tangency. When using a CAD system, select a point close to the tangent location you intend.

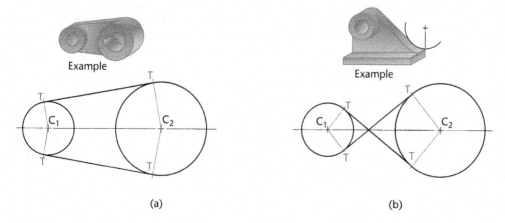

4.23   Drawing Tangents to Two Circles

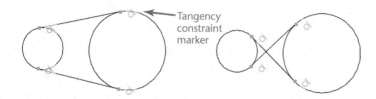

4.24   *Tangency constraints for two identical sets of circles are shown in AutoCAD.*

4.3 DRAWING AN ARC TANGENT TO A LINE OR ARC AND THROUGH A POINT

Given line *AB*, point *P*, and radius *R* (Figure 4.25a), draw line *DE* parallel to the given line and distance *R* from it. From *P* draw an arc with radius *R*, cutting line *DE* at *C*, the center of the required tangent arc.

Given line *AB*, with tangent point *Q* on the line and point *P* (Figure 4.25b), draw *PQ*, which will be a chord of the required arc. Draw perpendicular bisector *DE*, and at *Q* draw a line perpendicular to the line to intersect *DE* at *C*, the center of the required tangent arc.

Given an arc with center *Q*, point *P*, and radius *R* (Figure 4.25c), from *P*, draw an arc with radius *R*. From *Q*, draw an arc with radius equal to that of the given arc plus *R*. The intersection *C* of the arcs is the center of the required tangent arc.

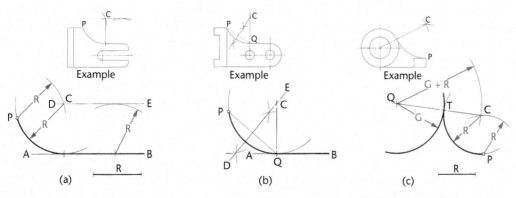

4.25   Tangents. *These are often easy constructions using CAD and object snaps.*

DRAWING AN ARC TANGENT TO TWO ARCS

Creating Construction Geometry

CAD software typically provides a command option to draw a circle or arc tangent to two entities (any combination of arcs, circles, or lines) given the radius. For example, the AutoCAD **Circle** command has an option called Ttr (tangent, tangent, radius). When you use this command, you first select the two drawing objects to which the new circle will be tangent and then enter the radius.

Take a look at the shift lever drawing. To draw this figure you must use a geometric construction to find the center of the 1.00-radius tangent arc. Before the lower 4.20-radius arc can be drawn, the smaller 1.00-radius arc must be constructed tangent to the 1.50 diameter circle. When an arc is tangent to a circle, its center must be the radius distance away from that circle.

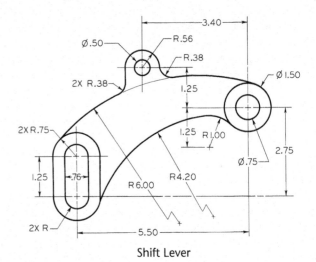

Shift Lever

1 Use basic CAD commands to draw the portions shown.

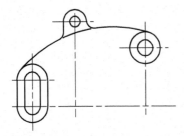

2 Construct circle B with a radius 1.00 larger than circle A. You can use the AutoCAD **Offset** command to do this quickly. The desired tangent arc must have its center somewhere on circle B. The vertical dimension of 1.25 is given between the two centers in the drawing. Construct line C at this distance. The only point that is on both the circle and the line is the center of the desired tangent arc.

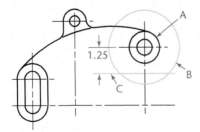

3 Draw the 1.00-radius circle tangent to the 1.50-diameter circle and centered on the point just found.

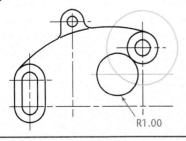

4 Next, construct the lower 4.20-radius arc to be tangent to the lower curve at the left and to the 1.00-radius circle. Then, trim the circles at their intersections to form the desired arcs.

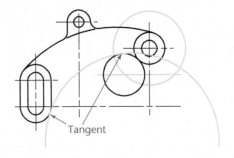

Tangent

Geometric Constraints

Using geometric constraints is another way to create this CAD geometry. When geometric constraints are used, a general-case arc can be drawn that is not perfectly tangent. Then, a tangent constraint, the vertical dimension between the arc center and the circle, and the required radius can be applied to the arc as drawn. The software will then calculate the correct arc based on these constraints.

If the desired distance changes, the dimensional constraint values can be updated, and the software will recalculate the new arc. Not all software provides constraint-based modeling, especially in a 2D drafting context. The AutoCAD software has had this feature since release 2010.

When using constraint-based modeling, you still must understand the drawing geometry clearly to create a consistent set of geometric and dimensional constraints.

> **TIP**
> Two different tangent circles with the same radius are possible—one as shown and one that includes both circles. To get the desired arc using AutoCAD, select near the tangent location for the correctly positioned arc.

4.4 BISECTING AN ANGLE

Figure 4.26a shows the given angle *BAC* to be bisected.

Step 1.   Lightly draw large arc with center at *A* to intersect lines *AC* and *AB*.

Step 2.   Lightly draw equal arcs *r* with radius slightly larger than half *BC*, to intersect at *D*.

Step 3.   Draw line *AD*, which bisects the angle.

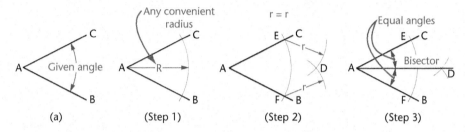

4.26   Bisecting an Angle

4.5 DRAWING A LINE THROUGH A POINT AND PARALLEL TO A LINE

With given point *P* as center, and any convenient radius *R*, draw arc *CD* to intersect the given line *AB* at *E* (Figure 4.27). With *E* as center and the same radius, strike arc *R′* to intersect the given line at *G*. With *PG* as radius and *E* as center, strike arc *r* to locate point *H*. The line *PH* is the required parallel line.

Using AutoCAD, you can quickly draw a new line parallel to a given line and through a given point using the **Offset** command with the **Through** option. Another method is to use the **Parallel** object snap while drawing the line as shown in Figure 4.28. You can also copy the original line and place the copy through the point.

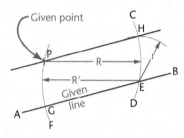

4.27   Drawing a Line through a Point

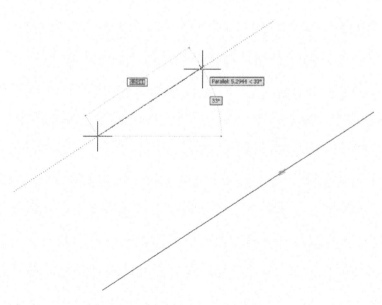

4.28   Drawing a Line through a Point

4.6 DRAWING A TRIANGLE WITH SIDES GIVEN

Given the sides *A*, *B*, and *C*, as shown in Figure 4.29a,

Step 1.   Draw one side, as *C*, in the desired position, and draw an arc with radius equal to side *A*.
Step 2.   Lightly draw an arc with radius equal to side *B*.
Step 3.   Draw sides *A* and *B* from the intersection of the arcs, as shown.

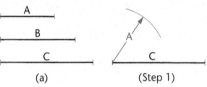 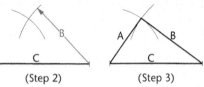

(a)   (Step 1)   (Step 2)   (Step 3)

> **TIP**
> Using AutoCAD, you can enter the relative length and angle from the previous endpoint using the format:
> *@lengthvalue<anglevalue*

4.29   Drawing a Triangle with Sides Given

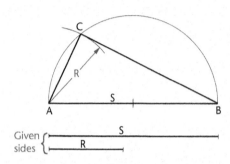

4.30   Drawing a Right Triangle

4.7 DRAWING A RIGHT TRIANGLE WITH HYPOTENUSE AND ONE SIDE GIVEN

Given sides *S* and *R* (Figure 4.30), with *AB* as a diameter equal to *S*, draw a semicircle. With *A* as center and *R* as radius, draw an arc intersecting the semicircle at *C*. Draw *AC* and *CB* to complete the right triangle.

4.8 LAYING OUT AN ANGLE

Many angles can be laid out directly with the triangle or protractor. For more accuracy, use one of the methods shown in Figure 4.31.

Tangent Method   The tangent of angle θ is *y/x*, and *y = x* tan θ. Use a convenient value for *x*, preferably 10 units (Figure 4.31a). (The larger the unit, the more accurate will be the construction.) Look up the tangent of angle θ and multiply by 10, and measure *y* = 10 tan θ.

EXAMPLE To set off 31-1/2°, find the natural tangent of 31-1/2°, which is 0.6128. Then, *y* = 10 units × 0.6128 = 6.128 units.

Sine Method   Draw line *x* to any convenient length, preferably 10 units (Figure 4.31b). Find the sine of angle θ, multiply by 10, and draw arc with radius *R* = 10 sin θ. Draw the other side of the angle tangent to the arc, as shown.

EXAMPLE To set off 25-1/2°, find the natural sine of 25-1/2°, which is 0.4305. Then *R* = 10 units × 0.4305 = 4.305 units.

Chord Method   Draw line *x* of any convenient length, and draw an arc with any convenient radius *R*—say 10 units (Figure 4.31c). Find the chordal length *C* using the formula *C* = 2 sin θ/2. Machinists' handbooks have chord tables. These tables are made using a radius of 1 unit, so it is easy to scale by multiplying the table values by the actual radius used.

EXAMPLE Half of 43°20′ = 21°40′. The sine of 21°40′ = 0.3692. C = 2 × 0.3692 = 0.7384 for a 1 unit radius. For a 10 unit radius, C = 7.384 units.

EXAMPLE To set off 43°20′, the chordal length *C* for 1 unit radius, as given in a table of chords, equals 0.7384. If *R* = 10 units, then *C* = 7.384 units.

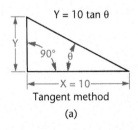 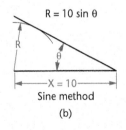 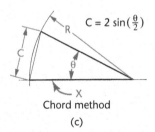

Tangent method   Sine method   Chord method
(a)   (b)   (c)

4.31   Laying Out Angles

4.9 DRAWING AN EQUILATERAL TRIANGLE

Side *AB* is given. With *A* and *B* as centers and *AB* as radius, lightly construct arcs to intersect at *C* (Figure 4.32a). Draw lines *AC* and *BC* to complete the triangle.

Alternative Method Draw lines through points *A* and *B*, making angles of 60° with the given line and intersecting *C* (Figure 4.32b).

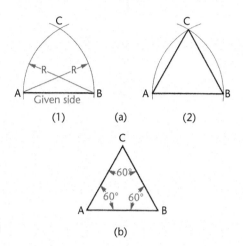

4.32 Drawing an Equilateral Triangle

4.10 POLYGONS

A polygon is any plane figure bounded by straight lines (Figure 4.33). If the polygon has equal angles and equal sides, it can be inscribed in or circumscribed around a circle and is called a regular polygon.

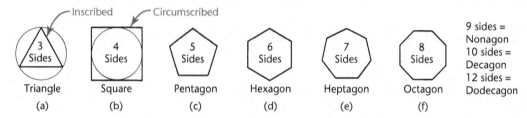

4.33 Regular Polygons

Polygon

Creates an equilateral closed polyline

You can specify the different parameters of the polygon including the number of sides. The difference between the inscribed and circumscribed options is shown.

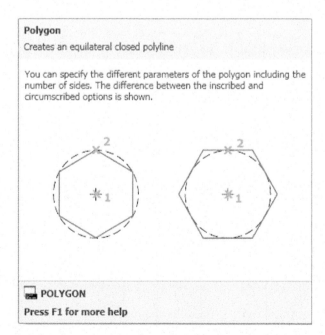

POLYGON

Press F1 for more help

TIP

The AutoCAD **Polygon** command is used to draw regular polygons with any number of sides. The polygon can be based on the radius of an inscribed or circumscribed circle. The length of an edge of the polygon can also be used to define the size. Figure 4.34 shows the quick help for the **Polygon** command. The **Rectangle** command is another quick way to make a square in AutoCAD.

4.34 *Polygons can be defined by the number of sides and whether they are inscribed in or circumscribed around a circle. (Autodesk screen shots reprinted courtesy of Autodesk, Inc.)*

4.11 DRAWING A REGULAR PENTAGON

Dividers Method: Divide the circumference of the circumscribed circle into five equal parts with the dividers, and join the points with straight lines (Figure 4.35a).

Geometric Method:

Step 1.   Bisect radius *OD* at *C* (Figure 4.35b).

Step 2.   Use *C* as the center and *CA* as the radius to lightly draw arc *AE*. With *A* as center and *AE* as radius, draw arc *EB* (Figure 4.35c).

Step 3.   Draw line *AB*, then measure off distances *AB* around the circumference of the circle. Draw the sides of the pentagon through these points (Figure 4.35d).

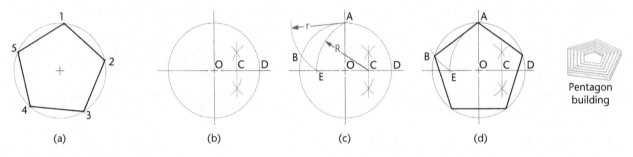

(a)   (b)   (c)   (d)   Pentagon building

4.35   Drawing a Pentagon

4.12 DRAWING A HEXAGON

Each side of a hexagon is equal to the radius of the circumscribed circle (Figure 4.36a). To use a compass or dividers, use the radius of the circle to mark the six points of the hexagon around the circle. Connect the points with straight lines. Check your accuracy by making sure the opposite sides of the hexagon are parallel.

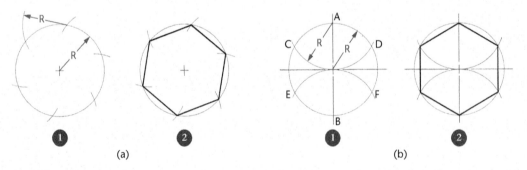

(a)   (b)

4.36   Drawing a Hexagon

Centerline Variation Draw vertical and horizontal centerlines (Figure 4.36b). With *A* and *B* as centers and radius equal to that of the circle, draw arcs to intersect the circle at *C*, *D*, *E*, and *F*, and complete the hexagon as shown.

Hexagons, especially when drawn to create bolt heads, are usually dimensioned by the distance across the flat sides (not across the corners). When creating a hexagon using CAD, it is typical to draw it as circumscribed about a circle, so that the circle diameter is defining the distance across the flat sides of the hexagon (see Figure 4. 32).

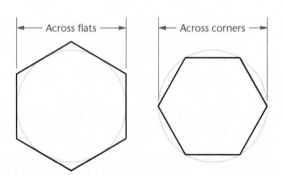

4.37   Across Flats vs. Across Corners

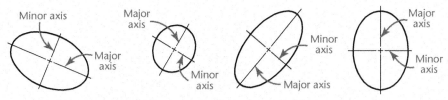

4.38 Major and Minor Axes of Some Ellipses

4.13 ELLIPSES

An ellipse can be defined by its major and minor axis distances. The major axis is the longer axis of the ellipse; the minor axis is the shorter axis. Some ellipses are shown and labeled in Figure 4.38.

An ellipse is created by a point moving along a path where the sum of its distances from two points, each called a focus of an ellipse (foci is the plural form), is equal to the major diameter. As an aid in understanding the shape of an ellipse, imagine pinning the ends of a string in the locations of the foci, then sliding a pencil along inside the string, keeping it tightly stretched, as in Figure 4.39. You would not use this technique when sketching, but it serves as a good illustration of the definition of an ellipse.

Most CAD systems provide an Ellipse command that lets you enter the major and minor axis lengths, center, or the angle of rotation for a circle that is to appear elliptical.

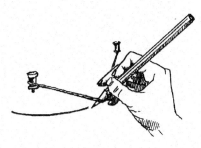

4.39 Pencil and String Method. *When an ellipse is created with the pencil-and-string method, the length of the string between the foci is equal to the length of the major axis of the ellipse. Any point that can be reached by a pencil inside the string when it is pulled taut meets the condition that its distances from the two foci sum to the length of the major diameter.*

SPOTLIGHT

Locating the Foci of an Ellipse

To locate the foci of an ellipse, draw arcs with their centers at the ends of the minor axis and their radii equal to half the major axis. The intersection of each pair of arcs is a focus of the ellipse.

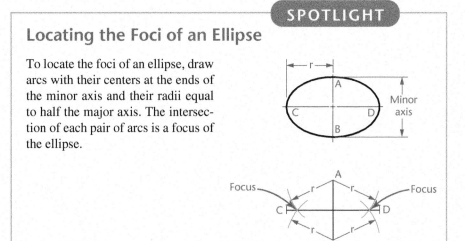

SPOTLIGHT

The Perimeter of an Ellipse

The perimeter, *P*, of an ellipse is a set of points defined by their distance from the two foci. The sum of the distances from any point on the ellipse to the two foci must be equal to the length of the major diameter. The perimeter of an ellipse may be approximated in different ways. Many CAD packages use infinite series to most closely approximate the perimeter. The mathematical relationship of each point on the ellipse to the major and minor axes may be seen in the approximation of the perimeter at right:

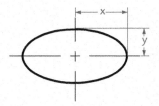

$$P = 2\pi \sqrt{\frac{x^2 + y^2}{2}}$$

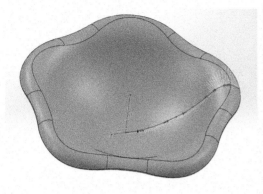

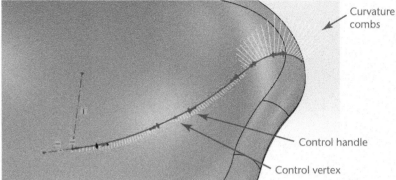

Curvature combs

Control handle

Control vertex

4.14 SPLINE CURVES

Splines are used to describe complex, or *freeform*, curves. Many surfaces cannot be easily defined using simple curves such as circles, arcs, or ellipses. For example, the flowing curves used in automobile design blend many different curves into a smooth surface. Creating lifelike shapes and aerodynamic forms may require spline curves (Figure 4.40).

The word *spline* originally described a flexible piece of plastic or rubber used to draw irregular curves between points. Mathematical methods generate the points on the curve for CAD applications.

One way to create an irregular curve is to draw curves between each set of points. The points and the tangencies at each point are used in a polynomial equation that determines the shape of the curve. This type of curve is useful in the design of a ship's hull or an aircraft wing. Because this kind of irregular curve passes through all the points used to define the curve, it is sometimes called an *interpolated spline* or a *cubic spline*. An example and its vertices are shown in Figure 4.41.

Other spline curves are approximated: they are defined by a set of vertices. The resulting curve does not pass through all the vertices. Instead, the vertices "pull" the curve in the direction of the vertex. Complex curves can be created with relatively few vertices using approximation methods. Figure 4.42 shows a 3D approximated spline curve and its vertices.

The mathematical definition for this type of spline curve uses the X- and Y- (and Z- for a 3D shape) coordinates and a parameter, generally referred to as *u*. A polynomial equation is used to generate functions in *u* for each point used to specify the curve. The resulting functions are then blended to generate a curve that is influenced by each point specified but not necessarily coincident with any of them.

4.40   Complex Curves. *The organic shape of this flowerlike bowl was created using SolidWorks splines. Splines can be controlled in a variety of ways. The enlarged view shows the curvature combs used to view the effect of the controlling curves that make up the spline. Dragging a control handle changes the direction of the curve at the control vertex. (Courtesy of Robert Kincaid.)*

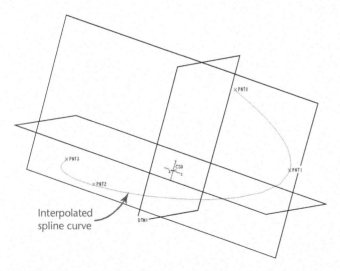

4.41   Interpolated Spline. *An interpolated spline curve passes through all the points used to define the curve.*

Interpolated spline curve

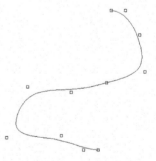

4.42   Approximated Spline. *Except for the beginning and endpoints, the fit points for the spline curve stored in the database do not always lie on the curve. They are used to derive the curve mathematically.*

B-Splines

The ***Bezier curve*** was one of the first methods to use spline approximation to create flowing curves in CAD applications. The first and last vertices are on the curve, but the rest of the vertices contribute to a blended curve between them. The Bezier method uses a polynomial curve to approximate the shape of a polygon formed by the specified vertices. The order of the polynomial is 1 degree less than the number of vertices in the polygon (see Figure 4.43).

4.43   Bezier Curve. *A Bezier curve passes through the first and last vertex but uses the other vertices as control points to generate a blended curve.*

The Bezier method is named for Pierre Bezier, a pioneer in computer-generated surface modeling at Renault, the French automobile manufacturer. Bezier sought an easier way of controlling complex curves, such as those defined in automobile surfaces. His technique allowed designers to shape natural-looking curves more easily than they could by specifying points that had to lie on the resulting curve, yet the technique also provided control over the shape of the curve. Changing the slope of each line segment defined by a set of vertices adjusts the slope of the resulting curve (see Figure 4.44). One disadvantage of the Bezier formula is that the polynomial curve is defined by the combined influence of every vertex: a change to any vertex redraws the entire curve between the start point and endpoint.

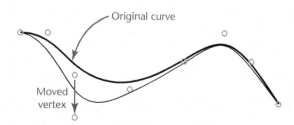

4.44   Editing a Bezier Curve. *Every vertex contributes to the shape of a Bezier curve. Changing the location of a single vertex redraws the entire curve.*

A ***B-spline*** approximation is a special case of the Bezier curve that is more commonly used in engineering to give the designer more control when editing the curve. A B-spline is a blended piecewise polynomial curve passing near a set of control points. The spline is referred to as ***piecewise*** because the blending functions used to combine the polynomial curves can vary over the different segments of the curve. Thus, when a control point changes, only the piece of the curve defined by the new point and the vertices near it change, not the whole curve (see Figure 4.45). B-splines may or may not pass through the first and last points in the vertex set. Another difference is that for the B-spline the order of the polynomial can be set independently of the number of vertices or control points defining the curve.

In addition to being able to locally modify the curve, many modelers allow sets of vertices to be weighted differently. The weighting, sometimes called tolerance, determines how closely the curve should fit the set of vertices. Curves can range from fitting all the points to being loosely controlled by the vertices. This type of curve is called a nonuniform rational B-spline, or ***NURBS*** curve. A rational curve (or surface) is one that has a weight associated with each control point.

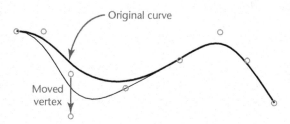

4.45   B-Spline Approximation. *The B-spline is constructed piecewise, so changing a vertex affects the shape of the curve near only that vertex and its neighbors.*

Splines are drawn in CAD systems based on the mathematical relationships defining their geometry. Figure 4.46 shows an approximated spline drawn using AutoCAD. Figure 4.47 shows an interpolated spline drawn using SolidWorks. Both curves are drawn with a spline command, and both provide a dialog box that allows you to change properties defining the curve; however, the properties that are controlled vary by the type of spline being created by the software package. You should be familiar with the terms used by your modeling software for creating different types of spline curves.

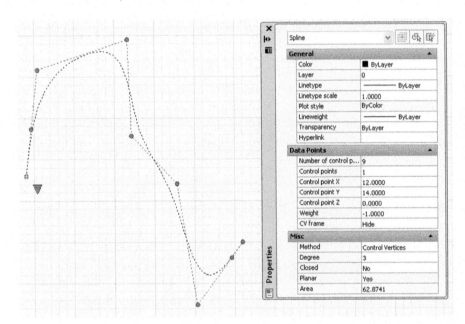

4.46   Approximated Spline. *This spline drawn in AutoCAD is pulled toward the defined control points. The Properties dialog box at the right allows you to change the weighting factor for each control point.* (Autodesk screen shots reprinted courtesy of Autodesk, Inc.)

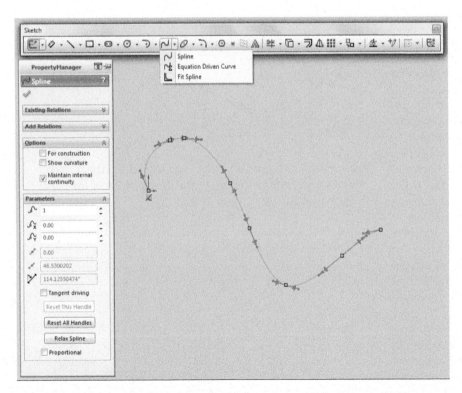

4.47   Interpolated Spline. *This SolidWorks spline passes through each control point. Software tools allow you to control spline properties. (Image courtesy of ©2016 Dassault Systèmes SolidWorks Corporation.)*

4.15 GEOMETRIC RELATIONSHIPS

When you are sketching, you often imply a relationship, such as being parallel or perpendicular, by the appearance of the lines or through notes or dimensions. When you are creating a CAD model you use drawing aids to specify these relationships between geometric entities.

Two lines or planes are *parallel* when they are an equal distance apart at every point. Parallel entities never intersect, even if extended to infinity. Figure 4.48 shows an example of parallel lines.

Two lines or planes are *perpendicular* when they intersect at right angles (or when the intersection that would be formed if they were extended would be a right angle), as in Figure 4.49.

Two entities *intersect* if they have at least one point in common. Two straight lines intersect at only a single point. A circle and a straight line intersect at two points, as shown in Figure 4.50.

When two lines intersect, they define an angle as shown in Figure 4.51.

The term *apparent intersection* refers to lines that appear to intersect in a 2D view or on a computer monitor but actually do not touch, as shown in Figure 4.52. When you look at a wireframe view of a model, the 2D view may show lines crossing each other when, in fact, the lines do not intersect in 3D space. Changing the view of the model can help you determine whether an intersection is actual or apparent.

Two entities are *tangent* if they touch each other but do not intersect, even if extended to infinity, as shown in Figure 4.53. A line that is tangent to a circle will have only one point in common with the circle.

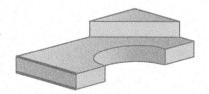

4.48   *The highlighted lines are parallel.*

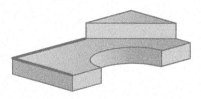

4.49   *The highlighted lines are perpendicular.*

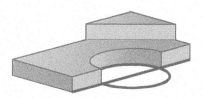

4.50   *The highlighted circle intersects the highlighted line at two different points.*

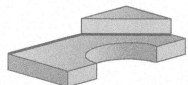

4.51   *An angle is defined by the space between two lines (such as those highlighted here) or planes that intersect.*

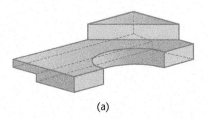

(a)

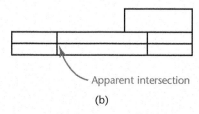

Apparent intersection

(b)

4.52   Apparent Intersection. *From the shaded view of this model in (a), it is clear that the back lines do not intersect the half-circular shape. In the wireframe front view in (b), the lines appear to intersect.*

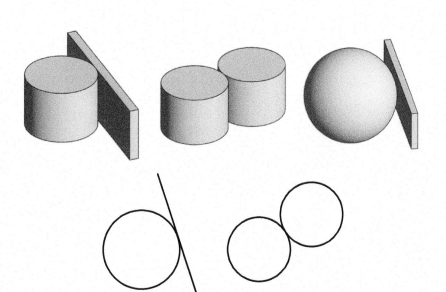

4.53   Tangency. *Lines that are tangent to an entity have one point in common but never intersect. 3D objects may be tangent at a single point or along a line.*

When a line is tangent to a circle, a radial line from the center of the circle is perpendicular at the point of tangency, as shown in Figure 4.54. Knowing this can be useful in creating sketches and models.

The regular geometry of points, lines, circles, arcs, and ellipses is the foundation for many CAD drawings that are created from these types of entities alone. Figure 4.55 shows a 2D CAD drawing that uses only lines, circles, and arcs to create the shapes shown. Figure 4.56 shows a 3D wireframe model that is also made entirely of lines, circles, and arcs. Many complex-looking 2D and 3D images are made solely from combinations of these shapes. Recognizing these shapes and understanding the many ways you can specify them in the CAD environment are key modeling skills.

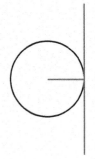

4.54 *A radial line from the point where a line is tangent to a circle will always be perpendicular to that line.*

4.55 A 2D Drawing Made of Only Lines, Circles, and Arcs

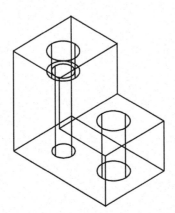

4.56 A 3D Model Made of Only Lines, Circles, and Arcs

4.16 SOLID PRIMITIVES

Many 3D objects can be visualized, sketched, and modeled in a CAD system by combining simple 3D shapes or primitives. They are the building blocks for many solid objects. You should become familiar with these common shapes and their geometry. The same primitives that are useful when sketching objects are also used to create 3D models of those objects.

A common set of primitive solids used to build more complex objects is shown in Figure 4.57. Which of these objects are polyhedra? Which are bounded by single-curved surfaces? Which are bounded by double-curved surfaces? How many vertices do you see on the cone? How many on the wedge? How many edges do you see on the box? Familiarity with the appearance of these primitive shapes when shown in orthographic views can help you in interpreting drawings and in recognizing features that make up objects. Figure 4.58 shows the primitives in two orthographic views.

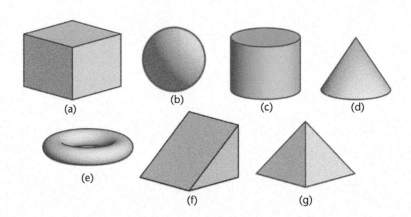

4.57 Solid Primitives. *The most common solid primitives are (a) box, (b) sphere, (c) cylinder, (d) cone, (e) torus, (f) wedge, and (g) pyramid.*

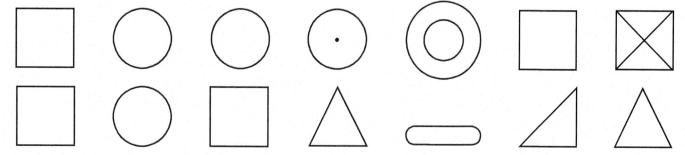

4.58 *Match the top and front views shown here with the primitives shown in Figure 4.57.*

Review the orthographic views and match each to the isometric of the same primitive shown in Figure 4.57.

Look around and identify some solid primitives that make up the shapes you see. The ability to identify the primitive shapes can help you model features of the objects using a CAD system (see Figure 4.59). Also, knowing how primitive shapes appear in orthographic views can help you sketch these features correctly and read drawings that others have created.

Making Complex Shapes with Boolean Operations

Boolean operations, common to most 3D modelers, allow you to join, subtract, and intersect solids. Boolean operations are named for the English mathematician George Boole, who developed them to describe how sets can be combined. Applied to solid modeling, Boolean operations describe how volumes can be combined to create new solids.

The three Boolean operations, defined in Table 4.1, are

- Union (join/add)
- Difference (subtract)
- Intersection

4.59 Complex Shapes. *The 3D solid primitives in this illustration show basic shapes that make up a telephone handset.* (Photo copyright Everything/Shutterstock.)

Table 4.1 Boolean Operations

Name	Definition	Venn Diagram
Union (join/add)	The volume in both sets is combined or added. Overlap is eliminated. Order does not matter: A union B is the same as B union A.	
Difference (subtract)	The volume from one set is subtracted or eliminated from the volume in another set. The eliminated set is completely eliminated—even the portion that does not overlap the other volume. The order of the sets selected when using difference *does* matter (see Figure 4.60). A subtract B is not the same as B subtract A.	
Intersection	The volume common to both sets is retained. Order does not matter: B intersect A is the same as A intersect B.	

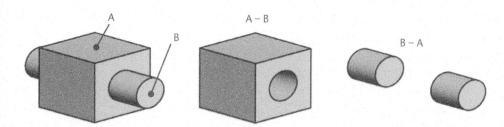

4.60 Order Matters in Subtraction. *The models here illustrate how A – B differs significantly from B – A.*

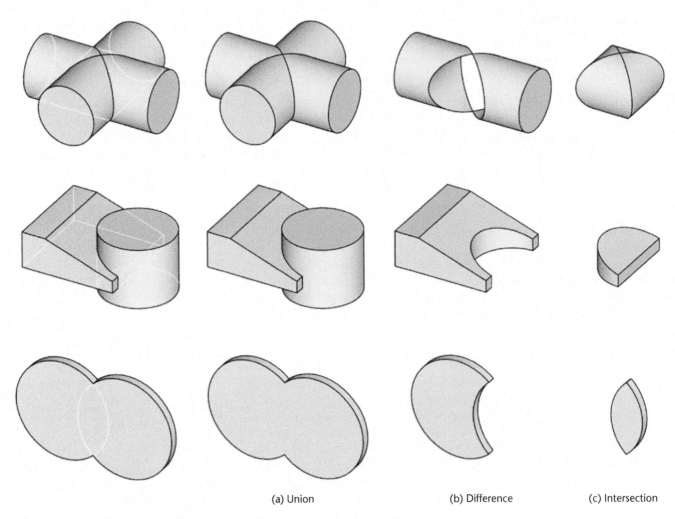

(a) Union   (b) Difference   (c) Intersection

4.61   Boolean Operations. *The three sets of models at left produce the results shown at right when the two solids are (a) unioned, (b) subtracted, and (c) intersected.*

Figure 4.61 illustrates the result of the Boolean operations on three pairs of solid models. Look at some everyday objects around you and make a list of the primitive solid shapes and Boolean operations needed to make them.

Figure 4.62 shows a bookend and a list of the primitives available in the CAD system used to create it, along with the Boolean operations used to make the part.

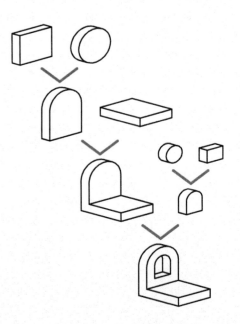

4.62   Shapes in a Bookend. *This diagram shows how basic shapes were combined to make a bookend. The box and cylinder at the top were unioned, then the resulting end piece and another box were unioned. To form the cutout in the end piece, another cylinder and box were unioned, then the resulting shape was subtracted from the end piece.*

4.17 RECOGNIZING SYMMETRY

An object is symmetrical when it has the same exact shape on opposite sides of a dividing line (or plane) or about a center or axis. Recognizing the symmetry of objects can help you in your design work and when you are sketching or using CAD to represent an object. Figure 4.63 shows a shape that is symmetrical about several axes of symmetry (of which two are shown) as well as about the center point of the circle.

Mirrored shapes have symmetry where points on opposite sides of the dividing line (or mirror line) are the same distance away from the mirror line. For a 2D mirrored shape, the axis of symmetry is the mirror line. For a 3D mirrored shape, the symmetry is about a plane. Examples of 3D mirrored shapes are shown in Figure 4.64.

4.63 Symmetrical Part. *Symmetrical parts can have symmetry about a line or point, or both.*

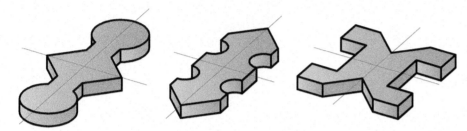

4.64 3D Mirrored Shapes. *Each of these symmetrical shapes has two mirror lines, indicated by the thin axis lines. To create one of these parts, you could model one quarter of it, mirror it across one of the mirror lines, then mirror the resulting half across the perpendicular mirror line.*

To simplify sketching, you need to show only half the object if it is symmetrical (Figure 4.65). A centerline line pattern provides a visual reference for the mirror line on the part.

Most CAD systems have a command available to mirror existing features to create new features. You can save a lot of modeling time by noticing the symmetry of the object and copying or mirroring the existing geometry to create new features.

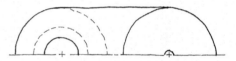

4.65 *Orthographic sketches of symmetrical parts may show only half of the object.*

Right- and Left-Hand Parts

Many parts function in pairs for the right and left sides of a device. A brake lever for the left side of a mountain bike is a mirror image of the brake lever for the right side of the bike (Figure 4.66). Using CAD, you can create the part for the left side by mirroring the entire part. On sketches you can indicate a note such as RIGHT-HAND PART IS SHOWN. LEFT-HAND PART IS OPPOSITE. Right-hand and left-hand are often abbreviated as RH and LH in drawing notes.

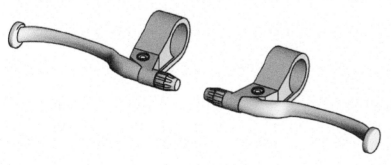

4.66 Right- and Left-hand Brake Levers

--- TIP ---
Using symmetry when you model can be important when the design requires it. When the design calls for symmetrical features to be the same, mirroring the feature ensures that the two resulting features will be the same.

Parting-Line Symmetry

Molded symmetrical parts are often made using a mold with two halves, one on each side of the axis of symmetry. The axis or line where two mold parts join is called a ***parting line***. When items are removed from a mold, sometimes a small ridge of material is left on the object. See if you can notice a parting line on a molded object such as your toothbrush or a screwdriver handle such as the one shown in Figure 4.67. Does the parting line define a plane about which the object is symmetrical? Can you determine why that plane was chosen? Does it make it easier to remove the part from the mold? As you are developing your sketching and modeling skills think about the axis of symmetry for parts and how it could affect their manufacture.

Parting
line

4.67 Parting Line. *The parting line on a molded part is often visible as a ridge of material.*

4.68 Two Halves of a Mold Used to Form a Strap (shown at left). *(Two straps can be molded at once.)*

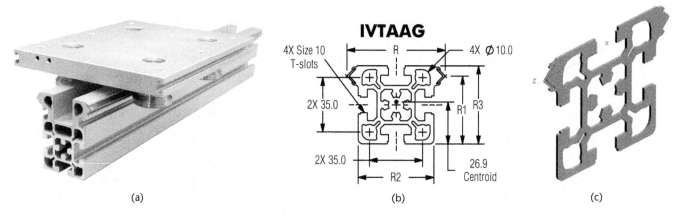

(a)   (b)   (c)

4.69 Extruded Shape. *Symmetry and several common geometric shapes were used to create this linear guide system. The rail in (a) was created by forcing aluminum through an opening with the shape of its cross section. The extruded length was then cut to the required length. The solid model in (c) was created by defining the 2D cross-sectional shape (b) and specifying a length for the extrusion. (Integrated configuration of Integral V™ linear guides courtesy of PBCLinear.)*

4.18 EXTRUDED FORMS

Extrusion is the manufacturing process of forcing material through a shaped opening (Figure 4.69). Extrusion in CAD modeling creates a 3D shape in a way similar to the extrusion manufacturing process. This modeling method is common even when the part will not be manufactured as an extrusion.

To create as shape by extrusion, sketch the 2D outline of the basic shape of the object (usually called a profile), and then specify the length for the extrusion. Most 3D CAD systems provide an Extrude command. Some CAD systems allow a taper (or draft) angle to be specified to narrow the shape over its length (Figure 4.70).

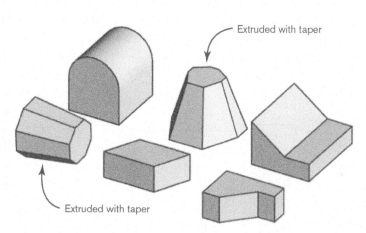

4.70 *These CAD models were formed by extruding a 2D outline. Two of the models were extruded with a taper.*

Swept Shapes

A swept form is a special case of an extruded form. Sweeping describes extruding a shape along a curved path. To sweep a shape in CAD, create the 2D profile and a 2D or 3D curve to serve as the path. Some swept shapes are shown in Figure 4.71.

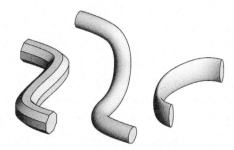

4.71 Swept Shapes. *These shapes started as an octagon, a circle, and an ellipse, then were swept along a curved path.*

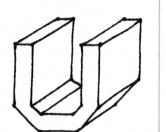

SPOTLIGHT

Sketching Extruded Shapes

Shapes that can be created using extrusion are often easily sketched as oblique projections. To sketch extruded shapes, show the shape (or profile) that will be extruded parallel to the front viewing plane in the sketch. Copy this same shape over and up in the sketch based on the angle and distance you want to use to represent the depth. Then, sketch in the lines for the receding edges.

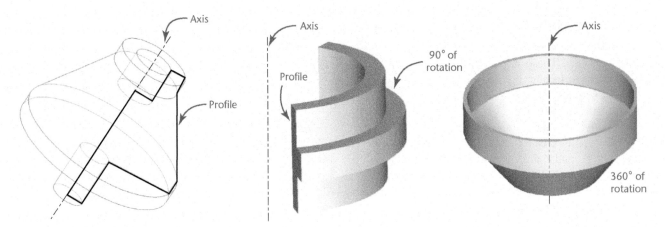

4.72 Revolved Shapes. *Each of the solids shown here was created by revolving a 2D shape around an axis.*

4.19 REVOLVED FORMS

Revolution creates 3D forms from basic shapes by revolving a 2D profile around an axis to create a closed solid object. To create a revolved solid, create the 2D shape to be revolved, specify an axis about which to revolve it, then indicate the number of degrees of revolution. Figure 4.72 shows some shapes created by revolution.

Often, a 2D sketch is used to create 3D CAD models. Look at the examples shown in Figure 4.73 and match them to the 2D profile used to create the part. For each part, decide whether extrusion, revolution, or sweeping was used to create it.

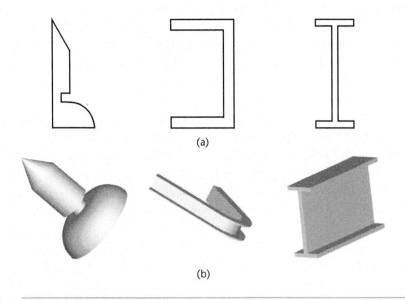

(a)

(b)

4.73 *What operation would you choose to transform the profiles shown in (a) into the models in (b)?*

4.20 IRREGULAR SURFACES

Not every object can be modeled using the basic geometric shapes explored in this chapter. Irregular surfaces are those that cannot be unfolded or unrolled to lie in a flat plane. Solids that have irregular or warped surfaces cannot be created merely by extrusion or revolution. These irregular surfaces are created using surface modeling techniques. Spline curves are frequently the building blocks of the irregular surfaces found on car and snowmobile bodies, molded exterior parts, aircraft, and other (usually exterior) surfaces of common objects, such as an ergonomic mouse. An example of an irregular surface is shown in Figure 4.74. You will learn more about modeling irregular surfaces in Chapter 5.

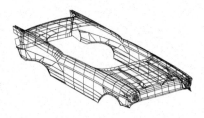

4.74 Irregular Surfaces

4.21 USER COORDINATE SYSTEMS

Most CAD systems allow you to create your own coordinate systems to aid in creating drawing geometry. These are often termed user coordinate systems (in Auto-CAD, for example) or local coordinate systems, in contrast with the default coordinate system (sometimes called the world coordinate system or absolute coordinate system) that is used to store the model in the drawing database. To use many CAD commands effectively, you must know how to orient a user coordinate system.

Most CAD systems create primitive shapes the same way each time with respect to the current X-, Y-, and Z-directions. For example the circular shape of the cylinder is always in the current X-Y plane, as shown in Figure 4.75.

To create a cylinder oriented differently, create a user coordinate system in the desired orientation (Figure 4.76).

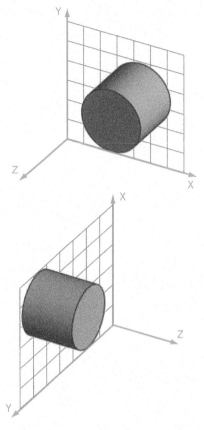

4.76 *These cylinders were created after the X-Y plane of the coordinate system was reoriented.*

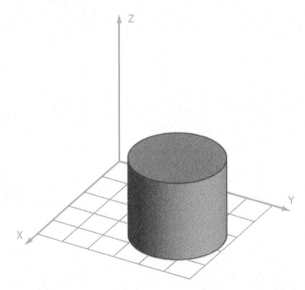

4.75 Cylinder Construction. *The cylinder is created with the circular base on the X-Y plane and the height in Z.*

To create the hole perpendicular to the oblique surface shown in Figure 4.77, create a new local coordinate system aligned with the inclined surface. After you have specified the location of the hole using the more convenient local coordinate system, the CAD software translates the location of the hole to the world (default) coordinate system.

> **TIP**
>
> All CAD systems have a symbol that indicates the location of the coordinate axes—both the global one used to store the model and any user-defined one that is active. Explore your modeler so you are familiar with the way it indicates each.

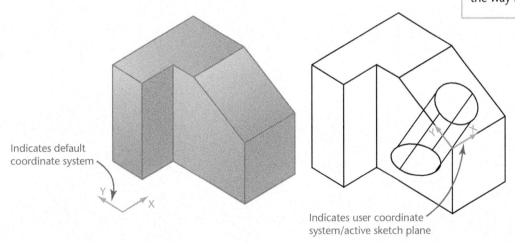

Indicates default coordinate system

Indicates user coordinate system/active sketch plane

4.77 Drawing on an Inclined Plane. *A new coordinate system is defined relative to the slanted surface to make it easy to create the hole.*

Many CAD systems have a command to define the plane for a user coordinate system by specifying three points. This is often an easy way to orient a new coordinate system—especially when it needs to align with an oblique or inclined surface. Other solid modeling systems allow the user to select an existing part surface on which to draw the new shape. This is analogous to setting the X-Y plane of the user coordinate system to coincide with the selected surface. With constraint-based modelers a "sketch plane" often is selected on which a basic shape is drawn that will be used to form a part feature. This defines a coordinate system for the sketch plane.

A user or local coordinate system is useful for creating geometry in a model. Changing the local coordinate system does not change the default coordinate system where the model data are stored.

4.22 TRANSFORMATIONS

A 3D CAD package uses the default Cartesian coordinate system to store information about the model. One way it may be stored is as a matrix (rows and columns of numbers) representing the vertices of the object. Once the object is defined, the software uses mathematical methods to transform the matrix (and the object) in various ways. There are two basic kinds of transformations: those that transform the model itself (called geometric transformations) and those that merely change the view of the model (called viewing transformations).

Geometric Transformations

The model stored in the computer is changed using three basic transformations (or changes): moving (sometimes called translation), rotating, and scaling. When you select a CAD command that uses one of these transformations, the CAD data stored in your model are converted mathematically to produce the result. Commands such as Move (or Translate), Rotate, and Scale transform the object on the coordinate system and change the coordinates stored in the 3D model database.

Figure 4.78 shows a part after translation. The model was moved over 2 units in the X-direction and 3 units in the Y-direction. The corner of the object is no longer located at the origin of the coordinate system.

Figure 4.79 illustrates the effect of rotation. The rotated object is situated at a different location in the coordinate system. Figure 4.80 shows the effect of scaling. The scaled object is larger dimensionally than the previous object.

> ── **TIP** ──
> The following command names are typically used when transforming geometry:
> - **Move**
> - **Rotate**
> - **Scale**

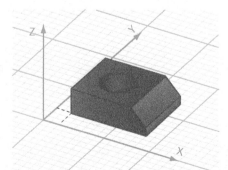

4.78   Translation. *This model has been moved 2 units in the X-direction and 3 units in the Y-direction.*

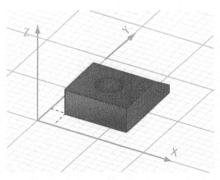

4.79   Rotation. *This model has been rotated in the X-Y plane.*

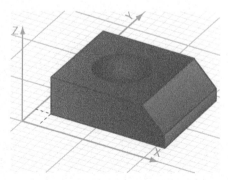

4.80   Scaling. *This model has been scaled to 1.5 times its previous size.*

4.81 Changing the View.
Note that the location of the model relative to the coordinate axes does not change in any of the different views. Changing the view does not transform the model itself.

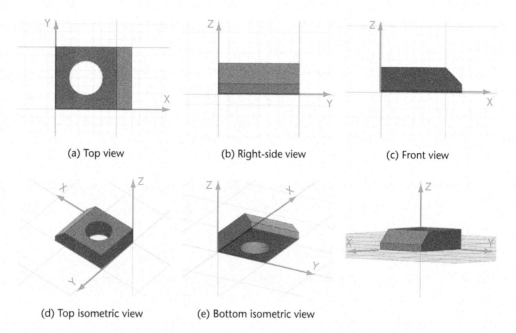

(a) Top view   (b) Right-side view   (c) Front view

(d) Top isometric view   (e) Bottom isometric view

Viewing Transformations

A viewing transformation does not change the coordinate system or the location of the model on the coordinate system; it simply changes your view of the model. The model's vertices are stored in the computer at the same coordinate locations no matter the direction from which the model is viewed on the monitor (Figure 4.81).

Although the model's coordinates do not change when the view does, the software does mathematically transform the model database to produce the new appearance of the model on the screen. This viewing transformation is stored as a separate

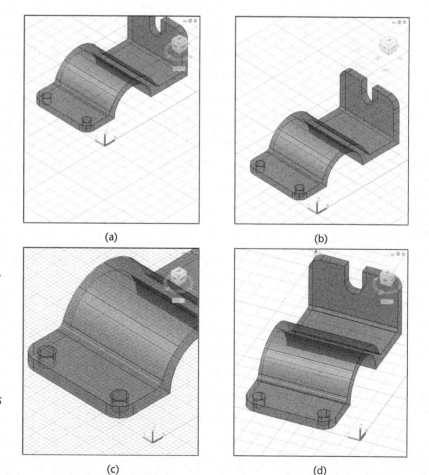

(a)   (b)

4.82 Common View Transformations.
Panning moved the view of the objects in (a) to expose a different portion of the part in (b). In (c), the view is enlarged to show more detail. In (d), the view is rotated to a different line of sight. In each case, the viewing transformation applies to all the objects in the view and does not affect the location of the objects on the coordinate system. (Notice that the position relative to the coordinate system icon does not change.)

(c)   (d)

part of the model file (or a separate file) and does not affect the coordinates of the stored model. Viewing transformations change the view on the screen but do not change the model relative to the coordinate system.

Common viewing transformations are illustrated in Figure 4.82. Panning moves the location of the view on the screen. If the monitor were a hole through which you were viewing a piece of paper, panning would be analogous to sliding the piece of paper to expose a different portion of it through the hole. Zooming enlarges or reduces the view of the objects and operates similar to a telephoto lens on a camera. A view rotation is actually a change of viewpoint; the object appears to be rotated, but it is your point of view that is changing. The object itself remains in the same location on the coordinate system.

Viewing controls transform only the viewing transformation file, changing just your view. Commands to scale the object on the coordinate system transform the object's coordinates in the database.

Examine the six models and their coordinates in Figure 4.83. Which are views that look different because of changes in viewing controls? Which look different because the objects were rotated, moved, or scaled on the coordinate system?

You will use the basic geometric shapes and concepts outlined in this chapter to build CAD models and create accurate freehand sketches. The ability to visualize geometric entities on the Cartesian coordinate system will help you manipulate the coordinate system when modeling in CAD.

> **TIP**
> The following are typical command names for view transformations:
> * **Pan**
> * **Spin** (or **Rotate View**)
> * **Zoom**

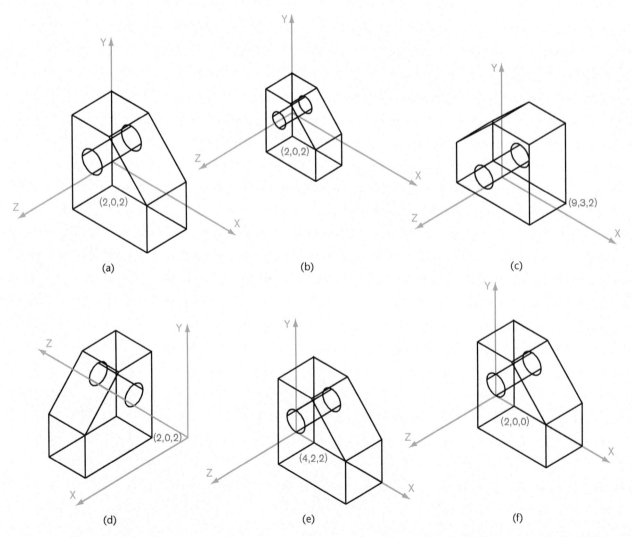

(a)   (b)   (c)

(d)   (e)   (f)

4.83 Geometric or Viewing Transformation? *Three of these models are the same, but the viewing location, zoom, or rotation has changed. Three have been transformed to different locations on the coordinate system.*

THE GEOMETRY OF 3D MODELING: USE THE SYMMETRY

Strategix ID used magnets to create a clean, quiet, zero maintenance brake for the exercise bike it designed for Park City Entertainment. When copper rings on the bike's iron flywheel spin past four rare-earth magnets, they create current in circular flow (an eddy current) that sets up a magnetic field.

This opposing magnetic field dissipates power and slows the wheel. Moving the magnets onto and off the copper rings varies the amount of resistance delivered. When Marty Albini, Senior Mechanical Engineer, modeled the plastic magnet carrier for the brake, he started with the magnets and their behavior as the carrier moved them onto and off the copper rings (see Figure 4.84). "There is no one way to think about modeling a part," Albini said. "The key is to design for the use of the part and the process that will be used to manufacture it." To make the magnet carrier symmetrical, Albini started by modeling half of it.

The magnet carrier was designed as a part in the larger flywheel assembly, parts of which were already completed.

Each pair of magnets was attached to a backing bar that kept them a fixed distance apart. To begin, Albini started with the geometry he was sure of: the diameter of the magnets, the space between them, and the geometry of the conductor ring. He sketched an arc sized to form a pocket around one of the magnets so that its center point would be located on the centerline of the conductor ring (see Figure 4.85). He then sketched another similar arc but with its center point positioned to match the distance between the centers of the two magnets. He connected the two arcs with parallel lines to complete the sketch of the inside of the carrier. This outline was offset to the outside by the thickness of the wall of the holder. (Because this is an injection-molded plastic part, a uniform wall thickness was used throughout.) One final constraint was added to position

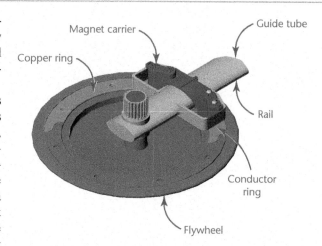

4.84 Flywheel Assembly. *The magnet carrier for the brake was designed to move onto and off the conductor ring by sliding along an elliptical guide tube, pulled by a cable attached to the small tab in the middle of the carrier.*

the carrier against the rail on the elliptical tube along which it would slide: the outside of the inner arc is tangent to this rail. With the sketch geometry fully defined, Albini extruded the sketch up to the top of the guide tube and down to the running clearance from the copper ring.

To add a lid to the holder, Albini used the SolidWorks **Offset** command to trace the outline of the holder. First, he clicked on the top of the holder to make its surface the active sketch plane. This is equivalent to changing the user coordinate system in other packages: it signals to SolidWorks that points picked from the screen lie on this plane. He then selected the

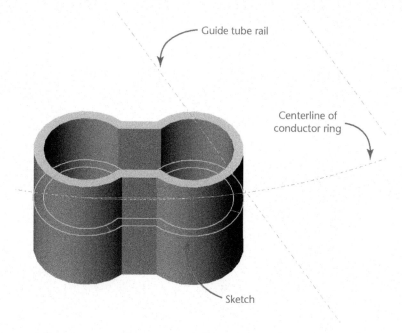

4.85 Extruding the Carrier. *The magnet carrier was extruded up and down from the sketch, shown here as an outline in the middle of the extruded part. Notice that the sketch is tangent to the guide tube rail, and the centers of the arcs in the sketch are located on the centerline of the conductor ring.*

top edges of the holder and used the **Offset** command with a 0 offset to "trace" the outline as a new sketch. To form the lid, he extruded the sketch up (in the positive Z-direction) the distance of the uniform wall thickness.

SolidWorks joined this lid to the magnet holder automatically because both features are in the same part and have surfaces that are coincident. This built-in operation is similar to a Boolean join in that the two shapes are combined to be one.

For the next feature, Albini created a "shelf" at the height of the rail on which the holder will slide. Using **Offset** again, he traced the outline of the holder on the sketch plane, then added parallel and perpendicular lines to sketch the outline of the bottom of the shelf. The outline was then extruded up by the wall thickness. The distance from the outside of the magnet holder to the edge of the shelf created a surface that would sit on the rail (see Figure 4.86).

Two walls were added by offsetting the edge of the shelf toward the magnet holder by the wall thickness, then offsetting the edge again by 0. Lines were added to connect the endpoints into an enclosed shape to be extruded. (In SolidWorks, an extrusion can be specified to extend in one or both directions, and to extend to a vertex, a known distance, the next surface, or the last surface encountered.) For the walls, Albini extruded them to the top surface of the magnet holder "lid."

The connecting web between the magnet holders needed to match the shape of the elliptical tube in the flywheel assembly (see Figure 4.87). To make it, Albini sketched an ellipse on the newly created wall. An ellipse is a sketching primitive that can be specified by entering the length of the major and minor axes. Albini used the dimensions from the tube for the first ellipse sketch, then drew a second one with the same center point but with longer axes so that a gap equal to the wall thickness between them would be formed. The two ellipses were trimmed off at the bottom surface of the shelf and at the midpoint, and lines were drawn to make a closed outline. The finished sketch was extruded to the outside surface of the opposite wall.

More walls were sketched and extruded from the bottom surface of the shelf. Then, the wall over the connecting web was sketched and extruded down to the web.

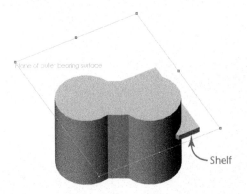

4.86 Changing the Sketch Plane. *The surface of the rail was used as the sketch plane for the "shelf" on which the magnet carrier will slide.*

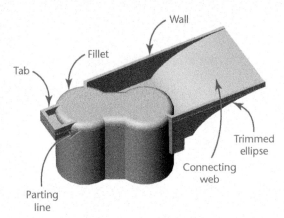

4.87 *This view of the magnet carrier shows the elliptical shape of the connecting web and the rectangular shape of the tab. The parting line for the part, shown here as a dotted white line, is located at the edge of the fillet on the top of the magnet chambers.*

The next step was to add the rounded edges for the top of the magnet holder. Albini invoked the **Fillet** command and selected to round all the edges of the top surface at once. As it created the fillet, SolidWorks maintained the relationship between the wall surfaces that intersected the top edge of the holder and extended them to the new location of the edge.

Next, Albini created a tab at the end of the part that would rest on the plastic collar in the assembly that went all the way around the magnet carrier. He first extruded a rectangular shape up from the top of the collar to form the "floor" of the tab. The walls of the tab required two additional extrusions.

The fillet at the top of the magnet holder provided the location for the parting line—the line where the two halves of the mold would come apart and release the part. Albini added a parting plane and used the built-in **Draft** option to add taper to the part so it would come out of the mold. After selecting all the surfaces below the parting plane, he specified a draft angle, and SolidWorks adjusted all the surfaces. This feature of SolidWorks makes it easy to add the draft angle after a part is finished. When draft is added, the geometry of the part becomes more complex and harder to work with. A cylinder with draft added becomes a truncated cone, for example, and the angles at which its edges intersect other edges vary along its length.

The next step was to add the bosses at the top of the magnet chambers that would support the bolts controlling the depth of the magnets. As it was a design goal to make the top of the chamber as stiff as possible to limit flex caused by the attraction of the magnets to the flywheel, the bosses were placed as far apart as possible, and ribs were added for rigidity. The bosses were sketched as circles on the top surface of the magnet holder with their centers concentric with the holes in the bar connecting the magnets below. Both bosses were extruded up in the same operation.

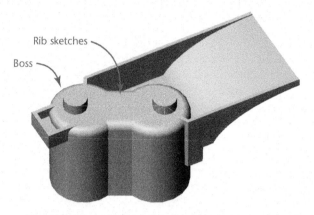

The result was a stiffer rib and a shape that could not be achieved with a single rib operation. To complete the part, circles were drawn concentric to the bosses and extruded to form holes that go through the part (see Figure 4.90). Draft was added to the ribs and walls to make the part release from the mold easily. Fillets were added to round all the edges, reducing stresses and eliminating hot spots in the mold. Then, the part was mirrored to create the other half. The center rib and tab for attaching the cable were added and more edges filleted. Draft was added to the inside of the holder, and the part was complete.

4.88 Bosses and Ribs. *Sketched circles were extruded to form the bosses on the top of the magnet chamber. The dotted lines shown here on the top of the chamber pass through the center point of the bosses and were used to locate the center rib and radial ribs.*

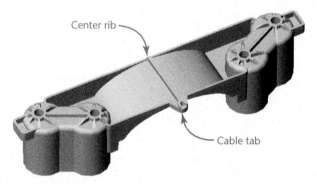

4.90 *Circles concentric with the bosses were extruded to form the holes before the part was mirrored and remaining features added to finish the magnet carrier.*

Ribs in SolidWorks are built-in features. To create a rib, you simply draw a line and specify a width, and SolidWorks creates the rib and ends it at the first surface it encounters. To create the center rib, Albini sketched a line on the plane at the top of the bosses and specified a width (ribs on a plastic part are usually two thirds of the thickness of the walls). The rib was formed down to the top surface of the holder lid. For the ribs around the bosses, Albini did as Obi Wan Kenobi might have advised: "Use the symmetry, Luke." He sketched the lines for ribs radially from the center points of the bosses (see Figure 4.88). To create the ribs, Albini created four of them on one boss, then mirrored them once to complete the set for one boss, then mirrored all the ribs from one boss to the other boss. Once all the ribs were formed, he cut the tops off the ribs and bosses to achieve the shape shown in Figure 4.89.

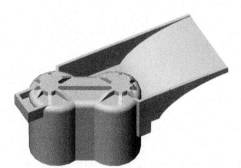

4.89 *This view of the magnet carrier shows the symmetry of the ribs and the shape that resulted from "slicing off" the top of the bosses after the ribs were formed.*

DEFINING DRAWING GEOMETRY

2D CAD programs may allow drawing geometry to be controlled through *constraints* or *parametric* definitions. AutoCAD is one software platform that now provides this tool. In AutoCAD, constraints are associations that can be applied to 2D geometry to restrict how the drawing behaves when a change is made.

Constraints are of two types:

- *Geometric constraints* create geometric relationships between drawing objects, such as requiring that a circle remain tangent to a line, even when its radius is updated.
- *Dimensional constraints* define distances, angles, and radii for drawing objects. These dimensional constraints typically can also be defined by equations, making them a powerful tool.

Usually, it is best to define the geometric constraints first and then apply dimensional constraints. This way the essential geometry of the shape is defined, and the dimensions can be changed as the size requirements vary.

Figure A shows an AutoCAD drawing that uses fixed and tangent constraints. The fixed constraint allows you to force a drawing object to stay in a permanent location on the coordinate system. The tangent constraint defines a relationship between two drawing objects, such as circles, arcs, and lines.

Understanding geometric relationships is a key skill for creating drawings that use parametric constraints. When geometric constraints are applied awkwardly or when the software does not provide a robust tool for constraining the shape, it can be difficult to get good results when updating drawings.

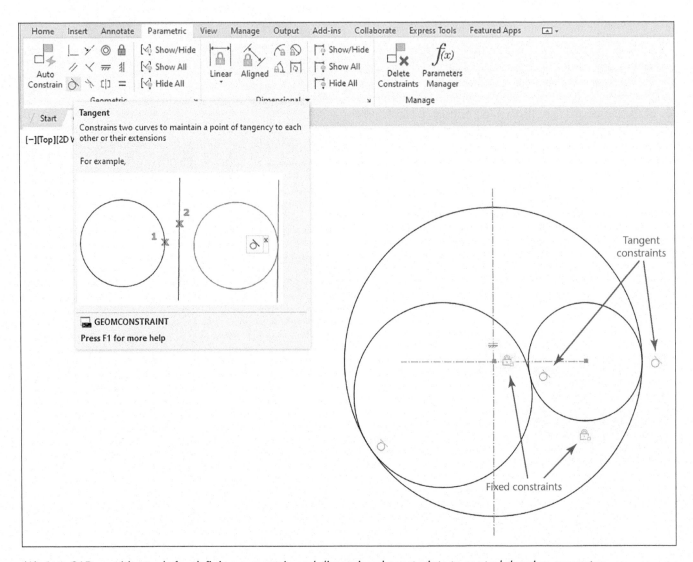

(A) *AutoCAD provides tools for defining geometric and dimensional constraints to control drawing geometry.*
(Autodesk screen shots reprinted courtesy of Autodesk, Inc.)

KEY WORDS

Absolute Coordinate System

Absolute Coordinates

Angle

Apparent Intersection

Bezier Curve

B-Spline

Cubic Spline

Cylindrical Coordinates

Default Coordinate System

Diameter

Extrusion

Focus of an Ellipse

Freeform

Interpolated Spline

Local Coordinate System

Mirrored

NURBS Curve

Parallel

Perpendicular

Piecewise

Polar Coordinates

Primitives

Radius

Relative Coordinates

Revolution

Right-Hand Rule

Spherical Coordinates

Spline

Sweeping

Symmetrical

Transformations

Translation

User Coordinate System

World Coordinate System

CHAPTER SUMMARY

- Understanding how to produce accurate geometry is required for technical drawings whether constructed by hand or using a CAD system.
- All drawings are made up of points, lines, arcs, circles, and other basic elements in relation to each other. Whether you are drawing manually or using CAD, the techniques are based on the relationships between basic geometric elements.
- CAD systems often produce the same result as a complicated hand construction technique in a single step. A good understanding of drawing geometry helps you produce quick and accurate CAD drawings as well as manual drawings.

SKILLS SUMMARY

You should be able to convert and interpret different coordinate formats used to describe point locations and be familiar with some of the basic geometry useful in creating CAD drawings. You should also be able to identify and sketch primitive shapes joined by Boolean operations. In addition, you should be able to visualize and sketch revolved and extruded shapes. The following exercises will give you practice using all these skills.

REVIEW QUESTIONS

1. What tools are useful for drawing straight lines?
2. What tools are used for drawing arcs and circles?
3. How many ways can an arc be tangent to one line? To two lines? To a line and an arc? To two arcs? Draw examples of each.
4. Draw an approximate ellipse with a major diameter of 6″ and a minor diameter of 3″. Draw a second approximate ellipse with a major diameter of 200 mm and a minor diameter of 100 mm.
5. Give one example of a construction technique for CAD that requires a good understanding of drawing geometry.
6. What is typical accuracy for manually created drawings?
7. What accuracies may be possible using a CAD system?
8. Sketch some objects that you use or would design that have right-hand and left-hand parts, such as a pair of in-line skates or side-mounted stereo computer speakers.
9. In solid modeling, simple 3D shapes are often used to create more complex objects. These are called primitives. Using an isometric grid, draw seven primitives.
10. What is a Boolean operation? Define two Boolean operations by sketching an example of each in isometric view.
11. Consider primitives and Boolean operations that could be used to create a "rough" model of each of the items shown below. Using the photos as underlays, sketch primitives that could be used to create items a–d.

    a. Handlebar-mount gun rack

    b. ACME Corporation reduction gear

c. Ashcroft Model 1305D deadweight pressure tester

d. Davis Instruments solar-powered digital thermometer

12. Use nothing but solid primitives to create a model of a steam locomotive. Sketch the shapes and note the Boolean operations that would be used to union, difference, or intersect them, or create the model using Boolean operations with your modeling software. Use at least one box, sphere, cylinder, cone, torus, wedge, and pyramid in your design.

CHAPTER EXERCISES

Exercise 4.1 Draw inclined line *AB* 65 mm long. Bisect it with line *CD*.

Exercise 4.2 Draw any angle. Label its vertex *C*. Bisect the angle and transfer half the angle to place its vertex at arbitrary point *D*.

Exercise 4.3 Draw an inclined line *EF*. Use distance *GH* equal to 42 mm. Draw a new line parallel to *EF* and distance *GH* away.

Exercise 4.4 Draw line *JK* 95 mm long. Draw a second line *LM* 58 mm long. Divide *JK* into five equal parts. Use a different method than you selected to divide line *JK* to divide line *LM* into three equal parts.

Exercise 4.5 Draw line *OP* 92 mm long. Divide it into three proportional parts with the ratio 3:5:9.

Exercise 4.6 Draw a line 87 mm long. Divide it into parts proportional to the square of *x*, where *x* = 1, 2, 3, and 4.

Exercise 4.7 Draw a triangle with the sides 76 mm, 85 mm, and 65 mm. Bisect the three interior angles. The bisectors should meet at a point. Draw a circle inscribed in the triangle, with the point where the bisectors meet as its center.

Exercise 4.8 Draw a right triangle that has a hypotenuse of 65 mm and one leg 40 mm. Draw a circle through the three vertices.

Exercise 4.9 Draw inclined line *QR* 84 mm long. Mark point *P* on the line 32 mm from *Q*. Draw a line perpendicular to *QR* at point *P*. Select any point *S* 45.5 mm from line *QR*. Draw a line perpendicular from *S* to line *QR*.

Exercise 4.10 Draw two lines forming an angle of 35.5°.

Exercise 4.11 Draw two lines forming an angle of 33.16°.

Exercise 4.12 Draw an equilateral triangle with sides of 63.5 mm. Bisect the interior angles. Draw a circle inscribed in the triangle.

Exercise 4.13 Draw an inclined line *TJ* 55 mm long. Using line *TJ* as one of the sides, construct a square.

Exercise 4.14 Create a 54-mm-diameter circle. Inscribe a square in the circle, and circumscribe a square around the circle.

Exercise 4.15 Create a 65-mm-diameter circle. Find the vertices of an inscribed regular pentagon. Join these vertices to form a five-pointed star.

Exercise 4.16 Create a 65-mm-diameter circle. Inscribe a hexagon, and circumscribe a hexagon.

Exercise 4.17 Create a square with 63.5 mm sides. Inscribe an octagon.

Exercise 4.18 Draw a triangle with sides 50 mm, 38 mm, and 73 mm. Copy the triangle to a new location and rotate it 180°.

Exercise 4.19 Make a rectangle 88 mm wide and 61 mm high. Scale copies of this rectangle, first to 70 mm wide and then to 58 mm wide.

Exercise 4.20 Draw three points spaced apart randomly. Create a circle through the three points.

Exercise 4.21 Draw a 58-mm-diameter circle. From any point *S* on the left side of the circle, draw a line tangent to the circle at point *S*. Create a point *T,* to the right of the circle and 50 mm from its center. Draw two tangents to the circle from point *T*.

Exercise 4.22 Open-Belt Tangents. Draw a horizontal centerline near the center of the drawing area. On this centerline, draw two circles spaced 54 mm apart, one with a diameter of 50 mm, the other with a diameter of 38 mm. Draw "open-belt"-style tangents to the circles.

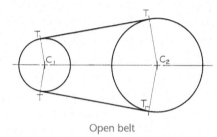

Open belt

Exercise 4.23 Crossed-Belt Tangents. Use the same instructions as Exercise 4.22, but for "crossed-belt"-style tangents.

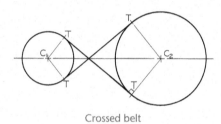

Crossed belt

Exercise 4.24 Draw a vertical line *VW*. Mark point *P* 44 mm to the right of line *VW*. Draw a 56-mm-diameter circle through point *P* and tangent to line *VW*.

Exercise 4.25 Draw a vertical line *XY*. Mark point *P* 44 mm to the right of line *XY*. Mark point *Q* on line *XY* and 50 mm from *P*. Draw a circle through *P* and tangent to *XY* at point *Q*.

Exercise 4.26 Draw a 64-mm-diameter circle with center *C*. Create point *P* to the lower right and 60 mm from *C*. Draw a 25-mm-radius arc through *P* and tangent to the circle.

Exercise 4.27 Draw intersecting vertical and horizontal lines, each 65 mm long. Draw a 38-mm-radius arc tangent to the two lines.

Exercise 4.28 Draw a horizontal line. Create a point on the line. Through this point, draw a line upward to the right at 60° from horizontal. Draw 35-mm-radius arcs in an obtuse and an acute angle tangent to the two lines.

Exercise 4.29 Draw two intersecting lines to form a 60° angle. Create point *P* on one line a distance of 45 mm from the intersection. Draw an arc tangent to both lines with one point of tangency at *P*.

Exercise 4.30 Draw a vertical line *AB*. In the lower right of the drawing, create a 42-mm-radius arc with its center 75 mm to the right of the line. Draw a 25-mm-radius arc tangent to the first arc and to line *AB*.

Exercise 4.31 With centers 86 mm apart, draw arcs of radii 44 mm and 24 mm. Draw a 32-mm-radius arc tangent to the two arcs.

Exercise 4.32 Draw a horizontal centerline near the center of the drawing area. On this centerline, draw two circles spaced 54 mm apart, one with a diameter of 50 mm, the other with a diameter of 38 mm. Draw a 50-mm-radius arc tangent to the circles and enclosing only the smaller one.

Exercise 4.33 Draw two parallel inclined lines 45 mm apart. Mark a point on each line. Connect the two points with an ogee curve tangent to the two parallel lines. (An ogee curve is a curve tangent to both lines.)

Exercise 4.34 Draw a 54-mm-radius arc that subtends an angle of 90°. Find the length of the arc.

Exercise 4.35 Draw a horizontal major axis 10 mm long and a minor axis 64 mm long to intersect near the center of the drawing space. Draw an ellipse using these axes.

Exercise 4.36 Create six equal rectangles and draw visible lines, as shown. Omit dimensions and instructional notes.

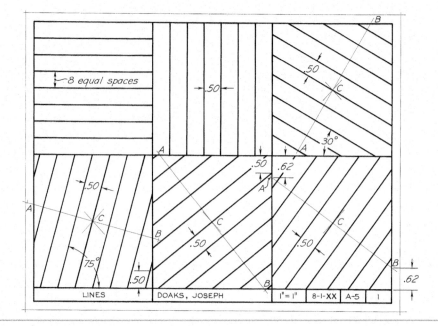

Exercise 4.37 Create six equal rectangles and draw lines as shown. In the first two spaces, draw examples of the standard line patterns used in technical drawings: visible, hidden, construction, centerlines, cutting-plane lines, and phantom. In the remaining spaces, locate centers *C* by diagonals, and then work constructions out from them. Omit the metric dimensions and instructional notes.

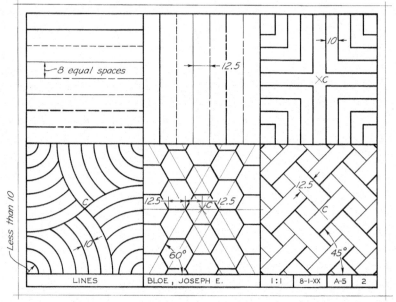

Exercise 4.38 Draw the figures as shown. Omit all dimensions.

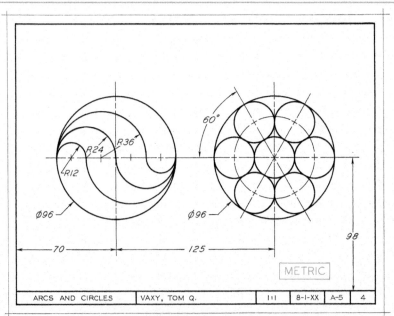

Exercise 4.39 Draw the friction plate. Omit dimensions and notes.

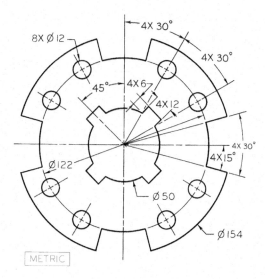

Exercise 4.40 Draw the Geneva cam. Omit dimensions and notes.

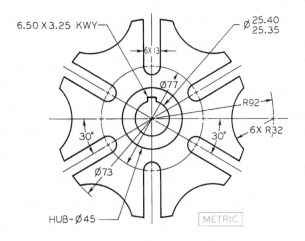

Exercise 4.41 Draw accurately in pencil the shear plate. Give the length of *KA*. Omit the other dimensions and notes.

AB = 94	FG = 61
BC = 40	GH = 48
CD = 35	HJ = 85
DE = 57	JK = 53
EF = 87	KA =

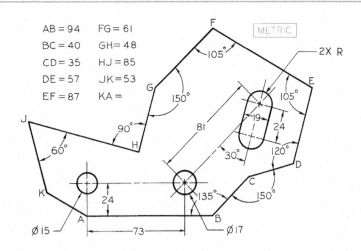

Exercise 4.42 Draw the ratchet wheel using pencil. Omit the dimensions and notes.

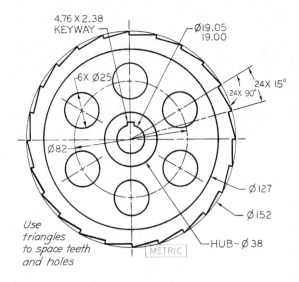

Exercise 4.43 Draw the latch plate using pencil. Omit the dimensions and notes.

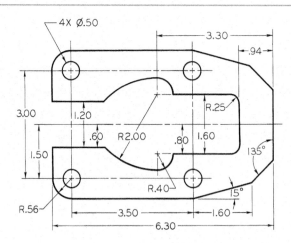

Exercise 4.44 Draw the parabolic floodlight reflector shown.

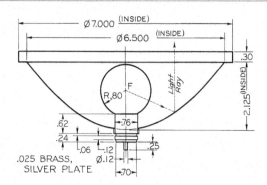

Exercise 4.45 Identify the solid primitives and Boolean operations you could use to create the following objects.

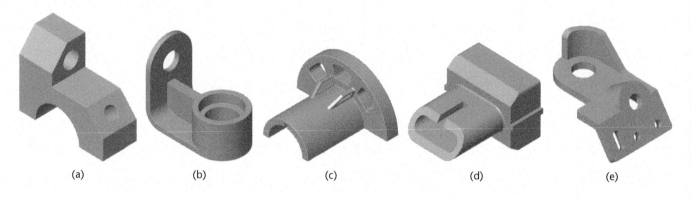

(a)   (b)   (c)   (d)   (e)

Exercise 4.46 Use an isometric grid to help sketch the solids formed by revolving the following shapes about the axis shown. Coordinates are defined by the X-Y-Z icon, with positive X to the right, positive Y up, and positive Z out of the page.

a.

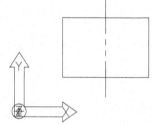

b.

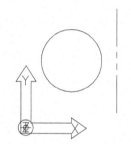

c.

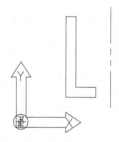

d.

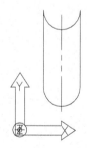

e.

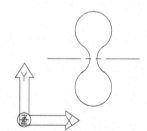

f.

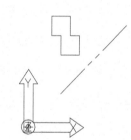

Exercise 4.47 Use an isometric grid to help sketch the solids formed by extruding the following shapes along the axis specified. Coordinates are defined by the X-Y-Z icon, with positive X to the right, positive Y up, and positive Z out of the page.

a. Extrude 6 inches in the positive Z-direction.

b. Extrude 4 inches in the positive Z-direction.

c. Extrude 6 inches in the positive Z-direction.

d. Extrude 4 inches in the positive Z-direction.

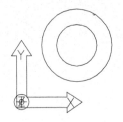 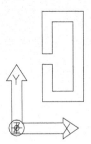 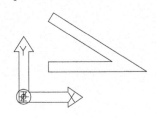 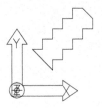

Exercise 4.48 Starting at point A in each of the figures, list the coordinates for each point in order as relative coordinates from the previous point.

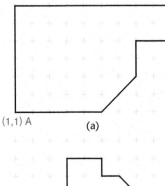

(1,1) A   (a)

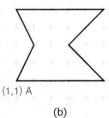

(1,1) A   (b)

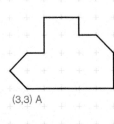

(3,3) A   (c)

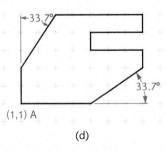

(1,1) A   (d)

Exercise 4.49 Plot the coordinates in each of the lists on grid paper. Each point represents the endpoint of a line from the previous point, unless otherwise indicated. Relative coordinates are preceded by @.

a. X, Y	b.	c.	d.
1.00, 1.00	0.00, 0.00	0,0	2,2
4.00, 1.00	3.00, 0.00	@2<0	@-1<0
4.00, 2.00	4.00, 1.00	@3<30	@3<90
6.00, 2.00	5.00, 0.00	@3<-30	@4<-30
6.00, 1.00	6.00, 1.00	@2<0	@3<30
8.00, 1.00	7.00, 0.00	@4<90	@1<0
8.00, 4.00	8.00, 1.00	0,4	@3.24<230
5.00, 4.00	9.00, 0.00	@4<-90	@4<180
4.00, 5.00	10.00, 1.00		
1.00, 5.00	10.00, 3.00		
1.00, 1.00	9.00, 4.00		
	8.00, 3.00		
	7.00, 4.00		
	6.00, 3.00		
	5.00, 4.00		
	4.00, 3.00		

Exercise 4.50 Using the information provided on the drawing, determine the coordinates you would use (absolute, relative, or polar) and the order in which you would enter them to create the figure.

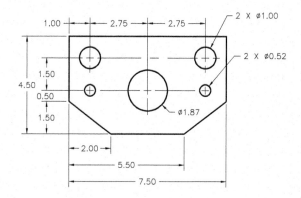

Exercise 4.51 Using the information provided on the drawing, determine the coordinates you would use (absolute, relative, or polar) and the order in which you would enter them to create the figure.

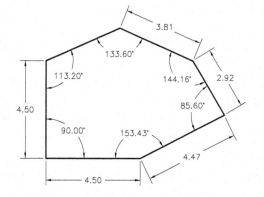

Exercise 4.52 Using the information provided on the drawing, determine the coordinates you would use (absolute, relative, or polar) and the order in which you would enter them to create the figure.

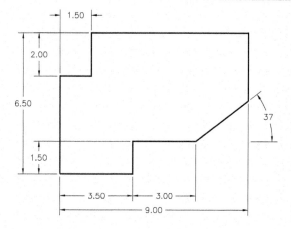

CHAPTER FIVE

MODELING AND DESIGN

───────── OBJECTIVES ─────────

After studying the material in this chapter, you should be able to:

1. Describe modeling methods available to represent your design.

2. List model qualities that can help you select among them.

3. Describe how models can be used in refining designs.

4. Describe which modeling method contains the most information about a design.

5. Describe how a constraint-based modeler differs from a traditional solid modeler.

6. Define design intent and how it is reflected in a constraint-based model.

7. Define the basic functions of a constraint-based modeler.

8. Identify the role of a base feature.

9. Identify constraint relationships and driving dimensions.

Refer to the following standards:
- *ANSI/ASME Y14.100 Engineering Drawing Practices*
- *ASME Y14.41 Digital Product Definition Data Practices*

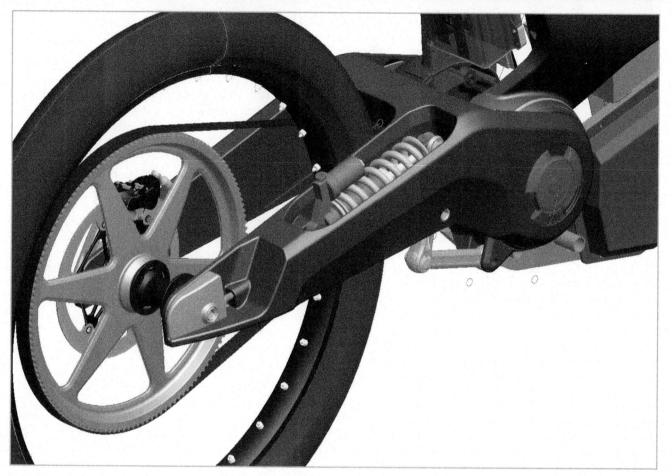

The ENV hydrogen fuel cell motorbike was designed from the fuel cell outward. During its development many refinements were made both technologically and visually. Models in this phase must represent the design accurately enough to be used for testing as well as to convey the details of the design for implementation. (Courtesy of Seymourpowell.)

OVERVIEW

Graphic tools are selected for their ability to capture a design idea and to help team members visualize solutions to the design problem. Freehand sketches and conceptual representations are the best way to generate and explore a wide range of options. You cannot model what you have not planned and thought about.

For design refinement, you need to include the detail necessary to define it for manufacture, as well as to test it against the design specifications. At the same time, you need to preserve your ability to modify the design as it evolves.

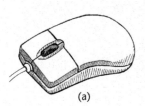

(a)

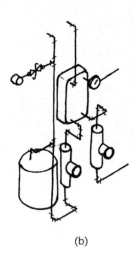

(b)

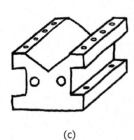

(c)

5.1   *The same modeling software may be used to model (a) the ergonomic mouse, (b) the piping system, and (c) the V-block, but different modeling methods may be best suited to each.*

REFINEMENT AND MODELING

From the solutions generated during ideation, only a few are selected for further consideration. The design review process determines whether money will be committed for further development of a design.

The process of refining and analyzing the design is iterative. As the refined design is tested, the test results suggest modifications to the design, and once the design is changed, it needs further analysis.

Creating a CAD model is an important step in the refinement process. A huge amount of design information can be stored in CAD models that are easily modified. The CAD model can be used to test and evaluate the design. By making changes easy—and in some cases, automating the update process—CAD modeling can eliminate some barriers to a thorough review and refinement of the design.

CAD models also encourage refinement by making it easier and less costly to get feedback about a design while it is in development. Accurate part descriptions allow you to test how well parts will fit together. Customer acceptance and styling issues can be assessed early in the design process using realistically shaded models. Analysis programs can import 3D CAD files or run as part of the CAD software, saving much time. Some analysis packages suggest optimizations to incorporate directly in the CAD model. Animation and kinematic analysis uses CAD data to determine whether the design will function properly before any parts are actually built.

Many different methods are used to create CAD models, each with its strengths and weaknesses for capturing design information. Each item shown in Figure 5.1 may be modeled differently, possibly requiring different software and techniques.

In this chapter, you will learn how different modeling methods represent and store design information, and the advantages and disadvantages of each. This information will aid you in choosing the most effective method for a particular design problem.

What Is a Model?

In general, a *model* is a representation of a system, device, or theory that allows you to predict its behavior. A dictionary definition for model is as follows:

1. A small object, usually built to scale, that represents in detail another, often larger object.
2. (a) A preliminary work or construction that serves as a plan from which a final product is to be made: *a clay model ready for casting.* (b) Such a work or construction used in testing or perfecting a final product: *a test model of a solar-powered vehicle.*
3. A schematic description of a system, theory, or phenomenon that accounts for its known or inferred properties and may be used for further study of its characteristics: *a model of generative grammar; a model of an atom; an economic model.*

This definition defines three key qualities that are shared to varying degrees by models used in engineering design:

- They represent in detail another object: the product or system to be produced.
- They are a plan from which a final product will be made.
- They are used for studying and testing the design to provide an approximation of how it will behave.

KINDS OF MODELS

Under the broad umbrella term model are several types.

Descriptive Models

Descriptive models represent a system or device in either words or pictures. Descriptive models sometimes use representations that are simplified or analogous to something that is more easily understood. The key function of a descriptive model is to describe; that is, to provide enough detail to convey an image of the final product.

A set of written specifications for a design is a descriptive model. If all the specifications are followed, the system will perform correctly. Sketching is also a type of descriptive model for your design ideas on paper. 2D and 3D CAD drawings are also descriptive models. A physical model or prototype is another type of descriptive model, although sometimes physical models are made to a smaller scale (called a scale model).

The figures at right show a scale model of a design for the Next Generation Space Telescope (NGST) developed by NASA. A model helps you visualize the design. It has the added benefit of being easy for non-engineers to understand while decisions are being made about the next step in the project.

A 1:10 Scale Model

This scale model represents a design by Ball Aerospace for the Next Generation Space Telescope (NGST). The mock-up was the largest and most complex scale model created by Ball Aerospace. At 1:10 scale, it represents a telescope that stands over 9 feet tall with a primary mirror 8 meters in diameter when fully deployed (Figure b). Because the primary mirror is so large, it must be able to fold in on itself to fit inside a launch vehicle, as shown in Figure a. This scale model demonstrated the deployment using seventeen computer-controlled motors. Because of the improbability of servicing this telescope in space, this design is also partially functional even if the mirrors fail to fully deploy.

(a)

(b)

(Photos courtesy of Ball Aerospace & Technologies Corporation.)

Analytical Models

An *analytical model* captures the behavior of the system or device in a mathematical expression or schematic that can be used to predict future behavior. The electrical circuit model shown in Figure 5.2 is an example of an analytical model. The circuit and its properties are represented in the model by equations and relations that simulate the way the component would behave in a real circuit. The designer can change values to make predictions about what will happen in a real circuit that is wired the same way as the model. This makes it easier, less expensive, and faster to test the design.

Part of creating an effective analytical model is determining which aspects of the system's behavior to model. In the circuit model, some information, such as interference between some components, is left out because it is too complex to represent effectively. A *finite element analysis* (FEA) model, such as that used to generate the stress plot shown in Figure 5.3a, simplifies the CAD model in a similar way. The FEA model breaks the model into smaller elements; reducing a complicated system to a series of smaller systems allows the stresses more easily to be solved. Understanding and using analytical models effectively requires knowing how the model differs from the actual system so the results can be interpreted correctly.

In the design process, use different types of models where they are appropriate. During the ideation phase of the design, sketching is often the best technique to use. As you begin to refine the design, you will use both descriptive and analytical models to represent the design more accurately and to provide insight into its behavior.

A 3D CAD model combines qualities of descriptive and analytical models. Because a 3D CAD model accurately depicts the geometry of a device, it can fully describe its shape, size, and appearance as a physical or scale model would. Additional information about the final product, such as the materials from which it will be made, can also be added to the model description stored

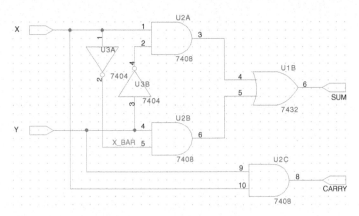

5.2 *A simple circuit design model allows simulation of its function. (Courtesy of Cadence® Design Systems, Inc.)*

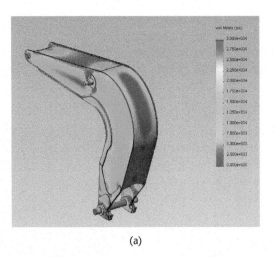

(a)

5.3 *Finite element analysis (a) is used to calculate the stresses on the gooseneck shown in (b) in designing this heavy-duty equipment. (Courtesy of TowHaul Corporation.)*

Gooseneck

(b)

(a)

5.4 Descriptive and Analytical.
This rendered view of the preliminary CAD model of the SIRTF assembly, shown in (a), looks very similar to the photograph of its 1:10 scale model, shown in (b) next to a 1:10 model of the Hubble Space Telescope.
(Courtesy of Ball Aerospace and Technologies Corporation.)

(b)

in the computer database. Figure 5.4 shows a CAD model of NASA's Space Infrared Telescope Facility (SIRTF).

A 3D CAD model can also be used for analytical modeling. The 3D model of the device can be used to study its characteristics (see Figure 5.5). Sophisticated software allows you to analyze, animate, and predict the behavior of the design under various physical conditions. The 3D CAD model is a detailed representation of the final object, suited for testing and study.

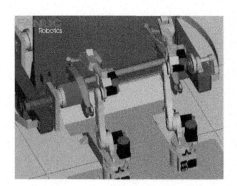

5.5 Motion Analysis. *These welding robots are programmed with code developed with 3D model data. The motion of the robots is simulated with a 3D model of the part to be welded and 3D models of the robots. Motion paths are then exported and used to program the actual robots. (Courtesy of FANUC America Corporation.)*

SPOTLIGHT

Model Qualities

Each modeling method has strengths and weaknesses. Models have general qualities that make them more or less useful for certain purposes and phases in the design process. Because design is an iterative process, being able to change the model easily can be important. Also, there can be a significant investment in equipment and effort in creating CAD models, so it is important for them to be useful for a variety of purposes. What are the qualities that can make models more or less useful?

Good models are

- visual (presenting information graphically);
- understandable (contain detail in a format suited to the audience);
- flexible (allow quick and easy updates and changes);
- cost-effective (provide benefits worth the cost of creating the model);
- measurable (able to extract size, shape, and other information);
- accurate (provide information with useful precision); and
- robust (contain information depicting the necessary aspects of the system and reflecting the design intent).

5.1 2D MODELS

Paper Drawings

2D sketches and multiview drawings are representations of the design. All the information defining the object may be shown in a paper drawing (see Figure 5.6), although it may require many orthographic views.

Multiview drawing techniques were designed to improve the robustness, measurability, and accuracy of paper drawings. These same techniques require some skill to be understood, however, and make multiview drawings harder to understand than a 3D model.

Equipment costs for paper drawings are minimal, but they take as long or longer to create than CAD drawings. Changes involve considerable erasing and redrawing, making them difficult to modify as the design changes. Because paper drawings are difficult to change, the labor costs associated with them usually outweigh the equipment savings.

Paper drawing accuracy is about plus or minus one fortieth the drawing scale. For example, a paper drawing of a map drawn at a scale of 1 inch = 400 feet has good accuracy if you can measure from it to plus or minus 10 feet. This makes paper drawings not particularly measurable or accurate—which is why proper dimensioning technique was developed. Proper dimensioning overcomes this limitation and provides measure-ments to the desired accuracy on the drawing. It is not good practice to make measurements from paper drawings.

Paper drawings can be very effective for quickly communicating the design of small parts for manufacturing. A properly dimensioned sketch can quickly convey all the information needed to make a part that is needed only one time (see Figure 5.7). Also, manufacturing facilities occasionally are not able to read electronic files and require paper drawings.

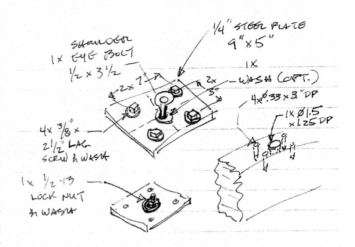

5.7 Computation Sketch Detail *(Courtesy of Jeffrey J. Zerr.)*

2D CAD Models

2D CAD models share the visual characteristics of paper drawings but are more accurate and easier to change. CAD systems have a large variety of editing tools that allow quick editing and reuse of drawing geometry. Standard symbols are easy to add and change.

2D CAD drawings can quickly be printed to different scales. Different types of information can be separated onto different *layers* that can either be displayed or turned off, making the model more flexible than a paper drawing.

Using CAD, you can accurately define the locations of lines, arcs, and other geometry. In AutoCAD, for example, you can store these locations to at least fourteen decimal places. You can query the database, and the information will be returned as accurately as you originally created it. Of course, the adage Garbage In, Garbage Out (GIGO) applies. If your endpoints do not connect, or you locate distances by eye instead of entering them precisely, you will not have accurate results.

CAD models represent the object full size, unlike paper drawings, so you can make measurements and calculations from 2D CAD models. Also, you can "snap" to locations on objects to determine sizes and distances that may not be dimensioned on a paper drawing. If there must be a clearance of 10 feet from the center of a tank to the location of another piece of equipment, you can measure from the CAD file to determine whether proper clearance is provided in the design.

Text and other information can be saved in a database and linked to the drawing information for later retrieval. The 2D

5.6 *This fully dimensioned paper drawing contains all the information needed to manufacture this part, which will be flame cut from a 96 × 156-inch sheet of steel. (Courtesy of Smith Equipment, USA.)*

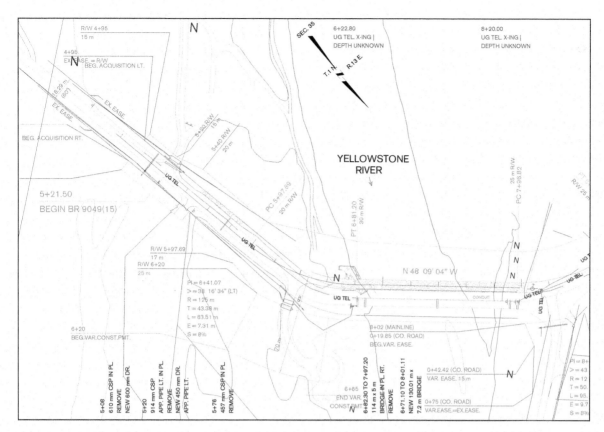

5.8 *Large-scale projects such as this highway plan are often modeled in 2D CAD. Most 2D CAD systems associate dimension values with the entities they describe, so dimensions can be updated if the drawing changes. (Courtesy of Montana Department of Transportation, MSU Design Section, Bozeman, MT.)*

database is limited, however, in its ability to represent information that depends on a 3D definition (such as the volume inside the object), so it is not generally useful for determining mass and other physical properties of the object.

The strengths and weaknesses of paper drawing are shared by 2D CAD models. To create them and read them you must be able to interpret the 2D views to "see" the 3D object. To measure from a 2D CAD model, you must show distances and angles true length in a view. Orthographic projection and descriptive geometry are needed to create these views. **Descriptive geometry** is the study of producing views of an object that show true lengths, shape, angles, and other information about an engineering design. Mastering these subjects enables you to use auxiliary views created with a 2D CAD system along with the traditional methods of descriptive geometry to solve many engineering problems.

Flexibility and accuracy make 2D CAD systems a cost-effective tool in a wide variety of businesses. For many civil engineering projects, the difficulty of capturing all the 3D information needed to model irregular surfaces, such as terrain, may not be worth the benefits of working in 3D. For projects such as highway design, civil mapping, electrical distribution, and building systems, 2D CAD models may provide enough information and be created more quickly from the information at hand (see Figure 5.8). Areas and perimeters can be calculated accurately, and drawings can be revised quickly. 2D CAD models are more accurate than paper drawings.

TIP

If lines and shapes in a 2D CAD drawing are not drawn using methods that connect exact geometry, they may not actually connect. This can cause a number of different problems. For example, when crosshatching inside a boundary, even a small gap can cause the hatching to "leak" out.

The drawing of the geneva cam below appears fine here and on screen. But when the corner is enlarged, it is clear that the line that should be tangent to the arc does not connect. Because of the algorithm used to generate circles and arcs, line segments used to represent them may not appear to connect when zoomed. But when the CAD drawing is regenerated from the data in the file, the line will—if tangent—clearly touch the arc, as shown in (c).

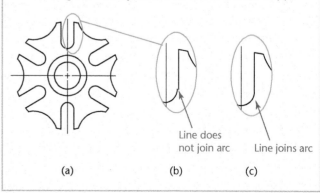

Line does   Line joins arc
not join arc

(a)   (b)   (c)

2D Constraint-Based Modeling

Constraint-based modeling originally started as a method for creating 3D models. Constraint-based 2D models provide a mechanism for defining a 2D shape based on its geometry. Relationships like concentricity and tangency can be added between entities in the drawing. For example, once a concentric constraint is added between two circles, they will remain concentric, and you will be alerted if you attempt to make a change that will violate this geometric constraint. Dimensions in the drawing constrain the sizes of features.

Relationships defined between parts of the 2D model are maintained by the software when you make changes to the drawing. Geometric constraints can be a valuable tool, but to benefit from them, you must apply them with a good understanding of basic drawing geometry and the behavior desired when changes are made to the shape.

2D CONSTRAINTS

2D Constraints in AutoCAD

2D drawing geometry defined using constraints must behave so as to satisfy the conditions placed on the drawing elements. Small constraint symbols indicate on-screen which conditions have been defined for the shape. The following constraints are available for defining AutoCAD geometry:

- *Horizontal:* Lines or pairs of points on objects must remain parallel to the X-axis.
- *Vertical:* Lines or pairs of points on objects must remain parallel to the Y-axis.
- *Perpendicular:* Two selected lines must maintain a 90° angle to one another.
- *Parallel:* Two selected lines must remain parallel.
- *Tangent:* Two curves must maintain tangency to each other or to their extensions.
- *Smooth:* A spline must be contiguous and maintain G2 curvature continuity with another entity.
- *Coincident:* Two points must stay connected.
- *Concentric:* Two arcs, circles, or ellipses must maintain the same center point.
- *Collinear:* Two or more line segments must remain along the same line.
- *Symmetric:* Two selected objects must remain symmetrical about a specified line.
- *Equal:* Selected entities must maintain the same size.
- *Fix:* Points, line endpoints, or curve points must stay in fixed position on the coordinate system.

The following size constraints are also available:

- *Linear:* The distance between two points along the X- or Y-axis must be maintained.
- *Aligned:* A distance between two points must be maintained.
- *Radius:* The radius for a curve must be maintained.
- *Diameter:* The diameter of a circle must be maintained.
- *Angular:* The angle between two lines must be maintained.

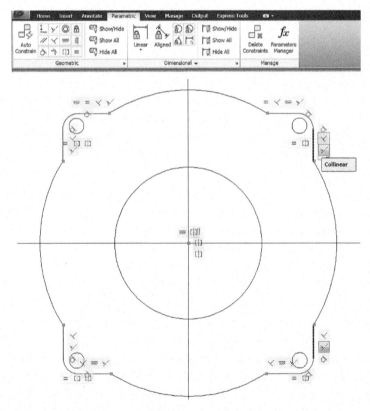

(Autodesk screen shots reprinted courtesy of Autodesk, Inc.)

5.2 3D MODELS

2D models must be interpreted to visualize a 3D object. To convey the design to individuals unfamiliar with orthographic projection—or to evaluate properties of the design that are undefined in 2D representations—3D models are used.

Physical Models

Physical models provide an easy visual reference. Physical models are called **prototypes** when they are made full size or used to validate a nearly final design for production. People can interact with them and get a feel for how the design will look and how it will function. Many problems with designs are discovered and corrected when a physical prototype is made.

The robustness and cost effectiveness of physical models are often linked. A simple model made of clay or cardboard may be enough for some purposes (see Figure 5.9), but determining the fit of many parts in a large-scale assembly, or producing a model realistic enough for market testing, may be cost prohibitive until very late in the design process. A full-size prototype of the BMW 850I cost more than $1 million to produce. The amount of information and detail built into the model adds to its cost.

5.9   *This physical clay model of the Romulus Predator was used to evaluate the aerodynamics of its lines in a wind tunnel at the University of Michigan. (Courtesy of Mark Gerisch.)*

The accuracy of a physical prototype also drives up its cost. Many objects are designed to be mass produced so that the cost of individual parts is reduced. When each part in the model must be produced one at a time, the cost of the prototype can be many times greater than the manufacturing cost of the final product. The more the model must match the final product in terms of materials used and final appearance, the greater the cost. Rapid prototyping systems offer quick and relatively inexpensive means of generating a physical model of smaller parts without the cost of machining or forming parts one at a time (see Figure 5.10).

Physical models are a very good visual representation of the design, but if they are not made from the materials that will be selected for the design, their weight and other characteristics will not match the final product. Sometimes, owing to the size of the project, the physical model must be made to a smaller scale than the final design. The accuracy of the final part also may not be possible with the materials and processes used for the prototype.

Probably the least attractive feature of a physical prototype is its lack of flexibility. Once a physical prototype has been created, changing it is expensive, difficult, and time-consuming. Consequently, full-size physical models are not usually used until fairly late in the design process—when major design changes are less likely. This can limit the usefulness of the model even though it provides important feedback about items that are not working well. When the information comes late in the design process, it can be too expensive to return to a much earlier stage of the design to pursue a different approach. Only critical

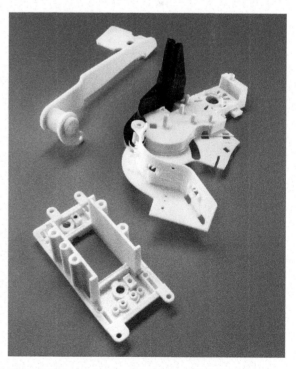

5.10   *Prototype parts created using a fused deposition modeling system are useful for design verification. (Courtesy of Stratsys, Inc.)*

problems may be fixed. Solutions to problems found late in the process are generally constrained to cause the least amount of redesign while fixing the problem. When a prototype is created late in the process, there may not be time or resources to create a new prototype for the new solution. New problems introduced by the change may not be seen until actual parts are produced.

Despite the trade-offs, even very costly physical models have been a cost-effective way for companies to avoid much more costly errors in manufacturing.

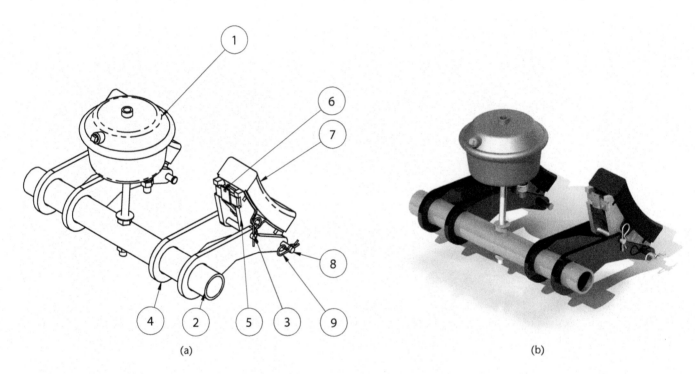

(a)   (b)

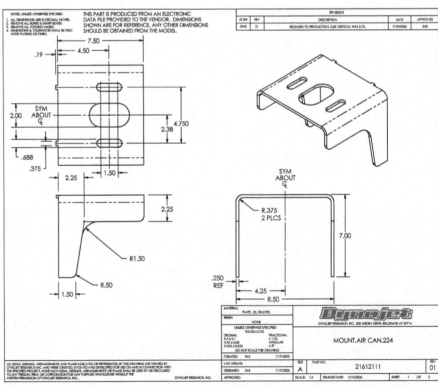

5.11 *The 3D model, shown as outline in (a), can also be rendered to produce the realistic view shown in (b) and to generate accurate 2D views for multiview drawings (c). (Courtesy of Dynojet Research, Inc.)*

(c)

3D CAD Models

A 3D CAD model offers all the benefits of a 2D model and a physical model. As a visual representation, 3D CAD models can generate standard 2D multiview drawings as well as realistically shaded and rendered views. Because a 3D CAD model accurately depicts the geometry of the device, it may eliminate the need for a prototype—or make it easy to create one from the data stored in the model. Options for viewing the model make it understandable to a wide range of individuals who might be involved with the design's refinement (see Figure 5.11).

Virtual Reality

Virtual reality (VR) refers to interacting with a 3D CAD model as if it were real—the model simulates the way the user would interact with a real device or system. Using a virtual reality display, users are immersed in the model so that they can move around (and sometimes through) it and see it from different points of view. The headset display shown in Figure 5.12 uses two displays set about 3 inches apart (the typical distance between a person's eyes). Each display shows a view of the object as it would be seen from the eye looking at it, which creates a stereoscopic view similar to the one sent to the brain by our two eyes. Some headsets let you control the viewpoint by moving your eyes or head, so that as you look around, a new view is created to correspond with the new direction.

Some 3D interfaces, such as a 3D mouse or haptic (meaning sense of touch) controller, let the user interact with the items in the 3D model in a way that enhances the illusion of reality. Some haptic devices (similar to the gloves shown in Figure 5.13) even use model data to provide physical feedback to the user when an object is encountered. If a virtual object is squeezed, feedback to the device provides the feeling of the resistance a solid object would give when squeezed. Systems may even interpret how much force would crush the object and provide this sensation to the user.

The term *virtual prototype* describes 3D CAD systems that represent the object realistically enough for users, designers, and manufacturers to get the same type of information they get from creating a physical prototype.

As more sophisticated software becomes available to analyze, animate, and predict the behavior of the design under

5.12 Virtual Reality Headset. *Cybermind's Visette45 has both closed and see-through versions offering an effective screen size of 80 inches at 2 meters. (Courtesy of Cinoptics.)*

various physical conditions, the 3D CAD model becomes a better representation of the final object—and better suited for testing and study.

3D CAD models offer a high degree of accuracy and measurability and a high degree of flexibility. Each new generation of CAD software automates more common tasks, allowing the designer to focus more on the design and less on the mechanics of changing the model. This flexibility allows the CAD model to become a preliminary work that is refined and tested until it is ready to be used as a plan for the final product.

The ability of 3D CAD models to be used throughout the process, serve in lieu of a physical model, and be reused and modified indefinitely makes them very cost effective, especially in designing mechanical assemblies. However, not all 3D CAD models are the same. Familiarity with different types of 3D modeling systems lets you select the method and software most suitable for your design project.

5.13 Virtual Reality Gloves. *These 5DT Ultra series of data gloves are controlled via a belt-worn wireless kit designed to transmit data for two gloves simultaneously. (Courtesy of 5DT/Fifth Dimension Technologies.)*

5.3 TYPES OF 3D MODELS

Each of the major 3D modeling methods—wireframe modeling, surface modeling, solid modeling, and parametric constraint-based modeling—has its advantages and disadvantages. Many CAD systems incorporate all these modeling methods into one single software package. Other software may provide only one or two of these methods.

Wireframe Models

Wireframe modeling represents the edges and contours of an object using lines, circles, and arcs oriented in 3D space. 3D wireframe drawings can be easy to create, are handled by many low-cost software packages, and provide a good tool for modeling simple 3D shapes. The method gets its name from the appearance of the model, which resembles a sculpture made of wires, as shown in Figure 5.14.

You create a wireframe model in much the same way that you create a 2D CAD drawing. Each edge where surfaces on the object intersect is drawn in 3D space using simple geometric tools, such as a 3D line or arc. The X-, Y-, and Z-coordinates for the endpoints are stored in the database along with the type of entity.

3D wireframes can quickly display process control, piping, sheet metal parts, mechanical linkages, and layout drawings showing critical dimensions that use relatively simple geometric shapes. Interferences and clearance distances are difficult to visualize in 2D piping drawings. It can be critical that they are not overlooked in the design. For example, to quickly check clearances for the design of an electrical substation, the engineer may create a wireframe model of the high-voltage conductors to ensure that conductors are not too close to other equipment that could produce an electrical arc, causing a short.

A 3D wireframe can be useful for piping layout around other 3D equipment, which can be difficult to visualize in 2D. The centerline of the pipe is easy to represent in a 3D wireframe, as shown in Figure 5.14. This prevents problems with clearances that are acceptable in two dimensions, but not in a third. For a system with moving parts or where complex shapes need to fit, a different 3D modeling method may better allow you to assess interferences.

Wireframe models do not include surfaces that can be shaded, so they are not realistic looking. Because you can see through the model, some shapes cannot be represented unambiguously, and it may be difficult to see from a single view which areas are holes and which are surfaces. The model in Figure 5.15 shows a wireframe

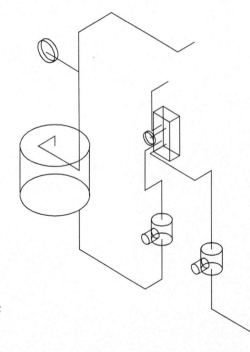

5.14   A Wireframe Model. *Edges and contours of an object are represented by lines, circles, and arcs oriented in 3D space. 3D wireframe is a suitable method for modeling this snow-melting system.*

model. Without rotating or checking coordinate locations, you may visualize the part as showing the hole from the top or the bottom (Figure 5.16).

Before you can measure oblique edges and surfaces in a 2D drawing, you must first create an auxiliary view showing that feature true size. The true size is already contained in the 3D wireframe and can be measured directly. For example, the length of edge A in Figure 5.17 can be determined from this 2D AutoCAD drawing only in the auxiliary view. The 3D wireframe model of the same part can show the length of the edge directly.

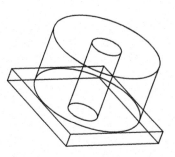

5.15 *Are you looking at the model from above or from below?*

5.16 *Adding faces to a wireframe model removes the ambiguity about the features.*

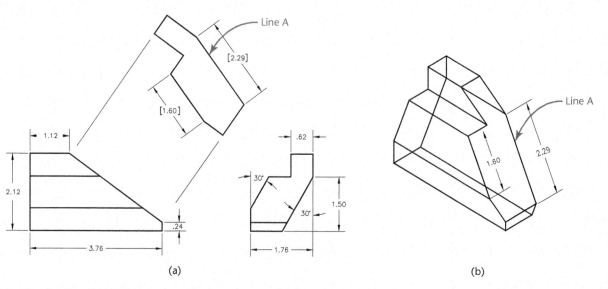

(a)   (b)

5.17 *(a) The 2D CAD drawing displays the true length of line A in an auxiliary view. (b) The length of the line in the 3D wireframe model can be determined directly from the model.*

Wireframe Modeler versus Wireframe Display

Wireframe modeling was the first 3D modeling method. Its depiction of edges and contours grew out of 2D modeling practices. The term "wireframe" is also used to describe an economical way of displaying a model on the computer screen in which just the edges and contours are shown. Representing objects on the screen using wireframe display is simpler and faster than showing shaded views. The computing power needed to generate and display a model was a constraint in the design of CAD modeling systems. Wireframe representation was developed when multimedia displays common on home computers today were available only on powerful mainframes. As computers evolved, computationally intensive modeling techniques became feasible. Display methods such as shaded views, shaded views with

edges, hidden line-removed views, and others can be generated from the data. There is still a trade-off between complexity and speed; more complex and detailed information means more processor time.

CAD modelers address this trade-off by representing the model data in two ways: first, as it is stored in the database (the coordinate locations for each entity in the model, for example) and second, as it will be displayed on the screen. The economy of wireframe display makes it a good choice for working with computer models—whatever the underlying modeling method. Surface, solid, and constraint-based modelers all offer a wireframe display and a range of tools for controlling that display. Each of them, however, creates a database with more information than can be found in that created by a wireframe modeler, which stores only vertex and edge information.

Surface Models

CAD surface models define a shape by storing its surface information. A surface model is similar to an empty box. The outer surfaces of the part are defined (although unlike an actual box, these surfaces do not have any material thickness). Because the surfaces are defined, they can be shaded to provide a realistic appearance.

Surface modelers are traditionally used by industrial designers and stylists who create the outside envelope for a device. These designers need modeling tools that convey a realistic image of the final product. Software tools developed for their use focused first on the challenge of modeling the exterior of the product, not the mechanical workings within. Many surface modelers offer specialized tools for lighting and rendering a model, so designers can create photorealistic images that cannot be distinguished from the actual product (see Figure 5.18).

Concurrent engineering and the use of the 3D CAD database as the product description contributed to the development of modeling software that satisfies the aesthetic needs of industrial designers as well as the functional information needed by engineers. Understanding surface modeling techniques will help you assess the kinds of features that are available in your modeler—and whether a dedicated surface modeler is required.

Surface Information in the Database

Most surface modeling software stores a list of a part's vertices and how they connect to form edges in the CAD database. The surfaces between them are generated mathematically from the lines, curves, and points that define them. Some surface modelers store additional information to indicate which is the inside and which is the outside of the surface. This is often done by storing a **surface normal**, a directional line perpendicular to the outside of the surface. This allows the model to be shaded and rendered more easily.

Storing the definitions of the surfaces in the CAD digital database is termed **boundary representation** (BREP), meaning that the information contained in the database represents the external boundaries of the surfaces making up the 3D model. Remember that these surfaces have no thickness.

The following are basic methods used to create surface models:

- Extrusion and revolution
- Meshes
- Spline approximations

Extruded and Revolved Surfaces

You can define a surface by a 2D shape or profile and the path along which it is revolved or extruded.

Figure 5.19 shows a surface model created by revolution, and the profile and axis of revolution used to generate it. Regular geometric entities can be revolved or extruded to create surface primitives such as cones, cylinders, and planes. Surface primitives are sometimes built into surface modeling software to be used as building blocks for complex shapes.

5.18   A Rendered Surface Model. *The industrial designer for the Timex TurnAndPull alarm was concerned that the inner rings would look too deep or too busy. A rendered surface model allowed team members to see how it would look when manufactured. (Courtesy of Timex Group USA, Inc.)*

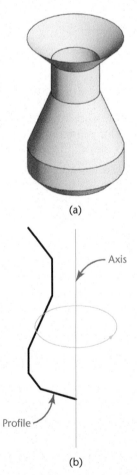

(a)

Axis

Profile

(b)

5.19   Revolved Surface. *The surface model in (a) was created by revolving the profile about the axis shown in (b).*

Meshes

Mesh surfaces are defined by the 3D location of each vertex stored in the CAD database. Each group of vertices is used to define a flat plane surface. Figure 5.20 shows a mesh surface and a list of some of its vertices.

Some mesh surfaces are called **triangulated irregular networks** (TINs), because they connect sets of three vertices with triangular faces to serve as the surface model. A mesh surface can be useful for modeling uneven surfaces, such as terrain, where a completely smooth surface is not necessary. A sufficiently large matrix will result in correspondingly smaller triangles that can better approximate a smooth surface. Refining the mesh will produce a smoother surface, but the size of the CAD file will increase and result in slower software performance. Some modeling packages allow you to define a smoothed representation of the surface instead of the somewhat bumpy appearance of a strictly mesh surface.

```
481,5066,4485
482,5066,4483
483,5066,4485
484,5066,4490
485,5066,4500
486,5066,4510
487,5066,4510
488,5066,4505
489,5066,4500
490,5066,4495
491,5066,4500
492,5066,4520
493,5066,4530
```

(a)   (b)   (c)

5.20 A Mesh Surface. *A mesh surface is composed of a series of planar surfaces defined by a matrix of vertices, as shown in (c). The wireframe view of the mesh in (a) appears more like a surface in the rendered view shown in (b).*

NURBS-Based Surfaces

The mathematics of nonuniform rational B-spline (NURBS) curves underlies the method used to create surfaces in most surface modeling systems. A NURBS surface is defined by a set of vertices in 3D space that are used to define a smooth surface mathematically.

Rational curves and surfaces have the advantage that they can be used to generate not only free-form curves but also analytical forms such as arcs, lines, cylinders, and planes. This is an advantage for surface modelers that use NURBS techniques, as the database does not need to accommodate different techniques for surfaces created using a surface primitive, mesh, extrusion, or revolution.

Spline curves can be used as input for revolved and extruded surfaces that can be lofted or swept. **Lofting** is the term used to describe a surface fit to a series of curves that do not cross each other. Sweeping creates a surface by sweeping a curve or cross section along one or more "paths." In both cases, the surface blends from the shape of one curve to the next (see Figure 5.21).

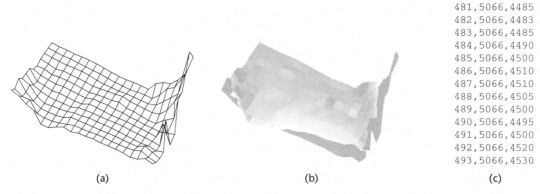

(a)

(b)

5.21 Lofting. *A lofted surface (a) blends a series of curves that do not intersect into a smooth surface. A swept surface (b) sweeps a curve along a curved path and blends the influence of both into a smooth surface model.*

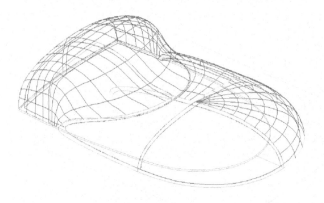 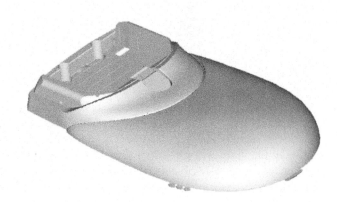

5.22   *When the spline curves shown here are used to generate a NURBS surface, the functions defining each curve are blended.* (Courtesy of Robert Mesaros.)

NURBS surfaces can also be created by meshing curves that run perpendicular to each other, as illustrated in Figure 5.22.

Visible Embryo Heart Model

By modeling embryonic hearts at different stages, researchers were able to use the models to examine the way different tissue layers expand and move as the heart develops. To study blood flow in developing hearts that are only 0.8 millimeter across, Kent Thornburg and Jeffrey Pentecost created models from which they generated a 5-centimeter-wide stereolithography physical model.

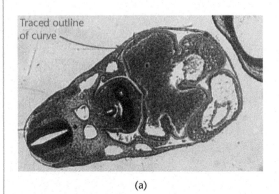

(a)

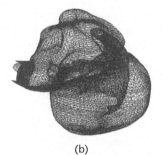

(b)

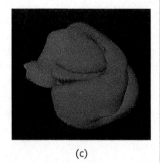

(c)

(a) Using cross sections of embryos from the Carnegie Collection of Human Embryos, the team made digital photomicrographs of each slide. Using the computer, they traced the outlines of heart tissues at each level.

(b) Lofting combined the cross sections into a surface model of the heart, shown in wireframe.

(c) The model made by stereolithography.

(Images courtesy of Dr. Jeffrey O. Pentecost, Director, Visible Embryo Heart Project, and Dr. Kent Thornburg, Director, Congenital Heart Research Center, at Oregon Health Sciences University, with the cooperation of Alias Wavefront and Silicon Graphics, Inc.)

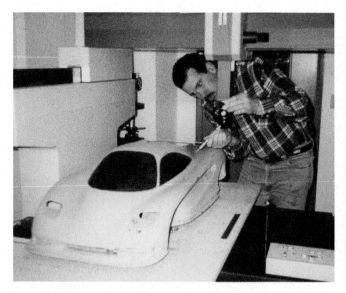

5.23 Digitizing a Model. *A coordinate measuring system was used to digitize the clay model of the Romulus Predator. Seventeen hundred data points were captured by digitizing half of the quarter-scale clay model of the Predator. Digitizing the data and mirroring it in the model ensured side-to-side symmetry. (Courtesy of Mark Gerisch.)*

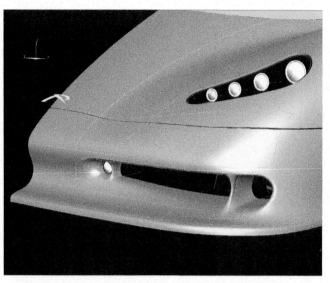

5.24 Surface Patches. *The lines on the surface model of the Predator prototype indicate individual surface patches that make up the model. Areas of the car with drastic curvature changes are divided into smaller patches, which keeps the mathematical order of the patches lower and reduces the overall complexity of the surface. (Courtesy of Mark Gerisch.)*

Reverse Engineering

Most reverse engineering software traces a physical object to generate mesh data, or data points for a surface model. Points on the object are captured as vertices, then translated into a digital surface representation. Reverse engineering can be an easy way to capture the surface definition of an existing model. Designers might use traditional surface sculpting methods and then digitize the physical model to create a digital database. An existing part might be reverse engineered so that it can be added to the CAD database. (Figure 5.23 shows data for the surface model in Figure 5.24 being created using a reverse engineering process.)

Complex Surfaces/Combining Surfaces

To create a surface model, you do not create the entire surface at once—just patches to combine into a continuous model. Just as curves can be made of individual segments that are smoothed into a continuous curve, surfaces can be made of entities referred to as **patches**. Like a spline curve, a patch can be **interpolated**, or approximated.

A **Coon's patch** is a simple interpolated surface that is bounded by four curves. Mathematical methods interpolate the points on the four boundary curves to determine the vertices of the resulting patch (see Figure 5.25).

Surface patches are joined by blending the edges of the patches. Areas created by blending, or the surfaces created by fillets, corners, or offsets, are called **derived surfaces**. They are defined by mathematical methods that combine the edges of the patches to create a smooth joint.

Sometimes, complex surface patches are created by trimming. For example, a circular patch may start with a rectangular patch, then be trimmed to a circle, and finally be blended with other surface patches.

Some surface modeling systems include the use of Boolean operations, whereas others do not. Systems that do not include Boolean operations or good tools for trimming surfaces can be difficult to use to create a feature such as a round hole through a curved surface because the exact shape of the surface, including the hole, must be defined by specifying its edges.

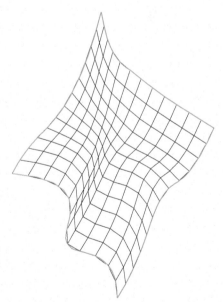

5.25 Coon's Patch. *The lines between the boundary curves in this Coon's patch surface represent the shape of the surface and illustrate the influence of the boundary curves on the interpolated surface between them.*

5.26 *The roof scoop on the Predator's clay model was not visible enough, so the designer adjusted the control points in the surface model in real time until the scoop looked just right on screen.* (*Courtesy of Mark Gerisch.*)

Editing Surfaces

Once a surface has been defined, editing depends on the method used by the surface modeler to create and store the surface. Usually, the information describing the locations of vertices is editable, and each vertex can be changed. If the surface modeling software retains the original 2D profile that was extruded or revolved to produce the surface, it can be used to facilitate changes to these surfaces. If not, it can be difficult to efficiently edit the surfaces.

For NURBS surfaces, each control point can be edited to produce local changes in the surface model. (Editing Bezier surfaces, by the same token, produces global changes to the surface.) Grabbing and relocating vertices is a highly intuitive way to edit a surface model that contributes to its usefulness in refinement. The term "tweaking" is used to describe editing a model by adjusting control points individually to see the result. For example, the NURBS surfaces used to define the shape of the Predator's exterior made it easy to use the surface model to explore design options in several areas (Figure 5.26).

Surface Model Accuracy

Surface model information can be stored with more or less accuracy. Compare the meshes shown in Figure 5.27. The mesh at left contains fewer vertices than the mesh shown in 5.27b. Although the surface shown in 5.27b is more accurate, the additional information makes its file size larger. This requires more computer processing to store and interact with the model. Depending on your purpose, the smaller number of vertices may be satisfactory.

Surface models used for computer-aided manufacturing (CAM) require a high degree of accuracy to produce smooth surfaces. The trade-off between speed and accuracy may be resolved by setting the surface display to a less accurate faceted representation and storing a smoothed or more highly defined surface definition in the database. It is important to distinguish between the screen display of the model and the surface definition stored in the database.

Splines used to create surfaces can also vary in accuracy. Splines can have more or fewer control points that you can use to shape the surface. To model surfaces smoothly, fewer control points may allow more fluid curves. A mesh surface used to calculate area may not be as accurate as one created using a smoothing algorithm such as NURBS or Bezier.

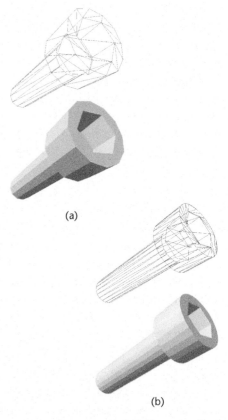

(a)

(b)

5.27 Accuracy and Surface Mesh. *The mesh in (a) has fewer vertices and larger facets than the mesh used in (b). The finer mesh in (b) more accurately represents the cylindrical shape of the bolt.*

Tessellation lines are used to indicate surfaces in a wireframe view, and they may or may not reflect the accuracy of the surface (see Figure 5.28). It is important to distinguish when tessellation lines represent the accuracy of the view of the model, and when they represent the accuracy of the model stored in the database. If the software accurately represents the actual geometry of the model in the model database, the tessellations simply represent the model in the on-screen view.

Using Surface Models

The primary strength of a surface model is improved appearance of surfaces and the ability to convey these complex definitions for computer-aided manufacturing. Customers purchase products not only on their function but also on their styling. A realistically shaded model can be used with potential customers to determine their reactions to its appearance. Lighting and different materials can be applied in most surface modeling software to create very realistic looking results (Figure 5.29). Many consumer products often start with the surface model, then the interior parts are engineered to fit the shape of the styled exterior. When surface models can be used in place of a physical prototype—or in place of the product itself for promotional purposes—the savings add to their cost effectiveness.

Because the relative locations of surfaces from a particular direction of sight can be calculated, surface modeling systems can automatically remove back edges (or represent them as hidden lines). Surface definitions remove the ambiguity inherent in some wireframe models and allow you to see holes and front surfaces by hiding the nonvisible parts of the model.

The complex surfaces defined by a surface model can be exported to numerically controlled machines, making it possible to manufacture irregular shapes that would be difficult to document consistently in 2D views. Both surface and solid models can be used to check for fit and interference before the product is manufactured. Often, surface models can be converted to solid models and vice versa.

Because surface models define surfaces, they can often report the surface area of a part. This information can be useful in calculating heat transfer rates, for example, and can save time, particularly when the surface is complex. The accuracy of the calculations may depend on the method used by the software to store the surface data.

Complex surfaces can be difficult to model. The cost-effectiveness of surface modeling depends on the difficulty of the surface, the accuracy required, and the purpose for which the model will be used. Many modeling software systems offer a combination of wireframe, surface, and solid modeling capabilities, making it possible to weigh the benefits against the difficulties and the time required to create each type of model.

5.28 Tesselation Lines. *The faceted representation on the left uses planar surfaces to approximate smooth curves.*

5.29 *This docking station illustrates the complex curves possible in a surface model. (Image courtesy of ©2016 Dassault Systèmes SolidWorks Corporation.)*

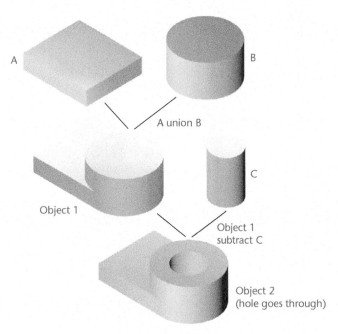

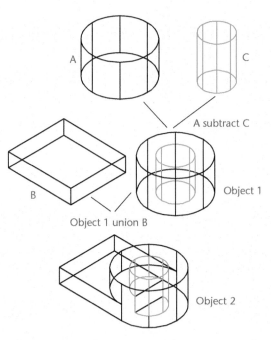

5.30   Order Matters. *The order of operations matters when you use Boolean operations to create a solid model— and when you edit it (see Figure 5.31).*

5.31   *Joining A and B after the hole is created by subtracting C changes the design—the hole no longer goes through the entire part.*

Solid Models

Solid models go beyond surface models to store information about the volume contained inside the object. They store the vertex and edge information of the 3D wireframe modeler, the surface definitions of the surface modeler, plus volume information. Many solid modelers also store the operations used to create features, which makes it possible to edit them quickly (see Figures 5.30 and 5.31). Solid models closely approximate physical models, making them especially useful for defining, testing, and refining the designs they represent.

Using 3D Solid Models

Many of the examples so far illustrated how accurate representation of a 3D object provides valuable engineering information. Solid models are highly visual and easy to understand and measure. They are also highly accurate if modeled accurately. Solid models are often able to replace physical models, as well as control CAM equipment, which adds to their cost-effectiveness.

In addition, 3D solid models are particularly suited for use with analysis packages. They contain all the information about an object's volume, and volume is important to many engineering calculations. Mass properties, centroid, moments of inertia, and weight can be calculated from the solid model as often as needed during the refinement process. The system behavior can be simulated from the wealth of information available in the model.

Solid models provide information needed for other analyses. Finite element analysis (FEA) methods break up a complex object into smaller shapes to make stress, strain, and heat transfer easier to calculate. Because the solid model defines the entire object, FEA software can use this information to generate an FEA mesh automatically for a part. This allows inclusion of this type of analysis earlier in the design process, incorporation of changes, and testing of the new model with FEA analysis again. Some FEA and solid modeling packages are integrated to provide this analysis within the modeling software. Others even allow direct model optimization based on the FEA results, creating a new version of the model that the designer can then revise further.

TIP

Understanding basic modeling methods will help you assess the modeling software of tomorrow. Some new modelers, referred to as "direct" or "explicit" modelers, such as Creo and SpaceClaim, offer a broad command set that adopts features from traditional surface *and* solid modelers.

5.4 CONSTRAINT-BASED MODELING

Constraint-based modeling has several advantages for engineering design. As the design evolves, constraint-based models can be updated by changing the sizes and relationships that define the model. In traditional solid modeling methods, changing the size of one feature may require several others to be changed, or the model may need to be totally re-created. Because of the iterative nature of the design process, a design is repeatedly modified as it is refined. The model's responsiveness can result in more cycles during the refinement stage (or more cycles in less time) and, ultimately, a better design.

Neptune Seatech Oy made the decision to switch from a 2D design method to a constraint-based 3D modeler, SolidWorks, so it could get its products to market faster while preserving the iterations needed for complex, accurate designs. Neptune Seatech is a Finnish engineering company that specializes in the design of vehicles for subsea applications—passenger and research submarines. To meet increasingly rigorous design, performance, and safety standards, the company found 2D methods made it hard to complete the desired number of design iterations and still meet product development deadlines. Its first project using the constraint-based 3D modeler, a floating bridge for ferries, took only 18 weeks to produce (see Figure 5.32).

The company enjoyed two other benefits of constraint-based modeling. First, the ease with which constraint-based models can be updated makes it possible to create families of designs. Neptune's floating bridge allows cars to pass from the ferry to land and vice versa during loading and unloading. Because each landing site is slightly different, the main dimensions of a given bridge vary slightly from one site to another. The bridge manufacturer that hired Neptune had several designs previously created for specific landing sites. To eliminate confusion in manufacturing, the customer wanted a design that could be updated for new bridges. Neptune proposed to design one bridge, then produce the others by changing the length and width factors. The constraint-based model of the bridge made it easy to change the

5.32 *Neptune Seatech's parametric model of the floating bridge for ferries was modified to create a family of designs for the variations in ferry landings.* (Courtesy of Neptune Seatech Oy.)

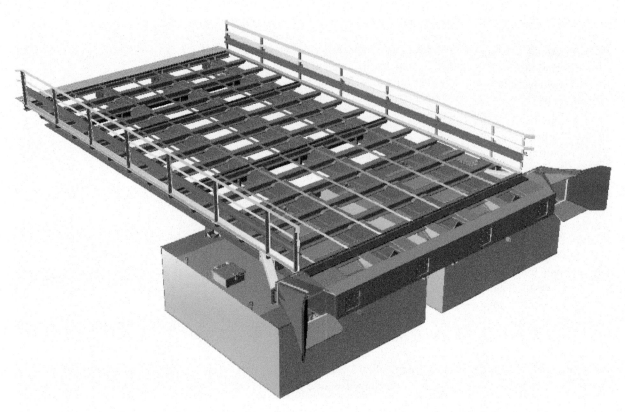

5.33   *Neptune Seatech's bridge model, created in SolidWorks, involved more than 1700 parts.* *(Courtesy of Neptune Seatech Oy.)*

pertinent dimensions and have the software update the related parts to a new size. The investment in the bridge model was used to refine the original bridge design, then used again as a starting point for variations in the product family (see Figure 5.33).

Neptune also enjoyed the software's ability to analyze mass properties. The weight and volume data for a floating bridge need to be evaluated during design so that the resulting bridge floats at the correct level. Calculating the weight of a floating bridge design would have taken 1 to 2 weeks using Neptune's previous methods, but the built-in capabilities of SolidWorks made it possible to monitor this data throughout the design process. The ease with which the model could be modified made it possible to analyze the model, make changes, and analyze the model again. The software also made it possible for analysis to occur earlier in the design process, allowing more time to optimize the design.

Constraint-based modeling also improves designs by focusing the modeler on the design intent for the product. If a constraint-based model is to be updated successfully when changes are made, the rules for building the model must capture the intended design solution for the system or device. The extra attention and planning required to capture design intent in the model makes the designer carefully consider the function and purpose of the item being designed, which in turn results in better designs.

5.5 CONSTRAINTS DEFINE THE GEOMETRY

In a constraint-based model, an object's features are defined by sizes and geometric relationships stored in the model and used to generate the part. Two basic kinds of constraints are used to drive the model geometry.

- *Size constraints* are the dimensions that define the model. The choice of dimensions and their placement is an important aspect of capturing the design intent.
- *Geometric constraints* define and maintain the geometric properties of an object, such as tangency, verticality, and so on. These geometric constraints are equally important in capturing design intent.

In constraint-based modeling, a *parameter* is a named quantity whose value can change; it is similar to a variable. Like a variable, a parameter can be used to define other parameters. If the length of a part is always twice the width, you can define its size as "2 × *Width*," where *Width* is the name of the dimension.

Unlike a variable, a parameter is never abstract: it always has a value assigned to it, so that the model can be represented. For example, the parameter *Width* is defined by a value, such as 3.5. The value for the length parameter is calculated based on the *Width*, so in this case *Length* is 7. If the width value is changed to 5, the length is automatically updated to the new value of "*Width* * 2," or 10 (see Figure 5.34).

Even something as simple as this rectangular block may have design intent built into its model. As it is being updated, do you want the center of the part to stay fixed and the part to elongate in both directions, or do you want it to lengthen all in one direction? If so which end should stay put?

Figure 5.35 shows a part that has been modeled in a 3D constraint-based design package. The parameters driving the geometry of the model are indicated on the drawing. When the parameter value for the length of the part was changed, the part was updated automatically, as shown in part b of the figure. Notice that the threaded length did not increase. If you wanted the thread length to increase as the bolt was lengthened, you would need to define the constraints and parameters differently.

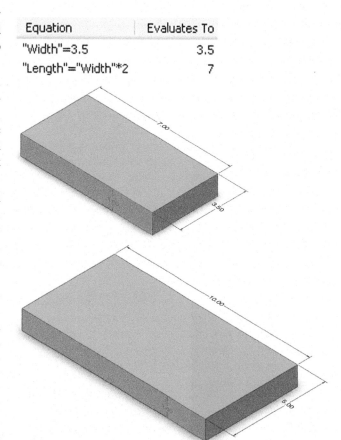

Equation	Evaluates To
"Width"=3.5	3.5
"Length"="Width"*2	7

5.34   *Once the parameter changes, the shape is updated.*

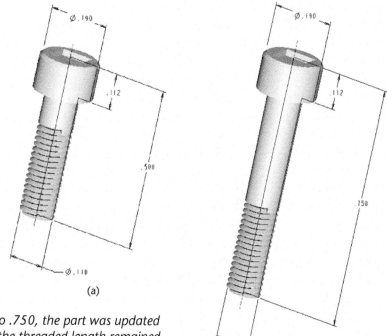

(a)

(b)

5.35   *When the length dimension increased to .750, the part was updated to reflect this new size constraint. Notice that the threaded length remained the same and the bolt head remained attached after the update. The modeler maintained the size and geometric relationships that were defined.*

Feature Dimensions

Dimensions in a constraint-based model can behave in different ways. A dimension can be:

- A size constraint: changing the dimension value updates the model feature. These are often called *driving dimensions*.
- A parameter used in an equation that "drives" the size of a model feature.
- A reference dimension, which gets its value from the model geometry, but is not a size constraint for the model. These are often called *driven dimensions.*
- A dimension that is purely a text note on a drawing or model view and whose value may not relate to the model geometry.
- A combination of the above.

Driving Dimensions

Driving dimensions control the size of a feature element in the model. Each driving dimension has two components: its name and its numerical value. Naming the dimensions allows them to be used in equations or relations that define other parts of the model geometry. The numerical value may be entered as a number in the definition of the dimension, or it may be derived from an equation. Figure 5.36a shows the shaft support part with its dimension values displayed; Figure 5.36b shows the same part with the dimension names. The constraint-based modeling software allows you to switch between display of numeric and named dimensions

in your model. Some modelers also allow you to show the dimensions so that they reveal the formulas used to relate dimensions to one another.

Formulas in Dimensions

Like the geometric constraints in the model, the size parameters create relationships between features of the part that can be captured in formulas. For example, if you wanted to maintain a constant material thickness around the outside of a central hole with diameter $d2$, you could enter the equation $d1 = d2 + 1.00$ for the diameter of the outer cylinder. Doing so ensures that the driven dimension ($d1$) will be 1.00 overall more than $d2$ no matter what value is entered for $d2$.

Another example is adding four holes to a rectangular base plate that should be centered 0.75 inch away from the edge of the plate. If the width of the plate changes, the hole locations should also. Defining the location of the holes using the equation $h\_location = width/2 - .75$, where *width* is the plate's width dimension and $h\_location$ is given from the center of the part, will make the holes stay in the same relative positions. To change the distance from the edge from .75 to 1.00, you would just update the equation and regenerate the model.

Equations in constraint-based dimensions generally use operators similar to those used in a spreadsheet or other programming notation. Many modelers make it easy to import to and export dimension values from an outside application, such as a spreadsheet. Complex formulas can be used to

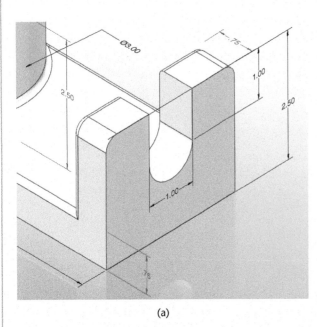
(a)

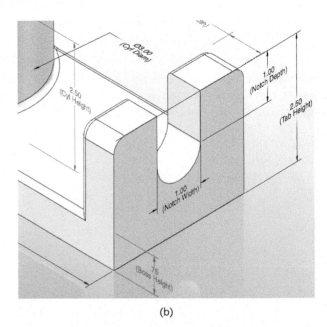
(b)

5.36 Two Ways to Display Dimensions in the Constraint-Based Model. *(a) The numerical display shows the current value for the dimensions. (b) Showing the parameter name can help you locate dimension names to be used in the dimension for another entity.*

calculate sizes in the spreadsheet or other program, and the resulting values can be imported back into the modeling package. Each modeling package has its own notation and syntax. Table 5.1 lists operators that can be used in equations in SolidWorks. Most modelers have a similar list.

It is important to keep track of the relationships you create. Most software allows you to name and document your constraint-based dimensions so you (and your colleagues) can interpret parameter names more readily. The software will generate a name for each dimension by default, but you should give key dimensions recognizable names so they are easier to interpret.

Parameters that are common to more than one part in an assembly are called **global parameters.** Naming global parameters that can be used throughout an assembly is a powerful means of ensuring that parts work together and that critical dimensions are updated in all parts of an assembly. With global parameters, it is even more important to choose names that are clear and to document their purpose in the notes field.

Driven and Cosmetic Dimensions

Driven or *reference* dimensions are associated with the model geometry but are not used to create the constraint-based model. Sometimes it is necessary to add a dimension to a drawing that was not needed to create the model. A driven dimension is a one-way link from the database; it cannot be used to change the model, but it will be updated if the model changes.

A **cosmetic dimension** has no link to the model; it is simply a text label. To dimension a feature at a size different from what is in the model, you must use a cosmetic dimension or otherwise break the link to the database value for the feature.

You should not often need driven dimensions. A well-created constraint-based model contains all the dimensional relationships needed.

Using the shaft support as an example again, a relationship can be defined so the diameter of the hole is always 1 inch smaller than the diameter of the cylinder. Changing the size of the cylinder will cause the diameter of the hole to change to preserve the size relationship.

Table 5.1 Operators

Operator	Name	Notes
+	plus sign	addition
–	minus sign	subtraction
*	asterisk	multiplication
/	forward slash	division
^	caret	exponentiation
sin (*a*)	sine	*a* is the angle; returns the sine ratio
cos (*a*)	cosine	*a* is the angle; returns the cosine ratio
tan (*a*)	tangent	*a* is the angle; returns the tangent ratio
sec (*a*)	secant	*a* is the angle; returns the secant ratio
cosec (*a*)	cosecant	*a* is the angle; returns the cosecant ratio
cotan (*a*)	cotangent	*a* is the angle; returns the cotangent ratio
arcsin (*a*)	inverse sine	*a* is the sine ratio; returns the angle
arccos (*a*)	inverse cosine	*a* is the cosine ratio; returns the angle
atn (*a*)	inverse tangent	*a* is the tangent ratio; returns the angle
arcsec (*a*)	inverse secant	*a* is the secant ratio; returns the angle
arccosec (*a*)	inverse cosecant	*a* is the cosecant ratio; returns the angle
arccotan (*a*)	inverse cotangent	*a* is the cotangent ratio; returns the angle
abs (*a*)	absolute value	returns the absolute value of *a*
exp (*n*)	exponential	returns *e* raised to the power of *n*
log (*a*)	logarithmic	returns the natural log of *a* to the base *e*
sqr (*a*)	square root	returns the square root of *a*
int (*a*)	integer	returns *a* as an integer
sgn (*a*)	sign	returns the sign of *a* as –1 or 1; For example: sgn (–21) returns –1
pi	pi	ratio of the circumference to the diameter of a circle (3.14...)

Feature-Based Modeling

Constraint-based modeling is also called **feature-based modeling** because its models are combinations of features. Creating a constraint-based model is similar to creating any other solid model. However, in constraint-based modeling the resulting part is derived from the dimensions and constraints that define the geometry of the features. Each time a change is made, the part is re-created from these definitions. Individual features and their relationships to one another make up the constraint-based model.

A *feature* is the basic unit of a constraint-based solid model. Each feature has properties that define it. When you create a feature, you specify the geometric constraints that apply to it, then specify the size parameters. The modeler stores these properties and uses them to generate the feature. If an element of the feature, or a related part of the model, changes, the modeling software regenerates the feature in accordance with the defining properties assigned to it. For example, an edge that is defined to be tangent to an arc will move to preserve the tangency constraint if the size of the arc is changed.

Some features, such as holes and fillets, may use predefined features with additional properties that are maintained as the model is updated. For example, a "through hole" (one that goes completely through the part feature) will be extended if the part thickness increases.

When you look at the fixed-height shaft support shown in Figure 5.37a, can you identify the features that make up its shape? Figure 5.37b shows the major cylinder, hole, plate, end plate, slot, and rounds that form the model of the shaft support.

Being able to update models easily to reflect changes in the design is a key ability of constraint-based modelers. If you are not using a constraint-based solid modeling program, you may have to re-create the feature just to change a size. This can result in considerable time and effort, especially for interrelated features.

In addition to defining relationships between features, constraint-based modeling software also allows you to use constraints and parameters across parts in an assembly. Thus, when a part changes, any related parts in the assembly can also be

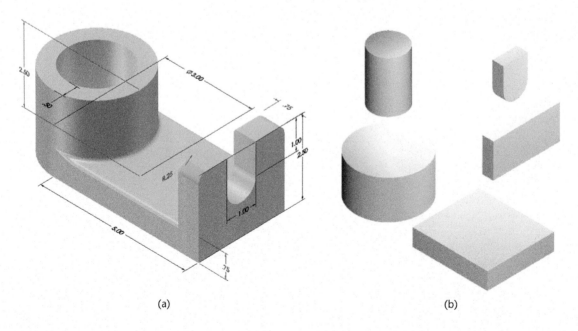

(a)   (b)

5.37 *The features that make up the support in (a) are shown individually in (b).*

5.38 Model Tree. *The window at the left side of the screen called the "model tree" (enlarged here) lists the features in the order in which they were created. The icon next to the feature indicates the operation used to create the feature. Extrusions and extruded cuts were used to form the cylinder, baseplate, and hole. Then, the end feature was extruded and the slot created using an extruded cut. Finally, fillets were added to round the edges.*

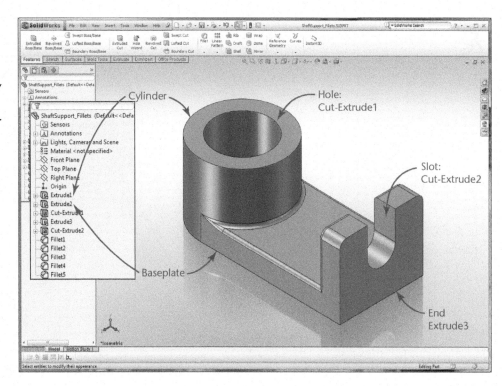

updated. Because the software regenerates the features and parts from the relationships stored in the database (see Figure 5.38), planning constraint-based relationships that reflect the design intent of the part or product is the key to efficient and useful constraint-based models.

5.6 PLANNING PARTS FOR DESIGN FLEXIBILITY

Design intent refers to the key dimensions and relationships that must be met by the part. Where does the part need to fit into other parts? Do certain features need to align with other features? How will the part change as the design evolves? By thinking about these relationships, you can organize the features so that the structure of the part and its relationships are the foundation for later features. Four key aspects of planning for design intent are summarized in Figure 5.39. Of course, you cannot know everything about a design before you begin, and there will be changes that will require more work than others; but starting your model with the geometric relationships in the design in mind will allow you to benefit from the power of constraint-based modeling. To see how a constraint-based model can reflect design intent, you should understand some basics about constraint-based modeling software.

Constraint-based modeling software in many ways parallels the design process. To start creating a part, you often start with a 2D sketch of the key shape of a feature, such as that shown in Figure 5.40. The initial sketch may be rough in appearance because the software will apply constraints to define the relationships between the simple 2D geometric elements of your sketch. This process is similar to the way one of your engineering colleagues interprets your hand-drawn sketches. If lines appear to be perpendicular or nearly so, your colleague assumes that you mean them to be perpendicular, without your having to mark the angular dimension between the lines. In a similar way, constraint-based modelers apply constraints to your rough sketch, so that lines that appear nearly perpendicular,

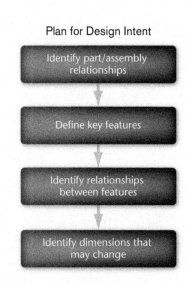

5.39 *Four Key Considerations When Planning a Constraint-Based Model*

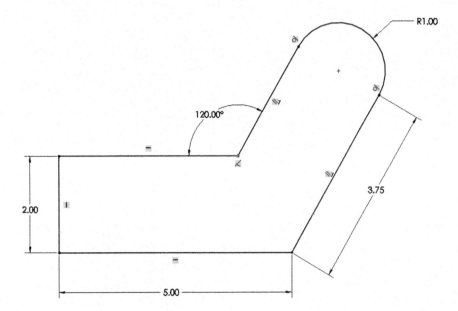

5.40 *A constrained sketch is used as the basis for a model feature. Geometric constraints are identified by the blue symbols.*

parallel, vertical, horizontal, concentric, or collinear will have a constraint relationship added to them so that they function that way in the model. This process is called "solving" the sketch in some modeling software, because the software is interpreting and assigning dimensions and constraints to generate a 2D "profile" of the feature. Before you generate the actual feature, you can review and change the dimensions and geometric constraints so they are what you intended. This step is key to defining your design intent. The sketch constraints in Figure 5.40 have already been added.

To generate a 3D feature, you then select a command to extrude, revolve, sweep, or blend the profile geometry. Figure 5.41 shows the profile in Figure 5.40 as it would appear after being (a) extruded, (b) swept, (c) revolved, and (d) lofted to create different types of features from the 2D sketch.

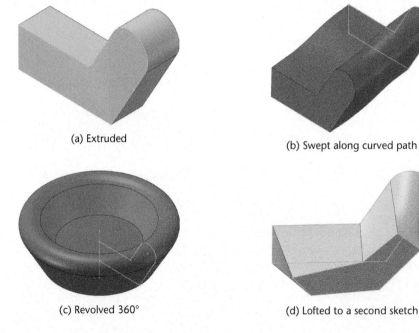

(a) Extruded

(b) Swept along curved path

(c) Revolved 360°

(d) Lofted to a second sketch

5.41 Same Sketch, Different Operations. *The same sketch was used to create each of these features. The sketch in (a) was extruded, in (b) swept along a curved path, in (c) revolved 360° about an axis, and in (d) lofted between the sketch and a second sketch with angled lines and a straight top.*

5.7 SKETCH CONSTRAINTS

Constraint-based modeling software starts by automatically interpreting your sketch, to define the constraints that it will hold constant. To do so, it evaluates your sketch against a set of rules stored in the software. A line, for example, that is drawn within 3° or 4° of being horizontal will be constrained to remain horizontal. Your sketch will be altered so the line you drew is, in fact, horizontal. The software will apply the constraints it needs to solve the sketch.

Constraint-based modeling programs allow you to review the constraints that are applied to the sketch geometry so you can change them to those needed to reflect your design intent. Table 5.2 describes some possible sketch constraints and shows symbols often used to indicate them on screen. (Different modelers use different symbols and means of displaying the constraints—see Table 5.3 and Figure 5.42). These constraints may create relationships to other lines in the sketch or to geometry in an existing feature.

Table 5.2 Sketch Constraints

Constraint	Rule	Symbol
Horizontal	Lines that are close to horizontal are constrained to be horizontal (usually you can control the number of degrees for this assumption, typically set to 3° or 4°).	H
Vertical	Lines that are close to vertical are constrained to be vertical (usually within 3° or 4°).	V
Equal length	Line segments that appear equal length are constrained to be equal.	L_1, L_2, etc.
Perpendicular	Lines that appear close to 90° apart are constrained to be perpendicular.	$\perp$
Parallel	Lines that appear close to parallel are constrained to be parallel.	//
Collinear	Lines that nearly overlap along the same line are assumed to be collinear.	No symbol displayed
Connected	Endpoints of lines that lie close together are assumed to connect.	Dot located at intersection
Equal coordinates	Endpoints and centers of arcs or circles that appear to be aligned horizontally or vertically will be constrained to have equal X- or equal Y-coordinates.	Small thick dashes between the points
Tangent entities	Entities that appear nearly tangent are constrained to be tangent.	T
Concentric	Arcs or circles that appear nearly concentric are concentric.	Dot at shared center point
Equal radii	Arcs or circles that appear to have similar radii are constrained to have equal radii.	R
Points coincide	Points sketched to nearly coincide with another entity are assumed to coincide.	No symbol displayed

CONSTRAINING A SKETCH

Like a hand-drawn sketch, the sketch for a constraint-based model captures the basic geometry of the feature as it would appear in a 2D view.

1 Sketch the basic shapes as you would see them in a 2D view. Many modelers will automatically constrain the sketch as you draw unless you turn this setting off in the software.

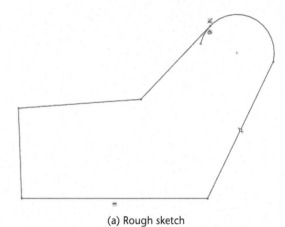

(a) Rough sketch

2 Apply geometric constraints to define the geometry of the sketch. If it is important to your design intent that lines remain parallel, add that constraint. If arcs must remain tangent to lines, apply that constraint. Here, lines A and B have been defined to be parallel; note the parallel constraint symbol.

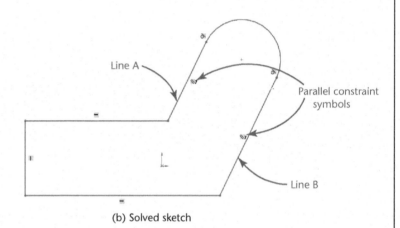

Line A

Parallel constraint symbols

Line B

(b) Solved sketch

3 Add dimensional constraints. The length of line B was sketched so that the software interpreted the dimensional constraint to be 3.34. The designer changed this dimension to 3.75 (the desired length), and the length of the line was updated to the new length.

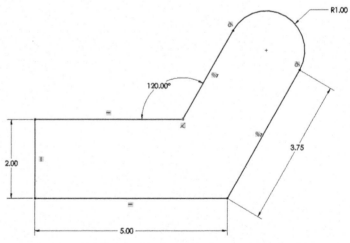

R1.00

120.00°

2.00

3.75

5.00

(c) Sketch with dimensional constraints

TIP

It is often useful to start drawing the feature near the final size required. Otherwise if the software is automatically constraining your sketch, a line segment that is proportionately much shorter may become hard to see or even considered effectively zero length and deleted by the software.

STEP by STEP

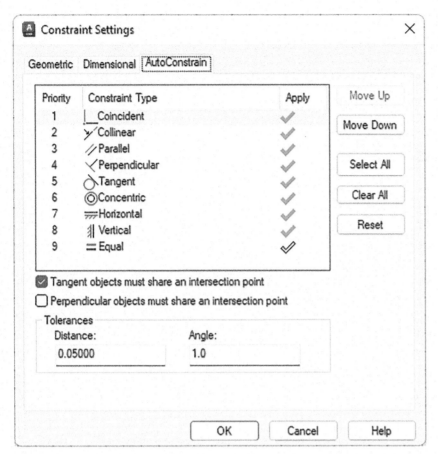

5.42 **Changing Constraint Defaults.** *The Constraint Settings dialog box in AutoCAD lets you change the priority in which the constraints are applied. You can also set the tolerance for sketched endpoints to be considered coincident, and lines to be assumed horizontal or vertical. Understanding which assumptions are being applied to your sketch can help you define the exact geometry you require. (Autodesk screen shots reprinted courtesy of Autodesk, Inc.)*

Not all constraint-based modeling programs apply all these constraints, nor do they apply them in the same fashion. Study the constraints available in the software you use and determine their effect on the sketch. You also may be able to set the threshold values for various constraints. For example, instead of having lines at 1° be automatically constrained as horizontal lines, you may wish to increase this value to 3° (Figure 5.42). If you are having difficulty getting the constraints you desire applied to the sketch, you may want to turn off automatic constraint application and select each specific constraint to apply to your sketch.

Most constraint-based modeling programs let you remove or override a constraint that is applied, or specify that the geometry is exact as drawn. Sometimes, you may have to force the sketch closer to the desired relationship. For example, if two lines are too far off in the sketch to be constrained as perpendicular by the software, you could add an angular dimension of 90° between them to force them to that relationship. With the dimensions driving the geometry to the condition you want, the software may apply the perpendicular constraint. Once the constraint is applied, you often can delete the dimension you added.

It is usually beneficial to let geometric constraints determine much of your sketch geometry, then dimension the sizes and relationships that cannot be defined using constraints. You could use a constraint-based modeler as you would a solid modeler, adding dimension values to define all the features, but this would not build in the intelligence that allows the software to automate updating the model.

Table 5.3 Selected Constraint Relations in SolidWorks

Symbol	Relation	Entities to Select	Result
	Horizontal or Vertical	One or more lines or two or more points	The lines become horizontal or vertical (as defined by the current sketch space). Points are aligned horizontally or vertically.
	Collinear	Two or more lines	The items lie on the same infinite line.
	Coradial	Two or more arcs	Items share the same center point and radius.
	Perpendicular	Two lines	The two items are perpendicular to each other.
	Parallel	Two or more lines. A line and a plane (or a planar face) in a 3D sketch	The items are parallel to each other. The line is parallel to the selected plane.
	ParallelYZ or ParallelZX	A line and a plane (or a planar face) in a 3D sketch	The line is parallel to the YZ (or ZX) plane with respect to the selected plane.
	Tangent	An arc, ellipse, or spline, and a line or arc	The two items remain tangent.
	Concentric	Two or more arcs, or a point and an arc	The arcs share the same center point.
	Midpoint	Two lines or a point and a line	The point remains at the midpoint of the line.
	Intersection	Two lines and one point	The point remains at the intersection of the lines.
	Coincident	A point and a line, arc, or ellipse	The point lies on the line, arc, or ellipse.
	Equal	Two or more lines or two or more arcs	The line lengths or radii remain equal.
	Symmetric	A centerline and two points, lines, arcs, or ellipses	The items remain equidistant from the centerline, on a line perpendicular to the centerline.

Overconstrained Sketches

Sketches used in constraint-based modeling may not be overconstrained. An overconstrained or overdimensioned sketch is one that has too many things controlling its geometry.

The sketch shown in Figure 5.43 is overconstrained. Because the top arc is constrained to be tangent to both vertical lines, and its radius is dimensioned (sd0), the width of the sketch is defined. The horizontal dimension shown at the bottom (sd2) defines this width again. If both the arc radius dimension and the overall width dimension were allowed in the model and one of them changed, it would be difficult or impossible for the part to be updated correctly. If the overall width changed and the tangent constraint or arc radius did not, the sketch geometry would be impossible.

Underconstrained Sketches

An underconstrained or underdimensioned sketch is one that has too few dimensions or constraints and is therefore not fully defined.

The sketch shown in Figure 5.44 is underconstrained. It lacks a height dimension controlling its vertical size. Without this dimension the sketch is not fully defined. Some software will allow you to create a 3D feature from an underconstrained sketch as long as the sketch follows basic rules—for example, the sketch does not cross itself, and the sketch encloses an area. If the sketch is underconstrained, the software assumes values for unspecified dimensions based on the sizes drawn. This can be helpful when you are trying out ideas, but it is best to plan to create a model that reflects your design intent.

Dimensions can easily be changed by typing a new value, so go ahead and guess the size and change it later if needed; but keep in mind that choosing which dimensions to use to define the sketch is a critical aspect of making sketches and features that will be updated as expected when a dimension changes.

Applying Constraints

You should select dimensions that define the proper relationships between the sketched geometry and other existing features in your model. The surfaces between which you choose to create the dimensions are a large factor in creating a model that will be updated in the desired manner. You should not let the rules of your software package determine the dimensions, as it is unlikely that they will reflect your design intent.

When you are dimensioning a sketch used to create a feature, place the dimensions where you can view them clearly. Later, if you create a drawing from your model, you will be able to clean up the appearance of the dimensions if needed. You can move dimensions, change their placement, and arrange them so they follow the standard practices. Good placement practices such as placing dimensions outside the object outline and keeping the dimensions a reasonable distance from one another will make the dimensions in your model easier to read.

3D models are accepted as final design documentation. When you are going to use the model as the design database and not provide drawings, it is even more important to ensure that dimensions and tolerances shown in the model are clear. You will learn more about practices for documenting inside the 3D model in Chapter 11.

If you do a good job selecting the dimensions that control the drawing geometry, you will have little cleanup work to do later when you are creating drawing views.

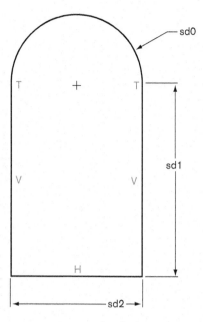

5.43   Overconstrained Sketch

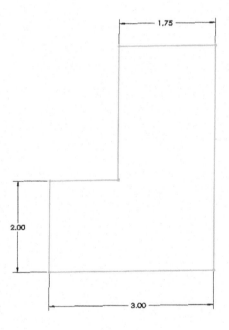

5.44   Underconstrained Sketch

Setting the Base Point

Some constraint-based modeling software assumes a ***base point*** in the sketch for the first feature you create. The base point is fixed on the coordinate system; the other sketch geometry is located on the coordinate system based on its relationship to this base point. The resulting feature will stay fixed on the coordinate system at this base point. When dimension values change, they will change relative to that point. There is only one base point per model.

The base point is indicated in Figure 5.45a by the × in the lower right corner of the sketch. When the width dimension changes, the sketch is updated to the new size while leaving the base point fixed on the coordinates. The rest of the sketch geometry is reoriented, as shown in Figure 5.45b.

If your software uses a base point, it should become the base point for the entire model. When the model is updated, all dimensions will be updated from this point. A good rule of thumb is to identify a fixed point on your model that you would use as a starting point for measuring the part for inspection purposes. Use this point as the base point, or locate your dimensions from it as if it were the base point.

Locating most of your dimensions from a common edge or major surface can be effective for two reasons. First, it helps you create dimensions that will be useful for inspecting the part after manufacture; the dimension values in your model will measure from the same point that an inspector will use to measure the finished part. Second, it helps you anticipate how the model will be updated. When a value is changed, the features on the model will be updated (move) relative to the edge referenced in their dimensions. When you locate dimensions relative to other features you may have difficulty predicting how the model will be updated because you have to add the effect of changes to the intermediate features.

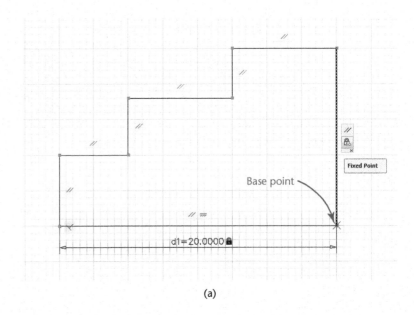

(a)

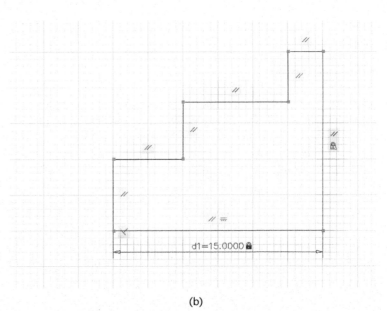

5.45   Base Point. *The base point fixes the sketch on the coordinate system in this underconstrained sketch. The base point serves as a fixed point when the model is updated. In AutoCAD, adding a Fixed Point constraint lets you identify the base point; otherwise, it is determined by software rules.*

(b)

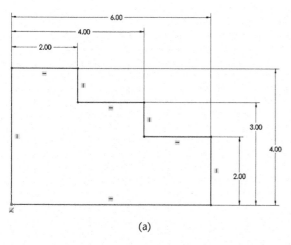

(a)

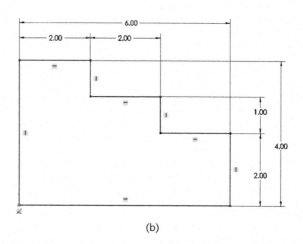

(b)

5.46 *These two sketches of the same part have very different relations built into the dimensions for the sketch. The sketch in (a) relates all dimensions to the left and bottom edges of the part. The sketch in (b) has a chain of relationships built into the dimensions.*

More important than any rule of thumb governing dimension selection or placement is to consider thoroughly the parts you are designing and to make the drawing geometry, constraints, and dimensions reflect the design intent for the part. In some cases, dimensioning a part from another feature is required to reflect the design intent. Figure 5.46 shows two sketches that have the same geometry but are dimensioned differently. When the 2.00 height dimension is changed to 2.50, how will each of these drawings be updated?

In the first case, shown in Figure 5.46a, the height of the 2.00 "step" will change to 2.50, narrowing the gap between it and the 3.00 step. In Figure 5.46b, the height of the 2.00 step will change to 2.50, and the height of the next step will be updated to 3.50 units so it remains 1.00 unit above it. In this case, the narrow gap will occur between the 3.50 and the 4.00 step. Either is correct to the extent that it reflects the intended design.

5.8 THE BASE FEATURE

To create useful relationships in a constraint-based model, it is helpful to start out your model with a good base feature. The **base feature** is the first feature you create. The other features are created using relationships that locate them to the base feature. Subsequent features are updated based on their relationships to the base feature or to one another. You should generally choose a fairly large, significant feature as the base feature.

Figure 5.47 shows the cylinder that could be created as the base feature for the shaft support and the other features that will relate to it. The major cylinder would make a good base feature because it is a significant feature of this part, and the other features make sense related to it. If the design intent of the part centers on the cylinder, its size and location determine the size and shape of other features. The width of the base plate will depend on the stability needed for the size of the cylinder. The hole for the shaft must be centered inside the cylinder and sized to leave enough remaining material for the wall thickness. Using the cylinder as the base feature also makes sense from the standpoint of the part's role within a larger assembly,

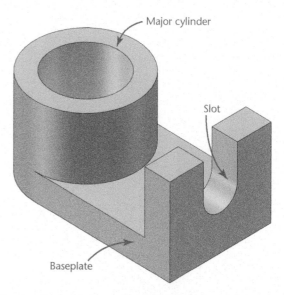

5.47 Base Feature. *The major cylinder for the shaft support makes a good base feature because the cylindrical shaft to be supported is an important aspect of this design.*

as its size could depend on the shaft being designed in a different part. By building your model around the major cylinder, you make it possible to update all features automatically if the cylinder size changes.

Adding Features to the Model

When you add features to the model, the way you constrain the sketch determines how it relates to the other features. Just as the base point serves to locate the base feature, at least one of the constraints applied to subsequent sketches must tell the software how the new feature relates to an existing feature.

To create the second feature, you can use a dimension to locate it relative to an existing edge or use a geometric constraint to align one of the sketch entities to the existing geometry. For example, you could dimension the center point of a hole to be a certain distance from the end of an existing feature or constrain the hole to be concentric to a cylinder or arc on an existing feature.

The way you dimension, constrain, or align your second feature determines how it will be updated with respect to the first feature. Use the things you know about the design to add features. Where are the fixed points on the model, and how does the feature you are adding relate to them? What are the conditions that the new feature needs to satisfy at all times? If existing features were to change, how would the feature you are adding need to change? In some cases, a simple dimension from an existing edge may be all that is needed to add the feature. In other cases, you will want to build in geometric or size relationships needed in the design. The basic process of constraint-based part modeling is illustrated in Figure 5.48. Starting with the base feature, you build a model by adding features and relating them to existing features. For each feature, the same basic process applies.

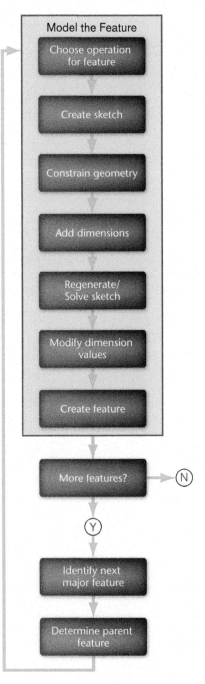

5.48 Flowchart of Constraint-Based Modeling

SPOTLIGHT

Use an Existing Edge

Pro/ENGINEER (as well as many other modelers) has a sketch command that allows you to specify an edge on an existing feature to project as a line in your sketch. This command creates the line in the sketch and constrains the sketched line to be collinear with the existing geometry in a single step. Even better, if the edge on the feature moves, the sketched entity moves with it to stay in alignment.

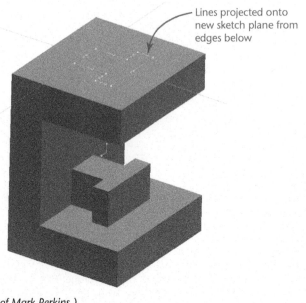

Lines projected onto new sketch plane from edges below

(Courtesy of Mark Perkins.)

Parent-Child Relationships

Constraint-based modeling software stores information about each feature and its relationship to its parent feature. The term **parent-child relationship** is used to describe how one feature is derived from another feature. This relationship is defined by the geometric constraints applied to the sketch as well as its dimensioned size constraints. Planning when creating a parent-child relationship is important.

The base feature is the parent feature for the next feature created from it. Just as real children depend on their parents, child features are dependent on their parent features. If a parent feature moves, the child feature moves in relation to it. For example, when the hole feature was added to the shaft support part, its location was defined as concentric with the major cylinder. When the cylinder's location changes, the hole feature remains concentric with the cylinder (Figure 5.49). If the hole is located relative to the baseplate or to some other feature and the cylinder is moved, the hole will not move with it (Figure 5.50).

If you delete a feature, you will also delete its child features unless you redefine them so that they are related to a different parent feature. This is another reason for selecting a good base feature; you do not want the first feature you create to be something that might be deleted later in the design. Not all features will have child features, but all features other than the base feature must be related to some parent feature.

5.49 *The hole is concentric with the cylinder. As the baseplate length increases, the hole remains concentric.*

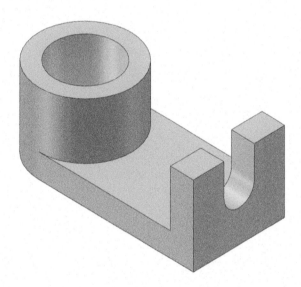

5.50 *The hole dimensioned from the right end of the part is in the wrong location when the baseplate length changes.*

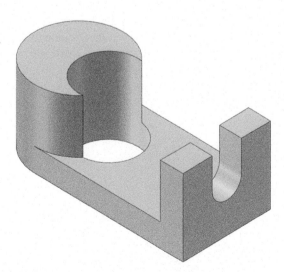

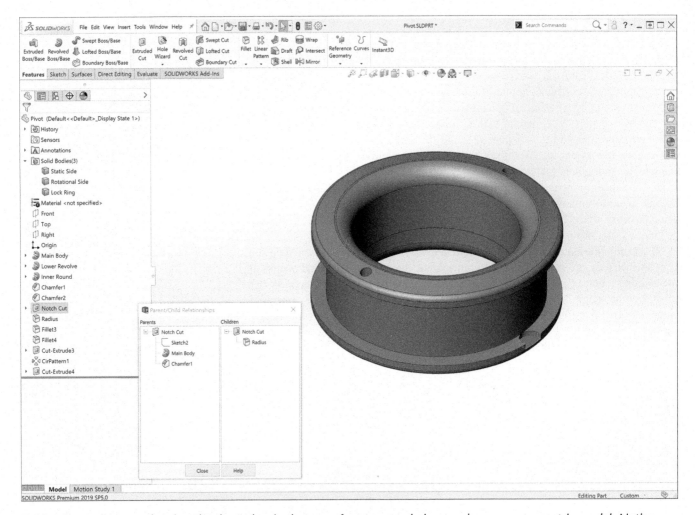

5.51   *A tree diagram showing the dependencies between features can help you plan your parametric model. Notice how the list of parent and child features from this SolidWorks model shows the dependencies between features.*
(Courtesy of Salient Technologies, Inc. (www.salient-tech.com))

One way to visualize the parent-child relationships as you plan your model is to build a tree diagram. The relationships in the Pivot model in Figure 5.51 are illustrated in the **Parent/Child Relationships** window. The panel labeled Children shows that the feature named Notch Cut has Radius as its child. These features may or may not have children (or "grandchildren") of their own. The panel labeled Parents shows that the parent features for Notch Cut are Sketch2, Main Body, and Chamfer1.

Many constraint-based modelers allow you to "play back" the model to see how it is being generated by the underlying parameters. The sequences shown in Figure 5.52 and Figure 5.53 illustrate how the features used to create the parts are ordered in relationships that reflect the design intent for the parts.

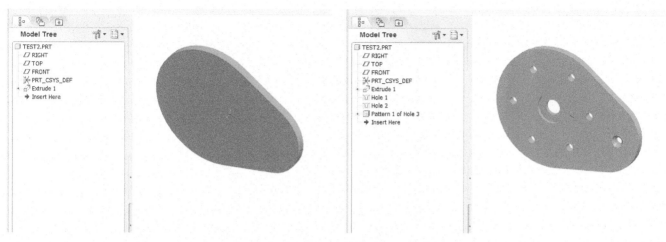

5.52 Base Feature. *The base feature (Extrude 1) is the first feature created. (Courtesy of Mark Perkins.)*

5.53 Child Features. *Subsequent features are children of previous features. (Courtesy of Mark Perkins.)*

Datum Planes and Surfaces

In engineering drawing, a ***datum*** is a theoretically exact point, axis, or plane. A datum provides a reference surface, axis, or point used for inspecting the manufactured part. Theoretically exact planes used in modeling are called ***datum planes***. They are planes used as a reference for model geometry. You can also create datum axes and datum points in 3D models. Features can be constrained and dimensioned relative to these planes, axes, and points, even though they are not solid objects and add no mass to the model. Some modeling packages provide a set of three mutually perpendicular datum planes, located so that they pass through the origin of the coordinate system, as a default. You typically may also create additional datum planes at other orientations and locations.

Often, it is very useful to use a set of datum planes (three mutually perpendicular planes) as the base feature in your drawing. In fact, most software provides them as the default starting features. Figure 5.54 shows the shaft support part with a set of datum planes used as the base feature.

One of the benefits of starting with a set of datum planes is that they can provide a set of normal surfaces that you can use to orient sketch geometry. This is particularly helpful when there are no planar surfaces on the part that you can use to build subsequent features easily. With a cylinder as the base feature for the shaft support, for example, there is no flat surface to which the end of the base plate can be constrained to be parallel. The datum plane "Right Plane" in Figure 5.54 provides a reference to which the plate is parallel.

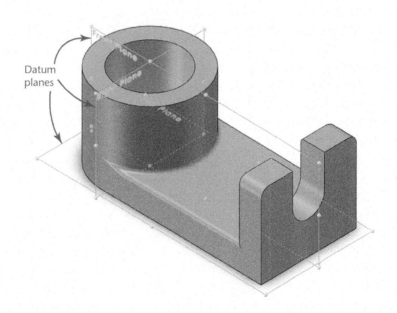

5.54 Datum Planes. *The three mutually perpendicular planes in this drawing serve as the base feature for the model.*

5.55 Datum Surface. *Surface C on this fixture is a datum surface or reference location that will be used to inspect the location of a part feature.* (Courtesy of Mark Perkins.)

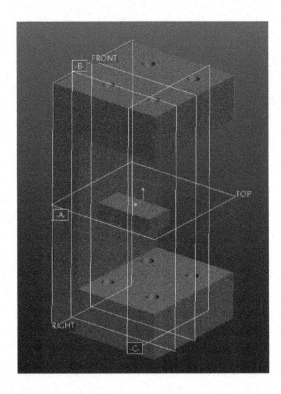

Whether or not you start with a set of datum planes as a base feature, consider the surfaces that will serve as datum surfaces on your part. Parts are inspected to see whether they were manufactured acceptably based on a similar set of three mutually perpendicular, theoretically exact planes. Measurements of the finished part are taken from surfaces coincident with one of the datum planes. As you define your features consider the dimensions that will determine whether the part will fit. How will the part be measured after manufacture? If there is a surface from which measurements will be taken, it can be advantageous to identify it as a datum surface in your part (see Figure 5.55).

Like the base point in a sketch, a datum plane serves as a reference from which the other features build. When you define a set of datum planes as the starting point for your model, you will be well on your way when deciding which datum surface to identify for use in inspecting the finished part.

Datum surfaces can also be helpful when defining tolerances for features. Defining your model using the dimensions that will be used to inspect the finished part will make it easier to determine the impact of variations from the stated dimension that occur during manufacture. (You will learn more about tolerances in Chapter 12.)

Datum planes also provide a common reference point for parts in an assembly. When parts share a set of datum planes, it is easier to align the part with other parts when you bring them together in an assembly model. If you do not use a set of datum planes as a base feature, you can locate new features from existing surfaces on the base feature.

Creating datum planes, lines, and points as base features can be used as a strategy called "skeleton modeling" (see Figures 5.56–5.58). Because the datums have no mass, they do not affect mass property calculations. They are easy to model and often do not change. For example, if you create a datum axis that is the centerline of the part, this is unlikely to change, whereas the shape of the part might. Even when some parts are not fully modeled or are represented only as a centerline, they can still be assembled using the datums as references.

Datum planes and datum surfaces can be added and identified at any time, but considering them as you plan your model will help you use them more effectively in capturing design intent in your model.

5.56 *This constrained sketch acts as the skeleton for the bike assembly. It is made only of circles, lines, and points, which have no mass. (Courtesy of Santa Cruz Bicycles.)*

5.57 *Dimensions are added to the constrained sketch defining the basic size relationships. These dimension values can easily be changed to try out different relationships. (Courtesy of Santa Cruz Bicycles.)*

5.58 *Parts can be assembled to, and even get their sizes directly from, the skeleton. This way parts can be viewed as assembled, even though all parts are not yet modeled. (Courtesy of Santa Cruz Bicycles.)*

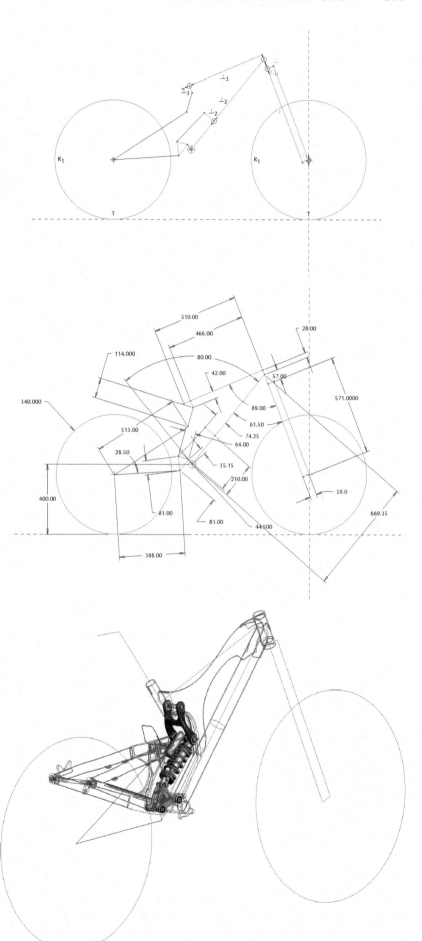

5.9 EDITING THE MODEL

One of the biggest advantages of constraint-based modeling is that you can edit the features after they are created. If you have several parts open at a time in your software, you may have to identify which is the active part, then select the feature you want to edit. Once you select the feature you wish to edit, the dimensions for the feature are displayed in a way that lets you change their values. Alternatively, you can also return to the original sketch that you used to create the feature and modify the sketch. Figure 5.59 shows the shaft support drawing with a change being made to the overall length of the part.

Depending on how the model was created, you may have more or less success in updating the model. For example, the baseplate that connects to the cylinder (indicated in the figure) can be created many different ways. Each way may have advantages or disadvantages for how the part will be updated.

Figure 5.60 shows three ways the baseplate could be generated:

a. Sketch the shape of the bottom surface on a sketch plane aligned with the bottom of the cylinder and extrude it upward.
b. Sketch the cross section on the midplane and extrude to both sides.
c. Sketch the rectangular end view on a plane offset parallel to the center datum plane and extrude the plate to meet the cylinder feature.

There are several other ways, too. Each of these methods works about the same when changing the length of the part. They vary if you decide to make the plate wider than the cylinder. Often, when a feature is extruded to an existing feature as in Figure 5.60c, the new feature cannot be updated so that it is wider than the surface to which it is extruded. The boundary, or end, of the feature is limited by the next surface. Where there is no portion of the surface at which the feature may end, it will continue to infinity and therefore be undefined.

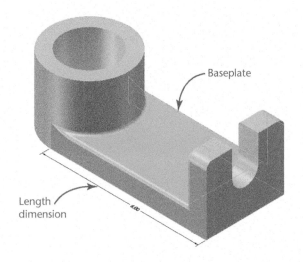

5.59 *The length of the shaft support is changed by editing the dimension value and updating the model.*

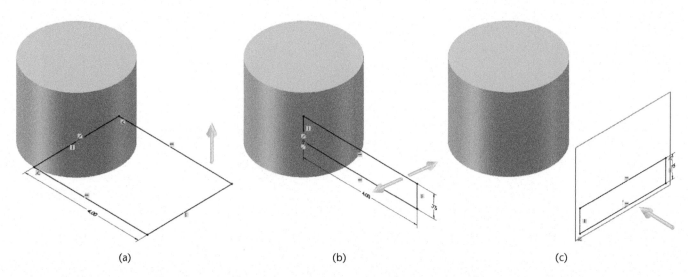

      (a)   (b)   (c)

5.60 *(a) Extruding upward; (b) extruding to both sides of a center plane; (c) extruding to the cylinder from an offset plane. All these methods could be used to generate the plate feature for the shaft support, but they update differently.*

Standard Features

Certain useful features are part of many engineering designs. Common features often have specific manufacturing processes developed to form them efficiently. For example, a **counterbore** is often used to create a recess for a bolt head or other fastener. Specific tools like the one shown in Figure 5.61 make it easy to form this feature.

Many constraint-based modeling programs use the same terminology for these features as that used in manufacturing and design. Review the standard feature types on the next page.

5.61   This counterbore tool on a milling machine makes a recess around the top of a hole. The center of the tool fits inside the hole to keep the counterbore concentric.

Working with Built-in Features

Many standard features, such as counterbored and countersunk holes, fillets, lugs, slots, and others may be available in the constraint-based modeling program as *built-in* or *placed features.* These features can be placed with a dedicated command on part surfaces. Some features are solids, and others are negative solids that are subtracted from the model (for example, a cylindrical hole). The features have properties built into them that the modeling software will preserve, just as it preserves the geometric and size relationships you set.

Many constraint-based modelers provide a number of options for quickly placing holes, often through a "hole wizard" or other dialog box. Properties that can often be set for holes are listed in Table 5.4.

A Hole command may also allow you to choose the specialized constraints for locating holes, such as concentric, placed by edge, and on point, as illustrated in Figure 5.62.

Table 5.4 Typical Hole Properties

Through	The hole goes all the way through the part or feature.
Blind	Material is removed to a specified depth to form the hole.
Countersunk	A conical shape is also removed to allow for a countersunk tapered screw head.
Counterbored	A cylindrical recess is formed, usually to receive a bolt head or nut.
Spotface	A shallow recess like a counterbore is formed, used to provide a good bearing surface for a fastener.

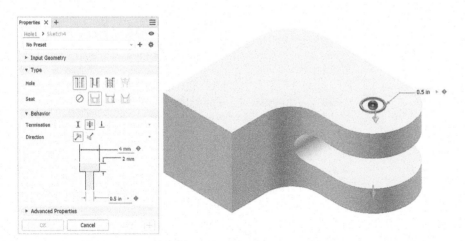

5.62   Autodesk Inventor's Hole Wizard has many placement options and offers many types of hole features to choose from. (Autodesk screen shots reprinted courtesy of Autodesk, Inc.)

Typical Features

Many CAD systems have aids to creating features that are a part of many engineering designs (see Figure 5.63) that can make creating your model even easier.

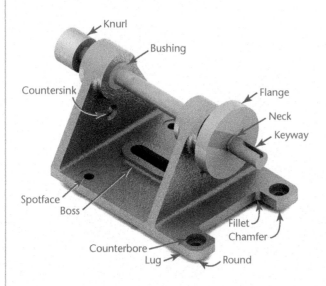

5.63   Commonly Manufactured Features

Feature	Example
Fillet: A rounded interior blend between surfaces; used, for example, to strengthen adjoining surfaces or to allow a part to be removed from a mold	
Round: A rounded exterior blend between surfaces; used to make edges and corners easier to handle, improve strength of castings, and allow for removal from a mold	
Counterbore: A cylindrical recess around a hole, usually to receive a bolt head or nut	
Countersink: A cone-shaped recess around a hole, often used to receive a tapered screw head	
Spotface: A shallow recess like a counterbore, used to provide a good bearing surface for a fastener	
Boss: A short raised protrusion above the surface of a part, often used to provide a strong flat bearing surface	
Lug: A flat or rounded tab protruding from a surface, usually to provide a method for attachment	
Flange: A flattened collar or rim around a cylindrical part to allow for attachment	
Chamfer: An angled surface, used on a cylinder to make it easier to start into a hole, or a plate to make it easier to handle	
Neck: A small groove cut around the diameter of a cylinder, often where it changes diameter	
Keyway/Keyseat: A shaped depression cut along the axis of a cylinder or hub to receive a key, used to attach hubs, gears, and other parts to a cylinder so they will not turn on it	
Knurl: A pattern on a surface to provide for better gripping or more surface area for attachment, often used on knobs and tool handles	
Bushing: A hollow cylinder that is often used as a protective sleeve or guide, or as a bearing	

A *fillet* is a common built-in feature that rounds the edge formed by two surfaces. Typically, a fillet can be created by selecting the edges to be filleted (several can be selected at once) and specifying the radius of the fillet. A round is another type of standard feature created in the same way, usually using the same Fillet command. When the surfaces move or are lengthened, the fillet or round adjusts automatically. Figure 5.64 shows a typical fillet and a typical round with a uniform radius.

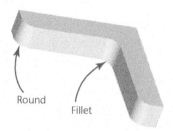

5.64   Fillet and Rounds

Sophisticated constraint-based modelers allow you to create uniform radius fillets and rounds, chained fillets and rounds that blend around a corner of a surface, constant-chord fillets and rounds, and variable-radius fillets and rounds (shown in Figure 5.65) using different methods. A constant-chord fillet is used in situations similar to Figure 5.65b, where a constant-radius fillet would result in thicker material on the uphill and downhill side of the blend. The constant-chord distance creates a fillet with a uniform amount of added material. More sophisticated blends between surfaces are also available in some software.

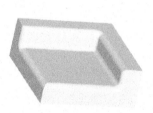      

(a) Chained fillets and rounds   (b) Constant-chord fillet   (c) Variable-radius round

5.65   Options for Fillets and Rounds

C0, C1, and C2 are terms used to describe the *geometric continuity* of surface blends (see Figure 5.66). (You may also see the letter G used as a designation for geometric continuity.)

- *C0:* Coincident surfaces meet but are not tangent. These are essentially intersecting surfaces, not ones that have a fillet.
- *C1:* Tangent surfaces meet and are tangent. This is the typical tangency produced by Fillet commands, and is suitable for most rounded edges.
- *C2:* Curvature continuous surfaces meet and are tangent, and where surfaces blend, they share a common center of curvature. Surface blends with this continuity do not have any abrupt change in radius. These blends are important for styling of surfaces such as automobile hoods and exterior plastic parts.
- *C3:* The next level above C2, except that the rate of change for the curvature is also continuous.

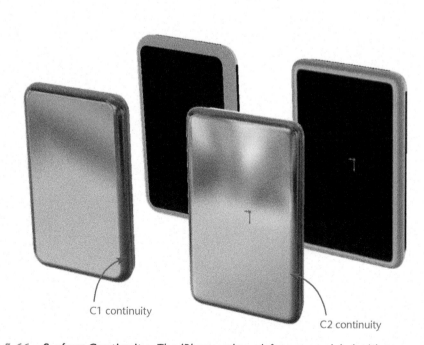

5.66   Surface Continuity. *The iPhones above left were modeled with tangent surfaces: C1 continuity. The smoother blends of the models on the right use C2 continuity. (Images courtesy of ©2016 Dassault Systèmes SolidWorks Corporation.)*

Complex Shapes

Complex shapes can often be made using special surface modeling commands that create surfaces that cannot easily be made with regular extrusion, revolution, sweeping, and blending. These surfaces can then be added to the model (see Figure 5.67). Once a surface has been added to the model and the edges completely matched (rather like being watertight), the object then can be "solidified" into a solid, which allows mass property calculations.

Because the complex surface can slow down model regeneration, an approximation of the surface may be used as a placeholder until later in the refinement process.

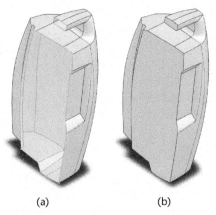

(a)   (b)

5.67   *The open-surface model in (a) is patched and then "solidified" into a solid model (b). (Courtesy of Strategix Vision.)*

5.10 CONSTRAINT-BASED MODELING MODES

Most constraint-based modelers have three main modes that link together to provide a full range of functionality in creating and documenting your designs: *part mode*, which allows you to create individually manufactured parts of a single material; *assembly mode*, which allows you to link multiple parts together into assemblies (Figure 5.68) or *subassemblies*; and *drawing mode*, which allows you to create orthographic, section, and pictorial drawings to document the design.

5.68   An Assembly Model of a Dynamometer
(Courtesy of Dynojet Research, Inc.)

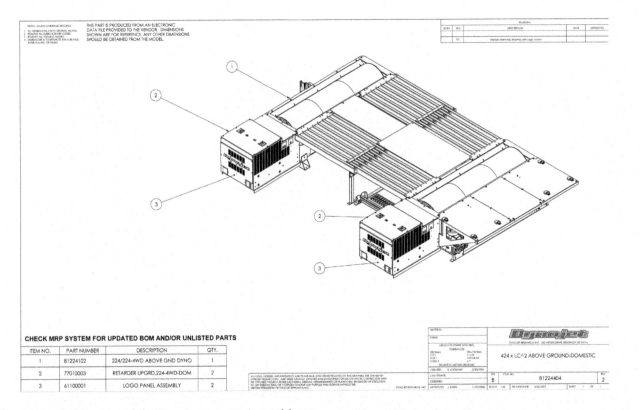

ITEM NO.	PART NUMBER	DESCRIPTION	QTY.
1	81224102	224/224-4WD ABOVE GND DYNO	1
2	77010003	RETARDER UPGRD,224-4WD-DOM	2
3	61100001	LOGO PANEL ASSEMBLY	2

5.69   A Drawing of the Dynamometer Assembly *(Courtesy of Dynojet Research, Inc.)*

Assemblies

Assembly capabilities in constraint-based modelers make concurrent engineering feasible. Companies can use the single design database as the hub of a collaborative environment for a cross-functional design team. Planning the critical relationships that capture the design intent of the assembly—just as would be done for each individual part—allows the constraint-based assembly to be used to coordinate efforts of several different individuals. The entire assembly and each part are stored in the design database for members of the design and manufacturing team to view, measure, or change (if authorized) while the parts are being designed.

The assembly provides a framework for the model. In the assembly, global parameters can be used to build intelligent assemblies. For example, if several parts assemble onto a shaft, the shaft diameter may be made a global parameter. The hole sizes on the parts that fit onto the shaft may be created by adding or subtracting a value from the global parameter for the shaft diameter. If the shaft diameter is changed, all the parts that fit with it may automatically be updated. Using global parameters can be an effective way to coordinate the design effort for a team. You will learn more about using assemblies to refine your design in Chapter 10.

(a)

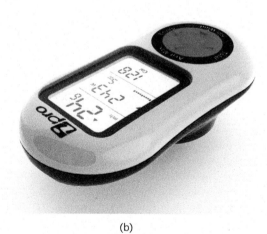

(b)

5.70 *The parts that make up the iBike Pro cycling computer were modeled individually as solids, then combined into a single assembly model to represent the finished product. The exploded view in (a) shows the individual parts clearly; the assembled view in (b) shows how the parts will fit together. (Courtesy of iBike and Salient Technologies, Inc.)*

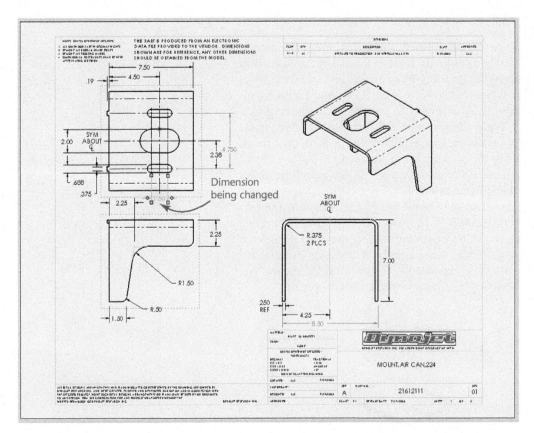

5.71 Associativity.
The 1.50 dimension for the slot highlighted in green in the top view is changed in the drawing to the new size, 2.00.
(Courtesy of Dynojet Research, Inc.)

Drawings from the Model

An advantage of solid modeling software is that drawings can be generated from the solid model. Creating drawings using constraint-based modeling software adds a significant dimension to this advantage: *associativity*.

Bidirectional Associativity

When a set of drawing views have been created from the model (Figure 5.71) and a change is made to the model, the drawing views will automatically be updated because they are associated with the actual model. Dimensions in most constraint-based modeling software control the sizes of the model features. The process of dimensioning a drawing can be automated because the software reports the dimension value for the entities in the CAD database.

If the size of a feature changes in the model, the value for the dimension in the drawing is automatically updated to show the correct values. When this is a one-way process—when changing the model causes the dimension value to be updated on the drawing—the dimensions are said to be ***associative***. When this is a one-way process, changing the dimension value on the drawing has no effect on the model geometry. In fact, it may break the link between the dimension value and the model geometry.

Most constraint-based modelers are ***bidirectionally associative***: changing a dimension in the drawing changes the model geometry, and vice versa (see Figures 5.71 and 5.72). Constraint-based modelers store and use the dimensions and constraints to generate the model. When dimensions are shown in a drawing, the values are the dimensions used to create the model. Whether these dimensions are changed in the part or on the drawing, the new values are stored in the database, and the model and all associated drawings are updated to reflect the new dimension values. Bidirectional associativity allows drawing changes to update the model, and model changes to update the drawings.

Before

After

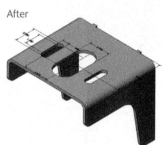

5.72 Bidirectional Associativity.
The model for the mounting bracket is shown before (slot at 1.50) and after the dimension on the drawing was changed to 2.00. (Courtesy of Dynojet Research, Inc.)

CONSTRAINT-BASED MODELING: CAPTURING DESIGN INTENT

When William Townsend was a Ph.D. student at MIT, he designed a four-axis robot arm that simulates the motion of the human arm. This human-scale dexterous arm works with the subsequently developed Barrett wrist and robot hand produced and manufactured by Townsend's engineering firm, Barrett Technology. To prepare the design for larger-scale production, the original 2D drawings were converted to constraint-based solid models, which enhanced Barrett Technology's ability to quickly make design changes and evaluate the results. By redesigning the robot arm, the company was able to make it the lightest one on the market and save 50% over previous manufacturing costs.

To benefit from constraint-based modeling, it was important to design the parts with the design goals in mind. "You need to keep your design intent in mind. Even though the software is a powerful tool, if you tie up a feature or overconstrain it, you are limiting the amount of flexibility you have in changing it easily later," said Brandon Larocque, project manager at Barrett Technology.

The top plate of the BarrettHand is a good example of how Larocque approaches constraint-based design (see Figure 5.73). The part has a total of fourteen features and took about 30 minutes to model in SolidWorks. When a new part is created, SolidWorks provides a default set of three orthogonal planes that intersect at the origin. The user can add more planes, but SolidWorks allows any surface to be used as a sketch plane. Larocque estimates that 80% to 90% of the parts he models do not need additional sketch planes.

The top plate of the hand began as half of a symmetrical sketch that was mirrored across the centerline (see Figure 5.74). The constraint-based relations in the mirrored half of the part were set up so they would be the same as those in the original half. To create the sketch, three radii were dimensioned to form the curved end of the plate: one in each corner and a larger one to form the curved end of the plate. The center of the largest radius is constrained to always lie on a horizontal construction line inserted into the base sketch. The other end-radii have tangency relationships where they meet the large radius and the straight lines that define the other edges of the plate. These tangency constraints were automatically created by SolidWorks when the radii were sketched in place. The three radii were constrained to be mutually tangent so the tool path generated by the model would be a single smooth curve through the three radii. The only other dimensions needed to define the part were those for the overall length of the part and the rectangular shape at the top of the part. All distances (dimensional constraints) were defined from the center of the part (which also coincided with the origin in SolidWorks). The sketch was then extruded to become the base feature for the part.

When Larocque thinks about selecting a base feature, he chooses one that will support additional features and reflect the way the part may be modified and eventually built. "I think

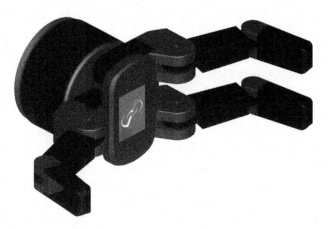

5.73 *This rendered view of the BarrettHand clearly shows the top plate in relation to the rest of the hand.*

modeling in 3D is similar to the way a machinist shapes a part. The modeling operations give you some intuition about the steps required to make the part and how many different setups a part will require. If you can make all of your features from the same surface of a part, chances are the machinist will be able to make them from a single setup as well. If you can form a part with a single revolution, you can probably make the part on a lathe in a single setup. Each time you add a sketching plane that is not normal or parallel to the default planes, you can assume the part may require an additional setup in order to machine it. Reducing a part's design from four setups to three can reduce the machining costs by 25%." In the case of the top plate, all its features except the bevel and the counterbores were created from the same side of the part.

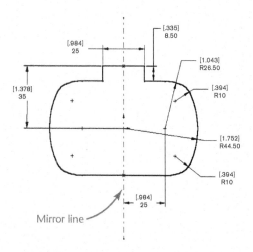

5.74 *The sketch for the base feature is symmetrical about the centerline. Dimensions are in SI units with inch units in brackets.*

(continued)

Because the plate is symmetrical, its center point also served as the design center of the part. The plate is designed to mate with two bearings set a specified distance apart. Dimensioning the part about a point at the intersection of the mirror line of the plate and a line through the center points of the two bearing bores means that any change in the distance between the bearings requires few changes to update the part.

The next step was to create the bevel around the outside of the base feature. Using the mirror plane (across which the first sketch was mirrored) as the sketching plane, Larocque sketched a triangular shape with a 30° angle (see Figure 5.75). This sketch was the profile for the bevel. A contour was sketched on the back surface of the plate to serve as the path for the triangular profile. After selecting both sketches, he used a sweeping operation to create the feature. SolidWorks prompted him to identify the profile (the triangle), the path (the contour sketch), and the sweep operation (a cut). The profile was dragged normal to the sweep path to cut the bevel on the plate. A machinist cutting this feature into actual metal would similarly use a 30° tapered mill to sweep out the same path defined in the model.

The next feature hollowed out the part. Sketching on the surface of the part that lies on the original sketch plane, Larocque created half of the shape of the area to be removed, dimensioned it from the centerline, and mirrored it to create the complete outline. The sketch was then extruded to the appropriate depth to be cut from the base feature (see Figure 5.76).

The fourth feature was a semicircular cutout to provide clearance for a motor pinion (see Figure 5.77). This circle was sketched on the original sketching plane, its diameter was dimensioned, and its center point was constrained to the center of the part (which corresponds to the distance from the centers of the bearings). Using a constraint to position the feature on the part's centerline guaranteed that the feature would stay centered even if the overall size of the part changed. To form the feature, Larocque specified a blind extrusion to a specified depth.

With the part hollowed out, the new interior surface was used as the sketch plane for the bosses that would be the bearing bores (see Figure 5.78). The bosses could have been formed on the initial sketching plane in the same operation that hollowed out the part, but their height would have been constrained by the depth of the part. If the depth were to change, the height of the bosses would, too. Using the new surface ensured that the relation of the bosses to the inside surface of the plate would remain constant, even if the depth of the surface changed.

To create the bosses, Larocque created symmetrical 20-millimeter circles with center points constrained to the horizontal centerline of the part. The circles were extruded, and two new concentric circles were sketched on the tops of the new features (see Figure 5.79). From the tops of the

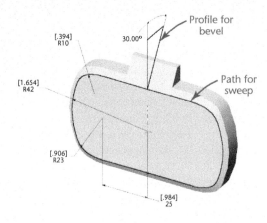

5.75 *The triangular shape of the bevel is a sketch on the mirror plane that was swept along the contour.*

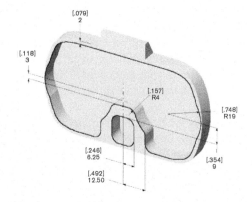

5.76 *The sketch for hollowing out the plate included two distinct outlines that were extruded as a single feature.*

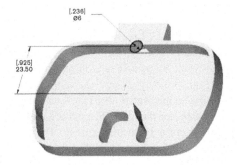

5.77 *The sketch for the motor pinion cutout was constrained to the center of the part.*

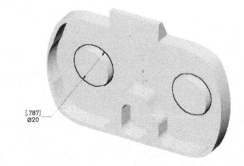

5.78 *The sketch for the bosses was drawn on the new surface created by the hollowing operation.*

bosses, Larocque extruded cuts back toward the bottom. Because the boss is to serve as a bearing bore, the depth of the hole in the middle must correspond to the width of the bearing, not the height of the boss. Extruding the hole from the top of the boss means that the hole will remain at the same depth even if the boss becomes taller or shorter. The same process was repeated to make the two smaller bosses.

The next feature was a chamfer on the inside edges of the bearing bores. SolidWorks allowed Larocque to multi-select all the bosses at once, then insert a chamfer (see Figure 5.80). A chamfer is a built-in feature with its own dialog box for setting its angle and depth. The single operation created the four chamfers, all to the same specifications. They constitute a single feature that cannot be decoupled into individual chamfers. Independent control of each chamfer would require creating four separate features.

Another built-in feature, a fillet, was added next. Larocque selected the two corners where the rectangular protrusion intersected the body of the part and added both fillets with the same operation.

The H-shaped pocket at the top of the plate was sketched next as a symmetrical feature. This feature is an alignment pocket that should move with the bearing bores. Its location and radii were dimensioned from the center of the part (to coincide with the centers of the two 20-mm bosses), and its length constrained to the centerline of the part (see Figure 5.81). "Most of the features after the base feature are dimensioned from the bearing bores because they are the defining characteristic of the part. I set up a relationship between the bearing bores and the alignment pocket because the alignment pocket determines where the bearings will fall."

The final features were the six holes and the counterbores to accommodate the fasteners to go into them. The first hole was given a diameter dimension, then the other holes were constrained to be the same size as the first (see Figure 5.82). All six were sketched on the sketch plane used for the bevel contour and extruded with the "through all" setting so they will always go all the way through the part, even if the part thickness changes. From the same side of the part, the counterbores were added to the holes as the final features. Larocque specified counterbores at the appropriate depth that are concentric with the hole (see Figure 5.83).

When asked about the degree to which he uses constraint-based relations, Larocque explained, "We like to keep the model somewhat segmented so we have more control over the updates, but we make sure to add relations where they make sense. For example, constraining symmetrical parts to a centerline as we did with the top plate of the hand can save enormous amounts of time when the part can update automatically. This aspect of the model was instrumental in our ability to make the BarrettHand lighter and less costly to manufacture."

(Designs courtesy of Barrett Technology, LLC, Newton, MA.)

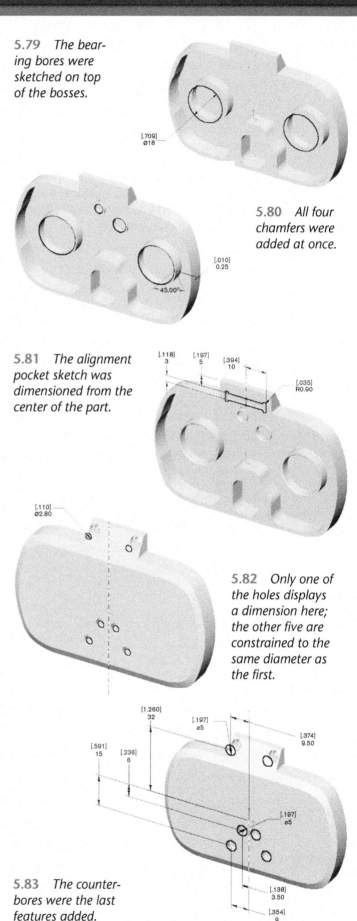

5.79 *The bearing bores were sketched on top of the bosses.*

5.80 *All four chamfers were added at once.*

5.81 *The alignment pocket sketch was dimensioned from the center of the part.*

5.82 *Only one of the holes displays a dimension here; the other five are constrained to the same diameter as the first.*

5.83 *The counterbores were the last features added.*

5.11 CHOOSING THE RIGHT MODELING METHOD

As you design, you will want to choose a modeling method that makes sense for your product, the stage in the design process, and the cost. Table 5.5 recaps the modeling methods according to the model qualities identified earlier in this chapter.

Key considerations are the time required to model the part and the purposes for which it will be used. A simpler method that provides all the needed information is more cost-effective than one that takes longer to model. However, time invested in a complete digital model of the product can pay for itself if it is used to generate visuals that help shape the design, reduce manufacturing difficulties, foster concurrent engineering—or promote the product later.

The accuracy of the modeling method is another key consideration. What types of analysis must be or could be completed with a model? What level of accuracy will be required to interface with CAM programs?

Table 5.5 Characteristics of Modeling Methods

Characteristic	Paper Drawings	2D Wireframe	Physical Model
Visual	2D views require interpretation and may be less understandable to a nonengineer.	2D views require interpretation and may be less understandable to a nonengineer.	Similar to actual object. Can be seen from all angles. May be smaller scale, unrealistic material.
Understandable	May require experience interpreting multiview drawing technique to be understood.	May require experience interpreting multiview drawing technique and descriptive geometry to be understood.	Can interact in a way similar to real object to aid in understanding. May be different scale, material than real object.
Flexible	Changes require erasure; difficult to accommodate large changes without redrawing.	Editing capabilities and layers make models more flexible than paper drawings.	Can be modified to a degree, but substantial changes may require a new model.
Cost-effective	Low equipment costs, but man-hours may be greater than with other methods. Cost effective for visualization and documenting simple parts. May be necessary if electronic formats cannot be read.	Useful for projects where the information gained from a 3D model is outweighed by the cost of capturing it, as in civil mapping and electrical circuit and distribution design.	Varies with the information contained in the model (where more information is usually more expensive) and the cost of manufacturing errors that could be prevented by the model.
Measurable	Not suited to be measured from.	Because objects are drawn full size, measurements may be taken from the model; knowledge of descriptive geometry required to derive information not shown in standard views.	Depends on how closely the model matches the materials and processes to be used to create the actual product.
Accurate	Requires proper dimensions to reflect design accurately.	Offers a high degree of accuracy when orthographic drawing techniques are understood.	Depends on how closely the model matches the materials and processes to be used to create the actual product.
Robust	May require multiple views to fully define the shape of an object.	More robust than paper drawings and can include links to large amounts of data; lacks information about volume found in 3D models.	Can include as much information as the actual product.
Application	Effective for sketches and quickly conveying the design of simple parts for manufacturing.	Useful for largely 2D information such as maps, layout drawings, and electrical circuits.	Good for testing fit of parts, interaction with other products and people, and analyzing aspects that cannot be simulated.

As you have seen, 3D modeling packages that are strong in surface modeling are needed to model the geometry of smoothly contoured features such as the ergonomic mouse shown earlier in the chapter. Piping systems and other structures of simple geometric shapes can sometimes be modeled very effectively using 3D wireframe modeling. Many inexpensive CAD packages support this type of modeling. However, a solid modeling package is required to create a model that can be used to check parts for fit and interference; calculate the weight of a final assembly from the many individual parts; generate a rendered view of the assembly that can be used in manufacturing, marketing, service and repair; and drive the computer-aided machinery to manufacture parts. The same assembly model created using constraint-based modeling methods would have the added advantage of being updated automatically when key dimensions change. It would also make it easy to create a family of similar parts.

Whether you choose the modeling package or learn to use the tools provided by your employer, you should be aware of the strengths and limitations of the software so you can use it most effectively.

Characteristic	3D Wireframe	Surface	3D Solid
Visual	Can be viewed from any direction and used to create standard 2D views; lack of surfaces may make views ambiguous.	Usually includes lighting and background options that can be used to create photo-realistic images of the model.	Shaded and rendered views present a realistic view of the object; offers automated 2D view generation; with most equipment only 2D view is available on monitor; part must be rotated to picture clearly.
Understandable	Requires viewer to mentally add surfaces to see the 3D shape.	Shaded views are easily understood by the viewer.	Shaded views are easily understood by the viewer.
Flexible	Editable, but changing individual objects more time-consuming than in other methods.	Each vertex is editable, but ease of changes depends on method used to create and store the surface.	CSG or hybrid models offer the most flexibility; can edit at the level of the solid object instead of individual geometric entity.
Cost-effective	Requires less computing power, and software is generally lower priced; good for modeling geometrically simple shapes.	Most cost-effective for modeling irregular surfaces that must be conveyed to manufacture with a high degree of accuracy; photo-realistic displays can offset modeling costs by adding value in marketing.	Completeness of the solid model cost-effective when model can be used for multiple purposes, such as testing, presentation, and CAM.
Measurable	Full-size entities are measurable without auxiliary views; can only measure between wireframe entities, however.	Can be used to calculate surface area.	Can be used to measure not just size but also weight, mass, and other physical properties.
Accurate	Offers a high degree of accuracy for the entities represented.	Depends on method used to store model data; smoothed surfaces generally more accurate than mesh surfaces.	Depends on method used to store model data; high degree of accuracy possible.
Robust	Model stores only vertices and edges; lacks surface or volume information; may be ambiguous as to voids or holes.	Fully defines the surfaces of a part; lacks volume information.	Includes volume as well as surfaces and vertices; can eliminate need for physical model.
Application	Good for applications where relationships in 3D space must be modeled, simple geometric shapes are sufficient for the objects to be modeled, and realistic views are not required.	Good for designs that include irregular or free-flowing surfaces and for those where the appearance of the product is a critical design criterion.	Good for applications where fit between parts and other engineering properties need to be evaluated before manufacture.

CHOOSING THE RIGHT METHOD: SURFACE MODELING

The Stryker SmartPump tourniquet system continuously monitors and controls tourniquet pressure during surgeries (Figure 5.84). When Kent Swendseid, Design Director at Strategix Vision, designed the enclosure for the product, he used surface modeling techniques to obtain the smooth curves envisioned for the case and built-in handle.

Before these outside surfaces were modeled, the internal components and user interface were worked out to determine the shape and volume required. Concept sketches were done (including rough models in 3D) to show various options for the enclosure. Once a concept was chosen and the internal configuration was known, surface modeling started in earnest.

Swendseid used a modeling approach that works well for complex molded assemblies: a "base part" controlling the overall shape and dimensions of the assembly is modeled first, then the component parts are derived from the base part. This way, if something in the design has to change, only the base part has to be modified to alter the exterior. The derived parts are updated accordingly. This approach also allows various parts to be modeled in parallel by a team rather than a single designer.

The case concept was a clamshell of two large molded parts with a molded-in handle. The first step was to identify key features, such as where and how the two molded parts would come together, and where mounting positions for things like the display would be. These were represented as planes in the model. Shapes and contours important to the shape were also created early in the modeling and are visible in the feature

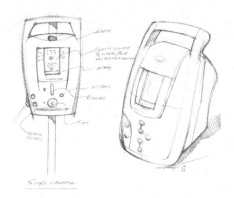

5.84 A Concept Sketch for the "Smart Tourniquet"

tree for the part (see Figure 5.85). These changed as modeling progressed, but because the model was built around them, it was simple to update.

The front face was modeled as a loft—a surface that morphs from one curve to another. The curvature was controlled by either guide curves or tangency constraints at the ends (Figure 5.86). Early surfaces are almost always modeled larger than the face that will end up on the part to simplify manipulation of the curvature—and to avoid unwanted edge effects.

The next surfaces added do not show up in the final model directly. These "helper surfaces" can be used to control the angle where two surfaces meet (Figure 5.87). To ensure that the surfaces of the mold will let go of the part when it is ejected, the surface has to have what's known as "draft"—the surface has to sit at an angle to the direction the mold opens.

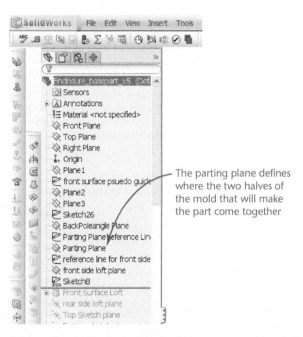

The parting plane defines where the two halves of the mold that will make the part come together

5.85 *The feature tree for the base part consists of planes and reference lines that other features are derived from and constrained to.*

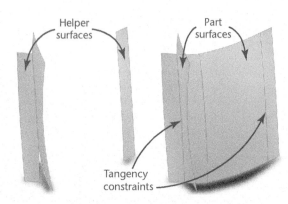

First loft curve

Second loft curve

5.86 *The front surface lofts between guide curves.*

Helper surfaces

Part surfaces

Tangency constraints

5.87 *Helper surfaces help position the surfaces and are trimmed off when no longer needed.*

Creating a simple helper surface at the parting plane provides a draft constraint to which to tie a more complex surface: if the surface is tangent to a surface with enough draft, it will have enough draft too. Helper surfaces are trimmed off, deleted, or hidden when no longer needed.

Additional faces were built using swept, extruded, and revolved surfaces to define half of the symmetrical shape of the case. Using the symmetry does more than save work; it also guarantees that the model will actually *be* symmetrical. For a surface model, it also ensures that there will be no visible artifact where the two parts join. This avoids distracting highlights and waviness in the finished part.

5.88   *Half the case is modeled to take advantage of the symmetry of the part.*

In Figure 5.88, you can see that the part surfaces were modeled to extend beyond their intersections with other surfaces, thus allowing the software to calculate the intersections mathematically to create the edges between surfaces. It also means that simpler profiles can be used to loft or sweep the surfaces. The mathematics of surface modeling favors using the fewest possible constraints, because more constraints require higher-order polynomials to describe the surface. If the spline defining the intersection were used to generate the surface, tiny perturbations in the driving geometry could result in ripples or other undesired effects in the surface.

Trimming forms the boundary between surfaces. This operation can be used to create hard edges, but in this case the shape required a rounded edge. This requirement could be met with a fillet, but the designer wanted to avoid the sudden change of curvature where the fillet meets the two surfaces it joins. This is a common desire in product modeling, especially with glossy surfaces that reveal the change of curvature as an unwanted highlight instead of a smooth 3D curve. The designer also wanted to "bulge" the rounded edge toward the top and bottom, which would have required a variable-radius fillet—at the time, an unreliable feature.

To create the rounded edge, the front and side surfaces were trimmed to helper surfaces that described the boundary (Figure 5.89, left) and the gap was filled with another loft, which allowed the result to be curvature-continuous. Note that the top and bottom of the two surfaces in Figure 5.89 (middle) still extend beyond where they will eventually end, again to minimize the number of constraints on the fill surface.

The order in which operations are done affects modeling efficiency. Sometimes it makes sense to leave trimming and joining surfaces to the very end, and sometimes it makes

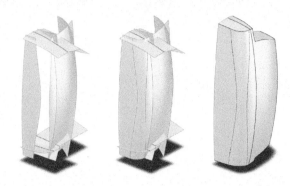

5.89   Trimming and Lofting a Surface to Create the Corner

sense to join them earlier to simplify selecting them for other operations.

For example, the device mounts by fitting around a vertical pole behind it, so the case needed an indentation to clear the pole. Because the pole clearance surface crossed several others, modeling this feature was delayed until the rest of the device had taken shape (see Figure 5.90).

When it came time to add the handle opening, ergonomic concerns and balance issues made it difficult to use the main parting plane of the base part. The handle does not symmetrically straddle the main parting plane, so where the two halves of the clamshell would come together would be very close to the front edge of the handle. Because this would make it uncomfortable to hold the unit, the boundary of the part inside the handle was shifted rearward toward the middle of the handle. The handle opening was given its own parting plane.

The front opening for the handle area was then modeled in one feature (Figure 5.91). The face at the front of the handle was deleted to open up the edges, and those edges were captured as a compound curved profile. The inner opening was sketched on the handle parting line plane, and a surface was lofted between the two curves. The rear opening was handled

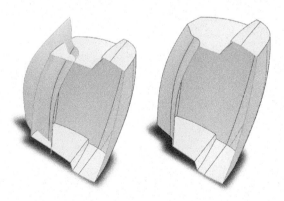

5.90   Adding the Clearance Surface for the Mounting Pole

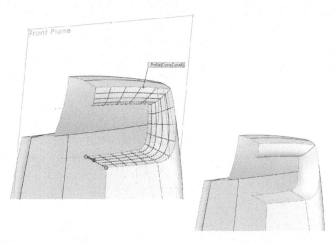

5.91   Modeling the Surface for the Front Half of the Handle Opening

5.93   Nonsymmetrical Detail Added to Back

similarly, as were the transition surfaces from the front of the case to the opening for the screen.

Once the surface half is complete, it can be "closed." This turns the surface model into a solid model. Actually, a solid model is a surface model, just an "airtight" one with no open edges.

With a symmetrical model, the easiest way to close the model is to knit (join at the edges) a planar surface at the symmetry plane to the open edges of the model (see Figure 5.92, middle). Some modelers then automatically assume the model is a solid, but some have to be told to check for edge gaps and missing faces before changing the status of the body.

Once the model is solidified, it can be mirrored, non-symmetrical features can be added, and the surface can be used in later design stages (see Figure 5.93). In some cases, it can make sense to mirror the surfaces themselves, but that can

increase the likelihood of small mathematical errors owing to the more complex nature of the boundary.

Building a model from a base part allows detail work to be started even before modeling of the base part is complete. As long as the surface can be closed and a solid formed, that solid can be shelled and split up into components. As additional features are added they are derived from the base part geometry so they will be updated if the base part changes. Figure 5.94 shows this kind of detailing in the rear half of the assembly.

5.94   Adding Features to the Shelled Model

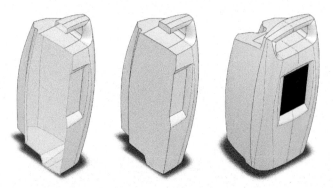

5.92   Closing the Model and Mirroring the Solid Part

(All figures courtesy of Strategix Vision team members Kent Swendseid, Marty Albini, and Aki Hirota.)

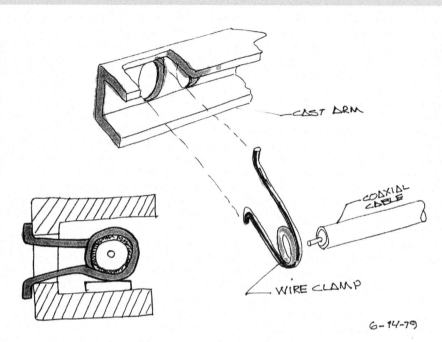

5.95 Solid modeling was Albert Brown's choice for refining the design of the parts shown in this sketch. The coaxial cable was formed by revolution; the cast arm was extruded and the holes formed with a Boolean operation. The wire clamp was created by sweeping its cross-sectional shape along a curved path. The resulting solid model allowed Brown to check the fit of the wire clamp. *(Courtesy of Albert W. Brown, Jr.)*

5.96 Concept sketches for this surgical device reveal several options for the enclosure, which was modeled using surface techniques. *(Courtesy of Strategix Vision.)*

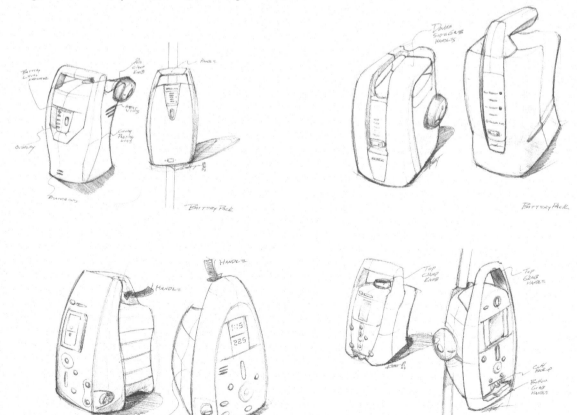

KEY WORDS

Analytical Model

Assembly Mode

Associative

Base Feature

Base Point

Bidirectionally Associative

Boundary Representation

Built-in or Placed Features

Chamfer

Constraint-Based or Parametric Modeling

Coon's Patch

Cosmetic Dimension

Counterbore

Datum

Datum Planes

Derived Surfaces

Descriptive Geometry

Descriptive Models

Design Intent

Drawing Mode

Driven Dimensions

Driving Dimensions

Feature

Feature-Based Modeling

Fillet

Finite Element Analysis

Geometric Constraints

Global Parameters

Interpolated

Layers

Lofting

Model

Parameter

Parent-Child Relationship

Part Mode

Patches

Prototypes

Size Constraints

Subassemblies

Surface Normal Vector

Tessellation Lines

Triangulated Irregular Networks

Virtual Prototype

Virtual Reality

Wireframe Modeling

CHAPTER SUMMARY

Now that you have completed this chapter you should be able to list the qualities that models have that make them useful in the design process. You should be able to describe four CAD modeling methods that you might use to refine your design ideas. Not all modeling methods capture the same amount of information about the parts or device. You should be able to select the best modeling method to use for a particular design problem. The exercises allow you to test your understanding of the modeling process, ask you to apply a particular CAD modeling process to a design problem, provide practice with your modeling package, and ask you to decide which modeler you would choose to design a particular object.

You should be able to list advantages of constraint-based modeling over solid modeling. You should be able to correctly use the term parent-child relationships as applied to part features. Associativity between drawing views and the 3D model is an key characteristic of sophisticated constraint-based modeling programs. Selecting the base feature of the model is important, as it is the first parent feature. The exercises ask you to demonstrate your understanding of parent-child relationships and base features by capturing design intent in a number of part models. They also provide additional practice with your constraint-based modeling package.

REVIEW QUESTIONS

1. You are a member of a team designing an automatic door-opening device so wheelchair users can enter and exit buildings on campus. Which of the modeling methods available to your design team are appropriate in each of the following situations:
   a. Preliminary design review with your immediate engineering (technical) supervisor
   b. Discussions of installation details with the campus architectural staff
   c. Meeting with a group of nontechnical advocates for accessibility by persons with disabilities
   d. Meeting with machine shop technicians who will fabricate your prototype
2. Which modeling method contains the most information about a design? Identify a situation in which this would not be the best model to use.
3. Recent developments in Global Positioning System (GPS) technology have resulted in small, relatively inexpensive, handheld GPS receivers (Figure 5.97).
   a. A need exists for a mount to attach the system to mountain bikes in such a way that the display is visible while the rider is mounted. It is not desirable to modify the GPS to provide attachment. Consideration should be given to protecting the electronics and display from damage during rugged use while providing a clear sky

view for the built-in antenna. What types of CAD models could be used to develop this mounting attachment?

  b. At what stage of the process would each type of model be appropriate?

4. For the following situations, choose a modeling method and explain why you would use it.

  a. Designing a prosthetic limb

  b. Routing a piping system for a building

  c. Designing a one-of-a-kind machined part

  d. Verifying clearances for an electrical substation located near an airfield

  e. Mapping an oil reservoir

5. Not all machines have moving parts. A wedge is an example of a simple machine. Use each of the modeling methods discussed in the chapter to model a wedge. Use the same size wedge for each model.

6. Constraint-based, or feature-based, modeling uses defined relationships between model elements to control various features. What two basic types of constraints are used to control features?

7. Why are the linear, angular, or other physical dimensions of a constraint-based model feature given a name? Give an example where this practice might be useful.

8. An acronym sometimes used to describe the process of preparing for the creation of a constraint-based model is TAP, representing the steps Think, Analyze, and Plan. Consider what it means to think, analyze, and plan a constraint-based model. Why are these steps especially important prior to beginning the constraint-based model?

9. What is meant by *parent-child relationship* in constraint-based modeling?

10. Define bidirectional associativity with respect to a constraint-based modeling program's drawing mode. How does this program feature enhance ease of use of the program?

11. You are considering modifying a model by changing dimensions in a drawing view. What problems might you encounter when using a constraint-based modeler without bidirectional associativity? What problems might you anticipate when using a constraint-based modeler with bidirectional associativity in this task?

5.97 A handheld GPS receiver.
(Courtesy of Garmin ©.)

CHAPTER EXERCISES

Exercise 5.1 The toy building blocks in the photos are assembled by inserting the posts on top of one block into the space around the central circular extrusion on the bottom of another block The parts are made of molded plastic. Consider the design intent for these blocks. What dimensions are critical so these blocks will fit together in different arrangements? Create a model of a six-post block (2 × 3). Update your model to contain eight posts (2 × 4), as in the block at right.

Exercise 5.2 For each part shown, list the modeling method you would choose to create it if you were creating the original product definition for mass-producing these items. Give the reasons for your choices.

a. (Copyright Aptyp_koK/Shutterfly.)

b. (Copyright grynold/Shutterfly.)

c. (Copyright a_v_d/Shutterstock.)

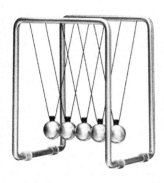

d. (Copyright bikeriderlondon/Shutterfly.)

e. (Copyright Tatiana Katsai/Shutterstock.)

f. (Copyright Africa Studio/Shutterstock.)

g. (Copyright homydesign/Shutterstock.)

h. (Copyright Sergiy Kuzmin/Shutterstock.)

i. (Copyright koya979/Shutterstock.)

j. *(Copyright ppl/Shutterstock.)*

k. *(Copyright Tim Scott/Shutterstock.)*

l. *(Copyright mrHanson/Shutterstock.)*

m. *(Copyright xiaorui/Shutterstock.)*

n. *(Copyright kezza/Shutterstock.)*

o. *(Copyright worananphoto/ Shutterstock.)*

p. *(Copyright Dennis Steen/Shutterstock.)*

q. *((top) Copyright FabrikaSimf/ Shutterstock; (bottom) Copyright Winai Tepsuttinun/Shutterstock.)*

r. *(Copyright StockPhotosArt/ Shutterfly.)*

s. *(Copyright Ivan Smuk/Shutterstock.)*

t. *(Copyright Cristina Annibali/ Shutterstock.)*

u. *(Copyright montego/ Shutterstock.)*

CHAPTER SIX

ORTHOGRAPHIC PROJECTION

OBJECTIVES

After studying the material in this chapter, you should be able to:

1. Recognize and sketch the symbol for third-angle projection.

2. List the six principal views of projection.

3. Sketch the top, front, and right-side views of an object with normal, inclined, and oblique surfaces.

4. Understand which views show depth in a drawing that shows top, front, and right-side views.

5. Know the meaning of normal, inclined, and oblique surfaces.

6. Compare using a 2D CAD program with sketching on a sheet of paper.

7. List the dimensions that transfer between top, front, and right-side views.

8. Transfer depth between the top and right-side views.

9. Label points where surfaces intersect.

10. Select a good arrangement of generated 2D drawing views to place from a 3D model.

Refer to the following standard:
- *ANSI/ASME Y14.3 Orthographic and Pictorial Views*

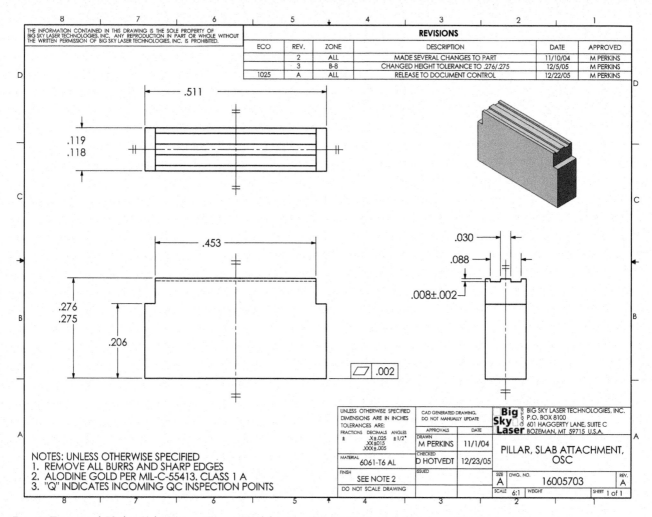

Front, Top, and Right-Side Views Generated from a 3D CAD Model *(Courtesy of Big Sky Laser.)*

OVERVIEW

A view of an object is called a *projection.* By projecting multiple views from different directions in a systematic way, you can completely describe the shape of 3D objects.

There are certain standard practices that you must know to create sketches and documentation drawings that can be easily interpreted. For example, you need to know which views to show, how they should be oriented in your drawing, and how to represent key information such as edges, surfaces, vertices, hidden lines, centerlines, and other crucial details.

The standard published in *ANSI/ASME Y14.3* is common in the United States, where third-angle projection is used. Europe, Asia, and many other places use the first-angle projection system.

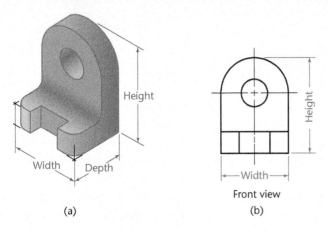

6.1   Front View of an Object

(a)   (b)
Front view

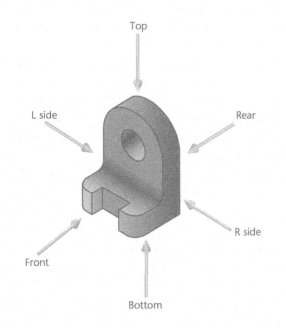

6.2   The Six Principal Views

UNDERSTANDING PROJECTION

To make and interpret drawings, you need to understand projection and the standard arrangement of views. You also need to be familiar with the geometry of solid objects and be able to visualize a 3D object that is represented in a 2D sketch or drawing. The ability to identify whether surfaces are normal, inclined, or oblique in orientation can help you visualize. Common features such as vertices, edges, contours, fillets, holes, and rounds are shown in a standard way, which makes drawings simpler to create and helps prevent them from being misinterpreted.

Views of Objects

A photograph shows an object as it appears to the observer but not necessarily as it is. It cannot describe the object accurately, no matter what distance or which direction it is taken from, because it does not show the exact shapes and sizes of the parts. It would be impossible to create an accurate 3D model of an object using only a photograph for reference because it shows only one view. It is a 2D representation of a 3D object.

Drawings are 2D representations as well, but unlike photos, they allow you to record sizes and shapes precisely. In engineering and other fields, a complete and clear description of the shape and size of an object is necessary to be sure that it is manufactured exactly as the designer intended. To provide this information about a 3D object, typically a number of systematically arranged views are used.

The system of views is called *multiview projection.* Each view provides certain definite information. For example, a front view shows the true shape and size of surfaces that are parallel to the front of the object. An example of a 3D object and its front view projection is shown in Figure 6.1. Figure 6.2 shows the same part and the six principal viewing directions. Figure 6.3 shows the same six views of a house.

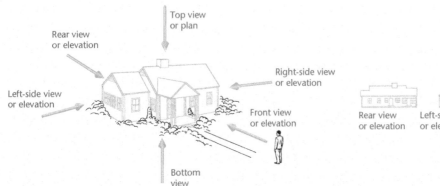

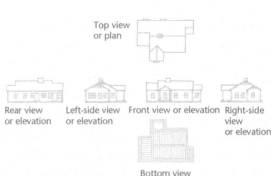

6.3   Six Views of a House

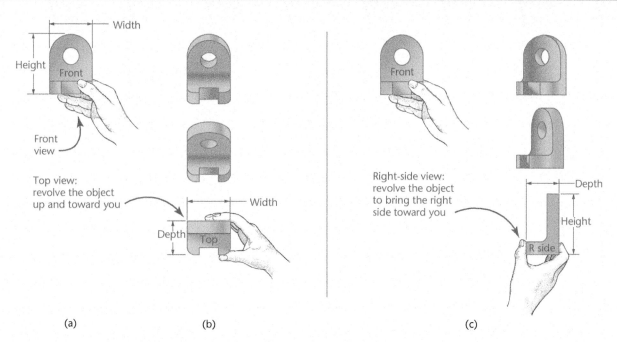

(a)   (b)   (c)

6.4 Revolving the Object to Produce Views. *You can experience different views by revolving an object, as shown. (a) First, hold the object in the front view position. (b) To get the top view, tilt the object toward you to bring the top of the object into your view. (c) To get the right-side view, begin with the object's front view facing you and revolve it to bring the right side toward you. To see views of the rear, bottom, or left side, you would simply turn the object to bring those sides toward you.*

The Six Standard Views

Any object can be viewed from six mutually perpendicular directions, as shown in Figure 6.2. These are called the six ***principal views.***

You can think of the six views as what an observer would see by moving around the object. As shown in Figure 6.3, the observer can walk around a house and view its front, sides, and rear. You can imagine the top view as seen by an observer from an airplane and the bottom, or worm's-eye view, as seen from underneath. The term *plan* may also be used for the top view. The term *elevation* is used for all views showing the height of the building. These terms are regularly used in architectural drawing and occasionally in other fields.

To make drawings easier to read, the views are arranged on the paper in a standard way. The views in Figure 6.3 show the American National Standard arrangement. The top, front, and bottom views align vertically. The rear, left-side, front, and right-side views align horizontally. To draw a view out of place is a serious error and is generally regarded as one of the worst mistakes in drawing. See Figure 6.4 for an illustration of how to visualize the different views.

Principal Dimensions

The three principal dimensions of an object are ***width, height,*** and ***depth*** (Figure 6.5). In technical drawing, these fixed terms are used for dimensions shown in certain views, regardless of the shape of the object. The terms *length* and *thickness* are not used because they may be misleading.

The front view shows only the height and width of the object and not the depth. In fact, any principal view of a 3D object shows only two of the three principal dimensions; the third is found in an adjacent view. Height is shown in the rear, left-side, front, and right-side views. Width is shown in the rear, top, front, and bottom views. Depth is shown in the left-side, top, right-side, and bottom views.

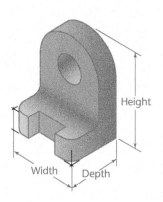

6.5 The Principal Dimensions of an Object

Projection Method

Figure 6.6 illustrates the front view of an object drawn using an orthographic projection. Imagine a sheet of glass parallel to the front surfaces of the object. This represents the *plane of projection.* The outline on the plane of projection shows how the object appears to the observer. In orthographic projection, rays (or projectors) from all points on the edges or contours of the object extend parallel to each other and perpendicular to the plane of projection. The word *orthographic* means "at right angles."

Examples of top and side views are shown in Figure 6.7. Specific names are given to the planes of projection. The front view is projected to the *frontal plane.* The top view is projected to the *horizontal plane.* The side view is projected to the *profile plane.*

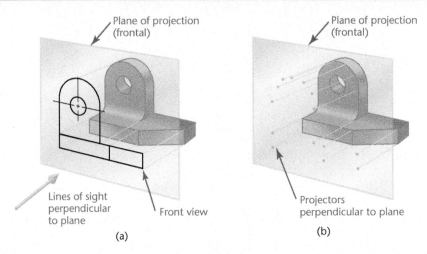

(a)   (b)

6.6   Projection of an Object

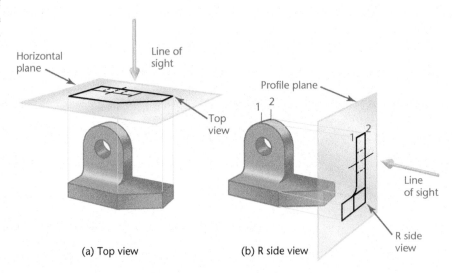

(a) Top view   (b) R side view

6.7   Horizontal and Profile Projection Planes

The Glass Box

One way to understand the standard arrangement of views on the sheet of paper is to envision a *glass box.* If planes of projection were placed parallel to each principal face of the object, they would form a box, as shown in Figure 6.8. The outside observer would see six standard views (front, rear, top, bottom, right side, left side) of the object through the sides of this imaginary glass box.

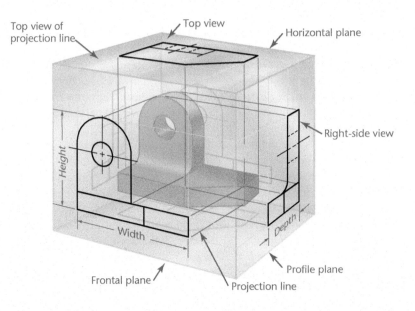

6.8   The Glass Box

To organize the views of a 3D object on a flat sheet of paper, imagine the six planes of the glass box being unfolded to lie flat, as shown in Figure 6.9. Think of all planes except the rear plane as hinged to the frontal plane. The rear plane is usually hinged to the left-side plane. Each plane folds out away from the frontal plane. The representation of the hinge lines of the glass box in a drawing are known as *folding lines.* The positions of these six planes after they have been unfolded are shown in Figure 6.10.

Carefully identify each of these planes and corresponding views with the planes' original position in the glass box.

In Figure 6.10, lines extend around the glass box from one view to another on the planes of projection. These are the projectors from a point in one view to the same point in another view. The size and position of the object in the glass box does not change. This explains why the top view is the same width as the front view and why it is placed directly above the front view. The same relation exists between the front and bottom views. Therefore, the front, top, and bottom views all line up vertically and are the same width. The rear, left-side, front, and right-side views all line up horizontally and are the same height.

Objects do not change position in the box, so the top view must be the same distance from the folding line *O/Z* as the right-side view is from the folding line *O/Y*. The bottom and left-side views are the same distance from their respective folding lines as are the right-side and the top views. The top, right-side, bottom, and left-side views are all the same distance from the respective folding lines and show the same depth.

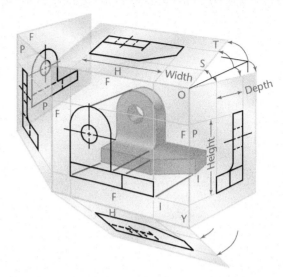

6.9   Unfolding the Glass Box

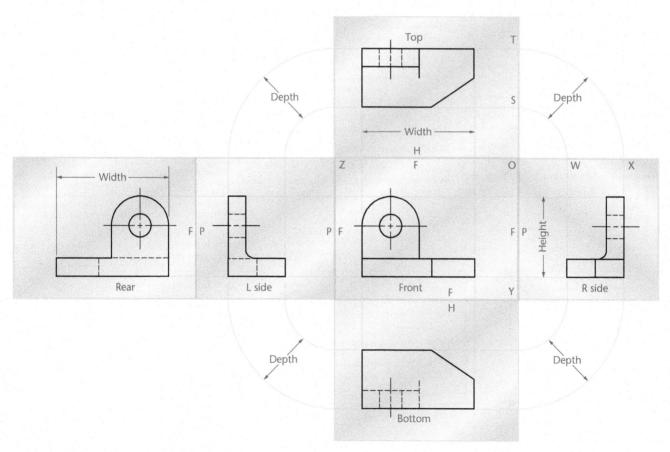

6.10   The Glass Box Unfolded

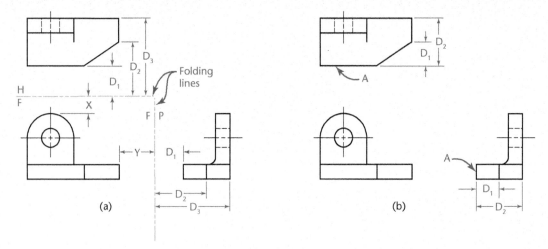

6.11   Views Shown with and without Folding Lines

The front, top, and right-side views of the object shown in the previous figures are shown in Figure 6.11a, but instead of a glass box, folding lines are shown between the views. These folding lines correspond to the hinge lines of the glass box.

The *H/F* folding line, between the top and front views, is the intersection of the horizontal and frontal planes. The *F/P* folding line, between the front and side views, is the intersection of the frontal and profile planes.

Although you should understand folding lines, particularly because they are useful in solving problems in descriptive geometry, they are usually left off the drawing, as in Figure 6.11b. Instead of using the folding lines as reference lines for marking depth measurements in the top and side views, you may use the front surface (A) of the object as a refer-

ence line. Note that D_1, D_2, and all other depth measurements correspond in the two views as if folding lines were used.

Spacing between Views

Spacing between views is mainly a matter of appearance. Views should be spaced well apart but close enough to appear related to each other. You may need to leave space between the views to add dimensions.

Transferring Depth Dimensions

The depth dimensions in the top and side views must correspond point-for-point. When using 2D CAD or instruments, transfer these distances accurately.

You can transfer dimensions between the top and side views either with dividers or with a scale, as shown

in Figures 6.12a and 6.12b. Marking the distances on a scrap of paper and using it like a scale to transfer the distance to the other view is another method that works well when sketching.

You may find it convenient to use a 45° miter line to project dimensions between top and side views, as shown in Figure 6.12c. Because the miter line is drawn at 45°, depths shown vertically in the top view can be transferred to be shown as horizontal depths in the side view and vice versa.

Measuring from a Reference Surface

To transfer a dimension from one view to a related view (a view that shares that dimension), measure from a plane that shows on edge in both views as in Figure 6.13.

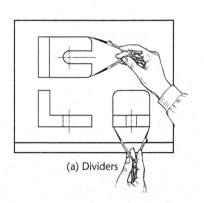
(a) Dividers

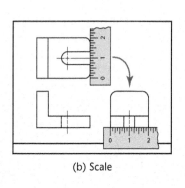
(b) Scale

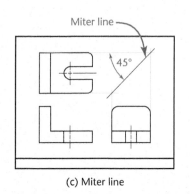
(c) Miter line

6.12   Transferring Depth Dimensions

Necessary Views

Figure 6.14 shows that right- and left-side views are essentially mirror images of each other, only with different lines appearing hidden. Hidden lines use a dashed-line pattern to represent portions of the object that are not directly visible from that direction of sight. Both the right and left views do not need to be shown, so usually the right-side view is drawn. This is also true of the top and bottom views, and of the front and rear views. The top, front, and right-side views, arranged together, are shown in Figure 6.15. These are called the *three regular views* because they are the views most frequently used.

A sketch or drawing should contain only the views needed to clearly and completely describe the object. These minimally required views are referred to as the *necessary views.* Choose the views that have the fewest hidden lines and show essential contours or shapes most clearly. Complicated objects may require more than three views or special views such as partial views.

Many objects need only two views to clearly describe their shape. If an object requires only two views, and the left-side and right-side views show the object equally well, use the right-side view. If an object requires only two views, and the top and bottom views show the object equally well, choose the top view. If only two views are necessary and the top view and right-side view show the object equally well, choose the combination that fits best on your paper. Some examples are shown in Figure 6.16.

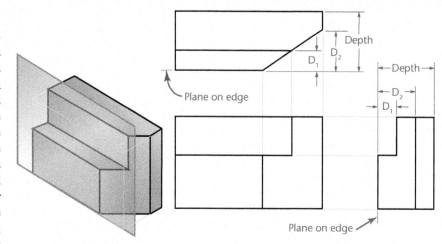

6.13 Transferring Depth Dimensions from a Reference Surface

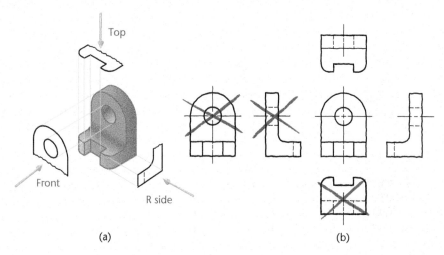

6.14 Opposite Views Are Nearly Identical

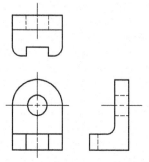

6.15 The Three Regular Views

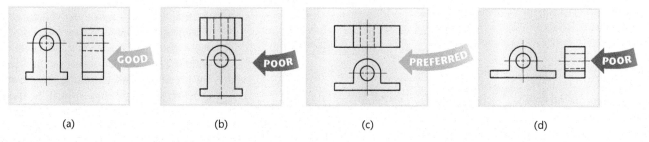

(a)   (b)   (c)   (d)

6.16 Choice of Views to Fit Paper

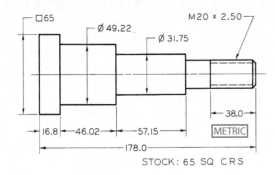

□65   Ø 49.22   M20 × 2.50   Ø 31.75
38.0
METRIC
16.8 — 46.02 — 57.15
178.0
STOCK: 65 SQ CRS

6.17 One-View Drawing of a Connecting Rod

GOOD

(Shows shape clearly)

POOR

(No! Show large surfaces parallel to the view)

POOR

(No! Other views show shapes better)

POOR

(No! Use a usual, stable, or operating position)

6.18 Choice of Front View

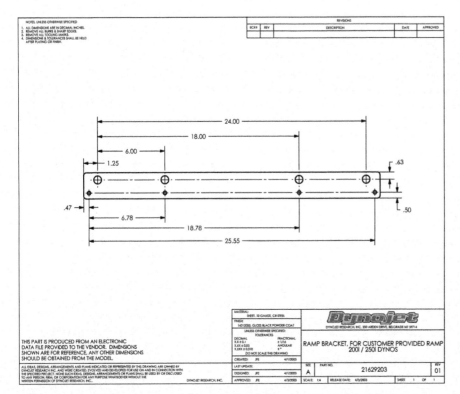

6.19 *A long part looks best oriented with the long axis horizontal on the sheet. (Courtesy of Dynojet Research, Inc.)*

Often, a single view supplemented by a note or by lettered symbols is enough, as shown in Figure 6.17. Objects that can be shown using a single view usually have a uniform thickness. This connecting rod is an exception. It is possible to show it in a single view owing to the way it is dimensioned.

Orientation of the Front View

Four views of a compact automobile are shown in Figure 6.18. The view chosen for the front view in this case is the side, not the front, of the automobile.

- The front view should show a large surface of the part parallel to the front viewing plane.
- The front view should show the shape of the object clearly.
- The front view should show the object in a usual, stable, or operating position, particularly for familiar objects.
- When possible, a machine part is drawn in the orientation it occupies in the assembly.
- Usually, screws, bolts, shafts, tubes, and other elongated parts are drawn in a horizontal position, as shown in Figure 6.19.

CAD software can be used to generate orthographic views directly from a 3D model, as shown in Figure 6.20. The pictorial view of this model is shown in Figure 6.21. When using CAD you still need to select a good orientation so that the part shows clearly in the front view. The standard arrangement of views shown in Figure 6.15 should be used. Do not be tempted to rearrange the views of your CAD drawing to fit the sheet better, unless you are using removed views.

First- and Third-Angle Projection

As you saw earlier in this chapter, you can imagine projecting views as unfolding a glass box made from the viewing planes. There are two main systems used for projecting and unfolding the views: *third-angle projection,* which is used in the United States, Canada, and some other countries, and *first-angle projection,* which is used primarily in Europe

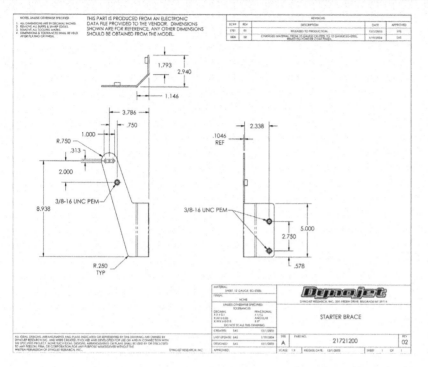

6.21 Pictorial View of the CAD Model Shown in Figure 6.20
(Courtesy of Dynojet Research, Inc.)

6.20 Computer-Generated Multiview Drawing from a CAD Model
(Courtesy of Dynojet Research, Inc.)

and Asia. Difficulty in interpreting the drawing and manufacturing errors can result when a first-angle drawing is confused with a third-angle drawing.

Because of the global nature of technical drawings, you should thoroughly understand both methods. However, since it can be confusing to try to learn both methods intermixed, this text presents third-angle projection throughout. When you are comfortable with creating third-angle projection drawings, revisit this section. You will see that the two drawing methods are very similar, and you should be able to extend the same skills to either type of drawing.

Third-Angle Projection

Figure 6.22a shows the concept of third-angle orthographic projection. To avoid misunderstanding, international *projection symbols* have been developed to distinguish between first-angle and third-angle projections on drawings. The symbol in Figure 6.22b shows two views of a truncated cone. You can examine the arrangement of the views in the symbol to determine whether first- or third-angle projection was used. On international drawings you should be sure to include this symbol.

To understand the two systems, think of the vertical and horizontal planes of projection, shown in Figure 6.22a, as indefinite in extent and intersecting at 90° with each other; the four angles produced are called the first, second, third, and fourth angles (similar to naming quadrants on a graph.) If the object to be drawn is placed below the horizontal plane and behind the vertical plane, as in the glass box you saw earlier, the object is said to be in the third angle. In third-angle projection, the views are produced as if the observer is outside, looking in.

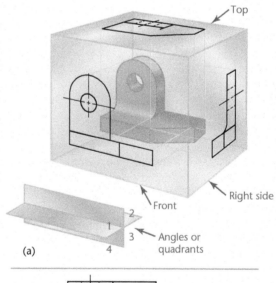

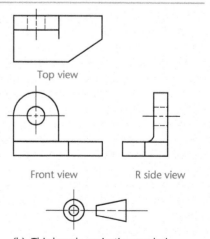

(b) Third-angle projection symbol

6.22 Third-Angle Projection

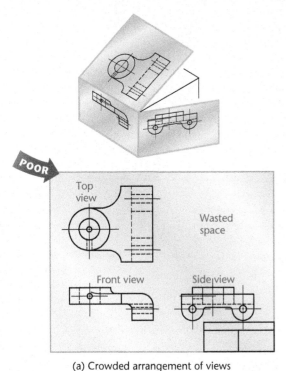

(a) Crowded arrangement of views

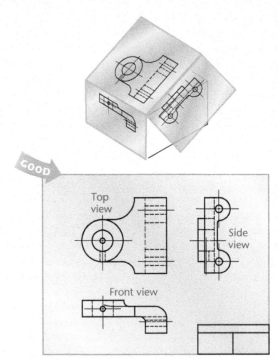

(b) Approved alternative arrangement of views

6.23   Position of Side View

Alternative Arrangements for Third-Angle Projection

Sometimes, drawing three views using the conventional arrangement wastes space. (For example, see the wide, flat object in Figure 6.23a.) Using the space on the paper efficiently may prevent the need to use a reduced scale.

For these cases, there is another acceptable arrangement of third-angle projection views. Imagine unfolding the glass box as shown in Figure 6.23b. The views are arranged differently, with the right-side view aligned with the top view. These views are still using third-angle projection.

In this case, the profile (side view) is hinged to the horizontal plane (top view) instead of to the frontal plane (front view) so that the side view is beside the top view when unfolded (Figure 6.23b). Notice that the side view is rotated 90° from the orientation shown in the side view in Figure 6.23a in this placement. Now you can directly project the depth dimension from the top view into the side view.

If necessary, you may place the side view horizontally across from the bottom view (so the profile plane is hinged to the bottom plane of the projection).

Similarly, the rear view may be placed directly above the top view or under the bottom view. In this case, the rear plane is considered hinged to the horizontal or bottom plane and rotated to coincide with the frontal plane.

First-Angle Projection

If the object is placed above the horizontal plane and in front of the vertical plane, the object is in the first angle. In first-angle projection the observer looks through the object to the planes of projection. The right-side view is still obtained by looking toward the right side of the object, the front by looking toward the front, and the top by looking down toward the top; but the views are projected from the object onto a plane behind the object in each case.

The biggest difference between third-angle projection and first-angle projection is how the planes of the glass box are unfolded, as shown in Figure 6.24. In first-angle projection, the right-side view is to the left of the front view, and the top view is below the front view, as shown.

You should understand the difference between the two systems and know the symbol that is placed on drawings to indicate which has been used. Keep in mind that you will use third-angle projection throughout this book.

Projection System Drawing Symbol

The symbol shown in Figure 6.25 is used on drawings to indicate which system of projection is used. Whenever drawings will be used internationally, you should include this symbol in the title block area.

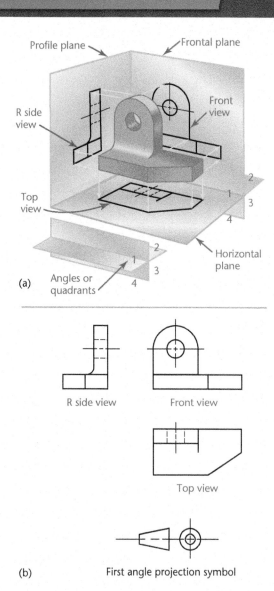

Profile plane

Frontal plane

R side view

Front view

Top view

Horizontal plane

2
1
3
4

2
1
3
4

(a)   Angles or quadrants

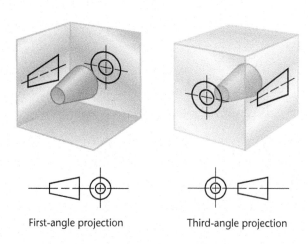

R side view

Front view

Top view

(b)   First angle projection symbol

6.24   First-Angle Projection. *An object that is above the horizontal plane and in front of the vertical plane is in the first angle. An observer looks through the object to the planes of projection.*

First-angle projection   Third-angle projection

6.25   Drawing Symbols for First- and Third-Angle Projection

Hidden Lines

One advantage of orthographic views over photographs is that each view can show the entire object from that viewing direction. A photograph shows only the visible surface of an object, but an orthographic view shows the object all the way through, as if it were transparent.

Thick, dark lines represent features of the object that are directly visible. Dashed lines represent features that would be hidden behind other surfaces.

Figure 6.26 shows a part that has internal features. When a 3D view of this model is rendered using a transparent material, as shown in Figure 6.27, you can see the internal features. Figure 6.28 shows this part from the front as it would be oriented in an orthographic drawing. The features that are hidden from view are shown in orthographic views using the hidden line pattern as shown in Figure 6.29.

Whenever possible, choose views that show features with visible lines. Use hidden lines where they are needed to make the drawing clear.

Some practices for representing intersections of hidden lines with other lines may be difficult to follow when using CAD. In CAD, adjust the line patterns so that the hidden lines in your drawing have the best appearance possible.

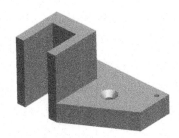

6.26   Shaded Model with Hidden Features

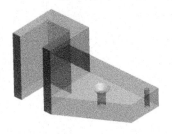

6.27   Transparent Model Showing Hidden Features

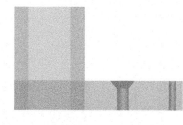

6.28   Front View of Transparent Model

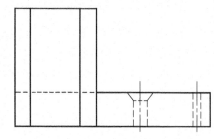

6.29   Front View Projection

Centerlines

The centerline pattern is used to:

- Show the axis of symmetry for a feature or part.
- Indicate a path of motion.
- Show the location for bolt-hole circles and other circular patterns.

The centerline pattern is composed of three dashes: one long dash on each end with a short dash in the middle. In the drawing, centerlines are shown thin and black. Because a centerline is not an actual part of the object, it extends beyond the symmetrical feature as shown in Figure 6.30.

The most common shape that needs a centerline is a cylindrical hole. Figure 6.30b shows centerlines in a drawing. In the circular view of a hole, the centerline should form a cross to mark the center location. When a feature is too small for the centerline pattern to be shown with the long-short-long dash pattern, it is acceptable to use a straight line. You will learn more about showing hidden lines and centerlines in the technique sections.

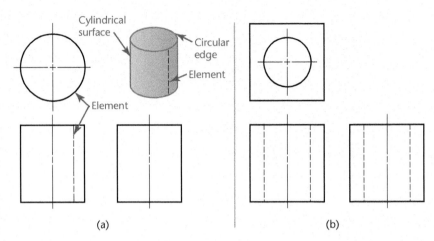

6.30   Cylindrical Surfaces and Holes

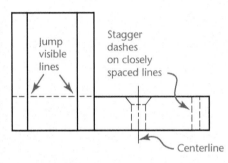

6.31   Hidden Lines

6.1 HIDDEN LINE TECHNIQUE

You can save time and reduce clutter by leaving out hidden lines that aren't necessary as long as you are certain that the remaining lines describe the object clearly and completely. If you omit unnecessary hidden lines, add a note to let the reader know that the lines were left out intentionally and that it is not an error in the drawing.

Sketch hidden lines by eye, using thin dark dashes about 5 mm long and spaced about 1 mm apart. Hidden lines should be as dark as other lines in the drawing, but should be thin.

When hidden lines intersect each other in the drawing, their dashes should meet. In general, hidden lines should intersect neatly with visible lines at the edge of an object. Leave a gap when a hidden line aligns with a visible line, so that the visible line's length remains clear.

6.2 PRECEDENCE OF LINES

Visible lines, hidden lines, and centerlines often coincide on a drawing. There are rules for deciding which line to show. A visible line always takes precedence over and covers up a centerline or a hidden line when they coincide in a view, as shown at *A* and *B* in Figure 6.32. A hidden line takes precedence over a centerline, as shown at *C*. At *A* the ends of the centerline are shown separated from the view by short gaps, but the centerline is usually left off entirely. Figure 6.33 shows examples of correct and incorrect hidden lines.

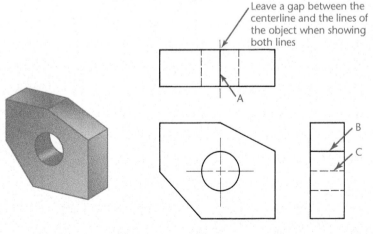

6.32   Precedence of Lines

Correct and Incorrect Practices for Hidden Lines

Make a hidden line join a visible line, except when it causes the visible line to extend too far, as shown here.

Leave a gap whenever a hidden line is a continuation of a visible line.

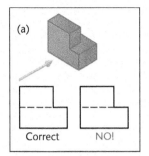

When two or three hidden lines meet at a point, join the dashes, as shown for the bottom of this drilled hole.

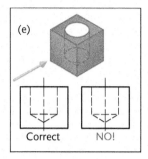

Make hidden lines intersect at L and T corners.

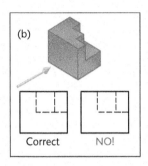

The same rule of joining the dashes when two or three hidden lines meet at a point applies for the top of this countersunk hole.

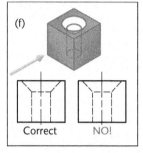

Make a hidden line "jump" a visible line when possible.

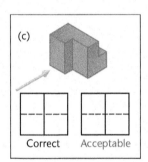

Hidden lines should not join visible lines when this makes the visible line extend too far

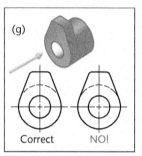

Draw parallel hidden lines so that the dashes are staggered, as in bricklaying.

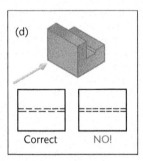

Draw hidden arcs with the arc joining the centerline, as in upper example. There should not be a gap between the arc and the centerline, as in the lower example with the straightaway joining the centerline.

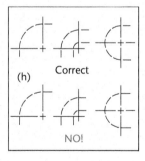

6.33 Correct and Incorrect Practices for Hidden Lines

TIP

When sketching, accent the beginning and end of each dash by pressing down on the pencil. Make hidden lines as tidy as you can so they are easy to interpret. Be sure to make hidden line dashes longer than gaps so they clearly represent lines. Your CAD system may have limitations that make it impractical to comply with these requirements. If so, strive for hidden lines that are clear and easy to interpret.

6.3 CENTERLINES

Centerlines (symbol: ℄) are used to indicate symmetrical axes of objects or features, bolt circles, and paths of motion as shown in Figure 6.34. Centerlines are useful in dimensioning. They are not needed on unimportant rounded or filleted corners or on other shapes that are self-locating.

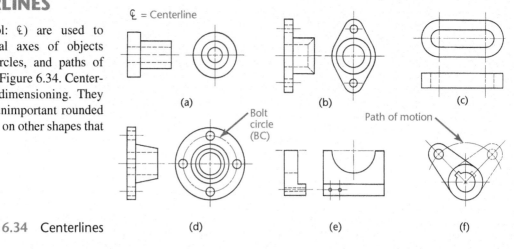

℄ = Centerline

(a)   (b)   (c)

Bolt circle (BC)   Path of motion

6.34   Centerlines

(d)   (e)   (f)

6.4 LAYING OUT A DRAWING

If you use 2D CAD, you can move the views later, keeping them in alignment, so you do not need to give as much attention to placement of the views in the beginning as if you were laying them out by hand. When using 3D CAD to generate views, you should still plan how the sheet will show the information clearly and select the necessary views to best represent the shape of the part. Although you can easily change the scale of a CAD drawing after it is created, placing the dimensions and views on the sheet requires some planning. If you consider the purpose of the drawing, the planned scale, and the space that will be required for adding notes and dimensions, you will save the time of having to rearrange their placement later.

HAND LAYOUT OF A METRIC THREE-VIEW DRAWING

1 Determine space desired between the front and right-side views (C), say 32 mm. Add this space to the sum of the length of the views that will be aligned along the long edge of the sheet (108 + 58 + 32 = 198). To set equal distances to the paper edge, subtract this total from the sheet width, then divide the remaining number by two (280 − 198 = 82, and 82 ÷ 2 = 41). Do the same for the views to be aligned along the short side of the paper, selecting a desired space between the views. Space D need not match C. Remember to leave space for dimensions as you plan your sheet.

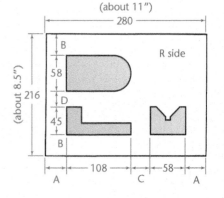

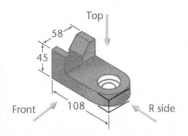

2 Set off vertical and horizontal spacing measurements with light tick marks along the edge of the sheet as shown. Locate centerlines from these spacing marks, and construct arcs and circles.

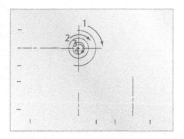

3 Construct the views, drawing horizontal, vertical, and then inclined construction lines in the order shown above.

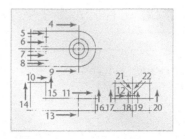

4 Add hidden lines and darken final lines.

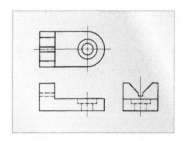

6.5 DEVELOPING VIEWS FROM 3D MODELS

For most 3D software, creating orthographic views from the model is simple. Two basic steps are required: selecting a location on the page where the orthographic view will be placed and selecting the viewing direction. Adding more orthographic views is even easier, as they may be automatically placed in relation to the initial view.

Even if your CAD package does not automate the creation of orthographic drawing views to this extent, creating orthographic views directly from the 3D model still offers an advantage. Even people trained in orthographic projection of views have difficulty visualizing complex orthographic views correctly all the time—and the views can be time-consuming to create. Using the 3D object to develop the views helps get the projection right.

When you are selecting which views to show, keep in mind the same practices that make a good sketch:

- Show the shape of the object clearly in the front view, which is placed in a central location on the drawing sheet (see Figure 6.35).
- For objects with uniform thickness, use a single view and specify the thickness in a note (see Figure 6.36).
- For complicated parts, show at least two drawing views in the standard arrangement to make it easy to interpret the views. The reader is not as familiar with the

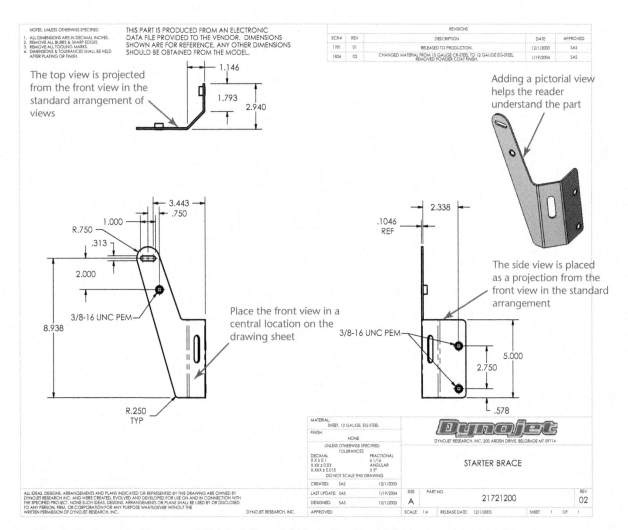

6.35 Orthographic Views and Shaded Pictorial View Generated from the Part Model *(Courtesy of Dynojet Research, Inc.)*

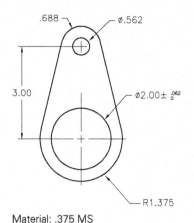

Material: .375 MS

6.36 *This object is fully defined with a single view and a note. (Courtesy of Implemax Equipment Co., Inc.)*

shape of the part as you are. Place additional views on a second drawing sheet if necessary; it is preferred to have all the views on one sheet if they are clear. When multiple sheets are used, indicate this in the title block with a note such as "Sheet 1 of 3."

- Make the drawing clear and easy to interpret. Use different line thicknesses to make the object stand out clearly.
- Show the object at a size so that its features are visible, or include an enlarged detail view at a larger scale (see Figure 6.37).
- Except for enlarged details, show all views at the same scale.
- Clearly note the difference in scale for enlarged detail views.
- Show only as many views as necessary. Do not add unnecessary views. They confuse the reader. At times additional views are needed for clear placement of dimensions. You can simplify views by leaving out hidden lines that do not add to the interpretation of the view. If you leave out lines, it is a good idea to label the view as a partial view.

Placing the Views

As you plan the views to be included, allow for plenty of white space on the drawing. Leave room for dimensions between the views, and separate the views from one another with white space. The space between drawing views does not have to be equal, yet the views should appear to be related. Do not space them too far apart. If there is not enough white space in your drawing, or if the views are too small to see the details clearly, consider using a larger sheet size (see Figure 6.38).

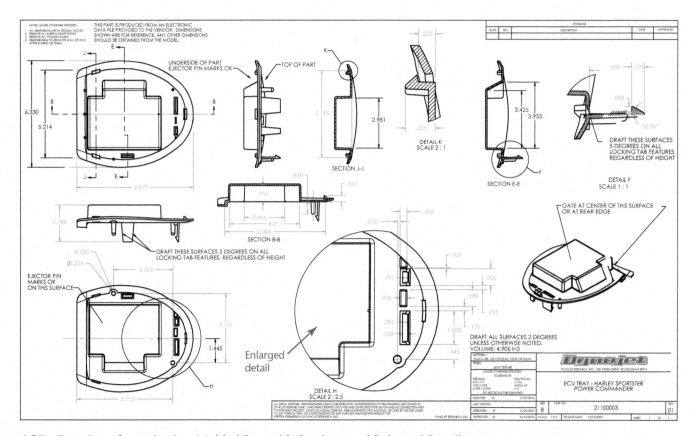

6.37   Drawing of an Injection-Molded Part with Sections and Enlarged Details *(Courtesy of Dynojet Research, Inc.)*

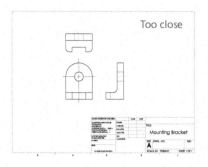
Too close

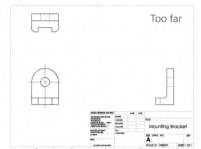
Too far

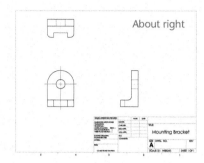
About right

6.38 Spacing Drawing Views

Isometric Views

Including isometric views in detail drawings helps others easily interpret the drawing. Isometric views are often shown in the upper right-hand area of the drawing, as there is often room there. The isometric view does not have to be at the same scale as the other views. Often, a smaller scale is just as clear and fits on the sheet better. It is not necessary to indicate the scale of the isometric view on the drawing. Figure 6.39 shows an example of an isometric view added to a part drawing. Remember that hidden lines are not usually shown in isometric views. Most modern CAD packages have preset isometric viewing directions that you can select for the model.

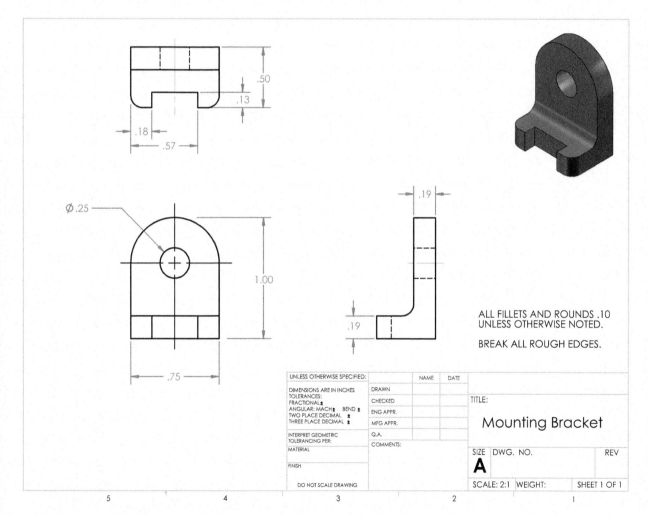

6.39 *The isometric view provides an easy visual reference for the part described in the orthographic views.*

6.6 VISUALIZATION

Along with having an understanding of the system for projecting views, you must be able interpret multiple views to picture the object that they show. In addition to being an indispensable skill to help you capture and communicate your ideas, technical sketching is also a way for others to present their ideas to you.

Even experienced engineers, technicians, and designers can't always look at a multiview sketch and instantly visualize the object represented. You will learn to study the sketch and interpret the lines in a logical way to piece together a clear idea of the whole. This process is sometimes called *visualization*.

Surfaces, Edges, and Corners

To effectively create and interpret multiview projections, you have to consider the elements that make up most solids. *Surfaces* form the boundaries of solid objects. A *plane* (flat) surface may be bounded by straight lines, curves, or a combination of the two.

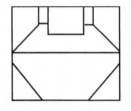
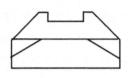
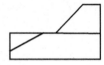
6.7 VIEWS OF SURFACES

A plane surface that is perpendicular to a plane of projection appears on edge as a straight line (Figure 6.41a). If it is parallel to the plane of projection, it appears true size (Figure 6.41b). If it is angled to the plane of projection, it appears foreshortened or smaller than its actual size (Figure 6.41c). A plane surface always projects either on edge (appearing as a single line) or as a surface (showing its characteristic shape) in any view. It can appear foreshortened, but it can never appear larger than its true size in any view.

There are terms used for describing a surface's orientation to the plane of projection. The three orientations that a plane surface can have to the plane of projection are *normal*, *inclined*, and *oblique*. Understanding these terms will help you picture and describe objects.

TIP
Using Numbers to Identify Vertices

Add lightly drawn numbers to your sketches to keep track of each vertex on the surface you are considering. Each vertex is unique on the part, so each numbered vertex will appear only once in each view. Sometimes two vertices will line up one behind the other, as in Figure 6.41a. When this happens you can list them in order with the closest first, as in 1, 2, or sometimes it is useful to put numbers for the closest visible vertex outside the shape, and the farthest hidden vertex inside the shape outline.

EV = Edge view
TS = True size
FS = Foreshortened

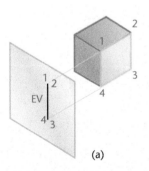
(a)

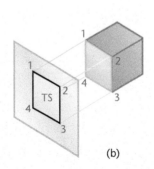
(b)

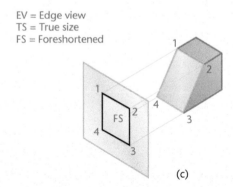
(c)

6.41   Projections of Surfaces

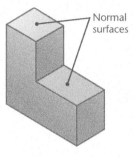

6.42   Normal Surfaces

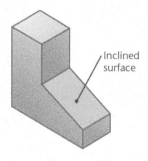

6.43   Inclined Surface

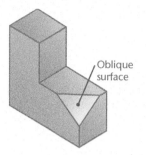

6.44   Oblique Surface

6.8 NORMAL SURFACES

A *normal surface* is parallel to a plane of projection. It appears true size and true shape on the plane to which it is parallel, and it appears as a true-length vertical or a horizontal line on adjacent planes of projection. Figure 6.42 shows an illustration of normal surfaces.

6.9 INCLINED SURFACES

An *inclined surface* is perpendicular to one plane of projection but inclined (or tipped) to adjacent planes. An inclined surface projects on edge on the plane to which it is perpendicular. It appears foreshortened on planes to which it is inclined. An inclined surface is shown in Figure 6.43. The degree of foreshortening is proportional to the inclination. Although the surface may not appear true size in any view, it will have the same characteristic shape and the same number of edges in the views in which you see its shape.

6.10 OBLIQUE SURFACES

An *oblique surface* is tipped to all principal planes of projection. Because it is not perpendicular to any projection plane, it cannot appear on edge in any standard view. Because it is not parallel to any projection plane, it cannot appear true size in any standard view. An oblique surface always appears as a foreshortened surface in all three standard views. Figures 6.44 and 6.45 show oblique surfaces.

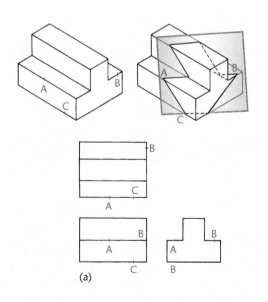

(a)

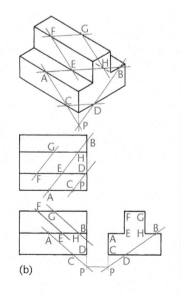

(b)

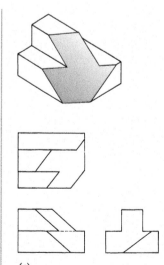

(c)

6.45   Adding an Oblique Surface to an Isometric Sketch

6.11 EDGES

The intersection of two plane surfaces of an object produces an *edge*, which shows as a straight line in the drawing. An edge is common to two surfaces, forming a boundary for each. If an edge is perpendicular to a plane of projection, it appears as a point; otherwise it appears as a line. If it is parallel to the plane of projection, it shows true length. If it is not parallel, it appears foreshortened. A straight line always projects as a straight line or as a point. The terms *normal, inclined,* and *oblique* describe the relationship of an edge to a plane of projection.

6.12 NORMAL EDGES

A *normal edge* is a line perpendicular to a plane of projection. It appears as a point on that plane of projection and as a true-length line on adjacent planes of projection (Figure 6.46).

6.13 INCLINED EDGES

An *inclined edge* is parallel to one plane of projection but inclined to adjacent planes. It appears as a true-length line on the plane to which it is parallel and as a foreshortened line on adjacent planes. The true-length view of an inclined line always appears as an angled line, but the foreshortened views appear as either vertical or horizontal lines (Figure 6.47).

6.14 OBLIQUE EDGES

An *oblique edge* is tipped to all planes of projection. Because it is not perpendicular to any projection plane, it cannot appear as a point in any standard view. Because it is not parallel to any projection plane, it cannot appear true length in any standard view. An oblique edge appears foreshortened and as an angled line in every view (Figure 6.48).

6.15 PARALLEL EDGES

When edges are parallel to one another on the object, they will appear as parallel lines in every view, unless they align one behind the other. This information can be useful when you are laying out a drawing, especially if it has a complex inclined or

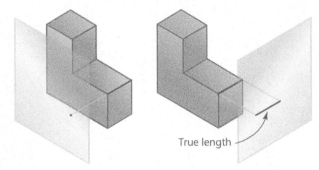

True length

6.46   Projections of a Normal Edge

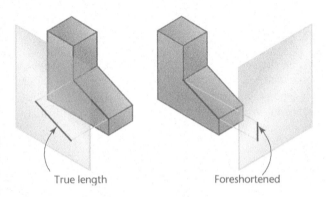

True length   Foreshortened

6.47   Projections of an Inclined Edge

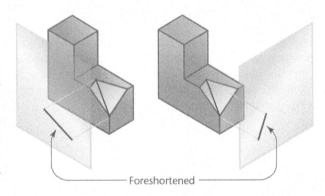

Foreshortened

6.48   Projections of an Oblique Edge

oblique surface that has parallel edges. Figure 6.49 shows an example of parallel lines in drawing views.

(a) Parallel planes intersected by another plane

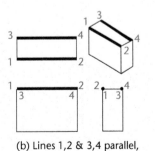

(b) Lines 1,2 & 3,4 parallel, and parallel to horizontal plane

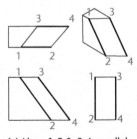

(c) Lines 1,2 & 3,4 parallel, and parallel to frontal plane

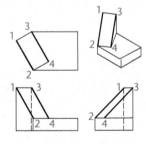

(d) Lines 1,2 & 3,4 parallel, and oblique to all planes

6.49   Parallel Lines

6.16 ANGLES

If an angle is in a normal plane (a plane parallel to a plane of projection), it will show true size on the plane of projection to which it is parallel (Figure 6.50). If an angle is in an inclined plane, it may be projected either larger or smaller than the true angle, depending on its position. The 45° angle is shown oversize in the front view in Figure 6.50b, and the 60° angle is shown undersize in both views in Figure 6.50c.

A 90° angle will project as true size, even if it is in an inclined plane, provided that one leg of it is a normal line.

In Figure 6.50d, the 60° angle is projected oversize, and the 30° angle is projected undersize. Try this on your own using a 30° or 60° triangle as a model, or even the 90° corner of a sheet of paper. Tilt the triangle or paper to look at an oblique view.

6.50   Angles

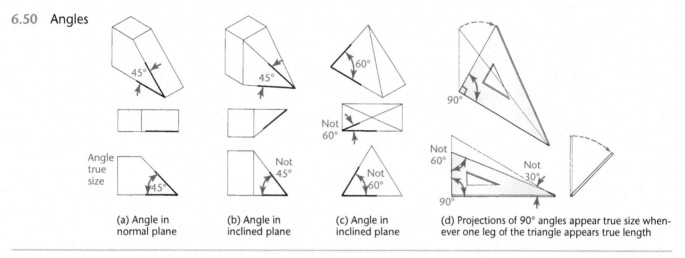

(a) Angle in normal plane

(b) Angle in inclined plane

(c) Angle in inclined plane

(d) Projections of 90° angles appear true size whenever one leg of the triangle appears true length

6.17 VERTICES

A corner, or *point*, is the common intersection of three or more surfaces, which is called a *vertex* on the part. A point appears as a point in every view. An example of a point on an object is shown in Figure 6.51.

6.18 INTERPRETING POINTS

A point located in a sketch can represent two things:

- A vertex
- The point view of an edge (two vertices lined up one directly behind the other)

6.51   Views of a Point

6.19 INTERPRETING LINES

A straight visible or hidden line in a drawing or sketch has three possible meanings, as shown in Figure 6.52:

- An edge (intersection) between two surfaces
- The edge view of a surface
- The limiting element of a curved surface

Because no shading is used on orthographic views, you must examine all the views to determine the meaning of the lines. If you were to look at only the front and top views in Figure 6.52, you might believe line *AB* is the edge view of a flat surface. From the right-side view, you can see that there is a curved surface on top of the object.

If you look at only the front and side views, you might believe the vertical line *CD* is the edge view of a plane surface. The top view reveals that the line actually represents the intersection of an inclined surface.

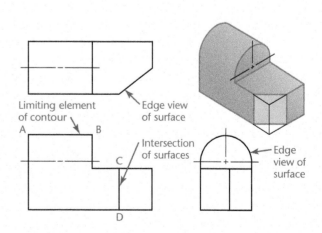

6.52   Interpreting Lines

6.20 SIMILAR SHAPES OF SURFACES

If a flat surface is viewed from several different positions, each view will show the same number of sides and a similar shape. This consistency of shapes is useful in analyzing views. For example, the L-shaped surface shown in Figure 6.53 appears L-shaped in every view in which it does not appear as a line. A surface will have the same number of sides and vertices and the same characteristic shape whenever it appears as a surface. Note how the U-shaped, hexagonal, and T-shaped surfaces in Figure 6.54 are recognizable in different views.

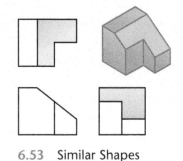

6.53   Similar Shapes

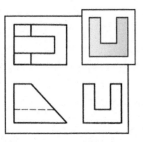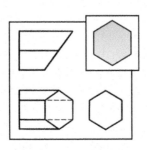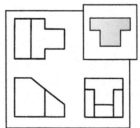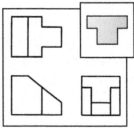

6.54   Similar Shapes

6.21 INTERPRETING VIEWS

One method of interpreting sketches is to reverse the mental process used in projecting them. The views of an angle bracket are shown in Figure 6.55a.

The front view (Figure 6.55b) shows the object's L-shape, its height, and its width. The meanings of the hidden lines and centerlines are not yet clear, and you do not know the object's depth.

The top view (Figure 6.55c) shows the depth and width of the object. It also makes it clear that the horizontal feature is rounded at the right end and has a round hole. A hidden line at the left end indicates some kind of slot.

The right-side view (Figure 6.55d) shows the height and depth of the object. It reveals that the left end of the object has rounded corners at the top and clarifies that the hidden line in the front view represents an open-end slot in a vertical position.

Each view provides certain definite information about the shape of the object, and all are necessary to visualize it completely.

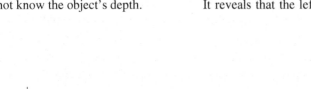

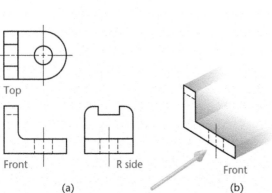

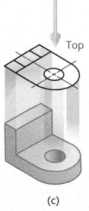

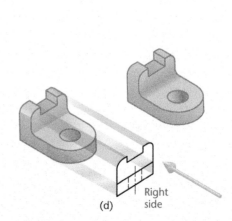

(a)   (b)   (c)   (d)

6.55   Visualizing from Given Views

READING A DRAWING

1 Visualize the object shown by the three views at left. Because no lines are curved, the object must be made up of plane surfaces.

The shaded surface in the top view is a six-sided L-shape. Because you do not see its shape in the front view—and every surface appears either as its shape or as a line—it must be showing on edge as a line in the front view. The indicated line in the front view also projects to line up with the vertices of the L-shaped surface.

Because we see its shape in the top view and because it is an angled line in the front view, it must be an inclined surface on the object. This means it will show its foreshortened shape in the side view as well, appearing L-shaped and six-sided. The L-shaped surface in the right-side view must be the same surface that was shaded in the top view.

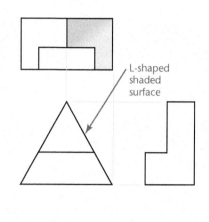

L-shaped shaded surface

2 The front view shows the top portion as a triangular surface, but no triangular shapes appear in either the top or the side view. The triangular surface must appear as a line in the top view and in the side view.

Sketch projection lines from the vertices of the surface where you see its shape. The same surface in the other views must line up along the projection lines. In the side view, it must be the line indicated. That can help you to identify it as the middle horizontal line in the top view.

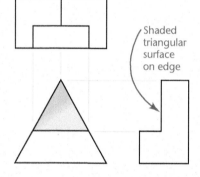

Shaded triangular surface on edge

3 The trapezoidal surface shaded in the front view is easy to identify, but there are no trapezoids in the top and side views. Again, the surface must be on edge in the adjacent views.

4 On your own, identify the remaining surfaces using the same reasoning. Which surfaces are inclined, and which are normal? Are there any oblique surfaces?

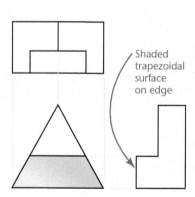

Shaded trapezoidal surface on edge

If you are still having trouble visualizing the object, try picturing the views as describing those portions of a block that will be cut away, as illustrated below.

6.22 MODELS

One of the best aids to visualization is an actual model of the object. Models don't necessarily need to be made accurately or to scale. They may be made of any convenient material, such as modeling clay, soap, wood, wire, or Styrofoam, or any material that can easily be shaped, carved, or cut. Some examples of soap models are shown in Figure 6.56.

Rules for Visualizing from a Drawing: Putting It All Together

Reading a multiview drawing is like unraveling a puzzle. When you interpret a drawing, keep these things in mind:

- The closest surface to your view must have at least one edge showing as a visible line.
- A plane surface has a similar shape in any view or appears on edge as a straight line.
- Lines of the drawing represent either an intersection between two surfaces, a surface perpendicular to your view that appears "on edge," or the limiting element of a curved surface.
- No two adjacent areas divided by a visible line in an orthographic view can be the same plane in the actual object. Areas not adjacent in a view may lie in the same plane on the object.
- If a line appears hidden, a closer surface is hiding it.
- Your interpretation must account for all the lines of the drawing. Every line has a meaning.

TIP

Making a Model

Try making a soap or clay model from projected views:

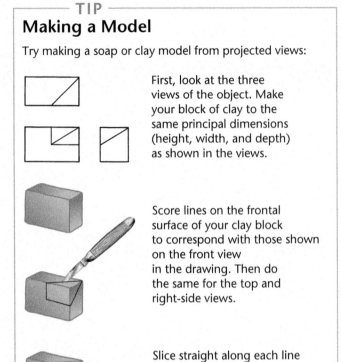

First, look at the three views of the object. Make your block of clay to the same principal dimensions (height, width, and depth) as shown in the views.

Score lines on the frontal surface of your clay block to correspond with those shown on the front view in the drawing. Then do the same for the top and right-side views.

Slice straight along each line scored on the clay block to get a 3D model that represents the projected views.

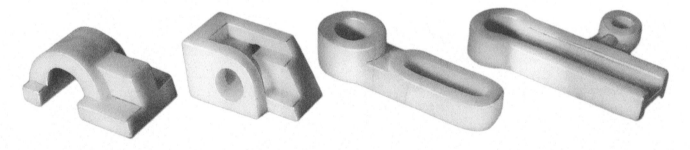

6.56   Soap Models

6.23 PROJECTING A THIRD VIEW

Ordinarily, when you are designing a product or system, you have a good mental picture of what it will look like from different directions. However, skill in projecting a third view can be useful for two reasons. First, views must be shown in alignment in the drawing and projected correctly. Second, practice in projecting a third view from two given views is an excellent way to develop your visual abilities.

Numbering the vertices on the object makes projecting a third view easy. Points that you number on the drawing represent points on the object where three surfaces come together to form a vertex (and sometimes a point on a contour or the center of a curve).

Once you have located a point in two drawing views, its location in the third view is known. In other words, if a point is located in the front and top view, its location in the side view is a matter of projecting the height of the point in the glass box from the front view and the depth of the point in the glass box from the top view.

To number the points or vertices on the object and show those numbers in different views, you need to be able to identify surfaces on the object. Then, project (or find) the points in each new view, surface by surface. You can use what you know about edges and surfaces to identify surfaces on the object when you draw views. This will help you interpret drawings created by others as well as project your own drawings correctly.

MANUALLY PROJECTING A THIRD VIEW

The figure below is a pictorial drawing of an object to be shown in three views. It has numbers identifying each corner (vertex) and letters identifying some of the major surfaces. You are given the top and front view. You will use point numbers to project the side view.

1 To number points effectively, first identify surfaces and interpret the views that are given. Start by labeling visible surfaces whose shapes are easy to identify in one view. Then, locate the same surface in the adjacent view. (The surfaces on the pictorial object have been labeled to make it easier.)

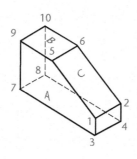

2 Surface A in the front view is a normal surface. It will appear as a horizontal line in the top view. The two rectangular surfaces B and C in the top view are a normal surface and an inclined surface. They will show as a horizontal line and an inclined line in the front view, respectively.

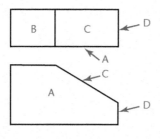

3 After identifying the surfaces, label the vertices of a surface that has an easily recognized shape, in this case, surface A.

Label its vertices with numbers at each corner as shown. If a point is directly visible in the view, place the number outside the corner.

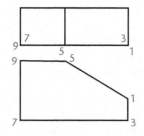

If the point is not directly visible in that view, place the numeral inside the corner. Using the same numbers to identify the same points in different views will help you project known points in two views to unknown positions in a third view.

4 Continue, surface by surface, until you have numbered all the vertices in the given views as shown. Do not use two different numbers for the same vertex.

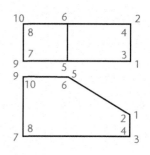

5 Try to visualize the right-side view you will create. Then, construct the right-side view point by point, using very light lines. Locate point 1 in the side view by drawing a light horizontal projection line from point 1 in the front view. Use the edge view of surface A in the top view as a reference plane to transfer the depth location for point 1 to the side view as shown.

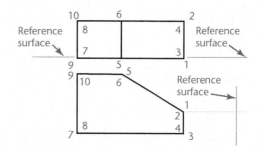

6 Project points 2, 3, and 4 in a similar way to complete the vertical end surface of the object.

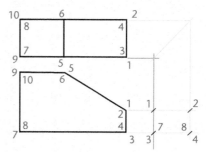

7 Project the remaining points using the same method, proceeding surface by surface.

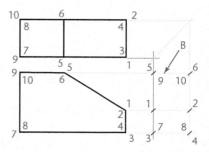

(continued)

STEP by STEP

MANUALLY PROJECTING A THIRD VIEW (CONT.)

8 Use the points that you have projected into the side view to draw the surfaces of the object as in this example.

If surface A extended between points 1-3-7-9-5 in the front view where you can see its shape clearly, it will extend between those same points in every other view.

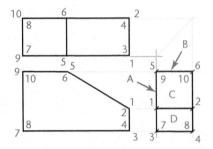

When you connect these points in the side view, they form a vertical line.

This makes sense, because A is a normal surface. As is the rule with normal surfaces, you will see its shape in one standard view (the front in this case) and it will appear as a horizontal or vertical line in the other views.

Continue connecting vertices to define the surfaces on the object, to complete the third view.

9 Inspect your drawing to see if all the surfaces are shown, and darken the final lines.

Consider the visibility of surfaces. Surfaces that are hidden behind other surfaces should be shown with hidden lines.

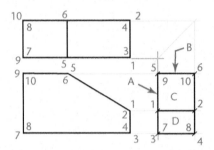

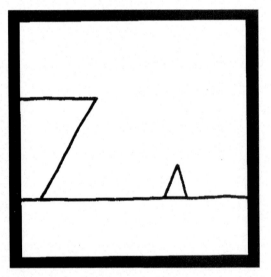

Ship Arriving Too Late to Save Drowning Witch. *This well-known drawing by artist Roger Price is an example of how a single orthographic view can be difficult to interpret. (Ship Arriving Too Late to Save Drowning Witch excerpted from The Ultimate Droodles Compendium by Roger Price ©2019 by Tallfellow Press. Used by permission. All rights reserved.)*

6.24 BECOMING A 3D VISUALIZER

To the untrained person, orthographic projections might not convey the idea of a 3D shape, but with some practice you should now be able to look at projected front, top, and right-side views and envision that they represent the width, depth, and height of an object. Understanding how points, lines, and surfaces can be interpreted and how normal, inclined, or oblique surfaces appear from different views helps you interpret orthographic views to form a mental image of the object.

Understanding how orthographic views represent an object gives you the power to start capturing your own concepts on paper in a way that others can interpret. Keep in mind the idea of an unfolded "glass box" to explain the arrangement of views. This clarifies how the views relate to one another and why you can transfer certain dimensions from adjacent views. Using standard practices to represent hidden lines and centerlines helps you further define surfaces, features, and paths of motion.

The better you understand the foundation concepts of projected views, the more fluent you will be in the language of 3D representation and the skill of spatial thinking, regardless of whether you sketch by hand or use CAD.

Key to Figure 6.40
Normal Surfaces: A, D, E, H
Inclined Surfaces: B, C
Oblique Surface: F

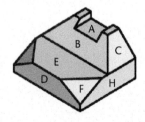

USING A MITER LINE

Given two completed views, you can use a miter line to transfer the depths and draw the side view of the object shown at right.

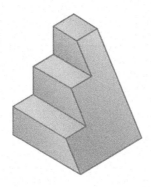

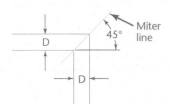

1 Locate the miter line a convenient distance away from the object to produce the desired spacing between views.

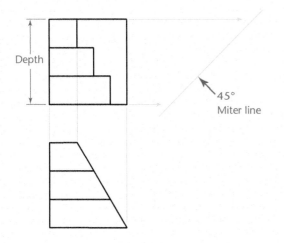

2 Sketch light lines projecting depth locations for points to the miter line and then down into the side view as shown.

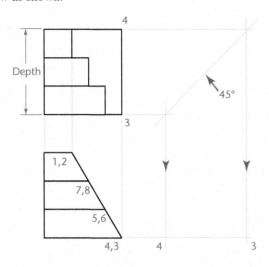

3 Project the remaining points.

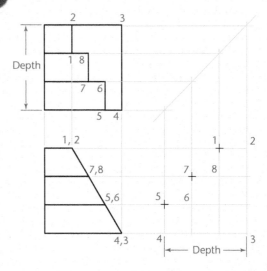

4 Draw the view by locating each vertex of the surface on the projection line and across the miter line.

To move the right-side view to the right or left, move the top view upward or downward by moving the miter line closer to or farther from the view. You don't need to draw continuous lines between the top and side views via the miter line. Instead, make short dashes across the miter line and project from these. The 45° miter-line method is also convenient for transferring a large number of points, as when plotting a curve.

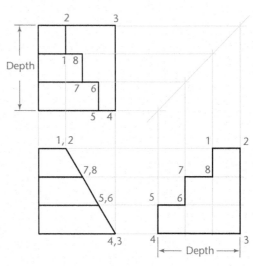

PORTFOLIO

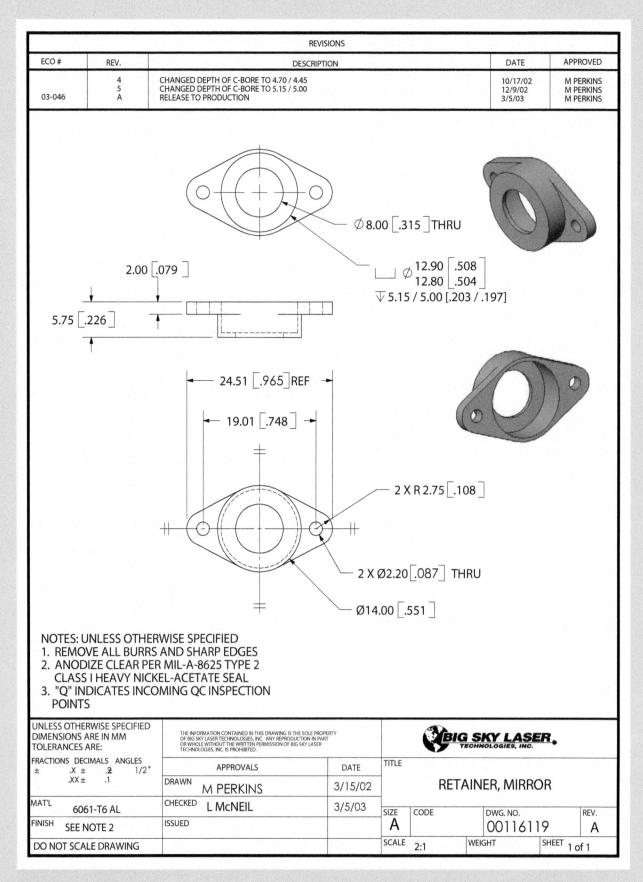

REVISIONS					
ECO #	REV.	DESCRIPTION		DATE	APPROVED
03-046	4	CHANGED DEPTH OF C-BORE TO 4.70 / 4.45		10/17/02	M PERKINS
	5	CHANGED DEPTH OF C-BORE TO 5.15 / 5.00		12/9/02	M PERKINS
	A	RELEASE TO PRODUCTION		3/5/03	M PERKINS

Ø 8.00 [.315] THRU

⌴ Ø 12.90 [.508]
      12.80 [.504]
▽ 5.15 / 5.00 [.203 / .197]

2.00 [.079]

5.75 [.226]

24.51 [.965] REF

19.01 [.748]

2 X R 2.75 [.108]

2 X Ø2.20 [.087] THRU

Ø14.00 [.551]

NOTES: UNLESS OTHERWISE SPECIFIED
1. REMOVE ALL BURRS AND SHARP EDGES
2. ANODIZE CLEAR PER MIL-A-8625 TYPE 2
   CLASS I HEAVY NICKEL-ACETATE SEAL
3. "Q" INDICATES INCOMING QC INSPECTION
   POINTS

UNLESS OTHERWISE SPECIFIED
DIMENSIONS ARE IN MM
TOLERANCES ARE:

FRACTIONS DECIMALS ANGLES
±   .X ±   .2   1/2°
         .XX ±   .1

THE INFORMATION CONTAINED IN THIS DRAWING IS THE SOLE PROPERTY OF BIG SKY LASER TECHNOLOGIES, INC. ANY REPRODUCTION IN PART OR WHOLE WITHOUT THE WRITTEN PERMISSION OF BIG SKY LASER TECHNOLOGIES, INC. IS PROHIBITED.

BIG SKY LASER, TECHNOLOGIES, INC.

APPROVALS	DATE	TITLE
DRAWN M PERKINS	3/15/02	RETAINER, MIRROR
CHECKED L McNEIL	3/5/03	
ISSUED		

MAT'L   6061-T6 AL

FINISH   SEE NOTE 2

DO NOT SCALE DRAWING

SIZE	CODE	DWG. NO.	REV.
A		00116119	A
SCALE 2:1	WEIGHT	SHEET 1 of 1	

Top, Front, and Bottom Views of a Mirror Retainer. *The bottom view is shown for ease of dimensioning.*
(Courtesy of Big Sky Laser.)

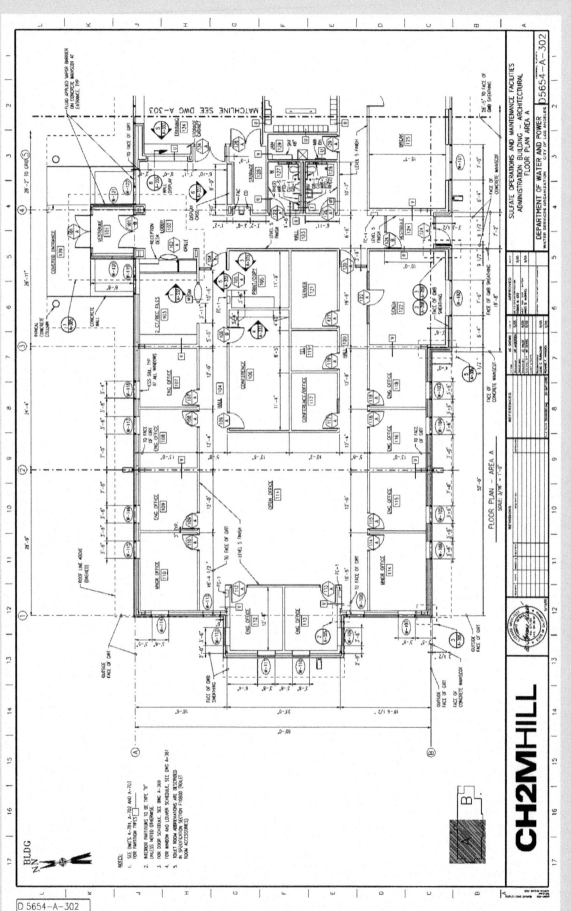

Architectural floor plans show the building as though the roof were cut off and the top orthographic view was projected.
(Courtesy of CH2M HILL.)

KEY WORDS

Depth

Edge

First-Angle Projection

Folding Lines

Frontal Plane

Glass Box

Height

Horizontal Plane

Inclined Edge

Inclined Surface

Multiview Projection

Necessary Views

Normal Edge

Normal Surface

Oblique Edge

Oblique Surface

Orthographic

Plane

Plane of Projection

Point

Principal Views

Profile Plane

Projection Symbols

Surfaces

Third-Angle Projection

Three Regular Views

Width

CHAPTER SUMMARY

- Orthographic drawings are the result of projecting the image of a 3D object onto one of six standard planes of projection. The six standard views are often thought of as an unfolded glass box. The arrangement of the views in relation to one another is important. Views must line up with adjacent views, so that any point in one view projects to line up with that same point in the adjacent view. The standard arrangement of views shows the top, front, and right side of the object.

- Visualization is an important skill. You can build your visual abilities through practice and through understanding terms describing objects. For example, surfaces can be normal, inclined, or oblique. Normal surfaces appear true size in one principal view and as an edge in the other two principal views. Inclined surfaces appear as an edge in one of the three principal views. Oblique surfaces do not appear as an edge in any of the principal views.

- Choice of scale is important for representing objects clearly on the drawing sheet.

- Hidden lines are used to show the intersections of surfaces, surfaces that appear on edge, and the limits of curved surfaces that are hidden from the viewing direction.

- Centerlines are used to show the axis of symmetry for features and paths of motion, and to indicate the arrangement for circular patterns.

- Creating CAD drawings involves applying the same concepts as in paper drawing. The main difference is that drawing geometry is stored more accurately using a computer than in any hand drawing. CAD drawing geometry can be reused in many ways and plotted to any scale as necessary.

REVIEW QUESTIONS

1. Sketch the symbol for third-angle projection.
2. List the six principal views of projection.
3. Sketch the top, front, and right-side views of an object of your design having normal, inclined, and oblique surfaces.
4. In a drawing that shows the top, front, and right-side view, which two views show depth? Which view shows depth vertically on the sheet? Which view shows depth horizontally on the drawing sheet?
5. What is the definition of a normal surface? An inclined surface? An oblique surface?
6. What are three similarities between using a CAD program to create 2D drawing geometry and sketching on a sheet of paper? What are three differences?
7. What dimensions are the same between the top and front view: width, height, or depth? Between the front and right-side view? Between the top and right-side view?
8. List two ways of transferring depth between the top and right-side views.
9. If surface A contains corners 1, 2, 3, 4, and surface B contains 3, 4, 5, 6, what is the name of the line where surfaces A and B intersect?

CHAPTER EXERCISES

The multiview projection exercises are intended to be sketched freehand on graph paper or plain paper. Sheet layouts such as A1, found inside the front cover, are suggested, but your instructor may prefer a different sheet size or arrangement. Use metric or decimal inch as assigned. The marks shown on some exercises indicate rough units of either 1/2″ and 1/4″ (or 10 mm and 5 mm). All holes are through holes. If dimensions are required, study Chapter 11, and use metric or decimal-inch dimensions as assigned by the instructor.

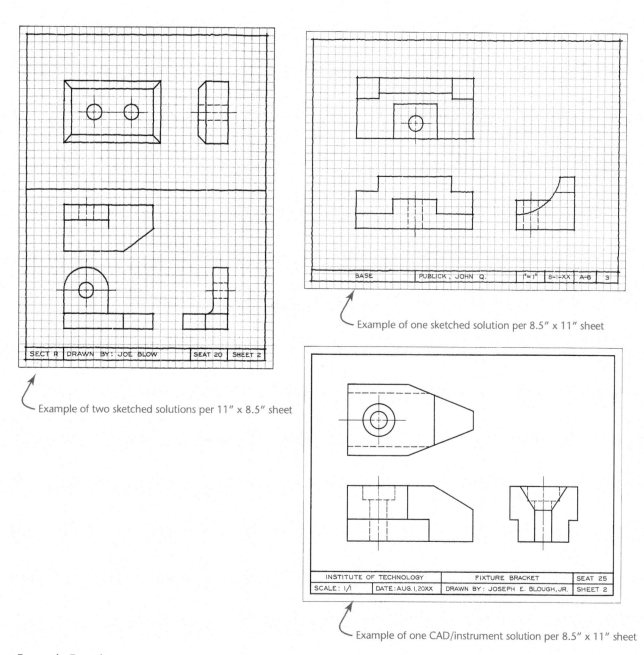

Example of two sketched solutions per 11″ x 8.5″ sheet

Example of one sketched solution per 8.5″ x 11″ sheet

Example of one CAD/instrument solution per 8.5″ x 11″ sheet

Example Exercise

Exercise 6.1 Spacer. Draw or sketch all necessary views.

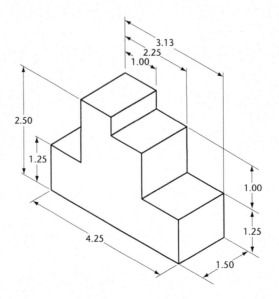

Exercise 6.2 Slide. Draw or sketch all necessary views.

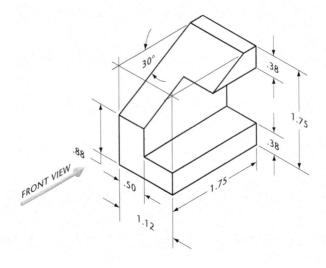

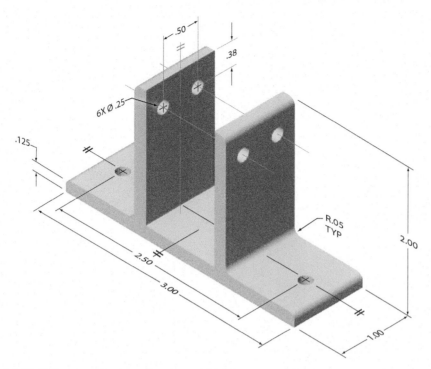

Exercise 6.3 Wall Bracket. Create a drawing with the necessary orthographic views for the wall bracket.

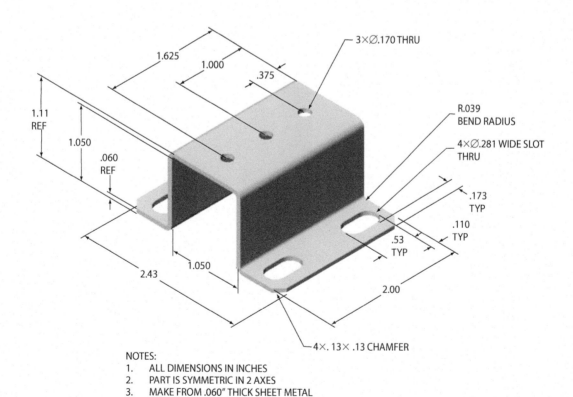

NOTES:
1.   ALL DIMENSIONS IN INCHES
2.   PART IS SYMMETRIC IN 2 AXES
3.   MAKE FROM .060" THICK SHEET METAL

Exercise 6.4 Sheet Metal Bracket. Create a drawing of the necessary orthographic views for the sheet metal bracket.

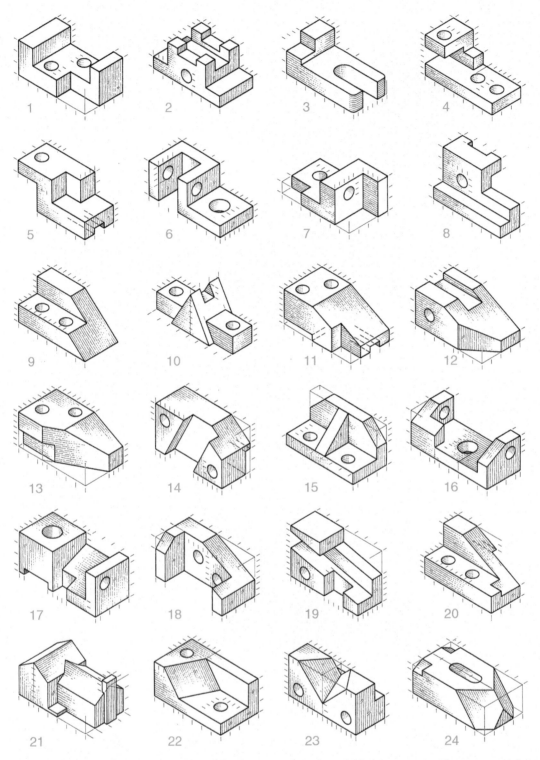

Exercise 6.5 Multiview Sketching Problems. Sketch necessary orthographic views on graph paper or plain paper, showing either one or two problems per sheet as assigned by your instructor. These exercises are designed to fit on 8.5″ × 11″ size A or metric A4 paper. The units shown may be either .500″ and .250″ or 10 mm and 5 mm. All holes are through holes.

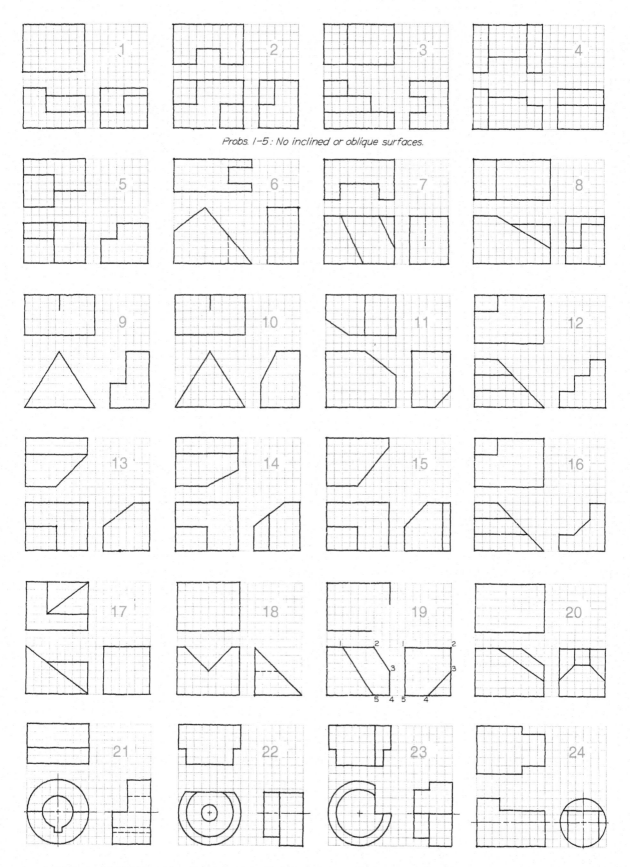

Probs. 1–5: No inclined or oblique surfaces.

Exercise 6.6 Missing-Line Sketching Problems. (1) Sketch the given views on graph paper or plain paper showing either one or two problems per sheet as assigned by your instructor. See the examples at the beginning of this chapter's exercises. These exercises are designed to fit on 8.5″ × 11″ size A or metric A4 paper. Add the missing lines. The squares may be either .250″ or 5 mm. (2) Sketch in isometric on isometric paper or in oblique on cross-section paper, if assigned.

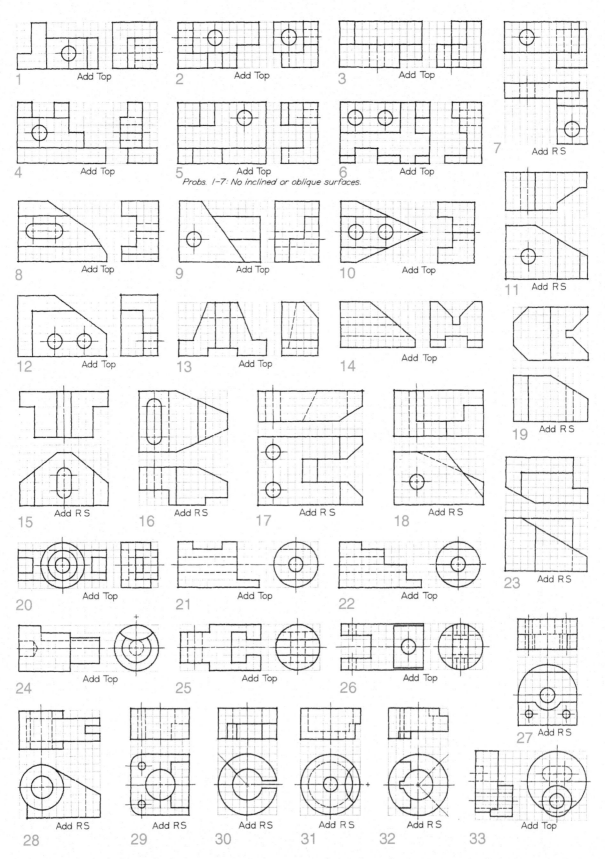

Probs. 1–7: No inclined or oblique surfaces.

Exercise 6.7 Third-View Sketching Problems. Sketch the given views and add the missing views as indicated on graph paper or plain paper. These exercises are designed to fit on 8.5″ × 11″ size A or metric A4 paper. The squares may be either .25″ or 5 mm. The given views are either front and right-side views or front and top views. Hidden holes with centerlines are drilled holes.

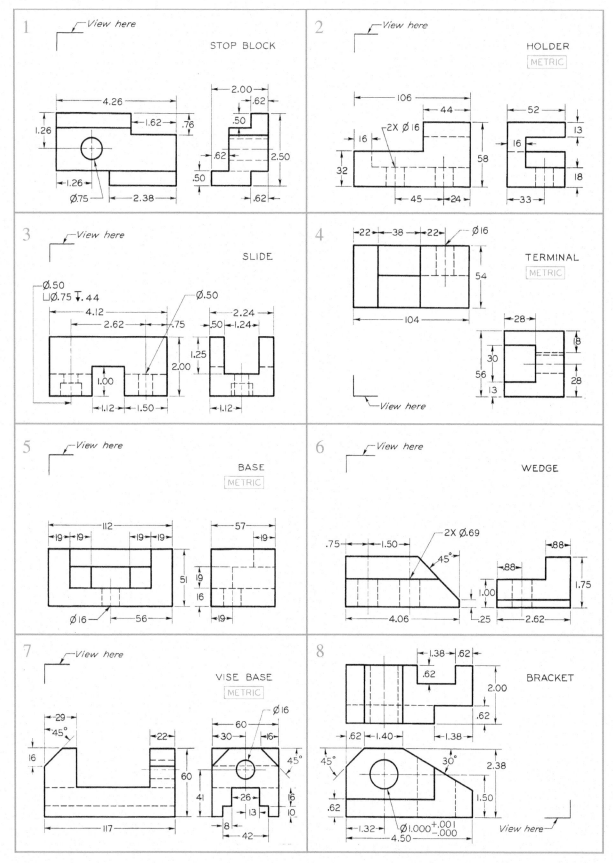

Exercise 6.8 Missing-View Problems. Sketch or draw the given views, and add the missing view. If dimensions are required, study Chapter 11. These exercises are designed to fit on 8.5″ × 11″ size A or metric A4 paper. Use metric or decimal-inch dimensions as assigned by the instructor. Move dimensions to better locations where possible. In problems 1–5, all surfaces are normal surfaces.

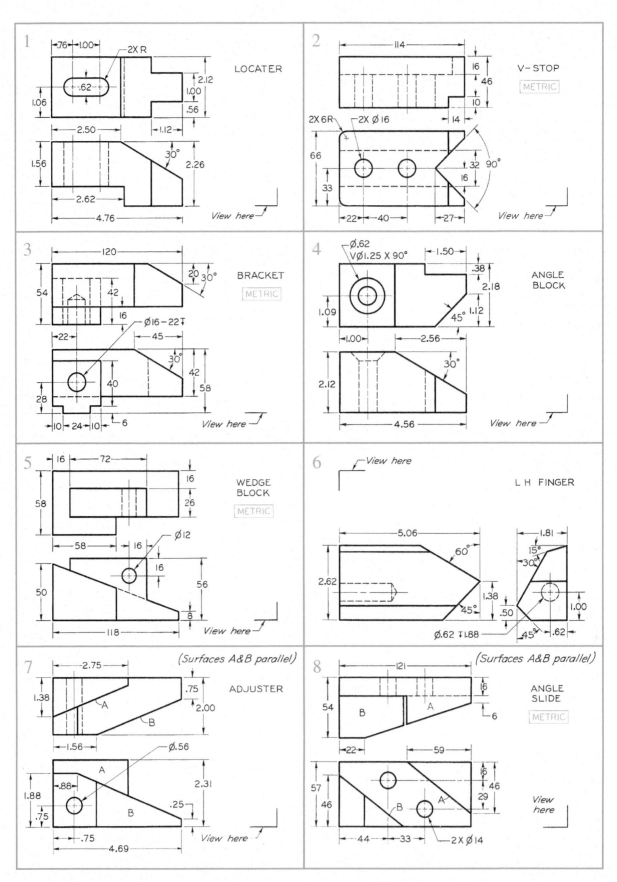

Exercise 6.9 Missing-View Problems. Sketch or draw the given views, and add the missing view. These exercises are designed to fit on 8.5″ × 11″ size A or metric A4 paper. If dimensions are required, study Chapter 11. Use metric or decimal-inch dimensions as assigned by the instructor. Move dimensions to better locations where possible.

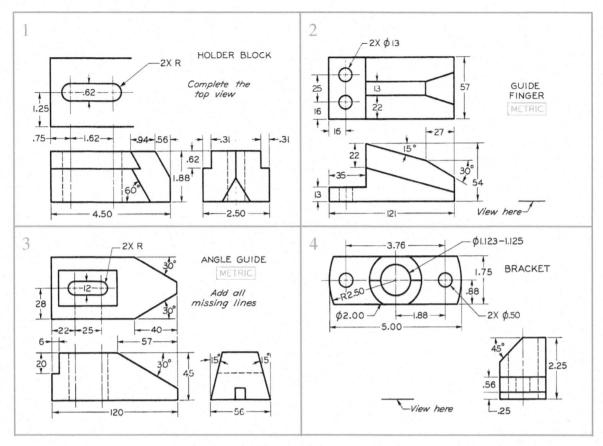

1 HOLDER BLOCK

2X R

.62

1.25

.75   1.62   .94   .56   .31   .31

Complete the top view

.62

1.88

60°

4.50   2.50

2 2X ⌀13

25   13   57

16   22

16   27

22   15°

35   30°   54

13

121   View here

GUIDE FINGER
METRIC

3 2X R

30°

12

28

30°

22   25   40

6

20   57   30°

45

120   56

15°   15°

ANGLE GUIDE
METRIC

Add all missing lines

4 3.76   ⌀1.123–1.125

R2.50   1.75

.88

⌀2.00   1.88   2X ⌀.50

5.00

View here

BRACKET

45°

2.25

.56

.25

Exercise 6.10 Missing-View Problems. Sketch or draw the given views, and add the missing view. These exercises are designed to fit on 8.5″ × 11″ size A or metric A4 paper. If dimensions are required, study Chapter 11. Use metric or decimal-inch dimensions as assigned by the instructor. Move dimensions to better locations where possible.

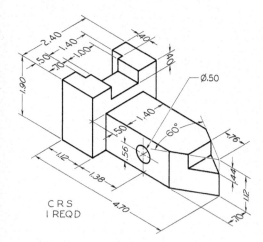

Exercise 6.11 Safety Key. Draw the necessary orthographic views on 8.5″ × 11″ size A or metric A4 paper. Use a title block or title strip as assigned by your instructor.

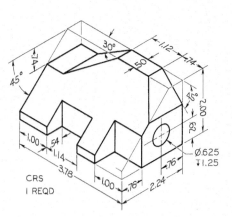

Exercise 6.12 Tool Holder. Draw the necessary orthographic views on 8.5″ × 11″ size A or metric A4 paper. Use a title block or title strip as assigned by your instructor.

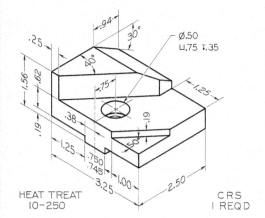

Exercise 6.13 Index Feed. Draw the necessary orthographic views on 8.5″ × 11″ size A or metric A4 paper. Use a title block or title strip as assigned by your instructor.

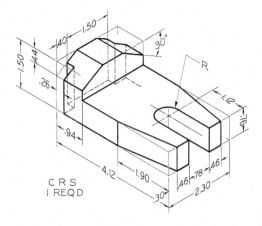

Exercise 6.14 Finger Guide. Draw the necessary orthographic views on 8.5″ × 11″ size A or metric A4 paper. Use a title block or title strip as assigned by your instructor.

Exercise 6.15 Draw the views as shown. Omit all dimensions.

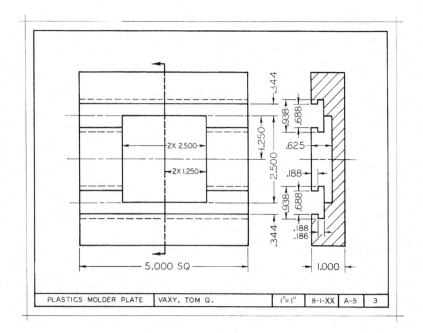

Exercise 6.16 Draw the views as shown. Omit all dimensions.

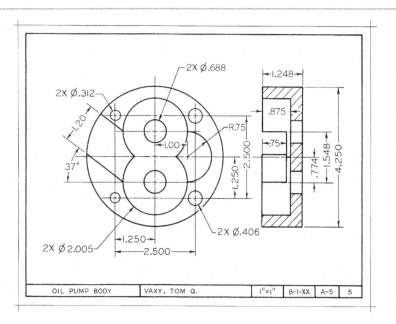

Exercise 6.17 Draw views of the seal cover. Omit the dimensions and notes.

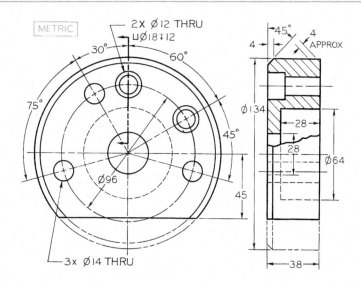

Exercise 6.18 Model each of the parts shown. Before starting, carefully consider which feature to use as the base feature and how you will create the model so it will be updated as specified.

a. Design intent: The length and width of the slot must be able to change to accommodate fit with a different part. The four holes must remain equally spaced around the wider/longer slot.

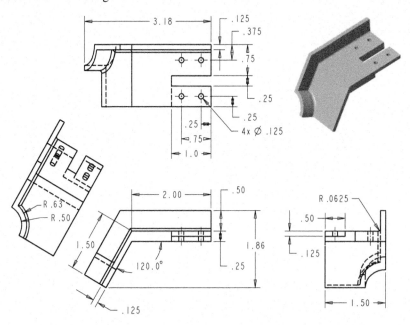

b. Model the hand weight shown. Determine the weight if this part is cast from ASTM class 20 gray iron. Update the model to create a set of three hand weights of different weights, but maintain the diameter and length of the crossbar grip.

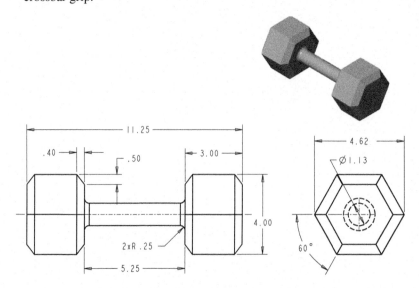

c. Model the part so that when the overall height, width, depth of the part are changed, the other features are updated proportionally to them.

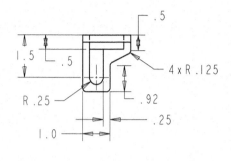

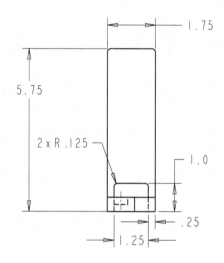

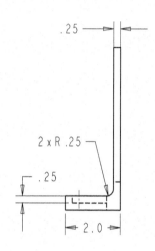

d. Create a model for the decorative corner cap shown.

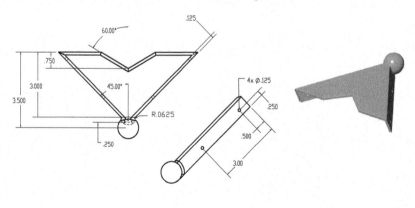

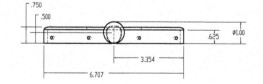

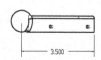

e. Model the rail bracket shown so that the diameter for the central hole can change to accommodate different diameters of railing. The height, width, and depth for the bracket should remain the same when the central hole size is updated. The mounting holes should also remain the original size.

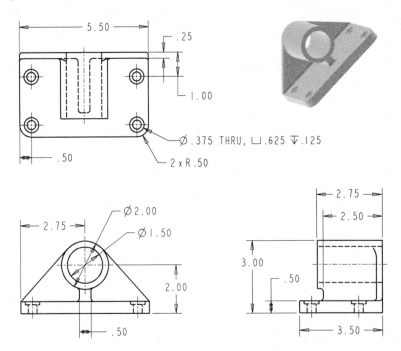

ALL ROUNDS = .125

f. Model the plastic speaker housing shown. Start by sketching the speaker housing and noting the dimensions that will control the shape. Once you have a sketch, use your sketched plan to model the speaker housing according to your plan.

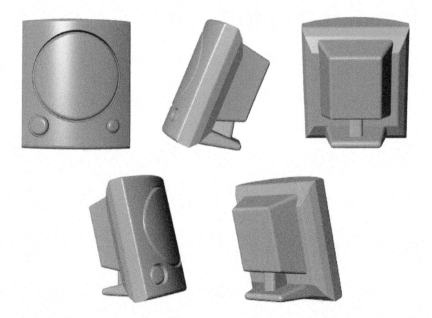

Exercise 6.19 Create a constraint-based model of the four-spoke hand wheel shown such that it can be resized to match the dimensions in the table.

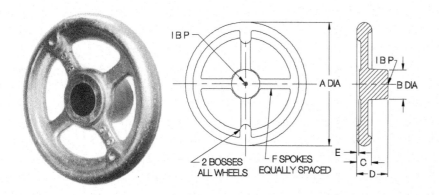

STRAIGHT SPOKES

PART NO. CAST IRON	A DIA	B DIA	C	D	E	F
CL-4-HWSF	4	1-1/4	5/8	1-11/16	1/8	4
CL-5-HWSF	5	1-1/2	3/4			
CL-6-HWSF	6	1-5/8		1-13/16		
CL-8-HWSF	8	1-7/8		2-1/16	5/32	
CL-10-HWSF	10	2-1/4	1	2-1/2		8
CL-12-HWSF	12	3		3-1/4	1/8	
CL-14-HWSF	14			3-3/4	3/32	

Exercise 6.20 Create a constraint-based model of the swing washer shown such that it can be resized to match the dimensions in the table. Capture size relationships between features in the constraint-based dimensions wherever possible.

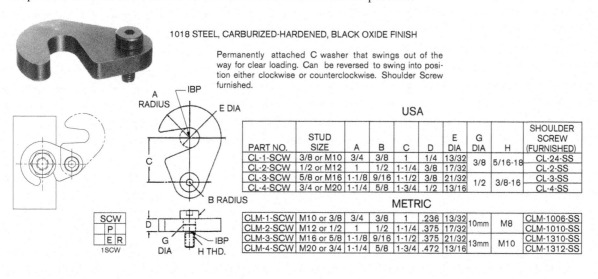

1018 STEEL, CARBURIZED-HARDENED, BLACK OXIDE FINISH

Permanently attached C washer that swings out of the way for clear loading. Can be reversed to swing into position either clockwise or counterclockwise. Shoulder Screw furnished.

USA

PART NO.	STUD SIZE	A	B	C	D	E DIA	G DIA	H	SHOULDER SCREW (FURNISHED)
CL-1-SCW	3/8 or M10	3/4	3/8	1	1/4	13/32	3/8	5/16-18	CL-24-SS
CL-2-SCW	1/2 or M12	1	1/2	1-1/4	3/8	17/32			CL-2-SS
CL-3-SCW	5/8 or M16	1-1/8	9/16	1-1/2	3/8	21/32	1/2	3/8-16	CL-3-SS
CL-4-SCW	3/4 or M20	1-1/4	5/8	1-3/4	1/2	13/16			CL-4-SS

METRIC

PART NO.	STUD SIZE	A	B	C	D	E DIA	G DIA	H	SHOULDER SCREW (FURNISHED)
CLM-1-SCW	M10 or 3/8	3/4	3/8	1	.236	13/32	10mm	M8	CLM-1006-SS
CLM-2-SCW	M12 or 1/2	1	1/2	1-1/4	.375	17/32			CLM-1010-SS
CLM-3-SCW	M16 or 5/8	1-1/8	9/16	1-1/2	.375	21/32	13mm	M10	CLM-1310-SS
CLM-4-SCW	M20 or 3/4	1-1/4	5/8	1-3/4	.472	13/16			CLM-1312-SS

Exercise 6.21 **Create a constraint-based model of the electronics bracket shown.**

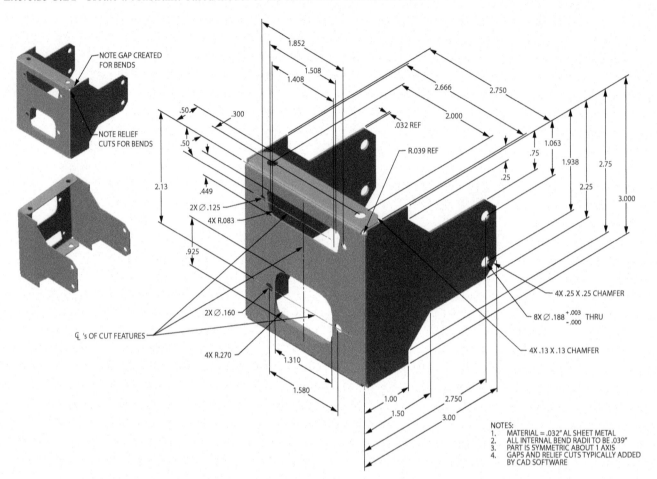

NOTE GAP CREATED
FOR BENDS

NOTE RELIEF
CUTS FOR BENDS

℄'s OF CUT FEATURES

1.852
1.508
1.408
.50
.300
.032 REF
2.666
2.750
2.000
R.039 REF
.50
1.063
.75
1.938
2.75
.25
2.25
3.000
2.13
.449
2X ∅.125
4X R.083
.925
2X ∅.160
4X R.270
4X .25 X .25 CHAMFER
8X ∅.188 +.003/-.000 THRU
4X .13 X .13 CHAMFER
1.310
1.580
1.00
2.750
1.50
3.00

NOTES:
1.   MATERIAL = .032" AL SHEET METAL
2.   ALL INTERNAL BEND RADII TO BE .039"
3.   PART IS SYMMETRIC ABOUT 1 AXIS
4.   GAPS AND RELIEF CUTS TYPICALLY ADDED
     BY CAD SOFTWARE

Exercise 6.22 Create a constraint-based model of the gyroscope base shown.

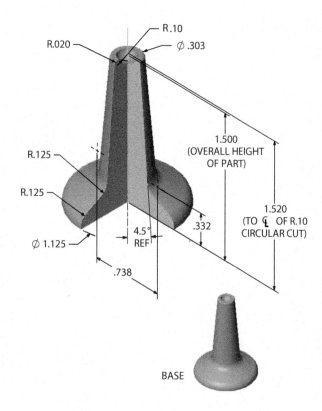

R.10
R.020
∅ .303
1.500
(OVERALL HEIGHT
OF PART)
R.125
R.125
1.520
(TO ⅊ OF R.10
CIRCULAR CUT)
.332
∅ 1.125
4.5°
REF
.738

BASE

Exercise 6.23 Create a constraint-based model of the pry bar shown.

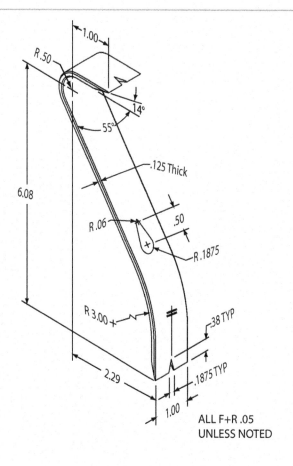

1.00
R.50
14°
55°
.125 Thick
6.08
R.06
.50
R.1875
R 3.00
.38 TYP
2.29
.1875 TYP
1.00
ALL F+R .05
UNLESS NOTED

Exercise 6.24 Create a constraint-based model of this ice cube tray.

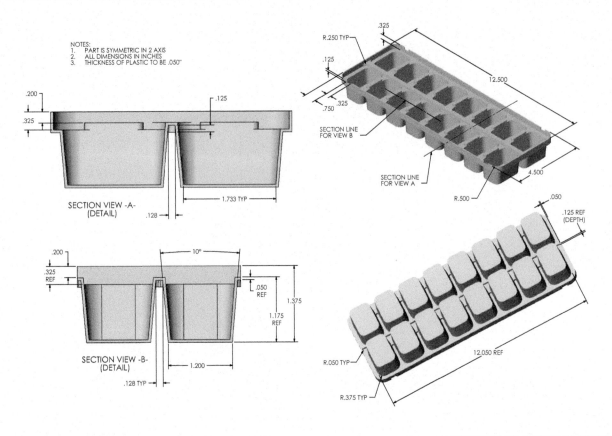

Exercise 6.25 Create a constraint-based model of this simple knob.

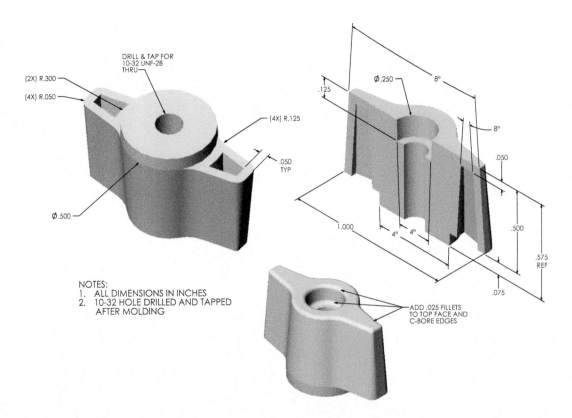

Exercise 6.26 Create a constraint-based model of the first part in each set, save the part, then edit the part to create the other configurations in each set. Save all part files.

a. Saw Blade

b. Calculator

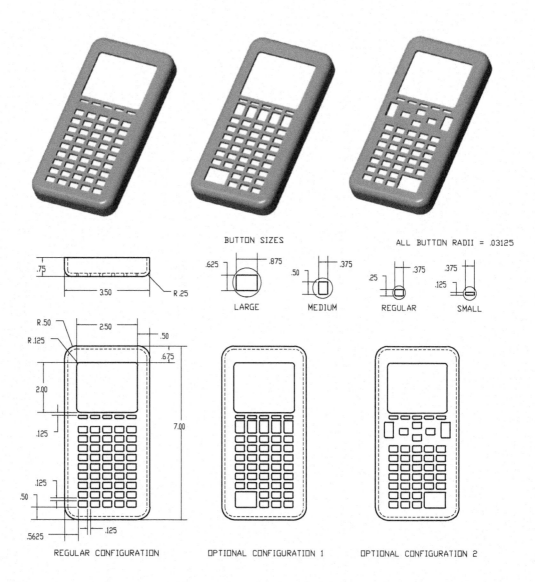

BUTTON SIZES

ALL BUTTON RADII = .03125

LARGE   MEDIUM   REGULAR   SMALL

REGULAR CONFIGURATION   OPTIONAL CONFIGURATION 1   OPTIONAL CONFIGURATION 2

NOTE: CALCULATOR BODY THICKNESS = .125

c. Geneva Cam

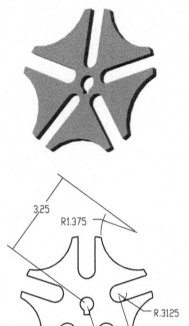

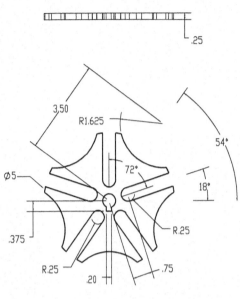

.25

GENEVA GEAR CONFIGURATION # 1

R1.625
3.50
72°
54°
18°
Ø5
R.25
.375
R.25
.20
.75

GENEVA GEAR CONFIGURATION # 2

3.25
R1.375
R.3125
1.25

d. Brace

BASE FEATURE W/ REGULAR RIB

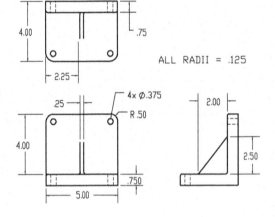

4.00
.75
2.25

ALL RADII = .125

.25
4x Ø.375
R.50
4.00
.750
5.00

2.00
2.50

STRENGTHENED RIB # 1

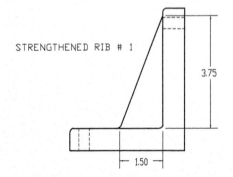

3.75
1.50

STRENGTHENED RIB # 2

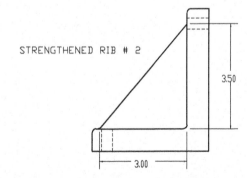

3.50
3.00

NOTE: RIB THICKNESS REMAINS .25

Exercise 6.27 Create a constraint-based model of the wall hanger.

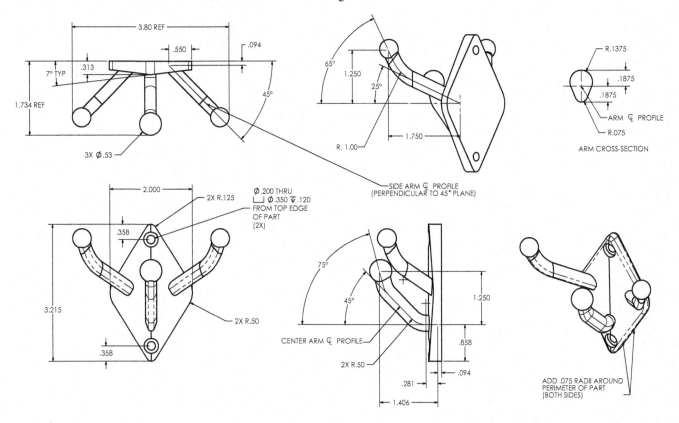

CHAPTER SEVEN

2D DRAWING REPRESENTATION

OBJECTIVES

After studying the material in this chapter, you should be able to:

1. Represent curved surfaces in multiview drawings.

2. Show intersections and tangencies of curved and planar surfaces.

3. Represent common types of holes.

4. Show fillets, rounds, and runouts in a 2D drawing.

5. Use partial views.

6. Apply revolution conventions when necessary for clarity.

7. Show removed views and projected views.

8. Show right- and left-hand parts.

9. Project curved surfaces by points.

10. Show and label an enlarged detail.

11. Show conventional breaks.

Refer to the following standards:
• *ANSI/ASME Y14.3 Orthographic and Pictorial Views*

Many consumer products, such as the robotic vacuum cleaner pictured here, use durable affordable plastic parts. The lifecycle of the product is something to keep in mind. Is there a path for reusing or recycling the plastic used, or for upgrading the product, or will it end in a landfill? (kostasgr/Shutterstock.)

OVERVIEW

An object with molded plastic parts like the one shown above has curved surfaces on inside and outside corners to make it easier to remove the part from the mold. There are a number of practices for showing curved surfaces in your drawings.

Learning the names of typical features and hole types that are used in part design and how they are represented in drawing views will make it easier for you to communicate about designs and to understand their documentation requirements.

At times, conventional practices are used that are not standard orthographic projections. This is to make it easier to represent or interpret objects in drawings. An example is revolving certain features when it adds to the clarity of the drawing. Another example is showing "breaks" when a part does not fit well on the sheet because of its long shape, or to avoid unnecessary detail.

There is an art to creating drawings that show the information clearly and provide all the detail necessary to manufacture it. People can read drawings most easily when views, dimensions, and lines are placed in logical locations that aid in the reader's comprehension of the part and the design intent for the part.

PRACTICES FOR 2D DOCUMENTATION DRAWINGS

Now that you are familiar with the basics of orthographic projection and visualizing objects from the information presented in orthographic views, you are ready to make and read more complex 2D drawings. Although you might sketch complex designs by hand, it is more likely that you would create these types of drawings using CAD, either as 2D CAD drawings, or as 2D CAD drawings generated from a 3D solid model.

Sometimes, practices used to create drawings with 3D CAD differ from those used to create hand-drawn or 2D CAD drawings. You must understand the standards and practices for creating good drawings even when using 3D CAD. The software will not do everything for you.

Common Manufactured Features

Certain features are a part of many engineering designs. Learning their names and shapes, as shown in Figure 7.1 and detailed in Table 7.1, helps you visualize and communicate about them. Some CAD systems may even have prebuilt features that you can place onto a 3D part to create them quickly.

Table 7.1 Common Manufactured Features

Feature	Example
Fillet: A rounded interior blend between surfaces; used, for example, to strengthen adjoining surfaces or to allow a part to be removed from a mold	
Round: A rounded exterior blend between surfaces; used to make edges and corners easier to handle, improve strength of castings, and allow for removal from a mold	
Counterbore: A cylindrical recess around a hole, usually to receive a bolt head or nut	
Countersink: A cone-shaped recess around a hole, often used to receive a tapered screw head	
Spotface: A shallow recess like a counterbore, used to provide a good bearing surface for a fastener	
Boss: A short raised protrusion above the surface of a part, often used to provide a strong flat bearing surface	
Lug: A flat or rounded tab protruding from a surface, usually to provide a method for attachment	
Flange: A flattened collar or rim around a cylindrical part to allow for attachment	
Chamfer: An angled surface, used on a cylinder to make it easier to start into a hole, or a plate to make it easier to handle	
Neck: A small groove cut around the diameter of a cylinder, often where it changes diameter	
Keyway/Keyseat: A shaped depression cut along the axis of a cylinder or hub to receive a key, used to attach hubs, gears, and other parts to a cylinder so they will not turn on it	
Knurl: A pattern on a surface to provide for better gripping or more surface area for attachment, often used on knobs and tool handles	
Bushing: A hollow cylinder that is often used as a protective sleeve or guide, or as a bearing	

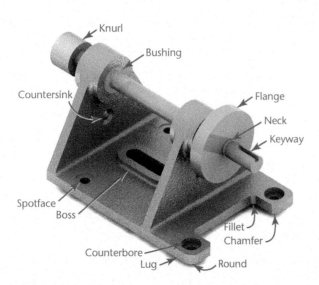

7.1   Commonly Manufactured Features

Conventional Representations

Standard orthographic projections don't always show complex shapes as clearly and simply as you may wish, so certain alternative practices, referred to as *conventions,* are accepted. Although "convention" is usually a general term for an accepted method, in the case of technical drawing it refers particularly to a simplified representation that enhances economy and clarity in a drawing. Although conventional representations do deviate from true orthographic projection, their methods of simplification are generally recognized and accepted. (See *ASME Y14.3.*) In other words, conventions are like rules for breaking the rules.

Intersections and Tangencies

To represent complex objects, multiview drawings use standard methods for depicting the way planar and curved surfaces meet. A plane surface can *intersect* or be *tangent* to a contoured surface, as shown in Figures 7.2 and 7.3. When a plane surface intersects the contoured surface, a line is drawn to represent the edge formed by that intersection. When the plane surface is tangent to the contoured surface, no line or a thin phantom line pattern is drawn where the surfaces meet, depending on whether the phantom line is needed to aid in visualization.

Removed Views

It is not always possible to show all the drawing views in alignment on the sheet. This is particularly true of civil and architectural drawings where the size and complexity of the object make it hard to show the level of detail necessary and still fit the views on one sheet. When this is the case, a removed view can be used. There are two different ways to indicate the viewing direction for removed views. One is to use a view indicator arrow to show the direction of sight, as shown in Figure 7.4a. The other is to use a viewing-plane line, as shown in Figure 7.4b. Clearly label the removed view.

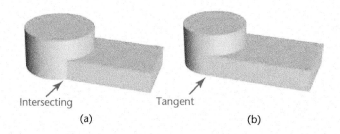

7.2 Intersecting and Tangent Surfaces

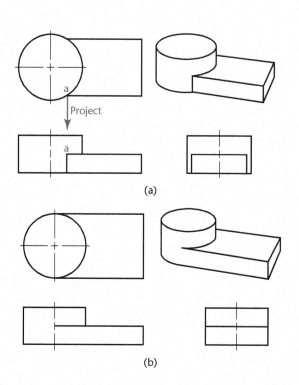

7.3 Orthographic Views of Intersecting and Tangent Surfaces

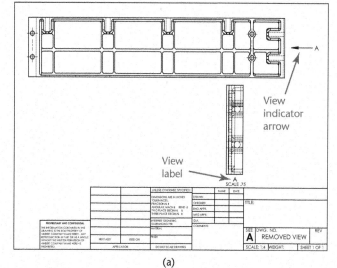

(a)

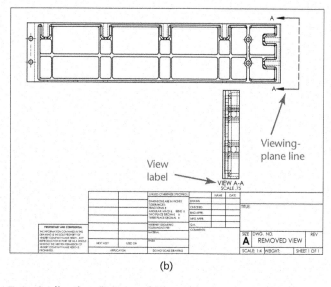

(b)

7.4 Indicating Removed Views

7.1 VISUALIZING AND DRAWING COMPLEX CYLINDRICAL SHAPES

The illustrations in Figure 7.5 show how to visualize cylindrical features being cut from a rectangular block (prism). Compare each illustration showing the material being removed with the drawing.

In Figure 7.5a there is no line where the contoured surface of the rounded top joins the straight planar sides. The top view appears as a rectangle. The centerline for the rounded top is shown in all three views. Consider these questions as you look at Figure 7.5a:

- In this drawing, how many views are necessary?
- Which views are repetitive?
- Is the centerline required to locate the rounded top?

In Figure 7.5b, the material for the center hole is removed. Then, hidden lines are added to the top and side view showing the limiting elements of the cylindrical hole. As you look at Figure 7.5b note:

- In the front view the hole appears round.
- The centerlines in the drawing locate the hole as well as the rounded top, since they are concentric.

In Figure 7.5c the counterbored holes are created. As you look at Figure 7.5c ask yourself:

- How many lines are used to show the counterbore in the side and top views?
- How many views are necessary?

In Figure 7.5d a portion of the top surface is removed. Notice how those lines appear in the top and side views. How many views are necessary now?

In Figures 7.5a and 7.5b only one view is required.

In Figure 7.5c, the side view or top view or a note specifying the depth of the counterbore is needed. The counterbore is five lines.

In Figure 7.5d the top or side view or a note is required. The side view is probably a better choice, because it shows more about the shape than the top view.

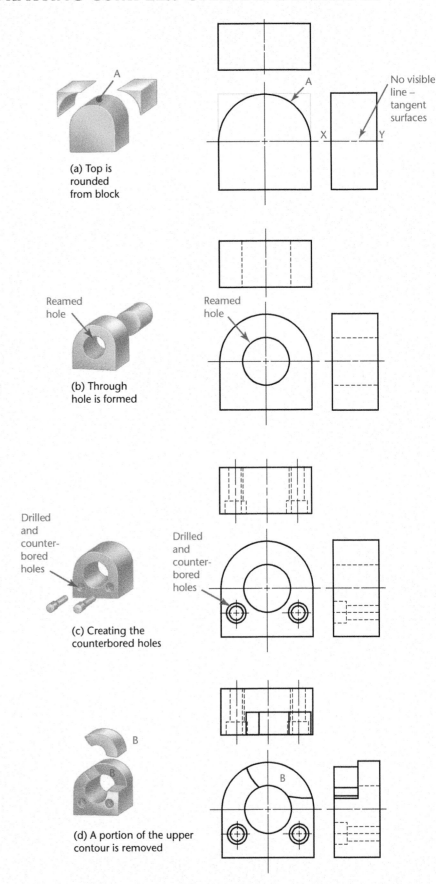

(a) Top is rounded from block

No visible line – tangent surfaces

Reamed hole

Reamed hole

(b) Through hole is formed

Drilled and counter-bored holes

Drilled and counter-bored holes

(c) Creating the counterbored holes

B

(d) A portion of the upper contour is removed

7.5   Visualizing and Drawing Cylindrical Shapes

7.2 CYLINDERS WHEN SLICED

Cylinders are often machined to form plane or other types of surfaces. Figure 7.6a shows a single machined cut that created two normal surfaces. Normal surfaces appear true shape in the view where the line of sight is perpendicular to the surface. In the two other views that normal surface appears on edge. The back half remains unchanged.

In Figure 7.6b, two stepped cuts form four normal surfaces. Note that surface 7–8 (top view) is through the center of the cylinder, producing in the side view line 21–24 and in the front view surface 11–14–16–15, which is equal in width to the diameter of the cylinder. Surface 15–16 (front view) shows in the top view as 7–8–Arc 4. Surface 11–14 (front view) shows in the top view as 5–6–Arc 3–8–7–Arc 2.

Figure 7.6c shows a part with two coaxial cylindrical features, which is cut to form a normal surface parallel to the axis of the cylinders.

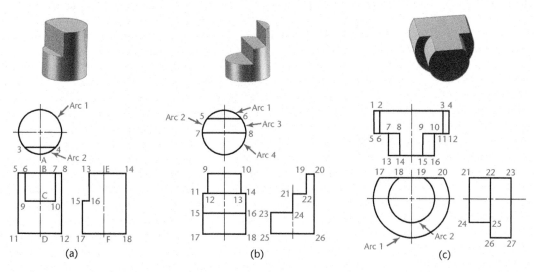

7.6   Showing Views of Cylinders with Planar Surfaces Cut Away

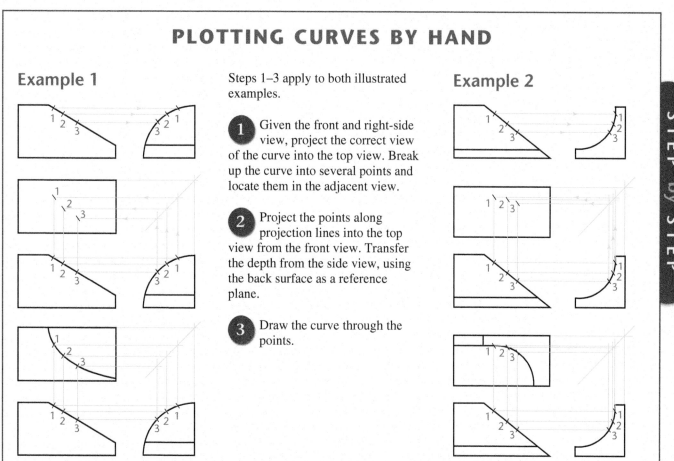

PLOTTING CURVES BY HAND

Example 1

Steps 1–3 apply to both illustrated examples.

1 Given the front and right-side view, project the correct view of the curve into the top view. Break up the curve into several points and locate them in the adjacent view.

2 Project the points along projection lines into the top view from the front view. Transfer the depth from the side view, using the back surface as a reference plane.

3 Draw the curve through the points.

Example 2

STEP by STEP

7.3 CYLINDERS AND ELLIPSES

If a cylinder is cut by an inclined plane, as shown in Figure 7.7a, the inclined surface is bounded by an ellipse. This ellipse will appear as a circle in the top view, as a straight line in the front view, and as an ellipse in the side view. Note that circle 1 appears circular in the top view regardless of the angle of the cut. If the cut is at 45° from horizontal, it would also appear as a circle in the side view.

When a circular shape is shown inclined in another view and projected into the adjacent view as shown in Figure 7.7b, it will appear as an ellipse, even though the shape is a circle. The inclined ellipse in Figure 7.7c is not shown true size and shape in any of the standard views given. You will learn in Chapter 9 how to create auxiliary views to show the true size and shape of inclined surfaces like these.

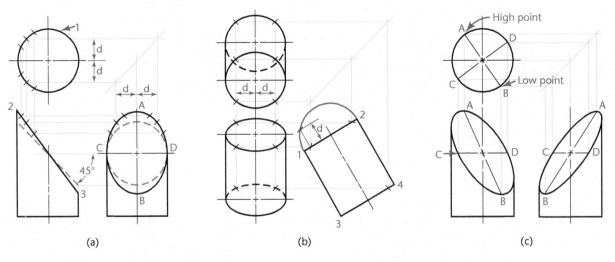

(a)   (b)   (c)

7.7 Elliptical Surfaces on Cylinders

7.4 INTERSECTIONS AND TANGENCIES

Where a curved surface is tangent to a plane surface (Figure 7.8a) no line is drawn, but when it intersects a plane surface, as in Figure 7.8b, a definite edge is formed.

Figure 7.8c shows that when curves join each other or plane surfaces smoothly (i.e., they are tangent) a line is not drawn to show where they come together. If a combination of

curves creates a vertical surface, as in Figure 7.8d, the vertical surface is shown as a line (here in the top view).

When plane surfaces join a contoured surface, a line is not shown if they are tangent, but is shown if they intersect. Figures 7.8e–h show examples of planes joining contoured surfaces.

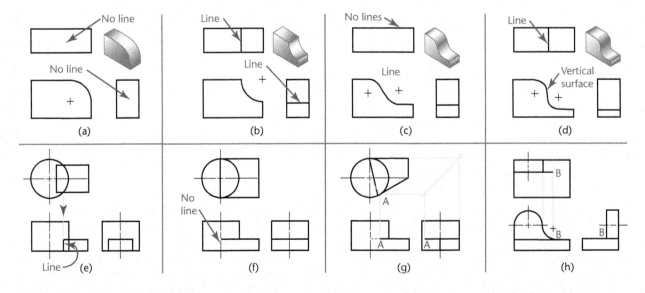

(a)   (b)   (c)   (d)

(e)   (f)   (g)   (h)

7.8 Intersections and Tangencies

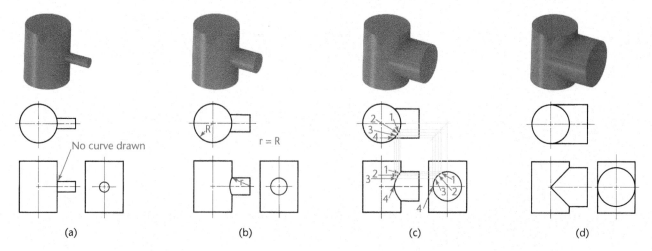

7.9 Intersections of Cylinders

Intersections of Cylinders

Figure 7.9a shows an example of a small cylinder intersecting a large cylinder. When the intersection is small, its curved shape is not plotted accurately because it adds little to the sketch or drawing for the time it takes. Instead it is shown as a straight line.

When the intersection is larger, it can be approximated by drawing an arc with the radius the same as that of the large cylinder, as shown in Figure 7.9b.

Large intersections can be plotted accurately by selecting points along the curve to project, as shown in Figure 7.9c.

When the cylinders are the same diameter, their intersections appear as straight lines in the adjoining view, as shown in Figure 7.9d. When you are using 3D modeling, the accurate intersection of the surfaces is typically represented (see Figure 7.10).

> **TIP**
>
> Using CAD tools you can locate the center and points on the major and minor axis and use the CAD software's ellipse tool to draw the whole ellipse through the points. Then, trim off the extra portion.
>
> A similar technique works when using a template.

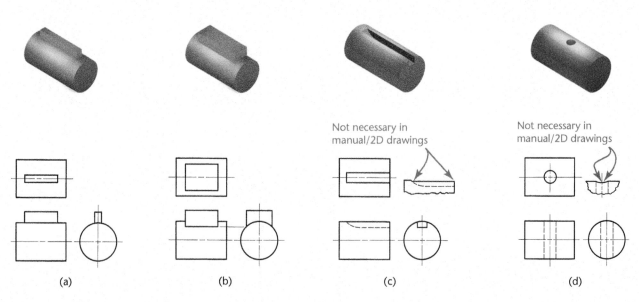

7.10 Intersections. *(a) and (b) Examples of a narrow prism intersecting a cylinder. (c) and (d) Intersections of a keyseat and cylinder and a small hole and cylinder.*

TO SHOW OR NOT TO SHOW:
TANGENT SURFACES IN SOLID MODELS

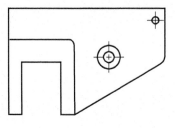

Orthographic drawing views
do not show tangent edges

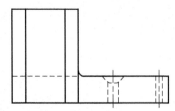 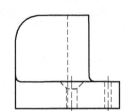

Best: Tangent edges shown as
phantom lines in pictorial view

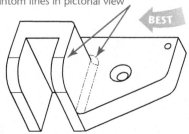

Okay: Tangent edges shown
as solid lines in pictorial view

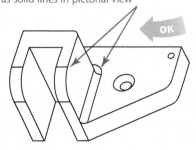

Poor: View is unclear without
tangent edges in pictorial view

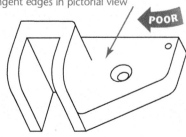

When you are creating solid models of contoured surfaces, it can be very useful to show the "tangent edges" where the contoured surface intersects the model. These lines that depict where the contoured surface ends and where the planar surface begins are not typically drawn in orthographic drawing views, unless the drawing might be confusing without them. When it is necessary to show the tangent edges, use a phantom line for them.

Using a phantom line to show the tangent edges of the model in the pictorial view is often necessary on parts that have many fillets and rounds; otherwise, the view generated by the software may not show the part clearly.

Most CAD software allows you to set the display of tangent edges both for the entire drawing and for individual views.

Even when you are creating drawings using a CAD system you should follow standard drawing conventions. Knowing your CAD software well is important so that you can manage settings like those for tangent edges to show your drawing clearly.

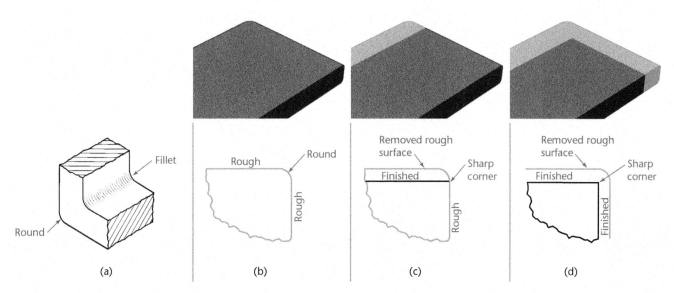

7.11 Rough and Finished Surfaces

7.5 FILLETS AND ROUNDS

A rounded interior corner is called a ***fillet.*** A rounded exterior corner is called a ***round*** (Figure 7.11a). Sharp corners are usually avoided in designing parts to be cast or forged because they are difficult to produce and can weaken the part.

Two intersecting rough surfaces produce a rounded corner (Figure 7.11b). If one of these surfaces is machined, as shown in Figure 7.11c, or if both surfaces are machined, as shown in Figure 7.11d, the corner becomes sharp. In drawings, a rounded corner means that both intersecting surfaces are rough. A sharp corner means that one or both surfaces are machined. Do not shade fillets and rounds on multiview drawings. The presence of the curved surfaces is indicated only where they appear as arcs, unless it is done to call attention to them.

3D CAD software varies in its ability to create complex blends for fillets and rounds. Figure 7.12 shows a CAD model with complex fillets. Figure 7.13 shows complex 3D CAD rounds.

7.12 Fillets on a CAD Model *(Courtesy of Ross Traeholt.)*

7.13 Rounds on a CAD Model of a Design for a Three-Hole Punch *(Courtesy of Douglas Wintin.)*

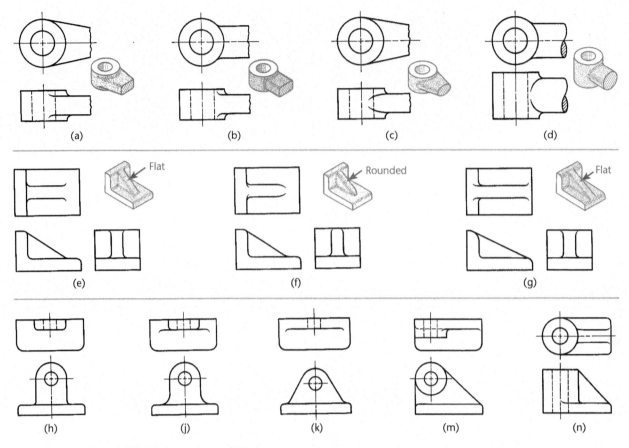

7.14 Conventional Fillets, Rounds, and Runouts

7.6 RUNOUTS

Small curves called *runouts* are used to represent fillets that connect with plane surfaces tangent to cylinders, as shown in Figures 7.14a–d. The runouts should have a radius equal to that of the fillet and a curvature of about one eighth of a circle, as shown in Figure 7.15c. Figures 7.14e–n show more examples of conventional representations for fillets, rounds, and runouts.

Runouts from different filleted intersections will appear different owing to the shapes of the horizontal intersecting members. In Figures 7.14e and 7.14f, the runouts differ because the top surface of the web is flat in Figure 7.14e, whereas the top surface of the web in Figure 7.14f is considerably rounded.

When two different sizes of fillets intersect, the direction of the runout is dictated by the larger fillet, as shown in Figures 7.14g and 7.14j.

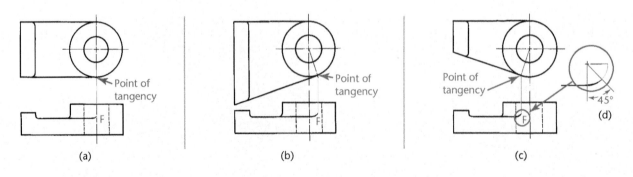

7.15 Runouts

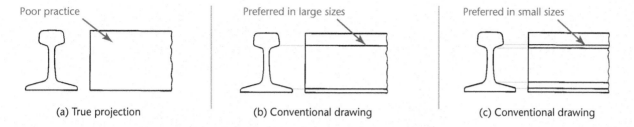

(a) True projection   (b) Conventional drawing   (c) Conventional drawing

7.16 Conventional Representation of a Rail

7.7 CONVENTIONAL EDGES

Rounded and filleted intersections eliminate sharp edges and can make it difficult to present the shape clearly. In some cases, as shown in Figure 7.16a, the true projection may be misleading. There is a conventional way of showing rounded and filleted edges for the sake of clarity. Added lines depicting rounded and filleted edges, as shown in Figures 7.16b and 7.16c, give a clearer representation, even though it is not the true projection. Project the added lines from the intersections of the surfaces as if the fillets and rounds were not present.

Figure 7.17 shows top views for each given front view. The first set of top views have very few lines, even though they are the true projection. The second set of top views, where lines are added to represent the rounded and filleted edges, are quite clear. Note the use of small Y shapes where rounded or filleted edges meet a rough surface. If an edge intersects a finished surface, no Y shape is shown.

George Washington Crossing the Delaware as Seen by a Trout
(Excerpted from The Ultimate Droodles Compendium by Roger Price ©2019 by Tallfellow Press. Used by permission. All rights reserved.)

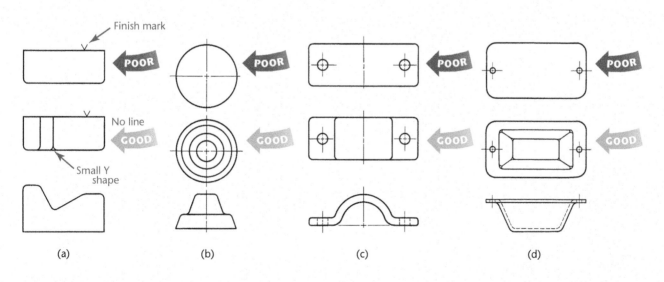

(a)   (b)   (c)   (d)

7.17 Conventional Edges

7.8 NECESSARY VIEWS

What are the absolutely minimum views required to completely define an object?

As you have already seen, sometimes only a single view with a note about the part's thickness is enough to define the shape (Figure 7.18). Sometimes two views are required (Figure 7.19). For complex parts three or more views may be required (Figure 7.20).

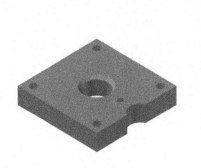

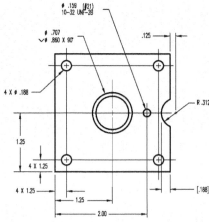

7.18 One-View Drawing

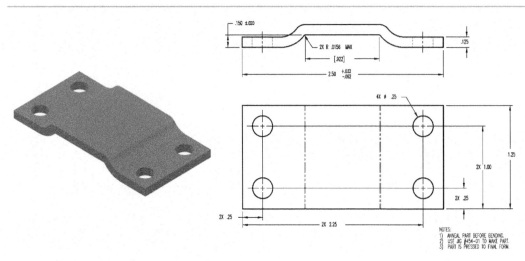

7.19 Two-View Drawing

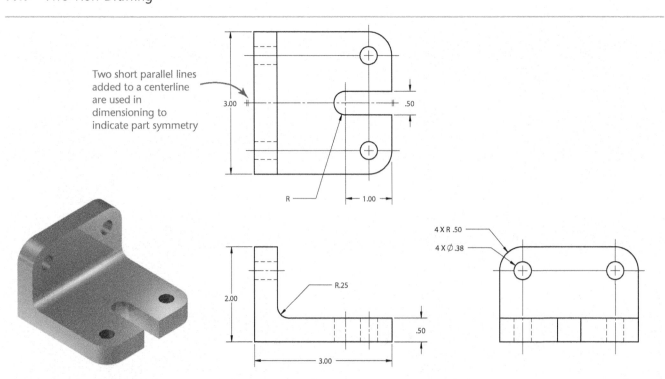

Two short parallel lines added to a centerline are used in dimensioning to indicate part symmetry

7.20 Three-View Drawing

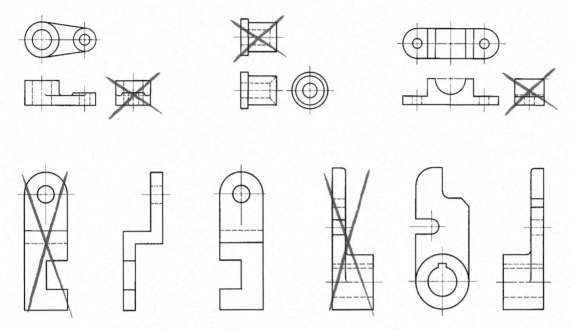

7.21 Three-View Drawings Showing Unnecessary Views Eliminated

In each set of views shown in Figure 7.21, three views are shown, but only two of the three are required.

When deciding which views to show, keep in mind the following:

- Show sufficient views to completely describe the shape.
- Show the right-hand view instead of the left-hand view if both show the object equally well.
- Choose the top view rather than the bottom view.

- Show long parts horizontally on the sheet for two reasons: (1) they fit better; (2) they tend to appear even longer when shown vertically.
- Make it your goal to communicate the information clearly. If an additional view helps toward this goal, show it. Keep in mind that drawings are easier to read and update if they are simpler, rather than more complex.

7.9 PARTIAL VIEWS

A view may not need to be complete to show what is necessary to clearly describe the object. This is called a *partial view* and is used to save sketching time and make the drawing less confusing to read. You can use a break line to limit the partial view, as shown in Figure 7.22a, or limit a view by the contour of the part shown, as shown in Figure 7.22b. If the view is symmetrical, you can draw a half-view on one side of the centerline, as shown in Figure 7.22c, or break out a partial view, as shown in Figure 7.22d. The half-views should be the near side, as shown.

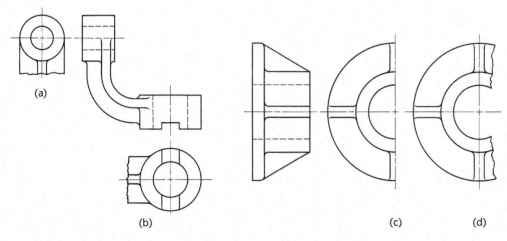

(a)

(b)   (c)   (d)

7.22 Partial Views

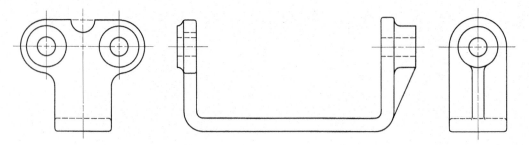

7.23 Partial Side Views

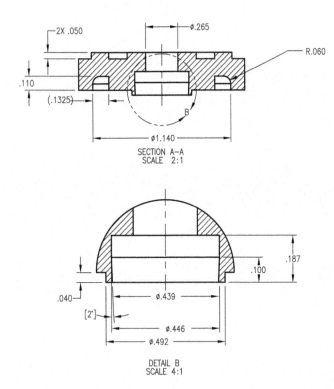

SECTION A–A
SCALE 2:1

DETAIL B
SCALE 4:1

7.24 Enlarged Detail

When you are drawing a partial view, do not place a break line where it will coincide with a visible or hidden line, as this may cause the drawing to be misinterpreted.

Occasionally, the distinctive features of an object are on opposite sides. In either complete side view there will be a considerable overlapping of shapes. In cases like this, two side views are often the best solution, as shown in Figure 7.23. The views are partial views, and certain visible and hidden lines have been omitted for clarity.

Showing Enlarged Details

Figure 7.24 shows drawing details clearly by including detail views drawn at a larger scale. When adding a detail, draw a circle around the features that will be included in the detail as shown in Figure 7.24 (top). Place the detail view on the sheet as you would a removed view. Label successive details with the word DETAIL followed by a letter, as in DETAIL A, DETAIL B, and so on, and note the scale for the detail below its name.

Enlarged details are easy to generate using CAD software.

Conventional Breaks

To shorten the view of a long object, you can use break lines as shown in Figure 7.25. Figure 7.26 shows two views of a garden rake. When the long handle of the rake is shown to scale, the details of the drawing are small and hard to read. Using a break to leave out a portion of the handle allows the scale for the ends to be increased to show the details clearly.

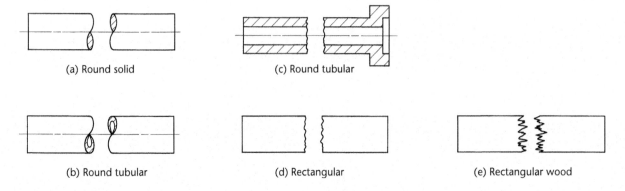

(a) Round solid

(c) Round tubular

(b) Round tubular

(d) Rectangular

(e) Rectangular wood

7.25 Conventional Break

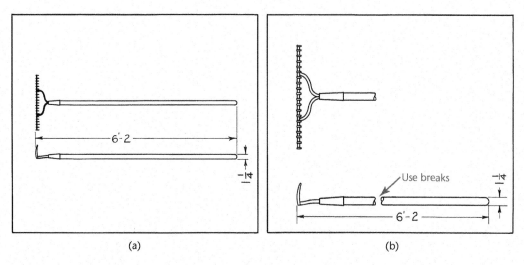

7.26 *Conventional breaks allow for increased scale to show detail.*

7.10 ALIGNMENT OF VIEWS

Always draw views in the standard arrangement shown in Figure 7.27 to be sure that your drawings are not misinterpreted. Figure 7.27a shows an offset guide that requires three views. Their correct arrangement is shown in Figure 7.27b. The top view should be directly above the front view, and the right-side view directly to the right of the front view—not out of alignment, as in Figure 7.27c, unless absolutely necessary and then the viewing directions must be clearly labeled in a pictorial view.

Never draw the views in reversed positions, with the bottom over the front view or the right side to the left of the front view, as shown in Figure 7.27d. Even though the views do line up with the front view, this arrangement could be misread.

Figure 7.28 shows three views in the correct alignment, but this drawing has a poor choice for the front view. The front view should show the shape of the object clearly. One way to consider this is that the front view shows the most information about the material that would have to be removed from a block.

After design sketches are completed, you will usually follow them with detailed CAD models and drawings. In CAD drawings, you should apply the same rules for arranging views, clearly depicting the subject of the drawing, using the proper line patterns and lineweights, and following all the necessary standards as used in drawings created by hand.

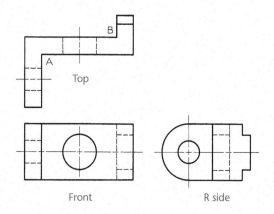

7.28 Three Views in Correct Alignment but Poor Choice of Front View

--- **TIP** ---

Because CAD makes it easy to move whole views, it is tempting to place views where they fit on the screen or plotted sheet and not in the standard or alternative projected arrangement. This is not acceptable, unless you label the viewing direction and show a removed view. Use removed views only when they are really necessary and be sure to label them clearly.

(a) Offset guide

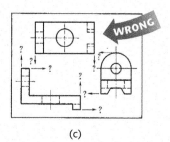

(b)   (c)

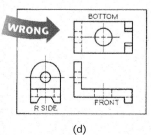

(d)

7.27 Alignment of Views for Third-Angle Projection

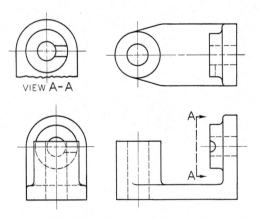

VIEW A-A

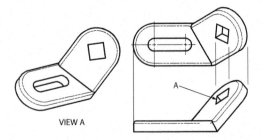

VIEW A

7.29   Removed View Using Viewing-Plane Line

7.30   Removed View Using View Indicator Arrow

7.11 REMOVED VIEWS

A ***removed view*** is a complete or partial view removed to another place on the sheet so that it is no longer in direct projection with any other view, as shown in the upper left corner of Figure 7.29. A removed view may be used to show a feature of the object more clearly, possibly to a larger scale, or to save drawing a complete regular view. A viewing-plane line is used to indicate the part being viewed. The arrows at the corners show the direction of sight. The removed views should be labeled View A–A or View B–B and so on; the letters refer to those placed at the corners of the viewing-plane line. A view indicator arrow can also be used to show the viewing direction for the removed view, as shown in Figure 7.30. Be sure to label the removed view clearly and provide its scale if it is different from the overall drawing scale.

Architectural drawings often cannot fit even two standard views on the sheet. The sheets are typically labeled to indicate the standard views, as in Figure 7.31. Views are labeled, for example, "Plan" for the top view, "East Elevation" for the side view seen from the east compass direction, and so forth. Additional views use a viewing-plane line or arrow to indicate the direction of sight.

In large civil drawings and other complex drawings such as the electrical drawing in Figure 7.32, one entire view may not be able to be shown clearly on a single sheet. For projects that extend sheet to sheet, match lines are often drawn showing how one sheet matches to the previous one.

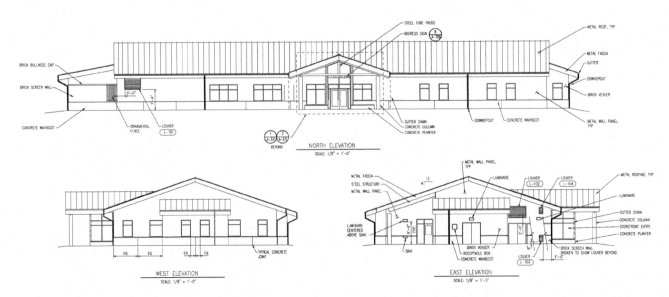

7.31   Architectural Drawing with Views Labeled *(Courtesy of CH2M HILL.)*

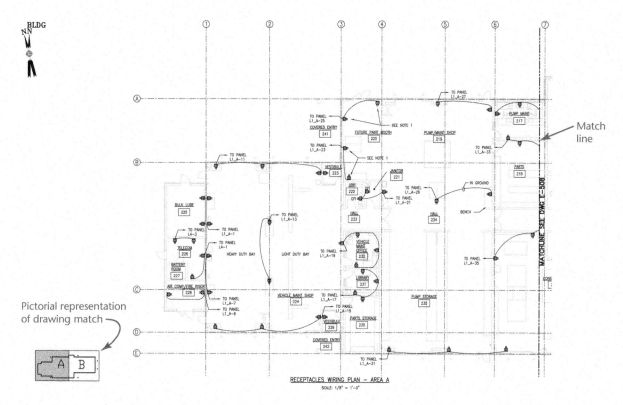

7.32 A Portion of a Building System Electrical Drawing Using Match Lines *(Courtesy of CH2M HILL.)*

7.12 RIGHT-HAND AND LEFT-HAND PARTS

Often, parts function in pairs of similar opposite parts, but opposite parts can rarely be exactly alike. For example, the right-front fender of an automobile cannot be the same shape as the left-front fender. A *left-hand part* is not simply a right-hand part turned around; the two parts are mirror images and are not interchangeable.

On sketches and drawings a left-hand part is noted as LH, and a *right-hand part* as RH. In Figure 7.33a, the part in front of the mirror is a right-hand part, and the image shows the left-hand part. No matter how the object is turned, the mirror image will show the left-hand part. Figures 7.33b and c show left-hand and right-hand drawings of the same object.

Ordinarily you draw only one of two opposite parts and label the one that is drawn with a note, such as LH PART SHOWN, RH OPPOSITE. If the opposite-hand shape is not clear, you should make a separate sketch or drawing to show it clearly and completely.

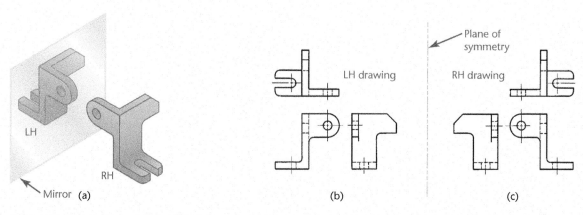

7.33 Right-Hand and Left-Hand Parts

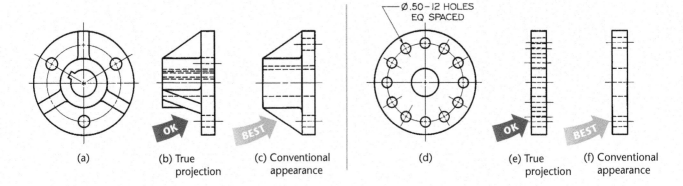

(a)   (b) True   (c) Conventional
              projection   appearance

Ø.50 – 12 HOLES
EQ SPACED

(d)   (e) True   (f) Conventional
              projection   appearance

7.34   Revolution Conventions

7.13 REVOLUTION CONVENTIONS

Regular multiview projections are sometimes awkward, confusing, or actually misleading. For example, Figure 7.34a shows an object that has three triangular ribs, three holes equally spaced in the base, and a keyway. The right-side view is a regular projection, but is not recommended—the lower ribs appear in a foreshortened position, the holes do not appear in their true relation to the rim of the base, and the keyway is projected as a confusion of hidden lines.

The method shown in Figure 7.34c is preferred because it is simpler to read and requires less time to sketch. Each of the features mentioned has been revolved in the front view to lie along the vertical centerline, from which it is projected to the correct side view.

Figures 7.34d and 7.34e show regular views of a flange with several small holes. The hidden holes are confusing and take unnecessary time to show. Figure 7.34f shows the holes revolved for clarity.

Figure 7.35 shows a regular projection with a confusing foreshortening of its inclined arm. In Figure 7.35b, the lower arm is revolved to line up vertically in the front view so that it projects the true length in the side view and makes the object's symmetry clear.

Revolutions like these are frequently used in connection with sectioning. Revolved sectional views are called *aligned sections.*

In views generated from 3D CAD models, revolving the features to show their true size is not required, but it is preferred, especially in hand-drawn and 2D CAD drawings.

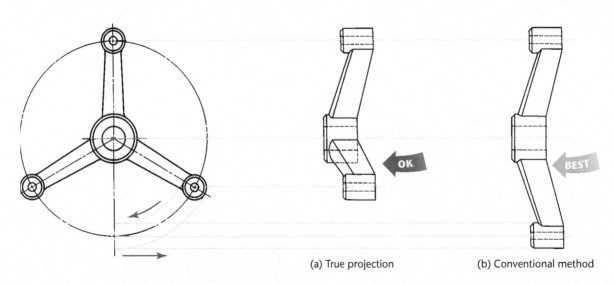

(a) True projection   (b) Conventional method

7.35   Revolution Conventions

Common Hole Features Shown in Orthographic Views

Orthographic views of common hole features are shown in Figure 7.36. See Table 7.1 on page 286 for descriptions of these common hole features.

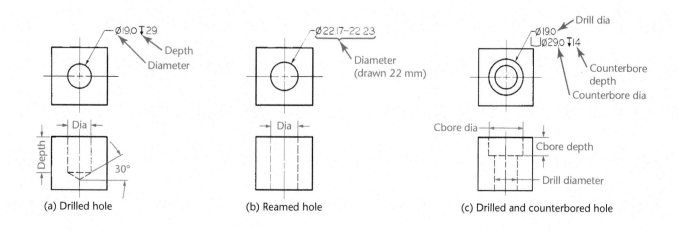

(a) Drilled hole   (b) Reamed hole   (c) Drilled and counterbored hole

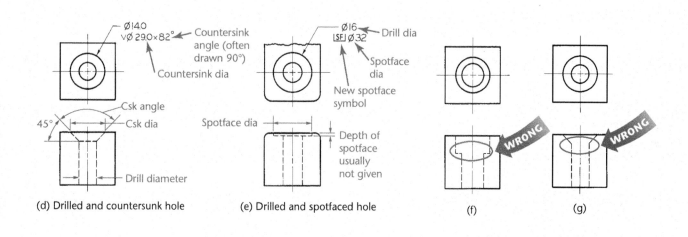

(d) Drilled and countersunk hole   (e) Drilled and spotfaced hole   (f)   (g)

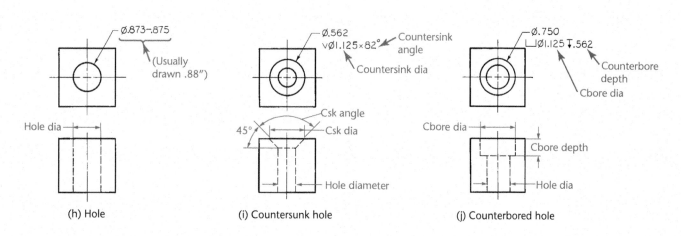

(h) Hole   (i) Countersunk hole   (j) Counterbored hole

7.36 Representing Holes in Orthographic Views; Dimensions for (a)–(e) in Metric, (h)-(j) in Inches

Common Features Shown in Orthographic Views

Orthographic views of common features are shown in Figure 7.37. See Table 7.1 on page 286 for descriptions of common features.

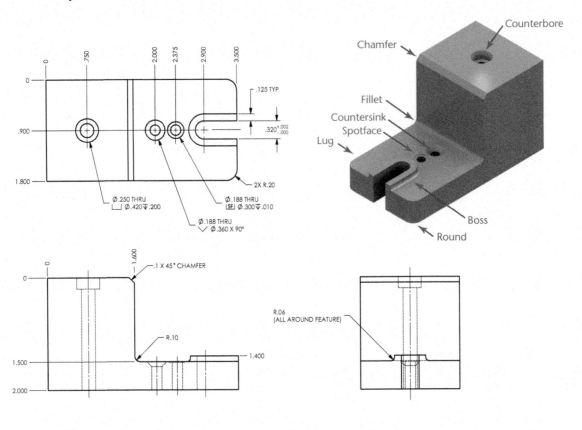

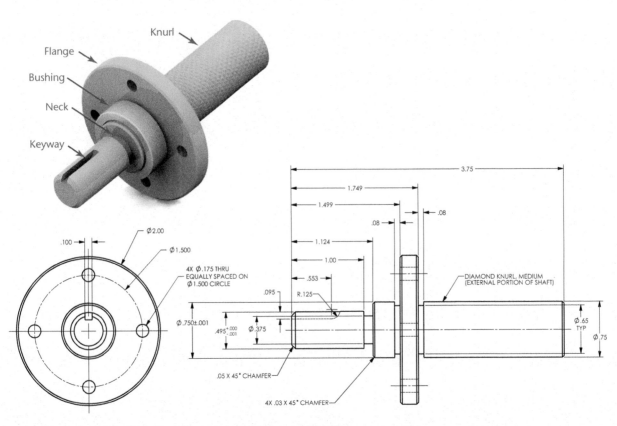

7.37 Representing Common Features in Orthographic Views

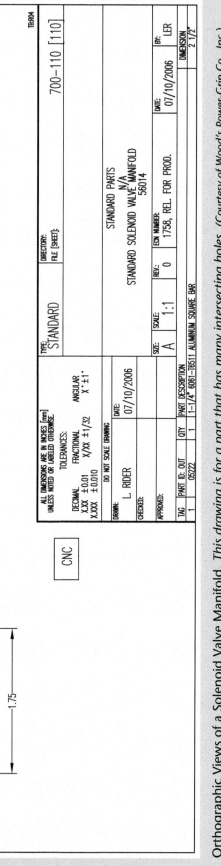

SECTION A-A

Ø 7/16"
2X 1/4 NPT

1.25

A

A

1.25

TBR04

700-110 [110]

ALL DIMENSIONS ARE IN INCHES [mm]
UNLESS NOTED OR LABELED OTHERWISE.
TOLERANCES:
DECIMAL   FRACTIONAL   ANGULAR
X.XX ±0.01   X/XX ±1/32   X° ±1°
X.XXX ±0.010

DO NOT SCALE DRAWING

DRAWN:	DATE:
L. RIDER	07/10/2006
CHECKED:	
APPROVED:	

| TAG | PART ID: OUT | QTY | PART DESCRIPTION |
| 1 | 05222 | 1 | 1-1/4" 6061-T6511 ALUMINUM SQUARE BAR |

DIRECTORY:
FILE [SHEET]:

TYPE:
STANDARD

STANDARD PARTS
N/A
STANDARD SOLENOID VALVE MANIFOLD
56014

| SIZE | SCALE: | REV.: | ECN NUMBER: |
| A | 1:1 | 0 | 1758, REL. FOR PROD. |

DATE:
07/10/2006

BY:
LER

DIMENSION
2 1/2"

CNC

4X Ø 7/32"

2X .1875

Ø 7/16 ▽ 3/4
1/4 NPT

2.5

1.25

2.25

2X .25

.625

2X Ø .339 (#R)
4X 1/8 NPT

1.75

.75

2X .75

Orthographic Views of a Solenoid Valve Manifold. *This drawing is for a part that has many intersecting holes. (Courtesy of Wood's Power-Grip Co., Inc.)*

PORTFOLIO

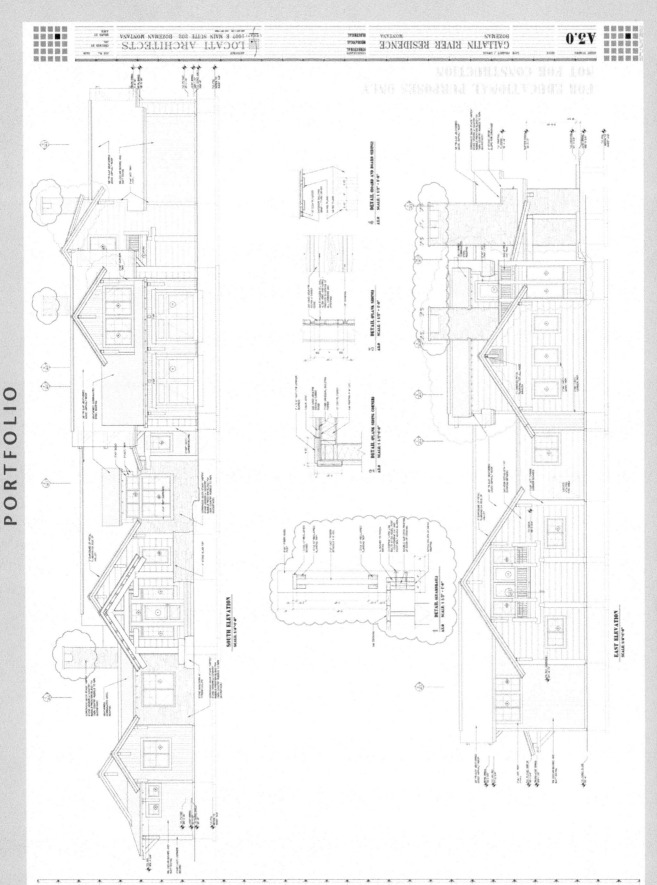

The views in this architectural drawing are too large to fit on a sheet in typical projection, so removed views are used. Notice that each view is clearly labeled as to its direction of sight, since the views are not in projection. (Courtesy of Locati Architects.)

KEY WORDS

Boss

Bushing

Counterbore

Countersink

Chamfer

Fillet

Flange

Intersect

Keyway/Keyseat

Knurl

Left-Hand Part

Lug

Neck

Partial View

Removed View

Revolutions

Right-Hand Part

Round

Runouts

Spotface

Tangent

CHAPTER SUMMARY

- Irregular curves can be plotted by identifying points on the object. The points can be projected to approximate the boundaries of the curved surface.
- Drawing conventions define usual practices for the representation of features such as holes, bosses, ribs, webs, lugs, fillets, and rounds.
- Use the same main practices to arrange drawing views on the sheet for both hand-drawn and CAD drawings. Show and label enlarged details and removed views. Use partial views and leave out hidden lines as long as the object is shown clearly.
- When curved and planar surfaces intersect, an edge is formed that is represented by a line in the drawing. When curved and planar surfaces are tangent, no edge is formed, so no line is needed. If the drawing is not clear without it, use a phantom line to show tangencies.
- Common types of holes are through, blind, countersunk, counterbored, and spotfaced.
- Fillets, rounds, and runouts are special types of tangent contours formed on parts with rounded edges.
- When necessary for clarity, features are sometimes shown in a revolved position using revolution conventions.
- Break lines can be used to leave out a section of a part where it is uniform or repetitive. Often, this is done to enlarge the scale of the remaining portions of the part so that details can be seen clearly.

REVIEW QUESTIONS

1. If the top view of an object shows a drilled through hole, how many hidden lines will be necessary in the front view to describe the hole? How many if the hole is counter-sunk? Counterbored?
2. If a plane surface intersects a contoured surface, should you show a line in the drawing to represent that intersection? What about when the plane is tangent?
3. What is a fillet? A round? A lug? A boss? Knurling?
4. How do you show right-hand and left-hand parts?
5. Which is easier, creating an enlarged detail by hand or using a CAD system?

CHAPTER EXERCISES

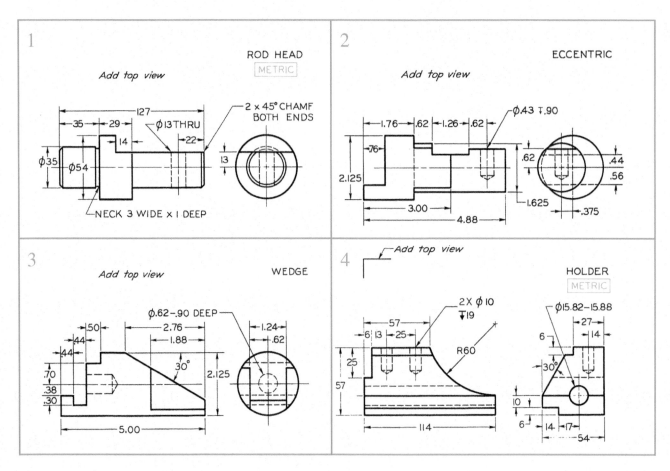

Exercise 7.1 Missing-View Problems. Sketch or draw the given views, and add the missing view. These exercises are designed to fit on 8.5″ × 11″ A-size or A4 metric size paper. Use a title block or title strip as assigned by your instructor. If dimensions are required, study Chapter 11 and use metric or decimal-inch dimensions as assigned by your instructor. Move dimensions to better locations where possible.

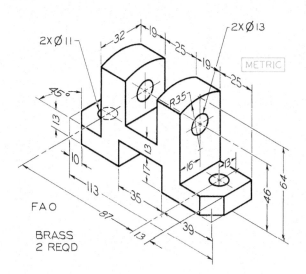

Exercise 7.2 Rod Support*

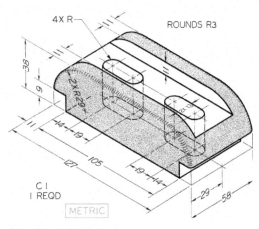

Exercise 7.3 Tailstock*

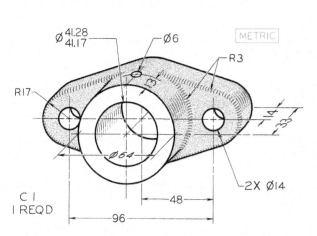

Exercise 7.4 Bearing*

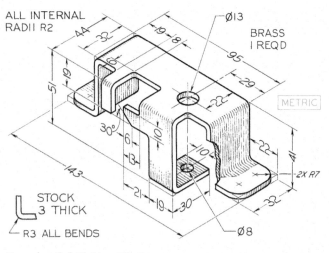

Exercise 7.5 Holder Clip*

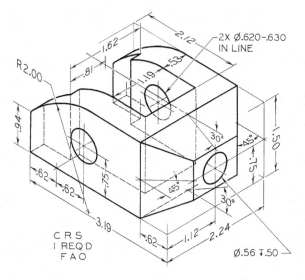

Exercise 7.6 Cam*

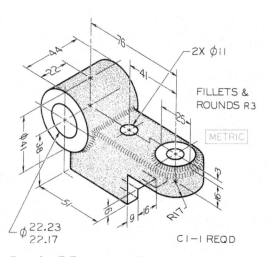

Exercise 7.7 Index Arm*

*Sketch or draw necessary views. These exercises are designed to fit on 8.5″ × 11″ A-size or A4 metric size paper. Use a title block or title strip as assigned by your instructor. If dimensions are required, study Chapter 11 and use metric or decimal-inch dimensions as assigned by your instructor. Move dimensions to better locations where possible.

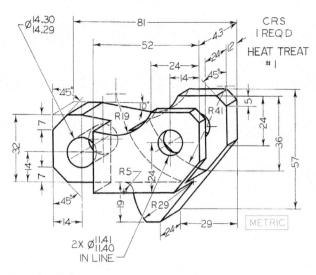

Exercise 7.8 Roller Lever*

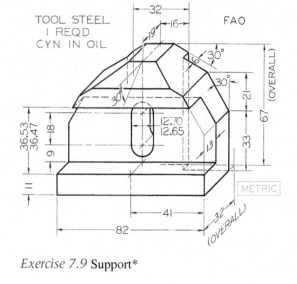

Exercise 7.9 Support*

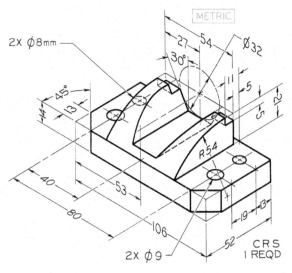

Exercise 7.10 Locating Finger*

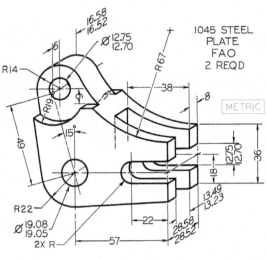

Exercise 7.11 Toggle Lever*

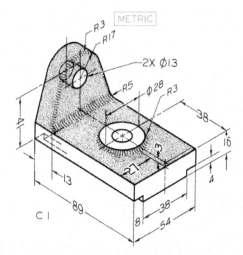

Exercise 7.12 Cut-off Holder*

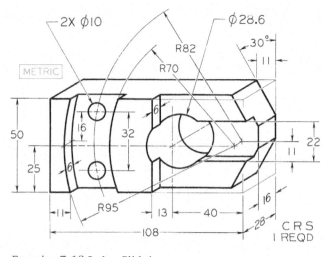

Exercise 7.13 Index Slide*

*Sketch or draw necessary views. These exercises are designed to fit on 8.5″ × 11″ A-size or A4 metric size paper. Use a title block or title strip as assigned by your instructor. If dimensions are required, study Chapter 11 and use metric or decimal-inch dimensions as assigned by your instructor. Move dimensions to better locations where possible.

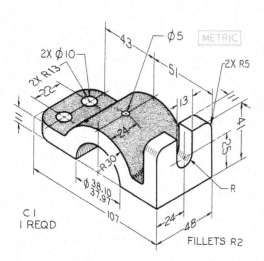

Exercise 7.14 Frame Guide*

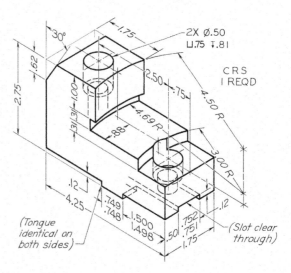

Exercise 7.15 Chuck Jaw*

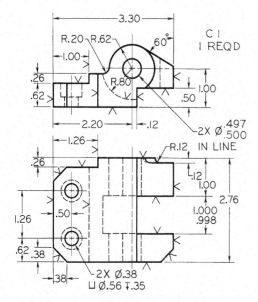

Exercise 7.16 Hinge Bracket.* Given: Front and bottom views. Required: Front, top, and right-side views.

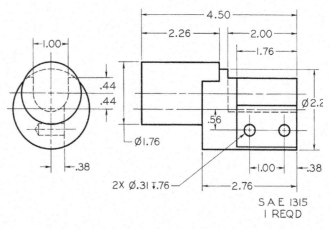

Exercise 7.17 Tool Holder.* Given: Front and left-side views. Required: Front, top, and right-side views.

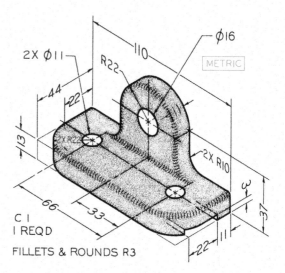

Exercise 7.19 Cross-feed Stop*

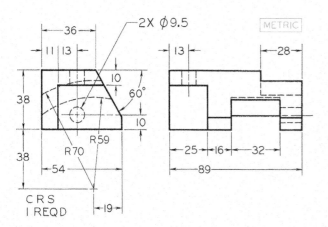

Exercise 7.18 Shifter Block.* Given: Front and left-side views. Required: Front, top, and right-side views.

*Sketch or draw necessary views. These exercises are designed to fit on 8.5″ × 11″ A-size or A4 metric size paper. Use a title block or title strip as assigned by your instructor. If dimensions are required, study Chapter 11 and use metric or decimal-inch dimensions as assigned by your instructor. Move dimensions to better locations where possible.

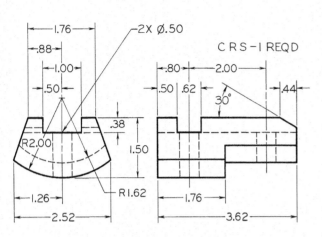

Exercise 7.20 Cross Cam.* Given: Front and left-side views. Required: Front, top, and right-side views.

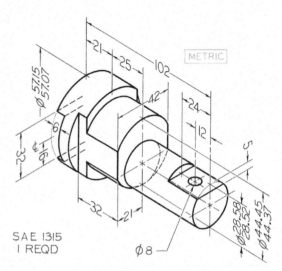

Exercise 7.21 Roller Stud*

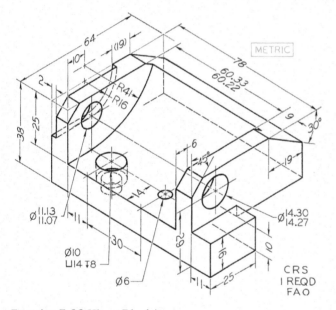

Exercise 7.22 Hinge Block*

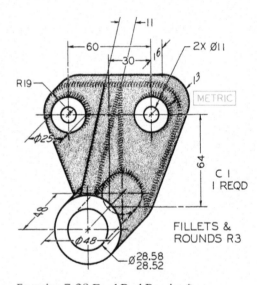

Exercise 7.23 Feed Rod Bearing*

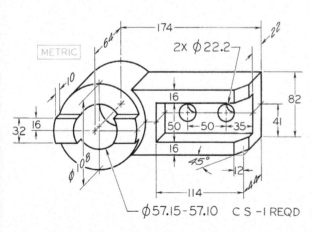

Exercise 7.24 Lever Hub.* Draw half size.

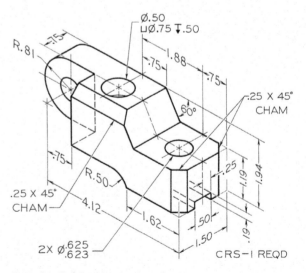

Exercise 7.25 Vibrator Arm*

*Sketch or draw necessary views. These exercises are designed to fit on 8.5″ × 11″ A-size or A4 metric size paper. Use a title block or title strip as assigned by your instructor. If dimensions are required, study Chapter 11 and use metric or decimal-inch dimensions as assigned by your instructor. Move dimensions to better locations where possible.

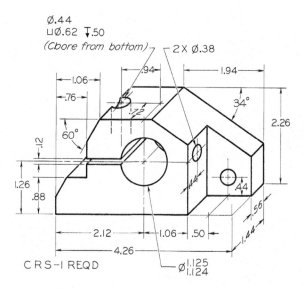

Exercise 7.26 Clutch Lever*

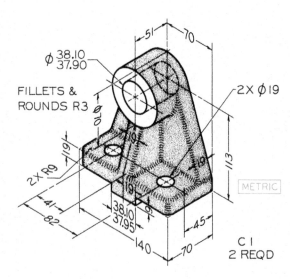

Exercise 7.27 Counter Bearing Bracket.* Draw half size.

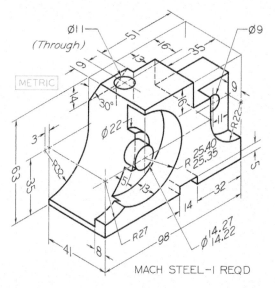

Exercise 7.28 Tool Holder*

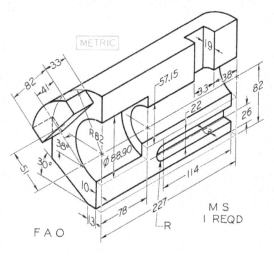

Exercise 7.29 Control Block*

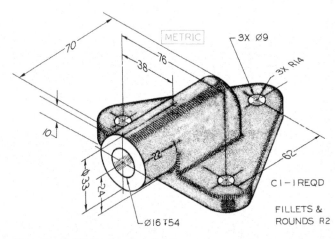

Exercise 7.30 Socket Bearing*

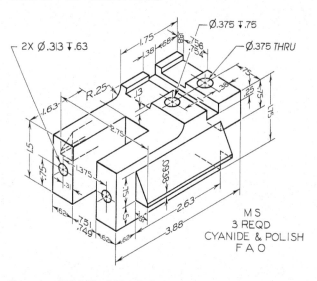

Exercise 7.31 Tool Holder*

*Sketch or draw necessary views. These exercises are designed to fit on 8.5″ × 11″ A-size or A4 metric size paper. Use a title block or title strip as assigned by your instructor. If dimensions are required, study Chapter 11 and use metric or decimal-inch dimensions as assigned by your instructor. Move dimensions to better locations where possible.

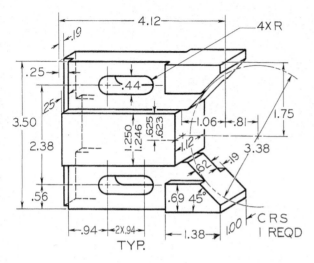

Exercise 7.32 Locating V-Block*

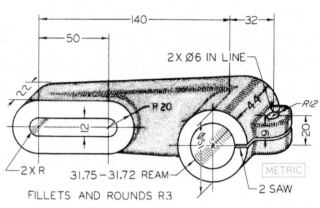

Exercise 7.33 Anchor Bracket*

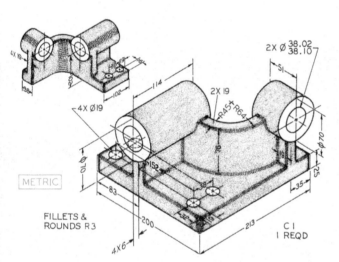

Exercise 7.34 Lead Screw Bracket.** Draw half size.

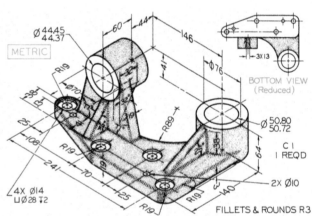

Exercise 7.35 Lever Bracket.** Draw half size.

**Sketch or draw necessary views. Larger and more detailed parts show the details more clearly when drawn on larger sheet sizes. Consider using B, C, or A3 or A2 sheets. Use a title block or title strip as assigned by your instructor. If dimensions are required, study Chapter 11 and use metric or decimal-inch dimensions as assigned by your instructor. Move dimensions to better locations where possible.

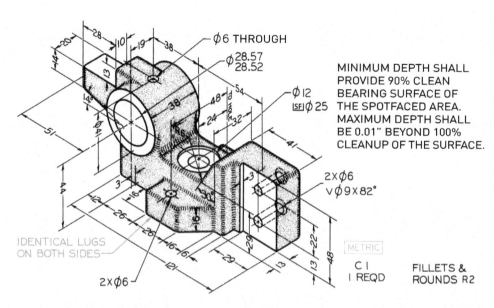

φ6 THROUGH

φ 28.57
  28.52

φ 12
|SF| φ 25

MINIMUM DEPTH SHALL
PROVIDE 90% CLEAN
BEARING SURFACE OF
THE SPOTFACED AREA.
MAXIMUM DEPTH SHALL
BE 0.01" BEYOND 100%
CLEANUP OF THE SURFACE.

2×φ6
∨φ9×82°

IDENTICAL LUGS
ON BOTH SIDES

2×φ6

METRIC

C I
I REQD

FILLETS &
ROUNDS R2

Exercise 7.36 Gripper Rod Center*

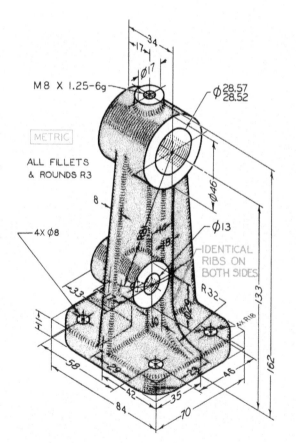

M8 X 1.25-6g

METRIC

ALL FILLETS
& ROUNDS R3

φ17

φ 28.57
  28.52

4X φ8

8

φ46

φ13

IDENTICAL
RIBS ON
BOTH SIDES

R 32

133

162

33

58   29

42   35   46

84   70

Exercise 7.37 Bearing Bracket*

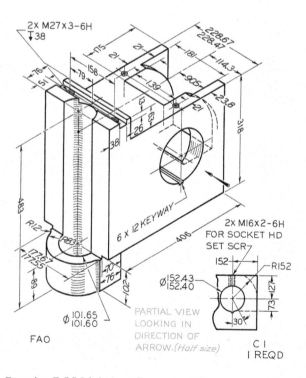

2× M27x3-6H
↧ 38

6 × 12 KEYWAY

2x MI6x2-6H
FOR SOCKET HD
SET SCR

152   RI52

φ 152.43
  152.40

73   127

30

PARTIAL VIEW
LOOKING IN
DIRECTION OF
ARROW. *(Half size)*

C I
I REQD

φ 101.65
  101.60

FAO

Exercise 7.38 Link Arm Connector.* Draw one-quarter size.

*Sketch or draw necessary views. Larger and more detailed parts show the details more clearly when drawn on larger sheet sizes. Consider using B, C, or A3 or A2 sheets. Use a title block or title strip as assigned by your instructor. If dimensions are required, study Chapter 11 and use metric or decimal-inch dimensions as assigned by your instructor. Move dimensions to better locations where possible.

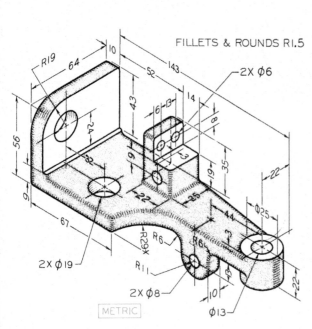

FILLETS & ROUNDS R1.5

Exercise 7.39 Mounting Bracket*

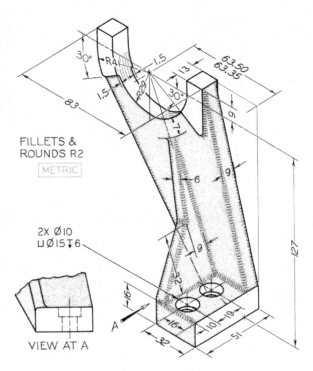

FILLETS & ROUNDS R2
METRIC

2X Ø10
⊔Ø15↧6

VIEW AT A

Exercise 7.40 LH Shifter Fork*

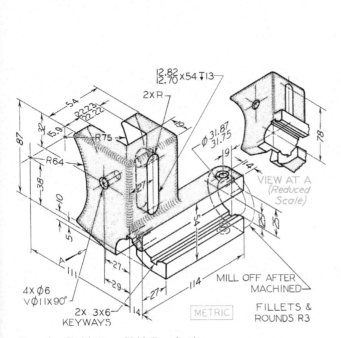

VIEW AT A
(Reduced Scale)

4X Ø6
∨Ø11X90°

2X 3X6
KEYWAYS

MILL OFF AFTER
MACHINED

FILLETS &
ROUNDS R3

METRIC

Exercise 7.41 Gear Shift Bracket*

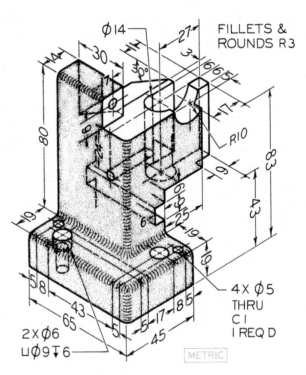

FILLETS &
ROUNDS R3

4X Ø5
THRU
C1
1 REQ D

2X Ø6
⊔Ø9↧6

METRIC

Exercise 7.42 Fixture Base*

*Sketch or draw necessary views. Larger and more detailed parts show the details more clearly when drawn on larger sheet sizes. Consider using B, C, or A3 or A2 sheets. Use a title block or title strip as assigned by your instructor. If dimensions are required, study Chapter 11 and use metric or decimal-inch dimensions as assigned by your instructor. Move dimensions to better locations where possible.

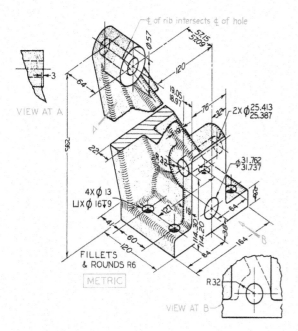

Exercise 7.43 Ejector Base.* Draw half size.

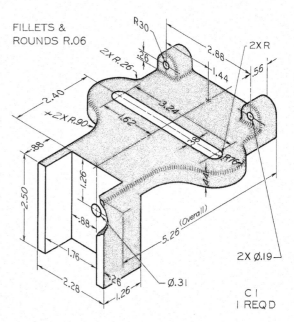

Exercise 7.44 Tension Bracket*

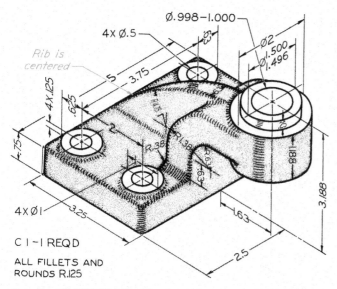

Exercise 7.45 Offset Bearing*

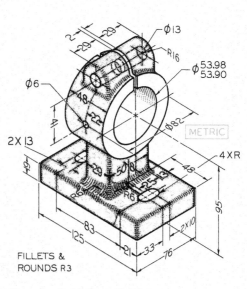

Exercise 7.46 Feed Guide*

*Sketch or draw necessary views. Larger and more detailed parts show the details more clearly when drawn on larger sheet sizes. Consider using B, C, or A3 or A2 sheets. Use a title block or title strip as assigned by your instructor. If dimensions are required, study Chapter 11 and use metric or decimal-inch dimensions as assigned by your instructor. Move dimensions to better locations where possible.

Exercise 7.47 Feed Shaft Bracket.
Given: Front and top views. Required:
Front, top, and right-side views,
half size.*

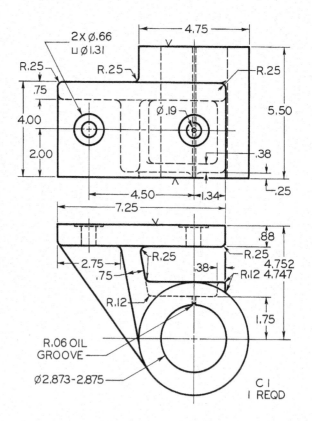

Exercise 7.48 Trip Lever. Given: Front,
top, and partial side views. Required:
Front, bottom, and left-side views,
drawn completely.*

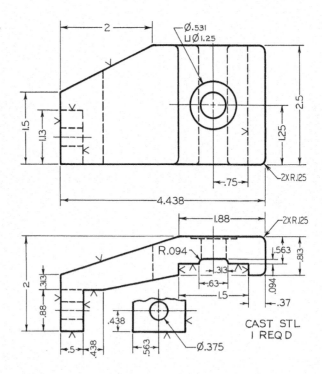

*Sketch or draw necessary views. Larger and more detailed parts show the details more clearly when drawn on larger sheet sizes. Consider using B, C, or A3 or A2 sheets. Use a title block or title strip as assigned by your instructor. If dimensions are required, study Chapter 11 and use metric or decimal-inch dimensions as assigned by your instructor. Move dimensions to better locations where possible.

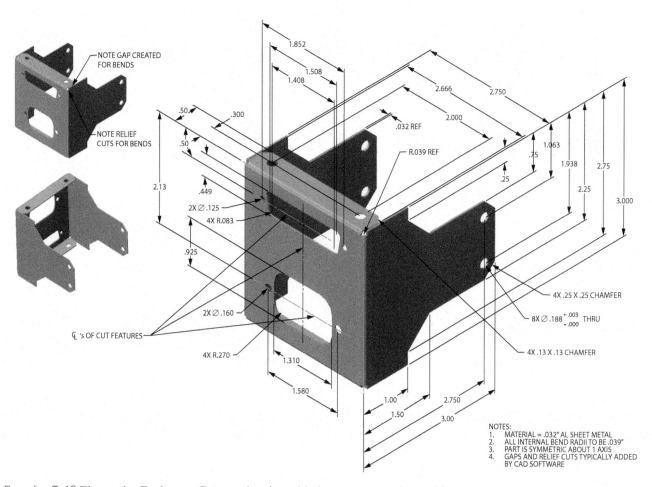

Exercise 7.49 Electronics Enclosure. Create a drawing with the necessary orthographic views for the sheet metal electronics mount.

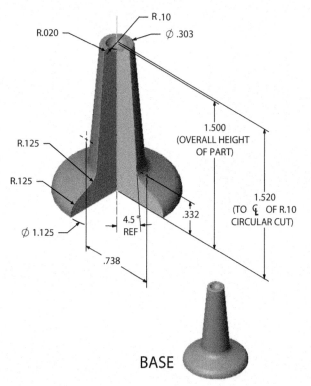

BASE

Exercise 7.50 Gyroscope Base. Create a drawing with the necessary orthographic views.

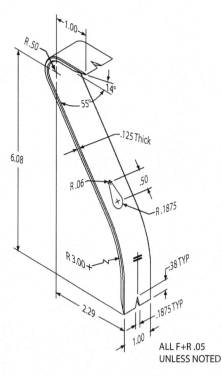

Exercise 7.51 Pry Bar. Create a drawing with the necessary orthographic views for the pry bar.

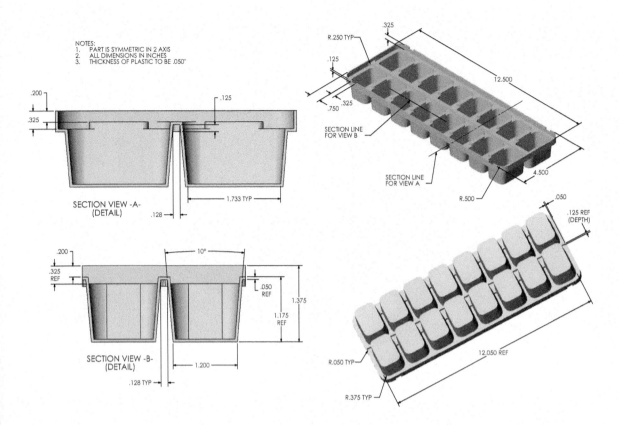

Exercise 7.52 Ice Cube Tray. Create a drawing showing the necessary orthographic views of the ice cube tray.

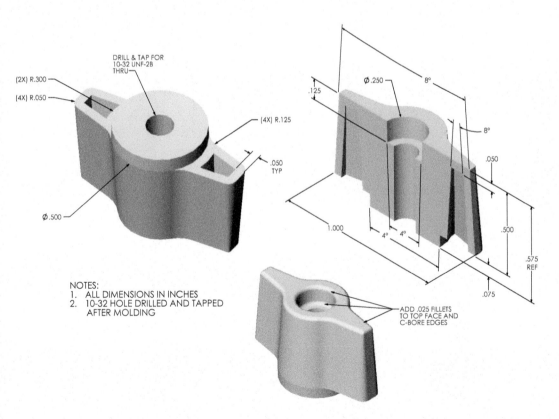

Exercise 7.53 Simple Knob. Create a drawing showing the necessary orthographic views of the knob.

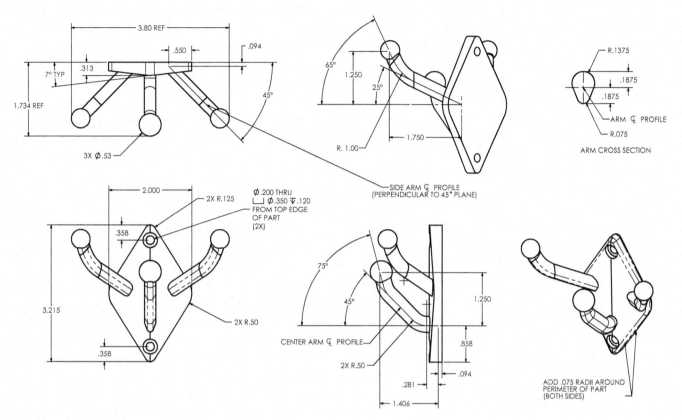

Exercise 7.54 Wall Hanger. Create a drawing showing the necessary orthographic views of the wall hanger. If assigned, create a 3D model and generate the drawing views from the model.

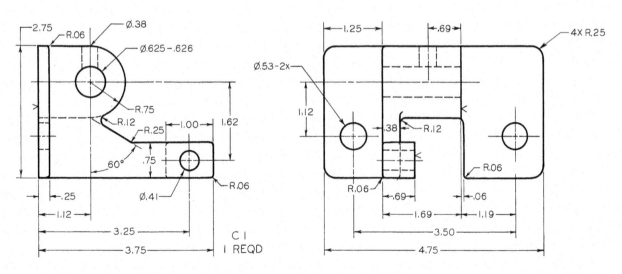

Exercise 7.55 Knurl Bracket Bearing. Given: Front and left-side views. Required: Take front as top view on new drawing, and add front and right-side views. (Use layout B or A3 with a title block as in Fig III or Fig IV, shown on inside front cover, or as directed by your instructor.)*

*Draw or sketch necessary views. Use metric or decimal-inch dimensions as assigned by the instructor.

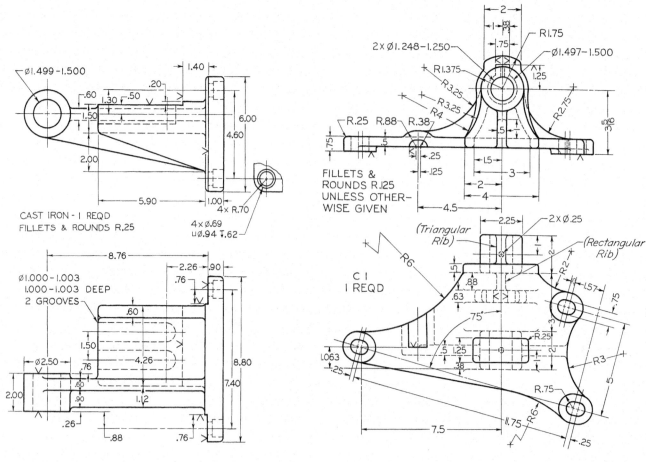

Exercise 7.56 Horizontal Bracket for Broaching Machine. Given: Front and top views. Required: Take top as front view in new drawing; then add top and left-side views. (Use layout C or A2 with a title block as in Fig IV, shown on inside front cover, or as directed by your instructor.)*

Exercise 7.57 Boom Swing Bearing for a Power Crane. Given: Front and bottom views. Required: Front, top, and left-side views. (Use layout C or A2 with a title block as in Fig IV, shown on inside front cover, or as directed by your instructor.)*

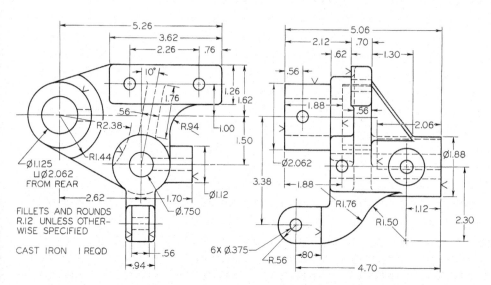

Exercise 7.58 Power Feed Bracket for Universal Grinder. Given: Front and right-side views. Required: Front, top, and left-side views, full size. (Use layout C or A2 with a title block as in Fig IV, shown on inside front cover, or as directed by your instructor.)*

*Draw or sketch necessary views. If dimensions are required, study Chapter 11 and use metric or decimal-inch dimensions as assigned by the instructor.

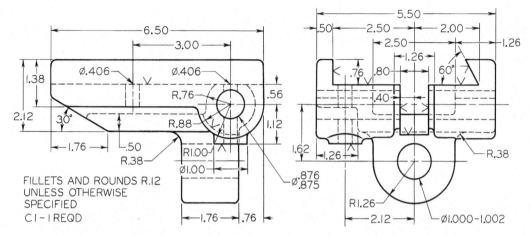

Exercise 7.59 Sliding Nut for Mortiser. Given: Top and right-side views. Required: Front, top, and left-side views, full size. (Use layout C or A2 with a title block as in Fig IV, shown on inside front cover, or as directed by your instructor.)*

*Draw or sketch necessary views. If dimensions are required, study Chapter 11 and use metric or decimal-inch dimensions as assigned by the instructor.

Exercise 7.60 Create a set of orthographic views generated from a solid model for the part shown. Change the overall width of the part from 3.18 to 3.75 inches. Change the angle from 120 to 135 degrees. Keep the remaining dimensions as given.

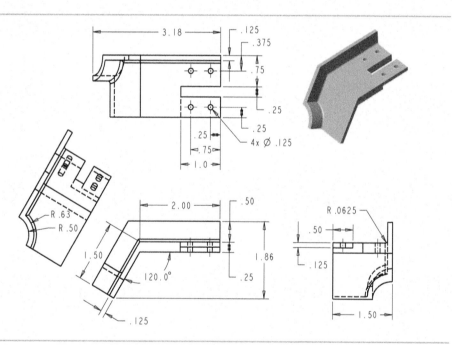

Exercise 7.61 Create a set of orthographic views generated from a solid model for the decorative corner cap part. Change the hole diameters from .125 to .1625. Change the spherical diameter to 1.25.

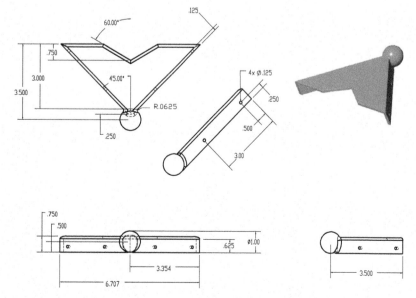

Exercise 7.62 Carefully consider which feature to use as the base feature and how you will create the model for the hand weight so it will update as specified. Determine the weight if this part is cast from ASTM class 20 gray iron. Update the model to create a set of three hand weights of different weights, but maintain the diameter and length of the crossbar grip. Create a set of orthographic views generated from your solid models for each of the three hand weights.

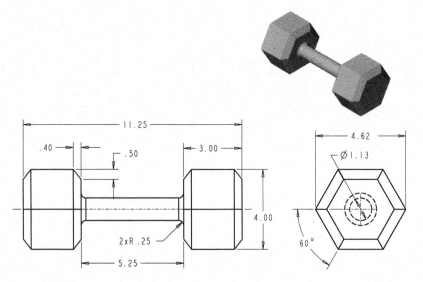

Exercise 7.63 Model the part so that as the overall height, width, depth of the part are changed the other features are updated proportionally to them. Before starting, carefully consider which feature to use as the base feature and how you will create the model so it will be updated as specified. Create a set of orthographic views generated from the solid model for the part as shown. Update the part so the overall height is 6.5″, the overall width is 2.5″ and the depth is 2.25″. Produce a second set of orthographic views showing the updated part.

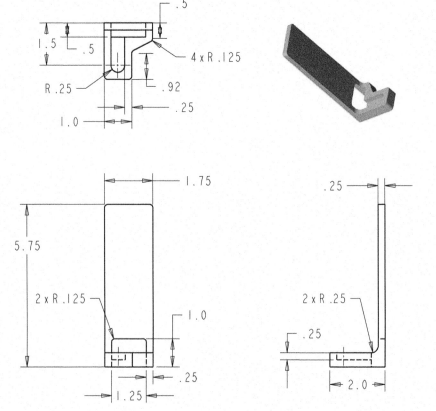

Exercise 7.64 Create a constraint-based model of the first configuration, save the part, then edit the part to create the second configuration shown. Before starting, carefully consider which feature to use as the base feature and how you will create the model so it will update as specified. Save all part files. Create a set of orthographic views generated from the solid model for each version of the geneva gear.

NOTE: THICKNESS = .25

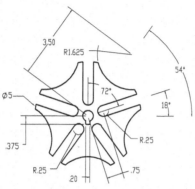

GENEVA GEAR CONFIGURATION # 1

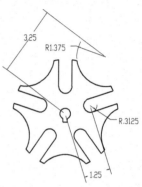

GENEVA GEAR CONFIGURATION # 2

Exercise 7.65 Create a constraint-based model of the first configuration, save the part, then edit the part to create the second configuration shown. Before starting, carefully consider which feature to use as the base feature and how you will create the model so it will be updated as specified. Save all part files. Create a set of orthographic views for each version of the part.

BASE FEATURE W/ REGULAR RIB

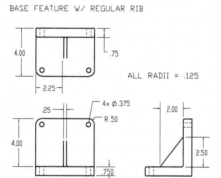

ALL RADII = .125

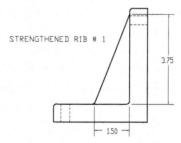

STRENGTHENED RIB # 1

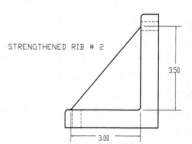

STRENGTHENED RIB # 2

NOTE: RIB THICKNESS REMAINS .25

CHAPTER EIGHT

SECTION VIEWS

OBJECTIVES

After studying the material in this chapter, you should be able to:

1. Understand sections and cutting-plane lines.

2. Apply correct section-lining practices.

3. Recognize and draw section lining for 10 different materials.

4. Draw a section view given a two-view drawing.

5. Demonstrate correct hidden-line practices for section views.

6. Identify seven types of sections.

7. Apply section techniques to create clear, interpretable drawings.

8. Demonstrate the proper techniques for sectioning ribs, webs, and spokes.

9. Use hatching when using conventional breaks to show elongated objects.

10. Interpret drawings that include section views.

Refer to the following standards:
* *ANSI/ASME Y14.3 Orthographic and Pictorial Views*

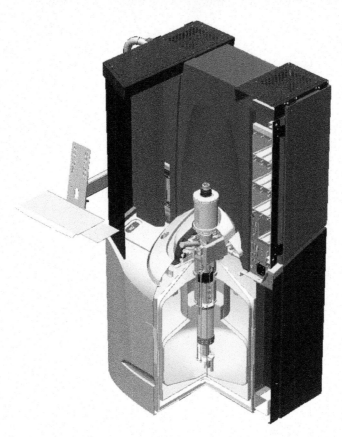

3D Section View of the Superconducting Quantum Interference Device (SQUID). *This isometric section view shows the interior details.* *(Courtesy of Quantum Design.)*

OVERVIEW

Technical drawings often represent a single part with a complex interior structure, or many different parts in a mechanical assembly, building, bridge, toy, or other product. When you are creating a drawing, if the interior structure cannot be shown clearly by using hidden lines, you should use a section view to reveal the internal features of the part.

To visualize a section view, think of slicing through the object as if you were cutting through an apple or melon. This familiar cutaway view—looking onto the cut portion of the object—is called a section view, or sometimes a cross section.

Special conventions, some that depart from the practices you have learned for orthographic projection, are used to make section views easier to understand. 3D CAD modeling software often cannot generate section views that meet all these special conventions, so current practice allows for direct sections of the 3D model. 2D and 3D CAD users need to understand section views thoroughly to use them effectively.

Selecting the section view that best shows the drawing information is a skill that takes practice.

8.1   Full Section of a Melon

UNDERSTANDING SECTIONS

Section views are used for three main purposes:

- To document the design and manufacture of single parts that are manufactured as one piece.
- To document how multiple parts are to be assembled or built.
- To aid in visualizing the internal workings of a design.

Sections of Single Parts

If you have ever cut a melon in half, you have created a full section in real life (Figure 8.1). To visualize a section of a single part is no different. Think of the part as being sliced through by the cutting plane, as if the plane were a giant cleaver. Once the object is cut, the closer half is pulled away, showing the inside construction of the part.

Full Sections

When the part is cut fully in half, the resulting view is called a *full section,* as shown in Figure 8.2. Figure 8.3 shows a technical drawing of the part from Figure 8.2 that does not use a section view. Notice how confusing all the hidden lines look.

Figure 8.4 shows the same drawing, but this time the right-side view is replaced with a right section view. Now it is much easier to understand.

In a drawing with a section view, the missing half is imagined to be removed and is not actually shown removed in any view except the section view. A line called the *cutting-plane line* provides the information necessary for understanding where the part was cut. The arrows at the ends of the cutting-plane line indicate the direction of sight for the section view.

In the section view, the areas that would have been in actual contact with the cutting plane (refer to the example shown in Figure 8.2) are shown with *section lining.* Those areas are crosshatched with thin parallel section lines.

The Cutting Plane

The cutting plane is shown in a view adjacent to the section view, in this case the front view. In this view, the cutting plane appears edgewise as a thick dashed line—the cutting-plane line.

The arrows at the ends of the cutting-plane line indicate the direction of sight for the section view, as shown in Figure 8.4. The arrows point *toward the section being viewed* as shown in Figures 8.4 and 8.5, not away from it, as in Figure 8.6.

Lines behind the Cutting Plane

The now-exposed visible edges of the object behind the cutting plane are shown, but they are not crosshatched with section lining, because they were not cut. Figure 8.7 shows an example of object edges exposed by the cutting plane appearing as visible lines in the section view. In a full section, the location of the cutting plane is obvious from the section itself, so the cutting-plane line is often omitted. You will learn about other section types that require the cutting-plane line to be understood later in this chapter. Cutting-plane lines should be used wherever necessary for clarity.

8.2   Slicing a Single Part

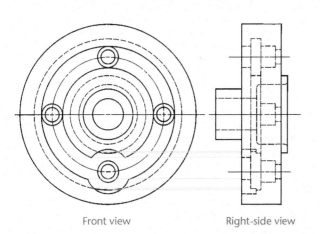

8.3   Front and Right-Side Views. *Parts with a lot of interior detail may have so many hidden lines that their views are confusing.*

8.4   Front and Right-Side View in Full Section. *Using a section view makes it easier to see interior details.*

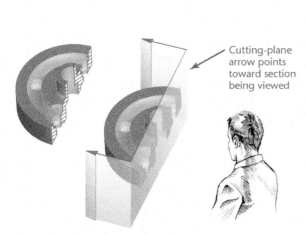

Cutting-plane arrow points toward section being viewed

8.5   Cutting-plane Line Indicates Direction of Sight

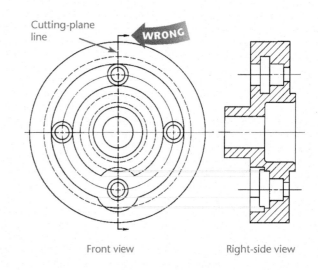

8.6   *Arrows should not point to removed portion.*

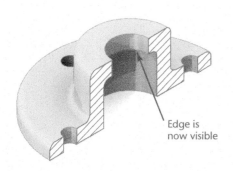

Edge is now visible

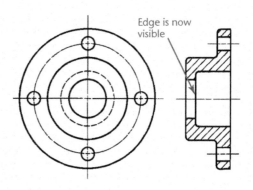

8.7   *Some previously hidden edges of the part are visible in the section view.*

VISUALIZING A FULL SECTION

Choose a Cutting Plane

1 This illustration shows a collar to be sectioned. To produce a clear section showing both the counter-bored recess and the smaller hole near the top of the object, choose a cutting plane that will pass through the vertical centerline in the front view, and imagine the right half of the object removed.

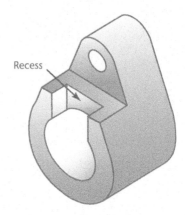

Identify the Surfaces

2 The pictorial drawing of the remaining half is shown at right. The first step in projecting the section view is making sure that you interpret the object correctly. Identifying the surfaces on the object can help.

Surfaces R, S, T, U, and V have been labeled on the given views and the pictorial view.

Which surface is R in the front view?

Which surface is U in the top view?

Are they normal, inclined, or oblique surfaces?

Can you identify the counterbored recess in each view?

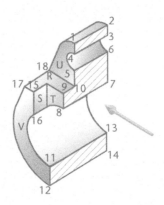

Draw the Section View

3 To draw the section view, omit the portion of the object in front of the cutting plane. You will be drawing only the portion that remains.

Determine which are solid parts of the object the cutting plane will pass through. *Hint: The outside of an object can never be a hole; it must be solid, unless the cutting plane passes through a slot to the exterior.*

The points that will be projected to create the section view have been identified for you in the example shown.

The three surfaces produced by the cutting plane are bounded by points 1-2-3-4 and 5-6-7-8-9-10 and 13-14-12-11. These are shown hatched.

Each sectioned area is completely enclosed by a boundary of visible lines. In addition to the cut surfaces, the section view shows all visible parts behind the cutting plane.

No hidden lines are shown. However, the corresponding section shown in this step is incomplete, because visible lines are missing.

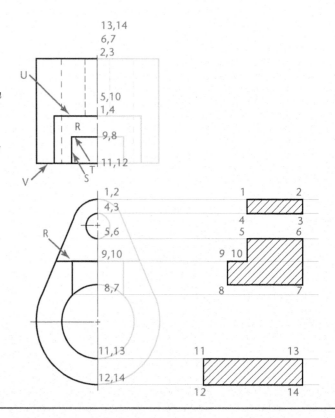

(continued)

Project the Visible Lines

4 From the direction the section is viewed, the top surface (V) of the object appears in the section as a visible line (12-11-16-15).

The bottom surface of the object appears similarly as 14-13-7-6-3-2. The bottom surface of the counterbored recess appears in the section as line 19-20.

Also, the back half of the counterbored recess and the drilled hole appear as rectangles in the section at 19-20-15-16 and 3-4-5-6. These points must also be projected. The finished view is shown at right.

Notice that since all cut surfaces are part of the same object, the hatching must all run in the same direction.

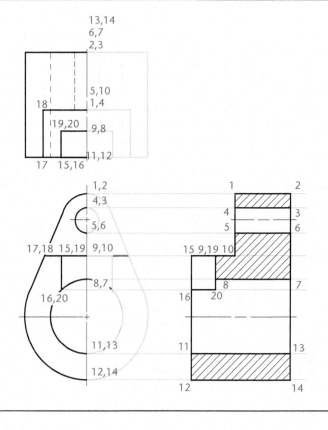

8.1 PLACEMENT OF SECTION VIEWS

Section views can replace the normal top, front, side, or other standard orthographic views in the standard view arrangement. Figure 8.8 shows an example. In this drawing, the front view of the object is shown in section. Only two views are necessary. The front view is shown as a section view, and the cutting-plane line is shown in the right-side view.

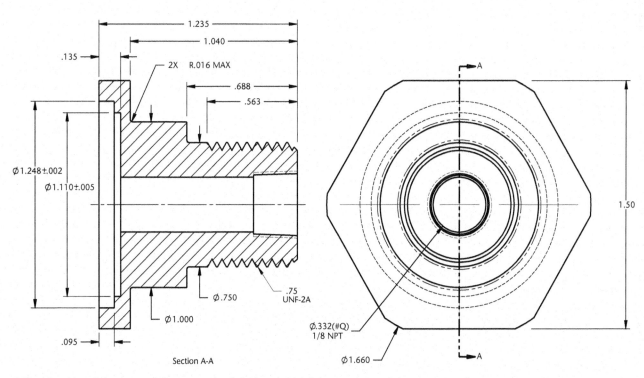

8.8 *Section views can replace standard orthographic views.* (Courtesy of Wood's Power-Grip. Co. Inc.)

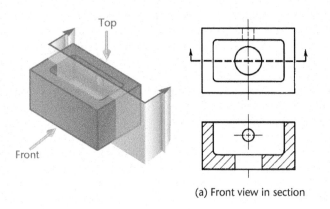

(a) Front view in section

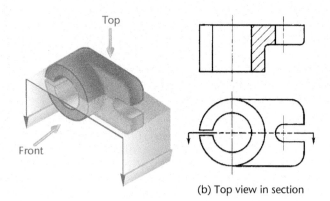

(b) Top view in section

8.9 Front and Top Views in Section

In Figure 8.9a, the object is cut through with a plane parallel to the front view. The front half of the object is imagined removed. The resulting full section may be referred to as the "front view in section" because it occupies the front view position.

In Figure 8.9b, the cutting plane is a horizontal plane (which would appear as a line in the front view). The upper half of the object is imagined removed. The resulting full section is shown in place of the top view.

When adding a section view to your drawing, keep in mind that your purpose is to document and convey information about your design and show the information in the way that best achieves this objective.

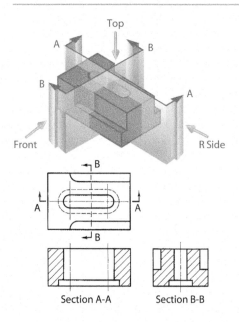

8.10 Front and Side Views in Section

8.2 LABELING CUTTING PLANES

In Figure 8.10, two cutting planes are shown, one a plane parallel to the front view and the other a plane parallel to the side view, both of which appear edgewise in the top view. Each section is completely independent of the other and drawn as if the other were not present.

For section A–A, the front half of the object is imagined removed. The back half is then viewed in the direction of the arrows for a front view, and the resulting section is a front view in section.

For section B–B, the right half of the object is imagined removed. The left half is then viewed in the direction of the arrows for a right-side view, and the resulting section is a right-side view in section. The cutting-plane lines are preferably drawn through an exterior view (in this case the top view, as shown) instead of a section view.

The cutting-plane lines in Figure 8.10 are shown for purposes of illustration only. They are generally omitted in cases where the location of the cutting plane is obvious.

8.3 LINE PRECEDENCE

When a cutting-plane line coincides with a centerline, the cutting-plane line takes precedence. When the cutting-plane line would obscure important details in the view, just the ends of the line outside the view and the arrows can be shown as in Figure 8.11. When you do this, be sure to leave a small but visible gap between the lines of the view and the small portion of the cutting-plane line.

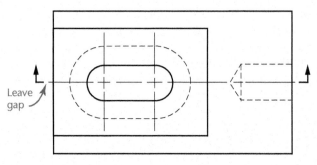

8.11 *The cutting-plane line takes precedence over the centerline unless it obscures important detail.*

8.4 RULES FOR LINES IN SECTION VIEWS

When creating section views follow these general rules:

- Show *edges and contours that are now visible behind the cutting plane*; otherwise a section will appear to be made up of disconnected and unrelated parts. (Occasionally, visible lines behind the cutting plane may be omitted, particularly from those generated from 3D models.)
- Omit *hidden lines in section views*. Section views are used to show interior detail without a confusion of hidden lines, so add them only if necessary to understand the part.
- Sometimes hidden lines are necessary for clarity and should be used in such cases, especially if their use will make it possible to omit a view (Figure 8.12d).
- A sectioned area is always completely bounded by a visible outline—never by a hidden line, because in every case the cut surfaces will be the closest surface in the section view and therefore their boundary lines will be visible (Figure 8.12e).
- In a section view of an object, the section lines in all hatched areas for that object must be parallel, not as shown in Figure 8.12f. The use of section lining in opposite directions is an indication of different parts, as when two or more parts are adjacent in an assembly drawing.
- A visible line can never cross a sectioned area in a view of a single part. This would be impossible on the full section of a single part because the section lines are all in the same plane. A line across it would indicate a change of plane (Figure 8.12g). In an assembly section, this would be possible. You will learn about assemblies later in the chapter.

TIP

Learning the rules for section lining saves time. Extra hidden lines and hatching that is denser than necessary take longer to draw and make drawings slower to print. They also make drawings harder to read.

TIP

In CAD, when views can be placed by projection from a 3D model, saving time by omitting a view is not a big concern, but saving space on the drawing sheet by leaving out a view often may be.

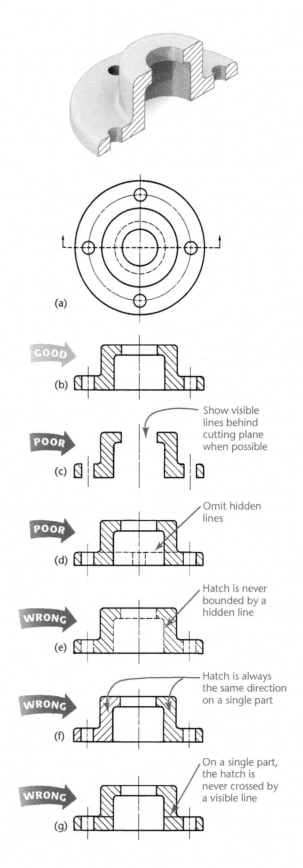

(a)

GOOD   (b)

POOR   (c)   Show visible lines behind cutting plane when possible

POOR   (d)   Omit hidden lines

WRONG   (e)   Hatch is never bounded by a hidden line

WRONG   (f)   Hatch is always the same direction on a single part

WRONG   (g)   On a single part, the hatch is never crossed by a visible line

8.12 Right and Wrong Lines in Section Views

8.5 CUTTING-PLANE LINE STYLE

Figure 8.13a shows the preferred style of line to use for the cutting-plane line. It is made up of equal dashes, each about 6 mm (1/4″) long ending in arrowheads. This form works especially well for drawings. The alternative style, shown in Figure 8.13b, uses alternating long dashes and pairs of short dashes and ends with arrowheads. This style has been in general use for a long time, so you may still see it on drawings. Both lines are drawn the same thickness as visible lines. The arrowheads at the ends of the cutting-plane line indicate the direction in which the cutaway object is viewed (as was shown in Figure 8.5).

Use capital letters at the ends of the cutting-plane line when necessary to help the drawing's reader match each cutting-plane line to its section view. Figure 8.10 showed an example where the cutting plane is labeled and the resulting section view is labeled to match. This most often occurs in the case of multiple sections or removed sections, which are discussed later in the chapter.

An alternative method for showing the cutting plane is to draw the cutting-line pattern and then draw reference arrows pointing to it in the direction of sight (Figure 8.14a).

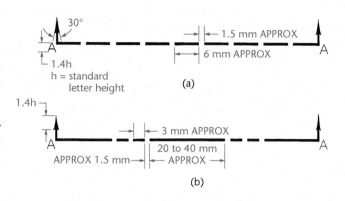

8.13 Cutting-Plane Lines (Full Size)

Especially on architectural drawings, the center of the cutting-plane line is often left out and stylized arrows are used to identify the cutting plane (Figure 8.14b).

The arrows on the cutting-plane lines are made larger than the dimension arrowheads to call attention to the location of sections and removed views. Make the arrows 1.4 times the drawing letter height. Make the view label text 1.4 times the drawing letter height also. For example, an 8.5″ × 11″ drawing uses text that is .125″ (1/8″) tall as a minimum, so for this sheet size, use arrows on the cutting plane .175″ (about 3/16″, or about 4.5 mm) tall (Figure 8.13).

Visualizing Cutting-Plane Direction

Correct and incorrect relations between cutting-plane lines and corresponding section views are shown in Figure 8.15.

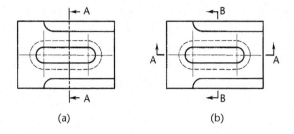

8.14 Alternative Methods for Showing a Cutting Plane

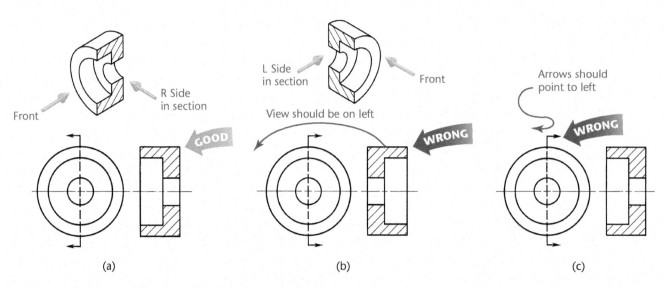

8.15 Correct and Incorrect Cutting-Plane Line Placement

8.6 SECTION-LINING TECHNIQUE

The correct method of drawing section lines is shown in Figure 8.16a. When drawing by hand, use a sharp, medium-grade pencil (H or 2H) to draw uniformly thin section lines, or *hatching* (a term meaning closely spaced parallel lines). There should be a marked contrast between the thin section lines and the thick visible outlines of the part.

Draw section lines at 45° from horizontal unless they would be parallel or perpendicular to major edges of the part, in which case use a different angle. Figure 8.16b shows an example of section lines drawn at a different angle to prevent them from being parallel or perpendicular to visible outlines.

Space the lines as evenly as possible by eye (for most drawings, about 2.5 mm (1/10″) apart). The spacing interval depends on the size of the drawing or of the sectioned area, with larger drawings having wider spacing. In a smaller draw-

ing the spacing interval may be as small as 1.5 mm (1/16″); in a large drawing, it may be 3 mm (1/8″) or more. As a rule, space the lines as generously as possible, yet close enough to clearly distinguish the sectioned areas.

Keep extension lines and dimension values off sectioned areas. If there is no alternative, omit the section lines behind the dimensions (Figure 8.16c).

> **TIP**
>
> Beginners tend to draw section lines too close together. This is tedious and makes small inaccuracies in spacing obvious. After the first few lines, look back repeatedly at the original spacing to avoid gradually increasing or decreasing the intervals between the lines.

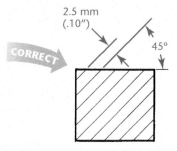

2.5 mm (.10″)   45°   CORRECT

- Uniformly spaced by an interval of about 2.5 mm
- Not too close together
- Uniformly thin, not varying in thickness
- Distinctly thinner than visible lines
- Neither running beyond nor stopping short of visible outlines

(a) Correctly drawn section lines

NO!	NO!	NO!	NO!	NO!
Spacing irregular	Lines too close	Varying line widths	Lines too thick	Lines short or overrunning

(b) Direction of Section Lines

If section lines drawn at 45° from horizontal would be parallel or perpendicular (or nearly so) to a prominent visible outline, the angle should be changed to 30°, 60°, or some other angle.

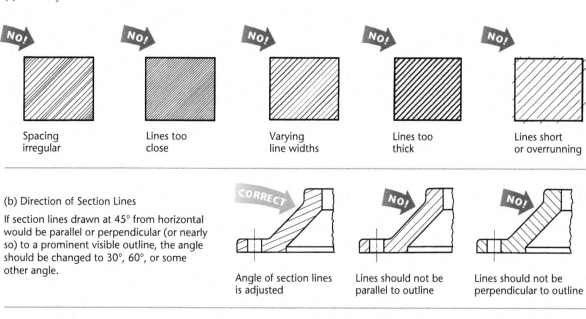

CORRECT — Angle of section lines is adjusted

NO! — Lines should not be parallel to outline

NO! — Lines should not be perpendicular to outline

(c) Dimensions and Section Lines

Keep extension lines and values for dimensions off crosshatched areas, but when this is unavoidable, the cross-hatching should be omitted where the dimension value is placed.

BEST — Extension lines and dimension values are not on hatched area

O.K. — Section lines are omitted behind dimensioning

NO! — Dimensioning should not be on hatched area

8.16   Correct and Incorrect Section-Lining Technique

Section Lining Large Areas

When adding section lines to a large area, use outline sectioning, where the center portion of the hatched area is left blank to save time and make the view more legible, as shown in Figure 8.17.

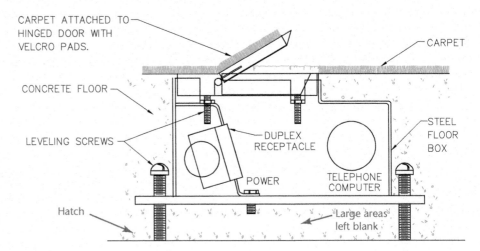

8.17 Outline Sectioning
(Courtesy of Associated Construction Engineering.)

Section-Lining Symbols

Section-lining symbols (Figure 8.18) may be used to indicate specific materials. These symbols represent general material types only, such as cast iron, brass, and steel. Because there are so many different types of materials (there are hundreds of types of steel, for example), a general name or symbol is not enough. A detailed specification listing the material must be lettered in the form of a note or in the title strip.

The general-purpose section lining (which is the same as that for cast iron) may be used to represent any material on the detail drawing for a single part.

Using different section-lining patterns helps you distinguish different materials, especially on assembly drawings, but it is acceptable to use the general-purpose symbol shown at different angles for different parts.

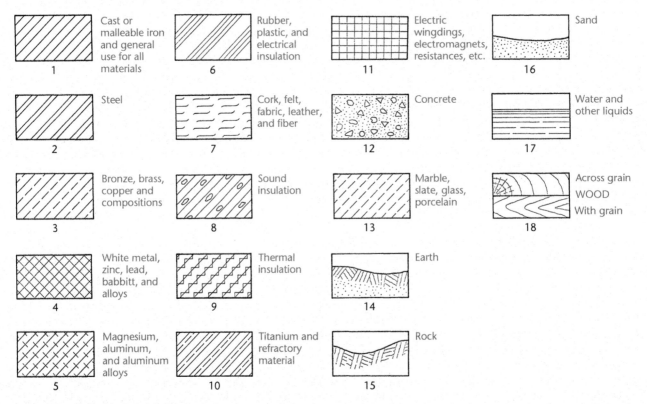

8.18 Symbols for Section Lining

Section Lining in CAD

CAD programs usually include libraries that allow you to select from a variety of section-lining patterns, making it easy to use different patterns, angles, and scales for the spacing of the pattern. When using CAD software to hatch an area in the drawing, be careful to specify a scale that relates to the printed drawing scale for that sheet. Otherwise, the hatching may turn out so dense that the object appears to be filled in solid, or so sparse that you do not see any hatching (Figure 8.19).

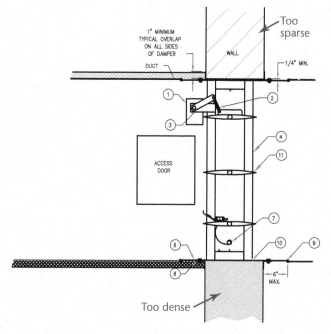

8.19   Incorrect Hatching in a CAD Drawing

8.7 HALF SECTIONS

Symmetrical objects can be shown effectively using a special type of section view called a **_half section_** (Figure 8.20). A half section exposes the interior of half of the object and the exterior of the other half. This is done by removing one quarter of the object. Half sections are not widely used to create detail drawings showing how to make a single part because it can be difficult to show all the dimensions clearly when some internal features are only partly shown in the sectioned half (Figure 8.20b).

In general,

- Omit hidden lines from both halves of a half section, whenever possible.
- Use a centerline to divide the sectioned half and the unsectioned half, as shown in Figure 8.20b.

Half-section drawings are most useful in showing an assembly where it is often necessary to show both internal and external construction in one drawing view and usually without dimensioning. A broken-out section may be preferred in some cases.

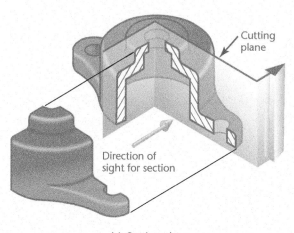

(a) Cutting plane

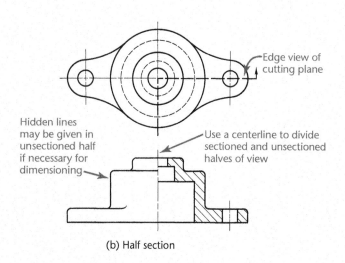

(b) Half section

8.20   Half Section

8.8 BROKEN OUT SECTIONS

It often happens that only a partial section of a view is all that is needed to expose interior shapes. Such a section, limited by a break line, is called a ***broken out section.***

In Figure 8.21, a full or half section is not necessary, and a small broken out section is sufficient to explain the construction.

In Figure 8.22, a half section would have caused the removal of half the keyway. The keyway is preserved by breaking out around it. In this case, the section is limited partly by a break line and partly by a centerline in the drawing.

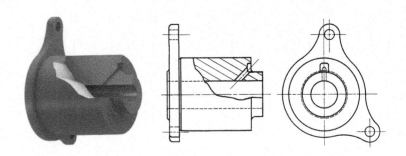

8.21   Broken Out Section

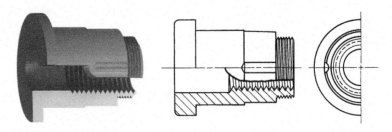

8.22   Break around Keyway

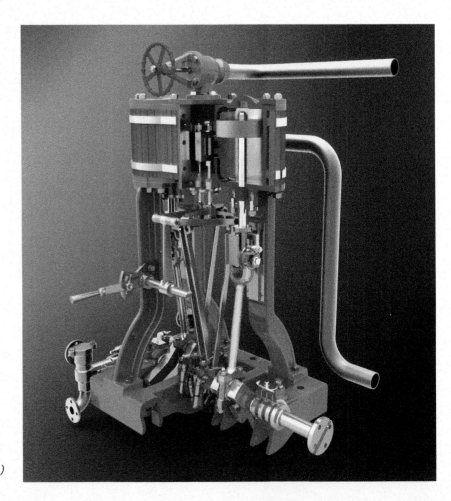

Steam Launch Engine, Modeled Actual Size and Sectioned to Illustrate Assembly and Function. *This CAD model was created by William L. Gould from an 1879 "drafting exercise handbook."*
(© www.gouldstudios.com Used with permission.)

8.9 REVOLVED SECTIONS

The shape of the cross section of a bar, arm, spoke, or other elongated object can be shown in the longitudinal view by using a *revolved section.*

To create a revolved section, first imagine a cutting plane perpendicular to the centerline or axis of the object, as shown in Figure 8.23a. Next, revolve the plane 90° about a centerline at right angles to the axis, as shown in Figures 8.23b and c.

The visible lines adjacent to a revolved section may be broken out if desired, as shown in Figure 8.24.

When you superimpose the revolved section over the top of the view, be sure that any original lines of the view covered by the revolved view are removed (Figure 8.25a).

Show the true shape of the revolved section, regardless of the direction of the lines in the view (Figure 8.25b).

Figure 8.26 shows examples of how revolved sections look in a drawing.

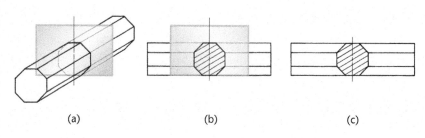

(a)   (b)   (c)

8.23   Using the Cutting Plane in Revolved Sections

8.24   Conventional Breaks Used with Revolved Sections

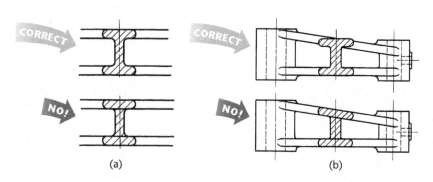

(a)   (b)

8.25   Common Errors in Drawing Revolved Sections

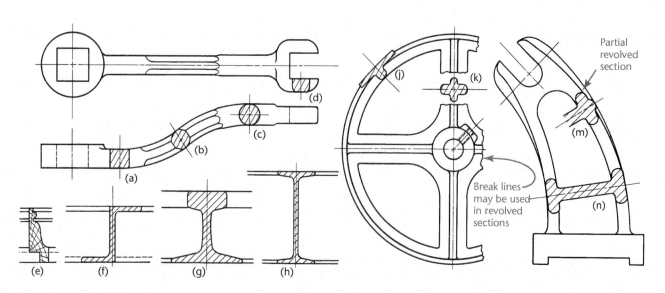

8.26   Revolved Sections

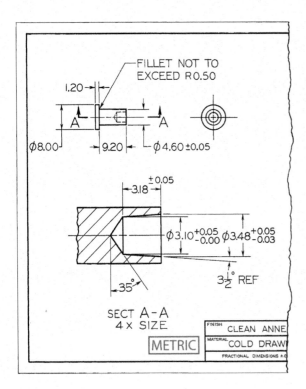

8.27 Removed Section

8.10 REMOVED SECTIONS

A *removed section* (Figure 8.27) is one that is not in direct projection from the view containing the cutting plane—that is, it is not positioned in agreement with the standard arrangement of views. Be sure to keep the section in its normal orientation and do not turn it a different direction on the sheet. If you must rotate the view, use a *rotation arrow* as shown in Figure 8.28 and note the angle the view was rotated.

Removed sections should be labeled, such as section A–A and section B–B, corresponding to the letters at the ends of the cutting-plane line (Figure 8.27). They should be arranged in alphabetical order from left to right on the sheet. Section letters should be used in alphabetical order, but letters I, O, and Q should not be used because they are easily confused with the numeral 1 or zero. Figure 8.29 shows several removed sections.

8.28 Rotation Arrow Symbol. *Use this to label a view that has been rotated (h = letter height in the drawing).*

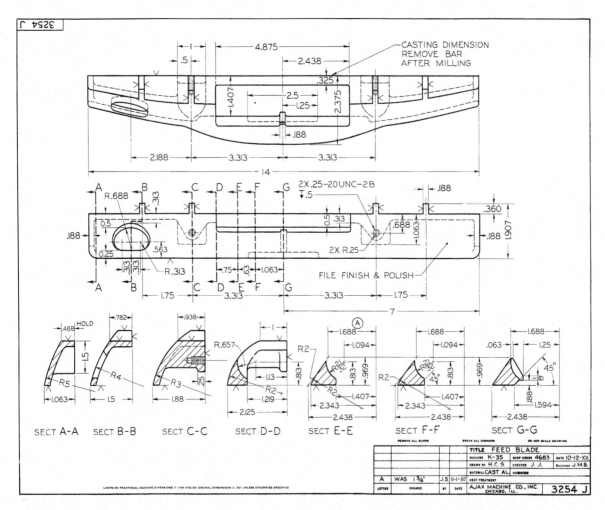

8.29 Removed Sections

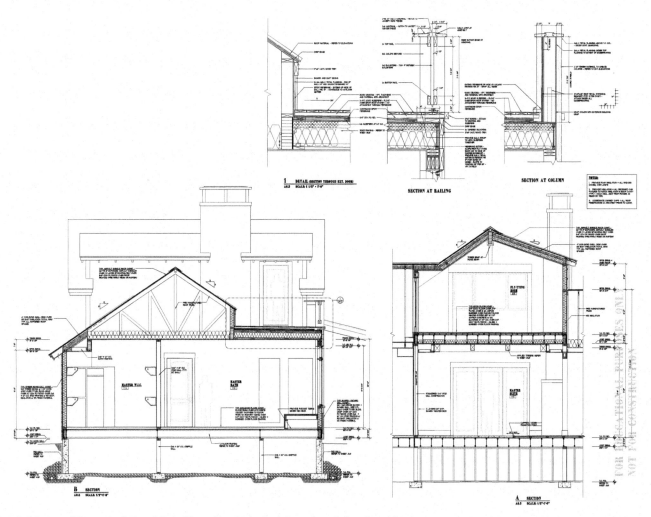

8.30 Architectural Drawing Showing Labeled Removed Section Views *(Courtesy of Locati Architects.)*

A removed section is often a ***partial section,*** in which only a portion of the section view is drawn. Removed sections are frequently drawn to an enlarged scale (Figure 8.29) to show detail and provide space for dimensions. When using an enlarged scale be sure to indicate the scale below the section view's title, as in Figure 8.27.

A removed section should be placed so that it no longer lines up in projection with any other view. It should be separated clearly from the standard arrangement of views (see Figure 8.30). Whenever possible, removed sections should be on the same sheet as the regular views. If a section must be placed on a different sheet, cross-references should be given on the related sheets. A note should be given below the section title, such as

SECTION B-B ON SHEET 4, ZONE A3

A similar note should be placed on the sheet on which the cutting-plane line is shown, with a leader pointing to the cutting-plane line and referring to the sheet on which the section will be found. Sometimes it is convenient to place removed sections on centerlines extended from the section cuts (Figure 8.31).

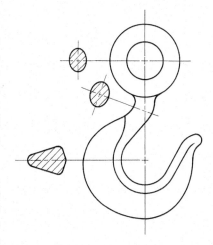

8.31 Removed Sections on Centerlines

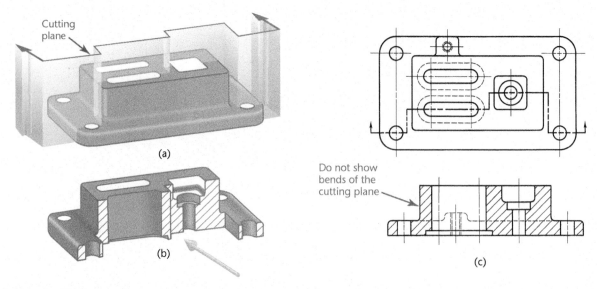

8.32 Offset Section

8.11 OFFSET SECTIONS

In sectioning complex objects, it is often desirable to show features that do not lie in a straight line by "offsetting" or bending the cutting plane. These are called ***offset sections.***

In Figure 8.32a the cutting plane is offset in several places to include the hole at the left end, one of the parallel slots, the rectangular recess, and one of the holes at the right end. The front portion of the object is then imagined to be removed (Figure 8.32b). The path of the cutting plane is shown by the cutting-plane line in the top view (Figure 8.32c), and the resulting offset section is shown in the front view.

- The offsets or bends in the cutting plane are all 90°.
- The bends in the cutting plane are never shown in the section view.

Figure 8.32 also illustrates how hidden lines in a section eliminate the need for an additional view. In this case, an extra view would be needed to show the small boss on the back if hidden lines were not shown.

Figure 8.33 shows an example of multiple offset sections. Notice that the visible background shapes appear in each section view without the use of hidden lines. It is also acceptable to show only the cut portion, but the views are easier to interpret when the lines that are visible behind the cutting plane are shown.

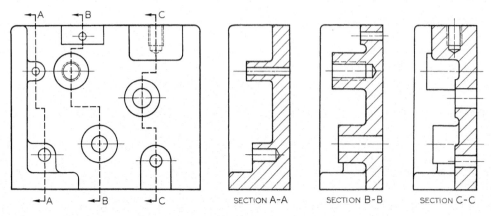

8.33 Three Offset Sections

8.12 RIBS IN SECTION

To avoid giving a false impression of thickness and solidity, ribs, webs, gear teeth, and other similar flat features are not hatched with section lining even though the cutting plane slices them. For example, in Figure 8.34, the cutting plane A–A slices through the center of the vertical web, or rib, and the web is not sectioned (Figure 8.34b). Thin features are not hatched even though the cutting plane passes lengthwise through them. The incorrect section is shown in Figure 8.34c. Note the false impression of thickness or solidity resulting from section-lining the rib.

If the cutting plane passes crosswise through a rib or any thin member, as in section B–B, section-line the feature in the usual manner, as in the top view of Figure 8.34a.

If a rib is not sectioned when the cutting plane passes through it flatwise, it is sometimes difficult to tell whether the rib is actually present, as, for example, ribs A in Figure 8.35a and b. It is difficult to distinguish spaces B as open spaces and spaces A as ribs. In such cases, double-spaced section lining of the ribs should be used (Figure 8.35c). This consists simply of continuing alternate section lines through the ribbed areas, as shown.

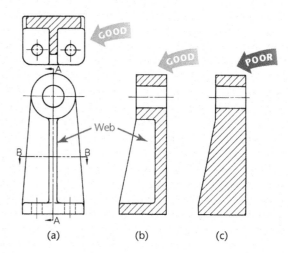

8.34 Web in Section

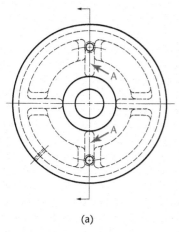

(a)

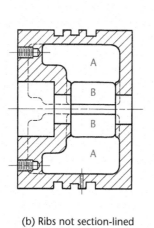

(b) Ribs not section-lined

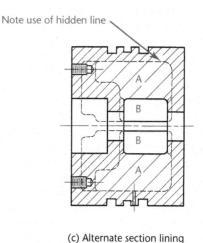

(c) Alternate section lining

8.35 Alternate Sectioning

8.13 ALIGNED SECTIONS

When parts with angled elements are sectioned, the cutting plane may be bent to pass through those features. The plane and features are then imagined to be revolved into the original plane. For example, Figure 8.36 shows an *aligned section.* The cutting plane was bent to pass through the angled arm and then revolved to a vertical position (aligned), from where it was projected across to the section view.

The angle of revolution should always be less than 90° for an aligned section.

Do not revolve features when the clarity of your drawing is not improved. In the exercises later in the chapter, you will see examples of when revolution should not be used.

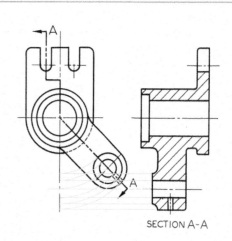

SECTION A-A

8.36 Aligned Section

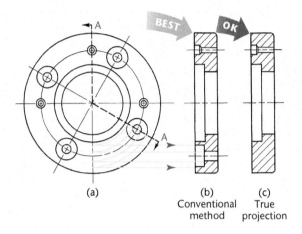

(a)

(b)
Conventional
method

(c)
True
projection

8.37   Aligned Section

In Figure 8.37 the cutting plane is bent to include one of the drilled and counterbored holes in the section view. The correct section view in Figure 8.37b gives a clearer and more complete description than does the section in Figure 8.37c, which is shown without any bend in the cutting plane.

In Figure 8.38a, the projecting lugs are not section-lined for the same reason that the ribs are not sectioned. In Figure 8.38b, the projecting lugs are located so that the cutting plane passes through them crosswise; therefore, they are section-lined.

Another example involving rib sectioning and aligned sectioning is shown in Figure 8.39. In the circular view, the cutting plane is offset in circular-arc bends to include the upper hole and upper rib, the keyway and center hole, the lower rib, and one of the lower holes. These features are imagined to be revolved until they line up vertically and are then projected from that position to obtain the section shown in Figure 8.39b. Note that the ribs are not section-lined. If a regular full section of the object were drawn without using the conventions

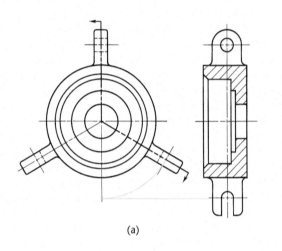

(a)

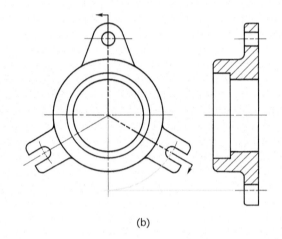

(b)

8.38   Aligned Section

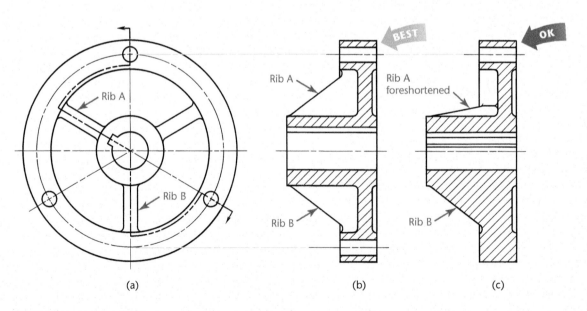

(a)

Rib A

Rib A

Rib B

Rib A
foreshortened

Rib B

(b)

(c)

8.39   Symmetry of Ribs

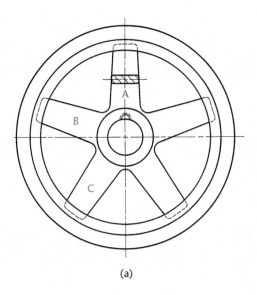
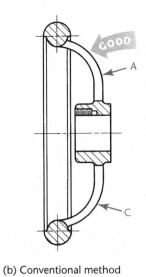
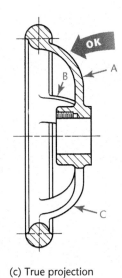

(a)   (b) Conventional method   (c) True projection

8.40   Spokes in Section

discussed here, the resulting section (Figure 8.39c) would be incomplete and confusing and would take more time to draw. Showing the actual section is acceptable when it is generated from a 3D model. When doing so, take care to provide clear views that can be interpreted by the reader.

In sectioning a pulley or any spoked wheel (Figure 8.40a), it is standard practice to revolve the spokes if necessary (if there are an odd number) and not to section-line the spokes (Figure 8.40b). If the spoke is hatched, the section gives a false impression of continuous metal (Figure 8.40c). If the lower spoke is not revolved, it will be foreshortened in the sectional view, in which it presents an "amputated" and a misleading appearance.

Figure 8.40 also illustrates correct practice in omitting visible lines in a sectional view. Notice that spoke B is omitted in Figure 8.40b. If it is included, as shown in Figure 8.40c, the spoke is foreshortened, difficult and time-consuming to draw, and confusing to the reader of the drawing.

8.14 PARTIAL VIEWS

If space is limited on the paper or to save time, partial views may be used with sectioning (Figure 8.41). Half views are shown in Figures 8.41a and b in connection with a full section and a half section, respectively. In each case the back half of the object in the circular view is shown, to remove the front portion of the object and expose the back portion in the section.

Another method of drawing a partial view is to break out much of the circular view, retaining only those features that are needed for minimum representation (Figure 8.41c).

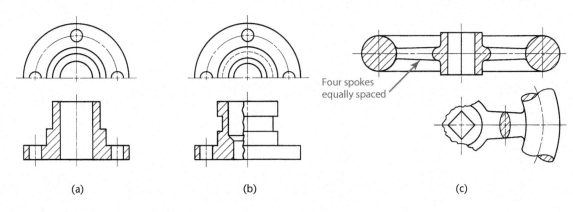

Four spokes equally spaced

(a)   (b)   (c)

8.41   Partial Views

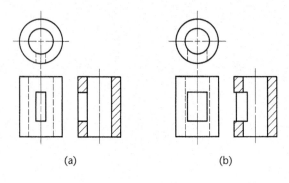

(a)   (b)

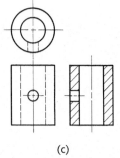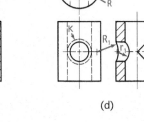

$R_1 = R$
$r_1 = r$

(c)   (d)

8.42 Intersections

8.15 INTERSECTIONS IN SECTIONS

Whenever an intersection is small or unimportant in a section, it is standard practice to disregard the true projection of the figure of intersection, as shown in Figures 8.42a and c. Larger intersections may be projected, as shown in Figure 8.42b, or approximated by circular arcs, as shown for the smaller hole in Figure 8.42d. Note that the larger hole K is the same diameter as the vertical hole. In such cases the curves of intersection (ellipses) appear as straight lines, as shown.

8.16 CONVENTIONAL BREAKS AND SECTIONS

Cross-hatching is often added when showing a conventional break. *Conventional breaks* are used to shorten the view of an object that is too long to show clearly at one scale on the drawing sheet. Figure 8.43 shows examples of hatching on conventional breaks. The parts to be broken must have the same section throughout, or if they are tapered, they must have a uniform taper.

The breaks used on cylindrical shafts or tubes are often referred to as "S-breaks" and are usually drawn by eye, although S-break templates are available.

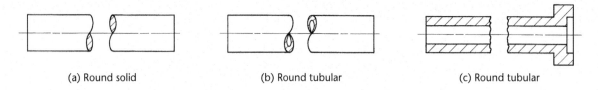

(a) Round solid   (b) Round tubular   (c) Round tubular

8.43 *Conventional breaks often show cross-hatching to show the cut material.*

8.17 ASSEMBLY SECTIONS

Section views are often used to create assembly drawings. Figure 8.44 shows an orthographic drawing for an assembly. Notice that the hatching on different parts varies; it has a different hatch pattern or is hatched at a different angle. On the same part, the hatching is always at the same angle to help you recognize the parts easily. Solid features that do not have interior structure are not hatched. You will learn more about these types of drawing in Chapter 14.

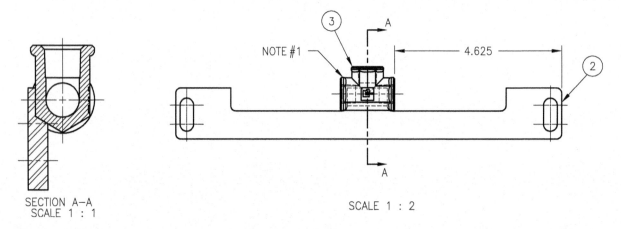

SECTION A–A
SCALE 1 : 1

SCALE 1 : 2

8.44 Assembly Section *(Courtesy of Wood's Power-Grip Co., Inc.)*

COMPUTER TECHNIQUES FOR SECTIONS

2D and 3D sectional views can be created using CAD. Most CAD systems have a "hatch" command to generate the section lining and hatch patterns to fill an area automatically. A wide variety of hatch patterns are generally available to show materials such as steel, bronze, sand, concrete, and many more.

Creating a full-section view from a 3D model is generally very easy. You often need to define only the cutting plane, viewing direction, scale, and where to place the view on the sheet. Often, the hatching for the cut surfaces is generated automatically. Sectioned views other than full sections can be more difficult to create. When you create an angled cutting plane line for a section view, Autodesk Inventor automatically generates the aligned section. Use this feature only when appropriate, such to show the internal structure of an angled feature. To create good section drawings, you should have a clear understanding of the standards for showing section views.

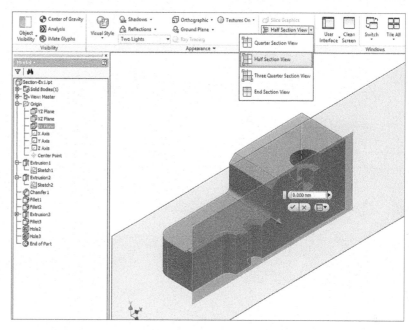

A Section Created in the 3D Model Using Autodesk Inventor *(Autodesk screen shots reprinted courtesy of Autodesk, Inc.)*

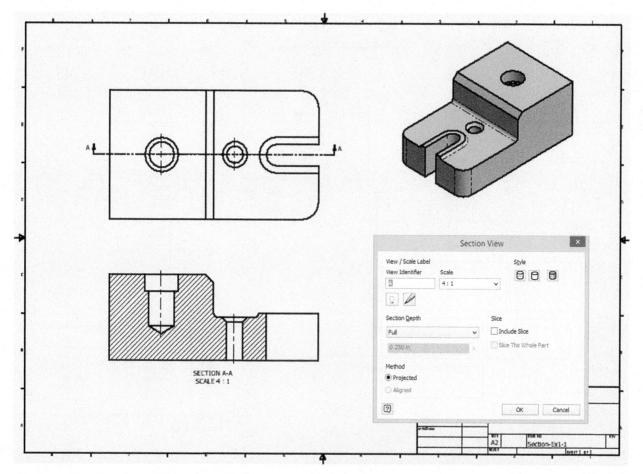

Sections can quickly be added to orthographic drawings generated from a 3D model.

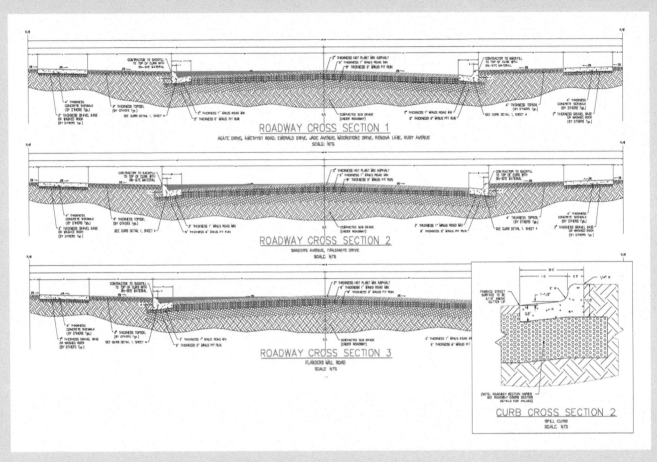

Roadway Sections *(Excerpted from a larger drawing) (Courtesy of Locati Architects.)*

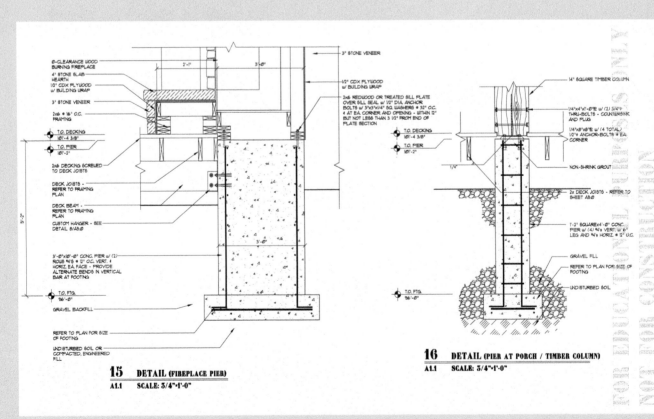

Section Detail *(Excerpted from a larger drawing) (Courtesy of Locati Architects.)*

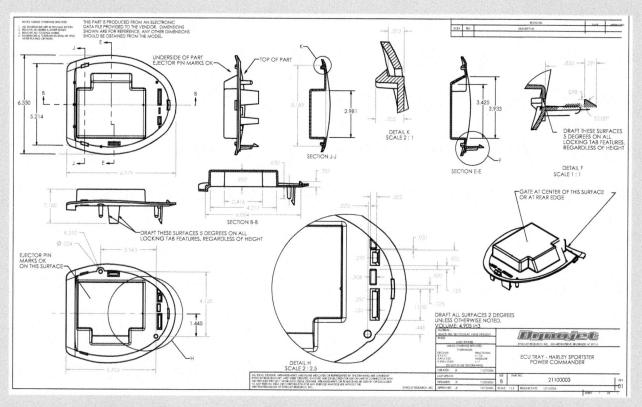

Detail Drawing for an Injection Molded Plastic Part with Removed Section Views *(Courtesy of Dynojet Research, Inc.)*

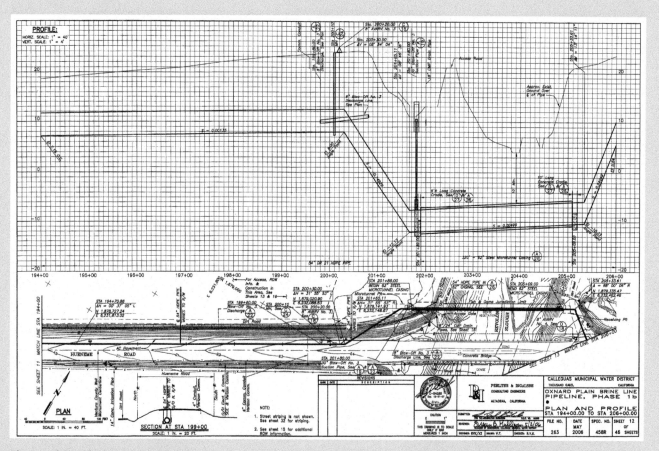

Plan and Profile Drawing with Sections *(Courtesy of Perliter & Ingalsbe Consulting Engineers.)*

KEY WORDS

Aligned Section

Broken Out Section

Conventional Breaks

Cutting-Plane Line

Full Section

Half Section

Hatching

Offset Section

Partial Section

Removed Section

Revolved Section

Rotation Arrow

Section Lining

Section-Lining Symbols

Section Views

CHAPTER SUMMARY

Now that you have finished this chapter, you should be able to:

- Show internal details of objects without the need for hidden lines by using section views.
- Imagine a variety of objects cut apart along a cutting-plane line.
- Show section lining (hatching) to indicate the solid parts of the object that would be cut by the cutting plane.
- Check that you are not showing hidden lines where they are no longer needed because the internal surfaces are exposed when the object is imagined cut.
- Use section-lining symbols to indicate the material of the object.
- Leave the section lining off ribs, webs, and spokes that are sectioned lengthwise.
- Revolve symmetrical features so the section view depicts the part's symmetry.
- Use conventional breaks on drawings to show object details when they would appear too small at a scale where the entire object would be shown on the sheet.
- Interpret assembly drawings that include section views.

REVIEW QUESTIONS

1. What does the cutting-plane line represent?
2. Sketch the section line symbols for 10 different materials.
3. List seven different types of sections and sketch an example of each.
4. Which section views are used to replace an existing primary view? Which section views are used in addition to the primary views?
5. How much of an object is imagined to be cut away in a half section?
6. What type of line is used to show the boundary of a broken out section?
7. Why are hidden lines generally omitted in a section view?
8. Why are some symmetrical features, like spokes and webs, revolved in the sectional view?
9. Why is a rib outlined with object lines and not filled with section lining?

CHAPTER EXERCISES

Any of the following exercises may be drawn freehand or with CAD. Study Chapter 11 on dimensioning first if you are going to add dimensions to your drawings. Show cutting-plane lines for practice.

Freehand Sectioning Problems

Exercises 8.1–8.4 are especially suited for sketching on 8.5″ × 11″ graph paper with appropriate grid squares. Sketch one or two problems per sheet, adding section views as indicated. To make your drawings fit on the paper easily, use each grid square as equal to either 6 mm or 1/4″.

Exercise 8.1 Redraw the given views and add the front section view.

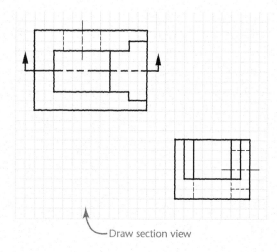

Draw section view

Exercise 8.2 Redraw the top view, rotate the side view, and move it into a position so that you can project the front view in section. Add the front section view.

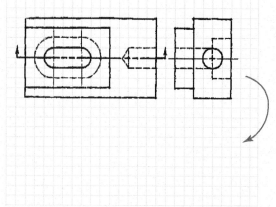

Rotate side view into position

Exercise 8.3 Redraw the top view, rotate the side view, and move it into a position so that you can project the front view in section. Add the front section view.

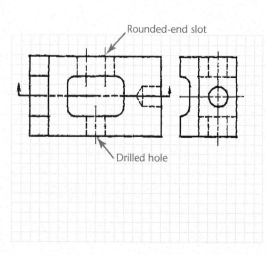

Rounded-end slot

Drilled hole

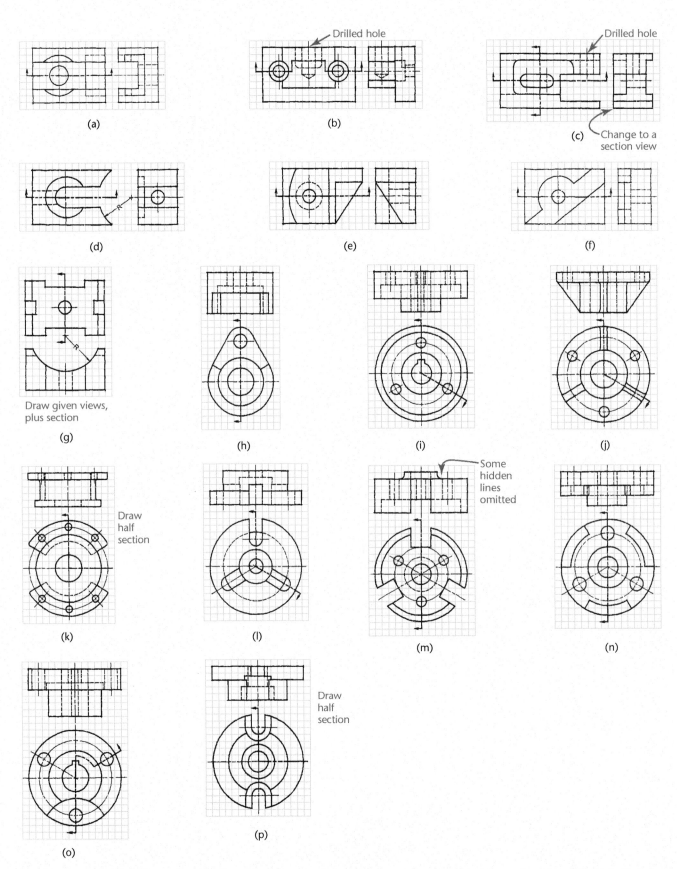

(a)

Drilled hole

(b)

Drilled hole

(c)   Change to a section view

(d)

(e)

(f)

Draw given views, plus section

(g)

(h)

(i)

(j)

Draw half section

(k)

(l)

Some hidden lines omitted

(m)

(n)

(o)

Draw half section

(p)

Exercise 8.4 Freehand Sectioning Problems. Sketch views and add sections as indicated by the cutting-plane lines. Cutting-plane lines can be omitted except for parts b and c. (*Note:* In freehand sketching, revolution conventions for aligned sections are generally observed. See Figure 8.39, Symmetry of Ribs, for an example.)

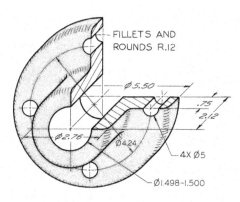

Exercise 8.5 Bearing. Draw necessary views, with full section.*

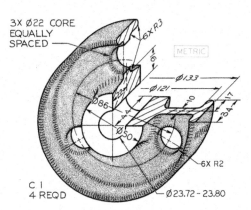

Exercise 8.6 Truck Wheel. Draw necessary views, with full section.*

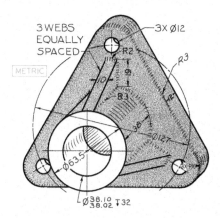

Exercise 8.7 Column Support. Draw necessary views, with broken out section.*

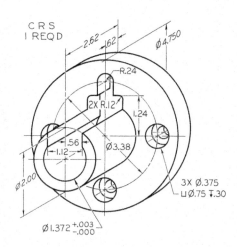

Exercise 8.8 Centering Bushing. Draw necessary views, with full section.*

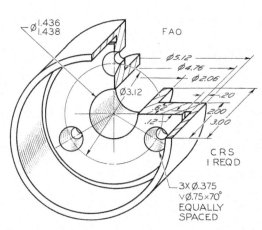

Exercise 8.9 Special Bearing. Draw necessary views, with full section.*

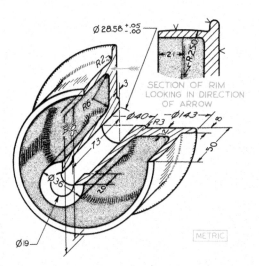

Exercise 8.10 Idler Pulley. Draw necessary views, with full section.*

*Leave out dimensions unless assigned by your instructor.

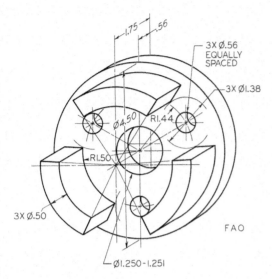

Exercise 8.11 Cup Washer. Draw necessary views, with full section.*

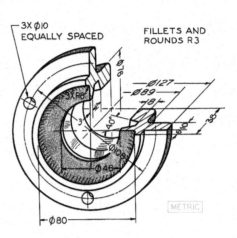

Exercise 8.12 Fixed Bearing Cup. Draw necessary views, with full section.*

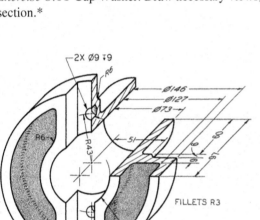

Exercise 8.13 Stock Guide. Draw necessary views, with half section.*

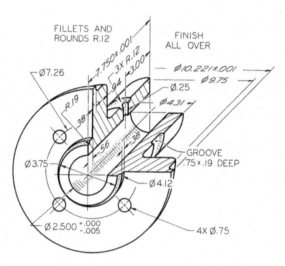

Exercise 8.14 Bearing. Draw necessary views, with half section. Scale: half size.*

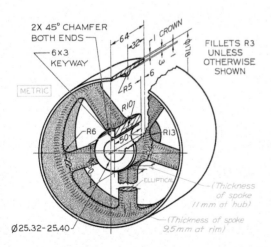

Exercise 8.15 Pulley. Draw necessary views, with full section, and revolved section of spoke.*

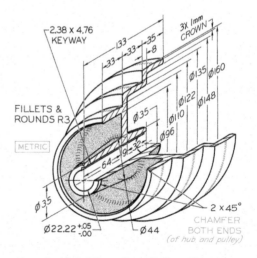

Exercise 8.16 Step-Cone Pulley. Draw necessary views, with full section.*

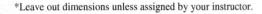

*Leave out dimensions unless assigned by your instructor.

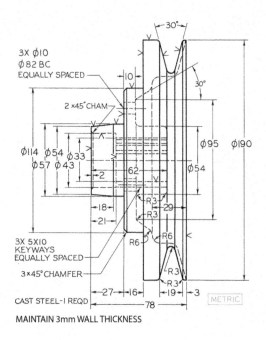

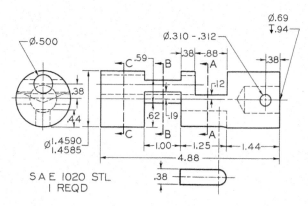

Exercise 8.17 Sheave. Draw two views, including half section.*

Exercise 8.18 Operating Valve. Given: Front, left-side, and partial bottom views. Required: Front, right-side, and full bottom views, plus indicated removed sections.*

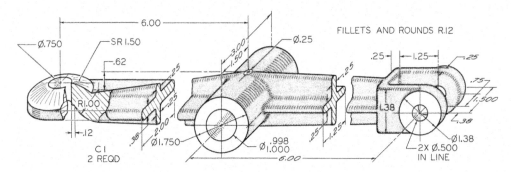

Exercise 8.19 Rocker Arm. Draw necessary views, with revolved sections.*

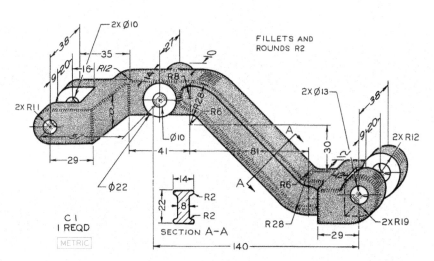

Exercise 8.20 Dashpot Lifter. Draw necessary views, using revolved section instead of removed section.*

*Leave out dimensions unless assigned by your instructor.

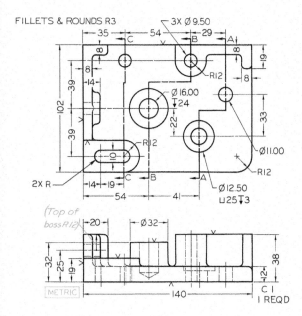

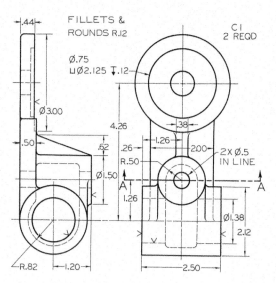

Exercise 8.21 Adjuster Base. Given: Front and top views. Required: Front and top views and sections A–A, B–B, and C–C. Show all visible lines.*

Exercise 8.22 Mobile Housing. Given: Front and left-side views. Required: Front view, right-side view in full section, and removed section A–A.*

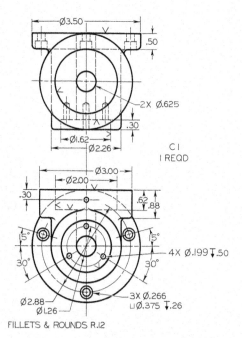

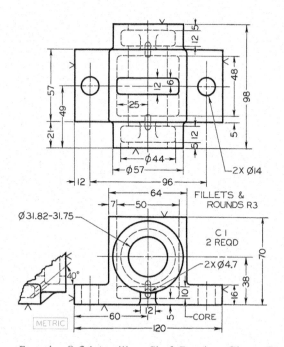

Exercise 8.23 Hydraulic Fitting. Given: Front and top views. Required: Front and top views and right-side view in full section.*

Exercise 8.24 Auxiliary Shaft Bearing. Given: Front and top views. Required: Front and top views and right-side view in full section.*

*Leave out dimensions unless assigned by your instructor.

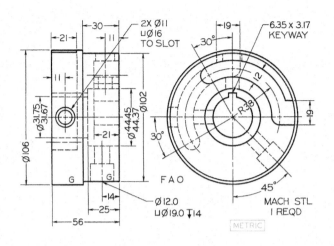

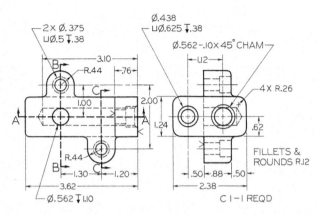

Exercise 8.25 Traverse Spider. Given: Front and left-side views. Required: Front and right-side views and top view in full section.*

Exercise 8.26 Bracket. Given: Front and right-side views. Required: Take front as new top; then add right-side view, front view in full section A–A, and sections B–B and C–C.*

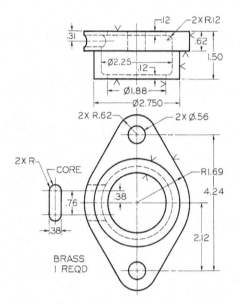

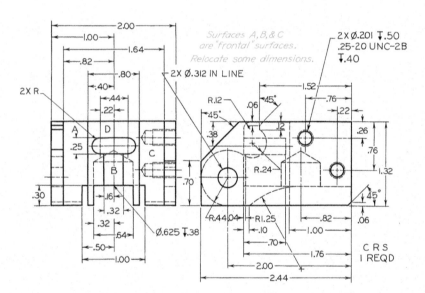

Exercise 8.27 Gland. Given: Front, top, and partial left-side views. Required: Front view and right-side view in full section.*

Exercise 8.28 Cocking Block. Given: Front and right-side views. Required: Take front as new top view; then add new front view, and right-side view in full section. Draw double size.*

*Leave out dimensions unless assigned by your instructor.

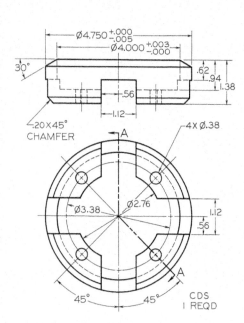

Exercise 8.29 Packing Ring. Given: Front and top views. Required: Front view and section A–A.*

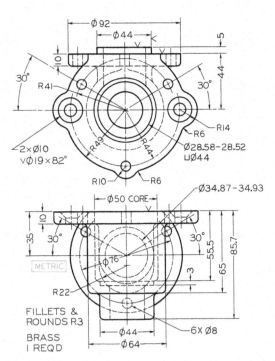

Exercise 8.30 Strainer Body. Given: Front and bottom views. Required: Front and top views and right-side view in full section.*

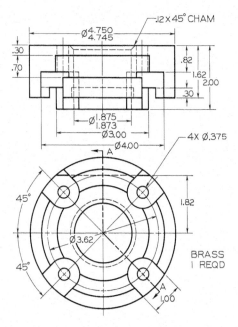

Exercise 8.31 Oil Retainer. Given: Front and top views. Required: Front view and section A–A.*

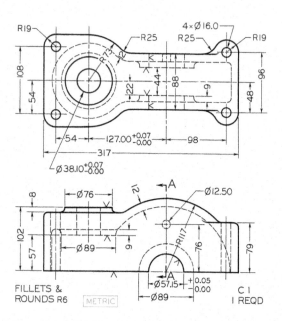

Exercise 8.32 Gear Box. Given: Front and top views. Required: Front in full section, bottom view, and right-side section A–A. Draw half size.*

*Leave out dimensions unless assigned by your instructor.

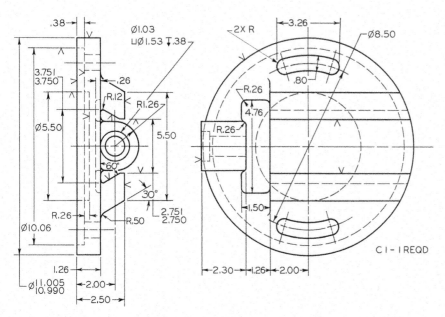

Exercise 8.33 Slotted Disk for Threading Machine. Given: Front and left-side views. Required: Front and right-side views and top full-section view. Draw half size.*

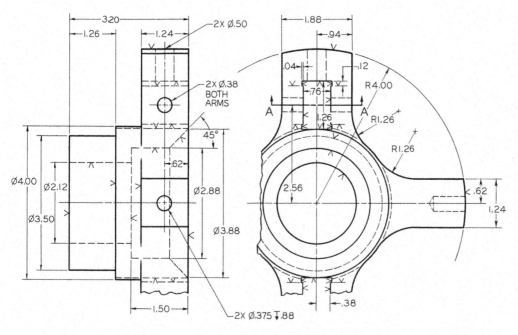

Exercise 8.34 Web for Lathe Clutch. Given: Partial front and left-side views. Required: Full front view, right-side view in full section, and removed section A–A.*

*Leave out dimensions unless assigned by your instructor.

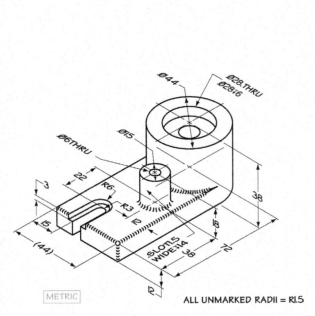

Exercise 8.35 Support. Draw necessary views adding a section view.

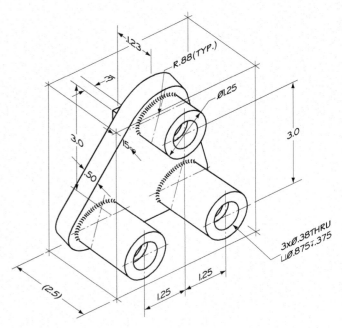

Exercise 8.36 Bushing. Draw necessary views with a broken out section.*

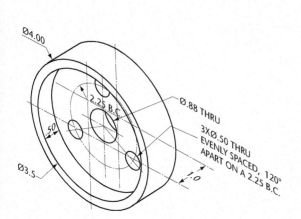

Exercise 8.37 Plastic Spacer. Draw all necessary views using an aligned section.*

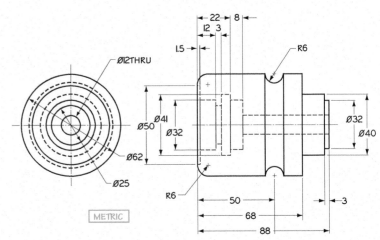

Exercise 8.38 Motor. Draw all required views with one half section.*

*Leave out dimensions unless assigned by your instructor.

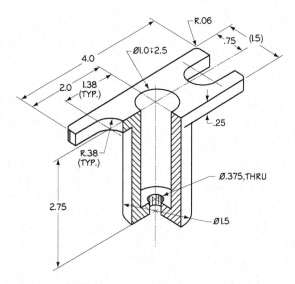

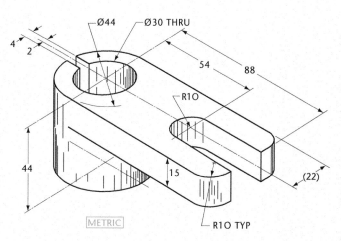

Exercise 8.39 Mounting Pin. Draw the necessary views showing the front view as a half section.*

Exercise 8.40 Clamp. Draw the necessary views showing the front view as a full section.*

*Leave out dimensions unless assigned by your instructor.

CHAPTER NINE

AUXILIARY VIEWS

─────── OBJECTIVES ───────

After studying the material in this chapter, you should be able to:

1. Create an auxiliary view from orthographic views.

2. Draw folding lines or reference-plane lines between any two adjacent views.

3. Construct depth, height, or width auxiliary views.

4. Plot curves in auxiliary views.

5. Construct partial auxiliary views.

6. Create auxiliary section views.

7. Produce views to show the true length of a line, point view of a line, edge view of a surface, and true-size view of a surface.

8. Show the true size of the angle between two planes (dihedral angle).

9. Construct the development of prisms, pyramids, cylinders, and cones.

10. Use triangulation to transfer surface shapes to a development.

11. Create the development of transition pieces.

12. Graphically solve for the intersection of solids.

13. Apply revolution to show true-length edges and true-size surfaces.

─────────────────────────

Refer to the following standard:
• *ANSI/ASME Y14.3 Orthographic and Pictorial Views*

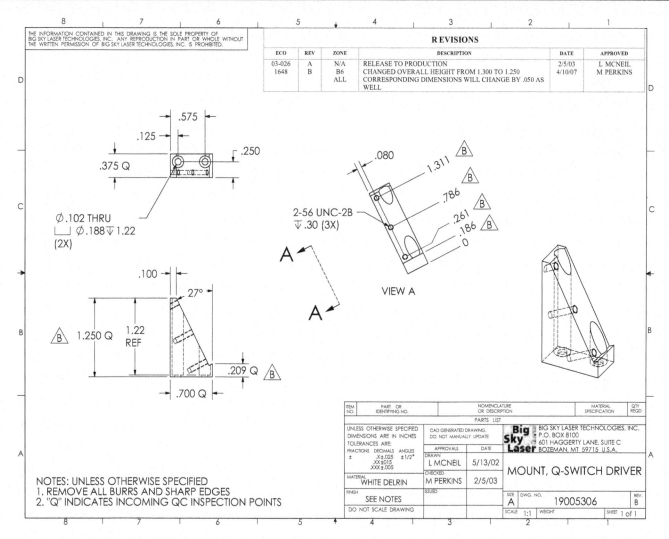

REVISIONS

ECO	REV	ZONE	DESCRIPTION	DATE	APPROVED
03-026	A	N/A	RELEASE TO PRODUCTION	2/5/03	L MCNEIL
1648	B	B6	CHANGED OVERALL HEIGHT FROM 1.300 TO 1.250	4/10/07	M PERKINS
		ALL	CORRESPONDING DIMENSIONS WILL CHANGE BY .050 AS WELL		

VIEW A

NOTES: UNLESS OTHERWISE SPECIFIED
1. REMOVE ALL BURRS AND SHARP EDGES
2. "Q" INDICATES INCOMING QC INSPECTION POINTS

BIG SKY LASER TECHNOLOGIES, INC.
P.O. BOX 8100
601 HAGGERTY LANE, SUITE C
BOZEMAN, MT 59715 U.S.A.

MOUNT, Q-SWITCH DRIVER

DWG. NO. 19005306   REV. B

SCALE 1:1   SHEET 1 of 1

Auxiliary View Drawing. *This switch mount uses an auxiliary view to show the true size of the inclined surface. (Courtesy of Big Sky Laser.)*

OVERVIEW

Inclined planes and oblique lines do not appear true size or true length in any of the principal planes of projection. When it is necessary to show the true length of an oblique line or the true size of an inclined plane, an auxiliary view must be created. The principles for creating auxiliary views are the same whether you are using traditional drawing, sketching, or CAD: a line of sight and reference plane are defined. With traditional drawing, the view is manually created along line-of-sight projectors. With CAD drawing, the computer generates the view automatically if a 3D model of the object was originally created.

Even if you are going to be using a CAD system to generate auxiliary views, it is important to understand the theory of developable surfaces. Some surfaces cannot be developed or "flattened out" to make an exact flat pattern for creating parts from sheet metal, cardboard packaging, or fabric. For example, a sphere can only be approximated. Understanding development methods can aid you in using your CAD software to the fullest extent.

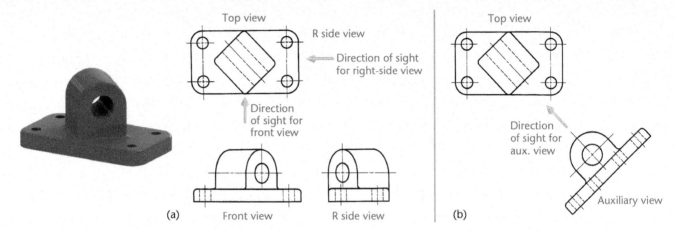

(a) Top view / R side view / Direction of sight for right-side view / Direction of sight for front view / Front view / R side view

(b) Top view / Direction of sight for aux. view / Auxiliary view

9.1 Regular Views and Auxiliary Views

UNDERSTANDING AUXILIARY VIEWS

Auxiliary views are useful for both design and documentation. Many objects are shaped so that their principal faces are not parallel to the standard planes of projection. For example, in Figure 9.1a the base of the design for the bearing is shown in its *true size* and shape, but the rounded upper portion is at an angle, so it does not appear true size and shape in any of the three regular views. When creating a drawing for documentation, you will often need to show the true size and shape of surfaces and angles. Likewise, you may need to create true-size flat patterns for sheet metal, packaging, and other purposes.

To show the true circular shapes, use a direction of sight perpendicular to the plane of the curve, to produce a view as shown in Figure 9.1b. The result is an *auxiliary view:* an orthographic view that is not a standard projection. This view, together with the top view, completely describes the object. The front and right-side views are not necessary.

The Auxiliary Plane

The object shown in Figure 9.2a has an inclined surface (P) that does not appear in its true size and shape in any regular view. To show the inclined surface true size, the direction of sight must be perpendicular to the inclined plane. Or using the glass box model, the auxiliary plane is aligned parallel to the inclined surface P to give a true-size view of it. The *auxiliary plane* in this case is perpendicular to the frontal plane of projection and hinged to it. It is angled to the horizontal (top) and profile (side) viewing planes.

The horizontal and auxiliary planes are unfolded into the plane of the front view, as shown in Figure 9.2b. Drawings do not show the planes of the glass box, but you can think of *folding lines* (H/F and F/A) representing the hinges that join the planes. The folding lines themselves are usually omitted in the actual drawing.

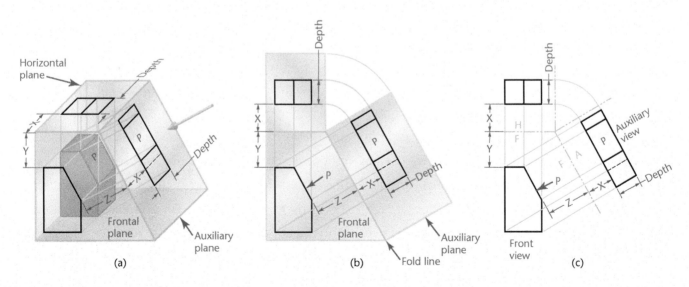

(a) Horizontal plane / Frontal plane / Auxiliary plane

(b) Frontal plane / Auxiliary plane / Fold line

(c) Auxiliary view / Front view

9.2 An Auxiliary View

Inclined surface P is shown in its true size and shape in the auxiliary view. Note that both the top and auxiliary views show the depth of the object. One dimension of the surface is projected directly from the front view, and the depth is transferred from the top view.

The locations of the folding lines depend on the size of the glass box and the location of the object within it. If the object is farther down in the box, distance Y is increased. If the object is moved back in the box, distances X increase but are still equal. If the object is moved to the left inside the glass box, distance Z is increased.

Primary Auxiliary Views

Any view obtained by orthographic projection onto a plane other than the horizontal, frontal, and profile projection planes is an auxiliary view. A *primary auxiliary view* is projected onto a plane that is perpendicular to one of the principal planes of projection and is inclined to the other two. Figure 9.3 shows examples of primary auxiliary views.

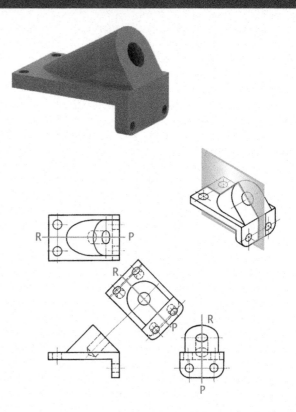

(a) Depth auxiliary view

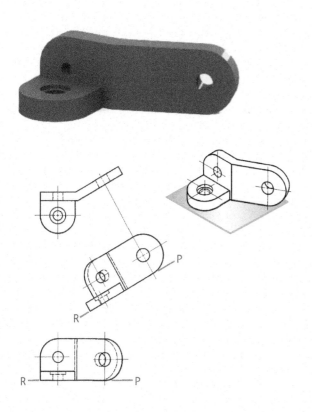

(b) Height auxiliary view

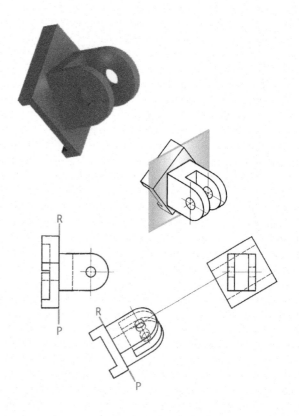

(c) Width auxiliary view

9.3 Primary Auxiliary Views

Visualizing an Auxiliary View as a Revolved Drawing

Figure 9.4a is a drawing showing top, front, and auxiliary views. Figure 9.4b shows the drawing revolved, as indicated by the arrows, until the auxiliary view and the front view line up horizontally. Although the views remain exactly the same, the names of the views are changed if drawn in this position. The auxiliary view now becomes a right-side view, and the top view becomes an auxiliary view. Sometimes it is easier to visualize and draw an auxiliary view when revolved to the position of a regular view in this manner. In any case, it should be understood that an auxiliary view is basically like any other view.

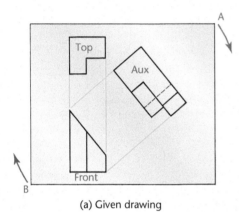

(a) Given drawing

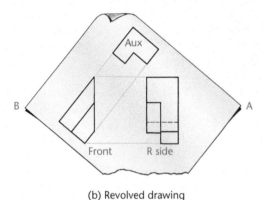

(b) Revolved drawing

9.4   Revolving a Drawing

Classification of Auxiliary Views

Auxiliary views are named for the principal dimension shown in the auxiliary view. For example, the auxiliary views in Figure 9.5 are **depth auxiliary views** because they show the object's depth. Any auxiliary view projected from the front view, also known as a *front adjacent view,* is a depth auxiliary view.

Similarly, any auxiliary view projected from the top view, also known as a *top adjacent view,* is a **height auxiliary view**; and any auxiliary view projected from a side view, also known as a *side adjacent view,* is a **width auxiliary view**.

Depth Auxiliary Views

An infinite number of auxiliary planes can be hinged perpendicular to the frontal plane (F) of projection. Five such planes are shown in Figure 9.5a. The horizontal plane is included to show that it is similar to the others. All these views show the object's depth and therefore are all depth auxiliary views.

The unfolded auxiliary planes, shown in Figure 9.5b, show how depth dimensions are projected from the top view to all auxiliary views. The arrows indicate the directions of sight.

The complete drawing, with the outlines of the planes of projection omitted, is shown in Figure 9.5c. Note that the front view shows the height and the width of the object, but not the depth. The principal dimension shown in an auxiliary view is the one not shown in the adjacent view from which the auxiliary view was projected.

Height Auxiliary Views

An infinite number of auxiliary planes can be hinged perpendicular to the horizontal plane (H) of projection. Several are shown in Figure 9.6a. The front view and all these auxiliary views show the height of the object. Therefore, all these auxiliary views are height auxiliary views.

The unfolded projection planes are shown in Figure 9.6b, and the complete drawing is shown in Figure 9.6c. Note that in the top view, the only dimension not shown is height.

Width Auxiliary Views

An infinite number of auxiliary planes can also be hinged perpendicular to the profile plane (P) of projection. Some are shown in Figure 9.7. The front view and all these auxiliary views are width auxiliary views.

The unfolded planes are shown in Figure 9.7b, and the complete drawing is shown in Figure 9.7c. In the right-side view, from which the auxiliary views are projected, the only dimension not shown is width.

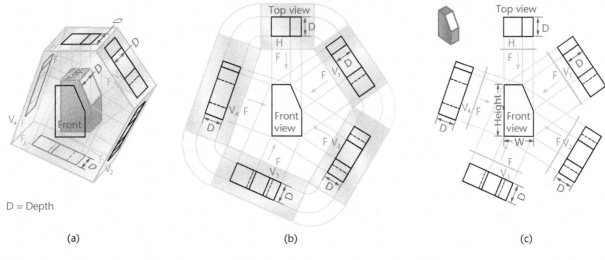

D = Depth

(a)   (b)   (c)

9.5   Depth Auxiliary Views

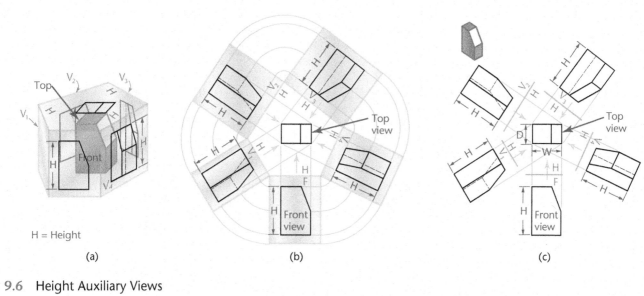

H = Height

(a)   (b)   (c)

9.6   Height Auxiliary Views

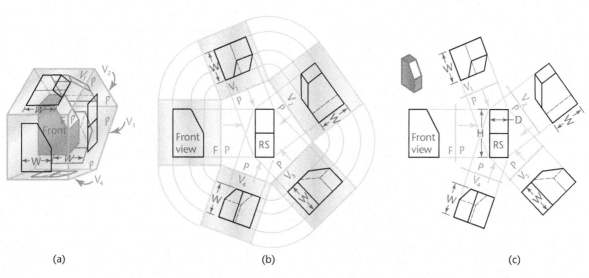

(a)   (b)   (c)

9.7   Width Auxiliary Views

Successive Auxiliary Views

Primary auxiliary views are projected from one of the principal views. In Figure 9.8, auxiliary view 1 is a primary auxiliary view projected from the top view.

From primary auxiliary view 1 a *secondary auxiliary view* 2 can be drawn, then from it a *third auxiliary view* 3, and so on. An infinite number of such successive auxiliary views may be drawn. However, secondary auxiliary view 2 is not the only one that can be projected from primary auxiliary view 1. As shown by the arrows around view 1, an infinite number of secondary auxiliary views, with different lines of sight, may be projected. Any auxiliary view projected from a primary auxiliary view is a secondary auxiliary view. Furthermore, any *succeeding auxiliary view* may be used to project an infinite series of views from it.

In this example, folding lines are more convenient than reference-plane lines. In auxiliary view 1, all numbered points of the object are the same distance from folding line H/V_1 as

they are in the front view from folding line H/F. These distances, such as distance *a*, are transferred from the front view to the auxiliary view.

To draw the secondary auxiliary view 2, ignore the front view and focus on the sequence of three views: the top view, view 1, and view 2. Draw light projection lines parallel to the direction of sight desired for view 2. Draw folding line V_1/V_2 perpendicular to the projection lines and at any convenient distance from view 1. Transfer the distances measured from folding line H/V_1 to locate all points in view 2. For example, transfer distance *b* to locate points 4 and 5 from folding line V_1/V_2. Connect points to draw the object and determine visibility. The closest corner (11) in view 2 will be visible, and the one farthest away (1) will be hidden, as shown.

To draw views 3, 4, and so on, use a similar process. Remember to use the correct sequence of three views.

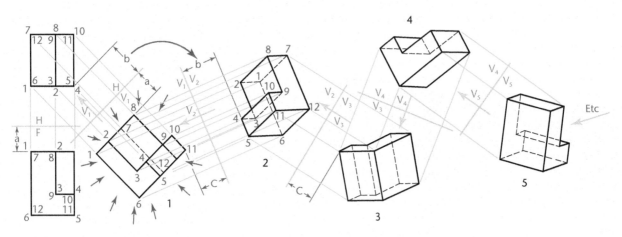

9.8 Successive Auxiliary Views

Secondary Auxiliary Views

A secondary auxiliary view is projected from a primary auxiliary view onto a plane that is inclined to all three principal projection planes. As shown in Figure 9.9, a part that has an oblique surface often requires a second auxiliary view to show that surface's true size and shape. In this case, the primary auxiliary view shows the oblique plane on edge.

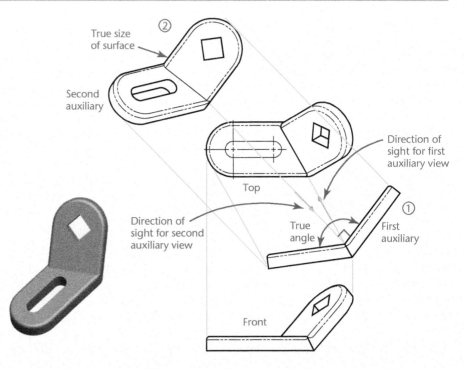

9.9 Second Auxiliary View, Showing the True Size of the Top Oblique Surface

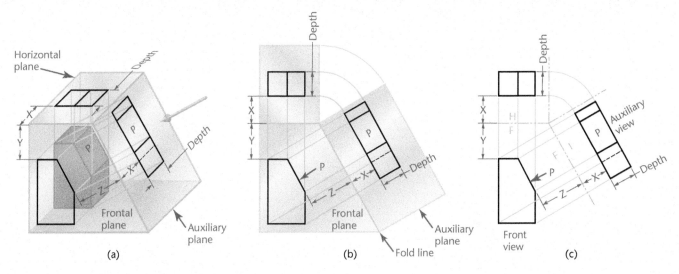

9.10 An Auxiliary View

Reference Planes

In the auxiliary view shown in Figure 9.10c, the folding line represents the edge view of the frontal plane of projection. In this case, the frontal plane is used for transferring distances—that is, depth measurements—from the top view to the auxiliary view.

Instead of using one of the planes of projection, you can use a *reference plane* parallel to the plane of projection that touches or cuts through the object. For example, in Figure 9.11a, a reference plane is aligned with the front surface of the object. This plane appears on edge, as a line, in the top and auxiliary views. Measurements are made from the reference lines. The depth dimensions in the top view and auxiliary views are equal. The advantage of the reference-plane method is that fewer measurements are required, because some points of the object lie in the reference plane. Make the reference plane using light lines similar to construction lines.

You can use a reference plane that coincides with the front surface of the object, as shown in Figure 9.11a. When an object is symmetrical, it is useful to select the reference plane to cut through the object, as shown in Figure 9.11b. This way you have

> **TIP**
> If you are using 2D CAD, you can draw half of the view and then mirror the object.

to make only half as many measurements to transfer dimensions because they are the same on each side of the reference plane. You can also use the back surface of the object, as shown in Figure 9.11c, or any intermediate point that would be advantageous.

Position the reference plane so it is convenient for transferring distances. Remember the following:

1. Reference lines, like folding lines, are always at right angles to the projection lines between the views.
2. A reference plane appears as a line in two *alternate views,* never in *adjacent views.*
3. Measurements are always made at right angles to the reference lines or parallel to the projection lines.
4. In the auxiliary view, all points are at the same distances from the reference line as the corresponding points are from the reference line in the alternate view, or the second previous view.

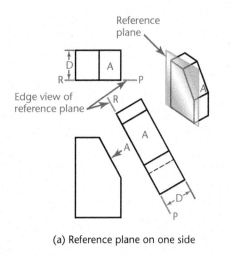

(a) Reference plane on one side

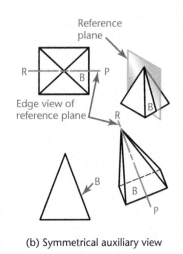

(b) Symmetrical auxiliary view

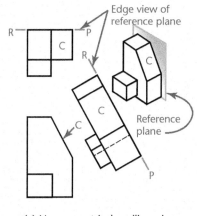

(c) Nonsymmetrical auxiliary view

9.11   Position of the Reference Plane

PROJECTING AN AUXILIARY VIEW

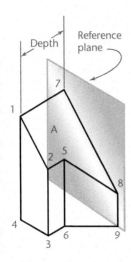

The object has been numbered in the pictorial view to aid in keeping track of the vertices. To create an auxiliary view of surface A, follow these steps.

1 Draw two views of the object and determine the direction of sight needed to produce a view that will show the true size of surface A.

Next, sketch projection lines parallel to the direction of sight.

Establish a reference plane. In this case the back surface of the object will work well. The reference lines in the top and auxiliary views are at right angles to the projection lines. These are the edge views of the reference plane, RP.

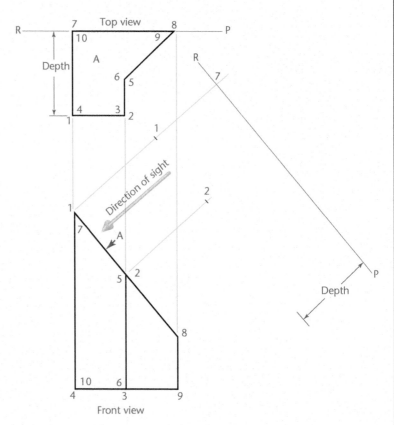

2 The auxiliary view of surface A will be true size and shape because the direction of sight is perpendicular to that surface. Transfer depth measurements from the top view to the auxiliary view. Each point in the auxiliary view will be on its projection line extended from the front view. The point will be the same distance from the reference line in the top view to the corresponding reference line in the auxiliary view. Finish projecting points 5 and 8.

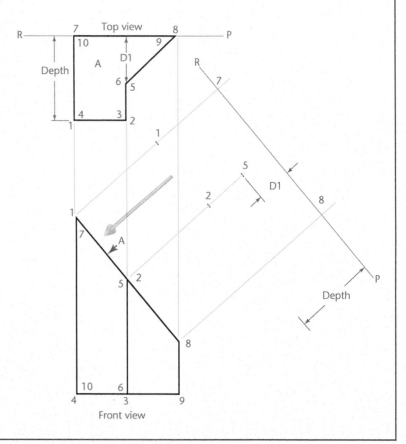

(continued)

3 Draw surface A true size in the auxiliary view by connecting the vertices in the same order as they are shown connecting in the top view (1-7-8-5-2-1).

Complete the auxiliary view by adding other visible edges and surfaces of the object. Each numbered point in the auxiliary view lies on its projection line from the front view and is the same distance from the reference line as it is in the top view. Note that two surfaces of the object appear as lines in the auxiliary view.

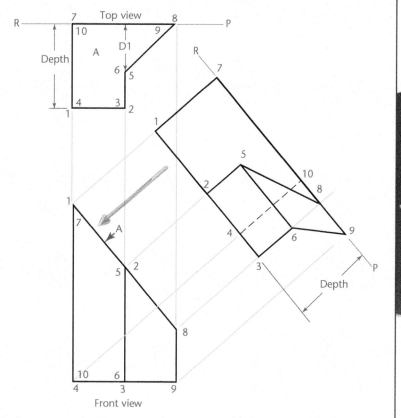

9.1 USING TRIANGLES TO SKETCH AUXILIARY VIEWS

You can use two triangles to quickly draw parallel and perpendicular lines for "accurate" sketches.

- Place two triangles together so that the 90° corners are on the outside, as shown in Figure 9.12.
- Slide them on your drawing until the outer edge of one triangle is along the line to which you want to sketch parallel.
- Hold down the triangle and slide the other along it.
- Draw parallel lines along one edge of the triangle. Draw perpendicular lines along the other edge.

This technique works well as an addition to freehand sketching when you want to show an auxiliary view.

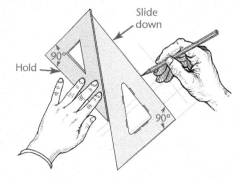

9.12 Triangles Being Used to Help Sketch Auxiliary Views

9.2 USING GRID PAPER TO SKETCH AUXILIARY VIEWS

You can use grid paper to help sketch auxiliary views by orienting the lines of the grid paper underneath your vellum or other semitransparent drawing sheet so that the grid is parallel to the inclined edge in the drawing, as shown in Figure 9.13. Use the grid to help sketch lines parallel and perpendicular to the edge in question.

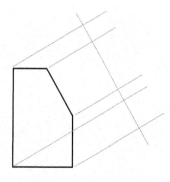

9.13 Sketching Auxiliary Views Using Grid Paper

SHOWING AN INCLINED ELLIPTICAL SURFACE TRUE SIZE

Given the front and side views shown, use these steps to project an auxiliary view showing the true size of the elliptical surface.

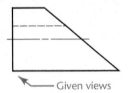

Given views

1 Because this is a symmetrical object, use a reference plane through the center of the object, as shown.

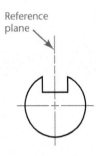

Reference plane

2 Select points on the circle in the side view.

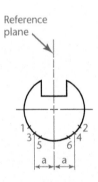

Reference plane

3 Locate the same points on the inclined surface and the left-end surface.

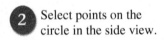

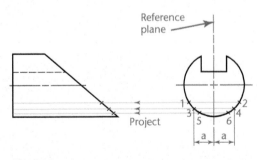

Given Views

4 Project each point to the auxiliary view along its projection line. In this case, the direction of sight is perpendicular to the edge view of the inclined surface. This will produce an auxiliary view showing the true shape of that surface.

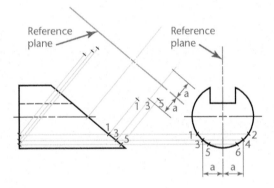

Reference plane   Reference plane

5 Transfer distances from the side view to the auxiliary view. Because the object is symmetrical, two points can be located with each measurement, as shown for points 1–2, 3–4, and 5–6. Project enough points to sketch the curves accurately.

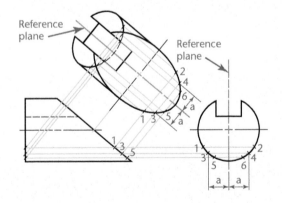

Reference plane   Reference plane

Because the major and minor axes are known, you can quickly create similar ellipses using CAD by locating the major and minor axes or the center and axes. For hand sketching, you may want to use an ellipse template.

STEP by STEP

9.3 USING CAD TO CREATE AUXILIARY VIEWS

Most CAD systems allow you to rotate the grid or to create a new coordinate system (often called a *user coordinate system*) so that it aligns with the inclined surface. If you are using 3D CAD, you can create true-size auxiliary views by viewing the object perpendicular to the surface you want to show true size (see Figure 9.14).

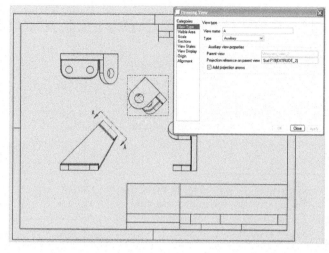

9.14 *CAD software provides tools for generating auxiliary views. (Courtesy of SolidWorks Corporation.)*

9.4 CIRCLES AND ELLIPSES IN AUXILIARY VIEWS

Circular shapes appear elliptical when viewed at an angle other than 90° (straight on to the circular shape). This is frequently the case when constructing auxiliary views (Figure 9.15).

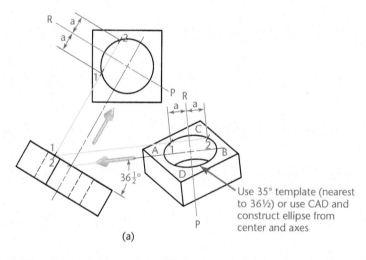

Use 35° template (nearest to 36½) or use CAD and construct ellipse from center and axes

(a)

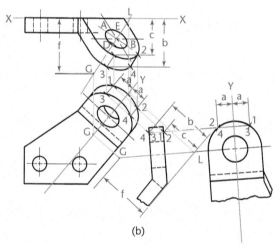

(b)

9.15 Circles Projected as Ellipses in Auxiliary Views

9.5 HIDDEN LINES IN AUXILIARY VIEWS

Generally, hidden lines should be omitted in auxiliary views, unless they are needed to clearly communicate the drawing's intent. Note the use of hidden lines in Figure 9.16.

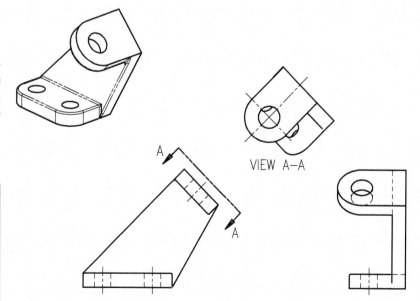

VIEW A–A

TIP

Your instructor may ask you to show all hidden lines for visualization practice, especially if the auxiliary view of the entire object is shown. Later, when you are familiar with drawing auxiliary views, omit hidden lines when they do not add needed information to the drawing.

9.16 *Omit hidden lines from auxiliary views whenever possible.*

PLOTTING CURVES MANUALLY IN AN AUXILIARY VIEW

Use the following steps to manually create an auxiliary view that shows the true size and shape of an inclined cut through a piece of molding. The method of plotting points is similar to that explained for the ellipse.

1 Identify some points along the curve shown in the side view. Locate those same points in the front view.

2 Locate the reference plane. Draw projectors perpendicular to the inclined surface in the front view and project the points into the auxiliary view.

3 Finish projecting all of the points on the inclined surface and draw its true shape in the auxiliary view.

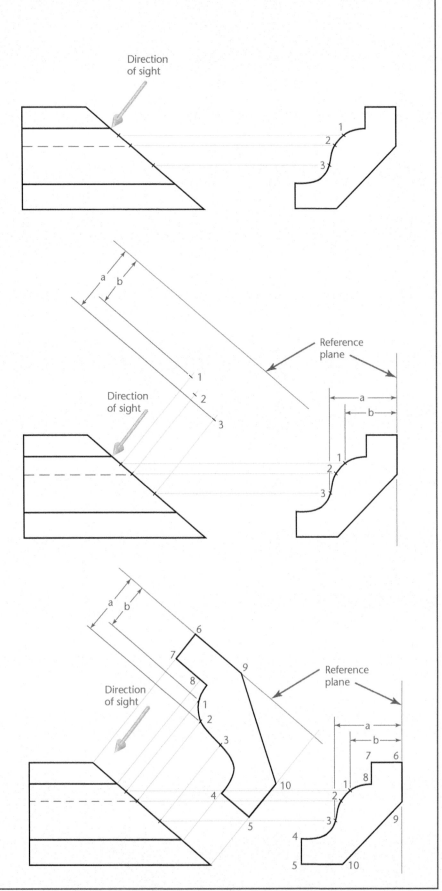

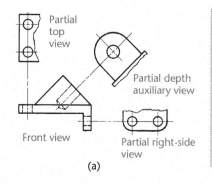

Partial top view

Partial depth auxiliary view

Front view

Partial right-side view

(a)

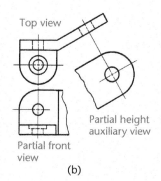

Top view

Partial height auxiliary view

Partial front view

(b)

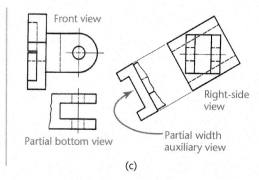

Front view

Right-side view

Partial bottom view

Partial width auxiliary view

(c)

9.17   Partial Views

9.6 PARTIAL AUXILIARY VIEWS

Using an auxiliary view often makes it possible to omit one or more regular views, but auxiliary drawings are time consuming to create and may even be confusing because of the clutter of lines.

Partial views are often sufficient and easier to read. Figure 9.17 shows partial regular views and *partial auxiliary views*. Usually, a break line is used to indicate the imaginary break in the views. Do not draw a break line coinciding with a visible line or hidden line.

So that partial auxiliary views (which are often small) do not appear "lost" and unrelated to any view, connect them to the views from which they project, either with a centerline or with one or two thin projection lines as shown in Figure 9.17.

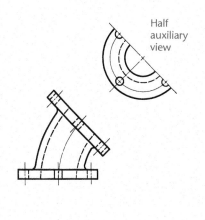

Half auxiliary view

9.7 HALF AUXILIARY VIEWS

If an auxiliary view is symmetrical, and if it is necessary to save space on the drawing or to save time, a *half auxiliary view* may be drawn, as shown in Figure 9.18. In this case, half of a regular view is also shown, since the bottom flange is also symmetrical. Note that in each case the near half is shown.

Half view

9.18   Half Views

9.8 REVERSE CONSTRUCTION

To complete the regular views, it is often necessary to first construct an auxiliary view where critical dimensions will be shown true size. For example, in Figure 9.19a, the upper part of the right-side view cannot be constructed until the auxiliary view is drawn. First, points are established on the curves and then projected back to the front view.

In Figure 9.19b, the 60° angle and the location of line 1–2 in the front view are given. To locate line 3–4 in the front view and lines 2–4, 3–4, and 4–5 in the side view, you must first construct the 60° angle in the auxiliary view and project it back to the front and side views, as shown.

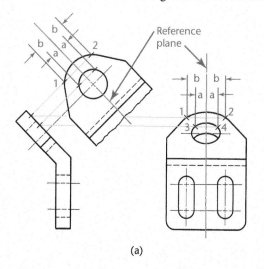

Reference plane

9.19   Reverse Construction

(a)

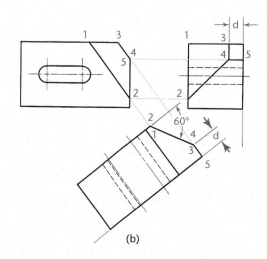

(b)

9.9 AUXILIARY SECTIONS

An *auxiliary section* is simply an auxiliary view in section (see Figure 9.20). A typical auxiliary section is shown in Figure 9.22. In this example, there is not sufficient space for a revolved section, although a removed section could have been used instead of an auxiliary section. Note the cutting-plane line and the terminating arrows that indicate the direction of sight for the auxiliary section. In an auxiliary section drawing, the entire portion of the object behind the cutting plane may be shown, or the cut surface alone may be shown.

The cutting-plane line indicates both the location of the cutting plane and the direction of sight for the auxiliary section. Figures 9.21 and 9.22 show examples of this. Notice that the auxiliary section is shown in alignment. Typically, a centerline is extended to locate the auxiliary sections or a few projection lines are shown in the drawing for this purpose.

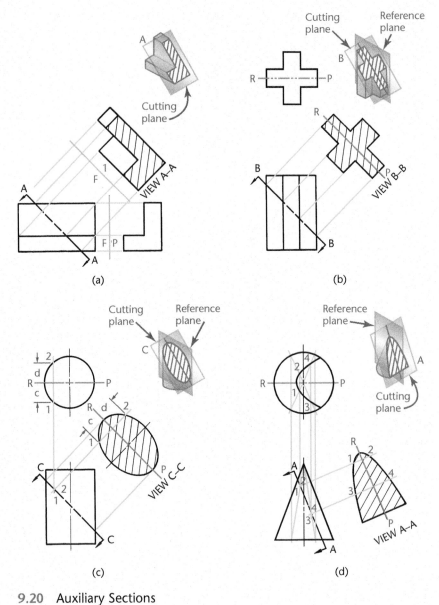

9.20   Auxiliary Sections

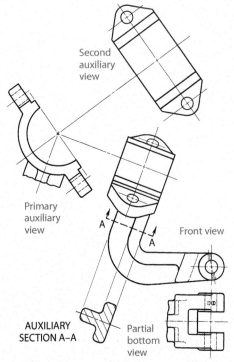

9.21   Secondary Auxiliary View—Partial Views

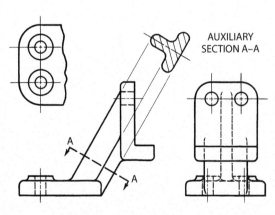

9.22   Auxiliary Section

9.10 VIEWING-PLANE LINES AND ARROWS

When the drawing sheet is too crowded to show the auxiliary view in direct projection you can use a *viewing-plane line* or a *viewing direction arrow* to indicate the direction of sight for the auxiliary view.

A viewing-plane line and a cutting-plane line look essentially the same. The arrows on either end of the line point in the direction of sight for the removed view. The ends of the line are labeled with letters, starting with A, then B, and so on. The auxiliary view, when placed in a removed location, should still be shown in the same orientation it would have if it were aligned in projection. Figure 9.23a shows a removed auxiliary view and viewing-plane line.

A viewing direction arrow for a removed auxiliary view is essentially the same as for any other removed view. Show an arrow pointing in the direction of sight for the removed auxiliary view. Label the removed view and place it in the same orientation it would have when projected, or if it is rotated, show a rotation arrow and specify the amount of rotation.

A centerline can be extended from a hole or other symmetric feature to indicate the alignment of the auxiliary view, as shown in Figure 9.23b.

Viewing direction arrows are particularly useful when showing a second auxiliary view in a drawing that is created from a 3D CAD model. Often, the primary auxiliary view is not necessary and can be left out if a viewing direction arrow is shown indicating the direction of sight for the second auxiliary view. An example of this use of a viewing direction arrow in a CAD drawing is shown in Figure 9.24.

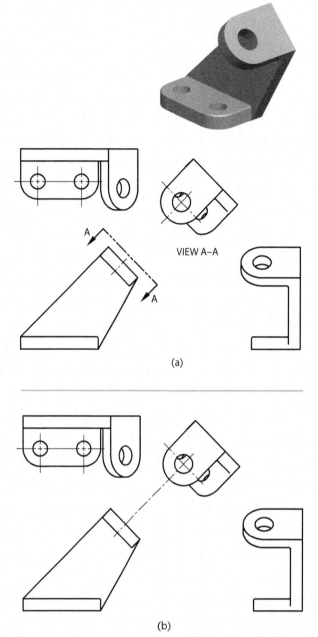

VIEW A–A

(a)

(b)

9.23 Using a Viewing-Plane Line to Show the Direction of Sight for an Auxiliary View. *Alternatively, a centerline can be extended to indicate the viewing direction.*

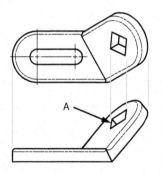

VIEW A

9.24 Using a Viewing Direction Arrow to Show the Direction of Sight for an Auxiliary View

9.11 USES OF AUXILIARY VIEWS

Generally, auxiliary views are used to show the true shape or true angle of features that appear distorted in the regular views. Auxiliary views are often used to produce views that show the following:

1. True length of line
2. Point view of line
3. Edge view of plane
4. True size of plane

You can use the ability to generate views that show the specific items listed to solve a variety of engineering problems. ***Descriptive geometry*** is the term for using accurate drawings to solve engineering problems. An accurate CAD drawing database can be used to solve many engineering problems when you understand the four basic views from descriptive geometry. Using 3D CAD, you can often model objects accurately and query the database for lengths and angles. Even so, you will often need the techniques described next to produce views that will help you visualize, create, or display 3D drawing geometry.

9.12 TRUE LENGTH OF A LINE

As shown in Figure 9.25, a line will show true length in a plane of projection that is parallel to the line. In other words, a line will show true length in an auxiliary view where the direction of sight is perpendicular to the line. To show a line true length, make the fold line parallel to the line you want to show true length in the auxiliary view. Whenever a line is parallel to the fold line between two views, it will be true length in the adjacent view.

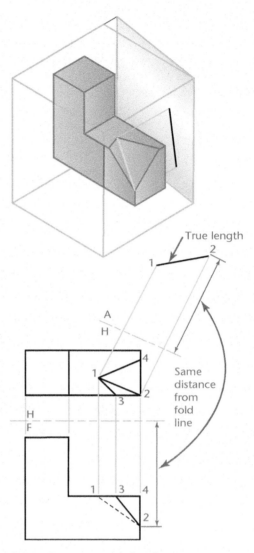

9.25   True Length of a Line

The Need to Show the True Length of a Line in CAD

Whether you are using 2D or 3D CAD or creating a sketch or drawing by hand, it is often necessary to create a view that shows a certain line true length. For example, a line must appear true length if you want to find its slope.

When you are working in a 3D CAD program, it is generally easy to list the true length of a line or an edge; but knowing the dimension is not the same as being able to show it on a drawing so that others can correctly interpret it.

To annotate the dimension on a drawing view where the line in question is shown true length you must understand how to create a view that is parallel to the line.

If you use 2D CAD, you will use the same methods explained in this chapter. If you use 3D CAD, reading about how to show a line at true length will help you understand how to create a plane parallel to that line in 3D CAD.

Understanding when a line is true length and when it is foreshortened in a view is also helpful in developing your ability to accurately visualize a 3D object from a 2D drawing.

SHOWING THE TRUE LENGTH OF A HIP RAFTER

The top and front views of the hip rafter (line 1–2) are shown. Use an auxiliary view to show the line true length.

1 Choose the direction of sight to be perpendicular to line 1–2 (front view).

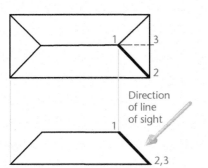

4 Draw projection lines from points 1, 2, and 3 to begin creating the auxiliary view.

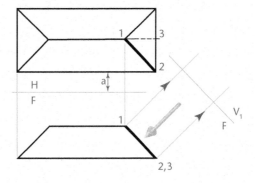

2 Draw the H/F folding line between the top and front views, as shown.

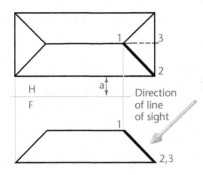

5 Transfer points 1 and 2 to the auxiliary view at the same distance from the folding line as they are in the top view, and along their respective projection lines. The hip rafter (line 1–2) is shown true length in the auxiliary view.

Also, triangle 1–2–3 in the auxiliary view shows the true size and shape of that portion of the roof because the direction of sight for the auxiliary view is perpendicular to triangle 1–2–3.

3 Draw the F/V₁ folding line parallel to line 1–2 and any convenient distance from line 1–2 (front view).

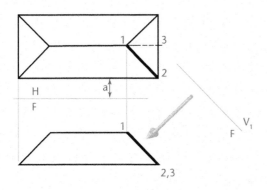

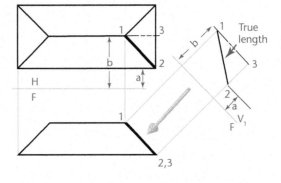

9.13 POINT VIEW OF A LINE

As shown in Figure 9.26, a line will show as a point view when projected to a plane perpendicular it. To show the point view of a line, choose the direction of sight parallel to the line where it is true length.

Showing the Point View of a Line

Refer to Figure 9.27 for the following steps:

1. Choose the direction of sight to be parallel to line 1–2.
2. Draw folding line H/F between the top and front views, as shown.
3. Draw folding line F/A perpendicular to line 1–2 where it is true length, and any convenient distance from line 1–2 (front view).
4. Draw projection lines from points 1 and 2 to begin creating the auxiliary view.
5. Transfer points 1 and 2 to the auxiliary view at the same distance from the folding line as they are in the top view and along their respective projection lines. They will line up exactly with each other to form a point view of the line.

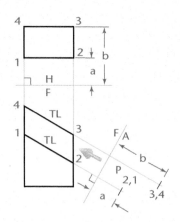

9.26   Point View of a Line

TIP

Viewing a Line as a Point

Draw a line in a plane—for example, a straight line on a sheet of paper. Then, tilt the paper to view the line as a point. You will see that when the line appears as a point, the plane containing it appears as a line. (Because your paper will end up being viewed on edge, it may be a little hard to see the line when it is oriented correctly.)

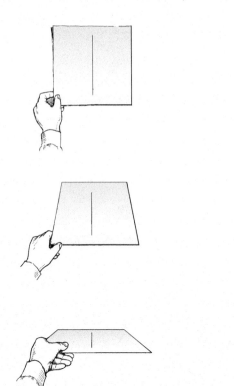

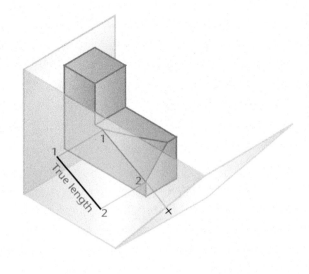

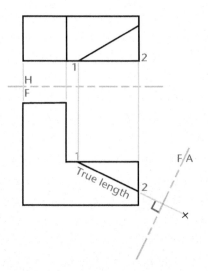

9.27   Point View of a Line

9.14 EDGE VIEW OF A PLANE

As shown in Figure 9.28, a plane will show on edge in a plane of projection that shows a point view of any line that lies entirely within the plane. To get the point view of a line, the direction of sight must be parallel to the line where it is true length. To show the edge view of a plane, choose the direction of sight parallel to a true-length line lying in the plane.

Finding the edge view of a plane is a useful tool for the following types of problems:

- Finding the shortest line from a point to a plane. The shortest line will be perpendicular from the point to the plane. This is easiest to show in a view showing the plane on edge.
- Finding the slope of a plane. When you are working in a 3D CAD program, it is easy to create a view from any direction. Understanding how to choose a direction that will produce the most useful view for your purposes is easier yet when you understand these basic principles. Even though you can use CAD inquiry tools to quickly determine the angle between planes, often you may need to document the angle of a plane in a view showing the plane on edge.

Showing the Edge View of a Plane

Refer to Figure 9.29 for the following steps:

1. Choose the direction of sight to be parallel to line 1–2 in the front view where it is already shown true length.
2. Draw folding line H/F between the top and front views, as shown.
3. Draw folding line F/A perpendicular to true-length line 1–2 and any convenient distance.
4. Draw projection lines from points 1, 2, and 3 to begin creating the auxiliary view.
5. Transfer points 1, 2, and 3 to the auxiliary view at the same distance from the folding line as they are in the top view and along their respective projection lines. Plane 1–2–3 will appear on edge in the finished drawing.

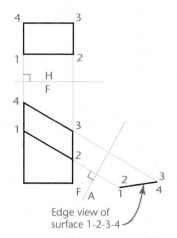

9.28 Edge View of a Surface

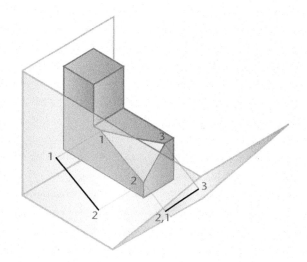

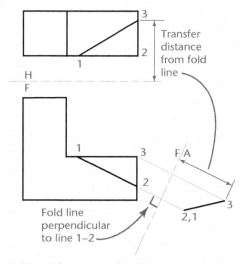

9.29 Edge View of a Plane

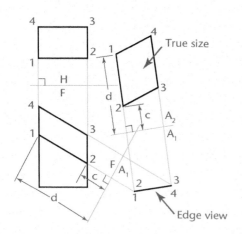

9.30   True Size of an Oblique Surface

9.15 TRUE SIZE OF AN OBLIQUE SURFACE

As shown in Figure 9.30, a plane will show true size when the plane of projection is parallel to it.

To show the true size view of a plane, choose the direction of sight perpendicular to the edge view of the plane.

Showing the true size of a surface continues from the method presented for showing inclined surfaces true size, where the edge view is already given. But to show an oblique surface true size, you need first to show the oblique surface on edge and then construct a second auxiliary view to show it true size.

Showing the True Size and Shape of an Oblique Surface

To show the true size and shape of an oblique surface, such as surface 1–2–3 in Figure 9.31, create a second auxiliary view. In this example folding lines are used, but you can achieve the same results for all of the preceding examples using reference lines.

1. Draw the auxiliary view showing surface 1–2–3 on edge, as explained previously.
2. Create a second auxiliary view with the line of sight perpendicular to the edge view of plane 1–2–3 in the primary auxiliary view. Project lines parallel to the arrow. Draw folding line A_1/A_2 perpendicular to these projection lines at a convenient distance from the primary auxiliary view.
3. Draw the secondary auxiliary view. Transfer the distance to each point from folding line F/A_1 to the second auxiliary view—for example, dimensions d_1, d_2, and d_3. The true size TS of the surface 1–2–3 is shown in the secondary auxiliary view, because the direction of sight is perpendicular to it.

Figure 9.32 shows an example of the steps to find the true size of an oblique surface. The first step, illustrated in Figure 9.32a, shows the oblique surface on edge. Figure 9.32b establishes the direction of sight perpendicular to the edge view. The final true size view of the surface is projected in Figure 9.32c.

Figure 9.33 shows a similar example using the reference-plane method.

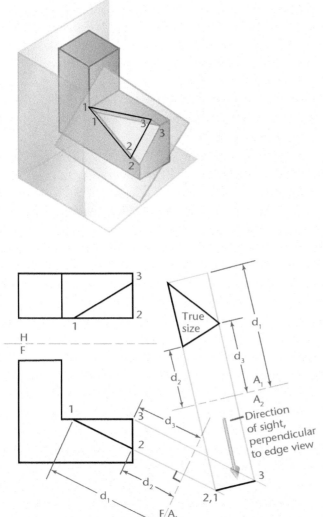

9.31   True-Size View of an Oblique Surface

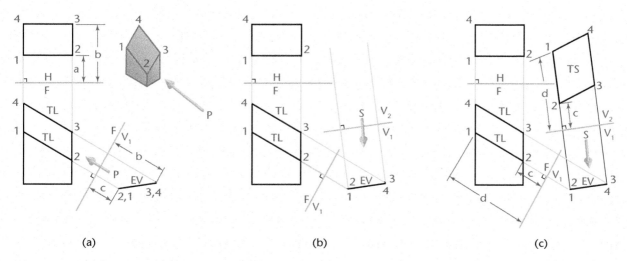

9.32 True Size of Oblique Surface—Folding Line Method

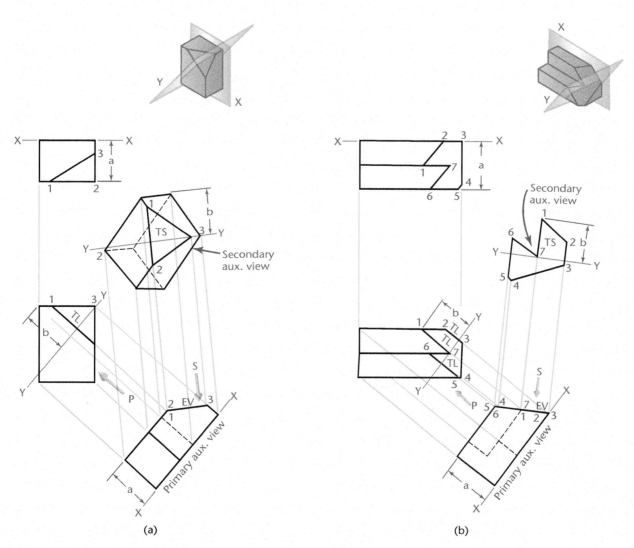

9.33 True Size of an Oblique Surface—Reference-Plane Method

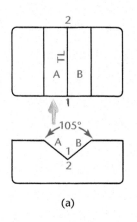
(a)

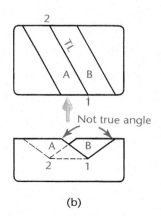
(b)

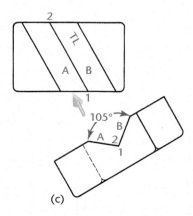
(c)

9.34 Dihedral Angles

9.16 DIHEDRAL ANGLES

The angle between two planes is called a ***dihedral angle.*** Auxiliary views often need to be drawn to show dihedral angles true size, mainly for dimensioning purposes. In Figure 9.34a, a block with a V-groove is shown where the dihedral angle between inclined surfaces A and B is shown true size in the front view.

In Figure 9.34b, the V-groove on the block is at an angle to the front surface so that the true dihedral angle is not shown. Assume that the actual angle is the same as in Figure 9.34a. Does the angle appear larger or smaller than in Figure 9.34a?

To show the true dihedral angle, the line of intersection (in this case 1–2) must appear as a point. Because the line of intersection for the dihedral angle is in both planes, showing it as a point will produce a view which shows both planes on edge. This will give you the true-size view of the dihedral angle.

In Figure 9.34a, line 1–2 is the line of intersection of planes A and B. Now, line 1–2 lies in both planes at the same time; therefore, a point view of this line will show both planes as lines, and the angle between them is the dihedral angle between the planes. To get the true angle between two planes, find the point view of the line of intersection of the planes.

In Figure 9.34c, the direction of sight is parallel to line 1–2 so that line 1–2 appears as a point, planes A and B appear as lines, and the true dihedral angle is shown in the auxiliary view.

Figure 9.35 shows a drawing using an auxiliary view to show the true angle between surfaces.

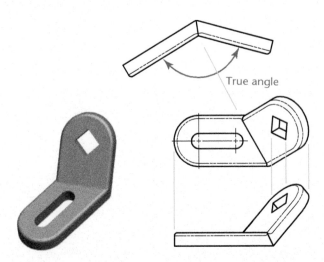
True angle

9.35 Using an Auxiliary View to Show the True Angle between Surfaces (Dihedral Angle)

UNDERSTANDING DEVELOPMENTS AND INTERSECTIONS

A *development* is a flat representation or pattern that when folded together creates a 3D object (Figure 9.36). An *intersection* is the result of two objects that intersect each other (Figure 9.37). Sheet metal construction is the most common application for developments and intersections. A development of surfaces, such as those found in sheet metal fabrication, is a flat pattern that represents the unfolded or unrolled surface of the form. The resulting flat pattern gives the true size of each connected area of the form so that the part or structure can be fabricated. Auxiliary views are a primary tool for creating developments, but many specialized software packages are available to automate creating developments and intersections. You can also apply what you have learned about auxiliary views to create developments and intersections using your CAD system.

Surface Terminology

The following terminology describes objects and concepts used in developments and intersections:

A *ruled surface* is one that may be generated by sweeping a straight line, called the *generatrix,* along a path, which may be straight or curved (Figure 9.38). Any position of the generatrix is an *element* of the surface. A ruled surface may be a plane, a single-curved surface, or a warped surface.

A *plane* is a ruled surface that is generated by a line, one point of which moves along a straight path while the generatrix remains parallel to its original position. Many geometric solids are bounded by plane surfaces (Figure 9.39).

A *single-curved surface* is a developable ruled surface; that is, it can be unrolled to coincide with a plane. Any two adjacent positions of the generatrix lie in the same plane. Examples are the cylinder (Figure 9.40) and the cone.

A *double-curved surface* is generated by a curved line and has no straight-line elements (Figure 9.41). A surface generated by revolving a curved line about a straight line in the plane of the curve is called a *double-curved surface of revolution.* Common examples are the *sphere*, *torus*, *ellipsoid,* and *hyperboloid.*

A *warped surface* is a ruled surface that is not developable. Some examples are shown in Figure 9.42. No two adjacent positions of the generatrix lie in a flat plane. Warped surfaces cannot be unrolled or unfolded to lie flat. Many exterior surfaces on an airplane or automobile are warped surfaces.

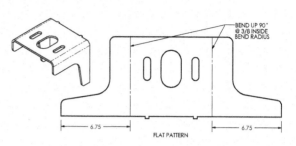

9.36 A Flat Pattern *(Courtesy of Dynojet Research, Inc.)*

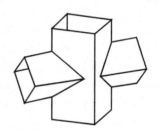

9.37 Intersecting Prisms

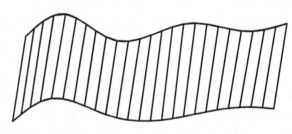

9.38 Ruled Surface

9.39 Plane Surfaces

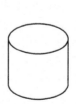

9.40 Single-Curved Surface

9.41 Double-Curved Surface

(a) Cylindroid

(b) Conoid

(c) Helicoid

(d) Hyperboloid

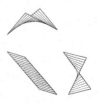

(e) Hyperbolic paraboloid

9.42 Warped Surfaces

Developable Surfaces

A *developable surface* may be unfolded or unrolled to lie flat. Surfaces composed of single-curved surfaces, of planes, or of combinations of these types are developable.

Warped surfaces and double-curved surfaces are not directly developable. They may be developed by approximating their shape using developable surfaces. If the material used in the actual manufacturing is sufficiently pliable, the flat sheets may be stretched, pressed, stamped, spun, or otherwise forced to assume the desired shape. Nondevelopable surfaces are often produced by a combination of developable surfaces that are then formed slightly to produce the required shape. Figure 9.43 shows examples of developable surfaces.

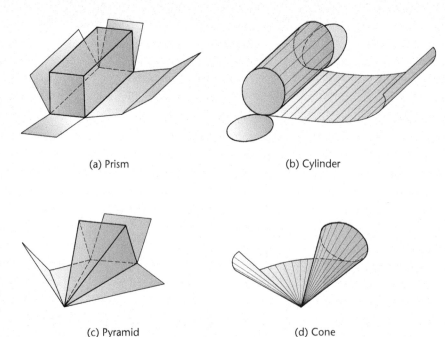

(a) Prism   (b) Cylinder

(c) Pyramid   (d) Cone

9.43   Development of Surfaces

Principles of Intersections

Accurate drawings showing the intersections of planes and solids are needed for openings in roof surfaces for flues and stacks; openings in wall surfaces for pipes, chutes, and so on; and the building of sheet metal structures such as tanks and boilers. In such cases, you generally need to determine the true size and shape of the intersection of a plane and one of the more common geometric solids. Figure 9.44 shows an example in which you would need to determine the intersection of a solid and a plane to create the correctly shaped opening in the vertical prism—the main flue—where the horizontal prism joins it.

For solids bounded by plane surfaces, you need find only the points of intersection of the edges of the solid with the plane and to join these points, in consecutive order, with straight lines.

For solids bounded by curved surfaces, it is necessary to find the points of intersection of several elements of the solid with the plane and to trace a smooth curve through these points. The intersection of a plane and a circular cone is called a *conic section.* Some typical conic sections are shown in Figure 9.45.

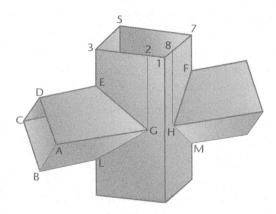

9.44   Intersecting Prisms

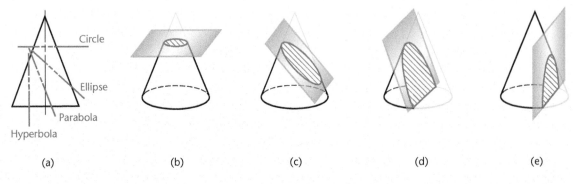

Circle

Ellipse

Parabola

Hyperbola

(a)   (b)   (c)   (d)   (e)

9.45   Conic Sections

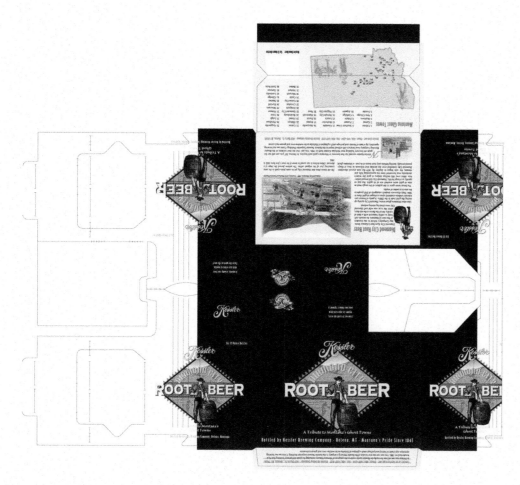

9.46 Flat Pattern for a Root Beer Package *(Courtesy of Kessler Brewing Co.)*

9.17 DEVELOPMENTS

The ***development of a surface*** is that surface laid out on a plane. Practical applications of developments occur in sheet metal work, stone cutting, pattern making, packaging, and package design. See Figure 9.46.

Single-curved surfaces and the surfaces of polyhedra can be developed. Developments for warped surfaces and double-curved surfaces can only be approximated.

In sheet metal layout, extra material must be provided for laps and seams. If the material is heavy, the thickness may be a factor, and the crowding of metal in bends must be considered. Stock sizes must also be taken into account and layouts made to economize on material and labor. In preparing developments, it is best to put the seam at the shortest edge and to attach the bases at edges where they match; this will minimize processing such as soldering, welding, and riveting.

It is common to draw development layouts with the inside surfaces up. This way, all fold lines and other markings are related directly to inside measurements, which are the important dimensions in all ducts, pipes, tanks, and vessels. In this position they are also convenient for use in the fabricating shop. See Sections 10.6 and 11.43 for more information about sheet metal bends.

Finding the Intersection of a Plane and a Prism and Developing the Prism

To create flat patterns for sheet metal, packaging, and other purposes, you must first determine the true size of the surface. The true size and shape of the intersection of a plane and a prism is shown in the auxiliary view in Figure 9.47. The length *AB* is the same as *AB* in the front view, and the width *AD* is the same as *AD* in the top view.

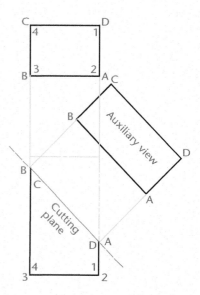

9.47 Auxiliary View Showing True Size and Shape of the Intersection of a Plane and a Prism

DEVELOPING A PRISM

These are the steps for creating the development for the prism shown here.

1 Draw the stretchout line, which represents the axis along which the part is unfolded or unrolled. On the stretchout line, transfer the true sizes of faces 1–2 and 2–3, which are shown true length in the top view. Remember that a line appears true length when the view is perpendicular to the line. In other words, when a line is parallel to the fold line between views, the line is true length in the adjacent view.

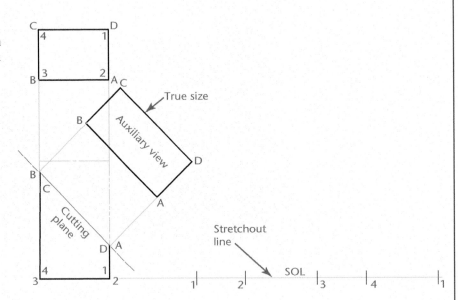

2 Where two surfaces join, draw perpendiculars to the stretchout line and transfer the true height of each respective edge. The front view shows the true heights in this case. Project the heights from the front view, as shown. Complete the development of these surfaces using straight lines to join the points you have plotted. Identify other surfaces that are connected to these and attach their true sizes to the development of the lower base and the upper base. Use an auxiliary view to find the true size of the surface and then draw it in place.

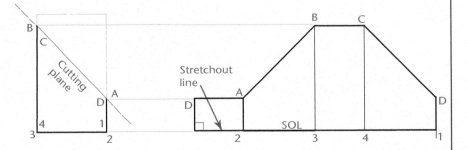

3 When you finish, you will have drawn the development of the entire prism, as shown. If needed, add tabs so that there is material to connect the surfaces when folded up.

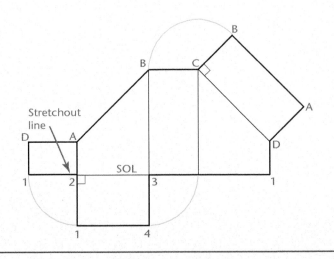

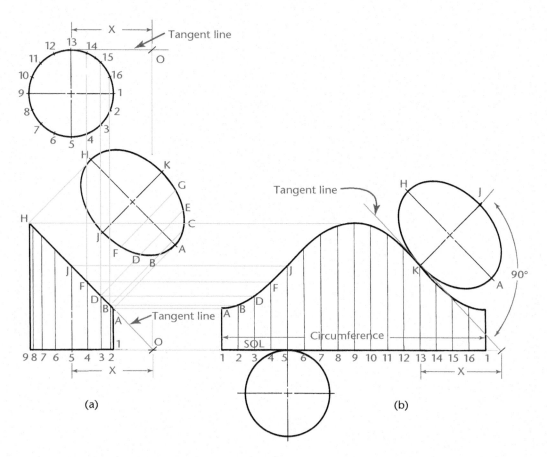

9.48 Plane and Cylinder

Finding the Intersection of a Plane and a Cylinder and Developing the Cylinder

The intersection of a plane and a cylinder is an ellipse whose true size is shown in the auxiliary view of Figure 9.48. The steps for developing a cylinder are as follows:

- Draw elements of the cylinder. It is usually best to divide the base of the cylinder into equal parts, shown in the top view and then projected into the front view.
- In the auxiliary view, the widths *BC, DE,* and so on, are transferred from the top view at 2–16, 3–15, respectively, and the ellipse is drawn through these points. The major axis *AH* shows true length in the front view, and the minor axis *JK* shows true length in the top view. You can use this information to quickly draw the ellipse using CAD.
- Draw the stretchout line for the cylinder. It will be equal to the circumference of the base, whose length is determined by the formula πd.
- Divide the stretchout line into the same number of equal parts as the circumference of the base, and draw an element through each division perpendicular to the line.
- Transfer the true height by projecting it from the front view, as shown in Figure 9.48b.
- Draw a smooth curve through the points *A, B, D,* and so on.
- Draw the tangent lines and attach the bases as shown in Figure 9.48b.

9.18 HEMS AND JOINTS FOR SHEET METAL AND OTHER MATERIALS

Figure 9.49 shows a wide variety of hems and joints used in fabricating sheet metal parts and other items. Hems are used to eliminate the raw edge as well as to stiffen the material. Joints and seams may be made for sheet metal by bending, welding, riveting, and soldering and for package materials by gluing and stapling.

You must add material for hems and joints to the layout or development. The amount you add depends on the thickness of the material and the production equipment. A good place to find more information is from manufacturers. They can be extremely helpful in identifying specifications related to the exact process that will be used to make the part.

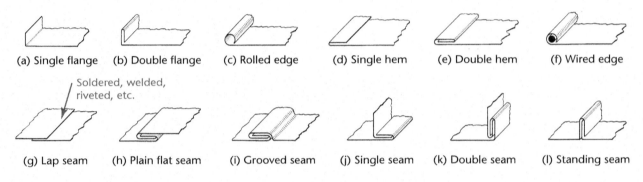

(a) Single flange   (b) Double flange   (c) Rolled edge   (d) Single hem   (e) Double hem   (f) Wired edge

(g) Lap seam   (h) Plain flat seam   (i) Grooved seam   (j) Single seam   (k) Double seam   (l) Standing seam

9.49   Sheet Metal Hems and Joints

9.19 MORE EXAMPLES OF DEVELOPMENTS AND INTERSECTIONS

Developing a Plane and an Oblique Prism

The intersection of a plane and an oblique prism is shown in Figure 9.50a. Where the plane is normal to the prism formed by plane *WX* (called a right section) it appears as a regular hexagon, as shown in the auxiliary view labeled "Right section." The oblique section cut by horizontal plane *YZ* is shown true size in the top view.

The development for this oblique prism is shown in Figure 9.50b. Use the right section to create stretchout line *WX*.

On the stretchout line, set off the true widths of the faces 1–2, 2–3, and so on, which are shown true size in the auxiliary view. Draw perpendiculars through each division. Transfer the true heights of the respective edges, which are shown true size in the front view. Join the points *A*, *B*, *C*, and so on with straight lines. Finally, attach the bases, which are shown in their true sizes in the top view, along an edge.

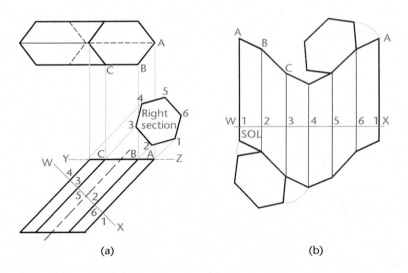

(a)   (b)

9.50   Plane and Oblique Prism

Developing a Plane and an Oblique Cylinder

The development of the intersection of a plane and an oblique cylinder is similar to that for a plane and an oblique prism, as shown in Figure 9.51.

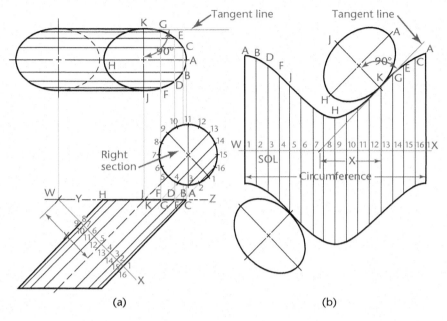

(a)   (b)

9.51   Plane and Oblique Circular Cylinder

Developing a Plane and a Pyramid

The intersection of a plane and a pyramid is a trapezoid, as shown in Figure 9.52.

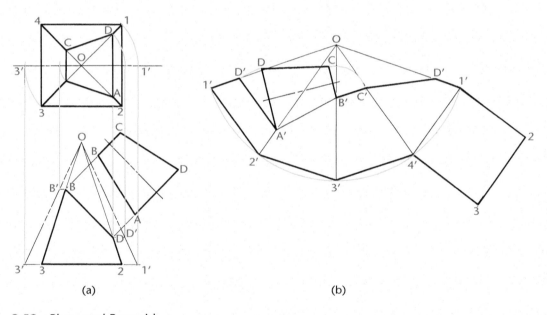

(a)   (b)

9.52   Plane and Pyramid

Developing a Plane and a Cone

The intersection of a plane and a cone is an ellipse, as shown in Figure 9.53. If a series of horizontal cutting planes are passed perpendicular to the axis, each plane will cut a circle from the cone that will show as true size and shape in the top view. Points in which these circles intersect the original cutting plane are points on the ellipse. Because the cutting plane is shown on edge in the front view (Figure 9.53a), all these piercing points can be projected from there to the others, as shown in Figure 9.53b.

To develop the lateral surface of a cone, think of the cone as a pyramid having an infinite number of edges. The development is similar to that for a pyramid.

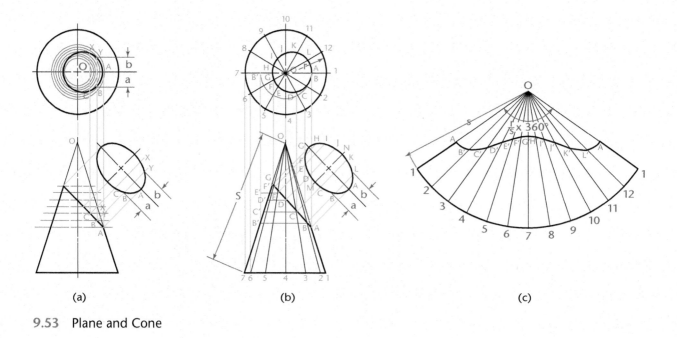

9.53   Plane and Cone

Developing a Hood and Flue

The development of a hood and flue is shown in Figure 9.54. Because the hood is a conical surface, it may be developed as shown in Figure 9.53. The two end sections of the elbow are cylindrical surfaces. The two middle sections of the elbow are cylindrical surfaces, but their bases are not perpendicular to the axes, so they will not develop into straight lines.

Develop them similar to an oblique cylinder. Make auxiliary planes *AB* and *DC* perpendicular to the axes so they cut right sections from the cylinders, which will develop into the straight lines *AB* and *CD* in the developments. Arranging the developments as shown allows the elbow to be constructed from a rectangular sheet of metal without wasting material. The patterns are shown in the right top portion of Figure 9.54 as they will be separated after cutting.

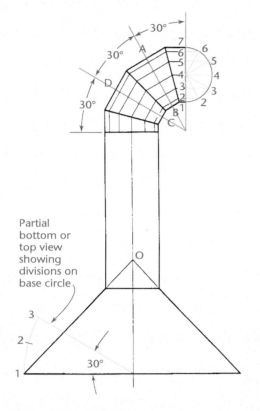

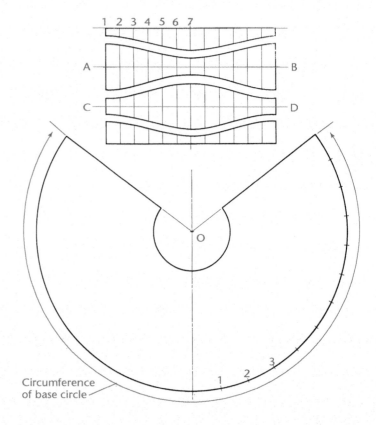

9.54   A Hood and Flue

   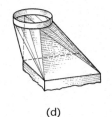 

(a)   (b)   (c)   (d)   (e)

9.55   Transition Pieces

9.20 TRANSITION PIECES

A *transition piece* is one that connects two different-shaped, different-sized, or skewed position openings. In most cases, transition pieces are composed of plane surfaces and conical surfaces, as shown in Figure 9.55. You will learn about developing conical surfaces by triangulation next. Triangulation can also be used to develop, approximately, certain warped surfaces. Transition pieces are used extensively in air conditioning, heating, ventilating, and similar construction.

9.21 TRIANGULATION

Triangulation is simply a method of dividing a surface into a number of triangles and transferring them to the development. To find the development of an oblique cone by triangulation, divide the base of the cone in the top view into any number of equal parts and draw an element at each division point, as shown in Figure 9.56. Find the true length of each element. If the divisions of the base are comparatively small, the lengths of the chords may be used in the development to represent the lengths of the respective arcs. Because the development is symmetrical, it is necessary to lay out only half the development, as shown at the right side of Figure 9.56.

DUCTWORK PARTS

Heating, ventilating, and air conditioning (HVAC) systems often use ductwork to transfer air through the system. The standard parts shown above are made of 26 gauge galvanized steel and can be purchased "off the shelf." When ducts must connect at odd angles to fit into existing spaces, custom designed developments and intersections are required.

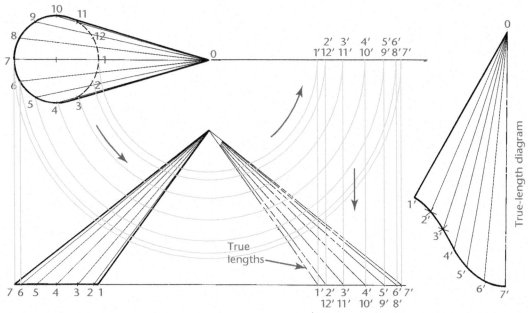

9.56   Development of an Oblique Cone by Triangulation

True-length diagram

9.22 DEVELOPING A TRANSITION PIECE CONNECTING RECTANGULAR PIPES ON THE SAME AXIS

The transition piece can be a frustum of a pyramid that connects rectangular pipes on the same axis, as shown in Figure 9.57. As a check on the development, lines parallel on the surface must also be parallel on the development.

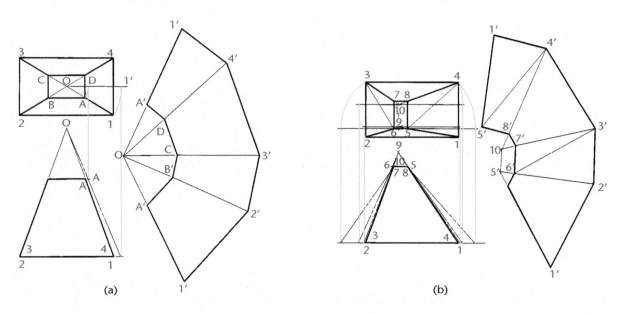

(a)   (b)

9.57   Development of a Transition Piece—Connecting Rectangular Pipes on the Same Axis

9.23 DEVELOPING A PLANE AND A SPHERE

The intersection of a plane and a sphere is a circle. The diameter of the circle depends on where the plane is located. Any circle cut by a plane through the center of the sphere is called a *great circle*. If a plane passes through the center and is perpendicular

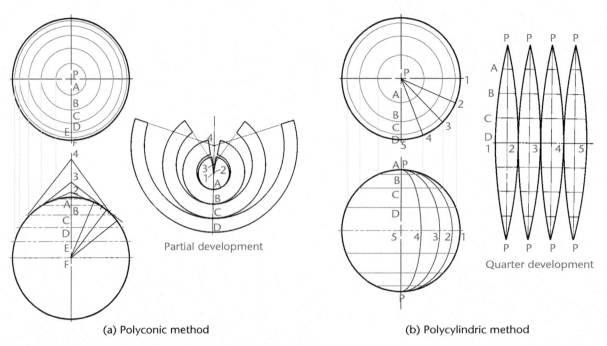

(a) Polyconic method   (b) Polycylindric method

9.58   Approximate Development of a Sphere

to the axis, the resulting great circle is called the **equator.** If a plane contains the axis, it will cut a great circle called a **meridian.**

The surface of a sphere is double curved and is not developable, but it may be developed approximately by dividing it into a series of zones and substituting a portion of a right-circular cone for each zone. If the conical surfaces are inscribed within the sphere, the development will be smaller than the spherical surface, but if they are circumscribed about the sphere, the development will be larger. If the conical surfaces are partly inside and partly outside the sphere, the resulting development is closely approximate to the spherical surface. This method of developing a spherical surface, the **polyconic** method, is shown in Figure 9.58a. It is used on government maps of the United States.

Another method of making an approximate development of the double-curved surface of a sphere is to divide the surface into equal sections with meridian planes and substitute cylindrical surfaces for the spherical sections. The cylindrical surfaces may be inscribed within the sphere, circumscribed about it, or located partly inside and partially outside. This method, the **polycylindric** method (sometimes called the *gore* method) is shown in Figure 9.58b.

9.24 REVOLUTION

Revolution, like auxiliary view projection, is a method of determining the true length and true size of inclined and oblique lines and planes. To create the auxiliary view, imagine that the object remains stationary and a new viewing plane is added as shown by the arrow in Figure 9.59a. Surface A shows true size and shape in the auxiliary view.

The same view of the object can be obtained by moving the object with respect to the viewing planes, as shown in Figure 9.59b. Here the object is revolved until surface A appears in its true size and shape in the right-side view. Revolution determines true length and true size without creating another view. Instead, revolution positions an object in space to create standard views that show the true size and shape of the inclined or oblique surface.

Axis of Revolution

Imagine the axis of revolution to be perpendicular to the front plane of projection in Figure 9.59b. The **axis of revolution** appears as a point in this view. The object revolves but does not change shape in this view. In the adjacent views in which the axis of revolution, if it were drawn, would show as a line in true length, the dimensions of the object that are parallel to the axis of revolution do not change. Other dimensions may appear foreshortened.

Creating a Revolved Drawing

To make a drawing using revolution to show the true size of a surface, use the following procedure:

1. Select the view that has the feature of interest, such as the inclined surface showing as an edge, that you want to revolve to produce a true-size feature in the adjacent view.
2. Select any point at any convenient position on or outside that view about which to draw the view revolved either clockwise or counterclockwise. That point is the end view, or point view, of the axis of revolution.
3. Draw this first view on the plane of projection. This is the only view that remains unchanged in size and shape.
4. Project the other views from this view using standard orthographic projection techniques.

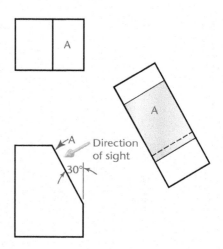

(a) Auxiliary view

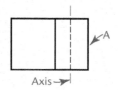

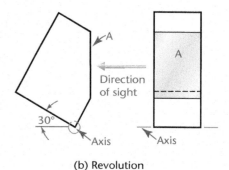

(b) Revolution

9.59 Auxiliary View and Revolution Compared

9.25 PRIMARY AND SUCCESSIVE REVOLUTIONS

The axis of revolution is usually perpendicular to one of the three principal planes of projection. A *primary revolution* is one in which the object is revolved about an axis perpendicular to the horizontal, frontal, or profile planes of projection. *Successive revolutions* are drawings that use multiple revolutions of the same object to produce a final revolved drawing with the desired result. Figure 9.60 shows an example. As you can imagine, this is accomplished in one step using CAD.

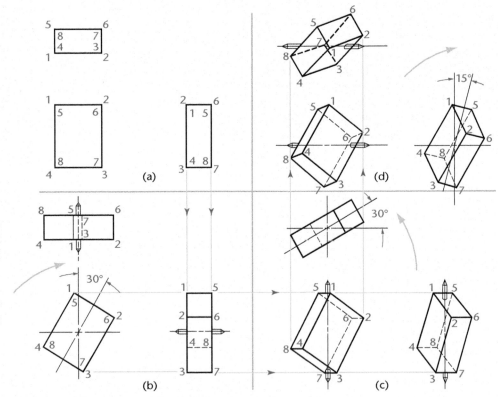

9.60   Successive Revolutions of a Prism

9.26 TRUE LENGTH OF A LINE: REVOLUTION METHOD

A line (edge) appears true length when it is parallel to one of the planes of projection. In Figure 9.61a, line *AB* (an element of the cone) is oblique to the planes of projection. Line *AB* appears foreshortened, not true length. If *AB* is revolved about the axis of the cone until it coincides with either of the contour elements (for example, AB_R), it will be shown in its true length in the front view because it will then be parallel to the front plane of projection.

In Figure 9.61b, to show the edge of the pyramid *CD* true length, it is revolved about the axis of the pyramid until it is parallel to the frontal plane of projection and therefore

shows true length in the front view. In Figure 9.61c, line *EF* is shown true length in the front view because it has been revolved about a vertical axis until it is parallel to the front plane of projection.

The true length of a line may also be found by constructing a right triangle or a true-length diagram (Figure 9.61d) with the base of the triangle equal to the top view of the line, for example, the distance from *E* to *F* in the top view in c, drawn as *XF* in d; and the height of the triangle equal to the projected height, *XE*, of the line taken from the front view. The hypotenuse of the triangle is equal to the true length of the line.

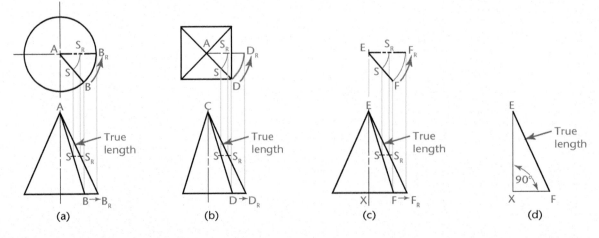

9.61   True Length of a Line—Revolution Method

CREATING AUXILIARY VIEWS USING 3D CAD

3D CAD can be used to generate any view in one or two steps, eliminating the need to project auxiliary views and revolve views manually. It is still very important to have a clear understanding of which line of sight will produce a true-size view or a view that shows a true dihedral angle. When a view from a CAD screen is measured or dimensioned, if the surface or angle is not true size, the automatic dimension from the CAD system may be that of the apparent, or projected, distance. Incorrectly dimensioned dihedral angles can be an error in CAD drawings created by inexperienced operators. Drawings should show angles true size where they are dimensioned or note it clearly if this is not the case.

Solid modeling techniques can be used to create accurate intersections between various solids. Some CAD programs have commands for creating transition pieces that blend solids of two differing shapes, for example, a sweep/join operation. Not all CAD software is capable of producing developments (flat patterns) of surfaces. Some surfaces, such as spheres or tori, can only be approximated by a flattened shape.

Views of the Solid Model from Which the Detail Drawings Were Created *(Courtesy of Dynojet Research, Inc.)*

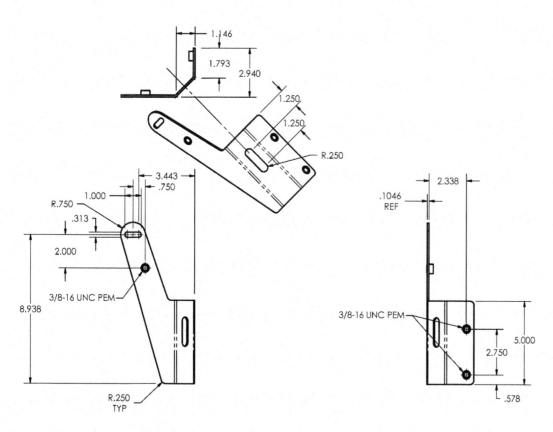

An auxiliary view is used on the drawing for this sheet metal part so that dimensions are shown where the feature is true size. (Courtesy of Dynojet Research, Inc.)

KEY WORDS

Adjacent View
Alternate View
Auxiliary Plane
Auxiliary Section
Auxiliary View
Axis of Revolution
Conic Section
Depth Auxiliary Views
Descriptive Geometry
Developable Surface
Development
Development of a Surface
Dihedral Angle
Double-Curved Surface
Double-Curved Surface of Revolution
Element
Ellipsoid
Equator
Extruded Solid
Folding Lines
Generatrix
Great Circle
Half Auxiliary View
Height Auxiliary Views
Hyperboloid
Intersection
Meridian
Partial Auxiliary Views
Plane
Polyconic
Polycylindric
Primary Auxiliary View
Primary Revolution
Reference Plane
Revolution
Revolved Solid
Ruled Surface
Secondary Auxiliary View
Single-Curved Surface
Sphere
Succeeding Auxiliary View
Successive Revolutions
Third Auxiliary View
Torus
Transition Piece
Triangulation
True Size
Viewing Direction Arrow
Viewing-Plane Line
Warped Surface
Width Auxiliary Views

CHAPTER SUMMARY

- An auxiliary view can be used to create a projection that shows the true length of a line or true size of a plane.
- An auxiliary view can be directly produced using CAD if the original object was drawn as a 3D model.
- Folding lines or reference lines represent the edge views of projection planes.
- Points are projected between views parallel to the line of sight and perpendicular to the reference lines or folding lines.
- A common use of auxiliary views is to show dihedral angles true size.
- Curves are projected to auxiliary views by plotting them as points.
- A secondary auxiliary view can be constructed from a previously drawn (primary) auxiliary view.
- The technique for creating the development of a solid is determined by the basic geometric shape. Prisms, pyramids, cylinders, and cones have their own particular development techniques.
- The intersection of two solids is determined by plotting the intersection of each surface and transferring the intersection points to each development.
- Cones and pyramids use radial development. Prisms and cylinders use parallel development.
- Truncated solids, cones, and pyramids are created by developing the whole solid and then plotting the truncated endpoints on each radial element.
- Transition pieces are developed by creating triangular surfaces that approximate the transition from rectangular to circular. The smaller the triangular surfaces, the more accurate the development.
- Revolution moves an object in space, to reveal what would normally be an auxiliary view of the object in a primary view (top, front, right side).
- The main purpose of revolution is to reveal the true length and true size of inclined and oblique lines and planes in a primary view.

REVIEW QUESTIONS

1. What is meant by true length? By true size?
2. Why is a true-length line always parallel to an adjacent reference line?
3. If an auxiliary view is drawn from the front view, what other views would show the same depth dimensions?
4. Describe one method for transferring depth between views.
5. What is the difference between a complete auxiliary view and a partial auxiliary view?
6. How many auxiliary views are necessary to draw the true size of an inclined plane? Of an oblique plane?
7. What is the angle between the reference plane line (or folding line) and the direction-of-sight lines?

8. How is the development of a pyramid similar to the development of a cone?

9. When a truncated cone or pyramid is developed, why is the complete solid developed first?

10. What descriptive geometry techniques are used to determine the intersection points between two solids?

11. What is a transition piece?

12. What is a stretchout line?

13. Which parts of a development are true size and true shape?

14. Which building trades use developments and intersections?

15. What is the purpose of revolution?

16. What is the axis of revolution? What determines where the axis is drawn?

17. What are successive revolutions?

CHAPTER EXERCISES

Design Project

Exercise 9.1 Breakfast cereal has traditionally been sold in a rectangular box. The packaging must keep the product fresh, be reasonably durable, look attractive on the shelf, and be useful for dispensing the product. Create an innovative new packaging for breakfast cereal that meets these requirements. Make your design a sensible candidate for mass production, striving for a low consumer price and conservation of raw materials. Consider whether to make your packaging reusable, disposable, or refillable. Use the graphic communication skills you have learned so far to represent your design clearly.

Auxiliary View Projects

Exercises 9.2–9.43 are to be drawn with CAD or freehand. If partial auxiliary views are not assigned, the auxiliary views are to be complete views of the entire object, including all necessary hidden lines. Make sure to provide enough space for the auxiliary view.

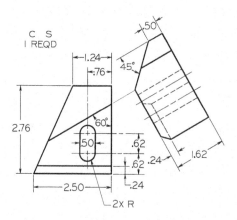

Exercise 9.2 RH Finger. Given: Front and auxiliary views. Required: Complete front, auxiliary, left-side, and top views.

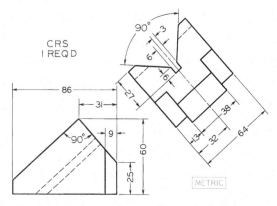

Exercise 9.3 V-Block, Given: Front and auxiliary views. Required: Complete front, top, and auxiliary views.

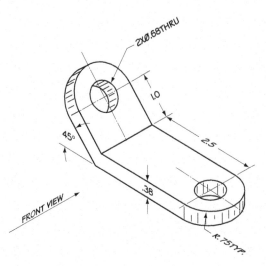

Exercise 9.4 Clamp

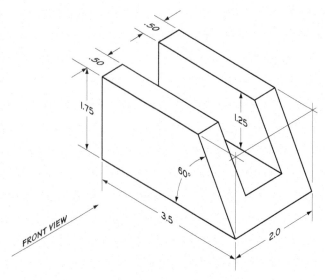

Exercise 9.5 Plastic Slide

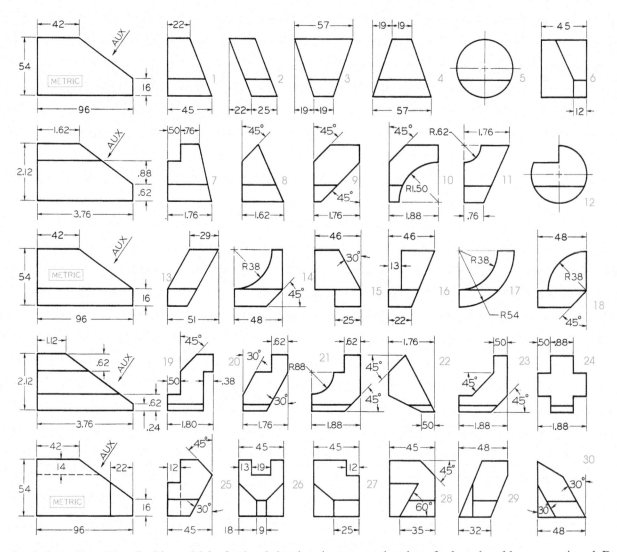

Exercise 9.6 Auxiliary View Problems. Make freehand sketch or instrument drawing of selected problems as assigned. Draw given front and right-side views, and add incomplete auxiliary view, including all hidden lines. If assigned, design your own right-side view consistent with given front view, then add complete auxiliary view.

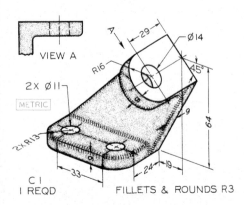

Exercise 9.7 Anchor Bracket. Draw necessary views or partial views.*

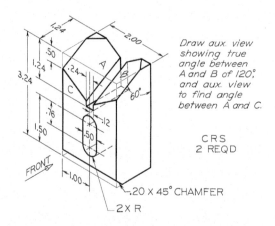

Exercise 9.8 Centering Block. Draw complete front, top, and right-side views, plus indicated auxiliary views.*

---

*If dimensions are required, study Chapter 11. Use metric or decimal-inch dimensions if assigned.

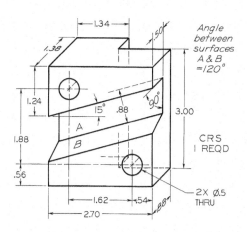

Exercise 9.9 Clamp Slide. Draw necessary views completely.*

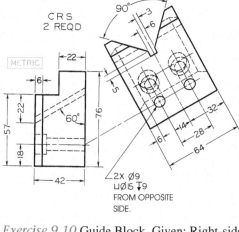

Exercise 9.10 Guide Block. Given: Right-side and auxiliary views. Required: Right-side, auxiliary, plus front and top views—complete.*

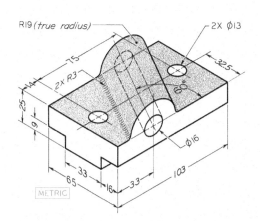

Exercise 9.11 Angle Bearing. Draw necessary views, including complete auxiliary view.*

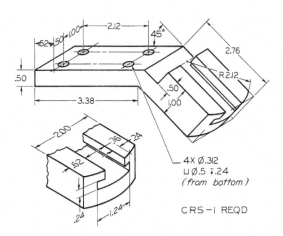

Exercise 9.12 Guide Bracket. Draw necessary views or partial views.*

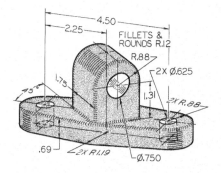

Exercise 9.13 Rod Guide. Draw necessary views, including complete auxiliary view showing true shape of upper rounded portion.*

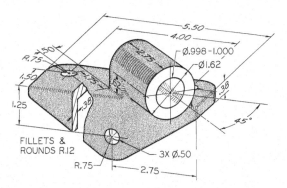

Exercise 9.14 Brace Anchor. Draw necessary views, including partial auxiliary view showing true shape of cylindrical portion.*

*If dimensions are required, study Chapter 11. Use metric or decimal-inch dimensions if assigned.

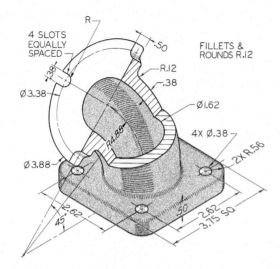

Exercise 9.15 45° Elbow. Draw necessary views, including a broken section and two half views of flanges.*

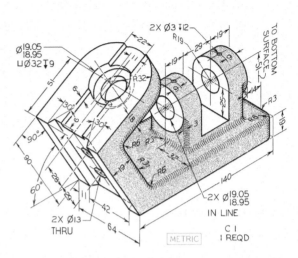

Exercise 9.16 Control Bracket. Draw necessary views, including partial auxiliary views and regular views.*

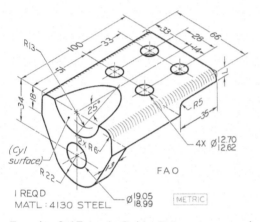

Exercise 9.17 Angle Guide. Draw necessary views, including a partial auxiliary view of cylindrical recess.*

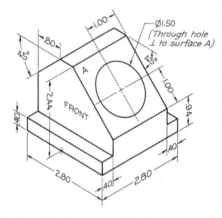

Exercise 9.18 Holder Block. Draw front and right-side views (2.80″ apart) and complete an auxiliary view of entire object showing the true shape of surface A and all hidden lines.*

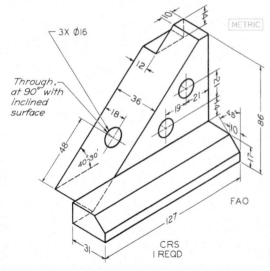

Exercise 9.19 Adjuster Block. Draw the necessary views, including a complete auxiliary view showing the true shape of inclined surface.*

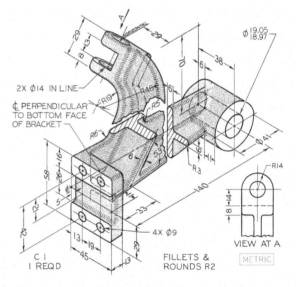

Exercise 9.20 Guide Bearing. Draw necessary views and partial views, including two partial auxiliary views.*

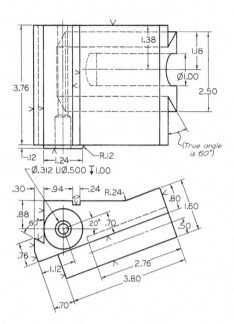

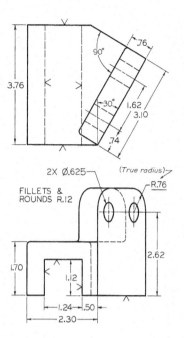

Exercise 9.21 Tool Holder Slide. Draw given views, and add complete a auxiliary view showing the true curvature of the slot on the bottom.*

Exercise 9.22 Drill Press Bracket. Draw given views and add complete auxiliary views showing the true shape of the inclined face.*

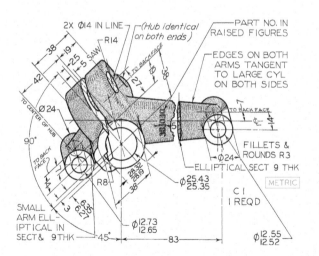

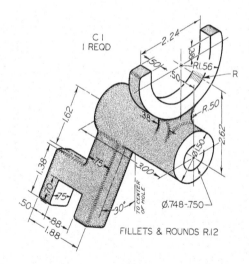

Exercise 9.23 Brake Control Lever. Draw necessary views and partial views.*

Exercise 9.24 Shifter Fork. Draw necessary views, including a partial auxiliary view showing the true shape of the inclined arm.*

*If dimensions are required, study Chapter 11. Use metric or decimal-inch dimensions if assigned.

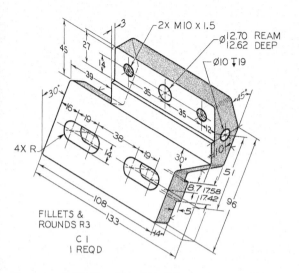

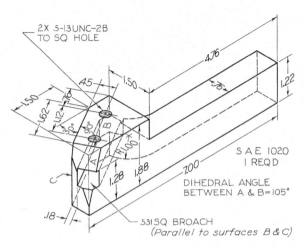

Exercise 9.25 Cam Bracket. Draw necessary views or partial views as needed.*

Exercise 9.26 RH Tool Holder. Draw necessary views, including partial auxiliary views showing the 105° angle and square hole true size.*

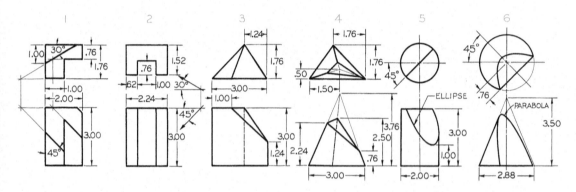

Exercise 9.27 Draw complete secondary auxiliary views, showing the true sizes of the inclined surfaces (except for Problem 2). In Problem 2 draw a secondary auxiliary view as seen in the direction of the arrow given in the problem.*

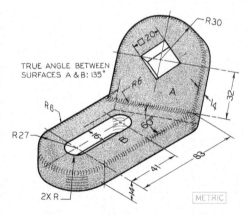

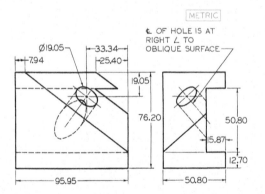

Exercise 9.28 Control Bracket. Draw necessary views including primary and secondary auxiliary views so that the latter shows the true shape of oblique surface A.*

Exercise 9.29 Holder Block. Draw given views and primary and secondary auxiliary views so that the latter shows the true shape of the oblique surface.*

*If dimensions are required, study Chapter 11. Use metric or decimal-inch dimensions if assigned.

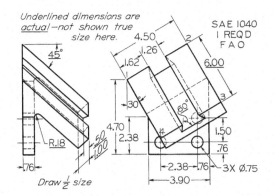

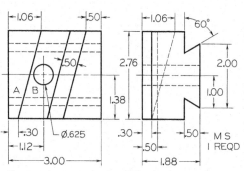

Exercise 9.30 Dovetail Slide. Draw complete given views and auxiliary views, including a view showing the true size of surface 1–2–3–4.*

Exercise 9.31 Dovetail Guide. Draw given views plus complete auxiliary views as indicated.*

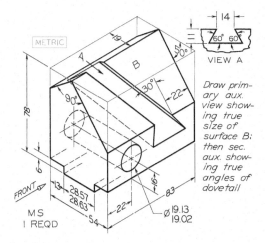

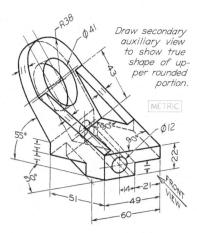

Exercise 9.32 Adjustable Stop. Draw complete front and auxiliary views plus a partial right-side view. Show all hidden lines.*

Exercise 9.33 Tool Holder. Draw complete front view and primary and secondary auxiliary views as indicated.*

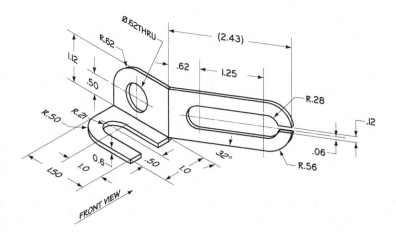

Exercise 9.34 Mounting Clip. Draw all required views. Include at least one auxiliary view.*

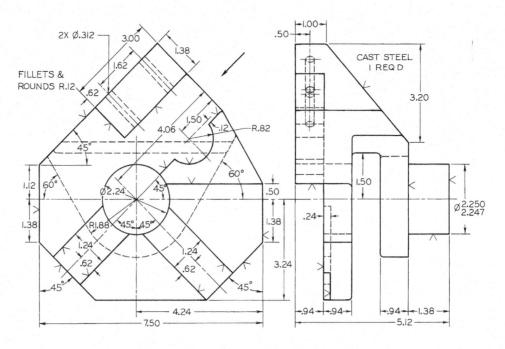

Exercise 9.35 Box Tool Holder for Turret Lathe. Given: Front and right-side views. Required: Front and left-side views, and complete auxiliary view as indicated by arrow.*

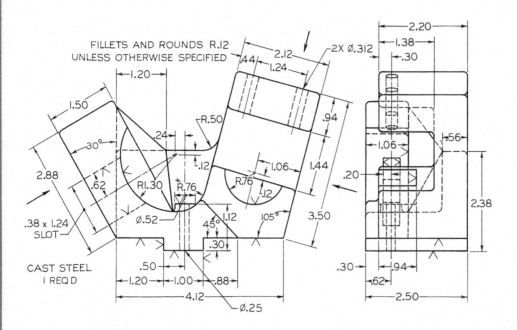

Exercise 9.36 Pointing Tool Holder for Automatic Screw Machine. Given: Front and right-side views. Required: Front view and three partial auxiliary views.*

*If dimensions are required, study Chapter 11. Use metric or decimal-inch dimensions if assigned.

Revolution Exercises

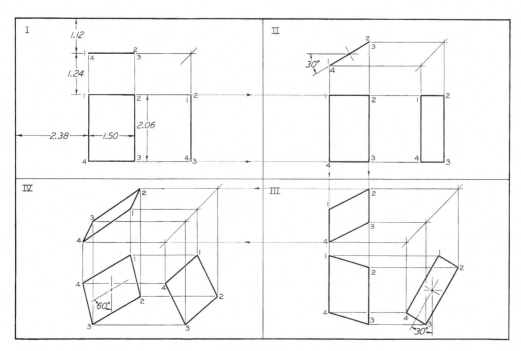

Exercise 9.37 Divide the working area into four equal parts, as shown. Draw given views of the rectangle, and then the primary revolution in space II, followed by successive revolutions in spaces III and IV. Number points as shown. Omit dimensions. Use a title strip as shown in Fig III, inside front cover.

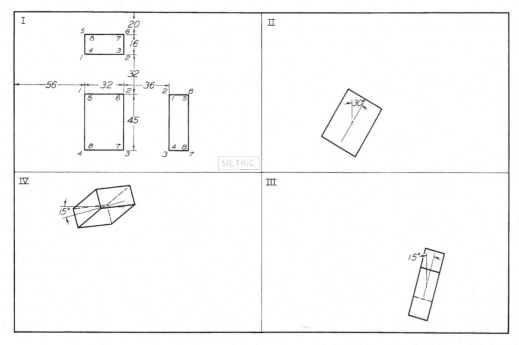

Exercise 9.38 Divide the working area into four equal parts, as shown. Draw given views of prism as shown in space I, then draw three views of the revolved prism in each succeeding space, as indicated. Number all corners. Omit dimensions. Use a title strip as shown in Fig III, inside front cover.

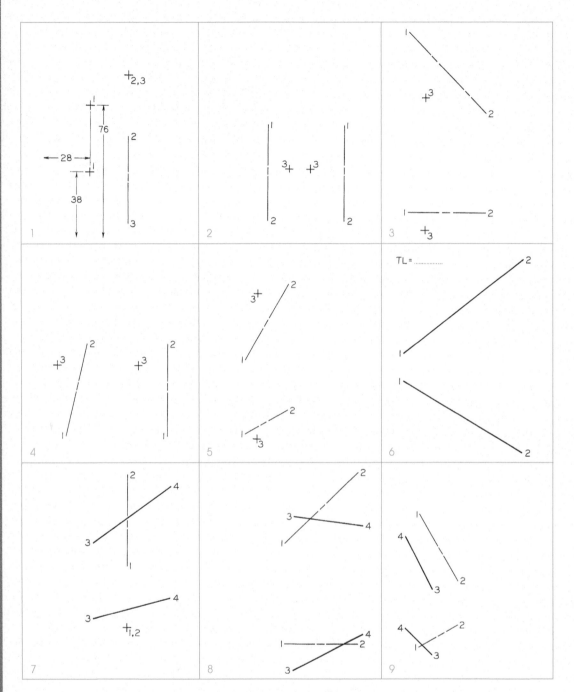

Exercise 9.39 Divide the working area into four equal areas for four problems per sheet to be assigned by the instructor. Data for the layout of each problem are given by a coordinate system in metric dimensions. For example, in Problem 1, point 1 is located by the scale coordinates (28 mm, 38 mm, 76 mm). The first coordinate locates the front view of the point from the left edge of the problem area. The second one locates the front view of the point from the bottom edge of the problem area. The third one locates either the top view of the point from the bottom edge of the problem area or the side view of the point from the left edge of the problem area. Inspection of the given problem layout will determine which application to use.

1. Revolve clockwise point 1(28, 38, 76) through 210° about axis 2(51, 58, 94)–3(51, 8, 94).
2. Revolve point 3(41, 38, 53) about axis 1(28, 64, 74)–2(28, 8, 74) until point 3 is at the farthest distance behind the axis.
3. Revolve point 3(20, 8, 84) about axis 1(10, 18, 122)–2(56, 18, 76) through 210° and to the rear of line 1–2.
4. Revolve point 3(5, 53, 53) about axis 1(10, 13, 71)–2(23, 66, 71) to its extreme position to the left in the front view.

5. Revolve point 3(15, 8, 99) about axis 1(8, 10, 61)–2(33, 25, 104) through 180°.

6. By revolution find the true length of line 1(8, 48, 64)–2(79, 8, 119). Scale: 1:100.

7. Revolve line 3(30, 38, 81)–4(76, 51, 114) about axis 1(51, 33, 69)–2(51, 33, 122) until line 3–4 is shown true length and below axis 1–2.

8. Revolve line 3(53, 8, 97)–4(94, 28, 91) about axis 1(48, 23, 81)–2(91, 23, 122) until line 3–4 is in true length and above the axis.

9. Revolve line 3(28, 15, 99)–4(13, 30, 84) about axis 1(20, 20, 97)–2(43, 33, 58) until line 3–4 is level above the axis.

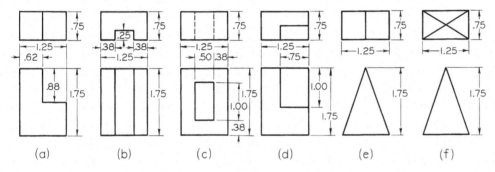

Exercise 9.40 Divide your sheet into four equal parts. In the upper left space draw the original drawing. In the upper right draw a simple revolution, and in the lower two spaces draw successive revolutions. Alternative assignment: Divide into two equal spaces. In the left space draw the original views. In the right space draw a simple revolution.

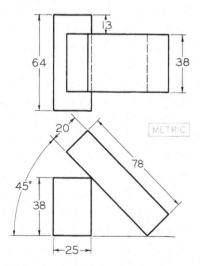

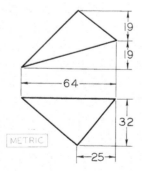

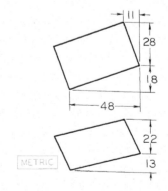

Exercise 9.41 Draw three views of the blocks but revolved 30° clockwise about an axis perpendicular to the top plane of projection. Do not change the relative positions of the blocks.

Exercise 9.42 Draw three views of a right prism 38 mm high that has as its lower base the triangle shown above.

Exercise 9.43 Draw three views of a right pyramid 51 mm high, having as its lower base the parallelogram shown above.

Development Exercises

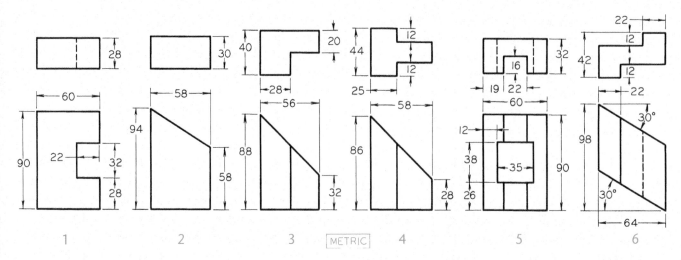

Exercise 9.44 Draw the given views and develop the lateral surface.

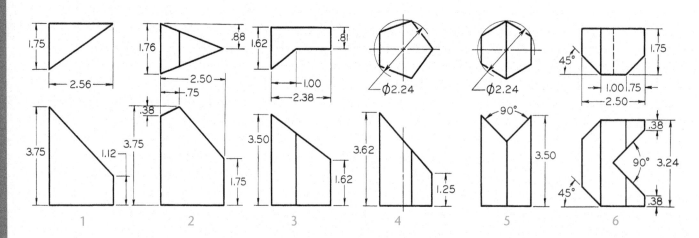

Exercise 9.45 Draw the given views and develop the lateral surface.

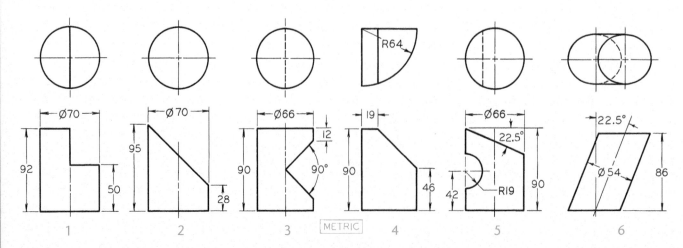

Exercise 9.46 Draw the given views and develop the lateral surface.

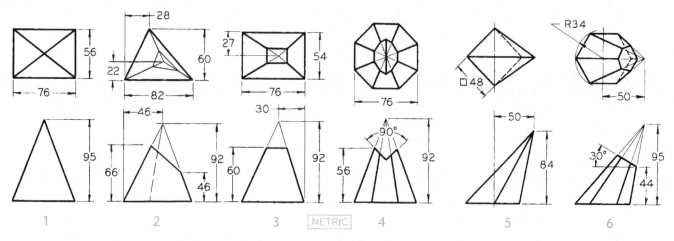

Exercise 9.47 Draw the given views and develop the lateral surface. (Use layout B or A3 with a title block as in Fig III or Fig IV, shown on inside front cover, or as directed by your instructor.)

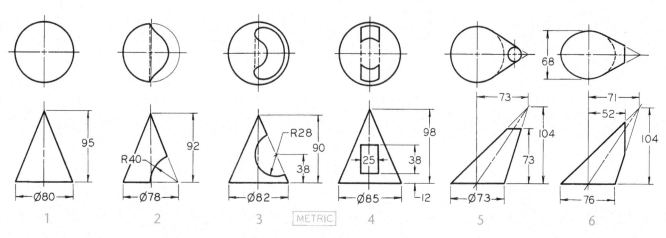

Exercise 9.48 Draw the given views and develop the lateral surface. (Use layout B or A3 with a title block as in Fig III or Fig IV, shown on inside front cover, or as directed by your instructor.)

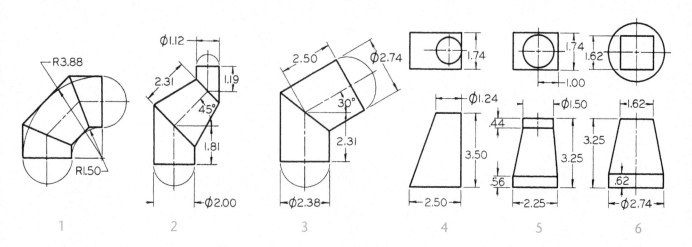

Exercise 9.49 Draw the given views of the forms and develop the lateral surface. (Use layout B or A3 with a title block as in Fig III or Fig IV, shown on inside front cover, or as directed by your instructor.)

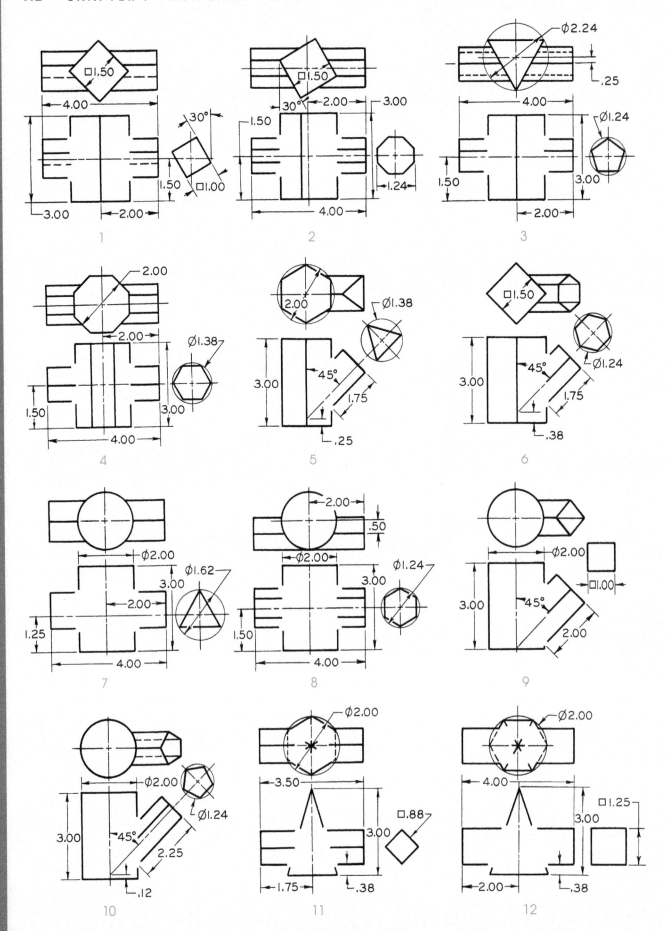

Exercise 9.50 Draw the given views of assigned form and complete the intersection, then develop the lateral surfaces.

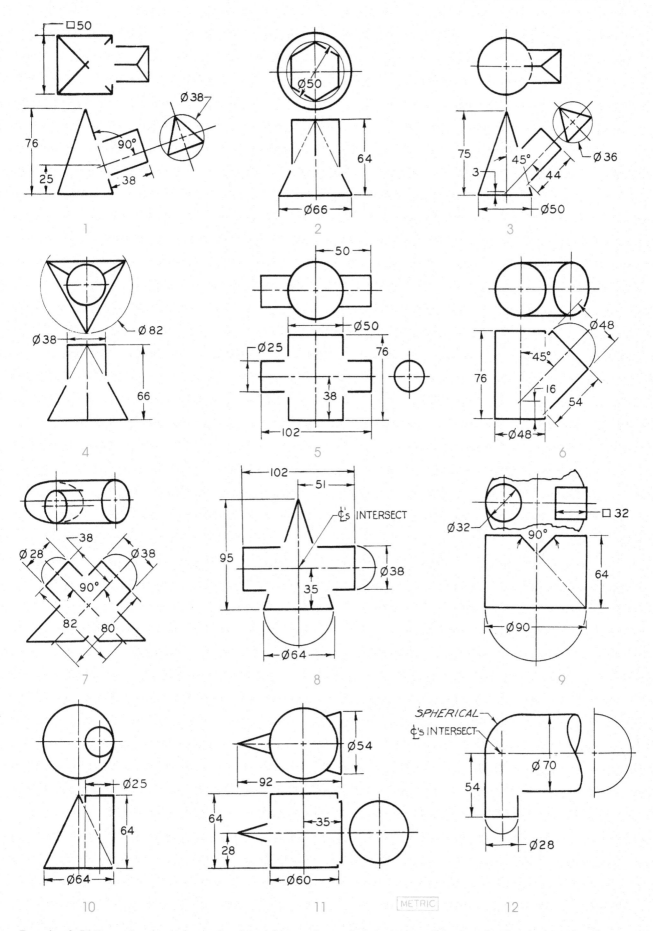

Exercise 9.51 Draw the given views of assigned form and complete the intersection, then develop the lateral surfaces.

CHAPTER TEN

MODELING FOR MANUFACTURE AND ASSEMBLY

OBJECTIVES

After studying the material in this chapter, you should be able to:

1. Describe the role of design in manufacture, assembly, disassembly, and service.

2. List the major manufacturing processes.

3. Look up accuracy and surface finishes for manufacturing processes.

4. Describe the role of measuring devices in production.

5. List factors that determine the cost of manufactured goods.

6. Define computer-integrated manufacturing.

7. Distinguish between static and dynamic assemblies.

8. Describe the role of intelligent assemblies in top-down design.

9. Identify how standard and static parts are used in assembly models.

10. Discuss methods of constraining assemblies made using solid modeling and parametric modeling.

11. Describe issues in modeling fasteners and springs.

12. Use an assembly model to test for fit and interference.

13. Evaluate the accuracy of mass properties calculations.

14. Define the file formats used for exporting CAD data.

15. List analysis methods that can use the CAD database.

16. Describe how rapid prototyping systems create physical models from CAD data.

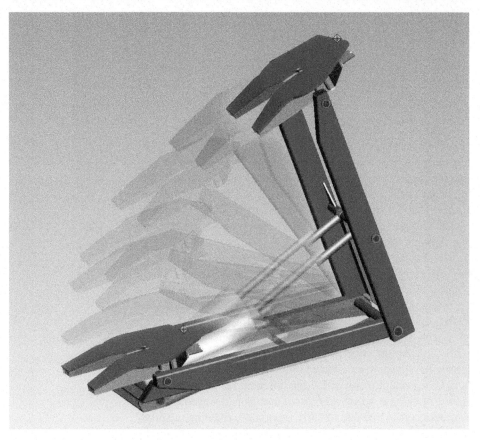

This 3D assembly model can be used to simulate the mechanism's range of motion.
(Courtesy of Leo Greene, www.e-Cognition.net.)

OVERVIEW

Look at the objects around you: your pen, watch, phone, chair, and light fixtures. All of these things have been transformed from various raw materials and assembled into the items you see. Some items, such as plastic coat hangers, forks, nails, bolts, and metal brackets are made of a single part. However, most objects are assembled from several parts made from different materials.

Assembly modeling shows how parts fit and function in the final product. Considering the design intent of the entire assembly makes it easier to work with others concurrently and to model complex and ever changing designs effectively.

An understanding of basic manufacturing processes helps you design affordable products. Communicate with the manufacturing team early in the design process and work together to ensure your models and drawings provide the necessary information.

Tools such as spreadsheets, equation solvers, motion simulation, and finite element software allow you to use model data to check for fit and interference issues, perform tolerance studies, perform failure and vibration analysis, determine stress concentrations, deflections, shear forces, bending moments, heat transfer properties, and natural frequencies, and make many other calculations. Parts can be checked at a range of sizes to see if they interfere with others in the assembly. Test results feed back into model changes, and the revised model is used for further testing.

Rapid prototyping allows you to create physical parts to test the fit, feel, and function of parts, or even produce usable parts through rapid manufacturing.

DESIGN FOR MANUFACTURE, ASSEMBLY, DISASSEMBLY, AND SERVICE

Design and manufacturing are interrelated, not separate, activities. Each part or component of a product must be designed so that it meets design requirements and specifications, and can be manufactured economically and efficiently. This improves productivity and allows a manufacturer to remain competitive.

This area is termed *design for manufacture* (DFM). DFM is a comprehensive approach to producing goods that integrates the design process with materials, manufacturing methods, process planning, assembly, testing, and quality assurance. Effectively implementing DFM requires a fundamental understanding of the characteristics, capabilities, and limitations of materials, manufacturing processes, and related operations, machinery, and equipment. This includes such considerations as variability in machine performance, dimensional accuracy and surface finish of the workpiece, processing time, and the effect of processing method on part quality.

You must be able to assess the impact of design modifications on manufacturing process selection, assembly, inspection, tools and dies, and product cost. Establishing quantitative relationships is essential for optimizing the design for ease of manufacturing and assembly at minimum product cost (also called *producibility*). Computer-aided design, engineering, manufacturing, and process planning techniques, using powerful computer programs, allow such analysis. Expert systems provide capabilities to expedite the traditional iterative process in design optimization.

After individual parts have been manufactured, they have to be assembled into a product. Assembly is an important phase of the overall manufacturing operation and requires consideration of the ease, speed, and cost of putting parts together. Also, many products must be designed so that disassembly is possible, enabling the products to be taken apart for maintenance, servicing, or recycling of their components. Because assembly operations can contribute significantly to product cost, *design for assembly* (DFA) as well as design for disassembly are now recognized as important aspects of manufacturing. Typically, a product that is easy to assemble is also easy to disassemble. Design for service, ensuring that individual parts or subassemblies in a product are easy to reach and service, is another piece of the puzzle.

(Copyright Dmitry Kalinovsky/Shutterstock.)

Methodologies and computer software (CAD) for DFA utilize 3D conceptual designs and solid models. In this way, subassembly and assembly times and costs are minimized while maintaining product integrity and performance; the system also improves the product's ease of disassembly. Combining design for manufacture and design for assembly into the more comprehensive design for manufacture and assembly (DFMA) recognizes the inherent interrelationships between design and manufacturing.

There are several methods of assembly, such as using fasteners or adhesive, or by welding, soldering, and brazing, each with its own characteristics and requiring different operations. The use of a bolt and nut, for example, requires preparation of holes that must match in location and size. Hole generation requires operations such as drilling or punching, which take additional time, require separate operations, and produce scrap. In contrast, products assembled with bolts and nuts can be taken apart and reassembled with relative ease.

Parts can also be assembled with adhesives. This method, which is being used extensively in aircraft and automobile production, does not require holes. However, surfaces to be assembled must match properly and be clean, because joint strength is adversely affected by the presence of contaminants such as dirt, dust, oil, and moisture. Unlike mechanically fastened parts, adhesively joined components, as well as those that are welded, are not usually designed to be taken apart and reassembled, hence are not suitable for the important purposes of recycling individual parts of the product.

Parts may be assembled by hand or by automatic equipment and robots. The choice depends on factors such as the complexity of the product, the number of parts to be assembled, the protection required to prevent damage or scratching of finished surfaces of the parts, and the relative costs of labor and machinery required for automated assembly.

Sometimes seemingly small decisions and variations in the design can add to the cost of the part. Even a small amount per part can be important when thousands or millions of the part will be produced. During the process of designing a part, communicate with the people responsible for having it manufactured and work together to produce the best design possible.

The processes used to manufacture parts may change over the production lifetime of a part. As a device becomes more and more accepted by consumers and production volumes increase owing to demand, it may become cost-effective to produce the device in new ways. Molded plastics, cast parts, machined parts, and sheet metal parts are common low-cost production methods. Design and modeling for these types of parts will alert you to issues you should consider and investigate as you model parts.

10.1   Car Bodies Crushed for Recycling
(Huguette Roe/Shutterstock)

10.1 ASSEMBLY MODELS

Individual part files make up a large part of the digital database for a design. Parts within the database may be organized by levels. At the highest level, all the parts are shown in the final assembly. (Figure 10.2 shows the many individual parts in a coffee brewer assembly.) Within a large assembly, subgroups may be broken out into sub-assemblies. *Subassemblies* are groups of parts that fit together to create one functional unit, often one that can be pre-assembled in some fashion to fit into the assembly as a unit. Breaking a design into levels can make it easier to divide tasks among different groups working on the same project. It can help in presenting, managing, and under-standing large, complex assemblies. Some subassemblies may even be reused in other designs as a unit.

You can combine individual parts into assemblies using your 3D CAD software in different ways. One method is to insert copies of your solid parts into a single assembly model. Assemblies that are created by copying 3D solid parts like these are *static assemblies*; that is, they do not change to reflect alterations in the individual parts. Because there is no link established between the part files and the assembly, if the individual parts are changed, they must be recopied or reinserted into the assem-bly model to update it. The two are completely separate, and changes made to either one will not affect the other. In contrast, in a *dynamic assembly*, parts are imported into the assembly through a linking process that allows the software to update the assembly as individual part files are modified.

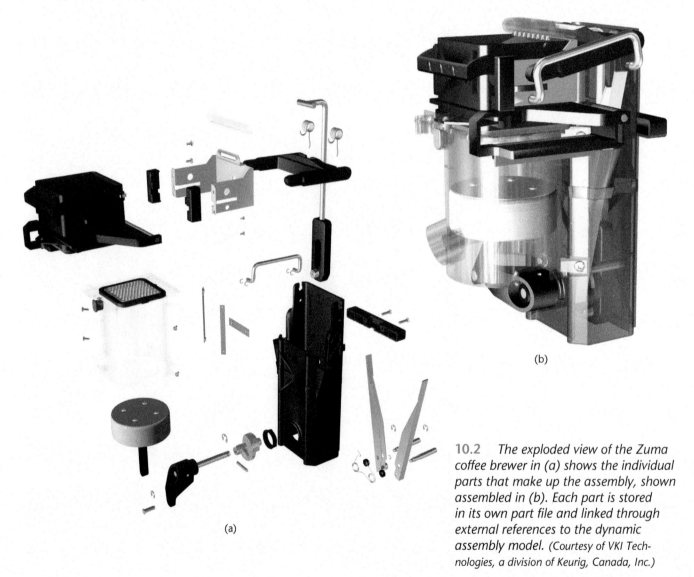

(b)

(a)

10.2   *The exploded view of the Zuma coffee brewer in (a) shows the individual parts that make up the assembly, shown assembled in (b). Each part is stored in its own part file and linked through external references to the dynamic assembly model. (Courtesy of VKI Tech-nologies, a division of Keurig, Canada, Inc.)*

Constraint-Based Assemblies

Constraint-based assemblies rely on subassembly and part files to be available for you to view them or make changes to the assembly. If you lose the file for a part, it will not show up in the assembly.

The associativity built into many constraint-based modelers may allow you to make changes to parts while viewing the assembly model or to alter a model by making changes to a drawing view. These changes update and modify the individual part files. This two-way updating capability is illustrated in Figure 10.3.

With constraint-based modeling software, you use assembly constraints to create the relationships between parts. The first part you add to the assembly is the parent part. As you add parts, you specify the constraints between the parent part and the added child part that reflect the design intent for the assembly. Mating parts have features that should fit together in an assembly. For example, if you want two holes to line up, you can use an assembly constraint to align them. If a part changes, it will still be oriented in the assembly so that the holes align.

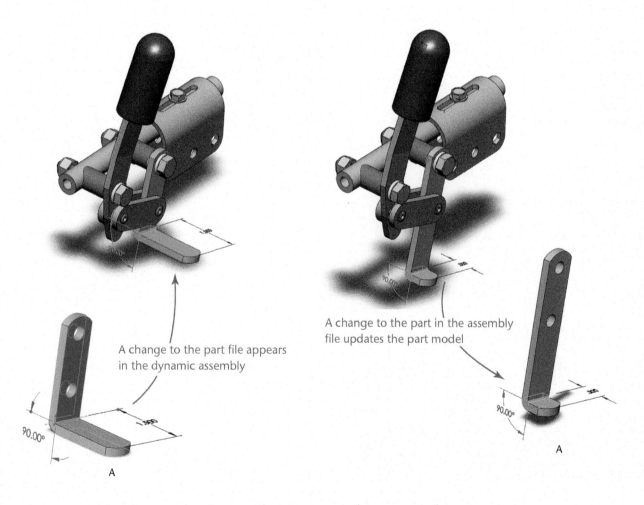

A change to the part file appears in the dynamic assembly

A change to the part in the assembly file updates the part model

10.3   *The links between part and assembly files are analogous to the bidirectional associativity between model and drawing. A change made to part A in the assembly updates the part file, and vice versa.*

Choosing the Parent Part

Constraint-based assemblies differ in the parent-child relationships that are built into the model. The first part that is added to the assembly acts as the parent part for other added parts, just as the base feature is the parent for any other features in the part model. These parent-child relationships are critical. If the parent is moved, the children move along with it. This can be a great advantage: if one of the parts in the assembly moves or changes, the child parts move to update their positions relative to it.

If you delete a part that is the parent of some other part in the assembly, then the location of the child part is undefined. As the modeling software tries to generate the assembly from the parts and relationships stored in the database, undefined locations require you to redefine the placement of the child parts and may, in the worst case, cause the file to fail to open or the software to crash.

One strategy is to use a standard set of datum planes as the first part in your assembly so that all other parts are children of this blank part that never changes (see Figure 10.4). Using a set of datum planes as the parent part in the assembly also helps fix your assembly on the coordinate system. Assemblies that are not fixed on the coordinate system may move in undesired ways when you are later trying to animate assembly motions.

When choosing the parent part to start out your assembly:

- Consider adding a blank set of datum planes as the first part in the assembly, particularly if your modeler does not already start with assembly datums. These can often be handy even for small tasks like reorienting subassembly parts. Additional datums are rarely detrimental. Manage the display of the datums to hide them when they are not needed.
- Start with major parts to which other parts connect.
- Start with key parts that are unlikely to be eliminated from the design or to be drastically changed.
- Mate the first part to datum planes to fix it on the coordinate system, so that it does not move.
- Assemble functional units into subassemblies first before adding them to the main assembly.

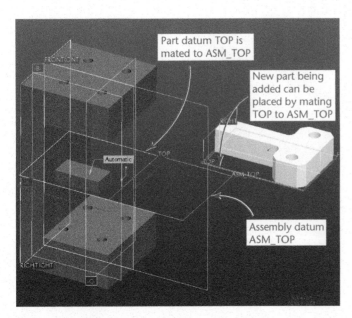

10.4   Assembly Datums. *Using assembly datums and establishing logical parent-child relations are key to assemblies that are updated easily. (Courtesy of Mark Perkins.)*

Assembly Constraints

Different software packages offer a similar set of constraint options. Become familiar with those available to you in your software. Table 10.1 on page 422 lists some of the common assembly constraints and their definitions.

Just as feature relationships are important to the way you create a model, assembly relationships can make your assembly model work for you. Consider the following as you add parts to the assembly:

- Use constraints to orient the new part that reflect relationships that will persist in the assembly.
- Think about the mechanism and the types of connections that parts should have to be a working device.
- Leave fasteners until last and insert them in manageable groups.

You can create a subassembly in much the same way that you create an assembly: by making an assembly of the subassembly components. This subassembly can be added to the main assembly in the same way you add a part. Organizing the model so that it comes together as it will on the assembly line aids in visualizing assembly difficulties. If a group of components are likely to be changed or replaced, linking all the subparts to a main component can make it easy to substitute an alternative design for that group of parts.

Dynamic Assemblies: The Zuma Brewer

Dynamic assemblies provide an advantage to design teams sharing files over a network. The assembly model brings together individual part design with the overall product effort. Most systems let you dynamically update your view of a part in the assembly even while someone else is actively changing it. This keeps the assembly current and ensures that the part you are designing fits with the other parts in the assembly.

Many benefits of constraint-based modeling directly related to assembly capabilities. VKI Technologies' single-cup coffee brewers require many moving parts and sophisticated electronics all contained in a compact, easy-to-use coffee maker. Using constraint-based modeling helped them fit the many components into smaller machines while reducing design time almost 50%.

The Zuma brewer assembly pulled together 62 different parts, shown in Figure 10.5. The assembly allowed the designer to be sure the components fit compactly yet did not interfere with one another. Moving parts were rotated through their range of motion in the assembly model to analyze and eliminate conflicts with other parts.

A big advantage of an assembly model is its role as a virtual prototype. For the Zuma brewer, the ability to visualize parts in 3D and evaluate them for fit with other parts almost eliminated the need to create physical models of the parts. When the brewer design was complete, the model was used to generate molds for the 15 plastic parts in the brewer. When the first real molded parts were available, they fit together well enough to make a functional brewer. In the past, with many parts and a limited amount of time, it was not uncommon for fit problems to be discovered after manufacture, not before.

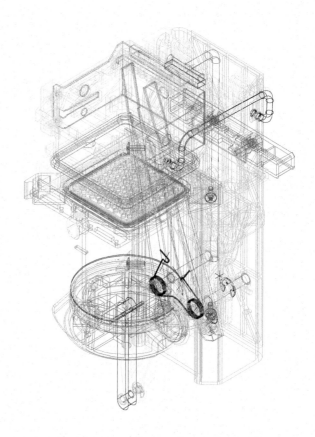

10.5 *The 62 individual parts in the assembly model of the Zuma brewer are shown in a wireframe view.*
(Courtesy of VKI Technologies, a division of Keurig, Canada, Inc.)

Table 10.1 Common Assembly Constraints.

Name	Definition	Illustration
Mate	Mates two planar surfaces together	
Mate Offset	Mates two surfaces together so they have an offset between them	
Insert (Concentric)	Inserts a "male" revolved surface into a "female" revolved surface, aligning the axes	
Align (Coincident)	Aligns two surfaces, datum points, vertices, or curve ends to be coplanar; also aligns revolved surfaces or axes to be coaxial	
Align Offset	Aligns two planar surfaces with an offset distance between them	
Parallel (Orient)	Aligns two surfaces, edges, or axes to be parallel (equal distance apart over their entire length)	
Perpendicular	Aligns two surfaces, edges, or axes to be perpendicular (at 90° to one another)	
Tangent	Aligns plane and curved surfaces, or two curved surfaces or edges to be tangent to one another	
Offset	An option for an assembly constraint that allows you to specify the relationship with distance between the entities	
Flip	An option for an assembly constraint that allows you to choose the opposite orientation for a plane, axis, or other entity	

Managing Assembly Files

The links between files that make dynamic assemblies possible also make it important to manage your files effectively. Use directory structures and naming conventions to keep your files organized. The extra time it takes to name and store your file in the appropriate directory can save hours of searching for the file at a later date.

File management is especially important when you are working in a design team using networked computers. Manage your files so that everyone can easily find them. Without good communication and an organized system for storing files, it is not unusual for one engineer to spend considerable time modifying a part only to have the latest modification not be used in the assembly because it was stored in the wrong directory.

It can happen that two different people modify the same part, undoing each other's changes. If you work as part of a team, make it clear who has the responsibility for changing different parts. One person should have "ownership" and the ability to make changes to the part file. If a change in another part requires a change to a part for which you are responsible, you should be notified of the changes so you can update your part accordingly. Some systems allow other team members to work with the file in read-only mode. This way, everyone can view the part, and perhaps even indicate changes, but changes are not made until the owner of the part approves them. This prevents different designers from concurrently changing the part.

Your software may manage how files are linked or externally referenced and how others access the files (see Figure 10.6). As you create assembly models, be aware of these options and how your work group uses them. Some companies invest in Product Data Management (PDM) systems that organize the design database and control the work flow process.

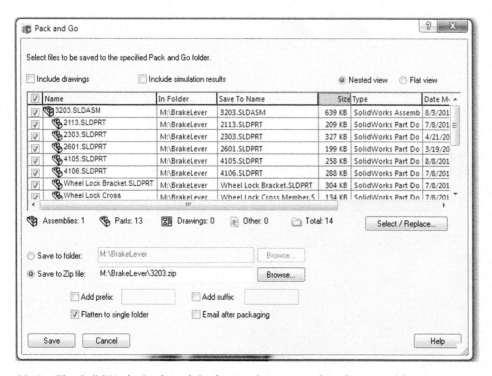

10.6   *The SolidWorks Pack and Go feature lets you gather the assembly, parts, drawings, and other model information to copy or move a project, without losing the linked files. If you did not use this feature, you would need to remember to copy or move each of the individual files to open the assembly file. (Image courtesy of ©2016 Dassault Systèmes SolidWorks Corporation.)*

10.2 ASSEMBLIES AND DESIGN

To work efficiently and concurrently, it is important that each designer be clear on the design intent so that problems of fit are minimized at later stages. Constraint-based modeling software also allows you to start with an assembly framework that can be used to define the design intent or parameters for individual parts and to help coordinate the work of different team members.

With this method, parts are designed so they link to a framework that defines major relationships in the assembly. This may be a skeleton using lines, arcs, curves, and points to show the assembly relationships. When you create the framework for each part up front, all parts do not have to be finished before they can be assembled. Parts can be assembled onto the skeleton at any stage of completion. Allowing the assembly to evolve as the parts are designed and refined allows each designer to see the parts the others are creating—or at least the critical relationships between parts—by looking at the assembly.

Top-down design starts the design by examining the function of the entire system, breaking that down into subassemblies or component groups based on their major functions, and, finally, defining each part that must be manufactured and assembled to create the design.

Bottom-up design starts at the part level, sizing individual components and building the design up from them. This is typically the approach used when components are standardized parts.

Middle-out design combines these two methods: some major standardized parts are used in the assembly to begin the design. The new components are designed to fit with these parts and function in the overall assembly.

An example of middle-out design is the Romulus Predator prototype, which was planned to combine racing capability with everyday street driving (Figure 10.7). This vehicle was never intended for mass production; the design and production costs would be recouped from a small manufacturing run. The design team used commercially available components such as brakes, steering column, steering wheel, and engine components to keep development costs down. These off-the-shelf parts were modeled in 3D and added to the assembly model. The custom parts were designed to work with these stock parts.

10.7   *The Predator's use of off-the-shelf components is an example of middle-out design. This view of the Predator was taken from the surface model created in ICEM Surf. (Courtesy of Mark Gerisch.)*

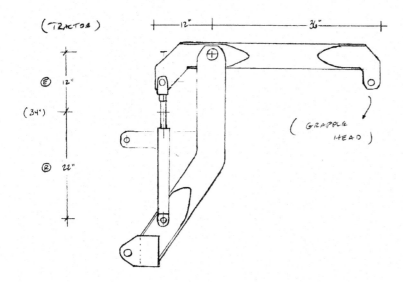

10.8 Layout Drawing *(Courtesy of Implemax Equipment Co., Inc.)*

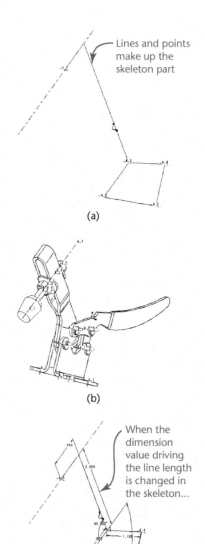

Layout Drawings

Traditionally, top-down design uses *layout drawings* to show the relationships between major functional items in the design. Layout drawings are especially useful when the product or system being designed has to fit with existing equipment. By defining the critical distances for fit with the existing equipment, the layout drawing documents the size constraints for the new equipment.

A typical layout drawing is shown in Figure 10.8. Note that the drawing is not complete in every detail but shows the major centerlines, sizes, and relationships between parts.

Assembling to a Skeleton

A wireframe *skeleton* in a 3D model serves the same purpose as a layout drawing. It is a framework on which the individual components can be located. Figure 10.9 shows a skeleton model used to control the location and position of parts in the assembly model of a clamp.

To create a skeleton model, first define the critical dimensions in your assembly. What dimensions are fixed—because of a physical space requirement, sizing requirement, or some other relationship? What dimensions are likely to change later in the design process? How will each part relate to the others in the assembly? Begin your skeleton as a part model made up of a constraint-based framework of 3D planes, lines, curves, and points that identify the basic relationships between parts in the assembly.

Figure 10.10a shows a skeleton model created for a laser printer. The dimensions between the planes, lines, points, and other entities making up the skeleton can be changed as needed as the design evolves to preserve the interfaces between parts. Changing the dimensions of the skeleton also allows the clearances and interferences between parts to be checked when the device is in different positions. By establishing this framework initially, each designer can upload a part to the assembly at any time to see how it will operate within the constraints established by the framework. Because the skeleton is made up of lines, planes, points, and other entities that do not have volume, using a skeleton will not change the mass property analysis for the assembly.

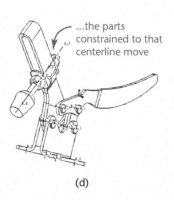

10.9 *(a) Skeleton model for the clamp assembly; (b) parts assembled onto the skeleton; (c) changing dimensions of the skeleton controls the positions in the assembly; (d) resulting change in the assembly. (Courtesy of Mark Perkins.)*

10.10 Printer Assembly. *(a) The skeleton model for this laser printer subassembly establishes a 3D framework for relationships between parts or groups of parts. (b) As parts are designed, their center points or edges are matched to the datum planes and axes of the skeleton. (c) In the completed subassembly all the parts are matched to their locations. (d) The completed printer assembly is shown with the covers removed. (e) The finished printer assembly.* (Courtesy of Xerox Corporation.)

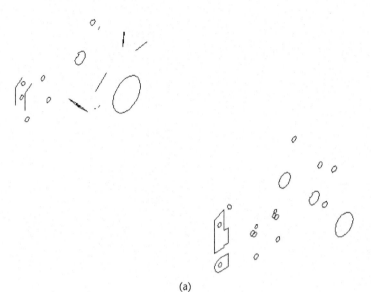

(a)

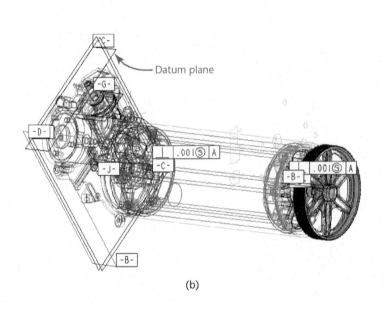

Datum plane

(b)

(d)

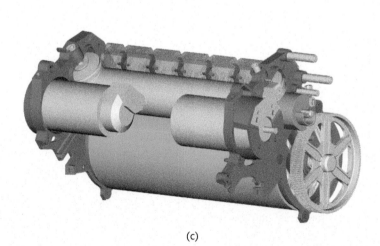

(c)

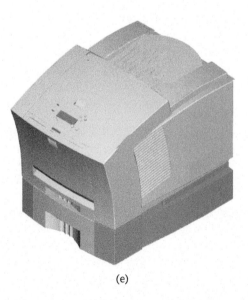

(e)

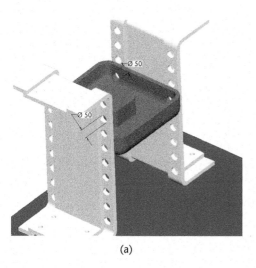

(a)

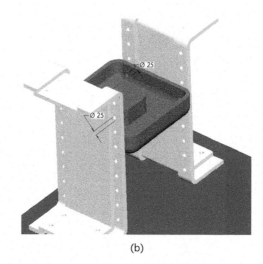

(b)

10.11   *(a) The holes in the brackets and tray are defined by the global parameter Hole_Size that has the value .50 to fit a .50-diameter round head machine screw. (b) The holes in both parts are changed to .25 by updating the global Hole_Size parameter value.*

Global Parameters

A *global parameter* is one that is the same across multiple parts. You can use global parameters to control the size of a feature so that mating features can be resized as a group.

Consider the fit between the mating parts shown in Figure 10.11. The holes on the mounting brackets and tray must align and must be roughly the same size so that a machine screw will fit through both parts. By creating a global parameter for the size of the hole, called in this case Hole_Size, you can change the size of the hole feature on both the brackets and the tray at once.

Global parameters can be defined for any dimension to be shared by parts in the assembly. You may define a global parameter from the skeleton itself to drive critical distances on part features.

Global parameters also make it possible to build relationships into the assembly as you would for an individual part. The drilling rig in Figure 10.12 contains more than five thousand parts but was designed to be resized to fit different drilling situations. Changes can be made at the assembly level (the top level) to change the width from any corner, the overall height, and the height of any bay. Equations in the dimension parameters for individual parts reference global parameters that when changed cause all parts in the assembly to be updated to the new size.

10.12   *IRI International has parametric models for different derrick styles. The basic rig structure is quickly reshaped to begin work on the design of custom parts for the new rig. (Courtesy of National Oilwell Varco (NOV).)*

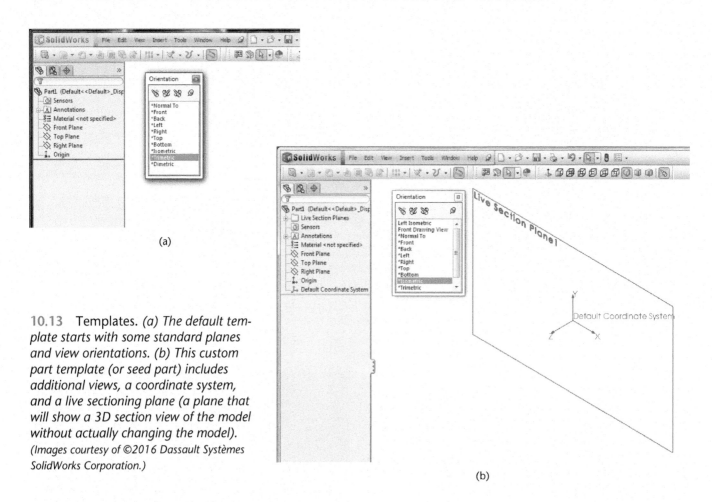

10.13 Templates. *(a) The default template starts with some standard planes and view orientations. (b) This custom part template (or seed part) includes additional views, a coordinate system, and a live sectioning plane (a plane that will show a 3D section view of the model without actually changing the model). (Images courtesy of ©2016 Dassault Systèmes SolidWorks Corporation.)*

Seed Parts

Seed parts, also called ***templates*** or ***prototype drawings***, are another technique for assembling parts effectively and for starting new drawings quickly and systematically. Seed part files contain elements you want every model to contain. A seed part might have a set of datum planes defined according to the company standard, named view orientations matched to the datum planes, unit settings, coordinate systems, layer names, and other items. Starting your new parts from a seed part saves you the time it would take to create these settings and elements in a new file.

Seed parts can help you assemble parts by providing a standard orientation. For example, when you assemble two parts, you may want a common datum surface to face the same direction on each part. Using a seed part, where standard datum planes have already been set up and named to make them easy to identify, can help you quickly insert your part in the correct orientation with respect to the rest of the assembly. Using standard view names as a part of your seed drawing helps you quickly produce views from your models (Figure 10.13).

Other members of the design team save time in creating a drawing from your model when you use consistent view-naming conventions.

Seed parts with consistent layer names can eliminate confusion in viewing assemblies. By starting parts with the same basic set of layers, you can keep the assembly organized and make it easy for other users to identify on which layer a feature would typically be shown.

If your company has a standard title block, tolerance block, notes, and set of required views, seed parts or prototype drawings can help produce drawings that all have the same high-quality appearance even when created by different users. Even if such a file is not a company standard, setting one up with this information eliminates having to re-create it each time. Standard notes that you can edit or delete if not appropriate also remind you to include important information on the drawing.

Modeling packages come with default settings for new files. Some settings that are stored with the drawing or model file may be included in a seed part. If you find that you are consistently changing a setting with every new drawing, the setting might be a candidate for inclusion into a seed part, template drawing, or stored custom interface. Scripts and macros are other great time savers when you have a repeated task.

Constraint-Based Drawing Elements

Another way to add borders, title blocks, and other drawing elements to your drawing is to link them parametrically as you would a part file. This allows you to create a title block and reuse it for all your drawings. This title block can prompt you for the engineer's name, approval date, material information, tolerances, and other information as parameters. If you use linked title blocks and other drawing information, you must manage the files for these linked items carefully as deleting the original title block makes it unavailable to any drawings where it was used.

> **TIP**
>
> You can save time creating new parts by adding often-used views and default settings to a seed part or template. Read about template files in your modeler's Help to determine which settings can be saved with such a file. Common items are the following:
>
> - Datum planes
> - Named 3D views
> - Unit settings
> - User coordinate systems
> - Layers and layer names
> - Drawing elements such as title and revision blocks and standard notes
> - Drawing styles and views
> - Customized workspace settings

10.3 ASSEMBLIES AND SIMULATION

An accurate and detailed assembly model allows simulation of the interactions between components in your design. Creating a skeleton model to drive the assembly geometry is one way to make a dynamic assembly that allows you to study component interactions. Another method is to assemble your parts using special "mechanism"-style assembly constraints. For example, instead of aligning the centers of a hole and a shaft, you can specify a "pin"-type joint. These joints restrict the degrees of freedom of the part in the assembly. Once you have the assembly defined in this way, you can use it to explore real-world behaviors of the mechanism. Figure 10.14 shows an example mechanism with forces applied to simulate the assembly function.

Depending on the software you have, you may be able to simulate part contacts; measure interference between parts; simulate gravity, springs, dampers, belts, gears, friction, and ergonomics; as well as perform kinematic analysis directly in your modeling environment. You will learn more about this later in this chapter.

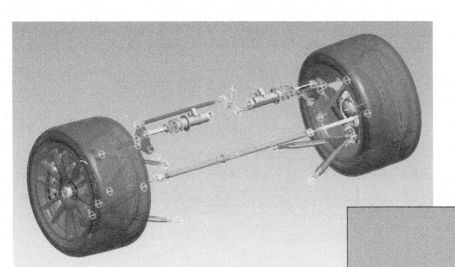

10.14 *This assembly model simulates the real-world forces on a Maserati MC12 race car suspension. Notice the yellow symbols showing the forces that are applied to the model. (Copyright © PTC Inc.)*

10.4 PARTS FOR ASSEMBLIES

To fully enjoy the benefits of a digital assembly model, your design database should include all the parts designed for the assembly. Most constraint-based modeling software allows you to add and import non-constraint-based parts to the constraint-based assembly so they can be represented during the design refinement process (see Figure 10.15).

Standard Parts

Using standard company parts (or purchased parts that are readily available) can be cost-effective for two reasons:

- They do not have to be designed. Many suppliers provide models of their parts in a variety of CAD formats that you can insert into your assembly model. Using standard company parts that were designed for another project saves design effort.
- Parts manufactured in quantity have a lower per-piece price. Some companies maintain a library of parts on the network that can easily be used. Sharing the part among more products helps increase the volume used. A parts database is useful even when manufacturing quantities are not high, as the company saves design time for every part reused.

When a company part is not available, a part that meets your need may be available from a supplier. Some engineers spend up to 20% of their time redrawing standard parts to show how they will fit with the newly designed parts in the assembly. Finding a model available from the supplier lets you spend your time designing the new components needed to get the job done.

Many sites provide their parts in standard 2D and 3D formats (such as .dxf, IGES, or STEP) and in the native formats for different modelers (such as AutoCAD and SolidWorks). Figure 10.16 shows a plastic knob available in 2D and 3D CAD formats from the vendor Davies Molding.

Common parts are also available in libraries that ship with your software or in third-party part libraries. These parts often have the advantage of being modeled using constraints so their sizes can easily be changed.

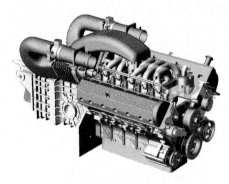

10.15   *All the components of this engine assembly were modeled as solids—whether they were new or off-the-shelf—so that the Predator assembly model would be complete and could serve as a virtual prototype for the car. (Courtesy of Mark Gerisch.)*

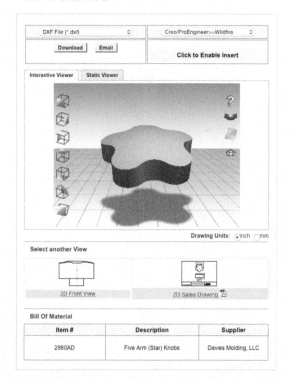

10.16   *CAD models of this plastic knob are available in a variety of formats. The CAD Drawings selection from ThomasNet.com makes it easy to find vendor part models like this one. (Courtesy of Davies Molding, LLC.)*

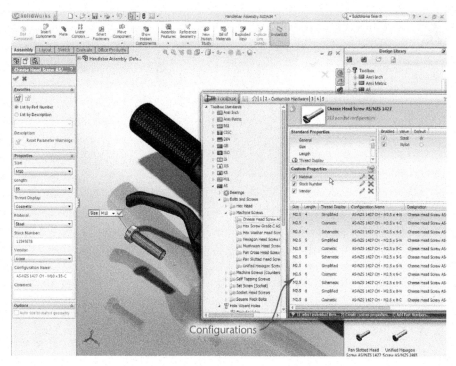

10.17 *SolidWorks provides drag-and-drop fasteners as a part of the Toolbox parts library. Notice the list of configurations for the fastener shown. These allow one model to serve different sets of parameter values stored. Because the basic shape of the fastener is the same, it can quickly be resized to different sizes. After a configuration is chosen, it can be further customized, as shown in this screen. (Image courtesy of ©2016 Dassault Systèmes SolidWorks Corporation.)*

Fastener Libraries

Many modeling packages provide part libraries for fasteners, bearings, and other items that are a frequent part of many designs (see Figure 10.17). If your software does not, you may want to build a library of typical fasteners used by your company so that you can quickly place them into assembly models. Many suppliers provide 3D models of their parts to make it easy to show them in your assemblies (Figure 10.18).

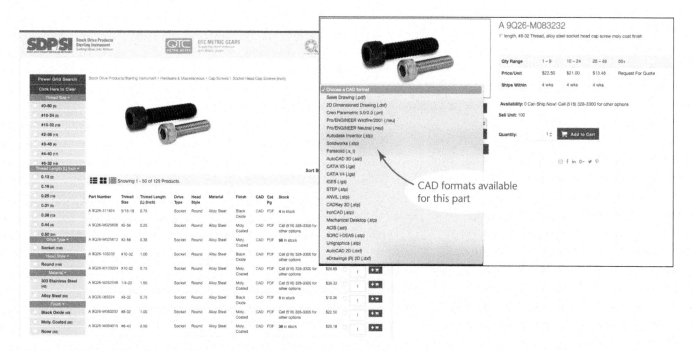

10.18 *CAD models of standard parts are available for download from companies like Stock Drive Products/Sterling Instrument. (Courtesy of Stock Drive Products/Sterling Instrument, sdp-si.com.)*

10.5 USING YOUR MODEL TO CHECK FITS

When parts are accurately modeled in 3D and organized into an assembly, you can use the assembly to perform fit and interference checking on the models. Doing a thorough study of how the parts will fit once assembled can save time and money. After tooling has already been produced to manufacture parts, changes to the design become very expensive.

Because the parts in the assembly can be shaded and viewed from any direction on the computer monitor, you can visually inspect the fits and clearances. You can also make measurements and list dimension values to compare parts with one another. Most solid and constraint-based modeling software also provides a command for checking the interference between two parts.

Interference Checking

Interference is the amount of overlap between one part and another. When you use a command to check the interference between two parts in an assembly, the solid

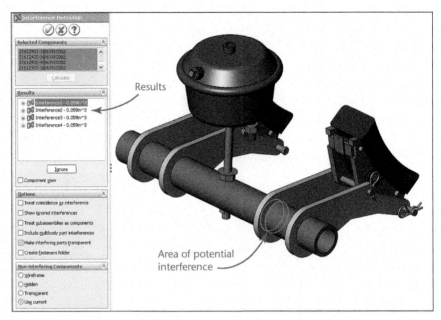

10.19   *The shaft is checked against the support arms to see whether these parts interfere. (Courtesy of Dynojet Research, Inc.)*

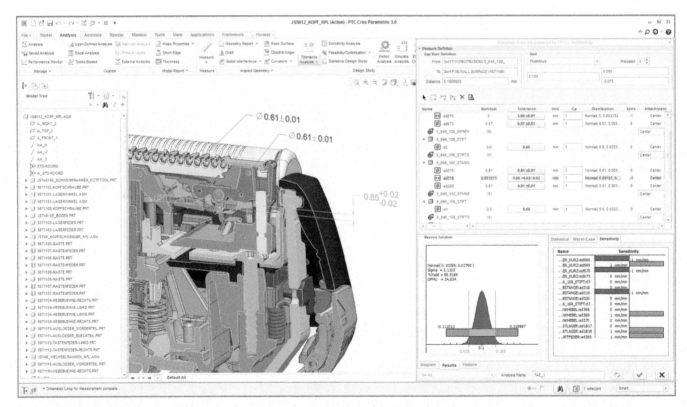

10.20   *PTC® Creo® provides a sophisticated interface for performing fit studies for a range of part tolerances. (Copyright © PTC Inc.)*

modeling software will report that the solids do not interfere or will indicate the amount of overlap—sometimes by creating a new solid to represent the overlap (see Figure 10.19).

Because constraint-based modeling software makes it easy to assemble parts early in the design process, interference checking tools can also facilitate more effective concurrent engineering. For example, Boeing's designers are responsible for checking their work in the digital pre-assembly model of the aircraft to identify places where the system or component they are designing will interfere with work in progress in other areas of the design. Each designer then takes steps to resolve the interference with the appropriate designers for the systems involved.

Manufacturing processes have certain ranges of accuracy. Requiring a high tolerance—one with very little allowable deviation—can limit the choice of manufacturing process to those that can be expected to meet that level of accuracy. Specifying very small tolerance values can increase the cost of the finished piece. In general, tolerances should allow as much variation as possible without affecting the functionality of the design.

Material selection also plays a role in the accuracy of the finished parts. Parts can be manufactured more accurately from some materials than others. In addition to determining the tolerance range for a part based on its function in the assembly, talk to personnel in manufacturing or the vendors who will make the parts. You should fully understand the issues in manufacturing the part to the dimensions and accuracy you specified and the effect this has on the price for the finished parts.

Some CAD software allows you to specify a tolerance range for a dimension and then apply that to the feature at either the upper or lower end of the dimension range. By doing so, you can run a check on how the parts will fit at the minimum and maximum clearance values. Figure 10.20 shows the options for analyzing tolerances using PTC® Creo®.

Even if your software does not provide functions for checking fits at the lower and upper limits of the tolerance range, you can systematically change the dimensions for mating features to represent the minimum clearance, then inspect the model to see how the parts fit.

Accessibility Checking

The assembly model can also be used to ensure that the design can be assembled. Whether the assembly will be done by robots or humans, parts and fasteners must be accessible. Many devices and systems also need to be repaired or upgraded later, requiring access well after the assembly phase. The 3D design database can be used to check whether people will be able to reach a part to remove or repair it after the system is assembled.

Ergonomic analysis software can help determine accessibility for assembly and repair. ***Ergonomics*** studies the ability of humans to use a system. Many ergonomic analysis packages have 3D models of human beings (anthropomorphic data) that you can position inside the designed system to see how people will fit.

Even if robots will assemble the components, people will often perform repairs. Evaluating repair issues can be even more difficult than assembly issues, because the assembly can proceed in such a way that interior parts are fitted together before their exteriors obscure access and visibility. You can use ergonomic analysis or human models to check whether parts can be reached to repair them, as shown in Figure 10.21.

 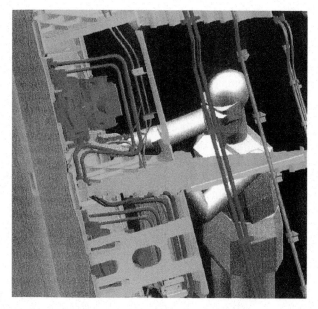

10.21 *Planning access to an airplane for service and repair is an important part of its design. This digital mannequin was imported into the CATIA software used by Boeing to evaluate the accessibility of its parts. (Copyright © Boeing.)*

10.6 MANUFACTURING PROCESSES

In this section you will learn some basic information about the impact that three manufacturing processes may have on the design of individual parts. Keep in mind that this is not intended to be a thorough presentation of everything you need to know about a particular process or all processes. You can learn more about manufacturing in engineering courses and from on the job experience.

10.22   *Injection molds have two halves that separate to release the plastic part.*

Designing Plastic Parts

Injection-molded plastic parts have characteristics you must consider when designing for them. Molded parts in general must include *draft*, or taper, that allows the part to be removed from the mold. Plastic shrinks as it cools, and the shrinkage plus the draft allows the parts to be removed from the mold into a collection bin. If the shape of the part requires it, ejector pins may be necessary to force the part out of the mold. Usually, the mold designer will determine the necessary cooling lines, ejector pins, and other features, but you should be aware of the general process. Ejector pins may leave a slight mark on the finished part. If these marks would negatively affect the cosmetics of your design, you may need to change the part shape so that it is removed from the mold easily and does not require ejector pins. You can identify important cosmetic surfaces on the part when you send drawings or files to the manufacturer so the mold maker can use this information when designing the mold.

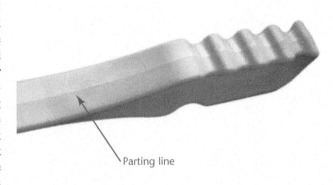

10.23   Parting Line. *Injection-molded parts may have a visible line where the mold halves joined.*

The **parting line** is where the two mold halves come together. If you look at common molded plastic parts, such as the one shown in Figure 10.23, you may see a fine line in the plastic where the two halves of the mold came together. You may also see marks where ejector pins pushed the part out of the mold (Figure 10.24).

When you model parts for injection molding, consider how the part will remove from the mold. Although there are some molding methods (such as slides) that allow you to make interior holes, the part cannot have a shape that will not allow it to be removed from the mold. Look at the part shape in Figure 10.25; the lip of the bowl makes it impossible to remove from the mold.

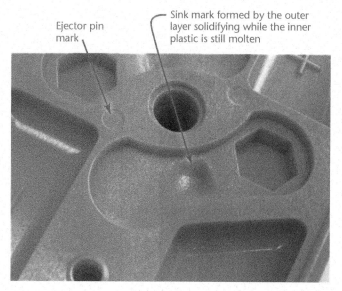

Ejector pin mark

Sink mark formed by the outer layer solidifying while the inner plastic is still molten

10.25 *Can you see why this part could not easily be removed from the mold?*

10.24 *Ejector pins may create marks on the surface. Surface defects such as sink marks are created when the mold fills or cools improperly. (Courtesy of Rebling Plastics.)*

As you design molded parts, plan for the parting line and design it so that both sides will be removed from the mold. You may want to add a construction plane to your CAD model, then project its edge onto the part as shown in Figure 10.26 to represent the parting line. Add draft to the surfaces of the part on each side of the parting line.

The amount of draft is decided by the size of the part, the finish of the mold, and the type of material and its shrink rate, among other factors. The Society of the Plastics Industry publishes guidelines to help you determine the exact amount of draft to add to the part. Usually, the mold designer will determine the shrinkage for the part and size the mold cavity so that the final parts will be to the size specified. Part shrinkage is not always uniform along the X-, Y-, and Z-directions. Many CAD packages can be used to size the part for shrinkage as well as add the draft.

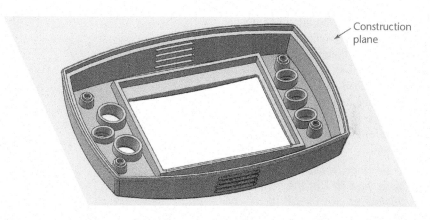

Construction plane

10.26 *The construction plane in this part identifies the location of the mold's parting line. The draft angle is added to the part on both sides of the parting line. (Courtesy of Robert Kincaid.)*

10.27 *Plastic parts such as these toys must be designed so they can be removed from the mold. (Ian Dikhtiar/ Shutterstock.)*

The following are four guidelines for designing injection molded plastic:

1. *Try to maintain a constant wall thickness.* See Figure 10.28a. The thickness of the plastic affects the rate at which it cools. Uniform wall thickness helps prevent sink marks in the plastic and keeps the part flat and uniform once molded. If wall thicknesses must change, make the change gradually instead of abruptly.

2. *Round all inside and outside corners* so parts will easily be removed from the mold. Rounded corners also improve uniform mold filling and help relieve stress concentrations in the mold. See Figure 10.28b.

3. *Use the maximum allowable draft angle, and never less than 1° per side.* See Figure 10.28c. Draft allows the parts to be removed from the mold. When parts are designed without enough draft, a vacuum can be created between the part and the side of the mold during removal. In extreme cases, this can damage the mold. When molded parts will have a surface texture, the draft angle must be increased to allow the part to be removed without damaging the texture.

4. *Projections typically should be not more than 70% of the normal wall thickness.* See Figure 10.28d. For best results, projections should be no more than two and a half to four times the wall thickness in length. A projection or rib that is too thick can cause sink marks on the opposite side of the part.

10.28 (a) *Maintain a constant wall thickness on injection-molded parts.*

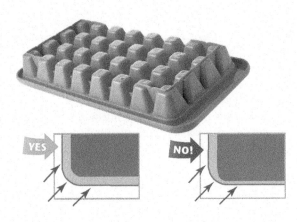

(b) *Round all inside and outside corners to improve release from the mold and relieve mold stress concentrations.*

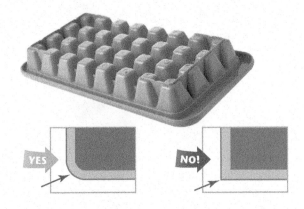

(c) *Use the maximum draft angle.*

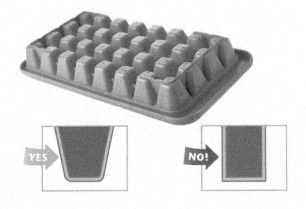

(d) *Size projections so they are no more than 70% of the wall thickness and no longer than four times the wall thickness.*

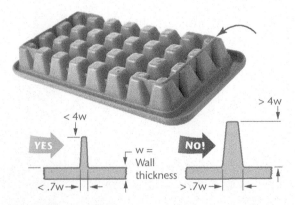

(Ice cube tray photo copyright Yossi James/Shutterstock.)

Cast Parts

Casting is the process of forming a part by pouring molten metal into a hollow mold. Many of the design issues for cast parts are similar to those for plastic parts. For example, surfaces must have draft and rounded corners to make it possible to remove the part from the mold.

In sand casting, you create a pattern to place in the sand to create the mold cavity. (The pattern may need to be larger than the finished part, as shrinkage occurs as the molded metal cools.) A gating system is added to allow the molten material to flow into the cavity and vents air when the molten metal is poured in. Sand is packed around the pattern and gating to create the mold. Then the pattern is removed to create the cavity. Molten metal is poured into the cavity, and once the metal is cooled, the mold is removed from the casting. Permanent molds are also possible, where the sand is bonded so the part may be removed without destroying the mold (Figure 10.29).

Like most molding processes, sand castings have two mold sides, called the *cope* and the *drag*. The *flask* is the term for the vessel that holds the packed sand around the part pattern. Cores can be added to form hollow recesses in the part. The final surface of the cast part is relatively rough where it touched the sand mold. The cast part may be machined to provide smoother surfaces on features where it is needed.

The Aluminum Association publishes the *Standard for Aluminum Sand and Permanent Mold Castings,* which is a useful guide to design requirements for these types of parts. Figure 10.30 shows two versions of a steel mounting bracket, (a) designed for casting and (b) designed for stamping from sheet metal.

10.29 A Permanent Mold Casting Cooling on the Exit Conveyor Belt *(Courtesy of Edelbrock Aluminum Foundries.)*

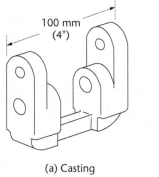 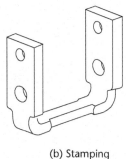

100 mm (4")

(a) Casting   (b) Stamping

10.30 Two Steel Mounting Brackets. *(a) Designed for Casting; (b) Designed for Stamping*

10.31 Milled Part (top); Part Turned on a Lathe (bottom) *(Courtesy of PENCOM.)*

Modeling Machined Parts

Machining processes remove material to produce the part shape desired. A rotating cutting tool shaves away material to form the shape of the part. These processes were some of the first to be computer controlled and are a common way to form metal parts.

Many machined parts start from common stock shapes such as round, square, plate, hex, block, and bar stock steel that come in standard sizes. When it is possible to use a standard size in your design, it may lower the cost to produce the part.

Some features, such as a perfectly square interior corner, are difficult to produce with this process. If you are planning your part for NC machining, avoid features that are difficult to machine or require multiple machine setups, unless they are needed. (You can make square interior corners using the electrodischarge machining process.) Fillets and rounds that result from machining methods provide additional strength and smooth the corners so they are not sharp when the part is handled. Figure 10.31 shows a part that has been milled (top) and a part that has been turned on a lathe (bottom).

10.32   *The 3D part in (a) will be formed by cutting the flat pattern (b) from a piece of sheet metal and bending it into shape. (Courtesy of J. E. Soares.)*

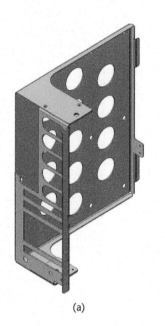
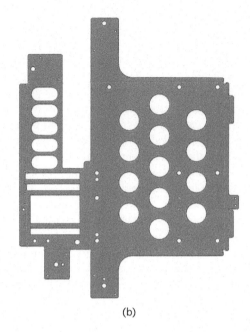

(a)   (b)

Modeling Sheet Metal Parts

Sheet metal parts, such as the one shown in Figure 10.32, are laid out as a flat pattern that is then bent into shape.

When modeling sheet metal parts, you may start by modeling them in 3D to visualize how they fit with mating parts. Each surface on the part must be shown true size in the flat pattern. Additional material for hems or overlaps to be welded must be added and the bend allowance factored in. The bend allowance is determined by how much the metal compresses and stretches when it is bent. Its value depends on the thickness and material of the metal. When the part is manufactured, it will start as a flat part cut from a sheet of uniform-thickness material. Sheet metal design features are available in most CAD modeling software that allow you to model the part with the bends and show the part in its flat or final shape.

Other sheet metal parts may be difficult to manufacture because of the way they must be bent. The brake press in Figure 10.33 is commonly used to form sheet metal parts by bending the metal along a straight line. Without special tooling, some parts may be impossible to bend without deforming other sections of the part.

Keep the following things in mind when modeling sheet metal parts:

- The bend location should allow enough material for the bend; material is compressed on the inside of the bend and stretched on the outside of the bend. Generally a flange (bent area) should be no smaller than 4 times the sheet thickness plus the allowance for the bend radius.

- Keep a single bend radius, when possible, to eliminate the need for tool changes or setups.
- The inside bend radius should be greater or equal to the sheet thickness. Compression of the material for a smaller radius is problematic.
- Do not locate holes, slots and similar features too near a bend or their shapes may be distorted during the bending process. Allow 3 times the sheet thickness plus the bending radius between a bend and a hole feature. In general, check with a sheet metal manufacturer who you are likely to be working with and inquire about their minimum allowance recommendations before your design is finalized.

10.33   **Brake Press** *(Copyright Prasit Rodphan/Shutterstock.)*

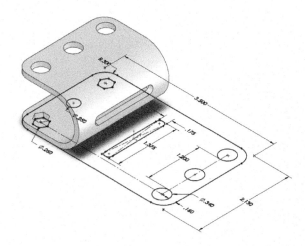

10.34 *The flat pattern sketch is bent to create the 3D sheet metal feature. (Courtesy of Salient Technologies, Inc. (www.salient-tech.com))*

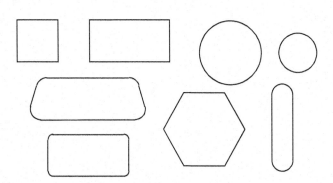

10.35 *These 2D outlines are a library of shapes that correspond to standard punches.*

Another consideration in sheet metal part design is arranging the flat pattern so that the parts nest together to waste the least amount of material. Software packages that can aid in the development of the flat pattern from a 3D wireframe, solid, or surface model (see Figure 10.34) oftentimes will help with pattern nesting to reduce waste material.

Holes in sheet metal parts are often created by a punch, such as an automated punch press. Standard punches can quickly create openings in the sheet metal part. Figure 10.35 shows a library of shapes corresponding to standard punches.

To help in designing sheet metal parts, you may want to keep a library of 2D outlines of standard punch shapes. You can then use these standard shapes to create 3D model geometry by importing the 2D section into your file and extruding and subtracting the feature to create the opening. Many CAD packages provide a variety of standard sheet metal features.

Some parts are possible to design but not possible to develop into a flat pattern. Figure 10.36 shows an example. This part cannot be created from a single flat sheet, as it would overlap itself.

Sheet metal parts are joined together by welding, soldering, or using hems. Figure 10.37 shows standard sheet metal hems.

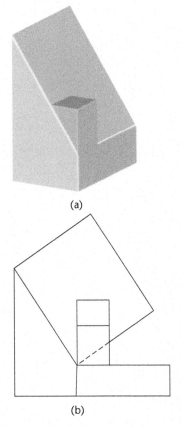

(a)

(b)

10.36 *(a) This 3D shape cannot be made of a single piece of sheet metal. (b) The flat pattern overlaps itself.*

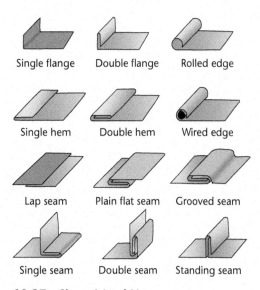

Single flange	Double flange	Rolled edge
Single hem	Double hem	Wired edge
Lap seam	Plain flat seam	Grooved seam
Single seam	Double seam	Standing seam

10.37 Sheet Metal Hems

This industrial reamer creates precise holes. Coolant is sprayed on the tool and part to prevent overheating. (Dmitry Kalinovsky/Shutterstock.)

Other Methods of Production

This is just an introduction to designing for plastic, molded, stamped, and sheet metal parts. Many options exist for achieving the qualities you want for your finished product. Table 10.2 presents some common methods you should be familiar with.

Table 10.2 Shapes and Some Common Methods of Production

Shape of Feature	Production Method
Flat surfaces	Rolling, planing, broaching, milling, shaping, grinding
Parts with cavities	End milling, electrical-discharge machining, electrochemical machining, ultrasonic machining, casting
Parts with sharp features	Permanent mold casting, machining, grinding, fabricating, powder metallurgy
Thin hollow shapes	Slush casting, electroforming, fabricating
Tubular shapes	Extrusion, drawing, roll forming, spinning, centrifugal casting
Tubular parts	Rubber forming, expanding with hydraulic pressure, explosive forming, spinning
Curvature on thin sheets	Stretch forming, peen forming, fabricating, assembly
Opening in thin sheets	Blanking, chemical blanking, photochemical blanking
Cross sections	Drawing, extruding, shaving, turning, centerless grinding
Square edges	Fine blanking, machining, shaving, belt grinding
Small holes	Laser, electrical discharge machining, electrochemical machining
Surface textures	Knurling, wire brushing, grinding, belt grinding, shot blasting, etching, deposition
Detailed surface features	Coining, investment casting, permanent-mold casting, machining
Threaded parts	Thread cutting, thread rolling, thread grinding, chasing
Very large parts	Casting, forging, fabricating, assembly
Very small parts	Investment casting, machining, etching, powder metallurgy, nanofabrication, micromachining

10.7 DOS AND DON'TS OF PRACTICAL DESIGN

Figures 10.38 and 10.39 show examples in which knowledge of manufacturing processes and limitations is essential for good design.

Casting Design

Figure 10.38 shows drawings of casting designs containing common design flaws alongside preferred alternatives.

Many difficulties in producing good castings result from abrupt changes in section or thickness. In Figure 10.38a, rib thicknesses are uniform so that the metal will flow easily to all parts. Fillet radii are equal to the rib thickness—a good general rule to follow. Whenever it is necessary to join a thin feature to a thicker feature, the thin feature should be thickened as it approaches the intersection, as shown in Figure 10.38b.

In Figures 10.38c, g, and h, coring is used to produce walls with more-uniform sections. In Figure 10.38d, an abrupt change in sections is avoided by making thinner walls and leaving a collar.

Figures 10.38e and f show examples in which the preferred design tends to allow the castings to cool without introducing internal stresses. The less desirable design is more likely to crack as it cools, since there is no give in the design. Curved spokes are preferable to straight spokes, and an odd number of spokes is better than an even number, because direct stresses along opposite spokes are avoided.

The design of a part may cause unnecessary trouble and expense for the pattern shop and foundry without any benefit to the design. For example, in the poor designs in Figures 10.38j and k, one-piece patterns would not withdraw from the sand, and two-piece patterns would be necessary. In the preferred examples, the design is just as useful and would be more economical in the pattern shop and foundry.

Practical Considerations

Figure 10.39 shows some basic practical considerations for manufacturing designs using various materials. In Figure 10.39a, a narrower piece of stock sheet metal can be used for certain designs that can be linked or overlapped. In this case, the stampings may be overlapped if dimension W is increased slightly, as shown, to save material.

The hardness of heat-treated steel depends on carbon content. To get maximum hardness, it is necessary to rapidly cool (quench) the steel after heating, so it is important that a design can be quenched uniformly. In Figure 10.39b, the solid piece will harden well on the outside but will remain soft and relatively weak on the inside. The hollow piece in the preferred example can be quenched from both the outside and inside. Thus, a hardened hollow shaft can actually be stronger than a solid one.

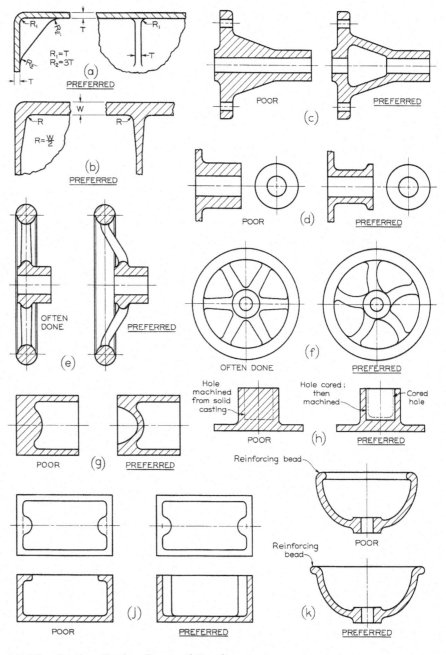

10.38   Casting Design Dos and Don'ts

In Figure 10.39c, a rounded groove (neck) around a shaft next to a shoulder eliminates a practical difficulty in precision grinding. Not only are sharp corners more expensive to grind, but sharp corners often lead to cracking and failure.

In Figure 10.39d the design at the right eliminates a costly reinforced weld, which would be needed in the design at left. The preferred example has strong virgin metal with a generous radius at the point where the stress is likely to be most severe. It is possible to make the design on the left as strong as that on the right, but it requires more expense, expertise, and special equipment.

It is difficult to drill into a slanting surface, as shown at the left in Figure 10.39e. Drilling is much easier if a boss is provided, as shown at right.

The design at the left in Figure 10.39f requires accurate boring or reaming of a blind hole all the way to a flat bottom, which is difficult and expensive. It is better to drill deeper than the hole is to be finished, as shown at the right, to provide room for tool clearance and chips.

In Figure 10.39g, the drill and counterbore in the upper example cannot be used for the hole in the centerpiece because of the raised portion at the right end. In the preferred example, the end is redesigned to provide access for the drill and counterbore.

In the top design in Figure 10.39h, the ends are not the same height, so each flat surface must be machined separately. In the design below, the ends are the same height, the surfaces are in line horizontally, and only two machining operations are necessary. It is always good to simplify and limit the machining as much as possible.

The design at the left in Figure 10.39j requires that the housing be bored for the entire length to receive a pressed bushing. Machining time can be decreased if the cored recess is made as shown, assuming that average loads would be applied in use.

The lower bolt in Figure 10.39k is encircled by a rounded groove no deeper than the root of the thread. This makes a gentle transition from the small diameter at the root of the threads to the large diameter of the body of the bolt, producing less stress concentration and a stronger bolt. In general, sharp internal corners should be avoided because these are points of stress concentration and possible failure.

In Figure 10.39m, a .25″ steel plate is being pulled, as shown by the arrows. Increasing the radius of the inside corners increases the strength of the plate by distributing the load over a greater area.

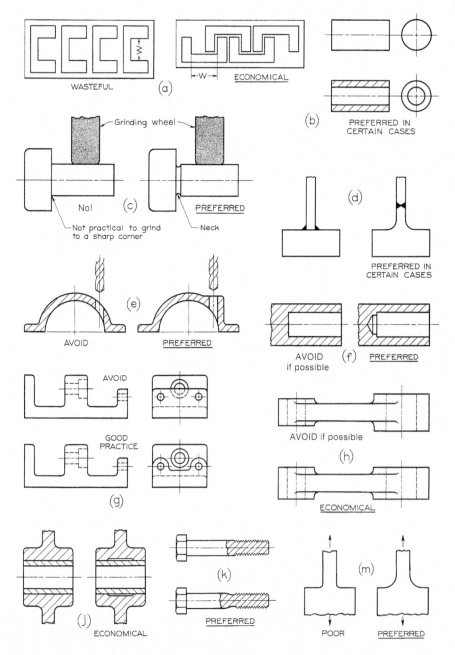

10.39   Practical Design Dos and Don'ts

10.8 MANUFACTURING MATERIALS

An ever-increasing variety of materials are available, each having its own characteristics, applications, advantages, and limitations. The following general types of materials are used in manufacturing.

- **Ferrous metals:** carbon, alloy, stainless, and tool and die steels.
- **Nonferrous metals:** aluminum, magnesium, copper, nickel, titanium, superalloys, refractory metals, beryllium, zirconium, low-melting alloys, and precious metals.
- **Plastics:** thermoplastics, thermosets, and elastomers.
- **Ceramics:** glass ceramics, glasses, graphite, diamond, and diamond-like materials.
- **Composite materials:** reinforced plastics, metal-matrix and ceramic-matrix composites. These are also known as engineered materials.
- **Nanomaterials:** shape-memory alloys, amorphous alloys, superconductors, and various others.

As new materials are developed, the selection of appropriate materials becomes even more challenging. There are constantly shifting trends in the usage of materials in all products, driven principally by economic needs.

Many examples of product failure can be traced to poor selection of material or manufacturing processes or poor control of process variables. A component or a product is generally considered to have failed when:

- It stops functioning (broken shaft, gear, bolt, cable, or turbine blade).
- It does not function properly or perform within required specification limits (worn bearings, gears, tools, and dies).
- It becomes unreliable or unsafe for further use (frayed cable in a winch, crack in a shaft, poor connection in a printed circuit board, or delamination of a reinforced plastic component).

When selecting materials for products, consider their mechanical properties: strength, toughness, ductility, hardness, elasticity, fatigue, and creep. The strength-to-weight and stiffness-to-weight ratios of material are also important, particularly for aerospace and automotive applications. Aluminum, titanium, and reinforced plastics, for example, have higher values of these ratios than steels and cast irons. The mechanical

This machine applies a pulling force to the specimen to measure its tensile strength. (N_Sakarin/Shutterstock.)

properties specified for a product and its components should, of course, be for the conditions under which the product is expected to function. Then, consider the physical properties of density, specific heat, thermal expansion and conductivity, melting point, and electrical and magnetic properties.

Chemical properties also play a significant role in hostile as well as normal environments. Oxidation, corrosion, general degradation of properties, toxicity, and flammability of materials are among the important factors to be considered. In some commercial airline disasters, for example, deaths occurred by toxic fumes from burning nonmetallic materials in the cabin.

Manufacturing properties of materials determine whether they can be cast, formed, machined, welded, and heat-treated with relative ease (Table 10.3). Methods used to process materials to the desired shapes can adversely affect the product's final properties, service life, and cost.

Cost and availability of raw and processed materials and manufactured components are major concerns in manufacturing. Competitively, the economic aspects of material selection are as important as the technological considerations of properties and characteristics of materials.

If raw or processed materials or manufactured components are not available in the desired shapes, dimensions, and

Table 10.3 General Manufacturing Characteristics of Various Alloys

Alloy	Castability	Weldability	Machinability
Aluminum	Excellent	Fair	Good/Excellent
Copper	Fair/Good	Fair	Fair/Good
Gray cast iron	Excellent	Difficult	Good
White cast iron	Good	Very Poor	Very Poor
Nickel	Fair	Fair	Fair
Steels	Fair	Excellent	Fair
Zinc	Excellent	Difficult	Excellent

quantities, substitutes and/or additional processing will be required, which can contribute significantly to product cost. For example, if a round bar of a certain diameter is not available in standard form, then a larger rod must be purchased and its diameter reduced by some means, such as machining, drawing through a die, or grinding. When possible, modify the product design to take advantage of standard dimensions of raw materials, thus avoiding additional manufacturing costs.

Different costs are involved in processing materials by different methods. Some methods require expensive machinery, others require extensive labor, and still others require personnel with special skills, a high level of education, or specialized training.

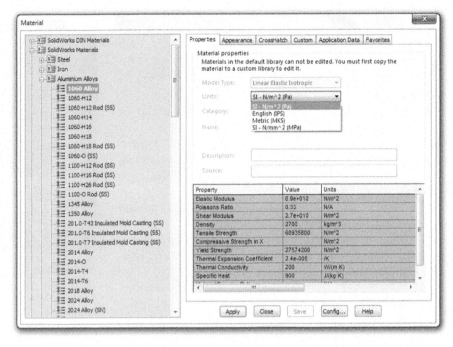

10.40   The Material Properties of 1060 Aluminum Alloy. *SolidWorks and other modelers provide preexisting materials that you can assign to parts. You also can set the properties of a material and save them in a custom material file that you can apply to your parts. (Image courtesy of ©2016 Dassault Systèmes SolidWorks Corporation.)*

Material Assignment in Models

When CAD software allows you to assign materials to your 3D parts, the materials can be used to calculate mass properties of parts and assemblies and for rendering appearances. This information is often stored in a database or in separate ***material files***. Once you have defined a material file, you can store and reuse it, saving you the effort of having to look up and redefine the material information each time it is needed. The calculated mass of your part depends on the density for the material that is entered in this file and the units for that density. The Material dialog box from SolidWorks in Figure 10.40 shows several standard materials predefined for you and the kinds of properties you can set.

When entering this information, match the units to the other units you are using. For example, if the mass density for the material is expected to be entered in slugs per cubic inch,

and you enter the value using slugs per cubic *feet*, the resulting calculations for the mass will be off by a significant factor—1728. When using material files from an existing library, you must take particular care to notice the units in which the information was entered and make sure that it matches the units you are using for your model.

Some CAD software uses a density of 1.00 for all materials or when parts have no material assigned and reports the mass based on this value. When a CAD system uses a density of 1.00 to calculate the mass of your model, you can calculate the actual mass by knowing the specific gravity of the material (which can be looked up in a materials table). If you do not check the calculations by hand and inadvertently use the density of 1.00 (as though your model were made of water), your incorrect mass value may cause a significant error.

SPOTLIGHT

Specific Gravity

Specific gravity is the value that can be used to relate the density of different materials by comparing them with the density of water. The mass density of distilled water at a temperature of 20° C is 1 gram per cubic centimeter, and its specific gravity is 1.00. Notice that specific gravity has no units. Gold has a specific gravity of 19. This essentially means that a volume of gold is 19 times as heavy as the same

volume of water. The specific gravities for some other common materials are as follows:

Aluminum alloys	2.8
Stainless steel	7.8
Brass	8.6
Titanium	4.4

10.9 APPEARANCE, SERVICE LIFE, AND RECYCLING

Color, feel, and surface texture determined by material appearance are all characteristics that we consider when making a decision about purchasing a product. Time- and service-dependent phenomena such as wear, fatigue, creep, and dimensional stability are also important. These phenomena can significantly affect a product's performance and, if not controlled, can lead to total failure of the product. Similarly, compatibility of materials used in a product is important. Friction, wear, and corrosion can shorten a product's life or cause it to fail prematurely. Another phenomenon that can cause failure is galvanic corrosion between mating parts made of dissimilar metals.

Recycling or proper disposal of materials at the end of their useful service lives has become increasingly important in an age when we are conscious of preserving resources and maintaining a clean and healthy environment. For example, many new products, such as decking materials, picnic tables, and even stylish interior panels are made from recycled HDPE (high-density polyethylene). The proper treatment and disposal of toxic wastes and materials is also a crucial consideration. Many CAD platforms provide database tools for analyzing the impact of materials selections on the design cost and its environmental impact.

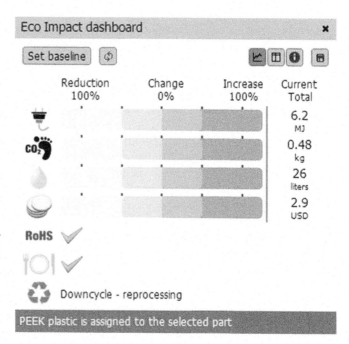

10.41 *Material advisor software compatible with CAD systems allows you to evaluate materials selections during the modeling process. (Autodesk screen shots reprinted courtesy of Autodesk, Inc.)*

10.10 DIMENSIONAL ACCURACY AND SURFACE FINISH

Size, thickness, and shape complexity of the part have a major bearing on the manufacturing process selected to produce it. Flat parts with thin cross sections, for example, cannot be cast properly. Complex parts may be formed easily and economically, but they may be cast or fabricated from individual pieces.

Tolerances and surface finish obtained in hot-working operations cannot be as good as those obtained in cold-working (room temperature) operations, because dimensional changes, warpage, and surface oxidation occur during processing at elevated temperatures. Some casting processes produce a better surface finish than others because of the different types of mold materials used and their surface finish.

10.42 Assembly of an Aircraft *(Courtesy AP Photo/Elaine.)*

The size and shape of manufactured products vary widely. For example, the main landing gear for a twin-engine, 400-passenger Boeing 777 jetliner is 4.3 m (14′) high, with three axles and six wheels, made by forging and machining processes (Figure 10.42). At the other extreme is the generation of a 0.05-mm (0.002″) diameter hole at one end of a 0.35-mm (0.014″) diameter needle, using a process called electrical-discharge machining. The hole is burr-free and has a location accuracy of ±0.003 mm (0.0001″).

Another small-scale manufacturing example is given in Figure 10.43, which shows microscopic gears as small as 100 μm (0.004″) in diameter. The center gear is smaller than a human hair. These gears may be used in applications such as powering microrobots to repair human cells, microknives in surgery, and camera shutters for precise photography. Such small-scale operations are called **nanotechnology** and **nanofabrication** ("nano" meaning one billionth).

Ultraprecision manufacturing techniques and machinery are now being developed and are coming into more common use. For machining mirrorlike surfaces, for example, the cutting tool is a very sharp diamond tip, and the equipment has very high stiffness and must be operated in a room where the temperature is controlled within 1°C. Highly sophisticated techniques such as molecular-beam epitaxy and scanning-tunneling microscopy are being implemented to obtain accuracies on the order of the atomic lattice, ±0.1 nm.

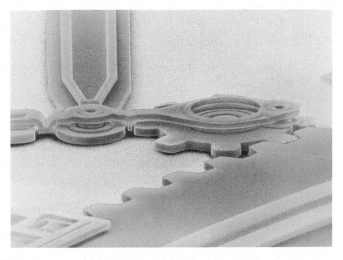

10.43   Colored Scanning Electron Micrograph of the Drive Gear (Orange) in a Micromotor. *The orange-colored gear in this colored scanning electron micrograph is smaller in diameter than a human hair and 100 times thinner than a sheet of paper. The whole micromotor device was etched into the surface of a wafer of silicon by the same techniques used to make silicon chips. (Alamy.)*

10.11 NET-SHAPE MANUFACTURING

Because not all manufacturing operations produce finished parts, additional operations may be necessary. For example, a forged part may not have the desired dimensions or surface finish, so additional operations such as machining or grinding may be necessary. Likewise, if it is difficult, impossible, or economically undesirable to produce a part with holes using just one manufacturing process, processes such as drilling may be needed. In another example, the holes produced by a particular manufacturing process may not have the proper roundness, dimensional accuracy, or surface finish, creating a need for additional operations such as honing.

Finishing operations can contribute significantly to the cost of a product. Consequently, the trend has been for **net-shape manufacturing** or near-net-shape manufacturing. In net-shape or near-net-shape manufacturing, the part is made as close to the final desired dimensions, tolerances, surface finish, and specifications as possible. Typical examples of these methods are near-net-shape forging and casting of parts, stamped sheet metal parts, injection-molded plastics, and components made by powder metallurgy techniques. Figure 10.44 shows a subassembly as originally designed (a), the redesign for ease of assembly (b), and finally as designed for net-shape manufacture as a single injection-molded part (c).

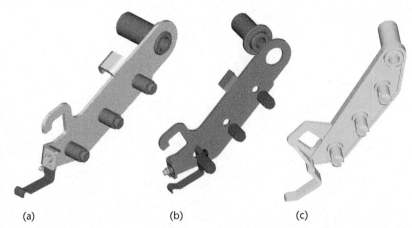

(a)   (b)   (c)

10.44   Net-Shape Manufacturing. *The original part shown in (a) required the assembly of several parts, the redesign shown in (b) made this part easier to assemble, but changing the design to (c), a single plastic part, requires no assembly. (Courtesy of Tektronix.)*

10.12 COMPUTER-INTEGRATED MANUFACTURING

The major goals of automation in manufacturing facilities are to integrate various operations to improve productivity, increase product quality and uniformity, minimize cycle times, and reduce labor costs. Since the 1940s, automation has accelerated because of rapid advances in control systems for machines and in computer technology.

Few developments in the history of manufacturing have had a more significant impact than computers. Computers are now used in a very broad range of applications, including control and optimization of manufacturing processes, material handling, assembly, automated inspection and testing of products, as well as inventory control and numerous management activities. Beginning with computer graphics and computer-aided design and manufacturing, the use of computers has been extended to computer-integrated manufacturing (CIM). Computer-integrated manufacturing is particularly effective because of its capability for

- responsiveness to rapid changes in market demand and product modification;
- better use of materials, machinery, and personnel, and reduced inventory;
- better control of production and management of the total manufacturing operation; and
- high-quality products at low cost.

Major Applications of Computers in Manufacturing

Computer numerical control (CNC) is a method of controlling the movements of machine components by direct insertion of coded instructions in the form of numerical data. Numerical control was first implemented in the early 1950s and was a major advance in the automation of machines.

Adaptive control (AC) automatically adjusts the parameters in a manufacturing process to optimize production rate and product quality, and to minimize cost. Parameters such as forces, temperatures, surface finish, and dimensions of the part are monitored constantly. If they move outside the acceptable range, the system adjusts the process variables until the parameters again fall within the acceptable range.

Industrial robots were introduced in the early 1960s, and they have been replacing humans in operations that are repetitive, boring, and dangerous, thus reducing the possibility of human error, decreasing variability in product quality, and improving productivity. Robots with sensory perception capabilities (intelligent robots) are being developed, with movements that simulate those of humans.

Automated handling of materials, controlled by computers, has allowed highly efficient handling of materials and products in various stages of completion (work in progress), such as from storage to machine, from machine to machine, and at the points of inspection, inventory, and shipment.

Automated and robotic assembly systems are replacing costly assembly by operators. Products are designed or redesigned so that they can be assembled more easily by machine.

Computer-aided process planning (CAPP) is capable of improving productivity in a plant by optimizing process plans, reducing planning costs, and improving the consistency of product quality and reliability. Functions such as cost estimating and work standards (time required to perform a certain operation) can also be incorporated into the system.

Group technology (GT) groups products by classifying them into families, according to similarities in design and similarities in manufacturing processes to produce the part. In this way, part designs and process plans can be standardized and families of parts can be produced efficiently and economically.

Just-in-time (JIT) production tries to deliver supplies just in time to be used, to produce parts just in time to be made into subassemblies and assemblies, and to finish products just in time to be delivered to the customer. In this way, inventory carrying costs are low, part defects are detected right away, productivity is increased, and high-quality products are made at low cost.

Cellular manufacturing involves workstations, which are manufacturing cells usually containing a central robot and

10.45 Car Frames Being Welded on a Robotic Assembly Line *(Jenson/Shutterstock.)*

several machines, each performing a different operation on the part.

Flexible manufacturing systems (FMS) integrate manufacturing cells into a large unit, all interfaced with a central computer. Flexible manufacturing systems have the highest level of efficiency, sophistication, and productivity in manufacturing. Although costly, they are capable of producing parts randomly and changing manufacturing sequences on different parts quickly; thus, they can meet rapid changes in market demand for various types of products.

Expert systems are basically intelligent computer programs. Expert systems are being developed rapidly with capabilities to perform tasks and solve difficult real-life problems as human experts would.

Artificial intelligence (AI) involves the use of machines and computers to replace human intelligence. Computer-controlled systems are becoming capable of learning from experience and making decisions that optimize operations and minimize costs. Artificial neural networks, which are designed to simulate the thought processes of the human brain, have the capability of modeling and simulating production facilities, monitoring and controlling manufacturing processes, diagnosing problems in machine performance, conducting financial planning, and managing a company's manufacturing strategy.

10.13 SHARED MANUFACTURING

Although large corporations can afford to implement current technology and take risks, smaller companies generally have difficulty in doing so owing to limited personnel, resources, and capital. More recently, the concept of ***shared manufacturing*** has been proposed. This consists of a regional or nationwide network of manufacturing facilities with state-of-the-art equipment for training, prototype development, and small-scale production runs to help small companies develop products that compete in the global marketplace.

In view of these advances and their potential, some experts envision a factory of the future in which production takes place with little or no direct human intervention. Although the discussion remains highly controversial, the human role in this system is expected to be confined to supervision, maintenance, and upgrading of machines, computers, and software.

10.14 MANUFACTURING METHODS AND THE DRAWING

In designing a part, consider what materials and manufacturing processes are to be used. These processes will determine the representation of the detailed features of the part, the choice of dimensions, and the machining or processing accuracy. The principal methods of metal forming are

- ***Casting***
- ***Machining*** from standard stock
- ***Welding***
- ***Forming*** from sheet stock
- ***Forging***

A knowledge of these processes, along with a thorough understanding of the intended use of the part, will help determine some basic manufacturing processes.

In sand casting, all cast surfaces remain rough textured, with all corners filleted or rounded. Sharp corners indicate that at least one of the surfaces is finished (i.e., machined further, usually to produce a flat surface), and finish marks are shown on the edge view of the finished surface. Plastic parts are similar in many ways to castings because they have filleted and rounded corners and draft to allow the parts to be removed from the mold.

In drawings of parts machined from standard stock, most surfaces are represented as machined. In some cases, as on shafting, the surface existing on the raw stock is often accurate enough without further finishing. Corners are usually sharp, but fillets and rounds are machined when necessary. For example, an interior corner may be machined with a radius to provide greater strength.

On welding drawings, several pieces are cut to size and welded together. Welding symbols (listed in Appendix 31) indicate the welds required. Generally, there are no fillets and rounds except those generated during the welding process itself. Certain surfaces may be machined after welding or, in some cases, before welding. Notice that lines are shown where the separate pieces are joined.

On sheet metal drawings, the thickness of the material is uniform and is usually given in the material specification note rather than by a dimension on the drawing. Bend radii and bend reliefs at corners are specified according to standard practice. For dimensions, either the decimal-inch or metric dimensioning systems may be used. Allowances of extra material for joints may be required when the flat blank size is being determined.

For forged parts, separate drawings may be made for the die maker and for the machinist. The forging drawing provides only the information to produce the forging, and the dimensions given are those needed by the die maker. All corners are rounded and filleted and are shown as such on the drawing. The draft is drawn to scale and is usually specified by degrees in a note. A separate shop drawing for the machinist may be used to show the locations and sizes of drilled holes and information for surface finishes.

MODELING SHEET METAL PARTS: THINK FLAT

When Stan McLean designs stainless steel sheet metal components manufactured by Ability Fabricators, he uses the sheet metal module in SolidWorks to model the multiple parts and optimize the fit of the various components.

"Ability Fabricators, Inc. specializes in custom equipment, mostly for the pharmaceutical and food industries," McLean explains. "Projects can be anything from fully automated equipment such as drum lifts and V-Blenders, to cabinets and tables, to a simple bracket to support a sensor on a bottling line. Modeling the complicated equipment involves inserting and positioning motors, actuators, sensors, bearings, and linear guides in the assembly, then building the required sheet metal brackets, supports, and covers around the components."

McLean usually has several files open at the same time as he works: the assembly model, subassemblies, and the individual part model he is working on. Each part in the assembly is stored in its own file and loaded into the assembly. When creating new sheet metal parts, McLean takes both a "top down" and "bottom up" approach. Certain parts are created on their

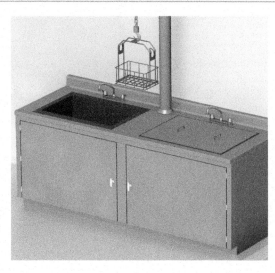

10.46 *This is the 3D model of the cabinet and countertop to be fabricated from sheets of 14 gauge stainless steel.*

own and then inserted into the assembly (bottom up design). Other sheet metal parts are created directly in the assembly based on the position of the various components (top down design).

With the individual components in place in the model, McLean can begin modeling the sheet metal parts needed to hold them. "A sheet metal part is a series of flanges or a box with various bends at various angles. I can sketch a rectangle, dimension it, extrude it to the gauge of the sheet metal I'm using, then add a flange by extruding another sketch—or by using the Insert Flange command in the sheet metal module." The sheet metal module contains a series of tools that are specifically designed to create the unique features of sheet metal parts, such as flanges, hem bends, sketched bends, corner seams, and more.

To ensure that all parts fit together correctly, McLean often sketches the base feature for a sheet metal part on one face of an existing component, then adds flanges by sketching on surfaces of other parts. "I'm always updating all of the parts in the assembly and modifying the sheet metal parts to make sure everything comes together as required."

When designing sheet metal structures such as the cabinet and countertop shown here, McLean models the parts one face at time and validates them in the assembly until it the part is complete. "By designing them one face at a time, I can adjust the faces as needed until everything is where it is supposed to be."

Sometime he creates subassemblies for single parts with multiple bodies to create weldments where more than one part or bodies are welded together. He adds regular fasteners or PEM fasteners (clinch nuts) to the assembly model as needed to fasten the parts together. He can also use tools in the sheet metal module to create lofted bends (for square to round transitions) or cylindrical or conical sections. When he adds a split line on one side of a complex form, Solidworks is capable of creating a flat pattern from the model.

The sheet metal module automatically creates and updates a flat pattern for the part. The flat pattern is the last feature shown in the feature

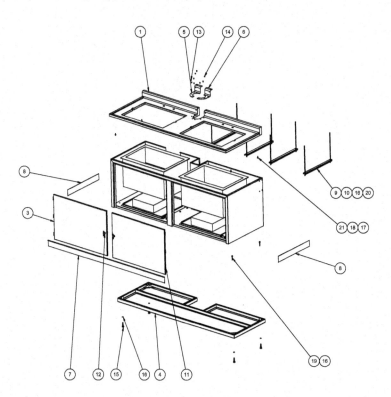

10.47 *An exploded wireframe view of the assembly model.*

browser. It can be toggled off and on as needed to display the flat pattern for verification. The software also checks automatically for collisions in the flat pattern.

McLean uses the sheet metal template in SolidWorks to carefully control the sheet metal parameters such as bend allowance (K-factor), sheet metal thickness, bend radius, corner relief, and other settings. He sets these values to make sure that the flat patterns calculated accurately reflect the real parts produced in the shop.

Sheet metal is defined by the gauge denoting its thickness and giving the type of material and finish. For example, 14 gauge stainless steel is 0.078″ thick. Sheets thicker than 3/16″ are usually referred to as plate. Although the tools in Solidworks are made for sheet metal, they work as well for creating thicker plate parts that will be rolled or brake formed. The thickness and gauge of the material affect the K-factor used to calculate the bend allowance—the amount the flat pattern will be adjusted for bending—and the location of the neutral line. Inside the neutral line the sheet metal part is in compression and made slightly smaller during forming on a brake press; outside the neutral line the metal is in tension and stretched. The neutral line represents the boundary where the part is the same length in both the flat and formed shape. Where the neutral line is on a given part is based on the bend radius and the ductility of the material and is not directly in the center of the bend.

Once the parts have been designed, McLean creates multiview, fully dimensioned 2D drawings of the 3D sheet metal part and a bill of materials for any fasteners it includes. Because the sheet metal parts will be cut with a numerically controlled machine, McLean saves the flat pattern as a separate .dxf file that can be imported by the software they use to generate the NC code for cutting the part. The result is a complete documentation drawing of the folded part and an electronic file of the flat shape that can be used to cut the shape from the sheet metal. Typical CNC machines for cutting sheet metal are a laser cutter, plasma cutter, or CNC-controlled punch press.

Although the software speeds up the modeling of sheet metal parts, it does not prevent the creation of impossible parts. "Because you're creating this bent-up enclosure, you have to think about the flat all the time," says McLean. "You can create a solid or sheet metal enclosure with flanges that, when

10.48 *Clinch nuts fasten the sheet metal parts together.*

unfolded, will overlap each other. You also have to know how the metal is going to be bent. If you have a part with several bends, and you do them in the wrong order, you can get to a point where you can't complete the bend because the part will either hit the machine or hit the die."

McLean's manufacturing background helps him "think flat" and allows him to optimize his designs in ways that others cannot. "Sometimes I look at a flat pattern and the formed part and need to make changes to optimize the fabrication. I also talk with the operators for the CNC laser cutter and press brake to make sure I have made the right decisions."

Short of manufacturing experience, however, McLean's advice for sheet metal parts is to "keep it simple." "Instead of welding three parts together, is it better to make a single, more complicated part? This is a trade-off with no simple answer. The question is, Where are you actually saving? If you get to the point where a part has 10 to 15 bends in it, you're probably better off going to two parts and welding them together."

(Courtesy of Ability Fabricators Inc.)

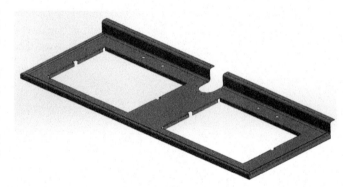

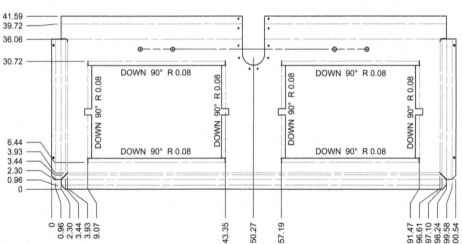

10.49 *The flat pattern for the part to be cut and formed into the countertop shown above right.*

10.15 MODELING FOR TESTING AND REFINEMENT

The refinement phase forms an iterative loop with the analysis phase of design. Test results feed back into model changes, and the revised model is used for further testing. Your 3D solid model database defines the geometry of the design and provides information for engineering analysis, such as determining mass, volume, surface area, and moments of inertia.

You can use tools such as a spreadsheet, equation solver, motion simulator, and finite element package with model data to check for stress concentrations; determine deflections, shear forces, bending moments, heat transfer properties, and natural frequencies; perform failure analysis and vibration analysis; and make many other calculations.

10.16 DETERMINING MASS PROPERTIES

The size, weight, surface area, and other properties available from a 3D model are frequently part of the design criteria your design must satisfy. The surface area of a part can determine whether a part cools as quickly as it should. The volume of a molded part will determine how much material is needed to fill the mold—which in turn determines a key component of the manufacturing cost.

When a satellite or other space vehicle is designed, the mass of the finished product is important for determining the thrust required for the vehicle to leave Earth's atmosphere. Accurate mass information can spell the difference between success and failure and, for manned space flights, the difference between life and death. At the same time, spacecraft designs seek to minimize the total mass of the system, so the built-in factors of safety cannot be as high as those for bridges built of heavy steel. When the margin for error is small, the importance of accurate mass properties information is even higher.

Calculating the mass of a model as complex as a satellite by hand is time-consuming and might add years to the design process. Most 3D CAD systems allow you to directly generate a wide range of mass property information about the model.

The following are mass property calculations commonly available in CAD modeling software:

- Volume
- Centroid or center of gravity
- Surface area
- Moments of inertia
- Mass
- Radii of gyration

Acquiring mass properties information directly from the model provides information that would be difficult to calculate accurately. Figure 10.50 shows the model of a bike brake assembly. Figure 10.53 on page 454 shows the mass properties generated from the model. Modeling software can report the volume of the part—regardless of its shape—with accuracies of up to plus or minus one hundred-millionth of a percent ($\pm$ 0.00000001).

10.50 *The volume of this brake assembly would be difficult to calculate by hand.*

MASS PROPERTY CALCULATIONS

Mass Properties of a Right Cylinder

You can learn more about using mass property calculations, such as moments of inertia, in engineering courses. The equations and illustrations in this example illustrate these properties as they would apply to a 1-inch diameter **right cylinder** (a cylinder in which the base is perpendicular to the height), shown in 10.51.

For this example cylinder:

π is approximately 3.14
r = .5 inch, the base's radius
d = 1 inch, the base's diameter
l = 2 inches, the height of the cylinder.

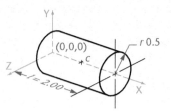

10.51   Right Cylinder

Volume

The **volume** of a solid is basically the amount of space it takes up; volume is measured in cubic units. For many basic geometric solids, like a cylinder, volume can be calculated using simple formulas. Complex shapes can be calculated either by breaking them down into simpler geometric solids—whose volumes are easier to calculate—and adding those volumes together or by using calculus-based methods. CAD software usually uses approximate methods to evaluate integrals to determine the volume and mass properties of any shape.

v = volume

The volume of a 1-inch-diameter cylinder, in which the 2-inch length is perpendicular to the circular base, is the area of the base times the length.

$$v = \pi \times r^2 \times l$$
$$= 3.14 \times (.5 \text{ in.})^2 \times 2 \text{ in.}$$
$$= 1.57 \text{ in.}^3$$

Surface Area

The **surface area** of a solid is the square measure of its exterior surface. It is also the total area of the boundary surfaces of a solid or surface model. You can think of the surface area as the measure of the exterior surface of the object flattened out into a plane (as shown in 10.52). Once again, it is easy to calculate for simple cases, but complex for irregular shapes. CAD software usually uses approximate methods to evaluate integrals to determine the surface area of any shape.

Sa = surface area

The surface area of the cylinder is the area of the rectangular shape that encloses the cylinder ($\pi d \times l$) plus the area of the two circular ends (πr^2).

$$Sa = \pi dl + 2(\pi r^2)$$
$$= (3.14 \times 1 \text{ in.} \times 2 \text{ in.})$$
$$+ 2 [3.14 \times (.5 \text{ in.})^2]$$
$$= 7.85 \text{ in.}^2$$

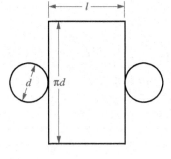

10.52   Surface Area

Mass

The **mass** is roughly the measure of the resistance that an object has to changing its steady motion.

m = mass
= volume $\times$ mass density
= $v \times$ mass density

MASS PROPERTY CALCULATIONS

Mass Density

Mass density for a given material is usually found by looking up the value in an engineering materials table. This is typically information you provide to calculate the mass for a given object. It is very important to make sure the units for your model (millimeters or inches, for example) match the units for the mass density that you provide (milligrams per cubic millimeter, for example). If they do not, you must convert the volume value reported from the software, or you will be off by a large factor in your calculations.

The mass of this cylinder, if made from copper, is its volume times the mass density of the material, which is 0.295.

$$m = 1.57 \text{ in.}^3 \times 0.295 \text{ lb/in.}^3$$
$$\quad = 0.46315 \text{ lb/in.}^3$$

Centroid or Center of Gravity

A *centroid* is a point defining the geometric center of an object. The centroid and center of gravity coincide when the part is made of a uniform material in a parallel gravity field. Most CAD software reports the centroid relative to the coordinate system that is selected. Make sure that you understand how the coordinate system is oriented when interpreting this value. Approximations of double integrals are used by the CAD software to calculate centroids.

C = centroid

The centroid for the cylinder is stated in terms of the three axes of the 3D coordinate system. Given the location of the origin at the center of one end of the cylinder, the centroid for this part is at (1,0,0) inches.

$$C = C_x, C_y, C_z$$
$$C_x = l/2 = 2/2 = 1$$
$$C_y = 0$$
$$C_z = 0$$
$$C = 1,0,0$$

Moments of Inertia

A *moment of inertia* is the measure of the resistance that an object has to changing its steady motion about an axis. A moment of inertia depends on the mass of the object and how that mass is distributed about the axis of interest. A moment of inertia is the second moment of mass of the object relative to the axis. Products of inertia are similar to moments of inertia, but they describe the mass distribution relative to two axes of interest. Make sure you understand how the coordinate system is oriented when interpreting this value.

I = moment of inertia
I = second moment of mass about an axis

For this cylinder,

$$I_x = \int (y^2 + z^2)dm$$
$$I_y = \int (x^2 + z^2)dm$$
$$I_z = \int (x^2 + y^2)dm$$

Radii of Gyration

The *radius of gyration* is the distance from the axis of interest where all the mass can be concentrated and still produce the same moment of inertia. Make sure you understand how the coordinate system is oriented when interpreting this value.

k = radius of gyration about an axis

For this cylinder,

$$k_x = \sqrt{\frac{I_x}{m}}$$
$$k_y = k_z = \sqrt{\frac{I_y}{m}}$$

Understanding Mass Property Calculations

Before you make use of the mass properties generated by your modeling software, it is important to understand how the values are derived. Modeling methods, algorithms, system variables, and units used by your CAD software make a difference in the accuracy of mass property calculations. For example, models that store the faceted representation of the part may produce less accurate calculations than models that store the accurate geometry.

Different modeling software uses different algorithms to calculate the volume of a solid. Some of them have error ranges of plus or minus 20%. One algorithm used to calculate the volume of a solid simply encloses the solid in a bounding box, then breaks it up into rectangular prisms parallel to the bounding box. (A bounding box is the smallest box inside which the solid will fit.) The lengths of the rectangular prisms are determined by the surface boundaries of the solid. The volumes of the prisms are then summed to find the volume of the solid. The accuracy of this method depends on the number of subdivisions into which the object is broken. The direction from which the prisms are created also affects the ability of the prisms to approximate the shape. Typically, both these settings are variables with ranges that you can set prior to calculating the mass properties.

Other systems use an iterative process to approximate the integral that describes the volume. These systems often let you specify a range of accuracy for the calculations. The more accurate you require the calculations to be, the more time they will take.

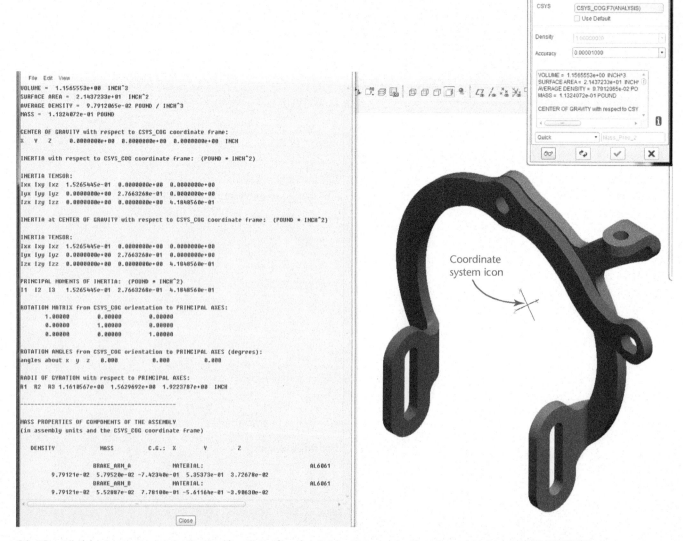

10.53   Highly Accurate Mass Properties Data for the Brake Assembly Generated Using Pro/ENGINEER

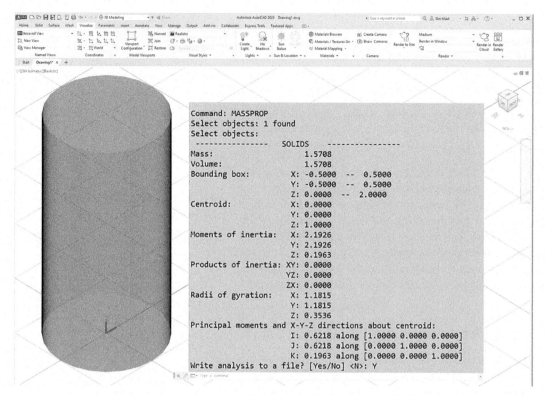

```
Command: MASSPROP
Select objects: 1 found
Select objects:
---------------    SOLIDS    ---------------
Mass:                    1.5708
Volume:                  1.5708
Bounding box:        X: -0.5000  --  0.5000
                     Y: -0.5000  --  0.5000
                     Z: 0.0000   --  2.0000
Centroid:            X: 0.0000
                     Y: 0.0000
                     Z: 1.0000
Moments of inertia:  X: 2.1926
                     Y: 2.1926
                     Z: 0.1963
Products of inertia: XY: 0.0000
                     YZ: 0.0000
                     ZX: 0.0000
Radii of gyration:   X: 1.1815
                     Y: 1.1815
                     Z: 0.3536
Principal moments and X-Y-Z directions about centroid:
                     I: 0.6218 along [1.0000 0.0000 0.0000]
                     J: 0.6218 along [0.0000 1.0000 0.0000]
                     K: 0.1963 along [0.0000 0.0000 1.0000]
Write analysis to a file? [Yes/No] <N>: Y
```

10.54 Mass Properties for the Cylinder from AutoCAD *(Autodesk screen shots courtesy of Autodesk, Inc.)*

Verifying Accuracy

A good way to verify the results you are getting for mass properties is to model a shape in which the geometry is known (such as the 1-inch-diameter cylinder used in the preceding example), then compare the properties calculated by hand with those given by the CAD system. Use your CAD software to model the cylinder shown in Figure 10.54: it has a diameter of 1 inch and a height of 2 inches. Calculate the volume by hand using the formula.

$$v = \pi \times r^2 \times l$$

$$= 3.14 \times (.5 \text{ in.})^2 \times 2 \text{ in.}$$

$$= 1.57 \text{ in.}^3$$

Then, list the same information from your solid modeling software. Is it the same? A modeler that stores an accurate representation, such as AutoCAD 2023 (Figure 10.54), will yield different results from one such as AutoCAD Release 12, which used faceted models and an approximate method to calculate volumes (Figure 10.55).

Even after checking the results with a simple object, you should routinely estimate the values for your models to make sure that the computed values from your system are reasonable. If there is a significant difference between the software report and your hand calculation, take time to determine what is producing the variation. Do not just believe the values reported by the software and base important decisions on those results. (There is a tendency to think the software values are right because they are printed neatly on the screen. Make sure you understand the values and their range of accuracy before you use them.)

Units and Assumptions

Some information reported under mass properties, such as the centroid, moments, and radii of gyration, is related to the coordinate system in which the model is stored or to a coordinate system you have selected. You must make sure that you understand the model orientation with respect to the coordinate system, or you may misinterpret the numbers reported.

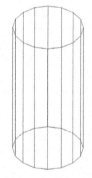

10.55 *The faceted models stored by AutoCAD Release 12, as shown here, produce a less accurate volume calculation than the more accurate form of the model stored by AutoCAD 2023.*

Pounds Mass versus Pounds Force

Don't confuse **pounds mass** with **pounds force** when using U.S. units. An object on Earth that has a mass of 1 pound also has a weight of 1 pound. If you send that object to the moon, where the gravitational force is about one sixth what it is on Earth, the object will still have 1 pound mass; however, its weight in pounds will be about one sixth of what it weighed on Earth. Mass equals weight divided by gravitational acceleration ($m = W/gc$).

The type of units specified or assumed is especially important in calculating mass properties. Using mismatched types of units is a common reason mass property values may not match your expected values. The common unit systems in the United States are the **inch-pound-second** (ips) and **foot-pound-second** (fps) systems. Elsewhere, the **Système International** (SI) is used, with meters, kilograms, and seconds (mks) as the basic units, although the **centimeter-gram-second** (cgs) system is also sometimes used, and machine parts are often modeled using millimeters. You must make sure that you understand the units that are used in the calculation of the mass properties.

10.17 EXPORTING DATA FROM THE DATABASE

In some cases, mass properties information provided by the solid model is enough to determine whether a key criterion is met; in other cases, the information from the model needs to be analyzed further or combined with additional information. The surface area of a model, for example, can be used with an estimate of paint per square foot to gauge the amount and cost of paint required.

Most solid and parametric modeling software allows you to export a wide range of data from the CAD database so it can be used in other applications. Mass properties data are commonly exported to text files that can be read by a spreadsheet, for example. Parameter data and the geometry of the model itself can also be exported to be used in other applications. Conversely, parameter information can be imported *into* constraint-based modeling software from spreadsheets or other analysis tools.

To use your CAD database with other applications, you should be aware of how data are transferred from one application to the other. Before selecting a particular CAD platform, you should investigate the export formats that are available and make sure that you can successfully transfer the information between the different software packages you may be using. Export a test part first to be sure the conversion will suit your needs. If you want to bring the data back into your CAD database from another application, this testing is even more important. Do not leave this testing to the last minute when you may be facing a critical deadline.

File Formats

Each software application has its own **native file format**. A native format is designed to store any and all information created with that application in an efficient form. Each application has its own codes stored with the data that are interpreted by the application when the file is opened. For this reason, file formats are identified by an extension. Microsoft Word, for example, creates .docx (or .doc) files. AutoCAD's native format is .dwg. If you try to open a .docx file in a different application—and do not get an error message—you may see strange characters on the screen. These are elements in the file used by Word that the other application does not know how to interpret.

Other file formats are standardized so they can be read by many different applications. A text-only or **ASCII** file (which often uses a .txt extension) uses nothing more than the standard 256 ASCII characters (the older ASCII standard had only 128 characters). ASCII is an acronym for American Standard Code for Information Interchange, an early standard that allows data to be shared reliably among all different kinds of computers. Each letter of the alphabet plus other common characters

— **TIP** —

Preparing for Mass Property Calculations

- Check the accuracy of your modeler by calculating values for a simple part by hand.
- Routinely estimate the values you expect and compare them with the modeler's results.
- Be sure the units used for a calculation are consistent with your model units.
- Note the coordinate system orientation used in certain calculations.
- Set materials properties for each part, taking care that units used fit your needs.
- Confirm the density used for materials in your modeler: does it use a default value?

— **TIP** —

Text-based tools and formats enabled the growth of the Internet and the World Wide Web. The HTML language used on the Web is a text-only format designed to allow formatted text and graphics to be displayed from a text-based file.

are coded the same way on any machine that reads and writes text files. If you have ever saved a formatted word processing document as a text file, you know that it does not save special formatting (such as bold and italic) or any graphics in the file. It does, however, create a copy of the words in your document that can be read on any computer.

Today, most software applications have filters that allow them to write or read nonnative file formats. These may be standardized formats, or they may be the native formats of other popular packages. AutoCAD's .dwg format, for example, can be read by many applications that make it easy for their users to work with these files.

Sometime, changing to a different format causes a loss of data—either in the new format or when you reconvert the data back into a form readable by your CAD software. You can never increase the amount of information in a file by translating it; you can only keep it the same or decrease it.

Common Formats for Export

Export formats for CAD data depend on what you are exporting. If you are exporting mass property data, attribute data, or dimension parameters, the export options offer a choice of formats, most of which are text-based. Some CAD packages export data to common spreadsheet formats, such as Microsoft Excel's .xls (or .xlsx) format. Almost all CAD software offers text export as an option.

When you export a table of data as text, you will commonly choose among *comma-delimited*, *space-delimited*, or *tab-delimited* text (see Figure 10.56). Tables of data are generally exported so that each record (or row of data in a table) is separated by a line break (signaling the software to go to the next line). Columns of data are separated (*delimited*) by a character—a space, comma, or tab. When the text file is read by the target application, you may have to specify which character was used to delineate the columns. If your data entries have many spaces in them, space-delimited would be a bad choice, as the target software would not be able to distinguish between the spaces in the entries and those between the columns. Tab-delimited is the most commonly used export format for tabular data. The comma-delimited format is also popular for importing to and exporting from CAD software.

If you plan to export your CAD model for analysis, to generate NC tool paths, or to do animation or kinematic analysis, you may need to use some kind of *graphics exchange format*. These are standardized formats that capture graphics information in the same way that a text file captures text data. Each

A1			*fx*	Pro/E Family Table								
	A	B	C	D	E	F	G	H	I	J	K	L
1	Pro/E Family Table											
2	BRAKE_ARM_A											
3												
4	INST NAME	COMMON NAME	d12	d5	d7	d1	d19	d23	d24	d4	d2	
5	!GENERIC	brake_arm_a.prt_INST	9	82	25	16.75	60	20	36	50	14.5	
6	A_1001	brake_arm_a.prt_INST	10	90	25	16.75	68.73	20	36	60	14.5	
7	A_1002	brake_arm_a.prt_INST	13	110	30	20	85	28	44	70	20	
8	A_1003	brake_arm_a.prt_INST	11	95	30	17	80	25	39.5	65 *		
9	A_1004	brake_arm_a.prt_INST	9	82 *	*		60 *	*		60 *		
10												
11												

Sheet1 / Sheet2 / Sheet3

```
Pro/E Family Table,,,,,,,,,,
BRAKE_ARM_A,,,,,,,,,,
,,,,,,,,,,
INST NAME,COMMON NAME,d12,d5,d7,d1,d19,d23,d24,d4,d2
!GENERIC,brake_arm_a.prt_INST,9,82,25,16.75,60,20,36,50,14.5
A_1001,brake_arm_a.prt_INST,10,90,25,16.75,68.73,20,36,60,14.5
A_1002,brake_arm_a.prt_INST,13,110,30,20,85,28,44,70,20
A_1003,brake_arm_a.prt_INST,11,95,30,17,80,25,39.5,65,*
A_1004,brake_arm_a.prt_INST,9,82,*,*,60,*,*,60,*
```

(b)

```
Pro/E Family Table
BRAKE_ARM_A

INST NAME       COMMON NAME    d12    d5    d7    d1    d19    d23    d24    d4    d2
!GENERIC        brake_arm_a.prt_INST  9   82   25   16.75  60   20   36   50   14.5
A_1001   brake_arm_a.prt_INST  10   90   25   16.75  68.73  20   36   60   14.5
A_1002   brake_arm_a.prt_INST  13   110  30   20     85   28   44   70   20
A_1003   brake_arm_a.prt_INST  11   95   30   17     80   25   39.5 65   *
A_1004   brake_arm_a.prt_INST  9    82   *    *      60   *    *    60   *
```

(c)

10.56 (a) Spreadsheet Showing the Parameter Data for the Brake Part Exported from Pro/ENGINEER. *The parameter data text file is shown exported in (b) comma-delimited text format and (c) tab-delimited text format.*

varies in the degree to which it captures the information in the model. The required accuracy for graphical data can also vary between graphics standards. This can be a problem because endpoints of lines that may have been considered connecting in one CAD package, where the accuracy indicates that endpoints connect if they are within 0.000001, may not connect when exported to a format that uses accuracies of 0.0000000001. The new format may not know how to interpret this difference in accuracy. The result may be that lines that previously connected no longer connect when translated.

The *Initial Graphics Exchange Specification* (IGES) is a graphics format capable of exporting wireframe, surface, or solid information. This format captures the 3D information and is commonly used to export the model for computer-aided manufacturing. It was developed to export engineering drawing data, with emphasis on the 2D and 3D wireframe model information, text, dimensions, and limited surface information typical of early CAD-drawn mechanical parts. The IGES standard is controlled by the National Computer Graphics Association (NCGA). The NCGA administers the National IGES User Group (NIUG), which provides access to information on

IGES. The volunteer organization IGES/PDES (Product Data Exchange using STEP) helps maintain the evolving IGES standard and publishes a specification for IGES. Because it is evolving, there are various versions of IGES in existence, with various capabilities. Because IGES has capabilities for exporting a wide variety of information, different *flavors* of it exist. You can often select options for how you want the information translated. You can find references on the Web that list the types of entities and how the information for them is stored in the IGES standard. A segment from an IGES file is shown in Figure 10.57.

The *STandard for the Exchange of Product model data* (STEP) is another 3D format that was agreed on more recently by the International Organization for Standardization (ISO). STEP may eventually allow more information to be transferred between CAD platforms than IGES.

Autodesk's *Drawing Exchange Format* (DXF) is popular for exporting 2D and 3D geometry between CAD platforms.

The *STereo Lithography* (STL) format is used to export 3D geometry to rapid prototyping systems. STL format translates the surface of the object into triangular facets. The size

```
                                                                        S0000001
1H,,1H;,23HMASTERCAM version 6.13a,10HSLTEST.GE3,9HMASTERCAM,1H1,16,8,
                                                                        G0000001
24,8,56,,1.,1,4HINCH,1,0.01,13H980608.150243,0.00005,100.,,,,8,0,;
                                                                        G0000002
       110       1       1       1       1              0      00000000D0000001
       110       0       3       1       0                            0D0000002
       110       2       1       1       1              0      00000000D0000003
       110       0       3       1       0                            0D0000004
       110       3       1       1       1              0      00000000D0000005
       110       0       3       1       0                            0D0000006
       110       4       1       1       1              0      00000000D0000007
       110       0       3       1       0                            0D0000008
       124       5       1       0       0              0      00010000D0000009
       124       0       3       1       0                            0D0000010
...
       100       0       3       2       0                            0D0000042
       110      34       1       1       1              0      00000000D0000043
       110       0       3       2       0                            0D0000044
       110      36       1       1       1              0      00000000D0000045
       110       0       3       1       0                            0D0000046
       110      37       1       1       1              0      00000000D0000047
       110       0       3       1       0                            0D0000048
       110      38       1       1       1              0      00000000D0000049
       110       0       3       2       0                            0D0000050
110,0.,-1.6974091509,-0.375,0.,-0.5,-0.375;                            1P0000001
110,0.75,0.,-0.375,0.5,0.,-0.375;                                      3P0000002
110,0.875,-1.8232830142,-0.375,0.875,-2.4167906074,-0.375;             5P0000003
110,0.75,-0.25,-0.375,0.5,-0.25,-0.375;                                7P0000004
124,1.,0.,0.,0.,0.,1.,0.,0.,0.,0.,1.,0.;                               9P0000005
100,-0.375,0.5,-0.5,0.5,0.,0.,-0.5;                                   11P0000006
100,-0.375,0.75,-0.5,1.2457224307,-0.5652630961,0.75,0.;              13P0000007
110,1.2457224307,-0.5652630961,-0.375,1.0008780126,-2.425041092,      15P0000008
-0.375;                                                               15P0000009
..
S0000001G0000002D0000050P0000039                                       T00000
```

10.57 *The IGES standard defines and codes entities in the CAD database using only comma- and space-delimited ASCII characters arranged in a standard format.*

SPOTLIGHT

Standard for the Exchange of Product Model Data

The STEP standard was developed by ISO to provide a format for representing and exchanging computer-readable product data. The initiative provides a neutral mechanism for describing product data throughout the life cycle of a product—not just its design, but also its manufacture, use, maintenance, and disposal. This means that the standard not only provides a neutral file format for exchange of 3D model information but also addresses additional product information such as that handled by a variety of database systems or a product data management (PDM) system. U.S. industry is represented in the process by PDES, a voluntary activity coordinated by the National Institute of Standards and Technology (NIST) (www.nist.gov).

and number of these facets determine how accurately the STL file matches the original object (see Figure 10.58).

Native versus Neutral Formats

Many CAD systems now allow you to read the native format file from another CAD system. This usually preserves the maximum amount of information in the translated file. When a native format is not available, only a more general format such as IGES may be available. These general formats are sometimes referred to as *neutral files*. Neutral files are useful both for exporting data and for importing files that have been created on a system other than your own.

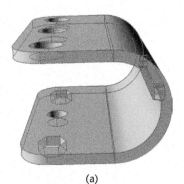

(a)

Vector versus Raster Data

Graphics programs are generally of two main types: *raster* or *vector*. CAD systems use vector-type data. This means that the information stored in the database contains the endpoints of lines, centers, radii of arcs, and other information based on the geometry of the objects. The CAD software draws a particular entity on the screen based on this vector information. The definition of the entities allows them to be drawn, printed, or converted to any size or format. All the previously mentioned graphics formats are used to exchange vector-type information.

Raster graphics programs (such as Photoshop) store information about the discrete pixels, or dots, that make up an image. Because this information is stored "dot by dot," it cannot contain useful information about the individual entities in the image, such as the center of a circle. Some examples of these formats are .bmp, .pcx, .tif, .png, .jpg, and .gif. These formats contain the information about the color and intensity of the pixels that should be formed to display the image. Images produced by scanning a picture or document are raster-type images. You cannot directly scan a drawing and use it in a vector-based CAD program. First, its raster-type information must be converted to vector information using a conversion algorithm. This is often unreliable, because the connectivity of endpoints, line types, and other information can be difficult to translate.

Many vector-type CAD programs allow you to export and import raster-type images. For example, a shaded model may be exported to a raster format, as in Figure 10.59, for printing or inclusion in a text document. Conversely, a scanned image, such as a company logo, or picture of an actual part, may be imported and placed in a vector drawing. Raster data in the CAD drawing remain a set of pixels; the entities in the drawing cannot be edited individually.

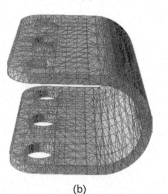

(b)

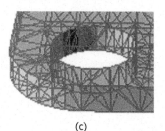

(c)

10.58   *The bracket was modeled in SolidWorks, then imported into (a) Rhino 3D and saved to (b) STL format. The enlarged view in (c) shows the faceted appearance of the rounded end in this file format.*

10.59   *This enlarged view of the raster image shows that it is made of pixels, not editable points, lines, and arcs.*

10.18 DOWNSTREAM APPLICATIONS

As the CAD model has evolved from a 2D drawing to a 3D database of design information, other software packages have evolved to facilitate engineering analysis of product and system design. These **downstream** applications may use data already created for the solid model. Increasingly, extensions for CAD packages offer analysis tools that operate within the 3D modeler so you don't have to define the model in another format. In this section, you will learn about analysis software that uses information from the CAD database.

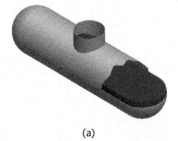

(a)

Spreadsheets

You are probably already familiar with spreadsheets. Values, text, and equations are entered into cells arranged in rows and columns. Each cell can be defined to store text and numeric data or to store the results of an action on data stored in other cells. Most spreadsheets offer a wide range of built-in functions— from finding a simple sum to more complex mathematical functions. Advanced users can create sophisticated problem-solving tools using spreadsheets, but a spreadsheet is handy for any kind of calculation.

Spreadsheets are an easy way to do "what-if" analysis. Once relationships have been set up, it is easy to change values and test many different scenarios with little effort. This ability to evaluate, modify, and reevaluate is integral to the iterative process of engineering design. The rows and columns make it easy to check the calculations done by the spreadsheet and easy to see results.

Many constraint-based modelers allow you to link the driven dimensions of the model to spreadsheet cells. Thus, you can use the spreadsheet to evaluate different options and then update the model dimensions based on the results.

Spreadsheets are an extremely helpful engineering tool not only for calculations but also for projecting and keeping track of costs. Creating parts that can be manufactured cost effectively and on time is an important aspect of design.

Equation Solvers

Equation-solving software, such as MathCAD and Matlab, is used to solve simultaneous equations and to visualize the results using built-in graphing functions. Equation solvers, like spreadsheets, allow you to change values easily and run different cases, but they also allow you to run a range of values to select an optimum solution from among several solutions. Their ability to optimize a solution makes them a valuable tool.

MathCAD's interface uses a standard notation, so you can type equations in the MathCAD editor the way you would ordinarily write them on paper. Most symbolic computation software lets you manipulate numbers, symbols, and math and logic expressions in a similar way.

You export data for use in an equation solver in the same way you would for a spreadsheet. In the example in Figure 10.60, information for the tank modeled was exported and loaded into MathCAD, where the convective heat loss for the tank was calculated from the surface area.

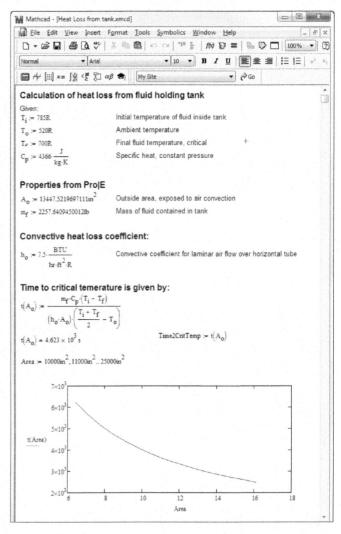

(b)

10.60 *The assembly model of the tank in (a) gives the combined mass properties of the tank and the fluid, which are different materials. Using the combined mass properties allows you to calculate the convective heat loss more accurately (b).*

Exporting from the Model for Cost Estimates

Model information, such as dimensions and surface area for the tank shown in Figure 10.61, was exported to a file named tank3.pls (shown in Figure 10.62).

This file was then imported into a spreadsheet (tank inf file.xlsx) to use the values for estimating the cost of producing the tank.

A second spreadsheet, costs.xlsx, shown in Figure 10.63, was created to multiply cost estimates for weld lengths, materials, and other information by the quantities and values in the tank data.

Once the calculations are complete, the same spreadsheet data can be used to produce a report, graph the costs, or recalculate the estimate based on updated cost or tank data.

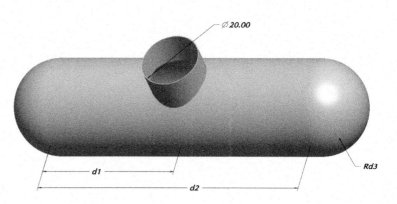

10.61   Tank Model

10.62   Tank Parameters

(continued)

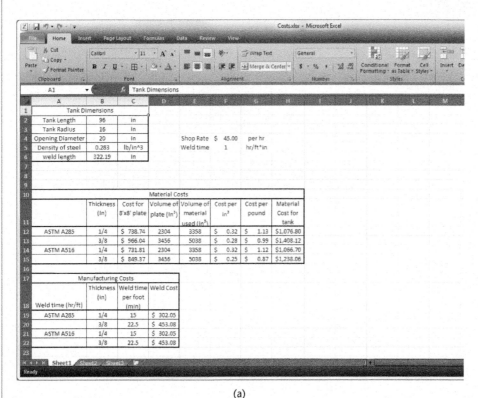

(a)

10.63 *The parameters from the tank were used to calculate cost information in Microsoft Excel, as shown in (a). The formulas used in the spreadsheet are visible in the view of the same spreadsheet shown in (b). Note that the formulas in cells B2–B4 and B6 relate directly to data in the tank inf file.xlsx, the spreadsheet into which the tank data were imported. If updated tank parameters are exported and imported into a new version of the tank inf file, the calculations in costs.xlsx will be updated with this new information.*

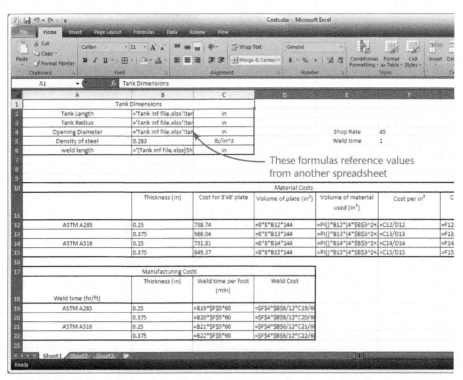

(b)

Finite Element Analysis

Finite element analysis (FEA) is a method of breaking up a complex shape into discrete smaller parts (**finite elements**) for which properties such as stress (see Figure 10.64), strain, temperature distribution, fluid flow, and electric and magnetic fields can more easily be found. The collective results for these smaller elements are linked together to determine the overall solution for the complex shape. The combination of smaller elements needed to cover a 2D or 3D shape is called a **mesh**. Many finite element analysis programs are available that can use CAD model geometry as the basis for FEA mesh.

Some FEA software is linked to or runs inside the CAD interface. For example, Creo Simulation (which has replaced Pro/Mechanica) is available in Pro/ENGINEER; SolidWorks Simulation is available within the SolidWorks interface. Other FEA software requires you to import or build your CAD model in the FEA software. Many FEA programs, such as ANSYS, will directly read CAD models from some of the more popular 3D software. Most FEA software will also import CAD geometry from neutral formats such as IGES, STEP, or DXF.

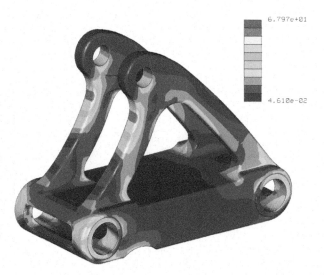

10.64   *This FEA stress plot makes it easy to visualize the distribution of stresses for the conditions applied to the model. (Courtesy of Santa Cruz Bicycles.)*

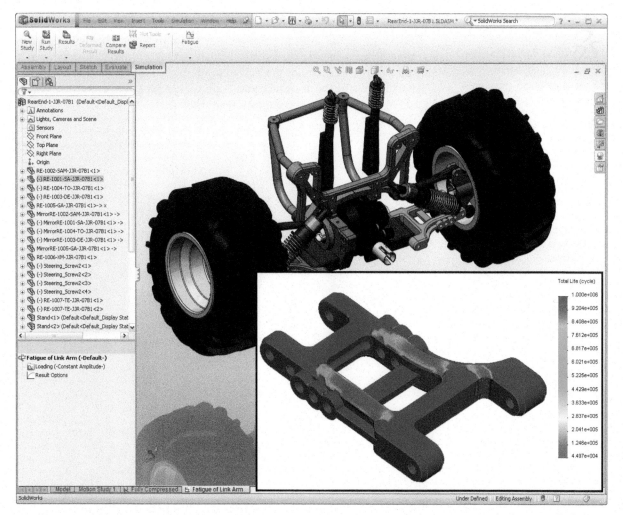

Fatigue analysis uses peak loads to estimate the lifetime of critical components. "Hot" colors in the link arm indicate sections that will fatigue soonest. (Image courtesy of ©2016 Dassault Systèmes SolidWorks Corporation.)

Meshing the Model

Selecting the proper element type when forming the mesh is essential to getting accurate results from the FEA program. Element types are shapes that will be used to make the mesh (see Figure 10.65). The choice of element type will depend on a number of factors, such as the material for the part, its geometric properties, and anticipated load.

A good understanding of material properties is necessary when using FEA methods. Material properties affect the appropriateness of the finite element type for your purposes. One property of a material is its *elasticity*. Only the simplest finite element types represent materials as entirely elastic. Most have capabilities that go far beyond simple elastic behavior. The element shape used in the mesh can determine how the material behavior is modeled. Some elements are used to represent elastic materials and small strain; some are elastic and include large strains; some are plastic; some are viscoelastic. Some elements even allow for coupled behavior. For example, temperature and stress can be coupled for thermoelastic problems in which temperature affects stress and vice versa. Similarly, electric current and stress couple for piezoelectric materials in which an electric current causes stress and vice versa. You must understand the range of material behavior likely to be encountered and select an appropriate element type to get good results from FEA analysis (see Figure 10.66).

Most modern finite element types have automatic mesh generation. The quality of your FEA results also depends on the quality (or refinement) of the mesh. For example, regions where stress gradients are steep require a finer mesh

10.65   *The mesh on the left is composed of one type of element, while the mesh on the right employs different element types to reduce processing time. A finer mesh is used where higher stresses are expected, but fewer elements where stress changes are more gradual. (Image credit: COMSOL.)*

to give good results. For symmetrical parts, where results will be the same on both sides of the axis of symmetry, time can be saved by cutting the model in half (or quarter) and analyzing only a portion of it. This keeps the file size and computation time down, which is particularly important when generating fine meshes.

After the mesh has been created, you use the FEA software to enter the forces.

Determining how to represent the forces on the object as they are applied to the mesh is another important consideration.

FEA software cannot tell when your assumptions, element type, or mesh density is not right for the problem you are analyzing. It will produce some type of result, but you must have the engineering background to interpret the validity of the result.

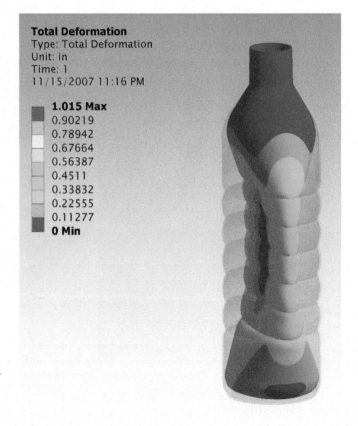

10.66   *This color plot shows the buckling of a plastic bottle in which the sides collapse from a negative internal pressure. This linear buckling model was created in ANSYS. The geometry is from a sample Autodesk Inventor part. (Image courtesy ANSYS, Inc.)*

ANALYZING THE BRAKE ASSEMBLY

The brake assembly in Figure 10.67 shows CAD data being used for FEA analysis. The brake arms are attached to the bike frame and to each other at the pivot point. Brake pads attach at the slots on each arm. In this example, Mechanica was used to analyze the brake arms to ensure that the arms can withstand the braking forces while still providing flexibility needed for smooth braking.

10.67   The Brake Assembly as Modeled in Pro/ENGINEER. *Note the attachment points for the brake pads and the bike frame.*

① Boundary conditions are applied to the model to constrain the axis of the hole for the pivot. It is fixed in the X-, Y-, Z-directions to model how this surface is used to attach the brake arms to the bike frame. This still allows the rotational motion of the arm during the analysis. Mechanica lets you select an entire region (surface) to use, then constrains the nodes at each point in the selected region of the mesh automatically. Figure 10.68 shows where constraints are applied to the left brake arm model.

10.68   *Constraints are applied to the part named BRAKE_ARM_A to represent the boundary conditions.*

(continued)

STEP by STEP

STEP by STEP

2 Next, loads are added to the model. The arrows pointing away from the selected regions in Figure 10.69 represent the applied loads that result when the brake cable pulls upward on the end of the brake arm, and the brake pad pushes against the wheel. (All the brake pad forces have not been shown here for easier visualization.)

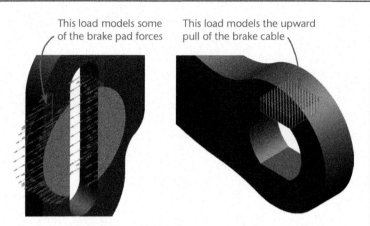

This load models some of the brake pad forces

This load models the upward pull of the brake cable

10.69 *Loads are applied representing the actions of the brake cable and pads.*

3 The type of element that will be used to form the mesh is set using the AutoGEM dialog box. Each element type has strengths and weaknesses for modeling particular features and material conditions. Figure 10.70 shows options that influence the mesh that will be generated automatically for the element type. In this case, the tetrahedron element type is selected for use with solids.

— **TIP** —

Pay close attention to units during any type of analysis. When values are input, make sure the units match the requested input as well as the units used in your model.

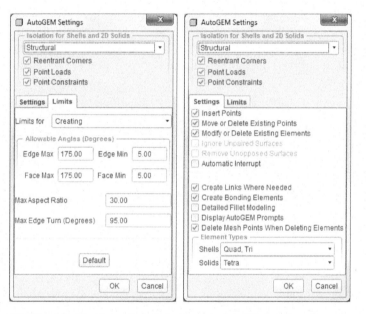

10.70 The Automatic Mesh Generation Dialog Box Panels. *Allowable angles for the mesh are input into a dialog box.*

4 Next, the material properties for the part are specified (if this has not already been done during modeling). In this case, AL 6061 has been chosen from a list of predefined materials (dialog box not shown.)

Mechanica's automatic mesh creation function fits a mesh to the part similar to that shown in Figure 10.71.

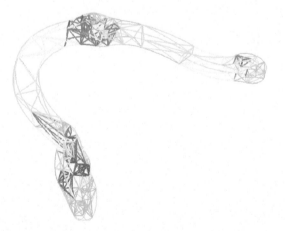

10.71 *The mesh breaks the part into elements that can be analyzed as discrete solvable parts.*

5 Now the model is ready for setting up the analysis (Figure 10.72). Mechanica uses a method called *interpolating polynomials* (P-elements) to solve for the results. Instead of refining the model by increasing the mesh density, using P-elements allows the mesh to remain the same, and the order of the interpolating polynomial for the element is increased. The hotter colors shown in Figure 10.71 represent areas where higher polynomial orders are used.

10.72   Setting Up the Analysis

6 In this case von Mises effective stress analysis was selected because it analyzes the combined results of stresses in all the different directions. This means that the analysis combines the various shear and normal stresses, then represents them as a single stress that you can relate to material properties. This is useful for determining maximum loading.

Next, the analysis is run and the results verified. Figure 10.73 shows the results of a quick check analysis. Hot colors (such as orange) are used to represent higher stresses. Cool colors (such as blue) represent lower stresses. Figure 10.74 shows a more refined analysis. The quick check might be used for base testing, but it is unlikely to yield useful analytical results.

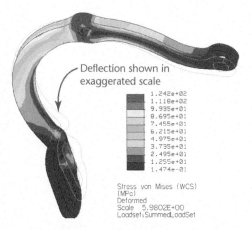

10.73   A Quick Check of the von Mises Plot for the Left Brake Arm. *The key indicates values for the stress regions.*

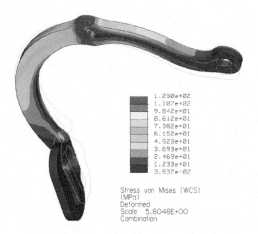

10.74   The Left Brake Arm Analysis Using Increased Model Density

STEP by STEP

Simulation Software

Simulation software allows you to simulate the function of a mechanism or mechanical system using rules that define how the parts will behave. Once you have modeled the mechanism's behaviors accurately you can set the simulation into motion to see how the model will behave under different conditions or in response to different inputs. Most simulations provide a visual representation of the action as well as numerical data about key behaviors. The ability to inspect the behavior of the device or system visually is a tool you can use to test designs early on—before prototyping—and to get a feel for how they will work. The data generated by the simulation can be used to assess how well the design meets criteria for the project. A simple 2D example is the four-bar linkage shown in Figure 10.75.

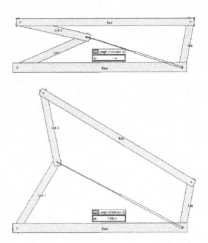

10.75   *This four-bar linkage was modeled in a 2D version of Working Model.*

Many 3D modelers today offer a motion analysis feature that allows you to see and measure a mechanical device in action. Adams and Working Model 3D are two simulation software packages that can work with the CAD data. Other simulation software exists for specific purposes such as wind tunnel simulations and manufacturing simulations. The broad term *simulation* can be applied to any program that reasonably mimics the behavior of a system.

In mechanical design, simulations can be especially effective in the area of kinematics, or the study of motion. Figure 10.76 shows a virtual prototype of a wind turbine simulated in MSC Software's Adams Multiphysics software. Although parts may be rotated through a range of motion in the CAD assembly model, simulating complex interactions among parts in an assembly may be accomplished better in a dedicated kinematics package.

In most cases, the CAD model can be imported directly or after being exported to a .dxf, STEP, or IGES file. Once the model is imported, part and assembly constraints are further constrained to model the kind of action allowed. Degrees of

10.76   *Simulation allows manufacturers to design better performing and more reliable systems by predicting how wind turbines will behave throughout their lifecycle. (Courtesy of MSC Software Corporation.)*

freedom define the directions in which a part can move. Materials and their properties are assigned to each part in the assembly (either in the CAD model or in the simulation software), as are motors and power sources. The appropriate forces are applied to the model, and other environmental settings (such as gravity) can be set to simulate action on the moon or in space.

Once the 3D model has been built, more complex analysis can be completed. The CAD model becomes a "virtual prototype" after joints and constraints are applied. In motorcycle design, for example, stability and safety of the design are a function of how the torque and stress induced by acceleration are handled by the vehicle. A designer can test the vehicle as if it were a real prototype and take accurate measurements of torque and tension. Variations on the design can be tested as the design is optimized.

In the example in Figure 10.77, robot actions are simulated in a 3D virtual world where process parameters critical to achieving system requirements are easy to visualize. For example, the transparent walls that define the working area of the robot are not visible in the real world, but they define the robot's work envelope in a way that is easy to understand. System users modify the virtual walls (and other parameters) and use ROBOGUIDE to optimize the performance of the system (Figure 10.78). The optimized parameters and motion paths can then be downloaded to the real robot system.

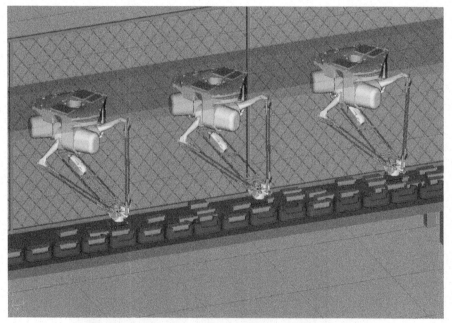

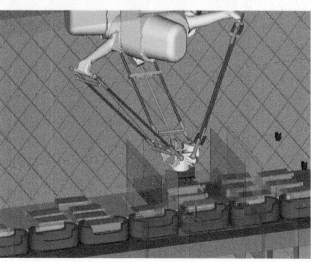

10.77   In these images, FANUC's ROBOGUIDE software is being used to validate high-speed picking and placing of parts by the robots shown. In the simulation, parts flow randomly into the robot work cell at 300 parts per minute. Multiple robots share the material-handling pick process and then place the parts into an outfeed packaging container. In the bottom figure, you can see the virtual transparent walls that define the working area of the robot. (Courtesy of FANUC America Corporation.)

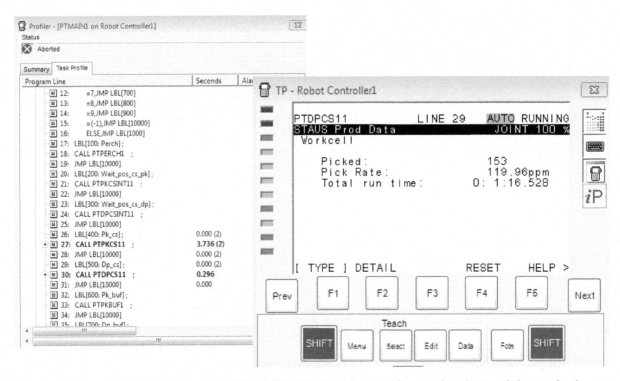

10.78   *Using metrics provided by FANUC's ROBOGUIDE, you can analyze and understand the result of process modifications. You can make changes to the simulated system and evaluate the result before implementing it in the real world. Changes to process parameters result in changes to characteristics such as motion cycle time and process throughput. The images above show detailed robot cycle time and process throughput information available in the software.* (Courtesy of FANUC America Corporation.)

When a simulation has been created directly from a CAD model, any change to the CAD model can automatically update the simulation. This interaction makes it even easier to use the simulation to guide the iterative process of design.

Human Factors

Human factors analysis considers how people will interact with a design. As you are designing, consider the qualities of the users of the system or product. Human populations have general characteristics, such as average height and language, that may affect their ability to use or operate the device you are designing. Operator visibility (see Figure 10.79), the complexity of the controls, and the ability of the operator to correctly map a control to its function are all ergonomic considerations. In addition, you also need to consider the people who will assemble, service, and repair the product. You can use your CAD model to help determine the sizes for access openings, critical distances that affect users' reach, and other important information for usability.

A variety of software products work with the CAD data to test human factors. The CAD model can be imported into the software, or human models can be imported into the CAD environment to see how they fit with the model (shown in Figure 10.80). NexGen's HumanCAD software models typical humans from 11 different populations, including databases of human sizes such as 1988 Natick US Army and NASA-STD-3000. These populations provide a range of ethnic

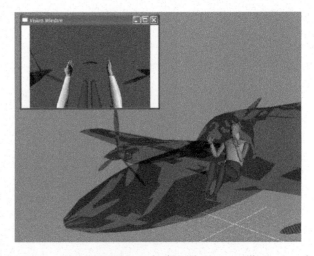

10.79   *This view through the pilot's eyes illustrates the ability of the pilot to see the runway from the airplane cockpit. Operator visibility is an important factor in meeting safety requirements as well as functional goals.* (Courtesy of NexGen Ergonomics, Inc., www.nexgenergo.com.)

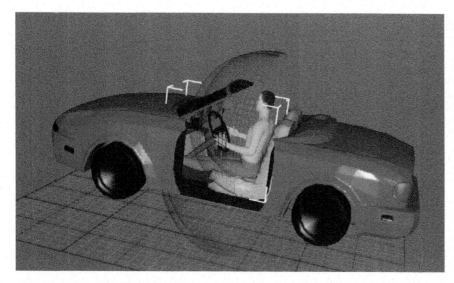
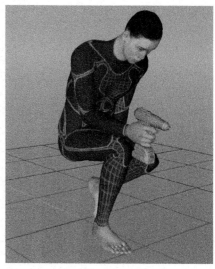

10.80   Human Models. *Models can be added to your CAD models to test human interactions using inverse and forward kinematics as well as to test reach, vision, and other criteria. Different hand tools can be evaluated for gripping and posture by simply importing them.* (Courtesy of NexGen Ergonomics, Inc., www.nexgenergo.com.)

groups, size percentiles, body types, ages, cultures, and gender that you can then fit with your CAD model to see how different categories of people might interact with the design. The library includes typical predefined body and hand positions, linked for realistic human motion ranges, that you can import and export among your design software using common file formats. It even provides physically challenged mannequins that you can use to test accessibility. You can also use mannequin software to "see" the view from the mannequin's eyes as it moves along

a path that you define, and to simulate lifting, pushing, and pulling by adding forces and torque in any direction on any body part.

Testing with a variety of virtual human sizes allows you to determine whether production line employees or machine operators can safely work by determining what they can see or reach (Figure 10.81). A variety of ergonomic analysis tools also enable you to analyze lifting, pushing, pulling, and other tasks in a virtual environment.

10.81   *Human factor analysis can determine whether controls are reachable.* (© 2016 Siemens Product Lifecycle Management System. Reprinted with permission.)

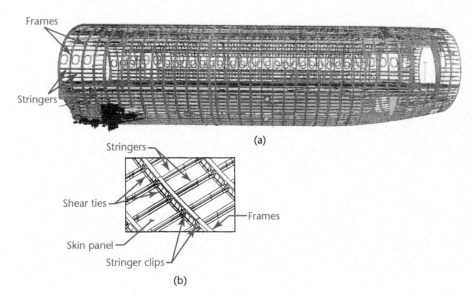

Frames

Stringers

Stringers

Shear ties

Skin panel

Stringer clips

Frames

(a)

(b)

10.82 *Design and manufacturing rules for the many similar parts in the aircraft fuselage were used to create a system that would automate much of the part modeling in CATIA, Boeing's 3D modeling system. The structural framework is visible in the assembly model of the fuselage in (a); the system of frames, stringers, stringer clips, and shear ties used to support the skin is illustrated in (b). (Copyright © Boeing.)*

Integrated Modeling and Design Software

The iterative nature of design refinement is fueling software tools that will allow the design to be modeled and analyzed in one software environment. Many analysis packages already provide tools that make it easier to alternate between the analysis package and the CAD model.

Design rules that can be used for design optimization have also generated a closer link between constraint-based modelers and equation solvers. Using design rules to automate the optimization and/or creation of model geometry has been successfully used at Boeing in the design of certain aspects of the fuselage system for commercial aircraft. The central fuselage of the Boeing 777, for example, is made of 50 skin panels, each of which contains more than four hundred parts. These four hundred–plus parts are the framework to which the aircraft's "skin" is attached. Each frame, stringer, stringer clip, and shear tie, illustrated in Figure 10.82, is very similar to the next one, but not exactly the same. Each is modeled individually because each may vary in the holes added to accommodate wiring, fasteners, and so on. Each is also individually designed to weigh as little as possible. Chemical milling is used to remove all unnecessary material from each part to reduce the weight of the aircraft. Rule-based design has eliminated much of the work of modeling these 20,000 parts. The Boeing knowledge-based engineering system uses both design rules and

10.83 *A manufacturing rule expresses the limits of the manufacturing process, such as chemical milling, that will be used. (Copyright © Boeing.)*

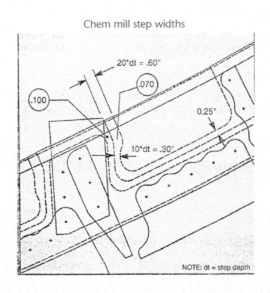

Chem mill step widths

20*dt = .60"

.070

.100

0.25"

10*dt = .30"

NOTE: dt = step depth

manufacturing rules to ensure that each part is structurally sound and optimized for weight (Figure 10.83). For example, one design rule is that chemical milling to reduce the thickness of the part must stop .75 inch from a hole in the part. This ensures that the strength of the area around the attachment will not be compromised. Manufacturing rules are derived from the limits of the manufacturing process used to remove excess weight. No part may be designed that cannot be milled. The parameters defining each feature of the part are evaluated against these rules both to optimize the design and to automate much of the part creation.

As you use your CAD database for analysis in downstream applications you should familiarize yourself with the options being developed that can facilitate the exchange of information among packages and the use of analytical tools in design refinement.

SPOTLIGHT

Getting Easier Being Green

SolidWorks Sustainability is a module that provides life cycle assessment (LCA) within the SolidWorks user interface. It gives you information about environmentally friendly options for your engineering design decisions. This software allows you to conduct life cycle analyses of parts and assemblies. You can use it to see the environmental impact in terms of air, carbon, energy, and water.

To see if you improve your design's environmental impact as you modify it, you can capture the existing baseline, then track how your new design compares. The Find Similar Material dialog box shown lets you search the material database for alternative materials based on their mechanical properties. As you choose them you can visually assess the magnitude and direction of their environmental impact with the charts in the panel at the bottom.

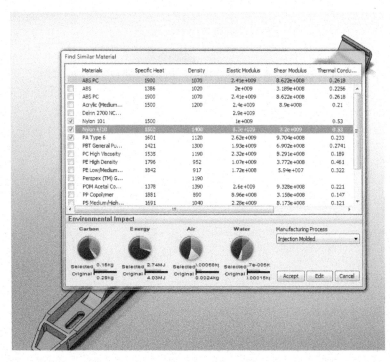

(Image courtesy of ©2016 Dassault Systèmes SolidWorks Corporation.)

10.19 PROTOTYPING YOUR DESIGN

No matter how accurate your CAD model, it is never exactly the same as the manufactured part. Traditionally, building a prototype was the best way to ensure that a design could be manufactured and that it would operate as desired when it was built. Today, the information in the 3D solid modeling database changed the role of the physical prototype in two key ways: it has made it possible to simulate a prototype with the 3D model, and it has made it faster and cheaper to create a physical prototype than ever before.

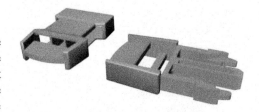

10.84 *Complex molded shapes can be prototyped cost effectively with rapid prototyping systems.*

A simulated prototype—often referred to as a *virtual* prototype—can serve many of the purposes of a physical model.

The same information in the CAD database can also be used to direct rapid prototyping processes that generate physical models relatively inexpensively.

Rapid Prototyping

Rapid prototyping (RP) systems let you create a prototype directly from a CAD design within minutes or hours instead of the days or weeks it might otherwise take.

What is it worth to the design process to have an actual part that people can hold in their hands? As a visualization tool and a means for checking the fit with other parts, a physical model is a valuable aid in reducing the time it takes a company to develop a product idea from a sketch to a product that is available in the marketplace. Approximately 10% of all manufacturing and design shops spend over $100,000 each year for prototypes. The resulting confidence in the design and improved ability to communicate with the customer about the design in an understandable way is an important advantage of rapid prototyping. Rapid tooling processes use the same 3D CAD information to produce molds and other tooling that can reduce the time to market even further.

Rapid prototypes are especially useful for prototypes of complex molded parts. Molds for fairly simple plastic parts can cost from $20,000 to $50,000, making them prohibitively expensive to create just for checking a design appearance. With rapid prototyping, single parts can be produced in a matter of hours and used to verify the design. In addition, complex shapes can be created as easily as simpler ones.

Despite its advantages over traditional processes, rapid prototyping is not lightning fast. A part that is $2 \times 3 \times 1$ inch may take an hour or longer to create. However, the time does not usually depend on the complexity of the part, just the size and accuracy built into the prototype file, and the type of process used. Parts that would ordinarily have to be molded or cast can be created in the same amount of time required for a rectangular block of about the same dimensions. The complexity of each slice does not have much effect on the time needed to create the part. Although a rectangular block is easy to manufacture using traditional machining methods, the buckle shown in Figure 10.84 is a good candidate for rapid prototyping because of its complex shape.

Translating the Model

Rapid prototyping systems all work on a similar principle: they slice the CAD model into thin layers, then create the model layer by layer from a material that can be fused to the next layer until the entire part is realized.

To send a CAD file to most rapid prototyping systems, you usually export a file in the STL file format. This file type was developed to export CAD data to an early rapid prototyping system. Since then, it has become the de facto standard for exporting CAD data to RP systems.

STL files define the boundaries of the CAD model using triangular facets. This format transforms any model into a standardized definition, but it has the disadvantage of generating a very large file when a realistic shape is required. You

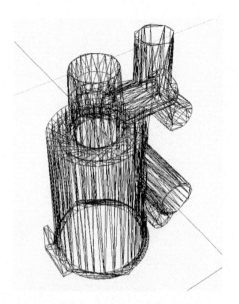

10.85 *Triangular facets that define the boundaries of the model will be more visible on curved surfaces and when the facet size used is large.*

usually have the option of setting the size of the facets when you export your model. If the facets are small and the model complex, the resulting STL file will be very large. If a larger size for the triangular facets is used, however, the prototyped part will have noticeable facets on its curved surfaces, as shown in Figure 10.85. Some exports can use smaller facets around more detailed features and larger facets around less detailed ones.

Once the CAD file has been exported, thin slices through the model are generated to create the layers (Figure 10.86). Generally speaking, the thinner the slice, the more accurate the part—however, thinner slices also mean that it will take longer to generate the prototype part.

The accuracy of the model's surface is limited by the material used in the process and how small the layers and features are that it can make. A prototype part created by depositing individual layers of material in the X-Y plane and dropping the table down in the Z-plane necessarily produces a jagged edge. The size of the *jaggies*, as these are often called, is dependent on the thickness of the layer of material that is deposited. This thickness is limited by the size of the smallest particles that can be fused together. RP systems that have more than three axes of movement can reduce or eliminate the jagged appearance by filling in material on angled edge surfaces.

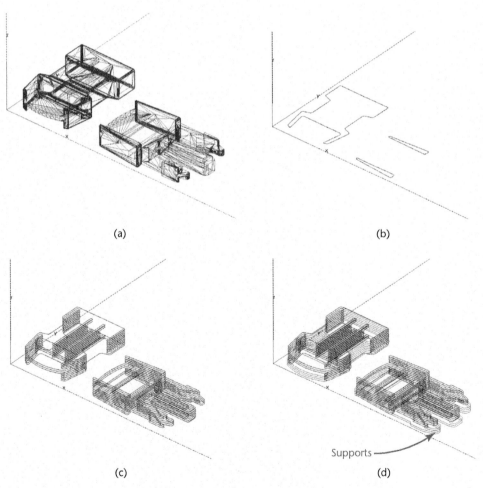

(a)

(b)

(c)

Supports

(d)

10.86   Slices. *(a) The model is imported as an STL file.*
(b and c) Slices through the model are generated (.01 intervals shown here).
(d) The software generates supports (shown here with lighter lines) for segments of the part that do not rest on one of the lower slices.

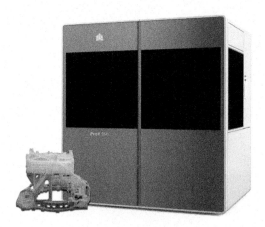

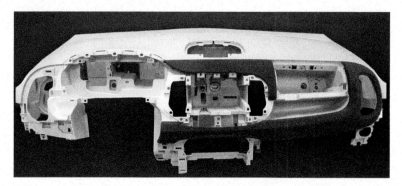

10.87 Stereolithography. *3D Systems ProX™ 950 SLA Production Printer makes it possible to directly manufacture precise plastic parts without CNC machining or injection molding. Part size can range from smaller than the eye of a needle to a full-size automobile dashboard. (Courtesy of 3D Systems, Inc.)*

Rapid Prototyping Systems

Rapid prototyping systems vary in the types of materials used, in the size of the model that can be created, and in the time it takes to generate a part. If your company owns a rapid prototyping system, the choice of system may be moot. If not, you should consider the design questions the prototype needs to answer when selecting an appropriate system. The accuracy, size, durability, and time it takes to create a prototype are dependent on the process and material used.

The main categories of rapid prototyping equipment are stereolithography, selective laser sintering, fused deposition modeling, and 3D printing. Most rapid prototyping systems can create parts up to about 10 cubic inches in size. Laminate object manufacturing and topographic shell fabrication are two less common methods that allow you to create prototypes of larger parts. 3D printing also offers options for large parts, such as the car being printed in Figure 10.88.

Stereolithography apparatus (SLA) uses laser-hardened resins to form the model. Figure 10.87 shows an SLA system. The system software controls a focused laser beam in a pool of light-sensitive polymer. The laser hardens each layer in the shape of the cross section or slice of the part. As successive layers are hardened they are submerged slightly into the resin pool and the next layer is hardened on top of them. Holes and pockets in the model are formed by uncured resin that easily pours out of the resulting part. SLA systems create durable parts that can be painted and finished to look very similar to the finished product. The range of accuracy for SLA parts can be up to ± 0.05 mm. Because of this accuracy, the prototype parts created using SLA can have relatively smooth surface finishes. SLA is an established technology, since it was the first method on the market.

Solid ground curing (SGC) systems are similar to SLA systems except that they use ultraviolet light to cure an entire cross section at once in the polymer pool. A negative of the shape of the cross section is created on a glass plate using electrostatic toner (similar to the process used in a copying machine), then used to mask ultraviolet light in the shape of

10.88 The Swim 3D Printed Car (top) as It Is Being Printed (bottom) *(Courtesy of Local Motors.)*

10.89 Cznger Vehicles 21C. *The Cznger 21C car was designed with the help of artificial intelligence and takes advantage of advances in additive manufacturing (AM) to produce the entire car without using tools. An SLS system using twelve lasers simultaneously is key to "printing" the chassis. Most automotive companies print a few components and then assemble them with other traditionally manufactured parts. (Photo of Cznger Vehicles' 21C courtesy of @iamted7.)*

10.90 *The 21C car was entirely modeled in 3D and designed for additive manufacturing, making it easy to produce printed prototypes of the vehicle in various scales. (Divergent 3D Factory photo courtesy of Marc Weisberg.)*

the cross section. With no lasers to replace, these systems are cost-effective and create accurate, durable parts.

Direct Light Processing (DLP), Continuous Liquid Interface Production (CLIP), Digital Light Synthesis™ (Carbon DLS™), and Daylight Polymer Printing (DPP) are updated takes on the general SLA concept.

DLP 3D uses a digital projector to cure a single layer at once. Some types of parts can be printed faster than SLA systems where the cured image layer is "drawn" using a laser, but the disadvantage can be the pixel shape in the rasterized image (or "voxel" as it is called in 3D).

CLIP's vat of resin is exposed to light through a window at the bottom of the vat, which solidifies the cross-section being projected onto it. The solidified shape is slowly raised and new liquid resin flows beneath it. Even though the printing is done in very fine layers, the resin flooding is continuous, allowing for much faster print times.

Daylight Polymer Printing (DPP) cures special daylight sensitive polymers using standard Liquid Crystal Display (LCD) screens.

All of the SLA type methods may require post process washing, spinning, or other methods to remove the excess resin and support structures needed in the build. Developing environmentally friendly polymers and reducing waste from uncured polymer and cleaning solvents is an ongoing area of improvement.

Selective laser sintering (SLS) uses a focused laser to fuse powdered metals, plastics, or ceramics. (Figure 10.93 shows an SLS-type rapid prototyping system.) The fused layer is covered with additional powder, and the next layer is fused to it. To form a hole in the prototyped piece, the powdered material is simply not fused in that area. The unfused powder still acts as a base for the next layer, but when the part is completed, the unfused portions are simply poured out (see Figure 10.94). This process has the advantage that models created from powdered metal can sometimes be machined for further refinement. The parts can also be strong enough to be used in certain types of assemblies as one-of-a-kind parts. When metals are used as the material the process may be termed Direct Metal Printing (DMP) or Direct Metal Laser Sintering (DMLS). When a high-energy electron beam is used instead of a laser, the process is termed Electron Beam Melting (EBM).

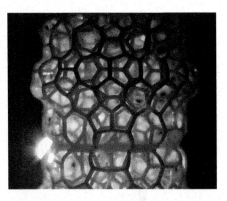

10.91 Carbon Digital Light Synthesis™ is similar to Digital Light Processing (DLP). *It uses a cassette to hold resin with a window below that projects the digital light image to cure the layer. The cassette provides a thin layer ready to polymerize and cure and allows fast print speeds. Advanced materials allow mixing of light and thermally cured materials, where the UV resin holds the thermally cured material in place for printing, and then is removed before curing. (Courtesy of Carbon, Inc.)*

10.92 *DLS allows for production of strong lightweight parts for direct manufacturing, such as this bicycle seat. (Courtesy of Carbon, Inc.)*

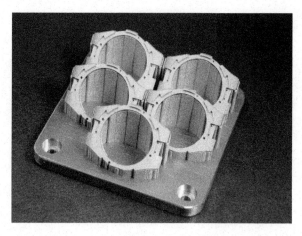

10.93   Selective Laser Sintering. *SLS fuses powdered metals and other materials to form parts. The ProX 300™ printer from 3D Systems lets you create dense metal and ceramic parts with fine machining tolerances and a repeatability of about 20 microns in all three axes. Materials include stainless steel, tool steel, super alloys, non-ferrous alloys, precious metals, and alumina. (Courtesy of 3D Systems, Inc.)*

An SLS system can create parts with accuracies of plus or minus 0.1 mm. Other materials, such as a glass-filled nylon, may be used with the sintering process to create parts with varying degrees of flexibility and durability. Elastomeric materials with rubberlike characteristics, for example, make it possible to prototype gaskets and athletic equipment.

Fused deposition modeling (FDM) systems use molten plastic deposited in layers corresponding to cross sections on the part. Because the soft molten plastic cannot be deposited in thin air, to make a hole or an overhang, a second type of plastic is used to create a support structure. Because the two plastics are different materials that do not readily adhere to one another, the support structure can be separated from the actual part. (Figure 10.86d shows these supports being formed by the RP software.) A part that is about 3 × 2 × 1 inch takes about three hours to create. MultiJet 3D Printers (MJP) print thin layers of liquid plastic onto a platform. Each layer is cured using UV light. A second wax material is used to build support structure. The build platform lowers for the next layer and the process continues layer by layer until the part is complete.

10.94   *This artist's laser sintered design would be very difficult to manufacture using traditional methods. (Courtesy of Vladimir Bulatov.)*

Laminated object manufacturing (LOM) produces solid parts from sheets of material, such as paper or vinyl. LOM systems can be used to create larger prototype parts. As in all rapid prototyping processes, software first generates cross-sectional slices through the model. Instead of fusing the slice, however, a computer-controlled laser cuts it from the first sheet of material. Then, a heated roller bonds the next sheet to the previous layer, and the next cross section is cut from this sheet. The material that will later be removed is cut into crosshatched shapes to make removal easier.

Topographic shell fabrication (TSF) uses layers of high-quality silica sand fused together with wax to build shells that can be used to mold rapid prototypes of large-scale parts. The sand is deposited in layers and then fused with molten wax sprayed from a computer-controlled three-axis nozzle. More sand is deposited and then the next layer is fused. The layers range from .05-inch to .15-inch thick and take about ten minutes per square foot of model to print. Once all the slices have been deposited, the sand/wax shell is smoothed, then lined with plaster or other material. The shell is then used as a temporary mold for creating parts of fiberglass, epoxy, foam, concrete, or other materials. This method is able to handle very large shapes up to 11 × 6 × 4 feet.

10.95   *An ever-increasing range of materials can be used in rapid prototyping systems, such as chocolate and sugar shown here, as well as materials suitable for prototyping integrated circuits. (Courtesy of 3D Systems, Inc.)*

10.96   A 3D Printer *(Courtesy of 3D Systems, Inc.)*

3D Printing/Material Jetting

Rapid prototyping systems referred to as 3D printing or material jetting systems "print" layers of molten thermoplastic material. These low-cost machines were designed to enable the use of prototypes early and often in the design cycle. The relatively low cost 3D printing systems (currently under $5,000) can be operated safely enough that they can sit next to the regular office printer or copier. Another advantage of 3D printer systems is that those having a three-axis print head can deposit the plastic on the edges of the part in a way that creates a smooth model surface (see Figure 10.97). Contemporary systems are being used with a wide variety of materials, such as carbon fiber-reinforced thermoplastics, that are strong enough for rapid manufacturing using 3D printing methods (Figure 10.98).

10.97   *Multiple materials and colors can be printed at the same time using different print heads. (Courtesy of 3D Systems, Inc.)*

(a)

(b)

10.98   *(a) This close-up view shows the print head of the 3D printer depositing a layer of material; (b) The fenders for the car in Figure 10.88 are being printed. (Courtesy of Local Motors.)*

Rapid Tooling

Rapid prototyping systems were developed to produce parts without having to create a mold or complete intermediate steps needed to manufacture a part. ***Rapid tooling*** is a similar process, but one that creates the *tool* (usually a mold for molded plastic or cast metal parts) through a rapid prototyping process, not the part itself (Figure 10.99). Metal injection molds and molds for cast metal parts are often one of the most expensive and time-consuming parts of the design process. Rapid tooling processes can reduce the amount of time involved in producing these tools. The resulting rapid tool can be used to produce test products and to get products to market early.

Rapid tooling can be accomplished by several different methods. One is direct mold design, in which the tool itself is created using a selective laser sintering–type process. Another method uses rapid prototyping to produce a master part from which a silicone rubber mold is formed. That mold is then used to make other parts. A third method (a more traditional process) uses computer-controlled machining technology to create the cavity in a mold blank to quickly create the mold.

Using a CAD file as input, the SLS process melts (or sinters) the powder to form a green mold shape consisting of metal particles bound by smaller areas of polymer. When the green mold is heated in a furnace, the plastic polymer burns off, leaving only the metal mold. The mold is then machined to a tolerance of $\pm.005$ inch to eliminate any defects and can be drilled, tapped, welded, and plated like a conventional mold.

With different materials, cores and molds for sand casting can be created directly using an SLS system, then cured (hardened) in a conventional sand casting oven. Another application is in ***investment casting***, in which an original shape called a master is used to create the proper-shaped opening in a mold. The master is typically made of a wax material so that it will melt out of the mold when molten metal is poured in. Investment casting masters can be produced using SLS processes.

Silicon rubber molds are another means of producing rapid tooling. This process uses an accurately prototyped part that is then coated with silicon rubber to form a mold from

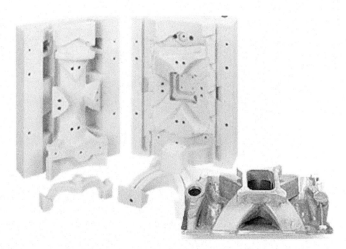

10.99   *This mold was created by a rapid tooling process.* (Courtesy of 3D Systems, Inc.)

which more parts can be molded. The MCP Vacuum Casting System, which uses this process, is capable of producing large plastic parts that weigh as much as 12 pounds and span 2 feet by 3 feet.

Rapid NC machining of mold inserts from a 3D CAD file also promotes rapid tooling. Even though this is more of a traditional process that creates the mold cavity by removing material, the NC-machined cavity combined with standard mold blanks can often lead to shorter tooling times for injection-molded parts. Metal spraying is another method that can be used in rapid tool production for less complex parts.

Despite the ease with which rapid tooling and rapid prototyping create physical models from CAD data, a strong understanding of traditional and current manufacturing methods will enable you to produce more cost-effective and producible parts.

SPOTLIGHT

Cores and Cavities

Molded parts are formed by cavities and cores. The ***cavity*** is the part of the mold that forms the outside shape of the object. The colloquial use of the term *mold* generally refers to the cavity. Holes that will be formed in molded parts are formed by cores. A ***core*** is a solid shape that fits inside the mold. It will form a hole in the cooled cast metal or molten plastic. Cores for cast metal parts are often made of packed sand. After the cast metal is cooled, the part is pounded to loosen the particles of sand from one another so they can be poured out through a small hole. This is similar to the way nonhardened resin or unfused powdered metal is poured out of holes in rapid prototypes.

TESTING THE MODEL: VIBRATION ANALYSIS

Lasers are subjected to some intense conditions. Installed in a wind tunnel, the assembly needs to withstand supersonic wind velocities. In a helicopter, the laser needs to function despite vibrations from the engine and rotors. Each of these generates vibrations at different frequencies. Before Quantel USA builds a prototype for testing, it uses the 3D model and SolidWorks Simulation to "shake up" the laser assembly to see how the parts will respond to vibrations at frequencies typical for the application.

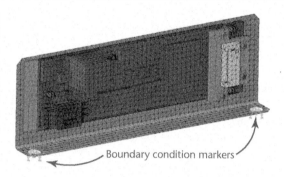

Boundary condition markers

10.101   The Mesh Applied to the Model

10.100   *The circuit board attaches to the sheet metal mount, which attaches via two bolts.*

The circuit board shown in Figure 10.100 generates a high-voltage pulse to a laser optic. It is mounted to a cantilevered sheet metal part that attaches to the laser assembly with two bolts. When the circuit board and mounting assembly are subjected to vibrations at different frequencies, will the resultant deflection (bending) result in failure? Laine McNeil, Senior Mechanical Engineer, set up a simulation to help find out.

First, he prepared the model for testing by generating a mesh appropriate for each part. Choosing the right kind of mesh and the right density (number of nodes) is a judgment call driven by the goals of the test. For example, the board components had been tested before, so McNeil could focus on the board and the cantilevered sheet metal part. For the circuit board, McNeil specified a 3D mesh to reflect the thickness of the board (see Figure 10.101). For the sheet metal mount, he chose a shell mesh and selected sheet metal as the material whose properties the mesh would use.

It is common to simplify the 3D model (by removing fillets, perhaps) to reduce the number of nodes in the mesh. Adding nodes improves accuracy, but it also increases the time needed for analysis. For example, the shell mesh chosen for the mount uses one surface of the part and applies the stiffness properties uniformly over the entire part. This generated fewer nodes, but provided enough complexity to adequately represent the sheet metal part.

McNeil next set up the boundary conditions for the assembly: what are the constraints on how the parts can move? First, how are the parts attached to each other? Parts can be bonded or attached in a way that they cannot move or slide (fixed geometry), hinged, connected via a roller/slider, or supported by a spring. The circuit board was mounted in place with three rubber interfacing pads. The rubber was bonded on one end to the sheet metal mount and to the circuit board at the other for this analysis.

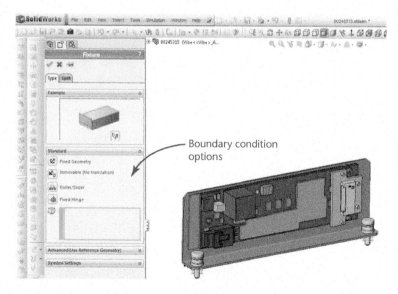

Boundary condition options

10.102   Choosing Boundary Conditions for the Circuit Board

Second, how are the parts connected to the outside world? The sheet metal mount is attached solely by its two bolts, so boundary conditions were set for the two bolt holes (shown in green in Figure 10.102). That is, only the bolt forces and friction are holding the mount; everything else can compress and deflect in the simulation. McNeil could have chosen "on flat surface" for the mount so that the part would not be allowed to deflect downward, only up, but that was not needed for this test.

The model was now analyzed at frequencies expected for its target use. Typical vibration frequencies range from 100 to 2000 hertz. Some clients have minimum standards that must be met, such as the U.S. military's "minimum integrity test." For the circuit board analysis, no deflection was detected in the sheet metal mount until almost 280 hertz. Figure 10.103c shows the deflection. The material between the bolt holes is shaded a lighter blue to indicate a small amount of movement, and the upper cantilevered portion of the sheet metal mount is colored red, indicating significantly higher motion. The circuit board had already been tested to conform to the minimum integrity test. Because the circuit board operated reliably despite the first resonant frequency mode shape showing that deformation occurred at as low as 120 hertz, McNeil could be confident that the assembly would be satisfactory as designed.

This result was not always the case. When the circuit board components were initially tested, the cube (representing a power supply) at the top left in Figure 10.103a fell off. It had been soldered onto the board, but the solder pads were not strong enough to hold at typical vibrations. Glue was added beneath the power supply to strengthen the bond.

In addition to simple resonant frequency shape generation, analysis can also simulate the energy driving the vibration and the associated displacement. Two examples of vibration-generating devices can readily demonstrate the difference. A cell phone vibrates, but the energy driving the vibration is not enough to shake a room. A hydraulically driven vibrator, used to dislodge material from the bed of a dump truck, has enough energy to shake a building one city block away. For the circuit board assembly, McNeil used the built-in capabilities of Solid-Works, so the energy behind the vibration was assumed to be infinite, and the displacement shown for the circuit board parts was not meaningful. In this instance, this was not the focus of the analysis. If determining actual displacement values is required, the model can be analyzed with a higher-end FEA package, in which a power spectral density curve can be used to define the energy levels causing motion.

At Quantel USA, testing the "virtual prototype" does not replace the need for a physical model. For each design a physical model is built and shaken at the frequencies expected during use. But if the model testing is done properly, the physical model passes the test and only one prototype is needed.

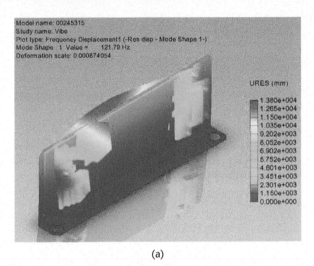

(a)

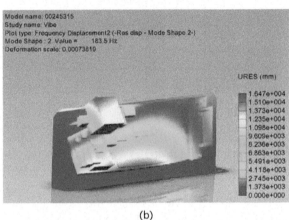

(b)

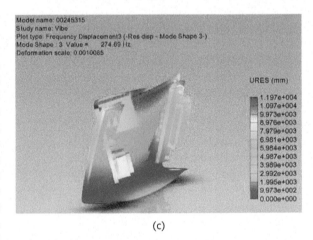

(c)

10.103 Results of Testing at (a) 121.70, (b) 183.5, and (c) 274.69 Hertz

(All images courtesy of Quantel USA.)

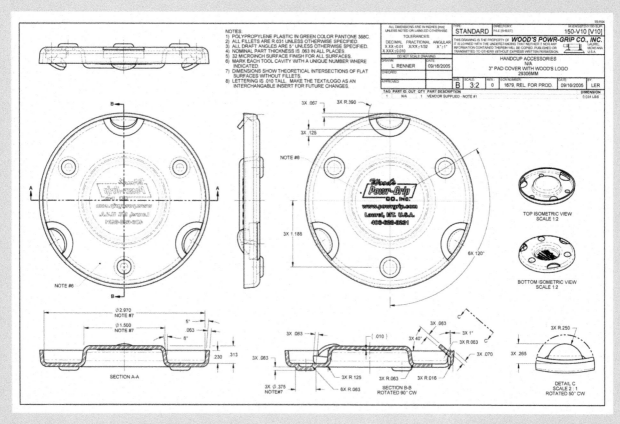

Drawing for a Molded Plastic Part *(Courtesy of Wood's Power-Grip Co., Inc.)*

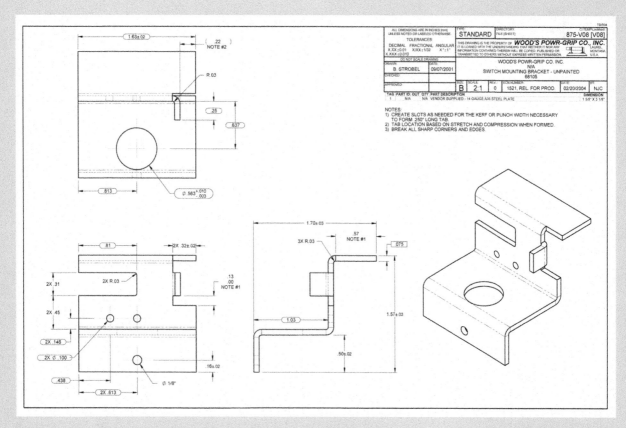

Drawing for a Sheet Metal Part *(Courtesy of Wood's Power-Grip Co., Inc.)*

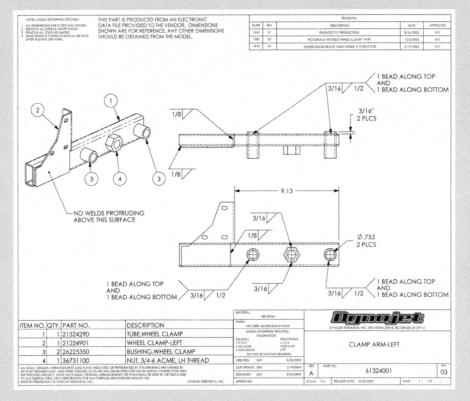

Drawing for a Welded Assembly *(Courtesy of Dynojet Research, Inc.)*

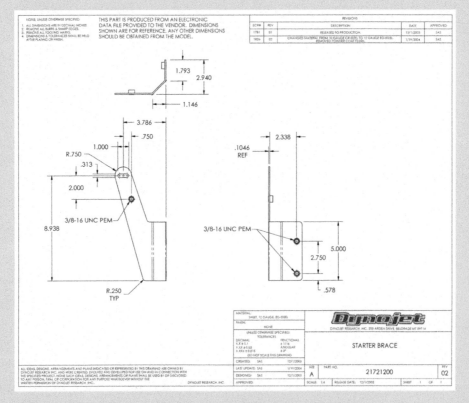

Drawing for a Sheet Metal Part *(Courtesy of Dynojet Research, Inc.)*

TELESCOPE PAINT $\boxed{15 \, DEC \, 97}$ 99

$V_{AMES \atop B.B.} = 5.35 m^2 \cdot 6.0 \times 10^{-4} m = 0.00321 m^3$

$M_{AMES \atop B.B.} = \left(1300 \frac{kg}{m^3} \cdot 0.00321 m^3 \cdot 0.8\right) + \left(3200 \frac{kg}{m^3} \cdot 0.00321 m^3 \cdot 0.2\right)$

$= 3.3384 kg + 2.0544 kg = 5.3928 kg$

$V_{AMES \atop M.T. \& A.T.} = 1.19 m^2 \cdot 6.0 \times 10^{-4} m = 0.000714 m^3$

$M_{AMES \atop M.T. \& A.T.} = \left(1300 \frac{kg}{m^3} \cdot 0.000714 m^3 \cdot 0.8\right) + \left(3200 \frac{kg}{m^3} \cdot 0.000714 m^3 \cdot 0.2\right)$

$= 0.74256 kg + 0.45696 kg = 1.1995 kg$

$V_{DESOTO \atop B.B.} = 5.35 m^2 \cdot 2.032E-4 m = 0.001087 m^3$

$M_{DESOTO \atop B.B.} = \left(1300 \frac{kg}{m^3} \cdot 0.001087 m^3 \cdot 0.8\right) + \left(3200 \frac{kg}{m^3} \cdot 0.001087 m^3 \cdot 0.2\right)$

$= 1.1306 kg + 0.6758 kg = 1.8264 kg$

$V_{DESOTO \atop M.T. \& A.T.} = 1.19 m^2 \cdot 2.032E-4 m = 0.000242 m^3$

$M_{DESOTO \atop M.T. \& A.T.} = \left(1300 \frac{kg}{m^3} \cdot 0.000242 m^3 \cdot 0.8\right) + \left(3200 \frac{kg}{m^3} \cdot 0.000242 m^3 \cdot 0.2\right)$

$= 0.2515 kg + 0.1548 kg = 0.4062 kg$

$\boxed{OUTER \, SHELL \, PAINT \quad DUST \, COVER}$

STANDARD DESOTO BLACK $\rho = 1300 \frac{kg}{m^3}$

DUST COVER -24 MILS   OUTER SHELL - BOTTOM   OUTER SHELL - MIDDLE

$A_{D.C.} = 1.56883 m^2$ $A_{0.S.b.} = 8.48329 m^2 / 4 = 2.12082 m^2$ $A_{0.S.M} = 9.24948 m^2 / 2$

                               $V_{0.S.b} = 2.12082 m^2 (2.032E-4 m)$ $= 4.62474 m^2$

                               $= 0.000431 m^3$ $= 4.41144 m^2 / 2$

                                                                                 $= 2.20572 m^2$

$V_{D.C.} = 1.56883 m^2 (2.032E-4 m) = 0.00039 m^3$ $V_{0.S.M} = 2.20572 m^2 (2.032E-4 m)$

                                                        $= 0.000448 m^3$

10.104 *Even the mass of the paint is calculated into the mass properties for space vehicles. For the SIRTF space telescope, the low-emissivity, silicon-grit-based coating was to be 24 mils thick. In the calculations shown here, the surface area data from the model were used to calculate the mass of the various "paints," one of which turned out to be almost 9 kg. This additional mass resulted in the use of a different coating to keep the mass of the telescope within the design constraints for the project. (Courtesy of Ball Aerospace & Technologies Corporation.)*

KEY WORDS

3D Printing

Adaptive Control (AC)

Allowance

ASCII

Bottom-Up Design

Casting

Cavity

Cellular Manufacturing

Centimeter-Gram-Second

Centroid

Ceramics

Comma-Delimited

Composite Materials

Computer Numerical Control (CNC)

Computer-Aided Manufacturing

Constraint-Based Assemblies

Core

Design for Manufacture (DFM)

Downstream

Draft

Drawing Exchange Format

Dynamic Assemblies

Elasticity

Ergonomics

Expert Systems

Exporting

External Reference

Factor of Safety

Ferrous Metals

Finishing

Finite Elements

Foot-Pound-Second

Forging

Forming and Shaping

Fused Deposition Modeling (FDM)

Global Parameter

Graphics Exchange Format

Group Technology (GT)

Inch-Pound-Second

Industrial Robots

Initial Graphics Exchange Specification

Interference

Investment Casting

Just-in-Time Production (JIT)

Laminated Object Manufacturing (LOM)

Layout Drawings

Life-Cycle Engineering

Machining

Mass Density

Material File

Mesh

Middle-Out Design

Moment of Inertia

Nanofabrication

Nanotechnology

Native File Format

Net-Shape Manufacturing

Neutral Files

Nonferrous Metals

Parting Line

Plastics

Pounds Force

Pounds Mass

Prototype Drawings

Radius of Gyration

Rapid Prototyping

Rapid Tooling

Raster

Right Cylinder

Seed Parts

Selective Laser Sintering (SLS)

Shared Manufacturing

Simulation

Skeleton

Solid Ground Curing (SGC)

Space-Delimited

Standard for the Exchange of Product Model Data (STEP)

Static Assemblies

Static Parts

Stereolithography Apparatus (SLA)

Subassemblies

Tab-Delimited

Templates

Top-Down Design

Topographic Shell Fabrication (TSF)

Vector

Virtual Prototype

Volume

Welding

CHAPTER SUMMARY

- Modern manufacturing involves product design, selection of materials, and selection of processes. The process of transforming raw materials into a finished product is called the manufacturing process.
- The design process requires a clear understanding of the functions and performance expected of that product.
- Concurrent engineering integrates the design process with production to optimize the life cycle of the product.
- Computer-aided design, engineering, and manufacturing are used to construct and study models (prototypes) allowing the designer to conceptualize objects more easily and more cost-efficiently.
- The selection of appropriate materials is key to successful product development.
- Manufacturing processing methods have changed dramatically over the last few decades. More cost- and time-efficient processes can be implemented using computer-integrated manufacturing.

SKILLS SUMMARY

Now that you have completed this chapter you should be able to distinguish between static and dynamic assembly models. Assembly constraints are used in constraint-based modeling to create "intelligent" assemblies. You should be familiar with several types of assembly constraints you may encounter in your software package.

Often, it is desirable to show stock parts in assemblies. Sometimes these parts can be acquired from a vendor. Thread, standard fasteners, and springs are among the stock parts that you may not want to model, as they can easily be indicated by a standard note.

Fit between mating parts in an assembly is an important design consideration. You should be familiar with ways that a CAD database can be used to check fit.

You should be able to list three manufacturing processes that are commonly used to manufacture parts and some of the considerations that may arise when modeling a part that will be manufactured using one of these methods.

When you create an assembly model, you may add standard parts, sheet metal parts, or use it to simulate the range of motion it is capable of. Now that you have completed this chapter, you should begin practicing using your CAD models for engineering analysis. You should be able to extract mass properties data from your CAD models and use them to solve simple engineering problems. You should also be familiar with exporting CAD data to various packages and selecting the best file format for the export. In addition, you should be able to describe how various rapid protoyping systems work to create physical models from CAD data.

REVIEW QUESTIONS

1. Parent-child relationships are important for assemblies built using a constraint-based modeler. What problems might occur, and how could you prevent drawing management problems when deleting or changing component parts in an assembly?

2. Define the differences between a *static assembly* and a *dynamic assembly*. Which method would offer advantages to design teams who access a common database of files through a network?

3. Many of the recent generation of computer modeling programs have capabilities for solid modeling and constraint-based modeling. Research the capabilities of the CAD program, solid modeler, or constraint-based modeler at your school or workplace. What nomenclature, commands, and procedures are used by the program to define capabilities in the following:
   a. External references
   b. Global parameters
   c. Interference checking
   d. Dynamic assemblies

4. A constraint-based modeler is used to create a gear cluster assembly by inserting modeled bicycle gear cogs and spacers onto a splined hub. Axial and radial alignment of the elements is critical to maintaining an accurate model. Define a sensible base point to use when adding individual cogs (gears) to the assembly.

5. Drawing templates, prototype drawings, and seed parts are one means to help assemble parts effectively. What are three advantages of using these file types when beginning a new model?

6. An entry-level engineer is given the job of creating a detailed assembly drawing of a trailer-mounted pump and motor assembly. The engineer models major components such as the diesel motor, the pump, and trailer frame as well as all the small parts such as wheels, tires, nuts, bolts, and lights. When the job is complete (after 10 solid weeks of work) and all the drawing elements are correct, the work is presented to the supervisor. What reaction would be expected from engineering management? Was this an efficient use of resources? Do you have suggestions that would streamline the process?

(Courtesy of REED.)

7. Although 3D modeling can describe part and assembly configuration in accurate detail, many parts or features are rarely included in a model until very late in the process if included at all. List four parts or features that fall into this category, and give reasons for omitting detail.

8. Component models of detail parts or assemblies can be obtained from suppliers and manufacturers. These models save the designer time and reduce the potential for error but can be difficult to use in a constraint-based model. Why? What advantage does the supplier gain from this service?

9. Constraint-based assemblies often have global parameters defined to assist in developing mating features of different parts. Identify which features of the two (mating) parts described in the following drawings would be candidates for shared parameters. (Note the different plotted scale of the parts!)

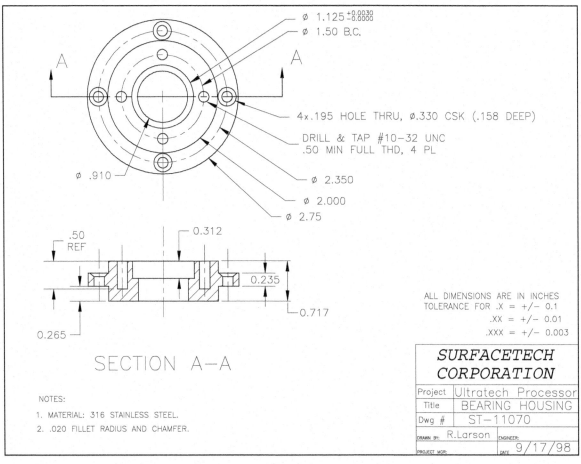

Ø 1.125 +0.0030/-0.0000
Ø 1.50 B.C.

A   A

4x.195 HOLE THRU, ø.330 CSK (.158 DEEP)

DRILL & TAP #10-32 UNC
.50 MIN FULL THD, 4 PL

Ø .910

Ø 2.350

Ø 2.000

Ø 2.75

.50 REF   0.312

0.235

0.717

0.265

SECTION A-A

ALL DIMENSIONS ARE IN INCHES
TOLERANCE FOR .X = +/- 0.1
             .XX = +/- 0.01
             .XXX = +/- 0.003

NOTES:

1. MATERIAL: 316 STAINLESS STEEL.
2. .020 FILLET RADIUS AND CHAMFER.

SURFACETECH CORPORATION

Project	Ultratech Processor
Title	BEARING HOUSING
Dwg #	ST-11070

DRAWN BY: R.Larson	ENGINEER:
PROJECT MGR:	DATE 9/17/98

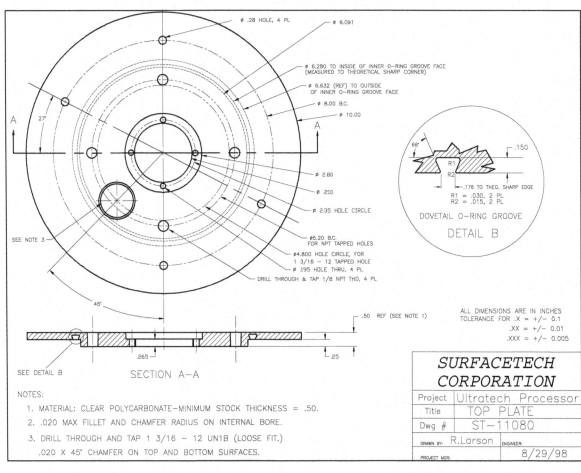

Ø .28 HOLE, 4 PL   Ø 6.091

Ø 6.280 TO INSIDE OF INNER O-RING GROOVE FACE
(MEASURED TO THEORETICAL SHARP CORNER)

Ø 6.632 (REF) TO OUTSIDE
OF INNER O-RING GROOVE FACE

Ø 8.00 B.C.

Ø 10.00

A   27°   A

Ø 2.80

Ø .210

Ø 2.35 HOLE CIRCLE

SEE NOTE 3

ø5.20 B.C.
FOR NPT TAPPED HOLES

ø4.800 HOLE CIRCLE, FOR
1 3/16 - 12 TAPPED HOLE

Ø .195 HOLE THRU, 4 PL

DRILL THROUGH & TAP 1/8 NPT THD, 4 PL

45°

66°   .150

R1
R2

.176 TO THEO. SHARP EDGE
R1 = .030, 2 PL
R2 = .015, 2 PL

DOVETAIL O-RING GROOVE

DETAIL B

.50 REF (SEE NOTE 1)

SEE DETAIL B   .265   .25

SECTION A-A

ALL DIMENSIONS ARE IN INCHES
TOLERANCE FOR .X = +/- 0.1
             .XX = +/- 0.01
             .XXX = +/- 0.005

NOTES:

1. MATERIAL: CLEAR POLYCARBONATE-MINIMUM STOCK THICKNESS = .50.

2. .020 MAX FILLET AND CHAMFER RADIUS ON INTERNAL BORE.

3. DRILL THROUGH AND TAP 1 3/16 - 12 UN1B (LOOSE FIT.)
   .020 X 45° CHAMFER ON TOP AND BOTTOM SURFACES.

SURFACETECH CORPORATION

Project	Ultratech Processor
Title	TOP PLATE
Dwg #	ST-11080

DRAWN BY: R.Larson	ENGINEER:
PROJECT MGR:	8/29/98

10. A designer must anticipate and understand the manufacturing processes that will be used to fabricate the created components. Describe differences in the model for a part designed for polyethylene (plastic) injection molding versus one for machined aluminum. Can you anticipate unique model requirements for a part created using hand lay-up resin-transfer molded composite (a process similar to that used for fiberglass)?

11. Material changes are common in the development phase of engineered parts. Consider a component part modeled first using 6061-T6 Aluminum, and then with 1020 Steel. No dimensional changes are made. Do each of the following properties of a solid change with changing material? How?
    a. Volume
    b. Mass
    c. Density
    d. Centroid
    e. Moment of inertia
    f. Radius of gyration

12. Vector data and raster data are both used in graphics programs. Which type of data format is better suited for CAD systems that have mass properties capability?

13. Define the steps involved in creating a stereolithographic rapid prototype part from a solid model. What are some of the considerations when deciding whether a CAD model is a good candidate for prototyping using stereolithography?

14. Give a brief explanation of the physical process used to create rapid prototype parts by each of the following methods. What are the advantages and disadvantages of each method?
    a. Stereolithography
    b. Fused deposition modeling
    c. Selective laser sintering
    d. 3D printing

15. How does *rapid tooling* differ from *rapid prototyping*? In what situations might either method be used to create actual working components rather than just shape-representative models?

CHAPTER EXERCISES

Exercise 10.1 As directed by your instructor, create a dimensioned sketch or skeleton model that defines the assembly relations for the following devices:

a. Vise grip

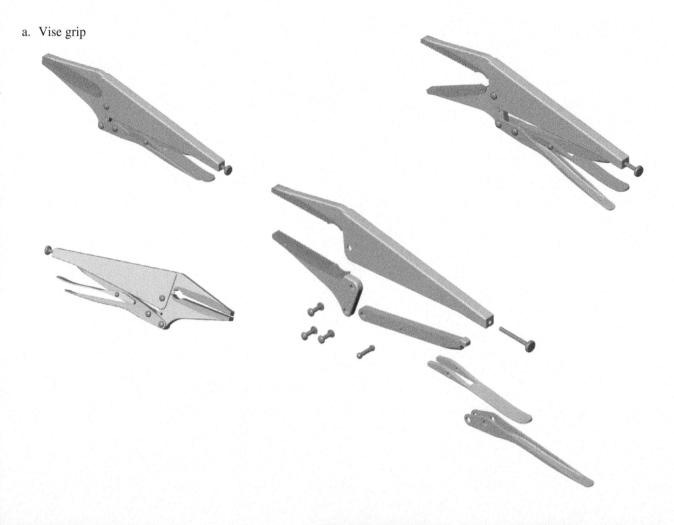

b. Jack

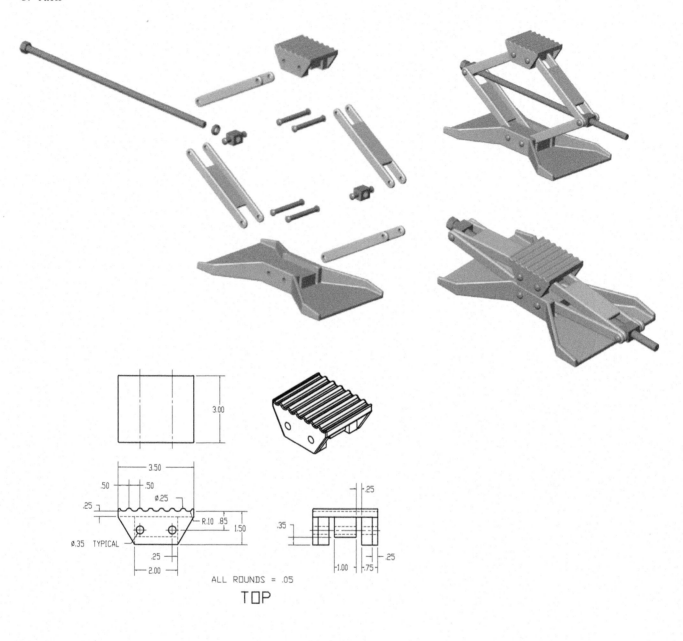

3.00

3.50
.50   .50
Ø.25
.25
Ø.35 TYPICAL
R.10 .85
1.50
.25
2.00

.25
.35
.25
1.00   .75

ALL ROUNDS = .05

TOP

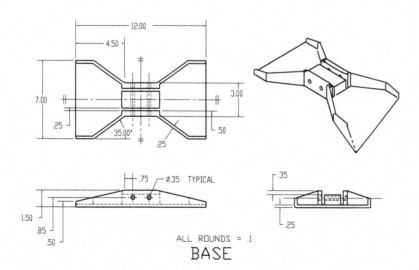

12.00
4.50
3.00
7.00
.25
35.00°
.50
.25

.75   Ø.35 TYPICAL

.35

1.50
.85
.50

.25

ALL ROUNDS = .1

BASE

b. Jack parts *(continued)*

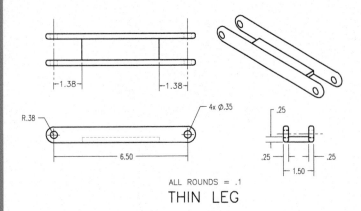

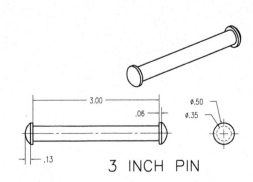

ALL ROUNDS = .1

THIN LEG

3 INCH PIN

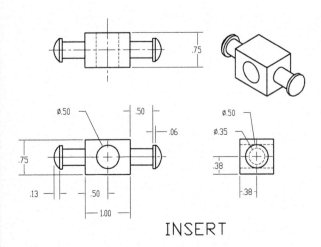

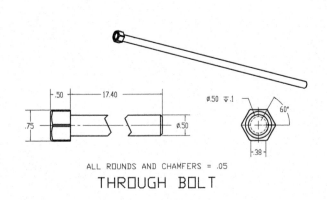

INSERT

ALL ROUNDS AND CHAMFERS = .05

THROUGH BOLT

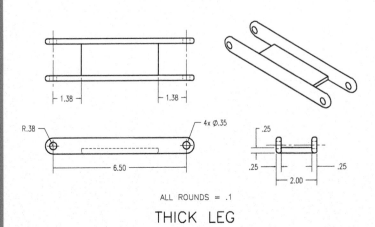

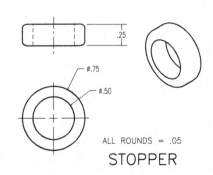

ALL ROUNDS = .1

THICK LEG

ALL ROUNDS = .05

STOPPER

c. Remote control

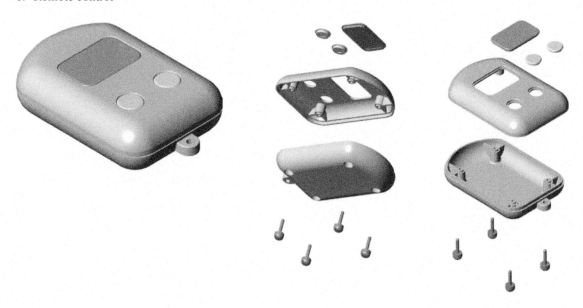

d. Compass

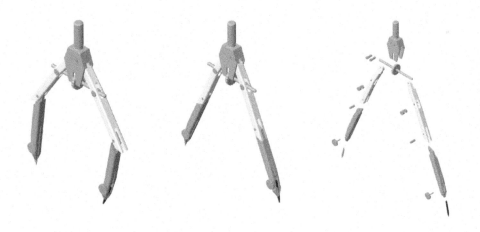

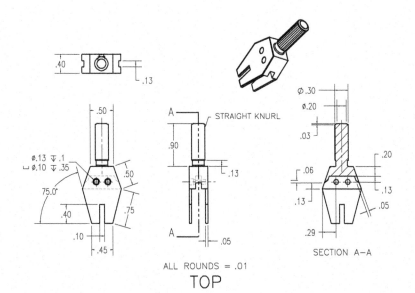

ø.13 ⌄ .1
⌐ ø.10 ⌄ .35

75.0°

.40

.10

.45

.50

.50

.75

A

.90

.13

A

STRAIGHT KNURL

.05

ALL ROUNDS = .01
TOP

ø.30
ø.20

.03

.06

.13

.29

.20

.13

.05

SECTION A—A

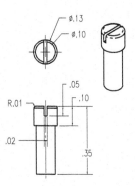

R.01

.02

ø.13
ø.10

.05

.10

.35

TOP SCREW

.40

.13

d. Compass parts *(continued)*

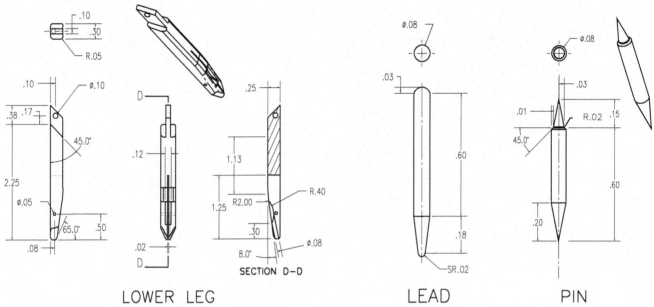

LOWER LEG LEAD PIN

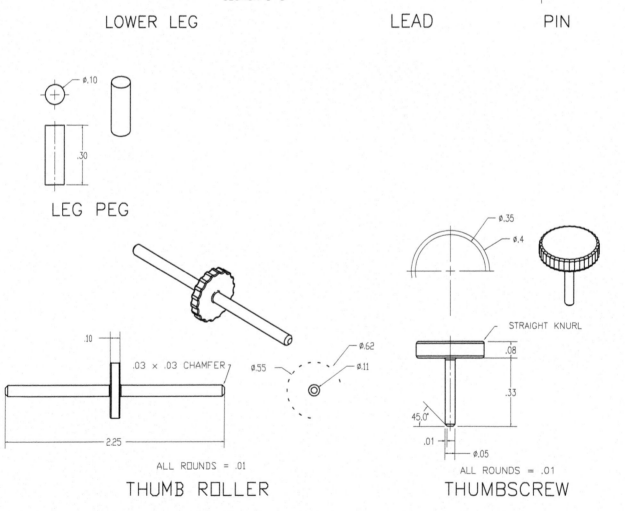

LEG PEG

THUMB ROLLER THUMBSCREW

d. Compass parts *(continued)*

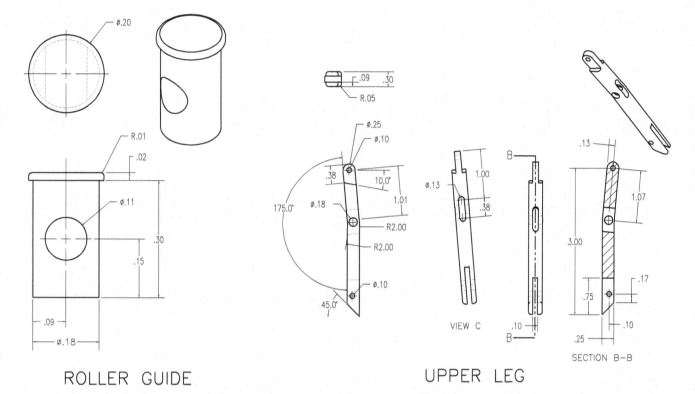

ROLLER GUIDE   UPPER LEG

Exercise 10.2 Purchase a clamp similar to the one shown from your local hardware store or online.

a. Make measurements and model each part.

b. Create an assembly model from the parts.

c. Create a skeleton and assemble the part models to the skeleton. Change the angle in the skeleton and investigate how the model changes.

d. Build the assembly as a mechanism so that you can simulate the motion of the mechanism by dragging the parts.

e. Investigate your software's capabilities for simulating the motion of a mechanism.

(Courtesy of POWERTEC Products.)

Exercise 10.3 Use the sheet metal features of your software to model the drill bit stand. Create different configurations of hole sizes, to accommodate different drill bits.

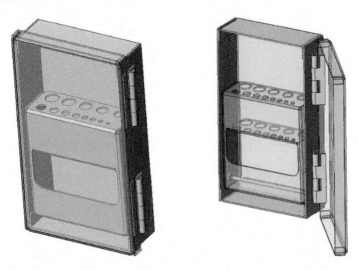

Exercise 10.4 Create part and assembly models for the clamp shown below and on the next page.

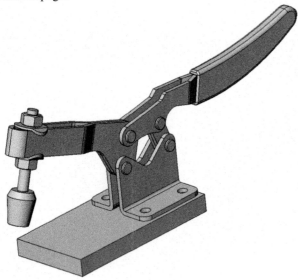

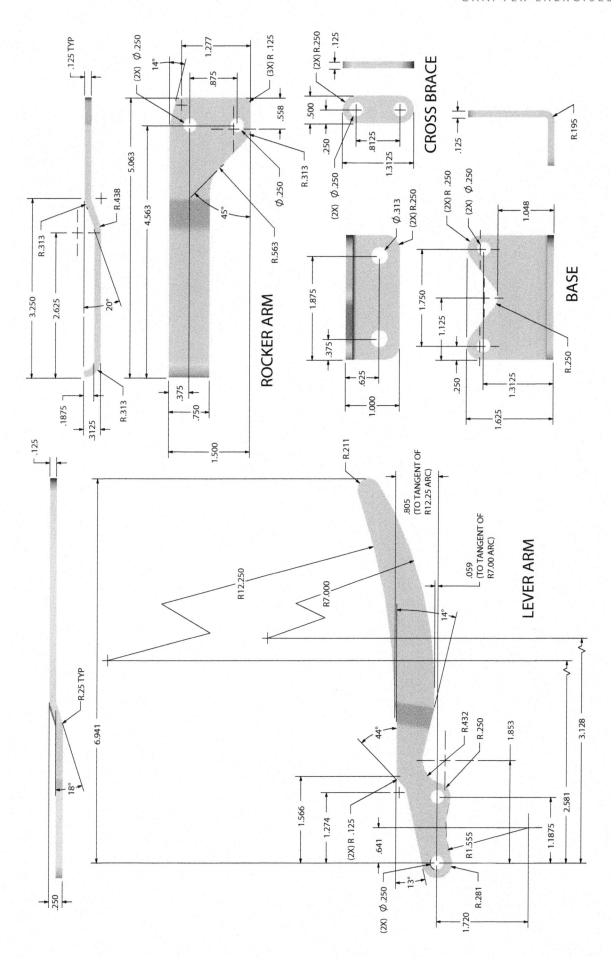

ROCKER ARM

CROSS BRACE

BASE

LEVER ARM

Exercise 10.5 Design a housing for the power and D-sub connector, like the one shown. Download part models for the standard parts.

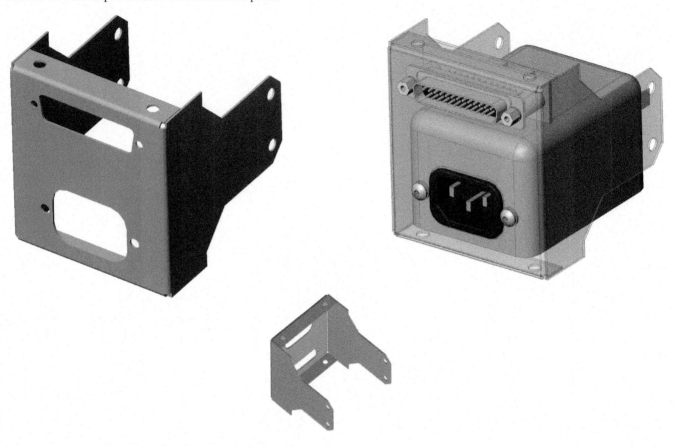

Exercise 10.6 Model and assemble the parts of the gyroscope. (See detail on next page.)

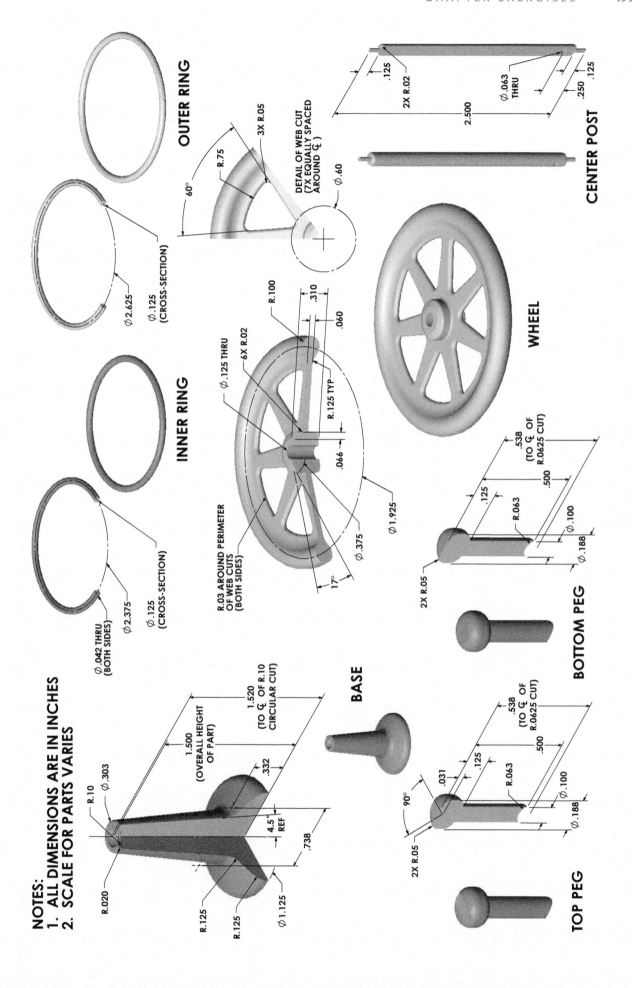

NOTES:
1. ALL DIMENSIONS ARE IN INCHES
2. SCALE FOR PARTS VARIES

OUTER RING

INNER RING

CENTER POST

WHEEL

BASE

BOTTOM PEG

TOP PEG

Mass Properties Exercises

Use your solid modeler to determine the mass of the following objects. Define a datum, then locate and dimension the centroid. Find the moment of inertia and radii of gyration about a defined major axis for each part.

Assume all objects are milled from 6061-T6 aluminum, with specific gravity of 0.28. Small fillets or chamfers do not significantly change your solution and can be neglected in the model, but do not neglect important machining details such as the internal radii formed by the .25″ or .50″ diameter cutters!

Dimensions shown are in inches.

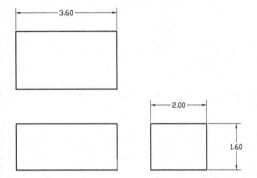

Exercise 10.7 Simple rectangular block

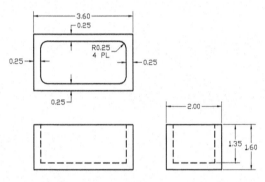

Exercise 10.8 Rectangular block with internal recess

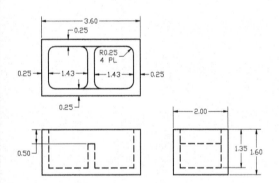

Exercise 10.9 Rectangular block with split internal recess

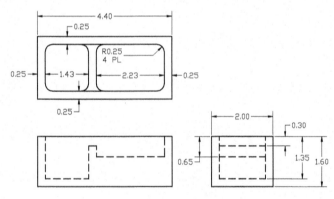

Exercise 10.10 Asymmetrically milled block

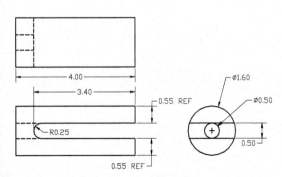

Exercise 10.11 Slotted tube

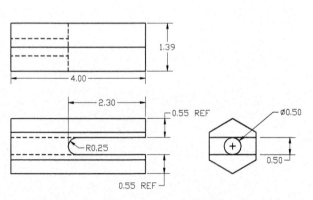

Exercise 10.12 Slotted hexagonal hollow rod

Exercise 10.13 Create a table in a spreadsheet program comparing the mass properties as calculated by your CAD modeler with hand-calculated exact values, for the following figures. Be sure to define a common datum for each figure, so that proper comparisons can be made. Include a column showing percent difference from the exact value. How does part-axis orientation affect your accuracy?

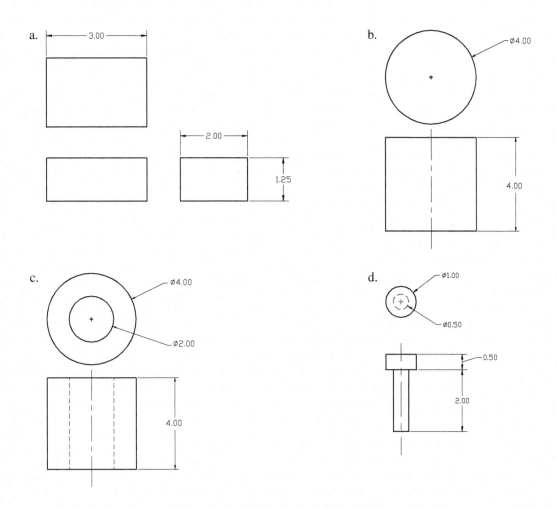

a.

3.00

2.00

1.25

b.

Ø4.00

4.00

c.

Ø4.00

Ø2.00

4.00

d.

Ø1.00

Ø0.50

0.50

2.00

Exercise 10.14 Use the mass properties data for the models in Exercise 10.13 to create a spreadsheet that computes the material, cost, and labor needed to coat the surface area of the parts.

Exercise 10.15 Find the center of gravity and total mass for the assembly that you created in Exercise 10.4.

CHAPTER ELEVEN

DIMENSIONING

OBJECTIVES

After studying the material in this chapter, you should be able to:

1. Use conventional dimensioning techniques to describe size and shape accurately on an engineering drawing.

2. Create and read a drawing at a specified scale.

3. Correctly place dimension lines, extension lines, angles, and notes.

4. Dimension circles, arcs, and inclined surfaces.

5. Apply finish symbols and notes to a drawing.

6. Dimension contours.

7. Use standard practices for dimensioning prisms, cylinders, holes, and curves.

8. List practices for dimensioning a solid model as documentation.

9. Identify guidelines for the dos and don'ts of dimensioning.

Refer to the following standards:
- *ANSI/ASME Y14.5 Dimensioning and Tolerancing*
- *ASME Y14.41 Digital Product Definition Data Practices*
- *ASME B4.2 Preferred Metric Limits and Fits*

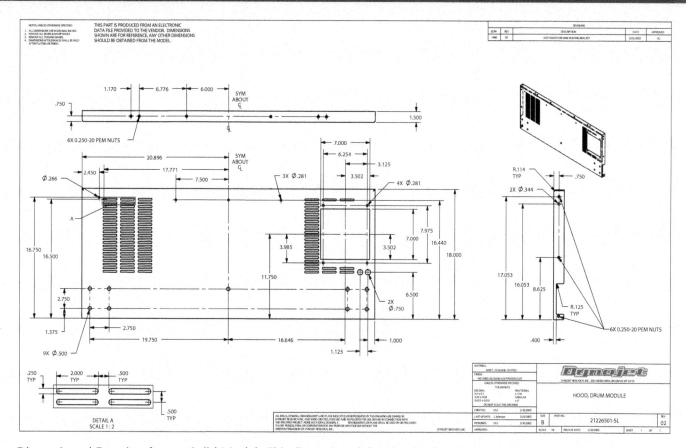

Dimensioned Drawing from a Solid Model. *This dimensioned drawing for the sheet metal drum module hood was created from a 3D model using SolidWorks. (Courtesy of Dynojet Research, Inc.)*

OVERVIEW

It is essential to describe not only the shape of the features you design but also their sizes and locations. Dimensions and notes define the size, finish, and other requirements to fully define what you want manufactured.

Standards organizations prescribe how dimensions should appear and the general rules for their selection and placement in the drawing and in digital models, but it takes skill and practice to dimension drawings so that their interpretation is clear and unambiguous.

Whether you are creating 2D drawings or 3D models, CAD systems are great for producing dimensions that follow standards for the appearance of the dimensions themselves. However, the job of selecting which dimension to show or where to place it in a drawing takes a level of intelligence that is not part of most CAD systems. Those important decisions are still up to the CAD user—or in other words, *you*.

Learning good practices for dimensioning and tolerancing to define part geometry can also help you create better 3D models. If you have a good understanding of how the sizes and locations of model features will be defined, you can plan how to capture this information clearly in the model.

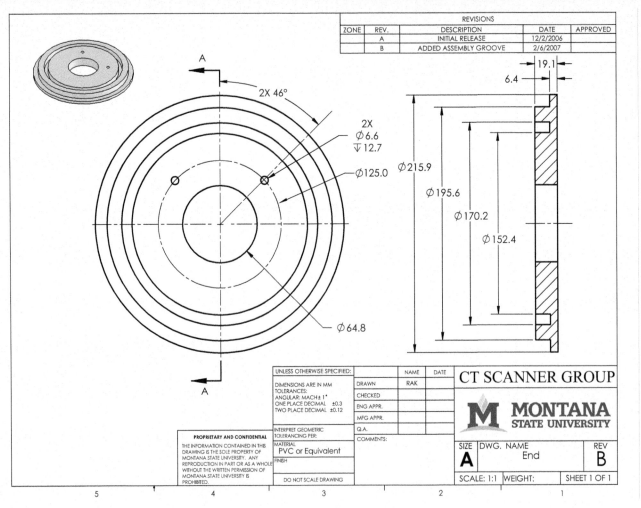

11.1   Automatically Generated Dimensions. *Views and dimensions can be generated automatically from a solid model. (Courtesy of Robert Kincaid.)*

UNDERSTANDING DIMENSIONING

You can describe an object's shape using different types of drawing views. By providing dimensions, you describe the sizes and locations of design features.

The need for interchangeability of parts is the basis for modern part dimensioning. Drawings for products must be dimensioned so that production personnel all over the world can make mating parts that will fit properly when assembled or when used to replace parts.

The increasing need for precision manufacturing and interchangeability has shifted responsibility for size control to the design engineer or detail drafter. The production worker must properly interpret the instructions given on the drawings to produce the required part or construct the building or system. You should be familiar with materials and methods of construction and with production requirements to create drawings that define exactly what you want to have manufactured.

Practices for dimensioning architectural and structural drawings are similar in many ways to those for dimensioning manufactured parts, but some practices differ. The portfolio section throughout this book shows a variety of drawings that you can use to familiarize yourself with practices from other disciplines.

Figure 11.1 shows a dimensioned CAD drawing created from a solid model. Although CAD can be a great help for proper dimensioning technique, you must provide the intelligence to choose and place the dimensions to create a drawing that conveys the design clearly. Even if you are going to transmit 3D CAD files as the product definition, you still need to consider how accurately the parts that you will eventually receive must match the model definition. Directly specifying tolerances in the model is one way to do this. You will learn more about tolerancing in Chapter 12.

Three Aspects of Good Dimensioning

Dimensions are given in the form of distances, angles, and notes regardless of the dimensioning units being used. For both CAD and hand drawing, the ability to create good dimensioned drawings requires the following:

1. Technique of dimensioning

The standards for the appearance of lines, spacing of dimensions, size of arrowheads, and so on, allow others to read your drawing. A typical dimensioned drawing is shown in Figure 11.2. Note the strong contrast between the visible lines of the object and the thin lines used for the dimensions. The dimensions are easily read because they follow the standards for dimensioning technique.

2. Placement of dimensions

Use logical placement for dimensions according to standard practices so that they are legible, easy to find, and easy for the reader to interpret. Notice that when dimensions are placed between two views, it is easier to see how the dimension relates to the feature as shown in each view.

3. Choice of dimensions

The dimensions you show affect how your design is manufactured. Dimension first for function and then review the dimensioning to see if you can make improvements for ease of manufacturing without adversely affecting the final result. 3D CAD models can be transmitted as all or part of a digital product definition, but this method still requires a thorough understanding of the sizes and relationships between the part features.

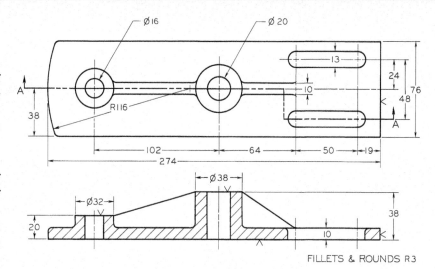

11.2   A Drawing Dimensioned in Millimeters

A drawing released for production should show the object in its completed state and contain all necessary information for specifying the final part. As you select which dimensions to show, provide functional dimensions that can be interpreted to manufacture the part as you want it built. Keep in mind:

- The finished piece.
- The function of the part in the total assembly.
- How you will inspect the final part to determine its acceptability.
- Production processes.

Also, remember the following points:

- Give dimensions that are necessary and convenient for producing the part.
- Give sufficient dimensions so that none must be assumed.
- Avoid dimensioning to points or surfaces inaccessible to the worker.
- Do not provide unnecessary or duplicate dimensions.

Tolerance

When a finished part is measured, it will vary slightly from the exact dimension specified. *Tolerance* is the total amount that the feature on the actual part is allowed to vary from what is specified by the drawing or model dimension. You will learn a number of ways to specify tolerances in Chapter 12.

A good understanding of tolerance is important to understanding dimensioning, especially when choosing which dimensions to show. For now, keep in mind that tolerance can be specified generally by giving a note on the drawing such as

ALL TOLERANCES ±.02 INCH
UNLESS OTHERWISE NOTED.

Another method of specifying tolerance is illustrated in the title block shown in Figure 11.3.

11.3   A Title Block Specifying Tolerances
(Courtesy of Dynojet Research, Inc.)

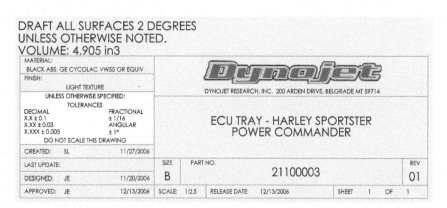

Geometric Breakdown

Engineering structures are composed largely of simple geometric shapes, such as the prism, cylinder, pyramid, cone, and sphere, although this is changing with the more organic shapes manufactured through various direct printing processes. These shapes may be exterior (positive) or interior (negative) forms. For example, a steel shaft is a positive cylinder, and a round hole is a negative cylinder.

The basic shapes result directly from design necessity—keeping forms as simple as possible—and from manufacturing operations. Forms having plane surfaces are produced by planing, shaping, milling, and so forth; forms having cylindrical, conical, or spherical surfaces are produced by turning, drilling, reaming, boring, countersinking, and other rotary operations. One way to consider dimensioning of engineering structures involves two basic steps:

1. Give the dimensions showing the sizes of the simple geometric shapes, called *size dimensions*.
2. Give the dimensions locating these elements with respect to one another, called *location dimensions*. Note that a location dimension locates a 3D geometric element and not just a surface; otherwise, all dimensions would have to be classified as location dimensions.

This process of geometric analysis helps you determine the features of the object and the features' relationships to one another, but it is not enough just to dimension geometry. You must also consider the function of the part in the assembly and the manufacturing requirements. This process is similar to that used when modeling designs in 3D CAD.

11.1 LINES USED IN DIMENSIONING

A *dimension line* is a thin, dark, solid line terminated by an arrowhead, indicating the direction and extent of a dimension (Figure 11.4). In a machine drawing, the dimension line is usually broken near the middle to place the dimension value in the line. In structural and architectural drawing, the dimension figure is placed above an unbroken dimension line.

As shown in Figure 11.5, the dimension line nearest the object outline should be spaced at least 10 mm (3/8″) away. All other parallel dimension lines should be at least 6 mm (1/4″) apart, and more if space is available. The spacing of dimension lines should be uniform throughout the drawing.

An *extension line* is a thin, dark, solid line that extends from a point on the drawing to which a dimension refers (Figure 11.5). The dimension line meets the extension lines at right angles, except in special cases. A gap of about 1.5 mm (1/16″) should be left where the extension line would join the object outline. The extension line should extend about 3 mm (1/8″) beyond the outermost arrowhead.

A *centerline* is a thin, dark line alternating long and short dashes. Centerlines are commonly used as extension lines in locating holes and other symmetrical features (Figure 11.6). When extended for dimensioning, centerlines cross over other lines of the drawing without gaps. Always end centerlines using a long dash. Refer to Figures 11.4–11.6 for examples of lines used in dimensioning.

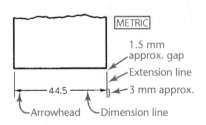

11.4   Dimension Line

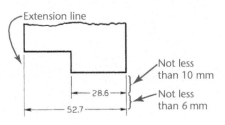

11.5   Extension Lines

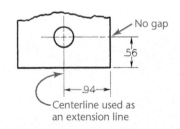

11.6   Centerlines

DIMENSIONING BY GEOMETRIC BREAKDOWN

To dimension the object shown in isometric at right, use the geometric breakdown as follows:

1 Consider the geometric features of the part.

In this case the features to be dimensioned include

- two positive prisms,
- one positive cylinder,
- one negative cone, and
- six negative cylinders.

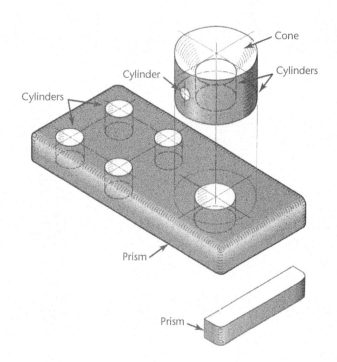

2 Specify the size dimensions for each feature by adding the dimension values as indicated. (In this illustration, the word "size" indicates the various dimension values.) Note that the four cylinders of the same size can be specified with one dimension.

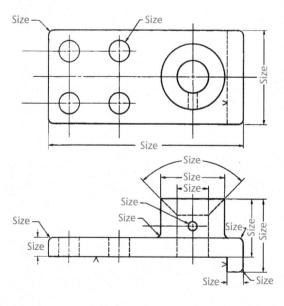

3 Finally, locate the geometric features with respect to one another. (Actual values would replace the words "size" and "location" in this illustration.) Always check to see that the object is fully dimensioned.

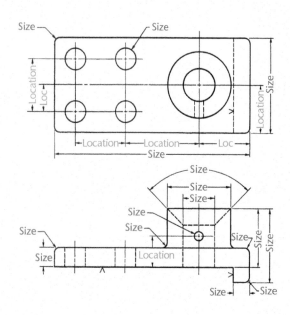

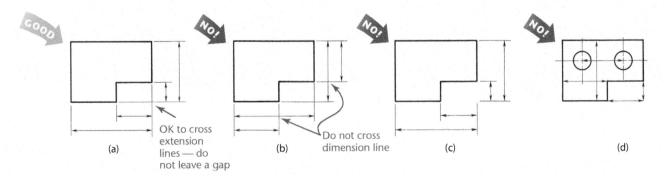

11.7   Dimension and Extension Lines

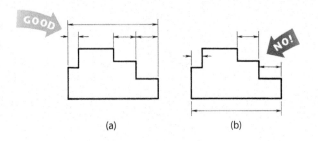

11.8   Grouped Dimensions

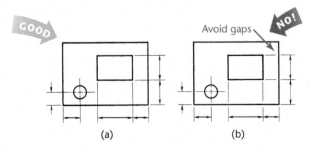

11.9   Crossing Lines

11.2 USING DIMENSION AND EXTENSION LINES

Dimension lines and extension lines should follow the guidelines shown in Figure 11.7a. The shorter dimensions are nearest to the object outline. Dimension lines should not cross extension lines, as in Figure 11.7b, which results from placing the shorter dimensions outside. Note that it is perfectly satisfactory to cross extension lines (Figure 11.7a), but they should not be shortened (Figure 11.7c). A dimension line should never coincide with or extend from any line of the drawing (Figure 11.7d). Avoid crossing dimension lines wherever possible.

Dimensions should be lined up and grouped together as much as possible, as in Figure 11.8a, and not as in Figure 11.8b.

In many cases, extension lines and centerlines must cross visible lines of the object (Figure 11.9a). When this occurs, gaps should not be left in the lines (Figure 11.9b).

Dimension lines are normally drawn at right angles to extension lines, but an exception may be made in the interest of clarity, as in Figure 11.10.

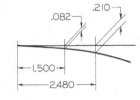

11.10   Oblique Extension

11.3 ARROWHEADS

Arrowheads, shown in Figure 11.11, indicate the extent of dimensions. They should be uniform in size and style throughout the drawing, not varied according to the size of the drawing or the length of dimensions. Sketch arrowheads freehand so that the length and width have a ratio of 3:1. The length of the arrowhead should be equal to the height of the dimension values (about 3 mm or 1/8″ long). For best appearance, fill in the arrowhead, as in Figure 11.11d. Figure 11.12 shows the preferred arrowhead styles for mechanical drawings. Most CAD systems allow you to select from a variety of styles.

> **TIP**
> When you are drawing by hand and using the arrowhead method in which both strokes are directed toward the point, it is easier to make the strokes toward yourself.

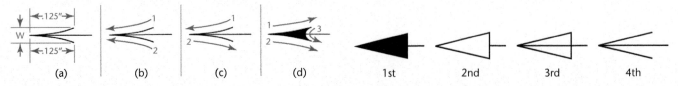

11.11   Arrowheads

11.12   Order of Preference for Arrowhead Styles

11.4 LEADERS

A *leader* is a thin, solid line directing attention to a note or dimension and starting with an arrowhead or dot.

A leader should be an inclined straight line drawn at a large angle, except for the short horizontal shoulder (about 3–6 mm or 1/8–1/4″) extending from the center of the first or last line of lettering for the note. A leader to a circle should be a radial line, which is a line that would pass through the center of the circle if extended. Figures 11.13a–d show examples of leader lines; radial lines are shown in Section 11.22.

Use an arrowhead to start the leader when you can point to a particular line in the drawing, such as the edge of a hole. Use a dot to start the leader when locating something within the outline of the object, such as an entire surface (see Figures 11.13e and f).

For the Best Appearance, Make Leaders

- Near each other and parallel.
- Across as few lines as possible.

Don't Make Leaders

- Parallel to nearby lines of the drawing.
- Through a corner of the view.
- Across each other.
- Longer than needed.
- Horizontal or vertical.

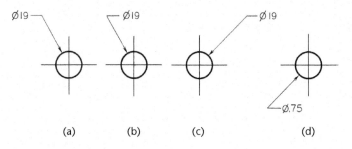
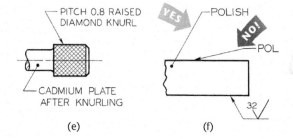

11.13 Leaders

11.5 DRAWING SCALE AND DIMENSIONING

Drawing scale is indicated in the title block, as described in Chapter 2. The scale is intended to help you visualize the object by giving an approximate idea of its size, but is not intended to communicate dimensions. Never scale measurements from drawings to find an unknown dimension. Many standard title blocks include a note such as DO NOT SCALE DRAWING FOR DIMENSIONS, as shown in Figure 11.14.

Draw a heavy straight line under any single dimension value that is not to scale (Figure 11.15). Before CAD was widely used, if a change made in a drawing was not important enough to justify correcting the drawing, the practice was simply to change the dimension value. If a dimension does not match the appearance in the drawing, the part is made as dimensioned, not as pictured. If there seems to be an error, many manufacturers check to confirm that the drawing is correct; however, it is your responsibility to specify exactly what you want built. If the entire drawing is not prepared to a standard scale, note NONE in the scale area of the title block. You may see the abbreviation NTS on older drawings, meaning "not to scale."

When you create a drawing using CAD, make sure to define dimensions according to the proper standards. Because it is easy to edit CAD drawings, you should generally fix the drawing geometry when making changes and not merely change dimension values. If you are using a digital model as the sole definition for the part, the model dimensions must be represented accurately.

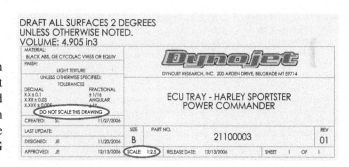

11.14 *Drawing scale is noted in the title block. The drawing should not be scaled for dimensions. (Courtesy of Dynojet Research, Inc.)*

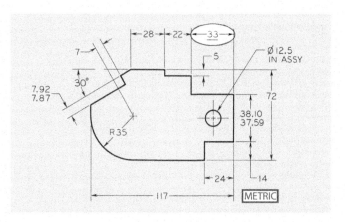

11.15 *Draw a heavy line under any dimension value that is not to scale.*

Keeping Dimensions and Lettering Legible at Smaller Scales

The sizes for lettering height, dimension line spacing, and so on, are to be shown that size on the plotted sheet. If you are going to use reduced-size working prints, increase the lettering, dimension arrows, and other sizes by approximately 50% (depending on the amount of reduction) to maintain legibility on the smaller print.

11.6 DIRECTION OF DIMENSION VALUES AND NOTES

All dimension values and notes are lettered horizontally to be read from the bottom of the sheet, as oriented by the title block. Figure 11.16 shows the direction for reading dimension values.

The exception is when dimensioning from a baseline as in coordinate dimensioning. Then dimension figures may be aligned with the dimension lines so that they may be read from

the bottom or right side of the sheet as shown in Figure 11.17. In both systems, general notes on the sheet and dimensions and notes shown with leaders are always aligned horizontally to read from the bottom of the drawing.

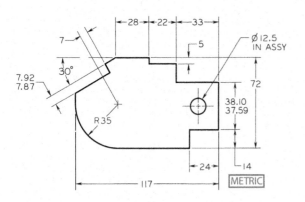

11.16   Unidirectional Dimension Figures

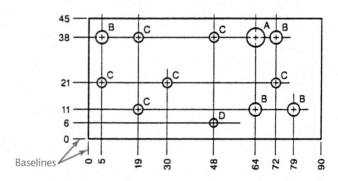

11.17   *Rectangular coordinate dimensioning may show values reading from the right. (Reprinted from ASME Y14.5M-1994 (R2004), by permission of The American Society of Mechanical Engineers. All rights reserved.)*

11.7 DIMENSION UNITS

Dimension values are shown using metric or decimal-inch values. Millimeters and decimal inches can be added, subtracted, multiplied, and divided more easily than fractions. For inch–millimeter equivalents of decimal and common fractions, see the inside back cover of this book.

When a note stating ALL MEASUREMENTS IN MILLIMETERS or ALL MEASUREMENTS IN INCHES UNLESS OTHERWISE SPECIFIED is used in the title block to indicate the measurement units, no units are needed with the dimension values. UNLESS OTHERWISE SPECIFIED is often abbreviated as UOS on drawings. When indicating dimensions:

- Millimeters are indicated by the lowercase letters mm placed to the right of the numeral, as in 12.5 mm.
- Meters are indicated by the lowercase m, as in 50.6 m.
- Inches are indicated by the symbol ″ placed slightly above and to the right of the numeral.
- Feet are indicated by the symbol ′ similarly placed. It is customary in feet-inch expressions to omit the inch mark.

It is standard practice to omit millimeter designations and inch marks on drawings and note the units in the title block except when there is a possibility of misunderstanding. For example, 1 VALVE should be 1″ VALVE.

Either meters or feet and inches and fractional inches are used in architectural and structural work where precision in the thousandths of an inch is not necessary and the steel tape or framing square is used to make measurements. Commodities such as pipe and lumber are identified by standard nominal sizes that are close to the actual dimensions.

In some industries, all dimensions, regardless of size, are given in inches; in others, dimensions up to and including 72″ are given in inches, and dimensions greater than 72″ are given in feet and inches. In U.S. structural and architectural drafting, all dimensions of 1′ or more are usually expressed in feet and inches.

11.8 MILLIMETER VALUES

The millimeter is the commonly used unit for most metric engineering drawings. One-place millimeter decimals are used when tolerance limits permit. Two (or more)-place millimeter decimals are used when higher tolerances are required. One drawing can combine dimensions shown with more and fewer decimal places depending on the necessary tolerance. Keep in mind that 0.1 mm is approximately equal to .004 in. If you are used to working in U.S. customary units, don't provide an

11.18 Millimeter
Dimension Values

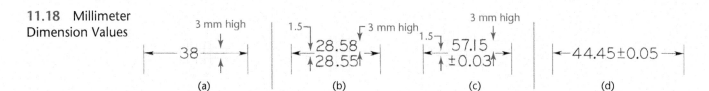

(a)   (b)   (c)   (d)

unrealistic precision when specifying millimeter values.

Figure 11.18 shows various ways that millimeter values can be shown for dimensioning. Figure 11.19 shows an example drawing dimensioned in millimeters.

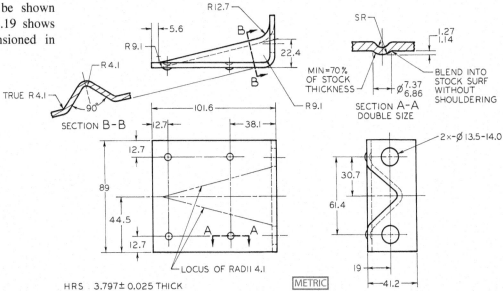

11.19 Complete
Millimeter Dimensioning

11.9 DECIMAL-INCH VALUES

Two-place inch decimals are typical when tolerance limits permit. Three or more decimal places are used for tolerance limits in the thousandths of an inch. In two-place decimals, the second place preferably should be an even digit (for example, .02, .04, and .06 are preferred to .01, .03, or .05) so that when the dimension is divided by 2 (for example, when determining the radius from a diameter), the result will still be a two-place decimal. However, odd two-place decimals are used when required for design purposes, such as in dimensioning points on a smooth curve or when strength or clearance is a factor. A typical example of the use of the complete decimal-inch system is shown in Figure 11.20.

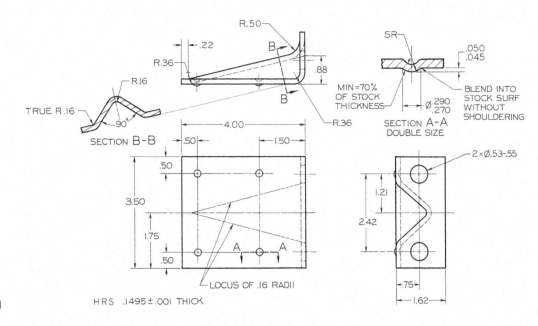

11.20 Complete
Decimal Dimensioning

11.10 RULES FOR DIMENSION VALUES

Good hand-lettering is important for dimension values on sketches. The shop produces according to the directions on the drawing, so to save time and prevent costly mistakes, make all lettering perfectly legible.

Make all decimal points bold, allowing ample space. When the metric dimension is a whole number, do not show either a decimal point or a zero. When the metric dimension is less than 1 mm, a zero precedes the decimal point.

When the decimal-inch dimension is used on drawings, a zero is not used before the decimal point of values less than 1 in. Typical values are shown to two decimal places even when they represent a whole number (e.g., use 2.00 instead of 2). Correct decimal-inch dimension values are shown in Figures 11.21a–e.

11.21   Decimal-Inch Dimension Values

11.11 RULES FOR ROUNDING DECIMAL DIMENSION VALUES

It is difficult to maintain tolerances smaller than a few thousandths of an inch in manufacturing. To provide reasonable tolerances that can be achieved in manufacturing, calculated dimension values for drawings sometimes need to be rounded. Unlike rounding rules used for statistical values, it is preferred to round drawing values to an even number.

When rounding a decimal value to fewer places, regardless of whether the dimension is expressed in inches or metric units, follow these rules:

- If the number following the rounding position is less than 5, make no change.
- If the number following the rounding position is more than 5, round up.
- If the number following the rounding position is a 5, round to an even number. (To do this, note whether the number in the rounding position is even or odd. If the 5 follows an odd number in the rounding position, round up to an even number. If the 5 follows an even number in the rounding position, make no change.)

Examples of Rounded Decimal Values

- 3.4632 becomes 3.463 when rounded to three places. (Make no change, because the 2 following the rounding position is less than 5.)
- 3.4637 becomes 3.464 when rounded to three places. (Round up, because the 7 following the rounding position is more than 5.)
- 8.37652 becomes 8.376 when rounded to three places. (Make no change, because the 6 in the rounding position is even and the number following the rounding position is a 5.)
- 4.375 becomes 4.38 when rounded to two places. (Round up to an even number, because the 7 in the rounding position is odd and the number following the rounding position is a 5.)

11.12 DUAL DIMENSIONING

Dual dimensioning is used to show metric and decimal-inch dimensions on the same drawing. Two methods of displaying the dual dimensions are described next.

Position Method

In the *position method* of dual dimensioning, the millimeter dimension is placed above the inch dimension, and the two are separated by a dimension line, or by an added line when the *unidirectional* system of dimensioning is used. An alternative arrangement is the millimeter dimension to the left of the inch dimension, with the two separated by a slash line, or virgule. Placement of the inch dimension above or to the left of the millimeter dimension is also acceptable. Each drawing should illustrate the dimension identification as $\frac{\text{MILLIMETER}}{\text{INCH}}$ or MILLIMETER/INCH.

Bracket Method

In the *bracket method* of dual dimensioning, the millimeter dimension is enclosed in parentheses. The location of this dimension is optional but should be uniform on any drawing—that is, above or below or to the left or the right of the inch dimension. Each drawing should include a note to identify the dimension values, such as DIMENSIONS IN () ARE MILLIMETERS.

11.13 COMBINATION UNITS

When more than one measurement system is used on the same drawing, the main units are indicated through a note in or near the title block. The alternative units are indicated with an abbreviation after the dimension value. Use mm after the dimension value if millimeters, or IN if inches, only when combining two measurement systems on one drawing. In the U.S. to facilitate the changeover to metric dimensions, some drawings are dual-dimensioned in millimeters and decimal inches, as shown in Figure 11.22. The second set of units shown in parentheses are for reference only.

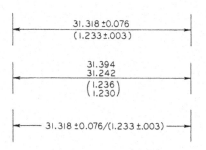

11.22 Dual-Dimensioned Drawing in Millimeters. *On drawing, inch values are given for reference only.*

11.14 DIMENSIONING SYMBOLS

A variety of dimensioning symbols are used to replace traditional terms or abbreviations (see Figure 11.23). The symbols are preferred because (1) they take less space in the drawing and (2) they are internationally recognized and therefore do not have translation issues if the part is manufactured in a country where a different language is spoken. Traditional terms and abbreviations found in Appendix 2 can be used if necessary.

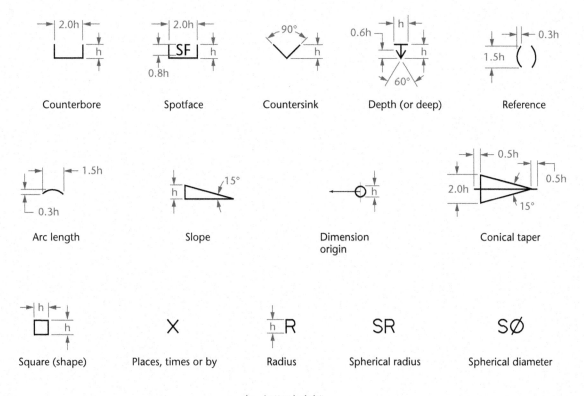

11.23 Form and Proportion of Dimensioning Symbols *(Reprinted from ASME Y14.5M-1994 (R2004), by permission of The American Society of Mechanical Engineers. All rights reserved.)*

11.15 PLACING AND SHOWING DIMENSIONS LEGIBLY

Rules for the placement of dimensions help you dimension your drawings so that they are clear and readable. They also help locate dimensions in standard places so that someone manufacturing the part doesn't have to search a complicated drawing to find a dimension. You cannot always follow every placement rule to the letter, so keep in mind that the ultimate goal is to dimension the drawing clearly so that the parts are built to your specifications.

Rules for Placing Dimensions Properly

- Never letter a dimension value over any line on the drawing; if necessary, break the line.
- In a group of parallel dimension lines, the dimension values should be staggered, as in Figure 11.24a, and not stacked up one above the other, as in Figure 11.24b.
- Do not crowd dimension figures into limited spaces, making them illegible. There are techniques for showing dimension values outside extension lines or in combination with leaders (Figure 11.25). If necessary, add a removed partial view or detail to an enlarged scale to provide the space needed for clear dimensioning.
- Place dimensions between views when possible, but attached to only a single view. This way it is clear that the dimension relates to the feature, which can be seen in more than one view.
- When a dimension must be placed in a hatched area or on the view, leave an opening in the hatching or a break in the lines for the dimension values, as shown in Figure 11.26b.
- Dimensions should not be placed on a view unless it promotes the clarity of the drawing, as shown in Figure 11.27. In complicated drawings such as Figure 11.27c, it is often necessary to place dimensions on a view.
- Avoid dimensioning to hidden lines (see Figure 11.28).

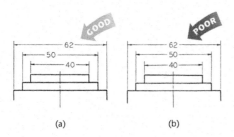

11.24   Staggered Numerals, Metric

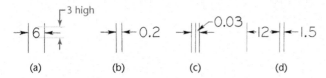

11.25   Fitting Dimension Values in Limited Spaces (Metric Dimensions)

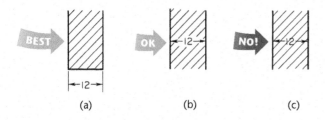

11.26   Dimensions and Section Lines

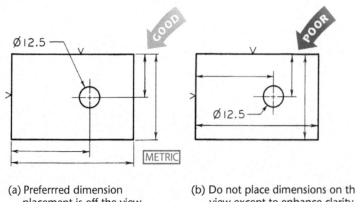

(a) Preferrred dimension placement is off the view

(b) Do not place dimensions on the view except to enhance clarity

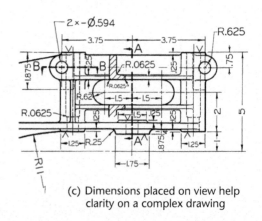

(c) Dimensions placed on view help clarity on a complex drawing

11.27   *Place dimensions on view only when clarity is enhanced.*

- Do not attach dimensions to visible lines where the meaning is not clear, such as the dimension 20 in the top view shown in Figure 11.29b.
- Notes for holes are usually placed where you see the circular shape of the hole, as in Figure 11.29a, but give the diameter of an external cylindrical shape where it appears rectangular. This way it is near the dimension for the length of the cylinder.
- Give dimensions where the shapes are shown—where the contours of the object are defined—as is shown in Figure 11.29.
- Locate holes in the view that shows the shape of the hole clearly.

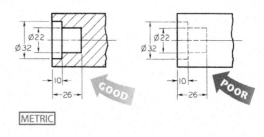

11.28 Placement of Dimensions

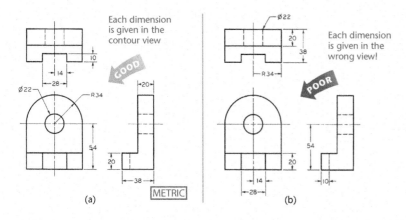

11.29 *Place dimensions where the contours of the object are defined.*

TIP

Thinking of Dimensioning in Terms of Material Removal

There are many ways to dimension a drawing. If you are having trouble getting started, it may help to consider the overall block of material and what features are to be removed from it, similar to the way you visualize for a sketch. This is especially true when the part is to be manufactured using a process that removes material, such as milling.

Look for the largest portions to be removed and give dimensions for their sizes and locations first. Next, add dimensions for the smaller features.

Because the overall dimensions will be the largest, they will be placed farthest from the view. If you are using CAD, it is easy to move dimensions later if you need more space. When you are sketching, block the overall dimension in lightly and leave substantial space between it and the drawing view for placement of shorter dimensions.

Use the rules that you have learned to place dimensions on the view that best shows the shape and close to where the feature is shown. This makes the drawing easier to read.

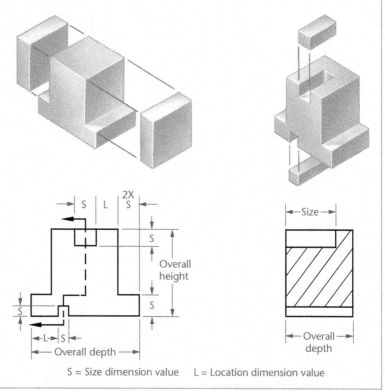

S = Size dimension value   L = Location dimension value

11.16 SUPERFLUOUS DIMENSIONS

All necessary dimensions must be shown, but do not give unnecessary or *superfluous dimensions.* Figure 11.30 shows examples of how to omit unnecessary dimensions. Do not repeat dimensions on the same view or on different views, or give the same information in two different ways.

As Figure 11.30b shows, it can be impossible to determine how the designer intended to apply the tolerance when a dimension is given two different ways. In chained dimensions, one dimension of the chain should be left out if the overall dimension is given, so that the machinist will work from one surface only. This is particularly important where an accumulation of tolerances can cause problems with how parts fit or function.

Do not omit dimensions, thinking, for example, that a hole is symmetrical and will be understood to be centered. Note in Figure 11.30b that one of the two location dimensions should be given for the hole at the right side of the part, even though it is centered. As the creator of the drawing, you should specify exactly how the part is to be built and inspected.

As shown in Figure 11.30e, when one dimension clearly applies to several identical features, or a uniform thickness, it need not be repeated, but the number of places should be indicated. Dimensions for fillets and rounds and other noncritical features need not be repeated, nor need the number of places be specified.

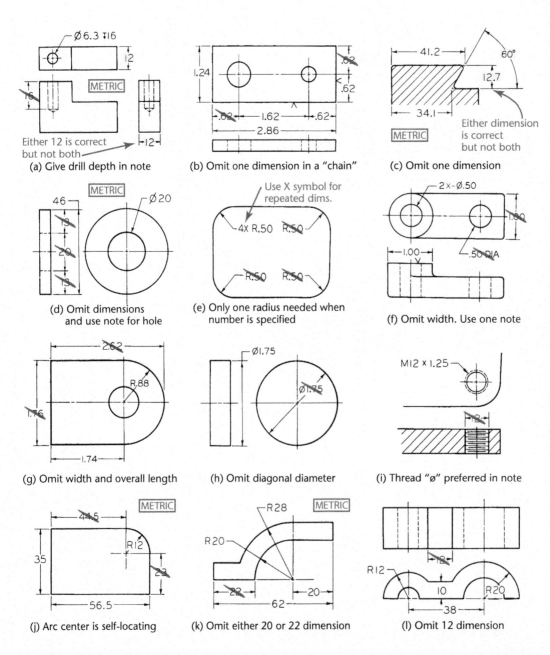

(a) Give drill depth in note

(b) Omit one dimension in a "chain"

(c) Omit one dimension

(d) Omit dimensions and use note for hole

(e) Only one radius needed when number is specified

(f) Omit width. Use one note

(g) Omit width and overall length

(h) Omit diagonal diameter

(i) Thread "ø" preferred in note

(j) Arc center is self-locating

(k) Omit either 20 or 22 dimension

(l) Omit 12 dimension

11.30 Superfluous Dimensions

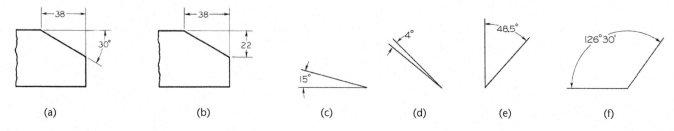

11.31   Dimensioning Angles

11.17 DIMENSIONING ANGLES

Angles are dimensioned by specifying the angle in degrees and a linear dimension, as shown in Figure 11.31a. Coordinate dimensions can also be given for two legs of a right triangle, as shown in Figure 11.31b. The coordinate method is better when a high degree of accuracy is required. Variations in degrees of angle are hard to control because the amount of variation increases with the distance from the vertex of the angle. Methods of indicating angles are shown in Figure 11.31. The tolerancing of angles is discussed in Chapter 12.

In civil engineering drawings, *slope* represents the angle with the horizontal, whereas *batter* is the angle with the vertical. Both are expressed by making one member of the ratio equal to 1, as shown in Figure 11.32. *Grade,* as of a highway,

is similar to slope but is expressed in percentage of rise per 100 feet of run. Thus a 20′ rise in a 100′ run is a grade of 20%. In structural drawings, angular measurements are made by giving the ratio of run to rise, with the larger size being 12″. These right triangles are referred to as *bevels.*

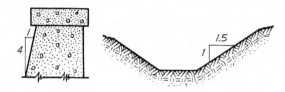

11.32   Angles in Civil Engineering Projects

11.18 DIMENSIONING ARCS

A circular arc is dimensioned in the view where its true shape in seen by giving the value for its radius preceded by the abbreviation R (Figure 11.33). The center is marked with a small cross to clarify the drawing, but not for small or unimportant radii or undimensioned arcs. When there is room enough, both the radius value and the arrowhead are placed inside the arc. If not, the arrowhead is left inside but the value is moved outside, or both the arrowhead and value are moved outside. When

section lines or other lines are in the way, the value and leader can be placed outside the sectioned or crowded area. For a long radius, when the center falls outside the available space, the dimension line is drawn toward the actual center, but a false center may be indicated and the dimension line "jogged" to it (Figure 11.33f).

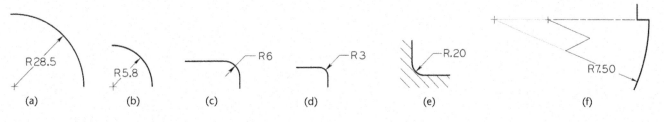

11.33   Dimensioning Arcs

11.19 FILLETS AND ROUNDS

Individual fillets and rounds are dimensioned like other arcs. If there are only a few and they are obviously the same size, giving one typical radius is preferred. However, fillets and rounds are often numerous on a drawing, and they usually are some standard size, such as metric R3 and R6, or R.125 and R.250 when using decimal-inch dimensions. In this case, give a general note in the lower portion of the drawing, such as:

FILLETS R6 AND ROUNDS R3 UNLESS OTHERWISE SPECIFIED

or

ALL CASTING RADII R6 UNLESS NOTED

or

ALL FILLETS AND ROUNDS R6.

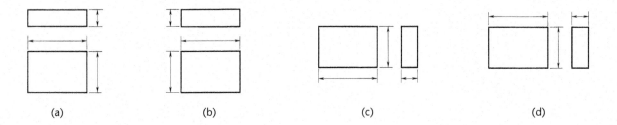

11.34   Dimensioning Rectangular Prisms

11.20 SIZE DIMENSIONING: PRISMS

The right rectangular prism is probably the most common geometric shape. Front and top views are dimensioned as shown in Figures 11.34a and b. The height and width are usually given in the front view, and the depth in the top view. The vertical dimensions can be placed on the left or right, usually in-line. Place the horizontal dimension between views as shown and not above the top or below the front view. Front and side views should be dimensioned as in Figures 11.34c and d. An example of size dimensions for a machine part made entirely of rectangular prisms is shown in Figure 11.35.

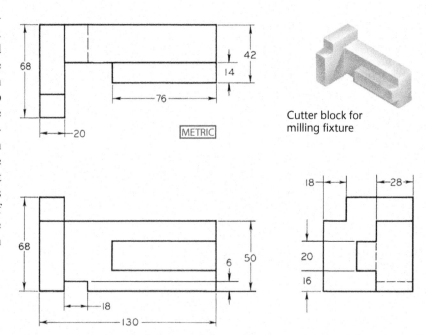

Cutter block for milling fixture

11.35   Dimensioning a Machine Part Composed of Prismatic Shapes

11.21 SIZE DIMENSIONING: CYLINDERS

The right circular cylinder is the next most common geometric shape and is commonly seen as a shaft or a hole. Cylinders are usually dimensioned by giving the diameter and length where the cylinder appears as a rectangle. If the cylinder is drawn vertically, give the length at the right or left, as in Figures 11.36a and b. If the cylinder is drawn horizontally, give the length above or below the rectangular view, as in Figures 11.36c and d.

Do not use a diagonal diameter inside the circular view, except when clarity is improved. Using several diagonal diameters on the same center becomes very confusing.

The radius of a cylinder should never be given, because measuring tools, such as the micrometer caliper, are designed to check diameters. Holes are usually dimensioned by means of notes

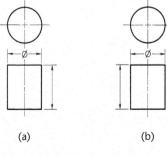

(a)   (b)

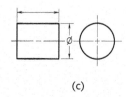

(c)

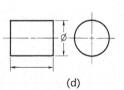

(d)

11.36   Dimensioning Cylinders

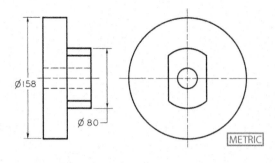

Use "∅" to indicate circular shape

(a)

Use "∅" to indicate circular view

(b)

11.37   Use of ∅ in Dimensioning Cylinders

specifying the diameter and the depth, as shown in Figure 11.37, with or without manufacturing operations.

Give the diameter symbol ∅ before all diameter dimensions, as in Figure 11.38a (*ANSI/ASME Y14.5*). In some cases, the symbol ∅ may be used to eliminate the circular view, as shown in Figure 11.38b. The abbreviation DIA following the numerical value was used on older decimal inch drawings.

When it is not clear that a hole goes all the way through the part, add the note THRU after the value.

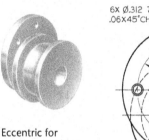

Eccentric for canning machine

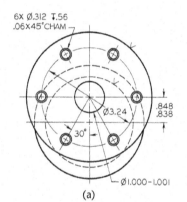

(a)

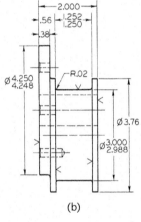

(b)

11.38   Dimensioning a Machine Part Composed of Cylindrical Shapes

11.22 SIZE DIMENSIONING: HOLES

Figure 11.39 shows standard symbols used in dimensioning holes. The order of items in a note corresponds to the order of procedure in the shop in producing the hole. The leader of a note should point to the circular view of the hole, if possible.

When the circular view of the hole has two or more concentric circles, as for counterbored, countersunk, spotfaced or tapped holes, the arrowhead should touch the outer circle. Draw a *radial leader line,* that is, one that would pass through the center

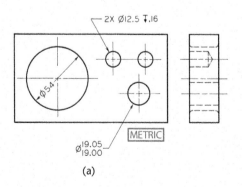

(a)

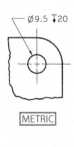

(b)

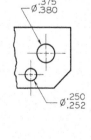

(c)

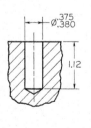

(d)

11.39   Dimensioning Holes

of the circle if it were extended. Figure 11.40 shows good and bad examples of radial leader lines.

Countersunk, counterbored, spotfaced, and tapped holes are usually specified by standard symbols or abbreviations, as shown in Figure 11.41.

Two or more holes can be dimensioned by a single note and by specifying the number of holes, as shown at the top of Figure 11.41. It is widely acceptable to use decimal fractions for both metric or inch drill sizes, as shown in Figure 11.41b. For numbered or letter-size drills (listed in Appendix 15), specify the decimal size or give the number or letter designation followed by the decimal size in parentheses—for example #28 (.1405) or "P" (.3230). Metric drills are all in decimal sizes and are not designated by number or letter.

Specify only the dimensions of the holes, without a note listing whether the holes are to be drilled, reamed, or punched,

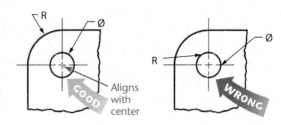

11.40 Good and Bad Examples of Radial Leader Lines

as shown in Figures 11.41c and d. The manufacturing technician or engineer is usually better suited to determine the least expensive process to use that will achieve the tolerance required.

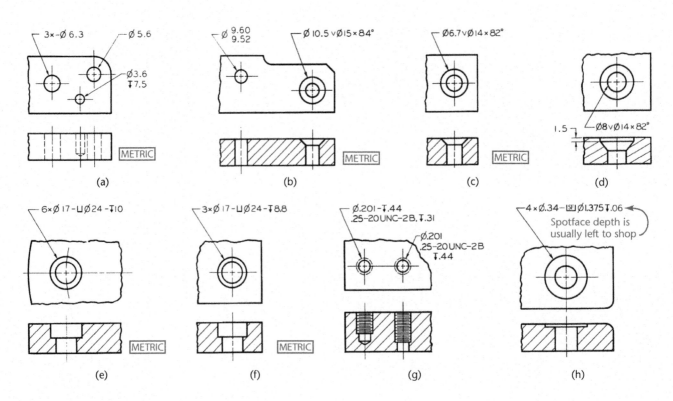

11.41 Standard Symbols for Hole Dimensions

11.23 APPLYING STANDARD DIMENSIONING SYMBOLS

Use standard dimensioning symbols when possible to save space and communicate dimensions clearly. (Refer to Figure 11.23 for details on how to draw the symbols.) Most CAD software contains a palette of standard symbols. Figure 11.42 shows the application of a variety of standard symbols. Note that Figure 11.42a shows the *basic dimension* symbol used in geometric dimensioning and tolerancing (GDT). In this case, "basic" does not mean "ordinary." You will learn more about the use of this special symbol in Chapter 12.

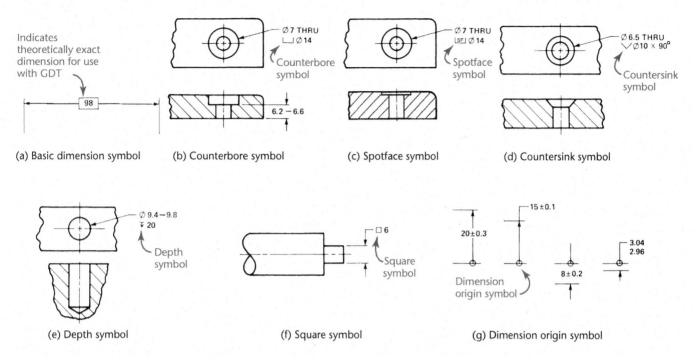

11.42   Use of Dimensioning Symbols. *(Reprinted from ASME Y14.5M-1994 (R2004), by permission of The American Society of Mechanical Engineers. All rights reserved.)*

11.24 DIMENSIONING COUNTERBORES AND SPOTFACES WITH FILLETS

At times a fillet radius is specified for a counterbored or spot-faced hole. Figure 11.43 shows an example of counterbored hole with a fillet radius specified. Note that the fillet radius is to the inside of the counterbore diameter.

When a fillet radius is specified for a spotface dimension, the fillet radius is added to the outside of the spotface diameter, as shown in Figure 11.44.

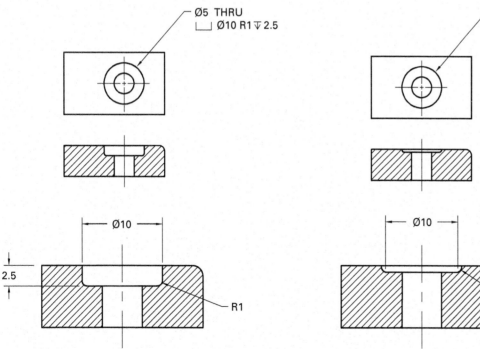

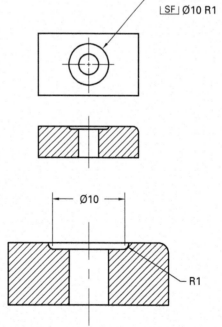

11.43   Counterbore with Fillet. *A note specifying a counterbore fillet radius defines a radius to the inside of the counterbore diameter.*

11.44   Spotface with Fillet. *A note specifying a spotface fillet radius defines a radius added to the outside of the spotface diameter.*

11.25 DIMENSIONING TRIANGULAR PRISMS, PYRAMIDS, AND CONES

To dimension a triangular prism, give the height, width, and displacement of the top edge in the front view, and the depth in the top view, as is shown in Figure 11.45a.

For a rectangular pyramid, give the heights in the front view and the dimensions of the base and the centering of the vertex in the top view, as in Figure 11.45b. If the base is square, you need give dimensions for only one side of the base, preceded by the square symbol, as in Figure 11.45c (or on older drawings you may see it labeled SQ).

For cones, give the altitude and the diameter of the base in the triangular view (Figure 11.45d). For a frustum of a cone, give the vertical angle and the diameter of one of the bases (Figure 11.45e). Another method is to give the length and the diameters of both ends in the front view. Still another is to give

the diameter at one end and the amount of taper per foot in a note.

Figure 11.45f shows a two-view drawing of a plastic knob. Overall, it is spherical and is dimensioned by giving its diameter preceded by the abbreviation and symbol for spherical diameter, S⌀ (in older notations it may be followed by the abbreviation SPHER). The torus-shaped bead around the knob is dimensioned by giving the thickness of the ring and the outside diameter.

Figure 11.45g shows a spherical end dimensioned by a radius preceded by the abbreviation SR. Internal shapes corresponding to the external shapes in Figure 11.45 would be dimensioned similarly.

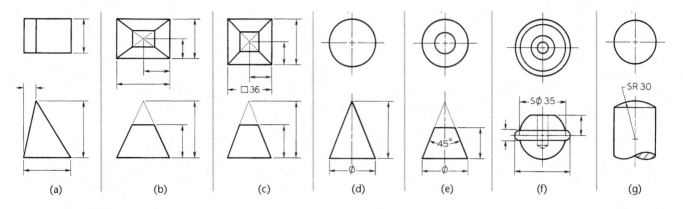

(a)   (b)   (c)   (d)   (e)   (f)   (g)

11.45   Dimensioning Various Shapes

11.26 DIMENSIONING CURVES

One way to dimension curves is to give a group of radii, as shown in Figure 11.46a. Note that in dimensioning the R126 arc, whose center is inaccessible, the center may be moved inward along a centerline and a jog made in the dimension line. Another method is to dimension the outline envelope of a curved shape so that the various radii are self-locating from "floating centers," as shown in Figure 11.46b. Both circular and noncircular curves may be dimensioned by using coordinate dimensions, or datums, as in Figure 11.46c.

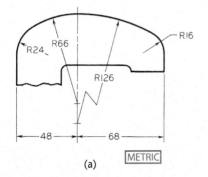

(a)

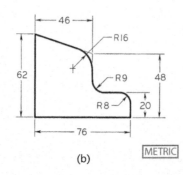

(b)

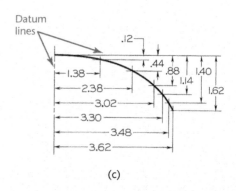

(c)

11.46   Dimensioning Curves

11.27 DIMENSIONING CURVED SURFACES

When angular measurements are unsatisfactory, you may give **chordal dimensions,** as shown in Figure 11.47a, or linear dimensions on the curved surfaces, as shown in Figure 11.47b.

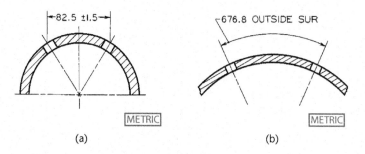

(a)   (b)

11.47 Dimensioning Along Curved Surfaces

11.28 DIMENSIONING ROUNDED-END SHAPES

The method for dimensioning rounded-end shapes depends on the degree of accuracy required. If precision is not necessary, use methods convenient for manufacturing, as in Figures 11.48a–c. Figures 11.48d–g show methods used when accuracy is required.

The link to be cast (or cut from sheet metal or plate) in Figure 11.48a is dimensioned as it would be laid out

for manufacture, giving the center-to-center distance and the radii of the ends. Note that only one radius dimension is necessary, and the number of places is included with the size dimension.

In Figure 11.47b, the pad on a casting with a milled slot is dimensioned from center to center to help the pattern maker and machinist in layout. This also gives the total travel of the milling cutter. The

width dimension indicates the diameter of the milling cutter, so give the diameter of a machined slot. A cored slot, however, would be dimensioned by radius to conform with the pattern-making procedure.

The semicircular pad in Figure 11.48c is laid out like the pad in Figure 11.48b, except that angular dimensions are used. Angular tolerances can be used if necessary.

11.48 Dimensioning Rounded-End Shapes. *For accuracy, in parts d–g, overall lengths of rounded-end shapes are given, and radii are indicated, but without specific values. The center-to-center distance may be required for accurate location of some holes. In part g, the hole location is more critical than the location of the radius, so the two are located.*

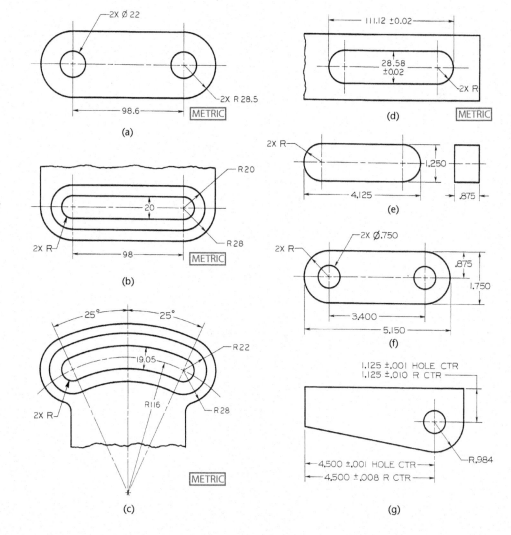

11.29 DIMENSIONING THREADS

Local notes are used to specify dimensions of threads. For tapped holes, the notes should, if possible, be attached to the circular views of the holes, as shown in Figure 11.49. For external threads, the notes are usually placed in the longitudinal views, where the threads are more easily recognized, as in Figure 11.49b and c. For a detailed discussion of thread notes, see Chapter 13.

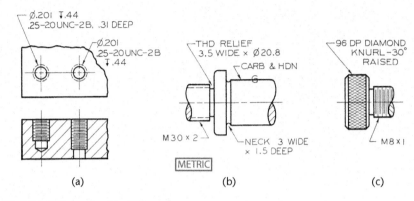

11.49 Dimensioning Threads

11.30 DIMENSIONING TAPERS

A *taper* is a conical surface on a shaft or in a hole. The usual method of dimensioning a taper is to give the amount of taper in a note, such as TAPER 0.167 ON DIA (with TO GAGE often added), and then give the diameter at one end with the length or give the diameter at both ends and omit the length. Taper on diameter means the difference in diameter per unit of length.

Standard machine tapers are used on machine spindles, shanks of tools,

or pins, and are described in "Machine Tapers" in *ANSI/ASME B5.10.* Such standard tapers are dimensioned on a drawing by giving the diameter (usually at the large end), the length, and a note, such as NO. 4 AMERICAN NATIONAL STANDARD TAPER as shown in Figure 11.50a.

For not-too-critical requirements, a taper may be dimensioned by giving the diameter at the large end, the length, and the included angle, all with proper

tolerances, as shown in Figure 11.50b. Alternatively, the diameters of both ends, plus the length, may be given with necessary tolerances.

For close-fitting tapers, the amount of taper per unit on diameter is indicated as shown in Figures 11.50c and d. A gage line is selected and located by a comparatively generous tolerance, and other dimensions are given appropriate tolerances as required.

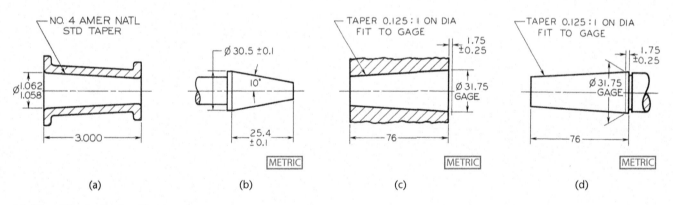

11.50 Dimensioning Tapers

11.31 DIMENSIONING CHAMFERS

A *chamfer* is a beveled or sloping edge. It is dimensioned by giving the length of the offset and the angle, as in Figure 11.51a. A 45° chamfer also may be dimensioned in a manner similar to that shown in Figure 11.51a, but usually it is dimensioned by note, as in Figure 11.51b.

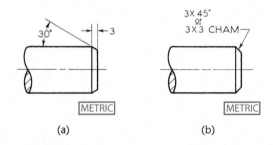

11.51 Dimensioning Chamfers

11.32 SHAFT CENTERS

Shaft centers are required on shafts, spindles, and other conical or cylindrical parts for turning, grinding, and other operations. Such a center may be dimensioned, as shown in Figure 11.52. Normally the centers are produced by a combined drill and countersink.

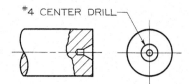

11.52 Shaft Center

11.33 DIMENSIONING KEYWAYS

The methods of dimensioning keyways for Woodruff keys and stock keys are shown in Figure 11.53. Note, in both cases, the use of a dimension to center the keyway in the shaft or collar. The preferred method of dimensioning the depth of a keyway is to give the dimension from the bottom of the keyway to the opposite side of the shaft or hole, as shown. The method of computing such a dimension is shown in Figure 11.53d. Values for A may be found in machinists' handbooks.

For general information about keys and keyways see Appendix 20.

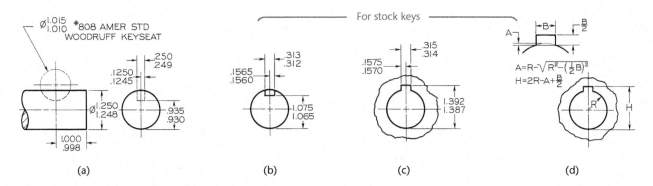

11.53 Dimensioning Keyways

11.34 DIMENSIONING KNURLS

A *knurl* is a roughened surface to provide a better handgrip or to be used for a press fit between two parts. For handgrip purposes, it is necessary only to give the pitch of the knurl, the type of knurling, and the length of the knurled area, as shown in Figures 11.54a and b. To dimension a knurl for a press fit, the toleranced diameter before knurling should be given, as shown in Figure 11.54c. A note should be added that gives the pitch and type of knurl and the minimum diameter after knurling (see *ANSI/ASME B94.6*).

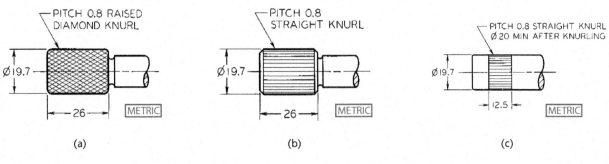

11.54 Dimensioning Knurls

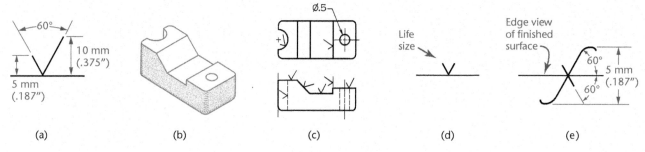

11.55 Finish Marks

11.35 FINISH MARKS

A *finish mark* is used to indicate that a surface is to be machined, or finished, as on a rough casting or forging. To the patternmaker or diemaker, a finish mark means that allowance of extra metal in the rough workpiece must be provided for the machining.

On drawings of parts to be machined from rolled stock, finish marks are generally unnecessary, because it is obvious that the surfaces are finished. Similarly, it is not always necessary to show finish marks when the dimension implies a finished surface, such as ⌀6.22–6.35 (metric) or ⌀2.45–2.50 (decimal-inch).

Figure 11.55 shows three styles of finish marks. The new basic symbol preferred by ANSI is shown in (a). The old general symbol ∨, shown in (d), and the old symbol ✗, shown in (e), are used to indicate an unspecified smooth machined surface. Due to more advanced inspection capabilities and the desire to build in quality processes, the old unspecified symbols are not used as much, unless used with a note, such as UOS ALL SURFACES 0.8/Ra 0.4. The old general symbol is like a capital V, made about 3 mm high, in conformity with the height of dimensioning lettering. The new basic symbol, preferred by ANSI, is like a larger capital with the right leg

extended. The short leg is made about 5 mm high, and the height of the long leg is about 10 mm. The basic symbol may be altered for more elaborate surface texture specifications.

Figure 11.55b shows a simple casting having several finished surfaces. In Figure 11.55c, two views of the same casting show how the finish marks are indicated on a drawing. The finish mark is shown only on the edge view of a finished surface and is repeated in any other view in which the surface appears as a line, even if the line is a hidden line.

If a part is to be finished all over, finish marks should be omitted, and a general note, such as FINISH ALL OVER or FAO, should be lettered on the lower portion of the sheet.

The several kinds of finishes are detailed in machine shop practice manuals. The following terms are among the most commonly used: finish all over, rough finish, file finish, sand blast, pickle, scrape, lap, hone, grind, polish, burnish, buff, chip, spotface, countersink, counterbore, core, drill, ream, bore, tap, broach, and knurl. When it is necessary to control the surface texture of finished surfaces beyond that of an ordinary machine finish, the symbol √ is used as a base for the more elaborate surface quality symbols. Older drawings may contain the previous style of surface finish symbol shown in Figure 11.55e.

Finished surfaces can be measured more accurately, so provide dimensions from these when possible, as in Figure 11.56.

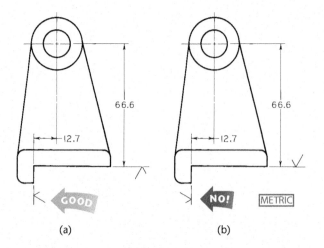

11.56 Correct and Incorrect Marks Showing Dimensions to Finished Surfaces. *The point of the symbol should be directed inward toward the body of metal similar to a tool bit, not upside down, as is shown in part b.*

11.36 SURFACE ROUGHNESS

The demands of automobiles, airplanes, and other machines that can stand heavy loads and high speeds with less friction and wear have increased the need for accurate control of surface quality by the designer, regardless of the size of the feature. Simple finish marks are not adequate to specify surface finish on such parts.

Surface finish is intimately related to the functioning of a surface, and proper specification of finish for surfaces such as bearings and seals is necessary. Surface quality specifications should be used only where needed, since the cost of producing a finished surface becomes greater as the quality of the surface called for is increased. Generally, the ideal surface finish is the roughest that will do the job satisfactorily.

	Symbol	Meaning
(a)	∨	Basic texture surface symbol. Surface may be produced by any method except when the bar or circle, (b) or (c), is specified.
(b)	∇	Material removal by machining is required. The horizontal bar indicates that material removal by machining is required to reproduce the surface and that material must be provided for that purpose.
(c)	∇̥	Material removal prohibited. The circle in the vee indicates that the surface must be produced by processes such as casting, forging, hot finishing, cold finishing, die casting, powder metallurgy, or injection molding without subsequent removal.
(d)	√	Surface texture symbol. To be used when any surface characteristics are specified above the horizontal line or to the right of the symbol. Surface may be produced by any method except when the bar or circle, (b) or (c), is specified.
(e)	√̥	All Around. The circle at the intersection of the angled and horizontal lines indicates the same finish applies to the entire surface. Point the callout for the surface finish where the surface indicated appears on edge. If it would be ambiguous, use separate callouts to each surface rather than the all around modifier.
(f)	√̊	All Over. The two concentric circles indicate that the same surface finish is required on all surfaces of the part.

Approx. 3X

3X

1.5X 60°

60°

1.5X

3X

Letter height = X

Drawing specifications

g   h

f   a / b / c / d

e   a₁ / b₁ / c₁ / d₁

Symbol method

a / b / c // d / a₁ / b₁ / c₁ / d₁ // e / f / g

Text method

Lower case letters represent the following surface requirements:

a = transmission band, meaning the shortest length or a range of the shortest and longest length for the sample to be measured and the filter types to use, if any. This must be specified at least in a note or specification, if not included in the symbol.

b = surface texture parameter and limits

c = evaluation length expressed as a number of samples (n = #) or a specified length. For example: n = 3 (meaning 3 samples), or 4 (meaning a sample length of 4 drawing units, either millimeters or inches depending on the drawing.)

d = calculation type

e = lay symbol

f = material removal modifiers, such as circle or bar

g = surface application modifier

h = processing notes

11.57 Surface Texture Symbols and Construction *(Reprinted from ASME Y14.36-2018, by permission of The American Society of Mechanical Engineers. All rights reserved.)*

The system of surface texture symbols recommended by ANSI/ASME (*Y14.36*) for use on drawings, regardless of the system of measurement used, is now broadly accepted by U.S industry. These symbols are used to define surface texture, roughness, and lay. See Figure 11.57 for the meaning and construction details for these symbols. The basic surface texture symbol in Figure 11.57 a indicates a finished or machined surface by any method, just as does the old general ∨ symbol. Modifications to the basic surface texture symbol, shown in Figures 11.57b–c, define restrictions on material removal for the finished surface. Where surface texture values other than average roughness are specified, the symbol must be drawn with the horizontal extension, as shown in Figure 11.57d.

Applications of Surface Roughness Symbols

Applications of the ***surface texture symbols*** are given in Figure 11.58. Note that the symbols read from the bottom and/or the right side of the drawing and that they are not drawn at any

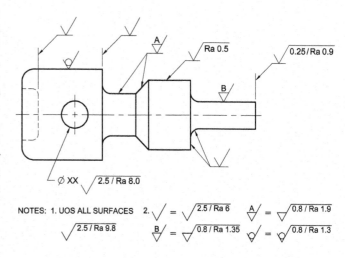

NOTES: 1. UOS ALL SURFACES

2. √ = √2.5 / Ra 6   A/ = √0.8 / Ra 1.9

√2.5 / Ra 9.8   B/ = ∇ 0.8 / Ra 1.35   ∇̥ = ∇̥ 0.8 / Ra 1.3

11.58 Application of Surface Texture Symbols *(Reprinted from ASME Y14.36-2018, by permission of The American Society of Mechanical Engineers. All rights reserved.)*

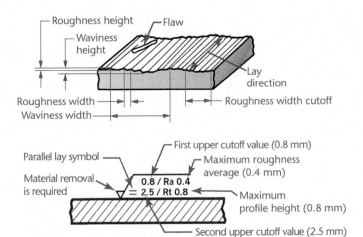

11.59 Surface Characteristics *(Reprinted from ASME Y14.36-2018, by permission of The American Society of Mechanical Engineers. All rights reserved.)*

angle or upside down. Measurements for roughness and waviness, unless otherwise specified, apply in the direction that gives the maximum reading, usually across the lay, as shown in Figure 11.59.

Recommended Roughness and Waviness Values

Recommended roughness height values are given in Table 11.1. When it is necessary to indicate the roughness-width cutoff values, the standard values used are listed in Table 11.2. If no value is specified, the 0.80 value is assumed.

When maximum waviness height values are required, the recommended values are given in Table 11.3.

Designations Used in Surface Texture Symbols

MRR Material Removal Required
NMR No Material Removed
APA Any Process Allowed
(G) Gaussian filter
Ra Mean roughness value
Rt Maximum peak to valley height
Rz Mean roughness depth
Rpk Mean height of the protruding peaks from the roughness profile
Rpm Mean maximum profile peak height
Rmr Material ratio of the profile
RMS Root Mean Square
UOS Unless Otherwise Specified

Lay Symbols and Surface Texture Symbols

Lay is the term for the dominant direction of the pattern formed by the cutting tool or grinding process used to manufacture a surface. When it is necessary to indicate lay, the lay symbols in Figure 11.60 are added to the surface texture symbols as shown in the given examples.

A typical range of surface roughness values that may be obtained from various production methods is included in Table 12.2.

Table 11.1 Preferred Series Roughness Average Values*
(Reprinted from ASME Y14.36M-1996 (R2002), by permission of The American Society of Mechanical Engineers. All rights reserved.)

Micrometers	Microinches
0.012	0.5
0.025	1
0.050	2
0.075	3
0.10	4
0.125	5
0.15	6
0.20	8
0.25	10
0.32	13
0.40	16
0.50	20
0.63	25
0.80	32
1.00	40
1.25	50
1.60	63
2.0	80
2.5	100
3.2	125
4.0	180
5.0	200
6.3	250
8.0	320
10.0	400
12.5	500
15	600
20	800
25	1000

* *Micrometers are the same as thousandths of a millimeter.*

Table 11.2 Standard Roughness Sampling Length (Cutoff) Values *(Reprinted from ASME Y14.36M-1996 (R2002), by permission of The American Society of Mechanical Engineers. All rights reserved.)*

Millimeters (mm)	Inches (″)
0.08	.003
0.25	.010
0.80	.030
2.5	.1
8.0	.3
25.0	1.0

Table 11.3 Preferred Series Maximum Waviness Height Values *(Reprinted from ASME Y14.36M-1996 (R2002), by permission of The American Society of Mechanical Engineers. All rights reserved.)*

Millimeters (mm)	Inches (″)
0.0005	.00002
0.0008	.00003
0.0012	.00005
0.0020	.00008
0.0025	.0001
0.005	.0002
0.008	.0003
0.012	.0005
0.020	.0008
0.025	.001
0.05	.002
0.08	.003
0.12	.005
0.20	.008
0.25	.010

This automotive aluminum part was manufactured through a low pressure die casting process and finished using high accuracy CNC machining. Some surfaces of the part may be left in a rough state, but other surfaces must be accurately finished in order to properly function for sliding, sealing, load bearing, etc. The drawing must communicate these requirements so that parts can be inspected to assure quality. (Mr. 1/Shutterstock.)

Symbol	Designation	Example
=	Lay parallel to the line representing the surface to which the symbol is applied	Direction of tool marks
⊥	Lay perpendicular to the line representing the surface to which the symbol is applied	Direction of tool marks
C	Lay approximately circular to the line representing the surface to which the symbol is applied	
P	Lay is nondirectional or protrudes like a "pebbly" cast surface	
X	Lay angular in both directions to the line representing the surface to which the symbol is applied	Direction of tool marks
M	Lay multidirectional	
R	Lay approximately radial to the line representing the surface to which the symbol is applied	

11.60   Lay Symbols *(Reprinted from ASME Y14.36-2018, by permission of The American Society of Mechanical Engineers. All rights reserved.)*

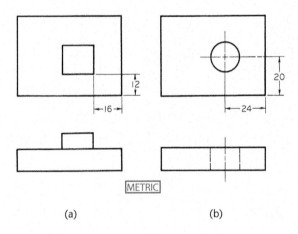

11.61   Location Dimensions

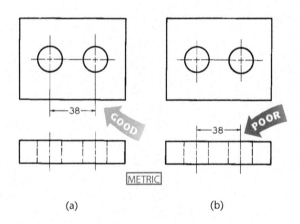

11.62   Locating Holes

11.37 LOCATION DIMENSIONS

After you have specified the sizes of the geometric shapes composing the structure, give *location dimensions* to show the relative positions of these geometric shapes. Figure 11.61a shows rectangular shapes located by their faces. In Figure 10.61b, cylindrical or conical holes or bosses, or other symmetrical shapes, are located by their centerlines. Location dimensions for holes are preferably given where the holes appear circular, as shown in Figures 11.62 and 11.63.

In general, location dimensions should be built from a finished surface or from an important center or centerline. Location dimensions should lead to finished surfaces wherever possible, because rough castings and forgings vary in size, and unfinished surfaces cannot be relied on for accurate measurements. The starting dimension, used in locating the first machined surface on a rough casting or forging, must necessarily lead from a rough surface or from a center or a centerline of the rough piece.

Holes equally spaced about a common center may be dimensioned by giving the diameter of the circle of centers, or bolt circle. Use a note such as 3X to indicate repetitive features or dimensions, where the X means *times*, and the 3 indicates the number of repeated features. Put a space between the letter X and the dimension as shown in Figure 11.63. Unequally spaced holes are located by means of the bolt circle diameter plus angular measurements with reference to only one of the centerlines. Examples are shown in Figure 11.63.

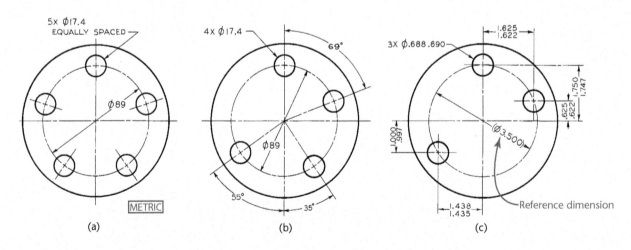

11.63   Locating Holes about a Center

Where greater accuracy is required, *coordinate dimensions* should be given, as shown in Figure 11.63c. In this case, the diameter of the bolt circle is enclosed in parentheses to indicate that it is to be used only as a reference dimension. Reference dimensions are given for information only. They are not intended to be measured and do not govern the manufacturing operations. They represent calculated dimensions and are often useful in showing the intended design sizes.

When several cylindrical surfaces have the same centerline (as in Figure 11.64b) you do not need location dimensions to show they are concentric; the centerline is enough.

When several nonprecision holes are located on a common arc, they are dimensioned by giving the radius and the angular measurements from a *baseline,* as shown in Figure 11.64a. In this case, the baseline is the horizontal centerline.

In Figure 11.64b, the three holes are on a common centerline. One dimension locates one small hole from the center; the other gives the distances between the small holes. Note that the dimension at *X* is left off. This method is used when the distance between the small holes is the important consideration. If the relation between the center hole and each of the small holes is more important, then include the distance at *X* and make the overall dimension a reference dimension.

Figure 11.64c shows another example of coordinate dimensioning. The three small holes are on a bolt circle whose diameter is given for reference purposes only. From the main center, the small holes are located in two mutually perpendicular directions.

Another example of locating holes by means of linear measurements is shown in Figure 11.64d. In this case, one measurement is made at an angle to the coordinate dimensions because of the direct functional relationship of the two holes.

In Figure 11.64e, the holes are located from two baselines, or datums. When all holes are located from a common datum, the sequence of measuring and machining operations is controlled, overall tolerance accumulations are avoided, and proper functioning of the finished part is assured. The datum surfaces selected must be more accurate than any measurement made from them, must be accessible during manufacture, and must be arranged to facilitate tool and fixture design. It may be necessary to specify accuracy of the datum surfaces in terms of straightness, roundness, flatness, and so on.

Figure 11.64f shows a method of giving, in a single line, all the dimensions from a common datum. Each dimension except the first has a single arrowhead and is accumulative in value. The overall dimension is separate.

These methods of locating holes are applicable to locating pins or other symmetrical features.

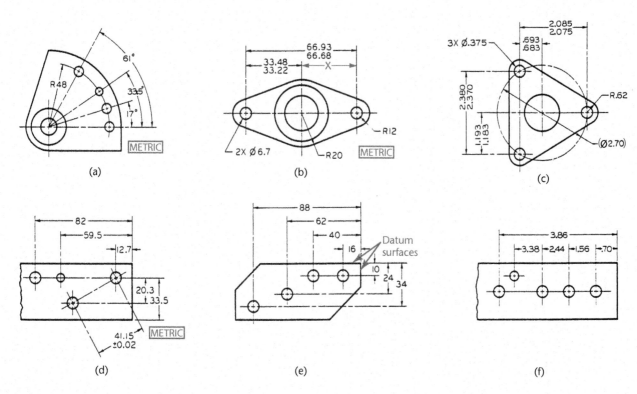

11.64 Locating Holes

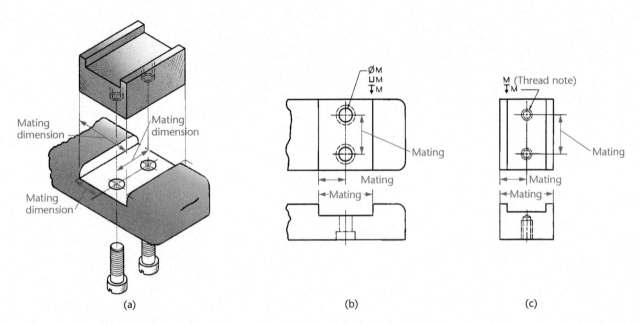

11.65   Mating Dimensions

11.38 MATING DIMENSIONS

In dimensioning a single part, its relation to mating parts must be taken into consideration. In Figure 11.65a, for example, a guide block must fit into a slot in a base. Those dimensions common to both parts, such as the distance between the holes, are mating dimensions. Other dimensions that do not control the accurate fitting together of two parts are not mating dimensions.

These *mating dimensions* should be given on the multiview drawings in the corresponding locations, as shown in Figures 11.65b and c. The actual values of two corresponding mating dimensions may not be exactly the same. For example, the width of the slot in Figure 11.65b may be dimensioned 1/32″ (0.8 mm) or several thousandths of an inch larger than the width of the block in Figure 11.65c, but these are mating

dimensions figured from a single basic width. Mating dimensions need to be specified in the corresponding locations on the two parts and toleranced to ensure proper fitting of the parts.

In Figure 11.66a, the dimension A is a necessary mating dimension and should appear on both the drawings of the bracket and of the frame. In Figure 11.66b, which shows a redesign of the bracket into two parts, dimension A is not used on either part because it is not necessary to closely control the distance between the cap screws. But dimensions F are now essential mating dimensions and should appear on the drawings of both parts. The remaining dimensions, E, D, B, and C, are not considered to be mating dimensions, since they do not directly affect the mating of the parts.

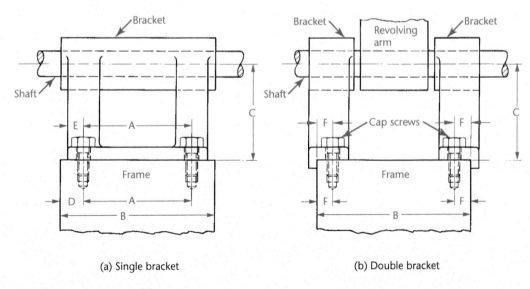

(a) Single bracket   (b) Double bracket

11.66   Bracket Assembly

11.39 COORDINATE DIMENSIONING

Coordinate dimensioning practices allow you to identify a corner of the part as the 0,0 location and dimension the remaining features relative to that position. This is very useful when numerically-controlled machines will be used in manufacturing the part, as the dimensions relate well to the manufacturing process. The lower-left corner on the part is often used as the 0,0 location (see Figure 11.67) as this is frequently the default for the numerically-controlled machine.

Rectangular coordinate dimensioning without dimension lines is shown in Figure 11.68.

Hole tables are often used in conjunction with coordinate dimensioning to save space when there are numerous holes of different sizes.

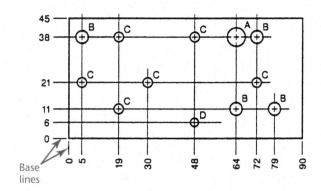

SIZE SYMBOL	A	B	C	D
HOLE Ø	7	4.8	3.6	3.1

11.67   Hole Table. *A hole table is often used to dimension complicated patterns of holes.* (Reprinted from ASME Y14.5M-1994 (R2004), by permission of The American Society of Mechanical Engineers. All rights reserved.)

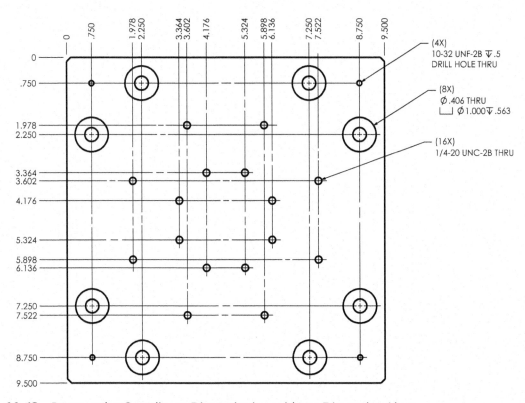

11.68   Rectangular Coordinate Dimensioning without Dimension Lines

11.40 TABULAR DIMENSIONS

A series of objects having like features but varying in dimensions may be represented by one drawing, as shown in Figure 11.69. Letters are substituted for dimension figures on the drawing, and the varying dimensions are given in tabular form. The dimensions of many standard parts are given in this manner in catalogs and handbooks.

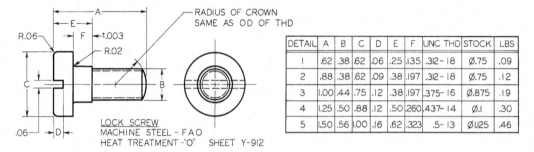

DETAIL	A	B	C	D	E	F	UNC THD	STOCK	LBS
1	.62	.38	.62	.06	.25	.135	.312-18	Ø.75	.09
2	.88	.38	.62	.09	.38	.197	.312-18	Ø.75	.12
3	1.00	.44	.75	.12	.38	.197	.375-16	Ø.875	.19
4	1.25	.50	.88	.12	.50	.260	.437-14	Ø.1	.30
5	1.50	.56	1.00	.16	.62	.323	.5-13	Ø1.125	.46

11.69 Tabular Dimensioning

11.41 DIMENSIONING FOR NUMERICALLY-CONTROLLED MACHINING

When dimensioning for numerically-controlled machining, follow these basic guidelines.

A set of three mutually perpendicular datum or reference planes is usually required. These planes either must be obvious, as shown in Figure 11.70, or must be clearly identified. (See Chapter 12 for information on identifying datums.)

The designer selects as origins for dimensions those surfaces or features most important to the function of the part. Enough of these features are selected to position the part in relation to the set of mutually perpendicular planes. All related dimensions are then made from these planes.

- All dimensions should be in decimals.
- Angles should be given, where possible, in degrees and decimal parts of degrees.
- Tools such as drills, reamers, and taps should be left up to the manufacturer unless a certain process is specifically required.
- All tolerances should be determined by the design requirements of the part, not by the capability of the manufacturing machine.

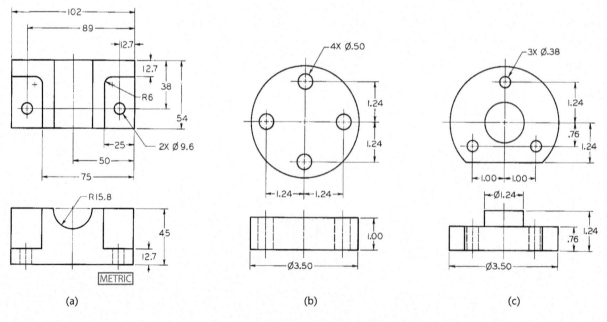

(a)   (b)   (c)

11.70 Dimensioning for Numerically-Controlled Machining

11.42 MACHINE, PATTERN, AND FORGING DIMENSIONS

The pattern maker is interested in the dimensions required to make the pattern, and the machinist is concerned only with the dimensions needed to machine the part. Frequently, a dimension that is convenient for the machinist is not convenient for the pattern maker, or vice versa. Because the pattern maker uses the drawing only once, while making the pattern, and the machinist refers to it continuously, the dimensions should be given primarily for the convenience of the machinist.

If the part is large and complicated, two separate drawings are sometimes made—one showing the pattern dimensions and the other the machine dimensions. The usual practice, however, is to prepare one drawing for both the pattern maker and the machinist.

For forgings, it is common practice to make separate forging drawings and machining drawings. A forging drawing of a connecting rod, showing only the dimensions needed in the forge shop, is shown in Figure 11.71. A machining drawing of the same part would contain only the dimensions needed in the machine shop.

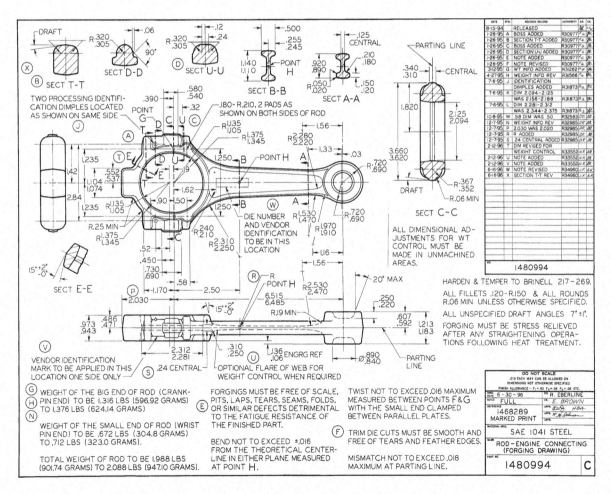

11.71 Forging Drawing of Connecting Rod *(Courtesy of General Motors LLC.)*

11.43 SHEET METAL BENDS

In sheet metal dimensioning, allowance must be made for bends. The intersection of the plane surfaces adjacent to a bend is called the *mold line,* and this line, rather than the center of the arc, is used to determine dimensions, as shown in Figure 11.72. The following procedure for calculating bends is typical. If the two inner plane surfaces of an angle are extended, their line of intersection is called the *inside mold line* or IML, as shown in Figures 11.73a–c. Similarly, if the two outer plane surfaces are extended, they produce the *outside mold line* or OML. The centerline of bend (₵B) refers primarily to the machine on which the bend is made and is at the center of the bend radius.

The length, or *stretchout,* of the pattern equals the sum of the flat sides of the angle plus the distance around the bend measured along the neutral axis. The distance around the bend is called the *bend allowance* or BA. When metal bends, it compresses on the inside and stretches on the outside. At a certain zone in between, the metal is neither compressed nor stretched, and this is called the *neutral axis,* as shown in Figure 11.73d. The neutral axis is usually assumed to be 0.44 of the thickness from the inside surface of the metal.

The developed length of material, or bend allowance, to make the bend is computed from the empirical formula

$$BA = (0.017453R + 0.0078T)N$$

where R = radius of bend, T = metal thickness, and N = number of degrees of bend, as in Figure 11.73c.

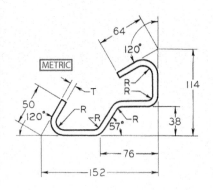

11.72   Profile Dimensioning

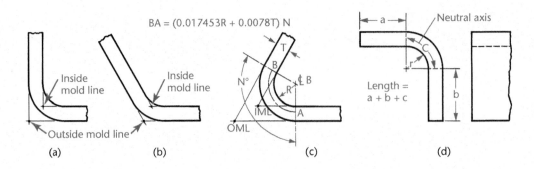

11.73   Bends

11.44 NOTES

It is usually necessary to supplement the direct dimensions with notes. Notes should be brief and carefully worded to allow only one interpretation. Notes should always be lettered horizontally on the sheet and arranged systematically. They should not be crowded and should not be placed between views, if possible. Notes are classified as **general notes** when they apply to an entire drawing and as **local notes** when they apply to specific items.

General Notes

General notes should be lettered in the lower right-hand corner of the first sheet of a set of drawings, above or to the left of the title block or in a central position below the view to which they apply. If notes are continued onto a second sheet, that sheet number should be given in a note on the first sheet of the drawing set, as in NOTES CONTINUED ON PAGE 4.

Here are some examples of general notes:

FINISH ALL OVER (FAO)

BREAK SHARP EDGES TO R0.8

G33106 ALLOY STEEL-BRINELL 340–380

ALL DRAFT ANGLES 3° UNLESS OTHERWISE SPECIFIED

DIMENSIONS APPLY AFTER PLATING

In machine drawings, the title strip or title block will carry many general notes, including those for materials, general tolerances, heat treatments, and patterns.

Local Notes

Local notes apply to specific operations only and are connected by a leader to the point at which such operations are performed, as shown in Figure 11.74. The leader should be attached at the front of the first word of a note, or just after the last word, and not at any intermediate place.

Use common abbreviations in notes (such as THD, DIA, MAX) only when they cannot be misunderstood. Avoid less common abbreviations. "When in doubt, spell it out" is a rule of thumb to avoid problems with misunderstood notes.

If a common symbol is available, it is preferred to the abbreviation because symbols are internationally recognized and not language dependent. All abbreviations should conform to *ANSI Y14.38*. See Appendix 2 for ANSI abbreviations.

In general, leaders and notes should not be placed on the drawing until the dimensioning is substantially completed. Notes and lettering should not touch lines of the drawing or title block. If notes are lettered first, they may be in the way of necessary dimensions and will have to be moved.

When using CAD to add text for drawing notes, keep in mind the final scale to which the drawing will be plotted. You may need to enlarge the text for it to be legible when plotted to a smaller scale.

Local notes and dimensions can also be placed in 3D CAD models. When doing so, take care to point the note to the surface in a place where it is unambiguous. Use an arrow at the end of the leader line to point to a feature. Use a dot at the end of the leader line when pointing a note onto the surface shape.

Flag Notes

Flag notes are another option for specific or local notes. These notes are identified with a flag note symbol, typically a rectangle, hexagon, or triangle containing the number of the note and placed with the general notes.

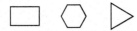

Flag notes apply only at each specific area of the drawing identified with the note symbol. See Fig. 11.74o for an example of a flag note.

Number the general notes and flag notes consecutively in a single list. Do not re-use note numbers of notes added in one revision and then subsequently deleted. If your PDM system assigns values, the notes it generates do not have to be in a continuous sequence.

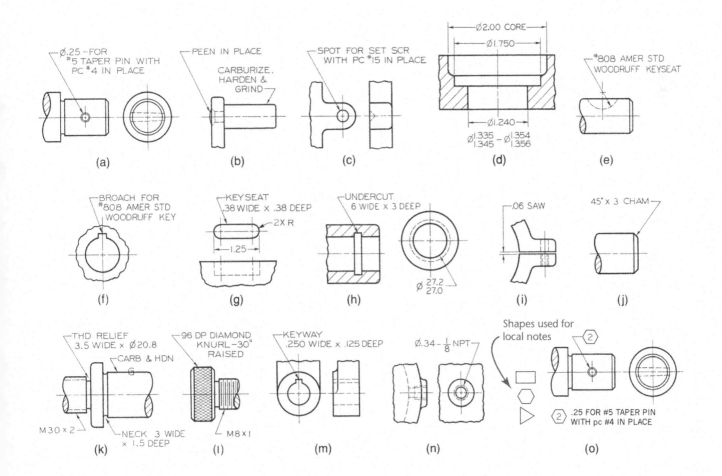

11.74 Local Notes

11.45 STANDARDS

Dimensions should be given, wherever possible, to make use of readily available materials, tools, parts, and gages. The dimensions for many commonly used machine elements—such as bolts, screws, nails, keys, tapers, wire, pipes, sheet metal, chains, belts, ropes, pins, and rolled metal shapes—have been standardized, and the drafter must obtain these sizes from company standards manuals, from published handbooks, from ANSI standards, or from manufacturers' catalogs. Tables of some of the more common items are given in the appendices.

Such standard parts are not delineated on detail drawings unless they are to be altered for use; they are conventionally drawn on assembly drawings and are listed in parts lists. Common fractions are often used to indicate the nominal sizes of standard parts or tools. If the complete decimal-inch system is used, all such sizes are ordinarily expressed by decimals—for example, .250 DRILL instead of 1/4 DRILL. If the all-metric system of dimensioning is used, then the preferred metric drill of the approximate same size (.2480″) will be indicated as 6.30 DRILL.

11.46 DOS AND DON'TS OF DIMENSIONING

The following checklist summarizes briefly most of the situations in which a beginning designer is likely to make a mistake in dimensioning. Students should check the drawing with this list before submitting it to the instructor.

1. Each dimension should be given clearly so that it can be interpreted in only one way.
2. Dimensions should not be duplicated, nor should the same information be given in two different ways—except for dual dimensioning—and no dimensions should be given except those needed to produce or inspect the part.
3. Dimensions should be given between points or surfaces that have a functional relation to each other or that control the location of mating parts.
4. Dimensions should be given to finished surfaces or important centerlines, in preference to rough surfaces, wherever possible.
5. Dimensions should be given so that it will not be necessary for the machinist to calculate, scale, or assume any dimension.
6. Dimension features should be attached to the view where the feature's shape is best shown.
7. Dimensions should be placed in the views where the features dimensioned are shown true shape.
8. Dimensioning to hidden lines should be avoided wherever possible.
9. Dimensions should not be placed on a view unless clarity is promoted and long extension lines are avoided.
10. Dimensions applying to two adjacent views should be placed between views, unless clarity is promoted by placing some of them outside.
11. The longer dimensions should be placed outside all intermediate dimensions so that dimension lines will not cross extension lines.
12. In machine drawing, all unit marks should be omitted, except when necessary for clarity; for example, 1″ VALVE or 1 mm DRILL.
13. Don't expect production personnel to assume that a feature is centered (as a hole on a plate), but give a location dimension from one side. However, if a hole is to be centered on a symmetrical rough casting, mark the centerline and omit the locating dimension from the centerline.
14. A dimension should be attached to only one view, not to extension lines connecting two views.
15. Detail dimensions should line up in chain fashion.
16. A complete chain of detail dimensions should be avoided; it is better to omit one. Otherwise add a reference to the overall dimension by enclosing it within parentheses.
17. A dimension line should never be drawn through a dimension figure. A figure should never be lettered over any line of the drawing. The line can be broken if necessary.
18. Dimension lines should be spaced uniformly throughout the drawing. They should be at least 10 mm (.38″) from the object outline and 6 mm (.25″) apart.
19. No line of the drawing should be used as a dimension line or coincide with a dimension line.
20. A dimension line should never be joined end to end with any line of the drawing.
21. Dimension lines should not cross, if avoidable.
22. Dimension lines and extension lines should not cross, if avoidable. (Extension lines may cross each other.)
23. When extension lines cross extension lines or visible lines, no break in either line should be made.
24. A centerline may be extended and used as an extension line, in which case it is still drawn like a centerline.
25. Centerlines should not extend from view to view.
26. Leaders for notes should be straight, not curved, and point to the center of circular views of holes wherever possible.
27. Leaders should slope at 45°, 30°, or 60° with horizontal, but may be made at any convenient angle except vertical or horizontal.

28. Leaders should extend from the beginning or the end of a note, with the horizontal "shoulder" extending from mid-height of the lettering.
29. Dimension figures should be approximately centered between the arrowheads, except in a stack of dimensions, where they should be staggered.
30. Dimension figures should be about 3 mm (.13″) high for whole numbers and 6 mm (.25″) high for fractions.
31. Dimension figures should never be crowded or in any way made difficult to read.
32. Dimension figures should not be lettered over lines or sectioned areas unless necessary, in which case a clear space should be reserved for the dimension figures.
33. Dimension figures for angles should generally be lettered horizontally.
34. Fraction bars should never be inclined except in confined areas, such as in tables.
35. The numerator and denominator of a fraction should never touch the fraction bar.
36. Notes should always be lettered horizontally on the sheet.
37. Notes should be brief and clear, and the wording should be standard in form.
38. Finish marks should be placed on the edge views of all finished surfaces, including hidden edges and the contour and circular views of cylindrical surfaces.
39. Finish marks should be omitted on holes or other features where a note specifies a machining operation.
40. Finish marks should be omitted on parts made from rolled stock.
41. If a part is finished all over, all finish marks should be omitted and the general note FINISH ALL OVER or FAO should be used.
42. A cylinder is dimensioned by giving both its diameter and length in the rectangular view, except when notes are used for holes. A diagonal diameter in the circular view may be used in cases where it increases clarity.
43. Manufacturing processes are generally determined by the tolerances specified, rather than specifically noted in the drawing. When the manufacturing process must be noted for some reason—such as for dimension holes to be bored, drilled, and reamed—use leaders that preferably point toward the center of the circular views of the holes. Give the manufacturing processes in the order they would be performed.
44. Drill sizes should be expressed in decimals, giving the diameter. For drills designated by number or letter, the decimal size must also be given.
45. In general, a circle is dimensioned by its diameter, an arc by its radius.
46. Diagonal diameters should be avoided, except for very large holes and for circles of centers. They may be used on positive cylinders for clarity.
47. A diameter dimension value should always be preceded by the symbol $\emptyset$.
48. A radius dimension should always be preceded by the letter R. The radial dimension line should have only one arrowhead, and it should pass through or point through the arc center and touch the arc.
49. Cylinders should be located by their centerlines.
50. Cylinders should be located in the circular views, if possible.
51. Cylinders should be located by coordinate dimensions in preference to angular dimensions where accuracy is important.
52. When there are several rough, noncritical features obviously the same size (fillets, rounds, ribs, etc.), it is necessary to give only typical (abbreviation TYP) dimensions or to use a note.
53. When a dimension is not to scale, it should be underscored with a heavy straight line or marked NTS or NOT TO SCALE.
54. Mating dimensions should be given correspondingly on both drawings of mating parts.
55. Pattern dimensions should be given in two-place decimals or in common whole numbers and fractions to the nearest 1/16″.
56. Decimal dimensions should be used for all machining dimensions.
57. Cumulative tolerances should be avoided where they affect the fit of mating parts.

THE CAD DATABASE AS DESIGN DOCUMENTATION

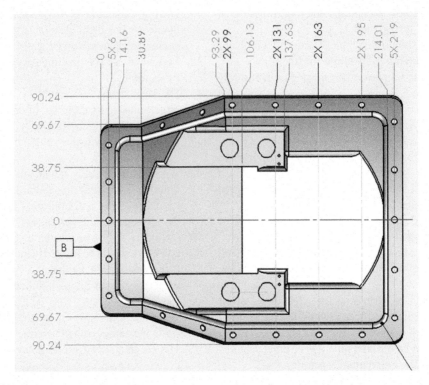

EDrawings software allows you to view 3D and 2D drawings. Many companies transmit and store eDrawings as their design record. (Courtesy of Zolo Technologies, Inc.)

An important advantage of producing an accurate CAD database is that you can use the model as a basis for manufacturing. Today's CAD packages offer tools for incorporating tolerances and manufacturing notes into the 3D CAD database itself that improve its ability to document the design. A good understanding of the type of information available in your CAD database combined with the knowledge of how to show critical dimensions and tolerances clearly are important in achieving the most benefit from 3D CAD software.

To use the CAD database as design documentation, companies must consider the legal requirements for maintaining a permanent record of the design. For some industries, a permanent record (or snapshot) of the design used for production must be maintained. A changeable record on the computer may not be considered a legally acceptable practice, or it may be acceptable only if a standard of model/drawing control is met.

ASME Y14.41, Digital Product Definition Data Practices, describes the standard for using a digital product definition to document designs. Some companies use the 3D model with electronic annotations stored in the file or a related database as the final documentation for the product. Other companies produce 2D original drawings from the 3D model to communicate the design for manufacturing and to provide design documentation for the project. For those companies the 3D model may be stored, but the design record is the fully dimensioned 2D drawings.

Other companies use a combination of the computer files and 2D drawings to document the design. The 2D drawings are used to communicate information about critical tolerances and other information that may not be easily visible in the 3D file. The CAD file serves as the interface to automated manufacturing processes, but the drawing allows the company to call attention to those elements of the design that are critical to its function. Because the manufacturer may not have the same software that was used to create the CAD model, the documentation needs to use a format that can be interpreted by the manufacturer, mold maker, or others who will create or inspect the parts. This is frequently a combination of electronic files in a common 3D format (such as IGES) for the model, and 2D CAD documentation drawings (either printed or in a common 2D file format such as DXF) showing critical dimensions.

Whether the 2D drawings are printed on paper or stored electronically, correctly shown orthographic views still provide much of the basis for communicating and documenting the design. Correctly shown drawing views are also used to communicate information for user manuals and repair manuals, as well as for manufacture and inspection.

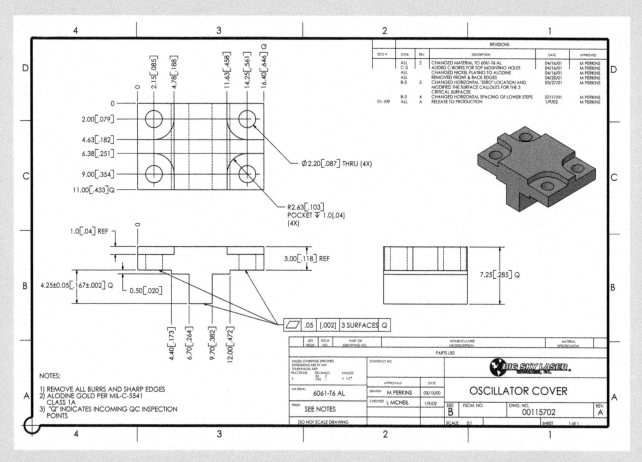

This drawing for a small part shows dimensions in millimeters with the inch values given [in brackets] for reference. (Courtesy of Big Sky Laser.)

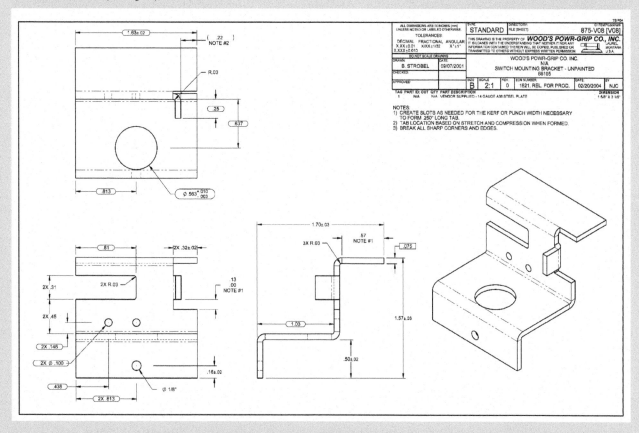

Dimensioned Drawing for a Sheet Metal Part *(Courtesy of Wood's Power-Grip Co., Inc.)*

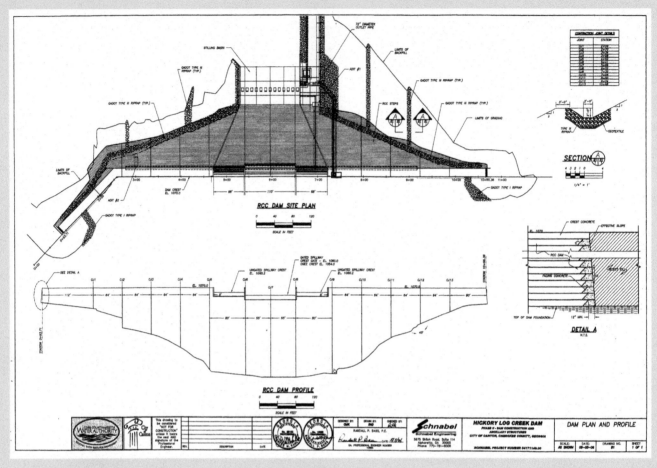

Plan and Profile for Dam Site *(Courtesy of Schnabel Engineering.)*

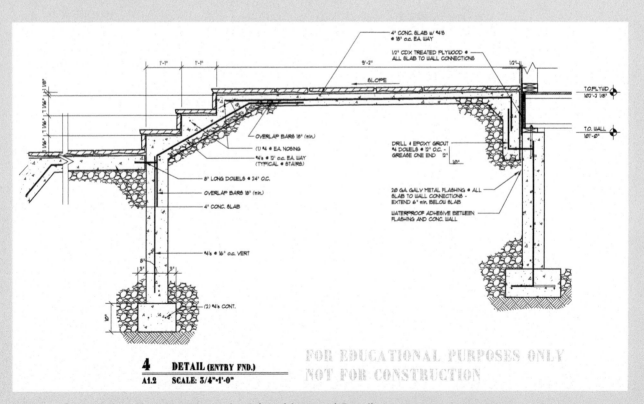

Portion of a Drawing Showing Dimensioned Architectural Details *(Courtesy of Locati Architects.)*

KEY WORDS

Arrowheads

Baseline

Batter

Bracket Method

Centerline

Chordal Dimensions

Coordinate Dimensions

Dimension Line

Dimensions

Dual Dimensioning

Extension Line

Finish Mark

General Notes

Grade

Leader

Local Notes

Location Dimensions

Mating Dimensions

Position Method

Radial Leader Line

Size Dimensions

Slope

Superfluous Dimensions

Surface Texture Symbols

Tolerance

Unidirectional

CHAPTER SUMMARY

- To increase clarity, dimensions and notes are added to a drawing to describe size, location, and manufacturing process precisely.
- Drawings are scaled to fit on a standard sheet of paper. Drawings created by hand are drawn to scale. CAD drawings are drawn full size and scaled when they are printed.
- Dimensions and notes are placed on drawings according to prescribed standards.
- Good placement practices are essential to making drawings easy to read.
- It is important to learn to dimension basic shapes. Complex drawings are usually made of many simpler features.
- Finish symbols and notes are a part of describing how the part is to be manufactured. They should be shown on the drawing as needed.
- The CAD database can serve as the design documentation, in which case drawings may not be necessary.
- Dimensioning dos and don'ts can provide guidelines for dimensioning practices, but overall, the dimensions that are necessary for the part to be manufactured and function in the assembly as intended must be shown.
- Special dimensioning techniques are used for surfaces that have been machined by one of the manufacturing processes.

REVIEW QUESTIONS

1. What are the different units used when a drawing is created using a metric scale? Using an architects' scale?
2. Explain the concept of contour dimensioning.
3. Which type of line is never crossed by any other line when dimensioning an object?
4. How is geometric analysis used in dimensioning?
5. What is the difference between a size dimension and a location dimension?
6. Which dimension system allows dimensions to be read from the bottom and from the right? When can a dimension be read from the left?
7. Draw an example of dimensioning an angle.
8. When are finish marks used? Draw two types.
9. How are negative and positive cylinders dimensioned? Draw examples.
10. How are holes and arcs dimensioned? Draw examples.
11. What are notes and leaders used for?
12. How does a counterbore dimension that specifies a fillet radius differ from a fillet radius specified as part of a spot-face dimension?
13. Why is it important to avoid superfluous dimensions?

CHAPTER EXERCISES

Most of your practice in dimensioning will be in connection with working drawings assigned from other chapters. However, some dimensioning problems are available here. The following problems are designed for 8.50″ × 11″ size sheets and are to be drawn and dimensioned to a full-size scale. Size 297 mm × 420 mm sheets may be used with appropriate adjustments in the title strip layout.

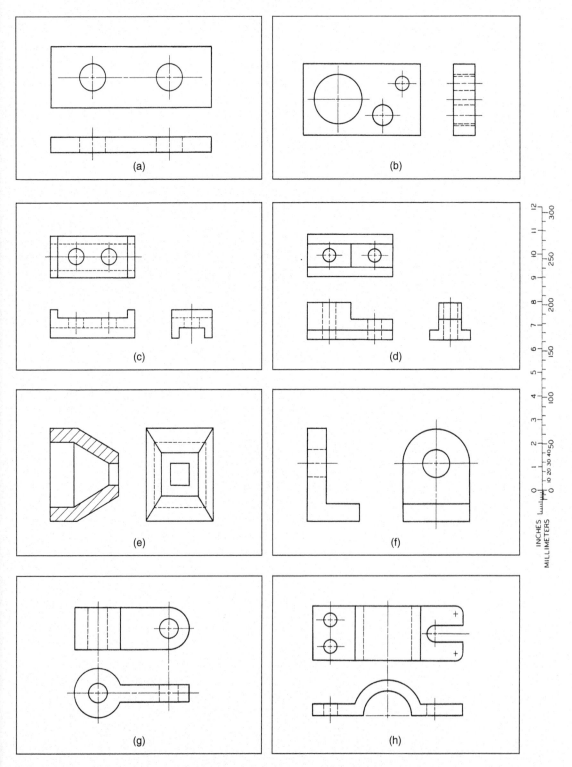

Exercise 11.1 To obtain sizes, use the views on this page and transfer them to the scale at the side to obtain values. Dimension drawings completely in one-place millimeters or two-place inches as assigned, full size. See the inside back cover for decimal-inch and millimeter equivalents.

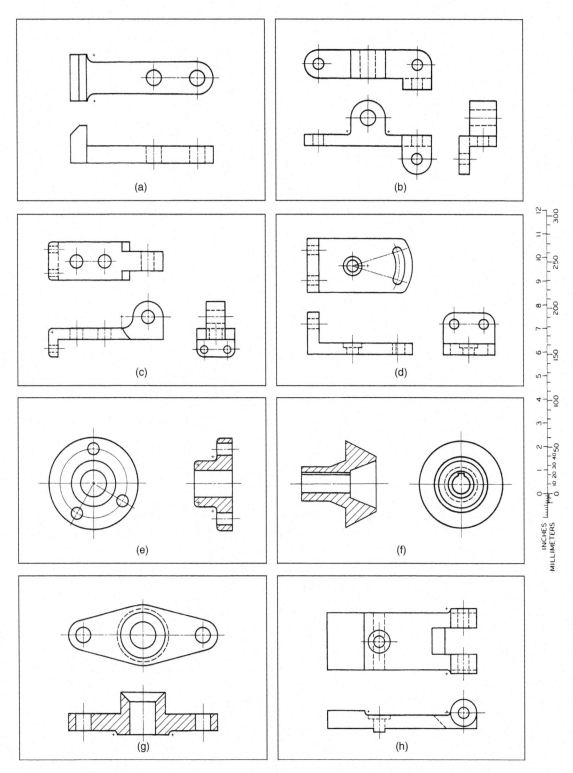

(a) (b)

(c) (d)

(e) (f)

(g) (h)

INCHES
MILLIMETERS

Exercise 11.2 To obtain sizes, use the views on this page and transfer them to the scale at the side to obtain values. Dimension drawings completely in one-place millimeters or two-place inches as assigned, full size. See the inside back cover for decimal-inch and millimeter equivalents.

Exercise 11.3 Draw both the finish texture symbol and the text designation to require the following surface finish: Upper cutoff value of 0.8mm, a maximum roughness average that does not exceed 1.6 μm, with 5 sample lengths used to find the average. Material removal on the surface is required.

CHAPTER TWELVE

TOLERANCING

---------- OBJECTIVES ----------

After studying the material in this chapter, you should be able to:

1. Describe the nominal size, tolerance, limits, and allowance of two mating parts.

2. Identify a clearance fit, interference fit, and transition fit.

3. Describe the basic hole and basic shaft systems.

4. Dimension mating parts using limit dimensions, unilateral tolerances, and bilateral tolerances.

5. Describe the classes of fit and give examples of each.

6. Draw geometric tolerancing symbols.

7. Specify geometric tolerances.

8. Relate datum surfaces to degrees of freedom.

Refer to the following standards:
- *ANSI/ASME Y14.5 Dimensioning and Tolerancing*
- *ANSI B4.1 Preferred Limits and Fits for Cylindrical Parts*
- *ANSI B4.2 Preferred Metric Limits and Fits*
- *ASME Y14.43 Dimensioning and Tolerancing Principles for Gages and Fixtures*
- *ISO 5459 Geometrical Product Specifications*
- *ISO 286-1; ISO 286-2*
- *ISO 1101*

Specifying Tolerance Is Essential to Ensuring that Interchangeable Parts Fit Together in Assemblies. *A worker uses an inside caliper to measure the hole diameter to ensure that it is within the specified tolerance range. (dotshock/Shutterstock.)*

OVERVIEW

Interchangeable manufacturing requires effective size control by the designer because, in mass production, all parts must fit together properly, regardless of where they are made.

For example, an automobile manufacturer might subcontract parts manufacturing to other companies—both parts for new automobiles and replacement parts for repairs. All parts must be enough alike that each can fit properly in any assembly.

The maximum acceptable amount that an actual part feature can vary from a specified dimension is called *tolerance*. On technical drawings, tolerances specify the degree of accuracy required for the provided dimensions.

Parts can be made to very precise dimensions, even to a few millionths of an inch or thousandths of a millimeter—as in gage blocks—but highly accurate parts are extremely expensive to produce and there is

still some variation between the exact dimension and the actual size of the part. Fortunately, perfectly exact sizes are not needed. The accuracy needed in a part depends on its function.

One aspect of quality is determined by manufacturing tolerances. Products with small variations in shape may fit together more precisely and command higher prices. However, it would not be practical for all products to be manufactured to high precision. For example, a manufacturer of children's tricycles might go out of business if the parts were made with jet engine accuracy—no one would be willing to pay the price.

Waste results when the manufacturing process cannot maintain shape and size within prescribed limits. By monitoring the manufacturing processes and reducing waste, a company can improve profits. This direct relationship to profit is one of the main reasons that tolerancing is critical to manufacturing success.

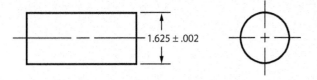

12.1   Direct Limits Used to Specify a Bilateral Tolerance

UNDERSTANDING TOLERANCE

Tolerancing is an extension of dimensioning. It allows you to specify a range of accuracy for the shape, size, and position of every feature of a product, so that the manufactured parts will fit together and function properly when assembled. CAD software often provide features for dimensioning, tolerancing, and checking fits and interferences that aid in the tolerancing process. To effectively provide tolerances in your drawings and CAD models, you must:

- Understand the fit required between mating parts.
- Have a clear picture of how inspection measurements are performed.
- Be able to apply tolerance symbols to a drawing or model.
- Apply functional tolerancing to individual part features.

Tolerance

Tolerance is the total amount a specific dimension is permitted to vary. Tolerances are specified so that any two mating parts will fit together. To keep part cost low, specify a tolerance as large as possible that still permits satisfactory function of the part. Tolerance can be stated several different ways on a drawing.

One method of providing a tolerance is to specify the dimension and give a plus or minus range after it. Figure 12.1 shows an example of a *bilateral tolerance*. A dimension given as 1.625 ± 0.002 means that the manufactured part may be 1.627 or 1.623 or anywhere between these maximum and minimum limit dimensions, as shown in Figure 12.2. The tolerance (the total amount the actual part feature is allowed to vary from what is specified) is 0.004.

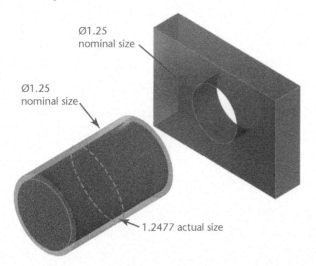

12.3   Nominal Size and Actual Size

Ø1.25
nominal size

Ø1.25
nominal size

1.2477 actual size

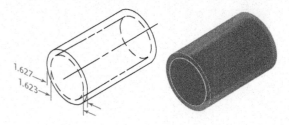

12.2   Upper and Lower Limits of Dimension

1.627
1.623

Quality Control

When you purchase parts or have them manufactured by another company, you must have a way to ensure that the parts are manufactured precisely enough.

Before paying for parts, most companies have a process to *quality certify (QC)* the parts against the drawing or model. Larger batches of parts may use statistical methods in which a relevant sample of the parts are inspected instead of all the parts. Some companies require certification from the part vendor rather than inspecting parts themselves.

A tolerance must be specified for each dimension so that it can be determined how accurately the part must be manufactured to be acceptable. The tolerances that you specify are based on the part's function and fit.

Unless otherwise stated, the dimensions and tolerances apply at 68 degrees F (20 degrees C) in a free state (not stretched or compressed, etc.). When inspected in other temperature conditions, the measurements may be appropriately compensated.

Definitions for Size Designation

You should become familiar with the size designation terms that apply in tolerancing.

Feature   A physical portion of a part, such as a pin, or a hole, or the representation of such a feature on a drawing or in a model.

Feature of size   The two types of features of size are regular and irregular. A regular feature of size is a cylindrical or spherical surface, a circular element (such as the cross section of a cylinder), or a set of two opposed parallel elements or opposed parallel surfaces that are associated with a directly toleranced dimension.

Actual local feature   The measured value of any individual cross section of a feature of size.

Nominal size   is used for general identification and is usually expressed in decimals or, less often, common fractions. In Figure 12.3, the nominal size of both hole and shaft, which is 1.25″, would be 1-1/4″ or 31.75 mm.

Allowance   is the minimum clearance space (or maximum interference) that is specified to achieve a fit between two mating parts. In Figure 12.3, the allowance is the difference between the size of the smallest hole and the size of the largest shaft. Allowance represents the tightest permissible fit. For clearance fits this difference will be positive, but for interference fits it will be negative.

12.4 *Part is waisted.*

12.5 *Part is bowed.*

12.6 *Part is tapered.*

12.7 *Part is barreled.*

Variations in Form

The dimensions of the cylinder in Figure 12.1 specify a bilateral tolerance that allows the part to be +.002 or –.002 from the 1.625 dimension specified. The drawing or model specifies the cylinder's shape, and the dimensions and tolerance specify its size and the allowable variation that the size may have.

But what about imperfections of the form? Some imperfections of form that may occur in manufacturing cylinders are shown in Figures 12.4–12.7. Of course, they are greatly exaggerated in the illustration. Because nothing can be made to exact perfection, some of these types of variations will occur in manufacturing. The objective of providing a tolerance is to indicate the acceptable amount of variation so that the parts will still fit and function.

You can think of tolerance as defining a ***perfect form envelope*** that the real produced part must fit inside in order to be acceptable.

TIP

You can sometimes notice variations in form by placing a machinists' scale along the edge of the part and checking to see whether you can slip a feeler gage between the scale and the edge of the part.

Tolerance Envelope

The following terms describe the tolerance envelope:

Actual mating envelope (AMC)   The envelope toward the outside of the material, in which the acceptable actual feature must fit. For external parts, like cylinders, this is the perfect feature at the largest permissible size; for internal features, like holes, this is the perfect feature at the smallest permissible size.

Actual minimum material envelope   This envelope is the counterpart to the actual mating envelope. For an acceptable external feature, it is the perfect feature at the smallest permissible size; for an internal feature this is the perfect feature at the largest permissible size.

Figure 12.8a illustrates the idea of a part fitting inside the perfect form envelope. The part (a shaft) is represented in green and the actual mating envelope and actual minimum material envelope are shown as blue areas. The part can be any size that is no larger than the actual mating envelope and no smaller than the actual minimum material envelope.

Figure 12.8c illustrates a bowed part that extends outside the actual mating envelope. Figure 12.8d shows a waisted part that extends beyond the actual minimum material envelope.

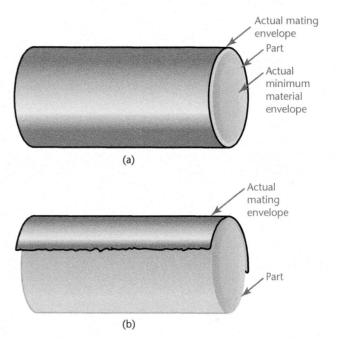

Actual mating envelope
Part
Actual minimum material envelope

(a)

Actual mating envelope

Part

(b)

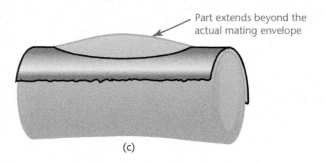

Part extends beyond the actual mating envelope

(c)

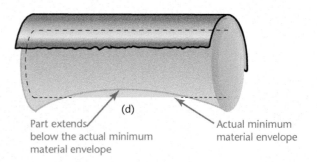

Part extends below the actual minimum material envelope

Actual minimum material envelope

(d)

12.8   (a) Acceptable Fit. (b) Section Showing Fit. (c) Unacceptable Part *(extends beyond the actual mating envelope)*. (d) Unacceptable Part *(extends beyond the actual minimum material envelope)*. *(Variations are exaggerated for the purpose of illustration.)*

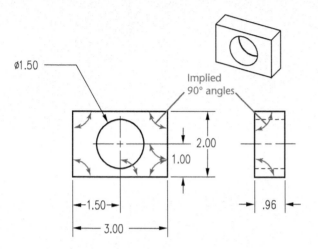

ALL TOLERANCES ±0.002 UNLESS OTHERWISE NOTED.
ANGULAR TOLERANCES ±1°.

12.9   *Noted tolerances apply to implied 90° angles the same as they do to dimensioned angles that are not noted otherwise.*

Implied Right Angles

When lines or centerlines intersect on a drawing at angles of 90°, it is customary not to dimension the angle. This situation is called an implied 90° angle. If the angle is something other than 90°, it must be dimensioned to be understood clearly.

Implied 90° angles have the same general tolerances applied to them as do any other angles covered by a general note. The exception is when a geometric tolerance is used for that feature. When geometric tolerances are specified, implied 90° or 0° angles between feature centerlines are considered basic dimensions to which no tolerance applies outside that stated by the geometric tolerance. Figure 12.9 shows a simple dimensioned drawing with a general tolerance note. The tolerance of plus or minus 1° applies to the implied 90° angles as well as to the dimensioned angles in the drawing. Figure 12.10 shows a drawing where implied 90° angles are controlled by the tolerance noted in the title block. Later in this chapter you will learn to use geometric dimensioning and tolerancing to control angles with greater precision.

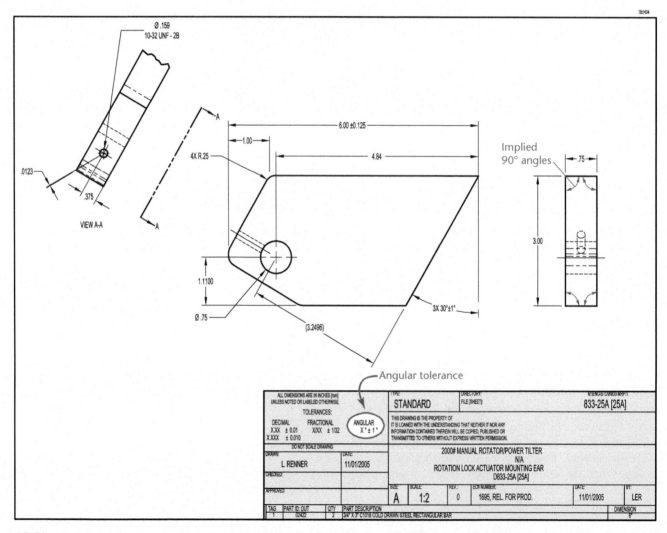

12.10   *Tolerance block note is applied to implied 90° angles in the drawing. (Courtesy of Wood's Power-Grip Co., Inc.)*

Fits between Mating Parts

Fit is the range of tightness or looseness resulting from the allowances and tolerances in mating parts. The loosest fit, or maximum clearance, occurs when the smallest internal part (shaft) is in the largest external part (hole), as shown in Figure 12.11a. The tightest fit, or minimum clearance, occurs when the largest shaft is in the smallest hole, as shown in Figure 12.11b. The difference between the largest allowable shaft size and the smallest allowable hole size (0.002″ in this case) is the allowance. There are three general types of fits between parts.

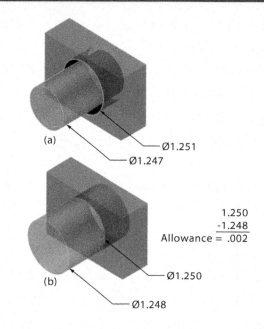

12.11 (a) Loosest and (b) Tightest Fit

Clearance Fit A *clearance fit* occurs when an internal part fits into an external part with space (or clearance) between the parts. In Figure 12.12, the largest shaft is 1.248″ and the smallest hole is 1.250″, giving a minimum space (allowance) of .002″ between the parts. In a clearance fit, the allowance is always positive.

 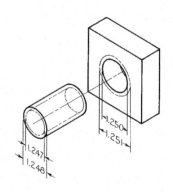 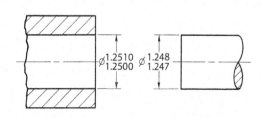

12.12 Clearance Fit

Interference Fit An *interference fit* occurs when the internal part is larger than the external part, so the parts must be forced together. In Figure 12.13, the smallest shaft is 1.2513″ and the largest hole is 1.2506″, so the interference of metal between parts is at least .0007″. For the largest shaft and smallest hole, the interference is 0.0019″. In an interference fit, the allowance is always negative.

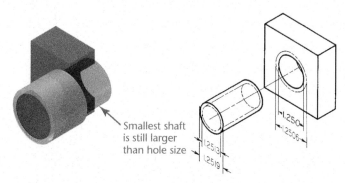 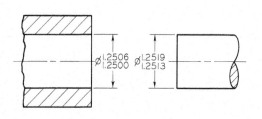

12.13 Interference Fit

Transition Fit A ***transition fit*** refers to either a tight clearance or interference. In Figure 12.14 the smallest shaft, 1.2503″, will fit into the largest hole, 1.2506″. But the largest shaft, 1.2509″, will have to be forced into the smallest hole, 1.2500″.

Line fit is sometimes used to indicate limits that are specified so that a clearance or surface contact results when mating parts are assembled.

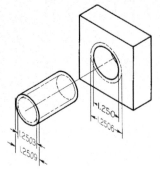

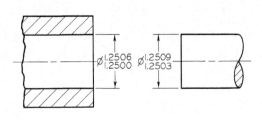

12.14   Transition Fit

Specifying Fit Using Limit Dimensions

Limit dimensions are a method of directly specifying tolerance by providing dimensions for the upper and lower limits of the feature's size. The high limit (maximum value) is placed above the low limit (minimum value) in place of the dimension value.

In the example shown in Figure 12.15, the actual hole may not be less than 1.250″ and not more than 1.251″. These are the limits for the dimension, and the difference between them (.001″) is the tolerance, as is indicated in Figure 12.16a.

Likewise, the shaft must be between limits 1.248″ and 1.247″. The difference between these limits is .001″ so the tolerance for the shaft is .001″. The minimum clearance is .002″, so any shaft will fit inside any hole interchangeably.

In metric dimensions, the limits for the hole are 31.75 mm and 31.78 mm. Their difference, 0.03 mm, is the tolerance (Figure 12.16b). Similarly, the limits for the shaft are 31.70 mm and 31.67 mm, and the difference between them, the tolerance, is 0.03 mm.

When parts are required to fit properly in assembly but are not required to be interchangeable, they are not always toleranced, but it is indicated on the drawing that they are to be made to fit at assembly. Figure 12.17 shows an example of this type of note.

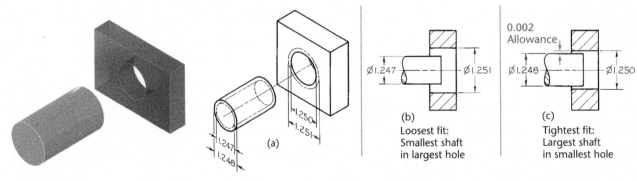

Shaft tolerance = 1.248 – 1.247 = 0.001   Allowance = 1.250 – 1.248 = 0.002

Hole tolerance = 1.251 – 1.250 = 0.001   Max clearance = 1.251 – 1.247 = 0.004

12.15   Specifying Fit through Limit Dimensions

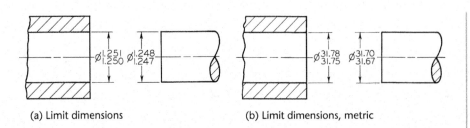

(a) Limit dimensions   (b) Limit dimensions, metric

12.16   Fits between Mating Parts

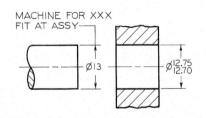

12.17   Noninterchangeable Fit

Selective Assembly

If allowances and tolerances are specified properly, mating parts are completely interchangeable, but for close fits, it is necessary to specify very small allowances and tolerances. The cost of manufacturing parts to such precision may be very high.

To avoid this expense, either manual or computer-controlled selective assembly is often used. In *selective assembly,* all parts are inspected and classified into several grades according to actual sizes, so that "small" shafts can be matched with "small" holes, "medium" shafts with "medium" holes, and so on. Figure 12.18 shows variation among the sizes of mating parts at an exaggerated size to illustrate the general idea.

Using selective assembly, acceptable fits may be obtained at less expense than by machining all mating parts to highly accurate dimensions. This method is often effective when using transition fits, since either clearance or interference is allowed. The use of selective assembly makes ordering replacement parts difficult.

The inner workings of a watch are an example of parts that must fit precisely to work. (alextan8/Shutterstock.)

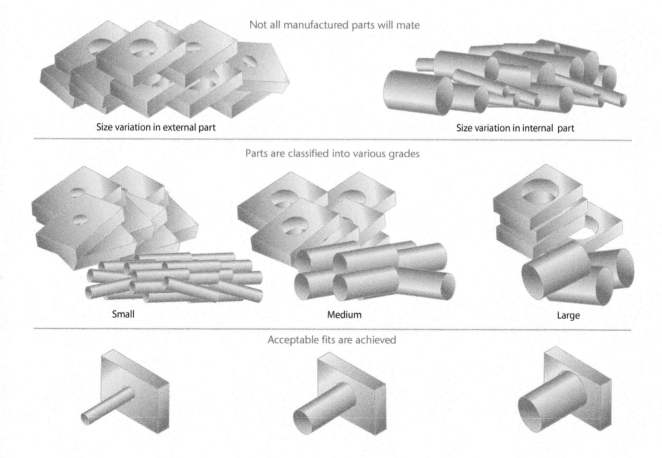

Not all manufactured parts will mate

Size variation in external part   Size variation in internal part

Parts are classified into various grades

Small   Medium   Large

Acceptable fits are achieved

12.18 Selective Assembly (*Difference between the sizes of mating parts is exaggerated for visibility.*)

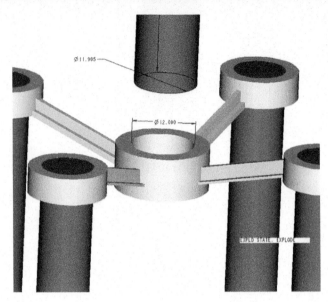

12.19 *Tolerances are usually based on the hole size, because holes are usually formed using standard tool sizes.*

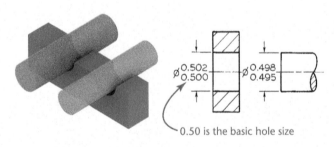

12.20   Hole System

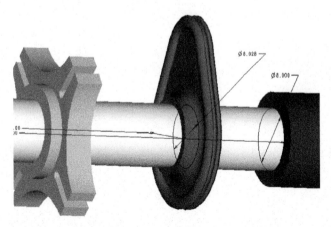

12.21 *When several parts fit to a single shaft, tolerances may be based on the shaft size.*

Hole System

Reamers, broaches, and other standard tools are often used to produce holes, and standard plug gages are used to check the actual sizes. In contrast, shafts are easily machined down to any size desired. Therefore, toleranced dimensions are commonly determined using the *hole system,* in which the minimum hole is taken as the feature size for the design. Then, the allowance is determined, and tolerances are applied. Figure 12.19 shows a CAD model where several shafts assemble into different holes. Figure 12.20 shows the fit between two parts sized based on the hole diameter.

Shaft System

In some industries, such as textile machinery manufacturing, which use a great deal of cold-finished shafting, the *shaft system* is used. It is advantageous when several parts having different fits are required on a single shaft, as in Figure 12.21, or when the shaft for some reason can't be machined to size easily. This system should be used only when there is a reason for it. In this system, the maximum shaft is taken as the feature size for the design and an allowance for each mating part is assigned, then tolerances are applied.

In Figure 12.22, the maximum size of the shaft, .500″, is the feature size for the design. For a clearance fit, an allowance of .002″ is decided on, giving the minimum hole size of .502″. Tolerances of .003″ and .001″, respectively, are applied to the hole and the shaft to obtain the maximum hole, .505″, and the minimum shaft, .499″. The minimum clearance is the difference between the smallest hole and the largest shaft, and the maximum clearance is the difference between the largest hole and the smallest shaft.

In the case of an interference fit, the minimum hole size is found by subtracting the desired allowance from the nominal shaft size.

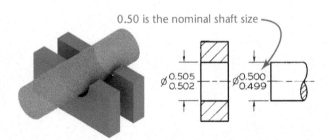

12.22   Shaft System

STEP by STEP

USING THE HOLE SYSTEM

1 Determine where mating parts fit. Because the hole will be machined with a standard-size tool, its size will be used to determine the fit. In the figure shown, the minimum size of the hole, .500″, is used.

2 Determine the type of fit and apply the allowance. For a clearance fit, an allowance of .002″ is subtracted from the hole size, making the maximum shaft size .498″, because it is easier to machine the shaft down to a smaller size than to apply the allowance to the hole.

3 Apply the tolerance. Tolerances of .002″ and .003″, in this example, are applied to the hole and the shaft, respectively, to obtain the maximum hole of .502″ and the minimum shaft of .495″. Thus, the minimum clearance is the difference between the smallest hole and the largest shaft, .002, and the maximum clearance is the difference between the largest hole and the smallest shaft, .007.

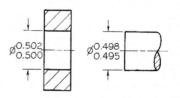

Clearance Fit

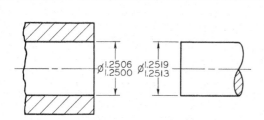

Interference Fit

In the case of an interference fit, find the maximum shaft size by adding the desired allowance (the maximum interference) to the hole size.

In the figure at left, the hole size is 1.2500″. The maximum interference decided on was .0019″, which when added to the hole size gives 1.2519″ as the largest shaft size.

MANUFACTURING TO ONE MILLIONTH OF AN INCH

Gage blocks, used for inspection and calibration, must be manufactured to extremely precise tolerances.

Gage blocks, also known as "Jo blocks" are made from steel, chrome, or ceramic and lapped and honed to accuracies of even just a few millionths of an inch (0.0000254 mm). These precise blocks are used in calibration and inspection. They are often used with a sine bar to measure angles precisely. Using the equation

sin angle = height/distance,

the fixed distance of the sine bar, and setting the precise height by raising one end of the sine bar on a gage block or stack of gage blocks, you can find precise angles. When the angle is known, the height of the gage blocks can be calculated from the equation. Often, tables are used to look up the needed height quickly to produce the required angle for setting up a machine.

Gage blocks are finished so precisely (flatness of around 1 microinch) that they "ring" when slowly slid together and aligned. These blocks are not magnetic. There is some debate as to the exact combination of air pressure, surface tension from the light film of oil or water vapor on the gage blocks, and/or the interchange of electrons between atoms of the surfaces of the two blocks that creates an attractive molecular force that holds the blocks together.

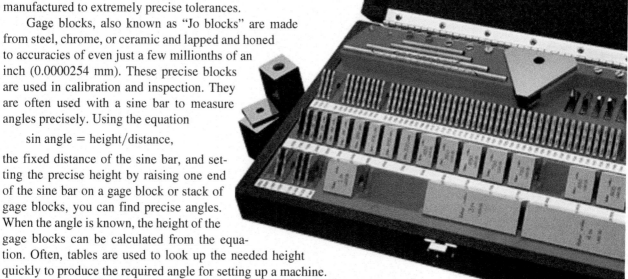

Set of Starrett-Weber Gage Blocks
(Courtesy of L.S. Starrett Company.)

12.1 SPECIFYING TOLERANCES

Every dimension on a drawing should have a tolerance, either direct or by a tolerance note. The primary ways to indicate tolerances in a drawing are

- A general tolerance note listed in a note or a table;
- A note providing a tolerance for a specific dimension;
- A reference on the drawing to another document that specifies the required tolerances;
- Adding limit tolerances to dimensions;
- Adding direct plus/minus tolerances to dimensions; and
- Geometric tolerances.

Many of these tolerancing methods can be used in combination in the same drawing.

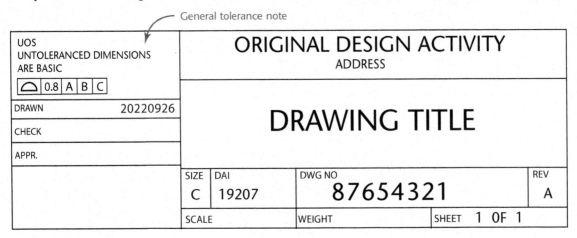

12.23   General Tolerance Note

12.2 GENERAL TOLERANCE NOTES

General notes are usually located in the lower right corner of the drawing sheet near the title block. Often, **general tolerance notes** are included in the title block itself. For example, a general tolerance note might state,

ALL TOLERANCES ±1 mm
UNLESS OTHERWISE NOTED.
ANGLES ±1 DEGREE.

This indicates that for a dimension value written as 25, for example, any measurement between 24 and 26 on the actual part would be acceptable.

Many companies have standard title blocks they insert into CAD drawing files containing general tolerancing standards for the type of production that is common to their industry. Figure 12.23 shows an example of a general tolerance note.

Another way general tolerances are stated is with a table on or near the title block indicating the tolerance by the number of digits used in the dimension, as shown in Figure 12.24. For example:

DIGITS	TOLERANCE
.X	±.2 INCH
.XX	±.02 INCH
.XXX	±.001 INCH
X°	±.1°

This type of table indicates that single-place decimal dimensions have a tolerance of ±.2. For example, a dimension value written as 3.5 could range anywhere from 3.3 to 3.7 on the actual part and still be acceptable. A dimension written as 3.55 could range from 3.53 to 3.57 on the actual part. And a value written as 3.558 could range from 3.557 to 3.559 and be acceptable. It is uncommon to see more than three decimal places listed for inch drawings, because precisions of ±.0001 are very high precision manufacturing and would be unlikely to be indicated merely by a general tolerance note.

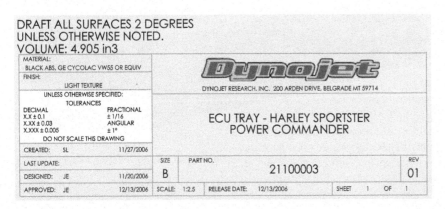

12.24   General Tolerance in Title Block *(Courtesy of Dynojet Research, Inc.)*

12.3 LIMIT TOLERANCES

Limit tolerances state the upper and lower limits for the dimension range in place of the dimension values, as shown in Figure 12.25. Figure 12.26 shows examples of limit tolerances in a drawing. The upper value is always placed above the lower value. In single-line note form, the low limit precedes the high limit, and the two values are separated by a dash, for example, 29–32.

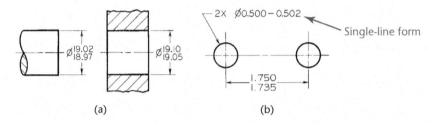

12.25   Methods of Stating Limits

Single-Limit Dimensioning

It is not always necessary to specify both limits when you use a single-limit tolerance. The note MIN or MAX is placed after a number to indicate the minimum or maximum dimension desired when other elements of design determine the other unspecified limit. For example, a thread length may be dimensioned as 1.500 MIN FULL THD or a radius dimensioned as R .05 MAX. Other applications of single-limit dimensions include depths of holes and chamfers.

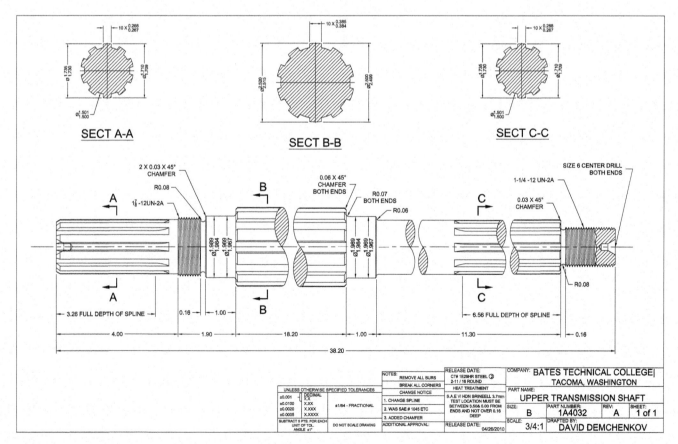

12.26   Limit Dimensions

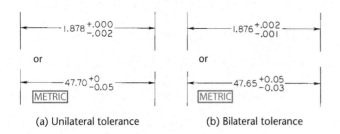

12.27   Plus/Minus Tolerance Expression

(a) Unilateral tolerance   (b) Bilateral tolerance

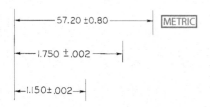

12.28   Bilateral Tolerances

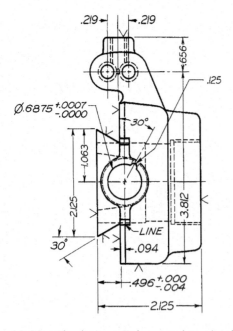

12.29   Plus/Minus-Toleranced Decimal Dimensions

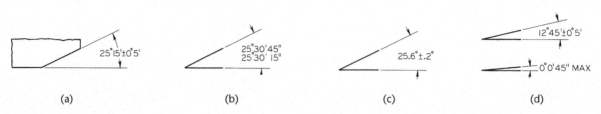

(a)   (b)   (c)   (d)

12.30   Angular Tolerances

12.4 PLUS-OR-MINUS TOLERANCES

In this method the basic size is followed by a plus-or-minus expression for the tolerance (Figure 12.27). The result can be:

- Unilateral when the tolerance applies in only one direction so that one value is zero; or
- Bilateral when either the same or different values are added and subtracted.

If two unequal tolerance numbers are given—one plus and one minus—the plus value is placed above the minus. One of the numbers may be zero. If the plus value and minus value are the same, a single value is given, preceded by the plus-or-minus symbol ($\pm$), as shown in Figure 12.28.

The *unilateral system* of tolerances allows variations in only one direction from the nominal size. This method is advantageous when a critical size is approached as material is removed during manufacture, as in the case of close-fitting holes and shafts. In Figure 12.27a, the nominal size is 1.878″ (47.70 mm). The tolerance of .002″ (0.05 mm) is all in one direction—toward the smaller size. If the dimension is for a shaft diameter, the nominal size of 1.878″ (47.70 mm) is nearer the critical size, so the tolerance is subtracted from the critical size. A unilateral tolerance is always all plus or all minus, but the zeros for the other tolerance value should be shown as in Figure 12.27a.

The *bilateral system* of tolerances allows variations in both directions from the nominal. Bilateral tolerances are usually given for location dimensions or any dimensions that can be allowed to vary in either direction. In Figure 12.27b, the nominal size is 1.876″ (47.65 mm), and the actual local feature may be larger by .002″ (0.05 mm) or smaller by .001″ (0.03 mm). If equal variation in both directions is allowed, the plus-or-minus symbol is used, as shown in Figure 12.28.

Angular tolerances are usually bilateral and given in terms of degrees, minutes, and seconds (Figure 12.30), unless geometric dimensioning and tolerancing is used. Limit tolerances for angles, as shown in Figure 12.30b, are less commonly used.

12.5 TOLERANCE STACKING

It is very important to consider the effect of one tolerance on another. When the location of a surface is affected by more than one tolerance value, the tolerances are cumulative. In some cases, for functional reasons, it may be desirable to define dimensions (such as X, Y, and Z shown in Figure 12.31a) chain fashion, without regard to the overall width of the part. This allows the tolerance to accumulate or "stack up." If the overall width dimension is shown in Figure 12.31a, the part is controlled in too many different ways—it is overdimensioned. In such cases, if it is shown, the overall dimension should be a *reference dimension* placed inside parentheses to indicate that it is for reference only.

In other cases it may be desired to hold two dimensions (such as X and Y in Figure 12.31a) and the overall width of the part closely by giving the overall width dimension. In that case, a dimension such as Z should be omitted or given as a reference dimension only. As a rule,

it is best to dimension each surface so that it is affected by only one dimension. This can be done by referring all dimensions to a single datum surface, such as B shown in Figure 12.31b.

Chained or Continuous Dimensioning

When dimensions are specified as a chain, the tolerances for the part may add up. A *chained dimension* uses the end of one dimension as the beginning of the next. *Tolerance stacking* refers to the way the tolerance for one dimension is added to the next dimension in the chain and so on from one feature to the next, resulting in a large variation in the location of the last feature in the chain. Figure 12.31a illustrates this effect where the surface labeled A is dimensioned chain fashion. Consider the location of the right end surface relative to the left end of the part. When features X, Y, and Z are at their maximum size,

the surface at the right end of the part can vary within a .015-wide zone. Tolerance stacking is not necessarily bad, if that is the intent for the relative locations of the features. You should be aware of the effect that tolerance has on chained dimensions and specify the tolerances this way only when you want the tolerance to accumulate.

Baseline Dimensioning

Baseline dimensioning locates a series of features from a common base feature. Tolerances do not stack up because dimensions are not based on other toleranced dimensions. Figure 12.31b illustrates how the same part in Figure 12.31a could be dimensioned using baseline dimensioning. Baseline dimensioning can make it easy to inspect the part, because features are measured from a common base feature. Dimensioning from a zero point as the base feature can also be a useful technique for dimensioning parts for NC machining.

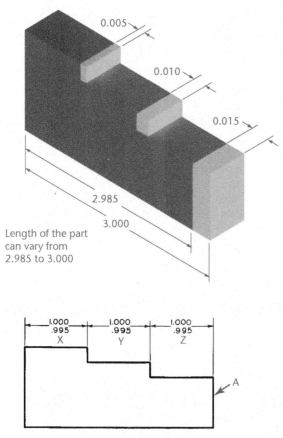

(a) Chained or continuous dimensioning

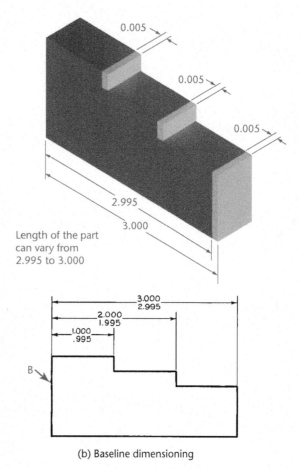

(b) Baseline dimensioning

12.31   Chained versus Baseline Dimensioning

12.6 USING AMERICAN NATIONAL STANDARD LIMITS AND FIT TABLES

The American National Standards Institute has issued *ANSI B4.1, Preferred Limits and Fits for Cylindrical Parts,* defining terms and recommending preferred standard sizes, allowances, tolerances, and fits in terms of the decimal inch. This standard gives a series of standard classes of fits on a unilateral-hole basis so that the fit produced by mating parts of a class of fit will produce approximately similar performance throughout the range of sizes. These tables give standard allowances for any given size or type of fit; they also prescribe the standard limits for the mating parts that will produce the fit.

The tables are designed for the hole system (see Appendices 4–8). For coverage of the metric system of tolerances and fits, see Appendices 10–13.

Table 12.1 gives the three general types of fits, the five subtypes, their letter symbols, and descriptions.

In the fit tables for each class of fit, the range of nominal sizes of shafts or holes is given in inches. To simplify the tables and reduce the space required to present them, the other values are given in thousandths of an inch as in the example shown in Figure 12.32. Minimum and maximum limits of clearance are given; the top number is the least clearance, or the allowance, and the lower number the maximum clearance, or loosest fit. Then, under the heading "Standard Limits," are the limits for the hole and for the shaft that are to be applied to the nominal size to obtain the limits of size for the parts, using the hole system.

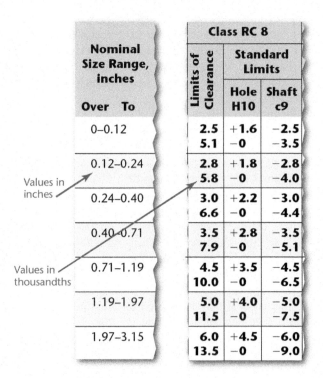

Values in inches

Values in thousandths

Nominal Size Range, inches		Class RC 8		
Over	To	Limits of Clearance	Standard Limits	
			Hole H10	Shaft c9
0–0.12		2.5 5.1	+1.6 −0	−2.5 −3.5
0.12–0.24		2.8 5.8	+1.8 −0	−2.8 −4.0
0.24–0.40		3.0 6.6	+2.2 −0	−3.0 −4.4
0.40–0.71		3.5 7.9	+2.8 −0	−3.5 −5.1
0.71–1.19		4.5 10.0	+3.5 −0	−4.5 −6.5
1.19–1.97		5.0 11.5	+4.0 −0	−5.0 −7.5
1.97–3.15		6.0 13.5	+4.5 −0	−6.0 −9.0

12.32 Portion of RC8 Fit Table. *The International Organization for Standardization (ISO) publishes a similar series of fit tables for metric values.*

Table 12.1 General Fit Types and Subtypes

Fit Type	Symbol	Subtype	Description
Clearance	RC	Running or sliding fits	Running and sliding fits (Appendix 4) are intended to provide a similar running performance, with suitable lubrication allowance, throughout the range of sizes. The clearances for the first two classes, used chiefly as slide fits, increase more slowly with diameter than the other classes, so that accurate location is maintained even at the expense of free relative motion.
Locational	LC	Clearance fits	Locational fits (Appendices 5–7) are fits intended to determine only the location of the mating parts; they may provide rigid or accurate location, as with interference fits, or provide some freedom of location, as with clearance fits. Accordingly, they are divided into three groups: clearance fits, transition fits, and interference fits.
	LT	Transition clearance or interference fits	
	LN	Locational interference fits	
Interference	FN	Force or shrink fits	Force or shrink fits (Appendix 8) constitute a special type of interference fit, normally characterized by the maintenance of constant bore pressures throughout the range of sizes. The interference therefore varies almost directly with diameter, and the difference between its minimum and maximum value is small to maintain the resulting pressures within reasonable limits.

Milling machines can produce parts within tolerances of 0.5 mm, or a few thousandths of an inch. (Nordroden/Shutterstock.)

12.7 TOLERANCES AND MACHINING PROCESSES

Tolerances should be as generous as possible and still permit satisfactory use of the part. The tighter the tolerance, the more expensive it is to manufacture the part. Great savings can be gained from the use of less expensive tools, from lower labor and inspection costs, and from reduced scrapping of material.

Table 12.2 is a chart to be used as a general guide to the tolerances achievable by the indicated machining processes. You can convert these to metric values by multiplying by 25.4 and rounding to one fewer decimal places.

Table 12.2 Tolerances Related to Machining Processes

Range of Sizes (in.)										
From	To and Including	Tolerances								
.000	.599	.00015	.0002	.0003	.0005	.0008	.0012	.002	.003	.005
.600	.999	.00015	.00025	.0004	.0006	.001	.0015	.0025	.004	.006
1.000	1.499	.0002	.0003	.0005	.0008	.0012	.002	.003	.005	.008
1.500	2.799	.00025	.0004	.0006	.001	.0015	.0025	.004	.006	.010
2.800	4.499	.0003	.0005	.0008	.0012	.002	.003	.005	.008	.012
4.500	7.799	.0004	.0006	.001	.0015	.0025	.004	.006	.010	.015
7.800	13.599	.0005	.0008	.0012	.002	.003	.005	.008	.012	.020
13.600	20.999	.0006	.001	.0015	.0025	.004	.006	.010	.015	.025

Process	1	2	3	4	5	6	7	8	9
Lapping and Honing	▓	▓	▓						
Grinding, Diamond Turning, and Boring	▓	▓	▓	▓					
Broaching		▓	▓						
Reaming			▓	▓	▓				
Turning, Boring, Slotting, Planing, and Shaping					▓	▓			
Milling						▓	▓		
Drilling							▓	▓	

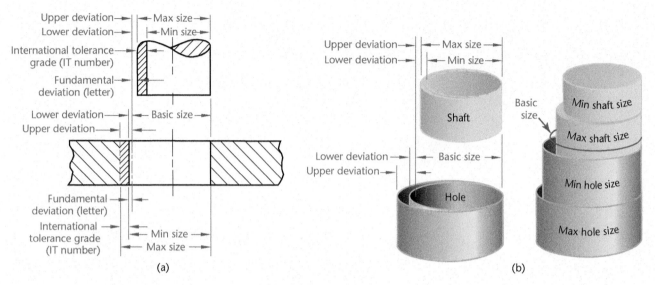

12.33   Terms Related to Metric Limits and Fits *(Reprinted from ASME B4.2-1978, by permission of The American Society of Mechanical Engineers. All rights reserved.)*

12.34   Specifying Tolerances with Symbols for Mating Parts

12.8 METRIC SYSTEM OF TOLERANCES AND FITS

The preceding material on limits and fits between mating parts applies for both systems of measurement. A system of preferred metric limits and fits by the International Organization for Standardization (ISO) is in the *ANSI B4.2* standard. The system is specified for holes, cylinders, and shafts, but it is also adaptable to fits between parallel surfaces of such features as keys and slots. The following terms for metric fits, shown in Figure 12.33a, are somewhat similar to those for decimal inch fits:

Basic size/nominal size   *Basic size/ nominal size* is the size from which limits or deviations are assigned. Basic sizes, usually diameters, should be selected from a table of preferred sizes, as shown in Table 12.3. Figure 12.34 shows examples of preferred and accceptable methods of specifying tolerances on a drawing.

Deviation   The *deviation* is the difference between the basic size and the hole or shaft size. This is equivalent to the tolerance in the decimal-inch system.

Upper deviation   The *upper deviation* is the difference between the basic size and the permitted maximum size of the part. This is comparable to the maximum tolerance in the decimal-inch system.

Lower deviation   The *lower deviation* is the difference between the basic size and the minimum permitted size of the part. This is comparable to the minimum tolerance in the decimal-inch system.

Fundamental deviation   The *fundamental deviation* is the deviation closest to the basic size. This is comparable to the minimum allowance in the decimal-inch system.

Tolerance   The *tolerance* is the difference between the permitted minimum and maximum sizes of a part.

International tolerance grade   The *international tolerance grade* (IT) is a set of tolerances according to the basic size that provides a uniform level of accuracy within the grade. For example, in the dimension 50H9 for a close-running fit in Figure 12.34, the IT grade is indicated by the numeral 9. (The letter H indicates that the tolerance is on the hole for the 50 mm dimension.) In all, there are 18 IT grades—IT01, IT0, and IT1 through IT16 (see Figures 12.35 and 12.36 for IT grades related to machining processes and for the practical use of the IT grades).

Tolerance zone   The *tolerance zone* refers to the relationship of the tolerance to the basic size. It is established by a combination of the fundamental deviation

12.35 International Tolerance Grades Related to Machining Processes (Reprinted from ASME B4.2-1978, by permission of The American Society of Mechanical Engineers. All rights reserved.)

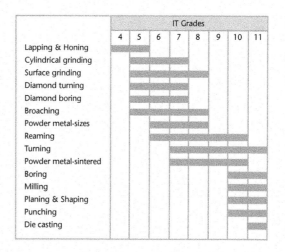

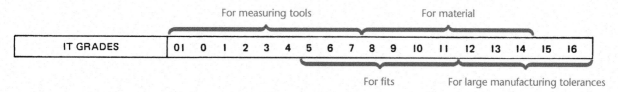

12.36 Practical Use of the International Tolerance Grades

indicated by a letter and the IT grade number. In the dimension 50H8, for the close-running fit, the H8 specifies the tolerance zone, as shown in Figure 12.37.

Hole system   The **hole system** of preferred fits uses the basic diameter as the minimum size. For the generally preferred hole-basis system, shown in Figure 12.37a, the **fundamental deviation** is specified by the uppercase letter H.

Shaft system   The shaft system of preferred fits is a system in which the basic diameter is the maximum size of the shaft. The fundamental deviation is given by the lowercase letter f, as shown in Figure 12.37b.

Interference fit   An interference fit results in an interference between two mating parts under all tolerance conditions.

Transition fit   A transition fit results in either a clearance or an interference condition between two assembled parts.

Tolerance symbols   *Tolerance symbols* are used to specify the tolerances and fits for mating parts, as shown in Figure 12.37c. For the hole-basis system, the 50 indicates the diameter in millimeters, the capital letter H indicates the fundamental deviation for the hole, and the lowercase letter f indicates the deviation for the shaft. The numbers following the letters indicate the IT grade. Note that the symbols for the hole and shaft are separated by a slash. Tolerance symbols for a 50-mm-diameter hole may be given in several acceptable forms, as shown in Figure 12.38. The values in parentheses are for reference only and may be omitted. For upper and lower limit values, see Appendix 10.

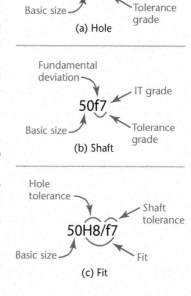

12.37 Applications of Definitions and Symbols to Holes and Shafts (Reprinted from ASME B4.2-1978, by permission of The American Society of Mechanical Engineers. All rights reserved.)

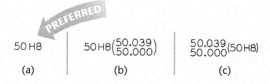

12.38 Acceptable Methods for Stating Tolerances (Reprinted from ASME Y14.5M-1994 (R2004), by permission of The American Society of Mechanical Engineers. All rights reserved.)

12.9 PREFERRED SIZES

The preferred basic sizes for computing tolerances are given in Table 12.3. Basic diameters should be selected from the "First Choice" column, because these are readily available stock sizes for round, square, and hexagonal products.

Table 12.3 Preferred Sizes
(Reprinted from ASME B4.2-1978, by permission of The American Society of Mechanical Engineers. All rights reserved.)

Basic Size, mm		Basic Size, mm		Basic Size, mm	
First Choice	Second Choice	First Choice	Second Choice	First Choice	Second Choice
1		10		100	
	1.1		11		110
1.2		12		120	
	1.4		14		140
1.6		16		160	
	1.8		18		180
2		20		200	
	2.2		22		220
2.5		25		250	
	2.8		28		280
3		30		300	
	3.5		35		350
4		40		400	
	4.5		45		450
5		50		500	
	5.5		55		550
6		60		600	
	7		70		700
8		80		800	
	9		90		900
				1000	

12.10 PREFERRED FITS

The symbols for either the hole-basis or shaft-basis preferred fits (clearance, transition, and interference) are given in Table 12.4. Fits should be selected from this table for mating parts where possible.

For values corresponding to the fits, see Appendices 10–13. Although second- and third-choice basic-size diameters are possible, they must be calculated from tables not included in this text. For the generally preferred hole-basis system, note that the ISO symbols range from H11/c11 (loose running) to H7/u6 (force fit). For the shaft-basis system, the preferred symbols range from C11/h11 (loose fit) to U7/h6 (force fit).

Suppose that you want to use the symbols to specify the dimensions for a free-running (hole-basis) fit for a proposed diameter of 48 mm. Because 48 mm is not listed as a preferred size in Table 12.3, the design is altered to use the acceptable 50-mm diameter when possible. From the preferred fit descriptions in Table 12.4, the free-running (hole-basis) fit is H9/d9. To determine the upper and lower deviation limits of the hole as given in the preferred hole-basis table (Appendix 10) follow across from the basic size of 50 to H9 under "Free Running." The limits for the hole are 50.000 and 50.062 mm. The upper and lower limits of deviation for the shaft are found in the d9 column under "Free Running." They are 49.920 and 49.858 mm, respectively. Limits for other fits are established in a similar way.

Limits for the shaft-basis dimensioning are determined similarly from the preferred shaft-basis table in Appendix 12. Refer to Figures 12.34 and 12.38 for acceptable methods of specifying tolerances by symbols on drawings. A single note for the mating parts (free-running fit, hole basis) would be H9/d9, as was shown in Figure 12.37.

Table 12.4 Preferred Fits
(Reprinted from ASME B4.2-1978, by permission of The American Society of Mechanical Engineers. All rights reserved.)

		ISO Symbol		
		Hole Basis	Shaft Basis*	Description
Clearance Fits		H11/c11	C11/h11	**Loose-running** fit for wide commercial tolerances or allowances on external members.
		H9/d9	D9/h9	**Free-running** fit not for use where accuracy is essential, but good for large temperature variations, high running speeds, or heavy journal pressures.
		H8/f7	F8/h7	**Close-running** fit for running on accurate machines and for accurate location at moderate speeds and journal pressures.
Transition Fits		H7/g6	G7/h6	**Sliding** fit not intended to run freely, but to move and turn freely and locate accurately.
		H7/h6	H7/h6	**Locational clearance** fit provides snug fit for locating stationary parts; but can be freely assembled and disassembled.
		H7/k6	K7/h6	**Locational transition** fit for accurate location, a compromise between clearance and interference.
		H7/n6	N7/h6	**Locational transition** fit for more accurate location where greater interference is permissible.
Interference Fits		H7/p6	P7/h6	**Locational interference** fit for parts requiring rigidity and alignment with prime accuracy of location but without special bore pressure requirements.
		H7/s6	S7/h6	**Medium drive** fit for ordinary steel parts or shrink fits on light sections, the tightest fit usable with cast iron.
		H7/u6	U7/h6	**Force** fit suitable for parts that can be highly stressed or for shrink fits where the heavy pressing forces required are impractical.

(Right margin: More Clearance ↑ ... ↓ More interference)

*The transition and interference shaft-basis fits shown do not convert to exactly the same hole-basis fit conditions for basic sizes in the range from 0 through 3 mm. Interference fit P7/h6 converts to a transition fit H7/p6 in the above size range.

12.11 GEOMETRIC DIMENSIONING AND TOLERANCING

Geometric tolerances state the maximum allowable variations of a form or its position from the perfect geometry implied on the drawing. The term "geometric" refers to various forms, such as a plane, a cylinder, a cone, a square, or a hexagon. Theoretically, these are perfect forms, but because it is impossible to produce perfect forms, it may be necessary to specify the amount of variation permitted. Geometric tolerances specify either the diameter or the width of a tolerance zone within which a surface or the axis of a cylinder or a hole must be if the part is to meet the required accuracy for proper function and fit. When tolerances of form are not given on a drawing, it is assumed that regardless of form variations, the part will fit and function satisfactorily.

Tolerances of form (shape) and position (location) control such characteristics as straightness, flatness, parallelism, perpendicularity (squareness), concentricity, roundness, angular displacement, and so on.

Methods of indicating geometric tolerances by means of geometric characteristic symbols, rather than by traditional notes, are recommended. See the latest dimensioning and tolerancing standard, *ANSI/ASME Y14.5*, for more complete coverage.

12.12 SYMBOLS FOR TOLERANCES OF POSITION AND FORM

Because traditional notes for specifying tolerances of position (location) and form (shape) may be confusing or unclear, may require too much space, and may not be understood internationally, most multinational companies have adopted symbols for such specifications (*ANSI/ASME Y14.5*). These symbols, shown in Table 12.5, provide an accurate and concise means of specifying *geometric characteristics* and tolerances in a minimum of space. A *feature control frame* (Figure 12.39) specifies the tolerance for the geometric characteristic to be controlled and any modifying conditions (see Table 12.6) that are required. The symbols may be supplemented by notes if the precise geometric requirements cannot be conveyed by the symbols.

Table 12.5 Geometric Characteristic Symbols
(Reprinted from ASME Y14.5M-1994 (R2004), by permission of The American Society of Mechanical Engineers. All rights reserved.)

Geometric Characteristic Symbols			
	Type of Tolerance	Characteristic	Symbol
For individual features	Form	Straightness	—
		Flatness	▱
		Circularity (roundness)	○
		Cylindricity	⌭
For individual or related features	Profile	Profile of a line	⌒
		Profile of a surface	⌓
For related features	Orientation	Angularity	∠
		Perpendicularity	⊥
		Parallelism	//
	Location	Position*	⌖
	Runout	Circular runout[†]	↗
		Total runout[†]	↗↗
	Location	Concentricity[††]	◎
	Runout	Symmetry[††]	≡

*May be related or unrelated.
[†]Arrowheads may be filled or not filled.
[††]Concentricity and Symmetry geometric characteristic symbols are no longer in use for ANSI standard drawings, although they have not been removed for ISO standard drawings.

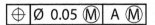

12.39 Feature Control Frame

Table 12.6 Modifying Symbols
(Reprinted from ASME Y14.5M-1994 (R2004), by permission of The American Society of Mechanical Engineers. All rights reserved.)

Modifying Symbols	
Term	**Symbol**
At maximum material condition/boundary	Ⓜ
At least material condition/boundary	Ⓛ
Projected tolerance zone	Ⓟ
Free state	Ⓕ
Tangent plane	Ⓣ
Independency	Ⓘ
Unequally disposed	Ⓤ
Statistical tolerance	⟨ST⟩
Continuous feature	⟨CF⟩
Between[†]	↔
From-To	→
All around	⟲
All over	⟲
Dimension origin	⊕→
Diameter	⌀
Spherical diameter	S⌀
Radius	R
Spherical radius	SR
Controlled radius	CR
Reference	( )
Arc length	⌒
Translation	▷
Square	□
Dynamic Profile	△

[†]Arrowheads may be filled or not filled.

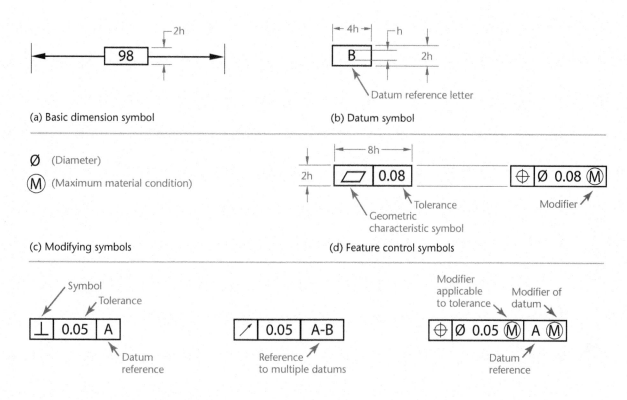

(a) Basic dimension symbol

(b) Datum symbol

(c) Modifying symbols

(d) Feature control symbols

(e) Feature control symbols with datum references

12.40   Use of Symbols for Tolerance of Position and Form *(Reprinted from ASME Y14.5M-1994 (R2004), by permission of The American Society of Mechanical Engineers. All rights reserved.)*

Figure 12.40 shows combinations of the various symbols and their meanings. The geometric characteristic symbols and the supplementary symbols are explained below with material adapted from *ANSI/ASME Y14.5:*

Basic dimension symbols use an enclosing frame, as shown in Figure 12.40a and below. The basic dimension is the value used to describe the theoretically exact size, shape, or location of a feature. It is the basis from which permissible variations are established either by specifying tolerances on other dimensions, by tolerances given in notes, or by using feature control frames.

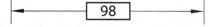

Datum identifying symbols consist of a capital letter in a square frame and a leader line extending from the frame to the concerned feature and terminating with a triangle. The triangle may be filled or not filled. Letters of the alphabet (except I, O, Q, X, Y, and Z) are used as datum identifying letters.

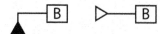

Supplementary symbols include the symbols for MMC (*maximum material condition*—or minimum hole diameter, maximum shaft diameter) and LMC (least material condition—or maximum hole diameter, minimum shaft diameter), as shown in Figure 12.40c. The abbreviations MMC and LMC are also used in notes (see also Table 12.6).

When needed, the symbol for diameter precedes the specified tolerance in a feature control symbol, as shown in

Figure 12.40d. For narrative notes, you can use the abbreviation DIA for diameter.

Combined symbols are found when individual symbols, datum reference letters, and needed tolerances are combined in a single frame, as shown in Figure 12.40e.

Form tolerance is given by a feature control symbol made up of a frame around the appropriate geometric characteristic symbol plus the allowable tolerance. A vertical line separates the symbol and the tolerance, as shown in Figure 12.40d. Where needed, the tolerance should be preceded by the symbol for the diameter and followed by the symbol for MMC or LMC.

Reference to a datum is indicated in the feature control frame by placing the datum reference letter after either the geometric characteristic symbol or the tolerance. Vertical lines separate the entries, and where applicable, the datum reference letter entry includes the symbol for MMC or LMC, as shown in Figure 12.40e.

Figure 12.41 shows how geometric dimensioning and tolerance symbols are applied to a drawing. Understanding datum surfaces and features is important to the application of geometric dimensioning and tolerancing.

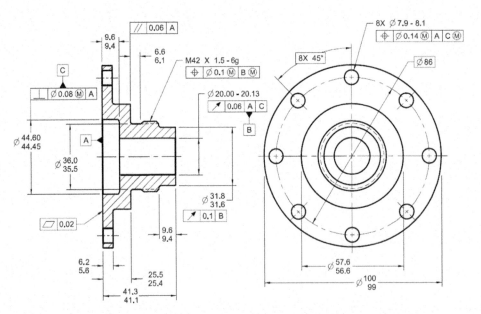

12.41 Application of Symbols to Position and Form Tolerance Dimensions *(Reprinted from ASME Y14.5-2009, by permission of The American Society of Mechanical Engineers. All rights reserved.)*

12.13 DATUM FEATURES

Datum features are used as references to control other features on the part. For example, when defining the location of a hole, you can specify its distance from a datum surface on the part.

Datums should be geometric features on the actual part, such as a point or a plane as shown in Figure 12.42. Centerlines on drawings are not used as datums.

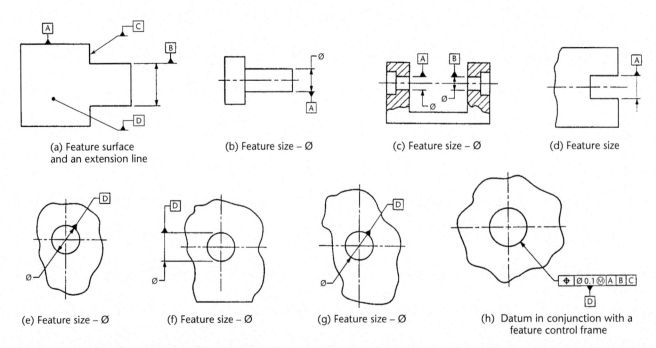

(a) Feature surface and an extension line

(b) Feature size – Ø

(c) Feature size – Ø

(d) Feature size

(e) Feature size – Ø

(f) Feature size – Ø

(g) Feature size – Ø

(h) Datum in conjunction with a feature control frame

12.42 Placement of Datum Feature Symbol *(Reprinted from ASME Y14.5M-1994 (R2004), by permission of The American Society of Mechanical Engineers. All rights reserved.)*

Datum Features versus Datum Feature Simulator

Datums are theoretically exact points, axes, lines, or planes. A *datum feature* is a physical feature on the part that is being manufactured or inspected. It is identified on the drawing by a datum feature symbol, such as shown in Figure 12.43. When specifying datum features keep in mind that the feature should

- Correspond to the mating feature on another part to which the fit is required,
- Be readily accessible on the part, and
- Be sufficiently large to permit its use for making measurements and alignments.

Datum features, because they are features of the actual part, are inherently imperfect. When a part is inspected to determine if it meets the tolerance requirement specified in relation to a datum, a datum feature simulator is used. The datum feature simulator is a boundary derived from the datum feature. It is typically the inverse of the datum feature. For example, if the datum feature is a hole, then the datum feature simulator is a positive cylinder, such as a go/no-go plug gage.

An example of a physical datum feature simulator is a precisely finished granite slab on which a part to be inspected is placed. Because physical datum feature simulators themselves cannot be exactly perfect, the tolerances defined for a feature must take into account the imperfections in precision gages and fixtures. Standards for these are specified in *ASME Y14.43*.

Datum Reference Frame

Imagine trying to measure the location of a hole in an air hockey puck while it is floating on an air hockey table. That would be difficult! A *datum reference frame* provides a framework for eliminating the translations (movement) and rotations of which the free part is capable.

A datum reference frame is often defined by three mutually perpendicular planes, used to immobilize the part to be

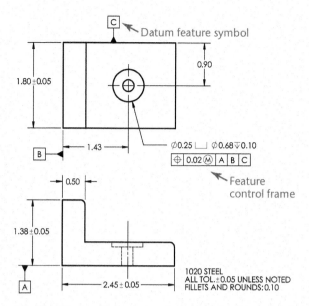

12.43 *Datum feature symbols identify datum surfaces on a drawing.*

inspected and provide a way to make accurate and repeatable measurements. The datum feature symbols on the drawing identify the ***primary datum***, ***secondary datum***, and ***tertiary datum*** (meaning first, second, and third) (Figure 12.43).

The datum reference frame is a theoretical construct that does not exist on the actual part. It is established from the datum features identified on the part drawing. Often, a fixture is used where the primary datum surface contacts the measurement fixture at three points, thus defining a plane. Once the primary datum plane is established, only two additional contact points are needed to establish the secondary datum plane. Once the primary and secondary planes are established, a single additional point will establish the tertiary datum plane (see Figure 12.44). The datum reference frame is established from the datum feature simulators, not from the datum features themselves.

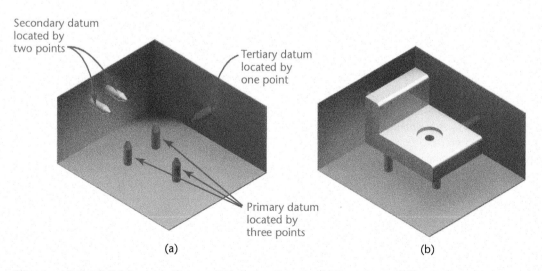

12.44 (a) Establishing the Datum Reference Frame; (b) Part Immobilized on Datum Reference Frame

CONSTRAINING DEGREES OF FREEDOM

Datums listed in a feature control frame are applied to constrain *degrees of freedom* of the part with respect to a datum reference frame. Datums can be identified to constrain the degrees of freedom of the part to immobilize it for inspection.

The free part shown here can translate (move) back and forth in the *x*, *y*, and *z* directions. It can also have rotations *u*, *v*, and *w*. It is said to have six degrees of freedom owing to these motions.

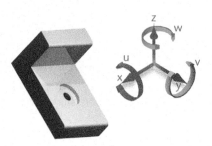

1 If the part rests on datum plane A, the part can no longer move in the *z* direction, nor can it rotate in *u* or *v* motions. Now it has three degrees of freedom. It can rotate in *w*, and move in *x* and *y*.

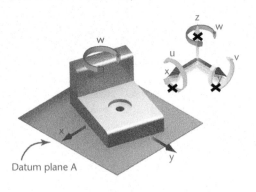

Datum plane A

2 Adding datum B further restricts the motion of the part. Now it can no longer move in the *y* direction or rotate in *w*. It has one remaining degree of freedom, motion in *x*.

Datum plane B

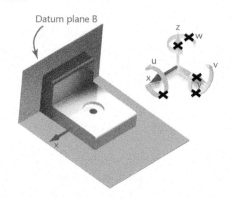

3 Adding datum C restricts the final motion to produce a part that is stationary. The *x*, *y*, and *z* axes may be specified on the drawing and in the feature control frame as needed for clarity.

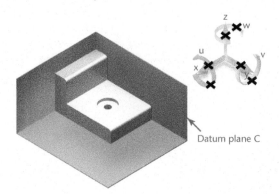

Datum plane C

Datum Targets

Datum targets, as shown in Figure 12.45, can be added to drawings when necessary to specify where points or areas of contact for the simulated datum should occur on the part. You can find detailed information on datum targets and inspection methods in standard geometric dimensioning and tolerancing texts.

Table 12.7 shows examples of typical datum features, how the feature is identified as a datum on the drawing, and a pictorial view of the theoretically exact datum feature simulator. The final column shows which motions would be constrained. In the application of a feature control frame, the degrees of freedom constrained will depend on whether the datum feature is referenced as a primary, secondary, or tertiary datum feature. The examples in the table show simple cases with single features.

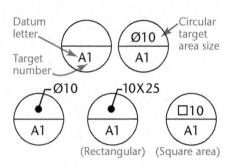

12.45 Datum Target Symbols

Table 12.7 Example Datum Features and Datum Feature Simulators

Feature Type	Feature	On the Drawing	Datum and Datum Feature Simulator	Datum and Constrained Motions
Planar		A	Plane	
Width		A	Center Plane	
Spherical		A	Point	
Cylindrical		A	Axis	
Conical		0.2 A	Axis and point	
Linear Extrusion		0.2	Axis and center plane	
Complex Shape		0.2 A	Axis, point, and center plane	

12.14 POSITIONAL TOLERANCES

Figure 12.46a shows a hole located from two surfaces at right angles to each other. The center may lie anywhere within a square tolerance zone, with sides equal to the tolerances. Using coordinate dimensioning, the total variation allowed along the diagonals of the square is 1.4 times the indicated tolerance. In contrast, when a circular area is used to specify the allowable variation for the center's location, up to 57% more parts may measure acceptable.

If four holes are dimensioned with rectangular coordinates, as in Figure 12.47a, the tolerance describes a square zone in which the center of the hole must be located (Figure 12.47b). This square-shaped zone allows the center of the hole to vary more in the diagonal direction than the stated tolerance value.

In Figure 12.47a, hole A is located from the corner of the part, and the other three are located from A. The tolerances applied to the locations for hole A result in a square tolerance zone. The other three holes are located from the previous hole. Their tolerances produce square zones whose locations vary according to the actual location of hole A. Two of the many possible zone patterns are shown in Figures 12.47b and c.

With the dimensions shown in Figure 12.47a, the resulting parts may not fit with mating parts, even though they meet the drawing tolerances.

Tolerancing features based on their geometry can prevent these problems. Geometric tolerancing controls the shape of the tolerance zone using geometric characteristics in the feature control frame. This is also called *true-position dimensioning*. Using it, the tolerance zone for holes can be circular, with the size of the circle depending on the variation permitted from true position as specified using a feature control frame (see Figure 12.48).

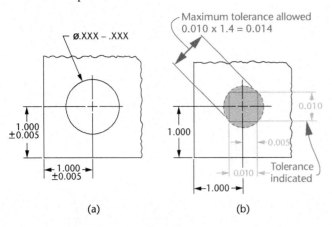

(a)   (b)

12.46   Tolerance Zones

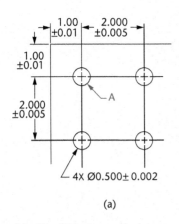

(a)

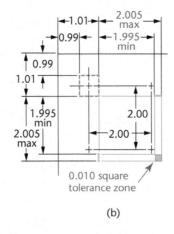

(b)

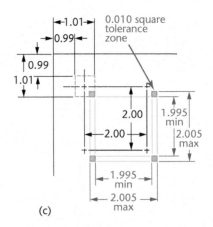

(c)

12.47   Tolerance Zones

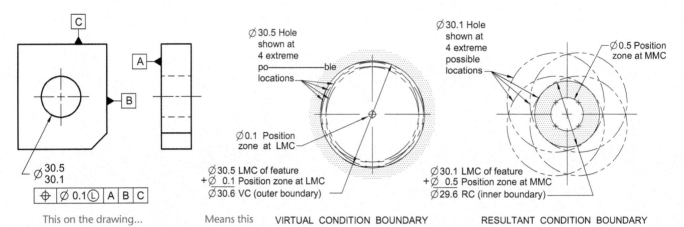

This on the drawing...   Means this   VIRTUAL CONDITION BOUNDARY   RESULTANT CONDITION BOUNDARY

12.48   True-Position Dimensioning *(Reprinted from ASME Y14.5-2018, by permission of The American Society of Mechanical Engineers. All rights reserved.)*

12.49 Cylindrical Tolerance Zone

(Reprinted from ASME Y14.5-2018, by permission of The American Society of Mechanical Engineers. All rights reserved.)

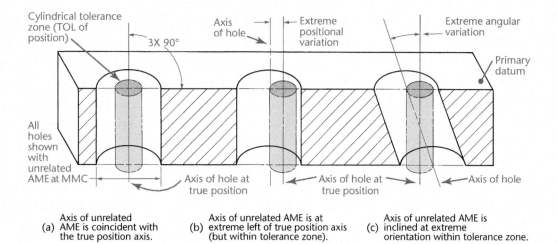

(a) Axis of unrelated AME is coincident with the true position axis.

(b) Axis of unrelated AME is at extreme left of true position axis (but within tolerance zone).

(c) Axis of unrelated AME is inclined at extreme orientation within tolerance zone.

Methods for relating feature control symbols to the feature were shown in Figure 12.41. The following are preferred:

1. Add the symbol to a feature's note or dimension.
2. Run a leader from the symbol to the feature.
3. Attach the side, end, or corner of the symbol frame to an extension line from the feature.
4. Attach a side or end of the symbol frame to the dimension line basic to the feature.

A basic dimension specifies the theoretically exact position of a feature. The location of each feature, such as a hole, slot, or stud, is given by untoleranced basic dimensions identified by an enclosing box. True position is usually established with respect to a datum.

A feature control frame for a positional tolerance describes a cylindrical tolerance zone with a diameter equal to the positional tolerance and a length equal to the length of the feature unless otherwise specified (Figure 12.48). The axis of the hole center must be within the cylindrical zone, as shown in Figure 12.49.

The centerline of the hole may coincide with the centerline of the cylindrical tolerance zone (Figure 12.49a). It may be parallel to it but displaced so that it remains within the tolerance cylinder (Figure 12.49b), or it may be inclined and remain within the tolerance cylinder (Figure 12.49c).

A positional tolerance specifies that all elements on the hole surface must be on or outside a cylinder whose diameter is equal to the minimum diameter or the maximum diameter of the hole minus the positional tolerance diameter, when the centerline of the cylinder is located at true position.

Special untoleranced basic dimensions locate features at true position, avoiding tolerance accumulation, as shown in Figure 12.50.

The exact locations of the true positions are given by untoleranced basic dimensions, ensuring that general tolerances are not applied to them. Basic dimensions are enclosed in a box to indicate that no tolerance applies to them, Alternatively, this information can be stated in a clearly worded note, such as UNTOLERANCED DIMENSIONS ARE BASIC.

Features such as slots may vary on either side of a true-position plane, as shown in Figure 12.51.

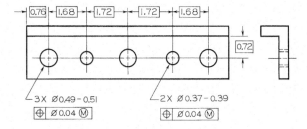

12.50 No Tolerance Accumulation

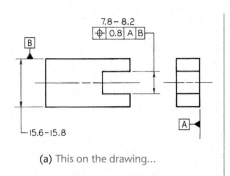

(a) This on the drawing...

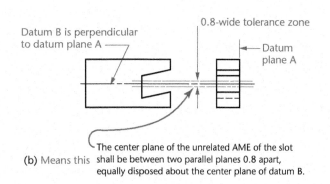

(b) Means this

12.51 Positional Tolerancing for Symmetry (Reprinted from ASME Y14.5-2018, by permission of The American Society of Mechanical Engineers. All rights reserved.)

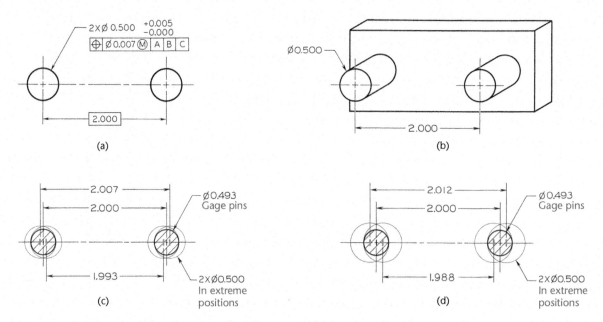

12.52   Maximum and Minimum Material Conditions—Two-Hole Pattern *(Reprinted from ASME Y14.5M-1994 (R2004), by permission of The American Society of Mechanical Engineers. All rights reserved.)*

12.15 MAXIMUM MATERIAL CONDITION

Maximum material condition, or MMC, means that a feature of a finished product contains the maximum amount of material permitted by the toleranced dimensions shown for that feature. Holes, slots, or other internal features are at MMC when at minimum size. Shafts, pads, bosses, and other external features are at MMC when at their maximum size. A feature is at MMC for both mating parts when the largest shaft is in the smallest hole and there is the least clearance between the parts.

In assigning positional tolerance to a hole, consider the size limits of the hole. If the hole is at MMC, or its smallest size, the positional tolerance is not affected, but if the hole is larger, the available positional tolerance is greater. In Figure 12.52a, two half-inch holes are shown. If they are exactly .500″ in diameter (MMC, or smallest size) and are exactly 2.000″ apart, a gage made of two round pins .500″ in diameter fixed in a plate 2.000″ apart, as shown in Figure 12.52b, should fit into them. However, the center-to-center distance between the holes may vary from 1.993″ to 2.007″ as specified by the ∅.007 positional tolerance in the feature control frame in Figure 12.52a.

If the .500″ diameter holes are at their extreme positions, as in Figure 12.52c, the pins in the gage would have to be .007″ smaller, or .493″ in diameter, to fit into the holes. If the .500″ diameter holes are located at the maximum distance apart, the .493″ diameter gage pins would contact the inner sides of the holes; and if the holes are located at the minimum distance apart, the .493″ diameter pins would contact the outer surfaces of the holes, as shown. If gage-maker's tolerances are not disregarded, the gage pins would have to be .493″ in diameter and exactly 2.000″ apart if the holes are .500″ in diameter, or MMC.

If the holes are .505″ in diameter—that is, at maximum size—the same .493″ diameter gage pins at 2.000″ apart will fit with the inner sides of the holes contacting the inner sides of the gage pins and the outer sides of the holes contacting the outer sides of the gage pins, as shown in Figure 12.52d. When the holes are larger, they may be farther apart and still fit the pins. In this case they may be 2.012″ apart, which is beyond the tolerance permitted for the center-to-center distance between the holes. Similarly, the holes may be as close together as 1.988″ from center to center, which again is outside the specified positional tolerance.

Thus, when holes are at maximum size, a greater positional tolerance becomes available. Because all features may vary in size, it is necessary to make clear on the drawing at what basic dimension the true position applies. In many cases, when the holes are larger, the additional positional tolerance is available without affecting the function. Parts can still be freely assembled whether or not the holes or other features are within the specified positional tolerance. This practice has been recognized and used in manufacturing for years in designing functional gages, used to inspect parts to ensure fit in the assembly. Keep in mind that MMC/LMC conditions only make sense applied to true position, straightness, parallelism, perpendicularity, and angularity geometric tolerances. For other boundaries, it would not make sense that any tolerance "bonus" would be allowed at the MMC or LMC. If so, you would just adjust the tolerance values themselves.

To avoid misinterpretation as to whether the MMC applies, it should be clearly stated by adding MMC symbols to each applicable tolerance on the drawing or by a document referenced on the drawing. When MMC is not specified on the drawing with respect to an individual tolerance, datum reference, or both, these rules apply:

1. Regardless of Feature Size (RFS) and Regardless of Feature Boundary (RFB) are the default conditions for tolerances unless MMC/MMB or LMC/LMB is applied to the particular geometric tolerance. RFS means that the tolerance applies independently of the actual measured size of the feature.
2. No element of the actual feature will extend beyond the envelope of the perfect form at MMC. Maximum material condition or least material condition must be specified on the drawing where it is required.

Virtual Condition (VC)

Virtual condition is a construct that applies when an MMC or LMC modifier is present in the feature control frame. VC is the constant boundary for the feature of size considering the geometric tolerance specified and the specified MMC or LMC for the feature. For example, when the feature is a shaft, its virtual condition is the maximum allowed shaft size plus the tolerance zone. This considers the largest allowed shaft (MMC) at the most extreme position. If this fit is acceptable, then smaller shafts in better position will also fit. The VC for a feature with a tolerance noted at MMC is calculated thusly:

VC of an internal feature = MMC (smallest size) − Geometric Tolerance
VC of an external feature = MMC (largest size) + Geometric Tolerance

Virtual condition is used in calculating "bonus tolerance" and designing inspection to qualify acceptable parts.

12.16 TOLERANCES OF ANGLES

Bilateral tolerances have traditionally been given on angles as shown in Figure 12.53. With bilateral tolerances, the wedge-shaped tolerance zone increases as the distance from the vertex of the angle increases.

If an angular surface is located by a linear and an angular dimension, as shown in Figure 12.54a, the surface must lie within a tolerance zone, as shown in Figure 12.54b. The angular zone will be wider as the distance from the vertex increases. To avoid the accumulation of tolerance farther out from the angle's vertex, the *basic angle tolerancing method,* shown in Figure 12.54c, is recommended. The angle is indicated as a basic dimension, and no angular tolerance is specified. The tolerance zone is now defined by two parallel planes, resulting in improved angular control, as shown in Figure 12.54d.

Use specific controls such as angular geometric controls or a basic dimension to prevent general tolerances from applying to implied right angles.

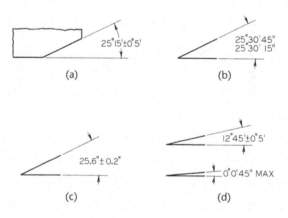

12.53 Tolerances of Angles

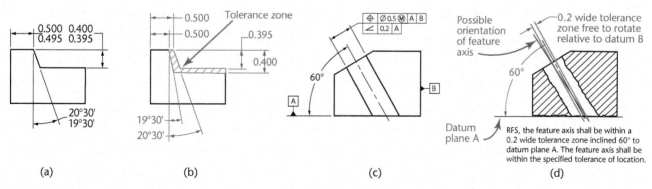

12.54 Angular Tolerance Zones *(Reprinted from ASME Y14.5-2018, by permission of The American Society of Mechanical Engineers. All rights reserved.)*

12.17 FORM TOLERANCES FOR SINGLE FEATURES

Straightness, flatness, roundness, cylindricity, and in some instances, profile, are form tolerances that apply to single features.

The *straightness tolerance* specifies a tolerance zone within which an axis or all points of the considered element must lie (Figure 12.55). Straightness is a condition in which an element of a surface or an axis is a straight line.

The *flatness tolerance* specifies a tolerance zone defined by two parallel planes within which the surface or derived median plane must lie (Figure 12.56). Flatness is the condition of a surface or derived median plane having all elements in one plane.

The *circularity (roundness) tolerance* specifies a tolerance zone bounded by two concentric circles within which each circular element of the surface must lie (Figure 12.57). Roundness is a condition of a cone or cylinder where all points of the surface intersected by any plane perpendicular to a common axis are equidistant from that axis. For a sphere, all points of the surface intersected by any plane passing through a common center are equidistant from that center.

The *cylindricity tolerance* specifies a tolerance zone bounded by two concentric cylinders within which the surface must lie (Figure 12.58). This tolerance applies to both circular and longitudinal elements of the entire surface. Cylindricity is a condition of a surface of revolution in which all points of the surface are equidistant from a common axis. When no tolerance of form is given, many possible shapes may exist within a tolerance zone (Figure 12.59).

The *profile tolerance* specifies a uniform boundary or nonuniform boundary (using the unequally disposed symbol) along the true profile within which all elements of the surface or single elements of the surface must lie (Figures 12.60 and 12.61). A profile is an outline of a surface, a shape made up of one or more features, or a two-dimensional element of one or more features. A digital file or drawing view defines the true profile.

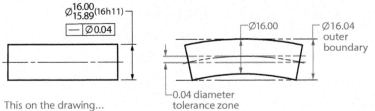

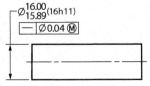

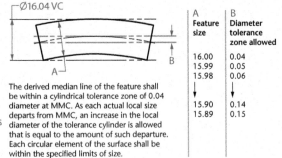

The derived median line of the feature shall be within a cylindrical tolerance zone of 0.04 diameter, regardless of the feature size. Each circular element of the surface shall be within the specified limits of size.

The derived median line of the feature shall be within a cylindrical tolerance zone of 0.04 diameter at MMC. As each actual local size departs from MMC, an increase in the local diameter of the tolerance cylinder is allowed that is equal to the amount of such departure. Each circular element of the surface shall be within the specified limits of size.

A Feature size	B Diameter tolerance zone allowed
16.00	0.04
15.99	0.05
15.98	0.06
↓	↓
15.90	0.14
15.89	0.15

12.55 Specifying Straightness *(Reprinted from ASME Y14.5-2018, by permission of The American Society of Mechanical Engineers. All rights reserved.)*

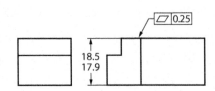

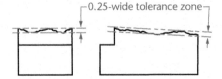

The surface shall be within two parallel planes 0.25 apart. The surface shall be within the specified limits of size.

12.56 Specifying Flatness *(Reprinted from ASME Y14.5-2018, by permission of The American Society of Mechanical Engineers. All rights reserved.)*

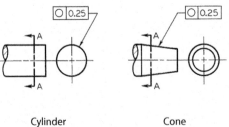

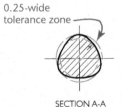

Each circular element of the surface in any plane perpendicular to a common axis must be within the specified tolerance of size and must lie between two concentric circles — one having a radius 0.25 larger than the other.

12.57 Specifying Roundness for a Cylinder or Cone *(Reprinted from ASME Y14.5M-1994 (R2004), by permission of The American Society of Mechanical Engineers. All rights reserved.)*

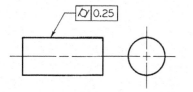

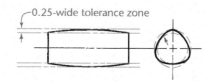

This on the drawing...   Means this   The cylindrical surface must be within the specified tolerance of size and must lie between two concentric cylinders — one having a radius 0.25 larger than the other.

12.58   Specifying Cylindricity

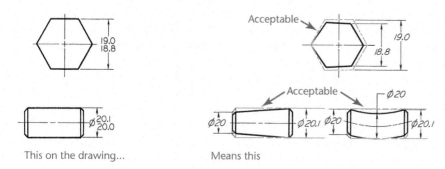

This on the drawing...   Means this

12.59   Acceptable Variations of Form—No Specified Tolerance of Form

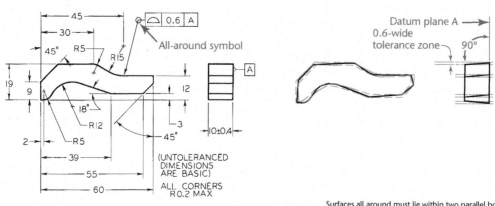

This on the drawing...   Means this   Surfaces all around must lie within two parallel boundaries 0.6 apart equally disposed about the true profile that are perpendicular to datum plane A. Radii of part corners must not exceed 0.2.

12.60   Specifying Profile of a Surface All Around

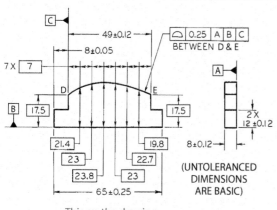

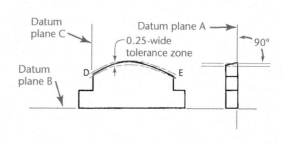

This on the drawing...   Means this   The surface between points D and E must lie between the two profile boundaries 0.25 apart equally disposed about the true profile, that are perpendicular to datum plane A and positioned with respect to datum planes B and C.

12.61   Specifying Profile of a Surface Between Points

12.18 ORIENTATIONS FOR RELATED FEATURES

Angularity, parallelism, perpendicularity, and in some instances, profile, are tolerances that apply to related features. These tolerances control the orientations of features to one another. Orientation tolerances do not control the location of the features.

Angularity specifies the condition of a surface, feature's center plane, or feature's axis at a specified angle from a datum plane or datum axis.

Perpendicularity specifies the condition of a surface, feature's center plane, or feature's axis at a right angle from a datum plane or datum axis. This is the same as angularity when specifying a 90° angle. Either method can be used.

Parallelism specifies the condition of a surface or feature's center plane equidistant from a datum plane or for a feature's axis, equidistant along its length from one or more datum planes or datum axes.

Orientation tolerances must be related to one or more datums. Only the rotational degrees of freedom are constrained when an orientation tolerance is specified. Orientation tolerances may specify the following:

- A zone defined by two parallel planes at the specified basic angle from, or perpendicular to, or parallel to one or more datum planes or a datum axis. The *surface* or *center plane* of the feature must lie within this zone.
- A zone defined by two parallel planes at the specified basic angle from, perpendicular to, or parallel to one or more datum planes or a datum axis. The *axis* of the feature must lie within this zone.
- A cylindrical zone at the specified base angle from, or perpendicular to, or parallel to one or more datum planes or a datum axis. The *axis* of the feature must lie within this zone.
- A zone defined by two parallel lines at the specified basic angle from, or perpendicular to, or parallel to one or more datum planes or a datum axis. Any *line element* of the feature must lie within this zone.

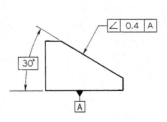

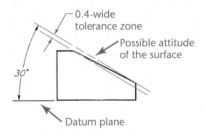

This on the drawing...   Means this

The surface must be within the specified tolerance of size and must lie between two parallel planes 0.4 apart that are inclined at 30° to the datum plane A.

12.62   Specifying Angularity for a Plane Surface
(Reprinted from ASME Y14.5M-1994 (R2004), by permission of The American Society of Mechanical Engineers. All rights reserved.)

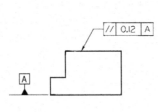

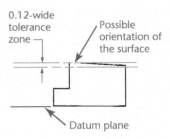

This on the drawing...   Means this

The surface must be within the specified tolerance of size and must lie between two planes 0.12 apart that are parallel to the datum plane A.

12.63   Specifying Parallelism for a Plane Surface
(Reprinted from ASME Y14.5M-1994, by permission of The American Society of Mechanical Engineers. All rights reserved.)

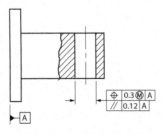

Parallelism for an axis (feature RFS)

This on the drawing...

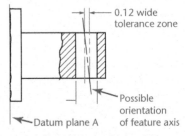

RFS, the featue axis shall be within two parallel planes 0.12 apart that are parallel to datum plane A. The feature axis shall be within the specified tolerance of location.

Means this

12.64   Specifying Parallelism for an Axis Feature
(Reprinted from ASME Y14.5-2018, by permission of The American Society of Mechanical Engineers. All rights reserved.)

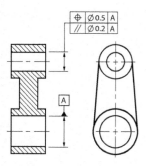

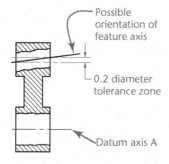

This on the drawing... Means this RFS, the feature axis shall be within a 0.2 diameter cylindrical zone parallel to datum axis A. The feature axis shall be within the specified tolerance of location.

12.65 Specifying Parallelism for an Axis Feature at MMC
(Reprinted from ASME Y14.5-2018, by permission of The American Society of Mechanical Engineers. All rights reserved.)

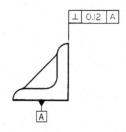

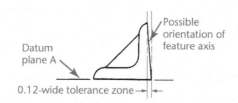

Perpendicularity for a plane surface

The surface must be within the specified tolerance of size and must lie between two parallel planes 0.12 apart that are perpendicular to the datum plane A.

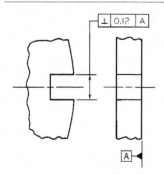

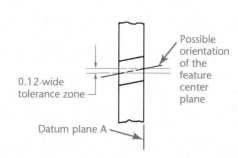

Perpendicularity for a median plane

The feature center plane must be within the specified tolerance of location and must lie between two parallel planes 0.12 apart, regardless of feature size, that are perpendicular to the datum plane A.

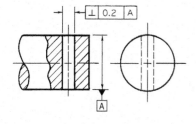

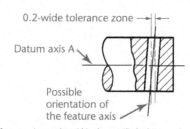

Perpendicularity for an axis

The feature axis must be within the specified tolerance of location and must lie between two planes 0.2 apart, regardless of feature size, that are perpendicular to the datum axis A.

12.66 Specifying Perpendicularity *(Reprinted from ASME Y14.5M-1994 (R2004), by permission of The American Society of Mechanical Engineers. All rights reserved.)*

The ***angularity tolerance*** specifies a tolerance zone defined by two parallel planes at the specified basic angle from a datum plane or axis within which the surface or the axis of the feature must lie (Figure 12.62).

The ***parallelism tolerance*** specifies a tolerance zone defined by two parallel planes or lines parallel to a datum plane or axis, respectively, within which the surface or axis of the feature must lie (Figures 12.63–12.65). Also, a parallelism tolerance may specify a cylindrical tolerance zone parallel to a datum axis within which the axis of the feature must lie.

The ***perpendicularity tolerance*** specifies one of the following:

1. A tolerance zone defined by two parallel planes perpendicular to a datum plane, datum axis, or axis within which the surface of the feature must lie.
2. A cylindrical tolerance zone perpendicular to a datum plane within which the axis of the feature must lie.

(Perpendicularity is the condition of a surface, median plane, or axis that is at 90° to a datum plane or axis.)

The ***concentricity tolerance*** specifies a cylindrical (or spherical for those applications) tolerance zone whose axis or center point coincides with a datum axis and within which all cross-sectional axes of the feature being controlled must lie. Concentricity is the condition in which the median points of all diametrically opposed elements of a surface of revolution are congruent with a datum axis.

Tabulated Tolerances

Tabulated tolerances may be used on drawings for a family of similar parts, where a table shows dimensions and tolerances for different part configurations. The notation TOL along with the table location for the tolerance is added to the tolerance block as shown in Figure 12.67.

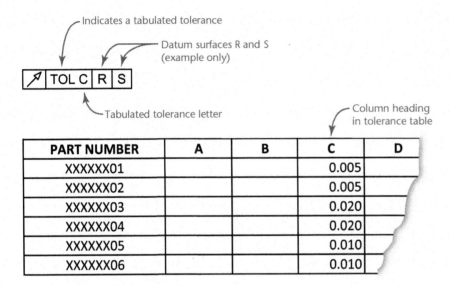

12.67   Tabulated Tolerances. *Use the abbreviation "TOL," followed by the letter indicating the heading in the table where that tolerance is listed. The example shows a portion of a table for a family of similar parts, where column C has different tolerances for different configurations of the part.*

12.19 USING GEOMETRIC DIMENSIONING AND TOLERANCING

Geometric dimensioning and tolerancing (GDT) has evolved over the last 40 years to become an indispensable tool for defining parts and features more accurately. GDT not only considers an individual part and its dimensions and tolerances but views that part in relation to its related parts. This allows the designer more latitude in defining the part's features more accurately by considering not only the part's dimensions but its tolerances at the initial design stage. GDT also simplifies the inspection process. This is accomplished through the use of ASME standards *(ASME-Y14.5)*, as we have discussed previously.

Individually manufactured parts and components must eventually be assembled into products. We take for granted that each part of a lawnmower, for example, will mate properly with its other components when assembled. The wheels will slip into their axles, the pistons will fit properly into their cylinders, and so on. Nothing should be too tight or too loose.

Geometric dimensioning and tolerancing, therefore, is important to both the design and manufacturing processes.

Applying GDT principles to the design process requires five steps.

Step 1   Define the part's functions. It is best to break the part down to its simplest functions. Be as specific as possible. For example, a lawnmower wheel's functions are to (a) give the product mobility; (b) lift the mowing deck off the ground; (c) add rigidity to the body, and so forth.

Step 2   List the functions by priority. Only one function should have top priority. This step can be difficult, because many parts are designed to incorporate multiple functions. In our lawnmower wheel example, the function with top priority would be to give the product mobility.

Step 3   Define the datum reference frame. This step should be based on your list of priorities. This may mean creating several reference frames, each based on a priority on your list. The frame should be set up in either one, two, or three planes.

Step 4   Select controls. In most cases, several controls will be needed (e.g., runout, position, concentricity, or roughness). Begin with the simplest control. By "simplest" we mean least restrictive. Work from the least restrictive to the most restrictive set of controls.

Step 5   Calculate tolerances. Most tolerances are mathematically based. This step should be the easiest. Apply MMC, RFS, or LMC where indicated. Avoid completing this step first; it should always be your final step.

12.20 TOLERANCES AND DIGITAL PRODUCT DEFINITION

Dimensioning and tolerancing can take place directly in the 3D digital database. The electronic file can be transmitted as the digital product definition specifying the shape, size, and finish to the company that will manufacture and/or assemble the parts.

When you create a 3D model, it represents the ideal geometric shape of the part. The part can be manufactured very precisely, but as precision is increased, so is the price of the part. Adding tolerances to the model informs the manufacturer of the accuracy that is required on the finished part for it to function in your design as you intend. Essentially, you need to tell the manufacturer when to stop trying to achieve the level of perfection that is represented in your model.

When you include annotations in the solid model, the annotation should:

- Be in a plane that is clearly associated with the corresponding surface or view;
- Be clearly associated with the corresponding model geometry;
- Be capable of being printed and meet applicable drawing standards; and
- Be possible to display on the screen or turn off.

In general, tolerances and annotations provided directly in the model need to be interpreted to achieve the result that you intend. A combination of drawings and the model, only drawings, or a fully annotated model are all available methods for documenting a design. Each method has its advantages and disadvantages. You should investigate which method is suitable for your use and understand the applicable standards. See Figure 12.68 for examples of tolerancing in CAD. Partially dimensioned drawings should note: SEE DATASET FOR FULL GEOMETRIC DESCRIPTION.

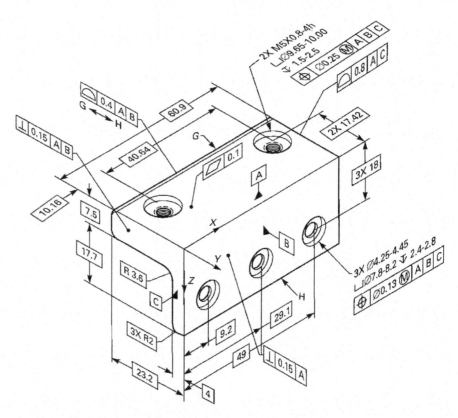

12.68 *Tolerances can be added directly to a 3D model so that it can be used as the digital product definition. (Reprinted from ASME Y14.41-2003, by permission of The American Society of Mechanical Engineers. All rights reserved.)*

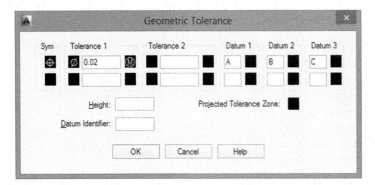

12.69   *This dialog box in CAD aids in creating geometric dimensioning and tolerancing symbols. (Autodesk screen shots reprinted courtesy of Autodesk, Inc.)*

12.21 COMPUTER GRAPHICS

CAD programs generally allow the user to add tolerances to dimension values in the drawings. Geometric dimensioning and tolerancing symbols, finish marks, and other standard symbols are typically available as a part of the CAD program or as a symbol library (see Figures 12.69–12.71).

Geometric dimensioning and tolerancing has become an essential part of today's manufacturing industry. To compete in today's marketplace, companies are required to develop and produce products of the highest quality, at lowest cost, and guarantee on-time delivery. Although considered by most to be a design specification language, GDT is a manufacturing and inspection language as well, providing a means for uniform interpretation and understanding by these various groups. It provides both a national and international contract base for customers and suppliers.

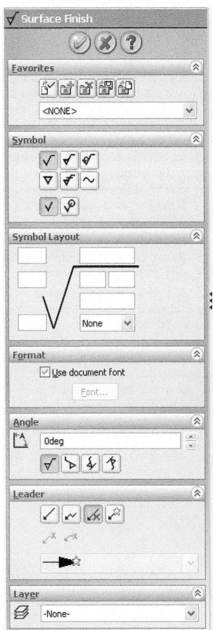

12.70   *SolidWorks software makes it easy to select surface finish symbols. (Courtesy of SolidWorks Corporation.)*

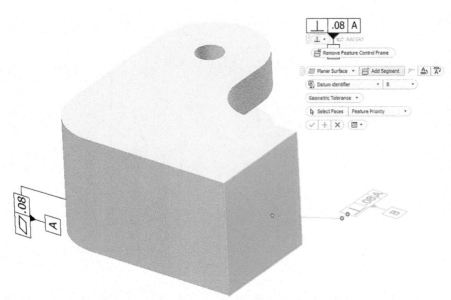

12.71   *With the tolerance command active, Autodesk Inventor suggests a likely choice for the feature and datum to use in the Feature Control Frame. You can set other options as needed. Its tolerance advisor provides information and warnings, such as "system of units is not compatible with the tolerance standard" you are using. (Autodesk screen shots reprinted courtesy of Autodesk, Inc.)*

USING SOLIDWORKS TO PERFORM A FIT STUDY

Tolerances are important to consider not just for each individual part but also for the entire assembly. Tolerance variations may accumulate from feature to feature of a part, and tolerances may also stack up from part to part in an assembly. One way to analyze the tolerances in the design of your assembly is to do a fit study. SolidWorks software is one modeler that has some useful tools for performing a fit study.

You can use the **Interference Detection** command in SolidWorks to show you where any two parts overlap in the model. To perform a fit study, modify the features of interest so they are at the upper size range of the allowable tolerance. Then, use the **Interference Detection** selection to display the dialog box shown in the figure. Click **Calculate** to display the names of components that overlap in the **Results** portion of the dialog box. Once you have checked the features sized at the upper extremes of the tolerance limits, set the feature to the lower size limit, and repeat the interference detection.

You can use SolidWorks to store configurations of each part. You can configure the model at the maximum material condition and at the minimum and store both. This allows you to quickly set the part model to a particular case for your fit study and then check the interferences.

As you can imagine, the more complex the assembly, the more valuable this CAD tool will be to you.

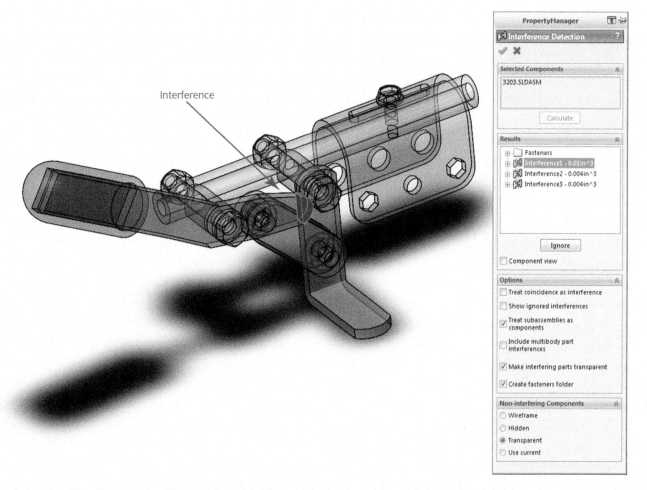

Areas that interfere in the assembly model are highlighted during interference detection. The length of this wheel lock lever part has been modified to exaggerate the material overlap when this part interferes. (Courtesy of Dynojet Research, Inc.)

PORTFOLIO

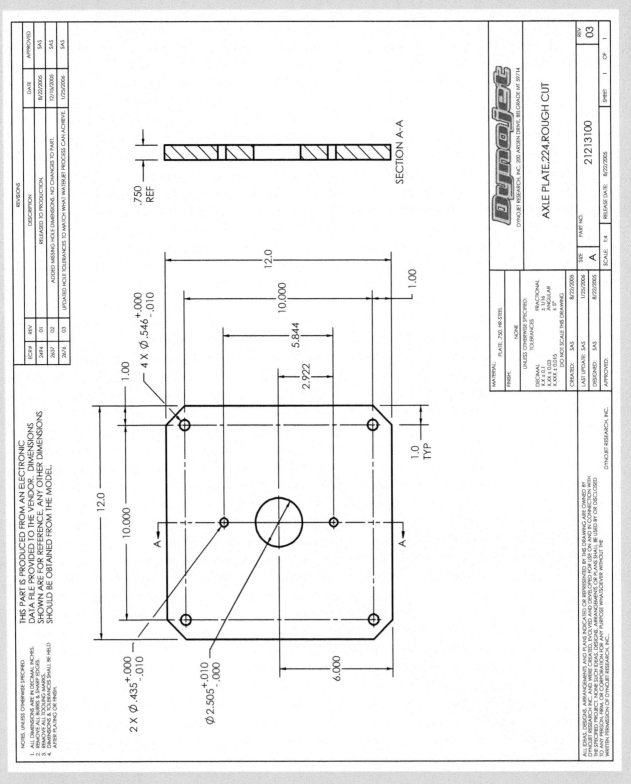

Unilateral tolerances are specified for hole sizes. (Courtesy of Dynojet Research, Inc.)

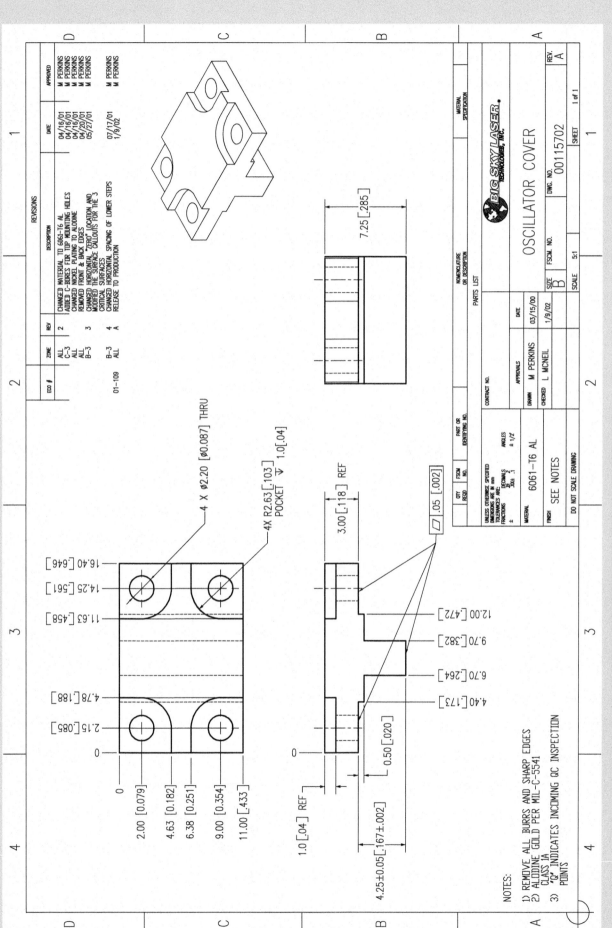

Form tolerances are specified on this dual-dimensioned drawing. (Courtesy of Big Sky Laser.)

PORTFOLIO

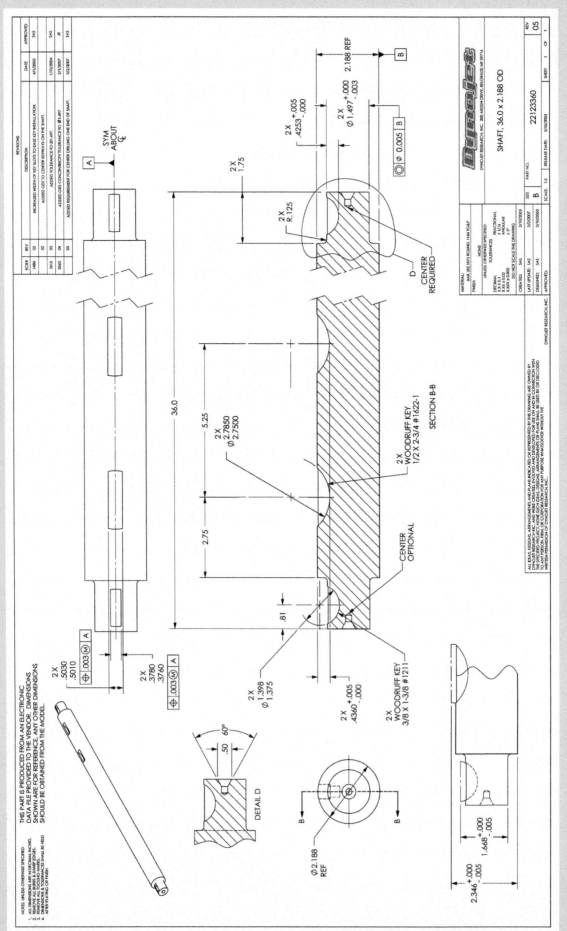

Dimensioned and Toleranced Part Drawing Using Limit, Variation, and Geometric Dimensioning and Tolerancing *(Courtesy of Dynojet Research, Inc.)*

KEY WORDS

Actual Local Feature
Actual Mating Envelope
Actual Minimum Material Envelope
Actual Size
Allowance
Angular Tolerances
Angularity Tolerance
Baseline Dimensioning
Basic Angle Tolerancing Method
Basic Dimension Symbol
Basic Size
Bilateral Tolerance
Bowed
Chained Dimension
Clearance Fit
Combined Symbols
Concentricity Tolerance
Cylindricity Tolerance
Datum Feature Symbol
Datum Features
Datum Reference Frame
Datum Targets
Degrees of Freedom
Deviation
Feature
Feature of Size
Feature Control Frame
Fit
Flatness Tolerance
Fundamental Deviation
General Tolerance Notes
Geometric Characteristics
Geometric Dimensioning and Tolerancing (GDT)
Geometric Tolerances
Hole System
Interference Fit
International Tolerance Grade (IT)
Limit Dimensions
Limit Tolerances
Line Fit
Lower Deviation
Maximum Material Condition
Nominal Size
Parallelism Tolerance
Perfect Form Envelope
Perpendicularity Tolerance

Primary Datum
Profile Tolerance
Quality Certify (QC)
Reference Dimension
Roundness (Circularity) Tolerance
Secondary Datum
Selective Assembly
Shaft System
Straightness Tolerance
Supplementary Symbols
Tertiary Datum
Tolerance
Tolerance Stacking
Tolerance Symbols
Tolerance Zone
Translation
Transition Fit
True-Position Dimensioning
Unilateral System
Upper Deviation
Virtual Condition
Waisted

CHAPTER SUMMARY

- Tolerance dimensioning describes the minimum and maximum limits for the size or the location of a feature.
- There are several types of dimensioning tolerances, including limit dimensions, unilateral tolerances, bilateral tolerances, and geometric tolerancing.
- Hole tolerance systems are the most commonly used tolerance systems because they assume the hole is nominal size and adjust the shaft to accommodate the tolerance.
- The amount of space between two mating parts at maximum material condition is called the allowance.
- Mating parts with large allowances are classified as having a clearance fit or a running and sliding fit.
- Mating parts with negative allowances are classified as having an interference fit or force fit.
- Mating parts are designed around a nominal size and class of fit. Other tolerances are calculated from these two values.
- High-quality parts are often dimensioned with geometric tolerancing to ensure that the size, shape, and relative geometric characteristics are properly defined.
- Datums can be used to define which degrees of freedom to restrict to make accurate and repeatable measurements.
- GDT has become an essential part of today's manufacturing industry. GDT is not only a design language but an inspection language as well.

REVIEW QUESTIONS

1. What do the two numbers of a limit dimension mean?
2. Draw three different geometric tolerances that reference a datum. Label the information in each box.
3. Why is the hole system more common than the shaft system for determining fits?
4. Give five examples of nominal sizes in everyday life. What is the purpose of a nominal size?
5. Give an example of two parts that would require a running and sliding fit. A force fit.
6. List five classes of fit.
7. Can one part have an allowance? Why?
8. Can two parts have a tolerance? Why?
9. Give an example of how GDT could be used as both a design and inspection tool.
10. Draw an isometric sketch of a cube and label the six degrees of freedom its motion can exhibit.
11. List the five steps required to apply GDT to the design process.

CHAPTER EXERCISES

Design Project

Exercise 12.1 Design a bike rack using standard tubing products and standard fittings. Provide a means for mounting the rack to concrete. What accuracy is required for your design to function? Research the manufacturing accuracy for the parts you specify. What is the maximum allowance your mounting can be off and still allow the parts to fit?

Tolerancing Projects

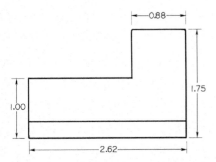

Exercise 12.2 Sketch the figure shown. Use either limit dimensions, bilateral tolerances, or geometric tolerancing to add a hole to the left end of the part, located .50″ from the bottom surface and 2″ from the right end of the part. The location should be accurate to ±.005 and its size accurate to within ±.002.

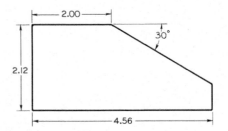

Exercise 12.3 Add geometric dimensioning and tolerancing symbols to the drawing to do the following: (a) Control the flatness of the bottom surface to a total tolerance of .001. (b) Control perpendicularity of the left surface and bottom surface to .003. (c) Control the tolerance for the 30° angle to .01.

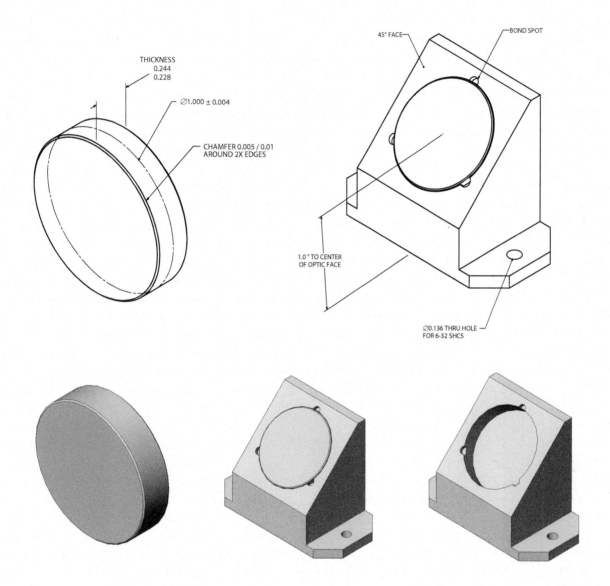

THICKNESS
0.244
0.228

Ø1.000 ± 0.004

CHAMFER 0.005 / 0.01
AROUND 2X EDGES

45° FACE

BOND SPOT

1.0 ° TO CENTER
OF OPTIC FACE

Ø0.136 THRU HOLE
FOR 6-32 SHCS

Exercise 12.4 You have been tasked with mounting a dielectric mirror at a 45° angle. This will be done by creating a mount out of 6061-T6 aluminum machined with a 45° face. The face will have a machined counterbore in which to mount the optic and three bond spots to attach the optic. The specifications for the design are:

- Reference the provided drawing for a stock 1″ dielectric mirror.
- The diameter for the counterbore must be .005″ to .010″ larger than the maximum diameter of the optic.
- The optic must sit at a minimum of .010″ and maximum of .020″ above the mounting surface.
- The optic will be bonded to the mount using ultraviolet curing adhesive. The adhesive bond spots will be .100″ diameter by .050″ deep, equally spaced around the perimeter of the optic counterbore.
- The center point of the outer surface of the optic will be located 1 ± .05″ from the bottom of the mount.
- The mount will be attached to a laser structure using two 6-32 socket head cap screws.

Answer these questions:

1. What diameter of counterbore is used to ensure the counterbore is .005″ to .010″ larger than the maximum diameter of the optic?
2. What depth of counterbore is used to ensure a .010″/.020″ protrusion height of the optic?
3. Create a full mechanical drawing with appropriate tolerances for the designed mount.

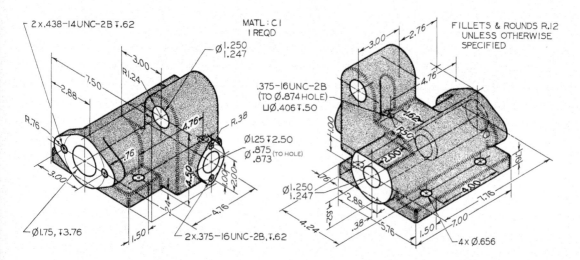

2x.438–14UNC–2B ⊤.62

MATL : C I
I REQD

FILLETS & ROUNDS R.12
UNLESS OTHERWISE
SPECIFIED

Ø1.250
1.247

3.00

7.50

R1.24

2.88

R.76

R.38

.76

4.76

.375–16UNC–2B
(TO Ø.874 HOLE)
⊔Ø.406 ⊤.50

Ø1.25 ⊤2.50
Ø.875 (TO HOLE)
.873

3.00

4.50

.24

4.76

.200

.100

1.50

Ø1.75, ⊤3.76

2x.375–16UNC–2B, ⊤.62

3.00

2.76

4.76

1.00

.62

R.50

2.00

Ø1.250
1.247

2.88

.76

.38

5.76

4.24

.52

1.50

7.00

7.16

4.00

.16

4x Ø.656

Exercise 12.5 Create a detail drawing for the automatic stop box shown in the two isometric views. Use standardized dimensioning and tolerancing symbols to replace notes as much as possible.

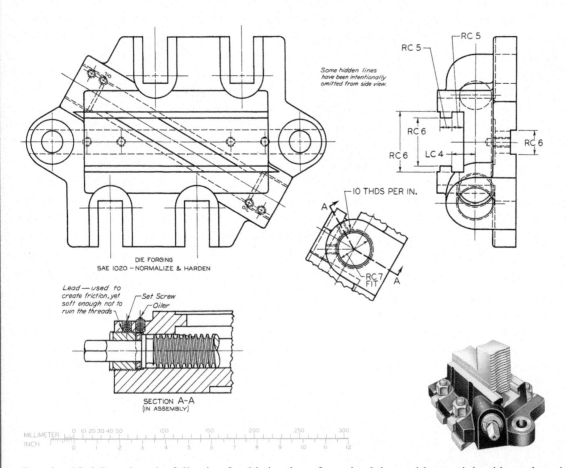

Some hidden lines
have been intentionally
omitted from side view.

.10

RC 5

RC 5

RC 5

RC 6

RC 6

RC 6

LC 4

RC 6

10 THDS PER IN.

A

A

RC7
FIT

DIE FORGING
SAE 1020 – NORMALIZE & HARDEN

Lead—used to
create friction, yet
soft enough not to
ruin the threads

Set Screw
Oiler

SECTION A-A
(IN ASSEMBLY)

MILLIMETER   0 10 20 30 40 50   100   150   200   250   300
INCH   0   1   2   3   4   5   6   7   8   9   10   11   12

Exercise 12.6 Complete the following for this jaw base for a chuck jaw, with top, right-side, and partial auxiliary views shown. (a) Create top, left-side (beside top), front, and partial auxiliary views complete with dimensions, if assigned. Use metric or decimal-inch dimensions. Use American National Standard tables for indicated fits or convert for metric values. See Appendices 4–13. (b) Create solid models for parts and assembly. Make detail drawings for parts and provide tolerances for critical fits. Use a general tolerance note for all other sizes.

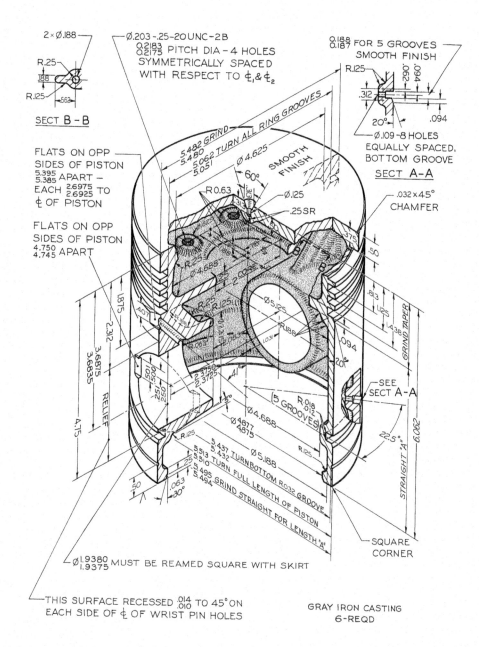

SECT B-B

2 × Ø.188

R.25

.188

R.125 .562

Ø.203 -.25 - 20 UNC - 2B
0.2183
0.2175 PITCH DIA - 4 HOLES
SYMMETRICALLY SPACED
WITH RESPECT TO ₵₁ & ₵₂

0.188
0.187 FOR 5 GROOVES
SMOOTH FINISH

R.125

.312 .290 .094

20° .094

Ø.109 -8 HOLES
EQUALLY SPACED,
BOTTOM GROOVE

SECT A-A

FLATS ON OPP
SIDES OF PISTON
5.395
5.385 APART -
EACH 2.6975
2.6925 TO
₵ OF PISTON

FLATS ON OPP
SIDES OF PISTON
4.750
4.745 APART

5.482 GRIND
5.480
5.062 TURN ALL RING GROOVES
5.051

Ø 4.625

60°

R 0.63

Ø.125

.25 SR

SMOOTH
FINISH

.032 × 45°
CHAMFER

.375

.50

R.25

Ø4.688

2 CORE

R.25 R.125

Ø5.125

R.188

.813

1.125

1.438

.094

20°

GRIND TAPER

.407

.063

.031

SEE
SECT A-A

R.018
.012

(5 GROOVES)

22.5°

6.062

STRAIGHT "A"

.500
.500

.250
.250

2 3.750
2.3725

41°

Ø4.688

Ø4.877
4.875

Ø5.188

R.125

R.125

5.437 TURN BOTTOM R.032 GROOVE
5.432

5.513 TURN FULL LENGTH OF PISTON
5.510

5.495 GRIND STRAIGHT FOR LENGTH "A"
5.494

.50

.063

30°

RELIEF

1.875

2.312

3.6875
3.6835

4.75

SQUARE
CORNER

Ø1.9380
1.9375 MUST BE REAMED SQUARE WITH SKIRT

THIS SURFACE RECESSED .014
.010 TO 45° ON
EACH SIDE OF ₵ OF WRIST PIN HOLES

GRAY IRON CASTING
6-REQD

Exercise 12.7 For this Caterpillar tractor piston, make a detail drawing full size. If assigned, use the unidirectional decimal-inch system, converting all fractions to two-place decimal dimensions, or convert all dimensions to metric. Use standard symbols for dimensioning and tolerancing to replace notes.

CHAPTER THIRTEEN

THREADS, FASTENERS, AND SPRINGS

---- OBJECTIVES ----

After studying the material in this chapter, you should be able to:

1. Define and label the parts of a screw thread.

2. Identify various screw thread forms.

3. Draw detailed, schematic, and simplified threads.

4. Define typical thread specifications.

5. Identify various fasteners and describe their use.

6. Draw various screw head types.

Refer to the following standards:
- *ANSI/ASME B1.1*
- *ANSI/ASME B1.7*
- *ANSI/ASME B1.13M*
- *ANSI/ASME B17.1*
- *ANSI/ASME Y14.6*

Fasteners *(Copyright Hellen Sergeyeva/Shutterstock.)*

OVERVIEW

Threaded fasteners are the principal devices used for assembling components. To speed production time and reduce costs, many new types of fasteners are created every year. Existing fasteners are also modified to improve their insertion in mass production. Many companies provide CAD drawings of their fasteners on the Web. When you are using standard fasteners in your designs, save time by downloading drawings or models.

Thread is usually dimensioned by giving a thread note in the drawing. This allows you to combine more information in a compact space.

The information in this chapter will prepare you to specify various types of thread and fasteners and to use the standard methods for representing them in your drawings.

13.1   Thread Used for Attachment
(Courtesy of Arthur S. Aubry/Stockbyte/ Getty Images.)

UNDERSTANDING THREADS AND FASTENERS

Screw threads are vital to industry. They are designed for hundreds of different purposes. The three basic applications are:

1. To hold parts together (Figure 13.1).
2. To provide for adjustment between parts (Figure 13.2).
3. To transmit power (Figure 13.3).

The shape of the helical (spiral shaped) thread is called the ***thread form.*** The metric thread form is the international standard, although the unified thread form is common in the United States. Other thread forms are used in specific applications.

3D CAD software may automatically depict fasteners inserted into the model using simplified thread representation in drawing views and may assist in creating proper callouts. The thread specification is a special leader note that defines the type of thread or fastener. This is an instruction for the shop technician so the correct type of thread is created during the manufacturing process.

13.2   Thread Used for Adjustment
(tritooth/123RF.)

13.3   Thread Used to Transmit Power *(ronen/123RF.)*

THE STANDARDIZATION OF SCREW THREADS

Once, there was no such thing as standardization. Nuts made by one manufacturer would not fit the bolts of another. In 1841 Sir Joseph Whitworth started crusading for a standard screw thread, and soon the Whitworth thread was accepted throughout England.

In 1864 the United States adopted a thread proposed by William Sellers of Philadelphia, but the Sellers nuts would not screw onto a Whitworth bolt or vice versa. In 1935 the American standard thread, with the same 60° V form of the old Sellers thread, was adopted in the United States.

Still, there was no standardization among countries. In peacetime it was a nuisance; in World War I it was a serious inconvenience; and in World War II the obstacle was so great that the Allies decided to do something about it. Talks began among the Americans, British, and Canadians, and in 1948 an agreement was reached on the unification of American and British screw threads. The new thread was called the Unified screw thread, and it represented a compromise between the American standard and Whitworth systems, allowing complete interchangeability of threads in three countries.

Sir Joseph Whitworth *(Courtesy of National Park Service.)*

In 1946 a committee called the International Organization for Standardization (ISO) was formed to establish a single international system of metric screw threads. Consequently, through the cooperative efforts of the Industrial Fasteners Institute (IFI), several committees of the American National Standards Institute, and the ISO representatives, a metric fastener standard was prepared.

*For a listing of ANSI standards for threads, fasteners, and springs, see page A-1.

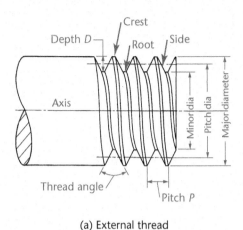

(a) External thread

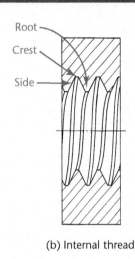

(b) Internal thread

13.4   Screw Thread Nomenclature

Close-Up View of Threaded Nut and Bolt *(Courtesy of Glen Jones/Shutterstock.)*

Screw Thread Terms

The following definitions apply to screw threads in general and are illustrated in Figure 13.4. For additional information regarding specific Unified and metric screw thread terms and definitions, refer to the appropriate standards.

Screw thread A ridge of uniform cross section in the form of a helix on the external or internal surface of a cylinder.

External thread A thread on the outside of a member, as on a shaft.

Internal thread A thread on the inside of a member, as in a hole.

Major diameter The largest diameter of a screw thread (for both internal and external threads).

Minor diameter The smallest diameter of a screw thread (for both internal and external threads).

Pitch The distance from a point on a screw thread to a corresponding point on the next thread measured parallel to the axis. In the United States, the pitch is equal to 1 divided by the number of threads per inch.

Pitch diameter The diameter of an imaginary cylinder passing through the threads where the widths of the threads and the widths of the spaces would be equal.

Lead The distance a screw thread advances axially in one turn.

Angle of thread The angle between the sides of the thread measured in a plane through the axis of the screw.

Crest The top surface joining the two sides of a thread.

Root The bottom surface joining the sides of two adjacent threads.

Side The surface of the thread that connects the crest with the root.

Axis of screw The longitudinal centerline through the screw.

Depth of thread The distance between the crest and the root of the thread measured normal to the axis.

Form of thread The cross section of thread cut by a plane containing the axis.

Series of thread The standard number of threads per inch for various diameters.

A HISTORICAL THREAD

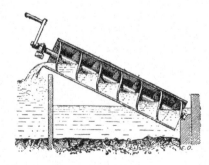

An Archimedean Screw
(Copyright Morphart Creation/ Shutterstock.)

The concept of the screw thread seems to have occurred first to Archimedes, the third-century-B.C. mathematician who wrote briefly on spirals and designed several simple devices applying the screw principle. By the first century B.C., the screw was a familiar element but was crudely cut from wood or filed by hand on a metal shaft. Not much was heard of the screw thread until the fifteenth century.

Leonardo da Vinci understood the screw principle, and created sketches showing how to cut screw threads by machine. In the sixteenth century, screws appeared in German watches and were used to fasten suits of armor. In 1669, the Frenchman Besson invented the screw-cutting lathe, but this method of production did not take hold for another century and a half; nuts and bolts continued to be made largely by hand. Screw manufacturing began in eighteenth-century England, during the Industrial Revolution.

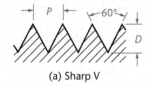

(a) Sharp V

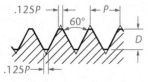

(b) American national

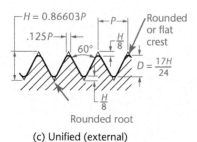

(c) Unified (external)

13.5 Sharp, American National, and Unified Screw Thread Forms

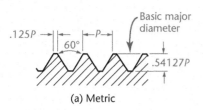

(a) Metric

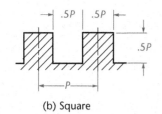

(b) Square

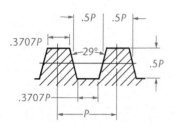

(c) Acme (general-purpose)

13.6 Metric, Square, and Acme Screw Thread Forms

Screw Thread Forms

The thread form is the cross-sectional shape of the thread. Various forms of threads are used for different purposes. Figures 13.5–13.7 show some of the typical thread forms.

Sharp-V thread (60°) is useful for certain adjustments because of the increased friction resulting from the full thread face. It is also used on brass pipe work (Figure 13.5a).

American national thread, with flattened roots and crests, is a stronger thread. This form replaced the sharp-V thread for general use (Figure 13.5b).

Unified thread is the standard thread agreed on by the United States, Canada, and Great Britain in 1948. It has replaced the American national form. The crest of the external thread may be flat or rounded, and the root is rounded; otherwise, the thread form is essentially the same as the American national. Some earlier American national threads are still included in the new standard, which lists 11 different numbers of threads per inch for the various standard diameters, together with selected combinations of special diameters and pitches. The 11 series includes the coarse thread series (UNC or NC), recommended for general use; the fine thread series (UNF or NF), for general use in automotive and aircraft work and in applications where a finer thread is required; the extra fine series (UNEF or NEF), which is the same as the SAE extra fine series, used particularly in aircraft and aeronautical equipment and generally for threads in thin walls; and the 8 series of 4, 6, 8, 12, 16, 20, 28, and 32 threads with constant pitch. The 8UN or 8N, 12UN or 12N, and 16UN or 16N series are recommended for the uses corresponding to the old 8-, 12-, and 16-pitch American national threads. In addition, there are three special thread series—UNS, NS, and UN— that involve special combinations of diameter, pitch, and length of engagement (Figure 13.5c).

Unified extra fine thread series (UNEF) has many more threads per inch for given diameters than any series of the American national or unified. The form of thread is the same as the American national. These small threads are used in thin metal where the length of thread engagement is small, in cases where close adjustment is required, and where vibration is great.

Metric thread is the standard screw thread agreed on for international screw thread fasteners. The crest and root are flat, but the external thread is often rounded if formed by a rolling process. The form is similar to the American national and unified threads but with less depth of thread. The preferred metric thread for commercial purposes conforms to the ISO basic profile M for metric threads. This M profile design is comparable to the unified inch profile, but the two are not interchangeable. For commercial purposes, two series of metric threads are preferred—coarse (general-purpose) and fine—much fewer than previously used (Figure 13.6a).

Square thread is theoretically the ideal thread for power transmission, since its face is nearly at right angles to the axis, but owing to the difficulty of cutting it with dies and because of other inherent disadvantages (such as the fact that split nuts will not readily disengage), square thread has been displaced to a large extent by the acme thread. Square thread is not standardized (Figure 13.6b).

Acme thread is a modification of the square thread and has largely replaced it. It is stronger than the square thread, is easier to cut, and has the advantage of easy disengagement from a split nut, as on the lead screw of a lathe (Figure 13.6c).

Standard worm thread (not shown) is similar to the acme thread but is deeper. It is used on shafts to carry power to worm wheels.

Whitworth thread was the British standard and has been replaced by the unified thread. The uses of Whitworth thread correspond to those of the American national thread (Figure 13.7a).

Knuckle thread is often used on electric bulbs. (Shahril KHMD/Shutterstock.)

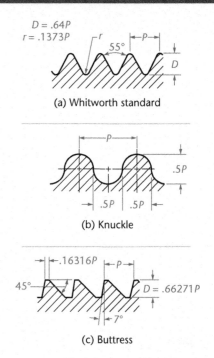

(a) Whitworth standard

(b) Knuckle

(c) Buttress

13.7 Whitworth Standard, Knuckle, and Buttress Screw Thread Forms

Knuckle thread is usually rolled from sheet metal but is sometimes cast. In modified forms, knuckle thread is used in electric bulbs and sockets, bottle tops, and the like (Figure 13.7b).

Buttress thread is designed to transmit power in one direction only. It is commonly used in large guns, in jacks, and in other mechanisms that have high strength requirements (Figure 13.7c).

A number of different thread forms are defined in various ASME standards that specify requirements for the design and selection of screw threads. For example, the old N thread series has been superseded by the UN series.

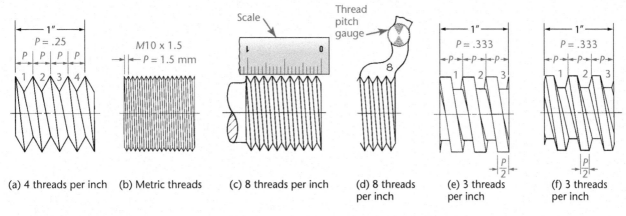

(a) 4 threads per inch   (b) Metric threads   (c) 8 threads per inch   (d) 8 threads per inch   (e) 3 threads per inch   (f) 3 threads per inch

13.8 Pitch

Thread Pitch

The pitch of any thread form is the distance parallel to the axis between corresponding points on adjacent threads, as shown in Figure 13.8.

For metric threads, this distance is specified in millimeters. The pitch for a metric thread that is included with the major diameter in the thread designation determines the size of the thread—for example, as shown in Figure 13.8b.

For threads dimensioned in inches, the pitch is equal to 1 divided by the number of threads per inch. See Appendix 14 for thread tables giving more information on standard numbers of threads per inch for various thread series and diameters. For example, a unified coarse thread of 1″ diameter has eight threads per inch, and the pitch P equals 1/8″ (.125″).

If a thread has only four threads per inch, the pitch and the threads themselves are quite large, as shown in Figure 13.8a. If there are 16 threads per inch, the pitch is only 1/16″ (.063″), and the threads are relatively small, similar to those in Figure 13.8b.

The pitch or the number of threads per inch can be measured with a scale or with a **thread pitch gage** (Figure 13.8d).

Thread Series

ASME/ANSI Y14.6, Screw Thread Representation, is a standard for drawing, specifying, and dimensioning threads on drawings.

A thread series is the detail of the shape and number of threads per inch composing different groups of fasteners. Table 13.1 shows the thread series for UN thread. (UNJ and UNR thread series have rounded root contours to aid in preventing stress concentrations that may result from the flat contour of the typical UN thread profile. Both are external thread specifications.)

Five series of threads were used in the old ANSI standards:

Coarse thread A general-purpose thread used for holding. It is designated NC (national coarse).

Fine thread With a greater number of threads per inch, it is used extensively in automotive and aircraft construction. It is designated NF (national fine).

8-pitch thread All diameters have 8 threads per inch. It is used on bolts for high-pressure pipe flanges, cylinder-head studs, and similar fasteners. It is designated 8N (national form, 8 threads per inch).

12-pitch thread All diameters have 12 threads per inch. It is used in boiler work and for thin nuts on shafts and sleeves in machine construction. It is designated 12N (national form, 12 threads per inch).

16-pitch thread All diameters have 16 threads per inch. It is used where necessary to have a fine thread regardless of diameter, as on adjusting collars and bearing retaining nuts. It is designated 16N (national form, 16 threads per inch).

The helical shape of thread is similar to the striping on a barber pole.

Table 13.1 Thread Series of UN Thread

Basic Thread Series	Constant Pitch	Coarse	Fine	Extra Fine	Special Diameter
UN	UN	UNC	UNF	UNEF	UNS
UNJ	UNJ	UNJC	UNJF	UNJEF	UNJS
N*	N	NC	NF	NEF	NS
UNR	UNR	UNRC	UNRF	UNREF	UNRS

This series is superseded by the UN series.

Right-Hand and Left-Hand Threads

A right-hand thread is one that advances into a nut when turned clockwise, and a left-hand thread is one that advances into a nut when turned counterclockwise, as shown in Figure 13.9. A thread is always considered to be right-hand (RH) unless otherwise specified. A left-hand thread is always labeled LH on a drawing.

This bottom bracket is used to attach the cranks on a bicycle to the frame. One end has right-hand thread and the other side left-hand thread so the pedal motion won't unscrew the bottom-bracket bearing cups.

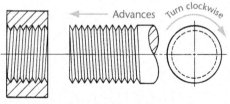

(a) Right-hand thread

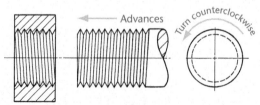

(b) Left-hand thread

13.9   Right-Hand and Left-Hand Threads

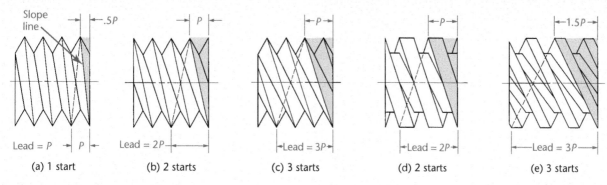

Slope line

| .5P | P | P | P | 1.5P |

Lead = P | P | Lead = 2P | Lead = 3P | Lead = 2P | Lead = 3P

(a) 1 start   (b) 2 starts   (c) 3 starts   (d) 2 starts   (e) 3 starts

13.10   Multiple Threads

Single and Multiple Threads

A *single thread,* as the name implies, is composed of one ridge, and the lead is therefore equal to the pitch. Multiple threads are composed of two or more ridges running side by side. As shown in Figures 13.10a–c, the slope is the hypotenuse of a right triangle whose short side equals .5P for single threads, P for double threads, 1.5P for triple threads, and so on. This relationship applies to all forms of threads. In double threads, the lead is twice the pitch; in triple threads, the lead is three times the pitch, and so on. On a drawing of a single or triple thread, a root is opposite a crest; in the case of a double or quadruple thread, a root is drawn opposite a root. There-

fore, in one turn, a double thread advances twice as far as a single thread, and a triple thread advances three times as far. RH double square and RH triple acme threads are shown in Figures 13.10d and e, respectively.

Multiple threads are used wherever quick motion, but not great power, is desired, as on ballpoint pens, toothpaste caps, valve stems, and so on. The threads on a valve stem are frequently multiple threads to impart quick action in opening and closing the valve. Multiple threads on a shaft can be recognized and counted by observing the number of thread starts on the end of the screw, as shown in Figure 13.11.

13.11   *This shaded model of a triple-threaded bolt makes it easy to see the three distinct threads. When you look at the end view of a bolt, you can count the number of starts.*

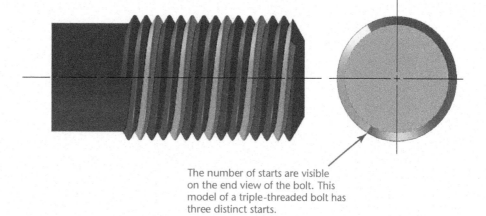

The number of starts are visible on the end view of the bolt. This model of a triple-threaded bolt has three distinct starts.

American National Thread Fits

For general use, three classes of fits between mating threads (as between bolt and nut) have been established by ANSI.

These fits are produced by the application of tolerances listed in the standard and are as follows:

Class 1 Fit   Recommended only for screw thread work where clearance between mating parts is essential for rapid assembly and where shake or play is not objectionable.

Class 2 Fit   Represents a high quality of commercial thread product and is recommended for the great bulk of interchangeable screw thread work.

Class 3 Fit   Represents an exceptionally high quality of commercially threaded product and is recommended only in cases where the high cost of precision tools and continual checking are warranted.

The standard for unified screw threads specifies tolerances and allowances defining the several classes of fit (degree of looseness or tightness) between mating threads. In the symbols for fit, the letter A refers to the external threads and B to internal threads. There are three classes of fit each for external threads (1A, 2A, 3A) and internal threads (1B, 2B, 3B). Classes 1A and 1B have generous tolerances, facilitating rapid assembly and disassembly. Classes 2A and 2B are used in the normal production of screws, bolts, and nuts, as well as in a variety of general applications. Classes 3A and 3B provide for applications needing highly accurate and close-fitting threads.

Metric and Unified Thread Fits

Some specialized metric thread applications are specified by tolerance grade, tolerance position, class, and length of engagement. There are a number of tolerance grades for metric thread fits. These are based on the diameter of the thread. The tolerance grade is given as a number and the position is given as a letter. Upper case letters are used for internal thread (like that on nuts) and lower case letters are used for external thread (like that on bolts).

Grade 6 is a medium tolerance. A number lower than 6 specifies a tighter, finer tolerance; a number larger than 6 indicates larger, coarser tolerances, which might be required for long lengths of thread engagement. A general-purpose application has a tolerance class of 6H for internal threads and a class of 6g for external threads. Metric thread tolerance classes of 6H/6g are generally assumed if not otherwise designated and are used in applications comparable to the 2A/2B inch classes of fits.

When a double designation is given, such as 5g6g, this indicates separate tolerance grades for the pitch diameter (given first, 5g) and the major diameter of the thread (given second, 6g), in this case external thread. A single-tolerance designation, such as 6H, indicates that both the tolerance grade and position for the pitch diameter and the minor diameter are the same (in this case internal thread) so it is listed only once.

The tolerance grade for the minor diameter and for the pitch diameter of internal thread may be 4, 5, 6, 7 or 8. The major diameter of external thread may be grade 4, 6, or 8 and the external pitch diameter may be grades 3 through 9.

The tolerance position is the range of the tolerance from the basic size of the thread profile. For internal thread, H has a zero fundamental deviation, and G has a positive fundamental deviation. External thread may be h (zero fundamental deviation), or e, f, or g, which all have negative fundamental deviations, meaning that the thread element will be smaller than the basic size, to assure it may be threaded into the hole.

Three Methods for Drawing Thread

There are three methods of representing screw threads on drawings—the schematic, simplified, and detailed methods. All three types may be combined on a single drawing.

Schematic and the more common simplified representations are used to show threads. The symbols are the same for all forms of threads, such as metric, unified, square, and acme, but the thread specification identifies which is to be used.

Detailed representation is a closer approximation of the exact appearance of a screw thread, in which the true profiles of the thread's form are drawn; but the helical curves are replaced by straight lines. The true projection of the helical curves of a screw thread is rarely used in practice. Detailed representation is shown in Figure 13.12. Do not use detailed representation unless the diameter of the thread on the drawing is more than 1″ or 25 mm and then only to call attention to the thread when necessary. Whether the crests or roots are flat or rounded, they are represented by single lines and not double lines. American national and unified threads are drawn the same way. Figure 13.13 shows schematic thread symbols, and Figure 13.14 shows simplified thread symbols.

Detailed directions for drawing and sketching schematic and simplified thread are shown on pages 602 and 603.

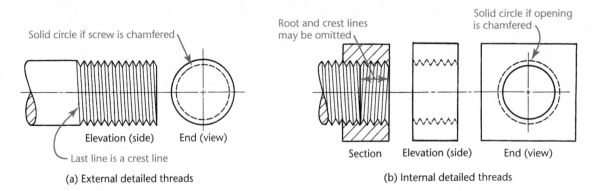

13.12   Detailed Metric, American National, and Unified Threads

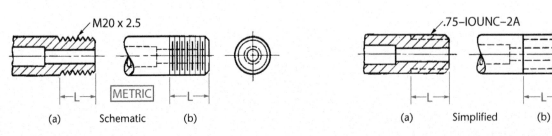

13.13   Schematic Thread Symbols

13.14   Simplified Thread Symbols

STEP by STEP

SHOWING DETAILED THREAD

1 Draw the centerline and lay out the length and major diameter as shown at right.

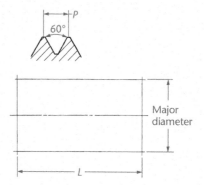

2 Find the number of threads per inch in the Thread Table for American National and Unified threads. This number depends on the major diameter of the thread and whether the thread is internal or external.

Find the pitch (P) by dividing 1 by the number of threads per inch. For example, .75–10 UNC has a major diameter of .75 inches and is 10 threads per inch. The pitch for metric threads is given directly in the thread designation. For example, in the designation M20 × 2, the 20 mm diameter thread has a pitch of 2 mm.

Establish the slope of the thread by offsetting the slope line .5P for single threads, P for double threads, 1.5P for triple threads, and so on. For right-hand external threads, the slope slants upward to the left; for left-hand external threads, the slope slants upward to the right.

By eye, mark off even spacing for the pitch. If using CAD, make a single thread and array the lines using the pitch as the spacing.

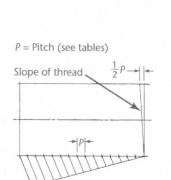

P = Pitch (see tables)

Slope of thread

TIP: Use slanted scale technique if sketching

3 From the pitch points, make crest lines parallel to the slope line. These should be dark, thin lines. Make two V's to establish the depth of the thread, and sketch light guidelines for the root of the thread, as shown.

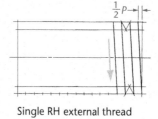

Single RH external thread

4 Finish the final 60° V's. The V's should be vertical; they should not lean with the thread.

Make root lines. Root lines will not be parallel to crest lines but should appear parallel to each other.

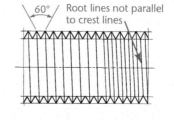

60° Root lines not parallel to crest lines

5 When the end is chamfered (usually 45° with the end of the shaft, sometimes 30°), the chamfer extends to the thread depth. The chamfer creates a new crest line, which you make between the two new crest points. It is not parallel to the other crest lines. When finished, all thread root and crest lines should be shown thin, but dark.

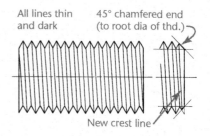

All lines thin and dark   45° chamfered end (to root dia of thd.)

New crest line

> **TIP**
>
> The thread depth table in Figure 13.15 gives approximate thread depths for a variety of common diameters. You can use thread depth tables to calculate the exact depth and spacing, but the calculated thread depth is often too small to show clearly on the drawing, so it is often shown larger than actual size for clarity.

MAJOR DIAMETER	#5 (125) TO #12 (216)	.25	.3125	.375	.4375	.5	.5625	.625	.6875	.75	.8125	.875	.9375	I.
DEPTH, D	.03125	.03125	.03125	.0468	.0468	.0625	.0625	.0625	.0625	.0781	.0937	.0937	.0937	.0937
PITCH, P	.0468	.0625	.0625	.0625	.0625	.0937	.0937	.0937	.0937	.125	.125	.125	.125	.125

Approximate thread depth table   *(For metric values: 1" = 25.4 mm or see inside back cover)*

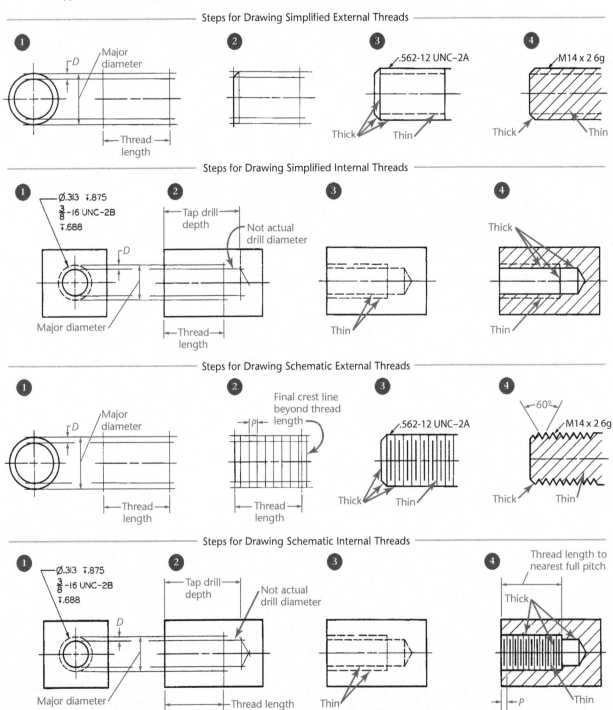

13.15   Steps for Drawing Thread Symbols—Simplified and Schematic

THREE WAYS TO SKETCH THREAD

Detailed Representation

Detailed representation is the most realistic looking, although it is a symbolic way of representing thread and does not show the helical shape accurately. Detailed representation is rarely ever sketched because it is time-consuming to draw the large number of lines making up its shape. Detailed representation does not reproduce well when the thread diameter on the sheet of paper is smaller than 1″ or 25 mm.

1 Lightly block in the threaded shaft. Draw a light vertical line to define the threaded portion. Add lines angled at 45° to represent the chamfer.

1/2 pitch distance

2 Make light ticks to mark the pitch distances.

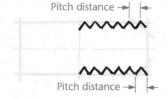

Pitch distance

Pitch distance

3 Sketch 60° V's representing the thread form.

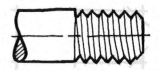

4 Connect crest to crest and root to root and darken in the final lines.

Simplified Representation

Simplified representation uses hidden lines to represent the depth of the thread. Because the thread depth is different for different pitches or thread series, and can sometimes be quite small, this hidden line is often shown at 1/16″ or 2 mm so it can easily be identified on a sketched or printed drawing. Notice the lines that represent the chamfer and the end of the threaded length. The chamfer makes it easier to get the bolt started in the hole.

1 Lightly block in the threaded shaft. Make a light vertical line to define threaded portion. Use a light line to mark the thread depth.

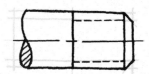

2 Sketch short dashes for the thread depth, then darken in the final lines.

Schematic Thread Representation

Schematic thread representation uses shorter thick parallel lines to represent the roots of the thread and longer thin lines to represent the crests. The ends of screws and bolts are shown chamfered, as they are in detailed and simplified representation. Distances from crest to crest or root to root are not always shown accurately; instead they are often shown about 1/8″ or 3 mm apart to give the appearance of thread.

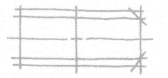

1 Lightly block in the threaded shaft. Make a light vertical line to define the threaded portion. Use a light line to mark the thread depth.

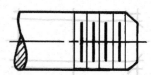

2 Use short thick lines to represent the roots and long thin lines to represent the crests.

13.1 THREAD NOTES

ASME/ANSI Y14.6, Screw Thread Representation, is a standard for representing, specifying, and dimensioning screw threads on drawings. Thread notes for metric, unified, and American national screw threads are shown in Figures 13.16 through 13.19. These same notes or symbols are used in correspondence, on shop and store-room records, and in specifications for parts, taps, dies, tools, and gages.

Metric screw threads are designated basically by the letter M (for metric thread) followed by the thread form and nominal size (basic major diameter) in millimeters and separated by the symbol × followed by the pitch, also in millimeters. For example, the basic thread note M10 × 1.5 is adequate for most commercial purposes, as shown in Figure 13.17. If needed, the class of fit and LH for left-hand designation is added to the note. (The absence of LH indicates a RH thread.)

If necessary, the length of the thread engagement is added to the thread note. The letter S stands for short, N means normal, and L means long. For example, the single note M10 × 1.5-6H/6g-N-LH combines the specifications for internal and external mating of left-hand metric threads of 10-mm diameter and 1.5-mm pitch with general-purpose tolerances and normal length of engagement.

For inch threads based on 60° forms, the thread designation should include (in order):

- Nominal diameter in inches
- Number of threads per inch
- Letter symbol of the thread series
- Number and letter of the thread class
- Any qualifying information needed, such as the class of fit or the thread gaging system

For example:

.750–16 UNF–2A(21)

A sample special thread designation is 1.50–7N-LH.

For multiple-start threads, use this format:

- Nominal diameter in inches
- Pitch in inches followed by the letter P
- Lead in inches followed by the letter L
- Number of starts in parentheses
- Letter symbol of the thread series
- Number and letter of the thread class
- Any qualifying information needed, such as the class of fit or the thread gaging system

For example:

.750–.0625P–.1875L (3 STARTS) UNF–2A(21)

Alternatively, the number of threads per inch can be given as is typical, followed by the lead in inches with the letter L afterward. Finally, the number of starts is given in parentheses, as in

.750–16–.1875L (3 STARTS) UNF–2A(21).

A thread note for a blind tapped hole is shown in Figure 13.16. A tap drill is sized to form a hole that will leave enough material for thread to be cut using a tap to form a threaded hole. In practice the tap drill size and depth are omitted and left up to the shop. At times it is desirable to state a tolerance range for the size of the hole prior to threading. This can be stated as follows:

⌀.656–.658 BEFORE THD .75–20–NEF–2B

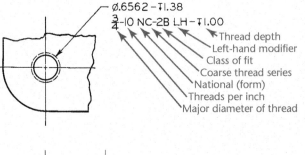

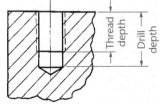

13.16 Thread Notes

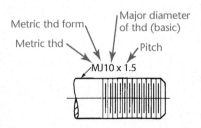

13.17 Metric Thread Notes

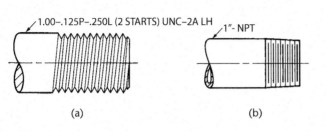

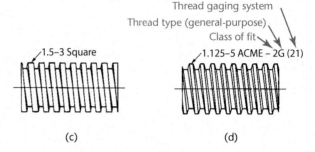

(a)   (b)   (c)   (d)

13.18   Thread Notes

Thread notes for holes are preferably attached to the circular views of the holes. Thread notes for external threads are preferably given where the threaded shaft appears rectangular, as shown in Figures 13.18a–d.

When converting typical fractional nominal diameter sizes to decimals, the decimal equivalent for the major diameter is given to four decimal places (omitting zero in the fourth place). For example, .1375–32 UNF-2A

Thread notes for unified threads are shown in Figures 13.19c and d. The letters A and B designate external or internal, respectively, after the numeral designating the class of fit. If the letters LH are omitted, the thread is understood to be right hand.

The following are some typical thread notes:

9/16–18 UNF–2B

1.75–16 UN–2A

.25–.050P–.015L (3 STARTS) UNC–2A

Acme Thread Notes

ACME screw threads use the following two classes of fit:

G *(general-purpose)* Provides clearance on the major and minor diameters of the thread.

C *(centralizing)* Provides for contact of the major diameters.

For many applications either specification is adequate, but the centralizing fit is preferred when the load will be transverse to the screw axis, as the thread major diameters then act as radial bearings. The G designation is not to be confused with the G used for metric fits. Some typical thread notes are:

1.75–4 ACME–2G

1.75–6 ACME–4C

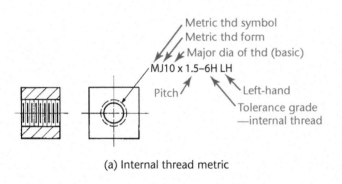

(a) Internal thread metric

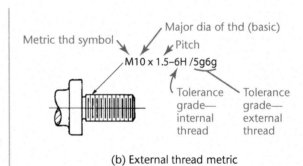

(b) External thread metric

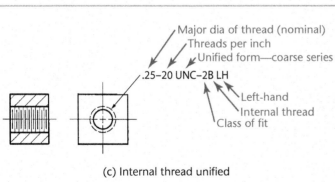

(c) Internal thread unified

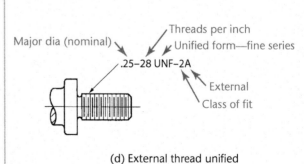

(d) External thread unified

13.19   Thread Notes

13.2 EXTERNAL THREAD SYMBOLS

Simplified representations for external threads are shown in Figures 13.20a and b. The threaded portions are indicated by hidden lines parallel to the axis at the approximate depth of the thread, whether the cylinder appears rectangular or circular. The depth shown is not always the actual thread depth, just a representation of it. Use the table in Figure 13.15 for the general appearance of these lines.

When the schematic form is shown in section, as in Figure 13.21a, show the V's of the thread to make the thread obvious. It is not necessary to show the V's to scale or to the actual slope of the crest lines. To draw the V's, use the schematic thread depth, as shown in Figure 13.16, and determine the pitch by drawing 60° V's.

Schematic threads are indicated by alternating long and short lines, as shown in Figure 13.21b. The short lines representing the root lines are thicker than the long crest lines. Theoretically, the crest lines should be spaced according to actual pitch, but this would make them crowded and tedious to draw, defeating the purpose, which is to save time in sketching them. Space the crest lines carefully by eye, then add the heavy root lines halfway between the crest lines. Generally, lines closer together than about 1/16″ are hard to distinguish. The spacing should be proportionate for all diameters. You do not need to use these actual measurements in sketching schematic threads, just use them to get a feel for how far apart to make the lines.

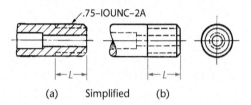

(a)   Simplified   (b)

13.20 External Thread Symbols for Simplified Thread

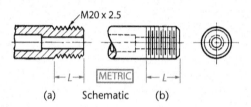

(a)   Schematic   (b)

13.21 External Thread Symbols for Schematic Thread

13.3 INTERNAL THREAD SYMBOLS

Internal thread symbols are shown in Figure 13.22. Note that the only differences between the schematic and simplified internal thread symbols occur in the sectional views. The representation of the internal schematic thread in section in Figures 13.22k, m, and o is exactly the same as the external representation shown in Figure 13.21b. Hidden threads, by either method, are represented by pairs of hidden lines. The hidden dashes should be staggered, as shown.

In the case of blind tapped holes, the drill depth normally is drawn at least three schematic pitches beyond the thread

length, as shown in Figures 13.22d, e, l, and m. The symbols in Figures 13.22f and n represent the use of a bottoming tap, when the length of thread is the same as the depth of drill. The thread length you sketch may be slightly longer than the actual given thread length. If the tap drill depth is known or given, draw the drill to that depth. If the thread note omits this information, as is often done in practice, sketch the hole three schematic thread pitches beyond the thread length. The tap drill diameter is represented approximately, not to actual size.

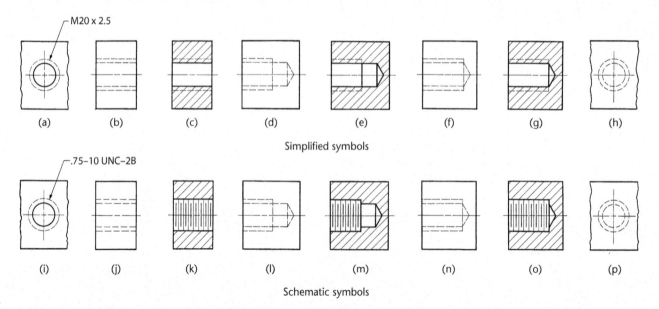

(a)   (b)   (c)   (d)   (e)   (f)   (g)   (h)

Simplified symbols

(i)   (j)   (k)   (l)   (m)   (n)   (o)   (p)

Schematic symbols

13.22 Internal Thread Symbols

DETAILED REPRESENTATION OF ACME THREADS

Detailed representation of acme threads is used only to call attention when details of the thread are important and the major diameter is larger than 1″ or 25 mm on the drawing. The steps are as follows.

1 Make a centerline and lay out the length and major diameter of the thread, as shown. For U.S. drawings, determine the pitch by dividing 1 by the number of threads per inch (see Appendix 21). Make construction lines for the root diameter, making the thread depth $P/2$. Make construction lines halfway between crest and root guidelines.

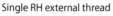
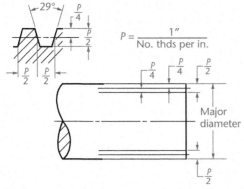

$$P = \frac{1''}{\text{No. thds per in.}}$$

2 Mark off spaces on the intermediate construction lines.

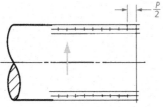

3 Through alternate points, make construction lines for the sides of the threads at 15° (instead of 14.5°).

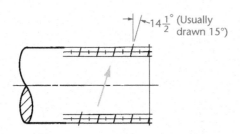

4 Make construction lines for the other sides of the threads, as shown. For single and triple threads, a crest is opposite a root; for double and quadruple threads, a crest is opposite a crest. Finish tops and bottoms of threads.

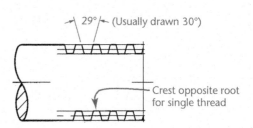

5 Make parallel crest lines.

6 Make parallel root lines, and finish the thread profiles. All lines should be thin and dark.

The internal threads in the back of the nut and the external threads on the front side of the screw will slope in opposite directions.

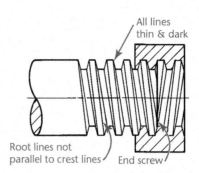

End views of acme threaded shafts and holes are drawn exactly like those for the square thread.

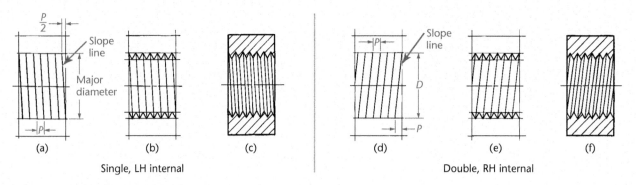

13.23 Detailed Representation—Internal Metric, Unified, and American National

13.4 DETAILED REPRESENTATION: METRIC, UNIFIED, AND AMERICAN NATIONAL THREADS

The detailed representation for metric, unified, and American national threads is the same, because the flats are disregarded.

Internal detailed threads in section are drawn as shown in Figure 13.23. Notice that for left-hand threads the lines slope upward to the left (Figures 13.23a–c); for right-hand threads the lines slope up to the right (Figures 13.23d –f).

Detailed Internal Square Thread

The internal thread construction is shown in Figure 13.24. Note that the thread lines representing the back half of the internal threads (because the thread is in section) slope in the opposite direction from those on the front side of the screw.

Steps in drawing a single internal square thread in section are shown in Figure 13.24. Note in Figure 13.24b that a crest is drawn opposite a root. This is the case for both single and triple threads. For double or quadruple threads, a crest is opposite a crest. Thus, the construction in Figures 13.24a and b is the same for any multiple of thread. The differences appear in Figure 13.24c, where the threads and spaces are distinguished and outlined.

The same internal thread is shown in Figure 13.24e from an external view. The profiles of the threads are drawn in their normal position, but with hidden lines, and the sloping lines are omitted for simplicity. The end view of the same internal thread is shown in Figure 13.24f. Note that the hidden and solid circles are opposite those for the end view of the shaft.

Detailed External Square Thread

Figure 13.25 is an assembly drawing showing an external square thread partly screwed into a nut. When the external and internal threads are assembled, the thread in the nut overlaps and covers up half of the V, as shown at B.

Sometimes in assemblies the root and crest lines may be omitted from the *nut only* portion of the drawing so that it is easier to identify the inserted screw.

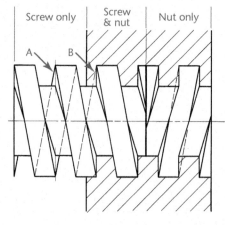

13.25 Square Threads in Assembly

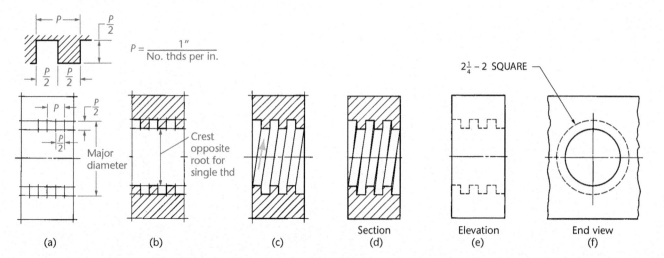

$$P = \frac{1''}{\text{No. thds per in.}}$$

13.24 Detailed Representation—Internal Square Threads

DETAILED REPRESENTATION OF SQUARE THREADS

Detailed representation of external square threads is used only when the major diameter is over about 1″ or 25 mm, and it is important to show the detail of the thread on the finished sketch or plotted drawing. The steps for creating a detailed square thread are as follows.

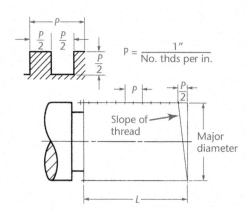

$$P = \frac{1''}{\text{No. thds per in.}}$$

1 Make a centerline and lay out the length and major diameter of the thread. For U.S. drawings, determine the pitch (*P*) by dividing 1 by the number of threads per inch. For a single right-hand thread, the lines slope upward to the left, and the slope line is offset as for all single threads of any form. On the upper line, use spacing equal to *P*/2, as shown.

2 From the points on the upper line, draw guidelines for the root of the thread, making the depth as shown.

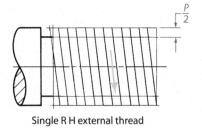

Single R H external thread

3 Make parallel visible back edges of threads.

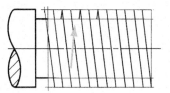

4 Make parallel visible root lines.

Root lines parallel

5 All lines should be thin and dark.

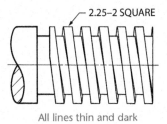

2.25–2 SQUARE

All lines thin and dark

TIP

End View of a Shaft

The end view of the shaft illustrated in this Step by Step feature is shown below. Note that the root circle is hidden. In a sketch, no attempt is made to show the true projection of any but the major diameter.

If the end of a shaft is chamfered, a solid circle is drawn instead of the hidden circle.

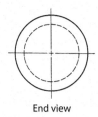

End view

13.5 THREADS IN ASSEMBLY

Threads in an assembly drawing are shown in Figure 13.26. It is customary not to section a stud or a nut or any solid part unless necessary to show some internal shapes. Show these items "in the round," as they would look if they were set in the hole after the assembly was cut to form the section. When external and internal threads are sectioned in assembly, the V's are required to show the threaded connection.

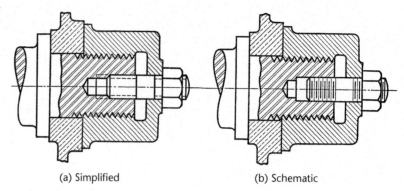

(a) Simplified   (b) Schematic

13.26   Threads in Assembly

13.6 MODELING THREAD

Thread is not typically modeled, because this complex helical surface adds greatly to the complexity and file size of the model without providing much useful manufacturing information. Many 3D modeling packages allow you to model thread accurately, but it is better to include this type of information as a note, or if you require this level of detail in the model, wait to add it after you have worked out the major details of the design.

Sometimes, the major and minor diameters of the thread are represented so they can be used in checking clearances and interferences. If not, the nominal size (the general size used to identify the fastener) of the threaded hole or shaft is modeled. A detailed list of fasteners and their proportions is included in Appendices 17–19.

SWEEP A THREAD FORM

Some modeling software allows you to define the helical path curve using an equation. Other software provides a helical sweep command that allows you to enter the number of revolutions and diameter parameters, which can be changed later.

To model thread:

a. Draw the cross-sectional shape of the thread.
b. Draw the helical path.
c. Sweep the cross section along the helical path to form the shape of the thread.

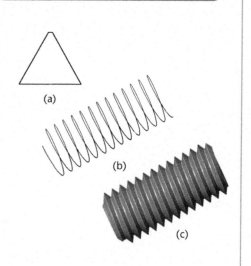

13.7 AMERICAN NATIONAL STANDARD PIPE THREADS

The American National Standard for pipe threads, originally known as the Briggs standard, was formulated by Robert Briggs in 1882. Two general types of pipe threads have been approved as American National Standard: tapered and straight.

The profile of the tapered pipe thread is illustrated in Figure 13.27. The taper of the standard tapered pipe thread is 1 in 16, or .75″ per foot measured on the diameter and along the axis. The angle between the sides of the thread is 60°. The depth of the sharp V is .8660p, and the basic maximum depth of the thread is .800p, where p = pitch. The basic pitch

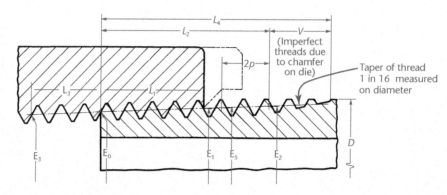

13.27   American National Standard Taper Pipe Thread *(Reprinted from ASME B1.20.1-1983 (R1992), by permission of The American Society of Mechanical Engineers. All rights reserved.)*

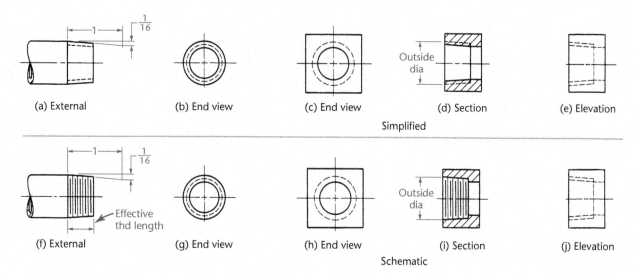

(a) External   (b) End view   (c) End view   (d) Section   (e) Elevation

Simplified

(f) External   (g) End view   (h) End view   (i) Section   (j) Elevation

Schematic

13.28 Conventional Pipe Thread Representation

diameters, E_0 and E_1, and the basic length of the effective external taper thread, L_2, are determined by the formulas

$$E_0 = D - (.050D + 1.1) \, 1/n$$
$$E_1 = E_0 + .0625L_1$$
$$L_2 = (.80D + 6.8) \, 1/n$$

where D = outer diameter of pipe, E_0 = pitch diameter of thread at end of pipe, E_1 = pitch diameter of thread at large end of internal thread, L_1 = normal engagement by hand, and n = number of threads per inch.

ANSI also recommends two modified tapered pipe threads for (1) dry-seal pressure-tight joints (.880 per foot taper) and (2) rail fitting joints. The former is used for metal-to-metal joints, eliminating the need for a sealer, and is used in refrigeration, marine, automotive, aircraft, and ordnance work. The latter is used to provide a rigid mechanical thread joint as is required in rail fitting joints.

Although tapered pipe threads are recommended for general use, there are certain types of joints in which straight pipe threads are used to advantage. The number of threads per inch, the angle, and the depth of thread are the same as on the tapered pipe thread, but the threads are cut parallel to the axis. Straight pipe threads are used for pressure-tight joints for pipe couplings, fuel and oil line fittings, drain plugs, free-fitting mechanical

joints for fixtures, loose-fitting mechanical joints for locknuts, and loose-fitting mechanical joints for hose couplings.

Pipe threads are represented by detailed or symbolic methods in a manner similar to that used to represent unified and American national threads. The symbolic representation (schematic or simplified) is recommended for general use regardless of the diameter, as shown in Figure 13.28. The detailed method is recommended only when the threads are large and when it is desired to show the profile of the thread, as for example, in a sectional view of an assembly.

As shown in Figure 13.28, it is not necessary to draw the taper on the threads unless there is some reason to emphasize it, because the thread note indicates whether the thread is straight or tapered. If it is desired to show the taper, it is sometimes shown exaggerated to make it more visible, as shown in Figure 13.28, where the taper is drawn 1/16″ per 1″ on *radius* (or 0.75″ per 1′ on diameter) instead of the actual taper of 1/16″ on *diameter*. American National Standard tapered pipe threads are indicated by a note giving the nominal diameter followed by the letters NPT (national pipe taper), as shown in Figure 13.29. When straight pipe threads are specified, the letters NPS (national pipe straight) are used. In practice, the tap drill size is normally not given in the thread note.

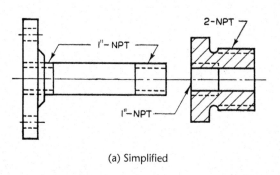

(a) Simplified

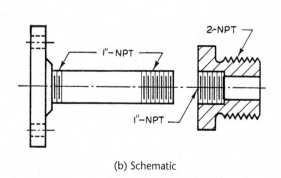

(b) Schematic

13.29 Conventional Representation of American National Standard Tapered Pipe Threads

13.8 USE OF PHANTOM LINES

Use phantom lines to save time when representing identical features, as shown in Figure 13.30. Threaded shafts and springs may be shortened without using conventional breaks but must be correctly dimensioned.

13.30   Use of Phantom Lines

13.9 TAPPED HOLES

The bottom of a drilled hole, formed by the point of a twist drill, is cone-shaped, as shown in Figures 13.31a and b. When an ordinary drill is used to make holes that will be tapped, it is referred to as a *tap drill*. When drawing the drill point, use an angle of 30° to approximate the actual 31° slope of the drill bit.

The thread length is the length of full or perfect threads. The tap drill depth does not include the cone point of the drill. In Figures 13.31c and d, the drill depth shown beyond the threads (labeled *A*) includes several imperfect threads produced by the chamfered end of the tap. This distance varies according to drill size and whether a plug tap or a bottoming tap is used to finish the hole.

A drawing of a tapped hole finished with a bottoming tap is shown in Figure 13.31e. Blind bottom-tapped holes are hard to form and should be avoided whenever possible. Instead, a relief with its diameter slightly greater than the major diameter of the thread is used, as shown in Figure 13.31f. Tap drill sizes for unified, American national, and metric threads can be found in tables. Tap drill sizes and lengths may be given in the thread note but are generally left to the manufacturer to determine. Because the tapped thread length contains only full threads, it is necessary to make this length only one or two pitches beyond the end of the engaging screw. In simplified or schematic representation, do not show threads in the bottoms of tapped holes. This way the ends of the screw show clearly.

The thread length in a tapped hole depends on the major diameter and the material being tapped. The minimum engagement length, when both parts are steel, is equal to the diameter (*D*) of the thread. Table 13.2 shows different engagement lengths for different materials.

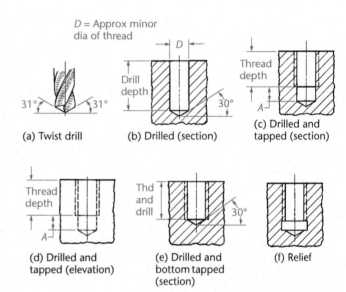

13.31   Drilled and Tapped Holes

Table 13.2 Thread Engagement Lengths for Different Materials

Screw Material	Part Material	Thread Engagement*
Steel	Steel	*D*
Steel	Cast iron	1.5*D*
Steel	Aluminum	2*D*

Requirements for thread engagement vary based on the specific materials. Use these rules of thumb only as guidelines.

TIP

Prevent tap breakage: A chief cause of tap breakage is insufficient tap drill depth. When the depth is too short, the tap is forced against a bed of chips in the bottom of the hole. Don't specify a blind hole when a through hole of not much greater length can be used. When a blind hole is necessary, the tap drill depth should be generous.

Clearance holes: When a bolt or a screw passes through a clearance hole, the hole is often drilled 0.8 mm larger than the screw for screws of 3/8" (10 mm) diameter and 1.5 mm larger for larger diameters. For more precise work, the clearance hole may be only 1/64" (0.4 mm) larger than the screw for diameters up to 10 mm and 0.8 mm larger for larger diameters.

Closer fits may be specified for special conditions. The clearance spaces on each side of a screw or bolt need not be shown on a drawing unless it is necessary to show clearly that there is no thread engagement. When it is necessary to show that there is no thread engagement, the clearance spaces should be drawn about 3/64" (1.2 mm) wide.

13.10 BOLTS, STUDS, AND SCREWS

The term *bolt* is generally used to denote a "through bolt" that has a head on one end, is passed through **clearance holes** in two or more aligned parts, and is threaded on the other end to receive a nut to tighten and hold the parts together, as shown in Figure 13.33a. A hexagon head *cap screw*, shown in Figure 13.33b, is similar to a bolt except it often has greater threaded length. It is often used when one of the parts being held together is threaded to act as a nut. The cap screw is screwed on with a wrench. Cap screws are not screwed into thin materials if strength is desired.

A *stud*, shown in Figure 13.33c, is a steel rod threaded on one or both ends. If threaded on both ends, it is screwed into place with a pipe wrench or with a stud driver. If threaded on one end, it is force-fitted into place. As a rule, a stud is passed through a clearance hole in one member, is screwed into another member, and uses a nut on the free end, as shown in Figure 13.33c.

A machine screw is similar to a slotted head cap screw but usually smaller. It may be used with or without a nut. Figure 13.34 shows different screw head types.

A set screw is a screw, with or without a head, that is screwed through one member and whose special point is forced against another member to prevent motion between the two parts.

(Courtesy of STILLFX/Shutterstock.)

Do not section bolts, nuts, screws, and similar parts when drawn in assembly because they do not have interior detail that needs to be shown.

13.32 Standard Bolt and Nut

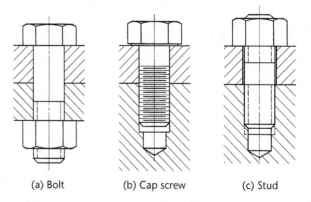

(a) Bolt   (b) Cap screw   (c) Stud

13.33 Bolt, Cap Screw, and Stud

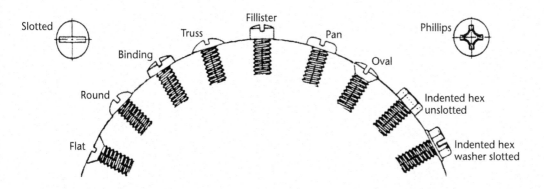

13.34 Types of Screw Heads

13.11 STANDARD BOLTS AND NUTS

American National Standard hexagon bolts and nuts are made in both metric and inch sizes. Square bolts and nuts, shown in Figure 13.35c, are produced only in inch sizes. Square heads and nuts are chamfered at 30°, and hexagon heads and nuts are chamfered at 15°–30°. Both are drawn at 30° for simplicity. Metric bolts, cap screws, and nuts also come in hexagon form.

Bolt Types Bolts are grouped into *bolt types* according to use: regular bolts for general use and heavy bolts for heavier use or easier wrenching. Square bolts come only in the regular type; hexagon bolts, screws, nuts, and square nuts are available in both regular and heavy.

Metric hexagon bolts are grouped according to use: regular and heavy bolts and nuts for general service and high-strength bolts and nuts for structural bolting.

Finish Square bolts and nuts, hexagon bolts, and hexagon flat nuts are unfinished. Unfinished bolts and nuts are not machined on any surface except for the threads. Hexagon cap screws, heavy hexagon screws, and all hexagon nuts, except hexagon flat nuts, are considered finished to some degree and have a "washer face" machined or otherwise formed on the bearing surface. The washer face is 1/64″ thick (drawn 1/32″ so that it will be visible on the plotted drawing), and its diameter is 1.5 times the body diameter for the inch series.

For nuts, the bearing surface may also be a circular surface produced by chamfering. Hexagon screws and hexagon nuts have closer tolerances and a more finished appearance but are not completely machined. There is no difference in the drawing for the degree of finish on finished screws and nuts.

Proportions Proportions for both inch and metric are based on the diameter (D) of the bolt body. These are shown in Figure 13.35.

For regular hexagon and square bolts and nuts, proportions are

$$W = 1\tfrac{1}{2}D \qquad H = \tfrac{2}{3}D \qquad T = \tfrac{7}{8}D$$

where W = width across flats, H = head height, and T = nut height.

For heavy hexagon bolts and nuts and square nuts, the proportions are

$$W = 1\tfrac{1}{2}D + \tfrac{1}{8}''\ (\text{or} + 3\text{ mm})$$
$$H = \tfrac{2}{3}D \qquad T = D$$

The washer face is always included in the head or nut height for finished hexagon screw heads and nuts.

Threads Square and hex bolts, hex cap screws, and finished nuts in the inch series are usually Class 2 and may have coarse, fine, or 8-pitch threads. Unfinished nuts have coarse threads and are Class 2B. For diameter and pitch specifications for metric threads, see Appendix 17.

Thread lengths For bolts or screws up to 6″ (150 mm) long,

$$\text{Thread length} = 2D + \tfrac{1}{4}''\ (\text{or} + 6\text{ mm})$$

For bolts or screws over 6″ in length,

$$\text{Thread length} = 2D + \tfrac{1}{2}''\ (\text{or} + 12\text{ mm})$$

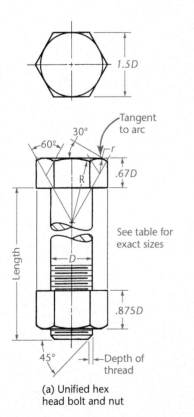

(a) Unified hex head bolt and nut

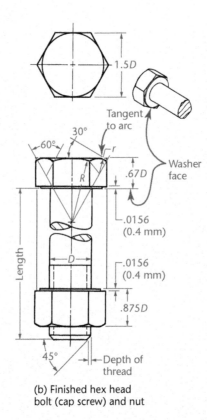

(b) Finished hex head bolt (cap screw) and nut

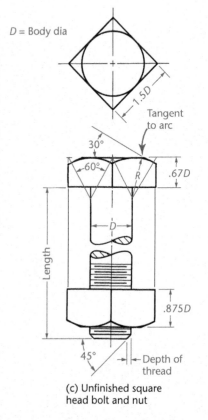

(c) Unfinished square head bolt and nut

13.35 Bolt Proportions (Regular)

Fasteners too short for these formulas are threaded as close to the head as practical. For drawing purposes, use approximately three pitches. The threaded end may be rounded or chamfered, but it is usually drawn with a 45° chamfer from the thread depth, as shown in Figure 13.35.

Bolt Lengths Bolt lengths have not been standardized because of the endless variety required by industry. Short bolts are typically available in standard length increments of 1/4″ (6 mm), and long bolts come in increments of 1/2″ to 1″ (12 to 25 mm). For dimensions of standard bolts and nuts, see Appendix 17.

13.12 DRAWING STANDARD BOLTS

Detail drawings show all the necessary information defining the shape, size, material, and finish of a part. Standard bolts and nuts do not usually require detail drawings unless they are to be altered (for example, by having a slot added through the end of a bolt), because they are usually stock parts that can easily be purchased, but you often need to show them on assembly drawings, which you will learn more about in Chapter 14.

Templates are available to help you add bolts quickly to sketches, or you can use the dimensions from tables if accuracy is important, as in figuring clearances. In most cases, a quick representation, where proportions are based on the body diameter, is sufficient. Three typical bolts illustrating the use of these proportions are shown in Figure 13.35.

Many CAD systems have fastener libraries that you can use to add a wide variety of nuts and bolts to your drawings. Often, these symbols are based on a diameter of 1 unit so that you can quickly figure a scale at which to insert them. Other systems prompt for the diameter and lengths and create a symbol to your specifications. In 3D models, when nuts and bolts are represented, the thread is rarely shown because it adds to the complexity and size of the drawing and is difficult to model. The thread specification is annotated in the drawing.

Generally, bolt heads and nuts should be drawn "across corners" in all views, regardless of projection. This conventional violation of projection is used to prevent confusion

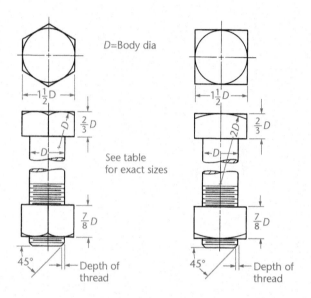

13.36   Bolts "Across Flats"

between the square and hexagon heads and nuts and to show actual clearances. Only when there is a special reason should bolt heads and nuts be drawn across flats, as shown in Figure 13.36.

13.13 SPECIFICATIONS FOR BOLTS AND NUTS

In specifying bolts in parts lists, in correspondence, or elsewhere, the following information must be covered in order:

1. Nominal size of bolt body
2. Thread specification or thread note
3. Length of bolt
4. Finish of bolt
5. Style of head
6. Name

Example (complete decimal inch)

.75–10 UNC–2A × 2.5 STAINLESS STEEL HEXAGON
CAP SCREW

Example (abbreviated decimal inch)

.75–10 UNC × 2.5 SS HEXCAP SCR

Example (metric)

M14–2 × 20 SS HEXCAP SCR

For either bolts or nuts, REGULAR or GENERAL PURPOSE are assumed if omitted from the specification. If the heavy series is intended, the word HEAVY should appear as the first word in the name of the fastener. Likewise, HIGH STRENGTH STRUCTURAL should be indicated for such metric fasteners and the particular grade may be specified. However, the number of the specific ISO standard is often included in the metric specifications—for example, M20–2.5 DIN 934 HEX NUT. Finish need not be mentioned if the fastener or nut is correctly named.

Nuts may be specified as follows:

Example (complete)

$\frac{5}{8}$–11 UNC–2B SQUARE NUT

Example (abbreviated)

$\frac{5}{8}$–11 UNC SQ NUT

Example (metric)

M20–2.5 HEX NUT

STEP by STEP

SKETCHING HEX BOLTS, CAP SCREWS, AND NUTS

1 Determine the diameter of the bolt, the length (from the underside of the bearing surface to the tip), the style of head (square or hexagon), the type (regular or heavy), and the finish before starting to draw.

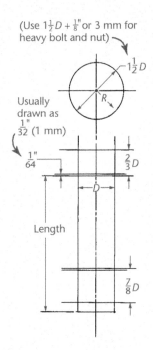

(Use $1\frac{1}{2}D + \frac{1}{8}$" or 3 mm for heavy bolt and nut)

Usually drawn as $\frac{1}{32}$" (1 mm)

$1\frac{1}{2}D$

R

$\frac{1}{64}$"

$\frac{2}{3}D$

D

Length

$\frac{7}{8}D$

2 Lightly sketch the top view as shown, where *D* is the diameter of the bolt. Project the corners of the hexagon or square to the front view. Sketch the head and nut heights. Add the washer face if needed. Its diameter is equal to the distance across flats of the bolt head or nut. Only the metric and finished hexagon screws or nuts have a washer face. The washer face is 1/64" (0.4 mm) thick but is shown at about 1/32" (1 mm) for clarity. The head or nut height includes the washer face.

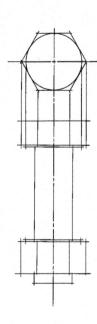

3 Represent the curves produced by the chamfer on the bolt heads and nuts as circular arcs, although they are actually hyperbolas. On drawings of small bolts or nuts under approximately 1/2" (12 mm) in diameter, where the chamfer is hardly noticeable, omit the chamfer in the rectangular view.

4 Chamfer the threaded end of the screw at 45° from the thread depth.

5 Show threads in simplified or schematic form for diameters of 1" (25 mm) or less on the drawing. Detailed representation is rarely used because it clutters the drawing and takes too much time.

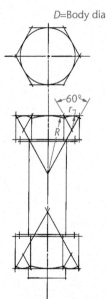

D=Body dia
60°
r
R

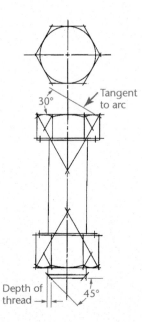

30°
Tangent to arc

Depth of thread
45°

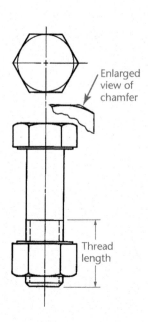

Enlarged view of chamfer

Thread length

HEX HEAD BOLT GRADES

Hex head bolts come in a variety of SAE grades. A system of marks on the head of the bolt indicates the grade, which is an indication of its minimum tensile strength.

The commonly used grades are 1 or 2 which are unmarked and are low to medium carbon steel. Grade 5 bolts provide higher minimum tensile strength. They are marked with 3 lines on the bolt head. Grade 8 bolts provide even higher minimum tensile strength and are marked with 6 lines.

Metric grades are marked with numerals in the format X.Y indicating the various grades, for example, 4.6 is a low carbon steel metric grade.

Bolt selection and the torques required to tighten them are based on your particular application.

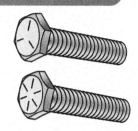

SAE grade 8 has 6 lines marked on the bolt head; SAE grade 5 has 3 lines marked on the bolt head.

13.14 LOCKNUTS AND LOCKING DEVICES

Many types of special nuts and devices to prevent nuts from unscrewing are available, and some of the most common are shown in Figure 13.37. The American National Standard jam nuts, as shown in Figures 13.37a and 13.37b, are the same as the hexagon or hexagon flat nuts, except that they are thinner. The application shown in Figure 13.37b, where the larger nut is on top and is screwed on more tightly, is recommended. They are the same distance across flats as the corresponding hexagon nuts (1-1/2D or 1″). They are slightly more than 1/2D in thickness but are drawn 1/2D for simplicity. They are available with or without the washer face in the regular and heavy types. The tops of all are flat and chamfered at 30°, and the finished forms have either a washer face or a chamfered bearing surface.

The lock washer, shown in Figure 13.37c, and the cotter pin, shown in Figure 13.37e, are very common (see Appendices 26 and 29). The set screw, shown in Figure 13.37f, is often made to press against a plug of softer material, such as brass, which in turn presses against the threads without deforming them. With cotter pins (see Appendix 29), it is recommended to use a hex slotted nut (Figure 13.37g), a hex castle nut (Figure 13.37h), or a hex thick slotted nut or a heavy hex thick slotted nut.

Similar metric locknuts and locking devices are available. See fastener catalogs for details.

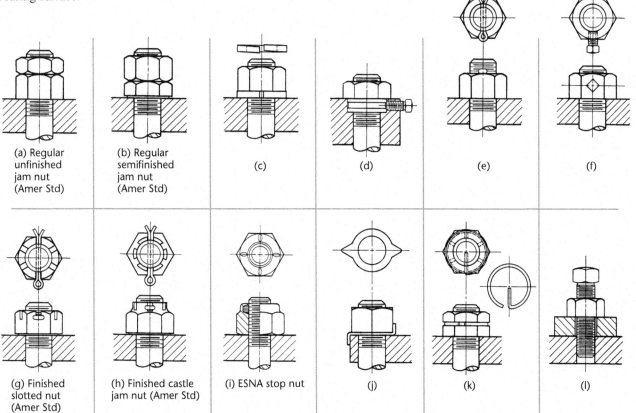

(a) Regular unfinished jam nut (Amer Std)　(b) Regular semifinished jam nut (Amer Std)　(c)　(d)　(e)　(f)

(g) Finished slotted nut (Amer Std)　(h) Finished castle jam nut (Amer Std)　(i) ESNA stop nut　(j)　(k)　(l)

13.37 Locknuts and Locking Devices

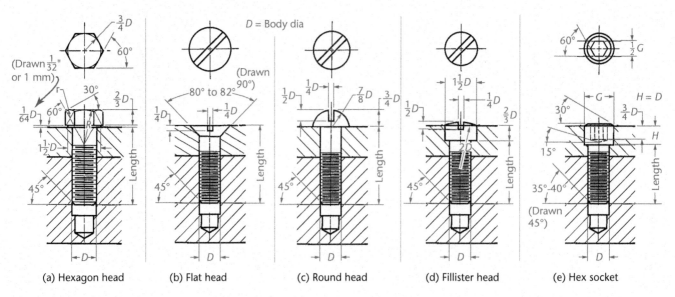

(a) Hexagon head   (b) Flat head   (c) Round head   (d) Fillister head   (e) Hex socket

13.38 Standard Cap Screws—See Appendices 17 and 18

Hexagon Head Screws Coarse, fine, or 8-thread series, 2A. Thread length $= 2D + \frac{1}{4}''$ up to 6″ long and $2D + \frac{1}{2}''$ if over 6″ long. For screws too short for formula, threads extend to within $2\frac{1}{2}$ threads of the head for diameters up to 1″. Screw lengths not standardized. For suggested lengths for metric hexagon head screws, see Appendix 17.

Slotted Head Screws Coarse, fine, or 8-thread series, 2A. Thread length $= 2D + \frac{1}{4}''$. Screw lengths not standardized. For screws too short for formula, threads extend to within $2\frac{1}{2}$ threads of the head.

Hexagon Socket Screws Coarse or fine threads, 3A. Coarse thread length $= 2D + \frac{1}{2}''$ where this would be over $\frac{1}{2}L$; otherwise thread length $= \frac{1}{2}L$. Fine thread length $= 1\frac{1}{2}D + \frac{1}{2}''$ where this would be over $\frac{3}{8}L$; otherwise thread length $= \frac{3}{8}L$. Increments in screw lengths $= \frac{1}{8}''$ for screws $\frac{1}{4}''$ to 1″ long, $\frac{1}{4}''$ for screws 1″ to 3″ long, and $\frac{1}{2}''$ for screws $3\frac{1}{2}''$ to 6″ long.

13.15 STANDARD CAP SCREWS

Five types of American National Standard cap screws are shown in Figure 13.38. The first four of these have standard heads, whereas the socket head cap screws, as shown in Figure 13.38e, have several different shapes of round heads and sockets. Cap screws are normally finished and are used on machine tools and other machines when accuracy and appearance are important. The ranges of sizes and exact dimensions are given in Appendices 17 and 18. The hexagon head cap screw and hex socket head cap screw are also available in metric.

Cap screws ordinarily pass through a clearance hole in one member and screw into another.

Cap screws are inferior to studs when frequent removal is necessary. They are used on machines requiring few adjustments. The slotted or socket-type heads are used for crowded conditions.

Actual dimensions may be used in drawing cap screws when exact sizes are necessary. Figure 13.38 shows the pro-

portions in terms of body diameter (*D*) that are usually used. Hexagonal head cap screws are drawn similar to hex head bolts. The points are chamfered at 45° from the schematic thread depth.

Note that screwdriver slots are drawn at 45° in the circular views of the heads, without regard to true projection, and that threads in the bottom of the tapped holes are omitted so that the ends of the screws may be clearly seen. A typical cap screw note is

Example (complete)

.375–16 UNC-2A × 2.5 HEXAGON HEAD CAP SCREW

Example (abbreviated)

.375 × 2.5 HEX HD CAP SCR

Example (metric)

M20 × 2.5 × 80 HEX HD CAP SCR

13.16 STANDARD MACHINE SCREWS

Machine screws are similar to cap screws but are usually smaller (.060″ to .750″ diameter) and the threads generally go all the way to the head. There are eight ANSI-approved forms of heads, which are shown in Appendix 19. The hexagonal head may be slotted if desired. All others are available in either slotted- or recessed-head forms. Standard machine screws are produced with a naturally bright finish, not heat treated, and have plain-sheared ends, not chamfered. For similar metric machine screw forms and specifications, see Appendix 19.

Machine screws are used for screwing into thin materials, and the smaller-numbered screws are threaded nearly to the head. They are used extensively in firearms, jigs, fixtures, and dies. Machine screw nuts are used mainly on the round head, pan head, and flat head types and are usually hexagonal.

Exact dimensions of machine screws are given in Appendix 19 tables, but they are seldom needed for drawing purposes. The four most common types of machine screws are shown in Figure 13.39, with proportions based on the diameter (D). Clearance holes and counterbores should be made slightly larger than the screws.

Typical machine screw notes are:

Example (complete)

$$\text{NO. 10 (.1900)–32 NF-3} \times \tfrac{5}{8} \text{ FILLISTER}$$
$$\text{HEAD MACHINE SCREW}$$

Example (abbreviated)

$$\text{NO. 10 (.1900)} \times \tfrac{5}{8} \text{ FILH MSCR}$$

Example (metric)

$$\text{M8} \times 1.25 \times 30 \text{ SLOTTED}$$
$$\text{PAN HEAD MACHINE SCREW}$$

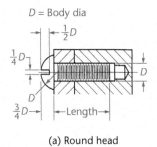

(a) Round head

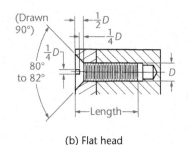

(b) Flat head

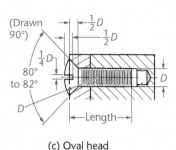

(c) Oval head

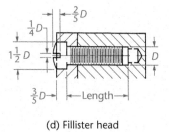

(d) Fillister head

13.39 Standard Machine Screws—See Appendix 19

13.17 STANDARD SET SCREWS

Set screws, shown in Figure 13.40, are used to prevent motion, usually rotary, between two parts, such as the movement of the hub of a pulley on a shaft. A set screw is screwed into one part so that its point bears firmly against another part. If the point of the set screw is cupped, or if a flat is milled on the shaft, the screw will hold much more firmly. Obviously, set screws are not efficient when the load is heavy or when it is suddenly applied. Usually they are manufactured of steel and case hardened (Figure 13.41).

Headless set screws have come into greater use because a projecting head on a set screw has caused many industrial casualties; this has resulted in legislation prohibiting their use in many states.

Metric hexagon socket headless set screws with the full range of points are available. Nominal diameters of metric hex socket set screws are 1.6, 2, 2.5, 3, 4, 5, 6, 8, 10, 12, 16, 20, and 24 mm.

Square-head set screws have coarse, fine, or 8-pitch threads and are Class 2A but are usually furnished with coarse threads, because the square-head set screw is generally used on the rougher grades of work. Slotted headless and socket set screws have coarse or fine threads and are Class 3A.

Nominal diameters of set screws range from number 0 up through 2″. Set screw lengths are standardized in increments of 1/32″ to 1″ depending on the overall length of the set screw.

Metric set screw length increments range from 0.5 to 4 mm, again depending on overall screw length.

Set screws are specified as follows:

Example (complete)

.375–16UNC-2A × .75 SQUARE HEAD FLAT POINT SET SCREW

Example (abbreviated)

.375 × 1.25 SQH FP SSCR

.4375 × .750 HEXSOC CUP PT SSCR

$\frac{1}{4}$–20 UNC 2A × $\frac{1}{2}$ SLTD HDLS CONE PT SSCR

Example (metric)

M10–1.5 × 12 HEX SOCKET HEAD SET SCREW

13.40   Set Screws

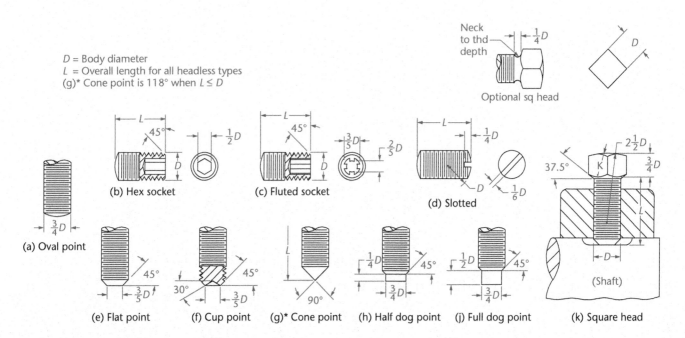

D = Body diameter
L = Overall length for all headless types
(g)* Cone point is 118° when $L \le D$

(a) Oval point

(b) Hex socket

(c) Fluted socket

(d) Slotted

(e) Flat point

(f) Cup point

(g)* Cone point

(h) Half dog point

(j) Full dog point

(k) Square head

13.41   Set Screw Proportions *(Courtesy of David M. Demchenkov)*

13.18 AMERICAN NATIONAL STANDARD WOOD SCREWS

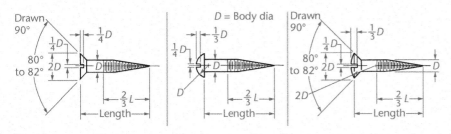

13.42 American National Standard Wood Screws

Wood screws with three types of heads—flat, round, and oval—have been standardized. The approximate dimensions sufficient for drawing purposes are shown in Figure 13.42.

The Phillips style recessed head is also available on several types of fasteners, as well as on wood screws. Three styles of cross recesses have been standardized by ANSI. A special screwdriver is used, as shown in Figure 13.43q, and this results in rapid assembly without damage to the head.

Wood Screws *(anborvl/123RF.)*

13.19 MISCELLANEOUS FASTENERS

Many other types of fasteners have been devised for specialized uses. Some of the more common types are shown in Figure 13.43. A number of these are American National Standard round head bolts, including carriage, button head, step, and countersunk bolts.

Helical-coil-threaded inserts, shown in Figure 13.43p, are shaped like a spring except that the cross section of the wire conforms to threads on the screw and in the hole. These are made of phosphor bronze or stainless steel, and they provide a hard, smooth protective lining for tapped threads in soft metals and plastics.

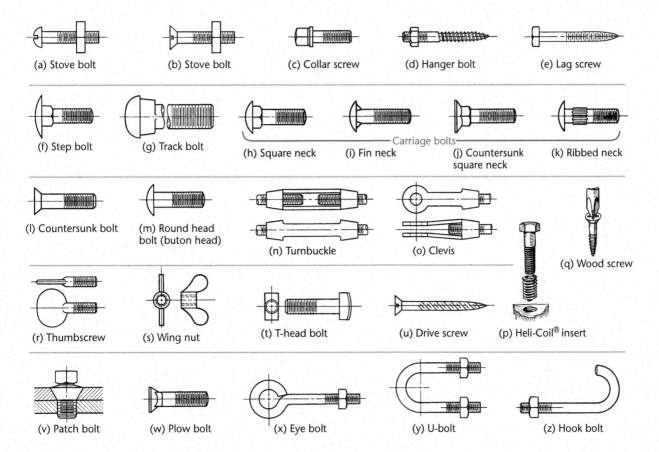

13.43 Miscellaneous Bolts and Screws

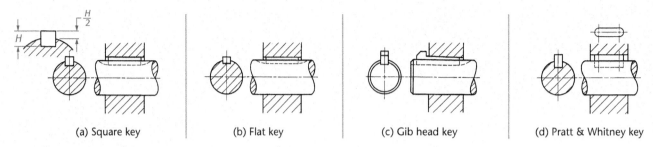

(a) Square key   (b) Flat key   (c) Gib head key   (d) Pratt & Whitney key

13.44   Square and Flat Keys

13.20 KEYS

Keys are used to prevent movement between shafts and wheels, couplings, cranks, and similar machine parts attached to or supported by shafts, as shown in Figure 13.44. A *keyseat* is in a shaft; a *keyway* is in the hub or surrounding part.

For heavy-duty functions, rectangular keys (flat or square) are used, and sometimes two rectangular keys are necessary for one connection. For even stronger connections, interlocking splines may be machined on the shaft and in the hole.

A *square key* is shown in Figure 13.44a.

A *flat key* is shown in Figure 13.44b. The widths of keys are generally about one fourth the shaft diameter. In either case, half the key is sunk into the shaft. The depth of the keyway or the keyseat is measured on the side—not the center—as shown in Figure 13.44a. Square and flat keys may have the top surface tapered 1/8″ per foot, in which case they become square taper or flat taper keys.

A *feather key* is rectangular to prevent rotary motion, but permits relative longitudinal motion. Usually, feather keys have gib heads, or are fastened so they cannot slip out of the keyway.

A *gib head key* (Figure 13.44c) is the same as a square taper or flat taper key except that a gib head allows its easy removal. Square and flat keys are made from cold-finished stock and are not machined. For dimensions, see Appendix 20.

A *Pratt & Whitney key* (P&W key) is shown in Figure 13.44d. It is rectangular, with semicylindrical ends. Two-thirds of its height is sunk into the shaft keyseat (see Appendix 24).

Woodruff keys are semicircular, as shown in Figure 13.45. This key fits into a semicircular key slot cut with a Woodruff cutter, as shown, and the top of the key fits into a plain rectangular keyway. Sizes of keys for given shaft diameters are not standardized. For average conditions, select a key whose diameter is approximately equal to the shaft diameter. For dimensions, see Appendix 23. See manufacturers' catalogs for specifications for metric counterparts.

Typical specifications for keys are

.25 × 1.50 SQ KEY

No. 204 WOODRUFF KEY

$\frac{1}{4} \times \frac{1}{6} \times 1\frac{1}{2}$ FLAT KEY

No. 10 P&W KEY

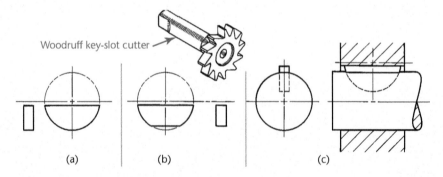

Woodruff key-slot cutter

(a)   (b)   (c)

13.45   Woodruff Keys and Key-Slot Cutter

13.21 MACHINE PINS

Machine pins include taper pins, straight pins, dowel pins, clevis pins, and cotter pins. For light work, taper pins can be used to fasten hubs or collars to shafts. Figure 13.46 shows the use of a taper pin where the hole through the collar and shaft is drilled and reamed when the parts are assembled. For slightly heavier duty, a taper pin may be used parallel to the shaft, as for square keys (see Appendix 28).

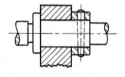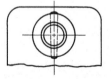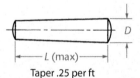

L (max)

Taper .25 per ft

13.46   Taper Pin

Dowel pins are cylindrical or conical and usually used to keep two parts in a fixed position or to preserve alignment. They are usually used where accurate alignment is essential. Dowel pins are generally made of steel and are hardened and ground in a centerless grinder.

Clevis pins are used in a clevis and held in place by cotter pins. For the latter, see Appendix 29.

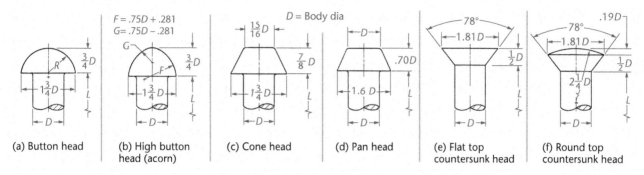

(a) Button head | (b) High button head (acorn) | (c) Cone head | (d) Pan head | (e) Flat top countersunk head | (f) Round top countersunk head

13.47 Standard Large Rivets

13.22 RIVETS

Rivets are regarded as permanent fastenings, unlike removable fastenings, such as bolts and screws. Rivets are generally used to hold sheet metal or rolled steel together and are made of wrought iron, carbon steel, copper, or occasionally other metals.

To fasten two pieces of metal together, holes are punched, drilled, or punched and then reamed, all slightly larger in diameter than the shank of the rivet. Rivet diameters are made from $d = 1.2\sqrt{t}$ to $d = 1.4\sqrt{t}$, where d is the rivet diameter and t is the metal thickness. The larger rivet diameter size is used for steel and single-riveted joints, and the smaller may be used for multiple-riveted joints. In structural work it is common to make the hole 1.6 mm (1/16″) larger than the rivet.

When the red-hot rivet is inserted, a "dolly bar" with a depression the shape of the driven head is held against the head. A riveting machine is used to drive the rivet and forms the head on the plain end. This causes the rivet to swell and fill the hole tightly.

Large rivets or heavy hex structural bolts are often used in structural work for bridges and buildings and in ship and boiler construction. They are shown in Figure 13.47 in their exact formula proportions. Button heads (Figure 13.47a) and countersunk heads (Figure 13.47e) are the rivets most commonly used in structural work. The button head and cone head are commonly used in tank and boiler construction.

Riveted Joints

Typical riveted joints are shown in Figure 13.48. Note that the rectangular view of each rivet shows the shank of the rivet with both heads made with circular arcs, and the circular view of each rivet is represented by only the outside circle of the head.

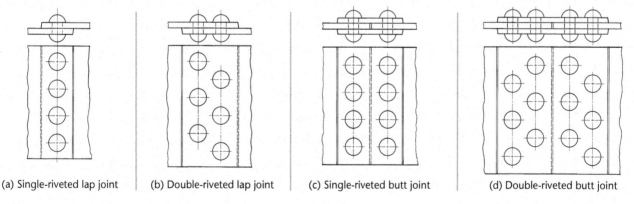

(a) Single-riveted lap joint | (b) Double-riveted lap joint | (c) Single-riveted butt joint | (d) Double-riveted butt joint

13.48 Common Riveted Joints

Rivet Symbols

Because many engineering structures are too large to be built in the shop, they are built in the largest units possible and then are transported to the desired location. Trusses are common examples.

The rivets driven in the shop are called *shop rivets,* and those driven on the job are called *field rivets.* However, heavy steel bolts are commonly used on the job for structural work. Solid black circles are used to represent field rivets, and other standard symbols are used to show other features, as shown in Figure 13.49.

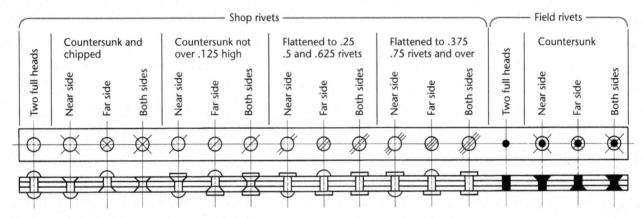

13.49   Conventional Rivet Symbols

Small Rivets

Small rivets are used for light work. American National Standard small solid rivets are illustrated with dimensions that show their standard proportions in Figure 13.50, from *ANSI/ASME B18.1.1.* Included in the same standard are tinners', coppers', and belt rivets. Metric rivets are also available. Dimensions for large rivets are in *ANSI/ASME B18.1.2.* See manufacturers' catalogs for additional details.

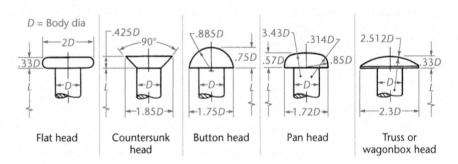

13.50   American National Standard Small Solid Rivet Proportions

Blind Rivets

Blind rivets, commonly known as *pop rivets* (Figure 13.51), are often used for fastening together thin sheet-metal assemblies. Blind rivets are hollow and are installed with manual or power-operated rivet guns that grip a center pin or mandrel, pulling the head into the body and expanding the rivet against the sheet metal. They are available in aluminum, steel, stainless steel, and plastic. As with any fastener, it is important to choose an appropriate material to avoid corrosive action between dissimilar metals.

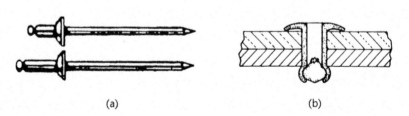

(a)   (b)

13.51   Blind Rivets (a) Before Installation and (b) Installed

13.23 SPRINGS

A spring is a mechanical device designed to store energy when deflected and to return the equivalent amount of energy when released (see *ANSI Y14.13M*). Springs are commonly made of spring steel, which may be music wire, hard-drawn wire, or oil-tempered wire. Other materials used for compression springs include stainless steel, beryllium copper, and phosphor bronze. Urethane plastic is used in applications where conventional springs would be affected by corrosion, vibration, or acoustic or magnetic forces.

Springs are classified as *helical springs* (Figure 13.52), or *flat springs*.

Springs *(Norton, Robert L., Machine Design: An Integrated Approach, 3rd, © 2006. Printed and electronically reproduced by permission of Pearson Education, Upper Saddle River, NJ.)*

Helical Springs

Helical springs are usually cylindrical but may also be conical. There are three types of helical springs:

- *Compression springs* offer resistance to a compressive force.
- *Extension springs* offer resistance to a pulling force.
- *Torsion springs* offer resistance to a torque or twisting force.

On working drawings, true projections of helical springs are not drawn because of the labor involved. Like screw threads, they are drawn in detailed and schematic methods, using straight lines to replace helical curves, as shown in Figure 13.52.

A square wire spring is similar to the square thread with the core of the shaft removed, as in Figure 13.52b. Use standard cross-hatching if the areas in section are large, as in Figures 13.52a and b. Small sectioned areas may be made solid black, as in Figure 13.52c.

In cases where a complete picture of the spring is not necessary, use phantom lines to save time in drawing the coils, as in Figure 13.52d. If the drawing of the spring is too small to be represented by the outlines of the wire, use schematic representation, shown in Figures 13.52e and f.

Compression springs have plain ends, as in Figure 13.53a, or squared (closed) ends, as in Figure 13.53b. The ends may be ground, as shown in Figure 13.53c, or both squared and ground, as in Figure 13.53d. Required dimensions are indicated in the figure. When required, RH or LH is specified for right-hand or left-hand coil direction.

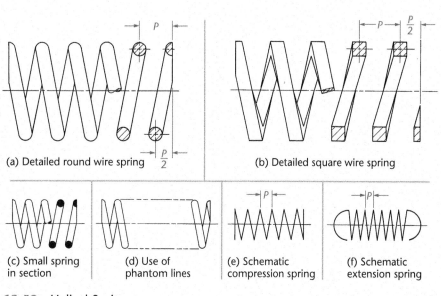

(a) Detailed round wire spring

(b) Detailed square wire spring

(c) Small spring in section

(d) Use of phantom lines

(e) Schematic compression spring

(f) Schematic extension spring

13.52   Helical Springs

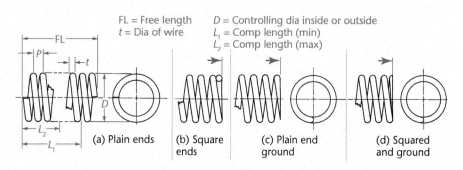

FL = Free length
t = Dia of wire
D = Controlling dia inside or outside
L_1 = Comp length (min)
L_2 = Comp length (max)

(a) Plain ends

(b) Square ends

(c) Plain end ground

(d) Squared and ground

13.53   Compression Springs

Extension springs may have many types of ends, so it is necessary to draw the spring or at least the ends and a few adjacent coils, as shown in Figure 13.54.

A typical torsion spring drawing is shown in Figure 13.55. A typical flat spring drawing is shown in Figure 13.56. Other types of flat springs are power springs (or flat coil springs),

Belleville springs (like spring washers), and leaf springs (commonly used in automobiles).

Many companies use a printed specification form to provide the necessary spring information, including data such as load at a specified deflected length, load rate, finish, and type of service.

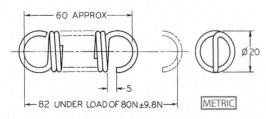

MATERIAL: 2.00 OIL TEMPERED SPRING STEEL WIRE
             14.5 COILS RIGHT HAND
             MACHINE LOOP AND HOOK IN LINE
             SPRING MUST EXTEND TO 110 WITHOUT SET
FINISH: BLACK JAPAN

13.54 Extension Spring Drawing

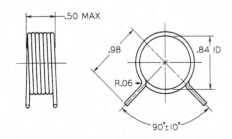

MATERIAL : .059 MUSIC WIRE
            6.75 COILS RIGHT HAND NO INITIAL TENSION
TORQUE : 2.50 INCH LB AT 155° DEFLECTION SPRING MUST
            DEFLECT 180° WITHOUT PERMANENT SET AND
            MUST OPERATE FREELY ON .75 DIAMETER SHAFT
FINISH : CADMIUM OR ZINC PLATE

13.55 Torsion Spring Drawing

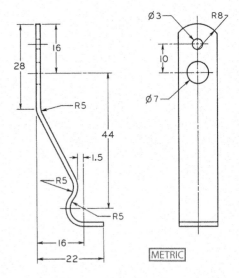

MATERIAL : 1.20 X 14.0 SPRING STEEL
HEAT TREAT : 44-48 C ROCKWELL
           FINISH : BLACK OXIDE AND OIL

13.56 Flat Spring Drawing

13.24 DRAWING HELICAL SPRINGS

The construction for a schematic elevation view of a compression spring with six total coils is shown in Figure 13.57a. Because the ends are closed, or squared, two of the six coils are "dead" coils, leaving only four full pitches to be set off along the top of the spring.

If there are six and a half total coils, as shown in Figure 13.57b, the $P/2$ measurement is set on opposite sides of the spring. The construction of an extension spring with six active coils and loop ends is shown in Figure 13.57c.

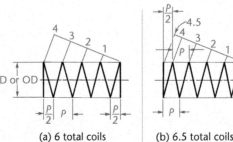

(a) 6 total coils
compression spring

(b) 6.5 total coils
compression spring

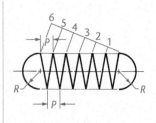

(c) 6.5 total coils
extension spring

13.57 Schematic Spring Representation

Figure 13.58 shows the steps in drawing a detailed section and elevation view of a compression spring. The spring is shown pictorially in Figure 13.58a. Figure 13.58b shows the cutting plane through the centerline of the spring. Figure 13.58c shows the section with the cutting plane removed. Steps to construct the sectional view are shown in Figures 13.58d–f. Figure 13.58g shows the corresponding elevation view.

If there are a fractional number of coils, such as the 5.5 coils in Figure 13.58h, the half-rounds of sectional wire are placed on opposite sides of the spring.

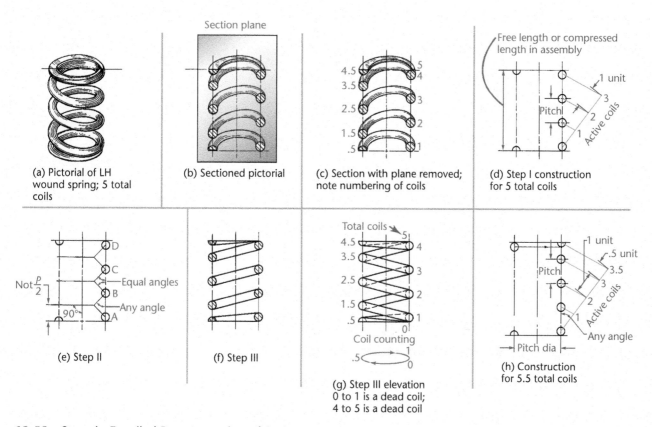

(a) Pictorial of LH wound spring; 5 total coils

(b) Sectioned pictorial

(c) Section with plane removed; note numbering of coils

(d) Step I construction for 5 total coils

(e) Step II

(f) Step III

(g) Step III elevation 0 to 1 is a dead coil; 4 to 5 is a dead coil

(h) Construction for 5.5 total coils

13.58 Steps in Detailed Representation of Spring

13.25 MODELING SPRINGS

Using 3D modeling, it is uncommon to model springs accurately, unless it is important to show them in the assembly. Springs are usually stock parts that are specified and purchased rather than designed individually. If you must show springs, they may sometimes be modeled as a single 3D curve, as shown in Figure 13.59. Because of their shape, springs are complex objects that greatly increase the file size of your models. You should model them accurately only when there is a design or production benefit to be gained from doing so.

13.59 *Springs are sometimes represented as a single 3D curve in a 3D model when the complexity of the shape outweighs the benefits of modeling it.*

DOWNLOADING STANDARD FASTENERS

Many stock fasteners are available to download in standard CAD formats ready to use in CAD drawings and models. For example, the PennEngineering company makes files available for the many PEM brand fasteners used to fasten sheet metal parts, such as the part shown in Figure B, on their site at www.pemnet.com.

The CAD files that you download can be inserted into your drawings to save drawing time. The stock fastener type is specified in a drawing note as shown in Figure B.

Data sheets in PDF format are also available from the PEM site. Figure C shows the cover of a 6-page PDF booklet that lists material, thread size, performance data, and other key data for unified and metric self-clinching flush nuts sold by PEM.

(A) *PEM brand fasteners, available from PennEngineering, are an example of the many stock fasteners that you can download in CAD file formats for easy insertion into drawings. (Courtesy of PennEngineering.)*

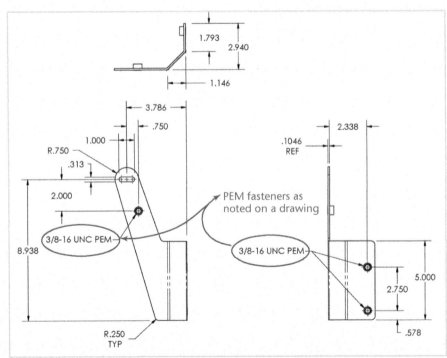

(B) PEM Stock Fasteners Shown on a Drawing *(Courtesy of Dynojet Research, Inc.)*

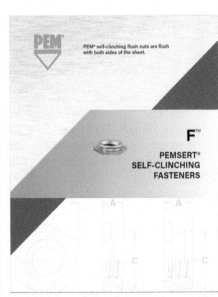

(C) *Data sheets are often available in PDF format. (Courtesy of PennEngineering.)*

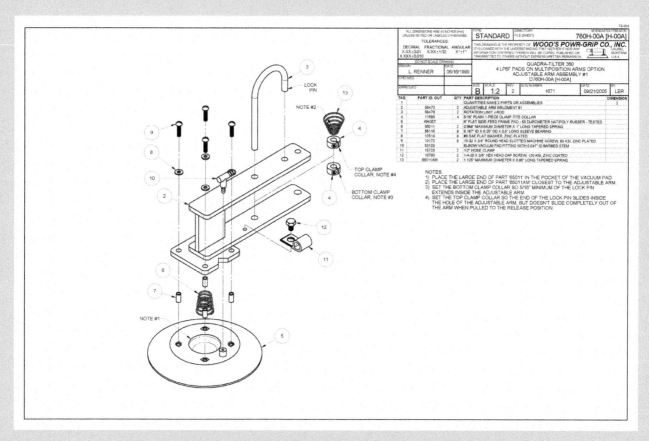

Assembly Drawing Showing Fasteners and Springs *(Courtesy of Wood's Power-Grip Co. Inc.)*

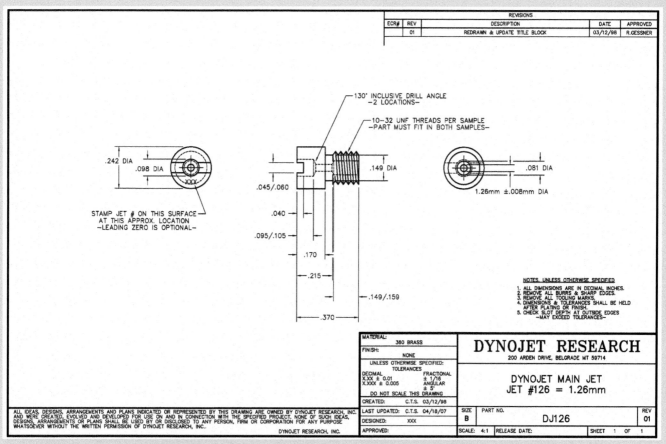

Part Drawing for a Special-Purpose Threaded Part (Scale 4:1) *(Courtesy of Dynojet Research, Inc.)*

PORTFOLIO

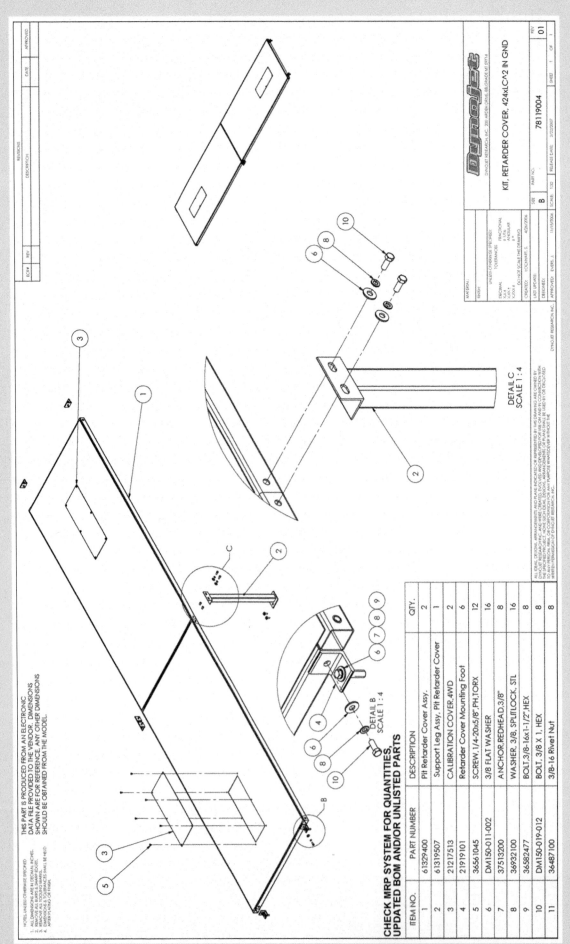

Enlarged details show the fasteners in this assembly drawing. (Courtesy of Dynojet Research, Inc.)

KEY WORDS

Acme Thread
American National Thread
Angle of Thread
Axis of Screw
Bolt Lengths
Bolt Types
Buttress Thread
Clearance Holes
Coarse Thread
Compression Springs
Crest
Depth of Thread
Extension Springs
External Thread
Feather Key
Fine Thread
Finish
Flat Key
Form of Thread
Gib Head Key
Internal Thread
Knuckle Thread
Lead
Major Diameter
Metric Thread
Minor Diameter
Multiple Threads
Pitch
Pitch Diameter
Pratt & Whitney Key
Root
Screw Thread
Series of Thread
Sharp-V thread
Side
Single Thread
Square Key
Square Thread
Standard Worm Thread
Thread Form
Thread Lengths
Thread Pitch Gage
Torsion Springs
Unified Extra Fine Thread Series
Unified Thread
Whitworth Thread
Woodruff Keys

CHAPTER SUMMARY

- There are many types of thread forms; however, metric and unified are the most common.
- The method of showing threads on a drawing is called the thread representation. The three types of thread representation are detailed, schematic, and simplified.
- The major diameter, pitch, and form are the most important parts of a thread specification.
- Thread specifications are dimensioned using a leader, usually pointing to the rectangular view of the threaded shaft or to the circular view of a threaded hole. The thread specification tells the manufacturing technician what kind of thread needs to be created.
- The nut and bolt is still the most common type of fastener. Many new types of fasteners are being created to streamline the production process.
- Keys and pins are special fasteners for attachment; for example, attaching a pulley to a shaft.
- The screw head determines what kind of tool will be necessary to install the fastener.

REVIEW QUESTIONS

1. Draw a typical screw thread using detailed representation, and label the parts of the thread.
2. Why are phantom lines used to represent the middle part of a long spring?
3. Draw several types of screw heads.
4. List five types of screws.
5. Why is the simplified thread representation the most commonly used drawing style?
6. List five fasteners that do not have any threads.
7. Write out a metric thread specification and a unified thread specification and label each part of the specification.
8. Which type of thread form is used on a lightbulb?
9. How are multiple threads designated in a thread note?
10. Using abbreviations, give a specification for a slotted headless flat point set screw.

CHAPTER EXERCISES

Design Project

Design a system that uses thread to transmit power, for use in helping transfer a handicapped person from a bed to a wheelchair. Use either schematic or detailed representation to show the thread in your design sketches.

Thread and Fastener Projects

Use the information in this chapter and in various manufacturers' catalogs to create the working drawings at the end of the next chapter, where many different kinds of threads and fasteners are required. Several other projects are included here (Exercises 13.1 to 13.5).

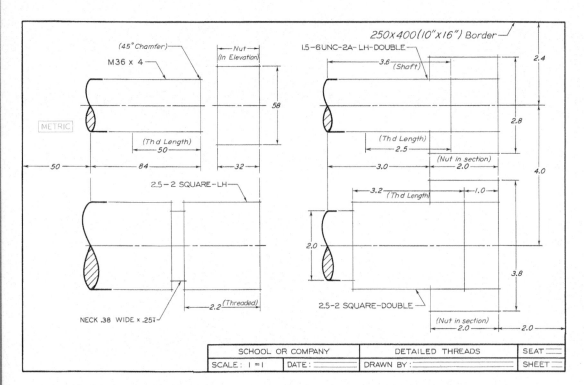

Exercise 13.1 Draw specified detailed threads arranged as shown. Omit all dimensions and notes given in inclined letters. Letter only the thread notes and the title strip. (Some dimensions are given to help you match the sheet layout.)

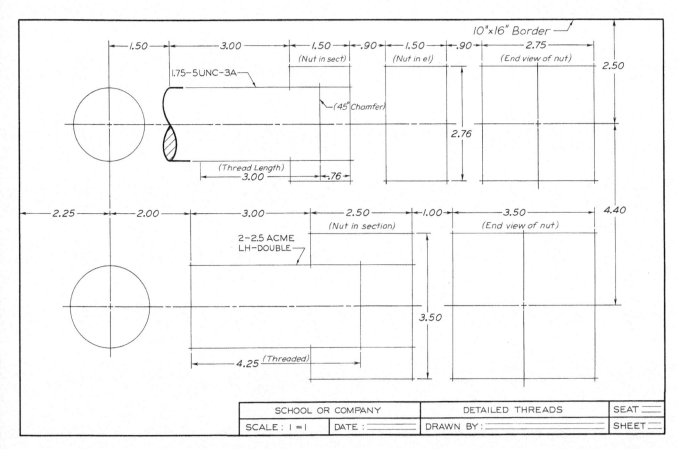

Exercise 13.2 Draw specified detailed notes given in inclined letters. Letter only the thread notes and the title strip. (Some dimensions are given to help you match the sheet layout.)

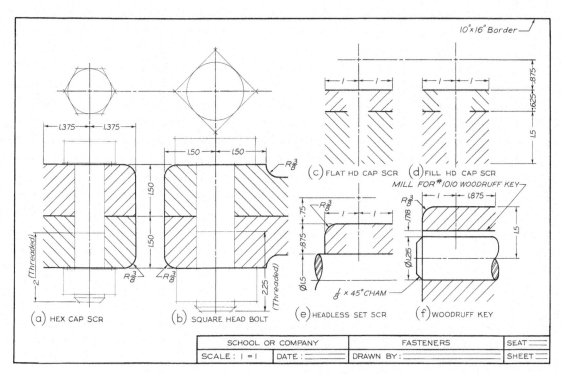

Exercise 13.3 Draw fasteners, arranged as shown. At (a) draw $\frac{7}{8}$–9 UNC-2A × 4 Hex Cap Screw. At (b) draw $1\frac{1}{8}$–7 UNC-2A × $4\frac{1}{4}$ Sq Hd Bolt. At (c) draw $\frac{3}{8}$–16 UNC-2A × $1\frac{1}{2}$ Flat Hd Cap Screw. At (d) draw $\frac{7}{16}$–14 UNC-2A × 1 Fil Hd Cap Screw. At (e) draw $\frac{1}{2}$ × 1 Headless Slotted Set Screw. At (f) draw front view of No. 1010 Woodruff key. Draw simplified or schematic thread symbols as assigned. Letter titles under each figure as shown. (Some dimensions are given to help you match the sheet layout.)

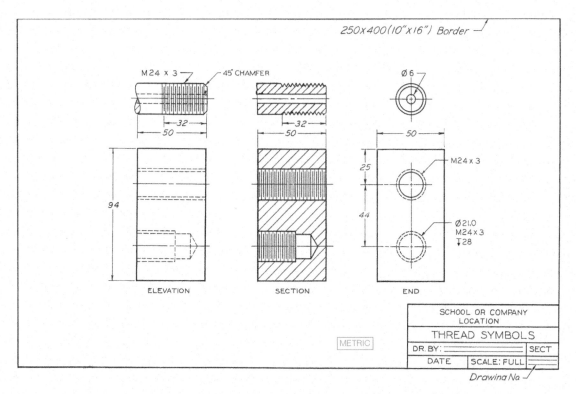

Exercise 13.4 Draw specified thread symbols, arranged as shown. Draw simplified or schematic symbols, as assigned by instructor, using layout B or A3 with a title block as in Fig III or Fig IV (see inside front cover). Omit all dimensions and notes given in inclined letters. Letter only the drill and thread notes, the titles of the views, and the title strip. (Some dimensions are given to help you match the sheet layout.)

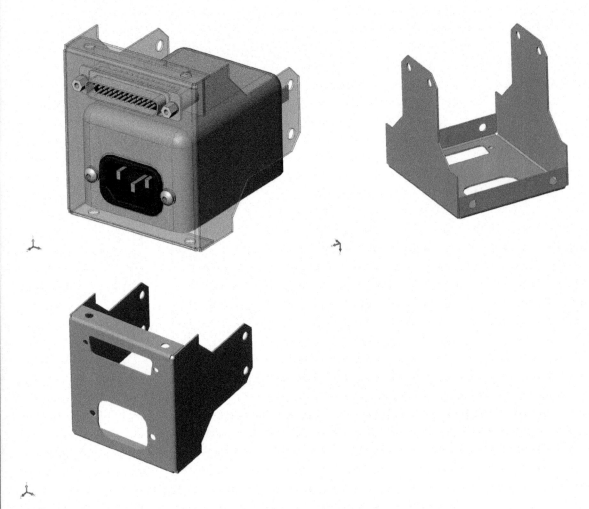

Exercise 13.5 Specify fasteners for attaching the sheet metal and standard electrical components shown. Use the Web to research power and electrical connectors.

Exercise 13.6 Captive hardware is a term for fasteners that, once installed, cannot be easily or accidentally removed. This is typically achieved by removing a portion of the threading on a screw shaft and then threading the captive hardware into a special sleeve that, once installed, prevents the hardware from backing out. Captive hardware is useful in situations where many fasteners are necessary—for example in sheet metal covers and large panels and when the fastener must be repeatedly unfastened and refastened.

For this exercise, modify a standard 6–32 × .75″ socket head cap screw (SHCS) so it can be installed into a sleeve that you will design. The dimensions for the lock and flat washer are provided on the facing page, and the dimensions from the screw to be modified are provided from a CAD file downloaded from the McMaster-Carr website. Provide dimensions for turning down the thread on the 6–32 SHCS and the missing callouts on the captive screw sleeve. Ensure the dimensions provided for the threaded portion of the screw and the clearance for the captive screw sleeve allow the screw to be fully inserted and allow it to be completely removed from the threaded blank material without causing interference.

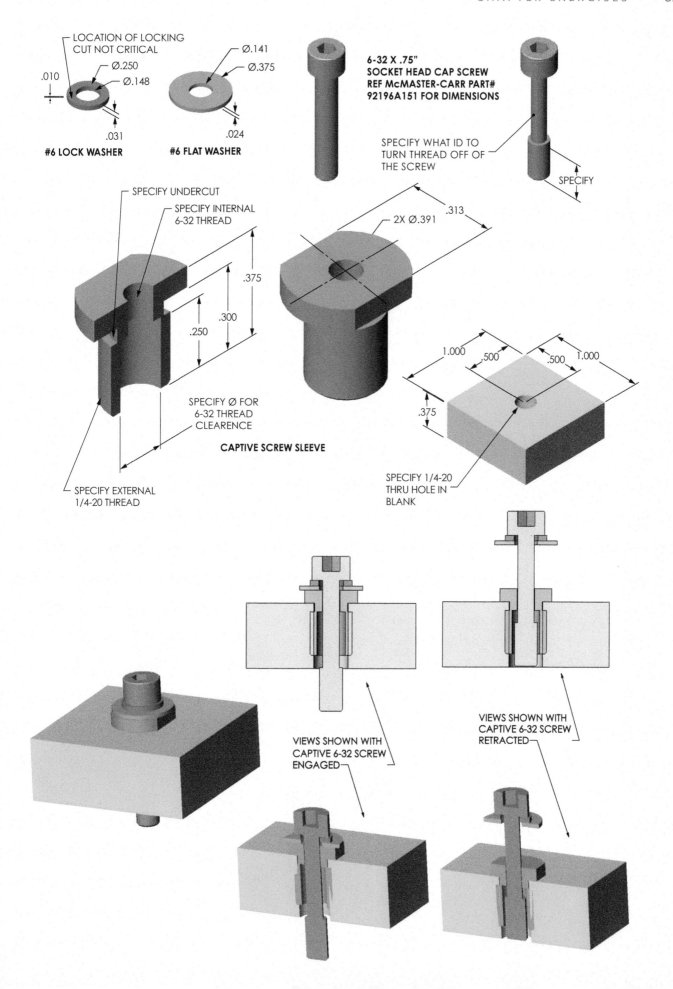

LOCATION OF LOCKING CUT NOT CRITICAL

Ø.250
Ø.148
.010
.031

#6 LOCK WASHER

Ø.141
Ø.375
.024

#6 FLAT WASHER

6-32 X .75"
SOCKET HEAD CAP SCREW
REF McMASTER-CARR PART#
92196A151 FOR DIMENSIONS

SPECIFY WHAT ID TO
TURN THREAD OFF OF
THE SCREW

SPECIFY

SPECIFY UNDERCUT

SPECIFY INTERNAL
6-32 THREAD

.375
.300
.250

2X Ø.391

.313

SPECIFY Ø FOR
6-32 THREAD
CLEARENCE

CAPTIVE SCREW SLEEVE

SPECIFY EXTERNAL
1/4-20 THREAD

1.000   .500   .500   1.000

.375

SPECIFY 1/4-20
THRU HOLE IN
BLANK

VIEWS SHOWN WITH
CAPTIVE 6-32 SCREW
RETRACTED

VIEWS SHOWN WITH
CAPTIVE 6-32 SCREW
ENGAGED

CHAPTER FOURTEEN

WORKING DRAWINGS

OBJECTIVES

After studying the material in this chapter, you should be able to:

1. Identify the elements of a detail drawing.

2. List the parts of an assembly drawing.

3. List six types of assembly drawings.

4. List the role of the record strip and title block in the approval process.

5. Describe the process for revising drawings.

6. Describe the special requirements of a patent drawing.

Refer to the following standards:
- *ASME Y14.24 Types and Applications of Engineering Drawings*
- *ASME Y14.34 Associated Lists*

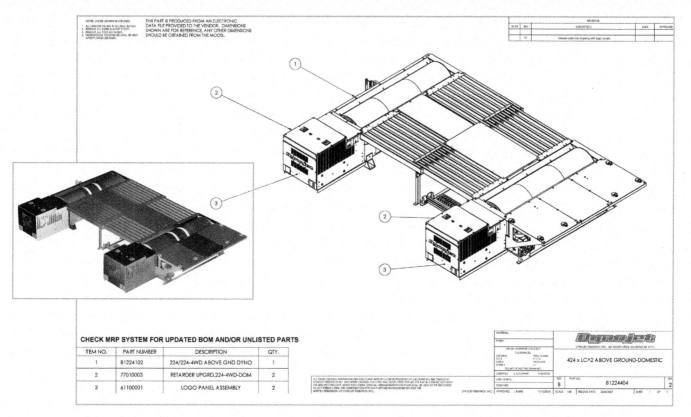

Upper Level Assembly Drawing for a Four-Wheel-Drive Dynamometer *(Inset shows 3D model.)* *(Courtesy of Dynojet Research, Inc.)*

OVERVIEW

Design professionals such as engineers and architects are creators or builders. They use graphics as a means to create, record, analyze, and communicate their design concepts or ideas so that they can be realized or made into products or structures. The ability to communicate verbally, symbolically, and graphically is essential to building the teams necessary to create large scale projects.

Different types of drawings are required at each stage of the design process. Early in the process, ideation sketches communicate and refine concepts for the project. Later, detailed layouts, analysis, and part drawings are created using 2D CAD or solid modeling techniques. Assembly drawings created in 3D CAD or using 2D methods show how multiple parts fit together. They describe the end result—how the individual pieces that must fit together to work.

Releasing and revising drawings is an important part of the design process. Revisions must be tracked, identified, logged, and saved for future reference. Understanding and using effective methods to manage paper and electronic documents is crucial for retaining important information and preventing costly and even dangerous mistakes.

Working Drawings or Construction Drawings

The term *working drawings* describes a set of *assembly drawings* and *detail drawings*. A set of civil drawings with site, grading plans, and the many structural details for building a dam or bridge is an example of a set of working drawings.

Architectural drawings are another type of working (or construction) drawings (Figure 14.1). They are given to the contractor to show how to construct the building envisioned by the architect. Working drawings for machines include assembly drawings showing how parts fit together and detail drawings showing how to manufacture the parts. Weldments are a type of assembly drawing showing the welds that must be used to form an assembly from separate pieces of metal.

Drawings, models, and supporting documentation are the specifications for design manufacture. They are given to contractors to perform the work or manufacture individual parts, so they must represent the design accurately. The drawing is a legal document describing what work is to be performed or what parts are to be produced.

A careful process of checking and approving drawings and models helps prevent errors. Take preparing or approving drawings as a serious responsibility. Overlooking what may seem to be small or insignificant details may result in large amounts of wasted money or, worse, a person's injury or death.

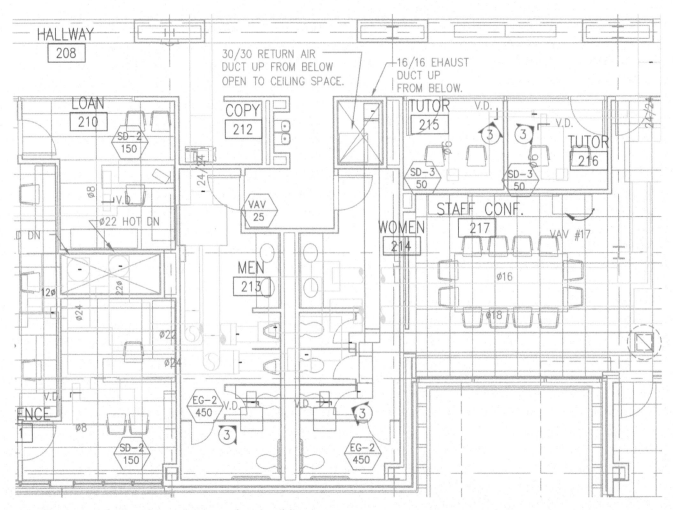

14.1   Portion of a Mechanical System for a Building *(Courtesy of Associated Construction Engineering, Inc.)*

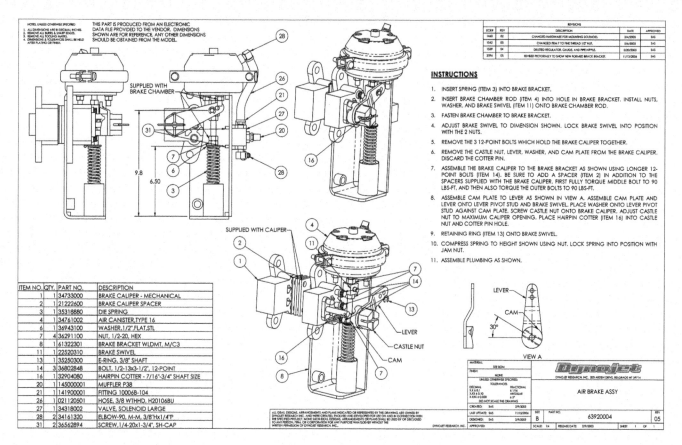

INSTRUCTIONS

1. INSERT SPRING (ITEM 3) INTO BRAKE BRACKET.

2. INSERT BRAKE CHAMBER ROD (ITEM 4) INTO HOLE IN BRAKE BRACKET. INSTALL NUTS, WASHER, AND BRAKE SWIVEL (ITEM 11) ONTO BRAKE CHAMBER ROD.

3. FASTEN BRAKE CHAMBER TO BRAKE BRACKET.

4. ADJUST BRAKE SWIVEL TO DIMENSION SHOWN. LOCK BRAKE SWIVEL INTO POSITION WITH THE 2 NUTS.

5. REMOVE THE 3 12-POINT BOLTS WHICH HOLD THE BRAKE CALIPER TOGETHER.

6. REMOVE THE CASTLE NUT, LEVER, WASHER, AND CAM PLATE FROM THE BRAKE CALIPER. DISCARD THE COTTER PIN.

7. ASSEMBLE THE BRAKE CALIPER TO THE BRAKE BRACKET AS SHOWN USING LONGER 12-POINT BOLTS (ITEM 14). BE SURE TO ADD A SPACER (ITEM 2) IN ADDITION TO THE SPACERS SUPPLIED WITH THE BRAKE CALIPER. FIRST FULLY TORQUE MIDDLE BOLT TO 90 LBS-FT, AND THEN ALSO TORQUE THE OUTER BOLTS TO 90 LBS-FT.

8. ASSEMBLE CAM PLATE TO LEVER AS SHOWN IN VIEW A. ASSEMBLE CAM PLATE AND LEVER ONTO LEVER PIVOT STUD AND BRAKE SWIVEL. PLACE WASHER ONTO LEVER PIVOT STUD AGAINST CAM PLATE. SCREW CASTLE NUT ONTO BRAKE CALIPER. ADJUST CASTLE NUT TO MAXIMUM CALIPER OPENING. PLACE HAIRPIN COTTER (ITEM 16) INTO CASTLE NUT AND COTTER PIN HOLE.

9. RETAINING RING (ITEM 13) ONTO BRAKE SWIVEL.

10. COMPRESS SPRING TO HEIGHT SHOWN USING NUT. LOCK SPRING INTO POSITION WITH JAM NUT.

11. ASSEMBLE PLUMBING AS SHOWN.

14.2 General Assembly Drawing for an Air Brake Created from a 3D CAD Model *(Courtesy of Dynojet Research, Inc.)*

Assembly Drawings

An assembly drawing shows the assembled machine or structure, with all detail parts in their functional positions or as an *exploded view* where you can relate the parts to their functional positions.

There are different types of assembly drawings:

1. Design assemblies, or layouts.
2. General assemblies.
3. Detail assemblies.
4. Working drawing assemblies.
5. Outline or installation assemblies.
6. Inseparable assemblies (as in weldments, and others).

Assembly drawings are often generated from 3D CAD models. For example, the assembly drawing for the air brake in Figure 14.2 was generated from the 3D CAD model of the air brake shown in a shaded view in Figure 14.3.

Views

Keep the purpose in mind when you select the views for an assembly drawing. The assembly drawing shows how the parts fit together and suggests the function of the entire unit. A complete set of orthographic views is not required. Often a single orthographic view will show all of the information needed when assembling the parts. The assembly drawing does not need to show how to make the parts, just how to put them together. The assembly worker receives the actual finished parts. The information for each individual part is shown on its detail drawing.

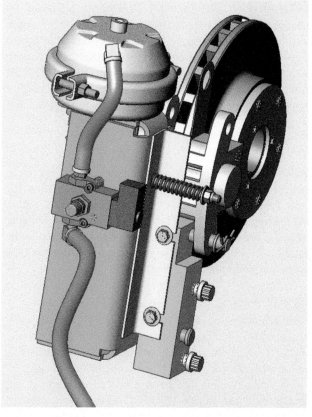

14.3 3D CAD Model for an Air Brake *(Courtesy of Dynojet Research, Inc.)*

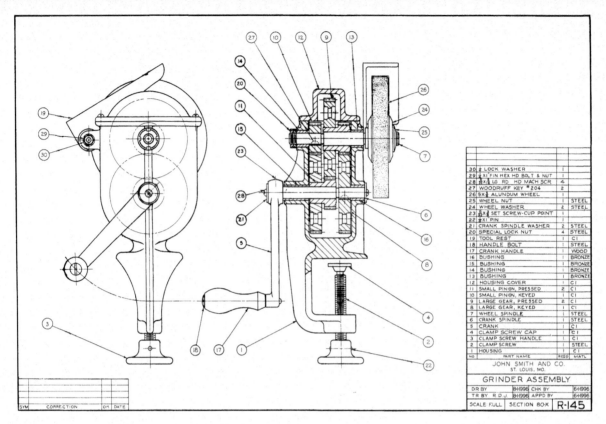

NO.	PART NAME	REQ'D	MATL
30	⅛ LOCK WASHER	1	
29	⅜X1 FIN HEX HD BOLT & NUT	1	
28	⅜X⅞ LG RD HD MACH SCR	4	
27	WOODRUFF KEY #204	2	
26	5X½ ALUNDUM WHEEL	1	
25	WHEEL NUT	1	STEEL
24	WHEEL WASHER	2	STEEL
23	⅜X⅜ SET SCREW-CUP POINT	1	
22	⅛X1 PIN	1	
21	CRANK SPINDLE WASHER	2	STEEL
20	SPECIAL LOCK NUT	4	STEEL
19	TOOL REST	1	CI
18	HANDLE BOLT	1	STEEL
17	CRANK HANDLE	1	WOOD
16	BUSHING	1	BRONZE
15	BUSHING	1	BRONZE
14	BUSHING	1	BRONZE
13	BUSHING	1	BRONZE
12	HOUSING COVER	1	CI
11	SMALL PINION, PRESSED	2	CI
10	SMALL PINION, KEYED	1	CI
9	LARGE GEAR, PRESSED	2	CI
8	LARGE GEAR, KEYED	1	CI
7	WHEEL SPINDLE	1	STEEL
6	CRANK SPINDLE	1	STEEL
5	CRANK	1	CI
4	CLAMP SCREW CAP	1	CI
3	CLAMP SCREW HANDLE	1	CI
2	CLAMP SCREW	1	STEEL
1	HOUSING	1	CI

JOHN SMITH AND CO.
ST. LOUIS, MO.

GRINDER ASSEMBLY

DR BY	8H996	CHK BY	6H996
TR BY R.D.J.	8H996	APPD BY	6H996
SCALE FULL	SECTION 80-X		R-145

SYM	CORRECTION	OK	DATE

14.4   Assembly Drawing of a Grinder

Hidden Lines in Assembly Drawings

Typically, hidden lines are not needed on assembly drawings. Keep in mind that the assembly drawing is often used by the worker who is putting the parts together. It needs to be easy to read and show the relationships between parts clearly. Hidden lines can make the drawing difficult to read, so use section or exploded views to show the interior parts in the assembly drawing.

Dimensions in Assembly Drawings

Assembly drawings are not usually dimensioned except to show the relative positions of one feature to the next when that distance must be maintained at the time of the assembly, such as the maximum height of a jack, or the maximum opening between the jaws of a vise. When machining is required in the assembly operation, the necessary dimensions and notes may be given on the assembly drawing.

Assembly Sections

Because assemblies often have parts fitting into or overlapping other parts, 2D and 3D sections are useful views. For example, in Figure 14.4, try to imagine the right-side view drawn in elevation with interior parts represented by hidden lines.

Any kind of section may be used as needed. A broken-out section is shown in Figure 14.4. Half sections and removed sections are also frequently used. Pictorial sections are helpful in creating easy-to-read assembly drawings.

Detail Drawings or Piece Part Drawings

Drawings of the individual parts are called *piece part drawings, part drawings,* or *detail drawings.* Detail drawings contain all of the necessary information to manufacture any specific part being created for a product or design. Figures 14.5 and 14.6 show detail drawings. The information provided on detail drawings includes:

- All necessary drawing views or accurate 3D model information to fully define the shape.
- Dimensions that can be specified in a drawing or can be measured accurately from a 3D model.
- Tolerances either specified in a drawing or annotated in a 3D model so that how the tolerance applies can be clearly understood.
- The material for the manufactured part.
- Any general or specific notes including heat treatment, painting, coatings, hardness, pattern number, estimated weight, and surface finishes, such as maximum surface roughness.
- Approval or release and revision tracking, whether part of a 2D drawing title and revision block or part of a digital signature system.

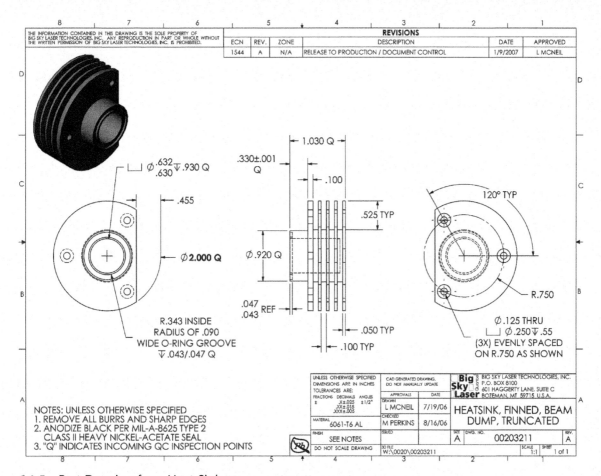

14.5   Part Drawing for a Heat Sink *(Courtesy of Big Sky Laser.)*

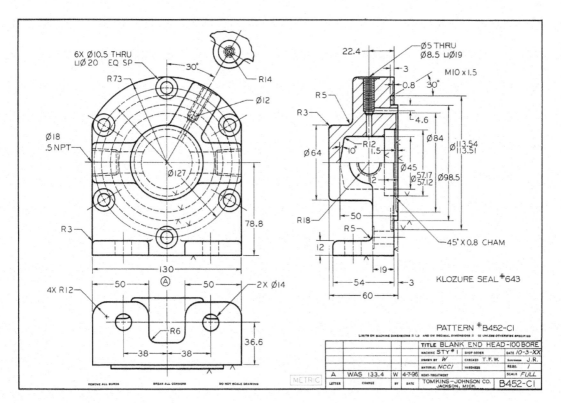

14.6   A Detail Drawing

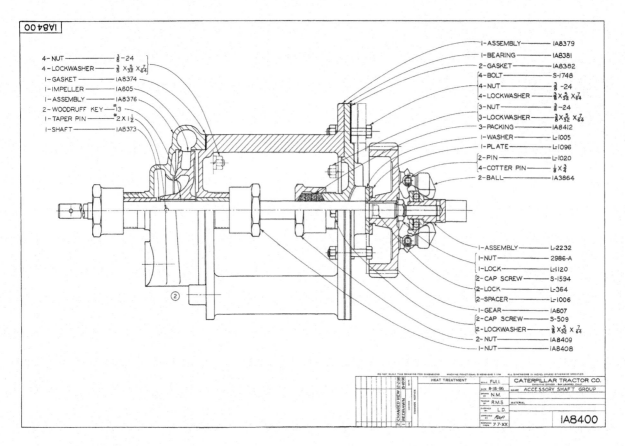

14.7   Subassembly of Accessory Shaft Group

14.1 SUBASSEMBLIES

A set of working drawings includes detail drawings of individual parts and the assembly drawing showing the assembled unit. Often, an entire subassembly may be reused in a different design. It is easier to reuse the group of parts in a new design if they are grouped together logically and contained in separate drawings. Your top-level assembly drawing will appear cleaner if you keep subassemblies well organized, as the entire subassembly can be identified as a single item on a higher-level assembly drawing. Fasteners for the subassembly that attach it to its mating parts in the next higher level assembly drawing are usually shown or listed on the bill of materials (sometimes referred to as BOM) at the higher level.

Structuring a product into assemblies and subassemblies requires thoughtful decision making to facilitate retrieving part, subassembly, and assembly drawings later on. If your company uses a product data management system (PDM), planning is essential to seeing downstream results.

An example of a subassembly is shown in Figure 14.7. A subassembly is drawn the same way as an assembly drawing, just for a subgroup that assembles to other parts.

14.2 IDENTIFICATION

Circled numbers called *balloon numbers* or *ball tags* are used to identify the parts in the assembly (Figure 14.8). Circles containing the part numbers are placed adjacent to the parts, with leaders terminated by arrowheads touching the parts as shown in Figure 14.9.

Place the circles in orderly horizontal or vertical rows and not scattered over the sheet. Draw leader lines at an angle, not horizontally or vertically. Do not let leaders cross. Make adjacent leaders parallel or nearly so. For multiple small parts that are easily distinguished, a single leader may have multiple circle item numbers as shown in Figure 14.9.

The circled item number identifies each part. Show information for the part in the parts list. The parts list is usually included on the drawing sheet but may also be a separate document.

Another method of identification is to letter the part names, quantity required, and part numbers at the end of leaders, as shown in Figure 14.7. More commonly, only the part numbers are given, together with standard straight-line leaders.

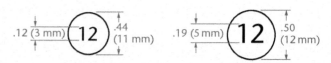

14.8   Identification Numbers

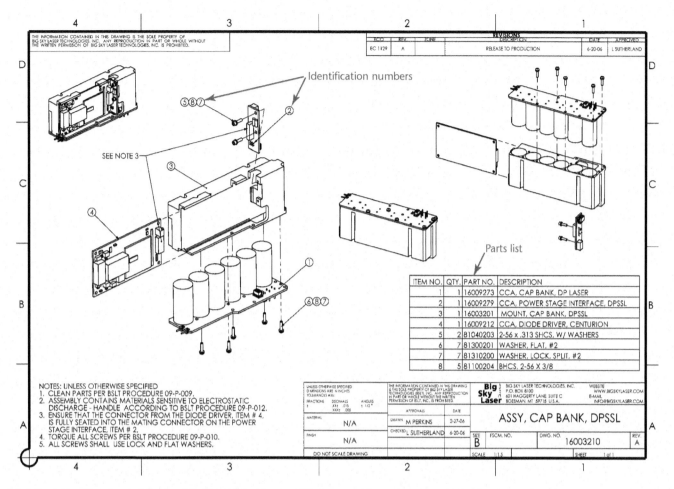

14.9 Identification of Assembly Drawing Items with a Parts List *(Courtesy of Big Sky Laser.)*

Multidetail Drawings

When multiple detail drawings are shown on one sheet, label each part with identification similar to that used on any detail drawings. A portion of a multidetail drawing is shown in Figure 14.10. It is highly preferred to show only one part per sheet. This provides a unique drawing number for each part, which is very important for retrieving information from a PDM system. Often the part number is used as the drawing number.

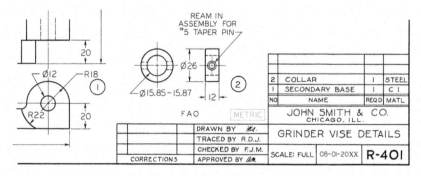

14.10 Portion of a Drawing Showing Identification of Details with a Parts List

14.3 PARTS LISTS

A *parts list* or *bill of materials* (BOM) itemizes the parts of a structure shown on an assembly drawing (*ANSI Y14.34*). The title strip alone is sufficient on detail drawings of only one part, but a parts list is necessary on assembly drawings or detail drawings of several parts. Parts can be listed in general order of size or importance or grouped by types.

ITEM NO.	QTY.	PART NO.	DESCRIPTION
1	1	16009273	CCA, CAP BANK, DP LASER
2	1	16009279	CCA, POWER STAGE INTERFACE, DPSSL
3	1	16003201	MOUNT, CAP BANK, DPSSL
4	1	16009212	CCA, DIODE DRIVER, CENTURION
5	2	81040203	2-56 x .313 SHCS, W/ WASHERS
6	7	81300201	WASHER, FLAT, #2
7	7	81310200	WASHER, LOCK, SPLIT, #2
8	5	81100204	BHCS, 2-56 X 3/8

14.11 Parts List *(Courtesy of Big Sky Laser.)*

Parts lists for machine drawings (Figure 14.11) contain:

- Part identification number (PIN).
- Description of each part.
- Quantity required in the assembly.

The following abbreviations can be used to indicate quantities that are not exactly known: AR indicates *as required*; EST followed by a number specifies an *estimated quantity*.

Parts lists that contain application data must include information for the next assembly level.

Frequently, other information is supplied in the parts list, such as material, DAI code, pattern numbers, stock sizes, and weights of parts.

Automatic BOM Generation

CAD software often allows you to generate the parts list automatically or somewhat automatically. Some CAD software uses the terminology Parts List, others BOM, and some use both terms but have different command features based on which is selected (they will be considered interchangeable here). Figure 14.12 shows a dialog box used to automate generation of a parts list.

If you created a 3D assembly model by inserting CAD models for the parts, the software can query the assembly model for quantities and the file names that were inserted to generate the parts list. This is another good reason to use good file management practices and name your parts logically. Most software allows you to type in information, but overriding the information this way makes it harder to automatically update files, losing some of the advantage of using 3D CAD.

Locating the Parts List

If the parts list rests on top of the title box or strip, the order of the items should be from the bottom upward so that new items can be added later, if necessary. If the parts list is placed in the upper-right corner, the items should read downward.

Listing Standard Parts

Standard parts, whether purchased or company produced, are not drawn but are included in the parts list. Bolts, screws, bearings, pins, keys, and so on are identified by the part number from the assembly drawing and are specified by name and size or number.

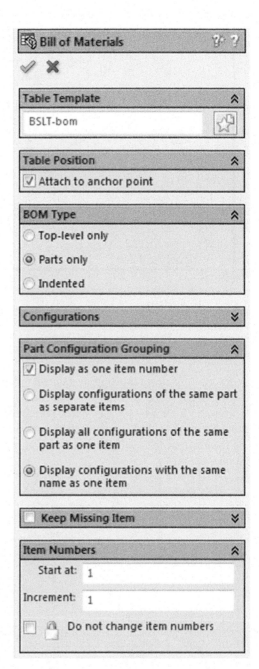

14.12 SolidWorks Dialog Box Showing Options for Automatically Inserting a Bill of Materials Table *(Image courtesy of ©2016 Dassault Systèmes SolidWorks Corporation.)*

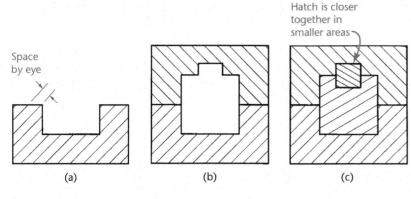

Space by eye

Hatch is closer together in smaller areas

(a)   (b)   (c)

14.13   Section Lining in Assemblies (Full Size)

14.4 ASSEMBLY SECTIONS

In assembly sections it is necessary not only to show the cut surfaces but also to distinguish between adjacent parts. Do this by drawing the section lines in opposing directions, as shown in Figure 14.13. The first large area is sectioned at 45° (Figure 14.13a). The next large area is sectioned at 45° in the opposite direction. Additional areas are then sectioned at other angles, such as 30° or 60°, as shown in Figure 14.13c, or at other angles.

In small areas it is necessary to space the section lines closer together. In larger areas, space section lining more widely or use outline section lining.

Use the general-purpose section lining for assemblies. You can also give a general indication of the materials used by using symbolic section lining (Figure 14.14). Refer to Chapter 8 to review section drawing practices.

In sectioning relatively thin parts in an assembly, such as gaskets and sheet metal parts, section lining is ineffective and should be left out or shown in solid black, as in Figure 14.15.

In architectural drawings, filling sectioned areas solidly is called *poche,* as shown in Figure 14.16. It is often used to show walls that have been cut through, as on floor plans.

Often solid objects, or parts that do not show required information, are sliced by the cutting plane. Leave these parts unsectioned, or "in the round." This includes bolts, nuts, shafts, keys, screws, pins, ball or roller bearings, gear teeth, spokes, and ribs, among others. See Figure 14.17.

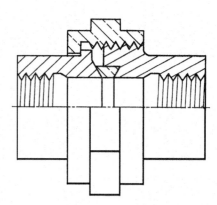

14.14   Symbolic Section Lining

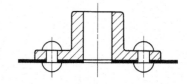

14.15   Solidly Hatching Small Parts

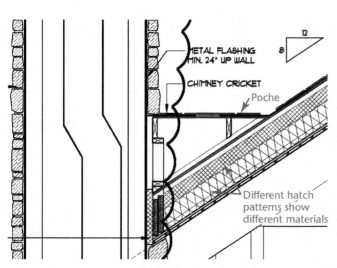

METAL FLASHING MIN. 24" UP WALL

CHIMNEY CRICKET

Poche

Different hatch patterns show different materials

14.16   Architectural Drawing Detail. *Use hatch patterns to indicate material and poche small features. (Courtesy of Locati Architects.)*

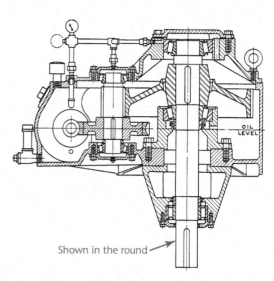

OIL LEVEL

Shown in the round

14.17   Assembly Section

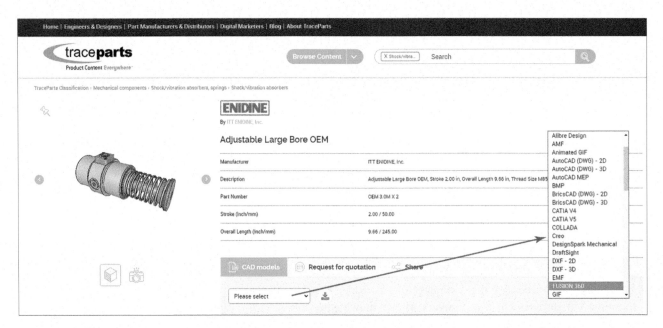

You can save time in creating assemblies by downloading models of stock parts from vendors online. Sites such as TraceParts.com make it easy to locate stock parts from many different manufacturers. (Courtesy of TraceParts.com.)

14.5 WORKING DRAWING ASSEMBLY

A *working drawing assembly* is a combined detail and assembly drawing (Figure 14.18). These drawings are often used in place of separate detail and assembly drawings when the assembly is simple enough for all of its parts to be shown clearly in the single drawing. In some cases, all but one or two parts can be drawn and dimensioned clearly in the assembly drawing, in which event these parts are detailed separately on the same sheet. This type of drawing is common in valve drawings, locomotive subassemblies, aircraft subassemblies, and drawings of jigs and fixtures.

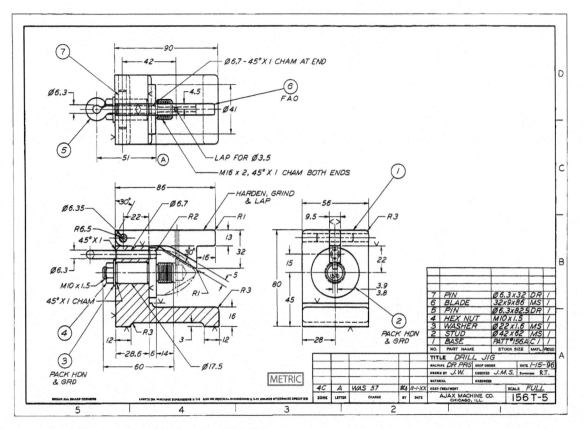

14.18   Working Drawing Assembly of Drill Jig

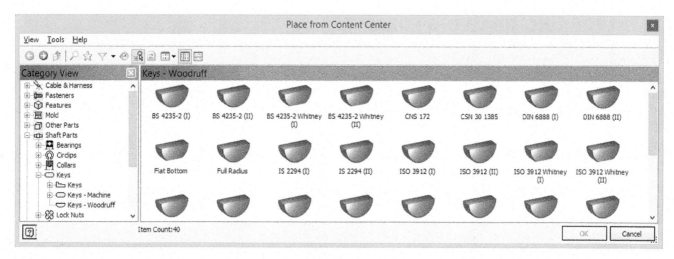

Autodesk Inventor is an example of a software package that features stock parts useful for creating assemblies.
(Autodesk screen shots reprinted courtesy of Autodesk, Inc.)

14.6 INSTALLATION ASSEMBLIES

An assembly made specifically to show how to install or erect a machine or structure is an ***installation assembly.*** This type of drawing is also often called an *outline assembly*, because it shows only the outlines and the relationships of exterior surfaces. A typical installation assembly is shown in Figure 14.19. In aircraft drafting, an installation drawing (assembly) gives complete information for placing details or subassemblies in their final positions in the airplane.

14.7 CHECK ASSEMBLIES

After all detail drawings of a unit have been made, it may be necessary to make a ***check assembly,*** especially if a number of changes were made in the details. Such an assembly is shown accurately to scale to graphically check the correctness of the details and their relationship in assembly. After the check assembly has served its purpose, it may be converted into a general assembly drawing.

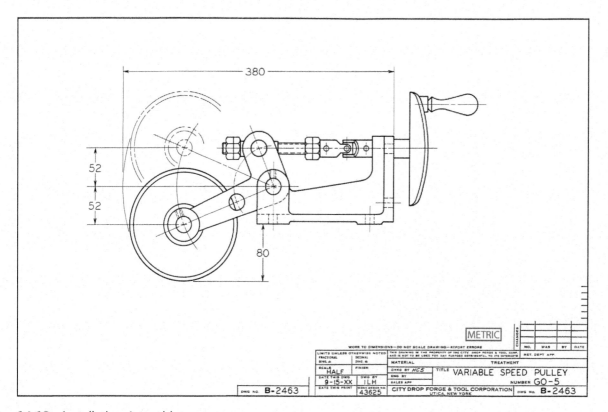

14.19   Installation Assembly

14.8 WORKING DRAWING FORMATS

Number of Details Per Sheet

There are two general methods for grouping detailed parts on sheets. Showing one detailed part per sheet is typically preferred because it is easier to repurpose drawings for other uses and to track revision data when the sheet does not contain extra parts.

Small machines or structures composed of few parts sometimes show all the details on one large sheet. Showing the assembly and all its details on one sheet can be convenient, but it is generally more difficult to revise and maintain. The same scale should be used for all details on a single sheet, if possible. When this is not possible, clearly note the scale under each dissimilar detail.

Most companies show one detail per sheet, however simple or small it may be. For many parts the basic 8.5″ × 11″ or 210 mm × 297 mm sheet works well. Because it is easy to lose a few drawings on smaller sheets from a set that is mostly on larger sheets, some companies use 11″ × 17″ (or the equivalent metric size) sheets for all parts.

Digital Drawing Transmittal

Electronic file formats such as Portable Document Format (PDF), originally developed by Adobe Systems in 1993, allow the originator to send a document that can be commented on without allowing the original document to be changed.

Several search engines allow you to search for text embedded in the PDF file. This means that PDF can provide advantages not just for storing, but also for retrieving the information later. Adobe Systems provides a useful document (in PDF format) on using PDF as an archiving standard. Dassault Systèmes' eDrawings Viewer is a popular format for viewing, printing, and marking up drawings produced in

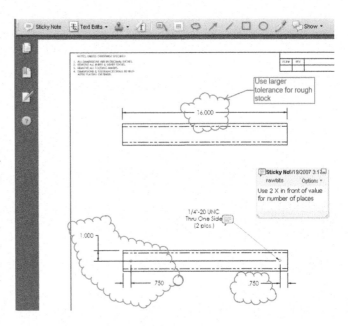

14.20   A Portion of a PDF File Showing Redlined Markups *(Courtesy of Dynojet Research, Inc.)*

SolidWorks and AutoCAD. It runs on Windows, Mac OS, and mobile platforms and does not require the user to have any CAD software installed.

Using electronic files saves trees, makes it quicker to distribute and store documents, and allows others to review documents from various applications. Figure 14.20 shows a drawing stored in PDF format with comments and redlined markups.

(Copyright Mykola Mazuryk/Shutterstock.)

PAPER CONSERVATION

The U.S. Environmental Protection Agency (EPA) reported that in 2018 the U.S. paper and paperboard industry generated over 67 million tons of product. About 25% of this ended up in landfills. Although paper and paperboard products were among the largest contributors to municipal solid waste at about 23% (with food at 21%) of the total weight, this volume is down from the EPA estimate of paper at 38% just a few years ago. The really good news is that the largest component of municipal waste being recycled is paper—at nearly 67%. Since 2020, Covid masks and PPEs have increased the amount of paper used even though recycling has improved. Deforestation is still a looming problem as trees are cleared to make way for agriculture and housing developments.

Websites related to paper conservation include:
- www.lesk.com/mlesk/ksg97/ksg.html
- www.environmentalpaper.org
- www.epa.gov

14.21 Title Strip

14.22 Title Block with Parts List *(Courtesy of Dynojet Research, Inc.)*

Title and Record Strips

Drawings constitute important and valuable information regarding products, so carefully designed, well-kept, systematic files are important.

The function of the title and record strip is to show, in an organized way, all necessary information not given directly on the drawing with its dimensions and notes. The type of title block or strip used depends on the filing system in use, the manufacturing processes, and the requirements of the product. The following should generally be given in the title form:

1. Name and address of the company originating the design.
2. Drawing title.
3. Drawing number.
4. Revision.
5. Approval sign offs for the Drafter, Checker, Engineer and the dates of approval.
6. Drawing scale. Use "NONE" when no scale is used. Sheets in a set may be to different scales.
7. Sheet size.
8. Sheet number. Such as 1 of 8, if the drawing has multiple sheets.

Other information may be included, such as material, quantity, heat treatment, finish, hardness, pattern number, estimated weight, superseding and superseded drawing numbers, symbol of machine, and so on, depending on the plant organization and unique aspects of the product. Some typical title blocks are shown in Figures 14.21, 14.22, and 14.23.

The title form is usually placed along the bottom of the sheet or in the lower right-hand corner of the sheet, because drawings are often filed in flat, horizontal drawers, and the title must be easily found. However, as many filing systems are in use, the location of the title form depends on a company's organizational preference. Many companies adopt their own title forms or those preferred by ANSI.

To letter items in a title form:

- Use a font such as Arial that provides easy to read Gothic capitals.
- Letter items according to their relative importance. Use heavier, larger or more widely spaced type (or a combination of these) to indicate important items.
- Give the drawing number the most emphasis, followed by the name of the object and name of the company. (Date, scale, and originator's and checker's names are important, but do not need to be prominent.)
- Refer to Chapter 2 for detailed information on title forms and standard letter heights.

14.23 Title Block *(Courtesy of Quantel USA.)*

14.9 DRAWING NUMBERS

Every drawing should be numbered. Some companies use numbers, such as 19530056, or a number with a prefix or suffix letter, such as A60412 or 60412-A. The drawing number is usually the same as the product identification number (PIN). To make information retrieval easy, these identification number cannot have spaces. Letters that can be mistaken for numbers, such as I, O, Q, S, X, and Z, are not used.

In different numbering schemes, various parts of the drawing number indicate different things, such as model number of the machine and the nature or use of the part. In general, it is best to use a simple numbering system and not to load the number with too many indications.

The drawing number should be lettered 7 mm (.2500″) high in the lower-right and upper-left corners of the sheet.

To benefit from a CAD system, you must be able to store and retrieve your drawings efficiently. Drawing tracking software allows users to search by part number or by text items to locate and retrieve drawing files and CAD models.

14.10 ZONING

To help people locate a particular item on a large or complex drawing, regular ruled intervals are labeled along the margins, often in the right and lower margins only. The intervals on the horizontal margin are labeled from right to left with numerals, and the intervals on the vertical margin are labeled from bottom to top with letters, similar to road maps. Note the zone letters and numbers around the border of Figure 14.24.

14.11 CHECKING DRAWINGS

The importance of accuracy in technical drawing cannot be overstated. Errors sometimes cause tremendous unnecessary expenditures. The signature on the drawing identifies who is responsible for its accuracy.

In small offices, checking is usually done by the designer or by one of the drafters. In large offices, experienced engineers may be employed to devote a major part of their time to checking drawings.

A drawing is carefully checked and signed by the person who made it. It is then checked by the lead designer for function, economy, practicability, fit, tolerances, and so on. Corrections, if any, are then made by the original drafter.

The final checker should systematically review the drawing for any remaining errors. They should study the drawing with particular attention to:

1. Soundness of design, with reference to function, strength, materials, economy, manufacturability, serviceability, ease of assembly and repair, lubrication, and so on.
2. Choice of views, partial views, auxiliary views, sections, lettering, and so on.
3. Dimensions, with special reference to repetition, ambiguity, legibility, omissions, errors, and finish marks. Special attention should be given to tolerances.
4. Standard parts. In the interest of economy, as many parts as possible should be standard.
5. Notes, with special reference to clear wording and legibility.
6. Clearances. Moving parts should be checked in all possible positions to ensure freedom of movement.
7. Title form information.

14.12 DRAWING REVISIONS

Design changes, error correction, and customer input may require drawing changes. An accurate record of all changes made to released drawings is tracked via a revision block. This is important so that the sources of all changes may be understood, verified, and approved.

The record of revisions should show the change, by whom, when, and why the change was made. An engineering change order (ECO) or engineering change request (ECR) is processed to approve and track changes to drawings once they have been released for production.

Any changes or additions made to a drawing are tracked by a *revision number.* A symbol can be added to the drawing showing the item affected by the revision (Figure 14.24).

It is not recommended to remove information by crossing it out. In rare cases when a dimension is not noticeably affected by a change, it may be underlined with a heavy line to indicate that it is not to scale.

It is important to keep permanent CAD files, prints, or microfilms of each issue to show how the drawing appeared before the revision. Issue new prints each time a change is made. If the revision history block on the actual drawing becomes too cumbersome, the older items can be removed, leaving only the three most recent. The information for the previous revisions must still be stored as part of the permanent record.

Digital systems absolutely must use careful backup procedures and, due to data loss concerns, are still not approved in some industries.

If considerable change on a drawing is necessary, it may be necessary to make a new drawing and stamp the old one OBSOLETE and store it in an "obsolete" file. In the title block of the old drawing, enter the words "SUPERSEDED BY" or "REPLACED BY" followed by the number of the new drawing. On the new drawing, under "SUPERSEDES" or "REPLACES," enter the number of the old drawing.

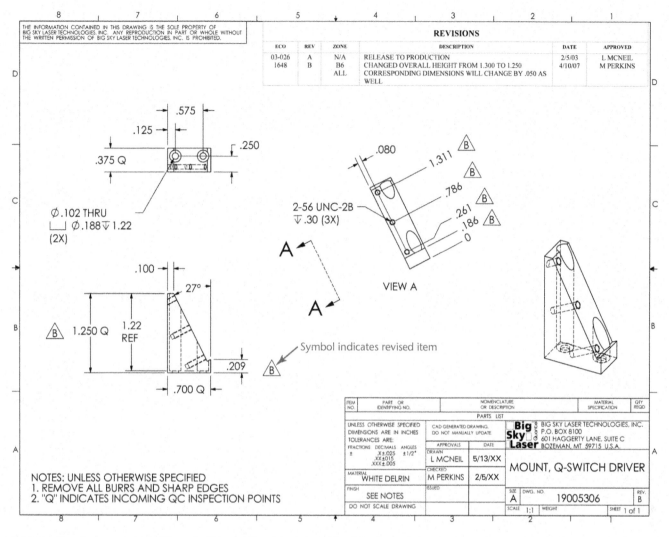

14.24 *Symbols match the item in the revision block to revised features on a drawing. (Courtesy of Big Sky Laser, Inc.)*

People use various methods to link the area on a drawing where the change is made to the entry in the revision block. The most common is to place numbers or letters in a small circle or triangle near each place where the changes were made and to use the same numbers or letters in the revision block, as shown in Figure 14.24. On zoned drawings, the zone of the correction is shown in the revision block. The change should also be described briefly, along with the date and initials of the person making the change.

14.13 SIMPLIFYING DRAWINGS

Drawing time is a considerable part of the total cost of a product. It makes sense to reduce drawing costs by using practices to simplify your drawings without losing clarity. For example, use partial views, half views, thread symbols, piping symbols, and single-line spring drawings when appropriate. Omit lines or lettering on a drawing that are not needed for clarity. In addition to saving production time, this makes drawings easier to read. To simplify drawings:

1. Use word descriptions when practical.
2. Do not show unnecessary views.
3. Use standard symbols such as ∅ and standard abbreviations (see Appendix 2) when appropriate.
4. Avoid elaborate, pictorial, or repetitive details. Use phantom lines to avoid drawing repeated features.
5. List rather than draw standard parts such as bolts, nuts, keys, and pins.
6. Omit unnecessary hidden lines.
7. Use outline section lining in large areas to save time and improve legibility.
8. Omit unnecessary duplication of notes and lettering.
9. Use symbolic representation for piping and thread.
10. Use CAD libraries and standard parts when feasible for design and drawings.

Some industries have simplified their drafting practices even more. Learn the practices appropriate to the industry for which you are creating drawings.

14.14 PATENT DRAWINGS

The patent application for a machine or device must include drawings to illustrate and explain the invention. All patent drawings must be mechanically correct and constitute complete illustrations of every feature of the invention claimed. The strict requirements of the U.S. Patent Office facilitate the examination of applications and the interpretation of patents issued. Examples of patent drawings are shown in Figure 14.25.

Drawings for patent applications are pictorial and explanatory in nature; therefore they are not as detailed as working drawings for production purposes. Centerlines, hidden lines, dimension notes, and so forth, are omitted, since specific dimensions, tolerances, and notes are often not required to patent the general design or innovation.

The drawings must contain as many figures as necessary to show the invention clearly. There is no limit on the number of sheets that may be submitted. The drawings can be produced by hand or from the same CAD database used to create the design documentation.

Figures should be numbered consecutively (e.g., Figure 1, Figure 2, Figure 3A, Figure 3B, etc.). Views, features, and parts are identified by numbers that refer to the descriptions and explanations given in the specification section of the patent application. The reference number for a part or feature should remain the same in every diagram.

Exploded isometric or perspective drawings with reference numbers identifying the parts (i.e., assembly drawings) are preferred. Centerlines are used to illustrate how parts are aligned in exploded views. While the drawing must show every feature that is listed in the patent claims, if standardized parts are used, they can be represented symbolically and do not have to be drawn in detail.

The figures may be plan, elevation, section, pictorial, and detail views of portions or elements, and they may be drawn to an enlarged scale if necessary.

The U.S. Patent Office has basic standards for drawings:

- All sheets within a single application must be the same size, and two sheet sizes are accepted:
  - U.S. size: 8.5″ by 11″ (216 mm × 279 mm).
  - International size: 210 mm × 297 mm.
- Paper must be single sided.
- Paper must be oriented vertically, so that the short side of the sheet is at the top (called portrait style in printing options).
- No border lines are permitted on the sheets.
- The following minimum margins must be maintained:
  - Top margin: 1″ (25 mm).
  - Left margin: 1″ (25 mm).
  - Right margin: .675″ (15 mm).
  - Bottom margin: .375″ (10 mm).
- No labels or drawing lines may extend into the margin except for the specific identification required at the top of each sheet and two scan target points.
- All drawings must be submitted in black and white—no color drawings or photos except in very limited cases.
- Lines must be solid black and suitable for reproduction at a smaller size.
- Shading (either cross hatch or stippling) is used whenever it improves readability. In rare cases when it is necessary to show a feature hidden behind a surface, a lighter solid line is used.
- Sketches are acceptable for the application process, but formal drawings will have to be created if accepted.

Photocopies are accepted, because three copies of each drawing must be submitted. The drawings will not be returned so it is *not* a good idea to send an original with the initial patent application. Drawings may also be submitted via the electronic filing system.

While the above gives you a basic idea of the standards for patent drawings, the strict requirements of the U.S. Patent Office are carefully documented on their website. Be sure to follow their requirements exactly if you are preparing drawings for a patent application.

For more information, log on to the U.S. Patent and Trademark Office's website at www.uspto.gov.

You can also consult the *Guide for Patent Draftsmen*, which can be obtained from the Superintendent of Documents, U.S. Government Printing Office, Washington, D.C. 20402.

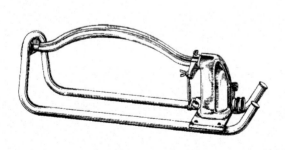

14.25 Patent Drawing Examples. *Although two examples are shown here, each drawing is shown on a separate sheet in the patent application. (Courtesy of US. Patent and Trademark Office.)*

CONVEY THE ESSENCE OF THE DESIGN

Ryan Cargo graduated from Montana State University in 2005 with a B.S. in Mechanical Engineering and soon was hired by a NASA contractor to work on aircraft and satellite-based earth-science research systems, where he helped build the camera shutters for the James Webb Space Telescope. After a move to bike-friendly Berlin, Germany, he helped design a new high-speed FDM (fused deposition modeling) print head at a large-format 3D printing startup. Ryan's passion for bicycle touring and the sight of thousands of bicycles on the streets of Berlin sparked his interest in designing a new type of bike frame.

Ryan wanted to get away from the typical triangle tube frame construction. He pictured the axles, handlebars, seat, and cranks all hanging in free space and began imagining all the ways to connect those components with more interesting materials. Taking measurements from his road bike, Ryan drew the locations of all the key points to scale on paper. Using tracing paper over this "location template," Ryan sketched all sorts of novel shapes until an idea emerged for a structure with gently curving surfaces that could easily be made from laminated plywood reinforced with composites.

From the hand sketches, Ryan cut full-size plywood shapes and fixed them at the key points where the axle, head tube, seat tube, and bottom bracket would attach, otherwise letting the plywood take on its natural and aesthetically pleasing bend. Using calipers to get X-, Y-, and Z-coordinates of the resulting surface, he created a surface model using Rhinoceros 3D CAD software, then used SolidWorks to add critical interfaces, such as bores for bearings, recesses for chain clearance and brake calibers, and the internal passages for cable and hydraulic lines. Ryan used the model to 3D print full-scale molds for laying up the carbon fiber and wood veneers of the real bike frame.

Thinking of turning his bike-building hobby into a business, Ryan decided to protect the design by getting a patent. He was curious about the patent process anyway. "I'm used to focusing on every detail on engineering drawings—a clear dimensioning strategy, tolerances that ensure the real part works, making every detail about material and coatings clear, and so on. I found patent drawings (especially for this design patent) to be a refreshing break from this, allowing me some flexibility to be artistic and to convey the essence of how the design feels," said Ryan.

The patent office drawing requirements state, "One of the views should be suitable for inclusion on the front page of the patent application publication and patent as the illustration of the invention." Ryan chose a front-right isometric view of the bike frame for this, with the frame itself stippled and major components (such as the wheels and handlebars) shown as

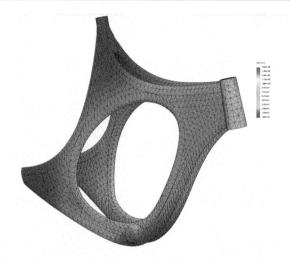

14.26 *Ryan's aerospace background came in handy when he modelled forces on the pedals and the fork to identify stress concentrations on the frame. He used this information to determine the type and number of layers of carbon fiber cloth needed. Arrow plots of the principal stresses across the frame surface helped him determine the direction to orient the carbon cloth pieces with the fibers in pure tension to contribute to the frame's rigidity.*

faint, dashed lines, to convey that the design is for a bicycle that anyone could ride but with a very novel frame (Figure 14.27). Ryan submitted his patent drawings electronically as high-resolution images embedded in Microsoft Word files. From start to finish, the patent process took about 18 months. Ryan was granted the patent in 2018. You can see more about his unique design at www.juliet-designs.com.

Ryan currently works at Meta, designing robots and industrial automation products for data centers, and enjoys riding his uniquely designed bicycles with his wife and young son.

(All images courtesy of Ryan Christopher Cargo.)

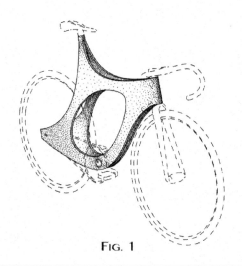

14.27 *This pictorial view was submitted as part of the patent process. Hidden lines show equipment that is not a part of the patent, but which serves to convey its function.*

FIG. 1

ASSEMBLY DRAWINGS USING 3D CAD

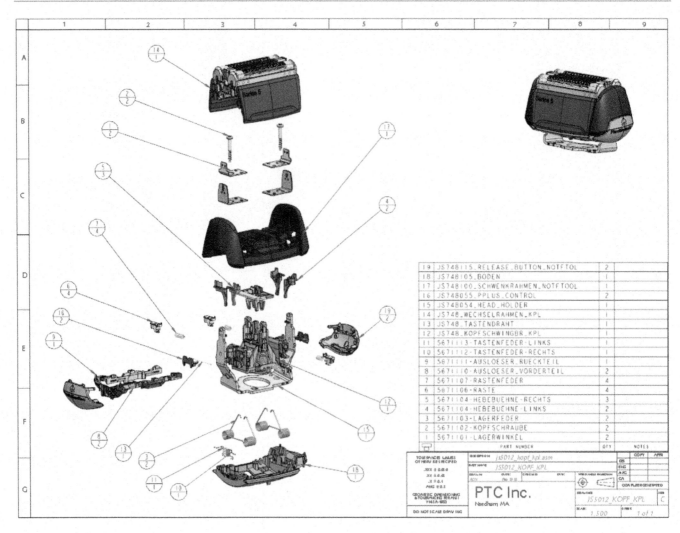

Example of a Color Shaded Exploded View Assembly from PTC® Creo® *(Copyright © PTC Inc.)*

Great looking assembly drawings are only one of the benefits of using 3D CAD for your designs. You can also check to see how parts fit together, perform tolerance studies, and even see how mechanisms you are designing will behave. Additionally, you can analyze the mass properties of your design, determine the volume and surface area of complicated shapes, and produce documentation drawings directly from the part models.

Software such as PTC® Creo® allows you to use color shaded views of models in the exploded view assembly drawing, as shown in the figure above.

As you decide whether to use a color shaded drawing or a black and white line drawing for an assembly drawing, consider whether and how the drawing will be reproduced. Shaded color views make it easy to identify and visualize the parts, but require color printing and copying to look their best on paper. This does not present a problem if you are distributing files electronically.

Even though color shaded drawings look great, there are times when black and white drawings are preferable, or required. For example, patent drawings must be black and white, showing visible lines and not hidden lines. Black and white drawings are also helpful in user manuals, which may be copied or printed in black and white.

With 3D CAD software, it is not difficult to switch between color shaded views, outlines, and views that show hidden lines to suit the particular need that the drawing will meet.

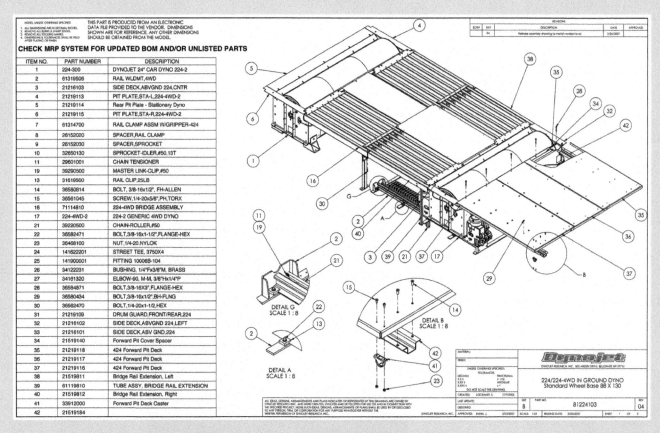

Assembly Drawing for Four Wheel Drive Pit Dyno *(Courtesy of Dynojet Research, Inc.)*

A cover sheet for architectural plans lists drawings in the set and abbreviations used. (Courtesy of Locati Architects.)

PORTFOLIO

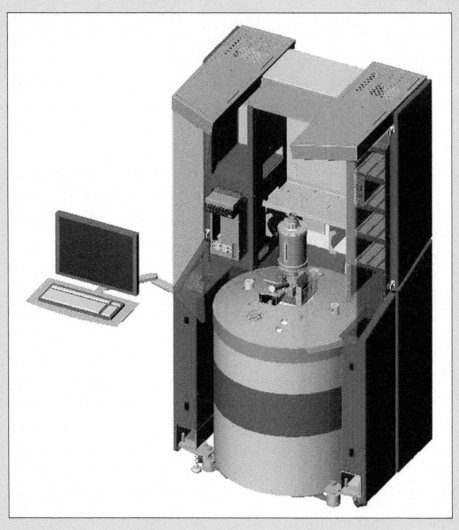

Fully Assembled 3D CAD Model Showing How Parts Fit in Assembly
(Courtesy of Quantum Design.)

KEY WORDS

Assembly Drawings

Assembly Layout

Ball Tags

Balloon Numbers

Bill of Materials

Check Assembly

Detail Drawings

Exploded View

Installation Assembly

Part Drawings

Parts List

Piece Part Drawings

Poche

Revision Number

Subassembly

Working Drawing Assembly

Working Drawings

CHAPTER SUMMARY

- The final drawings created during the design process include assembly drawings, working drawings, design drawings, and patent drawings.
- There are many revisions to drawings during the design process. The drafter must keep track of each version and what changes were made.
- Managing complex projects often involves considering how parts are grouped into subassemblies. Subassembly drawings are similar to assembly drawings, but show a group of parts rather than the entire project.
- Assembly drawings may use one of several different types of views, such as sections, exterior views, exploded views, pictorial views.
- A parts list or bill of materials tracks the items in the assembly or subassembly. As a minimum, it typically contains the item number, description, quantity, and material for the parts.

REVIEW QUESTIONS

1. What kinds of information are included in an assembly drawing?
2. How is a detail drawing different from an assembly drawing?
3. Why are drawings numbered? Why is this numbering so important?
4. Describe the drawing revision process. Why is it so important to keep track of revisions?
5. How are revised paper drawings stored? How are revised CAD drawings stored?
6. How does inserting parts to form subassemblies save time in documenting designs?
7. What are the special requirements of a patent drawing?

CHAPTER EXERCISES

Design Exercises

The following suggestions for project assignments are of a general and very broad nature, and it is expected that they will help generate many ideas for specific design projects. Much design work is undertaken to improve an existing product or system by utilization of new materials, new techniques, or new systems or procedures. In addition to the design of the product itself, another large amount of design work is essential for the tooling, production, and handling of the product. You are encouraged to discuss with your instructor any ideas you may have for a project.

Each solution to a design problem, whether prepared by an individual student or formulated by a group, should be in the form of a report, which should be typed or carefully lettered, assembled, and bound. It is suggested that the report contain the following (or variations of the following, as specified by your instructor):

1. A title sheet. The title of the design project should be placed in approximately the center of the sheet, and your name or the names of those in the group in the lower right-hand corner. The symbol PL should follow the name of the project leader.
2. Table of contents with page numbers.
3. Statement of the purpose of the project with appropriate comments.
4. Preliminary design sketches, with comments on advantages and disadvantages of each, leading to the final selection of the best solution. All work should be signed and dated.
5. An accurately made pictorial and/or assembly drawing(s), using traditional drawing methods or CAD as assigned, if more than one part is involved in the design.
6. Detail working drawings, freehand, mechanical, or CAD-produced as assigned. The 8.5″ × 11″ sheet size is preferred for convenient insertion in the report. Larger sizes may be bound in the report with appropriate folding.
7. A bibliography or credit for important sources of information, if applicable.

Exercise 14.1 Design new or improved playground, recreational, or sporting equipment. For example, a new child's toy could be both recreational and educational. Create an assembly drawing.

Exercise 14.2 Design new or improved health equipment. For example, physically handicapped people need special equipment.

Exercise 14.3 Design a cup holder attachment to retrofit cars. It must accommodate a range of cup sizes from 8 oz to 64 oz.

Exercise 14.4 Design a guitar stand to support either an acoustic or electric guitar. It should be convenient and stable, suitable for use on stage. Allow for quick change of guitars by the musician.

Exercise 14.5 Break up into design teams. See how many different ideas each team can come up with for a new layout of your classroom. Time limit is 20 minutes.

Exercise 14.6 Design a new or improved bike safety lock and chain. Integrate the locking devices into the bike's frame, if possible. Create an assembly drawing showing the features of your design.

Working Drawing Exercises

The problems in Exercises 14.7–14.62 are presented to give you practice in making the type of regular working drawings used in industry. Many exercises, especially assemblies, offer an opportunity to exercise your ability to redesign or improve on the existing design. Due to the variations in sizes and in scales that may be used, you are required to select the sheet sizes and scales, when these are not specified, subject to the approval of the instructor. Standard sheet layouts are shown inside the front cover of this book. (Any of the title forms shown inside the front cover of this book may be used, with modification if desired, or you may design the title block if assigned by the instructor.)

The statements for each problem are intentionally brief, and your instructor may vary the requirements. Use the preferred metric system or the acceptable complete decimal-inch system, as assigned.

In problems presented in pictorial form, the dimensions and finish marks are to provide you the information necessary to make the orthographic drawing or solid model. The dimensions given are in most cases those needed to make the parts, but due to the limitations of pictorial drawings they are not in all cases the dimensions that should be shown on the working drawing. In the pictorial problems, the rough and finished surfaces are shown, but finish marks are usually omitted. You should add all necessary finish marks and place all dimensions in the preferred places in the final drawings.

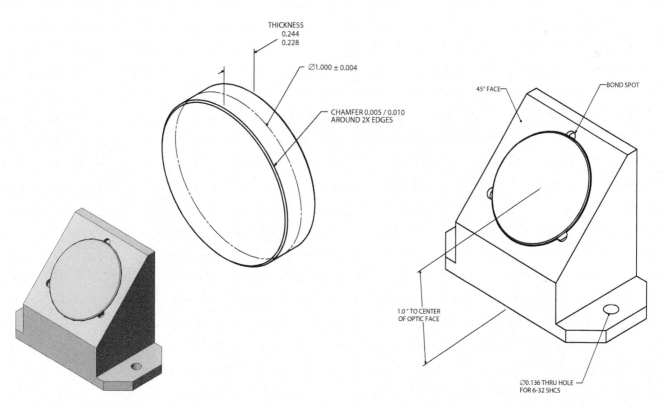

Exercise 14.7 Create part drawings and an assembly for the optical lens and mount. Maintain the critical distances and precise 45° angle for the lens.

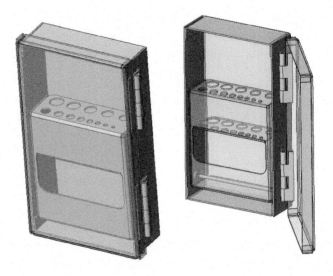

Exercise 14.8 Design the sheet metal housing for the power and D-sub connectors shown. Download stock models for standard parts. Create the flat patterns for the sheet metal if assigned by your instructor.

Exercise 14.9 Design a sheet metal drill bit case. Create detailed part and assembly drawings. Develop the flat patterns if assigned. Use "relations" in your model so that you can change the sizes for the holes and overall height, width and depth for the case and automatically update your design to different configurations.

Exercise 14.10 Create an exploded assembly drawing for the gyroscope. Create detail drawings for the parts as assigned by your instructor. Dimensioned parts are shown on the facing page.

Exercise 14.11 Create an exploded assembly drawing for the clamp. Dimensioned parts are shown on pages 662–663.

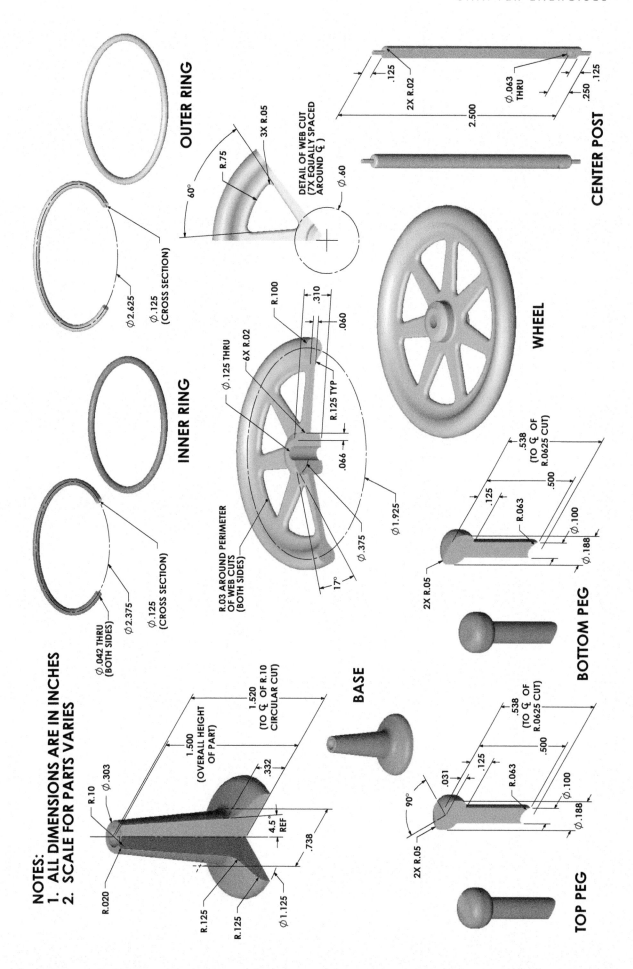

NOTES:
1. ALL DIMENSIONS ARE IN INCHES
2. SCALE FOR PARTS VARIES

OUTER RING

3X R.05

R.75

60°

DETAIL OF WEB CUT
(7X EQUALLY SPACED
AROUND ℄)

⌀.60

⌀2.625

⌀.125
(CROSS SECTION)

INNER RING

⌀.042 THRU
(BOTH SIDES)

⌀2.375

⌀.125
(CROSS SECTION)

CENTER POST

.125

2X R.02

2.500

⌀.063
THRU

.250

.125

WHEEL

R.100

.310

.060

⌀.125 THRU

6X R.02

R.125 TYP

.066

R.03 AROUND PERIMETER
OF WEB CUTS
(BOTH SIDES)

⌀1.925

⌀.375

17°

BASE

1.500
(OVERALL HEIGHT
OF PART)

1.520
(TO ℄ OF R.10
CIRCULAR CUT)

⌀.303

R.10

.332

4.5°
REF

.738

R.020

R.125

R.125

⌀1.125

BOTTOM PEG

.538
(TO ℄ OF
R.0625 CUT)

.500

.125

R.063

⌀.100

⌀.188

2X R.05

TOP PEG

.538
(TO ℄ OF
R.0625 CUT)

.500

.031

.125

R.063

⌀.100

⌀.188

90°

2X R.05

Exercise 14.10 Gyroscope, continued

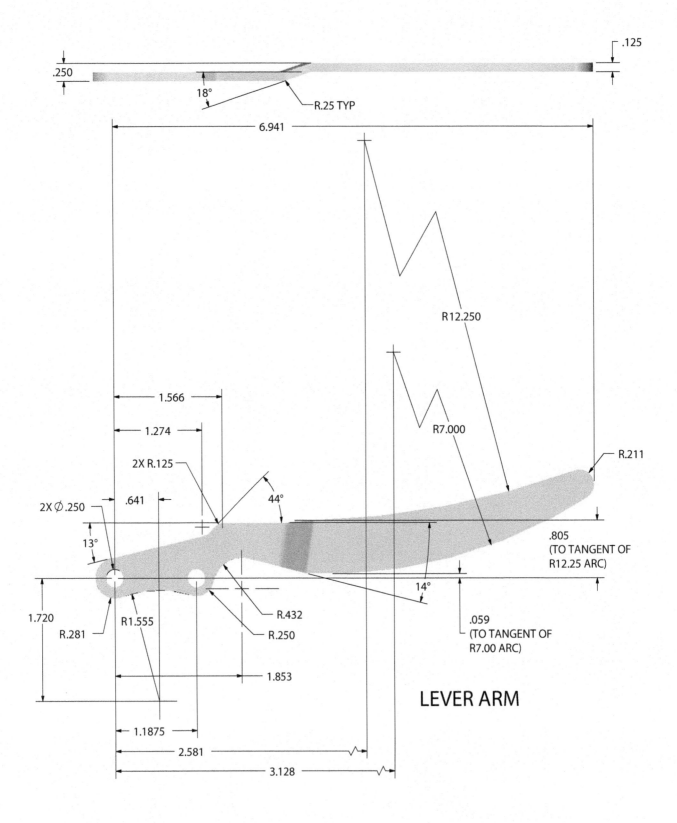

.125

.250

18°

R.25 TYP

6.941

R12.250

R7.000

R.211

1.566

1.274

2X R.125

44°

2X Ø.250

.641

13°

.805
(TO TANGENT OF
R12.25 ARC)

14°

1.720

R.432

R.281

R1.555

R.250

.059
(TO TANGENT OF
R7.00 ARC)

1.853

LEVER ARM

1.1875

2.581

3.128

Exercise 14.11 Clamp, continued

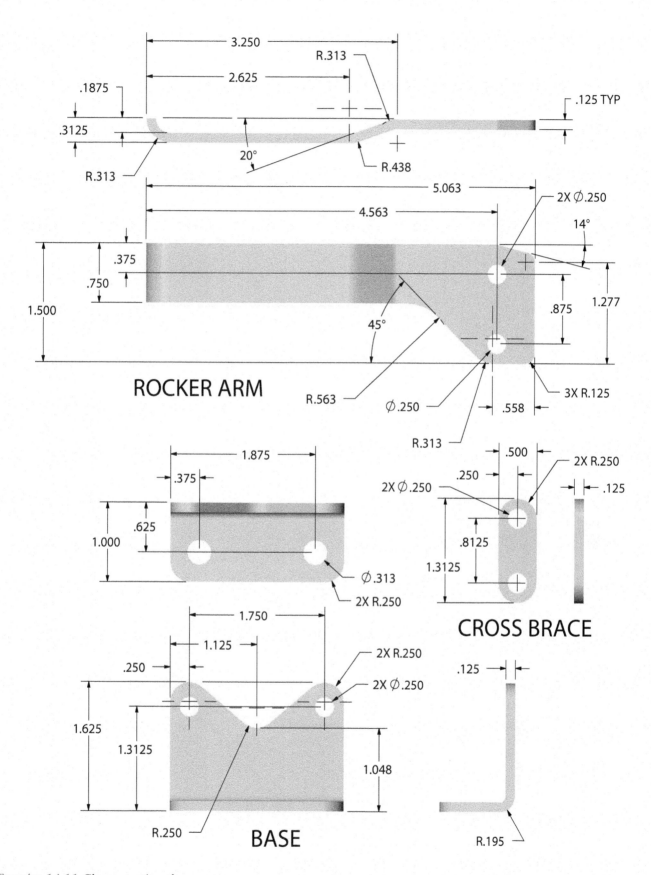

ROCKER ARM

CROSS BRACE

BASE

Exercise 14.11 Clamp, *continued*

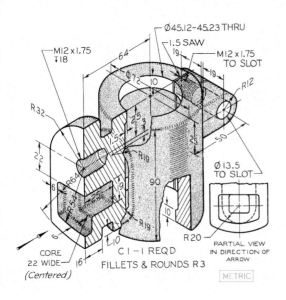

Exercise 14.12 Make a detail drawing for the table bracket.

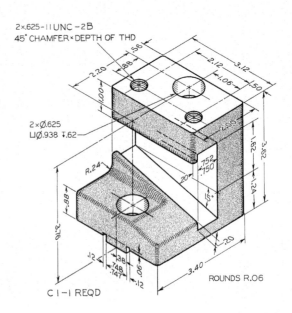

Exercise 14.13 Make a detail drawing for the RH tool post. If assigned, convert dimensions to metric.

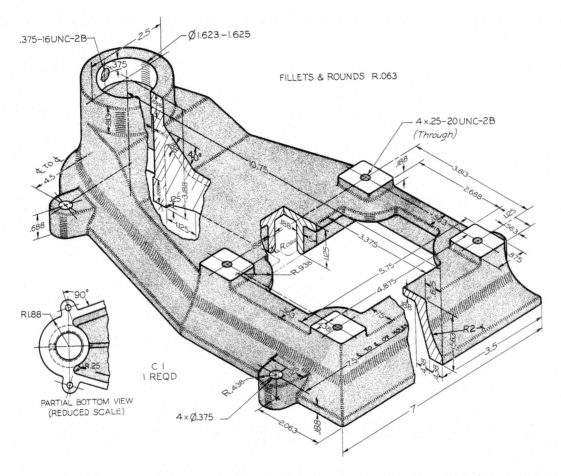

Exercise 14.14 Make a detail drawing for the drill press base. Use unidirectional metric or decimal-inch dimensions.

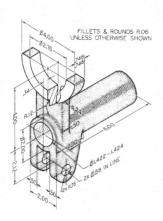

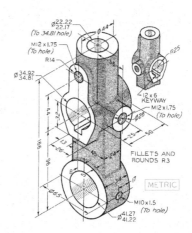

Exercise 14.15 Make a detail drawing for the shifter fork. If assigned, convert dimensions to metric system.

Exercise 14.16 Make a detail drawing for the idler arm.

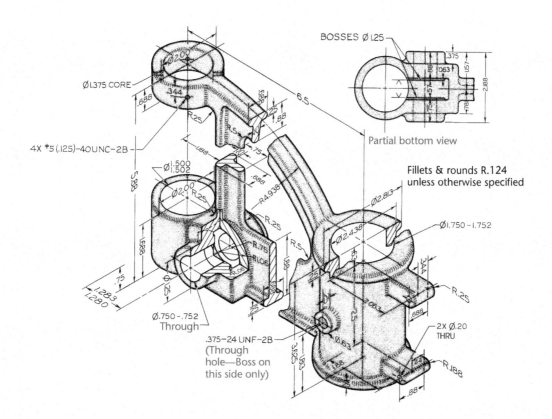

Exercise 14.17 Make a detail drawing for the drill press bracket. If assigned, convert dimensions to decimal inches or redesign the part with metric dimensions.

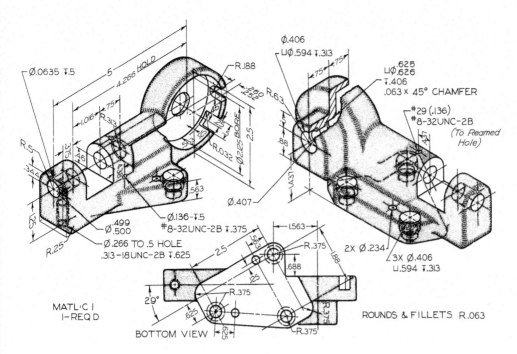

Exercise 14.18 Make a detail drawing for the dial holder. If assigned, convert dimensions to decimal inches or redesign the part with metric dimensions.

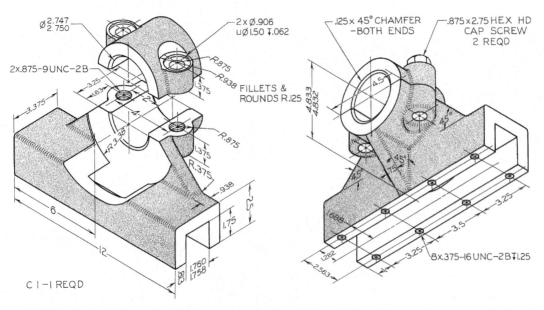

Exercise 14.19 Make detail drawings half size for the rack slide. If assigned, convert dimensions to decimal inches or redesign the part with metric dimensions.

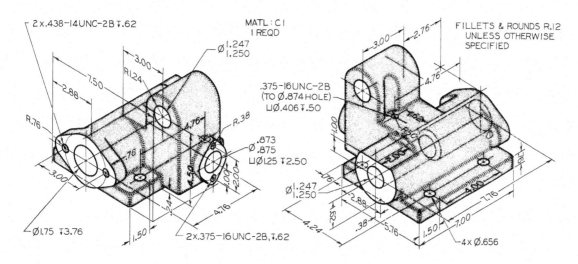

Exercise 14.20 Make a detail drawing half size for the automatic stop box. If assigned, redesign the part with metric dimensions.

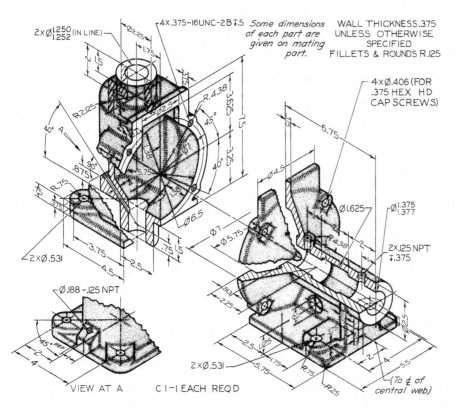

Exercise 14.21 Make detail drawings half size for the conveyer housing. If assigned, convert dimensions to decimal inches or redesign the parts with metric dimensions.

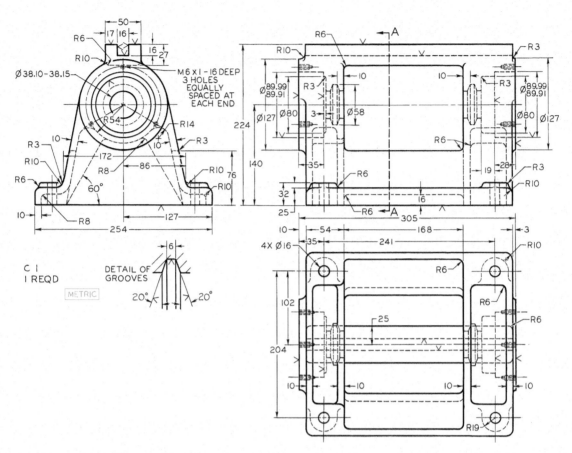

Exercise 14.22 For the spindle housing, draw as follows. Given: Front, left-side, and bottom views, and partial removed section. Required: Front view in full section, top view, and right-side view in half section on A-A. Draw half size. If assigned, dimension fully.

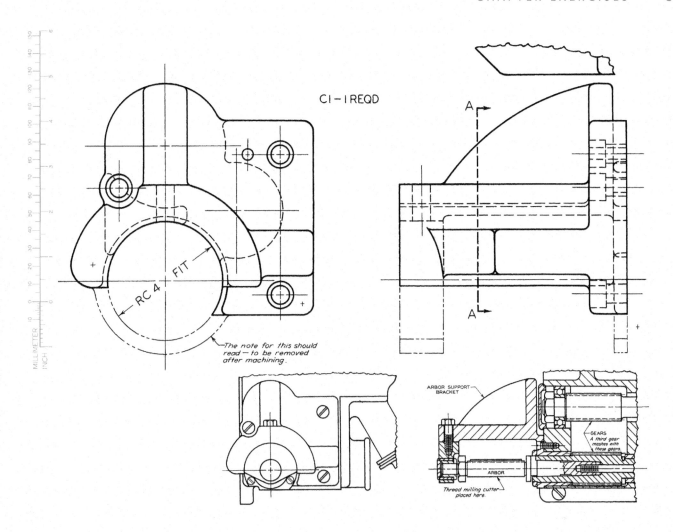

CI – I REQD

The note for this should read — to be removed after machining.

ARBOR SUPPORT BRACKET

GEARS
A third gear meshes with these gears.

ARBOR

Thread milling cutter placed here.

Exercise 14.23 For the arbor support bracket, draw the following. Given: Front and right-side views. Required: Front, left-side, and bottom views, and a detail section A-A. Use American National Standard tables for indicated fits and, if required, convert to metric values (see Appendices 4–13). If assigned, dimension in the metric or decimal-inch system.

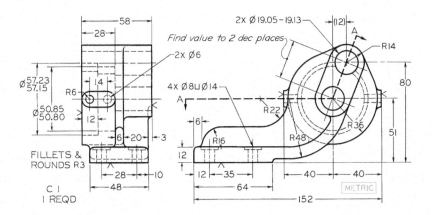

FILLETS & ROUNDS R3

C I
I REQD

METRIC

Exercise 14.24 For the pump bracket for a thread milling machine, draw the following. Given: Front and left-side views. Required: Front and right-side views, and top view in section on A-A. Draw full size. If assigned, dimension fully.

Exercise 14.25 For the support base for planer, draw the following. Given: Front and top views. Required: Front and top views, left-side view in full section A-A, and removed section B-B. Draw full size. If assigned, dimension fully.

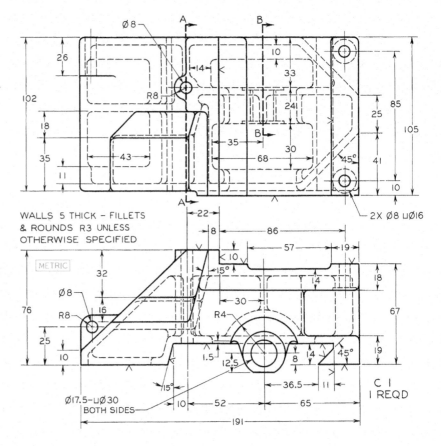

Exercise 14.26 For the jaw base for chuck jaw, draw the following. Given: Top, right-side, and partial auxiliary views. Required: Top, left-side (beside top), front, and partial auxiliary views complete with dimensions, if assigned. Use metric or decimal-inch dimensions. Use American National Standard tables for indicated fits, or convert to metric values (see Appendices 4–13).

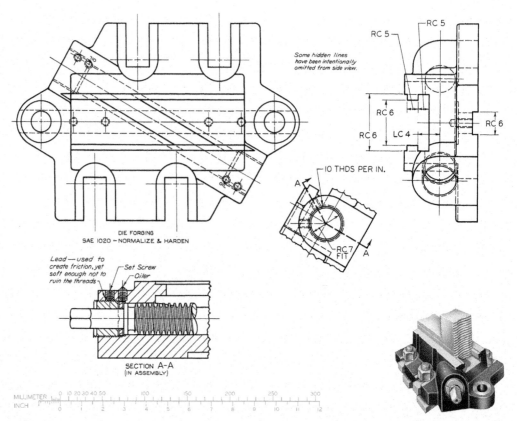

Exercise 14.27 For the fixture base for 60-ton vertical press, draw the following. Given: Front and right-side views. Required: Revolve front view 90° clockwise, then add top and left-side views. Draw half size. If assigned, complete with dimensions.

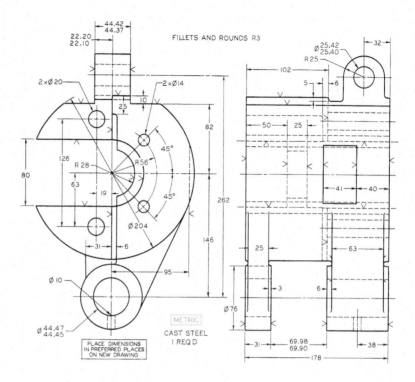

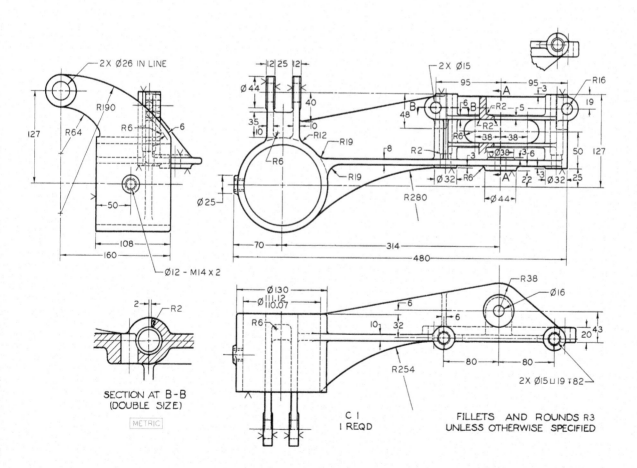

Exercise 14.28 For the bracket, draw the following. Given: Front, left-side, and bottom views, and partial removed section. Required: Make detail drawing. Draw front, top, and right-side views, and removed sections A-A and B-B. Draw half size. Draw section B-B full size. If assigned, complete with dimensions.

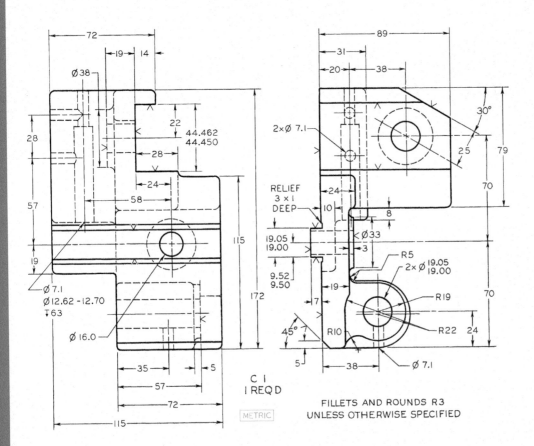

Exercise 14.29 For the roller rest bracket for automatic screw machine, draw the following. Given: Front and left-side views. Required: Revolve front view 90° clockwise, then add top and left-side views. Draw half size. If assigned, complete with dimensions.

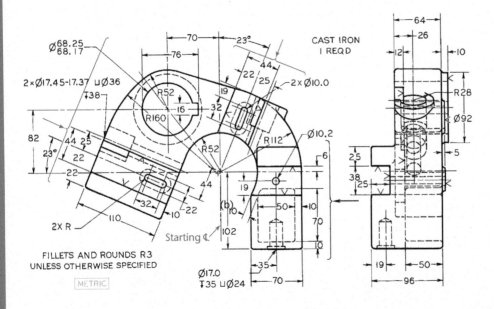

Exercise 14.30 For the guide bracket for gear shaper, draw the following. Given: Front and right-side views. Required: Front view, a partial right-side view, and two partial auxiliary views taken in direction of arrows. Draw half size. If assigned, complete with unidirectional dimensions.

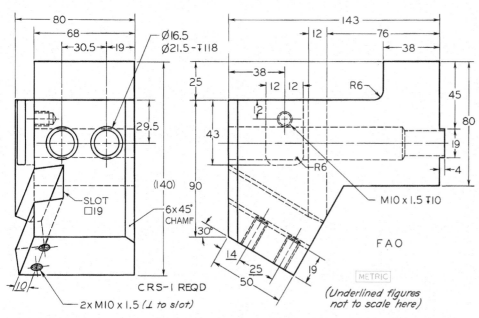

Exercise 14.31 For the rear tool post, draw the following. Given: Front and left-side views. Required: Take left-side view as new top view; add front and left-side views, approx. 215 mm apart, a primary auxiliary view, then a secondary view taken so as to show true end view of 19 mm slot. Complete all views, except show only necessary hidden lines in auxiliary views. Draw full size. If assigned, complete with dimensions.

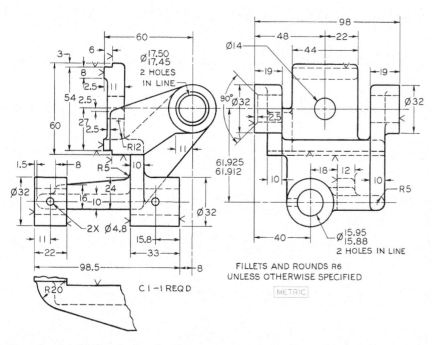

Exercise 14.32 For the bearing for a worm gear, draw the following. Given: Front and right-side views. Required: Front, top, and left-side views. Draw full size. If assigned, complete with dimensions.

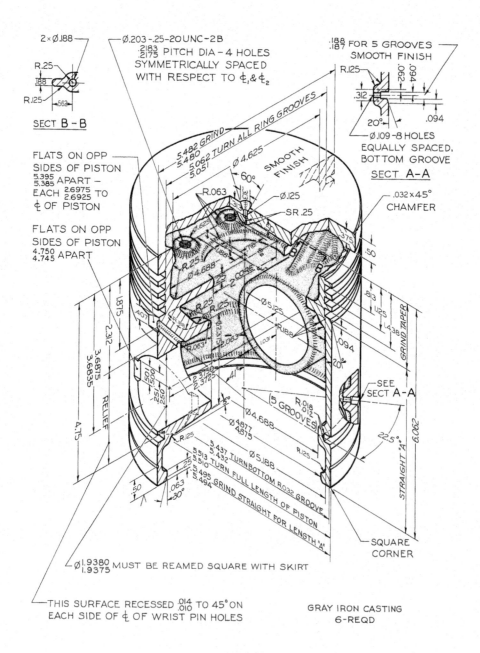

Exercise 14.33 For the caterpillar tractor piston, draw the following. Make detail drawing full size. If assigned, use unidirectional decimal-inch system, converting all fractions to two place decimal dimensions, or convert all dimensions to metric.

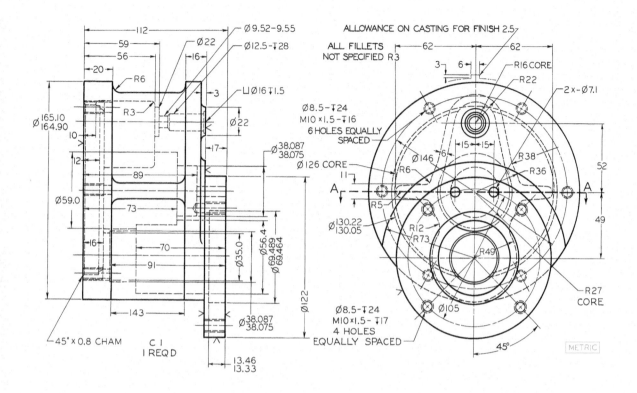

Exercise 14.34 For the generator drive housing, draw the following. Given: Front and left-side views. Required: Front view, right-side view in full section, and top view in full section on A-A. Draw full size. If assigned, complete with dimensions.

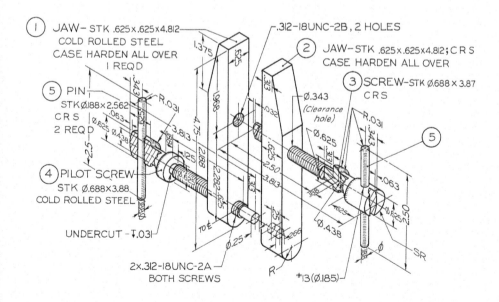

Exercise 14.35 For the machinist's clamp, draw the following. Draw details and assembly. If assigned, use unidirectional two place decimal-inch dimensions or redesign for metric dimensions.

Exercise 14.36 For the hand rail
column, draw the following.
(1) Draw details. If assigned, complete
with dimensions.
(2) Draw assembly.

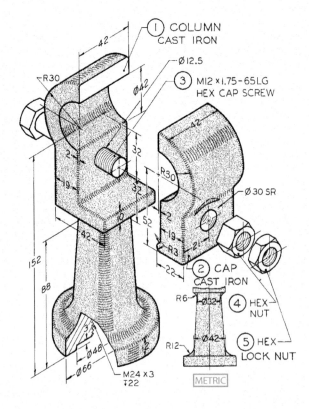

Exercise 14.37 For the drill jig, draw
the following.
(1) Draw details. If assigned, complete
with dimensions.
(2) Draw assembly.

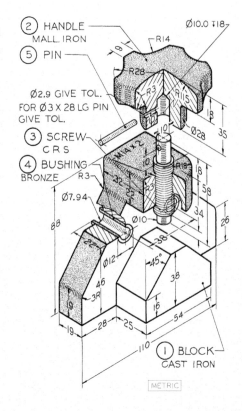

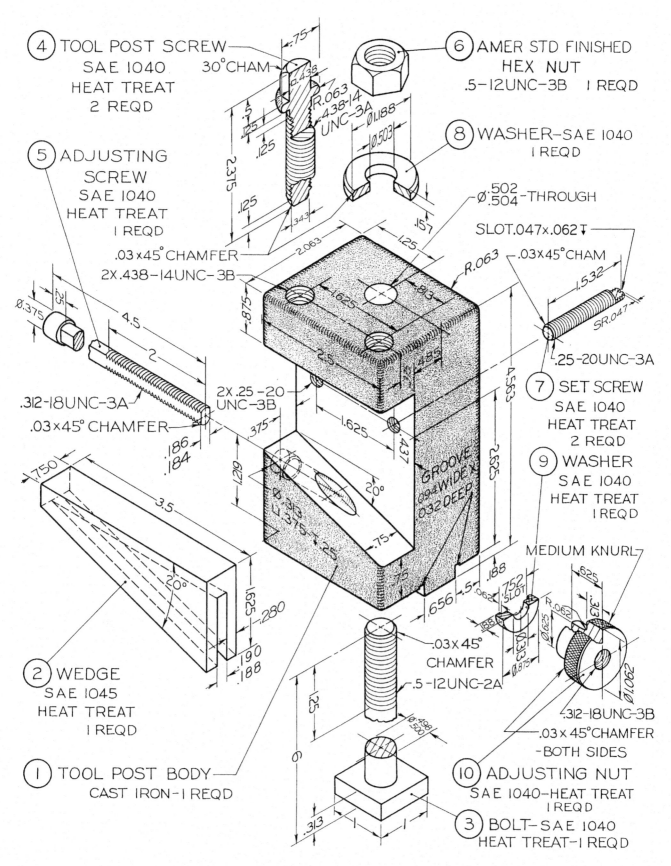

Exercise 14.38 For the tool post, draw the following. (1) Draw details. (2) Draw assembly. If assigned, use unidirectional two place decimals for all fractional dimensions or redesign for all metric dimensions.

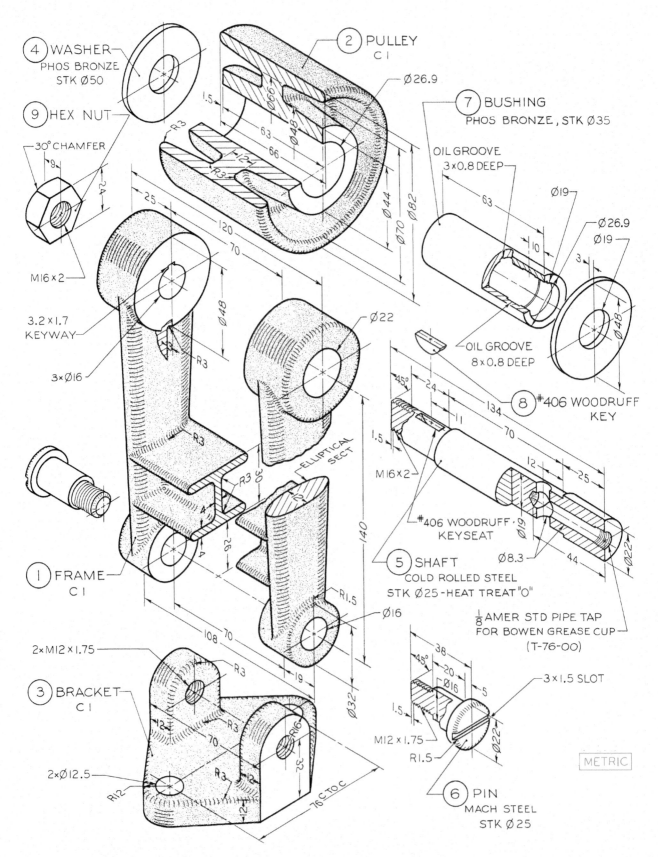

Exercise 14.39 For the belt tightener, draw the following. (1) Draw details. (2) Draw assembly. It is assumed that the parts are to be made in quantity, and they are to be dimensioned for interchangeability on the detail drawings. Use tables in Appendices 4–7 for limit values. Design as follows. (a) Bushing fit in pulley: locational interference fit. (b) Shaft fit in bushing: free-running fit. (c) Shaft fits in frame: sliding fit. (d) Pin fit in frame: free-running fit. (e) Pulley hub length plus washers fit in frame: allowance 0.13 and tolerances 0.10. (f) Make bushing 0.25 mm shorter than pulley hub. (g) Bracket fit in frame: Same as (e).

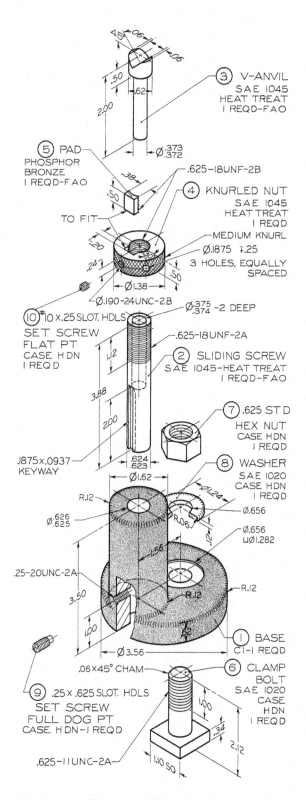

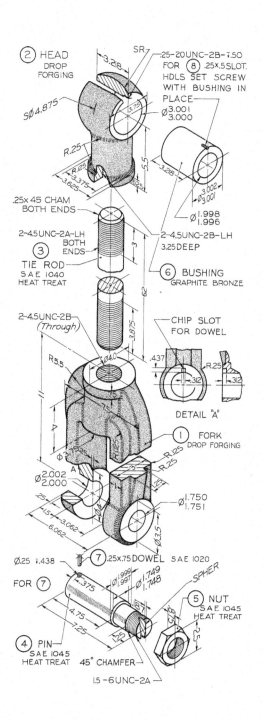

Exercise 14.40 For the milling jack, draw the following. (1) Draw details. (2) Draw assembly. If assigned, convert dimensions to metric or decimal-inch system.

Exercise 14.41 For the connecting bar, draw the following. (1) Draw details. (2) Draw assembly. If assigned, convert dimensions to metric or decimal-inch system.

Exercise 14.42 For the clamp stop, draw the following. (1) Draw details. (2) Draw assembly. If assigned, convert dimensions to decimal-inch system or redesign for metric dimensions.

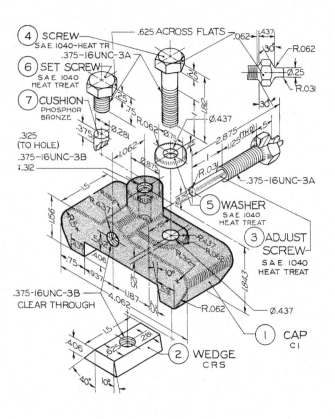

Exercise 14.43 For the pillow block bearing, draw the following. (1) Draw details. (2) Draw assembly. If assigned, complete with dimensions.

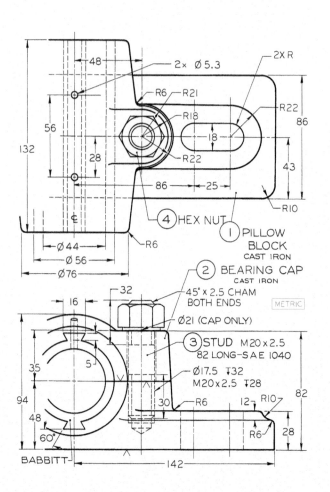

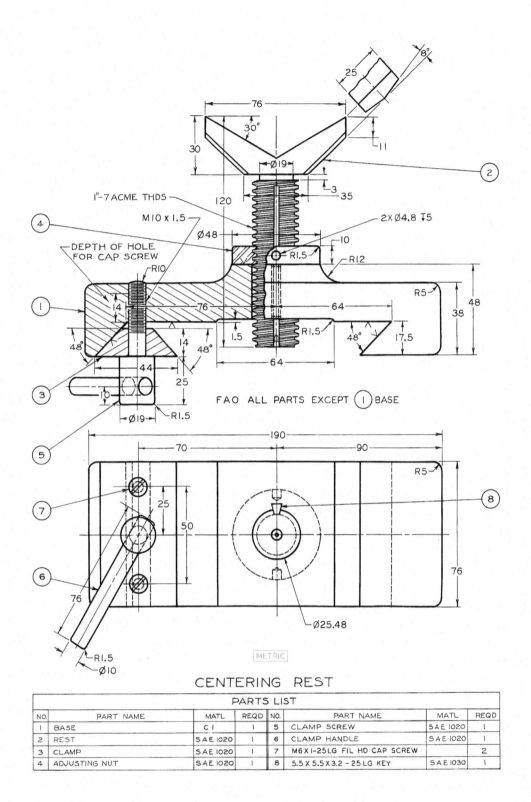

CENTERING REST

METRIC

PARTS LIST							
NO.	PART NAME	MATL	REQD	NO.	PART NAME	MATL	REQD
1	BASE	C I	1	5	CLAMP SCREW	SAE 1020	1
2	REST	SAE 1020	1	6	CLAMP HANDLE	SAE 1020	1
3	CLAMP	SAE 1020	1	7	M6X1-25LG FIL HD CAP SCREW		2
4	ADJUSTING NUT	SAE 1020	1	8	5.5X5.5X3.2-25LG KEY	SAE 1030	1

Exercise 14.44 For the centering rest, draw the following. (1) Draw details. (2) Draw assembly. If assigned, complete with dimensions.

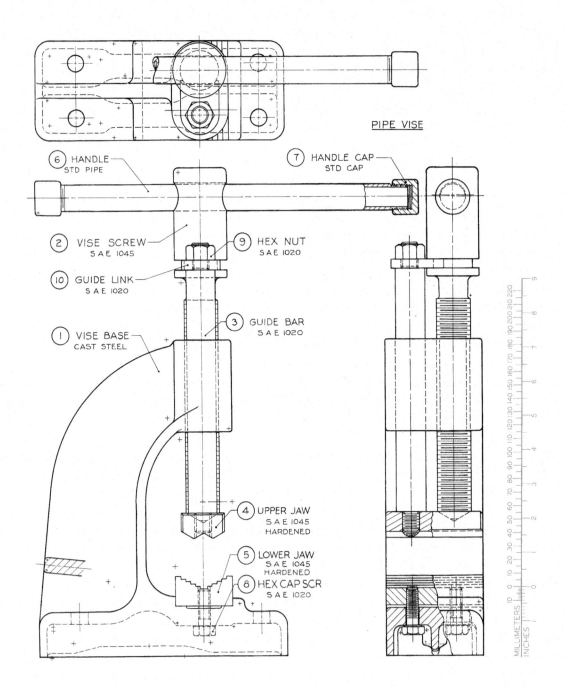

PIPE VISE

⑥ HANDLE
STD PIPE

⑦ HANDLE CAP
STD CAP

② VISE SCREW
S A E 1045

⑨ HEX NUT
S A E 1020

⑩ GUIDE LINK
S A E 1020

③ GUIDE BAR
S A E 1020

① VISE BASE
CAST STEEL

④ UPPER JAW
S A E 1045
HARDENED

⑤ LOWER JAW
S A E 1045
HARDENED

⑧ HEX CAP SCR
S A E 1020

MILLIMETERS
INCHES

Exercise 14.45 For the pipe vise, draw the following. (1) Draw details. (2) Draw assembly. To obtain dimensions, take distances directly from figure with dividers; then set dividers on printed scale and read measurements in millimeters or decimal inches as assigned. All threads are general-purpose metric threads (see Appendix 14) or unified coarse threads except the American National Standard pipe threads on handle and handle caps.

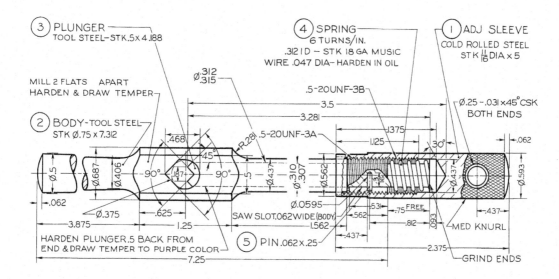

Exercise 14.46 For the tap wrench, draw the following. (1) Draw details. (2) Draw assembly. If assigned, use unidirectional two place decimals for all fractional dimensions or redesign for metric dimensions.

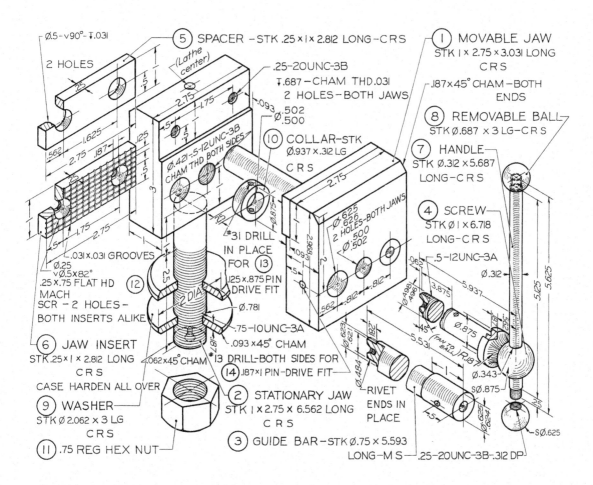

Exercise 14.47 For the machinist's vise, draw the following. (1) Draw details. (2) Draw assembly. If assigned, use standard symbols and unidirectional two-place decimals for all fractional dimensions or redesign for metric dimensions.

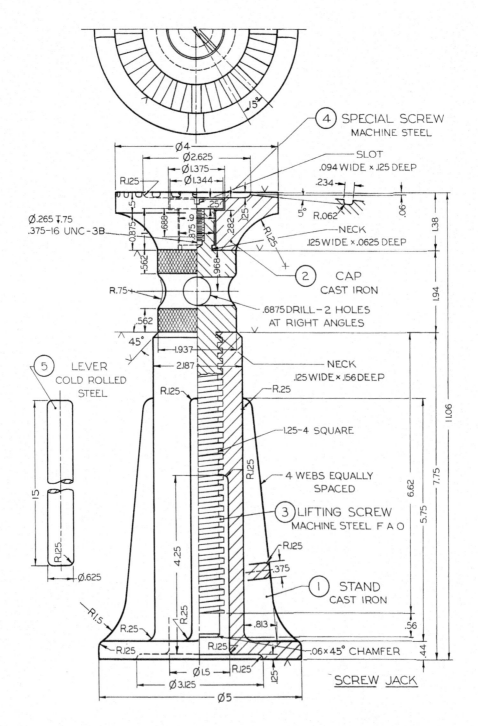

Exercise 14.48 For the screw jack, draw the following. (1) Draw details. (2) Draw assembly. If assigned, convert dimensions to decimal inches or redesign for metric dimensions.

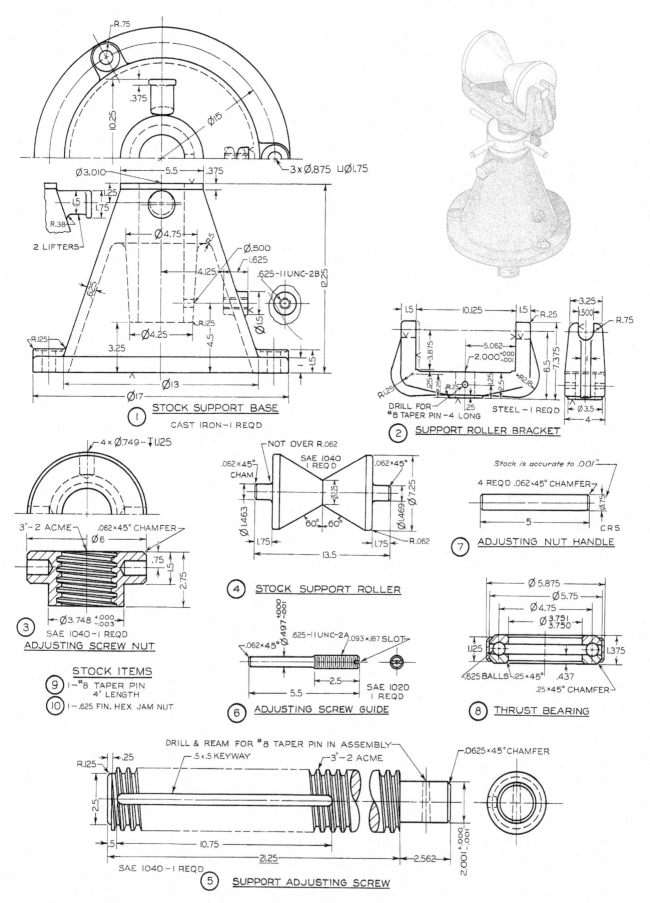

① **STOCK SUPPORT BASE**
CAST IRON—1 REQD

② **SUPPORT ROLLER BRACKET**
STEEL — 1 REQD

③ **ADJUSTING SCREW NUT**
SAE 1040 — 1 REQD

④ **STOCK SUPPORT ROLLER**
SAE 1040 1 REQD

⑥ **ADJUSTING SCREW GUIDE**
SAE 1020 1 REQD

⑦ **ADJUSTING NUT HANDLE**
CRS

⑧ **THRUST BEARING**

STOCK ITEMS
⑨ 1—#8 TAPER PIN 4" LENGTH
⑩ 1—.625 FIN. HEX JAM NUT

⑤ **SUPPORT ADJUSTING SCREW**
SAE 1040—1 REQD

Exercise 14.49 For the stock bracket for cold saw machine, draw the following. (1) Draw details. (2) Draw assembly. If assigned, use unidirectional decimal dimensions or redesign for metric dimensions.

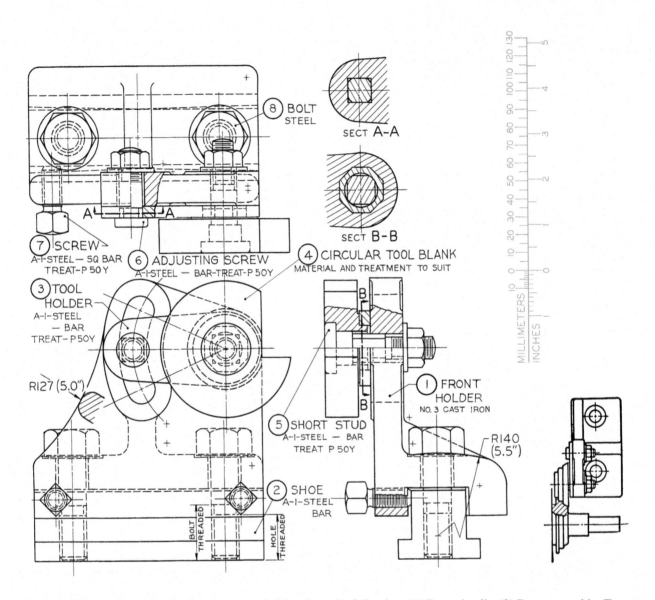

Exercise 14.50 For the front circular forming cutter holder, draw the following. (1) Draw details. (2) Draw assembly. To obtain dimensions, take distances directly from figure with dividers and set dividers on printed scale. Use metric or decimal-inch dimensions as assigned.

Exercise 14.51 For the machine vise on the facing page, draw the following. (1) Draw details. (2) Draw assembly. If assigned, convert dimensions to the decimal-inch system or redesign with metric dimensions.

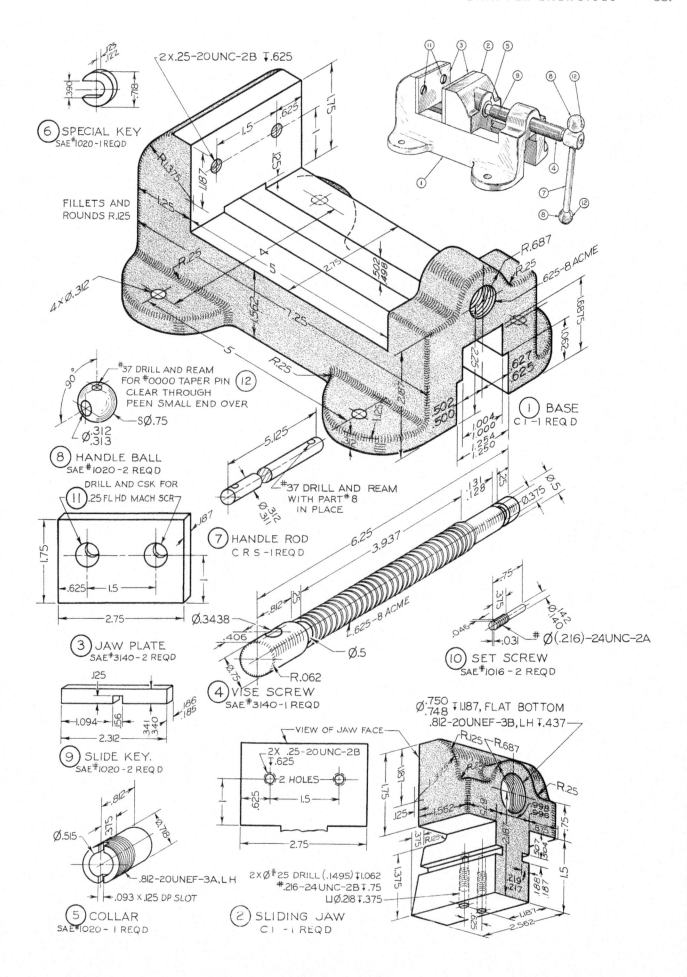

.125
.122
.390
.718

2 x .25-20UNC-2B ⊤.625

⑥ SPECIAL KEY
SAE #1020 - 1 REQD

FILLETS AND
ROUNDS R.125

.625
1.5
1.75
.125
.187
R.1375
1.25
R.25
4 x Ø.312
5
4
7.25
R.25
2.75
.502
.498
.562
.562
.2.87
.125
3.12

R.687
R.25
.625-8 ACME
1.6875
1.062
.627
.625
.502
.500
2.25
1.004
1.000
1.254
1.250
.25

① BASE
C I - 1 REQ D

90°
#37 DRILL AND REAM
FOR #0000 TAPER PIN ⑫
CLEAR THROUGH
PEEN SMALL END OVER
S Ø.75
Ø.312
.313

⑧ HANDLE BALL
SAE #1020 - 2 REQD

5.125
Ø.312
.311

#37 DRILL AND REAM
WITH PART #8
IN PLACE

⑦ HANDLE ROD
C R S - 1 REQ D

.131
.128
.25
Ø.375
Ø.5
6.25
3.937
.625-8 ACME

DRILL AND CSK FOR
⑪ .25 FL HD MACH SCR
.187
1.75
.625
1.5
2.75

③ JAW PLATE
SAE #3140 - 2 REQD

Ø.3438
.812
.25
.406
Ø.75
R.062

④ VISE SCREW
SAE #3140 - 1 REQD

.75
.375
Ø.142
.140
.046
.031
Ø(.216)-24UNC-2A

⑩ SET SCREW
SAE #1016 - 2 REQD

.125
.186
.185
1.094
.156
.341
.340
2.312

⑨ SLIDE KEY.
SAE #1020 - 2 REQD

— VIEW OF JAW FACE —
2X .25-20UNC-2B
⊤.625
2 HOLES
.625
1.5
.625
2.75
2 x Ø #25 DRILL (.1495) ⊤1.062
#.216-24UNC-2B ⊤.75
⊔ Ø.218 ⊤.375

Ø.750 ⊤1.187, FLAT BOTTOM
.748
.812-20UNEF-3B, LH ⊤.437
R.125 R.687
R.25
R.25
.187
1.75
.125
1.562
.875
.375 R.125
.998
.996
.75
2.87
.507
.504
.219
.217
.188
.187
1.187
2.562
1.375
.625
1.5

② SLIDING JAW
C I - 1 REQ D

.812
.375
Ø.515
.718
.812-20UNEF-3A, LH
.093 x .125 DP SLOT

⑤ COLLAR
SAE #1020 - 1 REQD

Exercise 14.52 For the grinder vise, draw the following. (1) Draw details. (2) Draw assembly. If assigned, convert dimensions to decimal inches or redesign with metric dimensions. See part details on the following pages.

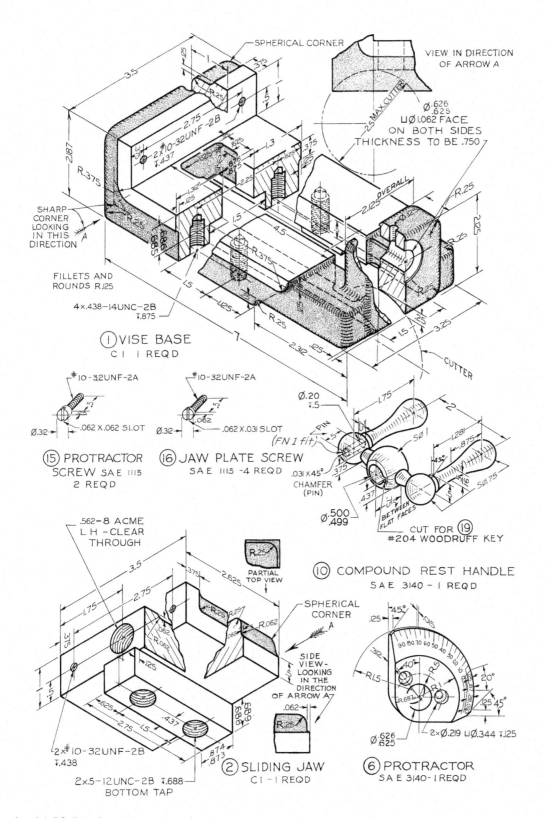

SPHERICAL CORNER

VIEW IN DIRECTION
OF ARROW A

Ø.626
.625
⊔Ø1.062 FACE
ON BOTH SIDES
THICKNESS TO BE .750

2.5 MAX CUTTER

2×#10-32UNF-2B
⊤.437

R.375

SHARP
CORNER
LOOKING
IN THIS
DIRECTION

FILLETS AND
ROUNDS R.125

4×.438-14UNC-2B
⊤.875

①VISE BASE
C I   I REQD

OVERALL

R.25

R.25

#10-32UNF-2A

#10-32UNF-2A

Ø.20
⊤.5

PIN

Ø.312   .062×.062 SLOT

Ø.312   .062   .062×.031 SLOT

(FN 1 fit)

⑮ PROTRACTOR
SCREW SAE 1115
2 REQD

⑯ JAW PLATE SCREW
SAE 1115 -4 REQD

Ø.500
.499

.031×45°
CHAMFER
(PIN)

.437

CUT FOR ⑲
#204 WOODRUFF KEY

SØ.75

U
BETWEEN
FLAT FACES

⑩ COMPOUND REST HANDLE
SAE 3140 - 1 REQD

CUTTER

.562-8 ACME
L H - CLEAR
THROUGH

PARTIAL
TOP VIEW

SPHERICAL
CORNER

SIDE
VIEW-
LOOKING
IN THE
DIRECTION
OF ARROW A

R.062

R.25

2×#10-32UNF-2B
⊤.438

2×.5-12UNC-2B ⊤.688
BOTTOM TAP

② SLIDING JAW
C I - I REQD

⑥ PROTRACTOR
SAE 3140-1 REQD

Ø.626
.625

2×Ø.219 ⊔Ø.344 ⊤.125

Exercise 14.52 Grinder vise, continued.

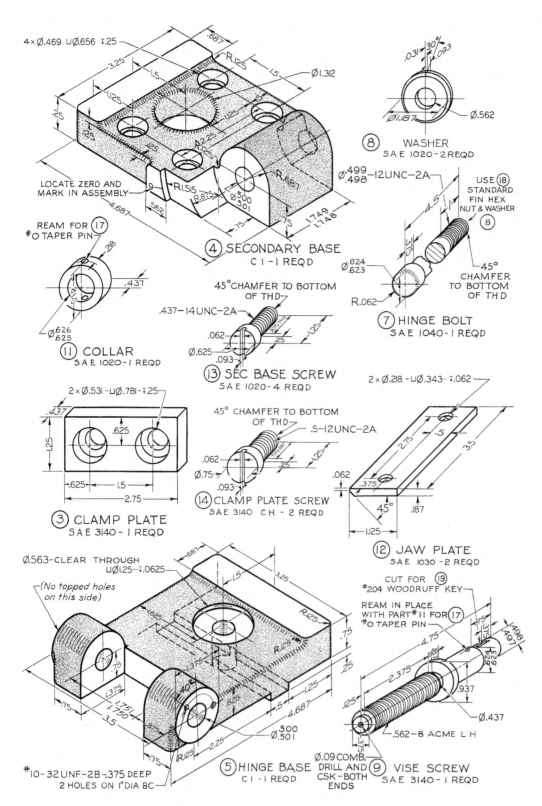

Exercise 14.52 Grinder vise, continued.

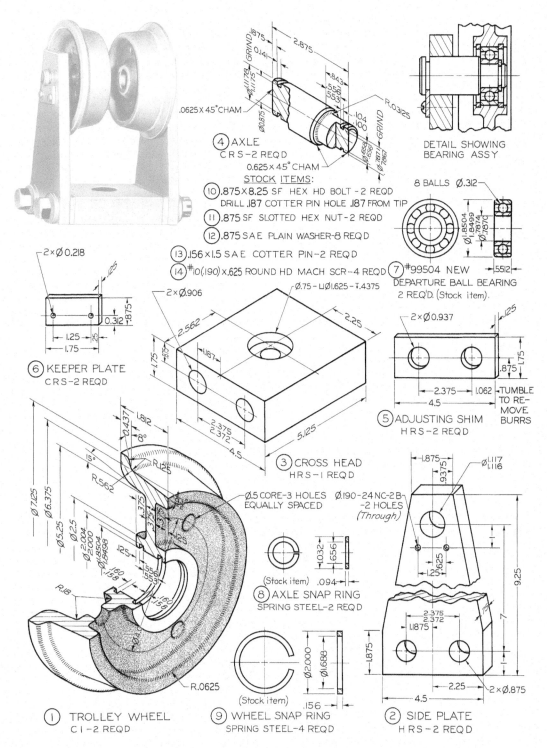

(4) AXLE
C R S – 2 REQ D

.0625 X 45° CHAM

0.625 X 45° CHAM

GRIND

R.03I25

**DETAIL SHOWING
BEARING ASS'Y**

STOCK ITEMS:

(10) .875 X 8.25 SF HEX HD BOLT – 2 REQD
DRILL .187 COTTER PIN HOLE .187 FROM TIP

(11) .875 SF SLOTTED HEX NUT – 2 REQD

(12) .875 SAE PLAIN WASHER – 8 REQD

(13) .156 X I.5 SAE COTTER PIN – 2 REQD

(14) #I0 (.190) X .625 ROUND HD MACH SCR – 4 REQD

8 BALLS Ø.312

(7) #99504 NEW
DEPARTURE BALL BEARING
2 REQ'D. (Stock item).

2 × Ø 0.218

(6) KEEPER PLATE
C R S – 2 REQ D

2 × Ø.906

Ø.75 – IIØI.625 – ⊤.4375

(3) CROSS HEAD
H R S – I REQ D

2 × Ø 0.937

(5) ADJUSTING SHIM
H R S – 2 REQ D

TUMBLE
TO RE-
MOVE
BURRS

Ø.5 CORE – 3 HOLES
EQUALLY SPACED

Ø.190 – 24 NC – 2 B
– 2 HOLES
(Through)

(8) AXLE SNAP RING
SPRING STEEL – 2 REQ D

(Stock item)

Ø2.000
Ø1.688

(9) WHEEL SNAP RING
SPRING STEEL – 4 REQ D

(Stock item)

(1) TROLLEY WHEEL
C I – 2 REQ D

R.0625

R.I8

(2) SIDE PLATE
H R S – 2 REQ D

2 × Ø.875

Exercise 14.53 For the trolley, draw the following. (1) Draw details, omitting parts 7–14. (2) Draw assembly. If assigned, convert dimensions to decimal inches or redesign for metric dimensions.

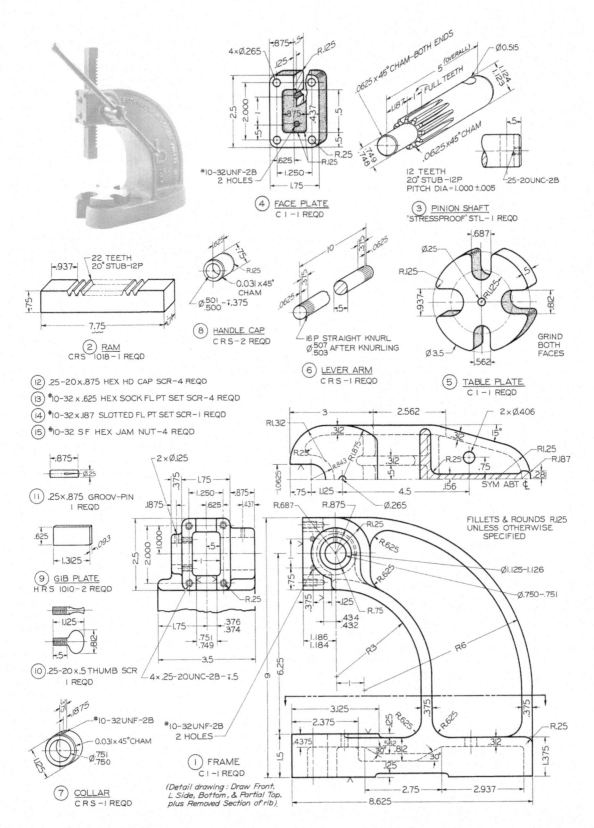

Exercise 14.54 For the arbor press, draw the following. (1) Draw details. (2) Draw assembly. If assigned, convert dimensions to decimal inches or redesign for metric dimensions.

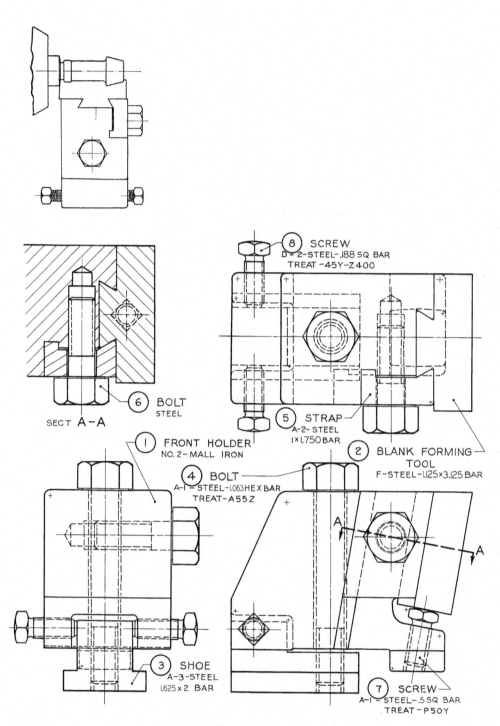

8 SCREW
D-2-STEEL-.188 SQ BAR
TREAT-45Y-Z400

6 BOLT
STEEL

SECT A-A

5 STRAP
A-2- STEEL
I×1.750 BAR

1 FRONT HOLDER
NO. 2- MALL IRON

2 BLANK FORMING
TOOL
F-STEEL-1.125×3.125 BAR

4 BOLT
A-I - STEEL-1.063 HEX BAR
TREAT-A55Z

A A

3 SHOE
A-3-STEEL
1.625 × 2 BAR

7 SCREW
A-I - STEEL-.5 SQ BAR
TREAT-P50Y

Exercise 14.55 For the forming cutter holder, draw the following. (1) Draw details using decimal or metric dimensions. (2) Draw assembly. Above layout is half size. To obtain dimensions, take distances directly from figure with dividers and double them. At top-left is shown the top view of the forming cutter holder in use on the lathe.

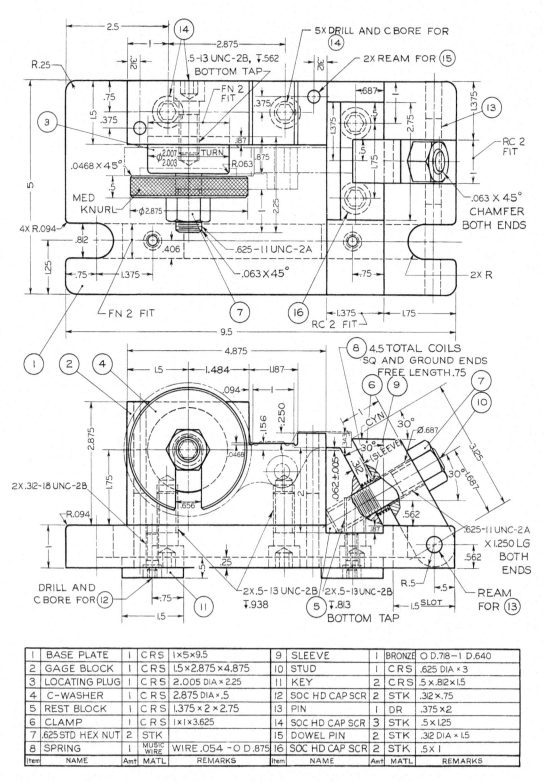

Item	NAME	Amt	MATL	REMARKS	Item	NAME	Amt	MATL	REMARKS
1	BASE PLATE	1	CRS	1×5×9.5	9	SLEEVE	1	BRONZE	O D.718–1 D.640
2	GAGE BLOCK	1	CRS	1.5×2.875×4.875	10	STUD	1	CRS	.625 DIA × 3
3	LOCATING PLUG	1	CRS	2.005 DIA × 2.25	11	KEY	2	CRS	.5×.812×1.5
4	C-WASHER	1	CRS	2.875 DIA×.5	12	SOC HD CAP SCR	2	STK	.312×.75
5	REST BLOCK	1	CRS	1.375 × 2 × 2.75	13	PIN	1	DR	.375×2
6	CLAMP	1	CRS	1×1×3.625	14	SOC HD CAP SCR	3	STK	.5×1.25
7	.625 STD HEX NUT	2	STK		15	DOWEL PIN	2	STK	.312 DIA × 1.5
8	SPRING	1	MUSIC WIRE	WIRE .054 – O D.875	16	SOC HD CAP SCR	2	STK	.5×1

Exercise 14.56 For the milling fixture for clutch arm, draw the following. (1) Draw details using the decimal-inch system or redesign for metric dimensions, if assigned. (2) Draw assembly.

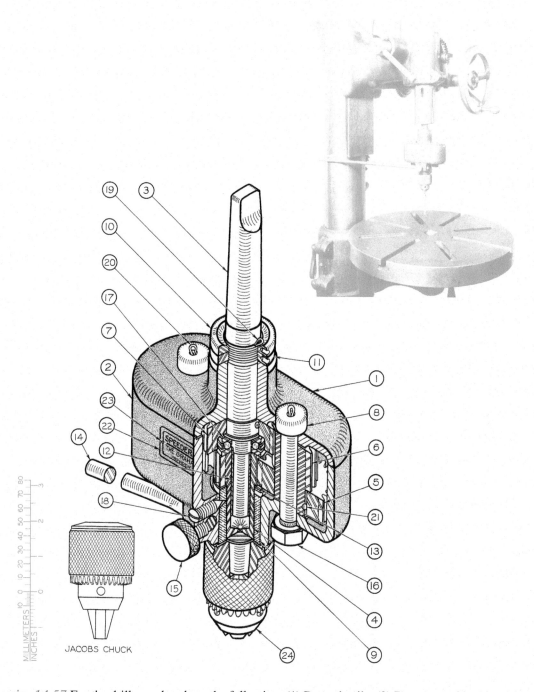

JACOBS CHUCK

Exercise 14.57 For the drill speeder, draw the following. (1) Draw details. (2) Draw assembly. If assigned, convert dimensions to decimal inches or redesign with metric dimensions. See part details on the following pages.

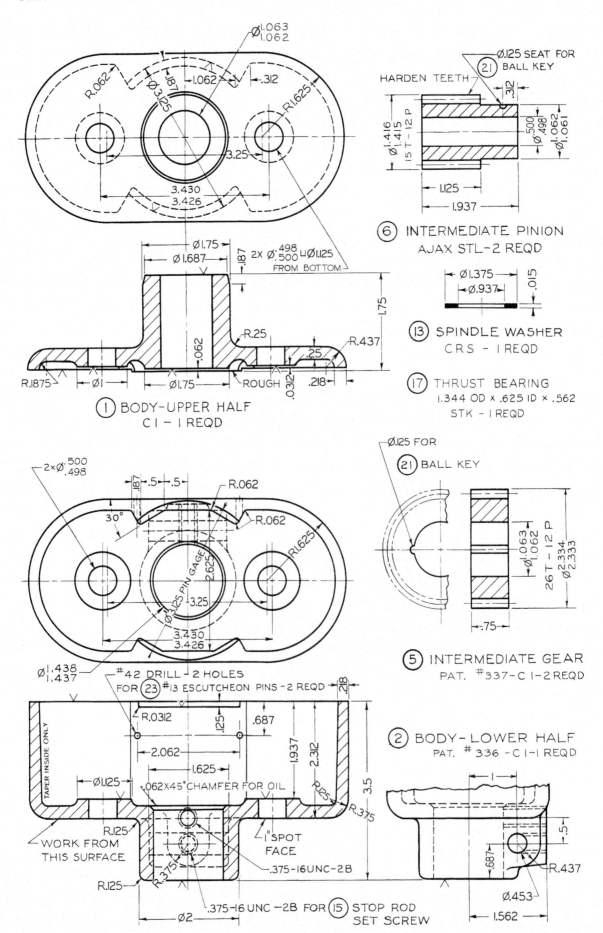

Exercise 14.57 Drill speeder, continued.

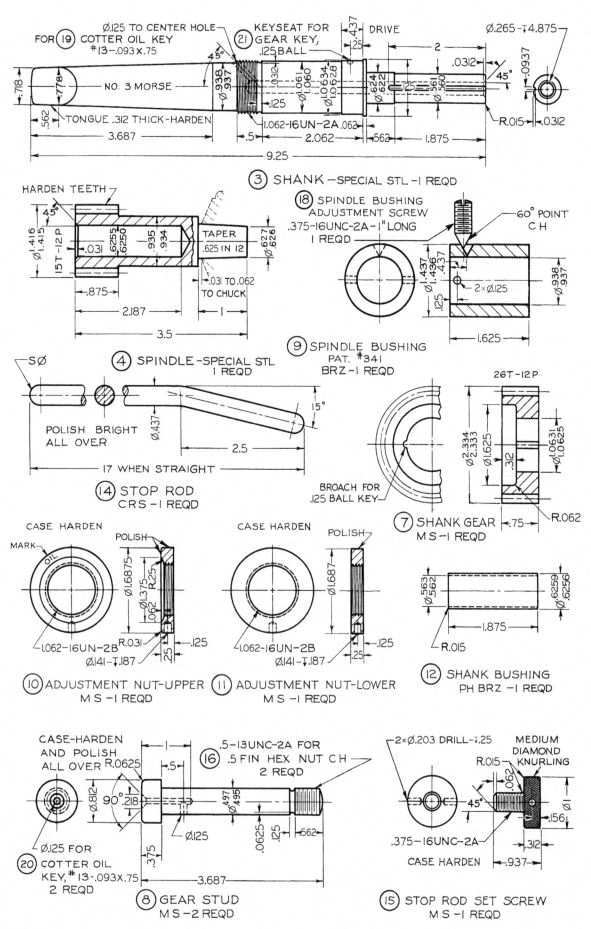

Exercise 14.57 Drill speeder, continued.

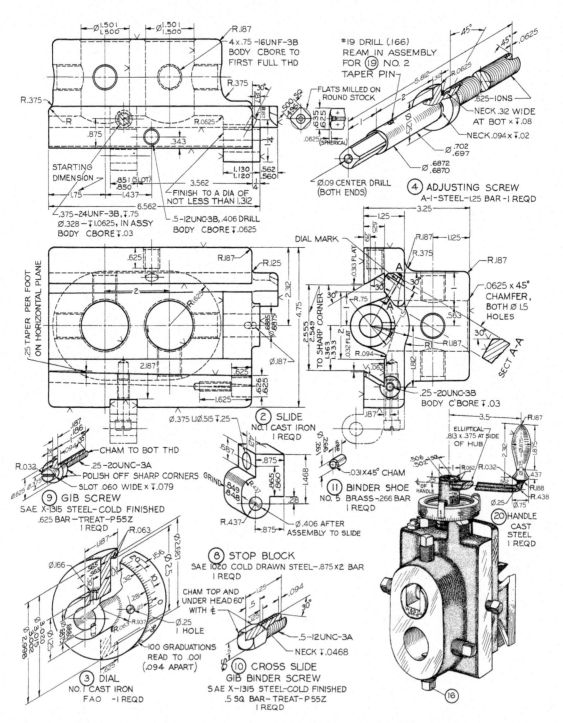

Exercise 14.58 For the vertical slide tool, draw the following. (1) Draw details. If assigned, convert dimensions to decimal inches or redesign for metric system. (2) Draw assembly. Take given top view as front view in the new drawing; then add top and right-side views. If assigned, use unidirectional dimensions. See more part details on the following page.

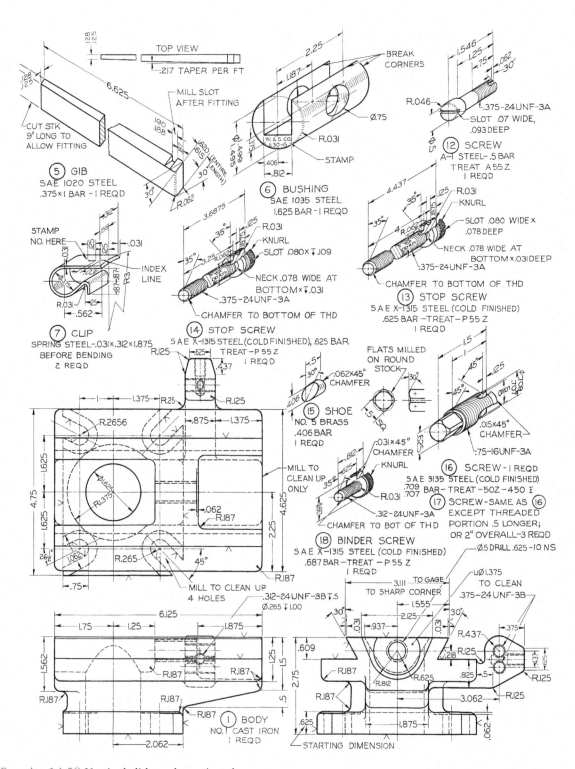

Exercise 14.58 Vertical slide tool, continued.

Exercise 14.59 For the slide tool, draw the following. Consult part information on the following pages to: (1) Draw details using decimal inch dimensions or redesign with metric dimensions, if assigned. (2) Make an assembly drawing of this slide tool.

TOTAL ON MACH.	NO. PCS.	NAME OF PART	PART NO.	CAST FROM PART NO.	TRACING NO.	MATERIAL	ROUGH WEIGHT PER PC.	DIA.	LENGTH	MILL	PART USED ON	NO.REQ. FINISH
	1	Body	219-12		D-17417	A-3-S D F						
	1	Slide	219-6		D-19255	A-3-S D F					219-12	
	1	Nut	219-9		E-19256	#10 BZ					219-6	
	1	Gib	219-1001		C-11129	S A E 1020					219-6	
	1	Slide Screw	219-1002		C-11129	A-3-S					219-12	
	1	Dial Bush.	219-1003		C-11129	A-1-S					219-1002	
	1	Dial Nut	219-1004		C-11129	A-1-S					219-1002	
	1	Handle	219-1011		E-18270	(Buy from Cincinnati Ball Crank Co.)					219-1002	
	1	Stop Screw (Short)	219-1012		E-51950	A-1-S					219-6	
	1	Stop Screw (Long)	219-1013		E-51951	A-1-S					219-6	
	1	Binder Shoe	219-1015		E-51952	#5 Brass					219-6	
	1	Handle Screw	219-1016		E-62322	X-1315 C.F.					219-1011	
	1	Binder Screw	219-1017		E-63927	A-1-S					219-6	
	1	Dial	219-1018		E-39461	A-1-S					219-1002	
	2	Gib Screw	219-1019		E-52777	A-1-S		$\frac{1}{4}$-20	1		219-6	
	1	Binder Screw	280-1010		E-24962	A-1-S					219-1018	
	2	Tool Clamp Screws	683-F-1002		E-19110	D-2-S					219-6	
	1	Fill Hd Cap Scr	1-A			A-1-S		$\frac{3}{8}$	$1\frac{3}{8}$		219-6 219-9	
	1	Key	No.404 Woodruff								219-1002	

PARTS LIST NO. OF SHEETS __2__ SHEET NO. __1__ MACHINE NO. M-219 LOT NUMBER NO. OF PIECES
NAME __NO. 4 SLIDE TOOL (SPECIFY SIZE OF SHANK REQ'D.)__

Exercise 14.59 Slide tool, continued. Parts List.

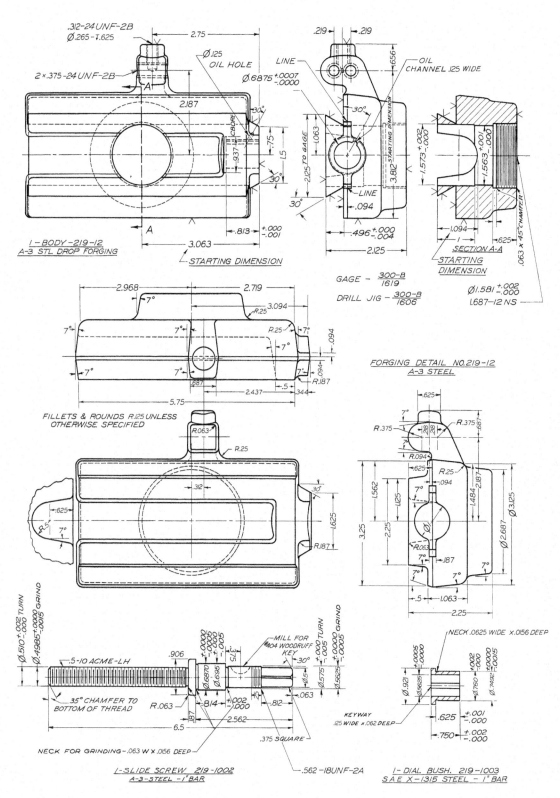

Exercise 14.59 *Slide tool, continued.*

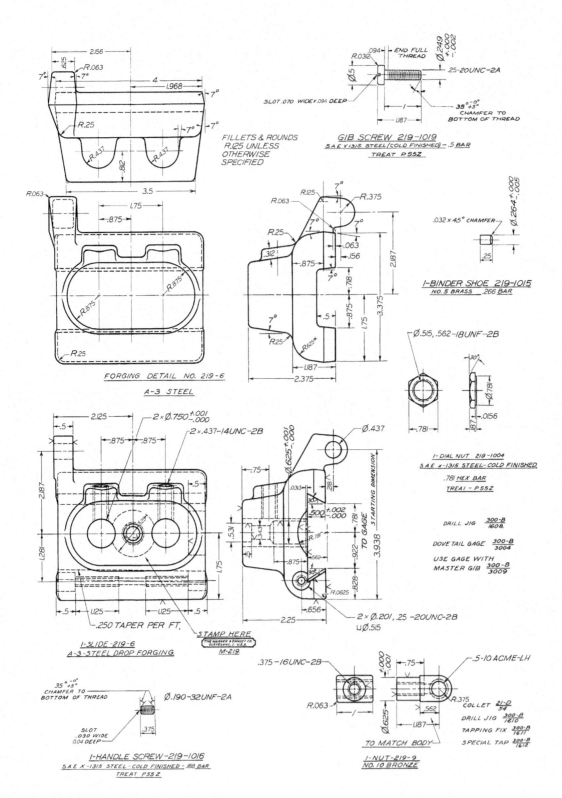

Exercise 14.59 Slide tool, continued.

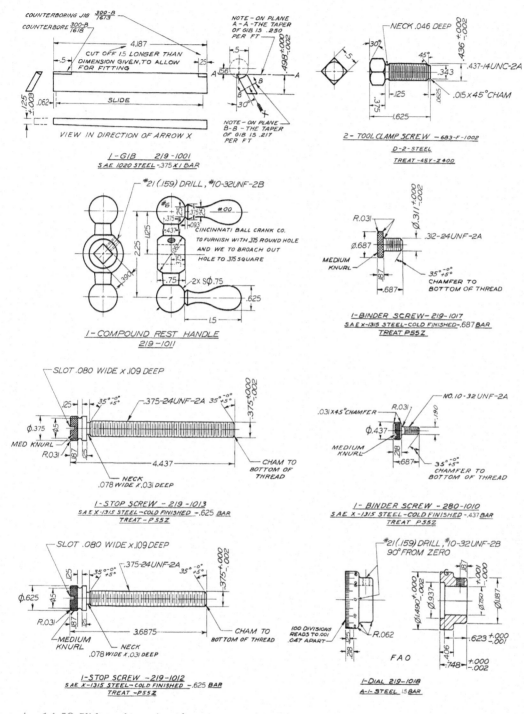

Exercise 14.59 Slide tool, continued.

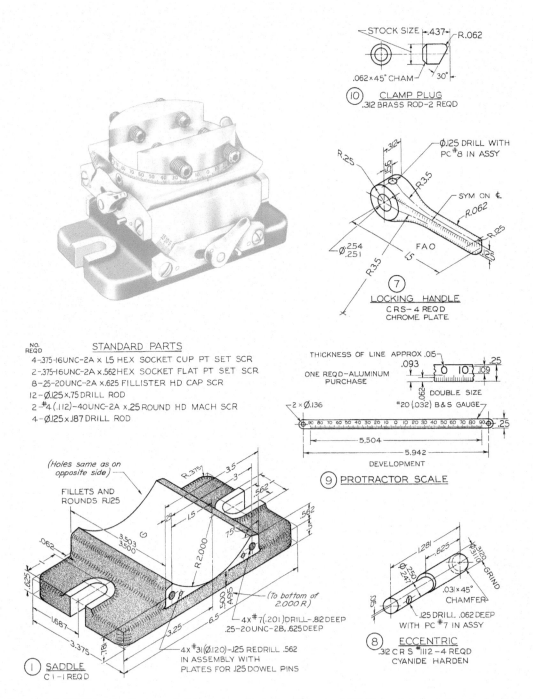

STOCK SIZE .437 R.062

.062×45° CHAM 30°

10 CLAMP PLUG
.312 BRASS ROD-2 REQD

Ø.125 DRILL WITH
PC #8 IN ASSY

R.25
.312
.150
R3.5
SYM ON ₵
R.062
R.125
Ø.254 FAO
.251 .125
R3.5 1.5

7 LOCKING HANDLE
C R S- 4 REQD
CHROME PLATE

STANDARD PARTS

NO. REQD
4 -.375-16UNC-2A x 1.5 HEX SOCKET CUP PT SET SCR
2 -.375-16UNC-2A x.562 HEX SOCKET FLAT PT SET SCR
8 -.25-20UNC-2A x.625 FILLISTER HD CAP SCR
12 -Ø.125 x.75 DRILL ROD
2 -#4 (.112)-40UNC-2A x.25 ROUND HD MACH SCR
4 -Ø.125 x.187 DRILL ROD

THICKNESS OF LINE APPROX .015
.093 .25
ONE REQD-ALUMINUM .062 .109
PURCHASE
DOUBLE SIZE
2 × Ø.136 #20 (.032) B&S GAUGE
90 80 70 60 50 40 30 20 10 0 10 20 30 40 50 60 70 80 90 .25
5.504
5.942
DEVELOPMENT

9 PROTRACTOR SCALE

(Holes same as on opposite side)
FILLETS AND ROUNDS R.125
R.375
3.5
3
.562
.062
.29
1.5
.562
1.5
75°
R2.000
.625
3.503
3.500
G
.500
.495
(To bottom of 2.000 R)
1.687
6.5
4x #7(.201)DRILL-.812 DEEP
.25-20UNC-2B,.625 DEEP
3.25
3.375
.181
4x #31(Ø.120)-.125 REDRILL .562
IN ASSEMBLY WITH
PLATES FOR .125 DOWEL PINS

1 SADDLE
C 1 - 1 REQD

1.281
.625
Ø.3120 GRIND
Ø.250
.247
.03I×45°
CHAMFER
.375
.125 DRILL .062 DEEP
WITH PC #7 IN ASSY

8 ECCENTRIC
.312 C R S #1112 - 4 REQD
CYANIDE HARDEN

Exercise 14.60 For the "any angle" tool vise, draw the following. (1) Draw details using decimal-inch dimensions or redesign with metric dimensions, if assigned. (2) Draw assembly. See more part details on the following page.

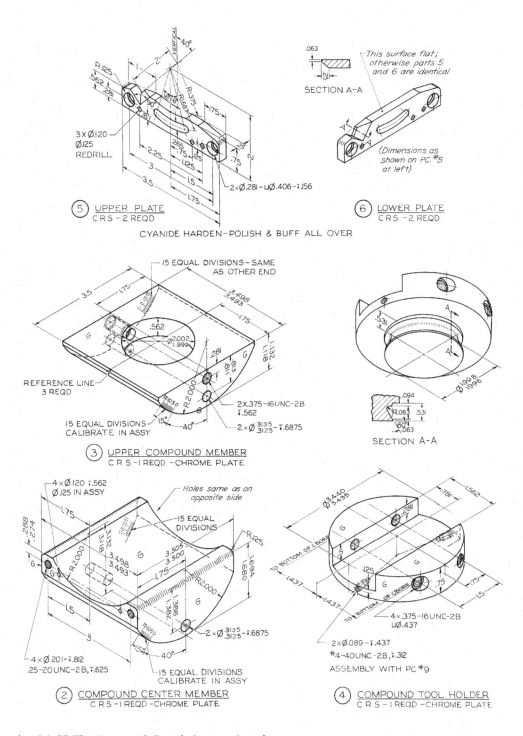

Exercise 14.60 The "any angle" tool vise, continued.

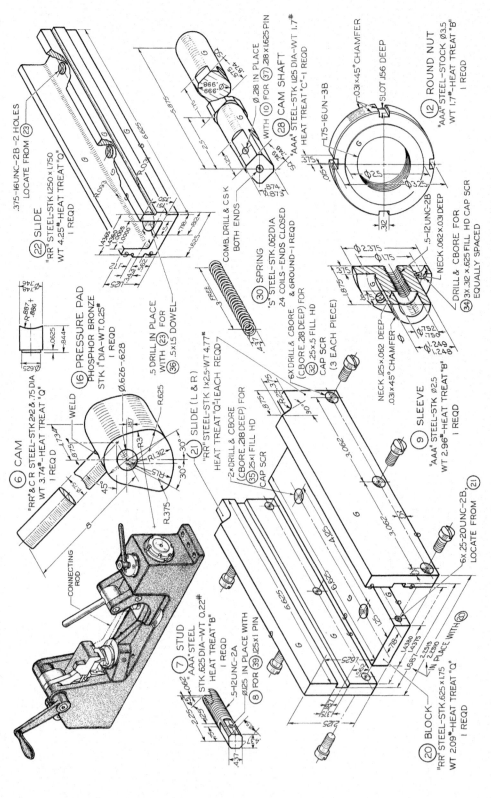

Exercise 14.61 For the fixture for centering connecting rod, draw the following. Consult part information on the following pages to: (1) Draw details using decimal-inch dimensions or redesign with metric dimensions, if assigned. (2) Draw assembly.

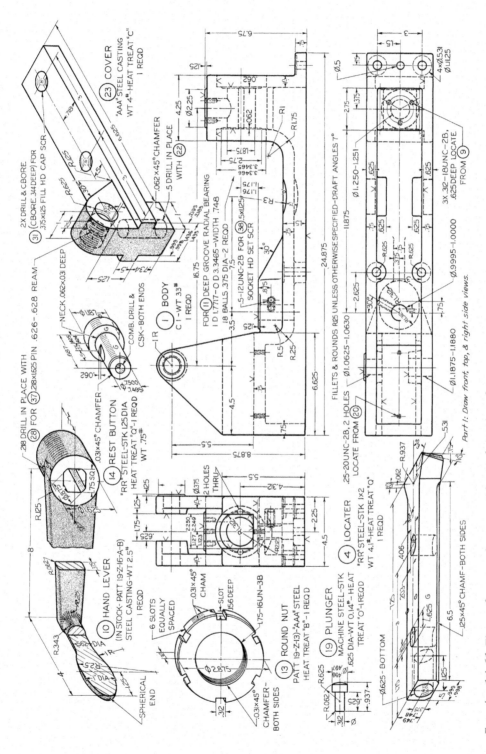

Exercise 14.61 Fixture for centering connecting rod, continued.

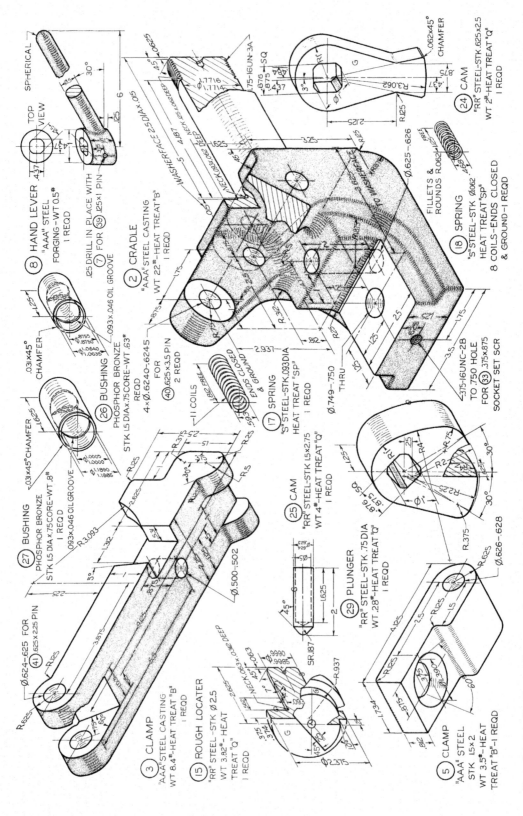

Exercise 14.61 Fixture for centering connecting rod, continued.

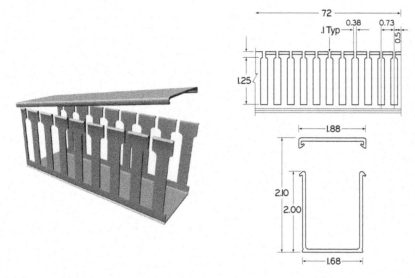

Exercise 14.62 For the plastic open slot wiring duct, front and side views, redraw with metric dimensions, reducing the size by 3.

CHAPTER FIFTEEN

DRAWING CONTROL AND DATA MANAGEMENT

--- OBJECTIVES ---

After studying the material in this chapter, you should be able to:

1. Present the rationale for controlling engineering documents.

2. Describe the role of the drawing or CAD file in engineering documentation.

3. List the basic steps in approving and controlling CAD data.

4. Organize your files and directories in a consistent manner.

5. Practice good file handling and backup procedures.

6. Describe the basic principles of product data management.

Refer to the following standards:
- *ASME Y14.100 Engineering Drawing Practices*
- *ASME Y14.41 Digital Product Definition Data Practices*

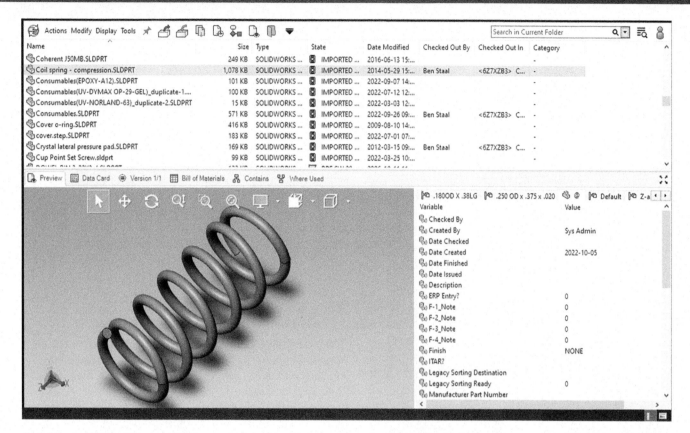

SolidWorks PDM offers a realistic view of each part so users can quickly identify and select a component from within an assembly. Notice the options for checking in and checking out the component. This ensures that two different people are not modifying the same part. The software provides many document control features, including the ability to track who made changes to a part or assembly. (Courtesy of Ben Staal, Quantel USA.)

OVERVIEW

Technical drawings are an important part of the engineering design process. The drawing's role in documenting engineering design was developed to satisfy the need for control in several areas. Legally, designs must be documented—for the life of the product at least, but in many cases permanently. Drawings serve as a contract with the manufacturer that will produce the design. To control how drawings are released for manufacture, companies and industries follow procedures to eliminate misunderstandings and costly mistakes. When decisions are made to change a design, engineering change orders document these changes so they become a part of the permanent record of the design. Regulatory bodies, standards organizations, and case law have all contributed to the rules for retaining and producing documentation for your engineering designs. You should become familiar with the requirements for designs in the industry in which you work.

DOCUMENTATION AND THE DESIGN DATABASE

Companies using computer-aided design tools must address issues of document management. When paper drawings were used throughout the design process as well as for documentation, practices for approving and releasing drawings, making drawing changes, and distributing and storing drawings were developed over time to fit the use of "hard copy" as a medium. With the advent of design databases stored on computer systems, these practices were updated to use electronic files. Companies had to adapt their practices from paper drawings to electronic files to retain their engineering design records in a systematic and permanent way.

Companies must also address document sharing issues. Concurrent engineering depends on the ability of a team of individuals to work together on interrelated tasks and with the design database. The team's access to current and accurate information is crucial to its members' ability to work simultaneously on different aspects of the same project.

Managing the flow of design database information to and among members of the team is a contemporary aspect of drawing control.

Today's commercial systems use a central database to store and serve data to a wide range of other software tools. Whether you work at a large or small company, you need to be aware of the issues in document management and the tools being developed to save you time and facilitate your involvement in team-based concurrent engineering.

DRAWING MANAGEMENT IN ENGINEERING ETHICS

The Hyatt Regency Walkways Collapse provides a vivid example of the importance of accuracy and detail in engineering design and shop drawings (particularly regarding revisions), and the costly consequences of errors.

On July 17, 1981, the Hyatt Regency Hotel in Kansas City, Missouri, held a videotaped tea-dance party in their atrium lobby. With many party-goers standing and dancing on the suspended walkways, connections supporting the ceiling rods that held up the second and fourth-floor walkways across the atrium failed, and both walkways collapsed onto the crowded first-floor atrium below. The fourth-floor walkway collapsed onto the second-floor walkway, while the offset third-floor walkway remained intact. The collapse left 114 dead and in excess of 200 injured. Millions of dollars in costs resulted from the collapse, and thousands of lives were adversely affected. The ensuing investigation of the accident revealed some unsettling facts.

During January and February 1979, the design of the hanger rod connections was changed in a series of events and disputed communications between the fabricator (Havens Steel Company) and the engineering design team (G.C.E. International, Inc., a professional engineering

firm). The fabricator changed the design from a one-rod to a two-rod system to simplify the assembly task, doubling the load on the connector, which ultimately resulted in the walkways' collapse.

The fabricator, in sworn testimony after the accident, claimed that his company (Havens) telephoned the engineering firm (G.C.E.) for change approval. G.C.E. denied ever receiving such a call from Havens.

On October 14, 1979 (more than one year before the walkways collapsed), while the hotel was still under construction, more than 2700 square feet of the atrium roof collapsed because one of the roof connections at the north end of the atrium failed.

In testimony, G.C.E. stated that on three separate occasions they requested on-site project representation during the construction phase; however, these requests were not acted on by the owner (Crown Center Redevelopment Corporation), owing to additional costs of providing on-site inspection.

Even as originally designed, the walkways were barely capable of holding up the expected load and would have failed to meet the requirements of the Kansas City Building Code.

Owing to evidence supplied at the hearings, a number of principals involved lost their engineering licenses, several firms went bankrupt, and many expensive legal suits were settled out of court. The case serves as an excellent example of the importance of meeting professional responsibilities and what the consequences are for professionals who fail to meet those responsibilities.

(Excerpted from "Negligence, Risk and the Professional Debate over Responsibility for Design" A Case History of the Kansas City Hyatt Regency Walkways Collapse. Department of Philosophy and Department of Mechanical Engineering, Texas A&M University.)

15.1 REQUIREMENTS FOR ENGINEERING DOCUMENTATION

The information contained in the 3D design database used to produce drawings and to send files for NC machining, mold design, or other manufacturing processes is an important part of the engineering design record. The ASME standard *Y14.41, Digital Product Definition Data Practices,* outlines documentation practices for digital designs and types of digital data that may be associated with them. This standard augments traditional documentation practices developed for paper drawings to encompass all the design information companies must manage.

Companies must manage the design record so they can produce documentation for various purposes, such as defending themselves against product safety liability and patent infringement lawsuits. In the event of legal issues, you must be able to produce the document as it existed and in a method that is admissible in a court of law. Because electronically stored files can be altered, they may not be considered an acceptable method for documenting engineering designs unless there is a clear process in place for storing and managing the digital data. In addition, most legal requests are for copies of all versions of the design, and all copies stored and used within the company. It can be costly and embarrassing if they are not well organized and correct, or if there are multiple versions in use that vary from one to the other.

Legal standards for the length of time engineering drawings need to be retained vary from state to state and industry to industry. In most cases, industry standards groups weigh the risk of record destruction in the context of product and public safety and make recommendations for its members. American Records Management Association (ARMA) is one source of information about engineering drawing retention. Even if the legal standard is less stringent, a court may rule that a firm should meet the industry's common practice to avoid a finding of negligence.

Industries regulated by the Food and Drug Administration (FDA) should also be aware of its Guidelines for Electronic Records and Signatures. Regulatory agencies such as the FDA consider engineering drawings "specifications" or "documents" and have clarified their record-keeping guidelines to include electronic forms such as graphics files. Military standards, such as MIL-PRF-5480, define practices for communicating digital product data when contracting with the U.S. military. Companies that are undertaking records management guidelines should be aware of the most current rulings and recommendations for electronic media from their industry's standards and regulatory groups.

In addition to complying with legal requirements for documenting engineering designs, effective storage and retrieval of engineering design documentation can make a difference in a company's ability to succeed in today's world marketplace. The effective use of a digital design database can provide many benefits outside of just reduced drafting time or a shortened product development cycle.

15.2 DRAWING CONTROL METHODS

Understanding the process that drawings go through for approval, release, and storage is the first step toward good practices for the approval, release, and storage of your electronic design data.

Drawing Approval and Release

The title block on the drawing is used to document the change from a draft to a finished drawing. Blocks for signing and dating *drawn by*, *checked by*, and *approved by* are used to release the drawing to manufacturing or to a contractor to be produced. Often, the part number is assigned during the initial release of the drawing or model. The released drawing and or model are stored for the permanent record. Figure 15.1 shows a title block used to gather approval signatures.

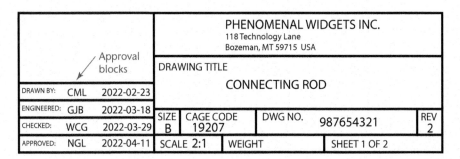

15.1   Title Block with Approval Signatures

SHEET ___1___ OF ___1___   №. H10547

FORM 686 REVISED 10-28-68

ENGINEERING CHANGE DATE: 6-9-98		PART NO.	HE0004-AV-01-01					DRAFT.	WTG
		ON HAND						CK'D.	JMN
WARNING CHANGE DATE: 6-9-98		ON ORD.						APPR.	FB
		RES.						REL. BY	FB

| COPIES TO: | IND. ENG. | X | PROD. CON. | X | INSP. | X | SERVICE | | OTHER | |

ENG. APPR.	
REQ. BY DEPT. – NAME	
PART NO.	HE0004-AV-01-01 REV. A
CHANGE	CORRECTED BOM ITEMS 19,20,34,35 & 36
REASON	DRAWING CORRECTION
ACTION REQUIRED	PROD. CON. ON HAND	PAMPA- BUILD
	ON ORD.	PEMEX
	EFF. ON UNIT	20794-95-96
	TOOLING	
	SERVICE	

15.2   ECO. *This engineering change order is an electronic document that is completed for each change to a released drawing. (Courtesy of National Oilwell Varco (NOV).)*

Change Orders

In the imperfect real world, released drawings often require some type of correction during construction or manufacture. After a drawing has been released, however, it should not be changed unless an ***engineering change order*** (ECO), shown in Figure 15.2, is approved. An ECO, also called an *engineering change notification* (ECN) or *engineering change request* (ECR), details the nature of the change in a separate document. After the ECO is approved, the drawing is revised and a revision noted on the drawing.

Revision Block

After revision, a dated ***revision block***, shown in Figure 15.3, is updated on the drawing. A revision block describes briefly what the change was and may also indicate the number of the engineering change order (which contains more information about the change). The drawing is then approved again. A small number (circled or contained in a triangle) is added to call attention to the revision on the drawing. An easily visible revision number is located in the title block. Annotating the revision number in the title block helps ensure that two people discussing the print from two different locations can verify that each is looking at the same revision of the drawing.

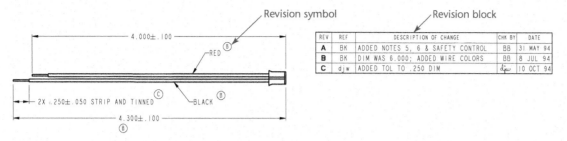

15.3   Revision Block. *The revision block shown here identifies the change made to the drawing, but the change is also marked with a revision symbol to make it easy to locate. (Courtesy of Xerox Corporation.)*

A Drawing as a Snapshot in Time

Each revision of the released drawing serves to document the design at a particular point in time. Some companies continue to print and store a paper copy of the CAD file as their permanent record. If the electronic CAD file is updated and no longer matches the drawing, the paper copy acts to preserve the design documentation. In this kind of system, the same approval and archival practices just described are applied to the paper drawings generated from the CAD database. This is a perfectly acceptable practice if you can retrieve these paper drawings later as needed.

Today, similar practices allow the same level of control around electronic files that store the design data. Stored digital documents may also serve as the permanent record if they are properly controlled. For example, a company may store the electronic file using a process in which the CAD documents are "frozen" at each approval, in the same way a paper drawing would be archived.

Releasing drawings as electronic files covers only a portion of the design and product information that a company needs to control. In the rest of this chapter, you will learn more about sharing, controlling, and storing the electronic files used to document engineering design.

15.3 GOOD PRACTICES FOR ELECTRONIC DRAWING STORAGE

Organized practices for storage, approval, retrieval, file naming, and tracking revision history for electronic CAD data are important. Chances are, you will work in a company that has developed and articulated its standards of data management, and you will be expected to adhere to them. The company may have invested in a product data management system (PDM). In either case, much of the responsibility for managing data will be yours. Understanding the issues in personal file management will help you devise your own system, if you must, and help you appreciate the pros and cons of various approaches.

Storing Electronic Files

The advent of personal computers on each designer's desktop may have contributed to the difficulty of managing electronic data. Each designer may organize the files he or she is working on differently, or keep multiple copies of a file in different directories. When others need to view or edit the file, it may be hard to be sure which is the current version. Without a thorough approval process for release of drawings, the designer may neglect to track and store the revision history. Even when previous revisions are stored electroni-

cally, they may not be useful because they do not satisfy the requirements for a static snapshot of the design at the time of release.

Many companies run into difficulties with their CAD data because they start out small and do not implement an organized system for managing the files. By the time they realize that they require better organization, they have thousands of poorly organized files and many CAD users with poor file storage habits. It is a very important part of your job to manage the engineering design records that you produce. Design documents, models, and drawings are the property of the company, not the individual designer (unless you specifically have some other written agreement). As such, their usefulness should not depend on the ability of a single individual to locate or interpret them.

Organized Directory Structures

Using an organized directory structure makes it easier to retrieve your CAD files and other electronically stored design data. Think of a directory on the disk as a kind of file folder. You would not put all your paperwork loose in your file cabinet; neither should you scatter files over your drive.

15.4 *Organize directories and files in logical groups.*

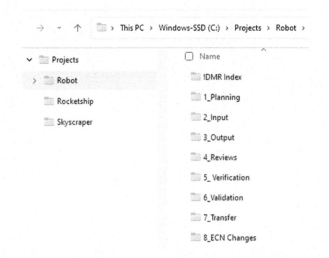

Most people create a directory structure in a way that makes sense for the types of projects they do. A project-based directory structure, such as the one shown in Figure 15.4, allows you to store all files related to a particular project in the same directory.

Within each project, you may want to have subdirectories for different parts or different kinds of data associated with the project. A good rule of thumb is to think about situations when you (or others) will want to retrieve the data. Will you think of it in terms of the project? (Remember that a key to working with assemblies is the availability of the individual part files associated with it.) Or will you think of it in terms of another characteristic? Your CAD file directories may be project based, whereas other files may be organized differently. Making the directories work as you do will help you find what you need easily. You can use search functions to find documents, but that can be a time-consuming process compared with knowing where to look.

It is not a good idea to have a single "My Documents" directory where you store all your files, even if you intend to move them to another project-based directory later. This chore may not get done, or you may not remember which version of the file is current. Nor is it a good practice to store your work files in the directory that contains the application software. (When you install software upgrades, you may accidentally overwrite or delete your work files.)

If you are using a networked computer system, you can store company documents on the network in a directory that others in the company can access. Because CAD files require large amounts of storage space, you need to manage the space on the drives available to you. Keeping copies of all files on your personal system should be weighed against the frequency with which you need those files, the time involved in retrieving the files as needed, and the likelihood that the copy of the file on your system will still be current the next time you need it.

If you work for a company that has implemented a system to control its electronic data, you may be required to keep all your CAD files in a workspace allotted to you on the network server. This makes it possible for the company to control (and regularly back up) these data, and it removes the burden of doing so from each individual employee.

TIP

Although your operating system provides a "My Documents" folder as the default where files are stored, this is usually not a good choice for important project files. The folder may be difficult for a different user logged onto the same computer to locate. The best choice for files is a network folder where everyone who needs access can locate the files.

File Naming Conventions

Naming your files systematically is as important as organizing them. If a company-wide policy for naming files does not exist, you should develop one for your own files to make them easy to find.

Each released part and assembly drawing should have a unique part identification number (PIN). You may want to assign PINs in a systematic way so that users familiar with the system can search for types of documents. For example, you may have a pseudo–Dewey decimal system for types of drawings or documents your company typically produces, so that numbers starting with 100 are electrical schematics, 200s are assemblies, and so forth. The next set of numbers can further identify the type of file by another set of characteristics, such as project group numbers.

To make it easy to retrieve files, usually the drawing name/number is the same as the released CAD file name. When drawing numbers are assigned in a random way, maintain an organized database where users can look to find the particular project, drawing, part model, file name, and other information.

Additional data in the form of metadata may be stored with the file name. The revision number can be added as drawings are revised. Once a company has file retention guidelines in place, file names can also incorporate a tag that indicates when it may be removed from long-term storage. This kind of tag is generally added by the group that manages the company's archives, but it demonstrates the role of the file name in encapsulating information and aiding in file management. Whatever organized system a company uses is an improvement over having each employee name drawings as he or she pleases.

15.4 DRAWING STANDARDS

Like file naming standards, drawing standards can help you work more productively and can contribute to the usefulness of the drawings as company records.

Company standards maintain consistency in the way drawings and models are constructed. Standardizing the layers in a CAD drawing, for example, can make them more navigable. Architectural engineering firms use layers to organize the many systems, such as plumbing and electrical, that are part of building design. Each of these systems is assigned a set of layers and layer names so that each drawing can be manipulated in the same way. Notes and drawing text are commonly stored on a separate layer across drawings so this information can be turned on and off as needed when working with the model. Because CAD software carries layer information along with parts, standardizing layer names can prevent unnecessary confusion when files are combined. The colors used for layers and different drawing elements can also be standardized. For example, the proposed elements of the design may be magenta, the electrical wiring may be blue, and so on.

Many other aspects of creating a drawing can be standardized. The borders required for each different sheet size, the information contained in the title block (and how it is to appear), and the fonts and letter sizes to be used for different items are frequently spelled out in a company's drawing standards. The text of certain notes—such as manufacturing standards or safety control notices—is often standardized so that legally appropriate and consistent information is provided in all cases. In addition, libraries of symbols and stock parts may be provided to help you work more efficiently and produce drawings that can easily be understood and reused by others.

Starting with a "seed" part for a model may allow you to use standardized view names, datum planes, and other information to make it easy to navigate the model and assemble parts quickly.

The guidelines for drawing standards can be codified and may even be stored within the CAD system (Figure 15.5). In some cases, a drawing checker helps ensure that drawings meet company standards; in others, it is the responsibility of the designer to check the company's published standards. The standards may be enforced by the records management group responsible for archiving design documents, which will refuse to accept drawings that are not prepared according to standards. Although it may be easy to rename a file after it is created to make it consistent with company standards, you should address drawing standards by starting new drawings from a prototype file or seed part that provides the company's common framework.

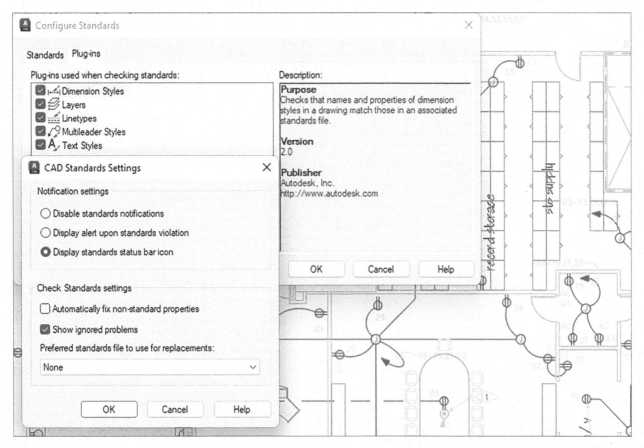

15.5 *The AutoCAD Batch Standards Checker can be used to verify that files meet some basic company standards.*
(Autodesk screen shots reprinted courtesy of Autodesk, Inc.)

15.5 PERMISSION AND OWNERSHIP

File use in a networked environment adds a dimension of ownership to file management. *Ownership* is a term used to refer to the security systems built into network operating systems that allow the system to restrict access to data on the network. Personal computers allow some form of file protection to prevent files from being erased, but networked systems allow for more sophisticated security for files and directories.

To control access to data over a network, the network administrator gives different kinds of *permission* to different users. Permission defines a user's level of access to a file. For example, some users may have *read-only* permission. They can read or view a file but cannot save changes to it. *Write* permission allows a user to create and change files. *Change* permission allows a user to read and change files or folders but not to delete them. The permission can be set globally or for each set of files to provide the level of access needed.

Using the operating system's built-in file protection is a low-cost way to require approval for edits to electronic files.

You can discuss security with your network administrator and use it to allow others to view your files but not change them. This can be effective when others need to remain current with your work.

In a concurrent, team-based environment, you may need a more elaborate system to regulate the use of shared files. Operating system permissions are generally allocated by user for groups of files in a directory. To change permission based on the file type requires a different kind of software. For example, a file that has been approved and released may have its new status reflected in its file name, and all users may have read-only access to the file from that point forward. The network itself may be configured into work groups that allow easy access to files among team members until the project's control passes to another group, say, from engineering to manufacturing.

15.6 BACKING UP DRAWING FILES

It is an important responsibility to back up the models, drawings, and other data that you create. Losing your files is equivalent to losing the hours it took to create the files. In a small company, data loss can be catastrophic, but in any company, data loss can severely affect the profitability of a project or product. You should save your files frequently while you are working. A good rule of thumb is to save approximately every 15 minutes so you will lose only 15 minutes of work if the power goes down or the system crashes.

Several different methods are available for backing up your data. Simply copying the data to a removable disk is one approach that works well for single documents, but it is too time-consuming for routine backups. There are companies that provide affordable storage for off-site backups via the Web. These are an excellent choice for small, low-security compa-

nies. For CAD data, you may want to keep previous versions as well as the current version of files. Some CAD software provides this feature automatically, but you must pay attention to whether you have this turned on in the configuration.

If you work for a large company, it will usually be the network administrator's responsibility to ensure that a workable backup system is in place. Larger companies usually back up changed files nightly and do full backups daily, weekly, or monthly, depending on their needs. A secure copy of the data should be stored off-site so that in the event of a disaster, the backup files can be recovered. There are many horror stories of companies whose hard drives and backup copies were destroyed in an earthquake. Because backups are frequently made on magnetic media, you also need to consider the conditions under which the backups are being stored.

15.7 STORAGE MEDIA

New kinds of storage media for electronic files are being developed every day, offering different combinations of stability, shelf life, speed, and capacity. Electronic CAD files can require sizable amounts of storage space. The choice of media for backing up files on a daily or weekly basis and those used for long-term storage should make best use of the options available. For backup media, the data transfer rate from the system to the backup and the cost per megabyte of storage may be more important than the shelf life of the medium (as it will be replaced periodically and must accommodate large amounts of data). For archival media, on the other hand, stability and shelf life may make a more

expensive medium a better choice in the long run and may even outweigh the fact that it may take longer to write files to the storage media. Considerations for migrating data from one system to another are also important aspects of long-term storage and use of your digital design data.

Some companies use service companies to provide their storage and backup, or store data in the "cloud" (which is really the Internet). Analyzing the risks and benefits of storing your data in the "cloud" versus using in-house servers is an important decision. The cloud storage provider may host your data in a country that has differing privacy laws, for example, or they may go out of business.

15.8 USING THE 3D DESIGN DATABASE IN CONCURRENT ENGINEERING

So far this chapter has focused on the methods used to preserve engineering data stored in graphics files. But effective use of the digital design database goes beyond thinking of it as documentation needed to transfer manufacturing information to the shop floor, or to be stored as the design record for the product. To fully realize the role of the design database in concurrent engineering, document management and drawing control become enterprise-wide concepts that mirror and support the goals of the company in getting high-quality products to market more quickly and at less expense.

Concurrent engineering teams are composed of members from many diverse groups. Individuals within the company at the same location interact regularly with others in remote locations as well as external team members, such as multinational manufacturing suppliers and contractors. Team members may represent engineering design, marketing, manufacturing, engineering, the shop floor, procurement, service and support, and clients, each interacting with the 3D design database in different ways.

The sharing required for effective concurrent engineering poses unique challenges for electronic file management and control. Companies that wish to succeed at concurrent engineering need ways for a diverse and geographically distributed group of individuals to work with and contribute to a common database of information. By providing access to information that does not depend on time zones, telephone accessibility, or geographic location, the design database can eliminate time spent in making connections to get data and free up time for the team to work together with the information. Making it easier to find needed information can also contribute to better decision making. Finally, controlling the accuracy of the information used by various team members can eliminate wasted effort. To realize these benefits, companies use software tools and methodologies that not only provide document control but also facilitate access to complete information about a product.

15.9 QUALITY MANAGEMENT

A key motivation for many companies that undertake systematic data management is quality certification. Managing engineering documents and electronic data is one step in a quality management system. Many companies become ISO 9000 certified as an indication of their quality manufacturing processes.

ISO 9000/9001

The *International Organization for Standardization* (which is always abbreviated ISO regardless of its translation) is a worldwide federation of national standards bodies from some one hundred countries. ISO publishes many standards, most of which are specific to nuts, bolts, and standard parts. The ISO 9000 family of standards is different. It is a generic management system standard designed to help companies that manufacture their own products ensure a consistent level of quality in design, production, installation, and service. When the European Community (EU) agreed to unify trade regulations, they adopted ISO 9000 as the standard to be met by companies that wished to manufacture products to be sold in the EU. ISO 9001 updates and clarifies how companies are to monitor the effectiveness of their quality measures.

ISO 9000 encompasses procedures and documentation across an organization, but two areas set out the criteria for practices used to create, approve, store, retrieve, and revise engineering drawings: design control as well as document and data control.

To fulfill the design control requirement, a company must show that all its designs are being controlled to meet quality requirements spelled out in the standard. The standard envisions a process that includes clear design criteria, good communication among team members, testing and verification of designs, and well-defined approval processes. The standard is very similar to the design process that you have been learning about in this text and that is practiced by many of the companies profiled in the examples and cases. The following checklist was prepared by the ISO

9000/QS-9000 Support Group for companies to use in evaluating how close they are to meeting the design control standard:

1. Do you have a written design development procedure that your company follows religiously?
2. Are you using a project management-type approach to design development?
3. Are properly trained, educated, and experienced staff assigned to the design teams? Are these teams properly supported?
4. Is a product brief updated and transmitted regularly among interested parties?
5. Are the relationships among departments and teams spelled out in some form of document (usually an organizational chart)?
6. Are product requirements documented and reviewed for clarity and consistency?
7. Are design outputs published as calculations, requirements, and prints, and are these verified by an independent source?
8. Do the design outputs meet regulatory, safety, health, environmental, and other external requirements?
9. Are acceptance criteria also part of the design output?
10. Are the acceptance criteria and other product requirements tested or otherwise verified?
11. Is a documented system of design verification used with qualified personnel to assure that design outputs meet customer requirements?
12. Do you have a written procedure for the modification of an existing design that requires formal approvals?

This checklist suggests a broad range of documents in addition to CAD data that supports quality assurance. The ISO 9000 document and data control standards further define the documents a company must control. These include:

- drawings
- specifications
- blueprints
- inspection instructions
- test procedures
- work instructions
- operation sheets
- quality manuals
- operational procedures
- quality assurance procedures

The document control standard specifically allows for documents to be stored digitally but calls for clear procedures for storing and revising documents. These procedures apply the same principles of control discussed in the paper drawing control process at the beginning of this chapter. Another checklist from the ISO 9000/QS-9000 Support Group identifies some of the qualities of this type of document control:

- Document has central approval authority.
- There is a master list of documents.
- The right documents are in the right place.
- There are no obsolete documents in circulation.
- The nature of any change shall be explained.
- Documents are reissued after a specified number of revisions.
- Documents are signed, dated, and numbered.
- Time-sensitive documents are removed when out of date.
- Approval is needed to revise, remove, or copy a controlled document.
- All corrections are signed and dated.
- A separate procedure is used to initiate corrections.

ISO 9000 does not specify an exact standard to which registered companies must conform; rather, it requires the company to develop, implement, and certify its own quality process. ISO 9001:2008 extends the standard and clarifies that the company's effort needs to go beyond quality measurement; it needs to include a process for implementing changes based on the information and on customer satisfaction that has been measured. ISO 9000 criteria, then, are another consideration when developing a data management system.

15.10 PRODUCT DATA MANAGEMENT

One way to achieve the goals of data storage and to expand the use of the database in a concurrent environment is to develop or invest in a software tool called a *product data management* (PDM) system. PDM refers to computer systems that provide organized management, storage, and retrieval of not just engineering data but all documents related to managing a product.

Data management systems can be implemented at different levels in the organization. Many organizations start out with a system at the *work group level*. For example, CAD files may be controlled and shared with a system that serves just the engineering and manufacturing group. These people have similar needs for information and work with many of the same documents, so the system needed is relatively simple. At the *enterprise level*, the data management system would include the CAD files as well as many other documents, and would serve them to users across the company (see Figure 15.6). As you might guess, an enterprise-level PDM has many more issues of access and control than a work group–level system. The ability of different team members to use the database according to their needs—for financial or manufacturing data, for example—can make them more productive and creative members of the team.

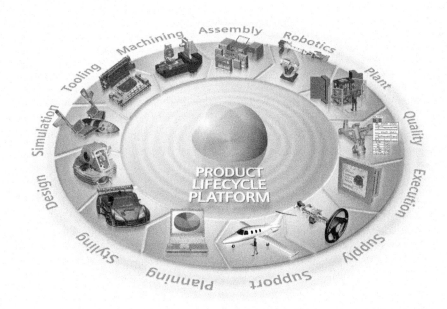

15.6 Enterprise-wide Product Data Management. *The Siemens PLM System is designed to serve data inside and outside the organization. This illustration shows types of information centered around a 3D design database available to design, marketing, manufacturing, engineering, procurement, service and support team members, as well as to external team members, such as multinational manufacturing suppliers and contractors. Data from the database would be provided to external users over the Internet (for public data) or via a secure, password-protected site (to share nonpublic information with suppliers and other partners in remote locations). (©2016 Siemens Product Lifecycle Management System. Reprinted with permission.)*

Organized by Product

The PDM system attempts to manage all the product-related information—specifications, part information, NC programs, CAD drawings, models, spreadsheets, test results, electronic images, and paper documents—throughout the life cycle of the product. This information includes release to manufacturing forms, change orders, and approval documentation. Traditional approaches to recording and preserving part and assembly files do not capture other pieces of data related to the project, or they capture it in a way that is difficult to obtain. For example, the weight of a component may be derived from the model file document in the system but not stored separately where it could be retrieved as an attribute of that component. Product data management systems allow users to store documents—be they CAD files, spreadsheets, or memos—as well as attribute data about a product.

The *produc*t in PDM relates to how the information is organized. A database, like your file system, can be organized in many ways. The information managed by a PDM system has traditionally been stored by functional area: manufacturing has the programs used to control the manufacturing machinery, marketing has the written specifications for the final product, and purchasing may have the final bill of materials. To obtain one of these pieces of information, the user needs to know how it is stored and by whom. Each may be stored in a different database. A PDM system uses the product as the organizing principle. To find a piece of information, the user can start with the product to which it relates.

A Relational Database

All data management systems use some type of database to store the data they control. Because product data management systems are organized around a product, they generally use a ***relational database*** to allow the system to serve information in many different ways.

Some data management systems use a simpler kind of database to organize data, often referred to as ***flat files***. Flat-file databases are analogous to a filing cabinet. Each record is like a card in the cabinet. If each record is a document, then the attributes of the document can be stored as searchable fields on the card. For example, a CAD file might have fields for the project name, the type of part, material, the designer, revision, change order number, and so on. Any data field can be used to search the database. The database is called a flat file because it is like a stack of cards, as shown in Figure 15.7.

A drawback of a flat-file database is the difficulty of showing multiple relationships. A drawing of a standard part, for example, should be stored only once in the database, although it is a part that appears in many different projects. If the project name for a part is a single field, with which project should the standard part be associated? If more fields are added to accommodate multiple project names, each of these fields will have to be searched anytime the user wants to find a list of parts by project.

A relational database overcomes this limitation by breaking data into tables of data that are related to each other through a common field. Figure 15.8 shows how

Project A		Project B		Project C	
Client: Acme Incorporated		Client:		Client:	
Project Manager: Albert Washington		Project Manager:		Project Manager:	
Assembly No.: 004412		Assembly No.:		Assembly No.:	
Part No.: 416		Part No.:		Part No.:	
Part No.: 212		Part No.:		Part No.:	

15.7 *The structure of a flat file is like an index card. The top-level structure—the document—is the card, and any data pertaining to the document are fields on the card. If the top level of the database were a project, then the fields associated with it would be the individual documents that relate to the project.*

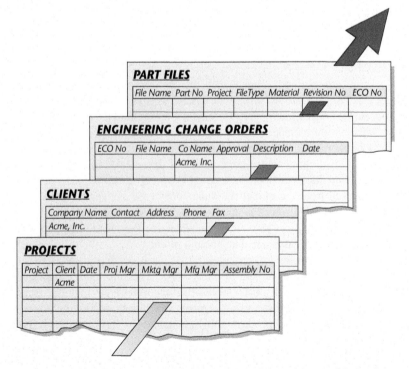

15.8 *Each entity in a relational database is stored in a table and linked to other entities by the fields they have in common.*

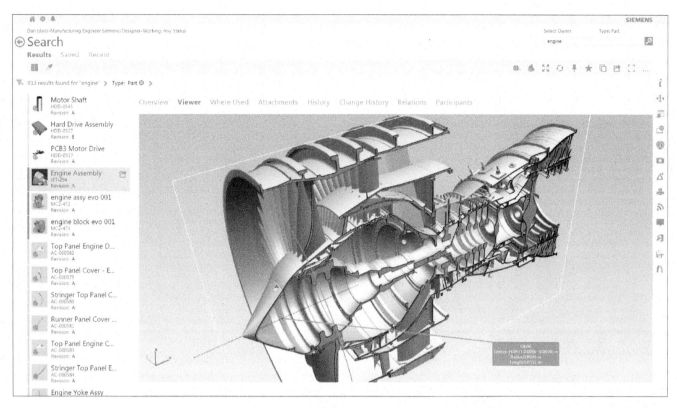

15.9 *Search features like those in Siemens Teamcenter PLM let users search to quickly find and view CAD files as well as other project information. (©2016 Siemens Product Lifecycle Management System. Reprinted with permission.)*

data might be organized in a relational database. A client table could assign a unique client ID to each client and contain fields for all the information about a client. A project table would assign a unique project ID to every project and include other fields of information related to the project, such as the client ID. Both tables share the client ID field, making it possible to link the data between the two tables. This allows a user to search any table of data and retrieve information from related tables through the common link.

Relational capabilities make it possible to search for and view data in the system in many different ways. Each document in the system is stored in one location, but it can belong to several different groups of documents at the same time through the relationships defined in the database. A table of standard parts, for example, could be linked by ID number to any number of projects yet reside in the database in a single location.

The relational capability makes it possible to query the system in a variety of ways. A product-based structure, for example, relates every document to a product manufactured by the company. Documents can be stored in separate tables by document type, such as drawing, 3D model, technical publication, or spreadsheet file. Each kind of file can be stored with attributes relevant to its type, such as title block information for a drawing, or publication date for a technical manual. The relations in the database make it possible to search for data in almost any combination (Figure 15.9). A user could locate, for example, all the sheet metal parts fabricated by a particular vendor for a particular customer, or all stainless steel fasteners less than 10 mm long.

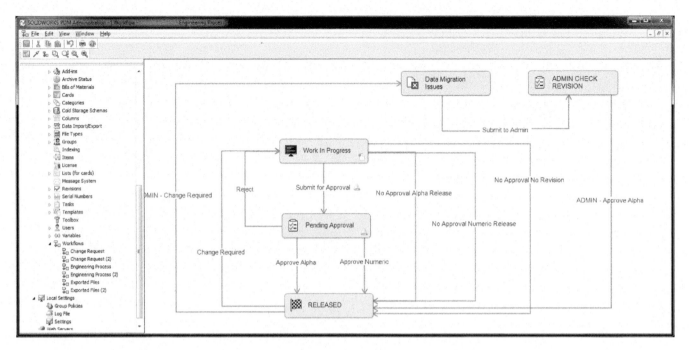

15.10 Workflow in a PDM

15.11 MANAGING WORK FLOW

Storage and retrieval of data is the key aspect of a product data management system, but its contribution to concurrent engineering is its ability to control access to and ensure accuracy of shared data. *Work flow* is the term used to describe how information moves through the system's checkpoints and out and back to team members.

The key to any electronic document control system is that a master record of all product data is stored securely on a networked computer system. The system provides access to the documents according to the user's defined level of permission. To work with a document, a user must check it out, as one would check out a book from a library. Changes that are made to the electronic file must be approved before the document is returned to the system. The earlier version of the document is stored as it appeared before the revision in order to provide a design history.

Most PDM systems allow for sophisticated levels of access that fit the organization and how they work. Only certain individuals will have the authority to create or change documents for a particular project. In a concurrent environment, the checkpoints corresponding to drawing approval may not be enough. Coding drawings according to their status— submitted, checked, approved, released—may offer more flexibility in how files are shared (Figure 15.10).

Many PDM systems also provide for tools that allow input from members who do not have permission to change a model but may "redline" a document (mark possible changes that are flagged and that can be implemented if they are approved by someone with permission to change the file) or add "sticky notes" that can be reviewed by the file's owner and other team members. This capability can improve team communication and interaction without adding meeting time or paperwork.

Archiving Work History

The controls built into work-flow systems in the product data management system function similarly when data are to be archived for long-term storage. PDM systems generally offer more information about the project history than a simple archive of files would. The system might capture time spent in each phase of the project, the number of revisions made at each stage, a list of team members who were involved, and other information that may be used to measure and improve productivity.

The system can also expand the snapshot in time that an engineering drawing represents. At any given point in time, the system can produce not just the drawing or CAD model but also a complete set of data for a project at that moment in time. This kind of archive can make it possible to backtrack to a problem point in the design or revisit a key decision point and pursue an alternative line with the design from that point.

Individual Productivity

One of the benefits that companies expect from an enterprise-wide PDM system is improved productivity that translates to reduced time-to-market for their products. Rockwell Corporation reported that implementing a PDM system reduced the time it took its project managers to cost a product from 4–5 days to 4–5 minutes because all the data were easily available. Similarly, design engineers can spend up to 25% to 30% of their time looking for information, retrieving information, waiting for copies of drawings, and archiving new data. An effective PDM system can eliminate this unproductive time because the designer knows where and how to look for released designs and other data. By providing easier access, the system can also promote reuse of existing designs and reduce the time spent "reinventing the wheel."

Many of the issues of file management can also be automated or aided by PDM software. By establishing work groups in the system that are linked to projects, the system can be designed to notify members of the group whenever a file is updated or changed. Designers who have downloaded copies of files can work with them until notified that they need to download a later version. Other PDM and file management systems, especially those implemented over distance networks, seek to reduce download times by comparing file dates and versions on the server and the receiving machine. For any set of files, the system will download only those that are more current than those already available. Graphical preview capabilities built into many systems also make it easier to identify files, especially large CAD files, before downloading them.

Instant-messaging tools, project e-mail grouped around thematic threads that team members can read and review as needed, automated file management tools, file transfer routines, and data query tools all help capture and disseminate data with the least amount of effort on the part of the user.

15.12 DATA MANAGEMENT AND THE WEB

Implementing a product data management system, or even a simpler document database, is a significant investment in capturing information, defining the use of various documents, and specifying the hardware and software needed. For smaller companies, the investment in a full-blown PDM system may not be necessary, but the strategy of organizing and retrieving engineering design data is still applicable.

Smaller companies, or those that must interact regularly with suppliers and partners in distant locations, can use the Internet to distribute access to project data. By creating a secure website, a company can provide network users access to the project data. Many of the same messaging and document management functions provided by a PDM system can be provided through browser and Internet-based tools (Figure 15.11).

Database servers that automate product websites also can provide access to the most current information and files. In addition, the Web has spawned a full range of tools for previewing graphical information that can be used to navigate through and select from CAD information.

CAD Files on the Web

One of the most useful developments for publishing CAD data on the Web is a *viewer*. A viewer is a small application that allows you to open and view CAD drawings without having the application package itself. Most CAD platforms offer a viewer that allows you to zoom, pan, and print the model. Without the cost of printing or mailing, a viewer makes it possible to make your CAD data viewable to a wider audience—including customers and nonengineers who want to preview a design but may not be able to interpret a 2D drawing.

The graphical nature of the Web and the rapid pace at which tools are being developed for it make it an ideal environment for sharing data among team members and for publishing CAD data. By preserving the interactivity of the model and the complexity of the data, yet making the model available to individuals who do not have a CAD workstation on their desktop, Web viewers overcome many of the limitations of paper drawings for those not familiar with technical drawings.

15.11   *Basecamp provides management tools using a Web browser format.*

ENGINEERING DOCUMENTATION:
MAKE IT WITHSTAND THE TEST OF TIME

"People often don't understand why there are such strict requirements for engineering documentation within the company," says Cliff Moore, Engineering Document Control Manager at Delta Design, the largest manufacturer of semiconductor test-handling equipment used by IC manufacturers around the world.

Delta Design is an ISO 9000–compliant company that uses a worldwide network of suppliers and has manufacturing and assembly facilities in the United States, the Philippines, Mexico, Singapore, and China. However, ISO guidelines do not tell a company how to manage and control its documents. Each company must have its own system that assures the quality of the product. Proper engineering documentation is one important aspect of this overall system.

At Delta Design, engineers use SolidWorks software to create 3D part models and assemblies. Drawings are created from the models to provide detailed manufacturing information. One aspect of Cliff's job is to manage the release and storage of the database of drawings and models.

New projects often start with a concept from the technical sales force or from an existing customer. From the concept, design specifications are written to guide the development of the new machine or subsystem. After the initial design specification is approved, engineers work freely on concepts and models, storing them on areas of the network devoted to their work group. As the design develops, new part identifying numbers may be tracked using an engineering revision code that Delta Design calls an X-rev. Once the design has been refined, tested, prototyped, and retested for fatigue and other long-term failure issues, and cost analysis performed, successful designs move on to the engineering release process. This is where Cliff and his team get involved.

15.12 *Delta Design's digital ECO form is used to release new parts or to approve changes to existing parts.*

To receive the necessary approvals to release the design, the engineer provides 3D models for each designed-for-manufacture part, an assembly model, and a set of drawings. An assembly drawing lists the bill of materials (BOM), which identifies each item and its part number (also in the title block of the part drawing) and illustrates how the device assembles. Separate work instructions may need to be included for complicated processes. Off-the-shelf purchased parts, such as connectors, washers, and screws, are also assigned part numbers and cross referenced with the manufacturer part number. In most cases the suppliers or manufacturers have solid models that can be downloaded, but if not, the engineer creates those models as needed. Test results and engineering notes are also a part of the release package.

The files for the project are then copied to a temporary directory, where they are reviewed by the individuals who will approve the release for manufacturing. The files in the temporary directory can be read by anyone but only changed or moved by a document control technician. The engineer completes an ECO requesting approval to release the new parts and assembly (see Figure 15.12). Cliff reviews the drawing package to ensure "due diligence" on the part of the designer. Cliff reminds them, "Someone may need to come back to this information five or ten years later, long after the 'tribal knowledge' about the project is gone."

Even though the approval process is digital, a face-to-face meeting is also held to review all new part releases and revisions to existing parts. This ensures good communication among all the different departments involved. Members from manufacturing, purchasing, product management, various engineering disciplines, and document control must give their final approval. Once everyone has signed off, the parts are ready for release and get the go-ahead for manufacture.

At this point, Cliff moves the part and assembly files into the master file storage area for released parts. Each file is named with its part number. Delta Design makes complex automated equipment for semiconductor test handling. They have tens of thousands of released parts. To make retrieval quicker, the files are stored in separate directories for assembly models, part models, and drawing files. Subfolders group the parts using the first few digits of the part number (Figure 15.13). Cliff and his staff verify that the links to parts within the assembly are working by opening the files after they are moved to the master directory. The same part may be used in many different assemblies and subassemblies. Opening each assembly file after it is moved ensures that all the correct part files are available and that the paths to them within the assembly are correct.

The other side of the equation is the Enterprise Resource Planning (ERP) software that the company uses. Information about parts, such as number, cost, purchasing agent responsibility, number on hand, reordering quantities, and where the part is used, is stored in a large database. PDFs of the part drawings are linked to the part information in the database. Anyone needing the information can search the database and view the linked part drawings.

Soon, Cliff hopes to move to an enterprise-wide PDM system that provides integrated work-flow tools, model checkout management, and automated notifications. Delta Design currently uses its own "homegrown" tools for these, which may require checking in several different places to ensure that two different project teams do not work on designs that change the same model. Cliff currently keeps a spreadsheet of all the ongoing projects and the part numbers that are involved. He looks forward to being even more efficient when these steps are automated.

(Case study images courtesy of Delta Design, a Cohu Company.)

15.13 *Released part models are stored in a master directory where they can be read but not erased or changed by anyone except document control personnel.*

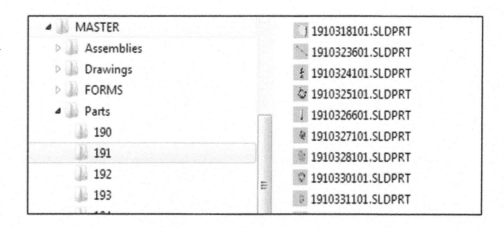

KEY WORDS

Approved By

Checked By

Drawn By

Engineering Change Order (ECO)

Enterprise Level

Flat Files

International Organization for Standardization (ISO)

Ownership

Permission

Product Data Management

Relational Database

Revision Block

Work Flow

Work Group Level

CHAPTER SUMMARY

- Models and drawings are detailed and expensive to create. It is important to understand how to manage product data for maximum advantage.
- Engineering documents have requirements for control and long term storage.
- Drawings, documented models, and other design data play an important function in engineering documentation.
- Some basic steps are typical for approving and controlling CAD data. You should also be able to describe various systems for producing engineering drawing numbers.
- Good file-handling and backup procedures require organization and a systematic approach.
- Terminology related to engineering documentation includes some commonly used acronyms such as PDM, ECN, and ECO and you should be familiar with the use of these terms.

SKILLS SUMMARY

You should understand issues in managing engineering drawings and product data. The exercises presented here allow you to describe how engineering documents are controlled and the role of drawings and CAD data in engineering documentation. You should be able to list the basic steps in approving and controlling CAD data and to describe various systems for producing engineering drawing numbers. Good file-handling and backup procedures require organization and a systematic approach. You should be able to describe how to use folders to organize files and directories in a consistent manner. You should be familiar with terminology related to engineering documentation and be able to define commonly used acronyms.

REVIEW QUESTIONS

1. How can CAD files be cataloged for future use?
2. List at least three ways in which you can use the Internet to communicate to other people involved in the product development or design process.
3. What is an ECO? What approval steps might be associated with it in a CAD drawing?
4. How can an engineer or designer determine whether a drawing is the most up-to-date when they are reviewing it on a printed sheet?
5. What is the role of a PDM system?

CHAPTER EXERCISES

Exercise 15.1 Develop a file naming convention and directory structure that would work for the documents related to your course work. Consider all the courses you are likely to take over your college years and how you might want to access documents from them. What different kinds of documents would you want to include? Anticipate making the documents available over a network to your prospective employer, and create a naming structure that will convey meaningful information about the document file. Draw a flowchart of the directory structure you would use to organize the files. Show the steps needed to access a particular type of document.

Exercise 15.2 A three-person company designs, fabricates, and sells a line of biological laboratory equipment. All drawings are produced using a CAD system. The company sells products to about twelve labs, with each user needing small custom features on the base product line. Contrast this company's document control needs with that of a large company that must keep track of multiple part source vendors, and uses dispersed teams of designers. What are the differences and similarities between the drawing control requirements of the two companies?

Exercise 15.3 Why might you wish to store electronic files in a directory different from the one containing your application software?

Exercise 15.4 Provide the source words and a one- or two-sentence definition of the following common engineering and computer acronyms (some research or investigation may be required):

PDM	FEA	ISO	ECO	ECN	VRML
CAD	EDMS	WORM	ASTM	HTML	.DXF

Exercise 15.5 What is the key to a successful product data management system?

Exercise 15.6 It is common to begin a project with a *drawing tree* or *drawing breakdown structure* (DBS) to identify the relationships among detail components, subassemblies, and assemblies. Create a DBS for a simple device, such as a stapler, doorknob, or vise.

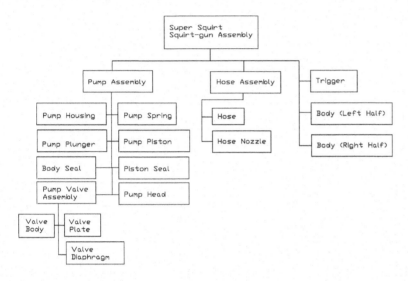

Exercise 15.7 A block diagram of drawing release process steps for a conventional paper drawing has been started for you on the right. Complete this flowchart and then create a block diagram of typical steps in the drawing release process for a computerized part in a digital database.

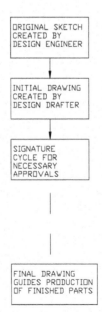

Exercise 15.8 A designer creates two original mating part drawings on a CAD system and stores them digitally in a specific folder on her PC. The drawings are printed and the prints are issued to the machine shop to guide part fabrication. After about 100 parts of the expected 300-part run have been produced, a change is requested by the shop to permit a larger bolt size to be used for assembly. The bolt size request affects both mating parts, so that interchangeability between the old and new parts will be lost. The designer complies and issues new drawings.

a. How should these new drawings be stored? Distributed? Labeled?
b. What procedure would you recommend to identify both drawings and parts produced?
c. Can you anticipate problems that might arise if good practices are not followed?

Exercise 15.9 ISO 9000 requirements for document and quality control are listed in a 12-item checklist in this chapter. State the logical reason for each of these 12 items, including potential consequences of ignoring each of the recommendations.

Exercise 15.10 Visit the company website for your CAD package and download the viewer software (if available). What types of files can the viewer open? What viewing and annotation options are built into the viewer?

CHAPTER SIXTEEN

GEARS AND CAMS

—— **OBJECTIVES** ——

After studying the material in this chapter, you should be able to:

1. Define the characteristics of a spur gear, worm gear, and bevel gear.

2. Calculate the gear ratio and rpm of two mating gears, given the pitch diameters.

3. Define the principal spur gear terms.

4. Draw a spur gear.

5. Describe the relationship between a cam profile and a displacement diagram.

6. Draw a cam profile, given a displacement profile drawing.

7. List the types of cam followers.

Refer to the following standards:
- *ANSI Y14.7.1 Gear Drawing Standards, Part 1: For Spur, Helical, Double Helical, and Rack*
- *ANSI Y14.7.2 Gear and Spline Drawing Standards, Part 2: Bevel and Hypoid Gears*
- *AGMA 933-B03 Basic Gear Geometry*

Two Spur Gears with Meshing Teeth *(Milos Luzanin/Shutterstock.)*

OVERVIEW

Gears, pulleys and belts, chains and sprockets, cams, linkages, and other devices are commonly used to transmit power and motion from one machine member to another. Understanding the function of these devices will help you create correct models, drawings, and specifications for them.

Gears are one of the most common drive transfer mechanisms. Gears can change rotation direction, rotation speed, and axis orientation. The complex shape of a gear tooth is the result of mathematical computation. Drawing gears exactly on paper or with CAD requires considerable theoretical knowledge; however, it is often not necessary to represent details of gear teeth. Advanced CAD software programs often can generate gear models based on the parameters for the gear. Hav-

ing an understanding of gear terminology before you start drawing a gear will help you provide the necessary information.

Cams change rotational motion into reciprocating motion. Both gears and cams are commonly used in automobile engines and transmissions.

The American Gear Manufacturers Association (AGMA) was founded in 1916. AGMA produces standards for gear design and manufacture for American and global markets. The association publishes specific standards for gear types such as spur gears used in vehicles, plastic gears, bevel gears, and many others. AGMA 933-B03 is the standard for basic gear geometry. For more information when designing gears, check their website at www.agma.org for relevant standards.

Spur Gear *(Courtesy of Big Sky Laser.)*

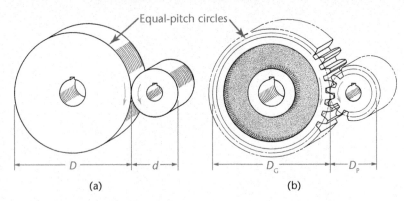

Equal-pitch circles

(a)   (b)

16.1   Friction Wheels and Toothed Gears

UNDERSTANDING GEARS

Gears are used to transmit power and rotating or reciprocating motion from one machine part to another. They may be classified according to the position of the shafts that they connect. Parallel shafts, for example, may be connected by *spur gears*, *helical gears*, or *herringbone gears*. Intersecting shafts may be connected by *bevel gears* having either straight, skew, or spiral teeth. Nonparallel, nonintersecting shafts may be connected by *helical gears*, *hypoid gears*, or a worm and *worm gear.* A spur gear meshed with a rack will convert rotary motion to reciprocating motion.

ASME/AGMA publishes detailed standards for gear design and drawing. Refer to these standards for current design specification and inspection practices for all gear types discussed in this chapter.

Using Gears to Transmit Power

The *friction wheels* shown in Figure 16.1a transmit motion and power from one shaft to another parallel shaft. However, friction wheels are subject to slipping, and a great deal of pressure is required between them to create the necessary frictional force; therefore, they are usually used for low-power applications, such as CD ROM drives. Spur gears (Figure 16.1b) have teeth on the cylindrical surfaces that fit together and transmit the same motion and power without slipping and with reduced bearing pressures.

If a friction wheel of diameter D turns at n **rpm** (revolutions per minute), the linear velocity, v, of a point on its periphery will be $\pi D n$, because $\pi D = c$ (circumference).

Example

Let

$D = 3$ in.
$n = 100$ rpm

Then

$v = \pi D n = \pi(3)(100)$ in./min
$= 942$ in./min

or

$\dfrac{942}{12} = 78.5$ ft/min

The *pitch circles* of a pair of mating spur gears correspond exactly to the outside diameters of the friction wheels, and because the gears turn in contact without slipping, they must have the same linear velocity at the pitch line.

Therefore $\pi D_G n_G = \pi D_P n_P$

or

$$\frac{D_G}{D_P} = \frac{n_P}{n_G} = m_G$$

where D_G = *pitch diameter* larger gear (called the gear)
D_P = pitch diameter of smaller gear (called the *pinion*)
n_G = rpm of gear
n_P = rpm of pinion
m_G = *gear ratio*

The gear ratio is also expressed as n_P/n_G or D_G/D_P.

Example

Let $D_G = 27''$ and $D_P = 9''$

Then

Gear ratio $= m_G = 27{:}9$

$= 3{:}1$ (read as 3 to 1)

Example

For the same gear pair, let $n_P = 1725$ rpm. Find n_G.

$$\frac{n_P}{n_G} = \frac{D_G}{D_P} \qquad \frac{n_G}{n_P} = \frac{D_P}{D_G}$$

$$n_G = n_P \frac{D_P}{D_G} = 1725 \cdot \frac{9}{27}$$

$$= \frac{1725}{3}$$

$$= 575 \text{ rpm}$$

The teeth on mating gears must be of equal width and spacing, so the number of teeth on each gear, N, is directly proportional to its pitch diameter, or

$$\frac{N_G}{N_P} = \frac{D_G}{D_P} = \frac{n_P}{n_G} = m_G$$

Spur Gear Definitions and Formulas

Proportions and shapes of gear teeth are well standardized, and the terms illustrated and defined in Figure 16.2 are common to all spur gears. The dimensions relating to tooth height are for full-depth 14.5° (which are becoming outmoded) or for 20° or 25° involute teeth. Of course, meshing gears must have the same pressure angle.

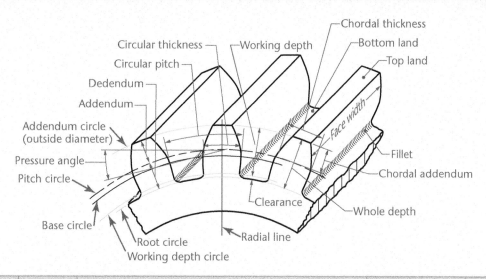

Term	Symbol	Definition	Formula for 20°/25° Pressure Angles	Formula for 14.5° Pressure Angle
Addendum	a	Radial distance from pitch circle to top of tooth	$a = 1/P$	$a = 1/P$
Base circle	D_B	Circle from which involute profile is generated	$D \cos(20° \text{ or } 25°)$	$D \cos(14.5°)$
Chordal addendum	a_c	Radial distance from the top of a tooth to the chord of the pitch circle	$a_c = a + \frac{1}{2}D$ $[1 - \cos(90°/N)]$	$a_c = a + \frac{1}{2}D$ $[1 - \cos(90°/N)]$
Chordal thickness	t_c	Thickness of a tooth measured along a chord of the pitch circle	$t_c = D \sin(90°/N)$	$t_c = D \sin(90°/N)$
Circular pitch	p	Distance measured along pitch circle from a point on one tooth to corresponding point on the adjacent tooth; includes one tooth and one space	$p = \pi D/N$ $p = \pi/P$	$p = \pi D/N$ $p = \pi/P$
Circular thickness	t	Thickness of a tooth measured along the pitch circle: equal to half the circular pitch	$t = p/2 = \pi/2P$ $t = \pi/2P$	$t = p/2 = \pi/2P$ $t = \pi/2P$
Clearance	c	Distance between top of a tooth and bottom of mating space, equal to the dedendum minus the addendum	$c = b - a$ $c = 0.25/P$	$c = b - a$ $c = 0.157/P$
Dedendum	b	Radial distance from pitch circle to bottom of tooth space	$b = 1.250/P$	$b = 1.157/P$
Diametral pitch	P	Ratio equal to the number of teeth on the gear per inch of pitch diameter	$P = N/D$	$P = N/D$
Number of teeth	N_G or N_P	Number of teeth on the gear or pinion	$N = P \times D$	$N = P \times D$
Outside diameter	D_o	Diameter of addendum circle, equal to pitch diameter plus twice the addendum	$D_o = D + 2a$ $D_o = (N + 2)/P$	$D_o = D + 2a$ $D_o = (N + 2)/P$
Pitch circle		An imaginary circle with the circumference of the friction gear from which the spur gear is derived		
Pitch diameter	D_G or D_P	Diameter of pitch circle of gear or pinion	$D = N/P$	$D = N/P$
Pressure angle	ϕ	Angle that determines direction of pressure between contacting teeth and designates shape of involute teeth—e.g. 14.5°, 20° or 25° involute; also determines the size of base circle		
Root diameter	D_R	Diameter of the root circle; equal to pitch diameter minus twice the dedendum	$D_R = D - 2b =$ $(N - 2.5)/P$	$D_R = D - 2b =$ $(N - 2.314)/P$
Whole depth	h_t	Total height of the tooth; equal to the addendum plus the dedendum	$h_t = a + b =$ $2.250/P$	$h_t = a + b =$ $2.157/P$
Working depth	h_k	Distance a tooth projects into mating space; equal to twice the addendum	$h_k = 2a = 2/P$	$h_k = 2a = 2/P$

16.2   Spur Gear Terminology

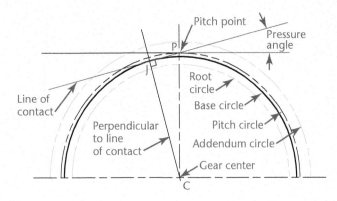

16.3   Construction of a Base Circle

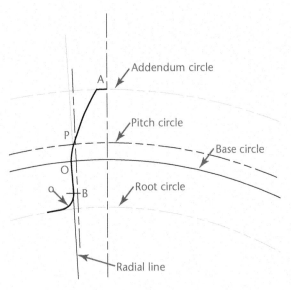

16.4   The Involute Profile

16.5   Shaded Model of Involute Shaped Spur Gear Teeth. *It is not typical to model gear teeth in detail, as doing so creates an unnecessarily large and complex model.*

To make gears operate smoothly with a minimum of noise and vibration, the curved surface of the tooth profile uses a definite geometric form. The most common form in use today is the **involute** profile shown in Figure 16.4. (The word *involute* means "rolled inward.")

16.1 CONSTRUCTING A BASE CIRCLE

The involute tooth form depends on the pressure angle, which was ordinarily 14.5° and is now typically 20° or 25°. This pressure angle determines the size of the **base circle;** from this the involute curve is generated.

To calculate the base circle for the spur gear as shown in Figure 16.3, follow these steps. At any point on the pitch circle, such as point *P* (the pitch point) draw a line tangent to the pitch circle; draw a second line through *P* at the required pressure angle (frequently approximated at 15° on the drawing). This line is called the *line of contact*. Next, draw a line perpendicular to the line of contact from the center, *C*. Then, draw the base circle with radius *CJ* tangent to the line of contact at *J*.

16.2 THE INVOLUTE TOOTH SHAPE

If the exact shape of the tooth is desired, the portion of the profile from the base circle to the **addendum circle** (outside diameter) can be drawn as the involute of the base circle. In Figure 16.4, the tooth profile from *A* to *O* is an involute of the base circle. The part of the profile below the base circle, line *OB*, is drawn as a radial line (a straight line drawn from the gear center) that terminates in the fillet at the **root circle.** The fillet should be equal in radius to one and a half times the clearance from the tip of the tooth to the bottom of the mating space.

16.3 APPROXIMATE INVOLUTE USING CIRCULAR ARCS

Involute curves can be closely approximated with two circular arcs, as shown in Figure 16.6. This method, originally devised by G. B. Grant, uses a table of arc radii, an involute odontograph, for gears with various numbers of teeth. To use this method, draw the base circle as described above, and set off the spacing of the teeth along the pitch circle. Then, draw the face of the tooth from *P* to *A* with the face radius *R*, and draw the portion of the flank from *P* to *O* with the flank radius *r*. Draw both arcs from centers located on the base circle. The table in Figure 16.6 gives the correct face and flank radii for gears of one **diametral pitch.** For other pitches, divide the values in the table by the diametral pitch. For gears with more than 90 teeth, use a single radius (let *R = r*) computed from the appropriate formula given in Figure 16.6, then divide by diametral pitch. Below the base circle, complete the flank of the tooth with a radial line *OB* and a fillet. (A typical fillet radius is 1.5 times the clearance.)

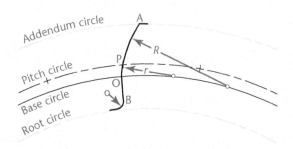

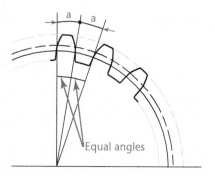

16.7 Spacing Gear Teeth

No. of Teeth (N)	14.5°		20°	
	R (in.)	r (in.)	R (in.)	r (in.)
12	2.87	0.79	3.21	1.31
13	3.02	0.88	3.40	1.45
14	3.17	0.97	3.58	1.60
15	3.31	1.06	3.76	1.75
16	3.46	1.16	3.94	1.90
17	3.60	1.26	4.12	2.05
18	3.74	1.36	4.30	2.20
19	3.88	1.46	4.48	2.35
20	4.02	1.56	4.66	2.51
21	4.16	1.66	4.84	2.66
22	4.29	1.77	5.02	2.82
23	4.43	1.87	5.20	2.98
24	4.57	1.98	5.37	3.14
25	4.70	2.08	5.55	3.29
26	4.84	2.19	5.73	3.45
27	4.97	2.30	5.90	3.61
28	5.11	2.41	6.08	3.77
29	5.24	2.52	6.25	3.93
30	5.37	2.63	6.43	4.10
31	5.51	2.74	6.60	4.26
32	5.64	2.85	6.78	4.42
33	5.77	2.96	6.95	4.58
34	5.90	3.07	7.13	4.74
35	6.03	3.18	7.30	4.91
36	6.17	3.29	7.47	5.07
37–39	6.36	3.46	7.82	5.32
40–44	6.82	3.86	8.52	5.90
45–50	7.50	4.46	9.48	6.76
51–60	8.40	5.28	10.84	7.92
61–72	9.76	6.54	12.76	9.68
73–90	11.42	8.14	15.32	11.96
91–120	0.118N		0.156N	
121–180	0.122N		0.165N	
Over 180	0.125N		0.171N	

16.6 Wellman's Involute Odontograph for Drawing Gear Teeth Using Circular Arcs

16.4 SPACING GEAR TEETH

Suppose that number of teeth $(N) = 20$ and diametral pitch $(P) = 4$ for a 14.5° involute tooth. The values from Figure 16.6 are $R = 4.02$ and $r = 1.56$. These must be divided by P; yielding $R = 4.02/4 = 1.005''$ and $r = 1.56/4 = 0.39''$.

Space the teeth around the periphery by laying out equal angles (Figure 16.7). The number of spaces should be $2N$, twice the number of teeth, to make the space between teeth equal to the tooth thickness at the pitch circle. In the example, because $N = 20$, $a = 360°/2N = 360°/40 = 9°$, the angle subtended by each tooth and each space.

> **TIP**
>
> The Divide command in the AutoCAD software is very handy for dividing a circle or other geometry into any number of equal divisions. You can also use it to insert a block at the same time. A polar array is another useful tool for creating gears.

Involute Gear Hob. *Spur gears with involute tooth shapes are usually manufactured using a hobbing machine. This machine cuts gear teeth by rotating the gear blank and a cutter like the one shown at a fixed speed ratio. The cross-sectional profile of the sides of the teeth on the cutter generates the involute tooth shape for the gear. Very small gears normally must be milled instead. (Dmitry Kalinovsky/ Shutterstock.)*

16.5 RACK TEETH

Gear teeth formed on a flat surface are called a **rack.** In the involute system, the sides of rack teeth are straight and are inclined at an angle equal to the pressure angle. To mesh with a gear, the **linear pitch** of the rack must be the same as the **circular pitch** of the gear, and the rack teeth must have the same height proportions as the gear teeth (see Figure 16.8).

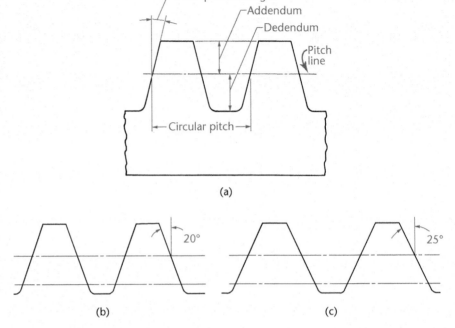

16.8 Involute Rack Teeth. *(a) 14.5° Pressure Angle, (b) 20° Pressure Angle, (c) 25° Pressure Angle*

16.6 WORKING DRAWINGS OF SPUR GEARS

A typical working drawing of a spur gear is shown in Figure 16.9. Because the teeth are cut to standard shape, it is not necessary to show individual teeth on the drawing. Instead, draw the addendum and root circles as phantom lines and the pitch circle as a centerline.

The drawing actually shows only a **gear blank**—a gear complete except for teeth. Because the machining of the blank and the cutting of the teeth are separate operations, the necessary dimensions are arranged in two groups: the blank dimensions are shown on the views, and the cutting data are given in a note or table.

Before laying out the working drawing, calculate the gear dimensions. For example, if the gear must have 48 teeth of 4 diametral pitch, with 14.5° full-depth involute profile, as in Figure 16.9, calculate the following items in this order: **pitch diameter, addendum, dedendum, outside diameter, root diameter, whole depth, chordal thickness,** and **chordal addendum.**

The dimensions shown in Figure 16.9 are the minimum requirements for the spur gear. The chordal addendum and chordal thickness are given to aid in checking the finished gear. Other special data may be given in the table, according to the degree of precision required and the manufacturing method.

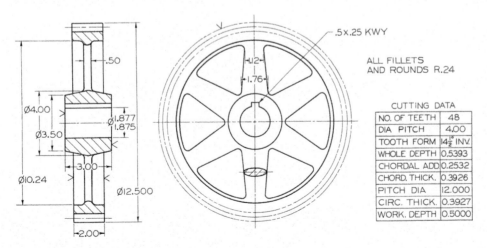

.5×.25 KWY

ALL FILLETS
AND ROUNDS R.24

CUTTING DATA	
NO. OF TEETH	48
DIA PITCH	4.00
TOOTH FORM	14½° INV.
WHOLE DEPTH	0.5393
CHORDAL ADD	0.2532
CHORD. THICK.	0.3926
PITCH DIA	12.000
CIRC. THICK.	0.3927
WORK. DEPTH	0.5000

16.9 Working Drawing of a Spur Gear

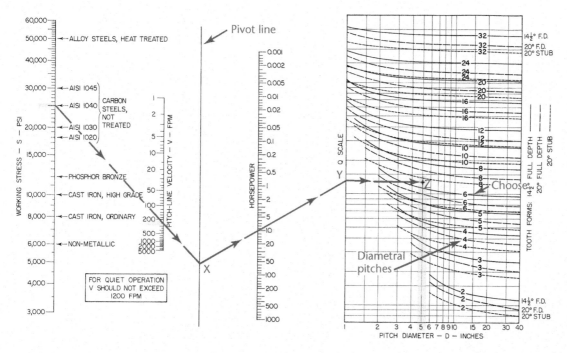

16.10 Chart for Design of Cut Spur Gears. *The chart is based on the Lewis equation, with the Barth velocity modification, and assumes gear face width equal to three times the circular pitch.*

16.7 SPUR GEAR DESIGN

Spur gear design normally begins with selecting pitch diameters to suit the required speed ratio, center distance, and space limitations. The size of the teeth (the diametral pitch) depends on the gear speeds, gear materials, horsepower to be transmitted, and the selected tooth form. The complete analysis and design of precision gears is complex and beyond the scope of this textbook, but the chart in Figure 16.10 gives suitable diametral pitches for ordinary cut spur gears.

Example Determine the diametral pitch and face width for a 5″ pitch diameter (G10400 carbon steel) pinion with 14.5° full-depth teeth that must transmit 10 hp (horsepower) at 200 rpm.

Calculate the pitch in line velocity V as follows:

$$V = \pi/12\left(D_{\mathrm{P}}n_{\mathrm{P}}\right)$$
$$= 0.262 \times 5 \times 200 = 262 \text{ fpm}\left(\text{ft/min}\right)$$

On the chart, draw a straight line from 25,000 psi on the working stress scale through 262 fpm on the velocity scale to

intersect the pivot line at X. From X, draw a second straight line through 10 on the horsepower scale to intersect the Q scale at Y. From this point, enter the graph of pitches and go to the ordinate for 5″ pitch diameter. The junction point Z falls slightly above the curve for 14.5° full-depth teeth of 6 diametral pitch; hence, choose 6 diametral pitch for the gears.

For good proportions, the face width of a spur gear should be about three times the circular pitch, and this proportion is incorporated in the chart. For 6 diametral pitch, the circular pitch is $\pi/6$ or .5236″, and the face width is $3 \times .5236$ or 1.5708″. This width should be rounded to 1-5/8″ (1.625″).

When both the pinion and the gear are of the same material, the smaller gear is the weaker, and the design should be based on the pinion. When the materials are different, the chart should be used to determine the horsepower capacity of each gear.

16.11 Worm

A Waverly Guitar Tuner. *Worms are often designed so they can easily turn the gear, but the gear cannot turn the worm. Guitar machines, often called tuners, use worm gears so that the guitar can be tuned by turning the worm, but the strings are kept taut, as the gear cannot turn the worm.*
(Courtesy of Stewart-MacDonald Company.)

16.8 WORM GEARS

Worm gears are used to transmit power between nonintersecting shafts that are at right angles to each other. A worm (Figure 16.11) is a screw with a thread shaped like a rack tooth. The worm wheel is similar to a helical gear that has been cut to conform to the shape of the worm for more contact. Worm gearing offers a large speed ratio, since with one revolution a single-thread worm advances the worm wheel only one tooth and a space.

Figure 16.12 shows a worm and a wheel engaged. The section taken through the center of the worm and perpendicular to the axis of the worm wheel shows that the worm section is identical to a rack and that the wheel section is identical to a spur gear. Consequently, in this plane the height proportions of thread and gear teeth are the same as for a spur gear of corresponding pitch.

Pitch (*p*) The axial *pitch* of the worm is the distance from a point on one thread to the corresponding point on the next thread measured parallel to the worm axis. The pitch of the worm must be exactly equal to the circular pitch of the gear.

Lead *(L)* The *lead* is the distance that the thread advances axially in one turn. The lead is always a multiple of the pitch. Thus, for a single-thread worm, the lead equals the pitch; for a double-thread worm, the lead is twice the pitch, and so on.

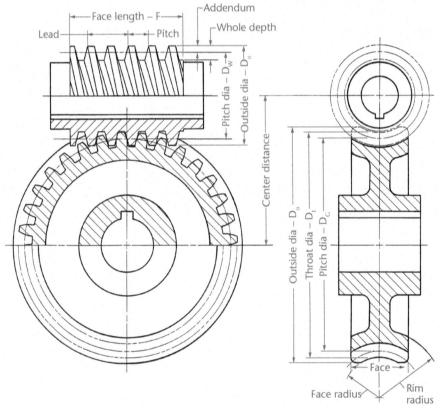

16.12 Double-Thread Worm and Worm Gear

Lead angle (λ)

The lead angle is the angle between a tangent to the helix at the pitch diameter and a plane perpendicular to the axis of the worm. The lead angle can be calculated from

$$\tan \lambda = \frac{L}{\pi D_W}$$

where

D_W = pitch diameter of the worm

The speed ratio of worm gears depends only on the number of threads on the worm and the number of teeth on the gear. Therefore,

$$m_G = \frac{N_G}{N_W}$$

where

N_G = number of teeth on the gear
N_W = number of threads on the worm

For 14.5° standard involute teeth and single-thread or double-thread worms, the following proportions are the recommended practice of the AGMA. All formulas are expressed in terms of circular pitch p instead of diametral pitch P. It is easier to machine the worm and the hob used to cut the gear if the circular pitch has an even rational value such as 5/8″.

For the worm:

Pitch diameter	$D_W = 2.4p + 1.1*$
Whole depth	$h_t = 0.686p$
Outside diameter	$D_o = D_W + 2a$
Face length	$F = p(4.5 + N_G/50)$

For the gear:

Pitch diameter	$D_G = p(N_G/\pi)$
Throat diameter	$D_t = D_G + 0.636p$
Outside diameter	$D_o = D_t + 0.4775p$
Face radius	$R_f = .5D_W - 0.318p$
Rim radius	$R_r = .5D_W + p$
Face width	$F = 2.38p + 0.25$
Center distance	$C = .5(D_G + D_W)$

Recommended value but may be varied.

16.9 WORKING DRAWINGS OF WORM GEARS

In an assembly drawing, the engaged worm and gear can be shown as in Figure 16.12, but usually the gear teeth are omitted and the gear blank represented conventionally, as shown in the lower half of the circular view. On detail drawings, the worm and gear are usually drawn separately, as shown in Figures 16.13 and 16.14. Although their dimensioning depends on the production method, it is standard practice to dimension the blanks on the views and give the cutting data in a table, as shown. Note dimensions that closely affect the engagement of the gear and worm have been given as three-place decimal or limit dimensions; other dimensions, such as rim radius, face lengths, and gear outside diameter, have been rounded to convenient two-place decimal values.

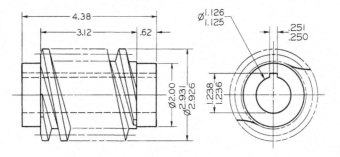

CUTTING DATA	
NO. OF THREADS	2
PITCH DIA	2.533
AXIAL PITCH	0.625
LEAD–R H	1.250
LEAD ANGLE	8° 56'
PRESSURE ANGLE	14½°
WHOLE DEPTH	0.429

16.13 Working Drawing of a Worm

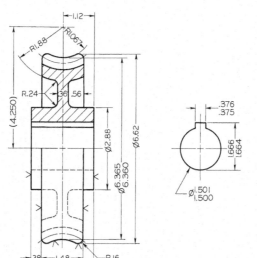

CUTTING DATA	
NO. OF TEETH	30
PITCH DIA	5.967
ADDENDUM	0.199
WHOLE DEPTH	0.429
NO. OF THREADS	2
AXIAL PITCH	0.625
LEAD–R H	1.250
LEAD ANGLE	8° 56'
PRESSURE ANGLE	14½°

16.14 Working Drawing of a Worm Gear

16.15   Bevel Gears *(Courtesy of Stock Drive Products/Sterling Instruments.)*

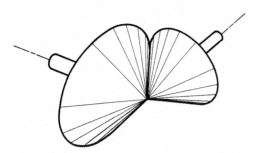

16.16   Friction Cones

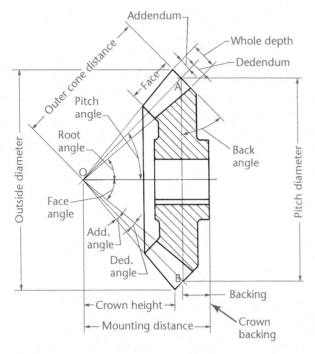

16.17   Bevel Gear Terminology

16.10 BEVEL GEARS

Bevel gears (Figure 16.15) are used to transmit power between shafts whose axes intersect. The analogous friction drive would consist of a pair of cones with a common apex at the point where their axes intersect, as in Figure 16.16. The axes may intersect at any angle, but right angles are most common. Bevel gear teeth have the same involute shape as teeth on spur gears, but they are tapered toward the cone apex; hence, the height and width of a bevel gear tooth vary with the distance from the cone apex. Spur gears are interchangeable (a spur gear of given pitch will run properly with any other spur gear of the same pitch and tooth form), but this is not true of bevel gears, which must be designed in pairs and will run only with each other.

The speed ratio of bevel gears can be calculated from the same formulas given for spur gears.

16.11 BEVEL GEAR DEFINITIONS AND FORMULAS

Because the design of bevel gears is very similar to that of spur gears, many spur gear terms are applied with slight modification to bevel gears. Just as in spur gears, the pitch diameter D of a bevel gear is the diameter of the base of the pitch cone, the circular pitch p to the teeth is measured along this circle and the diametral pitch P is also based on this circle.

The important dimensions and angles of a bevel gear are illustrated in Figure 16.17. The pitch cone is shown as the triangle AOB, and the pitch angle is half of angle AOB. The root and face angle lines do not actually converge at point O but are often drawn as if they do for simplicity. Figure 16.17 shows that the pitch angle of each gear depends on the relative diameters of the gears. When the shafts are at right angles, the sum of the pitch angles for the two mating gears equals 90°.

Therefore, the pitch angles, Γ (gamma), are determined from the following equations:

$$\tan \Gamma_G = \frac{D_G}{D_P} = \frac{N_G}{N_P}$$

and

$$\tan \Gamma_P = \frac{D_P}{D_G} = \frac{N_P}{N_G}$$

In the simplified formulas given here, tooth proportions are assumed equal on both gears, but in modern practice bevel gears are often designed with unequal addenda and unequal tooth thicknesses to balance the strength of gear and pinion. Refer to AGMA standards for more details.

Terms for bevel gear definitions and formulas are given in Table 16.1.

16.12 WORKING DRAWINGS OF BEVEL GEARS

Like those for spur gears, working drawings of bevel gears give only the dimensions of the gear blank. Data necessary for cutting the teeth are given in a note or table. A single sectional view will usually provide all necessary information (Figure 16.18). If a second view is required, only the gear blank is drawn, and the tooth profiles are omitted. Two gears are shown in their operating relationship. On detail drawings, each gear is usually drawn separately, as in Figure 16.17, and fully dimensioned. Placement of the gear-blank dimensions depends largely on the manufacturing methods used in producing the gear, but the scheme shown is commonly followed.

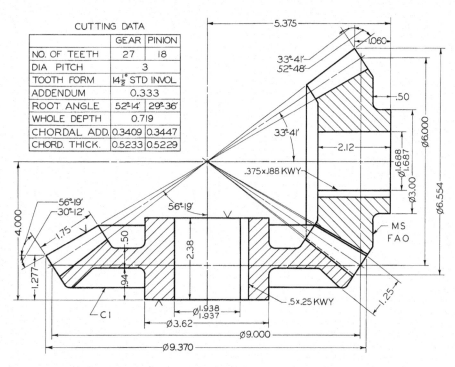

CUTTING DATA	GEAR	PINION
NO. OF TEETH	27	18
DIA PITCH	3	
TOOTH FORM	$14\frac{1}{2}°$ STD INVOL	
ADDENDUM	0.333	
ROOT ANGLE	52°14'	29°36'
WHOLE DEPTH	0.719	
CHORDAL ADD.	0.3409	0.3447
CHORD. THICK.	0.5233	0.5229

16.18   Working Drawing of Bevel Gears

Table 16.1 Bevel Gear Terms, Definitions, and Formulas

Term	Symbol	Definition	Formula
Addendum	a	Distance from pitch cone to top of tooth; measured at large end of tooth	$a = 1/P$
Addendum angle	α	Angle subtended by addendum; same for gear and pinion	$\tan \alpha = a/A$
Back angle		Usually equal to the pitch angle	
Backing	Y	Distance from base of pitch cone to rear of hub	
Chordal addendum Chordal thickness	a_c t_c	For bevel gears, the formulas given for spur gears can be used if D is replaced by $D/\cos \Gamma$ and N is replaced by $N \cos \Gamma$	
Crown backing	Z	More practical than backing for shop use; dimension Z given on drawings instead of Y	$Z = Y + a \sin \Gamma$
Crown height	X	Distance, parallel to gear axis, from cone apex to crown of the gear	$X = .5D_o/\tan \Gamma_o$
Dedendum	b	Distance from pitch cone to bottom of tooth; measured at large end of tooth	$b = 1.188/P$
Dedendum angle	δ	Angle subtended by dedendum; same for gear and pinion	$\tan \delta = b/A$
Face angle	Γ_o	Angle between top of teeth and the gear axis	$\Gamma_o = \Gamma + \alpha$
Face width	F	Should not exceed $A/3$ or $10/P$, whichever is smaller	
Mounting distance	M	A dimension used primarily for inspection and assembly purposes	$M = Y + .5D/\tan \Gamma$
Outer cone distance	A	Slant height of pitch cone; same for gear and pinion	$A = D/(2 \sin \Gamma)$
Outside diameter	D_o	Diameter of outside or crown circle of the gear	$D_o = D + 2a \cos \Gamma$
Pitch diameter	D_G	Diameter of base of pitch cone of gear	$D_G = N_G/P$
	D_P	Diameter of base of pitch cone of pinion	$D_P = N_P/P$
Root angle	Γ_R	Angle between the root of the teeth and the gear axis	$\Gamma_R = \Gamma - \delta$

STOCK GEAR MODELS AND DRAWINGS

A great website where you can find stock models for gears is the Stock Drive Products/Sterling Instrument site at sdp-si.com (Figure A). Once you have registered, you can search their site for useful standard parts that you might purchase for a design. After you have located a part, you can download 2D or 3D CAD data. Figure B shows the compatible file types available for download. Detailed data sheets are available for download in PDF format. You can even use a Web viewer to view and rotate the 3D model before you download it (Figure C).

When gears are ordered to use as standard parts in an assembly, a detailed gear drawing is not necessary. A table showing the gear information is often sufficient. Simplified representations of the shape—for example, the exterior envelope and/or base curves—may be used to represent the gear.

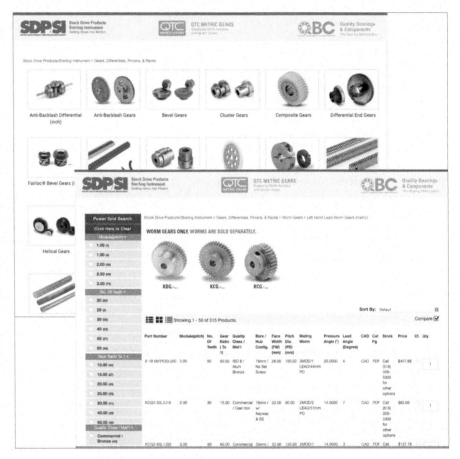

(A) *Stock Drive Product/Sterling Instrument provides downloadable CAD models for the parts they sell. (Courtesy of Stock Drive Products/Sterling Instrument, sdp-si.com.)*

(B) *Several CAD formats are available for download. (Courtesy of Stock Drive Products/Sterling Instrument, sdp-si.com.)*

(C) *An interactive viewer allows you to view and rotate the 3D model via the Web. (Courtesy of Stock Drive Products/Sterling Instrument, sdp-si.com.)*

Camshafts *(Courtesy of Andrew Wakeford/Getty Images, Inc.-Photodisc.)*

Billet Steel Cams for Ford 4.6/5.4L SOHC V-8 *(Courtesy of Crane Cams, Inc.)*

16.13 CAMS

Cams can produce unusual and irregular motions that would be difficult to produce otherwise. Figure 16.19a shows the basic principle of the cam. A shaft rotating at uniform speed carries an irregularly shaped disk called a cam; a reciprocating member, called the *cam follower*, presses a small roller against the curved surface of the cam. (The roller is held in contact with the cam by gravity or a spring.) Rotating the cam causes the follower to reciprocate with a cyclic motion according to the shape of the *cam profile.*

Figure 16.19b shows an automobile valve cam that operates a flat-faced follower. Figure 16.19c shows a disk cam with the roller follower attached to a linkage to transmit motion to another part of the device.

The following sections discuss how to draw a cam profile that will cause the follower to produce the particular motion that is needed.

Most CAD software provides tools to generate cams from design data, so you will not typically draw them manually. However the general principle is helpful when using these design tools.

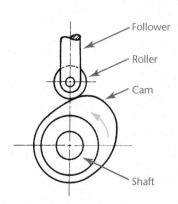

(a) Basic cam principle

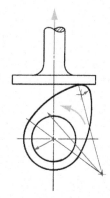

(b) Automobile valve cam with flat-faced follower

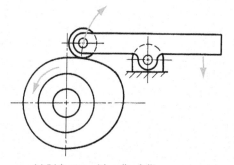

(c) Disk cam with roller follower attached to a linkage

16.19   Disk Cams

16.20 Displacement Diagram with Typical Curves

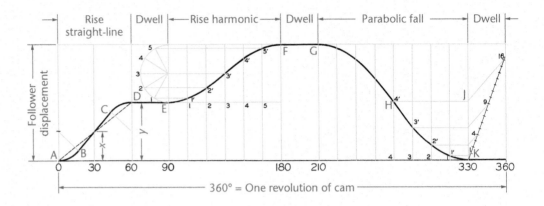

16.14 DISPLACEMENT DIAGRAMS

Because the motion of the follower is your first concern, its rate of speed and its various positions should be carefully planned in a displacement diagram before the cam profile is constructed. A *displacement diagram* (Figure 16.20) is a curve showing the displacement of the follower as ordinates on a baseline that represents one revolution of the cam. Draw the follower displacement to scale, but you can use any convenient length to represent the 360° of cam rotation.

The motion of the follower as it rises or falls depends on the shape of the curves in the displacement diagram. In this diagram, four commonly employed types of curves are shown. If a straight line is used, such as the dashed line *AD* in Figure 16.20, the follower will move

with a uniform velocity, but it will be forced to start and stop very abruptly, producing high acceleration and unnecessary force on the follower and other parts. This straight-line motion can be modified as shown in the curve *ABCD*, where arcs have been introduced at the beginning and at the end of the period.

The curve shown at *EF* gives harmonic motion to the follower. To manually construct this curve, draw a semicircle with a diameter equal to the desired rise. Divide the circumference of the semicircle into equal arcs. (The number of divisions should be the same as the number of horizontal divisions.) Then, find points on the curve by projecting horizontally from the divisions on the semicircle to the corresponding ordinates.

The parabolic curve shown at *GHK* gives the follower constantly accelerated and decelerated motion. The half of the curve from *G* to *H* is exactly the reverse of the half from *H* to *K*. To manually construct the curve *HK*, divide the vertical height from *K* to *J* into distances proportional to 1', 2', 3', or 1, 4, 9, and so on. The number of vertical divisions should be the same as the number of horizontal divisions. Find points on the curve by projecting horizontally from the divisions on the line *JK* to the corresponding ordinates. The parabolic curve and curves of higher polynomial equations produce smoother follower motion than those of the other curves discussed.

16.15 CAM PROFILES

The general method for manually constructing a cam profile is shown in Figure 16.21. The disk cam rotating counterclockwise on its shaft raises and lowers the roller follower, which is constrained to move along the straight line *AB*. The displacement diagram at the bottom of the figure shows the desired follower motion.

With the follower in its lowest or initial position, the center of the roller is at *A*, and *OA* is the radius of the base circle. The diameter of the base circle is determined from design parameters that are not discussed here.

Because the cam must remain stationary while it is being drawn, you can obtain an equivalent rotative effect by imagining that the cam stands still

while the follower rotates about it in the opposite direction. Therefore, the base circle is divided into 12 equal divisions corresponding to the divisions used in the displacement diagram. These divisions begin at zero and are numbered in the direction opposite the cam rotation.

The points 1, 2, and so on, on the follower axis *AB* indicate successive positions of the center of the roller and are located by transferring ordinates such as *X* and *Y* from the displacement diagram. Thus, when the cam has rotated 60°, the follower roller must rise a distance *X* to position 2, and after 90° of rotation, a distance *Y* to position 3, and so on.

Note that while the center of the roller moved from its initial position *A* to position 2, for example, the cam rotated

60° counterclockwise. Therefore, point 2 must be revolved clockwise about the cam center *O* to the corresponding 60° tangent line to establish point 2'. In this position, the complete follower would appear as shown by the phantom outline. Points represent consecutive positions of the roller center, and a smooth curve drawn through these points is called the *pitch curve*. To obtain the actual cam profile, the roller must be drawn in a number of positions, and the cam profile drawn tangent to the roller circles, as shown. The best results are obtained by first drawing the pitch curve very carefully and then drawing several closely spaced roller circles with centers on the pitch curve, as shown between points 5' and 6'.

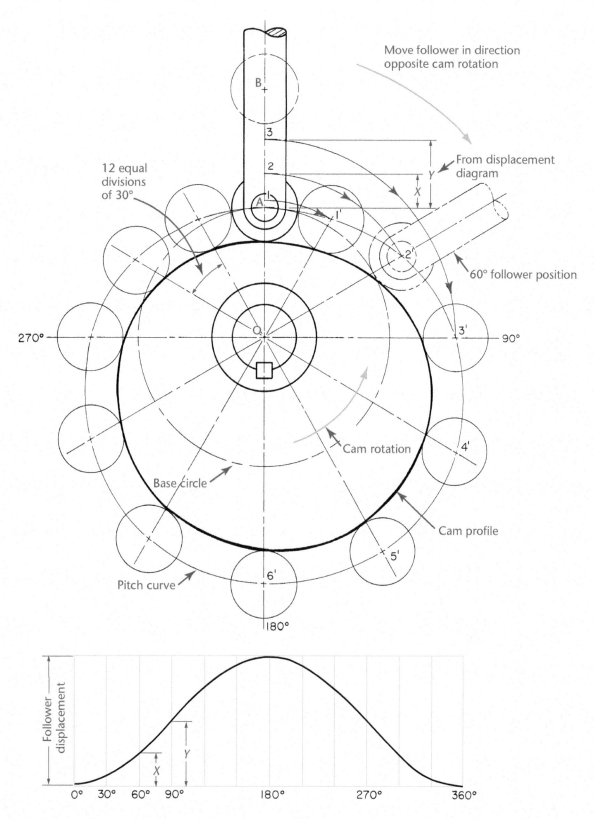

16.21 Disk Cam Profile Construction

16.16 OFFSET AND PIVOTED CAM FOLLOWERS

If the follower is offset as shown in Figure 16.22, an offset circle is drawn with center O and radius equal to the amount of offset. As the cam turns, the extended centerline of the follower will always be tangent to this offset circle. The equiangular spaces are stepped off on the offset circle, and tangent lines are then drawn from each point on the offset circle, as shown.

If the roller is on a pivoted arm, as shown in Figure 16.23a, then the displacement of the roller center is along the circular arc AB. The height of the displacement diagram (not shown) should be made equal to the rectified length of arc AB. Ordinates from the diagram are then transferred to arc AB to locate the roller positions 1, 2, 3, ... As the follower is revolved about the cam, pivot point C moves in a circular path of radius OC to the consecutive positions C_1, C_2, and so on. Length AC is constant for all follower positions; hence, from each new position of point C, the follower arc of radius R is drawn as shown at the 90° position. The roller centers 1, 2, 3 are now revolved about the cam center O to intersect the follower arcs at 1', 2', 3'. After the pitch curve is completed, the cam profile is drawn tangent to the roller circles.

The construction for a flat-faced follower is shown in Figure 16.23b. The initial point of contact is at A, and points 1, 2, 3, represent consecutive positions of the follower face. Then, for the 90° position, point 3 must be revolved 90°, as shown, to position 3', and the flat face of the follower is drawn through point 3' at right angles to the cam radius. When this procedure is repeated for each position, the cam profile will be enveloped by a series of straight lines, and the cam profile is drawn inside and tangent to these lines. Note that the point of contact, initially at A, changes as the follower rises. At 90°, for example, contact is at D, a distance X to the right of the follower axis.

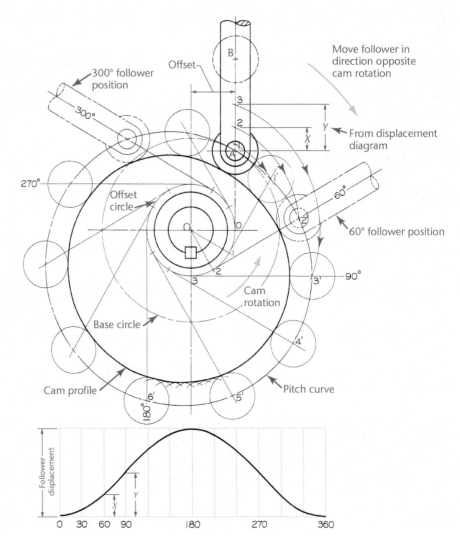

16.22   Disk Cam Profile with Offset Follower Construction

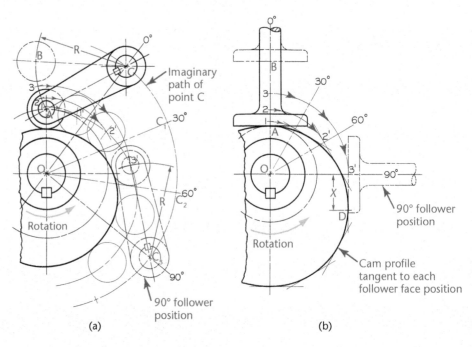

(a)   (b)

16.23   Pivoted and Flat-Faced Followers

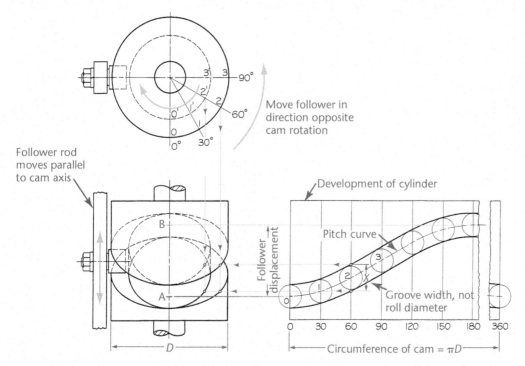

16.24   Cylindrical Cam

16.17 CYLINDRICAL CAMS

When the follower movement is in a plane parallel to the camshaft, some form of cylindrical cam must be employed. In Figure 16.24, for example, the follower rod moves vertically parallel to the cam axis as the attached roller follows the groove in the rotating cam cylinder.

A cylindrical cam of diameter D is required to lift the follower rod a distance AB with harmonic motion in 180° of cam motion and to return the rod in the remaining 180° with the same motion. The displacement diagram is drawn first and conveniently placed directly opposite the front view. The 360° length of the diagram must be made equal to πD so that the resulting curves will be a true

development of the outer surface of the cam cylinder. The pitch curve is drawn to represent the required motion, and a series of roller circles is then drawn to establish the sides of the groove tangent to these circles. This completes the development of the outer cylinder and actually provides all information needed for making the cam; hence, it is not uncommon to omit the curves in the front view.

To complete the front view, points on the curves are projected horizontally from the development. For example, at 60° in the development, the width of the groove measured parallel to the cam axis is X, a distance slightly greater than the

actual roller diameter. This width X is projected to the front view directly below point 2, the corresponding 60° position in the top view, to establish two points on the outer curves. The inner curves for the bottom of the groove can be established in the same manner, except that the groove width X is located below point 2', which lies on the inner diameter. The inner curves are only approximate because the width at the bottom of the groove is actually slightly greater than X, but the exact bottom width can be determined only by drawing a second development for the inner cylinder.

16.18 OTHER DRIVE DEVICES

When the distance between drive and driven shafts makes the use of gears impractical, devices such as belt and pulley or chain and sprocket drives are often employed. Layout and detailing standards vary somewhat from one company to another, but design procedures and specification methods may be obtained from almost any good textbook or handbook on mechanical design.

GEARS USING AUTODESK INVENTOR DESIGN ACCELERATOR

When you know the design requirements for a gear pair, you can use a CAD package, such as Autodesk Inventor, to automatically generate the 3D models from the information. It can be very time-consuming to create drawings of gears and cams by hand, whereas using CAD frees you to spend more time on other aspects of your designs.

Figure A shows the Autodesk Inventor software's **Spur Gear Component Generator** design tab, which you can use to enter the defining details for the gear pair. Clicking the **Preview** option shows the values and a pictorial representation of the dimensional features for the gear, as shown in Figure B. Once you have entered the data, select OK to generate the 3D models. They are automatically assembled so that the teeth mesh as shown in Figure C. Each gear is a separate part, for which you can list the data and generate the table of information necessary to manufacture the gear. You can also simulate motion to aid in inspecting how your design will function.

Gear drawings specify the information needed to manufacture the gear using a table. Figure D shows an example of the gear table that can be automatically generated using the software.

The Inventor software's Design Accelerator has similar tools for designing bolted connections, shafts, spur gears, bevel gears, worm gears, bearings, spring, belts, pins, welds, hubs, beams, and columns, among other useful items.

(A) Design Tab of the Autodesk Inventor Spur Gear Component Generator

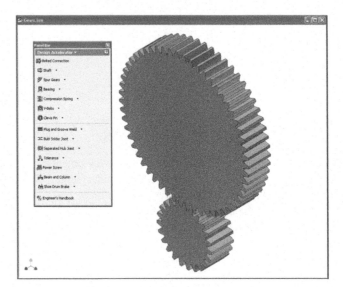

(C) 3D Gear Model

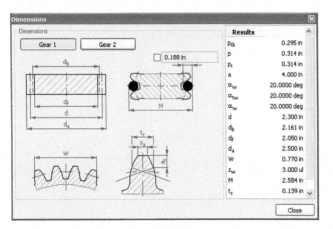

(B) Preview Showing Values and a Representation of Dimensional Features

(Autodesk screen shots reprinted courtesy of Autodesk, Inc.)

Gears

		Gear 1	Gear 2
Type of Model		Component	Component
Number of Teeth	N	23 ul	57 ul
Unit Correction	x	0.0000 ul	0.0000 ul
Pitch Diameter	d	2.300 in	5.700 in
Outside Diameter	d_a	2.500 in	5.900 in
Root Diameter	d_f	2.050 in	5.450 in
Base Circle Diameter	d_b	2.161 in	5.356 in
Work Pitch Diameter	d_w	2.300 in	5.700 in
Facewidth	b	1.000 in	1.000 in
Facewidth Ratio	b_r	0.4348 ul	0.1754 ul
Addendum	a^*	1.0000 ul	1.0000 ul
Clearance	c^*	0.2500 ul	0.2500 ul
Root Fillet	r_f^*	0.3500 ul	0.3500 ul

(D) Table of Information Needed to Manufacture the Spur Gear

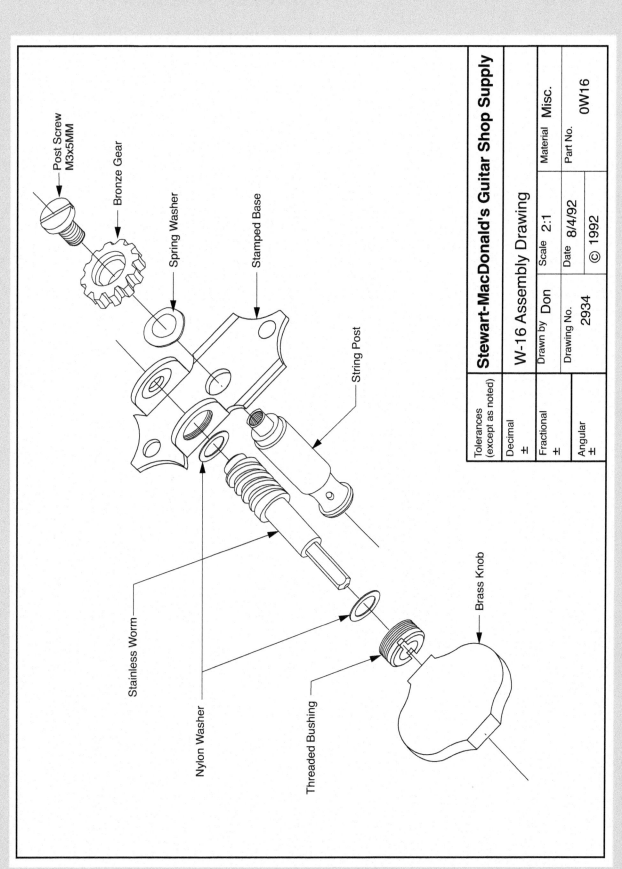

Post Screw
M3x5MM

Bronze Gear

Spring Washer

Stamped Base

String Post

Stainless Worm

Nylon Washer

Threaded Bushing

Brass Knob

Tolerances (except as noted)	Stewart-MacDonald's Guitar Shop Supply		
Decimal ±	W-16 Assembly Drawing		
Fractional ±	Drawn by Don	Scale 2:1	Material Misc.
Angular ±	Drawing No. 2934	Date 8/4/92	Part No. 0W16
		© 1992	

Assembly Drawing for Waverly Tuner (*Courtesy of the Stewart-MacDonald Company.*)

KEY WORDS

Addendum

Addendum Circle

Base Circle

Bevel Gears

Cam

Cam Follower

Cam Profile

Chordal Addendum

Chordal Thickness

Circular Pitch

Dedendum

Diametral Pitch

Displacement Diagram

Friction Wheels

Gear Blank

Gear Ratio

Gears

Helical Gears

Herringbone Gears

Hypoid Gears

Involute

Lead

Outside Diameter

Pinion

Pitch

Pitch Circles

Pitch Curve

Pitch Diameter

Rack

Root Circle

Root Diameter

rpm

Spur Gears

Stub Teeth

Whole Depth

Worm Gears

CHAPTER SUMMARY

- Gears transmit power from one rotating shaft to another. The purpose of a gear is to change the rpm, direction, or axis orientation.
- Exact drawings for gears are difficult to draw on paper or with CAD because of complex tooth shape. A table of gear data is typically all that is needed to define the shape.
- Once the mathematical calculations for a gear are complete, the construction of a gear profile is begun by constructing four circles: the addendum circle, pitch circle, base circle, and root circle.
- The involute profile is the most common gear tooth profile.
- Advanced CAD programs can automate the construction of gear teeth.
- The most common gear type is the spur gear. Spur gear axes are parallel to each other.
- The axes of worm gears and bevel gears are positioned 90° to each other.
- Cams change rotating motion into reciprocating motion. The displacement curve defines the linear follower movement as the cam rotates through 360° of rotary motion.
- When gears are ordered as standard parts to use in an assembly, a detailed drawing is not necessary. A table showing the gear information is often sufficient.

REVIEW QUESTIONS

1. What is the purpose of a gear?
2. What is the geometric shape most commonly used for a gear tooth profile?
3. What are the four circles used to draw a gear?
4. Which types of gears have shafts that are perpendicular to each other?
5. Describe how to draw a cam profile, given a displacement diagram.
6. What is the purpose of a cam follower?
7. How many total degrees of rotation are shown on a cam displacement diagram?
8. Why is the cam follower position always the same at the starting point and the ending point?

CHAPTER EXERCISES

Gearing and Cam Exercises

The following exercises provide practice in laying out and making working drawings of the common types of gears and cams. Where paper sizes are not given, select both scale and sheet layout. If assigned, convert the design layouts to metric dimensions. The instructor may choose to assign specific problems to be completed using CAD.

Gearing

Exercise 16.1 Draw the following by hand or using CAD, as assigned by your instructor.

a. A 12-tooth IDP pinion engages a 15-tooth gear. Make a full-size drawing of a segment of each gear showing how the teeth mesh. Construct the 14.5° involute teeth exactly, noting any points where the teeth appear to interfere. Label gear ratio m_G on the drawing. Include dimensions, notes, and cutting data as assigned by your instructor.

b. Follow the instructions for part a but use 13 or 14 teeth, or any number of teeth as assigned by your instructor.

c. Follow the instructions for part a but use 20° stub teeth instead of involute teeth.

d. Follow the instructions for part a but use a rack in place of the 12-tooth pinion.

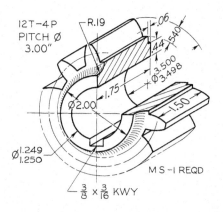

Exercise 16.2 Make a display drawing of the pinion shown in the figure above. Show two views, drawing the teeth by the odontograph method shown in Figure 16.6. Draw double size. Omit dimensions.

Exercise 16.3 A spur gear has 60 teeth of 5 diametral pitch. The face width is 1.50″. The shaft is 1.19″ in diameter. Make the hub 2.00″ long and 2.25″ in diameter. Calculate all dimensions accurately, and make a working drawing of the gear. Show six spokes, each 1.12″ wide at the hub, tapering to .75″ wide at the rim and .50″ thick. Use your own judgment for any dimensions not given. Draw half size.

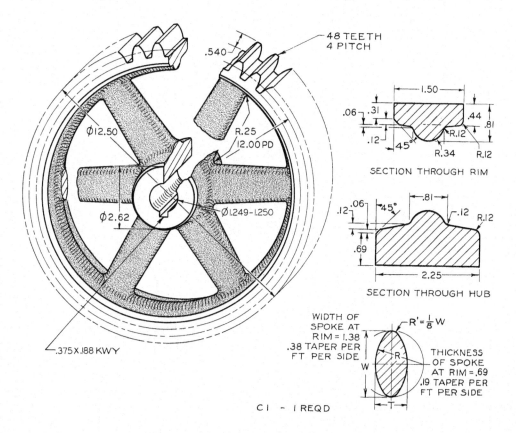

Exercise 16.4 Make a pictorial display of the spur gear shown above. Show the gear as an oblique half section, similar to Exercise 16.2. Draw four-times size, reducing the 30° receding lines by half, as in cabinet projection. Draw the teeth by the odontograph method.

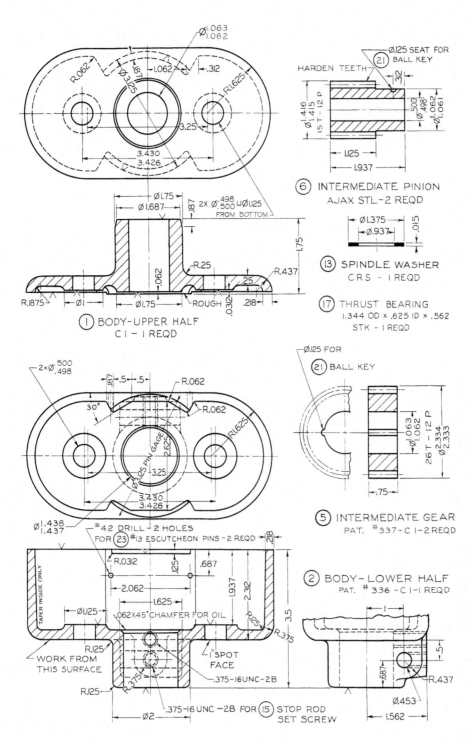

① BODY-UPPER HALF
C I – I REQD

⑥ INTERMEDIATE PINION
AJAX STL–2 REQD

⑬ SPINDLE WASHER
C R S – I REQD

⑰ THRUST BEARING
1.344 OD x .625 ID x .562
STK – I REQD

⑤ INTERMEDIATE GEAR
PAT. #337–C I–2 REQD

② BODY – LOWER HALF
PAT. # 336 – C I–I REQD

Exercise 16.5 Draw the following.

a. Make a pictorial display of the intermediate pinion shown in part 6 in the figure. Show the gear as an oblique half section, similar to Exercise 16.2. Draw four-times size, reducing the 30° receding lines by half, as in cabinet projection. Draw the teeth by the odontograph method.

b. Make a working drawing of the intermediate pinion shown in part 6 of the figure. Check the gear dimensions by calculation.

c. Make a working drawing of the intermediate gear shown in part 5 of the figure. Check the gear dimensions by calculation.

d. Follow instructions for part a, but use the pinion shown in Exercise 16.2.

Exercise 16.6 Draw the following by hand or using CAD, as assigned by your instructor.

a. A pair of bevel gears has teeth of 4 diametral pitch. The pinion has 13 teeth, the gear 25 teeth. The face width is 1.12″. The pinion shaft is .94″ in diameter, and the gear shaft is 1.19″ in diameter. Calculate all dimensions accurately, and make a working drawing showing the gears engaged as in Figure 16.18. Make the hub diameters approximately twice the shaft diameters. Select key sizes from Appendix 20. The backing for the pinion must be .62″, and for the gear 1.25″. Use your own judgment for any dimensions not given.

b. Make a working drawing of the pinion.

c. Make a working drawing of the gear.

d. Show two views of the pinion in part b. Follow the general instructions in that problem.

e. Follow instructions in part a but use 5 diametral pitch and 30 and 15 teeth. The face is 1.00″. Shafts: pinion, 1.00″ diameter; gear, 1.50″ diameter. Backing: pinion, .50″; gear, 1.00″.

f. Follow instructions in part a but use 4 diametral pitch, both gears 20 teeth. Select the correct face width. Shafts: 1.38″ diameter. Backing: 0.75″.

(a) Counter shaft end used on a trough conveyor

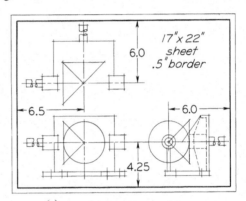

(b) Layout for an assembly drawing of a similar unit

Exercise 16.7 Make a half-scale assembly drawing of the complete unit (a suggested layout with full-size dimensions for view placement is shown). The following full-size dimensions are sufficient to establish the position and general outline of the parts; the minor detail dimensions, web and rib shapes, and fillets and rounds should be designed with the help of the photograph in part a of the figure

The gears are identical in size and are similar in shape to the one in Figure 16.17. There are 24 teeth of 3 diametral pitch in each gear. Face width, 1.50″. Shafts, 2.00″ diameter, extending 7.00″ beyond left bearing, 4.00″ beyond rear (break shafts as shown). Hub diameters, 2.75″. Backing, 1.00″. Hub lengths, 3.25″. The front gear is held by a square gib key and a .38″ set screw. The collar on front shaft next to right bearing is .75″ thick, 2.25″ outside diameter, with a .38″ set screw.

On the main casting, the split bearings are 2.75″ diameter, 3.00″ long, and 10.00″ apart. Each bearing cap is held by two 1/2″ bolts, 3.50″ apart, center to center. Oil holes have a layout for an assembly drawing of a similar unit. Pipe tap for plug or grease cup. Shaft centerlines are 6.50″ above bottom surface, 8.00″ from the rear surface of casting. The main casting is 11.50″ high, and its base is 16.00″ long, 8.75″ wide, and .75″ thick. All webs, ribs, and walls are uniformly .50″ thick. In the base are eight holes (not shown in the photograph) for 1/2″ bolts, two outside each end, and two inside each end.

First block in the gears in each view, then block in the principal main casting dimensions. Fill in details only after principal dimensions are clearly established.

Exercise 16.8
a. The worm and worm gear shown in Figure 16.12 have a circular pitch of .62",
   and the gear has 32 teeth of 14.5° involute form. The worm is double threaded.
   Make an assembly drawing similar to Figure 16.12. Draw the teeth on the gear
   by the odontograph method of Figure 16.6. Calculate dimensions accurately,
   and use AGMA proportions. Shafts: worm, 1.12" diameter; gear, 1.62"
   diameter.
b. Make a working drawing of the worm in part a.
c. Make a working drawing of the gear in part a.
d. Make a working drawing of the worm in part a, but make the worm single
   threaded.

Exercise 16.9
a. A single-thread worm has a lead of .75". The worm gear has 28 teeth of
   standard form. Make a working drawing of the worm. The shaft is 1.25" in
   diameter.
b. Make a working drawing of the gear in part a. The shaft is 1.50" in diameter.

Cams

Exercise 16.10 Draw the following for the 90° roller follower in the figure.
a. For the setup in the figure, draw the displacement diagram and determine the
   cam profile that will give the radial roller follower this motion: up 1.50" in
   120°, dwell 60°, down in 90°, dwell 90°. Motions are to be unmodified straight
   line and of uniform velocity. The roller is .75" in diameter, and the base circle
   is 3.00" in diameter. Note that the follower has zero offset. The cam rotates
   clockwise.
b. Instructions are the same as for part a, except that the straight-line motions are to
   be modified by arcs whose radii are equal to half the rise of the follower.
c. Instructions are the same as for part a, Except that the upward motion is to be
   harmonic and the downward motion parabolic.
d. Instructions are the same as for part c, except that the follower is offset 1.00" to
   the left of the cam centerline. Full-size dimensions for suggested view placement are given in the example layout.

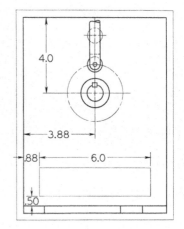

Exercise 16.11 For the 90° flat-faced follower in the figure, draw the displacement
diagram, and determine the cam profile that will give the flat-faced follower this
motion: dwell 30°, up 1.50" on a parabolic curve in 180°, dwell 30°, down with
harmonic motion in 120°. The base circle is 3.00" in diameter. After completing the
cam profile, determine the necessary width of face of the follower by finding the
position of the follower where the point of contact with the cam is farthest from the
follower axis. The cam rotates counterclockwise.

The minimum width of the follower face (2S) can be determined from

$$S = dy/d\theta$$

where

$$\theta = \text{the angular displacement}$$
$$y = \text{the corresponding lift}$$

The width of the follower face can also be determined by inspection of the widest
tangent. See the figure.

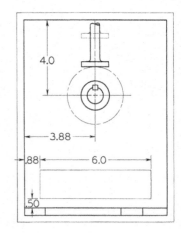

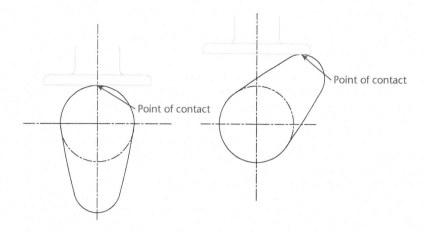

Point of contact

Point of contact

Exercise 16.12 Draw the following for the 45° roller follower at right.
  a. For the setup in the figure, draw the displacement diagram, and determine the cam profile that will swing the pivoted follower through an angle of 30° with the same motion as prescribed in Exercise 16.11. The radius of the follower arm is 2.75″, and in its lowest position the center of the roller is directly over the center of the cam. The base circle is 2.50″ in diameter, and the roller is .75″ in diameter. The cam rotates counterclockwise.
  b. Follow instructions for part a, except that the motion is up 1.50″ in 120°, dwell 60°, down in 90°, dwell 90°.
  c. Follow instructions for part a, except that the motion is to be dwell 30°, up 1.50″ on a parabolic curve in 180°, dwell 30°, down with harmonic motion in 120°.

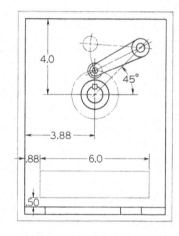

Exercise 16.13 Draw the following by hand or using CAD, as given by your instructor.
  a. Using an arrangement as in Figure 16.24, construct a half development and complete the front view for the following cylindrical cam. Cam, 2.50″ diameter, 2.50″ high. Roller, .50″ diameter; cam groove, .38″ deep. Camshaft, .62″ diameter; follower rod, .62″ wide, .31″ thick. Motion: up 1.50″ with harmonic motion in 180°, down with the same motion in remaining 180°. Cam rotates counterclockwise. Assume lowest position of the follower at the front center of cam.
  b. Follow instructions for part a, but construct a full development for the following motion: up 1.5″ with parabolic motion in 120°, dwell 90°, down with harmonic motion in 150°.

ELECTRONIC DIAGRAMS 17

CHAPTER SEVENTEEN

ELECTRONIC DIAGRAMS

OBJECTIVES

After studying the material in this chapter, you should be able to:

1. Identify common component symbols on an electronic schematic diagram.

2. Draw a schematic diagram using standardized symbols.

3. Draw connecting and crossover paths.

4. Identify interrupted and uninterrupted lines.

5. Designate terminals and numerical values of components.

Refer to the following standards:
- *ASME Y14.44 Reference Designations for Electrical and Electronics Parts and Equipment*
- *ANSI/IEEE 91/91A Graphic Symbols for Logic Functions*
  (Includes IEEE 91A Supplement)
- *ANSI/IEEE 315 Graphic Symbols for Electrical and Electronics Diagrams*
  (Includes IEEE 315A Supplement)
- *ASME 14.24 Types and Applications of Engineering Drawings*

A Mobile Phone Transmitter Atop a Building in Chicago, Illinois *(Courtesy of Roger Tully/Stone Allstock/ Getty Images.)*

OVERVIEW

As all types of designs become more closely integrated with computer controls it is becoming increasingly uncommon for a device to be purely mechanical. Embedded electronics, software, sensors, and network connectivity enables devices to collect and exchange data to communicate with and sense other devices in the "Internet of Things" (IoT). A wide variety of drawings are necessary for the fabrication of electrical machinery, switching devices, chassis for electronic equipment, cabinets, housings, and other "mechanical" elements associated with electrical equipment. Some of these drawings are based on the same principles as any typical mechanical drawing.

Although more and more circuits are contained in integrated circuit chips, many devices still require wired connections. These connections are represented on schematic diagrams, block diagrams, and wiring diagrams.

Every discrete component can be represented with a unique graphic symbol. Components with terminals or numeric values are labeled. Specialized circuit design software allows users to create drawings as well as conduct simulations and analyze electronic circuits.

Many standard CAD programs include libraries of electronic symbols that make drawing schematic diagrams easier and less time consuming. For sketching, plastic templates can be used to save drawing time.

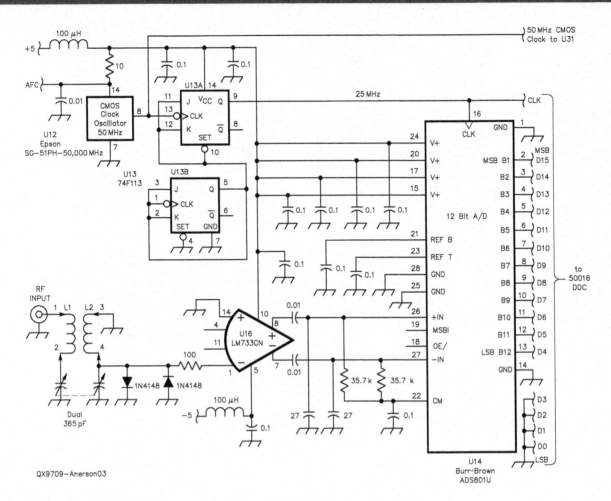

QX9709—Anerson03

17.1 Schematic Diagram *(Courtesy of September 1997 QEX: Copyright ARRL.)*

UNDERSTANDING ELECTRONIC DIAGRAMS

Figure 17.1 shows a schematic diagram. Figure 17.2 shows a first-floor lighting diagram for an architectural project. There are a wide variety of electrical and electronic drawings and diagrams. As is the case in all types of technical drawing, you will need to become familiar with specialized industrial practice for the drawings you prepare. A wiring diagram for a second-floor house plan looks quite different from a logic diagram. This chapter is intended to introduce you to the types of drawings and general practices and symbols used in electronic diagrams.

Standard Symbols

The symbols approved by the American National Standards Institute (ANSI) are published in *Graphic Symbols for Electrical and Electronic Diagrams, ANSI/IEEE 315*. In addition, modern printed circuitry techniques, which are used extensively in electronic equipment, require specially prepared diagrams or drawings. Much of the material in this chapter is extracted or adapted from that standard.

Other standards should be referred to as required. The U.S. government has developed a series of standards to be used by military contractors, for example *MIL-STD-681 Identification Coding and Application of Hook Up and Lead Wires*. In other applications, adherence to standards developed by Underwriters' Laboratory (UL) may be required, particularly where safety considerations may dictate a special printed circuit board layout or component spacing. Standards are updated as they evolve, so research the current applicable standards for the type of drawing you are creating.

CAD Symbol Libraries

You can create or purchase libraries of standard electronic symbols for use in electronic diagrams. CAD symbol libraries should follow approved standards just as manually created drawings would. When you create CAD drawings showing electronic symbols, consider the final size of the plotted drawing. Make sure that symbols you create or add to drawings meet minimum size standards as set out in *ASME Y14.2*.

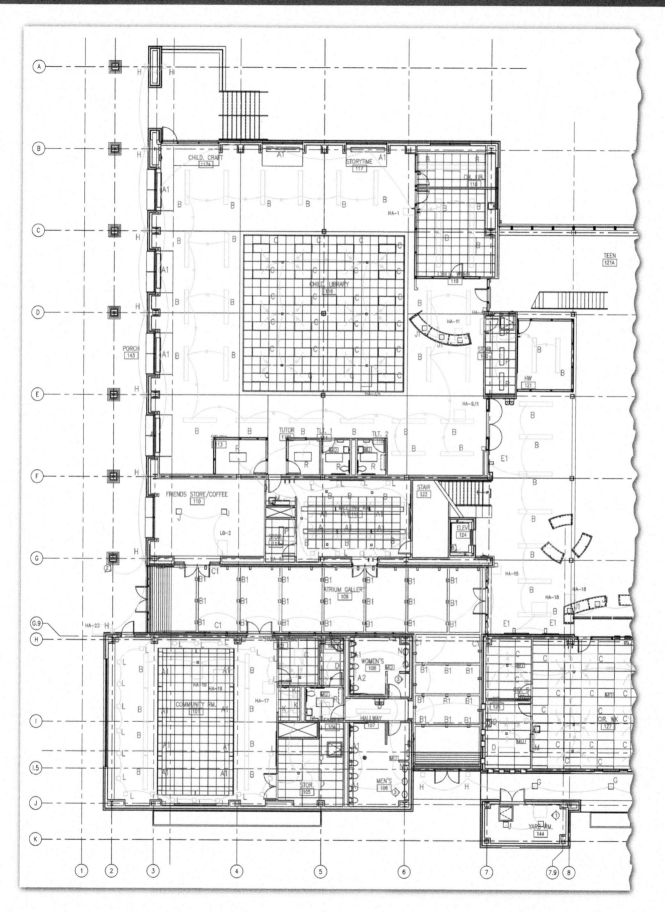

17.2 Portion of a Single-Line Diagram Showing the First-Floor Lighting Plan for a Public Library
(Courtesy of Associated Construction Engineering.)

Types of Electronic Diagrams

The following are types of diagrams defined in *ASME Y14.24* that are commonly used in the electronics industry.

Functional block diagram

A *functional block diagram* shows the functions of major elements in a circuit, assembly, or system using a simplified form. It is used to simplify the representation of complex equipment by using blocks or rectangles to depict stages, units, or groups of components in a system (Figure 17.3).

Single-line diagram

A *single-line diagram* shows the path of an electrical/ electronic circuit in a general format using single lines and symbols (Figure 17.4).

Schematic or circuit diagram

A *schematic diagram* or *circuit diagram* shows the electrical connections and functions of a specific circuit arrangement. It does not depict the physical shape, size, or arrangement of the elements. This type of drawing is used to communicate the design, construction, and maintenance information for electronic equipment. It facilitates tracing the circuit to convey its function (Figure 17.5).

Connection or wiring diagram

A *connection* or *wiring diagram* shows the connections of an installation or its component devices or parts. It may cover internal or external connections, or both, and contains the level of detail to show the connections involved. The connection diagram usually shows general physical arrangement of the component devices or parts. This type of diagram is used to represent the wiring between component devices in electrical or electronic equipment (Figure 17.6).

Interconnection diagram

An *interconnection diagram* shows only external connections between unit assemblies or equipment. The internal connections of the unit assemblies or equipment are usually omitted. This diagram is similar to the connection diagram; both serve to supplement schematic diagrams.

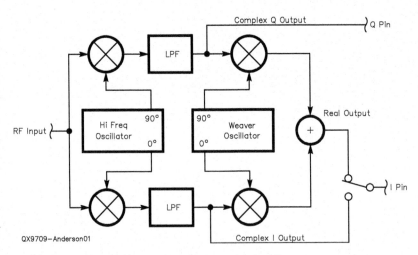

17.3   Functional Block Diagram for a Digital Downconverter *(Courtesy of September 1997 QEX: Copyright ARRL.)*

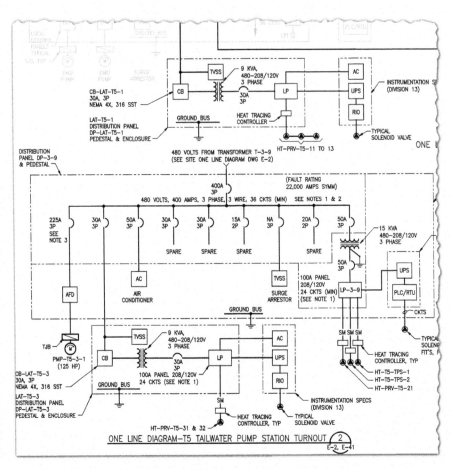

17.4   Single-Line Diagram *(Courtesy of CH2M HILL.)*

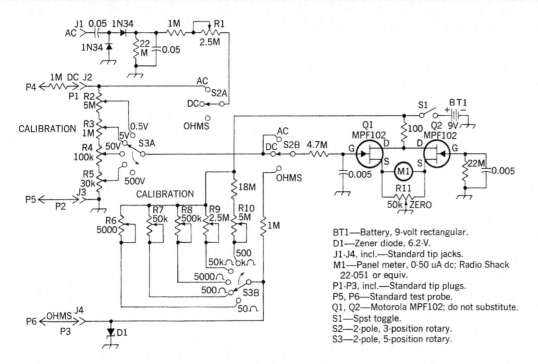

BT1—Battery, 9-volt rectangular.
D1—Zener diode, 6.2-V.
J1-J4, incl.—Standard tip jacks.
M1—Panel meter, 0-50 uA dc; Radio Shack
     22-051 or equiv.
P1-P3, incl.—Standard tip plugs.
P5, P6—Standard test probe.
Q1, Q2—Motorola MPF102; do not substitute.
S1—Spst toggle.
S2—2-pole, 3-position rotary.
S3—2-pole, 5-position rotary.

17.5   Schematic Diagram of a FET (field-effect transistor) VOM (volt-ohm-milliammeter)
(Courtesy of American Radio Relay League.)

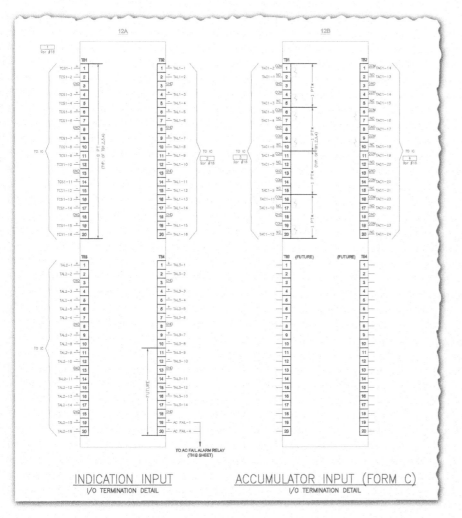

INDICATION INPUT
I/O TERMINATION DETAIL

ACCUMULATOR INPUT (FORM C)
I/O TERMINATION DETAIL

17.6   Portion of a Connection Diagram *(Courtesy of Golden Valley Electric Association.)*

17.1 DRAWING SIZE, FORMAT, AND TITLE

The title should include the standardized wording for the type of the drawing and a description of the application, for example:

SINGLE-LINE DIAGRAM—AM–FM RECEIVER SCHEMATIC DIAGRAM—250-WATT AMATEUR TRANSCEIVER

It is often useful to include some basic wiring information on schematic diagrams, such as connection details of transformers and switches. For combined forms such as this, do not alter the title, but describe the primary function of the diagram.

17.2 LINE CONVENTIONS AND LETTERING

As in any drawing for reproduction, select line thicknesses and letter sizes according to the amount of reduction or enlargement involved so that all parts of the drawing will be legible.

ASME recommends a line of medium thickness for general use on electrical diagrams. A thin line may be used for brackets, leader lines, and so on. To emphasize special features such as main *signal paths,* a thicker line may be used to provide the desired contrast. For recommended line thickness and lettering, refer to *ASME Y14.2.*

Line conventions for electrical diagrams are shown in Figure 17.7. Lettering on electrical diagrams should meet the same standards as for other drawings. For most sheet sizes, a letter height of 3 mm (.125″) is typical.

For general use	Medium
Mechanical connection, shielding, & future circuits line	Medium
Bracket-connecting dash-line	Medium

Use of these line thicknesses optional:

Brackets, leader lines, etc.	Thin (0.3 mm)
Boundary of mechanical grouping	Thin (0.3 mm)
For emphasis	Thick (0.6 mm)

17.7 Line Conventions for Electronic Diagrams
(Reprinted from ASME Y14.2, by permission of The American Society of Mechanical Engineers. All rights reserved.)

17.3 STANDARD SYMBOLS FOR ELECTRONIC DIAGRAMS

Symbols Symbols should conform to an internationally or nationally approved standard, such as *IEEE 315*, a portion of which is shown in Figure 17.8. On rare occasions when no standard symbol is available, you can devise a special symbol (or augment a standard symbol), provided that you include an explanatory note. Appendix 35 provides many common schematic symbols for electrical/electronic diagrams.

Size of symbols Symbols should be drawn roughly 1.5 times the size of those shown in the *IEEE 315* standard. The relative proportions of the symbols and relative sizes compared with one another should be maintained. If the drawing will be printed at a reduced scale, the symbols must be larger, so that when reduced they will still be completely legible. Following this recommendation, circular envelopes for semiconductors will be about 16 mm (or .62″) to 19 mm (or .75″) in diameter, although the envelope for semiconductors may be omitted if no confusion results.

Switches and relays Switches and relays should be shown in the "normal" position—with no operating force or applied energy. If exceptions are necessary, as for switches that may operate in several positions with no applied force, describe the conditions in an explanatory note on the drawing.

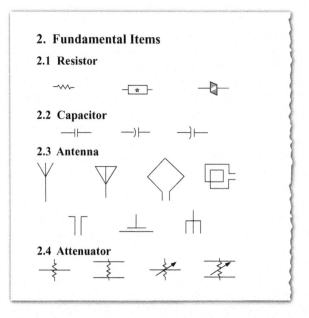

17.8 A Portion of the Standard Showing Graphic Symbols for Electrical and Electronics Diagrams
(Courtesy of IEEE.)

17.4 ABBREVIATIONS

Abbreviations on electrical diagrams should conform to *ASME Y14.38*. (See Appendix 2.)

17.5 GROUPING PARTS

When parts or components are naturally grouped, as in separately obtained sub-assemblies or assembled components such as relays, tuned circuit transformers, hermetically sealed units, and printed circuit boards, indicate the group using a dashed line to enclose them in a "box," as in Figure 17.9. You can also group components by showing extra space from adjacent circuitry.

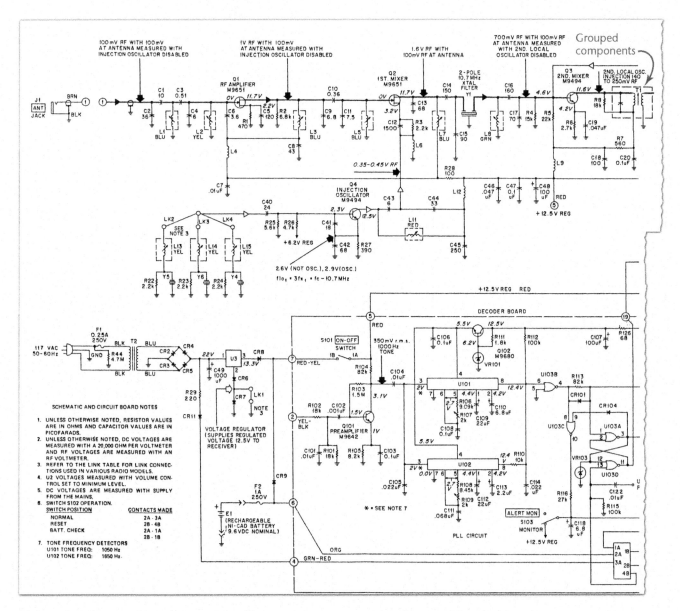

17.9 Portion of a Maintenance-Type Schematic Diagram of FM Weather Monitor Radio

17.6 ARRANGEMENT OF ELECTRICAL/ELECTRONIC SYMBOLS

Figure 17.10 shows a freehand sketch of a schematic diagram. It helps to use grid paper when sketching schematics, because it is easier to keep components lined up and makes a neater sketch. Rearrange details to improve the final diagram if it is redrawn. Templates, such as the one shown in Figure 17.11, save time when drawing symbols.

CAD can help you to produce complicated schematic drawings efficiently. As a minimum, CAD software provides standard symbol libraries that make it quick to place the symbols into a drawing. On the more complex side, CAD packages may automatically route traces and simulate the circuit function. Figure 17.12 shows an example drag-and-drop CAD symbol palette. Figure 17.13 shows symbols in circuit simulation software.

Symbol Arrangement

Arrange the various parts and symbols to balance blank areas and lines. Provide sufficient blank space adjacent to symbols to allow for reference designations and notes. Exceptionally large spaces give an unbalanced effect but may be necessary to provide for later circuit additions. Of course, using CAD, it is easy to move and stretch the existing drawing to add space.

Signal Path

Arrange schematic and single-line diagrams so that the signal or transmission path from input to output proceeds from left to right and from top to bottom when possible. Supplementary circuits, such as a power supply or an oscillator circuit, are usually drawn below the main circuit.

Stages of an electronic device are groups of components or a semiconductor, which together perform one function of the device. For example, the sketch in Figure 17.10 shows the RF (radio frequency) amplifier stage of the FM Weather Monitor Radio, whose schematic was shown in Figure 17.9. Other stages that can be seen in Figure 17.9 are the first and second mixer stages associated with transistors Q2 and Q3; the limiter/detector stage, containing integrated circuit U1; and finally the audio output stage, U2, and speaker. The power supply, which rectifies alternating current through **diodes** CR2–CR5 to produce direct current voltage, regulated through integrated circuit U3, is shown at the lower left, along with a rechargeable battery backup power supply, E1.

Also shown in the lower portion of the diagram is the circuitry contained on a separate tone decoder printed circuit board (within the dashed lines).

With experience in drawing electronic circuits you are able to visualize fairly accurately the space required by the circuitry involved in each stage. Generally, you should keep the semiconductor symbols arranged in horizontal lines and group the associated circuitry in a reasonably symmetrical arrangement about them. This way each stage is confined to an area of the drawing.

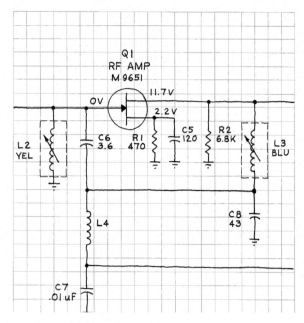

17.10 A Portion of a Preliminary Freehand Sketch of a Schematic Diagram

17.11 Electronic Symbol Template

Note that the signal path from input to output follows from left to right and top to bottom. The input is at the upper left and the output at the lower right in Figure 17.9. The signal path is clearly designated by a heavier-than-normal line. This is typical of maintenance-type schematic diagrams, which are drawn to be easily read and interpreted by service technicians. Heavier lines in the drawing are used for emphasis but do not have any other significance. Supplementary circuitry (in this case the power supply) is in the lower portion of the diagram.

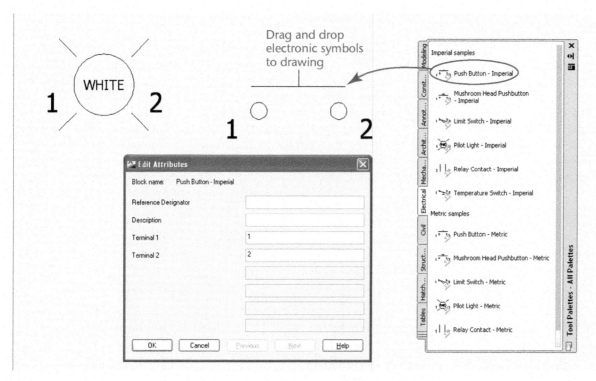

17.12 AutoCAD Software Provides a Convenient Tool Palette for Inserting Symbols *(Autodesk screen shots reprinted courtesy of Autodesk, Inc.)*

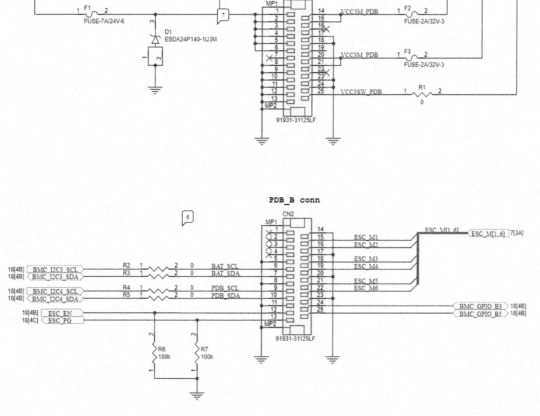

17.13 A Circuit Design Created in Altium Designer. *Circuits created in Altium allow simulation of their function. (Image ©2023 Altium LLC. All rights reserved. Used with permission.)*

17.7 CONNECTIONS AND CROSSOVERS

Connecting lines (for conductors) are typically drawn horizontally or vertically, minimizing bends and **crossovers.** Avoid using long interconnecting lines. You can use interrupted paths to prevent the need for long, awkward interconnecting lines or in cases where a diagram occupies more than one sheet. When parallel connecting lines must be drawn close together, the spacing between lines should not be less than .06″ *after reduction*. Group parallel lines with similar functions and with at least double spacing between groups to make the drawing easier to interpret.

At times it is impossible to avoid drawing a line representing a conductor wire across another conductor wire, where the wires cross but do not connect. These crossovers must clearly depict that the conductors *do not* make a connection. Figure 17.14a shows the recommended practice, in which the termination of a line signifies a connection. If more than three lines come together, as at Z, the dot symbol is necessary. You can avoid this by staggering the connecting lines, as in b. The looped crossovers in Figure 17.14c are no longer standard but are still used when there is possibility of confusion.

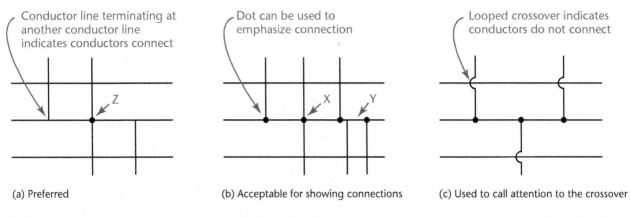

(a) Preferred

(b) Acceptable for showing connections

(c) Used to call attention to the crossover

17.14   Crossovers

17.8 INTERRUPTED PATHS

Interrupted paths may be used for either a single line or groups of lines to simplify a diagram (Figures 17.15 and 17.16). Label these carefully with letters, numbers, abbreviations, or other identification so that their destinations are unmistakable. Grouped lines are also bracketed as well as labeled (Figure 17.16). When convenient, interrupted grouped lines may be connected by dashed lines (Figure 17.17).

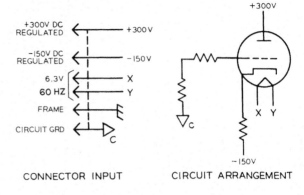

17.15   Identification of Interrupted Lines *(Courtesy of IEEE.)*

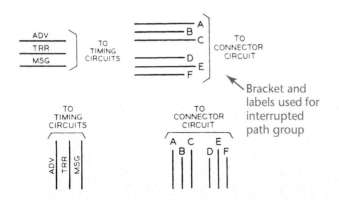

17.16   Typical Arrangement of Line Identifications and Destinations *(Courtesy of IEEE.)*

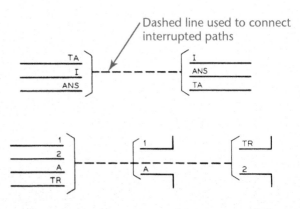

17.17   Interrupted Lines Interconnected by Dashed Lines *(Courtesy of IEEE.)*

17.9 TERMINALS

Terminal circles need not be shown unless they are needed for clarity and identification.

When actual physical markings appear on or near *terminals* of a component, they may be shown on the electrical diagram. Otherwise, assign arbitrary reference numbers or letters to the terminals and add a simple diagram that associates the numbers or letters with the actual arrangement of terminals on the component (Figures 17.18, 17.19, and 17.20b). Figure 17.20a is a pictorial explanation of Figure 17.20b.

Terminal identification for rotary variable resistors follows similar practices, but it is often desirable to indicate the direction of rotation as well, usually as clockwise or counterclockwise, as viewed from the knob or actuator end of the control. Any other arrangement must be explained by a note or diagram. The letters CW placed near the terminal adjacent to the movable contact identify the extreme clockwise position of the movable terminal (Figure 17.21a). When terminals are numbered, number 2 is assigned to the movable contact (Figure 17.21b). Additional fixed taps are assigned sequential numbers, as in Figure 17.21c.

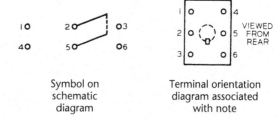

Symbol on schematic diagram

Terminal orientation diagram associated with note

17.18 Terminal Identification—Toggle Switch *(Courtesy of IEEE.)*

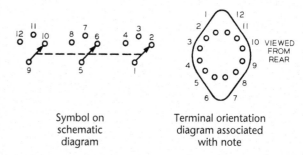

Symbol on schematic diagram

Terminal orientation diagram associated with note

17.19 Terminal Identification—Rotary Switch *(Courtesy of IEEE.)*

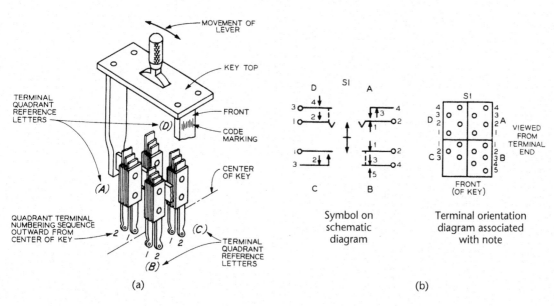

(a)

Symbol on schematic diagram

Terminal orientation diagram associated with note

(b)

17.20 Terminal Identification—Lever-Type Key *(Courtesy of IEEE.)*

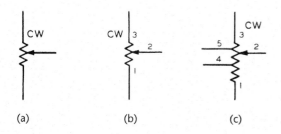

(a)   (b)   (c)

17.21 Terminal Identification for a Variable Resistor *(Courtesy of IEEE.)*

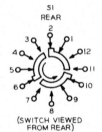

17.22 Terminal Identification and On-Off Switch *(Courtesy of Motorola, Inc.)*

17.23 Position–Function Relationship for Rotary Switches, Optional Methods *(Courtesy of IEEE.)*

SI VOLTAGE TEST	
FUNCTION	TERM
OFF	1-2
+100V REG	1-3
+150V REG	1-4
+300V UNREG	1-5
+450V UNREG	1-6

(a) Functions shown at symbol (b) Functions shown in tabular form

Switch S101 of Figure 17.22 illustrates the use of terminal symbols and their identification. Switch position, as it affects function, should also be shown on a schematic diagram. Depending on complexity, the designation may range from the simple on-off of switch S101 in Figure 17.22 to the functional labeling of the terminals in Figure 17.23a or to the tabular form of function listing in Figure 17.23b.

The tabular forms use dashes to indicate which terminals are connected for each position. For example, in Figure 17.24, position 2 connects terminal 1 to terminal 3, terminal 5 to terminal 7, and terminal 9 to terminal 11.

	SI		
POS	FUNCTION	TERM.	
1	OFF(SHOWN)	1-2,5-6,9-10	
2	STANDBY	1-3,5-7,9-11	
3	OPERATE	1-4,5-8,9-12	

(a) Symbol on schematic diagram (b) Functions shown in tabular form

17.24 Position–Function Relationships for Rotary Switches Using the Tabular Method *(Courtesy of IEEE.)*

17.10 COLOR CODING

Terminals or leads are frequently identified by colors or symbols, which should be indicated on the diagram. Figure 17.25 shows how the colors of the insulated wire leads are noted near each terminal. Colors are shown on the drawing using the following codes:

Black: BLK

Blue: BLU

Brown: BRN

Gray: GRA

Green: GRN

Orange: ORN

Red: RED

Violet: VIO

White: WHT

Yellow: YEL

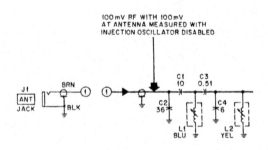

17.25 Color Coding *(Courtesy of Motorola, Inc.)*

17.11 DIVISION OF PARTS

For clarity, draw sections of multielement parts separately in a schematic diagram. Indicate subdivisions with suffix letters. For the rotary switch in Figure 17.26, the first portion S1A of switch S1 is identified as S1A FRONT and S1A REAR, viewed as usual from the actuator end.

An example using suffixes is shown in Figure 17.27. Here the two piezoelectric crystals A and B are enclosed in one unit, Y1. They are then referred to as Y1A and Y1B.

Another way to identify parts of components that are functionally separated on the diagram is with the PART OF prefix (Figure 17.28a). If the portion is indicated as incomplete by a short-break line, as in Figure 17.28b, the words PART OF may be omitted.

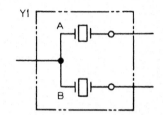

17.27 Identification of Parts by Suffix Letters *(Courtesy of IEEE.)*

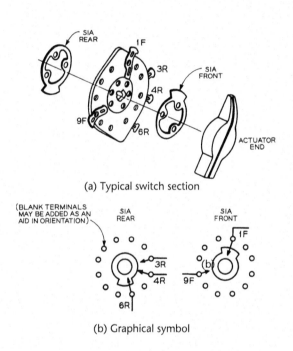

(a) Typical switch section

(b) Graphical symbol

17.26 Development of a Graphical Symbol—Rotary Switch *(Courtesy of IEEE.)*

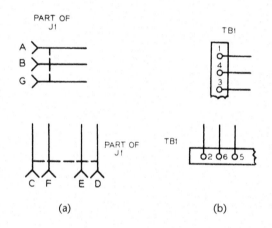

(a)   (b)

17.28 Identification of Portions of Items *(Courtesy of IEEE.)*

17.12 ELECTRON TUBE PIN IDENTIFICATION

Electron tubes are generally not used in new designs but are still commonly seen in high-power amplifiers. You may see their symbols in maintenance diagrams used while troubleshooting or modifying existing equipment. Electron tube pins are conventionally numbered clockwise from the tube base key or other point of reference, with the tube viewed from the bottom. In the recommended method of pin identification on a diagram, the corresponding numbers are shown immediately outside the tube envelope, adjacent to the connecting line (Figures 17.29 and 17.30).

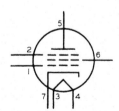

17.29 Terminal Identification for Electron Tube Pins *(Courtesy of IEEE.)*

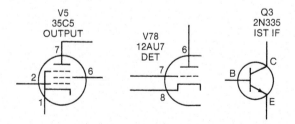

17.30 Reference Designation, Type Number, and Function for Electron Tubes and Semiconductors *(Courtesy of IEEE.)*

17.13 REFERENCE DESIGNATIONS

In electrical diagrams it is essential to identify each separately replaceable part with appropriate combinations of letters and numbers. Portions not separately replaceable are frequently identified, as in the previous examples. In electronics communications, the recognized form is the appropriate letter followed by a number (the same size and on the same line) with no separating hyphen or space. This is followed by any required suffix, again with no hyphen.

Numbers assigned for each category (resistances, capacitances, inductances, etc.) should start in the upper left corner of the diagram proceeding left to right, then top to bottom, ending at the lower right corner. If parts are deleted in revision, the remaining components should not be renumbered. The numbers not used should be listed in a table (Figure 17.31). If the circuit contains many parts, it may also be helpful to include, as shown, the highest numbers used in each category.

Semiconductors, such as transistors and integrated circuits, are identified by the reference designation and the type number. It is often helpful to include the function below the type number. All this information should be placed near (preferably above) the symbol.

HIGHEST REFERENCE DESIGNATIONS	
R65	C35
REFERENCE DESIGNATIONS NOT USED	
R7, R9 R60, R62	C11, C14 C19, C23

17.31   Highest and Omitted Reference Designations *(Courtesy of IEEE.)*

17.14 NUMERICAL VALUES

Multiplier	Prefix	Symbol	
		Method 1	Method 2
10^{12}	tera	T	T
10^9	giga	G	G
10^6 (1,000,000)	mega	M	M
10^3 (1,000)	kilo	k	K
10^{-3} (.001)	milli	m	MILLI
10^{-6} (.000001)	micro	μ	U
10^{-9}	nano	n	N
10^{-12}	pico	p	P
10^{-15}	femto	f	F
10^{-18}	atto	a	A

(a) Multipliers

Range in Ohms	Express as	Example
Less than 1,000	ohms	.031 470
1,000 to 99,999	ohms or kilohms	1800 15,853 10 k 22 K
100,000 to 999,999	kilohms or megohms	380 k .38 M
1,000,000 or more	megohms	3.3 M

(b) Resistance

Range in Picofarads	Express as	Example
Less than 10,000	picofarads	152.4 pF 4700 PF
10,000 or more	microfarads	.015 μF 30 UF

(c) Capacitance

17.32   Numerical Values for Components

Along with reference designations, numerical values for resistance, capacitance, and inductance should be shown, preferably in the form using the fewest numerals. To do this, you can combine the multipliers shown in Figure 17.32a and the symbols in Figure 17.32b and 17.32c. Note that commas are not used in four-digit numbers: 4700 is recommended, not 4,700.

Inductance

According to magnitude, inductance may be expressed in henries (H), millihenries (mH or MILLI H), or microhenries (μH or UH). Following the principle of minimizing the number of numerals, 2μH is preferable to .002 mH, and 5 mH is better than either .005H or 5000 UH.

To avoid repeating measurement units, use a note such as:

UNLESS OTHERWISE SPECIFIED, RESISTANCE VALUES ARE IN OHMS AND CAPACITANCE VALUES ARE IN MICROFARADS.

Part Value Placement

For clarity, locate numerical values immediately adjacent to the symbol. Suggested forms are shown in Figure 17.33.

17.33   Methods of Reference Designation and Part Value Placement *(Courtesy of IEEE.)*

17.15 FUNCTIONAL IDENTIFICATION AND OTHER INFORMATION

It sometimes contributes to the readability of a diagram to include special functional identification of certain parts or stages. In particular, where functional designations (TUNER, OUTPUT, etc.) are to be shown on a panel or *chassis* surface, they should also be shown on the electrical diagram in an appropriate place.

Test points may be identified by the words TEST POINT on the drawing. If several are to be shown, the abbreviated form TP1, TP2, or M1, M2, and so on may be used.

Still other information that may be shown on schematic diagrams, if desired, includes the following:

1. DC resistance of *transformer* windings and coils
2. Critical input or output impedance values
3. Voltage or current wave shapes at selected points
4. Wiring requirements for critical *ground* points, shielding pairing, and so on
5. Power or voltage ratings of parts
6. Indication of operational controls or circuit functions

17.16 INTEGRATED CIRCUITS

An *integrated circuit* is a semiconductor wafer or chip that has been processed to produce a microminiature replacement for discrete components, such as transistors, diodes, *resistors,* capacitors, and connecting wiring.

Integrated circuits are widely used in consumer products, such as calculators, personal computers, radios, and televisions, as well as in mainframe computers, microprocessors, and many other industrial applications.

A typical integrated circuit, housed in a DIP (dual in-line package) less than an inch in length (Figure 17.34a), contains circuitry replacing all the discrete components shown in Figure 17.34b. To simplify the representation of the circuitry, use a schematic symbol, as shown in Figure 17.34c.

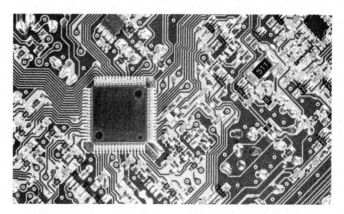

Detail of silicon wafer containing microchips (pedrosala/ Shutterstock.)

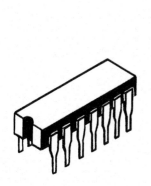

(a) Pictorial representation of component

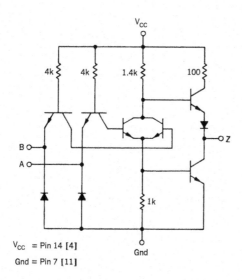

V_{cc} = Pin 14 [4]
Gnd = Pin 7 [11]

(b) Schematic representation (1/4 of circuit shown)

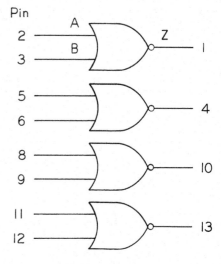

(c) Symbolic representation

17.34   A Typical Dual In-Line Package Integrated Circuit Representation *(Courtesy of Motorola, Inc.)*

17.17 PRINTED CIRCUITS

In the interests of miniaturization and mass production, ***printed circuit*** (PC) boards are widely used in the electronics industry, replacing expensive and tedious hand-wiring manufacturing methods (see Figure 17.35).

A variety of procedures have been developed for fabricating these boards. Their name is derived from an early method of production, depositing (printing) a pattern of conductive ink on a base of insulating material. The method now most commonly used consists of etching a wiring pattern on copper-coated phenolic, glass–polyester, or glass–epoxy material.

Single-sided PC boards have a component side and a foil side. The component side often has part designations silk-screened on the board; on the foil side, the component leads are soldered onto the copper foil.

If CAD is not being used, once the electronic designer has decided on the physical arrangement of components to be mounted on the printed circuit board, a free-hand layout sketch is made.

It is important to maintain close tolerances in the production of PC artwork, so that the various electronic components' leads will fit properly in the spaces provided for them on the finished board. CAD circuit design software should be utilized whenever possible to provide optimum PC board designs with minimal effort.

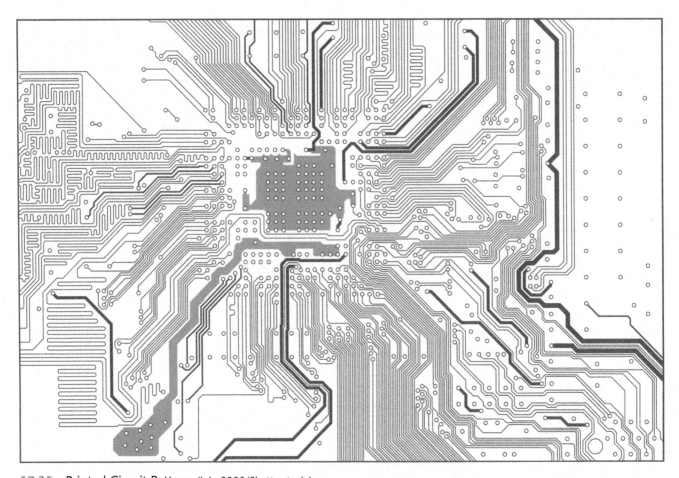

17.35   Printed Circuit Pattern *(jules2000/Shutterstock.)*

17.18 COMPUTER GRAPHICS

CAD greatly simplifies the process of producing printed circuit artwork. Sophisticated programs let you reduce the physical size of the board and minimize the need for crossover jumper wires.

Double-sided printed circuit boards are common, and many compact designs require multilayer boards, in which the conductive paths are sandwiched between insulating layers. These board layouts (Figure 17.36) require precise registration of the artwork for each layer to ensure proper alignment of corresponding features, such as holes that are to be "plated through" from side to side.

A CAD component layout program allows you to create the best possible parts placement in the shortest possible time. Microminiature surface-mount components, which have short solder tab connections instead of wire leads and so do not require drilled mounting holes, are used with increasing frequency. The small size of these parts requires a high degree of accuracy in board layout and design that CAD systems can easily provide.

CAD systems are capable of providing full-size or scaled artwork along with other data required to set up automated soldering and drilling equipment required to produce a finished printed circuit board.

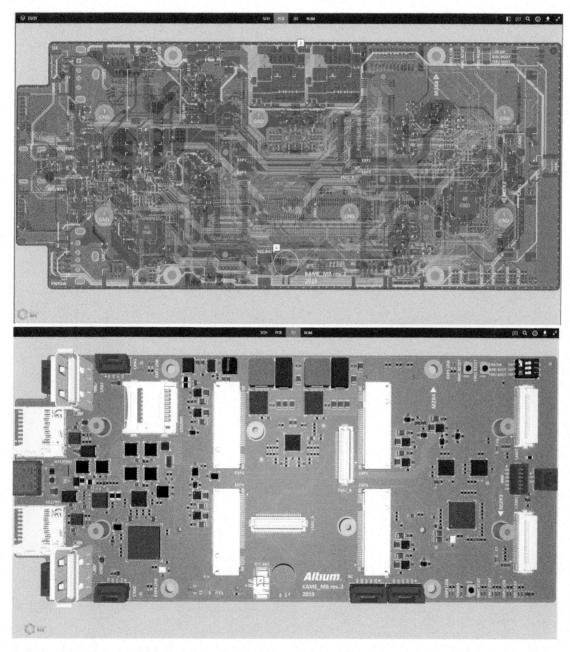

17.36 The Altium PCB Editor Provides an Interactive Routing Engine to Simplify Printed Circuit Board Design (*Images ©2023 Altium LLC. All rights reserved. Used with permission.*)

PORTFOLIO

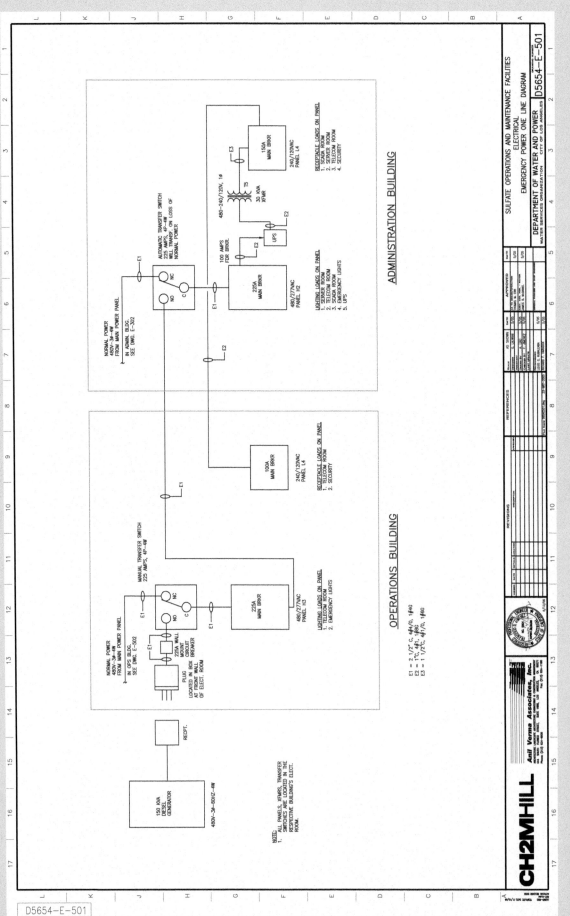

Block Diagram *(Courtesy of CH2M Hill.)*

KEY WORDS

Chassis

Connection or Wiring Diagram

Crossovers

Diodes

Functional Block Diagram

Ground

Integrated Circuit

Interconnection Diagram

Interrupted Paths

Printed Circuit

Resistors

Schematic Diagram or Circuit Diagram

Semiconductors

Signal Paths

Single-Line Diagram

Stages

Switches and Relays

Terminals

Transformer

CHAPTER SUMMARY

- Schematic diagrams show the signal path between discrete components.
- Wiring diagrams show point-to-point wiring connections.
- Block diagrams show simplified representations of subsystems. Each subsystem is designated by a separate rectangular box.
- Unique graphic symbols are assigned to every electronic component. CAD programs store these symbols in a library. Schematic sketches can be created using plastic template guides.
- Computer graphics programs can automate much of the drawing needed to generate a printed circuit board layout.
- Letters and numbers are placed next to components to indicate connection points, terminal pin designations, and reference values.

REVIEW QUESTIONS

1. In what direction does the signal path flow in a schematic diagram?
2. What is the difference between a block diagram and a schematic diagram?
3. What does each box represent in a block diagram?
4. In a schematic diagram, what does a large dot mean when two lines cross?
5. How are a component's terminal pins identified in a schematic diagram?
6. Draw the representation of a wire that stops and then continues at a different location.
7. What type of electronic drawing shows parts in three dimensions?
8. What are the names of each side of a printed circuit board? Which side contains the soldered connections?
9. Draw the schematic symbols for 10 electronic components.
10. What is the schematic symbol for chassis ground?

CHAPTER EXERCISES

All the following problems may also be solved using CAD or freehand. If freehand sketches are assigned, 8.5″ × 11″ grid paper with .25″ grid squares is suggested. Refer to Appendix 35 for standard graphical symbols.

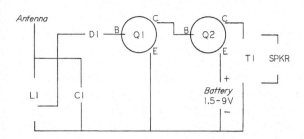

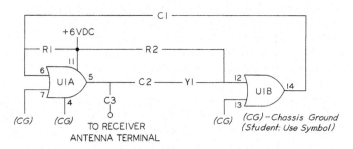

Exercise 17.1 The circuit shown is suitable for classroom or laboratory demonstrations. After a local radio station is tuned with a regular 9-V battery in place, other devices, such as photoelectric cells and homemade batteries, are substituted.

Make a freehand or CAD schematic diagram of the circuit, approximately twice the size of the figure. Use standard symbols and show component values and reference designations, following recommended practices.

Components List

C1	10-365 PF variable capacitor
D1	Germanium diode
L1	Loopstick antenna coil with center tap
T1	Output transformer: 2500 ohm primary, 3–4 ohm secondary
Q1	NPN type RF transistor (B = base, C = collector, E = emitter)
Q2	PNP type audio transistor

Exercise 17.2 The unit shown is used to calibrate the tuning dials of shortwave communications receivers by providing a check signal every 100 kHz throughout the commonly used bands.

Reproduce the schematic diagram approximately double size, freehand or using CAD, as assigned. Add standard symbols and include reference designations, component values, and other data following recommended practices.

Components List

Capacitors

C1	1000 PF
C2	7–45 PF trimmer
C3	10 PF

Crystal

Y1	100 kHz

Resistors (ohms)

R1	56K
R2	56K

Integrated Circuit

U1	HEP 570 (quad 2-input gate)

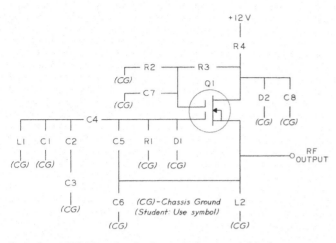

Exercise 17.3 The circuit shown is for a variable frequency oscillator (VFO) that may be used with transmitters operating in the 80-m amateur radio ("ham") band.

Make a freehand or CAD schematic diagram, approximately twice the size of the figure. Use standard symbols and include reference designations and component values, following recommended practices.

Components List

Capacitors

C1	100 PF trimmer
C2	50 PF
C3	150 PF variable
C4	470 PF
C5, C6	1000 PF
C7, C8	.1 UF

Resistors (ohms)

R1, R2, R3	22K
R4	270

Coils

L1	6 UH ceramic or air core
L2	1 MH RF choke

Semiconductors

D1	1N914 silicon diode
D2	6 V, 1 W zener diode
Q1	40673 dual-gate MOSFET transistor

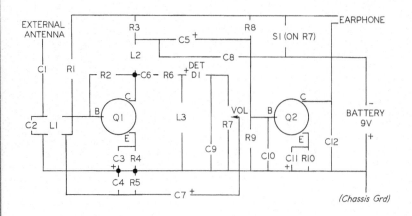

Exercise 17.4 Make a freehand or CAD schematic diagram of the circuit shown approximately double size. Use standard symbols and show reference designations and component values, following recommended practices.

Note: By rearranging slightly a few connecting lines, you can eliminate the three dot symbols.

Components List

Capacitors

C1	10 PF
C2	10–365 PF variable
C3	90 UF
C4	.005 UF
C5	5 UF
C6	.001 UF
C7	5 UF
C8	.01 UF
C9	.005 UF
C10	.005 UF
C11	90 UF
C12	.005 UF

Resistors (ohms)

R1	47K
R2	82K
R3	2200
R4	1000
R5	10K
R6	82
R7	10K variable (potentiometer)
R8	82K
R9	5600
R10	3900

Coils

L1	Loopstick antenna (same symbol as magnetic core transformer)
L2	Magnetic core, .5 MILLI H
L3	Magnetic core, 1.0 MILLI H

Transistors

(E = emitter, B = base, C = collector)

Q1	PNP type, RF-AF amplifier
Q2	PNP type, audio amplifier

Miscellaneous

S1	On-off switch (mounted on R7)
D1	Diode detector

Exercise 17.5 Figures a and b are pictorial wiring diagrams of a transistorized code-practice oscillator. The unit provides for practicing International Morse Code either by listening to an audible tone over headphones or speaker or by watching a flashing light.

Study the illustrations and the components list carefully, making preliminary sketches of connections. Then, make a complete schematic diagram of the circuit following recommended practices and including component values and reference designations.

Note: Terminal strips TS-1 and TS-2 and the battery holder are for mechanical function and convenience in wiring. They should not be shown in a schematic diagram.

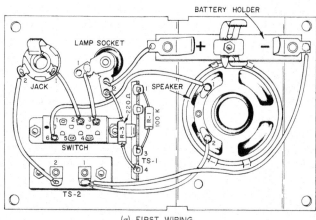

(a) FIRST WIRING

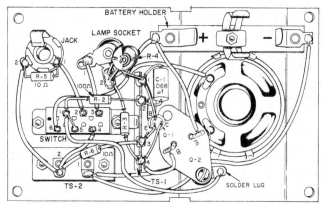

(b) FINAL WIRING

Components List

Capacitors
C1	.068 UF

Resistors (ohms)
R1	100K
R2	100
R3	220
R4	50K variable (potentiometer)
R5	10
R6	10

Transistors
(E = emitter, B = base, C = collector)
Q1	NPN type, oscillator
Q2	PNP type, amplifier

Miscellaneous
Battery	"C" Type, 1.5 V
Battery holder	
Jack	2-conductor (for headphones)
Key	Telegraph key (not shown—connected between terminals 1 and 2 of TS-2)
Lamp, 1.5 V	
Lamp socket	
Speaker	
Switch	3-position slide switch

Connections

Position one (OFF-LIGHT)—terminals 1–5, 3–4

Position two (SPEAKER)—terminals 1–6, 2–4

Position three (PHONES)—terminals 2–5

Terminal strips TS-1 and TS-2

CHAPTER EIGHTEEN

STRUCTURAL DRAWINGS

OBJECTIVES

After studying the material in this chapter, you should be able to:

1. Create a structural truss or floor plan drawing.

2. Label and specify the size and shape of steel structural members.

3. Identify, draw, and label various structural steel shapes.

4. Identify, draw, and label high-strength bolts used in structural joints.

5. Identify welding symbols used in steel fabrication of structural components.

6. Identify and read concrete and brick construction details.

Refer to the following standards:
- *www.ascelibrary.org Search and browse to view tables of contents and abstracts from this comprehensive online library of over 33,000 papers from ASCE journals for all disciplines of civil engineering. Full text is available to subscribers.*
- *www.awc.org American Wood Council design standards*

An engineer works with a laptop computer near an unfinished bridge. (Courtesy of Kaluzny & Thatcher/Stone Allstock/ Getty Images.)

OVERVIEW

Structural drawing consists of the preparation of design and construction drawings for buildings, bridges, domes, tanks, towers, and other civil structures. A structural member is essentially one that is bearing a load. Structural drawing is a very large field made up of a wide variety of disciplines. Although the basic drawing principles are the same as for those of machines and machine parts, some methods of representation are different in structural drafting.

Ordinarily, the structural engineer determines the form and shape of a structure, as well as the sizes of the main members to be used. Detail drawings are often made under the engineer's supervision. In many cases, creating detail drawings is a position that provides a stepping-stone to greater responsibility.

Structural drawing can appear in plan or elevation. The location, size, shape, material, and fastening details must be clearly defined. Inaccurate or ambiguous structural drawings can cause building failure and endanger human life. Structural drawings are an essential part of engineering design. Nearly every commercial building uses structural steel in its construction. Residential construction often uses structural wood members.

Many computer graphics programs can enhance the drawing process by providing structural strength calculations for each structural element in a drawing. To ensure safety, meticulous proofing and checking is performed by every member of the team.

STRUCTURAL DRAWINGS

A spider web is one of nature's fine examples of a structure. The web is made of many parts connected to form a unit strong enough to support the spider. Most building or civil project structures also have many interconnecting parts, such as beams, girders, and columns, that form a framework strong enough to support loads (Figures 18.1 and 18.2).

Structural drawings include foundation plans, wall section and framing details, structural steel framing and details, beam and column drawings and details, and others.

Structural drawings are created using either 2D or 3D CAD software. 3D CAD offers better visualization, as well as analytical and simulation capabilities, but owing to the complexity of large structures, 3D CAD requires a considerable modeling effort. Wireframe 3D models can sometimes reduce the amount of modeling effort and still provide sufficient information. Structural analysis of piping is an example where 3D wireframe models are used. 2D CAD provides the ability to make accurate orthographic drawings and easily reuse standard details.

The materials most commonly used in construction are wood, glass, structural steel, aluminum, concrete (plain, reinforced, and prestressed), structural clay products, and stone masonry (plain and reinforced). Each of these materials presents its own benefits and challenges as a construction material. Each material also has standard members that are manufactured in stock sizes and shapes. CAD software often provides libraries for these stock parts and features.

18.1   Spider Web. *A single thread of an orb web is only 0.15 μm thick and yet the strands are capable of stopping a flying bee because they are strong and also very elastic. (Copyright Sailplans/Shutterstock.)*

18.2   *The structure of this octagonal roof resembles a spider's web. (ananaline/ Shutterstock.)*

18.1 WOOD CONSTRUCTION

Many different types of wood are used as structural timber, including ash, birch, cedar, cypress, Douglas fir, elm, oak, pine, poplar, redwood, and spruce. Information concerning the strength properties of the various types and grades can be obtained from Wood Structural Design Data. The *ANSI/AF&PA NDS National Design Specification for Wood Construction,* published by the American Wood Council (AWC), contains detailed construction information, accessed at www.awc.org/codes-standards/publications/nds-2015 (see Figure 18.3).

Nominal Sizes for Wood Products

The surface of a wood product is finished, or "dressed," by milling or planing. Owing to wood loss in surfacing, a 1″ thick designation for a thickness is actually ¾″ for dry lumber and 25/32″ for **green lumber.** Lumber is considered "green" if its moisture content exceeds 19 percent. Table 18.1 shows dressed thickness for various sizes of dry and green wood.

Symbols for Finished Surfaces on Wood Products

Symbols are used to indicate requirements for finished surfaces on wood.

S2S: Surface two sides.
S2E: Surface two edges.
S4S: All four faces are to have finished surfaces.

The working drawings must show whether standard dressed, standard rough, or special sizes are to be used.

Wood is commonly used for sills, columns, studs, joists, rafters, **purlins, trusses,** and sheathing in homes and other buildings. Methods of fastening timber members include nails, screws, lag screws, drift bolts, bolts, steel plates, and various special timber connectors.

Ordinarily, a structural timber is cut so that the wood fibers, or grain, runs parallel to the length. The strength resistance of wood is not the same in a direction perpendicular to the grain as it is parallel to the grain. Therefore, in designing connections, the direction of the force to be transmitted must be taken into account. Also, proper spacing, edge distance, and end distance must be maintained for screws, bolts, and other connectors.

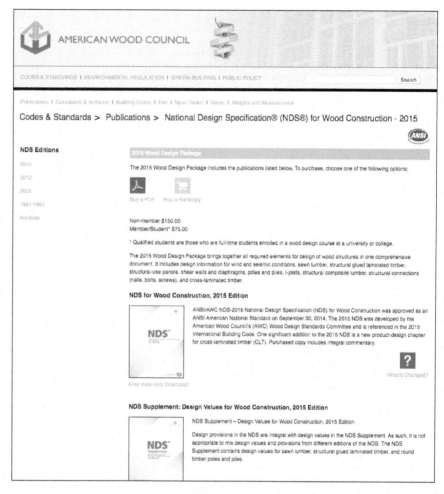

18.3 *The American Wood Council publishes the National Design Specification for Wood Construction (NDS). (Courtesy of the American Wood Council.)*

Table 18.1 Nominal and Dressed Sizes for Dry and Green Wood

Nominal Size	Dressed Thickness, Dry	Dressed Thickness, Green
1″	3/4″	25/32″
2″ to 4″	Subtract 1/2″	Subtract 7/16″
5″, 6″, and 7″	Subtract 1/2″	Subtract 3/8″
8″	Subtract 3/4″	Subtract 1/2″

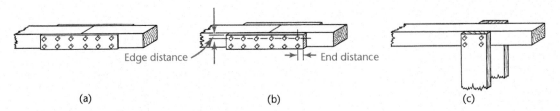

Edge distance   End distance

(a)   (b)   (c)

18.4 Typical Bolted Joints

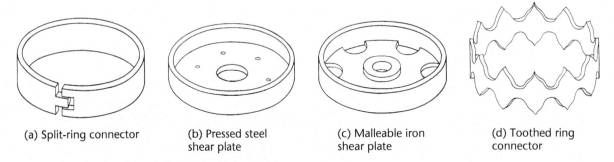

(a) Split-ring connector

(b) Pressed steel shear plate

(c) Malleable iron shear plate

(d) Toothed ring connector

18.5 Metal Connectors for Timber Structures

Wood Joints

Typical bolted *joints* are shown in Figure 18.4. Either steel or wood splice plates may be used to transmit the forces (Figures 18.4a and 18.4b). A detail without splice plates is shown in Figure 18.4c. Many specialty connectors and shear plates are available.

Connector Designs

Each type of connection requires a different design. Figure 18.5 shows split-ring metal connectors. Figure 18.6 shows how split-ring connectors are installed. Figure 18.7 shows a drawing of the left half of a timber roof truss using this type of connector. Only the left half is drawn, because the truss is symmetrical. The views of the top and bottom chords show the relative positions of the connecting members of the structure. In truss drawings, the view of the top chord is an auxiliary view (see Exercise 18.1). It is also customary to show the lower chord using a section taken just above the lower chord with the line of sight downward.

Metal Ring Connectors

Metal ring connectors can be installed in wood of proper grade and moisture content to provide increased resistance to shearing loads. The method consists of using either a toothed ring, called an *alligator,* or a split ring (Figure 18.5a) to connect wood to wood or wood to metal joints.

Toothed Rings

Place the toothed ring (Figure 18.5d) between two members to connect them. Draw the two members together by tightening the bolt so that the teeth of the ring are forced into the two members. The ring assists in transmitting stress from one member to the other.

Split Rings

Cut a groove into each of the two members to connect them. Place the ring in the grooves. Fasten the two members together using a bolt, as shown in Figure 18.6.

The open joint of the ring should be in a direction at right angles to that of the stress, so that as the stress is applied the ring is deformed slightly and transmits the pressure to the wood within the ring as well as to that outside the ring. With this connection, the tensile and shearing strengths of wood are developed to a higher degree than by other methods of connection, and it is possible to use timber in tension much more economically.

It is standard practice to show ring connectors by solid lines, as shown in Figure 18.7.

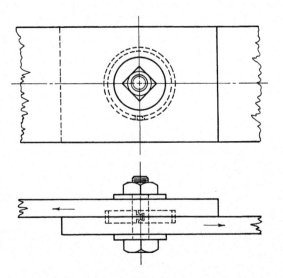

18.6 Method of Installing Split-Ring Connectors

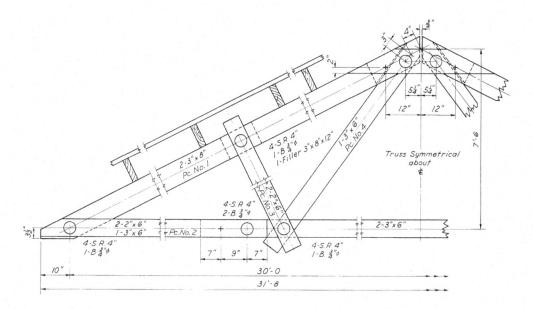

18.7   A Roof Truss *(See Exercise 18.1 for the complete drawing.)*

Straps and Plates

Many specialty straps and plates are available for connecting wood members to wood or other materials (Figure 18.8). Figure 18.9 shows a drawing detail specifying a strap tie holddown. Simpson Strong-Tie Co. is one manufacturer that provides a custom menu for AutoCAD that allows you to easily insert orthographic views of their connectors in your drawings. Use the resources available from manufacturing companies to save time and effort in drawing repetitive detail.

Another resource you can find on the Web is the Truss Plate Institute, which provides design and verification services as well as a variety of publications for connecting wood structural members. You can find their resources at www.tpinst.org.

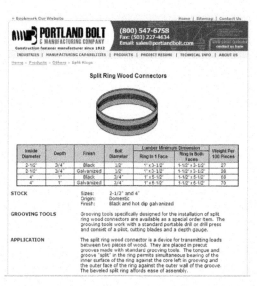

18.8   *Design and sizing information is easy to find on the World Wide Web. (Courtesy of Portland Bolt and Manufacturing Company, www.portlandbolt.com.)*

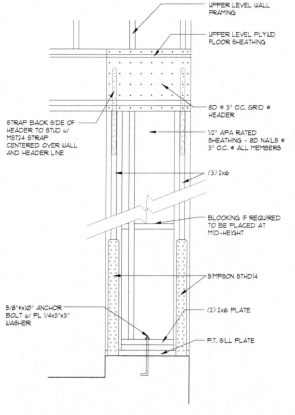

18.9   Drawing Detail Calling for Simpson STHD Strap Tie Hold-Down *(Courtesy of Locati Architects.)*

18.2 STRUCTURAL STEEL

Structural steel drawings are ordinarily one of two types: engineering *design drawings* made by the design engineer, and manufacturing (shop) drawings usually made by the steel fabricator. For a more complete treatment of this subject, consult *Detailing for Steel Construction* (published by the American Institute of Steel Construction, Chicago, IL).

Design drawings show the overall dimensions of the structure, such as the location of columns, beams, angles, and other structural shapes, and list the sizes of these members. Detail in the form of typical cross sections, special connections required, and various notes are also included.

For example, a building floor plan shows the steel columns in cross section and the beam or girder framing using single heavy lines, as shown in Figure 18.10. Members framing from column to column, providing end support for other beams, are called **girders;** smaller beams framing between girders are called **filler beams.** The designer's plans are sent to the steel fabricator who will furnish the steel for the job. From these plans the fabricator makes the necessary detailed shop drawings and erection plans. Before shop work begins, the fabricator's drawings are sent to the design engineer for final checking and approval. The design engineer is the authority who makes any changes necessary to ensure the required strength and safety of connections. Once the fabricator receives shop drawings approved by the engineer, the shop work can begin.

Shop drawings consist of detail drawings of all parts of the entire structure, showing exactly how the parts are to be made. These drawings show all dimensions necessary for fabrication, usually calculated to the nearest 1/16″. They also show the location of all holes needed for connections, the details of connection parts, and the required sizes of all material. Notes

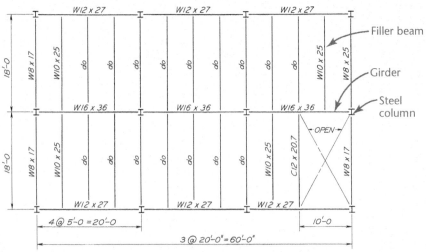

18.10 Typical Steel Floor Design Plan

specify fabrication or construction methods on the detail drawings whenever such items are not covered by separate written specifications. Fabrication, shop methods, and field construction methods must be fully understood by the detailer.

The design of details and connections is an important part of the engineering of the structure. The connections of the various members must be sufficient to transmit the forces in these members. Connection details should be drawn to a scale large enough to show them without crowding. Overall lengths of members are not always drawn to scale in order to show connections clearly. Break lines can be very useful. Show all necessary dimensions. Measurements should never be made from detail drawings by the shop or in the field by the workers making the piece.

Piece Marks

A system is used to mark each piece that is separately handled. This mark is called the **piece mark** and should be shown wherever the member appears on the drawings (Figure 18.11). The piece mark is also painted on the member in the shop and later serves as a shipping mark and erection mark in the field for final assembly of the member in the structure.

Erection Plans

Erection plans made by the steel fabricator are assembly drawings for the steel structure. They show how the steel parts fit together. The piece marks of the individual members are shown on the erection plan to make it easy to identify individual parts. Show only as much detail as needed so that a skilled worker can assemble the parts. The detail drawings fully describe each member and how it connects, so this information is not needed in the erection plan. Line diagrams show the steel members using heavy straight lines. When the assembly is complex, more detail is needed. Draw the assembly views to scale. As

18.11   Piece Marks

with detail shop drawings, workers should never measure from the drawing to obtain dimensions. Use notes on these drawings to indicate how the structure is to be assembled.

An erection plan for the roof steel framing on a building addition is shown in Figure 18.12. This structure is for a paper roofing products pulp mill. New steel is shown by full lines. Existing roof members are shown by dashed lines. Connections to existing steel members are shown in sectional views. The timber framing for the support of large roof ventilators is also shown.

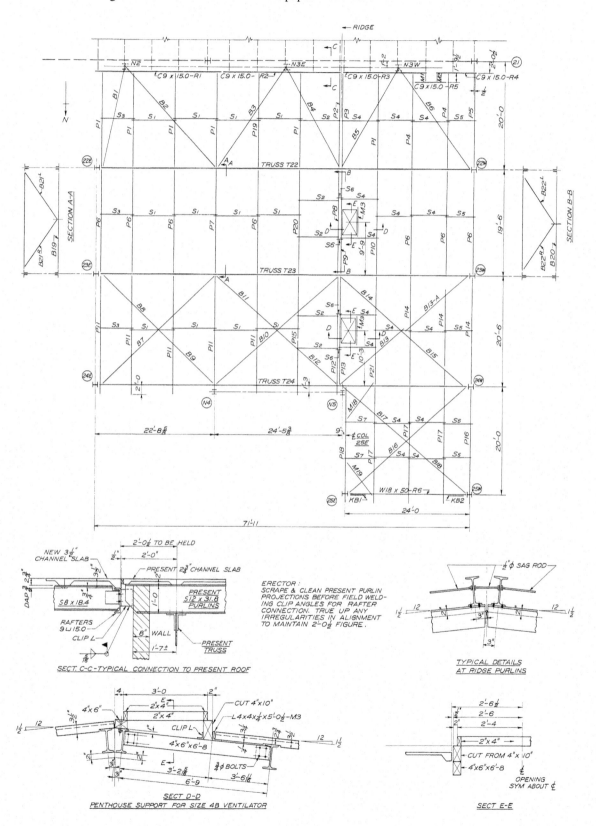

18.12 Roof Steel Erection Plan

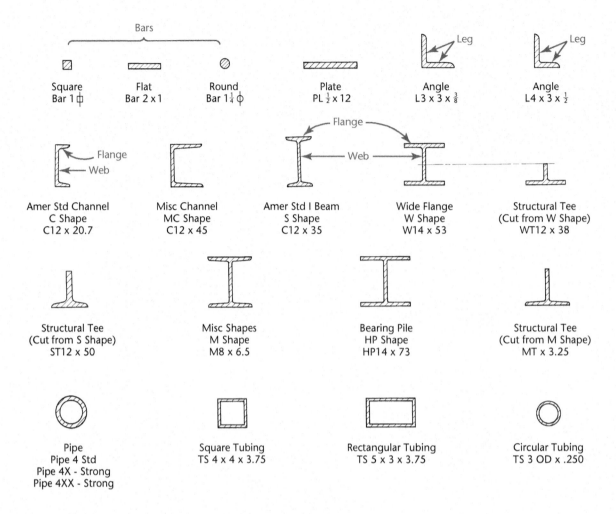

18.13   Structural Steel Shapes

18.3 STRUCTURAL STEEL SHAPES

Structural steel is available in many standard shapes that are formed by the mill by rolling steel billets under high temperatures. (Aluminum and magnesium shapes are also available but are not covered in this text.) Some of the available shapes are square, flat, round bars; plates; equal-leg and unequal-leg angles, American Standard and miscellaneous channels; S, W, M, and HP shapes for beams, columns, and bearing piles; structural tees mill cut from W, S, or M shapes; and standard strong and extra strong pipe and tubing in square, rectangular, or circular cross sections. Figure 18.13 shows some typical cross sections of these shapes and how they are designated or listed in the bill of materials. Use the correct designation on both the design and the detail drawings wherever the structural member appears. For example, designate a wide *flange* section of 14″ nominal depth, weighing 53 lb per foot and having an overall length of 26′-2 $\frac{1}{8}$″ as W14 × 53 × 26′-2 $\frac{1}{8}$″.

Most CAD programs have structural shape symbol libraries available. Templates are also available to save time in drawing structural symbols by hand.

18.4 SPECIFICATIONS

Dimensions, weights, and properties of rolled steel structural shapes, rolling mill practice, and miscellaneous data for designing and estimating is listed in the *Manual of Steel Construction* (American Institute of Steel Construction, AISC). This is the authoritative manual for structural steel drafting.

Fifteen types or grades of *structural steel* are available. These differ in chemical composition and physical properties. An ASTM (American Society for Testing Materials) specification defines each type. There are considerable variations in the strengths and costs of the various grades. Economical selection of steel grade depends on physical properties of steels, such as strength, ductility, corrosion resistance, and cost. Specify the type by giving the ASTM designation on the drawing. The most commonly used grade is ASTM A36; the number 36 specifies that the guaranteed minimum yield strength is 36 ksi (36,000 lb/in.^{2}). Many lightweight cold-formed C and Z section shapes are also available.

18.5 WELDED AND BOLTED CONNECTIONS

The main members of a steel structure are joined together in the field to build the structure. Most joints are welded connections to the main members. Open holes are provided for field bolts that join the members together. Connections are made of angles or connection plates that attach to the main members by riveting or by bolting with either ordinary or high-strength steel bolts in either bearing-type or slip-critical-type connections. High-strength bolts must be field tightened by a specific amount of torque applied to the wrench. Formerly, shop riveting and field riveting were used exclusively in structural work.

TIP

Scales for Detailing

Often, scales of 3/4" = 1'–0, or 1" = 1'–0 are convenient for showing steel details. The details need to be large enough to show clearly. Owing to the length of steel members, break lines may be necessary. In some cases, scale in any direction may need to be exaggerated to show details.

18.6 RIVETED CONNECTIONS

Although riveting is seldom used now, you may find reference to riveted joints in original plans of structures that require new additions or modifications. Structural rivets are made of soft carbon steel and are available in diameters ranging from 1/2" to 1-1/4". Rivets driven in the shop are called *shop rivets*, and those driven in the field (at the construction site) are called *field rivets*. Rivets are usually of the button-head type and are driven hot, into holes 1/16" larger than the rivet diameter. The length of a rivet is the thickness (grip) of the parts being connected, plus the length of the shank necessary to form the driven head and to fill the hole. Excess shank length will produce capped heads, whereas lengths too short will not permit the formation of a full head. Shop rivets are ordinarily driven by large riveting machines that are part of the permanent shop equipment.

Field rivets are heated in a forge at the construction site. The heated rivet is held firmly in the hole with a dolly bar while the pneumatic hammer or rivet gun forms a round, smooth head.

A shop drawing for a riveted roof truss is shown in Figure 18.14. Only the left half is drawn, because the truss is symmetrical about the centerline. Note the use of the gage lines (lines passing through rivets or holes like centerlines) of the members. Locate gage lines close to the centroid of the axes of the members, and at the joints where members intersect. These gage lines should intersect at a single point to avoid unnecessary moment stresses due to off-center locations (eccentricities). The open holes indicate where the field splices are to be—usually at the centerline of the truss (℄) for the top chord and at $5'-2\frac{5}{16}$ from the centerline for the bottom chord.

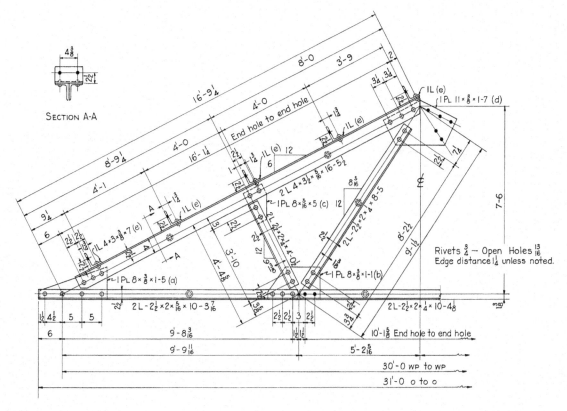

18.14 A Riveted Truss

18.7 FRAME BEAM CONNECTIONS

AISC recommends certain standard connections for attaching beams. These connections are ordinarily adequate to transmit the end forces that beams carry. You should know the strength of these connections and use them only when they are sufficient. For complete information, see the *AISC Manual of Steel Construction, Allowable Stress Design (ASD)*, and *Load Resistance Factor Design (LRFD)*. This manual provides details for standard framed beam connections using 3/4", 7/8" and 1" diameter bolted or riveted connections, and allowable loads for both slip-critical-type and bearing-type connections. The fasteners may have a regular or a staggered arrangement. The holes may be either standard round or oversized slotted ones.

Figure 18.15 shows standard two-angle framed beam connections in a typical detail drawing of a floor beam. This drawing illustrates several important features. Shop rivets are shown as open circles on shop drawings. Holes for field rivets or bolts are blacked in solid. Gage lines are always shown. Line up holes or rivets on these lines when possible rather than "breaking the gage."

It is necessary to locate the **gage line** of an angle for each leg, unless it has already been shown for the identical angle elsewhere on the drawing. The edge distance, from end rivet or hole to the end of the angle, must be given at one end; the billed length of the piece is worked out to provide the necessary edge distance at the other end. It is not necessary that the beam extend the full length of the back-to-back distance of end angles. It is shown "set back" at both ends; the length of beam called for is 1" less than the $13'-7\frac{3}{4}$ distance.

Below the drawing, the mark B25 is the piece or shipping mark that appears on the erection plan and is to be painted on the member in the shop for identification. The end connection angles are fully detailed at the left end of the beam and are given the assembly mark aa. At the right end where these same angles are again used, only the assembly mark 2–aa, to indicate two angles, is needed. The value $10'-1\frac{1}{4}$ is called an **extension figure.** This is the distance from the back of the left-end angles to the center of the group of four holes. Note that this dimension is on the same horizontal line as the $3'-4\frac{1}{2}$ figure just to the left. It is customary, in giving feet and inches, to give the foot mark (') after dimensions in feet, but not to give the (") inch mark, designating inches.

18.15 Floor Beam Shop Drawing

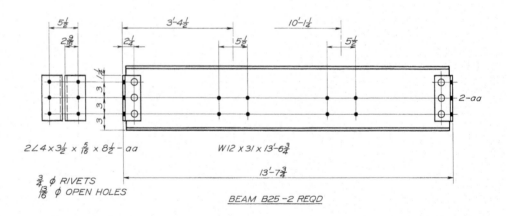

18.8 WELDING

Welding is a common method for connecting steel members of buildings and bridges. Most steel fabricators have bolt, welding, and riveting equipment available. Some handle only welded fabrication. The *fillet weld* is most common in structural steel fabrication. Use standard weld symbols to simplify making the shop drawings. For additional information, refer to Chapter 21 and to the relevant specification in the *AISC Manual of Steel Construction.* When a structure is to be welded, it should be designed throughout for this method of fabrication. It is not economical to merely substitute welding for riveting.

A beam with end connection angles shop welded to the *beam web* is shown in Figure 18.16. The remaining legs of the angles are to be welded to the connecting columns in the field, as shown in the end view. This view pertains only to field erection. Open holes in the far legs facilitate positioning for the bolts.

A shop drawing of a diagonal bracing between two columns is shown in Figure 18.17. Here the diagonal members are shop welded to gusset plates that are to be bolted to the column flanges as a permanent installation in the field.

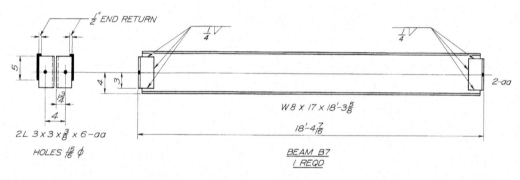

18.16   Detail of Welded Beam

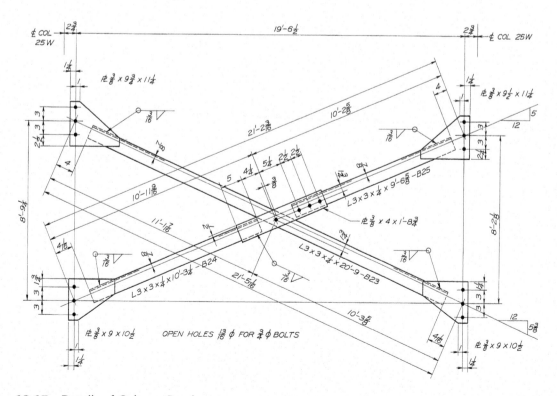

18.17   Details of Column Bracing

Figure 18.18 is the complete shop drawing for a symmetrical welded roof truss. Because it is symmetrical, only the left half of the structure needs to be shown. Symmetry is shown on the drawing by the note Sym. abt. ₵. In this drawing,

- The *clip angles* marked aa are to be used for the attachment of roof purlins to the truss.
- The only *plate material* is the small gusset plate marked pb.
- Most of the connections of web *members* to chords are made by fillet welding the angles to the webs of the chords.

- The *chords* are of structural tee (WT) type.
- The top chords are joined at the ridge by butt welding, which is also used at the end of the truss where the chords join.
- *Weld symbols* and *member marks* are used.
- Sizes and quantities are listed in the *bill of material* (BOM).
- The drawing is uncluttered and clear, with lots of important information conveyed under the heading "General Notes."

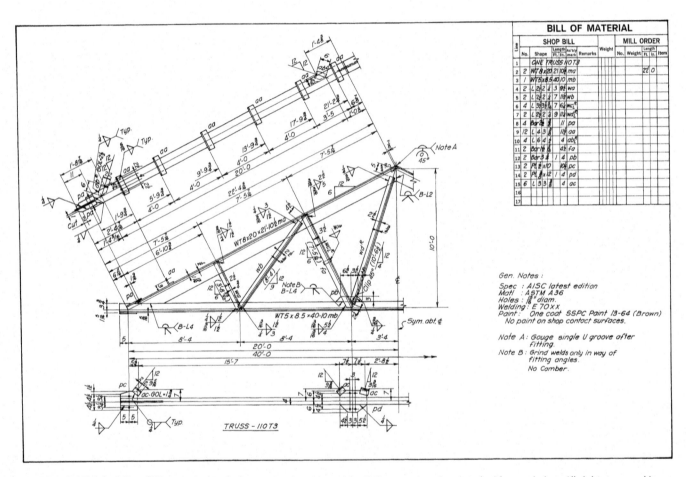

18.18   A Welded Roof Truss *(Copyright © American Institute of Steel Construction. Reprinted with permission. All rights reserved.)*

18.9 HIGH-STRENGTH BOLTING FOR STRUCTURAL JOINTS

Two common types of *high-strength steel bolts* are ASTM A325 and A490. The A449 type is physically similar to A325, except that A325 requires the use of special nuts. These bolts are treated by quenching and tempering. A325 bolts are made of medium carbon steel, whereas A490 are made of alloy steel. Metric high-strength structural bolts, nuts, and washers are available. Consult a manufacturer's catalog or Appendix 17

for specifications. During installation, these bolts are tightened a certain amount, either using the "turn of the nut method" or with a calibrated torque wrench.

Figure 18.19 shows a high strength steel bolt used to transmit a force from the center plate into the two outside plates. When the bolt is fully tightened, the connecting parts are held together by friction, preventing joint slip. This minimizes

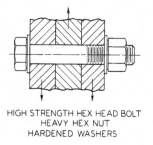

HIGH STRENGTH HEX HEAD BOLT
HEAVY HEX NUT
HARDENED WASHERS

18.19   High Tensile Strength Steel Bolt

fatigue failures due to impact or stress reversals. The slip resistance depends not only on the amount of clamping force but also on the nature of the contact surfaces.

Figure 18.19 shows hardened washers under both head and nut. Whether one or two washers are needed, or none, depends on the method of tightening, the yield stress of the material being joined, and whether the joint is to be the "slip-critical" or "bearing" type.

A bearing-type connection relies on the strength of the bolt shank bearing against the material, and no allowance is made for friction due to clamping action. Specifications for accepted practice, along with installation and inspection

procedures, design examples, and reference tables, are covered in *The Handbook of Bolts and Bolted Joints* (CRC Press).

Figure 18.20 shows the complete shop drawing of a steel column of two-floor height. The floors are indicated by reference lines B, 1, and 2 of the drawing. High-strength bolts are used to attach connection material to the W12 × 96 column shaft. The top views at levels 1 and 2 show the outstanding legs of the angles in section plan views. Open holes are shown by the round dots located by dimensions taken from the column centerlines. The open holes are for the insertion of field bolts in beam connections when the entire assembly is erected.

Faces A, B, C, and D are designated. Viewing a column from above, designate the faces in counterclockwise order, with faces A and C designating the flanges. For web faces B and D, usually only face B needs to be drawn. However, when the connections on face D are exceptionally complicated, it should be drawn as an additional *elevation* view.

Note how the drawing shows shop bolts and their designation "HSB" (high-strength bolts).

At the top of this column, splice connection material is provided by Bars (b), for attachment of the shaft above. All material for this column is listed in the bill of material on the drawing.

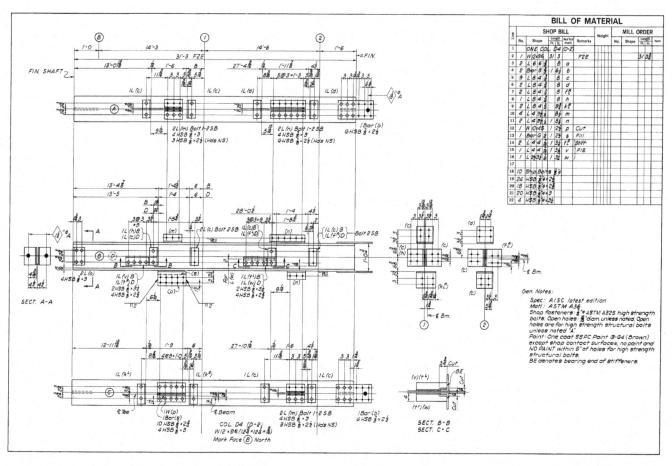

18.20   Steel Column Detail—Bolted Connections (*Copyright © American Institute of Steel Construction. Reprinted with permission. All rights reserved.*)

18.10 ACCURACY OF DIMENSIONS

An important part of the structural drawing is accurate dimensioning. If there are incorrect dimensions on the drawings, they will result in serious errors and misfits when members are assembled in the field. Correction of such errors not only entails considerable expense but often delays the completion of the work. Because in ordinary steel work dimensions are given to the closest 1/16″, considerable precision is demanded.

Consider the effect of tolerance stacking on the fit of steel members. Review the dimensioning and tolerancing practices in Chapters 11 and 12. Using baseline dimensioning can aid in defining the shape so that tolerances don't accumulate.

Using CAD, you can accurately list dimensions for the lengths of angled members that would have required trigonometric calculation prior to the advent of CAD.

Do not let the ability of CAD to list accurate dimensions cause you to overlook the fact that real-world fabrication will necessarily have some variation from the exact dimension value.

18.11 CONCRETE CONSTRUCTION

Concrete is made by mixing sand (fine aggregate) and gravel (coarse aggregate) or other fine and coarse aggregates with Portland cement and water. Its strength varies with the quality and relative quantities of the materials; the manner of mixing, placing, and curing; and the age of the concrete.

The compressive strength of concrete depends on the mix design, but concrete has been manufactured to develop an ultimate strength at 28 days as high as 7,000 psi. The material's tensile strength is limited to about one tenth its compressive strength. *High-strength concrete,* used in high-rise construction, has a compressive strength up to 17,000 psi.

Portland cement is a controlled, manufactured product, in contrast to natural cements. Its name is derived from its color, which resembles the color of a famous stone found on the island of Portland in southern England.

Because the tensile strength of plain concrete is very limited, its use as a building material can be improved by embedding steel reinforcing bars so that the steel resists the tension, and the concrete mainly resists the compression. The two materials act together in resisting forces and flexure. Concrete combined with steel in this way is called *reinforced concrete.*

When the steel is pretensioned before the superimposed load is applied, producing an interior force within the member, the material is called *prestressed concrete.* The type of steel used in prestressed concrete is flexible but very strong.

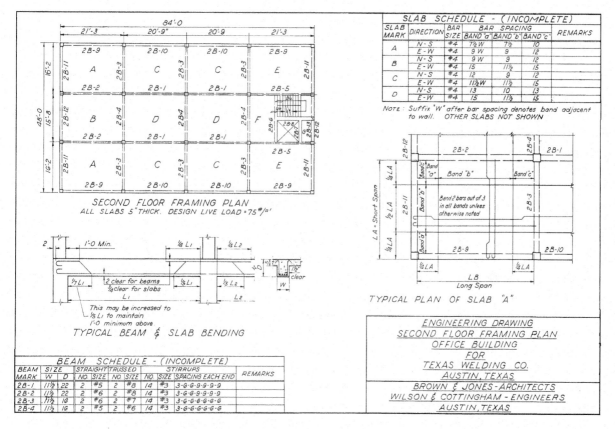

SLAB SCHEDULE - (INCOMPLETE)

SLAB MARK	DIRECTION	BAR SIZE	BAR SPACING BAND "a"	BAND "b"	BAND "c"	REMARKS
A	N-S	#4	7½ W	7½	10	
	E-W	#4	9 W	9	12	
B	N-S	#4	9 W	9	12	
	E-W	#4	15	11½	15	
C	N-S	#4	12	9	12	
	E-W	#4	11½ W	11½	15	
D	N-S	#4	13	10	13	
	E-W	#4	15	11½	15	

NOTE: Suffix "W" after bar spacing denotes band adjacent to wall. OTHER SLABS NOT SHOWN

SECOND FLOOR FRAMING PLAN
ALL SLABS 5" THICK. DESIGN LIVE LOAD = 75#/☐'

TYPICAL BEAM & SLAB BENDING

TYPICAL PLAN OF SLAB "A"

BEAM SCHEDULE - (INCOMPLETE)

BEAM MARK	SIZE W	D	STRAIGHT NO.	SIZE	TRUSSED NO.	SIZE	STIRRUPS NO.	SIZE	SPACING EACH END	REMARKS
2B-1	11½	22	2	#5	2	#8	14	#3	3-6-6-9-9-9-9	
2B-2	11½	22	2	#6	2	#8	14	#3	3-6-6-9-9-9-9	
2B-3	11½	16	2	#6	2	#7	14	#3	3-6-6-6-6-6-6	
2B-4	11½	16	2	#5	2	#6	14	#3	3-6-6-6-6-6-6	

ENGINEERING DRAWING
SECOND FLOOR FRAMING PLAN
OFFICE BUILDING
FOR
TEXAS WELDING CO.
AUSTIN, TEXAS

BROWN & JONES - ARCHITECTS
WILSON & COTTINGHAM - ENGINEERS
AUSTIN, TEXAS

18.21 Engineering Drawing for a Two-Way Slab and Beam Floor

18.12 REINFORCED CONCRETE DRAWINGS

The design of the reinforcing material for a reinforced concrete structure and preparation of the corresponding drawings are complicated. To simplify and to secure uniformity throughout engineering offices, the American Concrete Institute (ACI) at concrete.org publishes *PRC-315-18: Guide to Presenting Reinforcing Steel Design Details,* among many other useful code standards and documents.

Preparing two sets of drawings, an engineering drawing and a placing drawing, is common in order to present the information so that it is clear and unambiguous to both the steel fabricator and the placer. The engineering drawing is prepared for the manufacturer that fabricates the reinforcing steel. It shows the general arrangement of the structure, the sizes and reinforcements of the several members, and such other information as may be necessary for the correct interpretation of the designer's ideas. The drawing is also used for making forms with precise dimensions before placing the reinforcing bars and casting concrete. The placing drawing shows the sizes and shapes of the several rods, stirrups, hoops, ties, and so on, and arranges them in tabular forms for reference by the building contractor.

An engineering drawing for a two-way slab and beam floor of a multistory building is shown in Figure 18.21. For examples of placing drawings, consult the *Guide to Presenting Reinforcing Steel Design Details* referred to earlier.

Figure 18.22 shows detail views for the reinforced concrete intake for a hydroelectric site. Note that the steel bars, even though embedded in the concrete, are shown by solid lines and that the concrete is stippled in cross section. Unlike shop drawings for structural steel, concrete drawings are ordinarily made to the same scale in both directions. Often a scale of 1/4" to the foot is adequate, although when the structure is complicated, scales of 3/8" or 1/2" to the foot or larger may be used. Note the scale clearly below each detail view. Avoid a cluttered appearance (usually the result of crowding the drawing with notes) by using tables and schedules for listing bar sizes and other necessary data. Cover important points in a single detail drawing or a set of notes.

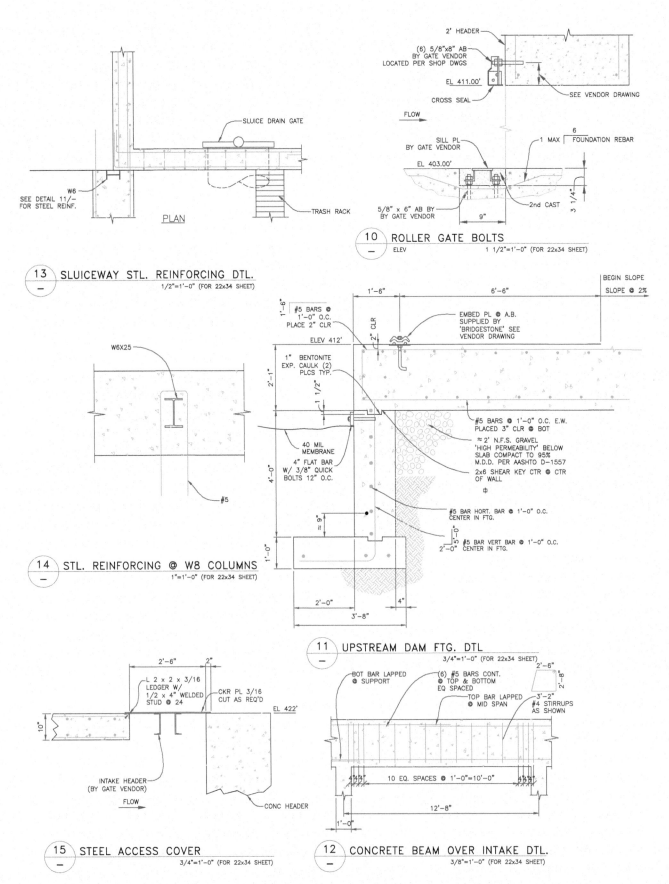

18.22 Reinforced Concrete. *Details for the intake for the Power Creek hydroelectric project near Cordova, Alaska, which has generation capacity of 30 average annual GWh of renewable energy. (Courtesy of Jason Cohn, Whitewater Engineering Corporation.)*

18.13 STRUCTURAL CLAY PRODUCTS

Brick and tile, which are manufactured clay products, have been in use for centuries and comprise some of the best known forms of building construction. They are made from different types of clay and in many different shapes, forms, and colors (Figure 18.23). Traditionally, they are built into masonry forms by skilled brick or tile masons, who place the units one at a time in a soft mortar. After the mortar hardens, it becomes an integral part of the structure. Typical mortars contain sand, lime, Portland cement, and water. Although the compressive and tensile strengths of the clay units themselves are considerable, the overall strength of the structure is limited by the strength of the mortar joints. The result is a structure of high compressible strength and relatively low tensile strength.

As with concrete, it is possible to reinforce brick and tile masonry by embedding steel rods, thus adding greatly to tension resistance and strength. This material is called reinforced brick (or tile) masonry (**RBM**).

Information on the manufacture, weight and strength properties, and various uses and applications of structural clay products can be found on the Brick Industry Association website. They also publish a reference guide, "Principles of Brick Masonry" and other technical notes and videos: https://www.gobrick.com/read-research/technical-notes.

Bricks are made in various sizes, with the $2\frac{1}{4} \times 3\frac{3}{4} \times 8''$ building brick being most common. Thickness of mortar joints usually varies from 1/4" to 3/4", with 3/8" and 1/2" most common. Of the several methods of bonding brick, the following are the most common (see Figure 18.23):

In *running bond,* all face brick are stretchers and are generally bonded to the backing by metal ties.

In *American bond,* the face brick are laid alternately, five courses of stretchers and one course of headers.

In *Flemish bond,* the face brick are laid with alternating stretchers and headers in every course.

In *English bond,* the face brick are laid alternately, one course of stretchers and one course of headers.

These standard methods of bonding are frequently modified to produce various artistic effects. Typical brick lintel arches are shown in Figure 18.24.

In addition to its use as a basic building material, tile is used in fireproofing structural steel members. Most building codes require that the steel members be enclosed in concrete or masonry so that fire will not cause collapse of the structure. Hollow tile units, which are light and relatively inexpensive, are well adapted to this use.

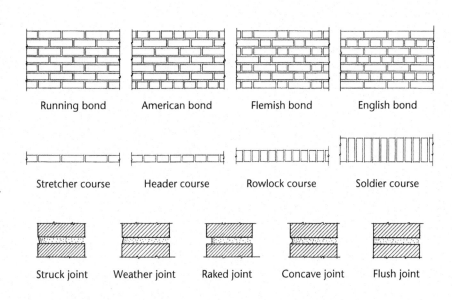

Running bond   American bond   Flemish bond   English bond

Stretcher course   Header course   Rowlock course   Soldier course

Struck joint   Weather joint   Raked joint   Concave joint   Flush joint

18.23   Methods of Laying and Bonding Brick, Tile, and Stone

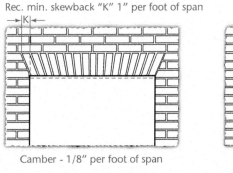

Rec. min. skewback "K" 1" per foot of span

Camber - 1/8" per foot of span

Brick units - tapered sides and ends

"r" = Rise

Brick units - tapered sides only

18.24   Typical Lintels

18.14 STONE CONSTRUCTION

Natural stone—generally limestone, marble, sandstone, or granite—is used in masonry construction, most commonly for ornamental facing.

Ashlar masonry (also spelled *ashler*) is formed of stones cut accurately to rectangular faces and laid in regular courses or at random with thin mortar joints.

Rubble masonry is formed of stones of irregular shapes laid in courses or at random with mortar joints of varying thickness.

Manufactured stone is concrete made of fine aggregate for the facing and coarse aggregate for the backing. The fine aggregate consists of screenings of limestone, marble, sandstone, or granite, to present an appearance similar to natural stone. Manufactured stone is made of any desired shape, with or without architectural ornament.

Architectural terra cotta is a hard-burned clay product and is used primarily for architectural decoration and for wall facing and wall coping.

Brick, stone, tile, and terra cotta are combined in many different ways in masonry construction. A few examples are shown in Figure 18.25.

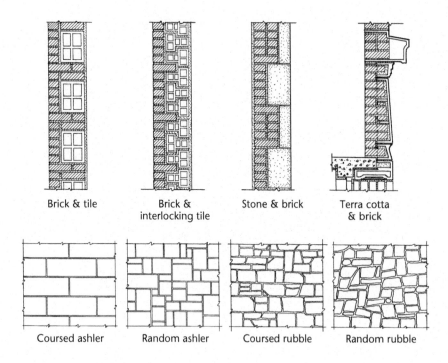

Brick & tile   Brick & interlocking tile   Stone & brick   Terra cotta & brick

Coursed ashler   Random ashler   Coursed rubble   Random rubble

18.25 Methods of Laying and Bonding Brick, Tile, and Stone

CAD TOOLS FOR STRUCTURAL DRAWINGS

Structural drawings use a variety of standard symbols and methods of representation. A number of CAD symbol libraries are available that allow users to quickly generate drawings of structural steel shapes, connecting members, and steel erection plans. Once plans have been created, other programs are available to automatically calculate areas and perform finite-element analysis on the design.

3D constraint-based software platforms often provide very sophisticated steel shapes that can be inserted to create assemblies that are easy to modify.

SDS/2 software from Design Data lets you designate the material edge distance, cope criteria, and other connection parameters to create 3D models of a structure. The software's automatic detailing feature makes it simple to produce 2D detail drawings, so the information can be communicated to the crew erecting the structure.

Construction of the 3rd Avenue Bridge over the Bronx River *(Courtesy of Design Data and GeniFab, Inc.)*

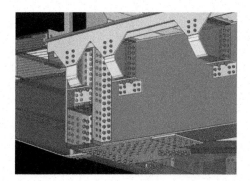

Detail of a Bolted Connection for the Bridge Structure *(Courtesy of Design Data and GeniFab, Inc.)*

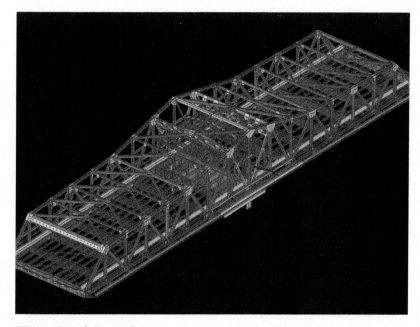

3D Model of the Bridge Structure Created in SDS/2 Software *(Courtesy of Design Data and GeniFab, Inc.)*

PORTFOLIO

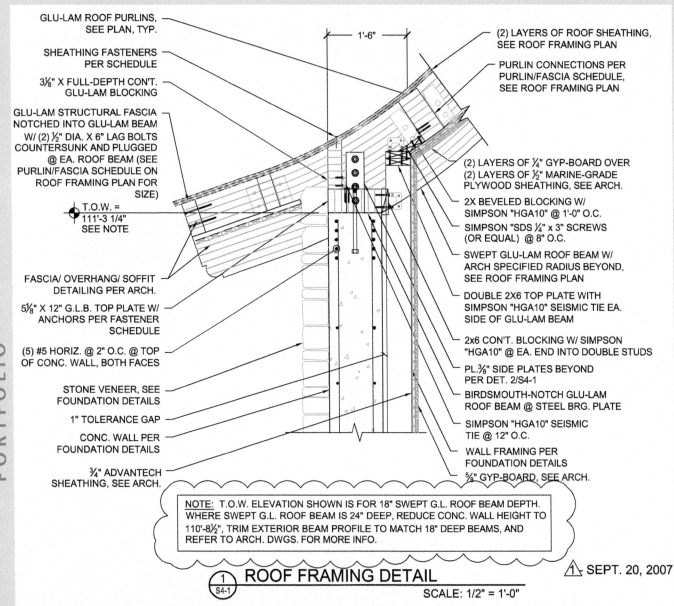

GLU-LAM ROOF PURLINS, SEE PLAN, TYP.

SHEATHING FASTENERS PER SCHEDULE

3⅛" X FULL-DEPTH CON'T. GLU-LAM BLOCKING

GLU-LAM STRUCTURAL FASCIA NOTCHED INTO GLU-LAM BEAM W/ (2) ½" DIA. X 6" LAG BOLTS COUNTERSUNK AND PLUGGED @ EA. ROOF BEAM (SEE PURLIN/FASCIA SCHEDULE ON ROOF FRAMING PLAN FOR SIZE)

T.O.W. = 111'-3 1/4" SEE NOTE

FASCIA/ OVERHANG/ SOFFIT DETAILING PER ARCH.

5⅛" X 12" G.L.B. TOP PLATE W/ ANCHORS PER FASTENER SCHEDULE

(5) #5 HORIZ. @ 2" O.C. @ TOP OF CONC. WALL, BOTH FACES

STONE VENEER, SEE FOUNDATION DETAILS

1" TOLERANCE GAP

CONC. WALL PER FOUNDATION DETAILS

¾" ADVANTECH SHEATHING, SEE ARCH.

1'-6"

(2) LAYERS OF ROOF SHEATHING, SEE ROOF FRAMING PLAN

PURLIN CONNECTIONS PER PURLIN/FASCIA SCHEDULE, SEE ROOF FRAMING PLAN

(2) LAYERS OF ¼" GYP-BOARD OVER (2) LAYERS OF ½" MARINE-GRADE PLYWOOD SHEATHING, SEE ARCH.

2X BEVELED BLOCKING W/ SIMPSON "HGA10" @ 1'-0" O.C.

SIMPSON "SDS ¼" x 3" SCREWS (OR EQUAL) @ 8" O.C.

SWEPT GLU-LAM ROOF BEAM W/ ARCH SPECIFIED RADIUS BEYOND, SEE ROOF FRAMING PLAN

DOUBLE 2X6 TOP PLATE WITH SIMPSON "HGA10" SEISMIC TIE EA. SIDE OF GLU-LAM BEAM

2x6 CON'T. BLOCKING W/ SIMPSON "HGA10" @ EA. END INTO DOUBLE STUDS

PL.⅜" SIDE PLATES BEYOND PER DET. 2/S4-1

BIRDSMOUTH-NOTCH GLU-LAM ROOF BEAM @ STEEL BRG. PLATE

SIMPSON "HGA10" SEISMIC TIE @ 12" O.C.

WALL FRAMING PER FOUNDATION DETAILS

⅝" GYP-BOARD, SEE ARCH.

NOTE: T.O.W. ELEVATION SHOWN IS FOR 18" SWEPT G.L. ROOF BEAM DEPTH. WHERE SWEPT G.L. ROOF BEAM IS 24" DEEP, REDUCE CONC. WALL HEIGHT TO 110'-8½", TRIM EXTERIOR BEAM PROFILE TO MATCH 18" DEEP BEAMS, AND REFER TO ARCH. DWGS. FOR MORE INFO.

1/S4-1 ROOF FRAMING DETAIL

⚠ SEPT. 20, 2007

SCALE: 1/2" = 1'-0"

Construction Detail for Attaching a Glu-Lam Beam to a Concrete Wall *(Courtesy of Hicks Engineering PC.)*

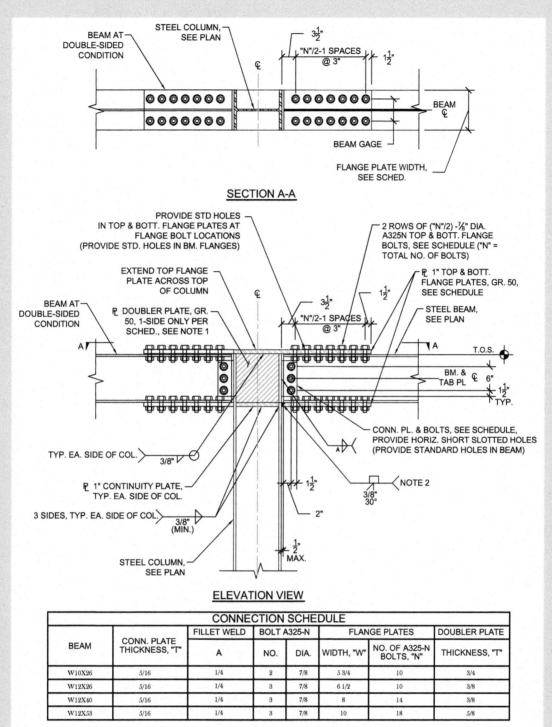

SECTION A-A

ELEVATION VIEW

CONNECTION SCHEDULE

BEAM	CONN. PLATE THICKNESS, "T"	FILLET WELD		BOLT A325-N		FLANGE PLATES		DOUBLER PLATE
		A	NO.	DIA.		WIDTH, "W"	NO. OF A325-N BOLTS, "N"	THICKNESS, "T"
W10X26	5/16	1/4	2	7/8		5 3/4	10	3/4
W12X26	5/16	1/4	3	7/8		6 1/2	10	3/8
W12X40	5/16	1/4	3	7/8		8	14	3/8
W12X53	5/16	1/4	3	7/8		10	18	5/8

NOTES:
1. PROVIDE C.J.P. WELD @ DOUBLER PLATE TO COLUMN FLANGES AND CONTINUITY PLATES (4-SIDES).

2. REMOVE BACK-UP BAR, GRIND BOTTOM OF WELD SMOOTH, & INSTALL 3/8" REINFORCING WELD. SHOP FULL PEN. WELDS TO BE 100 % INSPECTED IN ACCORDANCE WITH 2003 IBC. SECTIONS 1701.4.5 & 1703.

4 BOLTED FLANGE PLATE MOMENT CONN. DETAIL
S6-2   SCALE: 1/2" = 1'-0"

Detail Showing Welded and Bolted Connections (*Courtesy of Hicks Engineering PC.*)

P O R T F O L I O

KEY WORDS

American Bond

Architectural Terra Cotta

Ashlar Masonry

Beam Web

Bill of Material

Chords

Clip Angles

Design Drawings

Elevation

English Bond

Erection Plans

Extension Figure

Filler Beams

Fillet Weld

Flange

Flemish Bond

Gage Line

Girders

Green Lumber

High-Strength Concrete

High-Strength Steel Bolts

Joints

Manufactured Stone

Member Marks

Members

Piece Mark

Plate Material

Prestressed Concrete

Purlins

RBM

Reinforced Concrete

Rubble Masonry

Running Bond

Shop Drawings

Structural Drawings

Structural Steel

Trusses

Weld Symbols

CHAPTER SUMMARY

- The structural drawing is one of the most important elements in construction drawings.
- Cost and safety are important considerations when designing a structure that people will use, such as a building or bridge.
- Structural drawings are precise, detailed instructions for general contractors, who must create the structure according to the information in the drawings.
- Steel is commonly used in commercial construction because of its strength and durability. Steel shape and size designations are different from those for other materials, such as wood.
- Structural drawings show both plan and elevation views.
- Details about how structural members are connected and fastened to each other are critical parts of a structural drawing.
- Structural drawings use more notes about size, shape, location, and fastening details than other types of drawings.
- Safety is dependent on correctly following the engineer's design. Careful proofing and checking of every note and detail is an essential part of the engineering process.
- The list of materials, including their size, shape, and detail information, is often included in a material schedule that appears in table form in a corner of the drawing.
- When components are welded together, standard welding symbols and notes must be used.

REVIEW QUESTIONS

1. List five structural materials.
2. Draw four different structural steel shapes and label each shape.
3. How is reinforced concrete different from regular concrete?
4. What is shown in the plan view of a structural drawing?
5. What is shown in the elevation view of a structural drawing?
6. Would the spacing for steel roof trusses be shown in a plan view or an elevation view?
7. Would the individual members of a roof truss be shown in a plan view or an elevation view?
8. What are the most common fastening techniques for joining structural steel?

CHAPTER EXERCISES

The following problems are intended to offer practice in drawing and dimensioning simple structures and in illustrating methods of construction. They may be completed by hand or using CAD.

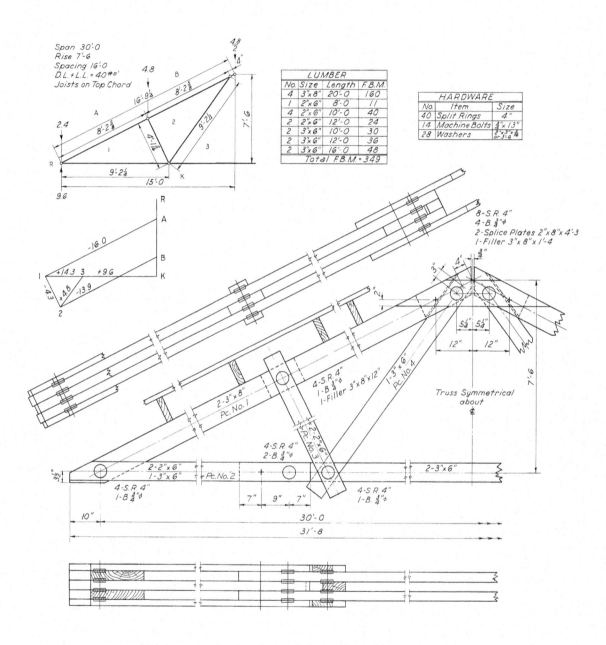

Exercise 18.1 Calculate point-to-point lengths (the distances between centers of joints) of the web members of the roof truss based on a design by Timber Engineering Company. Make a detailed drawing of web member piece No. 4.

Exercise 18.2 Make a complete detail of the top chord member of the truss shown for a 30° angle of inclination.

Exercise 18.3 Assuming riveted construction, with rivets of 3/4″ or 20 mm diameter, make a complete shop drawing for a typical filler beam of the steel floor design plan shown. Detail the same beam for welded construction. Consult the *AISC Manual of Steel Construction.*

Exercise 18.4 Assuming the column size to be W8 × 31, detail the W16 × 36 girder at the center of the drawing.

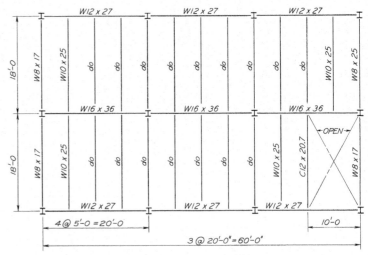

Typical Steel Floor Design Plan

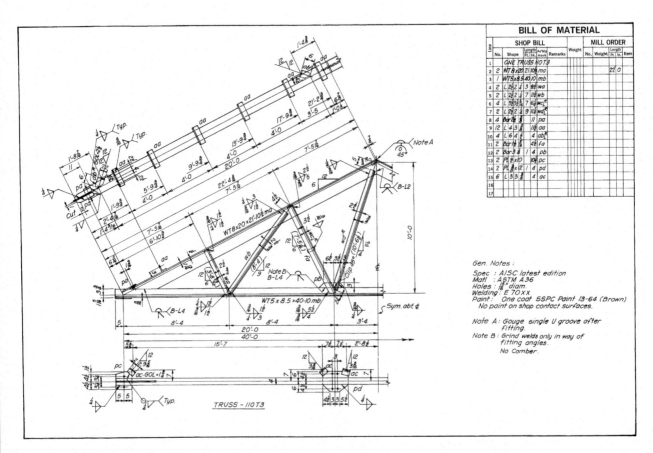

A Welded Roof Truss *(Copyright © American Institute of Steel Construction. Reprinted with permission.)*

Exercise 18.5 Make a complete detail for a truss of the same length, but change the height from 10′-0 to 6′-8. Use angle members of the same cross section sizes as those shown, but of different lengths, as needed.

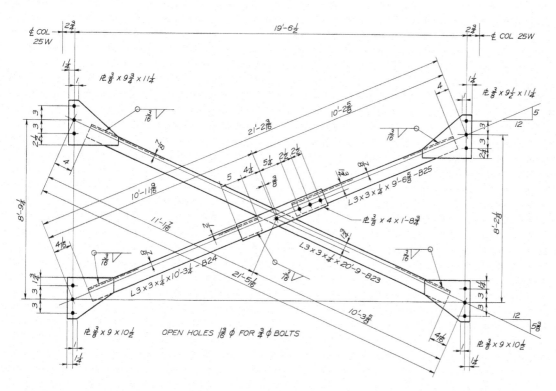

Exercise 18.6 Make a similar bracing detail as for the detail drawing of the column bracing shown, also changing the distance between column centers from 20'-0 to 18'-6.

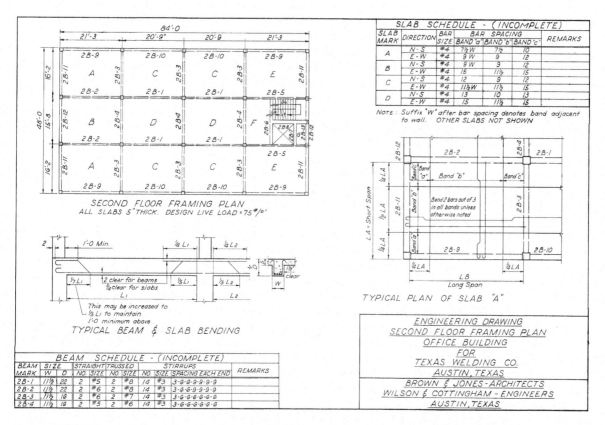

Exercise 18.7 Draw cross sections through panel D in both directions for the engineering drawing for a two-way slab and beam floor shown. Include the supporting beams in each cross section, and show all dimensions, size and spacing of reinforcing steel, and dimensions to locate the ends of bars and the points of bend for the bent bars. Also show and locate the stirrups in these views.

Exercise 18.8 Detail the brickwork surrounding a window frame for an opening 4'-7/8" wide by 6'-9" high. Use the type of curved arch lintel as shown. Assume standard-size building brick with mortar joints.

Exercise 18.9 Consult www.gobrick.com and draw a cross-sectional view through a 12" wall of composite brick and tile construction.

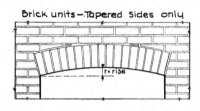
Brick units—Tapered sides only

r = rise

PROPOSED DECK

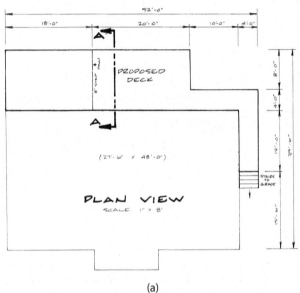

(a)

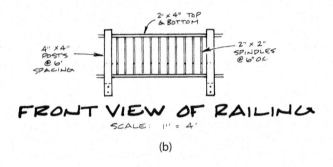
FRONT VIEW OF RAILING
SCALE: 1" = 4'

(b)

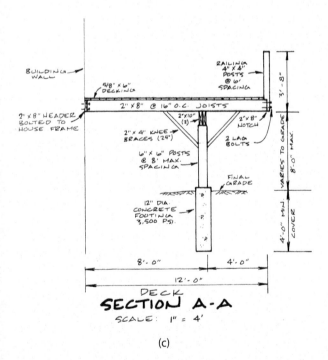
DECK SECTION A-A
SCALE: 1" = 4'

(c)

Exercise 18.10 Referring to the figure, redraw a complete detail of this proposed deck, changing the total width of the deck from 12' to 14' and the length from 52' to 54'.

Exercise 18.11 Referring to part b of the figure, adjust the dimensions on the posts from 4" × 4" to 6" × 6". Redraw a complete detail of the railing view and Section A–A.

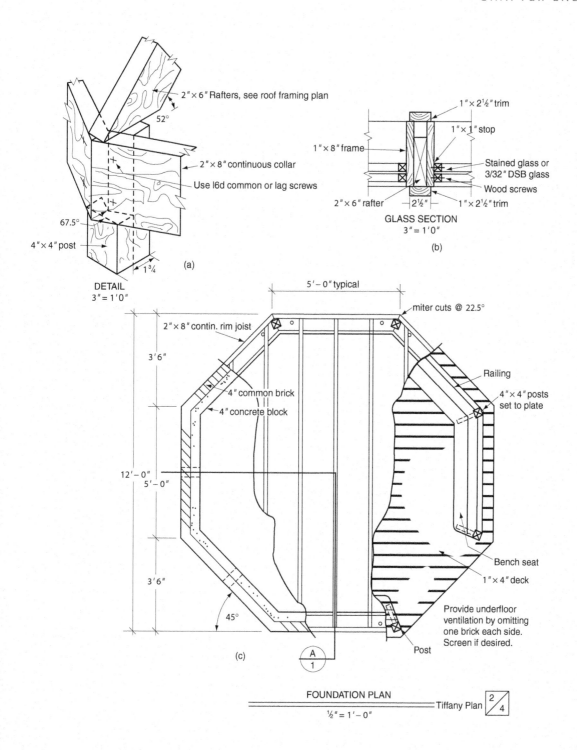

DETAIL
3″ = 1′0″

GLASS SECTION
3″ = 1′0″

(b)

(a)

(c)

FOUNDATION PLAN
½″ = 1′-0″
Tiffany Plan

Exercise 18.12 Referring to part a of the figure, adjust the post dimensions from 4″ × 4″ to 6″ × 6″. Redraw a complete detail of part a.

Exercise 18.13 Referring to part c of the figure, insert the adjustments made to the post detail in Exercise 18.12 and redraw the complete foundation plan.

CHAPTER NINETEEN

LANDFORM DRAWINGS

OBJECTIVES

After studying the material in this chapter, you should be able to:

1. Read and draw a plat, topographic contour map, street contour map, and highway plan and profile.

2. Read the elevation of a tract of land using contour lines.

3. Identify the scale and compass orientation of a topographic map.

4. Read and notate property boundaries on a land survey map.

5. Create a profile map from contour lines.

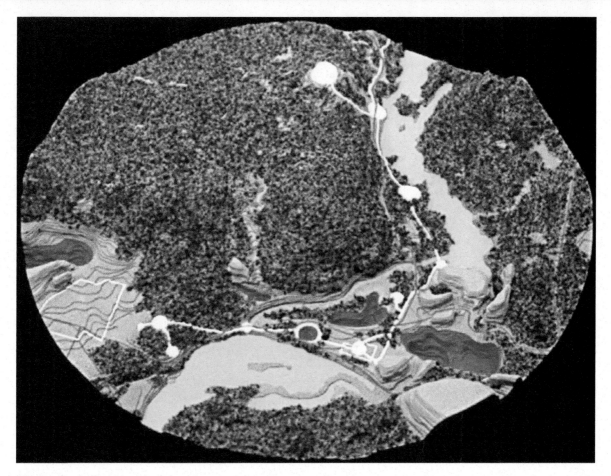

3D Geologic Terrain Model *(Courtesy of Howard Architectural Models, Inc.)*

OVERVIEW

Drawings and maps show natural and human-made features on the Earth's surface. Topographic drawings use orthographic projection, just as technical drawings do, in which the direction of sight is perpendicular to the plane of the map. Survey monuments placed on the ground allow features to be located with respect to definite point locations.

The U.S. Coast and Geodetic Survey, the U.S. Department of the Interior, and the U.S. Geological Survey (USGS) all produce contour maps of land boundaries. More detailed maps are created by local communities when subdividing property for residential and commercial construction. Highways and public works, such as dams and bridges, may require detailed topographic drawings of a given geographic area. Topographic drawings use contour lines to show elevation in the plan view. Profile drawings show the sectional elevation of a specified datum plane. Many topographic drawings become legal documents used in resolving disputes over property boundaries. USGS partners with businesses like TopoZone and Microsoft's TerraServer to provide map content online, and of course, Google Earth has excellent content.

UNDERSTANDING LANDFORM DRAWINGS

The purpose of a landform drawing or map determines the features and details to show on it and the scale to use. Many types of maps and drawings are used to locate features on the Earth's surface.

Because the shape of the Earth is spherical, any representation on a plane (such as a piece of paper) is distorted because spheres can be developed into a flat plane only by approximation. When drawing large areas, you can define control or reference points using spherical coordinates for latitude and longitude (meridians and parallels) as reference lines to minimize the distortion. In drawing small areas to a relatively large scale, the distortion due to the Earth's curvature is so slight that it may be neglected.

Definitions

Useful map and landform drawing terms include the following.

A *plat* is a map of a small area, plotted from a land *survey.* It does not ordinarily show elevations. Plats are drawn to calculate areas, locate property lines, and locate building projects and facilities (Figure 19.1).

A *traverse* consists of a series of intersecting straight lines of accurately measured lengths. At the points of intersection, the deflection angles between adjacent lines are measured and recorded. From the starting point you can calculate rectangular coordinates of the other intersection points using trigonometry. A closed traverse is a closed polygon that allows you to check the accuracy of the surveyed information based on whether or not the last angle and distance meet back at the starting point of the loop. The land survey plat of Figure 19.1 shows a closed traverse.

Elevations are vertical distances above a common *datum,* or reference plane or point. The elevation of a point on the surface of the ground is usually determined by differential leveling from some other point of known elevation. Commonly, elevations are referenced to the mean sea level.

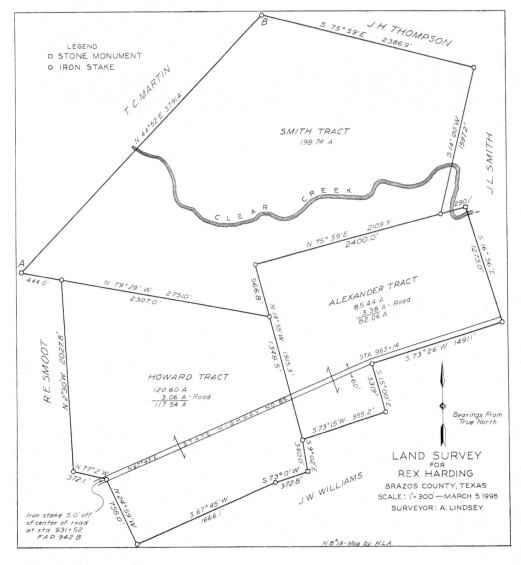

19.1 Land Survey Plat

A *profile* is a line contained in a vertical plane, and it depicts the relative elevations of various points along the line. For example, if a vertical section were to be cut into the Earth, the top line of this section would represent the ground profile (Figure 19.2).

Contours are lines drawn on a map to locate, in the plan view, points of equal ground elevation. On a single contour line, therefore, all points have the same elevation (Figure 19.2).

Hatchures are short, parallel, or slightly divergent lines drawn in the direction of the slope. They are closely spaced on steep slopes and converge toward the tops of ridges and hills. Hatchures are shade lines used to show relief on older maps.

Monuments are special installations of stone or concrete to mark the locations of points accurately determined by precise surveying. It is intended that monuments be permanent or nearly so, and they are usually tied in by references to nearby natural features, such as trees and large boulders.

Cartography is the science or art of mapmaking.

Topographic maps (Figure 19.3) depict:

1. Water, including seas, lakes, ponds, rivers, streams, canals, and swamps;
2. Relief, or elevations, of mountains, hills, valleys, cliffs, and the like;
3. Culture, or human constructions, such as towns, cities, roads, railroads, airfields, and boundaries.

Hydrographic maps convey information concerning bodies of water, such as shoreline locations; relative elevations of points of lake, stream, or ocean beds; and sounding depths.

Cadastral maps are accurately drawn maps of cities and towns, showing property lines and other features that control property ownership.

Military maps contain information of military importance in the area represented.

Nautical maps and charts show navigational features and aids, such as locations of buoys, shoals, lighthouses and beacons, and sounding depths.

Aeronautical maps and charts show prominent landmarks, towers, beacons, and elevations for the use of air navigators.

Engineering maps are made for special projects as an aid to locations and construction.

Landscape maps are used in planning installations of trees, shrubbery, drives, and other garden features in the artistic design of area improvements.

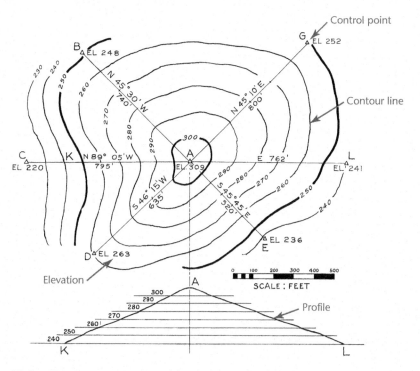

19.2   Contours Determined from Control Points

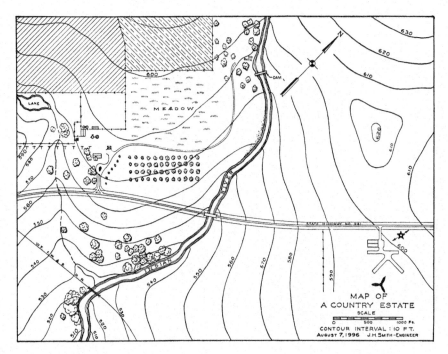

19.3   A Topographic Map

GETTING INFORMATION FOR MAPS

A survey is the basis of all maps and topographic drawings. Several surveying methods are used to obtain the information necessary to make a map.

Most surveys use *electronic survey instruments* to measure distances and angles. To measure to a distant point, the surveyor aims the instrument toward the point, where a passive reflector or prism has been set. The instrument generates either a modulated infrared light signal focused into a narrow beam, or a laser beam, aimed directly at the reflector. When the reflector bounces the beam back to the aiming head, the beam's travel time is measured electronically and directly converted into the distance to the point. One advantage of electronic measurement over the distance-taping method is that it is not necessary to stop traffic to take measurements. Electronic instruments measure distances of up to 4 mi with accuracies from .01′ to .03′, which is more than sufficient for topographic surveying. Figure 19.4 shows a Trimble VX spatial station. This type of instrument is often used to gather survey data.

Global positioning system (GPS) receivers calculate the receiver's position by interpreting data received from four different satellites concurrently through a process called *trilateration* (which is similar to triangulation).

Figure 19.5 shows a GPS satellite. Twenty-four satellites orbit the earth in a pattern called a *GPS satellite constellation* (see Figure 19.6). Each of these satellites broadcasts a signal that includes the precise time from the satellite's onboard atomic clock. The distance to the satellite from the position of a GPS receiver can be calculated based on the time delay in receiving the signal. From any position on Earth a receiver should be able to locate four satellites and using trilateration calculate very accurately the position of the receiver on the surface of the Earth. Most modern maps of large areas are prepared using GPS positioning and satellite imagery.

While GPS has revolutionized surveying, the vertical accuracy of GPS measurements (elevations) has not been as good as the horizontal accuracy (latitude and longitude). Knowledge of elevations is critical to surveyors, engineers, coastal managers, developers, and those who make resource or land-use management decisions.

Because forces such as sea level rise, subsidence (i.e., land sinking), and geological events constantly change the surface of the Earth, it is necessary to periodically resurvey areas to correct for changes. State and local governments spend tens of millions of dollars each year adjusting engineering proj-

19.4   *The Trimble VX Spatial Station* *(Courtesy of Trimble Navigation Ltd.)*

ects that are continually affected by changing land surfaces, so a fast, yet accurate, method for determining elevations is needed. Height Modernization, which uses GPS in conjunction with other new and existing technologies to increase the accuracy of elevation measurements, is one such method.

Photogrammetry and satellite imagery are widely used for map surveying. They use actual photographs of the Earth's surface and manufactured objects on the Earth. *Aerial photogrammetry,* via aircraft or satellite, is used for purposes such as governmental and commercial surveying, explorations, and property valuation. It has the advantage of being

19.5   GPS Satellite GPS IIR-M *(VTR/Alamy Stock Photo.)*

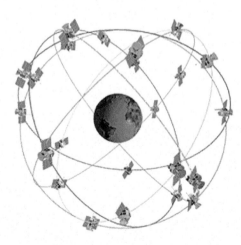

19.6   GPS Satellite Constellation *(Courtesy of Aerospace Corporation, http://www.aero.org.)*

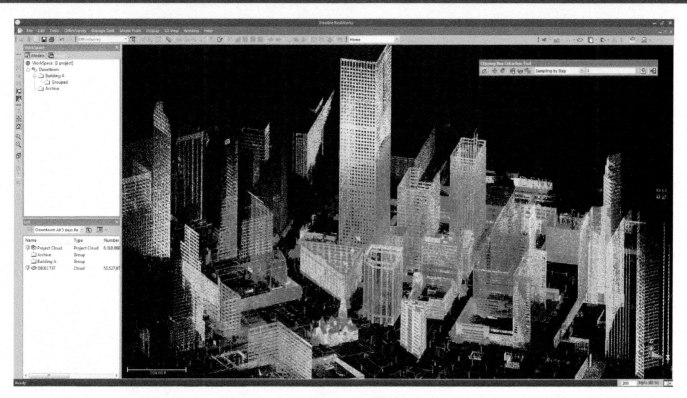

19.7   *3D laser scanning solutions such as Trimble RealWorks allow you to integrate point data and extract measurements inside a 3D CAD environment. (Courtesy of Trimble Navigation Ltd.)*

easy to use in difficult terrain with steep slopes, where ground surveying would be difficult or nearly impossible.

Taking photographs from ground stations with the axis of the camera lens nearly horizontal is called ***terrestrial photogrammetry.*** By combining the results of both aerial and terrestrial types of observations, it is possible to determine the relative positions of objects in a horizontal plane and their relative elevations.

Photogrammetry can be the basis of contour mapping as well as plan mapping. Generally, aerial photographs are used by forming a mosaic of photographs, which must overlap one another slightly. Photogrammetry offers the distinct advantage that a large area can be mapped from a single clear photograph. Photogrammetry can be used in connection with ground surveying by photographing control points already located on the ground by precise surveying.

For large land developments and large construction projects, new technologies for producing topographic maps have evolved. Some state highway departments and most engineering firms that specialize in surveying and map-

ping now make use of aerial photography with computers, terrain digitizers, stereoplotters, GIS, and various photolaboratory techniques. In high volume work situations, expensive equipment may save enough time to justify its cost.

Laser distance meters typically calculate distance based on the difference in phase between the internal reference laser pulse and the external laser pulse reflected from the targeted object or a reflector

19.8   *The Disto A8 Laser Distance Meter Allows Measurement of Distances up to 200 m (650′) with Precision of ±1.5 mm (.06″). (Courtesy of Leica Geosystems, Switzerland.)*

plate attached to it. An example of this type of device is shown in Figure 19.8.

NOAA's National Geodetic Survey (NGS) has a Height Modernization Program that is contributing to a state-of-the-art National Spatial Reference System (NSRS). NGS, in cooperation with the GPS community, developed standards, specifications, and techniques to enable GPS to attain the accuracy levels required for most applications using height information. These guidelines, which are available on the NGS website, provide detailed instructions for the amount of survey control required as a base from which to start the modernization of elevation data. NGS also provides instructions on how surveys must be carried out to ensure that results meet the requirements. Meeting these specifications is important to ensure that surveys can be tied to the NSRS.

19.9   Optical Mechanical System
(Courtesy of David White.)

Optical mechanical systems are less used today. Before electronic measurement systems became affordable, an optical instrumental method called the ***stadia method*** was used in mapmaking. A stadia transit is an optical instrument used with a stadia rod. The instrument reading obtained by sighting visually on the rod and using a conversion factor, could be converted to distance. An example of this type of device is shown in Figure 19.9.

Short distances are ordinarily measured by ***steel tape,*** with driven stakes marking the points between field measurements.

Scaled measurements are made on rare occasions. In this method, distances are determined by measuring aerial photographs, when the scale is known.

For additional information, refer to publications such as the *Manual of Surveying Instructions for the Survey of the Public Lands of the United States,* prepared and published by the Bureau of Land Management (online at blm.gov). Many governmental agencies also publicize information about maps and geographic data on the Web.

RISE OF THE THREE GORGES DAM

Completed in 2009, the Three Gorges Dam is the world's largest hydroelectric power generator and one of the few man-made structures so enormous that it's visible to the naked eye from space.

The dam is built along the Yangtze River, the third largest in the world, stretching more than 3,900 miles across China. Historically, the river has been prone to massive flooding, overflowing its banks about once every 10 years. The dam is designed to improve flood control on the river and protect the 15 million people and 3.7 million acres of farmland in the Yangtze flood plains.

Observations from the NASA-built Landsat satellites provide an overview of the dam's construction. The earliest data set, from 1987, shows the region prior to the start of construction. By 2000, construction along each riverbank was underway, but sediment-filled water still flowed through a narrow channel near the river's south bank. The 2004 data shows development of the main wall and the partial filling of the reservoir, including numerous side canyons. By mid-2006, construction of the main wall was completed and a reservoir more than 2 mi (3 km) across had filled just upstream of the dam.

November 7, 2006

Satellite Imagery of the Three Gorges Dam *(Courtesy of NASA.)*

April 17, 1987

19.1 SYMBOLS

Various natural and human-made features are designated by special symbols. A list of the most commonly used map symbols is given in Appendix 32. Figure 19.10 shows an example of some commonly used symbols. You can find a full set on the Web at www.usgs.gov/publications/topographic-map-symbols. Templates such as that shown in Figure 19.11 can save time in drawing map symbols by hand.

19.2 BEARINGS

The *bearing* of a line is its angle from magnetic north. Bearings are listed by referencing the angle the line makes departing from either the north or the south toward either the east or west. In Figure 19.12, the bearing for traverse line AB is N 44°52′ E, meaning that if you were standing at point A facing north, you would turn 44°52′ toward the east to face point B. (If you were at point B, you would use the opposite directions to face point A, facing south and turning 44°52′ toward the west.)

Once the bearings of the lines of a traverse have been determined, the angles between them can be computed by adding or subtracting. Electronic survey instruments are used to calculate the bearings of lines, because compass readings are not accurate. Magnetic north and true north are not the same, and local magnetism may affect the position of the compass needle.

19.3 ELEVATION

If GPS is not used to provide elevation, an optical instrument called a *level,* equipped with a telescope for sighting long distances, can be used to determine differences in elevation in the field. The process is called **differential leveling.** When the instrument is leveled, the line of sight of its telescope is horizontal. A level rod, graduated in feet and decimals of feet, may be held on various points. Instrument readings of the rod then serve to determine the differences in elevations of the points.

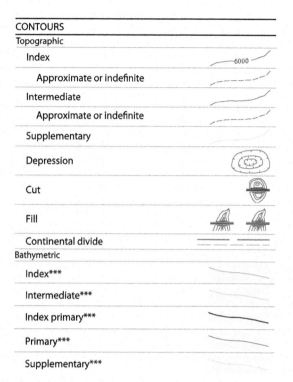

19.10   USGS Topographic Map Symbols *(Courtesy of USGS.)*

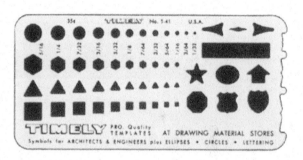

19.11   Timely Map Symbol Template *(Courtesy of Timely Products Co., Inc.)*

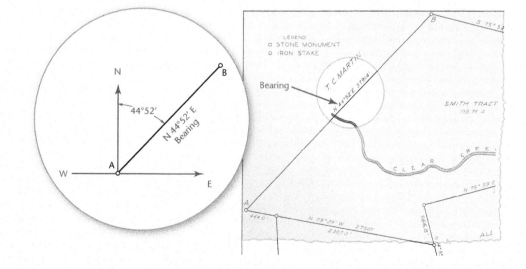

19.12   Bearings Specify an Angle and Direction from North or South toward East or West. *The bearing N 44°52′ E means that if you were at point A facing north, you would turn 44°52′ toward the east to face point B.*

19.4 CONTOURS

Contours are map lines showing points of equal ground elevation. Figure 19.13 shows a comparison between a contour map and a satellite image taken from the TopoZone website.

A *contour interval* is the vertical distance between horizontal planes passing through successive contours. For example, in Figure 19.14 the contour interval is 10′. The contour interval should not change on any one map. It is customary to show every fifth contour by a line heavier than those representing intermediate contours.

For contour lines keep in mind:

- If extended far enough, every contour line will close.
- At streams, contours form Vs pointing upstream.
- Even spacing between successive contours means that the ground slopes uniformly.
- Uneven spacing between contours means that the slope changes frequently.
- Widely spaced contours indicate a gentle slope.
- Closely spaced contours indicate steep slopes.

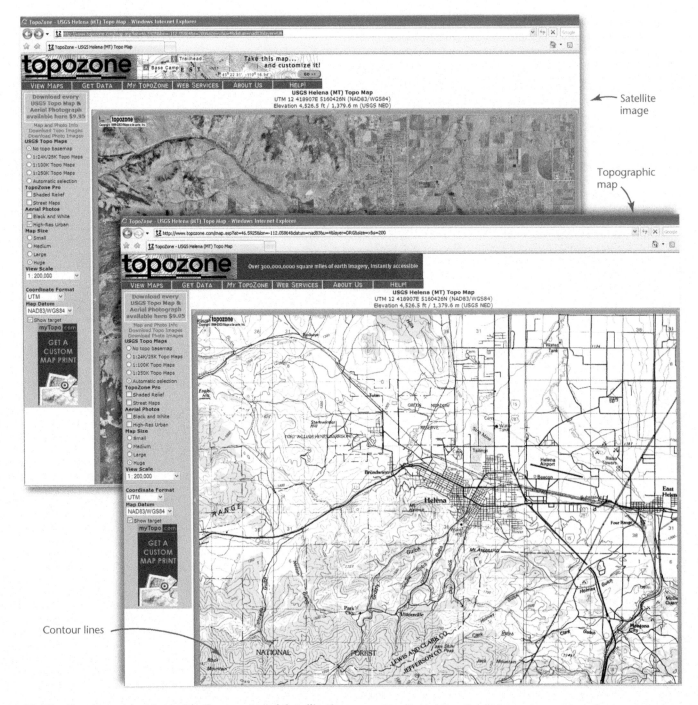

19.13 Topographic Map with Contours and Satellite Imagery *(Courtesy of TopoZone at www.topozone.com)*

Interpolating Elevation Data

Locations of points on contour lines are determined by interpolation. In Figure 19.14, the locations and elevations of seven control points have been determined. The goal is to draw the contour lines assuming the slope of the surface of the ground is uniform between station A and the six adjacent stations, using a contour interval of 10′. The locations of the intersections of the contour lines with the straight lines joining the point A and the six adjacent points, were calculated as follows.

The horizontal distance between stations A and B is 740′. The difference in elevation of those stations is 61′. The difference in elevation of station A and contour 300 is 9′; therefore, contour 300 crosses line AB at a distance from station A of 9/61 of 740, or 109.1′. Contour 290 crosses the line AB at a distance from contour 300 of 10/61 of 740, or 121.3′. This 121.3′ distance between contour lines is constant along the line AB and can be measured without more calculations.

You can interpolate points where the contours cross the other lines of the survey the same way. After interpolating the elevations you can draw the contour lines through points of equal elevation as shown.

After contours have been plotted, you can draw a profile of the ground line in any direction. In Figure 19.14, the profile of line KAL is shown in the lower or front view. It is customary, as shown here, to draw the profile using an exaggerated vertical scale to emphasize the varying slopes. Laser scanning combined with increasingly accurate GPS satellite data allows highly detailed depiction of terrain such as that shown in Figure 19.15.

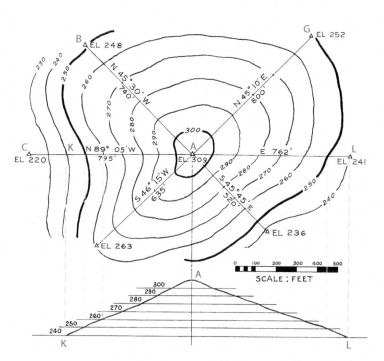

19.14   Contours Determined from Control Points

19.15   Elevation-Based Rendering. *Trimble RealWorks software will display the point cloud captured in a 3D scan using color to indicate elevation.* (Courtesy of Trimble Navigation Ltd.)

Contour lines may be plotted from recorded elevations of points on the ground, as in Figure 19.16a. This figure illustrates a checkerboard survey, in which lines are drawn at right angles to each other, dividing the survey into 100' squares, and where elevations have been measured at the corners of the squares. The contour interval is taken as 2', and the slope of the ground between adjacent stations is assumed to be uniform.

The points where the contour lines cross the survey lines can be located approximately by inspection, by graphical methods, or by the numerical method explained for Figure 19.14.

You can also find the points of intersection that contour lines make with survey lines by constructing a profile of each line of the survey, as shown for line 1 in Figure 19.16b. Draw horizontal lines at elevations where you want to show contours. The points where the profile line intersects these horizontal lines are the elevations of points where corresponding contour lines cross the survey line 1. These can be projected upward, as shown, to locate these points.

The profile of any line can be constructed from the contour map by the converse of the process just described.

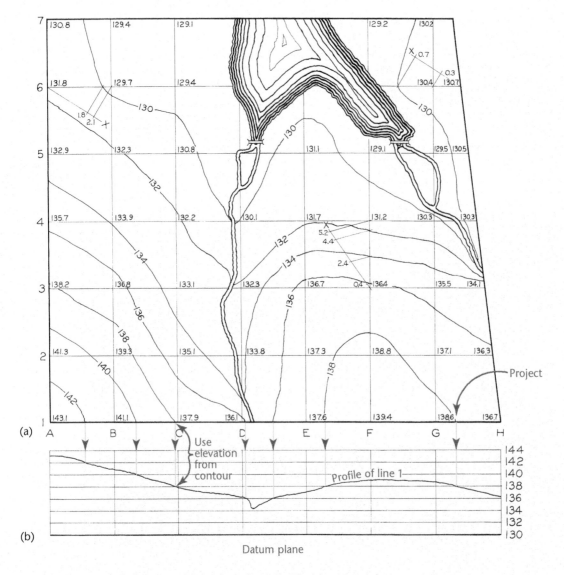

19.16 Contours Determined from Readings at Regular Intervals

3D Terrain Models

Electronic survey data containing elevations can often be downloaded directly to 3D terrain modeling software. Most of these software solutions produce a surface model of the terrain formed of many small triangles and are thus called a Triangulated Irregular Network, or TIN. Contours, profiles, cut-and-fill calculations, and other information can be generated semiautomatically from the TIN. An example is shown in Figure 19.17.

19.5 CITY MAPS

The particular use of a map determines what features are to be shown. Maps of city areas may be put to many uses. Figure 19.18, a city plan for location of new road construction, shows only those features of importance to the location and construction of the road. The transit line starts at the centerline intersection of Park St. and 5th Ave., and it is marked as station 0 + 00. From here it extends north over the railroad yard to cross the river. Features near the transit line, such as buildings, are shown and identified by name. Street widths are important and are shown. Contour lines between the railroad yard and the river indicate the steeply sloping terrain.

19.17 TIN 3D Terrain Model Produced in Autodesk Civil 3D

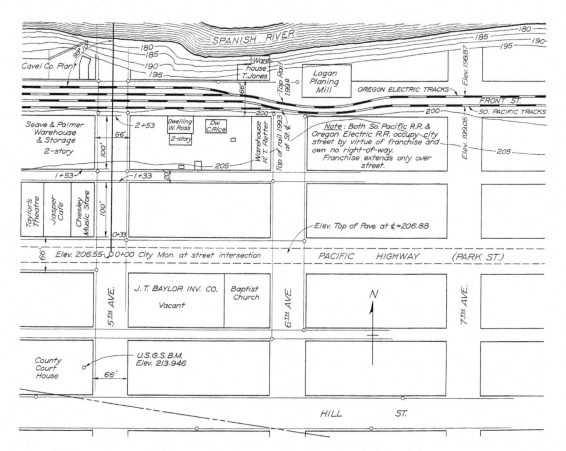

19.18 A City Plan for Location of a New Road Project

Subdivision Plats

Maps perform an important function for those who plan the layout of lots and streets. For example, Figure 19.19a shows an original layout of these features for a new residential area. An examination of the contours will show that this layout is not satisfactory, since the directions of the streets do not fit the natural ground slopes. Streets should be arranged so that the subdivision can be entered from a low point and so that a maximum number of lots will be above street grade. The layout in Figure 19.19b is a decided improvement, for in it the streets curve to fit the topography, and the entrance is located at a low point.

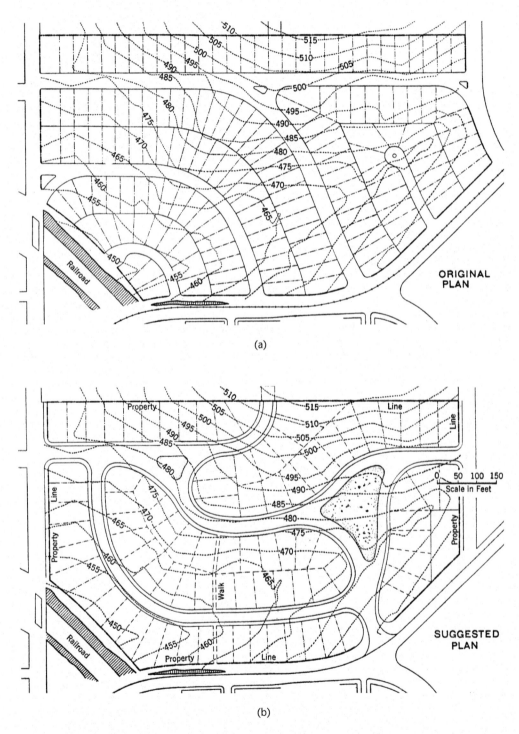

(a)

(b)

19.19 Adjustment of Streets to Topography *(From Land Subdivision, ASCE Manual No. 16 of Engineering Practice, with permission from ASCE.)*

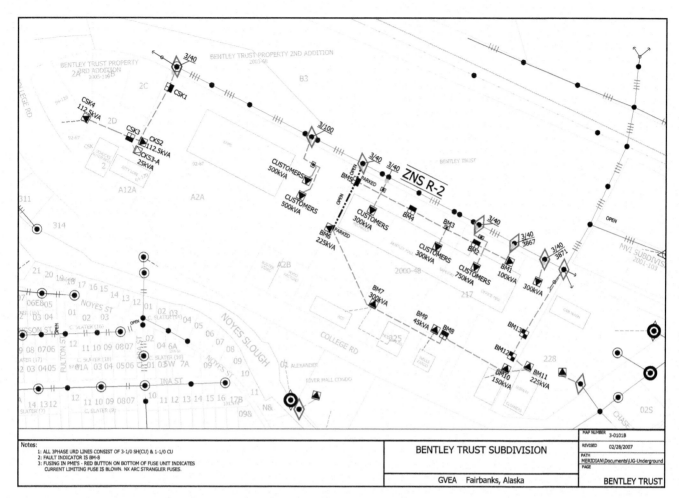

Notes:
1. ALL 3PHASE URD LINES CONSIST OF 3-1/0 SH(CU) & 1-1/0 CU
2. FAULT INDICATOR IS BM-8
3. FUSING IN PME'S - RED BUTTON ON BOTTOM OF FUSE UNIT INDICATES CURRENT LIMITING FUSE IS BLOWN. NX ARC STRANGLER FUSES.

BENTLEY TRUST SUBDIVISION

GVEA   Fairbanks, Alaska

MAP NUMBER 3-0101B
REVISED 02/28/2007
PATH MERIDIAN\Documents\UG-Underground
PAGE

BENTLEY TRUST

19.20 *Above-ground and underground power is located from subdivision plats.* (Courtesy of Golden Valley Electric Association.)

Uses for Subdivision Plats

Utilities and other information are often referenced to locations from subdivision plats. A subdivision plat showing the locations of above-ground and underground power is shown in Figure 19.20. Subdivision plats are recorded legal documents, and they are often available from county clerks and recorders' offices. These drawings are used as reference for property boundaries, for landscape development, and other uses.

Landscape Drawings

Maps have a definite use in landscape planning. Figure 19.21 is a landscape drawing showing a proposed layout of a deck, water feature, and trees for beautification of an outdoor space.

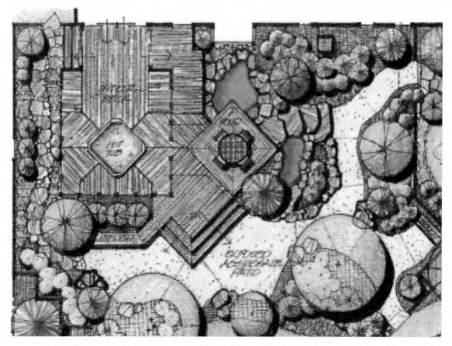

19.21 A Landscape Drawing (Courtesy of Hispanic Business, Inc.)

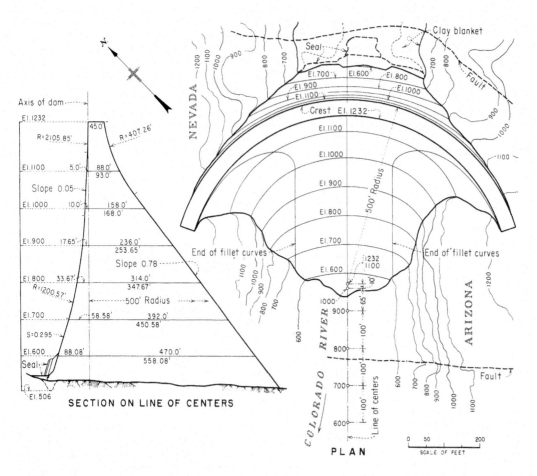

19.22   Plan for Hoover Dam *(From Treatise on Dams. Courtesy of U.S. Dept. of the Interior, Bureau of Reclamation.)*

19.6 STRUCTURE LOCATION PLANS

Maps are used to plan construction projects and locate construction features so they fit the topography of the area. A project location plan for a dam is shown in Figure 19.22. This map shows the important natural features, contours, a plan view of the structure, and a cross section through Hoover Dam.

To show the complete construction drawings for a large bridge project may take hundreds of drawings, but one of the most important early drawings is a general arrangement plan and elevation in the form of a line diagram. Figure 19.23 is an example—a plan and elevation of a large bridge structure.

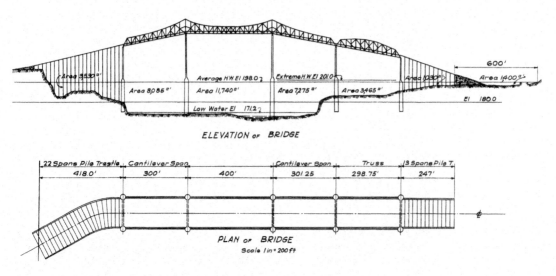

19.23   Plan and Elevation of a Bridge Structure

19.7 HIGHWAY PLANS

Before highway construction starts, it is necessary to plan the horizontal and vertical location and alignments. Commonly, both the plan view and profile are drawn on the same sheet, as in Figure 19.24.

The topographical plan at the top of Figure 19.24 shows such features as trees, fences, and farmhouses along the right of way. The transit line, locating the centerline of the new road, is drawn with stations located every 100 ft, 50 m, or some other convenient spacing. Data for creating the horizontal curves in the field are calculated and listed on the drawing.

Reading the information on the drawing, notice that the point of curve (P.C.) at station 17 + 00 is the point at which the line begins to curve with a 600' radius, for a curve length of 400'. The central angle is 38°12', and the degree of curve (the angle subtended by a 100' chord) is shown as 9°33'. The reverse curve of 800' radius begins at station 21 + 00. Note also the North point and the bearing N 73° E of the transit line.

The vertical alignment is shown in profile below the plan view. Note the station numbers listed below the profile. The scale of this view is larger in the vertical than in the horizontal direction to exaggerate the elevations so they show easily. The existing ground profile along the centerline of the road is shown, as well as the profile of the proposed vertical alignment. The symbol P. I. denotes the point of intersection of the grade lines, and grade slopes are given in percentages. A 1% grade would rise vertically 1' in each 100' of horizontal distance. Station 22 + 00, therefore, is the intersection point of an upgrade of 1.5% and a downgrade of −2%.

To provide a smooth transition between these grades, a vertical curve (V.C.) of 1100' length was used. This curve is parabolic and tangent to grade at stations 17 + 00 and 28 + 00. The

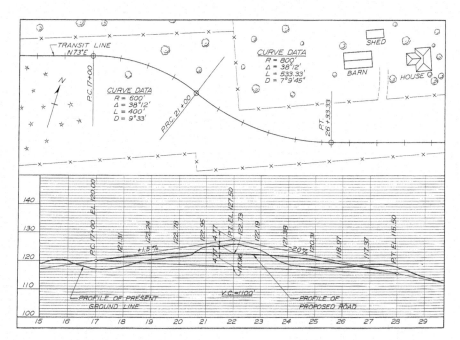

19.24 A Highway Plan and Profile

straight line joining these points has an elevation 117.96' directly below the P.I. At this point the parabolic curve must pass through the midpoint of the vertical distance, at a height of 4.77' below the P.I.

The final profile elevations are given in Figure 19.24. Calculations are given in Table 19.1.

> **TIP**
> Ordinates to parabolas, measured from tangents, are proportional to the squares of the horizontal distances from the points of tangency. Therefore, it is possible to calculate the elevations of points along the curve by first determining the grade elevations and then subtracting the parabolic curve ordinates.

Table 19.1 Calculation of Vertical Curve Elevations

Station	Tangent Elevations	Ordinate	Curve Elevations
18	121.50	.19*	121.31
19	123.00	.76	122.24
20	124.50	1.72	122.78
21	126.00	3.05	122.95
22	127.50	4.77	122.73
23	125.50	3.31	122.19
24	123.50	2.12	121.38
25	121.50	1.19	120.31
26	119.50	.53	118.97
27	117.50	.13	117.37

$$* \frac{(100)^2 - 4.779}{(500)^2}5 = .199$$

CONTOUR MAPS FROM 3D DATA

CAD software such as Autodesk's Civil 3D allows you to create contour maps by entering site data such as that shown in Figure A. Data can even be downloaded directly into the CAD software from a total station survey instrument.

Using Civil 3D software, you can show point descriptions, contour lines, grid lines, and features such as bodies of water or structures and produce topographic pictorial drawings.

Planners are able to lay out roads and subdivisions using specialized software features that provide the contractor with earthwork calculations for individual lots or the entire site.

The same survey data that produce contour maps can be used to produce profiles like those shown in Figure B. Profiles generated from a TIN can be used for earthwork calculations. Street intersections and features such as cul-de-sacs can be automatically generated.

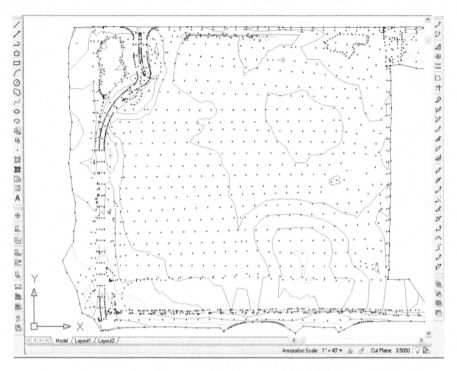

(A) *Autodesk Civil 3D software provides tools to generate contour maps from survey data.* (Autodesk screen shots reprinted courtesy of Autodesk, Inc.)

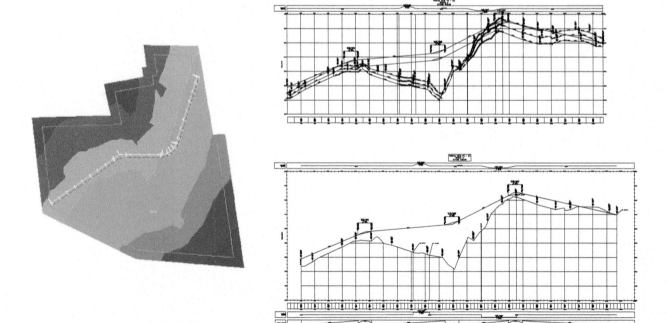

(B) *Profiles can be generated across any alignment once the TIN for the site has been created. The profiles shown above are from alignments shown in the colored contour map at left.* (Autodesk screen shots reprinted courtesy of Autodesk, Inc.)

PORTFOLIO

This portion of a site plan shows contours, lot boundaries, utility easement, and the primary view directions. (Courtesy of Locati Architects.)

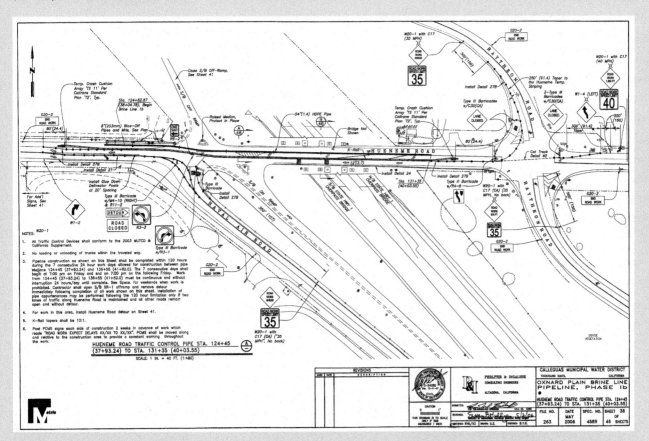

Highway signage and barricades, along with trees, shrubs, and fences, are located on this pipeline construction traffic control drawing. (Courtesy of Perliter and Ingalsbe Consulting Engineers and Calleguas Municipal Water District.)

KEY WORDS

Aerial Photogrammetry

Aeronautical Maps

Bearing

Cadastral Maps

Cartography

Contours

Datum

Differential Leveling

Electronic Survey Instruments

Elevations

Engineering Maps

Global Positioning System (GPS)

GPS Satellite Constellation

Hatchures

Hydrographic Maps

Landscape Maps

Laser Distance Meters

Military Maps

Monuments

Nautical Maps

Optical Mechanical Systems

Photogrammetry and Satellite Imagery

Plat

Profile

Quadrangle

Scaled Measurements

Stadia

Steel Tape

Survey

Terrestrial Photogrammetry

Topographic Maps

Traverse

CHAPTER SUMMARY

- Topographic drawings represent three dimensions on a 2D plan view.
- Land surveys denote the boundaries of tracts of land. Boundaries are defined by bearing and length.
- Contour lines are used to show elevation on a plan drawing. Each contour line represents one elevation level. Closely spaced contour lines indicate a steep slope. Widely spaced contour lines indicate a flatter slope.
- A profile drawing of elevation is created by drawing a cutting-plane datum on the plan view and transferring distances and elevation from the plan to the profile drawing. Profile drawings are often used to determine cut-and-fill slopes for roadways and railways.
- Land subdivision drawings show roads, property boundaries, and major landscape landmarks such as parks, streams, buildings, and large trees.
- Computer graphics workstations can model 3D surfaces from satellite photographs. Computers model surfaces by creating a wireframe structure and then applying solid color contours to the wireframe surface.

REVIEW QUESTIONS

1. What is the purpose of a plat drawing? Is it a plan or an elevation?
2. What is the topographic notation for a plat boundary that runs exactly east and west for 1503.4′?
3. What are the lines that indicate elevation on a topographic map?
4. What is the purpose of a profile drawing?
5. If contour lines are very close together, is the slope steep or gentle?

CHAPTER EXERCISES

The following problems are given to afford practice in topographic drawing. They may be completed by using either traditional drawing methods or a CAD program. The drawings are designed for a size B or A3 sheet. When adding text labels to your drawings, refer to Figure 19.1 for examples of text placement along lot lines and landform features.

Exercise 19.1 Draw symbols of six of the common natural surface features (streams, lakes, etc.) and six of the common development features (roads, buildings, etc.) shown in Appendix 32.

Exercise 19.2 Draw, to assigned horizontal and vertical scales, profiles of any three of the six lines shown in Figure 19.14.

Exercise 19.3 Assuming the slope of the ground to be uniform and assuming a horizontal scale of $1'' = 200'$ and a contour interval of $5'$, plot, by interpolation, the contours of Figure 19.14.

Exercise 19.4 Using the elevations shown in Figure 19.16a and a contour interval of $1'$, plot the contours to any convenient horizontal and vertical scales, and draw profiles of lines 3 and 5 and of any two lines perpendicular to them. Check, graphically, the points in which the contours cross these lines.

144.7	139.2	143.1	144.6	144.3	143.5	142.2
142.5	138.0	139.0	141.3	142.7	139.3	139.1
140.7	137.5	136.1	138.6	138.0	136.1	137.2
138.8	136.5	135.0	136.2	135.7	135.9	136.1
139.1	136.4	134.6	133.5	133.7	134.1	135.8
135.3	134.5	133.0	132.7	132.0	131.9	132.3
135.9	134.0	132.7	131.3	130.8	129.6	131.5

Exercise 19.5 Using a contour interval of $1'$ and a horizontal scale of $1'' = 100'$, plot the contours from the elevations given above at $100'$ stations. Check, graphically, the points in which the contours cross one of the horizontal lines and one of the vertical lines, using a vertical scale of $1'' = 10'$. Sketch, approximately, the drainage channels.

Exercise 19.6 Use CAD to draw a plat of the survey shown in Figure 19.1. If the drawing is accurate, the plat will close. Plot your final drawing on as large a sheet as practical. Determine a standard scale at which to show the drawing. Make sure the text labeling your drawing lines appears legible and at a standard height.

Exercise 19.7 Draw a topographic map of a country estate similar to that shown in Figure 19.3.

Exercise 19.8 Calculate profile elevations for a vertical curve $800'$ long to join grades of $+3.00\%$ and -3.00%. Assume grade elevations at points of tangency to be $100.00'$.

CHAPTER TWENTY

PIPING DRAWINGS

OBJECTIVES

After studying the material in this chapter, you should be able to:

1. Identify cast iron, brass, copper, and thermoplastic pipe and tubing fittings.

2. Draw and label common pipe joints using ANSI/ASME standard designations.

3. Draw the multiview or pictorial piping drawings using standard schematic symbols.

4. Draw the schematic symbols for valves and identify flow direction.

Refer to the following standards:
- ASME Y32.2.3 Graphic Symbols for Pipe Fittings, Valves, and Piping (Historical
- reference only.)
- AWWA C110/A21.10-03 Ductile-Iron and Grey-Iron Fittings for Water
- ISA 5.1 Instrumentation Symbols and Identification

A Complex Arrangement of Pipes and Tubes at a Gas Processing Plant *(Copyright Christian Lagerek/Shutterstock.)*

OVERVIEW

Pipe is made of aluminum, brass, clay, concrete (made both with ordinary aggregates and in combination with other materials), copper, glass, iron, lead, plastics, rubber, wood, and other materials or combinations of materials. Cast iron, steel, wrought iron, brass, copper, and plastic pipes are most commonly used for transporting water, steam, oil, or gases. Pipe is also used for structural elements such as columns and handrails.

Building plans for industrial plants, commercial buildings, and residences all use piping diagrams to describe the distribution path of the gases and liquids these buildings require. Special schematic symbols simplify each type of pipe connection. CAD libraries provide piping symbols for quick insertion into drawings. Piping symbol templates are also available for use in hand sketching.

Piping valves and joints such as those shown in this photo are typically shown using schematic symbols in technical drawings. (Tinnarat Suwanna/123RF.)

UNDERSTANDING PIPING DRAWINGS

Standard Symbols

To make drawings of piping systems quick to produce and easy to read, a standard set of symbols shown in Appendix 33 has been developed to represent the various pipe fittings and valves. Figure 20.1 shows a few of the standard symbols. CAD systems have standard symbols available, and templates for drawing piping symbols are a time-saver when you are sketching piping.

Types of Drawings

Two types of drawings are common for piping systems: single- and double-line.

    Single-line drawings show the centerline of the pipe as shown in Figure 20.2b.

    Double-line drawings show two lines representing the pipe diameter as shown in Figure 20.2a and Figure 20.8.

    Either type of drawing can be used in orthographic drawings, orthographic section views, or pictorial drawings. An example of an orthographic drawing of a piping system is shown in Figure 20.7. In complicated systems, where a large amount of piping of various sizes is run in close proximity and where clearances are important, the use of double-line multiview drawings, made accurately to scale, is desirable.

	Flanged	Screwed	Bell & Spigot	Welded	Soldered
Joint					
Elbow					
Elbow (45°)					

20.1   Standard Piping Symbols *(See Appendix 33)*

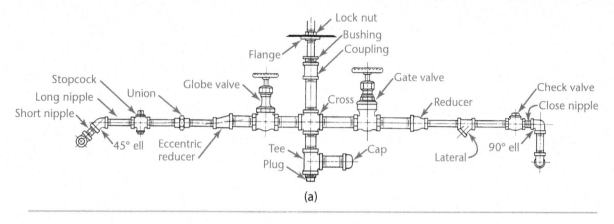

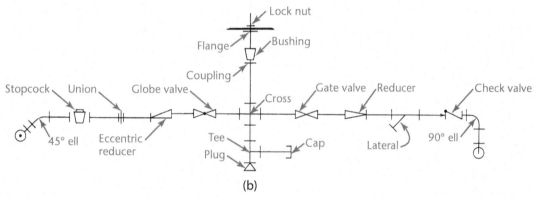

20.2 Piping Symbols Used in a (a) Double-Line Drawing; (b) Single-Line Drawing

20.3 Piping System Drawing Created Using CAD *(Courtesy of Softdesk, Inc.)*

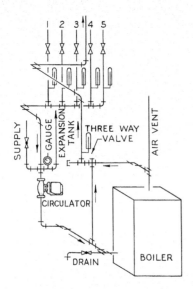

20.4   Schematic Drawing of Piping Connecting Boiler to Heating Coils

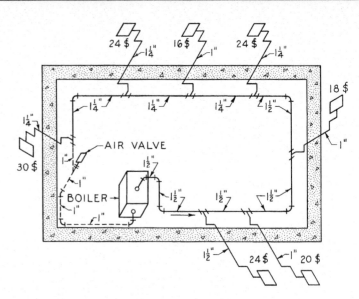

20.5   A One-Pipe Steam Heating System

Axonometric projections are also used for piping drawings. Figure 20.4 shows an oblique projection used for a piping diagram. The drawing shown in Figure 20.5 is a modified form of oblique projection generally used in representing the piping arrangement for heating systems. In these cases, the pipe mains are shown in plan and the risers in oblique projection in various directions to make the representation as clear as possible.

In most installations, some pipes are vertical and some are horizontal. If the vertical pipes are revolved into the hori-zontal plane or if the horizontal pipes are revolved into the vertical plane by turning some of the fittings, the entire installation can be shown in one plane, as shown in Figure 20.6c. This is called a *developed piping drawing.*

Showing the relative positions of component parts in all views reduces the probability of interference when the piping is erected and is almost a neces-sity when piping components are pre-fabricated in a shop and sent to the job in finished dimensions. Prefabrication is common for large systems and large pipe sizes. Most piping 2-1/2″ and larger is shop fabricated.

3D CAD is useful for creating pip-ing drawings. Showing the centerline of the pipe along with the valve may often be all that is necessary. Extrude the pipe diameter along the centerline to produce a drawing that shows the entire pipe when more detail is needed. Automated interference checking, available in 3D CAD, can help eliminate errors in the design.

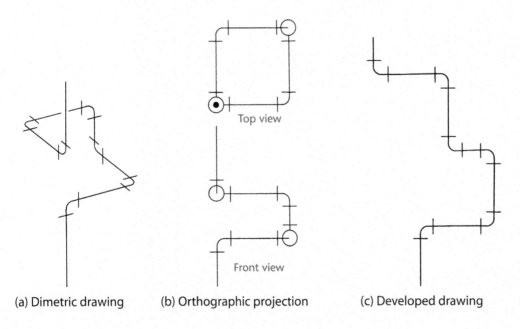

(a) Dimetric drawing   (b) Orthographic projection   (c) Developed drawing

20.6   Representations of Pipe Expansion Joint

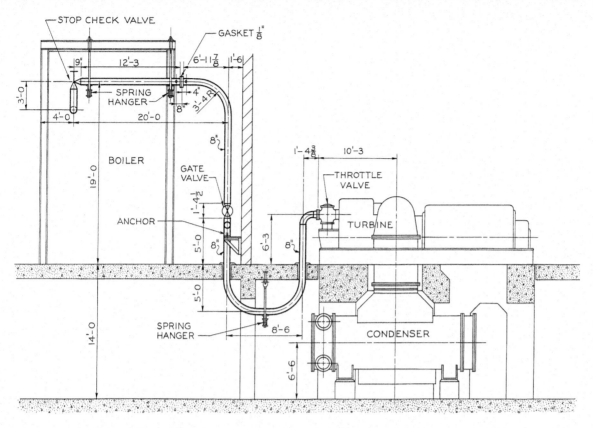

20.7 A Dimensioned Piping Drawing—Side View of Steam Piping

Dimensioning Piping Drawings

In dimensioning a piping drawing, give distances from center to center (c to c), center to end (c to e), or end to end (e to e) of fittings or valves and the lengths of all straight runs of pipe, as shown in Figure 20.7. Fully dimensioned single-line drawings are not always drawn to scale. You may find it useful to use break lines and omit portions of the straight pipe.

Allowances in pipe lengths for makeup in fittings and valves must be made in preparing a bill of materials.

Show the centerlines in double-line drawings if they are to be dimensioned.

Show the size of the pipe for each run by a numeral or by a note at the side of the pipe. Use a leader when necessary for clarity.

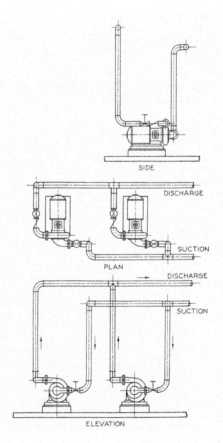

20.8 Two-Line Piping Drawing for a Pumping Plant

20.1 STEEL AND WROUGHT IRON PIPE

Steel or wrought iron pipe is used for water, steam, oil, and gas. Until the early 1930s, it was available in only three weights, known as "standard," "extra strong," and "double extra strong." At that time increasing pressures and temperatures, particularly for steam service, made the availability of more diversified wall thicknesses desirable.

The American National Standards Institute/American Society of Mechanical Engineers (ANSI/ASME) has developed dimensions for 10 different **schedules** of pipe (see Appendix 42). The table in Appendix 42 shows dimensions for nominal sizes from 1/8″ to 24″. Dimensions have not been established for all schedules. In the different schedules, the outside diameters (O.D.) are maintained for each nominal size to facilitate threading and the uniform use of fittings and valves.

Certain of the schedule dimensions correspond to the dimensions of "standard" and "extra strong" pipe. These are shown in boldface type in the appendix.

The schedule dimensions shown for Schedules 30 and 40 correspond to standard pipe, and those for Schedule 80 correspond to extra strong pipe. There are no schedule dimensions corresponding to double extra strong pipe. Some of the established schedule dimensions may not always be commercially available, so investigate before specifying pipe on drawings. Generally, schedules 40, 80, and 160 are readily available.

Note that the actual outside diameter of pipe in nominal sizes 1/8″ to 12″ inclusive is larger than the nominal size, whereas the outside diameter of pipe in nominal sizes 14″ and larger corresponds to the nominal size. Pipe in nominal sizes 14″ and larger is commonly referred to as O.D. pipe.

Pipe may be welded or seamless. Welded pipe is available in schedules 40 and 80 in the smaller sizes. Lap welded pipe is made in sizes up to and including 2″. Butt welded pipe is available as furnace-welded material, in which a formed length is heated in a furnace and then welded, in sizes up to and including 3″. Butt welded pipe is also available as continuous welded pipe, in which the finished pipe is continuously heated, formed, and welded from a roll of strip steel, in sizes up to and including 4″. Seamless pipe is made in both small and large sizes.

Many applications require the use of alloys to withstand pressure–temperature conditions without having to be excessively thick. Many alloys are available in both ferritic and austenitic material. Refer to the specifications of the American Society for Testing Materials (ASTM) for these alloys and for dimensional tolerances.

Steel pipe is available as **black pipe** or as **galvanized pipe.** Galvanized pipe is used for water distribution, and black pipe for natural gas.

Steel or wrought iron pipe comes in lengths up to about 40′ in the small sizes, with the length decreasing with increasing size and wall thickness.

20.2 CAST IRON PIPE

Cast iron (C.I.) pipe is used for water or gas service and as soil pipe. For water and gas pipe, it is generally available in sizes from 3″ to 60″ inclusive and in standard lengths of 12′. Various wall thicknesses satisfy different internal pressure requirements. The dimensions and the pressure ratings of the various classes are shown in Appendix 43.

Generally, water and gas pipes are connected with **bell and spigot joints** (Figure 20.9a) or **flanged joints** (Figure 20.9b), although other types of joints are also used (Figure 20.9c).

As soil pipe, cast iron pipe is available in sizes 2″ to 15″ inclusive, in standard lengths of 5′, and in service and extra heavy weights. Soil pipe is generally connected with bell and spigot joints, but soil pipe with threaded ends is available in sizes up to 12″.

Using cast iron pipe, designers consider both the internal pressure and the external loading, due to fill and other loadings, such as roads and tracks. Cast iron pipe is brittle, and settling can cause fracture unless the joints are sufficiently flexible. This is why flange joints are not usually used for buried pipes unless they are adequately supported.

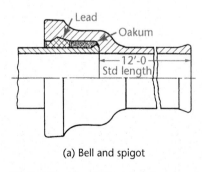
(a) Bell and spigot

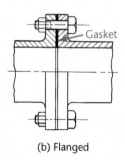
(b) Flanged

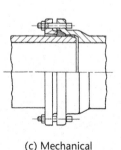
(c) Mechanical

20.9   Cast Iron Pipe Joints

90° elbow   90° elbow, plain   45° elbow   90° street elbow   Tee   Service tee   Cross   45° Y bend

Return bend   Reducer   Coupling   Cap   Bushing, outside hex.   Plug   Close nipple   Short nipple   Long nipple

20.10 Screwed Fittings

20.3 SEAMLESS BRASS AND COPPER PIPE

Pipe made of brass and copper is available in approximately the same dimensions as "standard" and "extra strong" steel pipe. It is used in plumbing for supply, soil, waste drain, and vent lines. It is also particularly suitable for process work where formation of scale or oxidation in steel pipe would be troublesome. Brass pipe and copper pipe are available in straight lengths up to 12′.

Brass pipe, generally known as ***red brass pipe,*** is an alloy of approximately 85% copper and 15% zinc. Copper pipe is practically pure copper with less than 0.1% of alloying elements.

Brass pipe and copper pipe should be joined with fittings of copper-base alloy to avoid galvanic action resulting in corrosion. Where screwed joints are used, fittings similar to cast or malleable iron fittings are available (Figure 20.10).

Flanged fittings of brass and copper are of different dimensions than fittings made of ferrous material. Refer to dimensional standards published by the American National Standards Institute *(ANSI/ASME B16.24)* for dimensions of brass and copper fittings.

20.4 COPPER TUBING

Copper tubing is often used in applications for nonferrous construction in sizes below 2″. It is suitable for process work, for plumbing, and for heating systems (particularly radiant heating).

Copper tubing is made as ***hard temper*** and as ***soft tubing.*** Hard temper tubing is much stiffer than soft tubing and is used when rigidity is desired. Soft tubing is easy to bend and is used where bending during assembly is required. Neither hard nor soft temper tubing has the rigidity of iron or steel pipe and

must be supported at frequent intervals. Where multiple runs of parallel tubes are used over distances of 20′ or more, parallel runs of soft tubing are laid in a trough to provide continuous support.

Copper tubing joints are usually made with ***flared joints*** (Figure 20.11a), or ***solder joints*** (Figure 20.11b). There are several types of flared joints, but the basic design of making a metal-to-metal joint is common to all. Fittings, such as tees, elbows, and couplings, are available for flared joints.

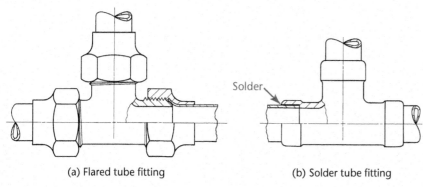

(a) Flared tube fitting   (b) Solder tube fitting

20.11 Copper Pipe Fittings

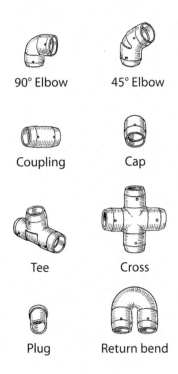

90° Elbow

45° Elbow

Coupling

Cap

Tee

Cross

Plug

Return bend

20.12   Solder Fittings

Solder joints are also known as *capillary joints* because the *annular space* between the tube and the fitting is so small that the molten solder is drawn into the space by capillary action. The solder may be introduced through a hole in the fitting (Figure 20.12) or through the outer end of the annular space. Fittings can be purchased with a factory-assembled ring of solder in the fitting. Solder joints may be made with soft solder (usually 50/50 or 60/40 tin and lead) or with silver solder. Silver solder has a higher melting point than soft solder, makes a stronger joint, and is suitable for higher operating temperatures.

Copper pipe or tubing has an upper operating temperature limit of 406 °F. If solder fittings are used, the upper temperature limit depends on the softening point of the solder rather than the temperature limit of the base material.

Copper tubing can be connected to threaded pipe or fittings using *adapters*. Adapters are available with either male or female pipe threads and with either flared or solder connections for

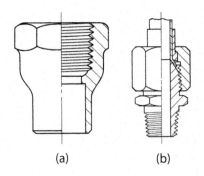

(a)   (b)

20.13   Adapters—Copper Tube to Threaded Pipe

the tubing. Two types are shown in Figure 20.13.

Copper tubing is available in straight lengths up to 20′ or in coils of 60′ for soft temper material. Hard temper material is available in straight lengths only, because it cannot be coiled. Installation costs for coiled material are lower, because fewer joints are needed. Copper tubing is available in both O.D. and nominal sizes.

20.5 PLASTIC AND SPECIALTY PIPES

Pipe and tubing of other material, such as aluminum and stainless steel, are also available. A wide variety of plastic pipe, both rigid and flexible, is used in construction. Plastic pipe is lightweight, corrosion proof, resistant to many chemicals, and has a smooth inner surface which offers low flow resistance.

PVC (polyvinyl chloride) pipe and fittings are available in Schedule 40 and extra heavy Schedule 80. Schedule 80 is used where higher working pressures are present and may be threaded. Schedule 40 should not be threaded, and is normally assembled with slip fittings and solvent. The maximum temperature rating for PVC is 140 °F (110 °C).

CPVC (chlorinated polyvinyl chloride) pipe is similar to PVC and has a higher maximum temperature rating, 180 °F (132 °C). Both PVC and CPVC pipe are commonly available in sizes ranging from 1/2″ to 4″ inside diameter (I.D.).

Black polyethylene flexible pipe, approved by the National Sanitation Foundation for use with drinking water, has a rated working pressure of 100 psi when not exposed to direct sunlight. It is available in sizes from 1/2″ to 2″ I.D. Black polyethylene pipe should not be used on hot-water lines or exposed to temperatures greater than 100 °F (88 °C). It is often used for underground lawn sprinkler systems.

HDPE (high-density polyethylene) is available in sizes from 1/2″ to 63″ in a variety of wall thicknesses and shapes.

The applications of these materials vary according to their physical properties and temperature–pressure limitations. Regardless of the material used in a piping system, the procedure followed in the design of the system and the creation of the necessary drawings remains basically the same.

20.6 PIPE FITTINGS

Pipe fittings are used to join lengths of pipe, to provide changes of direction, to provide branch connections at different angles, or to effect a change in size. They are made of cast iron, malleable iron, cast or forged steel, nonferrous alloys, and other materials for special applications. Pipe fittings are available in different weights and should be matched to the pipe they are used with. Ferrous fittings are made for threaded, welded, or flanged joints. Nonferrous fittings are made for threaded, solder, flared, or flanged joints. The common types of fittings for threaded joints were shown in Figure 20.10. Common fittings for solder joints were shown in Figure 20.12. Fittings for welded joints are shown in Figure 20.14, and for flanged joints in Figure 20.15.

Where both or all ends of a fitting are the same nominal size, the fitting is designated by the nominal size and the description—for example, a 2" *screwed tee.* Where two or more ends of a fitting are not the same nominal size, the fitting is designated as a *reducing fitting,* the dimensions of the run precede those of the branches, and the dimension of the larger opening precedes that of the smaller opening—for example, a 2" × 1-1/2" × 1" *screwed reducing tee.* See Figure 20.16 for typical designations.

The threads of screwed fittings conform to the pipe thread with which they are to be used, either male or female.

Dimensions of 125 lb cast iron screwed fittings, 250 lb cast iron screwed fittings, 125 lb cast iron flanged fittings, and 250 lb cast iron flanged fittings are shown in Appendices 46–47 and 49–50.

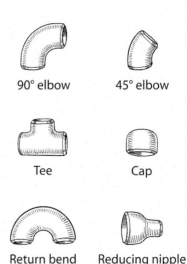

90° elbow   45° elbow

Tee   Cap

Return bend   Reducing nipple

Welding nipple

20.14   Butt Welded Fittings

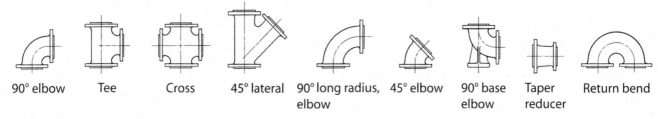

90° elbow   Tee   Cross   45° lateral   90° long radius, elbow   45° elbow   90° base elbow   Taper reducer   Return bend

20.15   Flanged Fittings

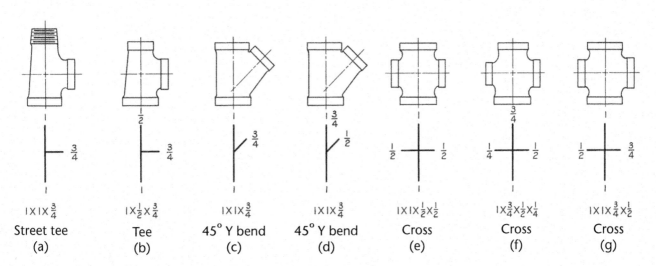

$1 \times 1 \times \frac{3}{4}$
Street tee
(a)

$1 \times \frac{1}{2} \times \frac{3}{4}$
Tee
(b)

$1 \times 1 \times \frac{3}{4}$
45° Y bend
(c)

$1 \times 1 \times \frac{3}{4}$
45° Y bend
(d)

$1 \times 1 \times \frac{1}{2} \times \frac{1}{2}$
Cross
(e)

$1 \times \frac{3}{4} \times \frac{1}{2} \times \frac{1}{4}$
Cross
(f)

$1 \times 1 \times \frac{3}{4} \times \frac{1}{2}$
Cross
(g)

20.16   Designating Sizes of Fittings

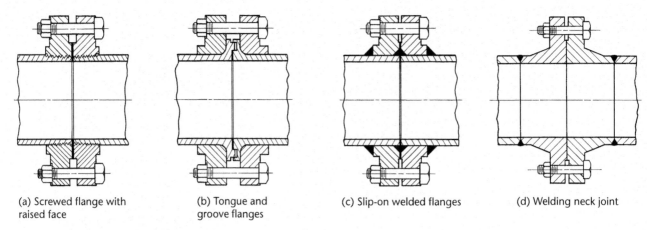

(a) Screwed flange with
raised face

(b) Tongue and
groove flanges

(c) Slip-on welded flanges

(d) Welding neck joint

20.17   Special Types of Flanged Joints

20.7 PIPE JOINTS

The joints between pipes, fittings, and valves may be *screwed, flanged, welded,* or, for nonferrous metallic materials, *soldered.* Plastic pipes may be screwed together or fastened with slip joints and solvent or with compression fittings.

The American National Standard pipe threads were illustrated in Figures 13.27–13.29, and tabular dimensions are shown in Appendix 42. The threads of the American Petroleum Institute (API) differ somewhat from the American National Standard pipe threads. Refer to the API Standards for these differences.

Threaded joints can be made up tightly by simply screwing the cleaned threads together. However, it is common practice to use *pipe compound,* as it lubricates the threads and enables them to be screwed together more tightly. It also serves to seal irregularities, providing a tighter joint. Pipe compound is applied to the male thread only, to avoid forcing it into the pipe and to prevent contamination or obstruction.

Flanged Joints

Flanged joints are made by bolting two flanges together with a resilient *gasket* between the flange faces. Flanges may be attached using a screwed joint or by welding, lapping the pipe, or being cast integrally with the pipe, fitting, or appliance.

The faces of the flanges between which the gasket is placed have different standard facings, such as flat face, 1/16″ raised face, 1/4″ raised face, male and female, tongue and groove, and ring joints. Flat face and 1/16″ raised face are standard for cast iron flanges in the 125 lb and 250 lb classes, respectively. The other types of facing are standard for steel flanges.

The number and size of the bolts joining these flanges vary with the size and the working pressure of the joint. Bolting for Class 125 cast iron and Class 250 cast iron flanges are shown in Appendices 46 and 49, respectively.

For dimensions of the various flange facings and for flange and bolting dimensions of the various sizes and pressure standards of steel flanges, refer to the ANSI standard for *Steel Pipe Flanges and Flanged Fittings (ANSI/ASME B16.5),* which is too extensive to be included here. Some special types of flanged joints are shown in Figure 20.17.

Welded Joints

Piping construction using welded joints is in almost universal use today, particularly for higher pressure and temperature conditions. Such joints may either be socket welded or butt welded (Figure 20.18). Socket welded joints are limited to use in small sizes. The contours of the butt welded joints shown in Figure 20.18b and c are those shown in *ANSI/ASME B16.25.*

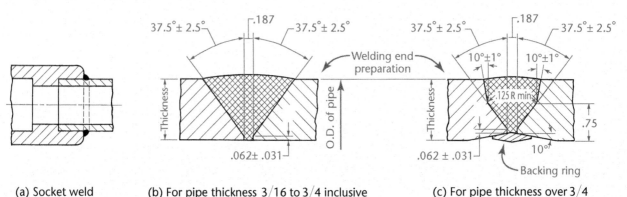

(a) Socket weld

(b) For pipe thickness 3/16 to 3/4 inclusive

(c) For pipe thickness over 3/4

20.18   Welded Joints

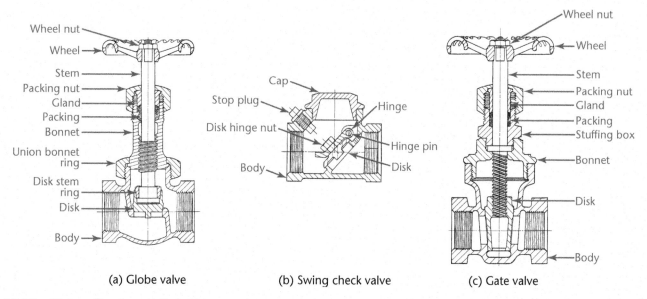

(a) Globe valve   (b) Swing check valve   (c) Gate valve

20.19   Globe, Check, and Gate Valves

20.8 VALVES

Valves are used to stop or regulate the flow of fluids in a pipeline. The more common types are *gate valves, globe valves,* and *check valves.* Other types, such as *pressure-reducing valves* and *safety valves,* are used to maintain a desired lower pressure on the downstream side of the valve or to prevent undesirable overpressure, respectively.

Globe Valves

Globe valves have approximately spherical bodies with the seating surface at either a right or an acute angle to the centerline of the pipe (Figure 20.19a). In a globe valve, the flowing fluid makes abrupt turns in the body resulting in higher pressure loss than in a gate valve.

Globe valves are commonly used for close regulation of flow and are less subject to cutting action in throttling service than gate valves.

Inside screw and outside screw and yoke (OS & Y) type valves are also available. Angle valves and needle valves are special designs of the general class of globe valves.

Check Valves

Check valves are used to limit fluid flow to only one direction. *Swing check valves* use a disk that may be hinged to swing partially out of the stream (Figure 20.19b). *Lift check values* use a disk that is guided so that it rises vertically from its seat.

Gate Valves

Gate valves have full-size straightway openings that offer small resistance to the flow of fluid. The gate, or disk, may rise on the stem (inside screw type) (Figure 20.19c), or the gate may rise with the stem, which in turn rises out of the body (rising stem, or outside screw and yoke type). Inside screw type valves are used in the smaller sizes and lower pressures.

Seating may be on nonparallel seats, in which case the disk is solid and wedge shaped. There is also a type of gate valve that uses parallel seats. In this type, two disks are hung loosely on the stem and are free of the seats until an adjusting wedge reaches a lug at the closed position of the valve, when further movement of the stem causes the wedge to spread the disks and form a tight joint on the parallel seats. These valves are used only on low-pressure and low-temperature services.

Solenoid-Actuated Valves

A thermostatically controlled heating system is an example of process control. When you set your home thermostat to a particular value, the heating system is typically controlled using solenoid actuated valves to try to meet the set temperature value. Solenoid valves are electromechanical devices often used to regulate the flow of liquid or gas. Drawings for process control often combine electronic and piping elements to show how the process is controlled. Figure 20.20a shows a cross-sectional view of a two-way, two-position, normally closed solenoid valve. Figure 20.20b shows a schematic diagram for a two-way, two-position, normally closed solenoid flow control valve.

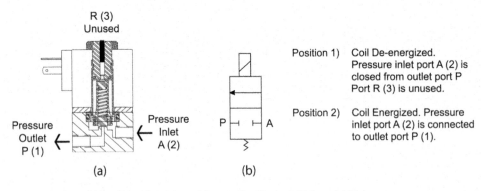

20.20   Two-Way Two-Position, Normally Closed Solenoid Valve
(Courtesy of Spartan Scientific.)

20.9 AMERICAN NATIONAL STANDARD CODE FOR PRESSURE PIPING

The American National Standards Institute has adopted an *American National Standard Code for Pressure Piping (ANSI/ASME B31)*. This compilation of recommended practices and minimum safety standards covers various types of piping, such as power piping, industrial gas and air piping, oil refinery piping, oil transportation piping, refrigerating piping, chemical industry process piping, and gas transmission and distribution piping.

PIPING DRAWING FOR A FIELD INSTRUMENT

MSE Technology Applications, Inc. (MSE) designed a field instrument to expedite the process of sorting drums containing volatile organic compounds (VOCs). The previous sorting process used a gas chromatograph/mass spectrometer (GC/MS) which was time consuming and relatively expensive. Drums were required to pass two independent field measurements before they could be transported. Figure A is a schematic diagram showing the valves, filters, piping and other features for the instrumentation.

From each drum a headspace gas sample was drawn and analyzed first by a field-ready flame ionization detector (FID) VOC meter. A second field instrument, a photo ionization detector (PID) VOC meter equipped with a 10.6-eV lamp analyzed the headspace gas a second time. If the sum of the two VOC measurements were less than 500 ppmv, the waste was designated less than 500 ppmv flammable VOCs and therefore allowed to be shipped. Tests of the device showed the portable field instruments provided a confident approach to sampling and analyzing headspace gas in drums, saving time and avoiding the costly GC/MS analysis previously used.

The actual equipment, when assembled, looked very similar to the 3D CAD model shown in Figure B.

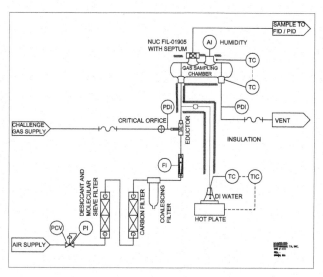

(A) Drum Simulation and Setup Diagram *(Courtesy of MSE Technology Applications, Inc.)*

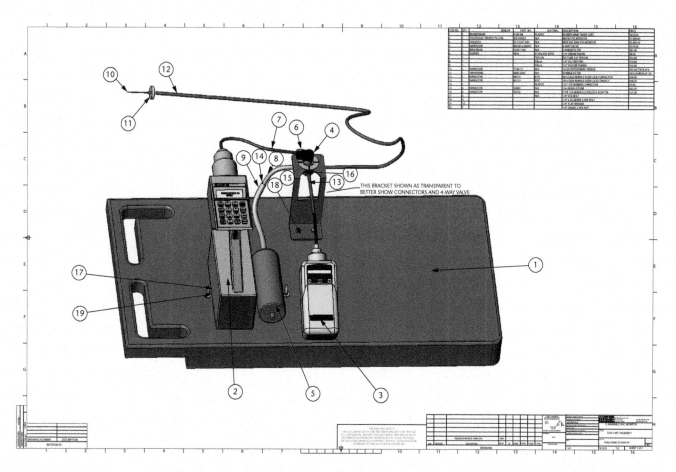

(B) Assembly Drawing and Parts List from the 3D CAD Model *(Courtesy of MSE Technology Applications, Inc.)*

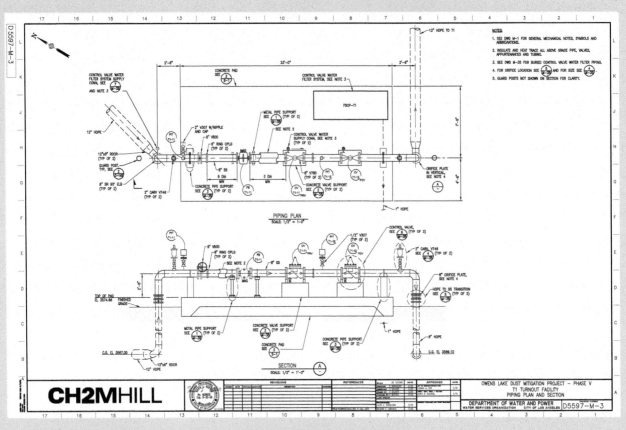

Double-Line Piping Plan and Elevation Drawing *(Courtesy of CH2M Hill.)*

PORTFOLIO

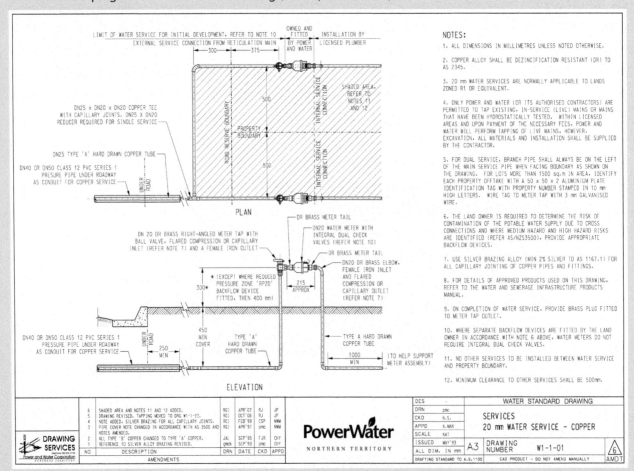

Water Service Drawing *(Courtesy of Power and Water Corporation.)*

KEY WORDS

Adapters

Annular Space

Bell and Spigot Joints

Black Pipe

Capillary Joints

Check Valves

CPVC

Developed Piping Drawing

Double-line Drawings

Flanged

Flanged Joints

Flared Joints

Galvanized Pipe

Gasket

Gate Valves

Globe Valves

Hard Temper

HDPE

Lift Check Values

Pipe Compound

Pressure-Reducing Valves

PVC

Red Brass Pipe

Reducing Fitting

Safety Valves

Schedules

Screwed

Screwed Reducing Tee

Screwed Tee

Single-line Drawings

Soft Tubing

Solder Joints

Soldered

Swing Check Valves

Welded

CHAPTER SUMMARY

- Steel and wrought iron pipes are commonly used for water, steam, oil, and gas. Steel provides the strength necessary for the high pressures commonly associated with these substances.
- Cast iron is primarily used for water, gas, and waste. Cast iron is durable for all but the highest pressures. Cast iron pipe typically uses threaded fittings.
- Copper tubing is typically used for water and compressed air. Copper tubing can be connected with solder joints or with compression fittings.
- Plastic pipe and fittings are lightweight, corrosion resistant, and have a smooth inner surface. They are often used as a substitute for metallic pipe.
- Single-line drawings and simplified symbols are commonly used to represent pipes and fittings on a pipe drawing. Piping drawings are usually not drawn to scale.
- Valves control the flow of material through a pipe.
- A library of computer piping symbols can speed the creation and modification of CAD piping drawings.

REVIEW QUESTIONS

1. Which pipe material would be used for the highest pressures?
2. Which types of fittings are commonly used with cast iron pipe? With copper tubing?
3. Which fitting would join two pipes at 90° or 45°?
4. Which fitting would join two pipes at 180°?
5. Which fitting would join four pipes together at one joint?
6. Which fitting would connect two pipes of different diameter?
7. What is the purpose of a valve?
8. How is flow direction indicated on a piping drawing?
9. Why is a library of piping symbols important when drawing with CAD?
10. Draw and label five single-line piping symbols.

CHAPTER EXERCISES

Exercise 20.1 Make a double-line drawing, similar to Figure 20.2a and Figure 20.8, showing the following fittings: a union, a 45° Y bend, an eccentric reducer, a globe valve, a tee, a stopcock, and a 45° ell. Use 1/2″ and 1″ wrought steel pipe and 125 lb cast iron screwed fittings.

Exercise 20.2 Make a single-line drawing, similar to Figure 20.2b, showing the following fittings: a 45° ell, a union, a 45° Y bend, an eccentric reducer, a tee, a reducer, a gate valve, a plug, a cap, and a cross.

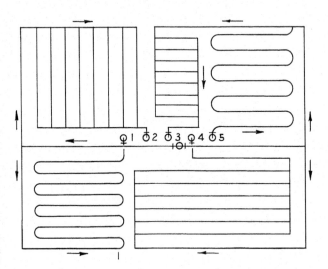

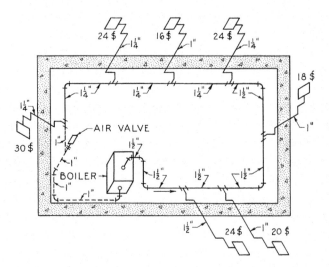

Exercise 20.3 Make a single-line drawing of the system of pipe coils and grids shown above. Show, by their respective standard symbols, the elbows and tees that must be used to connect pipes meeting at right angles if welding is not used to make the joints.

Exercise 20.4 Make an oblique projection, similar to that shown above, of the one-pipe steam heating system shown. Show the pipes by single lines, the fittings by their standard symbols, and the boiler and radiators as parallelepipeds.

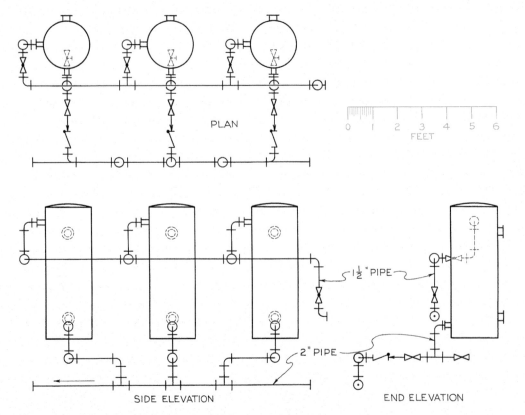

Exercise 20.5 Make a single-line isometric drawing of the piping layout shown. Use a scale of 3/4″ = 1′−0. (Make the drawing similar to the isometric layout shown in Exercise 20.6.)

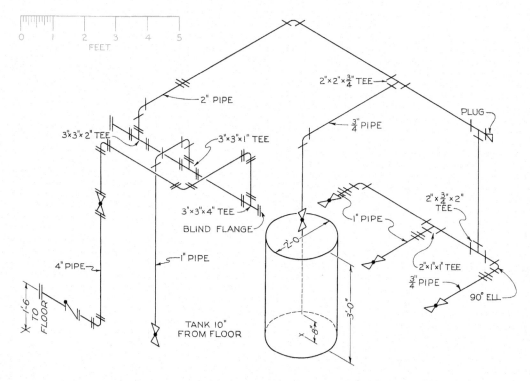

Exercise 20.6 Make a single-line multiview drawing of the piping layout shown above. Use a scale of $1'' = 1'-0$. (This drawing should be similar to the piping layout in Exercise 20.5.)

Exercise 20.7 Make a double-line multiview drawing of the piping layout in Exercise 20.5 to a scale of your own selection. (This drawing should be similar to the two-line piping drawing in Figure 20.2a, but you will create front, top, and side views.)

Exercise 20.8 Make a double-line multiview drawing of the piping layout in Exercise 20.6 to a scale of your own selection. Use Schedule 80 wrought steel pipe throughout, with Class 250 cast iron flanged fittings where pipe is larger than 2″ and Class 250 cast iron screwed fittings where pipe is 2″ and smaller. (This drawing should be similar to the two-line piping drawing in Figure 20.2a, but you will create front, top, and side views.)

CHAPTER TWENTY-ONE

WELDING REPRESENTATION

--- OBJECTIVES ---

After studying the material in this chapter, you should be able to:

1. Describe the various welding processes.

2. Draw the common welding symbols.

3. Dimension a welding drawing using standard ANSI welding notation.

4. Identify and draw a fillet weld, groove weld, back weld, spot weld, seam weld, projection weld, and flash weld.

5. Describe the use of welding symbols in CAD drawings.

Refer to the following standards:
- *AWS A2.4 Standard Symbols for Welding, Brazing, and Nondestructive Examination*
- *AWS A1.1 Metric Practice Guide for the Welding Industry*
- *AWS A3.0 Standard Welding Terms and Definitions*

An automobile frame is welded on a robotic automobile assembly line. (*Courtesy of Vladimir Pcholkin/Stone/Getty Images.*)

OVERVIEW

For fastening parts together permanently, rather than using bolts, screws, rivets, or other fasteners, welding is often the method of choice. Welding is widely used in fabricating machine parts or other structures that formerly would have been formed by casting or forging. Structural steel frames for buildings, ships, and other structures are often welded. Welding is one of few machine processes that adds material to a workpiece, rather than removing it.

Welding symbols on a mechanical drawing provide precise instructions for the welder. The weld type and the location of each weld must be clearly defined using standardized symbols. CAD libraries of welding symbols can simplify the drawing process. Welding templates can speed the process of drawing by hand.

UNDERSTANDING WELDMENT DRAWINGS

Welding is used extensively and for a wide variety of attachment purposes. A series of "Standard Welding Symbols" were developed in 1947 to provide an accurate method of showing the exact types, sizes, and locations of welds on construction drawings of machines or structures. Before these standards were developed, notes on the drawing such as "To be welded throughout" or "To be completely welded," gave responsibility for welding control to the welding shop. Such instruction was dangerously vague and could be unnecessarily expensive, because shops would often "play it safe" by welding more than necessary.

Welding Processes

The principal methods of welding are

- *Gas welding*
- *Arc welding*
- *Resistance welding*

Gas Welding The oxyacetylene method is generally known as gas welding. Gas welding originated in 1895, when the French chemist Le Châtelier discovered that the combustion of acetylene gas with oxygen produced a flame hot enough to melt metals. This discovery was soon followed by the development of practical methods to produce and transport oxygen and acetylene and the construction of torches and welding rods.

Arc Welding The electric arc method is generally known as arc welding. In arc welding, the heat of an electric arc is used to fuse the metals that are to be welded or cut. Gas metal arc welding *(GMAW)* is often known by its subtypes metal inert gas welding *(MIG)* and metal active gas welding *(MAG).*

Arc welding uses a wire electrode that is fed along with a shielding gas through the welding gun. Gas tungsten arc welding *(GTAW),* often known as tungsten inert gas welding *(TIG),* and plasma arc welding are processes that conduct the arc through a heated gas called a plasma to produce strong high-quality welds. Arc and gas welding are important construction processes in industry.

Resistance Welding Electric resistance welding is generally called resistance welding. In resistance welding, two pieces of metal are held together under some pressure, and a large amount of electric current is passed through the parts. The resistance of the metals to the passage of the current causes heat at the junction of the two pieces, resulting in the welding of the metals.

Standard Symbols

The text and illustrations of this chapter are based primarily on *ANSI/AWS A2.4, Standard Symbols for Welding, Brazing, and Nondestructive Examination.* You may also want to refer to *AWS A1.1, Metric Practice Guide for the Welding Industry,* and *ANSI/AWS A3.0, Standard Welding Terms and Definitions.*

Welding drawings are a special type of assembly drawing, as weldments are composed of a number of separate pieces fastened together as a unit. The welds themselves are not drawn but are clearly and completely indicated by the welding symbols. Figure 21.1 shows a drawing using standard welding symbols. Most CAD packages provide standard welding symbols that can quickly be inserted into your drawing.

The joints are all shown in the drawing as they would appear before welding. Dimensions are given to show the sizes of the individual pieces to be cut from stock. Each component piece is identified by encircled numbers and by specifications in the parts list.

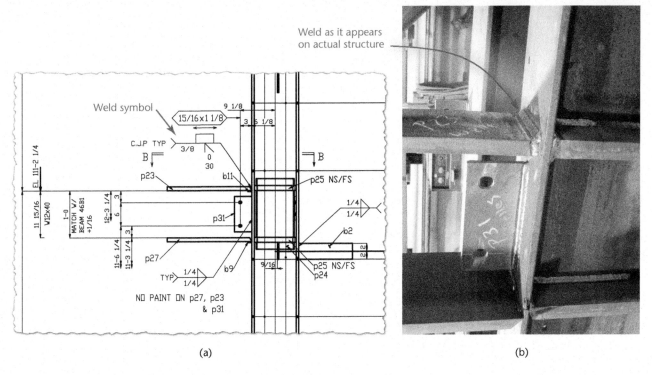

Weld as it appears on actual structure

(a) (b)

21.1 (a) Portion of a Weldment Drawing and (b) Welded Structure *(Photo has been rotated to the same orientation as the drawing in part a.) (Courtesy of Midwest Steel Industries.)*

UNDERSTANDING A WELDING SYMBOL

A welding symbol added to the drawing has many different features that specify each detail of the weld. The items that can be specified are:

- Type of weld
- Process
- Depth of bevel, size, or strength for some weld types
- Groove weld size
- Finishing designator
- Contour
- Groove angle
- Root opening
- Length of weld
- Number and *pitch* (center to center spacing) of welds
- Whether the weld is to be field welded (done on site)
- All-around indicator
- Which side of the material is to be welded

That is a lot of information contained in one symbol. The next sections provide more detail about the information contained in the symbol you will add to your drawings. Figure 21.1 shows an example of weld symbols used on a drawing and the actual welded part. Figure 21.2 points out features of a weld to which the symbol may refer.

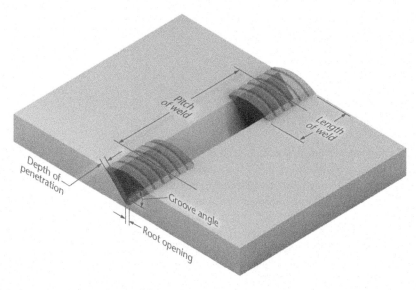

21.2 Features of a Weld

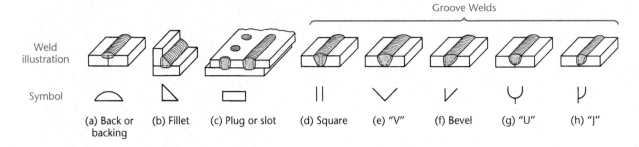

Weld illustration / Symbol

Groove Welds

(a) Back or backing   (b) Fillet   (c) Plug or slot   (d) Square   (e) "V"   (f) Bevel   (g) "U"   (h) "J"

21.3   Basic Welds and Symbols

21.1 TYPES OF WELDED JOINTS

There are five basic types of welded joints: *butt joint, corner joint, T-joint, lap joint,* and *edge joint.* They are classified according to the positions of the parts being joined. Table 21.1 shows illustrations of the types of welded joints.

A number of different types of welds are applicable to each type of joint, depending on the thickness of metal, the strength of joint required, and other considerations.

21.2 TYPES OF WELDS

The four types of arc and gas welds are shown in Figure 21.3:

- *Back or backing weld*
- *Fillet weld*
- *Plug or slot weld*
- *Groove weld*

Groove welds are further classified as square, V, bevel, U, and J, as shown in Figures 21.3d through h.

More than one type of weld may be applied to a single joint. For example, a V weld may be on one side and a back weld on the other side. Frequently, the same type of weld is used on opposite sides, forming such welds as a double-V, a double-U, or a double-J.

The four basic resistance welds are:

- *Spot weld*
- *Projection weld*
- *Seam weld*
- *Flash or upset weld*

Except for the flash or upset weld, the corresponding symbols for these welds and additional basic weld symbols for surfacing, groove, and flange joints are given in Figure 21.4. (See Section 21.12 for the use of the square groove weld symbol for the flash or upset resistance weld.) Supplementary symbols are shown in Figure 21.5. Depending on your field and the particular project, you may need to use only a simple symbol composed of the minimum elements (the arrow and the weld symbol) or you may need to use the additional components.

Table 21.1 Basic Types of Welded Joints

Type of Joint	Example
Butt joint	
Corner joint	
T-joint	
Lap joint	
Edge joint	

Spot or projection	Seam	Surfacing	Groove		Edge	Scarf
			Flare	Flare bevel		

Reference line

21.4 Additional Basic Weld Symbols

Weld all around	Field weld	Melt-thru	Consumable insert (square)	Backing or spacer matl	Contour		
					Flush	Convex	Concave

21.5 Supplementary Symbols

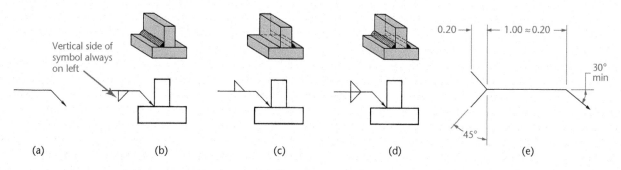

Vertical side of symbol always on left

0.20   1.00 ≈ 0.20

30° min

45°

(a)   (b)   (c)   (d)   (e)

21.6 Welding Symbols

21.3 WELDING SYMBOLS

The basic element of the symbol is the "bent" arrow, as shown in Figure 21.6a. The arrow points to the joint where the weld is to be made (Figure 21.6b). Attached to the reference line, or shank, of the arrow is the weld symbol for the desired weld. The symbol would be one of those illustrated in Figures 21.3 and 21.4. In this case, a fillet weld symbol has been used.

The weld symbol is placed below the reference line if the weld is to be on the *arrow side* of the joint, as in Figure 21.6b, or above the reference line if the weld is to be on the *other side* of the joint, as in Figure 21.6c. If the weld is to be on both the arrow side and the other side of the joint, weld symbols are placed on both sides of the reference line (Figure 21.6d). This rule for placement of the weld symbol is followed for all arc or gas weld symbols. Dimensions for creating a weld symbol are shown in Figure 21.6e.

When a joint is represented by a single line on a drawing, as in the top and side views of Figure 21.7b, the arrow side of the joint is regarded as the "near" side to the reader of the drawing, according to the usual conventions of technical drawing.

For the plug, slot, seam, and projection welding symbols, the arrow points to the outer surface of one of the members at

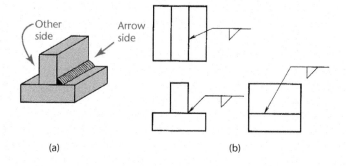

Other side

Arrow side

(a)   (b)

21.7 Arrow Side and Other Side

the centerline of the weld. In such cases, the arrow side of the joint is the one to which the arrow points, or the side "near" the reader (see Sections 21.8 and 21.12).

Note that for all fillet or groove symbols, the vertical side of the symbol is always drawn on the left, as shown in Figure 21.6b.

For best results, welding symbols should be drawn using CAD or a template, but in certain cases where necessary, they may be drawn freehand.

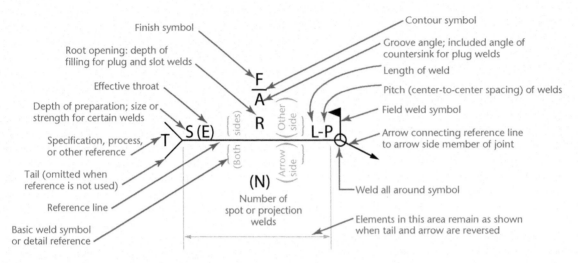

21.8   The Standard Locations for the Elements of the Welding Symbol

The complete welding symbol, enlarged, is shown in Figure 21.8. See Appendix 31 for additional welding symbol details.

Reference to a specification, process, or other supplementary information is indicated by a symbol in the tail of the arrow (Figure 21.9a). Otherwise, a general note may be placed on the drawing, such as

UNLESS OTHERWISE INDICATED, MAKE ALL WELDS PER SPECIFICATION NO. XXX

If no reference is indicated in the symbol, the tail may be omitted.

To avoid repeating the same information on many welding symbols on a drawing, general notes may be used, such as

FILLET WELDS .3125″ UNLESS OTHERWISE INDICATED

or

ROOT OPENINGS FOR ALL GROOVE WELDS .1875″ UNLESS OTHERWISE INDICATED

Welds extending completely around a joint are indicated by an open circle around the elbow of the arrow (Figure 21.9b). When the weld all around symbol is not used, the welding symbol is understood to apply between abrupt changes in direction of the weld, unless otherwise shown. A short vertical

staff with a solid triangular flag at the elbow of the arrow indicates a weld to be made "in the field" (on the site) rather than in the fabrication shop (Figure 21.9c).

Spot, seam, flash, or upset symbols usually do not have arrow-side or other-side significance and are simply centered on the reference line of the arrow (Figures 21.10a through c). Spot and seam symbols are shown on the drawing as indicated in Figures 21.10d and e. Note that the required process must be specified in the tail of the symbol (RSW = resistance spot weld, EBW = electron beam weld).

For bevel or J-groove welds, the arrow should point with a definite change of direction, or break, toward the member that is to be beveled or grooved (Figures 21.11a and b). In this case, the upper member is grooved. The break is omitted if the location of the bevel or groove is obvious.

Lettering for the symbols should be placed to read from the bottom or from the right side of the drawing in accordance with the aligned system (Figures 21.11c through e). Dimensions may be indicated on a drawing in the fractional, decimal-inch, or metric system.

When a joint has more than one weld, the combined symbols are used (Figures 21.11f through h).

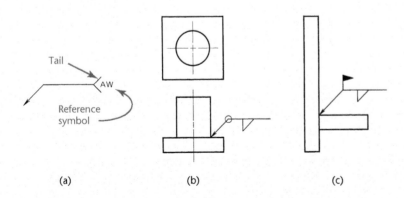

(a)   (b)   (c)

21.9   The Standard Locations for the Elements of the Welding Symbol

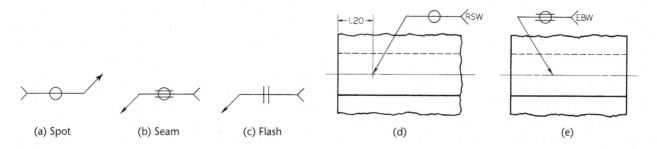

21.10 Spot, Seam, and Flash Welding Symbols

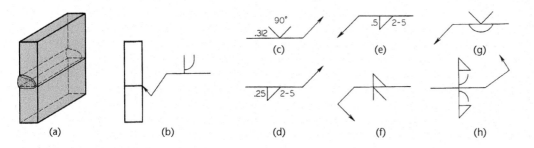

21.11 Welding Symbols

21.4 FILLET WELDS

The usual fillet weld has equal legs (Figure 21.12a). The size of the weld is the length of one leg, as indicated by a dimension figure (fraction, decimal-inch, or metric) at the left of the weld symbol (Figure 21.12b). For fillet welds on both sides of a joint, the dimensions should be indicated on both sides of the reference line, whether the dimensions are identical or different. (Figure 21.12c). The lengths of the welds and the pitch (center-to-center spacing of welds) are indicated as shown. When the welds on opposite sides are different in size, the sizes are given as shown in Figure 21.12d. If a fillet weld has unequal legs, the weld orientation is shown on the drawing, if necessary, and the lengths of the legs are given in parentheses to the left of the weld symbol, as in Figure 21.12e. If a general note is given on the drawing, such as

ALL FILLET WELDS .3125″ UNLESS OTHERWISE NOTED

the size dimensions are omitted from the symbols.

No length dimension is needed for a weld that extends the full distance between abrupt changes of direction. For each abrupt change in direction, an additional arrow is added to the symbol, except when the weld all around symbol is used.

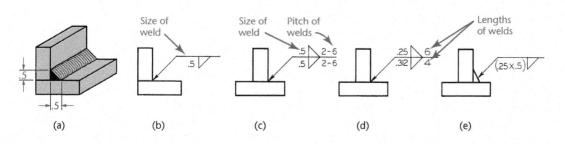

21.12 Dimensioning of Fillet Welds

Fillet Weld Length

Lengths of fillet welds may be indicated by symbols in conjunction with dimension lines (Figure 21.13a). The extent of fillet welding may be shown graphically with section lining if desired (Figure 21.13b).

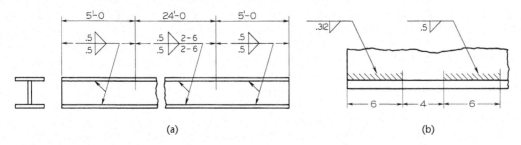

21.13   Lengths of Fillet Welds

Intermittent Fillet Welding

Chain intermittent fillet welding is indicated as shown in Figure 21.14a. If the welds are staggered, the weld symbols are staggered (Figure 21.14b).

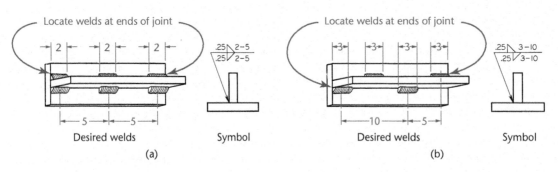

21.14   Intermittent Welds

Surface Contour and Fillet Welds

Unfinished flat-faced fillet welds are indicated by adding the *flush* symbol (see Figure 21.5), to the weld symbol (Figure 21.15a). If fillet welds are to be made flat-faced by mechanical means, add the flush-contour symbol and the user's standard finish symbol to the weld symbol (Figures 21.15b through d). These finish symbols indicate the method of finishing (C = chipping, G = grinding, M = machining, R = rolling, H = hammering) and not the degree of finish. If fillet welds are to be finished to a *convex contour*, the convex-contour symbol is added, together with the finish symbol (Figure 21.15e).

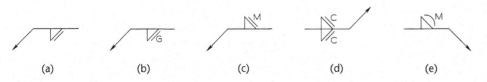

21.15   Surface Contour of Fillet Welds

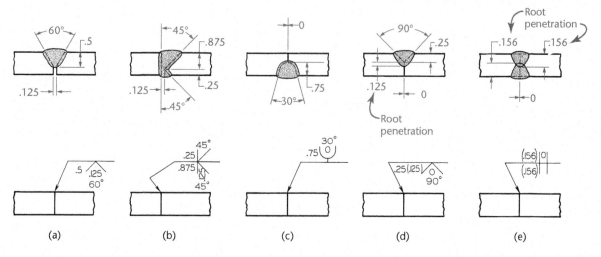

21.16 Groove Welds

21.5 GROOVE WELDS

In Figure 21.16, various groove welds are shown in the top row with their corresponding symbolic representations shown below. The sizes of the groove welds (depth of the V, bevel, U, or J) are indicated on the left of the weld symbol. For example, in Figure 21.16a, the size of the V-weld is .50″, in Figure 21.16b the sizes are .25″ and .875″, in Figure 21.16c the size is .75″, and in Figure 25.16d the size is .25″. For the symbol in Figure 21.16d the size is followed by .125″, which is the additional "root penetration" of the weld. In Figure 21.16e, the root penetration is .156″ from zero, or from the outside of the members. Note the overlap of the root penetration in this case.

The root opening or space between members, when not covered by a company standard, is shown within the weld symbol. In Figures 21.16a and b, the root openings are .125″. In Figures 21.16c through e, the openings are zero.

The groove angles, when not covered by a company standard, appear just outside the openings of the weld symbols (Figures 21.16a and b).

A general note may be used on the drawing to avoid repeating the symbols, such as

ALL V-GROOVE WELDS TO HAVE 60° GROOVE ANGLE
UNLESS OTHERWISE SHOWN

However, when the dimensions of one or both of two opposite welds differ from the general note, both welds should be completely dimensioned.

When single-groove or symmetrical double-groove welds extend completely through, the size need not be added to the welding symbol. For example, in Figure 21.16a, if the V-groove extended entirely through the joint, the depth or size would simply be the thickness of the stock and would not need to be indicated in the welding symbol.

Surface Contour and Groove Welds

When groove welds are to be approximately flush without finishing, add the flush-contour symbol (see Figure 21.5) to the weld symbols (Figures 21.17a and b). If the welds are to be machined, add the flush-contour symbol and the user's standard finish symbol to the weld symbol (Figures 21.17c and d). These finish symbols indicate the method of finishing (C = chipping, G = grinding, M = machining) and not the degree of finish. If a groove weld is to be finished with a convex-contour, add the convex-contour and finish symbols, as in Figure 21.17e.

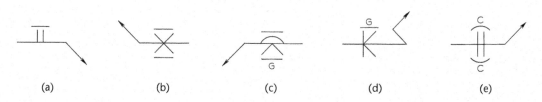

21.17 Surface Contour of Groove Welds

21.6 BACK OR BACKING WELDS

A back or backing symbol opposite the groove weld symbol indicates bead-type welds used as back or backing welds on single-groove welds (Figure 21.18a). Dimensions for back or backing welds are not shown on the symbol, but may be shown, if necessary, directly on the drawing.

A flush contour symbol included in the weld symbols indicates that the back or backing welds are to be approximately flush without machining (Figure 21.18b). If they are to be machined, the user's finish symbol is added (Figures 21.18c and d). If the welds are to be finished with a convex contour, the convex-contour symbol and the finish symbol are included in the weld symbol, as shown in Figure 21.18e.

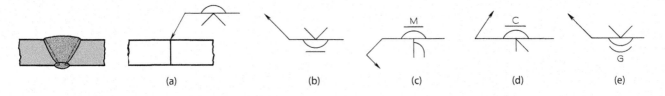

(a)   (b)   (c)   (d)   (e)

21.18   Back or Backing Weld Symbols

21.7 SURFACE WELDS

The surface weld symbol indicates a surface to be built up with single- or multiple-pass bead type welds (Figure 21.19). Because this symbol does not indicate a welded joint, there is no arrow-side or other-side significance, so the symbol is always drawn below the reference line. Indicate the minimum height of the weld deposit at the left of the weld symbol, except where no specific height is required. When a specific area of a surface is to be built up, give the dimensions of the area on the drawing.

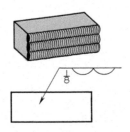

21.19   Surface Weld Symbol

21.8 PLUG AND SLOT WELDS

The same symbol is used for plug welds and slot welds. Figures 21.20a and d show the hole or slot that is made to receive the weld. If it is in the arrow-side member, place the weld symbol below the reference line, as shown Figures 21.20b and c. If it is in the other-side member, place the weld symbol above the line, as shown in Figures 21.20e and f.

Place the size of a plug weld (which is the smallest diameter of the hole, if countersunk) at the left of the weld symbol. If the included angle for the countersink of a plug weld is in accordance with the user's standard, omit it; otherwise, place it adjacent to the weld symbol as shown in Figures 21.20b and c.

A plug weld is understood to fill the depth of the hole unless its depth is indicated inside the weld symbol, as shown in Figure 21.21a. The pitch of plug welds is shown at the right of the weld symbol (Figure 21.21b). If the weld is to be approximately flush without finishing, add the flush-contour symbol, as in Figure 21.21c. If the weld is to be made flush by mechanical means, a finish symbol is added (Figure 21.21d). Flush-contour and finish symbols are used the same way for slot welds and for plug welds.

Indicate the depth of filling for slot welds the same way as for plug welds (Figure 21.21a). The size and location dimensions of slot welds cannot be shown on the welding symbol. Show them directly on the drawing (Figure 21.20f) or in a detail with a reference to it on the welding symbol, as shown in Figure 21.21e.

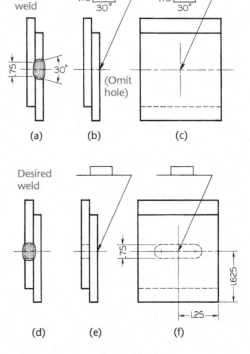

21.20   Plug and Slot Welds

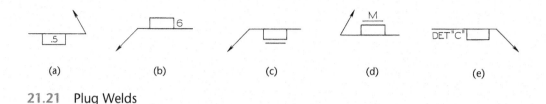

21.21   Plug Welds

21.9 SPOT WELDS

The spot weld symbol, with the required welding process indicated in the tail, may or may not have arrow-side or other-side significance. Show dimensions on the same side of the reference line as the symbol, or on either side when the symbol is centered on the reference line and no arrow-side or other-side significance is intended.

The size of a spot weld is its diameter. Show this value at the left of the weld symbol on either side of the reference line (Figure 21.22a). If you need to indicate the minimum acceptable shear strength in pounds per spot, instead of the size of the weld, place this value at the left of the weld symbol, and

indicate pitch at the right of the weld symbol, as shown in Figure 21.22b. In this case the spot welds are 3″ apart.

If a joint requires a certain number of spot welds, give the number in parentheses above or below the symbol, as in Figure 21.22c. If the exposed surface of one member is to be flush, add the flush-contour symbol above the symbol if it is the other-side member, and below it if it is the arrow-side member, as in Figure 21.22d. Figure 21.22e shows the welding symbol used in conjunction with ordinary dimensions.

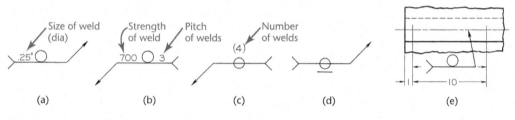

21.22   Spot Welds

21.10 SEAM WELDS

The seam weld symbol, with the welding process indicated in the tail, may or may not have arrow-side or other-side significance. Dimensions are shown on the same side of the reference line as the symbol, or on either side when the symbol is centered on the reference line and no arrow-side or other-side significance is intended.

The size of the seam weld is its width. Show this value at the left of the weld symbol, on either side of the reference line (Figure 21.23a). If you need to indicate the minimum acceptable shear strength in pounds per linear inch, instead of the size of the weld, place this value at the left of the weld symbol, and show the length of a seam weld at the right of the weld symbol,

as in Figure 21.23b. In this case, the seam weld is 5″ long. If the weld extends the full distance between abrupt changes of direction, no length dimension in the symbol is given.

The pitch of intermittent seam welding is the distance between centers of lengths of welding. Show the pitch at the right of the length value (Figure 21.23c). In this case, the welds are 2″ long and spaced 4″ center to center.

When the exposed surface of one member is to be flush, add the flush-contour symbol above the symbol if it is the other-side member and below it if it is the arrow-side member (Figure 21.23d). Figure 21.23e shows the welding symbol used in conjunction with ordinary dimensions.

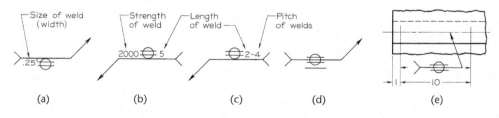

21.23   Seam Welds

21.11 PROJECTION WELDS

In projection welding, one member is embossed in preparation for the weld (Figure 21.24a). When welded, the joint appears in section, as in Figure 21.24b. In this case, the weld symbols are placed below the reference lines (Figure 21.24c) to indicate that the arrow-side member is the one that is embossed. The weld symbols would be placed above the lines if the other member were embossed.

Projection welds are dimensioned by either size or strength. The size is the diameter of the weld. This value is shown to the left of the weld symbol (Figure 21.24d). If you need to indicate the minimum acceptable shear strength in pounds per weld, place the value at the left of the weld symbol (Figure 21.24e). Indicate the pitch at the right of the weld symbol (Figure 21.24e). In this case, the

welds are spaced 6″ (152 mm) apart. If the joint requires a definite number of welds, give the number in parentheses (Figure 21.24e). If the exposed surface of one member is to be flush, add the flush-contour symbol (Figure 21.24f). Figure 21.24g shows the welding symbol used in conjunction with ordinary dimensions. The welding process reference is required in the tail of the symbol.

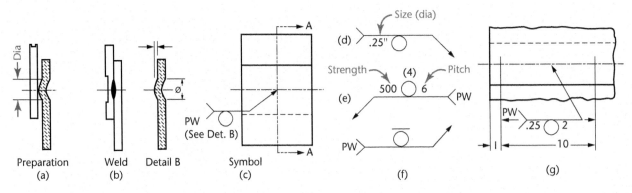

21.24   Projection Welds

21.12 FLASH AND UPSET WELDS

Flash and upset weld symbols have no arrow-side or other-side significance, but the supplementary symbols do. A flash-welded joint is shown in Figure 21.25a, and an upset-welded joint in Figure 21.25b. The joint after machining flush is shown in Figure 21.25c. The complete symbol (Figure 21.25d) includes the weld symbol together with the flush-contour and machining symbols.

If the joint is ground to smooth contours (Figure 21.25e), the resulting welding drawing and symbol would be constructed as in Figure 21.25f, which includes convex-contour and grind symbols. In either Figure 21.25d or f, the joint may be finished on only one side, if desired, by indicating the contour and machining symbols on the appropriate side of the reference line. The dimensions of flash and upset welds are not shown on the welding symbol. Note that the process reference for flash welding (FW) or upset welding (UW) must be placed in the tail of the symbol.

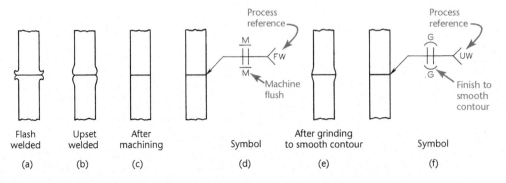

21.25   Flash and Upset Welds

21.13 WELDING APPLICATIONS

A typical example of welding fabrication for machine parts is shown in Figure 21.26. In many cases, especially when only one or a few identical parts are required, it is cheaper to produce by welding than to make patterns and sand castings and do the necessary machining. Thus, welding is particularly adaptable to custom-built constructions.

Welding is also suitable for large structures that are difficult or impossible to fabricate entirely in the shop, and it is coming into greater use for steel structures, such as building frames, bridges, and ships. A welded beam is shown in Figure 18.16, and a welded assembly of diagonal bracing between two columns is shown in Figure 18.17. A welded truss is shown in Figure 21.27. It is easier to place members in such a welded truss so that their center-of-gravity axes coincide with the working lines of the truss than is the case in a riveted truss. Compare this welded truss with the riveted truss in Figure 18.14.

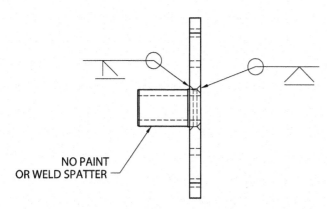

21.26 Application of Welding-Fabrication for Machine Parts
(Courtesy of Dynojet Research, Inc.)

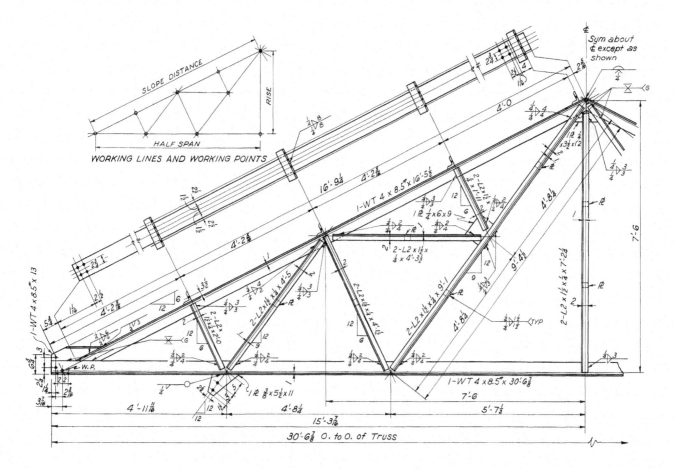

21.27 A Welded Truss

21.14 WELDING TEMPLATES

Welding templates can simplify drawing welding symbols by hand (which may be done in pencil or ink). They have all the forms needed for drawing the arrow, weld symbols, and supplementary symbols, as well as an illustration of the complete composite welding symbol for quick reference.

21.15 COMPUTER GRAPHICS

Welding symbol libraries available in CAD (Figure 21.29) allow for rapid application of accurate, uniform symbols that are in compliance with AWS standards (Figure 21.28). In addition to standard symbols, many CAD programs permit the operator to create custom symbols as required.

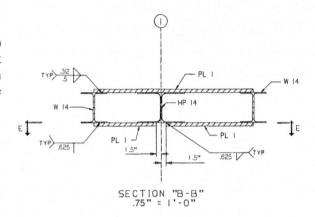

SECTION "B-B"
.75" = 1'-0"

21.28   CAD-Generated Welded Structural Detail

BASIC WELDING SYMBOLS AND THEIR LOCATION SIGNIFICANCE						
LOCATION SIGNIFICANCE	**FLANGE**	**GROOVE**				
	CORNER	SQUARE	V	BEVEL	U	J
ARROW SIDE						
OTHER SIDE						
BOTH SIDES	NOT USED					
NO ARROW SIDE OR OTHER SIDE SIGNIFICANCE	NOT USED		NOT USED	NOT USED	NOT USED	NOT USED

LOCATION SIGNIFICANCE	**GROOVE**		FILLET	PLUG OR SLOT	SPOT OR PROJECTION	SEAM
	FLARE-V	FLARE-BEVEL				
ARROW SIDE						
OTHER SIDE						
BOTH SIDES				NOT USED	NOT USED	NOT USED
NO ARROW SIDE OR OTHER SIDE SIGNIFICANCE	NOT USED	NOT USED	NOT USED	NOT USED		

LOCATION SIGNIFICANCE	**BACK OR BACKING**	**SURFACING**	**SCARF FOR BRAZED JOINT**	**FLANGE**	**SUPPLEMENTARY SYMBOLS**	
				EDGE		
ARROW SIDE	GROOVE WELD SYMBOL				ALL AROUND	ALL AROUND
OTHER SIDE	GROOVE WELD SYMBOL	NOT USED			FIELD	FIELD
BOTH SIDES	NOT USED	NOT USED		NOT USED	TAIL	
NO ARROW SIDE OR OTHER SIDE SIGNIFICANCE	NOT USED	NOT USED	NOT USED	NOT USED	TEXT	

21.29   Computervision Production Drafting Symbols

WELD SYMBOLS FROM CAD

Most CAD systems provide a way to quickly generate weld symbols to place in your drawing. The Autodesk Inventor dialog box shown in Figure A allows you to select the symbol for type and size of weld, field placement, whether to add the all-around symbol, and special indications for contour and finish method. Once you have made your selections, the weld symbol as shown in Figure B is automatically generated from them, and you have only to click to place the symbol in your drawing.

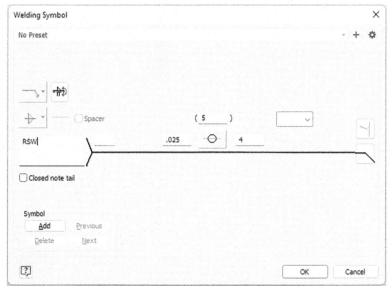

(A) Autodesk Inventor Weld Symbol Dialog Box *(Autodesk screen shots reprinted courtesy of Autodesk, Inc.)*

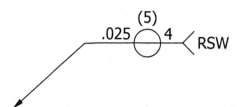

(B) Automatically Generated Weld Symbol *(Autodesk screen shots reprinted courtesy of Autodesk, Inc.)*

Specialized software such as Design Data's SDS/2 allows you to design and model connections between members based on parameters that you define for each job. You can designate the material, edge distance, cope criteria, and other connection specifications, and SDS/2 will automatically generate connections. You can model all the details, for example, the fillet welds shown in Figure C, using the software's 3D modeler. 2D drawings can be taken directly from the model, providing an accurate fit in the field.

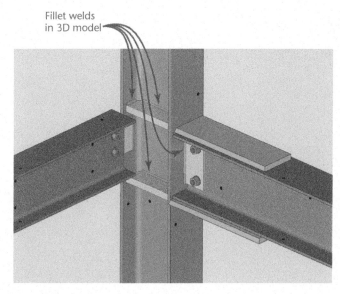

(C) Fillet Welds in a 3D Model *(Courtesy of Paul Hergett, Midwest Steel Industries.)*

PORTFOLIO

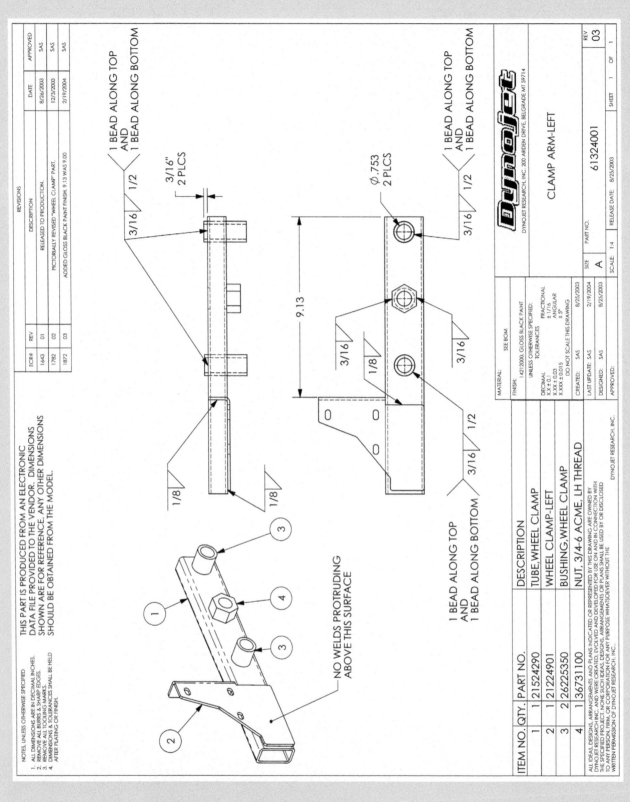

Welding symbols specify the welds for attaching the tube, bushings, nut, and plate for the clamp arm. (Courtesy of Dynojet Research, Inc.)

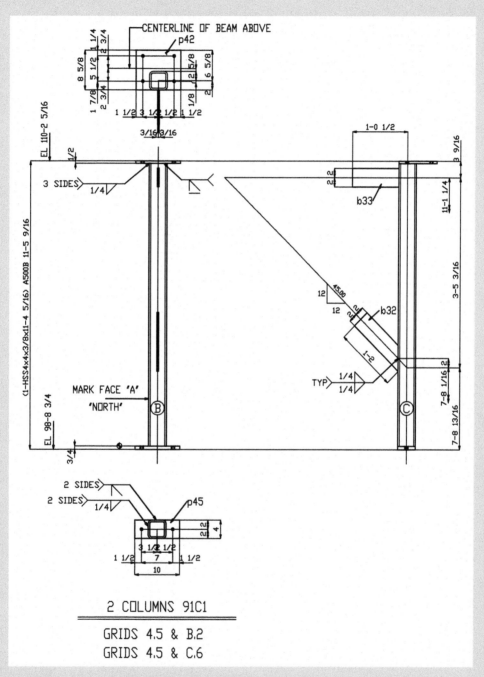

Welding symbols specify how plates attach to a structural beam in this drawing created from a 3D model using SDS/2 software. (Courtesy of Paul Hergett, Midwest Steel Industries.)

KEY WORDS

Arc Welding

Arrow Side

Back or Backing Weld

Butt Joint

Convex Contour

Corner Joint

Edge Joint

Fillet Weld

Flash or Upset Weld

Flush

Gas Welding

GMAW

Groove Weld

GTAW

Lap Joint

MAG

MIG

Other Side

Pitch

Plug or Slot Weld

Projection Weld

Resistance Welding

Seam Weld

Spot Weld

TIG

T-Joint

Welding Drawings

CHAPTER SUMMARY

- The four basic types of arc and gas welds are back, fillet, plug, and groove.
- The four basic types of resistance welds are spot, projection, seam, and flash.
- The welding symbol defines the location of the weld, the type of weld, and the welding process.
- Groove welds are classified as square, V, bevel, U, and J.
- A weld symbol below the leader line indicates that the weld is on the same side of the joint as the leader arrow.

REVIEW QUESTIONS

1. Which indicates the weld is on the opposite side: the weld type shown above the line, or below the line?
2. Draw the shapes for the following weld symbols: fillet, square, bevel, V, U, J.
3. List five names describing the ways the material can be oriented in forming a joint.
4. List the five types of groove welds.
5. Draw a typical welding symbol and label its parts.
6. Which type of weld would join two pieces at 90°?
7. What is a field weld?

CHAPTER EXERCISES

The following problems are given to familiarize you with some applications of welding symbols to machine construction and to steel structures.

For Exercises 21.1–21.21 Change to a welded part. Make working drawings, using appropriate welding symbols.

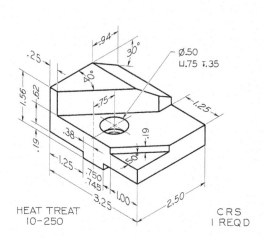

Exercise 21.1

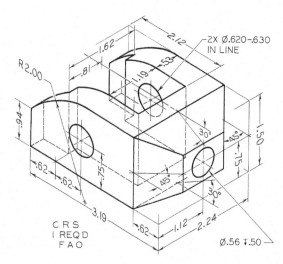

Exercise 21.2

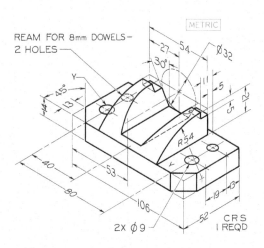

Exercise 21.3

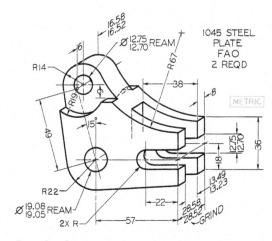

Exercise 21.4

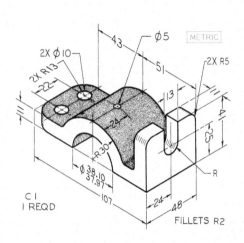

Exercise 21.5

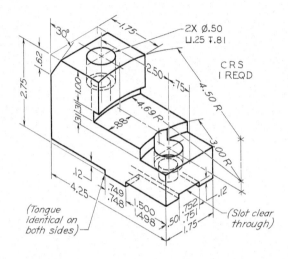

Exercise 21.6

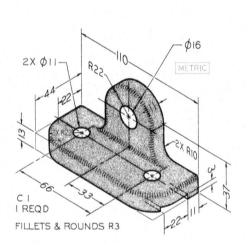

Exercise 21.7

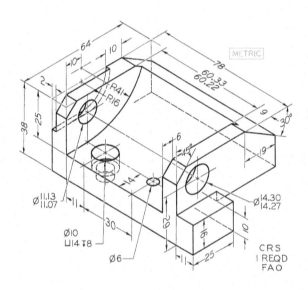

Exercise 21.8

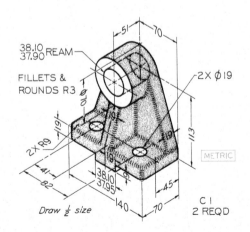

Exercise 21.9

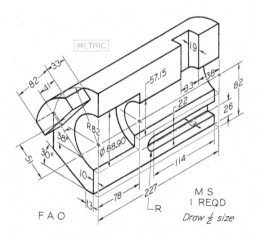

Exercise 21.10

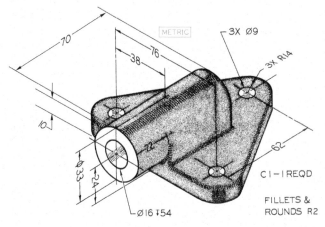

Exercise 21.11

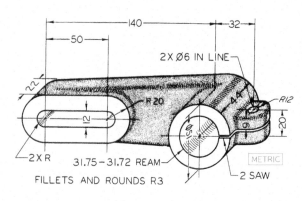

Exercise 21.12

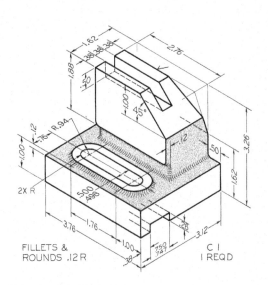

Exercise 21.13

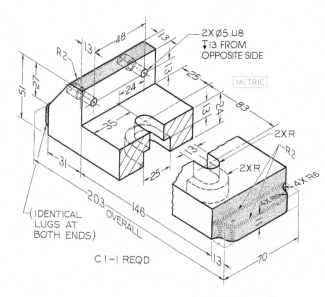

Exercise 21.14

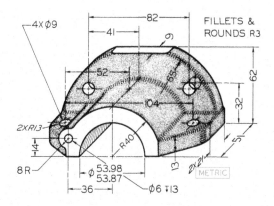

Exercise 21.15

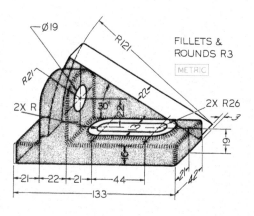

Exercise 21.16

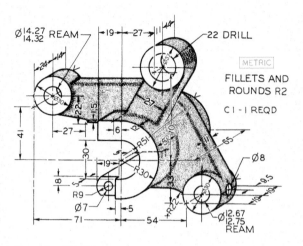

Exercise 21.17

METRIC

FILLETS AND
ROUNDS R2

C1 - 1 REQD

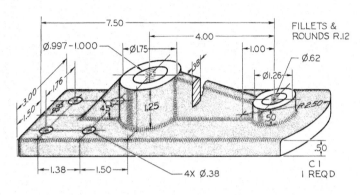

Exercise 21.18

FILLETS &
ROUNDS R.12

C1
1 REQD

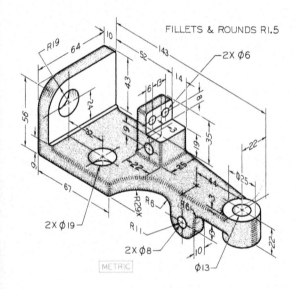

FILLETS & ROUNDS R1.5

Exercise 21.19

METRIC

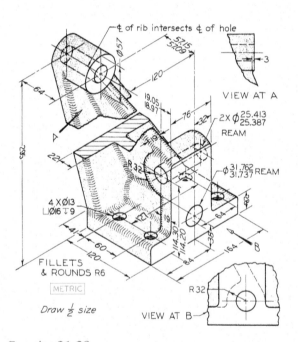

Exercise 21.20

Draw ½ size

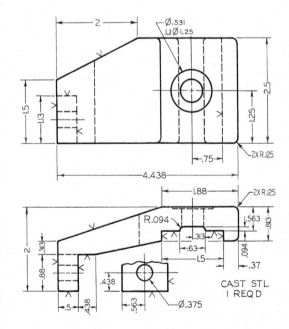

CAST STL
1 REQD

Exercise 21.21

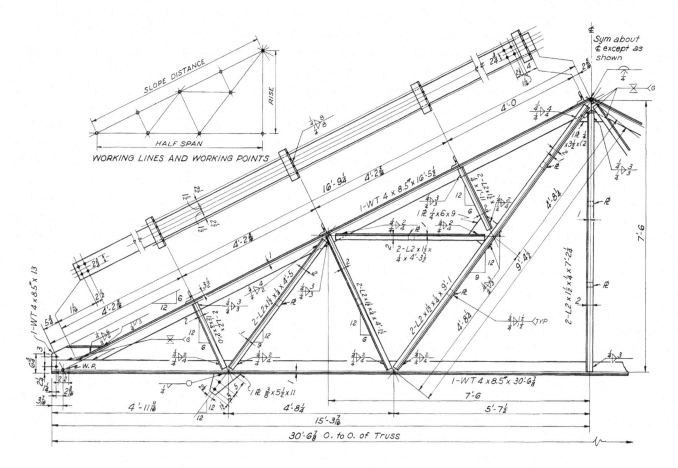

Roof Truss Exercises

For Exercises 21.22–21.24 refer to the Roof Truss drawing shown.

Exercise 21.22 Make a half-size drawing of the joint at the center of the lower chord of the truss where the chord is supported by two vertical angles. The chord is a structural tee, cut from an, 8″ × 5–1/4″, 17 lb, wide flange shape. Draw the front and side views, and show the working lines, the two angles, the structural tee, and all welding symbols.

Exercise 21.23 Make a half-size front view, showing the welding symbols, of any joint of the roof truss in which three or four members meet.

Exercise 21.24 Draw half-size front, top, and left-side views of the end joint of the truss in showing the welding symbols.

GLOSSARY

"The beginning of wisdom is to call things by their right names."

—CHINESE PROVERB

n means *noun*; *v* means *verb*

acme (n)   Screw thread form.

addendum (n)   Radial distance from pitch circle to top of gear tooth.

allen screw (n)   Special set screw or cap screw with hexagon socket in head.

allowance (n)   Minimum clearance between mating parts.

alloy (n)   Two or more metals in combination, usually a fine metal with a baser metal.

aluminum (n)   A lightweight but relatively strong metal. Often alloyed with copper to increase hardness and strength.

anneal (v)   To heat and cool gradually, to reduce brittleness and increase ductility.

arc weld (v)   To weld by electric arc. The work is usually the positive terminal.

babbitt (n)   A soft alloy for bearings, mostly of tin with small amounts of copper and antimony.

bearing (n)   A supporting member for a rotating shaft.

bevel (n)   An inclined edge, not at a right angle to the joining surface.

bolt circle (n)   A circular centerline on a drawing, containing the centers of holes about a common center.

bore (v)   To enlarge a hole with a boring mill.

boss (n)   A cylindrical projection on a casting or a forging.

BOSS

brass (n)   An alloy of copper and zinc.

braze (v)   To join with a hard solder of brass or zinc.

Brinell (n)   A method of testing hardness of metal.

broach (n)   A long cutting tool with a series of teeth that gradually increase in size that is forced through a hole or over a surface to produce a desired shape.

bronze (n)   An alloy of eight or nine parts copper and one part tin.

buff (v)   To finish or polish on a buffing wheel composed of fabric with abrasive powders.

burnish (v)   To finish or polish by pressure on a smooth rolling or sliding tool.

burr (n)   A jagged edge on metal resulting from punching or cutting.

bushing (n)   A replaceable lining or sleeve for a bearing.

calipers (n)   Instrument (of several types) for measuring diameters.

cam (n)   A rotating member for changing circular motion to reciprocating motion.

carburize (v)   To heat a low-carbon steel to approximately 2000 °F in contact with material that adds carbon to the surface of the steel, and to cool slowly in preparation for heat treatment.

case-harden (v)   To harden the outer surface of a carburized steel by heating and then quenching.

castellate (v)   To form like a castle, as a castellated shaft or nut.

casting (n)   A metal object produced by pouring molten metal into a mold.

cast iron (n)   Iron melted and poured into molds.

center drill (n)   A special drill to produce bearing holes in the ends of a workpiece to be mounted between centers. Also called a "combined drill and countersink."

COMBINED DRILL
& C SINK

chamfer (n)   A narrow inclined surface along the intersection of two surfaces.

CHAMFER

chase (v)   To cut threads with an external cutting tool.

chill (v)   To harden the outer surface of cast iron by quick cooling, as in a metal mold.

chip (v)   To cut away metal with a cold chisel.

chuck (n)   A mechanism for holding a rotating tool or workpiece.

coin (v)   To form a part in one stamping operation.

cold rolled steel (CRS) (n)   Open-hearth or Bessemer steel containing 0.12–0.20% carbon that has been rolled while cold to produce a smooth, quite accurate stock.

collar (n)   A round flange or ring fitted on a shaft to prevent sliding.

COLLAR

color-harden (v)   Same as *case-harden*, except that it is done to a shallower depth, usually for appearance only.

cotter pin (n)   A split pin used as a fastener, usually to prevent a nut from unscrewing.

counterbore (v)   To enlarge an end of a hole cylindrically with a counterbore.

COUNTERBORE

countersink (v)   To enlarge an end of a hole conically, usually with a countersink.

COUNTERSINK

crown (n)   A raised contour, as on the surface of a pulley.

cyanide (v)   To surface-harden steel by heating in contact with a cyanide salt, followed by quenching.

dedendum (n)   Distance from the pitch circle to the bottom of the tooth space.

development (n)   Drawing of the surface of an object unfolded or rolled out on a plane.

diametral pitch (n)   Number of gear teeth per inch of pitch diameter.

die (n)   (1) Hardened metal piece shaped to cut or form a required shape in a sheet of metal by pressing it against a mating die; (2) also used for cutting small male threads. In a sense, a die is the opposite of a tap.

die casting (n)   Process of forcing molten metal under pressure into metal dies or molds, producing a very accurate and smooth casting.

die stamping (n)   Process of cutting or forming a piece of sheet metal with a die.

dog (n)   A small auxiliary clamp for preventing work from rotating in relation to the face plate of a lathe.

dowel (n)   A cylindrical pin, commonly used to prevent sliding between two contacting flat surfaces.

DOWEL

draft (n)   The tapered shape of the parts of a pattern to permit it to be easily withdrawn from the sand or, on a forging, to permit it to be easily withdrawn from the dies.

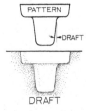

PATTERN
DRAFT
DRAFT

draw (v)   To stretch or otherwise to deform metal. Also to temper steel.

drill (v)   To cut a cylindrical hole with a drill. A *blind hole* does not go through the piece.

drill press (n)   A machine for drilling and other hole forming operations.

drop forge (v)   To form a piece while hot between dies in a drop hammer or with great pressure.

face (v)   To finish a surface at right angles, or nearly so, to the centerline of rotation on a lathe.

(FAO) (v)   An instruction on a drawing to employ the desired surface finish on all surfaces.

feather (key) (n)   A flat key, which is partly sunk in a shaft and partly in a hub, permitting the hub to slide lengthwise of the shaft.

file (v)   To finish or smooth with a file.

fillet (n)   An interior rounded intersection between two surfaces.

fin (n)   A thin extrusion of metal at the intersection of dies or sand molds.

fit (n)   Degree of tightness or looseness between two mating parts, as a *loose fit*, a *snug fit*, or a *tight fit*.

fixture (n)   A special device for holding the work in a machine tool, but not for guiding the cutting tool. Compare with *jig*.

flange (n)   A relatively thin rim around a piece.

FLANGE

flash (n)   Same as *fin*.

flask (n)   A box made of two or more parts for holding the sand in sand molding.

flute (n)   Groove, as on twist drills, reamers, and taps.

forge (v)   To force metal while it is hot to take on a desired shape by hammering or pressing.

galvanize (v)   To cover a surface with a thin layer of molten alloy, composed mainly of zinc, to prevent rusting.

gasket (n)   A thin piece of rubber, metal, or some other material, placed between surfaces to make a tight joint.

gate (n)   The opening in a sand mold at the bottom of the sprue through which the molten metal passes to enter the cavity or mold.

graduate (v)   To set off accurate divisions on a scale or dial.

grind (v)   To remove metal by means of an abrasive wheel, often made of carborundum. Use chiefly where accuracy is required.

harden (v)   To heat steel above a critical temperature and then quench in water or oil.

heat-treat (v)   To change the properties of metals by heating and then cooling.

interchangeable (adj.)   Refers to a part made to limit dimensions so that it will fit any mating part similarly manufactured.

jig (n)   A device for guiding a tool in cutting a piece. Usually it holds the work in position. Compare with *fixture*.

journal (n)   Portion of a rotating shaft supported by a bearing.

kerf (n)   Groove or cut made by a saw.

KERF

key (n)   A small piece of metal sunk partly into both shaft and hub to prevent rotation.

keyseat (n)   A slot or recess in a shaft to hold a key.

KEYSEAT

keyway (n)   A slot in a hub or portion surrounding a shaft to receive a key.

KEYWAY

knurl (v)   To impress a pattern of dents in a turned surface with a knurling tool to produce a better hand grip.

lap (v)   To produce a very accurate finish by sliding contact with a *lap*, or piece of wood, leather, or soft metal impregnated with abrasive powder.

lathe (n)   A machine used to shape metal or other materials by rotating against a tool.

lug (n)   An irregular projection of metal, but not round as in the case of a boss, usually with a hole in it for a bolt or screw.

malleable casting (n)   A casting that has been made less brittle and tougher by annealing.

mill (v)   To remove material by means of a rotating cutter on a milling machine.

mold (n)   The mass of sand or other material that forms the cavity into which molten metal is poured.

MS (n)   Machinery steel, sometimes called mild steel, with a small percentage of carbon; cannot be hardened.

neck (v)   To cut a groove called a *neck* around a cylindrical piece.

NECK

normalize (v)   To heat steel above its critical temperature and then to cool it in air.

pack-harden (v)   To *carburize*, then to *case-harden*.

pad (n)   A slight projection, usually to provide a bearing surface around one or more holes.

PAD

pattern (n)   A model, usually of wood, used in forming a mold for a casting. In sheet metal work a pattern is called a *development*.

peen (v)   To hammer into shape with a ballpeen hammer.

pickle (v)   To clean forgings or castings in dilute sulfuric acid.

pinion (n)   The smaller of two mating gears.

pitch circle (n)   An imaginary circle corresponding to the circumference of the friction gear from which the spur gear was derived.

plane (v)   To remove material by means of a planer.

planish (v)   To impart a planished surface to sheet metal by hammering with a smooth-surfaced hammer.

plate (v)   To coat a metal piece with another metal, such as chrome or nickel, by electrochemical methods.

polish (v)   To produce a highly finished or polished surface by friction, using a very fine abrasive.

profile (v)   To cut any desired outline by moving a small rotating cutter, usually with a master template as a guide.

punch (v)   To cut an opening of a desired shape with a rigid tool having the same shape, by pressing the tool through the work.

quench (v)   To immerse a heated piece of metal in water or oil to harden it.

rack (n)   A flat bar with gear teeth in a straight line to engage with teeth in a gear.

ream (v)   To enlarge a finished hole slightly to give it greater accuracy, with a *reamer*.

relief (n)   An offset of surfaces to provide clearance for machining.

RELIEF

rib (n)   A relatively thin flat member acting as a brace or support.

RIB

rivet (v)   To connect with rivets or to clench over the end of a pin by hammering.

round (n)   An exterior rounded intersection of two surfaces.

SAE   Society of Automotive Engineers.

sandblast (v)   To blow sand at high velocity with compressed air against castings or forgings to clean them.

scleroscope (n)   An instrument for measuring hardness of metals.

scrape (v)   To remove metal by scraping with a hand scraper, usually to fit a bearing.

shape (v)   To remove metal from a piece with a *shaper*.

shear (v)   To cut metal by means of shearing with two blades in sliding contact.

sherardize (v)   To galvanize a piece with a coating of zinc by heating it in a drum with zinc powder, to a temperature of 575 °F–850 °F.

shim (n)   A thin piece of metal or other material used as a spacer in adjusting two parts.

solder (v)   To join with solder, usually composed of lead and tin.

spin (v)   To form a rotating piece of sheet metal into a desired shape by pressing it with a smooth tool against a rotating form.

spline (n)   A keyway, usually one of a series cut around a shaft or hole.

SPLINED HOLE

spotface (v)   To produce a round spot or bearing surface around a hole, usually with a spotfacer. The spotface may be on top of a boss or it may be sunk into the surface.

SPOTFACE

sprue (n)   A hole in the sand leading to the gate, which leads to the mold, through which the metal enters.

steel casting (n)   Like cast iron casting except that in the furnace scrap steel has been added to the casting.

swage (v)   To hammer metal into shape while it is held over a *swage*, or die, which fits in a hole in the *swage block*, or anvil.

sweat (v)   To fasten metal together by the use of solder between the pieces and by the application of heat and pressure.

tap (v)   To cut relatively small internal threads with a *tap*.

taper (n)   Conical form given to a shaft or a hole. Also refers to the slope of a plane surface.

taper pin (n)   A small tapered pin for fastening, usually to prevent a collar or hub from rotating on a shaft.

TAPER PIN

taper reamer (n)   A tapered reamer for producing accurate tapered holes, as for a taper pin.

temper (v)   To reheat hardened steel to bring it to a desired degree of hardness.

template or templet (n)   A guide or pattern used to mark out the work, guide the tool in cutting it, or check the finished product.

tin (n)   A silvery metal used in alloys and for coating other metals, such as tin plate.

tolerance (n)   Total amount of variation permitted in limit dimension of a part.

trepan (v)   To cut a circular groove in the flat surface at one end of a hole.

tumble (v)   To clean rough castings or forgings in a revolving drum filled with scrap metal.

turn (v)   To produce, on a lathe, a cylindrical surface parallel to the centerline.

twist drill (n)   A drill for use in a drill press.

undercut (n)   A recessed cut or a cut with inwardly sloping sides.

UNDERCUT

upset (v)   To form a head or enlarged end on a bar or rod by pressure or by hammering between dies.

web (n)   A thin flat part joining larger parts. Also known as a *rib*.

weld (v)   Uniting metal pieces by pressure or fusion welding processes.

Woodruff (key) (n)   A semicircular flat key.

WOODRUFF KEYS

wrought iron (n)   Iron of low carbon content useful because of its toughness, ductility, and malleability.

APPENDICES

CONTENTS

1 LIST OF STANDARDS ORGANIZATIONS

American National Standards Institute, 25 West 43rd St., New York, NY, 10036. For complete listing of standards, see the ANSI catalog of American National Standards, or visit www.ansi.org.

Standards from the following developers are available at webstore.ansi.org.

AA	Aluminum Association
AAMI	Association for the Advancement of Medical Instrumentation
AARST	American Association of Radon Scientists and Technologists
ABMA	American Bearing Manufacturers Association
ABMA	American Brush Manufacturers Association
ABYC	American Boat & Yacht Council
ACC	American Chemistry Council
ADA	American Dental Association
AGA	American Gas Association
AGMA	American Gear Manufacturers Association
AGRSS	Automotive Glass Replacement Safety Standards
AHAM	Association of Home Appliance Manufacturers
AHRI	Air-Conditioning, Heating, and Refrigeration Institute
AIAA	American Institute of Aeronautics and Astronautics
AIAG	Automotive Industry Action Group
AIHA	American Industrial Hygiene Association
AIIM	Association for Information and Image Management
ALI	American Ladder Institute
AMCA	Air Movement and Control Association International, Inc.
ANS	American Nuclear Society
AORN	Association of periOperative Registered Nurses
APSP	Association of Pool and Spa Professionals
APT	Association for Print Technologies
APTA	American Public Transportation Association
ARMA	ARMA International
AS+	Austrian Standards Institute
ASA	Acoustical Society of America
ASABE	American Society of Agricultural and Biological Engineers
ASCA	Accredited Snow Contractors Association
ASCE	American Society of Civil Engineers

ASHRAE	American Society of Heating, Refrigerating and Air-Conditioning Engineers, Inc.
ASIS	ASIS International
ASME	American Society of Mechanical Engineers
ASQ	American Society for Quality
ASSE	The American Society of Sanitary Engineering
ASSP	The American Society of Safety Professionals
ASTM	ASTM International
ATCC	American Type Culture Collection
ATIS	Alliance for Telecommunications Industry Solutions, Inc.
AVIXA	Audiovisual and Integrated Experience Association
AWS	American Welding Society
AWWA	American Water Works Association
B11	B11 Standards, Inc.
BHMA	Builders Hardware Manufacturers Association
BOMA	Building Owners and Managers Association International
BSI	British Standards Institution
CEMA	Conveyor Equipment Manufacturers Association
CGA	Compressed Gas Association, Inc.
CITRA	Center for International Regulatory Assistance
CLSI	Clinical and Laboratory Standards Institute
CSA	Canadian Standards Association
CTA	Consumer Technology Association
DS	Danish Standards
DIN	German Institute for Standardization
DOD	U.S. Department of Defense
EIMA	EIFS Industry Members Association
ESDA	Electrostatic Discharge Association
ESTA	Entertainment Services and Technology Association
ETSI	European Telecommunications Standards Institute
GISC	Glazing Industry Secretariat Committee
GTEEMC	Georgia Tech Energy and Environmental Management Center
HFES	Human Factors and Ergonomics Society
HI	Hydraulic Institute
HL7	Health Level Seven
IACET	International Association for Continuing Education and Training

IAPMO	International Association of Plumbing and Mechanical Officials
ICBO	International Conference of Building Officials
ICC	International Code Council
IEC	International Electrotechnical Commission
IEEE	Institute of Electrical and Electronics Engineers
IES	Illuminating Engineering Society
IESO	Indoor Environmental Standards Organization
IEST	Institute of Environmental Sciences and Technology
IFI	Industrial Fasteners Institute
IICRC	Institute of Inspection, Cleaning and Restoration Certification
IKECA	International Kitchen Exhaust Cleaning Association
ILTVA	International Light Transportation Vehicle Association, Inc.
INCITS	Information Technology Industry Council
IPC	Association Connecting Electronics Industries
ISA	International Society of Automation
ISEA	International Safety Equipment Association
ISO	International Organization for Standardization
IS&T	Society for Imaging Science and Technology
ISTA	International Safe Transit Association
ITSDF	Industrial Truck Standards Development Foundation
JIS	Japanese Industrial Standards
LIA	Laser Institute of America
MHI	Material Handling Industry of America
MSS	Manufacturers Standardization Society of the Valve and Fittings Industry, Inc.
MTS	Institute for Market Transformation to Sustainability
NACE	National Association of Corrosion Engineers
NAESB	North American Energy Standards Board
NASPO	North American Security Products Organization
NECA	National Electrical Contractors Association
NEMA	National Electrical Manufacturers Association
NETA	International Electrical Testing Association
NFPA	National Fire Protection Association
NFPA	National Fluid Power Association
NIRMA	Nuclear Information and Records Management Association
NISO	National Information Standards Organization
NIST	National Institute of Standards and Technology
NPPC	National Pork Producers Council
NSAA	National Ski Areas Association
NSF	NSF International
NW&RA	National Waste & Recycling Association
OASIS	Advancing Open Standards for the Information Society
OEOSC	Committee for Optics and Electro-Optical Instruments
OPEI	Outdoor Power Equipment Institute
PCPC	Personal Care Products Council
PDA	Parenteral Drug Association
PLASTICS	The Plastics Industry Association
PMI	Project Management Institute
PMMI	Association for Packaging and Processing Technologies
PSAI	Portable Sanitation Association International
PSDA	Print Services and Distribution Association
RESNA	Rehabilitation Engineering and Assistive Technology Society of North America
RIA	Robotic Industries Association
SAE	SAE International
SAI	Standards Australia
SCTE	Society of Cable Telecommunications Engineers
SES	Society for Standards Professionals
SAIA	Scaffold & Access Industry Association
SIA	Security Industry Association
SIS	Swedish Standards Institute
SMACNA	Sheet Metal and Air Conditioning Contractors' National Association
SPC	Standards Press of China
TAPPI	Technical Association for the Pulp, Paper, and Converting Industry
TCATA	Textile Care Allied Trades Association
TCNA	Tile Council of North America
TIA	Toy Industry Association
UL	Underwriters Laboratories Inc.
VC	Vision Council
WCMA	Window Covering Manufacturers Association
WMMA	Wood Machinery Manufacturers Association
WPC	Washington Publishing Company
X9	Accredited Standards Committee X9, Inc.

2 ABBREVIATIONS FOR USE ON DRAWINGS AND IN TEXT—AMERICAN NATIONAL STANDARD

Selected abbreviations reprinted from ANSI/ASME Y14.38–2007, by permission of the American Society of Mechanical Engineers. All rights reserved.

A

abbreviation	ABBR	aeronautic	AERO	aluminum	AL
about	ABT	aeronautical national taper pipe thread	ANPT	aluminum conductor steel reinforced	ACRS
above	ABV	after	AFT	amalgam	AMLG
above baseline	ABL	aggregate	AGGR	ambient	AMB
abrasive	ABRSV	aileron	AIL	amendment	AMEND
absolute	ABS	air blast circuit breaker	ABCB	American	AMER
absorption	ABSORB	air circuit breaker	ACB	American Gage Design Standard	AGDS
accelerate	ACCEL	air cleaner	AIRCLNR	American Standard Code for Information Interchange	ASCII
accelerator	ACLTR	air condition	AIRCOND	American Standard Elevator Code	ASEC
accelerometer	ACCLRM	air cooled	ACLD	American Steel Wire Group	ASWG
acceptor	ACPTR	air escape	AE	American Wire Gage	AWG
access	ACS	air header	AHDR	ammeter	AMM
access opening	AO	air scoop	AS	ammonia	AMNA
access panel	AP	air shutoff	ASHOF	ammonium nitrate	AMNIT
accessory	ACCESS	air shutter	AIRSHTR	amount	AMT
account	ACCT	air starting	ASTRG	ampere	AMP
accumulate	ACCUM	air-break switch	ABSW	ampere hour	AMPHR
accumulator	ACC	aircraft	ACFT	ampere hour meter	AHM
acetate	ACTT	airframe	AFR	amplifier	AMPL
acetylene	ACET	airport	APRT	amplitude	AMPTD
acoustic	ACST	airtight	AT	amplitude modulation	AM
acoustical tile ceiling	ATC	alarm	ALM	analog	ANLG
across	ACR	alarm check valve	ACV	analog to digital	AD
across flats	ACRFLT	alclad	ALCD	analog to digital converter	ADC
acrylic	ACRYL	alcohol	ALC	analysis	ANAL
actual	ACTL	alignment	ALIGN	analyze	ANALY
actuate	ACTE	alkaline	ALK	anchor	ANC
actuating	ACTG	alkalinity	ALKY	anchor bolt	AB
actuator	ACTR	all terrain vehicle	ATV	anechoic	ANCH
adapter	ADPTR	allocate	ALLOC	angle order	ANLOR
addendum	ADD	allowance	ALLOW	angle stop valve	ASV
additional	ADDL	alloy	ALY	angular	ANLR
additive	ADDT	alloy steel protective plating	ASPP	anhydrous	ANHYD
address	ADRS	alphabetical	ALPHA	anneal	ANL
adhesive	ADH	alteration	ALTRN	announcing	ANCG
adjacent	ADJ	altered	ALTRD	annunciator	ANN
adjustable speed	ADJSP	alternate	ALTN	anode	A
administer	ADMIN	alternating current	AC	anodize	ANDZ
adsorbent	ADSORB	alternation	ALT	answer	ANS
advance	ADV	alternative	ALTNV		
advisory	ADVSY	alternator	ALTNTR		
aerodynamic	AERODYN	altimeter	ALTM		

antenna	ANT	asphalt	ASPH	auxiliary register	AUXR
antifriction bearing	AFB	asphalt plank floor	ASPHPF	auxiliary switch	ASW
antifriction metal	AFM	asphalt roof shingles	ASPHRS	auxiliary switch (breaker) normally closed	ASC
antilogarithm	ANTILOG	asphalt tile base	ATB		
apartment	APT	aspirator	ASPRTR	auxiliary switch (breaker) normally open	ASO
aperture	APERT	assemble	ASSEM		
apparatus	APPAR	assembly	ASM	availability	AVLBL
apparent	APRNT	assembly	ASSY	available	AVAIL
appearance	APP	assign	ASGN	avenue	AVE
appendix	APPX	assignment	ASGMT	average	AVG
application	APPL	assistance	ASSTN	average diameter	AVGDIA
applied	APLD	assistant	ASST	aviation	AVN
applique	APLQ	associate	ASSOC	avoirdupois	AVDP
approach	APRCH	association	ASSN	awning	AWN
approval	APPVL	assorted	ASRT	axial flow	AXFL
approve	APPV	astronomical unit	AU	axial pitch	AXP
approved	APVD	asymmetric	ASYM	axial pressure angle	APA
approximate	APPROX	asymptote	ASYMP	azimuth	AZ
April	APR	at a later date	ALD	**B**	
aqueous	AQ	atomic hydrogen weld	ATW	babbitt	BAB
arbitrary	ARB	atomic weight	ATWT	backview	BV
arc weld	ARCW	atomizing	ATMG	backwater valve	BWV
arccosecant	ARCCSE	attach	ATCH	baffle	BAF
arccosine	ARCCOS	attack	ATCK	baggage	BAG
arccotangent	ARCCOT	attention	ATTN	balance	BAL
architectural projected window	APW	attenuation	ATTEN	balanced line driver	BLD
		attitude	ATTD	balanced voltage	BALV
archive	ARCH	audible	AUD	balancing coil	BALCL
arcing	ARNG	audio frequency	AF	balancing rheostat	BALRHEO
arcsecant	ARCSEC	auditor	AUDTR	balancing set	BALS
arcsine	ARCSIN	augment	AGMT	ball stop	BSP
arctangent	ARCTAN	August	AUG	ballast	BLST
arithmetic	ARITH	authorize	AUTH	band elimination	BDELIM
arithmetic average	AA	automatic check valve	AUTOCV	band filter cutoff	BFCO
arithmetic logic unit	ALU	automatic phase control	APC	bandstop filter	BSFL
arithmetic unit	ARITHU			bandwidth	BW
armament	ARMT	automatic phase lock	APL	barred	BRRD
armature	ARM	automatic reclosing	AUTORECL	barrel tile roof	BTR
arrange	ARR	automatic starter	AUTOSTRT	barrier, waterproof	BWP
arrester	ARSR	automatic stop and check valve	AUTOSCV	base diameter	BDIA
arsine	ARS			base helix angle	BHA
article	ART	automatic transformer	AXFMR	base pitch	BP
articulated	ARTCLD	automatic volume control	AVC	basement	BSMT
artificial	ARTF	automatic zero set	AZS	basic	BSC
artillery	ARTY	automation	AUTOMN	basket	BSKT
as required	AR	automobile	AUTO	battery	BTRY
as soon as possible	ASAP	automotive	AUTOM	bearing	BRG
asbestos	ASB	auxiliary	AUX	before	BFR
asbestos covered metal	ACM	auxiliary power unit	APU	bell crank	BELCRK

belling	BLNG	blowtorch	BLWT	building	BLDG
bellmouth	BLMTH	blue	BLU	built in	BLTIN
bellows	BLWS	blue indicating light	BIL	bulkhead	BHD
below	BLW	blue tool steel	BTS	bulldozer	BDZR
bench	BNCH	board	BD	bulletin	BULL
benchmark	BM	bobbin	BOB	bulletproof	BPRF
bend down	BDN	body on chassis	BOC	bullnose	BN
bend radius	BR	boiler	BLR	bundle	BDL
bend up	BUP	boiler feed water	BFW	buoyant	BYNT
bending	BNG	boiler pressure	BOPRESS	burlap	BRLP
bent	BT	boiling	BOG	burner	BNR
berth	BTH	bolster	BOLS	burning	BRNG
Bessemer	BESS	bolted on base	BOBS	burnish	BNSH
between	BETW	bonded	BND	burster	BRSTR
bevel	BEV	bonding	BNDG	bus selector	BSLR
beveled wood siding	BWS	bonnet	BNT	bushel	BU
beverage	BVGE	booster	BSTR	bushing	BSHG
bidirectional	BIDIR	bootstrap	BTST	bushing potential device	BPD
billet steel	BLSTL	bottle	BTL	business	BUS
bimetallic	BMTLC	bottom	BOT	butane	BUTN
binary	BIN	bottoming	BOTMG	butt weld	BTWLD
binary digit	BIT	boundary	BDY	butterfly	BTFL
binary divide	BDV	bracket	BRKT	button	BTN
binder	BDR	braid	BRD	button head	BTNHD
binding	BDG	brake	BK	buzzer	BUZ
binding head	BDGH	brass	BRS	bypass	BYP
binocular	BNCLR	brass divider strip	BDS	C	
biological	BIOL	braze	BRZ	cable	CBL
biological electronics	BIONICS	brazier	BRAZ	cable television	CATV
biology	BIO	brazier head	BRAZH	cable termination equipment	CTE
biparting doors	BIPD	brazing	BRZG	calibration	CAL
bipost	BPT	break	BRK	cam timing contact	CTC
Birmingham Wire Gage	BWG	break jaw	BJ	camera control unit	CCU
bits per inch	BPI	breaker	BRKR	cannister	CSTR
bits per second	BPS	breaking	BRKG	capable	CPBL
bituminous	BITUM	bridge	BRDG	capacitance	CAP
black	BLK	bright	BRT	carbide steel	CS
black enamel slate	BES	brilliance	BRIL	carrier operated relay	COR
black iron	BI	Brinell hardness	BH	carrying	CRYG
black oil finish state	BOFS	Brinell hardness number	BHN	cartridge	CRTG
blacken	BLKN	British Standard	BSI	casing	CSG
blackening	BLKNG	British Standard Wire Gage	SWG	castellate	CSTL
blanket	BLKT	British thermal unit	BTU	casting	CSTG
blanking	BLKG	broach	BRCH	category	CAT
blanking die	BLKGD	broadband	BRDG	cathode ray oscilloscope	CRO
bleeder	BLDR	brown	BRN	cathode ray tube	CRT
blend	BLN	buckram	BUCK	caution	CAUT
blocking oscillator	BO	buffer amplifier	BA	Celsius	C
blower	BLO	buffing	BFG	center tap	CT

center to center	C to C	control shift register	CSR	deaerating	DEARTG
centerline	CL	control transmitter	CX	dealer	DLR
central processing equipment	CPE	controlled rectifier	CR	decelerate	DCLR
		convection	CONVN	decibel	DB
central processing unit	CPU	convector	CONVR	decimal	DEC
ceramic tile base	CTB	convergence	CONVG	decision	DECN
change in design	CID	corrosion	CRSN	declutch	DCLU
chrome vanadium	CRVAN	corrosive	CRSV	decode	DCD
chromium plate	CRPL	corrugated wire glass	CWG	decoder	DCDR
chronometer	CRNMTR	cosecant	CSC	decompression	DECOMPN
circuit switching unit	CSU	countersink	CSK	decontamination	DECONTN
circulating water pump	CWP	countersink other side	CSKO	decrease	DECR
coarse	CRS	countersunk head	CSKH	decrement	DECRT
coated	CTD	cradle	CRDL	dedendum	DED
coating	CTG	crankshaft	CSHAFT	deep drawn	DD
cold drawn copper	CDC	crash position indicator	CPI	defective	DEF
cold water	CW	crimp	CRP	deflating	DFL
color code	CC	cross bracing	XBRA	deflect	DEFL
combining	COMB	cross connection	XCO	defrost	DRF
commercial and government entity code	CAGE	cross connection	XCONN	degaussing	DEGUSG
		cross country	XCY	degree	DEG
commission	COMSN	cross point	XPT	dehydrator	DYHR
communication and data	C&D	cross section	XSECT	delay	DLY
communications satellite	COMSAT	crossarm	XARM	delete	DELE
compact disk	CD	crossbar	XBAR	delineation	DEL
comparator buffer	CB	crossbar tandem	XBT	delivery	DLVY
compatible single side band	CSSB	crosshair	XHAIR	deluxe	DLX
compiler	COMP	crossing	XING	demagnetize	DMGZ
compressor	COMPR	crosshead	CRSHD	demodulator	DEMOD
computer-aided design	CAD	crossover	CRSVR	demodulator band filter	DBF
computer-aided manufacturing	CAM	cruising	CRUIS	demolition	DML
concentric	CONC	cryogenics	CRYOG	denatured	DNTRD
concession	CON	cryptography	CRYPTO	denote	DEN
concrete splash block	CSB	crystal	XTAL	density	DENS
concurrent	CNCR	crystal oscillator	XTLO	dental	DNTL
condition	COND	crystalline	CRYST	department	DEPT
conference	CONF	cubic feet per minute	CFM	deposit	DEP
conical	CONL	cubic feet per second	CFS	depot installed	DEPINST
connection	CONN	curve	CRV	depression	DEPR
consecutive	CONSEC	cushing	CSHG	depth	D
console	CSL	cyanide	CYN	depth	DP
constant current transformer	CCT	cycle	CY	derivative	DERIV
constant output amplifier	COA	cylinder	CYL	derrick	DRK
constant speed drive	CSD			describe	DESCR
contact	CONT	**D**		description	DESCP
contact potential difference	CPD	damper	DMPR	desiccant	DSCC
continental horsepower	CONTHP	damping	DPG	design	DSGN
continued	CONTD	dated	DTD	design specification	DSPEC
control power switch	CSW	datum	DAT	designation	DES
control read only memory	CROM	daughterboard	DTRBD		

destination	DESTN	distill	DSTL	down	DN
destructive readout	DRO	distillate	DISTLT	downdraft	DNDFT
destructor	DESTR	distilled water	DW	dozen	DOZ
detached	DTCH	distinguish	DISTING	drafting	DFTG
detail	DET	distortion	DISTN	drafting machine	DFMACH
detent	DTT	distress	DTRS	draw bar pull	DBP
determination	DETN	distribution amplifier	DAMP	drawer	DWR
develop	DVL	distribution panel	DPNL	drawing	DWG
developed length	DEVLG	distributor	DISTR	drawing change notice	DCN
development	DEV	dither	DTER	drawn	DWN
deviation	DEVN	diver	DVR	dredger	DRGR
device	DVC	diverter	DIV	dressed (lumber)	DRS
dial indicating	DLINDG	do not use	DNU	dresser	DRSR
dial lock	DLOCK	docking	DCKG	dressing	DRSG
diameter bolt circle	DBC	document	DOC	drill	DR
diamond	DMD	does not apply	DNA	drill jig	DJ
diamond pyramid hardness	DPH	domestic	DOM	drive fit	DF
diazo print	DPR	door closer	DCL	drive unit	DRU
diesel	DSL	door stop	DST	driver	DRVR
diesel belt drive	DBD	door switch	DSW	drop manhole	DMH
diesel engine	DENG	Doppler velocity		drop wood siding	DWS
diesel mechanical	DM	and position	DOVAP	dry chemical	DCHEM
diesel oil	DO	dots per inch	DPI	dry pipe valve	DPV
diethanolamine	DEA	double	DBL	drying	DYG
differential thermocouple		double acting	DBLACT	dual speed drive	DSD
voltmeter	DTVM	double acting door	DAD	dull black finish slate	DBFS
digital analog converter	DAC	double based solid propellant	DBSP	dummy	DUM
digital block AND OR gate	DBAO	double end	DE	dumping	DMPG
digital to analog	DA	double extra strong	XXSTR	duplex	DX
digital voltmeter	DVM	double face	DBLF	damping	DPG
dimmer	DMR	double pole back connected	DPBC	duplexer	DPLXR
diode resistor transistor logic	DRTL	double pole double throw	DPDT	duplicate	DUP
diode transistor logic	DTL	double pole double throw		duty cycle	DTYCY
dipstick	DPSK	switch	DPDTSW	dwelling	DWEL
direct current	DC	double pole front connected	DPFC	dynamic	DYN
direct drive	DDR	double pole single throw	DPST	dynamometer	DYNMT
direct memory access	DMA	double pole single throw		dynamotor	DYNM
directly	DRCTY	switch	DPSTSW	**E**	
disable	DSBL	double pole switch	DPSW	each	EA
discontinue	DSCONT	double secondary current		each way	EW
discrete Fourier transform	DFT	transformer	DSCT	ebony asbestos	EBASB
discriminator	DSCRM	double side band	DSB	eccentric	ECC
disengaging	DSENGA	double sided	DS	economize	ECON
disk operating system	DOS	double single sideband	DSSB	edge thickness	ET
dispenser	DISP	double throw	DT	edgewise	EDGW
dispensing	DSPNSG	double wall	DBLW	education	EDUC
display	DSPL	double wall fiberboard	DWLFBD	effective	EFF
disposition	DISPN	doubler	DBLR	effective focal length	EFFL
distance	DIST	dovetail	DVTL	ejection	EJN
distance measuring equipment	DME	dowel	DWL		

ejector	EJCTR	emboss	EMB	exclusive	EXCL
elastic	ELAS	emergency power supply	EMPS	execute	EXEC
elbow	ELB	emission	EMSN	exercise	EXER
electric	ELEC	emitter	E	exhaust	EXH
electric contact	ELCTC	emitter	EMTR	exhaust gas temperature	EGT
electric contact ring	ELCTRG	emitter coupled logic	ECL	exhaust vent	EXHV
electric contact brush	ELCTCBR	empennage	EMP	existing	EXST
electric discharge tube	EDT	employee	EMPL	exit guide vane	EGV
electric dynamometer	EDYNMT	emulator	EMU	expand	EXP
electric motor driven	EMD	emulsion	EMUL	expanded binary coded decimal interchange	EBCDIC
electric water cooler	EWC	enable	ENBL	
electrical discharge machining	EDM	enamel	ENAM	expansion joint	EXPJT
		encapsulation	ENCAP	expedite	EXPED
electrical metallic tubing	EMT	enclose	ENCL	expendable	EXPEN
electrical resistance	ER	encode	ENCD	experimental testing	X
electrical specification	ESPEC	encoder	ENCDR	explanation	EXPL
electrical time, superquick	ETSQ	end cell switch	ECSW	explode	EXPLD
electrocardiogram	ECG	end half	EHF	explosion	EXPLN
electrode	ELCTD	end to end	EE	explosive	XPL
electrohydraulic	ELHYD	endless tangent screw	ETS	explotation	EXPLTN
electrolyte	ELCTLT	endstone	ESTN	exponent	EXPNT
electromagnetic	EM	engine drive	ED	exposure	EXPSR
electromechanical	ELMCH	engineering change notice	ECN	extender	EXTND
electromotive force	EMF	engineering change proposal	ECP	extension	EXT
electron	ELCTRN	engineering change request	ECR	extra	EX
electron coupled oscillator	ECO	engineering field change	EFC	extra fine	EF
electron type semiconductor material	N	engineering release notice	ERN	extra heavy	XHVY
		engineering support activity	ESA	extra long wheel base	XLWB
electronic control	ELECTC	engineering work order	EWO	extra strong	XSTR
electronic standard	ESTD	equivalent focal length	EQFL	extraordinary wave	XWAVE
electronic switching	ES	equivalent series resistance	ESR	extracting	EXTG
electronic voltmeter	EVN	erased	ERS	extreme	EXTM
electronic voltohmmeter	EVOM	erecting	ERCG	extremely low frequency	ELF
electronically operated valve	ELV	erector	ERCR	extrude	EXTR
electronics	ELEX	escape	ESC	eyelet	EYLT
electronics switching system	ESS	especially	ESP	eyepiece	EYPC
electronik	ELEK	estimate	EST	**F**	
electropneumatic	ELPNEU	estimated completion date	ECD	fabricate	FAB
electrostatic discharge	ESD	et cetera	ETC	face width	FW
electrostatic discharge resistive	ESOS	evacuate	EVAC	faceplate	FP
		evaluate	EVAL	facility	FACIL
element	ELEM	evaluation	EVLTN	facing	FCG
electrostatic discharge sensitive	ESDS	evaporate	EVAP	facsimile	FAX
		ever lock	EVRLK	factor	FAC
elevate	ELEV	examination	EXAM	factory	FCTY
elevation	EL	excavate	EXC	Fahrenheit	F
eliminate	ELIM	excessive	EXCSV	failure	FLR
elliptical	ELP	exchange	EXCH	failure rate	FR
elliptical head	ELPH	exciter	EXCTR	fairing	FAIR
elongate	ELNG				

familiar	FAM	file support equipment	FSE	flaring	FLRG
fan in	FNI	fillet	FIL	flashless	FLHLS
fan out	FNO	filling	FILL	flash welding	FLW
far side	FS	fillister head	FILH	flat bar	FB
fast operate (relay)	FO	film processing	FLMPRS	flat fillister head	FFILH
fast time constant	FTC	film sound	FLMSD	flat nose	FN
fastener	FSTNR	filter	FL	flat trim template	FTT
fault	FLT	filter	FLTR	flat work	FLWK
fault isolation test	FIT	final assembly	FA	flathead	FLH
feasible	FSBL	finger	FGR	flatten	FLN
February	FEB	finish	FNSH	flexible	FLEX
Federal	FED	finish all over	FAO	flip-flop complementary	FFC
Federal Stock Number	FSN	finish one side	F1S	floating	FLTG
Federal Supply Catalog Identification List	FSCIL	finish two sides	F2S	floating point instruction set	FIS
		fire alarm bell	FABL	flood light	FLDT
Federal Supply Code for Manufacturers	FSCM	fire control system	FCS	flooding	FLDNG
		fire extinguisher	FEXT	flotation	FLOT
feedback	FDBK	fire hose	FH	flow rate	FLRT
feedback potentiometer	FPOT	fire hose cabinet	FHC	flow switch	FLSW
feedback resistance	FBR	fire hose rack	FHR	fluid flow	FDFL
feeder	FDR	fire hydrant	FHY	fluid pressure line	FDPL
feedwater	FDW	fire resistant	FRES	fluked	FLKD
feedwater pump	FWP	fire room	FRM	fluorescent	FLUOR
feeler	FELR	firebrick	FBCK	flurry	FLRY
female pipe thread	FPT	fireplug	FPL	flush metal threshold	FMT
female	FEM	fireproof	FPRF	flush mount	FLMT
female flared	FFL	firmware	FMW	flush threshold	FT
female thread	FTHRD	first in first out	FIFO	flush type	FLTP
ferrule contact	FERCON	first reduction	1 RED	flush valve	FV
fiberboard	FBRBD	first stage	1 STG	fluted	FLTD
fiberboard, corrugated	FBDC	fiscal year	FY	fluted socket	FLUSOC
fiberboard, double wall	FDWL	fission	FSSN	fluted socket head	FLUSOCH
fiberboard, solid	FBDS	fitted	FTD	flutter	FLUT
fibrous	FBRS	fitting	FTG	flyweight	FLYWT
field	FLD	fixed	FXD	flywheel	FLYWHL
field decelerator	FDE	fixed autotransformer	FATR	focal	FOC
field discharge	FDI	fixed point	FXP	foggy	FGY
field dynamic braking	FDB	fixture	FXTR	folding	FLDG
field effect transistor	FET	flagstone	FLGSTN	follow	FOL
field force, decreasing	FFD	flame	FLM	follow up	FLWP
field force, increasing	FFI	flame resistant	FLMRES	foot per second	FPS
field manual	FM	flame tight	FLMTT	food service	FDSVC
field service modification work order	FSMWO	flameproof	FLMPRF	foot board	FBM
		flammable	FLMB	foot per minute	FPM
field switch	FSW	flange	FLG	foot-pound force	FTLB
field weakening	FWK	flapper	FLPR	for example	EG
figure	FIG	flared	FLRD	forced draft	FD
filament center tap	FCT	flared tube fitting	FTF	forged	FGD
filament ground	FG	flared tube fitting gasket seal	FTFGS	forged steel	FST
file finish	FF				

forging	FORG	full indicator movement	FIM	gear rack	GRK
forked	FKD	full load	FLLD	gear shaft	GRSHFT
forman	FMAN	full load amperes	FLA	gearbox	GRBX
formation	FORM	full scale	FSC	gearcase	GRC
former	FRMR	fully heat treated	FHT	gearing	GRG
formula translation	FORTRAN	function	FCTN	general	GENL
forward	FWD	fundamental	FUND	general contractor	GENCONT
foundation	FDN	funnel	FUNL	general note	GN
foundry	FDRY	furnish	FURN	general plan equipment	
four conductor	4/C	fuse	FZ	requirement	GPER
four dimensional	4D	fuse box	FUBX	generation	GEN
four pole	4P	fuse holder	FUHLR	generator field	GFLD
four pole double throw		fuselage	FUSLG	geological	GEOL
switch	4PDTSW	future	FUT	geomagnetism	GEOMAG
four pole single throw				geometry	GMTRY
switch	4PSTSW	**G**		German silver	GSIL
four pole switch	4PSW	gage	GA	gimbal	GMBL
four stage	4STG	gage board	GABD	glass	GL
four way	4WAY	gage code number	GCN	glass block	GLB
four wire	4W	gain time control	GTC	glaze	GLZ
foyer	FOY	gallery	GALL	glazed all tile base	GWTB
fractional	FRAC	galley	GALY	glazed facing unit	GFU
fragment	FRAG	gallon	GAL	glazed structural	
framework	FRWK	gallons per minute	GPM	facing unit	GSFU
free cutting brass	FCB	gallons per second	GPS	glazed structural	
free height	FRHGT	galvanize	GALV	unit base	GSUB
free machining steel	FMS	galvanized steel	GALVS	glazed structural units	GSU
freeboard	FREEBD	galvanized steel wire rope	GSWR	glazed wall tile	GWT
freezer	FRZR	galvannealed	GALVND	glazed wallboard	GLWB
freight	FRT	galvanometer	GALVNM	glide slope	GLS
french fry	FRFY	gang punch	GP	glider	GLI
frequency	FREQ	garage	GAR	globe stop valve	GSV
fresh water drain		garbage	GBG	globe valve	GLV
collecting tank	FWDCT	garbage in garbage out	GIGO	glossary	GLOSS
friction	FRICT	garboard	GARBD	glow plug	GLPG
fringe	FRNG	gas operated	GOPR	glycerin	GLYCN
from below	FRBEL	gas turbine	GTRB	gold	GLD
front connection	FC	gas weld	GASW	governing	GOVG
front end	FRTN	gas, nonpersistent	GNP	government	GOVT
front of board	FOB	gaseous mixture	GM	Government Industry Data	
front upset jaw	FUJ	gaseous oxygen	GOX	Exchange Program	GIDEP
fuel air ratio	FARATIO	gasket	GSKT	governor	GOV
fuel indicator reading	FIR	gasoline	GAS	grab rod	GR
fuel injection pump	FIP	gasoline engine	GENG	gradient	GRAD
fuel oil pump	FOP	gasproof	GPF	granite	GRAN
fuel tank	FTK	gastight	GT	grommet	GROM
fuel transfer pump	FTP	gate	G	granolithic base	GRB
fueling	FLNG	gate turnoff	GTO	granolithic finished floor	GFF
fulcrum	FUL	gate valve	GTV	granulated	GNLTD
full dog point	FDP	galvanized iron	GALVI	graphic	GRPH

graphic kilovolt ampere meter	GVA	hand control	HNDCONT	helical compression	HLCPS
graphic varmeter	GRVA	hand rail	HNDRL	helical extension	HLEXT
graphite	GPH	hand reset	HNDRST	helicopter	HLCPTR
grater	GRTR	handbook	HDBK	helipotentiometer	HPOT
grating	GRTG	handhold	HH	helix angle	HLXA
gravel	GVL	handicap	HDCP	helper	HLP
gravel surface buildup roof	GSBR	handle	HDL	herringbone	HGBN
gray	GRA	handling	HDLG	hertz	Hz
gray	GY	handling room	HR	heterodyne	HET
gray iron	GI	handshake	HDSHK	heavy machine gun	HMG
grease	GRS	handwheel	HNDWL	hexagon	HEX
grease nozzle	GNOZ	hanger	HGR	hexagonal head	HEXHD
greatest common divisor	GCD	hanging	HNG	hexagonal socket	HEXSOC
green	GRN	hard chromium	HDCR	hexagonal socket head	HEXSOCH
green indicating lamp	GIL	hard disk	HD	high altitude platform	HAP
Greenwich mean time	GMT	hard drawn	HDDRN	high carbon steel	HCS
grind	GRD	harden	HDN	high carbon steel, heat treated	HCSHT
groove	GRV	harden and grind	HG		
grooved	GRVD	hardness	HDNS	high fidelity	HFI
groover	GRVR	hardness assurance	HA	high frequency	HF
grooving	GRVG	hardness critical item	HCI	high frequency oscillator	HFO
gross combined weight rating	GCWR	hardness critical process	HCP	high grade plow steel	HGPS
		hardware	HDW	high humidity	HIHUM
gross vehicle weight	GVW	hardware cloth	HDWC	high intensity	HINT
gross weight	GRWT	hardwood	HDWD	high level language	HLL
ground	GND	harmonic	HMNC	high point	HPT
ground fault interrupter	GFI	harness	HARN	high potential	HIPOT
ground glass	GGL	hatch	H	high potential test	HIPOTT
grown junction	GJ	haversine	HAV	high pressure steam	HPS
guarantee	GUAR	hazardous	HAZ	high speed radar	HSR
guard rail	GDR	head crank	HC	high speed steel	HSS
guidance	GDNC	header	HDR	high temperature	HTM
guide	GDE	heading	HDG	high tensile	HTNSL
gunmetal	GMET	headless	HDLS	high tensile cast iron	HTCI
gusset	GUS	headlining	HLNG	high tensile strength	HTS
gutter	GUT	headquarters	HQ	high tension	HT
gymnasium	GYM	headset	HDST	high voltage	HV
gypsum	GYP	heat exchange	HE	high voltage regulator	HVR
gypsum plaster ceiling	GPC	heat resisting	HTRES	high-frequency current	HFCUR
gypsum plaster wall	GPW	heat shield	HTSHLD	highpass filter	HPFL
gypsum sheathing board	GSB	heat sink	HTSK	highway	HWY
gypsum wallboard	GWB	heat treat	HTTR	hinge jaw	HJ
gyrocompass	GCMPS	heated	HTD	hinge pillar	HPLR
gyroscope	GYRO	heater	HTR	hoist	HST
H		heating	HTG	holddown	HLDN
half dog point	1/2DP	heavy	HVY	holder	HLDR
half hard	1/2H	height	HGT	holding	HLDG
half round	1/2RD	height by width by length	HXWXL	hollow	HOL
hammer	HMR	helical	HLCL	homing	HOM

hone finish monolithic floor	HFMF	hyperfine structure	HFS	increase	INCR
honeycomb	HNYCMB	hypergolic clean	HGC	incubator	INCBR
honorary	HON	hypotenuse	HYP	indent	INDT
hookup	HKP	**I**		indentured parts list	IPL
hopper	HPR	ideal lowpass filter	ILPFL	independent	INDEP
horizon	HRZN	identification	IDENT	indeterminate	INDET
horizontal	HORIZ	idler	IDL	index	IDX
horizontal center of gravity	HCG	ignition	IGN	indicate	IND
horizontal centerline	HCL	current source	IGEN	indicator transmitter	INDTR
horizontal impulse	HZMP	ignitor	IGNTR	indirectly	IDRTY
horizontal impulse reaction	HIR	illuminate	ILLUM	individually	INDV
horizontal reaction	HZRN	illustrate	ILLUS	inductance	L
horizontal reference line	HRL	illustrated parts breakdown	IPB	inductance capacitance	LC
horizontal volute spring suspension	HVSS	illustrated parts catalog	IPC	inductance capacitance resistance	LCR
horn gap switch	HGSW	imaginary	IMAG	inductance regulator	INDREG
horsepower	HP	imitation	IMIT	induction compass	ICMPS
horsepower hour	HPHR	immediate	IMMED	inductor	IDCTR
hose connector	HCONN	immersion	IMRS	inductosyn	ISYN
hose thread	HSTH	impact	IMP	industrial	INDL
hospital	HOSP	impedance	IMPD	inert	INRT
hot brine pump	HBPUMP	impedor	IMPR	inert gas	INRTG
hot galvanize	HGALV	impeller	IMPLR	inertial	INRTL
hot leg	HLG	imperfect	IMPF	inertial guidance	IG
hot rolled pickled and oiled	HRPO	imperial	IMPRL	inertial measurement unit	IMU
hot rolled steel	HRS	impingement	IGMT	infinite	INF
hot side	HSD	implement	IMPL	inflatable	IFL
hot water heater	HWH	impose	IMPS	information	INFO
hot water, circulating	HWC	impression	IMPRSN	ingot	IGT
house	HSE	improved plow steel	IMPPS	inhibit	INHB
household	HSHLD	improvement	IMPROV	initial	INIT
housing	HSG	impregnate	IMPRG	initial velocity	IV
hovering	HVRNG	impulse	IMPLS	inject	INJ
howitzer	HOW	impulse conductor	IC	inlet	INL
humid	HMD	in accordance with	IAW	inner	INR
hunting	HNTG	inboard	INBD	inner back end	IBE
hybrid	HYB	incandescent	INCAND	inner bottom	IB
hydrated	HYDTD	incendiary	INCND	inner front end	IFE
hydraulic	HYDR	inch	IN	inoperative	INOP
hydrocyanic acid	HCN	inch-pound	INLB	inorganic	INORG
hydroelectric	HYDRELC	incinerator	INCIN	input	INP
hydro-form dye	HFD	inclined	INCLN	input output	IO
hydrogen ion concentration	pH	inclosure	INCLS	input output buffer	IOB
hydrometer	HYDM	include	INCL	input output element	IOE
hydrophone	HYPH	incoherent	INCOH	input output register	IOR
hydrostatic	HYDRST	incoming	INCM	input translator	INXLTR
hyperbola	HYPERB	incomplete	INCOMP	inquiry	INQ
hyperbolic sine	SINH	incomplete sequence (relay)	IS	inscription	INSC
hyperbolic tangent	TANH	incorporated	INC	insecticide	ICTDC
		incorrect	INCOR		

inseparate	INSEP	intermittent duty	IDTY	jackscrew	JKSCR
insert	INSR	intermodulation distortion	IMD	jamming	JAMG
insert screw thread	INST	internal	INTL	January	JAN
inside	INS	internal combustion		japanned	JAP
inside frosted	IF	engine	ICE	jet propelled	JP
inside mold line	IML	internal pipe thread	IPT	jettison	JTSN
inside of metal	IM	International Annealed		job order	JO
inside radius	IR	Copper Standard	IACS	joggle	JOG
inside trim template	ITT	International Organization for		joiner	J
insignia	ISGN	Standardization	ISO	joint	JT
insoluble	INSOL	International Pipe Standard	IPS	joint bar	JTB
inspect	INSP	International Standard		joint compound	JC
inspection check fixture	ICF	Thread (metric)	IST	journal	JNL
inspection check template	ICT	interphase transformer	INTPHTR	July	JUL
install	INSTL	interpolation	INTRPL	junction	JCT
installer	INSTLR	interpole	INTPO	junction box	JB
instantaneous automatic		interpret	INTPR	junction field effect transistor	JFET
gain control	IAGC	interrogate	INTRG	June	JUN
instantaneous automatic		interrupt	INTRPT	junior	JR
volume control	IAVC	interrupted continuous			
instantaneous overload	IOL	wave	ICW	**K**	
instantaneous relay	INSTRLY	intersect	INTSCT	cathode	K
instruct	INSTR	intership	INTSHP	Kalamein	KAL
instrumentation	INSTM	interstage	INTSTG	Kalamein door	KALD
insufficient	INSUF	interval	INTVL	Kalamein door and frame	KDF
insulate	INSUL	intervalometer	INTVLM	keene cement plaster	KCB
insulated gate field		intricate	INTRC	keene cement plaster ceiling	KCPC
effect transistor	IGFET	intrinsic i-type		keeping	KPG
intake	INTK	semiconductor material	I	kerosene	KRSN
integral	INT	introduction	INTRO	key locker	KL
integrating	INTEG	invariant	INVAR	key pulsing	KPLS
intelligence	INTEL	inventory	INVN	keyboard	KYBD
intensity	INTEN	inverse	INVS	keypunch	KP
intercept	INTCP	inverse time limit	ITL	keyseat	KST
interchangeable	INTCHG	inverse time relay	ITR	keyway	KWY
interchanger	INTCHGR	invert	INVT	kick plate	KPL
intercommunication	ICM	inverter	INV	kickoff (relay)	KO
intercommunication	INTERCOM	involute	INVLT	kiln dried	KD
interconnection	INTCON	inward	INWD	kilovolt ampere hour	KVAH
intercooler	INCLR	ionosphere	IONO	kilovolt ampere hour meter	KVAHM
intercylinder	INTCYL	iron core reactor	ICR	kilovolt ampere meter	KVAM
interface	INTFC	iron pipe	IP	kilowatt hour meter	KWHM
interface control drawing	ICD	irregular	IRREG	kinescope	KINE
interference	INFRN	isolate	ISOL	kinetic energy	KE
interference	INTRF	isolation	ISLN	knee brace	KB
interior	INTR	isosceles	ISOS	knife blade	KNBL
interlock	INTLK	issue	ISS	knife edge	KNED
intermediate	INTMD			knife switch	KNSW
intermediate power amplifier	IPA	**J**		Koroseal	KRAL
intermittent	INTMT	jacket	JKT		
		jacket water	JW		

L

label	LBL
laboratory	LAB
labyrinth	LBYR
labyrinth pack	LBYRPK
lacquer	LAQ
ladder	LAD
lagging	LAG
lampholder	LPHLDR
laminate	LAM
lampblack	LMPBLK
landing	LDG
landmark	LDMK
lantern	LTRN
lanyard	LNYD
lapping	LPG
large	LGE
last in first out	LIFO
latch	LCH
lateral	LATL
latitude	LAT
lattice	LTC
launch	LANH
launcher	LCHR
laundry	LAU
lavatory	LAV
layer	LYR
layout	LYT
lead angle	LA
lead coated metal	LCM
leader	LDR
leading edge radius	LER
leakoff	LOFF
least material condition	LMC
leather	LTHR
leaves	LVS
left bank	LBK
left hand	LH
left hand drive	LHDR
left hand side	LHS
left male	LM
left–right indicator	LRI
left side	LS
length	LG
length between perpendiculars	LBP
length of curve	LCRV
length of lead (actual)	LOL
length overall	LOA

length to diameter ratio	LGC
lengthening	LNG
letter	LTR
level	LVL
lever	LVR
library	LBRY
license	LIC
lifesaving	LSVG
lift up door	LUD
lifting	LFT
lifting eye	LE
light	LT
light activated semiconductor controlled rectifier	LASCR
light amplification (by) stimulated emission (of) radiation	LASER
light emitting diode	LED
light switch	LTSW
light tank	LTTK
lighter than air	LTA
lighting	LTG
lightproof louver	LPL
lightproof shade	LPS
lightproof vent	LPTR
lightweight concrete	LWC
lighweight insulating concrete	LWIC
lignum vitae	LGNMVTE
limit	LIM
limit switch	LIMSW
limited	LTD
limiting	LMTG
limiter	LMTR
line drawing	LD
line of sight	LOS
linear	LIN
linkage	LKGE
linoleum	LINOL
lintel	LNTL
liquid	LIQ
liquid fuel	LIQFL
liquid in glass	LQGLS
liquid oxygen	LOX
liquid rocket engine	LRE
liquor	LQR
lithograph	LITHO
litter	LIT
lizard	LIZ
load inducing relay	LIRLY

load limiting resistor	LLRES
load ratio control	LRC
load resistor (relay)	LR
load shifting ratio	LSR
load update subset	LUS
load waterline	LWL
local	LCL
local apparent time	LAPT
local area network	LAN
local oscillator	LO
local sidereal time	LSDT
local standard time	LST
localizer	LOC
locate	LCT
lock pillar	LPLR
lock washer	LKWASH
locked	LKD
locked closed	LKDC
locked in device	LID
locked open	LKDO
locked rotor	LKROT
locker	LKR
locking	LKG
locknut	LKNT
lockscrew	LKSCR
locksmith	LSMITH
lockup	LKUP
lockwire	LKWR
locomotive	LOCO
logarithm	LOG
logarithm, natural	LN
logarithmic amplifier	LOAMP
logic	LGC
logic unit	LU
long side	LSD
long taper	LTPR
long wheelbase	LWB
longeron	LONGN
longitude	LONG
longitudinal expansion joint	LEJ
longleaf yellow pine	LLYP
loop control (relay)	LPC
looper	LPR
louvered door	LVD
low alloy steel	LS
low coolant	LCOLNT
low frequency	LF
low frequency oscillator	LFO
low level	LL

low level logic	LLL	major	MAJ	matrix output amplifier	MOA
low pass	LP	makeup	MKUP	maximum	MAX
low power output	LPO	makeup feed	MUFD	maximum capacity	MAXCAP
low speed	LSP	male and female	MF	maximum material condition	MMC
low stream	LSTM	male flared	MFLRD	maximum permissible exposure	MPE
low temperature	LTEMPT	male pipe thread	MPT	maximum working pressure	MWP
low torque	LTQ	male thread	MTHRD	maximum working voltage	MWV
low voltage	LV	malfunction	MALF	mean aerodynamic chord	MAC
low voltage protection	LVP	malleable	MAL	mean effective pressure	MEP
lower	LWR	malleable iron	MI	mean time between failures	MTBF
lower deck	LDK	management	MGT	mean time to failure	MTTF
lower sideband	LSB	manager	MGR	mean time to first failure	MTTFF
lowest	LWST	managing	MNG	mean time to repair	MTTR
lowest usable frequency	LUF	mandrel	MDRL	mean variation	MV
lowest usable high frequency	LUHF	manhole	MH	mean width ratio	MWR
lowpass filter	LPFL	manifold	MANF	measure	MEAS
lubricant	LUBT	manual	MNL	mechanical	MECH
lubricate	LUB	manual change order	MCO	mechanize	MECZ
lubricating oil	LUBO	manual change request	MCR	median	MDN
lubricating oil pump	LOP	manual gain control	MGC	medical	MED
lumber	LBR	manual overload	MANOVLD	medium	MDM
lumens per watt	LPW	manual volume control	MVC	medium high frequency	MHF
luminous	LUM	manually operated	MNLOPR	medium pressure	MP
lunar orbit rendezvous	LOR	manufacture	MFR	megabyte	MEG
		manufactured	MFD	melamine	MEL
M		manufacturing	MFG	member	MBR
machine	MACH	manuscript	MS	membrane	MEMB
machine screw	MSCR	maneuvering	MANUV	memorandum	MEMO
machine steel	MST	marble base	MRB	memory	MEM
machined surface	MASU	marble floor	MRF	merchandise	MDSE
machinery	MCHRY	marble threshold	MRT	merchantable	MERCH
machinist	MCHST	March	MAR	mercurial	MRCL
magnesium thorium	MAGTHOR	margin	MARG	meridian	MER
magnetic	MAG	marginal (relay)	MGL	meshing	MSHG
magnetic amplifier	MAGAMP	marked	MKD	message	MSG
magnetic modulator	MAGMOD	marker	MKR	message generator	MSGG
magnetic particle inspection	MPI	markings	MKGS	messenger	MESS
magneto	MGN	masking	MASK	metal	MET
magnetohydrodynamics	MHD	masonry	MSNRY	metal anchor	MA
magnetometer	MGTMTR	master oscillator power		metal anchor slots	MAS
magnetomotive force	MMF	amplifier	MOPA	metal awning type window	MATW
magnetron	MAGN	master switch	MSW	metal base	METB
magnitude	MAGTD	mastic	MSTC	metal casement window	MCW
magnify	MGF	mastic joint	MJ	metal clad switch gear	MCSWGR
mahogany	MAH	matched	MTCHD	metal corner bead	MCB
mainframe	MNFRM	material	MATL	metal covered door	MCD
maintenance	MAINT	material test specification	MTS	metal curb	METC
maintenance and repair	MR	mathematical	MATH	metal door	METD
maintenance parts kit	MPK	matrix	MAT	metal flashing	METF
maintenance parts list	MPL				

metal grille	METG	miter	MIT	multiple	MULT
metal interface amplifier	MIA	miter end	ME	multiple unit	MU
metal lath and plaster	MLP	mixing	MXG	multiplex	MUX
metal mold	METM	mixing flow	MXFL	multispeed	MLTSP
metal mount	MMT	mixture	MXT	munitions	MUN
metal oxide semiconductor	MOS	mobile	MBL	music wire	MUW
metal oxide semiconductor field effect transistor	MOSFET	mode transducer	MXDCR	music wire gage	MWG
		model	MOD	muzzle	MZL
metal oxide semiconductor transistor	MOST	modification work order	MWO	**N**	
metal partition	METP	modulator demodulator	MODEM	nacelle	NAC
metal rolling door	MRD	moisture	MSTRE	name plate	NPL
metal roof	METR	mold line	ML	namely	VIZ
metal strip	METS	molded	MLD	narrow	NAR
metal thick oxide silicon	MTOS	molding	MLDG	narrow band	NB
metal through wall flashing	MTWF	molecular weight	MOLWT	narrow gage	NG
metallic	MTLC	molecule	MOL	national	NATL
metallize	MTLZ	momentary	MOM	National coarse thread	NC
meter	M	monitor	MON	National Electrical Code	NEC
meter	MTR	monograph	MONOG	National Electrical Code Standards	NECS
meter kilogram second	MKS	monophonic	MONO		
meteorological	METRL	Montana	MT	National Electrical Safety Code	NESC
method	MTHD	month	MO	National extra fine thread	NEF
mezzanine	MEZZ	mooring	MRG	National fine thread	NF
microammeter	MCAM	mop rack	MOPR	National gas outlet thread	NGO
microcomputer	MCMPTR	most significant bit	MSB	National pipe thread	NP
microcurrent	MCKT	mostly	MSLY	national stock number	NSN
microelectronics	MELEC	motherboard	MTHBD	National taper pipe thread	NPT
microelement	MELEM	motion	MTN	National Wire Gage	NWG
microfunctional circuit	MFC	motor	MOT	natural	NAT
micrometer	MIC	motor belt drive	MBD	natural black slate	NBS
microminiature	MMIN	motor can	MOCAN	nautical	NAUT
microprocessor	MIPRCS	motor circuit switch	MCSW	nautical mile	NMI
microscope	MICR	motor direct	MD	naval	NAV
microwave early warning	MEW	motor direct connected	MDC	naval bronze	NAVBRZ
middle	MDL	motor V-belt	MVB	Navy Primary Standards	NPS
midget	MDGT	motorcycle	MC	Navy Secondary Standards	NSS
miles per gallon	MPG	motorized	MTZ	navy standard flange	NFL
miles per hour	MPH	mounted	MTC	needle	NDL
military	MIL	mounting	MTG	negative	NEG
military standard	MIL-STD	mounting center	MTGC	negative positive intrinsic negative	NPIN
milliammeter	MAM	movable	MVBL		
mineral	MNRL	movement	MVT	negative positive negative positive	NPNP
mineral surface roof	MSR	moving	MVG		
miniature	MINTR	muffler	MUF	negative positive negative transistor	NPN
minimum	MIN	multifrequency pulsing	MFP		
minimum discernible signal	MDS	multigage	MG	negative temperature coefficient	NTC
mirror	MIR	multilith	MULTH		
miscellaneous	MISC	multimeter	MULTR	neon indicating light	NEIL
missile	MSL	multiplane	MLTPL	neoprene	NPRN

net weight	NTWT	normal	NORM	oil plug	OPLG
network	NTWK	normal charge	NLCHG	oil pressure	OPRS
neutral	NEUT	normal circular pitch	NCP	oil pump	OP
neutron	NTN	normal diametral pitch	NDP	oil ring	OR
next higher assembly	NHA	normal overload	NOL	oil seal	OSL
nickel	NKL	normal pressure angle	NPA	oil switch	OS
nickel copper	NICOP	normal temperature and		oiltight	OT
nickel copper alloy	NCA	pressure	NTP	on center	OC
nickel silver	NISIL	normally open	NO	one stage	OSTG
nickel steel	NS	not applicable	NA	one way	OW
nipple	NIP	not in contact	NIC	opaque	OPA
nitride steel	NITSTL	not to scale	NTS	open close open	OCO
no drawing	ND	notched	NCH	open end	OE
no load	NLD	notice of revision	NOR	open hearth	OH
no voltage release	NVR	November	NOV	open jointed	OJ
noise generator	NGEN	nozzle	NOZ	open type control circuit	
no lead	NL	nuclear	NUC	contacts	OTCCC
nomenclature	NOMEN	numeral	NUM	opening	OPNG
nominal	NOM	nut plate	NTPL	openside	OPSD
noncombustible	NCOMBLE	nylon	NYL	operate	OPR
noncorrosive metal	NCM	**O**		operational	OPNL
noncoupled	NCPLD	object	OBJ	opposite	OPP
nondestructive evaluation	NDE	objective	OBJV	optical character recognition	OCR
nondestructive inspection	NDI	oblique	OBL	optimum	OPT
nondestructive readout	NDRO	obscure	OB	optimum working frequency	OWF
nondestructive testing	NDT	observation	OBSV	optional	OPTL
nonelectric	NELEC	obsolete	OBS	orange	O
nonenclosure	NENCL	obstruction	OBSTN	orange	ORN
nonflammable	NFLMB	obverse	OBV	orange indicating light	OIL
nonfused	NFSD	occupy	OCC	order	ORD
nonhygroscopic	NH	octahedral	OCTAHDR	organization	ORG
nonlinear	NLNR	October	OCT	orientation	ORIENT
nonmetallic	NM	odometer	ODOM	orifice	ORF
nonoscillating	NOSC	of true position	OTP	origin	ORIG
nonpetroleum	NPET	office	OFC	original equipment	
locknut pipe thread	NPSL	officer	OFCR	manufacturer	OEM
straight thread pipe		official	OFCL	oscillating	OSCG
couplings	NPSC	offset	OFS	oscillator	OSC
tight joints	NPTF	ohmmeter	OHM	oscillogram	OSCGRM
taper pipe thread railing		oil circuit breaker	OCB	oscilloscope	SCOPE
fixtures	NPTR	oil cleaner	OCLNR	other design activity	ODA
thread for press-tight joins	NPSF	oil cooled	OCLD	ounce	OZ
nonreactive relay	NR	oil cooler	OCLR	ounce-inch	OZIN
nonreinforced concrete pipe	NRCP	oil dipstick	ODPSK	ouside helix angle	OHA
nonreversible	NRVSBL	oil filter	OFL	out to out	OO
nonself	NSLF	oil immersed	OI	outerback end	OBE
nonslip thread	NST	oil level	OLVL	outlet	OUT
nonstandard	NONSTD	oil nozzle	ONOZ	output transistor	OUTXLTR
nonsynchronous	NONSYN	oil pan	OPN	outside diameter	OD
nontight	NT			outside diameter tube	ODT

outside face	OF	part number	PN	phase shift driver	PSHD
outside mold line	OML	part of	PO	phenoic	PHEN
outside screw and yoke	OSY	partial	PART	Phillips head	PHH
outside trim template	OTT	partition	PTN	phonograph	PHONO
oval head	OVH	partly	PTLY	phosphor bronze	PHBRZ
oval point	OVP	parts kit	PRTKT	phosphorescent	PHOS
overall	OA	party	PTY	photocopy	PHOC
overflow	OVFL	passenger	PASS	photodiode	PDIO
overfrequency relay	OFR	passivate	PSV	photoelectric	PELEC
overhanging	OVHG	passive	PSIV	photoelectric cell	PEC
overhaul	OVHL	paste	PST	photograph	PHOTO
overhead	OVHD	patent	PAT	phototransistor	PXSTR
overload	OVLD	patent pending	PATPEND	physical	PHYS
overload relay	ORLY	pattern	PATT	physiological	PHYSIOL
overpower	OVPWR	peak inverse (reverse) voltage	PRV	pickup	PU
override	OVRD			picture	PIX
oversize	OVS	pedestal	PED	piece mark	PCMK
overspeed	OVSP	pencil	PCL	pierce	PRC
overtravel	OVTR	pendent	PEND	pierced aluminum plank	PAP
overvoltage	OVV	pendular	PNDLR	pierced steel plank	PSP
oxide	OXD	penetrate	PEN	pigment	PGMT
oxygen	OXY	pentaerythryte tetranitrate	PETN	pigtail	PGT
		pentagon	PNTGN	piling	PLG
P		pentode	PENT	pillow block	PLBLK
package	PKG	percent	PCT	pilot	PLT
padder capacitor	PAD	percussion	PERC	pilot light	PLTLT
paint	PNT	perforate	PERF	pinion end	PE
painted	PTD	performance	PRFM	pintle	PTL
pallet	PLL	performance evaluation and review technique	PERT	pioneer	PION
pan head	PNH			pipe plug	PPG
panel	PNL	Performance Operational Maintenance Site	POMSEE	pipe rail	PR
panic bolt	PANB			pipe sleeve	PSL
panoramic	PAN	perimeter acquisition radar	PACR	pipe tap	PT
paper	PPR	periodic	PERD	pipeline	PPLN
parabola	PRB	peripheral	PRPHL	pipette	PPE
parabolic	PRBLC	peripheral command indicator	PCI	piping	PP
paraboloid	PRBD			pistol	PSTL
parachute	PRCHT	periscope	PERIS	piston	PSTN
paragraph	PARA	permanent	PERM	pitch diameter	PD
parallax	PRX	permeability	PERMB	pivot	PVT
parallel	PRL	perpendicular	PERP	places	PL
parameter	PRMTR	person	PER	plain washer	PW
parametric amplifier	PARAMP	personnel	PERS	planar	PLNR
parchment	PCHT	perspective	PERSP	planar epitaxial passivated transistor	PEP
parenthesis	PAREN	petroleum	PETRO		
parity bit	PBIT	pewter	PWTR	plane	PLN
parkerized	PARK	phantom	PHM	planet	PLNT
parking	PRKG	pharmacy	PHAR	planetary	PLNTY
parkway	PKWY	phase	PH	plank	PLK
part identification number	PIN	phase shift	PSH	planning	PLNG

plaque	PLQ	pound force inch	LBIN	pressed	PRSD
plaster	PLAS	pound force per square foot	PSF	pressed metal	PRSDMET
plastic	PLSTC	pound force per square inch	PSI	presser	PRSR
plate glass	PLGL	pound per cubic foot	PCF	pressure	PRESS
plated	PLD	pound per horsepower	PHP	pressure gage	PG
platform	PLATF	powder	PDR	pressure vessel	PV
plating	PLTG	powder	PWD	pressurize	PRSRZ
pliers	PLR	power	PWR	prevent	PVNT
plotting	PLOT	power amplifier	PA	previous	PREV
plow steel rope	PSR	power circuit breaker	PCB	primary	PRI
plumbing	PLMB	power control unit	PCU	Primary Coolant System	PCS
plunger	PLGR	power driven	PDVN	prime	PRM
plus or minus	PORM	power factor	PF	prime mover	PMVR
pneumatic	PNEU	power supply	PWRSPLY	primer	PRMR
pnpn transistor magnetic logic	PTML	power supply unit	PSU	priming	PRM
pocket	PKT	power switchboard	PSWDB	printed circuit	PC
point of compound curve	PCC	power takeoff	PTO	printed wiring assembly	PWA
point of intersection	PI	powerhouse	PWRH	printed wiring board	PWB
polarity	PLRT	practice	PRAC	printer	PTR
polish	POL	preamplifier	PREAMP	printing	PRNTG
polyester	POLYEST	prebent	PRBNT	printout	PTOUT
polyethylene	POLTHN	precast	PRCST	prism	PSM
polyethylene insulated conductor	PIC	precedence	PREC	private automatic branch exchange	PABX
polystyrene	PS	precharge	PRCH	probability	PROB
polytetrafluorethylene	PTFE	precipitate	PPT	procedure	PROC
polyvinyl chloride	PVC	precipitation	PRECP	process	PRCS
pontoon	PON	precipitin	PRCPTN	processing	PRCSG
popping	POP	precision	PRCN	processing unit	PROCU
porcelain	PORC	prefabricated	PREFAB	procurement	PRCMT
porro	POR	preference	PREF	production	PROD
port side light	PSLT	preferred	PFD	program	PRGM
portable	PORT	prefocus	PRFCS	program register	PRGMRGTR
position	POSN	preformed	PREFMD	programmable logic array	PLA
positioner	PSNR	preformed beam	PFB	programmable logic controller	PLC
positive	POS	preheat	PHT	programmable unijunction transistor	PUJT
positive displacement	PDISPL	preheater	PHR	programming	PRGMG
positive negative intrinsic positive	PNIP	preinserted	PINSTD	progress	PROG
		preliminary	PRELIM	project	PROJ
positive negative positive negative	PNPN	premium	PREM	projectile	PJCTL
		premolded	PRMLD	projection	PJCTN
positive negative positive transistor	PNP	premolded expansion joint	PEJ	projector	PJTR
		preparation	PREP	proof	PRF
post indicator valve	PIV	prescription	PRESCR	proofread	PRFRD
potable water	POTW	present	PRES	propane	PRPN
potential	POT	preservation	PSVTN	propellant	PRPLT
potential switch	PSW	preservative	PSVTV	propeller	PROP
pound	LB	press	PRS	proportion	PROPN
pound force foot	LBFT	press fit	PRFT		
		pressboard	PBD		

proposal	PRPSL
proposed	PRPSD
propulsion	PRPLN
prosthetic	PRSTC
protect	PTCT
protection	PROT
protective device	PROTDEV
prototype	PROTO
protractor	PROTR
provision	PROV
proximity	PROX
p-type hole semi-conductor material	P
publication	PUBN
pull button	PLB
pull button switch	PBSW
pull rod	PLRD
pulley	PUL
pulsation	PLSN
pulsator	PLSR
pulse	PLS
pulse amplitude modulation	PAM
pulse code modulation	PCM
pulse count modulation	PCTM
pulse duration modulation	PDM
pulse frequency modulation	PFM
pulse interval modulation	PIM
pulse per minute	PPM1N
pulse position modulation	PPM
pulse time modulation	PTM
pulse time multiplex	PTMUX
pulse width modulation	PWM
pulverizer	PULV
pump discharge	PDISCH
punch	PCH
punching	PCHG
purchase	PURCH
purge	PRG
purging	PRNG
purification	PRFCN
purifier	PUR
purple indicating light	PIL
push button	PB
push pull plate	PPP
push rod	PRD
pyrogen unit	PYGN
pyrometer	PYROM
pyrotechnic	PYRO

Q

quadrangle	QUAD
quadrant	QDRNT
quadrature	QDRTR
quadruple	QUADR
qualified products list	QPL
quality	QUAL
quality assurance	QA
quality conformance inspection	QCI
quality control	QC
quantitative	QUANT
quantity	QTY
quantum amplification stimulated emission	QUASER
quarry	QRY
quarry tile base	QTB
quart	QT
quarter	QTF
quarter hard	QTH
quarter hard	1/4H
quarter phase	QTRPH
quarter phase	1/4PH
quarter round	QTRRD
quarter round	1/4RD
quartz	QTZ
quaternary	QUAT
question	QUEST
quick break	QB
quick disconnect	QDISC
quick firing	QF
quick opening device	QOD
quiescent	QUIES
quintuple	QUIN
quotation	QUOT

R

rabbet	RAB
rachet	RCHT
radial	RDL
radiated emission	RE
radiation	RADN
radiator	RDTR
radio detection and ranging	RADAR
radio direction finding	RDF
radio frequency	RF
radio frequency choke	RFC
radio frequency interference	RFI
radio inertial	RIN
radio telegraph	RTLG

radio telephony	RTEL
radio teletype	RTT
radioactive	RAACT
radioactive liquid waste	RALW
radius	RAD
railcar	RLCR
railing	RLG
railroad	RR
railway	RY
raised	RSD
raised face diameter	RFD
raised face height	RFH
ramjet	RMJ
random	RNDM
random access memory	RAM
range	RNG
rating	RTG
rattail	RTTL
raw material	RM
rayon	RYN
reacting volt ampere meter	RVA
reaction	RCTN
reactivate	REACTVT
reactive	REAC
reactive factor meter	RFM
reactive voltmeter	RVM
reactor core	RCO
read write	RW
reader	RDR
reading	RDNG
readout	RDOUT
ready	RDY
real time	RT
real time input output transducer	RIOT
reamer	RMR
rebabbit	RBBT
recall	RCL
receive	RCV
received	RCVD
receiver	RCVR
receiving	RCVG
receptacle	RCPT
reception	RCPTN
recess	REC
recharger	RECHRG
reciprocate	RECIP
recirculate	RECIRC
reclaiming	RCLMG

reclined	RCLD	reinforce	REINF	resistance	R
reclose	RECL	reinforced concrete		resistance capacitance	RC
recognition	RECOG	culvert pipe	RCCP	resistance capacitance	
recoilless	RCLS	reinforced concrete pipe	RCP	coupled	RCCPLD
recommend	RECM	reject	REL	resistance inductance	RL
recompression	RCMPRS	relate	RLT	resistance inductance	
recondense	RECOND	relation	RLTN	capacitance	RLC
recondition	RCNDT	relaxation	RLXN	resistor	RES
reconnaissance	RECON	relay	RLY	resistor capacitor transistor	
record	RCD	relay block	RB	logic	RCTL
record and report	RAR	reliability	RELBL	resistor transistor logic	RTL
recording ammeter	RAMM	relief	RLF	resolution	RESOLN
recording demand meter	RDM	relief valve	RV	resolver	RSLVR
recording kilovolt ampere		relieve	RLV	resonant	RESN
meter	RKVAM	relocated	RELOC	respective	RSPV
recording tachometer	RTM	remote	RMT	respectively	RESP
recording varmeter	RVARM	remote control system	RCS	respirator	RSPTR
recoverability	RECY	remove	RMV	respond	RSPD
recovery	RCVY	removable	REM	response	RSPS
recreation	RCN	renewable	RNWBL	restore	RST
rectangle	RECT	repair	RPR	restorer	RESTR
recurrent	RCUR	repeat	RPT	restrict	RSTR
red fuming nitric acid	RFNA	repeater	RPTR	retain	RET
red indicating lamp	RIL	repeating coil	RPTC	retainer	RTNR
redesignate	REDSG	repeller	RPLR	retard	RTD
reduce	RDC	repetition	RPTN	retardation coil	RTDC
reducer	RDCR	replace	REPL	retension	RETNN
reduction	RDCN	replenishing	RPLNG	reticle	RTCL
reduction of area	RA	replenishment	RPNSM	reticulated grating	RG
reentry	REY	report	RPRT	retract	RETR
refacer	RECR	reproduce	REPRO	retrieve	RTRV
reference	REF	reproducer	RPDR	retroactive	RETRO
reference designation	REFDES	reproducing unit	RU	retrogressive	RETROG
reference line	REFL	republic	REPB	return	RTN
refined	RFND	repulsion	RPLSN	return head	RHD
reflected	REFLD	request	REQ	return to zero	RZ
reflective insulation	RI	request for price quotation	RPQ	reverberation control	
reflex	RFLX	required	REQD	of gain	RCG
refractory	RFRC	requirement	REQT	reverse	RVS
refrigerant	RFGT	requisition	REQN	reverse acting	RACT
refrigerate	REFR	rescind	RESC	reverse current	REVCUR
regardless of feature size	RFS	rescue	RSQ	reversible	RVSBL
regenerate	REGEN	rescue boat	RSQB	revision	REV
register	RGTR	research and development	R&D	revolution indicating	
register drive	RD	reserve	RSV	system	RIS
regular	RGLR	reserve feed water	RFW	revolutions per minute	RPM
regulate	RGLT	reservoir	RSVR	revolutions per second	RPS
regulator	RGLTR	residual	RESID	revolve	RVLV
reheater	RHR	residual field	RESFLD	rewind	RWND
Reid vapor pressure	RVP	resiliant	RESIL	rheostat	RHEO

rhodium	RHOD	safe working pressure	SWP	self-destroying	SD
rhombic	RHOMB	safety	SAF	self-locking	SLFLKG
ribbed	RIB	safety valve	SV	self-propelled	SELFPROP
ribbon	RBN	salinity	SAL	self-sealing	SLFSE
ridge	RDG	salvage	SALV	self-tapping	SLFTPG
rigging	RGNG	same size	SS	selsyn	SELS
right angle	RTANG	sampling	SMPLG	semiconductor	SEMICOND
right hand drive	RHDR	sandblast	SDBL	semiconductor controlled switch	SCS
right hand side	RHS	sanitary	SAN	semiconductor unilateral switch	SUS
right side	RS	saponify	SAPON	semiconductor bilateral switch	SBS
rigid	RGD	satellite	SATL	semifireproof	SFPRF
ring counter	RCNTR	saturate	SAT	semifixed	SFXD
rivet	RVT	sawtooth	ST	semiflush	SFLS
roasting	RSTG	Saybolt Furol second	SSF	semaphore	SMPHR
rocker	RKR	Saybolt Universal second	SSU	semitrailer	STLR
rocker arm	RKRA	scale	SC	sender	SDR
rocket	RKT	scale model	SCMOD	sending	SNDG
Rockwell hardness	RH	scanning	SCNG	sense	SEN
rod control	RCONT	scanning electron microscope	SEM	sense amplifier	SA
rod drive	RDDR	scattered	SCTD	sensitive	SENS
Roebling Wire Gage	RWG	scavenge	SCAV	sensitized	SNTZD
rolled	RLD	schedule	SCHED	sensitizing	SNTZG
roller	RLR	schematic	SCHEM	sensor	SNSR
roofing	RFG	science	SCI	separate	SEP
root mean square	RMS	scintillator	SCINT	sequence	SEQ
root sum square	RSS	scleroscope	SCLER	sequential coding	SECO
rotary	RTRY	scooter	SCTR	serial	SER
rotate	ROT	scope	SCP	serial number	SERNO
rotator	ROTR	scraper	SRPR	serrate	SERR
rotometer	ROTOMT	screen door	SCD	server	SVR
rotor	RTR	screw	SCR	service	SVCE
rough	RGH	screw down	SCRDN	service bulletin	SB
rough opening	RO	screwdriver	SCDR	service ceiling	SRVCLG
round	RND	sealed	SLD	service factor amperes	SFA
round head	RDH	seamless	SMLS	serving	SERG
round trips per hour	RTPH	seamless steel tubing	SSTU	servomechanism	SERVO
route	RTE	secant, hyperbolic	SECH	servomotor	SVTR
routine	ROUT	second	SEC	set screw	SSCR
rubber	RBR	section	SECT	setter	SETR
rubber insulation	RINSUL	sector	SCTR	setting	SET
rubber tile floor	RTF	sector scan indicator	SSI	settling	SETLG
rudder	RUD	securing	SECRG	sewage	SEW
runway	RWY	security	SCTY	sexless (connector)	SXL
rust preventive	RPVNTV	sedan	SED	sextant	SXTN
rustproof	RSTPF	segment	SEG	sextuple	SXT
		select	SEL	shaft	SFT
S		self-cleaning	SLFCLN	shaft extension	SFTEXT
saddle	SDL	self-closing	SELFCL		
safe operating area	SOAR	self-contained	SCNTN		
safe practice data sheet	SPDS				

shaft gear	SHFGR	single base solid propellant	SBSP	soil stack	SSK
shank	SHK	single beam klystron	SBK	solder	SLDR
shape	SHP	single conductor	IC	solenoid	SOL
sharpener	SHRP	single conductor cable	SCC	solenoid valve	SOLV
shearing	SHRNG	single cylinder	SCYL	solid fiberboard	SFB
sheathing	SHTHG	single end	SE	solid height	SOLHGT
sheave	SHV	single face	SIF	solid neutral	SN
sheet	SH	single feeder	SFDR	soluble	SLBL
shell	SHL	single groove insulation	SG	solution	SOLN
shield	SHLD	single groove single		solvent	SLVT
shift	SHF	petticoat insulation	SGSP	sound	SND
shipment	SHPT	single pole	SP	sound navigation and	
shipping	SHPNG	single pole double throw	SPDT	ranging	SONAR
shipping center	SHCR	single pole double throw		sound recorder reproducer	SRR
shock absorber	SHABS	switch	SPDTSW	soundproof	SNDPRF
shop replaceable unit	SRU	single side band	SSB	source	SCE
short circuit	SHORT	single sideboard	SSBD	source control drawing	SOCD
short leaf yellow pine	SLYP	single signal	SSIG	source control number	SOCN
short taper	STPR	single swing blocking		spacer	SPCR
short time constant	SHTC	oscillator	SSBO	special	SPCL
short wheelbase	SWB	sinter	SNTR	special treatment steel	STS
shot blast	SHBL	situation	SIT	specific gravity	SPGR
shoulder	SHLDR	sketch	SK	specification	SPEC
shower and toilet	SHT	skirted	SKD	speedometer	SPDOM
shown	SHN	skylight	SLT	speed converter	SPCONV
shrapnel	SHRAP	slate shingle roof	SSR	spider	SPDR
shredder	SHRDR	sleeve	SLV	spooling	SPG
shroud	SHRD	sleeving	SLVG	spot face	SF
shroud fin	SHRDF	slice	SLC	spot face other side	SFO
shunt trip	SHTR	sliding	SL	sprayed acoustical ceiling	SAC
shut down	SHTDN	sliding expansion joint	SEJ	stabilization	STBLN
shut off valve	SOV	slinger	SLGR	stabilize	STAB
shuttle	SHTL	slip joint	SJ	stabilized local oscillator	STALO
side light	SILT	slope	SLP	stabilized meter oscillator	STAMO
siding	SDG	slotted	SLTD	stabilized shunt	STSH
signal	SIG	slow speed	SLSP	stable	STB
signal to noise ratio	SNR	sludge	SLG	stainless	STNLS
signaling	SNLG	small	SM	stainless steel	SST
silencing	SILG	smooth face structural		stairway	STWY
silicomanganese steel	SMS	clay tile	SFSCT	stamp	STP
silicon precision alloy		smooth neck	SMNK	stanchion	STAN
transistor	SPAT	smooth surface built		standard	STD
silicon unilateral diffused		up roof	SSBR	standard intruction set	SIS
transistor	SUDT	snatch	SNH	standard military drawing	SMD
silver	SIL	snubber	SNBR	standardization	STDZN
silver brazing union	SBU	socket	SLK	standby	STBY
silver solder	SILS	socket head	SCH	standoff	STDF
similar	SIM	socket welding	SWLDG	starboard	STBD
sine	SIN	soda fountain	SDFTN	start and stop	STSP
single	SGL	software	SFW	starter	START

starting	STG	structural carbon steel soft	SCSS	suspended plaster ceiling	SPC
statement	STMT	structural clay tile	SCT	suspended sprayed	
station	STA	structure	STRUCT	acoustical ceiling	SSAC
stator	STTR	stuffing	STFG	sustaining	STNG
statuary bronze	STBRZ	subassembly	SUBASSY	sweat	SWT
status	STAT	subcaliber	SUBCAL	swinging bracket	SWGBKT
steady	STDY	subject	SUBJ	swinging door	SWGD
steam generator	STGEN	submarine	SUB	switch	SW
steam working pressure	STWP	submerged	SUBMG	switch gear	SWGR
steaming	STMG	submersible	SBM	switch stand	SWS
steel	STL	subminiature	SUBMIN	switchboard	SWBD
steel basement window	SBW	subsequent	SUBQ	switchgear block	SGB
steel cadmium plated	SCDP	subsoil drain	SSD	switchover	SWOV
stellite	STLT	substation	SUBSTA	swivel	SWVL
stepdown	STPDN	substitute	SUBST	symbol	SYM
stepdown and stepup	SDNSU	substrate	SBSTR	symmetrical	SYMM
stepup	STU	substructure	SUBSTR	symposium	SYMP
stereophonic	STEREO	succeeding	SUC	synchro switch	SSW
sterilizer	STER	suction	SUCT	synchro tie	SYNTI
stiffener	STIF	sufficient	SUF	synchronize	SYNC
stimulate	STML	suffix	SUFF	synchronous	SYN
stirrup	STIR	summary	SMY	synthetic	SYNTH
stitch	STC	summing	SUM	system	SYS
stock	STK	sump tank	SMTK	Système International	
stock number	SNO	sunny	SNY	d'Unités	SI
stock order	SO	supercharge	SPCHG	**T**	
stoke	STRK	superheater	SUPHTR	table lookup	TLU
stone	STN	superheterodyne	SUPERHET	table solution	TABSOL
storage	STOR	superimposed current	SUPCUR	tables of equipment	TE
storage address register	SAR	superintendent	SUPT	tabulate	TAB
storeroom	STRM	supersede	SUPSD	tabulator simulator	TABSYM
stormwater	STW	supersensitive	SUPSENS	tachometer	TACH
stowage	STWG	superstructure	SUPERSTR	tachometer voltmeter	TVM
straight	STR	supervise	SUPV	tackle	TKL
straight line frequency	SLF	supplement	SUPPL	tactical	TAC
straight line wavelength	SLWL	suppression	SUPPR	tally	TLY
strand	STRD	surface	SURF	tandem	TDM
strapped	STRP	surface four sides	S4S	tangent	TAM
strategic	STRAT	surface one side	S1S	tanker	TKR
stratosphere	STRATO	surface one side and		taper	TPR
streamline	STRLN	one edge	S1SE	taper shank	TS
stringer	STGR	surface two sides	S2S	tappet	TPT
stripped	STPD	surgical	SURG	tapping	TPG
stroboscope	STBSCP	survey	SURV	technical bulletin	TB
strong	STRG	survival	SRVL	technical note	TN
strongback	STRBK	suspend	SUSP	technical report	TR
structural	STRL	suspended acoustical plaster		technical	TECH
structural carbon steel hard	SCSH	ceiling	SAPC	teeth	T
structural carbon steel		suspended acoustical tile		telecommunications	TELECOM
medium	SCSM	ceiling	SATC		

telemeter	TLM	thick film	THKF	tobin bronze	TOBBRZ
telemeter transmitter	TMX	thickener	THKNR	toboggan	TOB
telemetry	TLMY	thicker	THKR	toggle	TGL
telephone	TEL	thickness	THKNS	tolerance	TOL
telephone booth	TELB	thimble	TMB	tone and alarm	TNALM
telescope	TLSCP	thin film	TF	tongue	TNG
television	TV	thin film transistor	TFT	tongueless	TGLS
television interference	TVI	thinner	TNR	top and bottom bolt	TBB
temper	TEM	thread	THD	top of frame	TFR
temperature	TEMP	thread	TRD	topping	TOPG
temperature differential	TD	thread both ends	TBE	torpedo	TORP
temperature indicating controlling	TIC	thread cutting	TC	torpedo battery	TBATT
temperature meter	TM	thread one end	TOE	torque	TRQ
temperature switch	TSW	threaded neck	THDNK	torque differential receiver	TDR
tempered	TMPD	threaded piece	THDPC	torquemeter	TORM
tempering	TMPRG	three conductor	3C	torsion	TRSN
template	TEMPL	three phase	3PH	torsional	TORNL
tensile	TNSL	three pole	3P	total	TOT
tension	TNSN	three pole double throw	3PDT	total dynamic head	TDH
tentative	TNTV	three pole double throw switch	3PDTSW	total indicator reading	TIR
terminal	TERM	three pole single throw	3PST	total load	TLLD
terminal block	TBLK	three way	3WAY	total time	TT
terminal protective device	TPD	three wire	3W	totalize	TOTLZ
terneplate	TRPL	throat	THRT	totalizing relay	TOR
terohmmeter	TOHM	throttle	THROT	tower	TWR
tertiary	TER	through	THRU	tracer	TRCR
test equipment	TSTEQ	thrower	THWR	tracking	TRKG
test link	TLK	throwout	THWT	trade name	TRN
test specification	TSPEC	thrust	THR	traffic	TRFC
tester	TSTR	thrust line	TL	trailer	TRLR
testing	TSTG	thyristor	THYR	trailing	TRG
testing and popping	TSPOP	ticket	TKT	trainer	TRNR
tetrachloride	TET	tightening	TTNG	trajectory	TRAJ
tetrofluorethylene	TETFLEYNE	tile shingle roof	TSR	transparent	TRANS
textile	TXTL	tiller	TLR	transceiver	XCVR
that is	IE	tilting	TLG	transducer	XDCR
theoretical	THEOR	timber	TMBR	transcribe	TRSCB
theoretical point of fog	TPF	timed	TMD	transcriber	TRSBR
therm	THM	time delay closing	TDC	transcribing	TRSBG
thermal	THRM	time delay opening	TDO	transfer	XFR
thermal converter	THC	time meter	TIM	transformer	XFMR
thermal demand transmitter	TDX	time of flight	TMFL	translator	XLTR
thermistor	THMS	time opening	TO	transmission	XMSN
thermoid	TH	time since new	TSN	transmit	XMT
thermometer	THERM	time since overhaul	TSO	transmittal	XMTL
thermostat	THERMO	timer	TMR	transmitted	XMTD
thermostatic	THRMSTC	timing	TMG	transmitter	XMTR
thick	THK	tinned	TND	transferred electronic logic	TEDL

transistor driver core memory	TDCM	truss head	TRH	undersize	US
transistor-transistor logic	TTL	tubing	TBG	undervoltage	UNDV
transistor under test	TUT	tune controlled gain	TCG	undervoltage device	UVD
transistorized	TSTRZ	tuned plate tuned grid	TPTG	underwater	UWTR
transition	TRNSN	tuned radio frequency	TRF	underwater battery	UB
transmit gain control	TGC	tungsten	TUNG	undetermined	UNDETM
transportation	TRANSP	tuning	TUN	unfinished	UNFIN
transpose	TRNPS	tunnel	TNL	unglazed ceramic mosaic tile	UCMT
transposition	TPSN	tunnel diode	TNLDIO	unified	UN
transverse	TRANSV	tunnel diode logic	TDL	Unified coarse thread	UNC
transverse expansion joint	TEJ	turbine	TURB	Unified extra fine thread	UNEF
trapezoid	TRAP	turnbuckle	TRNBKL	Unified fine thread	UNF
travel limit	TRVLMT	turned	TRND	Unified sideband	USB
traveler	TRVLR	turning	TURN	Unified special thread	UNS
traveling	TRVLG	turning gear	TRNGR	uniform	UNIF
traveling wave tube	TWT	turning light	TRNLT	unijunction transistor	UJT
traversing	TRAV	turntable	TRNTBL	uninterruptible power supply	UPS
treated	TRTD	turret	TUR	union bonnet	UNB
treated hard pressed fiberboard	THPFB	twin sideband	TWSB	unit check	UK
treatment	TRTMT	twist drill gage	TDG	unit heater	UH
treble	TRB	twisted	TW	unit under test	UUT
triangle	TRNGL	twisted pair	TWPR	unit weight	UWT
tributary	TRIB	two conductor	2C	United States gage	USG
trick wheel	TRKWHL	two digit	2DIG	universal	UNIV
trigger	TRIG	two phase	2PH	universal product code	UPC
trim after forming	TAF	two stage	2STG	universal time coordinated	UTC
trimmer	TRMR	two way	2WAY	unknown	UNK
trinitrotoluene	TNT	two wire	2W	unless otherwise specified	UOS
triode	TRI	type mode series	TMS	unlimited	UNLIM
triple	TPL	type plate	TYPL	unloading	UNL
triple throw	3T	typesetting	TYPSTG	unlocking	UNLKG
triple wall	TPLW	typesetting lead	TSL	unmarked	UNMKD
triplex	TRX	typical	TYP	unmounted	UNMTD
tripped	TRP	**U**		unregulated	UNRGLTD
trolley	TRLY	ultimate	ULT	unsensitized	USTZD
troposphere	TROPO	ultrahigh frequency	UHF	unsuppressed	UNSUPPR
throttle reset	TRST	ultrasonic frequency	UF	until cooler	UC
truck	TRK	ultraviolet	UV	untreated	UTRTD
true airspeed	TAS	unbleached	UBL	untreated hard pressed fiberboard	UHPFB
true position	TP	unbleached muslin	UMUS	untwist	UNTW
true position tolerance	TPTOL	unclamp	UNCLP	updraft	UPDFT
truncated Whitworth coarse thread	TWC	undefined	UNDEF	upper	UPR
		under	UND	upper and lower	UL
truncated Whitworth fine thread	TWF	undercurrent	UNDC	upper control limit	UCL
		underfrequency	UNDF	upright	URT
truncated Whitworth special thread	TWS	underfrequency relay	UFR	upward	UPWD
		underground	UGND	USA standard	USAS
trunnion	TRUN	underheat	UHT		
		underload	UNDVD		

use as required	UAR	vertex	VTX
used on	UO	vertical	VERT
used with	UW	vertical center of buoyancy	VCB
utensil	UTN	vertical center of gravity	VCG
utility	UTIL	vertical centerline	VCL

V

vacuum	VAC	vertical centrifugal	VCE
vacuum induction melt		vertical impulse	VIMP
vacuum arc remelt	VIMVAR	vertical ladder	VL
vacuum tube	VT	vertical radius	VTR
vacuum tube voltmeter	VTVM	vertical reference line	VRL
value	VAL	vertical volute spring	
value engineering	VE	suspension	VVSS
valve	V	very high frequency	VHF
valve box	VB	very high frequency	
valve seat	VST	direction finding	VHFDF
valve stem	VSTM	very high frequency	
vane axial	VNXL	omnidirectional radio	VOR
vaporize	VPR	very high frequency	
vaporproof	VAPPRF	omnirange localizer	VORLOC
var hour meter	VARHM	very large scale integration	VLSI
varactor	VRCTR	very long range	VLR
variable	VAR	very low altitude	VLA
variable floating point	VFLPT	very low frequency	VLF
variable frequency	VF	vestibule	VEST
variable frequency		vestigial sideband	VSB
clock	VFREQCLK	vestigial sideband modulation	VSM
variable frequency oscillator	VFO	vibrate	VIB
variable gain amplifier	VGA	Vickers hardness	VH
variable resistor	VARISTOR	video	VID
variable threshold logic	VTL	video amplifier	VIDAMP
variable voltage		video display terminal	VDT
transformer	VARITRAN	video frequency	VIDF
varistor	VRIS	video integration	VINT
varmeter	VARM	village	VIL
varnish	VARN	violet	VIO
varying	VRYG	viscometer	VISMR
vegetable	VEG	viscosity index	VI
vehicle	VEH	visible	VSBL
velocity	VEL	visual	VIS
vendor item control drawing	VICD	visual flight rules	VFR
vent pipe	VP	visual glide slope	VGS
ventilate	VENT	vital load center	VLC
verbatim	VERB	vitreous	VIT
verification	VERIF	voice	VO
verify	VRFY	voice coil	VC
vernier	VERN	voice operated transmitter	
versatile	VERST	keyer	VOX
versed sine	VERS	volatile organic compound	VOC
versus	VS	volt ohm milliammeter	VOM
		volt per mil	VMIL

voltage adjusting rheostat	VADJR
voltage control transfer	VCT
voltage controlled oscillator	VCO
voltage detector	VDET
voltage drop	VD
voltage regulator	VR
voltage relay	VRLY
voltage standing wave ratio	VSWR
voltage tunable magnetron	VTN
voltage variable capacitor	VVC
voltammeter	VAM
voltmeter	VM
volume	VOL
volume unit	VU
volumetric	VLMTRC
volute	VLT
vulcanize	VULC

W

wafer	WFR
wagon	WAG
waiting	WTG
wake light	WKLT
wall receptacle	WR
wallboard	WLB
walseal	WLSL
wardrobe	WRB
warehouse	WHSE
warning	WRN
warping	WKPU
warranty	WARR
wash fountain	WF
Washburn and Moen Gage	WMGA
washer	WSHR
washing	WSHG
water	WTR
water chiller	WCHR
water closet	WC
water cooled	WCLD
water cooler	WCR
water jacket	WJ
water pump	WP
water turbine	WTURB
waterproof	WTRPRF
waterproof shroud	WPS
waterproofing	WPG
watertight	WTRTT
waterwheel	WWHL
watt demand meter	WDM
watthour	WH

watthour demand meter	WHDM	winch	WN	working steam pressure	WSP
watthour meter	WHM	wind direction	WDIR	working voltage	WV
watthour meter with contact device	WHC	winder	WNDR	workshop	WKS
		winding	WDG	worm gear	WMGR
wattmeter	WM	windlass	WNDLS	worm shaft	WMSFT
wavelength	WL	window	WDO	worm wheel	WMWHL
weakened plane joint	WPJ	window unit	WU	wound	WND
weapon	WPN	windshield	WSHLD	wrecker	WRK
weather	WEA	wire assembly	WA	wringer	WRGR
weather seal	WSL	wire bound	WBD	wrist pin	WSTPN
weather stripping	WS	wire gage	WG	wrong direction	WRDIR
weatherproof	WTHPRF	wire glass	WGL	wrought	WRT
weathertight	WEAT	wire wound	WW	wrought brass	WBRS
webbing	WBG	wiring	WRG	wrought iron	WI
week	WK	with blowout	WBL	**Y**	
weight	WT	without	WO	yard	YD
welded	WLD	without blowout	WOBO	year	YR
welder	WLDR	wood awning type window	WATW	yellow	Y
weldless	WLDS	wood block floor	WBF	yellow indicating lamp	YIL
West	W	wood boring	WDBOR	yellow light	YLT
wheel	WHL	wood casement window	WCW	yellow varnished cambric	YVC
wheelbase	WB	wood cutting	WCTG	yield point	YP
whistle	WSTL	wood furring strips	WFS	yield strength	YS
white	WHT	wood panel	WDP	**Z**	
white indicating lamp	WIL	wood shingle roof	WSR	zero adjusted	ZA
white scale	WHS	wooden box	WBX	zero temperature coefficient	ZTC
width	WD	Woodruff	WDF		
width across flats	WAF	working pressure	WPR		

3 USEFUL FORMULAS FOR GEOMETRIC ENTITIES

Formulas for Circles

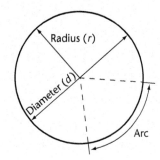

Circle*

Area $A = \pi r^2$
$A = 3.141 r^2$
$A = 0.7854 d^2$
Radius $r = d/2$
Diameter $d = 2r$
Circumference $C = 2\pi r$
$C = \pi d$
$C = 3.141 d$

*Note: 22/7 and 3.141 are different approximations for π.

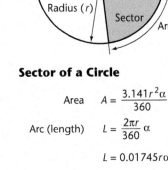

Sector of a Circle

Area $A = \dfrac{3.141 r^2 \alpha}{360}$

Arc (length) $L = \dfrac{2\pi r}{360} \alpha$

$L = 0.01745 r\alpha$

Angle $\alpha = \dfrac{L}{0.01745 r}$

Radius $r = \dfrac{L}{0.01745 \alpha}$

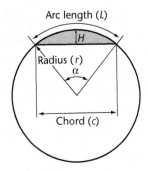

Segment of a Circle

Area $A = \frac{1}{2}(r \bullet L - c(r - h))$

Arc (length) $L = 0.01745 r\alpha$

Angle $\alpha = \dfrac{57.296 L}{r}$

Height $H = r - \frac{1}{2}\sqrt{4r^2 - c^2}$

Chord $c = 2r \sin \alpha$

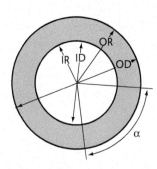

Circular Ring

Ring area $A = 0.7854 (OD^2 - ID^2)$
Ring sector area $a = 0.00873 \, \alpha(OR^2 - IR^2)$
$a = 0.00218 \, \alpha(OD^2 - ID^2)$
OD = outside diameter
ID = inside diameter
α = ring sector angle
OR = outside radius
IR = inside radius

Formulas for Triangles

Any Triangle

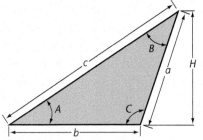

Obtuse angle triangle

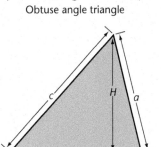

Acute angle triangle

Area

$$A = 1/2 bH = \frac{Hb}{2}$$

$$A = \sqrt{S(S-a)(S-b)(S-c)}$$

$$S = 1/2\ (a + b + c)$$

Perimeter $P = a + b + c$

Height $H = \frac{2}{b}\sqrt{S(S-a)(S-b)(S-c)}$

Sum of angles $180° = A + B + C$

Equilateral Triangle

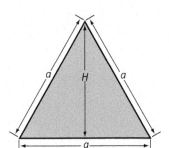

Area $A = a^2 \dfrac{\sqrt{3}}{4} = 0.433\,a^2$

$$A = 0.577 H^2$$

$$A = \frac{a^2}{2}\ \text{or}\ \frac{aH}{2}$$

Perimeter $P = 3a$

Height $H = \dfrac{a}{2}\sqrt{3} = 0.866a$

Right Triangle

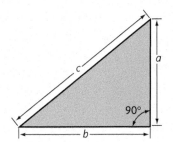

Area $A = \dfrac{ba}{2}$

Perimeter $P = a + b + c$

Height $a = \sqrt{c^2 - b^2}$

Base $b = \sqrt{c^2 - a^2}$

Hypotenuse $c = \sqrt{a^2 - b^2}$

Formulas for Four-Sided Polygons

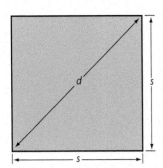

Square

Area $A = s^2$
$A = 0.5d^2$
Side $s = 0.707d$
Diagonal $d = 1.414s$
Perimeter $P = 4s$

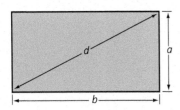

Rectangle

Area $A = ab$

Side a $a = \sqrt{d^2 - b^2}$

Side b $b = \sqrt{d^2 - a^2}$

Diagonal $d = \sqrt{a^2 - b^2}$

Perimeter $P = 2(a + b)$

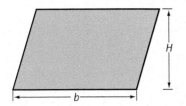

Parallelogram

Area $A = Hb$
Height $H = A/b$
Base $b = A/H$

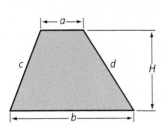

Trapezoid

Area $A = 1/2\,(a + b) \bullet H$
Perimeter $P = a + b + c + d$

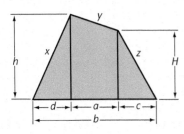

Trapezium

Area $A = \dfrac{a(H + h) + cH + dh}{2}$

Area Another method is to divide the area into two triangles, find the area of each, and add the areas together.

Perimeter $P = b + x + y + z$

Formulas for Ellipses and Parabolas

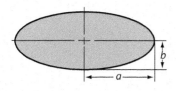

Ellipse

Area $A = \pi ab$
$A = 3.142ab$

Perimeter $P = 6.283 \cdot \dfrac{\sqrt{a^2 + b^2}}{2}$

Parabola

Area $A = 2/3\ ab$

Formulas for Regular Polygons

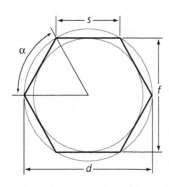

Multisided

Area $A = n\dfrac{s \cdot \frac{1}{2}f}{2}$

n = number of sides

Side $s = 2\sqrt{\frac{1}{2}d^2 - \frac{1}{2}f^2}$

Flats f = distance across flats; diameter of inscribed circle

Diagonal d = diameter of circumscribed circle
Perimeter P = sum of the sides
Angle $\alpha = 360/n$

Hexagon

Area	$A = 0.866f^2$
	$A = 0.650d^2$
	$A = 2.598s^2$
Side	$s = 0.577f$
	$s = 0.5d$
Flats	$f = 1.732s$
	$f = 0.866d$
Diagonal	$d = 2s$
	$d = 1.155f$
Perimeter	$P = 6s$
Angle	$\alpha = 60°$

Octagon

Area	$A = 0.828f^2$
	$A = 0.707d^2$
	$A = 4.828s^2$
Side	$s = 0.414f$
	$s = 0.383d$
Flats	$f = 2.414s$
	$f = 0.924d$
Diagonal	$d = 2.613s$
	$d = 1.083f$
Perimeter	$P = 8s$
Angle	$\alpha = 45°$

Formulas for 3D Shapes

Cube

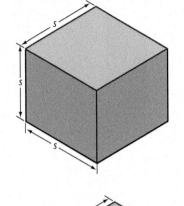

$$\begin{array}{ll}\text{Volume} & V = s^3 \\ \text{Surface area} & SA = 6s^2\end{array}$$

$$\text{Side} \quad s = \sqrt[3]{V}$$

Rectangular Prism

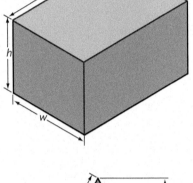

$$\begin{array}{ll}\text{Volume} & V = lwh \\ \text{Surface area} & SA = 2(lw + lh + wh) \\ \text{Length} & l = V/hw \\ \text{Width} & w = V/lh \\ \text{Height} & h = V/lw\end{array}$$

Cone (Right Circular)

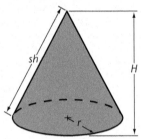

$$\begin{array}{ll}\text{Volume} & V = 1/3\ AH* \\ & A = \text{area of base} \\ & V = 1/3\pi r^2 H \\ & r = \text{radius of base}\end{array}$$

Slant height $\quad sh = \sqrt{r^2 + H^2}$

$$\begin{array}{ll}\text{Surface area} & SA = (1/2\ \text{perimeter of base} \bullet sh) + \pi r^2 \\ & SA = \pi r(sh) + \pi r^2 \\ \text{Lateral surface area} & LSA = \pi r(sh)\end{array}$$

*Note: True for any cone or pyramid

Pyramid

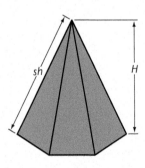

$$\begin{array}{ll}\text{Volume} & V = 1/3\ AH \\ & A = \text{area of base} \\ \text{Surface area} & SA = (1/2\ \text{perimeter of base} \bullet sh) + A\end{array}$$

Slant height $\quad sh = \sqrt{r^2 + h^2}$

r = radius of circle circumscribed around base

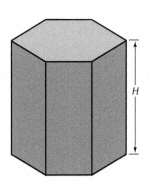

Prism

Volume $V = AH$*
          A = area of base
                (see multisided polygon)
Surface area SA = (area of each panel) + $2A$

*Note: True for any prism or cylinder with parallel bases.

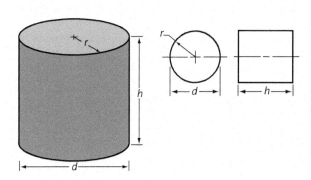

Cylinder (Right Circular)

Volume $V = Ah$
          $V = \pi r^2 h$
          $V = 0.7854 d^2 h$
Surface area $SA = \pi dh + 2\pi r^2$
               $SA = 2\pi rh + 2\pi r^2$
               $SA = 6.283 rh + 6.283 r^2$
Lateral surface area $LSA = 2\pi rh$

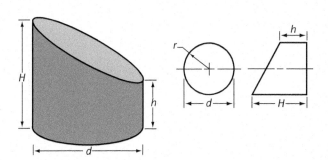

Frustum of a Cylinder

Volume $V = \pi r^2 \dfrac{H + h}{2}$

          $V = 1.5708 r^2 (H + h)$
          $V = 0.3927 d^2 (H + h)$
Lateral surface area $LSA = \pi r(H + h)$
                     $LSA = 1.5708 d(H + h)$

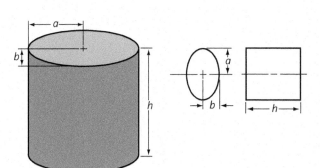

Elliptical Cylinder

Volume $V = \pi abh$

Lateral surface area $LSA = \pi h \sqrt{a^2 + b^2}$

4 RUNNING AND SLIDING FITS[a]—AMERICAN NATIONAL STANDARD

RC 1   *Close sliding fits* are intended for the accurate location of parts which must assemble without perceptible play.

RC 2   *Sliding fits* are intended for accurate location, but with greater maximum clearance than class RC 1. Parts made to this fit move and turn easily but are not intended to run freely, and in the larger sizes may seize with small temperature changes.

RC 3   *Precision running fits* are about the closest fits which can be expected to run freely and are intended for precision work at slow speeds and light journal pressures, but they are not suitable where appreciable temperature differences are likely to be encountered.

RC 4   *Close running fits* are intended chiefly for running fits on accurate machinery with moderate surface speeds and journal pressures, where accurate location and minimum play are desired.

Basic hole system. **Limits are in thousandths of an inch.** Limits for hole and shaft are applied algebraically to the basic size to obtain the limits of size for the parts. Data in **boldface** are in accordance with ABC agreements. Symbols H5, g5, etc., are hole and shaft designations used in ABC System.

Nominal Size Range, inches Over To	Class RC 1			Class RC 2			Class RC 3			Class RC 4		
	Limits of Clearance	Standard Limits		Limits of Clearance	Standard Limits		Limits of Clearance	Standard Limits		Limits of Clearance	Standard Limits	
		Hole H5	Shaft g4		Hole H6	Shaft g5		Hole H7	Shaft f6		Hole H8	Shaft f7
0–0.12	0.1 0.45	+0.2 −0	−0.1 −0.25	0.1 0.55	+0.25 −0	−0.1 −0.3	0.3 0.95	+0.4 −0	−0.3 −0.55	0.3 1.3	+0.6 −0	−0.3 −0.7
0.12–0.24	0.15 0.5	+0.2 −0	−0.15 −0.3	0.15 0.65	+0.3 −0	−0.15 −0.35	0.4 1.12	+0.5 −0	−0.4 −0.7	0.4 1.6	+0.7 −0	−0.4 −0.9
0.24–0.40	0.2 0.6	+0.25 −0	−0.2 −0.35	0.2 0.85	+0.4 −0	−0.2 −0.45	0.5 1.5	+0.6 −0	−0.5 −0.9	0.5 2.0	+0.9 −0	−0.5 −1.1
0.40–0.71	0.25 0.75	+0.3 −0	−0.25 −0.45	0.25 0.95	+0.4 −0	−0.25 −0.55	0.6 1.7	+0.7 −0	−0.6 −1.0	0.6 2.3	+1.0 −0	−0.6 −1.3
0.71–1.19	0.3 0.95	+0.4 −0	−0.3 −0.55	0.3 1.2	+0.5 −0	−0.3 −0.7	0.8 2.1	+0.8 −0	−0.8 −1.3	0.8 2.8	+1.2 −0	−0.8 −1.6
1.19–1.97	0.4 1.1	+0.4 −0	−0.4 −0.7	0.4 1.4	+0.6 −0	−0.4 −0.8	1.0 2.6	+1.0 −0	−1.0 −1.6	1.0 3.6	+1.6 −0	−1.0 −2.0
1.97–3.15	0.4 1.2	+0.5 −0	−0.4 −0.7	0.4 1.6	+0.7 −0	−0.4 −0.9	1.2 3.1	+1.2 −0	−1.2 −1.9	1.2 4.2	+1.8 −0	−1.2 −2.4
3.15–4.73	0.5 1.5	+0.6 −0	−0.5 −0.9	0.5 2.0	+0.9 −0	−0.5 −1.1	1.4 3.7	+1.4 −0	−1.4 −2.3	1.4 5.0	+2.2 −0	−1.4 −2.8
4.73–7.09	0.6 1.8	+0.7 −0	−0.6 −1.1	0.6 2.3	+1.0 −0	−0.6 −1.3	1.6 4.2	+1.6 −0	−1.6 −2.6	1.6 5.7	+2.5 −0	−1.6 −3.2
7.09–9.85	0.6 2.0	+0.8 −0	−0.6 −1.2	0.6 2.6	+1.2 −0	−0.6 −1.4	2.0 5.0	+1.8 −0	−2.0 −3.2	2.0 6.6	+2.8 −0	−2.0 −3.8
9.85–12.41	0.8 2.3	+0.9 −0	−0.8 −1.4	0.8 2.9	+1.2 −0	−0.8 −1.7	2.5 5.7	+2.0 −0	−2.5 −3.7	2.5 7.5	+3.0 −0	−2.5 −4.5
12.41–15.75	1.0 2.7	+1.0 −0	−1.0 −1.7	1.0 3.4	+1.4 −0	−1.0 −2.0	3.0 6.6	+2.2 −0	−3.0 −4.4	3.0 8.7	+3.5 −0	−3.0 −5.2

[a]From ANSI B4.1-1967 (R1994). For larger diameters, see the standard.

4 RUNNING AND SLIDING FITS[a]—AMERICAN NATIONAL STANDARD (cont.)

RC 5
RC 6 } *Medium running fits* are intended for higher running speeds, or heavy journal pressures, or both.

RC 7 *Free running fits* are intended for use where accuracy is not essential, or where large temperature variations are likely to be encountered, or under both these conditions.

RC 8
RC 9 } *Loose running fits* are intended for use where wide commercial tolerances may be necessary, together with an allowance, on the external member.

Nominal Size Range, inches Over To	Class RC 5			Class RC 6			Class RC 7			Class RC 8			Class RC 9		
	Limits of Clearance	Standard Limits Hole H8	Shaft e7	Limits of Clearance	Standard Limits Hole H9	Shaft e8	Limits of Clearance	Standard Limits Hole H9	Shaft d8	Limits of Clearance	Standard Limits Hole H10	Shaft c9	Limits of Clearance	Standard Limits Hole H11	Shaft
0–0.12	0.6 1.6	+0.6 −0	−0.6 −1.0	0.6 2.2	+1.0 −0	−0.6 −1.2	1.0 2.6	+1.0 −0	−1.0 −1.6	2.5 5.1	+1.6 −0	−2.5 −3.5	4.0 8.1	+2.5 −0	−4.0 −5.6
0.12–0.24	0.8 2.0	+0.7 −0	−0.8 −1.3	0.8 2.7	+1.2 −0	−0.8 −1.5	1.2 3.1	+1.2 −0	−1.2 −1.9	2.8 5.8	+1.8 −0	−2.8 −4.0	4.5 9.0	+3.0 −0	−4.5 −6.0
0.24–0.40	1.0 2.5	+0.9 −0	−1.0 −1.6	1.0 3.3	+1.4 −0	−1.0 −1.9	1.6 3.9	+1.4 −0	−1.6 −2.5	3.0 6.6	+2.2 −0	−3.0 −4.4	5.0 10.7	+3.5 −0	−5.0 −7.2
0.40–0.71	1.2 2.9	+1.0 −0	−1.2 −1.9	1.2 3.8	+1.6 −0	−1.2 −2.2	2.0 4.6	+1.6 −0	−2.0 −3.0	3.5 7.9	+2.8 −0	−3.5 −5.1	6.0 12.8	+4.0 −0	−6.0 −8.8
0.71–1.19	1.6 3.6	+1.2 −0	−1.6 −2.4	1.6 4.8	+2.0 −0	−1.6 −2.8	2.5 5.7	+2.0 −0	−2.5 −3.7	4.5 10.0	+3.5 −0	−4.5 −6.5	7.0 15.5	+5.0 −0	−7.0 −10.5
1.19–1.97	2.0 4.6	+1.6 −0	−2.0 −3.0	2.0 6.1	+2.5 −0	−2.0 −3.6	3.0 7.1	+2.5 −0	−3.0 −4.6	5.0 11.5	+4.0 −0	−5.0 −7.5	8.0 18.0	+6.0 −0	−8.0 −12.0
1.97–3.15	2.5 5.5	+1.8 −0	−2.5 −3.7	2.5 7.3	+3.0 −0	−2.5 −4.3	4.0 8.8	+3.0 −0	−4.0 −5.8	6.0 13.5	+4.5 −0	−6.0 −9.0	9.0 20.5	+7.0 −0	−9.0 −13.5
3.15–4.73	3.0 6.6	+2.2 −0	−3.0 −4.4	3.0 8.7	+3.5 −0	−3.0 −5.2	5.0 10.7	+3.5 −0	−5.0 −7.2	7.0 15.5	+5.0 −0	−7.0 −10.5	10.0 24.0	+9.0 −0	−10.0 −15.0
4.73–7.09	3.5 7.6	+2.5 −0	−3.5 −5.1	3.5 10.0	+4.0 −0	−3.5 −6.0	6.0 12.5	+4.0 −0	−6.0 −8.5	8.0 18.0	+6.0 −0	−8.0 −12.0	12.0 28.0	+10.0 −0	−12.0 −18.0
7.09–9.85	4.0 8.6	+2.8 −0	−4.0 −5.8	4.0 11.3	+4.5 −0	−4.0 −6.8	7.0 14.3	+4.5 −0	−7.0 −9.8	10.0 21.5	+7.0 −0	−10.0 −14.5	15.0 34.0	+12.0 −0	−15.0 −22.0
9.85–12.41	5.0 10.0	+3.0 −0	−5.0 −7.0	5.0 13.0	+5.0 −0	−5.0 −8.0	8.0 16.0	+5.0 −0	−8.0 −11.0	12.0 25.0	+8.0 −0	−12.0 −17.0	18.0 38.0	+12.0 −0	−18.0 −26.0
12.41–15.75	6.0 11.7	+3.5 −0	−6.0 −8.2	6.0 15.5	+6.0 −0	−6.0 −9.5	10.0 19.5	+6.0 −0	−10.0 13.5	14.0 29.0	+9.0 −0	−14.0 −20.0	22.0 45.0	+14.0 −0	−22.0 −31.0

[a]From ANSI B4.1-1967 (R1994). For larger diameters, see the standard.

5 CLEARANCE LOCATIONAL FITS[a]—AMERICAN NATIONAL STANDARD

LC *Locational clearance fits* are intended for parts which are normally stationary but which can be freely assembled or disassembled. They run from snug fits for parts requiring accuracy of location, through the medium clearance fits for parts such as spigots, to the looser fastener fits, where freedom of assembly is of prime importance.

Basic hole system. **Limits are in thousandths of an inch.** Limits for hole and shaft are applied algebraically to the basic size to obtain the limits of size for the parts. Data in **boldface** are in accordance with ABC agreements. Symbols H6, H5, etc., are hole and shaft designations used in ABC System.

Nominal Size Range, inches Over To	Class LC 1 Limits of Clearance	Class LC 1 Standard Limits Hole H6	Class LC 1 Standard Limits Shaft h5	Class LC 2 Limits of Clearance	Class LC 2 Standard Limits Hole H7	Class LC 2 Standard Limits Shaft h6	Class LC 3 Limits of Clearance	Class LC 3 Standard Limits Hole H8	Class LC 3 Standard Limits Shaft h7	Class LC 4 Limits of Clearance	Class LC 4 Standard Limits Hole H10	Class LC 4 Standard Limits Shaft h9	Class LC 5 Limits of Clearance	Class LC 5 Standard Limits Hole H7	Class LC 5 Standard Limits Shaft g6
0–0.12	**0** **0.45**	**+0.25** **−0**	**+0** **−0.2**	**0** **0.65**	**+0.4** **−0**	**+0** **−0.25**	**0** **1**	**+0.6** **−0**	**+0** **−0.4**	**0** **2.6**	**+1.6** **−0**	**+0** **−1.0**	0.1 0.75	**+0.4** **−0**	**−0.1** **−0.35**
0.12–0.24	**0** **0.5**	**+0.3** **−0**	**+0** **−0.2**	**0** **0.8**	**+0.5** **−0**	**+0** **−0.3**	**0** **1.2**	**+0.7** **−0**	**+0** **−0.5**	**0** **3.0**	**+1.8** **−0**	**+0** **−1.2**	0.15 0.95	**+0.5** **−0**	**−0.15** **−0.45**
0.24–0.40	**0** **0.65**	**+0.4** **−0**	**+0** **−0.25**	**0** **1.0**	**+0.6** **−0**	**+0** **−0.4**	**0** **1.5**	**+0.9** **−0**	**+0** **−0.6**	**0** **3.6**	**+2.2** **−0**	**+0** **−1.4**	0.2 1.2	**+0.6** **−0**	**−0.2** **−0.6**
0.40–0.71	**0** **0.7**	**+0.4** **−0**	**+0** **−0.3**	**0** **1.1**	**+0.7** **−0**	**+0** **−0.4**	**0** **1.7**	**+1.0** **−0**	**+0** **−0.7**	**0** **4.4**	**+2.8** **−0**	**+0** **−1.6**	0.25 1.35	**+0.7** **−0**	**−0.25** **−0.65**
0.71–1.19	**0** **0.9**	**+0.5** **−0**	**+0** **−0.4**	**0** **1.3**	**+0.8** **−0**	**+0** **−0.5**	**0** **2**	**+1.2** **−0**	**+0** **−0.8**	**0** **5.5**	**+3.5** **−0**	**+0** **−2.0**	0.3 1.6	**+0.8** **−0**	**−0.3** **−0.8**
1.19–1.97	**0** **1.0**	**+0.6** **−0**	**+0** **−0.4**	**0** **1.6**	**+1.0** **−0**	**+0** **−0.6**	**0** **2.6**	**+1.6** **−0**	**+0** **−1**	**0** **6.5**	**+4.0** **−0**	**+0** **−2.5**	0.4 2.0	**+1.0** **−0**	**−0.4** **−1.0**
1.97–3.15	**0** **1.2**	**+0.7** **−0**	**+0** **−0.5**	**0** **1.9**	**+1.2** **−0**	**+0** **−0.7**	**0** **3**	**+1.8** **−0**	**+0** **−1.2**	**0** **7.5**	**+4.5** **−0**	**+0** **−3**	0.4 2.3	**+1.2** **−0**	**−0.4** **−1.1**
3.15–4.73	**0** **1.5**	**+0.9** **−0**	**+0** **−0.6**	**0** **2.3**	**+1.4** **−0**	**+0** **−0.9**	**0** **3.6**	**+2.2** **−0**	**+0** **−1.4**	**0** **8.5**	**+5.0** **−0**	**+0** **−3.5**	0.5 2.8	**+1.4** **−0**	**−0.5** **−1.4**
4.73–7.09	**0** **1.7**	**+1.0** **−0**	**+0** **−0.7**	**0** **2.6**	**+1.6** **−0**	**+0** **−1.0**	**0** **4.1**	**+2.5** **−0**	**+0** **−1.6**	**0** **10**	**+6.0** **−0**	**+0** **−4**	0.6 3.2	**+1.6** **−0**	**−0.6** **−1.6**
7.09–9.85	**0** **2.0**	**+1.2** **−0**	**+0** **−0.8**	**0** **3.0**	**+1.8** **−0**	**+0** **−1.2**	**0** **4.6**	**+2.8** **−0**	**+0** **−1.8**	**0** **11.5**	**+7.0** **−0**	**+0** **−4.5**	0.6 3.6	**+1.8** **−0**	**−0.6** **−1.8**
9.85–12.41	**0** **2.1**	**+1.2** **−0**	**+0** **−0.9**	**0** **3.2**	**+2.0** **−0**	**+0** **−1.2**	**0** **5**	**+3.0** **−0**	**+0** **−2.0**	**0** **13.0**	**+8.0** **−0**	**+0** **−5**	0.7 3.9	**+2.0** **−0**	**−0.7** **−1.9**
12.41–15.75	**0** **2.4**	**+1.4** **−0**	**+0** **−1.0**	**0** **3.6**	**+2.2** **−0**	**+0** **−1.4**	**0** **5.7**	**+3.5** **−0**	**+0** **−2.2**	**0** **15.0**	**+9.0** **−0**	**+0** **−6**	0.7 4.3	**+2.2** **−0**	**−0.7** **−2.1**

[a]From ANSI B4.1-1967 (R1994). For larger diameters, see the standard.

5 CLEARANCE LOCATIONAL FITS[a]—AMERICAN NATIONAL STANDARD (cont.)

Nominal Size Range, inches Over To	Class LC 6 Limits of Clearance	Class LC 6 Hole H9	Class LC 6 Shaft f8	Class LC 7 Limits of Clearance	Class LC 7 Hole H10	Class LC 7 Shaft e9	Class LC 8 Limits of Clearance	Class LC 8 Hole H10	Class LC 8 Shaft d9	Class LC 9 Limits of Clearance	Class LC 9 Hole H11	Class LC 9 Shaft c10	Class LC 10 Limits of Clearance	Class LC 10 Hole H12	Class LC 10 Shaft	Class LC 11 Limits of Clearance	Class LC 11 Hole H13	Class LC 11 Shaft
0–0.12	0.3	+1.0	−0.3	0.6	+1.6	−0.6	1.0	+1.6	−1.0	2.5	+2.5	−2.5	4	+4	−4	5	+6	−5
	1.9	−0	−0.9	3.2	−0	−1.6	3.6	−0	−2.0	6.6	−0	−4.1	12	−0	−8	17	−0	−11
0.12–0.24	0.4	+1.2	−0.4	0.8	+1.8	−0.8	1.2	+1.8	−1.2	2.8	+3.0	−2.8	4.5	+5	−4.5	6	+7	−6
	2.3	−0	−1.1	3.8	−0	−2.0	4.2	−0	−2.4	7.6	−0	−4.6	14.5	−0	−9.5	20	−0	−13
0.24–0.40	0.5	+1.4	−0.5	1.0	+2.2	−1.0	1.6	+2.2	−1.6	3.0	+3.5	−3.0	5	+6	−5	7	+9	−7
	2.8	−0	−1.4	4.6	−0	−2.4	5.2	−0	−3.0	8.7	−0	−5.2	17	−0	−11	25	−0	−16
0.40–0.71	0.6	+1.6	−0.6	1.2	+2.8	−1.2	2.0	+2.8	−2.0	3.5	+4.0	−3.5	6	+7	−6	8	+10	−8
	3.2	−0	−1.6	5.6	−0	−2.8	6.4	−0	−3.6	10.3	−0	−6.3	20	−0	−13	28	−0	−18
0.71–1.19	0.8	+2.0	−0.8	1.6	+3.5	−1.6	2.5	+3.5	−2.5	4.5	+5.0	−4.5	7	+8	−7	10	+12	−10
	4.0	−0	−2.0	7.1	−0	−3.6	8.0	−0	−4.5	13.0	−0	−8.0	23	−0	−15	34	−0	−22
1.19–1.97	1.0	+2.5	−1.0	2.0	+4.0	−2.0	3.0	+4.0	−3.0	5	+6	−5	8	+10	−8	12	+16	−12
	5.1	−0	−2.6	8.5	−0	−4.5	9.5	−0	−5.5	15	−0	−9	28	−0	−18	44	−0	−28
1.97–3.15	1.2	+3.0	−1.2	2.5	+4.5	−2.5	4.0	+4.5	−4.0	6	+7	−6	10	+12	−10	14	+18	−14
	6.0	−0	−3.0	10.0	−0	−5.5	11.5	−0	−7.0	17.5	−0	−10.5	34	−0	−22	50	−0	−32
3.15–4.73	1.4	+3.5	−1.4	3.0	+5.0	−3.0	5.0	+5.0	−5.0	7	+9	−7	11	+14	−11	16	+22	−16
	7.1	−0	−3.6	11.5	−0	−6.5	13.5	−0	−8.5	21	−0	−12	39	−0	−25	60	−0	−38
4.73–7.09	1.6	+4.0	−1.6	3.5	+6.0	−3.5	6.0	+6	−6	8	+10	−8	12	+16	−12	18	+25	−18
	8.1	−0	−4.1	13.5	−0	−7.5	16.0	−0	−10	24	−0	−14	44	−0	−28	68	−0	−43
7.09–9.85	2.0	+4.5	−2.0	4.0	+7.0	−4.0	7.0	+7	−7	10	+12	−10	16	+18	−16	22	+28	−22
	9.3	−0	−4.8	15.5	−0	−8.5	18.5	−0	−11.5	29	−0	−17	52	−0	−34	78	−0	−50
9.85–12.41	2.2	+5.0	−2.2	4.5	+8.0	−4.5	7.0	+8	−7	12	+12	−12	20	+20	−20	28	+30	−28
	10.2	−0	−5.2	17.5	−0	−9.5	20.0	−0	−12	32	−0	−20	60	−0	−40	88	−0	−58
12.41–15.75	2.5	+6.0	−2.5	5.0	+9.0	−5	8.0	+9	−8	14	+14	−14	22	+22	−22	30	+35	−30
	12.0	−0	−6.0	20.0	−0	−11	23.0	−0	−14	37	−0	−23	66	−0	−44	100	−0	−65

[a]From ANSI B4.1-1967 (R1994). For larger diameters, see the standard.

6 TRANSITION LOCATIONAL FITS[a]—AMERICAN NATIONAL STANDARD

LT *Transition fits* are a compromise between clearance and interference fits, for application where accuracy of location is important, but either a small amount of clearance or interference is permissible.

Basic hole system. **Limits are in thousandths of an inch.** Limits for hole and shaft are applied algebraically to the basic size to obtain the limits of size for the mating parts. Data in **boldface** are in accordance with ABC agreements. "Fit" represents the maximum interference (minus values) and the maximum clearance (plus values). Symbols H7, js6, etc., are hole and shaft designations used in ABC System.

Nominal Size Range, inches, Over To	Class LT 1 Fit	Class LT 1 Hole H7	Class LT 1 Shaft js6	Class LT 2 Fit	Class LT 2 Hole H8	Class LT 2 Shaft js7	Class LT 3 Fit	Class LT 3 Hole H7	Class LT 3 Shaft k6	Class LT 4 Fit	Class LT 4 Hole H8	Class LT 4 Shaft k7	Class LT 5 Fit	Class LT 5 Hole H7	Class LT 5 Shaft n6	Class LT 6 Fit	Class LT 6 Hole H7	Class LT 6 Shaft n7
0–0.12	−0.10 / +0.50	+0.4 / −0	+0.10 / −0.10	−0.2 / +0.8	+0.6 / −0	+0.2 / −0.2							−0.5 / +0.15	+0.4 / −0	+0.5 / +0.25	−0.65 / +0.15	+0.4 / −0	+0.65 / +0.25
0.12–0.24	−0.15 / +0.65	+0.5 / −0	+0.15 / −0.15	−0.25 / +0.95	+0.7 / −0	+0.25 / −0.25							−0.6 / +0.2	+0.5 / −0	+0.6 / +0.3	−0.8 / +0.2	+0.5 / −0	+0.8 / +0.3
0.24–0.40	−0.2 / +0.8	+0.6 / −0	+0.2 / −0.2	−0.3 / +1.2	+0.9 / −0	+0.3 / −0.3	−0.5 / +0.5	+0.6 / −0	+0.5 / +0.1	−0.7 / +0.8	+0.9 / −0	+0.7 / +0.1	−0.8 / +0.2	+0.6 / −0	+0.8 / +0.4	−1.0 / +0.2	+0.6 / −0	+1.0 / +0.4
0.40–0.71	−0.2 / +0.9	+0.7 / −0	+0.2 / −0.2	−0.35 / +1.35	+1.0 / −0	+0.35 / −0.35	−0.5 / +0.6	+0.7 / −0	+0.5 / +0.1	−0.8 / +0.9	+1.0 / −0	+0.8 / +0.1	−0.9 / +0.2	+0.7 / −0	+0.9 / +0.5	−1.2 / +0.2	+0.7 / −0	+1.2 / +0.5
0.71–1.19	−0.25 / +1.05	+0.8 / −0	+0.25 / −0.25	−0.4 / +1.6	+1.2 / −0	+0.4 / −0.4	−0.6 / +0.7	+0.8 / −0	+0.6 / +0.1	−0.9 / +1.1	+1.2 / −0	+0.9 / +0.1	−1.1 / +0.2	+0.8 / −0	+1.1 / +0.6	−1.4 / +0.2	+0.8 / −0	+1.4 / +0.6
1.19–1.97	−0.3 / +1.3	+1.0 / −0	+0.3 / −0.3	−0.5 / +2.1	+1.6 / −0	+0.5 / −0.5	−0.7 / +0.9	+1.0 / −0	+0.7 / +0.1	−1.1 / +1.5	+1.6 / −0	+1.1 / +0.1	−1.3 / +0.3	+1.0 / −0	+1.3 / +0.7	−1.7 / +0.3	+1.0 / −0	+1.7 / +0.7
1.97–3.15	−0.3 / +1.5	+1.2 / −0	+0.3 / −0.3	−0.6 / +2.4	+1.8 / −0	+0.6 / −0.6	−0.8 / +1.1	+1.2 / −0	+0.8 / +0.1	−1.3 / +1.7	+1.8 / −0	+1.3 / +0.1	−1.5 / +0.4	+1.2 / −0	+1.5 / +0.8	−2.0 / +0.4	+1.2 / −0	+2.0 / +0.8
3.15–4.73	−0.4 / +1.8	+1.4 / −0	+0.4 / −0.4	−0.7 / +2.9	+2.2 / −0	+0.7 / −0.7	−1.0 / +1.3	+1.4 / −0	+1.0 / +0.1	−1.5 / +2.1	+2.2 / −0	+1.5 / +0.1	−1.9 / +0.4	+1.4 / −0	+1.9 / +1.0	−2.4 / +0.4	+1.4 / −0	+2.4 / +1.0
4.73–7.09	−0.5 / +2.1	+1.6 / −0	+0.5 / −0.5	−0.8 / +3.3	+2.5 / −0	+0.8 / −0.8	−1.1 / +1.5	+1.6 / −0	+1.1 / +0.1	−1.7 / +2.4	+2.5 / −0	+1.7 / +0.1	−2.2 / +0.4	+1.6 / −0	+2.2 / +1.2	−2.8 / +0.4	+1.6 / −0	+2.8 / +1.2
7.09–9.85	−0.6 / +2.4	+1.8 / −0	+0.6 / −0.6	−0.9 / +3.7	+2.8 / −0	+0.9 / −0.9	−1.4 / +1.6	+1.8 / −0	+1.4 / +0.2	−2.0 / +2.6	+2.8 / −0	+2.0 / +0.2	−2.6 / +0.4	+1.8 / −0	+2.6 / +1.4	−3.2 / +0.4	+1.8 / −0	+3.2 / +1.4
9.85–12.41	−0.6 / +2.6	+2.0 / −0	+0.6 / −0.6	−1.0 / +4.0	+3.0 / −0	+1.0 / −1.0	−1.4 / +1.8	+2.0 / −0	+1.4 / +0.2	−2.2 / +2.8	+3.0 / −0	+2.2 / +0.2	−2.6 / +0.6	+2.0 / −0	+2.6 / +1.4	−3.4 / +0.6	+2.0 / −0	+3.4 / +1.4
12.41–15.75	−0.7 / +2.9	+2.2 / −0	+0.7 / −0.7	−1.0 / +4.5	+3.5 / −0	+1.0 / −1.0	−1.6 / +2.0	+2.2 / −0	+1.6 / +0.2	−2.4 / +3.3	+3.5 / −0	+2.4 / +0.2	−3.0 / +0.6	+2.2 / −0	+3.0 / +1.6	−3.8 / +0.6	+2.2 / −0	+3.8 / +1.6

[a]From ANSI B4.1-1967 (R1994). For larger diameters, see the standard.

7 INTERFERENCE LOCATIONAL FITS[a]—AMERICAN NATIONAL STANDARD

LN   *Locational interference fits* are used where accuracy of location is of prime importance and for parts requiring rigidity and alignment with no special requirements for bore pressure. Such fits are not intended for parts designed to transmit frictional loads from one part to another by virtue of the tightness of fit, as these conditions are covered by force fits.

Basic hole system. **Limits are in thousandths of an inch.** Limits for hole and shaft are applied algebraically to the basic size to obtain the limits of size for the parts. Data in **boldface** are in accordance with ABC agreements. Symbols H7, p6, etc., are hole and shaft designations used in ABC System.

Nominal Size Range, inches Over To	Class LN 1			Class LN 2			Class LN 3		
	Limits of Interference	Standard Limits		Limits of Interference	Standard Limits		Limits of Interference	Standard Limits	
		Hole H6	Shaft n5		Hole H7	Shaft p6		Hole H7	Shaft r6
0–0.12	0 0.45	+0.25 −0	+0.45 +0.25	0 0.65	+0.4 −0	+0.65 +0.4	0.1 0.75	+0.4 −0	+0.75 +0.5
0.12–0.24	0 0.5	+0.3 −0	+0.5 +0.3	0 0.8	+0.5 −0	+0.8 +0.5	0.1 0.9	+0.5 −0	+0.9 +0.6
0.24–0.40	0 0.65	+0.4 −0	+0.65 +0.4	0 1.0	+0.6 −0	+1.0 +0.6	0.2 1.2	+0.6 −0	+1.2 +0.8
0.40–0.71	0 0.8	+0.4 −0	+0.8 +0.4	0 1.1	+0.7 −0	+1.1 +0.7	0.3 1.4	+0.7 −0	+1.4 +1.0
0.71–1.19	0 1.0	+0.5 −0	+1.0 +0.5	0 1.3	+0.8 −0	+1.3 +0.8	0.4 1.7	+0.8 −0	+1.7 +1.2
1.19–1.97	0 1.1	+0.6 −0	+1.1 +0.6	0 1.6	+1.0 −0	+1.6 +1.0	0.4 2.0	+1.0 −0	+2.0 +1.4
1.97–3.15	0.1 1.3	+0.7 −0	+1.3 +0.7	0.2 2.1	+1.2 −0	+2.1 +1.4	0.4 2.3	+1.2 −0	+2.3 +1.6
3.15–4.73	0.1 1.6	+0.9 −0	+1.6 +1.0	0.2 2.5	+1.4 −0	+2.5 +1.6	0.6 2.9	+1.4 −0	+2.9 +2.0
4.73–7.09	0.2 1.9	+1.0 −0	+1.9 +1.2	0.2 2.8	+1.6 −0	+2.8 +1.8	0.9 3.5	+1.6 −0	+3.5 +2.5
7.09–9.85	0.2 2.2	+1.2 −0	+2.2 +1.4	0.2 3.2	+1.8 −0	+3.2 +2.0	1.2 4.2	+1.8 −0	+4.2 +3.0
9.85–12.41	0.2 2.3	+1.2 −0	+2.3 +1.4	0.2 3.4	+2.0 −0	+3.4 +2.2	1.5 4.7	+2.0 −0	+4.7 +3.5

[a]From ANSI B4.1-1967 (R1994). For larger diameters, see the standard.

8 FORCE AND SHRINK FITS[a]—AMERICAN NATIONAL STANDARD

FN 1 *Light drive fits* are those requiring light assembly pressures, and produce more or less permanent assemblies. They are suitable for thin sections or long fits, or in cast-iron external members.

FN 2 *Medium drive fits* are suitable for ordinary steel parts, or for shrink fits on light sections. They are about the tightest fits that can be used with high-grade cast-iron external members.

FN 3 *Heavy drive fits* are suitable for heavier steel parts or for shrink fits in medium sections.

FN 4 }
FN 5 } *Force fits* are suitable for parts which can be highly stressed, or for shrink fits where the heavy pressing forces required are impractical.

Basic hole system. **Limits are in thousandths of an inch.** Limits for hole and shaft are applied algebraically to the basic size to obtain the limits of size for the parts. Data in **boldface** are in accordance with ABC agreements. Symbols H7, s6, etc., are hole and shaft designations used in ABC System.

Nominal Size Range, inches Over To	Class FN 1 Limits of Interference	Class FN 1 Hole H6	Class FN 1 Shaft	Class FN 2 Limits of Interference	Class FN 2 Hole H7	Class FN 2 Shaft s6	Class FN 3 Limits of Interference	Class FN 3 Hole H7	Class FN 3 Shaft t6	Class FN 4 Limits of Interference	Class FN 4 Hole H7	Class FN 4 Shaft u6	Class FN 5 Limits of Interference	Class FN 5 Hole H8	Class FN 5 Shaft x7
0–0.12	0.05 / 0.5	+0.25 / −0	+0.5 / +0.3	0.2 / 0.85	+0.4 / −0	+0.85 / +0.6				0.3 / 0.95	+0.4 / −0	+0.95 / +0.7	0.3 / 1.3	+0.6 / −0	+1.3 / +0.9
0.12–0.24	0.1 / 0.6	+0.3 / −0	+0.6 / +0.4	0.2 / 1.0	+0.5 / −0	+1.0 / +0.7				0.4 / 1.2	+0.5 / −0	+1.2 / +0.9	0.5 / 1.7	+0.7 / −0	+1.7 / +1.2
0.24–0.40	0.1 / 0.75	+0.4 / −0	+0.75 / +0.5	0.4 / 1.4	+0.6 / −0	+1.4 / +1.0				0.6 / 1.6	+0.6 / −0	+1.6 / +1.2	0.5 / 2.0	+0.9 / −0	+2.0 / +1.4
0.40–0.56	0.1 / 0.8	+0.4 / −0	+0.8 / +0.5	0.5 / 1.6	+0.7 / −0	+1.6 / +1.2				0.7 / 1.8	+0.7 / −0	+1.8 / +1.4	0.6 / 2.3	+1.0 / −0	+2.3 / +1.6
0.56–0.71	0.2 / 0.9	+0.4 / −0	+0.9 / +0.6	0.5 / 1.6	+0.7 / −0	+1.6 / +1.2				0.7 / 1.8	+0.7 / −0	+1.8 / +1.4	0.8 / 2.5	+1.0 / −0	+2.5 / +1.8
0.71–0.95	0.2 / 1.1	+0.5 / −0	+1.1 / +0.7	0.6 / 1.9	+0.8 / −0	+1.9 / +1.4				0.8 / 2.1	+0.8 / −0	+2.1 / +1.6	1.0 / 3.0	+1.2 / −0	+3.0 / +2.2
0.95–1.19	0.3 / 1.2	+0.5 / −0	+1.2 / +0.8	0.6 / 1.9	+0.8 / −0	+1.9 / +1.4	0.8 / 2.1	+0.8 / −0	+2.1 / +1.6	1.0 / 2.3	+0.8 / −0	+2.3 / +1.8	1.3 / 3.3	+1.2 / −0	+3.3 / +2.5
1.19–1.58	0.3 / 1.3	+0.6 / −0	+1.3 / +0.9	0.8 / 2.4	+1.0 / −0	+2.4 / +1.8	1.0 / 2.6	+1.0 / −0	+2.6 / +2.0	1.5 / 3.1	+1.0 / −0	+3.1 / +2.5	1.4 / 4.0	+1.6 / −0	+4.0 / +3.0

[a]ANSI B4.1-1967 (R1994).

8 FORCE AND SHRINK FITS[a]—AMERICAN NATIONAL STANDARD (cont.)

Nominal Size Range, inches Over / To	Class FN 1 Limits of Interference	Class FN 1 Hole H6	Class FN 1 Shaft	Class FN 2 Limits of Interference	Class FN 2 Hole H7	Class FN 2 Shaft s6	Class FN 3 Limits of Interference	Class FN 3 Hole H7	Class FN 3 Shaft t6	Class FN 4 Limits of Interference	Class FN 4 Hole H7	Class FN 4 Shaft u6	Class FN 5 Limits of Interference	Class FN 5 Hole H8	Class FN 5 Shaft x7
1.58–1.97	0.4 / 1.4	+0.6 / –0	+1.4 / –1.0	0.8 / 2.4	+1.0 / –0	+2.4 / +1.8	1.2 / 2.8	+1.0 / –0	+2.8 / +2.2	1.8 / 3.4	+1.0 / –0	+3.4 / +2.8	2.4 / 5.0	+1.6 / –0	+5.0 / +4.0
1.97–2.56	0.6 / 1.8	+0.7 / –0	+1.8 / +1.3	0.8 / 2.7	+1.2 / –0	+2.7 / +2.0	1.3 / 3.2	+1.2 / –0	+3.2 / +2.5	2.3 / 4.2	+1.2 / –0	+4.2 / +3.5	3.2 / 6.2	+1.8 / –0	+6.2 / +5.0
2.56–3.15	0.7 / 1.9	+0.7 / –0	+1.9 / +1.4	1.0 / 2.9	+1.2 / –0	+2.9 / +2.2	1.8 / 3.7	+1.2 / –0	+3.7 / +3.0	2.8 / 4.7	+1.2 / –0	+4.7 / +4.0	4.2 / 7.2	+1.8 / –0	+7.2 / +6.0
3.15–3.94	0.9 / 24	+0.9 / –0	+2.4 / +1.8	1.4 / 3.7	+1.4 / –0	+3.7 / +2.8	2.1 / 4.4	+1.4 / –0	+4.4 / +3.5	3.6 / 5.9	+1.4 / –0	+5.9 / +5.0	4.8 / 8.4	+2.2 / –0	+8.4 / +7.0
3.94–4.73	1.1 / 2.6	+0.9 / –0	+2.6 / +2.0	1.6 / 3.9	+1.4 / –0	+3.9 / +3.0	2.6 / 4.9	+1.4 / –0	+4.9 / +4.0	4.6 / 6.9	+1.4 / –0	+6.9 / +6.0	5.8 / 9.4	+2.2 / –0	+9.4 / +8.0
4.73–5.52	1.2 / 2.9	+1.0 / –0	+2.9 / +2.2	1.9 / 4.5	+1.6 / –0	+4.5 / +3.5	3.4 / 6.0	+1.6 / –0	+6.0 / +5.0	5.4 / 8.0	+1.6 / –0	+8.0 / +7.0	7.5 / 11.6	+2.5 / –0	+11.6 / +10.0
5.52–6.30	1.5 / 3.2	+1.0 / –0	+3.2 / +2.5	2.4 / 5.0	+1.6 / –0	+5.0 / +4.0	3.4 / 6.0	+1.6 / –0	+6.0 / +5.0	5.4 / 8.0	+1.6 / –0	+8.0 / +7.0	9.5 / 13.6	+2.5 / –0	+13.6 / +12.0
6.30–7.09	1.8 / 3.5	+1.0 / –0	+3.5 / +2.8	2.9 / 5.5	+1.6 / –0	+5.5 / +4.5	4.4 / 7.0	+1.6 / –0	+7.0 / +6.0	6.4 / 9.0	+1.6 / –0	+9.0 / +8.0	9.5 / 13.6	+2.5 / –0	+13.6 / +12.0
7.09–7.88	1.8 / 3.8	+1.2 / –0	+3.8 / +3.0	3.2 / 6.2	+1.8 / –0	+6.2 / +5.0	5.2 / 8.2	+1.8 / –0	+8.2 / +7.0	7.2 / 10.2	+1.8 / –0	+10.2 / +9.0	11.2 / 15.8	+2.8 / –0	+15.8 / +14.0
7.88–8.86	2.3 / 4.3	+1.2 / –0	+4.3 / +3.5	3.2 / 6.2	+1.8 / –0	+6.2 / +5.0	5.2 / 8.2	+1.8 / –0	+8.2 / +7.0	8.2 / 11.2	+1.8 / –0	+11.2 / +10.0	13.2 / 17.8	+2.8 / –0	+17.8 / +16.0
8.86–9.85	2.3 / 4.3	+1.2 / –0	+4.3 / +3.5	4.2 / 7.2	+1.8 / –0	+7.2 / +6.0	6.2 / 9.2	+1.8 / –0	+9.2 / +8.0	10.2 / 13.2	+1.8 / –0	+13.2 / +12.0	13.2 / 17.8	+2.8 / –0	+17.8 / +16.0
9.85–11.03	2.8 / 4.9	+1.2 / –0	+4.9 / +4.0	4.0 / 7.2	+2.0 / –0	+7.2 / +6.0	7.0 / 10.2	+2.0 / –0	+10.2 / +9.0	10.0 / 13.2	+2.0 / –0	+13.2 / +12.0	15.0 / 20.0	+3.0 / –0	+20.0 / +18.0
11.03–12.41	2.8 / 4.9	+1.2 / –0	+4.9 / +4.0	5.0 / 8.2	+2.0 / –0	+8.2 / +7.0	7.0 / 10.2	+2.0 / –0	+10.2 / +9.0	12.0 / 15.2	+2.0 / –0	+15.2 / +14.0	17.0 / 22.0	+3.0 / –0	+22.0 / +20.0
12.41–13.98	3.1 / 5.5	+1.4 / –0	+5.5 / +4.5	5.8 / 9.4	+2.2 / –0	+9.4 / +8.0	7.8 / 11.4	+2.2 / –0	+11.4 / +10.0	13.8 / 17.4	+2.2 / –0	+17.4 / +16.0	18.5 / 24.2	+3.5 / +0	+24.2 / +22.0

[a]From ANSI B4.1-1967 (R1994). For larger diameters, see the standard.

9 INTERNATIONAL TOLERANCE GRADES[a]

Dimensions are in millimeters.

Basic Sizes		Tolerance Grades[b]																	
Over	Up to and Including	IT01	IT0	IT1	IT2	IT3	IT4	IT5	IT6	IT7	IT8	IT9	IT10	IT11	IT12	IT13	IT14	IT15	IT16
0	3	0.0003	0.0005	0.0008	0.0012	0.002	0.003	0.004	0.006	0.010	0.014	0.025	0.040	0.060	0.100	0.140	0.250	0.400	0.600
3	6	0.0004	0.0006	0.001	0.0015	0.0025	0.004	0.005	0.008	0.012	0.018	0.030	0.048	0.075	0.120	0.180	0.300	0.480	0.750
6	10	0.0004	0.0006	0.001	0.0015	0.0025	0.004	0.006	0.009	0.015	0.022	0.036	0.058	0.090	0.150	0.220	0.360	0.580	0.900
10	18	0.0005	0.0008	0.0012	0.002	0.003	0.005	0.008	0.011	0.018	0.027	0.043	0.070	0.110	0.180	0.270	0.430	0.700	1.100
18	30	0.0006	0.001	0.0015	0.0025	0.004	0.006	0.009	0.013	0.021	0.033	0.052	0.084	0.130	0.210	0.330	0.520	0.840	1.300
30	50	0.0006	0.001	0.0015	0.0025	0.004	0.007	0.011	0.016	0.025	0.039	0.062	0.100	0.160	0.250	0.390	0.620	1.000	1.600
50	80	0.0008	0.0012	0.002	0.003	0.005	0.008	0.013	0.019	0.030	0.046	0.074	0.120	0.190	0.300	0.460	0.740	1.200	1.900
80	120	0.001	0.0015	0.0025	0.004	0.006	0.010	0.015	0.022	0.035	0.054	0.087	0.140	0.220	0.350	0.540	0.870	1.400	2.200
120	180	0.0012	0.002	0.0035	0.005	0.008	0.012	0.018	0.025	0.040	0.063	0.100	0.160	0.250	0.400	0.630	1.000	1.600	2.500
180	250	0.002	0.003	0.0045	0.007	0.010	0.014	0.020	0.029	0.046	0.072	0.115	0.185	0.290	0.460	0.720	1.150	1.850	2.900
250	315	0.0025	0.004	0.006	0.008	0.012	0.016	0.023	0.032	0.052	0.081	0.130	0.210	0.320	0.520	0.810	1.300	2.100	3.200
315	400	0.003	0.005	0.007	0.009	0.013	0.018	0.025	0.036	0.057	0.089	0.140	0.230	0.360	0.570	0.890	1.400	2.300	3.600
400	500	0.004	0.006	0.008	0.010	0.015	0.020	0.027	0.040	0.063	0.097	0.155	0.250	0.400	0.630	0.970	1.550	2.500	4.000
500	630	0.0045	0.006	0.009	0.011	0.016	0.022	0.030	0.044	0.070	0.110	0.175	0.280	0.440	0.700	1.100	1.750	2.800	4.400
630	800	0.005	0.007	0.010	0.013	0.018	0.025	0.035	0.050	0.080	0.125	0.200	0.320	0.500	0.800	1.250	2.000	3.200	5.000
800	1000	0.0055	0.008	0.011	0.015	0.021	0.029	0.040	0.056	0.090	0.140	0.230	0.360	0.560	0.900	1.400	2.300	3.600	5.600
1000	1250	0.0065	0.009	0.013	0.018	0.024	0.034	0.046	0.066	0.105	0.165	0.260	0.420	0.660	1.050	1.650	2.600	4.200	6.600
1250	1600	0.008	0.011	0.015	0.021	0.029	0.040	0.054	0.078	0.125	0.195	0.310	0.500	0.780	1.250	1.950	3.100	5.000	7.800
1600	2000	0.009	0.013	0.018	0.025	0.035	0.048	0.065	0.092	0.150	0.230	0.370	0.600	0.920	1.500	2.300	3.700	6.000	9.200
2000	2500	0.011	0.015	0.022	0.030	0.041	0.057	0.077	0.110	0.175	0.280	0.440	0.700	1.100	1.750	2.800	4.400	7.000	11.000
2500	3150	0.013	0.018	0.026	0.036	0.050	0.069	0.093	0.135	0.210	0.330	0.540	0.860	1.350	2.100	3.300	5.400	8.600	13.500

[a]From ANSI B4.2-1978 (R1994).
[b]IT Values for tolerance grades larger than IT16 can be calculated by using the formulas: IT17 = IT12 × 10, IT18 = IT13 × 10, etc.

10 PREFERRED METRIC HOLE BASIS CLEARANCE FITSª—AMERICAN NATIONAL STANDARD

Dimensions are in millimeters.

Basic Size		Loose Running Hole H11	Shaft c11	Fit	Free Running Hole H9	Shaft d9	Fit	Close Running Hole H8	Shaft f7	Fit	Sliding Hole H7	Shaft g6	Fit	Locational Clearance Hole H7	Shaft h6	Fit
1	Max	1.060	0.940	0.180	1.025	0.980	0.070	1.014	0.994	0.030	1.010	0.998	0.018	1.010	1.000	0.016
	Min	1.000	0.880	0.060	1.000	0.955	0.020	1.000	0.984	0.006	1.000	0.992	0.002	1.000	0.994	0.000
1.2	Max	1.260	1.140	0.180	1.225	1.180	0.070	1.214	1.194	0.030	1.210	1.198	0.018	1.210	1.200	0.016
	Min	1.200	1.080	0.060	1.200	1.155	0.020	1.200	1.184	0.006	1.200	1.192	0.002	1.200	1.194	0.000
1.6	Max	1.660	1.540	0.180	1.625	1.580	0.070	1.614	1.594	0.030	1.610	1.598	0.018	1.610	1.600	0.016
	Min	1.600	1.480	0.060	1.600	1.555	0.020	1.600	1.584	0.006	1.600	1.592	0.002	1.600	1.594	0.000
2	Max	2.060	1.940	0.180	2.025	1.980	0.070	2.014	1.994	0.030	2.010	1.998	0.018	2.010	2.000	0.016
	Min	2.000	1.880	0.060	2.000	1.955	0.020	2.000	1.984	0.006	2.000	1.992	0.002	2.000	1.994	0.000
2.5	Max	2.560	2.440	0.180	2.525	2.480	0.070	2.514	2.494	0.030	2.510	2.498	0.018	2.510	2.500	0.016
	Min	2.500	2.380	0.060	2.500	2.455	0.020	2.500	2.484	0.006	2.500	2.492	0.002	2.500	2.494	0.000
3	Max	3.060	2.940	0.180	3.025	2.980	0.070	3.014	2.994	0.030	3.010	2.998	0.018	3.010	3.000	0.016
	Min	3.000	2.880	0.060	3.000	2.955	0.020	3.000	2.984	0.006	3.000	2.992	0.002	3.000	2.994	0.000
4	Max	4.075	3.930	0.220	4.030	3.970	0.090	4.018	3.990	0.040	4.012	3.996	0.024	4.012	4.000	0.020
	Min	4.000	3.855	0.070	4.000	3.940	0.030	4.000	3.978	0.010	4.000	3.988	0.004	4.000	3.992	0.000
5	Max	5.075	4.930	0.220	5.030	4.970	0.090	5.018	4.990	0.040	5.012	4.996	0.024	5.012	5.000	0.020
	Min	5.000	4.855	0.070	5.000	4.940	0.030	5.000	4.978	0.010	5.000	4.988	0.004	5.000	4.992	0.000
6	Max	6.075	5.930	0.220	6.030	5.970	0.090	6.018	5.990	0.040	6.012	5.996	0.024	6.012	6.000	0.020
	Min	6.000	5.855	0.070	6.000	5.940	0.030	6.000	5.978	0.010	6.000	5.988	0.004	6.000	5.992	0.000
8	Max	8.090	7.920	0.260	8.036	7.960	0.112	8.022	7.987	0.050	8.015	7.995	0.029	8.015	8.000	0.024
	Min	8.000	7.830	0.080	8.000	7.924	0.040	8.000	7.972	0.013	8.000	7.986	0.005	8.000	7.991	0.000
10	Max	10.090	9.920	0.260	10.036	9.960	0.112	10.022	9.987	0.050	10.015	9.995	0.029	10.015	10.000	0.024
	Min	10.000	9.830	0.080	10.000	9.924	0.040	10.000	9.972	0.013	10.000	9.986	0.005	10.000	9.991	0.000
12	Max	12.110	11.905	0.315	12.043	11.950	0.136	12.027	11.984	0.061	12.018	11.994	0.035	12.018	12.000	0.029
	Min	12.000	11.795	0.095	12.000	11.907	0.050	12.000	11.966	0.016	12.000	11.983	0.006	12.000	11.989	0.000
16	Max	16.110	15.905	0.315	16.043	15.950	0.136	16.027	15.984	0.061	16.018	15.994	0.035	16.018	16.000	0.029
	Min	16.000	15.795	0.095	16.000	15.907	0.050	16.000	15.966	0.016	16.000	15.983	0.006	16.000	15.989	0.000
20	Max	20.130	19.890	0.370	20.052	19.935	0.169	20.033	19.980	0.074	20.021	19.993	0.041	20.021	20.000	0.034
	Min	20.000	19.760	0.110	20.000	19.883	0.065	20.000	19.959	0.020	20.000	19.980	0.007	20.000	19.987	0.000
25	Max	25.130	24.890	0.370	25.052	24.935	0.169	25.033	24.980	0.074	25.021	24.993	0.041	25.021	25.000	0.034
	Min	25.000	24.760	0.110	25.000	24.883	0.065	25.000	24.959	0.020	25.000	24.980	0.007	25.000	24.987	0.000
30	Max	30.130	29.890	0.370	30.052	29.935	0.169	30.033	29.980	0.074	30.021	29.993	0.041	30.021	30.000	0.034
	Min	30.000	29.760	0.110	30.000	29.883	0.065	30.000	29.959	0.020	30.000	29.980	0.007	30.000	29.987	0.000

ªFrom ANSI B4.2-1978 (R1994).

10 PREFERRED METRIC HOLE BASIS CLEARANCE FITS[a]—AMERICAN NATIONAL STANDARD (cont.)

Dimensions are in millimeters.

Basic Size		Loose Running			Free Running			Close Running			Sliding			Locational Clearance		
		Hole H11	Shaft c11	Fit	Hole H9	Shaft d9	Fit	Hole H8	Shaft f7	Fit	Hole H7	Shaft g6	Fit	Hole H7	Shaft h6	Fit
40	Max	40.160	39.880	0.440	40.062	39.920	0.204	40.039	39.975	0.089	40.025	39.991	0.050	40.025	40.000	0.041
	Min	40.000	39.720	0.120	40.000	39.858	0.080	40.000	39.950	0.025	40.000	39.975	0.009	40.000	39.984	0.000
50	Max	50.160	49.870	0.450	50.062	49.920	0.204	50.039	49.975	0.089	50.025	49.991	0.050	50.025	50.000	0.041
	Min	50.000	49.710	0.130	50.000	49.858	0.080	50.000	49.950	0.025	50.000	49.975	0.009	50.000	49.984	0.000
60	Max	60.190	59.860	0.520	60.074	59.900	0.248	60.046	59.970	0.106	60.030	59.990	0.059	60.030	60.000	0.049
	Min	60.000	59.670	0.140	60.000	59.826	0.100	60.000	59.940	0.030	60.000	59.971	0.010	60.000	59.981	0.000
80	Max	80.190	79.950	0.530	80.074	79.900	0.248	80.046	79.970	0.106	80.030	79.990	0.059	80.030	80.000	0.049
	Min	80.000	79.660	0.150	80.000	79.826	0.100	80.000	79.940	0.030	80.000	79.971	0.010	80.000	79.981	0.000
100	Max	100.220	99.830	0.610	100.087	99.880	0.294	100.054	99.964	0.125	100.035	99.988	0.069	100.035	100.000	0.057
	Min	100.000	99.610	0.170	100.000	99.793	0.120	100.000	99.929	0.036	100.000	99.966	0.012	100.000	99.978	0.000
120	Max	120.220	119.820	0.620	120.087	119.880	0.294	120.054	119.964	0.125	120.035	119.988	0.069	120.035	120.000	0.057
	Min	120.000	119.600	0.180	120.000	119.793	0.120	120.000	119.929	0.036	120.000	119.966	0.012	120.000	119.978	0.000
160	Max	160.250	159.790	0.710	160.100	159.855	0.345	160.063	159.957	0.146	160.040	159.986	0.079	160.040	160.000	0.065
	Min	160.000	159.540	0.210	160.000	159.755	0.145	160.000	159.917	0.043	160.000	159.961	0.014	160.000	159.975	0.000
200	Max	200.290	199.760	0.820	200.115	199.830	0.400	200.072	199.950	0.168	200.046	199.985	0.090	200.046	200.000	0.075
	Min	200.000	199.470	0.240	200.000	199.715	0.170	200.000	199.904	0.050	200.000	199.956	0.015	200.000	199.971	0.000
250	Max	250.290	249.720	0.860	250.115	249.830	0.400	250.072	249.950	0.168	250.046	249.985	0.090	250.046	250.000	0.075
	Min	250.000	249.430	0.280	250.000	249.715	0.170	250.000	249.904	0.050	250.000	249.956	0.015	250.000	249.971	0.000
300	Max	300.320	299.670	0.970	300.130	299.810	0.450	300.081	299.944	0.189	300.052	299.983	0.101	300.052	300.000	0.084
	Min	300.000	299.350	0.330	300.000	299.680	0.190	300.000	299.892	0.056	300.000	299.951	0.017	300.000	299.968	0.000
400	Max	400.360	399.600	1.120	400.140	399.790	0.490	400.089	399.938	0.208	400.057	399.982	0.111	400.057	400.000	0.093
	Min	400.000	399.240	0.400	400.000	399.650	0.210	400.000	399.881	0.062	400.000	399.946	0.018	400.000	399.964	0.000
500	Max	500.400	499.520	1.280	500.155	499.770	0.540	500.097	499.932	0.228	500.063	499.980	0.123	500.063	500.000	0.103
	Min	500.000	499.120	0.480	500.000	499.615	0.230	500.000	499.869	0.068	500.000	499.940	0.020	500.000	499.960	0.000

[a]From ANSI B4.2-1978 (R1994).

11 PREFERRED METRIC HOLE BASIS TRANSITION AND INTERFERENCE FITSª—AMERICAN NATIONAL STANDARD

Dimensions are in millimeters.

Basic Size		Locational Transn. Hole H7	Shaft k6	Fit	Locational Transn. Hole H7	Shaft n6	Fit	Locational Interf. Hole H7	Shaft p6	Fit	Medium Drive Hole H7	Shaft s6	Fit	Force Hole H7	Shaft u6	Fit
1	Max	1.010	1.006	0.010	1.010	1.010	0.006	1.010	1.012	0.004	1.010	1.020	−0.004	1.010	1.024	−0.008
	Min	1.000	1.000	−0.006	1.000	1.004	−0.010	1.000	1.006	−0.012	1.000	1.014	−0.020	1.000	1.018	−0.024
1.2	Max	1.210	1.206	0.010	1.210	1.210	0.006	1.210	1.212	0.004	1.210	1.220	−0.004	1.210	1.224	−0.008
	Min	1.200	1.200	−0.006	1.200	1.204	−0.010	1.200	1.206	−0.012	1.200	1.214	−0.020	1.200	1.218	−0.024
1.6	Max	1.610	1.606	0.010	1.610	1.610	0.006	1.610	1.612	0.004	1.610	1.620	−0.004	1.610	1.624	−0.008
	Min	1.600	1.600	−0.006	1.600	1.604	−0.010	1.600	1.606	−0.012	1.600	1.614	−0.020	1.600	1.618	−0.024
2	Max	2.010	2.006	0.010	2.010	2.010	0.006	2.010	2.012	0.004	2.010	2.020	−0.004	2.010	2.024	−0.008
	Min	2.000	2.000	−0.006	2.000	2.004	−0.010	2.000	2.006	−0.012	2.000	2.014	−0.020	2.000	2.018	−0.024
2.5	Max	2.510	2.506	0.010	2.510	2.510	0.006	2.510	2.512	0.004	2.510	2.520	−0.004	2.510	2.524	−0.008
	Min	2.500	2.500	−0.006	2.500	2.504	−0.010	2.500	2.506	−0.012	2.500	2.514	−0.020	2.500	2.518	−0.024
3	Max	3.010	3.006	0.010	3.010	3.010	0.006	3.010	3.012	0.004	3.010	3.020	−0.004	3.010	3.024	−0.008
	Min	3.000	3.000	−0.006	3.000	3.004	−0.010	3.000	3.006	−0.012	3.000	3.014	−0.020	3.000	3.018	−0.024
4	Max	4.012	4.009	0.011	4.012	4.016	0.004	4.012	4.020	0.000	4.012	4.027	−0.007	4.012	4.031	−0.011
	Min	4.000	4.001	−0.009	4.000	4.008	−0.016	4.000	4.012	−0.020	4.000	4.019	−0.027	4.000	4.023	−0.031
5	Max	5.012	5.009	0.011	5.012	5.016	0.004	5.012	5.020	0.000	5.012	5.027	−0.007	5.012	5.031	−0.011
	Min	5.000	5.001	−0.009	5.000	5.008	−0.016	5.000	5.012	−0.020	5.000	5.019	−0.027	5.000	5.023	−0.031
6	Max	6.012	6.009	0.011	6.012	6.016	0.004	6.012	6.020	0.000	6.012	6.027	−0.007	6.012	6.031	−0.011
	Min	6.000	6.001	−0.009	6.000	6.008	−0.016	6.000	6.012	−0.020	6.000	6.019	−0.027	6.000	6.023	−0.031
8	Max	8.015	8.010	0.014	8.015	8.019	0.005	8.015	8.024	0.000	8.015	8.032	−0.008	8.015	8.037	−0.013
	Min	8.000	8.001	−0.010	8.000	8.010	−0.019	8.000	8.015	−0.024	8.000	8.023	−0.032	8.000	8.028	−0.037
10	Max	10.015	10.010	0.014	10.015	10.019	0.005	10.015	10.024	0.000	10.015	10.032	−0.008	10.015	10.037	−0.013
	Min	10.000	10.001	−0.010	10.000	10.010	−0.019	10.000	10.015	−0.024	10.000	10.023	−0.032	10.000	10.028	−0.037
12	Max	12.018	12.012	0.017	12.018	12.023	0.006	12.018	12.029	0.000	12.018	12.039	−0.010	12.018	12.044	−0.015
	Min	12.000	12.001	−0.012	12.000	12.012	−0.023	12.000	12.018	−0.029	12.000	12.028	−0.039	12.000	12.033	−0.044
16	Max	16.018	16.012	0.017	16.018	16.023	0.006	16.018	16.029	0.000	16.018	16.039	−0.010	16.018	16.044	−0.015
	Min	16.000	16.001	−0.012	16.000	16.012	−0.023	16.000	16.018	−0.029	16.000	16.028	−0.039	16.000	16.033	−0.044
20	Max	20.021	20.015	0.019	20.021	20.028	0.006	20.021	20.035	−0.001	20.021	20.048	−0.014	20.021	20.054	−0.020
	Min	20.000	20.002	−0.015	20.000	20.015	−0.028	20.000	20.022	−0.035	20.000	20.035	−0.048	20.000	20.041	−0.054
25	Max	25.021	25.015	0.019	25.021	25.028	0.006	25.021	25.035	−0.001	25.021	25.048	−0.014	25.021	25.061	−0.027
	Min	25.000	25.002	−0.015	25.000	25.015	−0.028	25.000	25.022	−0.035	25.000	25.035	−0.048	25.000	25.048	−0.061
30	Max	30.021	30.015	0.019	30.021	30.028	0.006	30.021	30.035	−0.001	30.021	30.048	−0.014	30.021	30.061	−0.027
	Min	30.000	30.002	−0.015	30.000	30.015	−0.028	30.000	30.022	−0.035	30.000	30.035	−0.048	30.000	30.048	−0.061

ªFrom ANSI B4.2-1978 (R1994).

11 PREFERRED METRIC HOLE BASIS TRANSITION AND INTERFERENCE FITSᵃ—AMERICAN NATIONAL STANDARD (cont.)

Dimensions are in millimeters.

Basic Size		Locational Transn. Hole H7	Shaft k6	Fit	Locational Transn. Hole H7	Shaft n6	Fit	Locational Interf. Hole H7	Shaft p6	Fit	Medium Drive Hole H7	Shaft s6	Fit	Force Hole H7	Shaft u6	Fit
40	Max	40.025	40.018	0.023	40.025	40.033	0.008	40.025	40.042	−0.001	40.025	40.059	−0.018	40.025	40.076	−0.035
	Min	40.000	40.002	−0.018	40.000	40.017	−0.033	40.000	40.026	−0.042	40.000	40.043	−0.059	40.000	40.060	−0.076
50	Max	50.025	50.018	0.023	50.025	50.033	0.008	50.025	50.042	−0.001	50.025	50.059	−0.018	50.025	50.086	−0.045
	Min	50.000	50.002	−0.018	50.000	50.017	−0.033	50.000	50.026	−0.042	50.000	50.043	−0.059	50.000	50.070	−0.086
60	Max	60.030	60.021	0.028	60.030	60.039	0.010	60.030	60.051	−0.002	60.030	60.072	−0.023	60.030	60.106	−0.057
	Min	60.000	60.002	−0.021	60.000	60.020	−0.039	60.000	60.032	−0.051	60.000	60.053	−0.072	60.000	60.087	−0.106
80	Max	80.030	80.021	0.028	80.030	80.039	0.010	80.030	80.051	−0.002	80.030	80.078	−0.029	80.030	80.121	−0.072
	Min	80.000	80.002	−0.021	80.000	80.020	−0.039	80.000	80.032	−0.051	80.000	80.059	−0.078	80.000	80.102	−0.121
100	Max	100.035	100.025	0.032	100.035	100.045	0.012	100.035	100.059	−0.002	100.035	100.093	−0.036	100.035	100.146	−0.089
	Min	100.000	100.003	−0.025	100.000	100.023	−0.045	100.000	100.037	−0.059	100.000	100.071	−0.093	100.000	100.124	−0.146
120	Max	120.035	120.025	0.032	120.035	120.045	0.012	120.035	120.059	−0.002	120.035	120.101	−0.044	120.035	120.166	−0.109
	Min	120.000	120.003	−0.025	120.000	120.023	−0.045	120.000	120.037	−0.059	120.000	120.079	−0.101	120.000	120.144	−0.166
160	Max	160.040	160.028	0.037	160.040	160.052	0.013	160.040	160.068	−0.003	160.040	160.125	−0.060	160.040	160.215	−0.150
	Min	160.000	160.003	−0.028	160.000	160.027	−0.052	160.000	160.043	−0.068	160.000	160.100	−0.125	160.000	160.190	−0.215
200	Max	200.046	200.033	0.042	200.046	200.060	0.015	200.046	200.079	−0.004	200.046	200.151	−0.076	200.046	200.265	−0.190
	Min	200.000	200.004	−0.033	200.000	200.031	−0.060	200.000	200.050	−0.079	200.000	200.122	−0.151	200.000	200.236	−0.265
250	Max	250.046	250.033	0.042	250.046	250.060	0.015	250.046	250.079	−0.004	250.046	250.169	−0.094	250.046	250.313	−0.238
	Min	250.000	250.004	−0.033	250.000	250.031	−0.060	250.000	250.050	−0.079	250.000	250.140	−0.169	250.000	250.284	−0.313
300	Max	300.052	300.036	0.048	300.052	300.066	0.018	300.052	300.088	−0.004	300.052	300.202	−0.118	300.052	300.382	−0.298
	Min	300.000	300.004	−0.036	300.000	300.034	−0.066	300.000	300.056	−0.088	300.000	300.170	−0.202	300.000	300.350	−0.382
400	Max	400.057	400.040	0.053	400.057	400.073	0.020	400.057	400.098	−0.005	400.057	400.244	−0.151	400.057	400.471	−0.378
	Min	400.000	400.004	−0.040	400.000	400.037	−0.073	400.000	400.062	−0.098	400.000	400.208	−0.244	400.000	400.435	−0.471
500	Max	500.063	500.045	0.058	500.063	500.080	0.023	500.063	500.108	−0.005	500.063	500.292	−0.189	500.063	500.580	−0.477
	Min	500.000	500.005	−0.045	500.000	500.040	−0.080	500.000	500.068	−0.108	500.000	500.252	−0.292	500.000	500.540	−0.580

ᵃFrom ANSI B4.2-1978 (R1994).

12 PREFERRED METRIC SHAFT BASIS CLEARANCE FITS[a]— AMERICAN NATIONAL STANDARD

Dimensions are in millimeters.

Basic Size		Loose Running Hole C11	Loose Running Shaft h11	Loose Running Fit	Free Running Hole D9	Free Running Shaft h9	Free Running Fit	Close Running Hole F8	Close Running Shaft h7	Close Running Fit	Sliding Hole G7	Sliding Shaft h6	Sliding Fit	Locational Clearance Hole H7	Locational Clearance Shaft h6	Locational Clearance Fit
1	Max	1.120	1.000	0.180	1.045	1.000	0.070	1.020	1.000	0.030	1.012	1.000	0.018	1.010	1.000	0.016
	Min	1.060	0.940	0.060	1.020	0.975	0.020	1.006	0.990	0.006	1.002	0.994	0.002	1.000	0.994	0.000
1.2	Max	1.320	1.200	0.180	1.245	1.200	0.070	1.220	1.200	0.030	1.212	1.200	0.018	1.210	1.200	0.016
	Min	1.260	0.140	0.060	1.220	0.175	0.020	1.206	1.190	0.006	1.202	1.194	0.002	1.200	1.194	0.000
1.6	Max	1.720	1.600	0.180	1.645	1.600	0.070	1.620	1.600	0.030	1.612	1.600	0.018	1.610	1.600	0.016
	Min	1.660	0.540	0.060	1.620	0.575	0.020	1.606	1.590	0.006	1.602	1.594	0.002	1.600	1.594	0.000
2	Max	2.120	2.000	0.180	2.045	2.000	0.070	2.020	2.000	0.030	2.012	2.000	0.018	2.010	2.000	0.016
	Min	2.060	1.940	0.060	2.020	1.975	0.020	2.006	1.990	0.006	2.002	1.994	0.002	2.000	1.994	0.000
2.5	Max	2.620	2.500	0.180	2.545	2.500	0.070	2.520	2.500	0.030	2.512	2.500	0.018	2.510	2.500	0.016
	Min	2.560	2.440	0.060	2.520	2.475	0.020	2.506	2.490	0.006	2.502	2.494	0.002	2.500	2.494	0.000
3	Max	3.120	3.000	0.180	3.045	3.000	0.070	3.020	3.000	0.030	3.012	3.000	0.018	3.010	3.000	0.016
	Min	3.060	2.940	0.060	3.020	2.975	0.020	3.006	2.990	0.006	3.002	2.994	0.002	3.000	2.994	0.000
4	Max	4.145	4.000	0.220	4.060	4.000	0.090	4.028	4.000	0.040	4.016	4.000	0.024	4.012	4.000	0.020
	Min	4.070	3.925	0.070	4.030	3.970	0.030	4.010	3.988	0.010	4.004	3.992	0.004	4.000	3.992	0.000
5	Max	5.145	5.000	0.220	5.060	5.000	0.090	5.028	5.000	0.040	5.016	5.000	0.024	5.012	5.000	0.020
	Min	5.070	4.925	0.070	5.030	4.970	0.030	5.010	4.988	0.010	5.004	4.992	0.004	5.000	4.992	0.000
6	Max	6.145	6.000	0.220	6.060	6.000	0.090	6.028	6.000	0.040	6.016	6.000	0.024	6.012	6.000	0.020
	Min	6.070	5.925	0.070	6.030	5.970	0.030	6.010	5.988	0.010	6.004	5.992	0.004	6.000	5.992	0.000
8	Max	8.170	8.000	0.260	8.076	8.000	0.112	8.035	8.000	0.050	8.020	8.000	0.029	8.015	8.000	0.024
	Min	8.080	7.910	0.080	8.040	7.964	0.040	8.013	7.985	0.013	8.005	7.991	0.005	8.000	7.991	0.000
10	Max	10.170	10.000	0.260	10.076	10.000	0.112	10.035	10.000	0.050	10.020	10.000	0.029	10.015	10.000	0.024
	Min	10.080	9.910	0.080	10.040	9.964	0.040	10.013	9.985	0.013	10.005	9.991	0.005	10.000	9.991	0.000
12	Max	12.205	12.000	0.315	12.093	12.000	0.136	12.043	12.000	0.061	12.024	12.000	0.035	12.018	12.000	0.029
	Min	12.095	11.890	0.095	12.050	11.957	0.050	12.016	11.982	0.016	12.006	11.989	0.006	12.000	11.989	0.000
16	Max	16.205	16.000	0.315	16.093	16.000	0.136	16.043	16.000	0.061	16.024	16.000	0.035	16.018	16.000	0.029
	Min	16.095	15.890	0.095	16.050	15.957	0.050	16.016	15.982	0.016	16.006	15.989	0.006	16.000	15.989	0.000
20	Max	20.240	20.000	0.370	20.117	20.000	0.169	20.053	20.000	0.074	20.028	20.000	0.041	20.021	20.000	0.034
	Min	20.110	19.870	0.110	20.065	19.948	0.065	20.020	19.979	0.020	20.007	19.987	0.007	20.000	19.987	0.000
25	Max	25.240	25.000	0.370	25.117	25.000	0.169	25.053	25.000	0.074	25.028	25.000	0.041	25.021	25.000	0.034
	Min	25.110	24.870	0.110	25.065	24.948	0.065	25.020	24.979	0.020	25.007	24.987	0.007	25.000	24.987	0.000
30	Max	30.240	30.000	0.370	30.117	30.000	0.169	30.053	30.000	0.074	30.028	30.000	0.041	30.021	30.000	0.034
	Min	30.110	29.870	0.110	30.065	29.948	0.065	30.020	29.979	0.020	30.007	29.987	0.007	30.000	29.987	0.000

[a]From ANSI B4.2-1978 (R1994).

12 PREFERRED METRIC SHAFT BASIS CLEARANCE FITSᵃ— AMERICAN NATIONAL STANDARD (continued)

Dimensions are in millimeters.

Basic Size		Loose Running			Free Running			Close Running			Sliding			Locational Clearance		
		Hole C11	Shaft h11	Fit	Hole D9	Shaft h9	Fit	Hole F8	Shaft h7	Fit	Hole G7	Shaft h6	Fit	Hole H7	Shaft h6	Fit
40	Max	40.280	40.000	0.440	40.142	40.000	0.204	40.064	40.000	0.089	40.034	40.000	0.050	40.025	40.000	0.041
	Min	40.120	39.840	0.120	40.080	39.938	0.080	40.025	39.975	0.025	40.009	39.984	0.009	40.000	39.984	0.000
50	Max	50.290	50.000	0.450	50.142	50.000	0.204	50.064	50.000	0.089	50.034	50.000	0.050	50.025	50.000	0.041
	Min	50.130	49.840	0.130	50.080	49.938	0.080	50.025	49.975	0.025	50.009	49.984	0.009	50.000	49.984	0.000
60	Max	60.330	60.000	0.520	60.174	60.000	0.248	60.076	60.000	0.106	60.040	60.000	0.059	60.030	60.000	0.049
	Min	60.140	59.810	0.140	60.100	59.926	0.100	60.030	59.970	0.030	60.010	59.981	0.010	60.000	59.981	0.000
80	Max	80.340	80.000	0.530	80.174	80.000	0.248	80.076	80.000	0.106	80.040	80.000	0.059	80.030	80.000	0.049
	Min	80.150	79.810	0.150	80.100	79.926	0.100	80.030	79.970	0.030	80.010	79.981	0.010	80.000	79.981	0.000
100	Max	100.390	100.000	0.610	100.207	100.000	0.294	100.090	100.000	0.125	100.047	100.000	0.069	100.035	100.000	0.057
	Min	100.170	99.780	0.170	100.120	99.913	0.120	100.036	99.965	0.036	100.012	99.978	0.012	100.000	99.978	0.000
120	Max	120.400	120.000	0.620	120.207	120.000	0.294	120.090	120.000	0.125	120.047	120.000	0.069	120.035	120.000	0.057
	Min	120.180	119.780	0.180	120.120	119.913	0.120	120.036	119.965	0.036	120.012	119.978	0.012	120.000	119.978	0.000
160	Max	160.460	160.000	0.710	160.245	160.000	0.345	160.106	160.000	0.146	160.054	160.000	0.079	160.040	160.000	0.065
	Min	160.210	159.750	0.210	160.145	159.900	0.145	160.043	159.960	0.043	160.014	159.975	0.014	160.000	159.975	0.000
200	Max	200.530	200.000	0.820	200.285	200.000	0.400	200.122	200.000	0.168	200.061	200.000	0.090	200.046	200.000	0.075
	Min	200.240	199.710	0.240	200.170	199.885	0.170	200.050	199.954	0.050	200.015	199.971	0.015	200.000	199.971	0.000
250	Max	250.570	250.000	0.860	250.285	250.000	0.400	250.122	250.000	0.168	250.061	250.000	0.090	250.046	250.000	0.075
	Min	250.280	249.710	0.280	250.170	249.885	0.170	250.050	249.954	0.050	250.015	249.971	0.015	250.000	249.971	0.000
300	Max	300.650	300.000	0.970	300.320	300.000	0.450	300.137	300.000	0.189	300.069	300.000	0.101	300.052	300.000	0.084
	Min	300.330	299.680	0.330	300.190	299.870	0.190	300.056	299.948	0.056	300.017	299.968	0.017	300.000	299.968	0.000
400	Max	400.760	400.000	1.120	400.350	400.000	0.490	400.151	400.000	0.208	400.075	400.000	0.111	400.057	400.000	0.093
	Min	400.400	399.640	0.400	400.210	399.860	0.210	400.062	399.943	0.062	400.018	399.964	0.018	400.000	399.964	0.000
500	Max	500.880	500.000	1.280	500.385	500.000	0.540	500.165	500.000	0.228	500.083	500.000	0.123	500.063	500.000	0.103
	Min	500.480	499.600	0.480	500.230	499.845	0.230	500.068	499.937	0.068	500.020	499.960	5.020	500.000	499.960	0.000

ᵃFrom ANSI B4.2-1978 (R1994).

13 PREFERRED METRIC SHAFT BASIS TRANSITION AND INTERFERENCE FITSᵃ—AMERICAN NATIONAL STANDARD

Dimensions are in millimeters.

Basic Size		Locational Transn. Hole K7	Shaft h6	Fit	Locational Transn. Hole N7	Shaft h6	Fit	Locational Interf. Hole P7	Shaft h6	Fit	Medium Drive Hole S7	Shaft h6	Fit	Force Hole U7	Shaft h6	Fit
1	Max	1.000	1.000	0.006	0.996	1.000	0.002	0.994	1.000	0.000	0.986	1.000	−0.008	0.982	1.000	−0.012
	Min	0.990	0.994	−0.010	0.986	0.994	−0.014	0.984	0.994	−0.016	0.976	0.994	−0.024	0.972	0.994	−0.028
1.2	Max	1.200	1.200	0.006	1.196	1.200	0.002	1.194	1.200	0.000	1.186	1.200	−0.008	1.182	1.200	−0.012
	Min	1.190	1.194	−0.010	1.186	1.194	−0.014	1.184	1.194	−0.016	1.176	1.194	−0.024	1.172	1.194	−0.028
1.6	Max	1.600	1.600	0.006	1.596	1.600	0.002	1.594	1.600	0.000	1.586	1.600	−0.008	1.582	1.600	−0.012
	Min	1.590	1.594	−0.010	1.586	1.594	−0.014	1.584	1.594	−0.016	1.576	1.594	−0.024	1.572	1.594	−0.028
2	Max	2.000	2.000	0.006	1.996	2.000	0.002	1.994	2.000	0.000	1.986	2.000	−0.008	1.982	2.000	−0.012
	Min	1.990	1.994	−0.010	1.986	1.994	−0.014	1.984	1.994	−0.016	1.976	1.994	−0.024	1.972	1.994	−0.028
2.5	Max	2.500	2.500	0.006	2.496	2.500	0.002	2.494	2.500	0.000	2.486	2.500	−0.008	2.482	2.500	−0.012
	Min	2.490	2.494	−0.010	2.486	2.494	−0.014	2.484	2.494	−0.016	2.476	2.494	−0.024	2.472	2.494	−0.028
3	Max	3.000	3.000	0.006	2.996	3.000	0.002	2.994	3.000	0.000	2.986	3.000	−0.008	2.982	3.000	−0.012
	Min	2.990	2.994	−0.010	2.986	2.994	−0.014	2.984	2.994	−0.016	2.976	2.994	−0.024	2.972	2.994	−0.028
4	Max	4.003	4.000	0.011	3.996	4.000	0.004	3.992	4.000	0.000	3.985	4.000	−0.007	3.981	4.000	−0.011
	Min	3.991	3.992	−0.009	3.984	3.992	−0.016	3.980	3.992	−0.020	3.973	3.992	−0.027	3.969	3.992	−0.031
5	Max	5.003	5.000	0.011	4.996	5.000	0.004	4.992	5.000	0.000	4.985	5.000	−0.007	4.981	5.000	−0.011
	Min	4.991	4.992	−0.009	4.984	4.992	−0.016	4.980	4.992	−0.020	4.973	4.992	−0.027	4.969	4.992	−0.031
6	Max	6.003	6.000	0.011	5.996	6.000	0.004	5.992	6.000	0.000	5.985	6.000	−0.007	5.981	6.000	−0.011
	Min	5.991	5.992	−0.009	5.984	5.992	−0.016	5.980	5.992	−0.020	5.973	5.992	−0.027	5.969	5.992	−0.031
8	Max	8.005	8.000	0.014	7.996	8.000	0.005	7.991	8.000	0.000	7.983	8.000	−0.008	7.978	8.000	−0.013
	Min	7.990	7.991	−0.010	7.981	7.991	−0.019	7.976	7.991	−0.024	7.968	7.991	−0.032	7.963	7.991	−0.037
10	Max	10.005	10.000	0.014	9.996	10.000	0.005	9.991	10.000	0.000	9.983	10.000	−0.008	9.978	10.000	−0.013
	Min	9.990	9.991	−0.010	9.981	9.991	−0.019	9.976	9.991	−0.024	9.968	9.991	−0.032	9.963	9.991	−0.037
12	Max	12.006	12.000	0.017	11.995	12.000	0.006	11.989	12.000	0.000	11.979	12.000	−0.010	11.974	12.000	−0.015
	Min	11.988	11.989	−0.012	11.977	11.989	−0.023	11.971	11.989	−0.029	11.961	11.989	−0.039	11.956	11.989	−0.044
16	Max	16.006	16.000	0.017	15.995	16.000	0.006	15.989	16.000	0.000	15.979	16.000	−0.010	15.974	16.000	−0.015
	Min	15.988	15.989	−0.012	15.977	15.989	−0.023	15.971	15.989	−0.029	15.961	15.989	−0.039	15.956	15.989	−0.044
20	Max	20.006	20.000	0.019	19.993	20.000	0.006	19.986	20.000	−0.001	19.973	20.000	−0.014	19.967	20.000	−0.020
	Min	19.985	19.987	−0.015	19.972	19.987	−0.028	19.965	19.987	−0.035	19.952	19.987	−0.048	19.946	19.987	−0.054
25	Max	25.006	25.000	0.019	24.993	25.000	0.006	24.986	25.000	−0.001	24.973	25.000	−0.014	24.960	25.000	−0.027
	Min	24.985	24.987	−0.015	24.972	24.987	−0.028	24.965	24.987	−0.035	24.952	24.987	−0.048	24.939	24.987	−0.061
30	Max	30.006	30.000	0.019	29.993	30.000	0.006	29.986	30.000	−0.001	29.973	30.000	−0.014	29.960	30.000	−0.027
	Min	29.985	29.987	−0.015	29.972	29.987	−0.028	29.965	29.987	−0.035	29.952	29.987	−0.048	29.939	29.987	−0.061

ᵃFrom ANSI B4.2-1978 (R1994).

13 PREFERRED METRIC BASIS TRANSITION AND INTERFERENCE FITS[a]— AMERICAN NATIONAL STANDARD (continued)

Dimensions are in millimeters.

Basic Size		Locational Transn. Hole K7	Locational Transn. Shaft h6	Locational Transn. Fit	Locational Transn. Hole N7	Locational Transn. Shaft h6	Locational Transn. Fit	Locational Interf. Hole P7	Locational Interf. Shaft h6	Locational Interf. Fit	Medium Drive Hole S7	Medium Drive Shaft h6	Medium Drive Fit	Force Hole U7	Force Shaft h6	Force Fit
40	Max	40.007	40.000	0.023	39.992	40.000	0.008	39.983	40.000	−0.001	39.966	40.000	−0.018	39.949	40.000	−0.035
	Min	39.982	39.984	−0.018	39.967	39.984	−0.033	39.958	39.984	−0.042	39.941	39.984	−0.059	39.924	39.984	−0.076
50	Max	50.007	50.000	0.023	49.992	50.000	0.008	49.983	50.000	−0.001	49.966	50.000	−0.018	49.939	50.000	−0.045
	Min	49.982	49.984	−0.018	49.967	49.984	−0.033	49.958	49.984	−0.042	49.941	49.984	−0.059	49.914	49.984	−0.086
60	Max	60.009	60.000	0.028	59.991	60.000	0.010	59.979	60.000	−0.002	59.958	60.000	−0.023	59.924	60.000	−0.057
	Min	59.979	59.981	−0.021	59.961	59.981	−0.039	59.949	59.981	−0.051	59.928	59.981	−0.072	59.894	59.981	−0.106
80	Max	80.009	80.000	0.028	79.991	80.000	0.010	79.979	80.000	−0.002	79.952	80.000	−0.029	79.909	80.000	−0.072
	Min	79.979	79.981	−0.021	79.961	79.981	−0.039	79.949	79.981	−0.051	79.922	79.981	−0.078	79.879	79.981	−0.121
100	Max	100.010	100.000	0.032	99.990	100.000	0.012	99.976	100.000	−0.002	99.942	100.000	−0.036	99.889	100.000	−0.089
	Min	99.975	99.978	−0.025	99.955	99.978	−0.045	99.941	99.978	−0.059	99.907	99.978	−0.093	99.854	99.978	−0.146
120	Max	120.010	120.000	0.032	119.990	120.000	0.012	119.976	120.000	−0.002	119.934	120.000	−0.044	119.869	120.000	−0.109
	Min	119.975	119.978	−0.025	119.955	119.978	−0.045	119.941	119.978	−0.059	119.899	119.978	−0.101	119.834	119.978	−0.166
160	Max	160.012	160.000	0.037	159.988	160.000	0.013	159.972	160.000	−0.003	159.915	160.000	−0.060	159.825	160.000	−0.150
	Min	159.972	159.975	−0.028	159.948	159.975	−0.052	159.932	159.975	−0.068	159.875	159.975	−0.125	159.785	159.975	−0.215
200	Max	200.013	200.000	0.042	199.986	200.000	0.015	199.967	200.000	−0.004	199.895	200.000	−0.076	199.781	200.000	−0.190
	Min	199.967	199.971	−0.033	199.940	199.971	−0.060	199.921	199.971	−0.079	199.849	199.971	−0.151	199.735	199.971	−0.265
250	Max	250.013	250.000	0.042	249.986	250.000	0.015	249.967	250.000	−0.004	249.877	250.000	−0.094	249.733	250.000	−0.238
	Min	249.967	249.971	−0.033	249.940	249.971	−0.060	249.921	249.971	−0.079	249.831	249.971	−0.169	249.687	249.971	−0.313
300	Max	300.016	300.000	0.048	299.986	300.000	0.018	299.964	300.000	−0.004	299.850	300.000	−0.118	299.670	300.000	−0.298
	Min	299.964	299.968	−0.036	299.934	299.968	−0.066	299.912	299.968	−0.088	299.798	299.968	−0.202	299.618	299.968	−0.382
400	Max	400.017	400.000	0.053	399.984	400.000	0.020	399.959	400.000	−0.005	399.813	400.000	−0.151	399.586	400.000	−0.378
	Min	399.960	399.964	−0.040	399.927	399.964	−0.073	399.902	399.964	−0.098	399.756	399.964	−0.244	399.529	399.964	−0.471
500	Max	500.018	500.000	0.058	499.983	500.000	0.023	499.955	500.000	−0.005	499.771	500.000	−0.189	499.483	500.000	−0.477
	Min	499.955	499.960	−0.045	499.920	499.960	−0.080	499.892	499.960	−0.108	499.708	499.960	−0.292	499.420	499.960	−0.580

[a]From ANSI B4.2-1978 (R1994).

14 SCREW THREADS, AMERICAN NATIONAL, UNIFIED, AND METRIC

American National Standard Unified and American National Screw Threads.[a]

Nominal Diameter	Coarse[b] NC UNC Thds. per Inch	Tap Drill[d]	Fine[b] NF UNF Thds. per Inch	Tap Drill[d]	Extra Fine[c] NEF UNEF Thds. per Inch	Tap Drill[d]
0 (.060)			80	$\frac{3}{64}$		
1 (.073)	64	No. 53	72	No. 53	...	...
2 (.086)	56	No. 50	64	No. 50	...	...
3 (.099)	48	No. 47	56	No. 45	...	...
4 (.112)	40	No. 43	48	No. 42	...	...
5 (.125)	40	No. 38	44	No. 37	...	...
6 (.138)	32	No. 36	40	No. 33	...	...
8 (.164)	32	No. 29	36	No. 29	...	...
10 (.190)	24	No. 25	32	No. 21	...	...
12 (.216)	24	No. 16	28	No. 14	32	No. 13
$\frac{1}{4}$	20	No. 7	28	No. 3	32	$\frac{7}{32}$
$\frac{5}{16}$	18	F	24	I	32	$\frac{9}{32}$
$\frac{3}{8}$	16	$\frac{5}{16}$	24	Q	32	$\frac{11}{32}$
$\frac{7}{16}$	14	U	20	$\frac{25}{64}$	28	$\frac{13}{32}$
$\frac{1}{2}$	13	$\frac{27}{64}$	20	$\frac{29}{64}$	28	$\frac{15}{32}$
$\frac{9}{16}$	12	$\frac{31}{64}$	18	$\frac{33}{64}$	24	$\frac{33}{64}$
$\frac{5}{8}$	11	$\frac{17}{32}$	18	$\frac{37}{64}$	24	$\frac{37}{64}$
$\frac{11}{16}$	...	...	...	...	24	$\frac{41}{64}$
$\frac{3}{4}$	10	$\frac{21}{32}$	16	$\frac{11}{16}$	20	$\frac{45}{64}$
$\frac{13}{16}$	...	...	...	...	20	$\frac{49}{64}$
$\frac{7}{8}$	9	$\frac{49}{64}$	14	$\frac{13}{16}$	20	$\frac{53}{64}$
$\frac{15}{16}$	...	...	...	...	20	$\frac{57}{64}$

Nominal Diameter	Coarse[b] NC UNC Thds. per Inch	Tap Drill[d]	Fine[b] NF UNF Thds. per Inch	Tap Drill[d]	Extra Fine[c] NEF UNEF Thds. per Inch	Tap Drill[d]
1	8	$\frac{7}{8}$	12	$\frac{59}{64}$	20	$\frac{61}{64}$
$1\frac{1}{16}$	...	...	...	...	18	1
$1\frac{1}{8}$	7	$\frac{63}{64}$	12	$1\frac{3}{64}$	18	$1\frac{5}{64}$
$1\frac{3}{16}$	...	...	...	...	18	$1\frac{9}{64}$
$1\frac{1}{4}$	7	$1\frac{7}{64}$	12	$1\frac{11}{64}$	18	$1\frac{3}{16}$
$1\frac{5}{16}$	...	...	...	...	18	$1\frac{17}{64}$
$1\frac{3}{8}$	6	$1\frac{7}{32}$	12	$1\frac{19}{64}$	18	$1\frac{5}{16}$
$1\frac{7}{16}$	...	...	...	...	18	$1\frac{3}{8}$
$1\frac{1}{2}$	6	$1\frac{11}{32}$	12	$1\frac{27}{64}$	18	$1\frac{7}{16}$
$1\frac{9}{16}$	...	...	...	...	18	$1\frac{1}{2}$
$1\frac{5}{8}$	...	...	...	...	18	$1\frac{9}{16}$
$1\frac{11}{16}$	...	...	...	...	18	$1\frac{5}{8}$
$1\frac{3}{4}$	5	$1\frac{9}{16}$	...	...	...	...
2	$4\frac{1}{2}$	$1\frac{25}{32}$	...	...	...	...
$2\frac{1}{4}$	$4\frac{1}{2}$	$2\frac{1}{32}$	...	...	...	...
$2\frac{1}{2}$	4	$2\frac{1}{4}$	...	...	...	...
$2\frac{3}{4}$	4	$2\frac{1}{2}$	...	...	...	...
3	4	$2\frac{3}{4}$	...	...	...	...
$3\frac{1}{4}$	4	...	...	...	...	...
$3\frac{1}{2}$	4	...	...	...	...	...
$3\frac{3}{4}$	4	...	...	...	...	...
4	4	...	...	...	...	...

[a]ANSI/ASME B1.1-1989. For 8-, 12-, and 16-pitch thread series, see next page.
[b]Classes 1A, 2A, 3A, 1B, 2B, 3B, 2, and 3.
[c]Classes 2A, 2B, 2, and 3.
[d]For approximate 75% full depth of thread. For decimal sizes of numbered and lettered drills, see Appendix 15.

14 SCREW THREADS, AMERICAN NATIONAL, UNIFIED, AND METRIC (cont.)

American National Standard Unified and American National Screw Threads[a] (continued)

Nominal Diameter	8-Pitch[b] Series 8N and 8UN		12-Pitch[b] Series 12N and 12UN		16-Pitch[b] Series 16N and 16UN		Nominal Diameter	8-Pitch[b] Series 8N and 8UN		12-Pitch[b] Series 12N and 12UN		16-Pitch[c] Series 16N and 16UN	
	Thds. per Inch	Tap Drill[c]	Thds. per Inch	Tap Drill[c]	Thds. per Inch	Tap Drill[c]		Thds. per Inch	Tap Drill[c]	Thds. per Inch	Tap Drill[c]	Thds. per Inch[d]	Tap Drill[c]
$\frac{1}{2}$	...	...	12	$\frac{27}{64}$	...	...	$2\frac{1}{16}$	...	...	...	...	**16**	2
$\frac{9}{16}$	...	...	12[e]	$\frac{31}{64}$	...	...	$2\frac{1}{8}$	...	...	12	$2\frac{3}{64}$	16	$2\frac{1}{16}$
$\frac{5}{8}$	...	...	12	$\frac{35}{64}$	...	...	$2\frac{3}{16}$	...	...	...	...	**16**	$2\frac{1}{8}$
$\frac{11}{16}$	...	...	12	$\frac{39}{64}$	...	...	$2\frac{1}{4}$	8	$2\frac{1}{8}$	12	$2\frac{17}{64}$	16	$2\frac{3}{16}$
$\frac{3}{4}$	...	...	12	$\frac{43}{64}$	16[e]	$\frac{11}{16}$	$2\frac{5}{16}$	...	...	...	...	**16**	$2\frac{1}{4}$
$\frac{13}{16}$	...	...	12	$\frac{47}{64}$	16	$\frac{3}{4}$	$2\frac{3}{8}$	...	...	12	$2\frac{19}{64}$	16	$2\frac{5}{16}$
$\frac{7}{8}$	...	...	12	$\frac{51}{64}$	16	$\frac{13}{16}$	$2\frac{7}{16}$	...	...	...	...	**16**	$2\frac{3}{8}$
$\frac{15}{16}$	...	...	12	$\frac{55}{64}$	16	$\frac{7}{8}$	$2\frac{1}{2}$	8	$2\frac{3}{8}$	12	$2\frac{27}{64}$	16	$2\frac{7}{16}$
1	8[e]	$\frac{7}{8}$	12	$\frac{59}{64}$	16	$\frac{15}{16}$	$2\frac{5}{8}$	...	...	12	$2\frac{35}{64}$	16	$2\frac{9}{16}$
$1\frac{1}{16}$	...	...	12	$\frac{63}{64}$	16	1	$2\frac{3}{4}$	8	$2\frac{5}{8}$	12	$2\frac{43}{64}$	16	$2\frac{11}{16}$
$1\frac{1}{8}$	8	1	12[e]	$1\frac{3}{64}$	16	$1\frac{1}{16}$	$2\frac{7}{8}$	...	...	12	...	16	...
$1\frac{3}{16}$	...	...	12	$1\frac{7}{64}$	16	$1\frac{1}{8}$	3	8	$2\frac{7}{8}$	12	...	16	...
$1\frac{1}{4}$	8	$1\frac{1}{8}$	12	$1\frac{11}{64}$	16	$1\frac{3}{16}$	$3\frac{1}{8}$	...	...	12	...	16	...
$1\frac{5}{16}$	...	...	12	$1\frac{15}{64}$	16	$1\frac{1}{4}$	$3\frac{1}{4}$	8	...	12	...	16	...
$1\frac{3}{8}$	8	$1\frac{1}{4}$	12[e]	$1\frac{19}{64}$	16	$1\frac{5}{16}$	$3\frac{3}{8}$	...	...	12	...	16	...
$1\frac{7}{16}$	...	...	12	$1\frac{23}{64}$	16	$1\frac{3}{8}$	$3\frac{1}{2}$	8	...	12	...	16	...
$1\frac{1}{2}$	8	$1\frac{3}{8}$	12[e]	$1\frac{27}{64}$	16	$1\frac{7}{16}$	$3\frac{5}{8}$	...	...	12	...	16	...
$1\frac{9}{16}$	...	...	...	...	16	$1\frac{1}{2}$	$3\frac{3}{4}$	8	...	12	...	16	...
$1\frac{5}{8}$	8	$1\frac{1}{2}$	12	$1\frac{35}{64}$	16	$1\frac{9}{16}$	$3\frac{7}{8}$	...	...	12	...	16	...
$1\frac{11}{16}$	...	...	...	...	16	$1\frac{5}{8}$	4	8	...	12	...	16	...
$1\frac{3}{4}$	8	$1\frac{5}{8}$	12	$1\frac{43}{64}$	16[e]	$1\frac{11}{16}$	$4\frac{1}{4}$	8	...	12	...	16	...
$1\frac{13}{16}$	...	...	...	...	16	$1\frac{3}{4}$	$4\frac{1}{2}$	8	...	12	...	16	...
$1\frac{7}{8}$	8	$1\frac{3}{4}$	12	$1\frac{51}{64}$	16	$1\frac{13}{16}$	$4\frac{3}{4}$	8	...	12	...	16	...
$1\frac{15}{16}$	...	...	...	...	16	$1\frac{7}{8}$	5	8	...	12	...	16	...
2	8	$1\frac{7}{8}$	12	$1\frac{59}{64}$	16[e]	$1\frac{15}{16}$	$5\frac{1}{4}$	8	...	12	...	16	...

[a]ANSI/ASME B1.1-1989.
[b]Classes 2A, 3A, 2B, 3B, 2, and 3.
[c]For approximate 75% full depth of thread.
[d]Boldface type indicates Amrican National Threads only.
[e]This is a standard size of the Unified or American National threads of the coarse, fine, or extra fine series. See preceding page.

14 SCREW THREADS, AMERICAN NATIONAL, UNIFIED, AND METRIC (cont.)

Metric Screw Threads.[a]

Preferred sizes for commercial threads and fasteners are shown in **boldface** type.

Coarse (general purpose)		Fine	
Nominal Size & Thd Pitch	**Tap Drill Diameter, mm**	**Nominal Size & Thd Pitch**	**Tap Drill Diameter, mm**
M1.6 × 0.35	1.25	—	—
M1.8 × 0.35	1.45	—	—
M2 × 0.4	1.6	—	—
M2.2 × 0.45	1.75	—	—
M2.5 × 0.45	2.05	—	—
M3 × 0.5	2.5	—	—
M3.5 × 0.6	2.9	—	—
M4 × 0.7	3.3	—	—
M4.5 × 0.75	3.75	—	—
M5 × 0.8	4.2	—	—
M6 × 1	5.0	—	—
M7 × 1	6.0	—	—
M8 × 1.25	6.8	**M8 × 1**	7.0
M9 × 1.25	7.75	—	—
M10 × 1.5	8.5	**M10 × 1.25**	8.75
M11 × 1.5	9.50	—	—
M12 × 1.75	10.30	**M12 × 1.25**	10.5
M14 × 2	12.00	**M14 × 1.5**	12.5
M16 × 2	14.00	**M16 × 1.5**	14.5
M18 × 2.5	15.50	**M18 × 1.5**	16.5
M20 × 2.5	17.5	**M20 × 1.5**	18.5
M22 × 25[b]	19.5	**M22 × 1.5**	20.5
M24 × 3	21.0	**M24 × 2**	22.0
M27 × 3[b]	24.0	**M27 × 2**	25.0
M30 × 3.5	26.5	**M30 × 2**	28.0
M33 × 3.5	29.5	**M30 × 2**	31.0
M36 × 4	32.0	**M36 × 2**	33.0
M39 × 4	35.0	M39 × 2	36.0
M42 × 4.5	37.5	**M42 × 2**	39.0
M45 × 4.5	40.5	M45 × 1.5	42.0
M48 × 5	43.0	**M48 × 2**	45.0
M52 × 5	47.0	M52 × 2	49.0
M56 × 5.5	50.5	**M56 × 2**	52.0
M60 × 5.5	54.5	M60 × 1.5	56.0
M64 × 6	58.0	**M64 × 2**	60.0
M68 × 6	62.0	M68 × 2	64.0
M72 × 6	66.0	**M72 × 2**	68.0
M80 × 6	74.0	**M80 × 2**	76.0
M90 × 6	84.0	**M90 × 2**	86.0
M100 × 6	94.0	**M100 × 2**	96.0

[a]ANSI/ASME B1.13M-1995.
[b]Only for high strength structural steel fasteners.

15 TWIST DRILL SIZES—AMERICAN NATIONAL STANDARD AND METRIC

American National Standard Drill Sizes.[a] All dimensions are in inches. Drills designated in common fractions are available in diameters $\frac{1}{64}$" to $1\frac{3}{4}$" in $\frac{1}{64}$" increments, $1\frac{3}{4}$" to $2\frac{1}{4}$" in $\frac{1}{32}$" increments. $2\frac{1}{4}$" to 3" in $\frac{1}{16}$" increments and 3" to $3\frac{1}{2}$" in $\frac{1}{8}$" increments. Drills larger than $3\frac{1}{2}$" are seldom used, and are regarded as special drills.

Size	Drill Diameter	Size	Drill Diameter	Size	Drill Diameter	Size	Drill Diameter	Size	Drill Diameter	Size	Drill Diameter
1	.2280	17	.1730	33	.1130	49	.0730	65	.0350	81	.0130
2	.2210	18	.1695	34	.1110	50	.0700	66	.0330	82	.0125
3	.2130	19	.1660	35	.1100	51	.0670	67	.0320	83	.0120
4	.2090	20	.1610	36	.1065	52	.0635	68	.0310	84	.0115
5	.2055	21	.1590	37	.1040	53	.0595	69	.0292	85	.0110
6	.2040	22	.1570	38	.1015	54	.0550	70	.0280	86	.0105
7	.2010	23	.1540	39	.0995	55	.0520	71	.0260	87	.0100
8	.1990	24	.1520	40	.0980	56	.0465	72	.0250	88	.0095
9	.1960	25	.1495	41	.0960	57	.0430	73	.0240	89	.0091
10	.1935	26	.1470	42	.0935	58	.0420	74	.0225	90	.0087
11	.1910	27	.1440	43	.0890	59	.0410	75	.0210	91	.0083
12	.1890	28	.1405	44	.0860	60	.0400	76	.0200	92	.0079
13	.1850	29	.1360	45	.0820	61	.0390	77	.0180	93	.0075
14	.1820	30	.1285	46	.0810	62	.0380	78	.0160	94	.0071
15	.1800	31	.1200	47	.0785	63	.0370	79	.0145	95	.0067
16	.1770	32	.1160	48	.0760	64	.0360	80	.0135	96	.0063
										97	.0059

Letter Sizes

A	.234	G	.261	L	.290	Q	.332	V	.377
B	.238	H	.266	M	.295	R	.339	W	.386
C	.242	I	.272	N	.302	S	.348	X	.397
D	.246	J	.277	O	.316	T	.358	Y	.404
E	.250	K	.281	P	.323	U	.368	Z	.413
F	.257								

[a]ANSI/ASME B94.11M-1993.

15 TWIST DRILL SIZES—AMERICAN NATIONAL STANDARD AND METRIC
(continued)

Metric Drill Sizes. Decimal inch equivalents are for reference only.

Drill Diameter		Drill Diameter		Drill Diameter		Drill Diameter		Drill Diameter		Drill Diameter	
mm	in.	mm	in.	mm	in.	mm	in.	mm	in.	mm	in.
0.40	.0157	1.95	.0768	4.70	.1850	8.00	.3150	13.20	.5197	25.50	1.0039
0.42	.0165	2.00	.0787	4.80	.1890	8.10	.3189	13.50	.5315	26.00	1.0236
0.45	.0177	2.05	.0807	4.90	.1929	8.20	.3228	13.80	.5433	26.50	1.0433
0.48	.0189	2.10	.0827	5.00	.1969	8.30	.3268	14.00	.5512	27.00	1.0630
0.50	.0197	2.15	.0846	5.10	.2008	8.40	.3307	14.25	.5610	27.50	1.0827
0.55	.0217	2.20	.0866	5.20	.2047	8.50	.3346	14.50	.5709	28.00	1.1024
0.60	.0236	2.25	.0886	5.30	.2087	8.60	.3386	14.75	.5807	28.50	1.1220
0.65	.0256	2.30	.0906	5.40	.2126	8.70	.3425	15.00	.5906	29.00	1.1417
0.70	.0276	2.35	.0925	5.50	.2165	8.80	.3465	15.25	.6004	29.50	1.1614
0.75	.0295	2.40	.0945	5.60	.2205	8.90	.3504	15.50	.6102	30.00	1.1811
0.80	.0315	2.45	.0965	5.70	.2244	9.00	.3543	15.75	.6201	30.50	1.2008
0.85	.0335	2.50	.0984	5.80	.2283	9.10	.3583	16.00	.6299	31.00	1.2205
0.90	.0354	2.60	.1024	5.90	.2323	9.20	.3622	16.25	.6398	31.50	1.2402
0.95	.0374	2.70	.1063	6.00	.2362	9.30	.3661	16.50	.6496	32.00	1.2598
1.00	.0394	2.80	.1102	6.10	.2402	9.40	.3701	16.75	.6594	32.50	1.2795
1.05	.0413	2.90	.1142	6.20	.2441	9.50	.3740	17.00	.6693	33.00	1.2992
1.10	.0433	3.00	.1181	6.30	.2480	9.60	.3780	17.25	.6791	33.50	1.3189
1.15	.0453	3.10	.1220	6.40	.2520	9.70	.3819	17.50	.6890	34.00	1.3386
1.20	.0472	3.20	.1260	6.50	.2559	9.80	.3858	18.00	.7087	34.50	1.3583
1.25	.0492	3.30	.1299	6.60	.2598	9.90	.3898	18.50	.7283	35.00	1.3780
1.30	.0512	3.40	.1339	6.70	.2638	10.00	.3937	19.00	.7480	35.50	1.3976
1.35	.0531	3.50	.1378	6.80	.2677	10.20	.4016	19.50	.7677	36.00	1.4173
1.40	.0551	3.60	.1417	6.90	.2717	10.50	.4134	20.00	.7874	36.50	1.4370
1.45	.0571	3.70	.1457	7.00	.2756	10.80	.4252	20.50	.8071	37.00	1.4567
1.50	.0591	3.80	.1496	7.10	.2795	11.00	.4331	21.00	.8268	37.50	1.4764
1.55	.0610	3.90	.1535	7.20	.2835	11.20	.4409	21.50	.8465	38.00	1.4961
1.60	.0630	4.00	.1575	7.30	.2874	11.50	.4528	22.00	.8661	40.00	1.5748
1.65	.0650	4.10	.1614	7.40	.2913	11.80	.4646	22.50	.8858	42.00	1.6535
1.70	.0669	4.20	.1654	7.50	.2953	12.00	.4724	23.00	.9055	44.00	1.7323
1.75	.0689	4.30	.1693	7.60	.2992	12.20	.4803	23.50	.9252	46.00	1.8110
1.80	.0709	4.40	.1732	7.70	.3031	12.50	.4921	24.00	.9449	48.00	1.8898
1.85	.0728	4.50	.1772	7.80	.3071	12.50	.5039	24.50	.9646	50.00	1.9685
1.90	.0748	4.60	.1811	7.90	.3110	13.00	.5118	25.00	.9843		

16 ACME THREADS, GENERAL PURPOSE[a]

Size	Threads per Inch	Size	Threads per Inch	Size	Threads per Inch	Size	Threads per Inch
$\frac{1}{4}$	16	$\frac{3}{4}$	6	$1\frac{1}{2}$	4	3	2
$\frac{5}{16}$	14	$\frac{7}{8}$	6	$1\frac{3}{4}$	4	$3\frac{1}{2}$	2
$\frac{3}{8}$	12	1	5	2	4	4	2
$\frac{7}{16}$	12	$1\frac{1}{8}$	5	$2\frac{1}{4}$	3	$4\frac{1}{2}$	2
$\frac{1}{2}$	10	$1\frac{1}{4}$	5	$2\frac{1}{2}$	3	5	2
$\frac{5}{8}$	8	$1\frac{3}{8}$	4	$2\frac{3}{4}$	3	...	...

[a]ANSI/ASME B1.5-1988 (R1994).

17 BOLTS, NUTS, AND CAP SCREWS—SQUARE AND HEXAGON—AMERICAN NATIONAL STANDARD AND METRIC

American National Standard Square and Hexagon Bolts[a] and Nuts[b] and Hexagon Cap Screws.[c] **Boldface** type indicates product features unified dimensionally with British and Canadian standards. All dimensions are in inches.

Nominal Size D Body Diameter of Bolt	Regular Bolts					Heavy Bolts		
	Width Across Flats W		Height H			Width Across Flats W	Height H	
	Sq.	Hex.	Sq. (Unfin.)	Hex (Unfin.)	Hex Cap Scr.[c] (Fin.)		Hex. (Unfin.)	Hex Screw (Fin.)
$\frac{1}{4}$ 0.2500	$\frac{3}{8}$	$\frac{7}{16}$	$\frac{11}{64}$	$\frac{11}{64}$	$\frac{5}{32}$	...	...	...
$\frac{5}{16}$ 0.3125	$\frac{1}{2}$	$\frac{1}{2}$	$\frac{13}{64}$	$\frac{7}{32}$	$\frac{13}{64}$	...	...	...
$\frac{3}{8}$ 0.3750	$\frac{9}{16}$	$\frac{9}{16}$	$\frac{1}{4}$	$\frac{1}{4}$	$\frac{15}{64}$	...	...	...
$\frac{7}{16}$ 0.4375	$\frac{5}{8}$	$\frac{5}{8}$	$\frac{19}{64}$	$\frac{19}{64}$	$\frac{9}{32}$	...	...	...
$\frac{1}{2}$ 0.5000	$\frac{3}{4}$	$\frac{3}{4}$	$\frac{21}{64}$	$\frac{11}{32}$	$\frac{5}{16}$	$\frac{7}{8}$	$\frac{11}{32}$	$\frac{5}{16}$
$\frac{9}{16}$ 0.5625	...	$\frac{13}{16}$	...	...	$\frac{23}{64}$	...	...	...
$\frac{5}{8}$ 0.6250	$\frac{15}{16}$	$\frac{15}{16}$	$\frac{27}{64}$	$\frac{27}{64}$	$\frac{25}{64}$	$1\frac{1}{16}$	$\frac{27}{64}$	$\frac{25}{64}$
$\frac{3}{4}$ 0.7500	$1\frac{1}{8}$	$1\frac{1}{8}$	$\frac{1}{2}$	$\frac{1}{2}$	$\frac{15}{32}$	$1\frac{1}{4}$	$\frac{1}{2}$	$\frac{15}{32}$
$\frac{7}{8}$ 0.8750	$1\frac{5}{16}$	$1\frac{5}{16}$	$\frac{19}{32}$	$\frac{37}{64}$	$\frac{35}{64}$	$1\frac{7}{16}$	$\frac{37}{64}$	$\frac{35}{64}$
1 1.000	$1\frac{1}{2}$	$1\frac{1}{2}$	$\frac{21}{32}$	$\frac{43}{64}$	$\frac{39}{64}$	$1\frac{5}{8}$	$\frac{43}{64}$	$\frac{39}{64}$
$1\frac{1}{8}$ 1.1250	$1\frac{11}{16}$	$1\frac{11}{16}$	$\frac{3}{4}$	$\frac{3}{4}$	$\frac{11}{16}$	$1\frac{13}{16}$	$\frac{3}{4}$	$\frac{11}{16}$
$1\frac{1}{4}$ 1.2500	$1\frac{7}{8}$	$1\frac{7}{8}$	$\frac{27}{32}$	$\frac{27}{32}$	$\frac{25}{32}$	**2**	$\frac{27}{32}$	$\frac{25}{32}$
$1\frac{3}{8}$ 1.3750	$2\frac{1}{16}$	$2\frac{1}{16}$	$\frac{29}{32}$	$\frac{29}{32}$	$\frac{27}{32}$	$2\frac{3}{16}$	$\frac{29}{32}$	$\frac{27}{32}$
$1\frac{1}{2}$ 1.5000	$2\frac{1}{4}$	$2\frac{1}{4}$	1	1	$\frac{15}{16}$	$2\frac{3}{8}$	1	$\frac{15}{16}$
$1\frac{3}{4}$ 1.7500	...	$2\frac{5}{8}$	...	$1\frac{5}{32}$	$1\frac{3}{32}$	$2\frac{3}{4}$	$1\frac{5}{32}$	$1\frac{3}{32}$
2 2.0000	...	**3**	...	$1\frac{11}{32}$	$1\frac{7}{32}$	$3\frac{1}{8}$	$1\frac{11}{32}$	$1\frac{7}{32}$
$2\frac{1}{4}$ 2.2500	...	$3\frac{3}{8}$	...	$1\frac{1}{2}$	$1\frac{3}{8}$	$3\frac{1}{2}$	$1\frac{1}{2}$	$1\frac{3}{8}$
$2\frac{1}{2}$ 2.5000	...	$3\frac{3}{4}$	...	$1\frac{21}{32}$	$1\frac{17}{32}$	$3\frac{7}{8}$	$1\frac{21}{32}$	$1\frac{17}{32}$
$2\frac{3}{4}$ 2.7500	...	$4\frac{1}{8}$	...	$1\frac{13}{16}$	$1\frac{11}{16}$	$4\frac{1}{4}$	$1\frac{13}{16}$	$1\frac{11}{16}$
3 3.0000	...	$4\frac{1}{2}$	...	2	$1\frac{7}{8}$	$4\frac{5}{8}$	2	$1\frac{7}{8}$
$3\frac{1}{4}$ 3.2500	...	$4\frac{7}{8}$	...	$2\frac{3}{16}$	...	...	...	...
$3\frac{1}{2}$ 3.5000	...	$5\frac{1}{4}$	...	$2\frac{5}{16}$	...	...	...	...
$3\frac{3}{4}$ 3.7500	...	$5\frac{5}{8}$	...	$2\frac{1}{2}$	...	...	...	...
4 4.0000	...	6	...	$2\frac{11}{16}$	...	...	...	...

[a]ANSI B18.2.1-1981 (R1992).
[b]ANSI/ASME B18.2.2.-1987 (R1993).
[c]Hexagon cap screws and finished hexagon bolts are combined as a single product.

17 BOLTS, NUTS, AND CAP SCREWS—SQUARE AND HEXAGON— AMERICAN NATIONAL STANDARD AND METRIC (continued)

American National Standard Square and Hexagon Bolts and Nuts and Hexagon Cap Screws (continued). See ANSI B18.2.2 for jam nuts, slotted nuts, thick nuts, thick slotted nuts, and castle nuts.

Nominal Size D Body Diameter of Bolt		Regular Bolts					Heavy Nuts			
		Width Across Flats W		Thickness T			Width Across Flats W	Thickness T		
		Sq.	Hex.	Sq. (Unfin.)	Hex. Flat (Unfin.)	Hex. (Fin.)		Sq. (Unfin.)	Hex. Flat (Unfin.)	Hex. (Fin.)
$\frac{1}{4}$	0.2500	$\frac{7}{16}$	$\frac{7}{16}$	$\frac{7}{32}$	$\frac{7}{32}$	$\frac{7}{32}$	$\frac{1}{2}$	$\frac{1}{4}$	$\frac{15}{64}$	$\frac{15}{64}$
$\frac{5}{16}$	0.3125	$\frac{9}{16}$	$\frac{1}{2}$	$\frac{17}{64}$	$\frac{17}{64}$	$\frac{17}{64}$	$\frac{9}{16}$	$\frac{5}{16}$	$\frac{19}{64}$	$\frac{19}{64}$
$\frac{3}{8}$	0.3750	$\frac{5}{8}$	$\frac{9}{16}$	$\frac{21}{64}$		$\frac{21}{64}$	$\frac{11}{16}$	$\frac{3}{8}$	$\frac{23}{64}$	$\frac{23}{64}$
$\frac{7}{16}$	0.4375	$\frac{3}{4}$	$\frac{11}{16}$	$\frac{3}{8}$	$\frac{3}{8}$	$\frac{3}{8}$	$\frac{3}{4}$	$\frac{7}{16}$	$\frac{27}{64}$	$\frac{27}{64}$
$\frac{1}{2}$	0.5000	$\frac{13}{16}$	$\frac{3}{4}$	$\frac{7}{16}$	$\frac{7}{16}$	$\frac{7}{16}$	$\frac{7}{8}$a	$\frac{1}{2}$	$\frac{31}{64}$	$\frac{31}{64}$
$\frac{9}{16}$	0.5625	...	$\frac{7}{8}$	...	$\frac{31}{64}$	$\frac{31}{64}$	$\frac{15}{16}$	...	$\frac{35}{64}$	$\frac{35}{64}$
$\frac{5}{8}$	0.6250	1	$\frac{15}{16}$	$\frac{35}{64}$	$\frac{35}{64}$	$\frac{35}{64}$	$1\frac{1}{16}$a	$\frac{5}{8}$	$\frac{39}{64}$	$\frac{39}{64}$
$\frac{3}{4}$	0.7500	$1\frac{1}{8}$	$1\frac{1}{8}$	$\frac{21}{32}$	$\frac{41}{64}$	$\frac{41}{64}$	$1\frac{1}{4}$a	$\frac{3}{4}$	$\frac{47}{64}$	$\frac{47}{64}$
$\frac{7}{8}$	0.8750	$1\frac{5}{16}$	$1\frac{5}{16}$	$\frac{49}{64}$	$\frac{3}{4}$	$\frac{3}{4}$	$1\frac{7}{16}$a	$\frac{7}{8}$	$\frac{55}{64}$	$\frac{55}{64}$
1	1.0000	$1\frac{1}{2}$	$1\frac{1}{2}$	$\frac{7}{8}$	$\frac{55}{64}$	$\frac{55}{64}$	$1\frac{5}{8}$a	1	$\frac{63}{64}$	$\frac{63}{64}$
$1\frac{1}{8}$	1.1250	$1\frac{11}{16}$	$1\frac{11}{16}$	1	1	$\frac{31}{32}$	$1\frac{13}{16}$a	$1\frac{1}{8}$	$1\frac{1}{8}$	$1\frac{7}{64}$
$1\frac{1}{4}$	1.2500	$1\frac{7}{8}$	$1\frac{7}{8}$	$1\frac{3}{32}$	$1\frac{3}{32}$	$1\frac{1}{16}$	2a	$1\frac{1}{4}$	$1\frac{1}{4}$	$1\frac{7}{32}$
$1\frac{3}{8}$	1.3750	$2\frac{1}{16}$	$2\frac{1}{16}$	$1\frac{13}{64}$	$1\frac{13}{64}$	$1\frac{11}{64}$	$2\frac{3}{16}$a	$1\frac{3}{8}$	$1\frac{3}{8}$	$1\frac{11}{32}$
$1\frac{1}{2}$	1.5000	$2\frac{1}{4}$	$2\frac{1}{4}$	$1\frac{5}{16}$	$1\frac{5}{16}$	$1\frac{9}{32}$	$2\frac{3}{8}$a	$1\frac{1}{2}$	$1\frac{1}{2}$	$1\frac{15}{32}$
$1\frac{5}{8}$	1.6250	...	...	...	...	...	$2\frac{9}{16}$	...	...	$1\frac{19}{32}$
$1\frac{3}{4}$	1.7500	...	...	...	...	...	$2\frac{3}{4}$	...	$1\frac{3}{4}$	$1\frac{23}{32}$
$1\frac{7}{8}$	1.8750	...	...	...	...	...	$2\frac{15}{16}$	...	...	$1\frac{27}{32}$
2	2.0000	...	...	...	...	...	$3\frac{1}{8}$	...	2	$1\frac{31}{32}$
$2\frac{1}{4}$	2.2500	...	...	...	...	...	$3\frac{1}{2}$	...	$2\frac{1}{4}$	$2\frac{13}{64}$
$2\frac{1}{2}$	2.5000	...	...	...	...	...	$3\frac{7}{8}$	...	$2\frac{1}{2}$	$2\frac{29}{64}$
$2\frac{3}{4}$	2.7500	...	...	...	...	...	$4\frac{1}{4}$	...	$2\frac{3}{4}$	$2\frac{45}{64}$
3	3.0000	...	...	...	...	...	$4\frac{5}{8}$	...	3	$2\frac{61}{64}$
$3\frac{1}{4}$	3.2500	...	...	...	...	...	5	...	$3\frac{1}{4}$	$3\frac{3}{16}$
$3\frac{1}{2}$	3.5000	...	...	...	...	...	$5\frac{3}{8}$	...	$3\frac{1}{2}$	$3\frac{7}{16}$
$3\frac{3}{4}$	3.7500	...	...	...	...	...	$5\frac{3}{4}$	...	$3\frac{3}{4}$	$3\frac{11}{16}$
4	4.0000	...	...	...	...	...	$6\frac{1}{8}$	...	4	$3\frac{15}{16}$

aProduct feature not unified for heavy square nut.

17 BOLTS, NUTS, AND CAP SCREWS—SQUARE AND HEXAGON—AMERICAN NATIONAL STANDARD AND METRIC (continued)

Metric hexagon bolts, hexagon cap screws, hexagon structural bolts, and hexagon nuts.

Nominal Size D, mm	Width Across Flats W (max)		Thickness T (max)			
Body Dia and Thd Pitch	Bolts,[a] Cap Screws,[b] and Nuts[c]	Heavy Hex & Hex Structural Bolts[a] & Nuts[c]	Bolts (Unfin.)	Cap Screw (Fin.)	Nut (Fin. or Unfin.)	
					Style 1	Style 2
M5 × 0.8	8.0		3.88	3.65	4.7	5.1
M6 × 1	10.0		4.38	4.47	5.2	5.7
M8 × 1.25	13.0		5.68	5.50	6.8	7.5
M10 × 1.5	16.0		6.85	6.63	8.4	9.3
M12 × 1.75	18.0	21.0	7.95	7.76	10.8	12.0
M14 × 2	21.0	24.0	9.25	9.09	12.8	14.1
M16 × 2	24.0	27.0	10.75	10.32	14.8	16.4
M20 × 2.5	30.0	34.0	13.40	12.88	18.0	20.3
M24 × 3	36.0	41.0	15.90	15.44	21.5	23.9
M30 × 3.5	46.0	50.0	19.75	19.48	25.6	28.6
M36 × 4	55.0	60.0	23.55	23.38	31.0	34.7
M42 × 4.5	65.0		27.05	26.97	…	…
M48 × 5	75.0		31.07	31.07	…	…
M56 × 5.5	85.0		36.20	36.20	…	…
M64 × 6	95.0		41.32	41.32	…	…
M72 × 6	105.0		46.45	46.45	…	…
M80 × 6	115.0		51.58	51.58	…	…
M90 × 6	130.0		57.74	57.74	…	…
M100 × 6	145.0		63.90	63.90	…	…
High Strength Structural Hexagon Bolts[a] (Fin.) and Hexagon Nuts[c]						
M16 × 2	27.0	…	10.75	…	…	17.1
M20 × 2.5	34.0	…	13.40	…	…	20.7
M22 × 2.5	36.0	…	14.9	…	…	23.6
M24 × 3	41.0	…	15.9	…	…	24.2
M27 × 3	46.0	…	17.9	…	…	27.6
M30 × 3.5	50.0	…	19.75	…	…	31.7
M36 × 4	60.0	…	23.55	…	…	36.6

[a]ANSI/ASME B18.2.3.5M-1979 (R1995), B18.2.3.6M-1979 (R1995), B18.2.3.7M-1979 (R1995).
[b]ANSI/ASME B18.2.3.1M-1979 (R1995).
[c]ANSI/ASME B18.2.4.1M-1979 (R1995), B18.2.4.2M-1979 (R1995).

18 CAP SCREWS, SLOTTED[a] AND SOCKET HEAD[b]—AMERICAN NATIONAL STANDARD AND METRIC

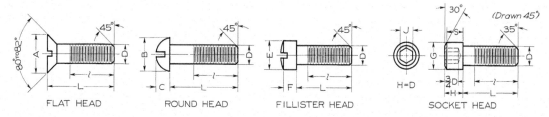

FLAT HEAD   ROUND HEAD   FILLISTER HEAD   SOCKET HEAD

Nominal Size D	Flat Head[a] A	Round Head[a] B	C	Fillister Head[a] E	F	Socket Head[b] G	J	S
0 (.060)	. . .	. . .	. . .	. . .	. . .	.096	.05	.054
1 (.073)	. . .	. . .	. . .	. . .	. . .	.118	$\frac{1}{16}$	.066
2 (.086)	. . .	. . .	. . .	. . .	. . .	.140	$\frac{5}{64}$	.077
3 (.099)	. . .	. . .	. . .	. . .	. . .	.161	$\frac{5}{64}$	.089
4 (.112)	. . .	. . .	. . .	. . .	. . .	.183	$\frac{3}{32}$	.101
5 (.125)	. . .	. . .	. . .	. . .	. . .	.205	$\frac{3}{32}$	.112
6 (.138)	. . .	. . .	. . .	. . .	. . .	.226	$\frac{7}{64}$	.124
8 (.164)	. . .	. . .	. . .	. . .	. . .	.270	$\frac{9}{64}$	.148
10 (.190)	. . .	. . .	. . .	. . .	. . .	.312	$\frac{5}{32}$	.171
$\frac{1}{4}$	.500	.437	.191	.375	.172	.375	$\frac{3}{16}$	.225
$\frac{5}{16}$	.625	.562	.245	.437	.203	.469	$\frac{1}{4}$	.281
$\frac{3}{8}$	.750	.675	.273	.562	.250	.562	$\frac{5}{16}$	.337
$\frac{7}{16}$	.812	.750	.328	.625	.297	.656	$\frac{3}{8}$	.394
$\frac{1}{2}$	.875	.812	.354	.750	.328	.750	$\frac{3}{8}$	.450
$\frac{9}{16}$	1.000	.937	.409	.812	.375	. . .	. . .	. . .
$\frac{5}{8}$	1.125	1.000	.437	.875	.422	.938	$\frac{1}{2}$	.562
$\frac{3}{4}$	1.375	1.250	.546	1.000	.500	1.125	$\frac{5}{8}$	.675
$\frac{7}{8}$	1.625	. . .	. . .	1.125	.594	1.312	$\frac{3}{4}$	.787
1	1.875	. . .	. . .	1.312	.656	1.500	$\frac{3}{4}$	.900
$1\frac{1}{8}$	2.062	. . .	. . .	. . .	. . .	1.688	$\frac{7}{8}$	1.012
$1\frac{1}{4}$	2.312	. . .	. . .	. . .	. . .	1.875	$\frac{7}{8}$	1.125
$1\frac{3}{8}$	2.562	. . .	. . .	. . .	. . .	2.062	1	1.237
$1\frac{1}{2}$	2.812	. . .	. . .	. . .	. . .	2.250	1	1.350

[a]ANSI/ASME B18.6.2-1995.
[b]ANSI/ASME B18.3-1986 (R1995). For hexagon-head screws, see Appendix 17.

18 CAP SCREWS, SLOTTED[a] AND SOCKET HEAD[b]—AMERICAN NATIONAL STANDARD AND METRIC (continued)

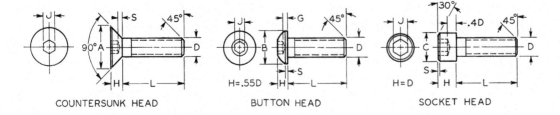

COUNTERSUNK HEAD   BUTTON HEAD   SOCKET HEAD

Metric Socket Head Cap Screws								
	Countersunk Head[a]			Button Head[a]			Socket Head[b]		Hex Socket Size
Nominal Size D	A (max)	H	S	B	S	G	C	S	J
M1.6 × 0.35	...	...	...	...	...	...	3.0	0.16	1.5
M2 × 0.4	...	...	...	...	...	...	3.8	0.2	1.5
M2.5 × 0.45	...	...	...	...	...	...	4.5	0.25	2.0
M3 × 0.5	6.72	1.86	0.25	5.70	0.38	0.2	5.5	0.3	2.5
M4 × 0.7	8.96	2.48	0.45	7.6	0.38	0.3	7.0	0.4	3.0
M5 × 0.8	11.2	3.1	0.66	9.5	0.5	0.38	8.5	0.5	4.0
M6 × 1	13.44	3.72	0.7	10.5	0.8	0.74	10.0	0.6	5.0
M8 × 1.25	17.92	4.96	1.16	14.0	0.8	1.05	13.0	0.8	6.0
M10 × 1.5	22.4	6.2	1.62	17.5	0.8	1.45	16.0	1.0	8.0
M12 × 1.75	26.88	7.44	1.8	21.0	0.8	1.63	18.0	1.2	10.0
M14 × 2	30.24	8.12	2.0	...	...	...	21.0	1.4	12.0
M16 × 2	33.6	8.8	2.2	28.0	1.5	2.25	24.0	1.6	14.0
M20 × 2.5	19.67	10.16	2.2	...	...	...	30.0	2.0	17.0
M24 × 3	...	...	...	...	...	...	36.0	2.4	19.0
M30 × 3.5	...	...	...	...	...	...	45.0	3.0	22.0
M36 × 4	...	...	...	...	...	...	54.0	3.6	27.0
M42 × 4.5	...	...	...	...	...	...	63.0	4.2	32.0
M48 × 5	...	...	...	...	...	...	72.0	4.8	36.0

[a]ANSI/ASME B18.3.4M-1986 (R1993).
[b]ANSI/ASME B18.3.1M-1986 (R1993).

19 MACHINE SCREWS—AMERICAN NATIONAL STANDARD AND METRIC

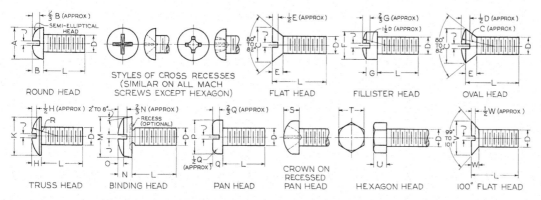

ROUND HEAD   STYLES OF CROSS RECESSES (SIMILAR ON ALL MACH SCREWS EXCEPT HEXAGON)   FLAT HEAD   FILLISTER HEAD   OVAL HEAD

TRUSS HEAD   BINDING HEAD   PAN HEAD   CROWN ON RECESSED PAN HEAD   HEXAGON HEAD   100° FLAT HEAD

American National Standard machine screws.

Length of Thread: On screws 2″ long and shorter, the threads extend to within two threads of the head and closer if practical; longer screws have minimum thread length of $1\frac{3}{4}$″.

Points: Machine screws are regularly made with plain sheared ends, not chamfered.

Threads: Either Coarse or Fine Thread Series, Class 2 fit.

Recessed Heads: Two styles of cross recesses are available on all screws except hexagon head.

Nominal Size	Max Diameter D	Round Head		Flat Heads & Oval Head		Fillister Head		Truss Head			Slot Width
		A	B	C	E	F	G	K	H	R	J
0	0.060	0.113	0.053	0.119	0.035	0.096	0.045	0.131	0.037	0.087	0.023
1	0.073	0.138	0.061	0.146	0.043	0.118	0.053	0.164	0.045	0.107	0.026
2	0.086	0.162	0.069	0.172	0.051	0.140	0.062	0.194	0.053	0.129	0.031
3	0.099	0.187	0.078	0.199	0.059	0.161	0.070	0.226	0.061	0.151	0.035
4	0.112	0.211	0.086	0.225	0.067	0.183	0.079	0.257	0.069	0.169	0.039
5	0.125	0.236	0.095	0.252	0.075	0.205	0.088	0.289	0.078	0.191	0.043
6	0.138	0.260	0.103	0.279	0.083	0.226	0.096	0.321	0.086	0.211	0.048
8	0.164	0.309	0.120	0.332	0.100	0.270	0.113	0.384	0.102	0.254	0.054
10	0.190	0.359	0.137	0.385	0.116	0.313	0.130	0.448	0.118	0.283	0.060
12	0.216	0.408	0.153	0.438	0.132	0.357	0.148	0.511	0.134	0.336	0.067
$\frac{1}{4}$	0.250	0.472	0.175	0.507	0.153	0.414	0.170	0.573	0.150	0.375	0.075
$\frac{5}{16}$	0.3125	0.590	0.216	0.635	0.191	0.518	0.211	0.698	0.183	0.457	0.084
$\frac{3}{8}$	0.375	0.708	0.256	0.762	0.230	0.622	0.253	0.823	0.215	0.538	0.094
$\frac{7}{16}$	0.4375	0.750	0.328	0.812	0.223	0.625	0.265	0.948	0.248	0.619	0.094
$\frac{1}{2}$	0.500	0.813	0.355	0.875	0.223	0.750	0.297	1.073	0.280	0.701	0.106
$\frac{9}{16}$	0.5625	0.938	0.410	1.000	0.260	0.812	0.336	1.198	0.312	0.783	0.118
$\frac{5}{8}$	0.625	1.000	0.438	1.125	0.298	0.875	0.375	1.323	0.345	0.863	0.133
$\frac{3}{4}$	0.750	1.250	0.547	1.375	0.372	1.000	0.441	1.573	0.410	1.024	0.149

Nominal Size	Max Diameter D	Binding Head			Pan Head			Hexagon Head		100° Flat Head		Slot Width
		M	N	O	P	Q	S	T	U	V	W	J
2	0.086	0.181	0.050	0.018	0.167	0.053	0.062	0.125	0.050	...	...	0.031
3	0.099	0.208	0.059	0.022	0.193	0.060	0.071	0.187	0.055	...	...	0.035
4	0.112	0.235	0.068	0.025	0.219	0.068	0.080	0.187	0.060	0.225	0.049	0.039
5	0.125	0.263	0.078	0.029	0.245	0.075	0.089	0.187	0.070	...	...	0.043
6	0.138	0.290	0.087	0.032	0.270	0.082	0.097	0.250	0.080	0.279	0.060	0.048
8	0.164	0.344	0.105	0.039	0.322	0.096	0.115	0.250	0.110	0.332	0.072	0.054
10	0.190	0.399	0.123	0.045	0.373	0.110	0.133	0.312	0.120	0.385	0.083	0.060
12	0.216	0.454	0.141	0.052	0.425	0.125	0.151	0.312	0.155	...	...	0.067
$\frac{1}{4}$	0.250	0.513	0.165	0.061	0.492	0.144	0.175	0.375	0.190	0.507	0.110	0.075
$\frac{5}{16}$	0.3125	0.641	0.209	0.077	0.615	0.178	0.218	0.500	0.230	0.635	0.138	0.084
$\frac{3}{8}$	0.375	0.769	0.253	0.094	0.740	0.212	0.261	0.562	0.295	0.762	0.165	0.094
$\frac{7}{16}$	.4375	...	...	...	.865	.247	.305	...	...	...	...	.094
$\frac{1}{2}$	.500	...	...	...	.987	.281	.348	...	...	...	...	.106
$\frac{9}{16}$	.5625	...	...	...	1.041	.315	.391	...	...	...	...	.118
$\frac{5}{8}$	.625	...	...	...	1.172	.350	.434	...	...	...	...	.133
$\frac{3}{4}$	.750	...	...	...	1.435	.419	.521	...	...	...	...	.149

19 MACHINE SCREWS—AMERICAN NATIONAL STANDARD AND METRIC

(continued)

Metric machine screws.[a]

Length of Thread: On screws 36 mm long or shorter, the threads extend to within one thread of the head: on longer screws the thread extends to within two threads of the head.

Points: Machine screws are regularly made with sheared ends, not chamfered.

Threads: Coarse (general purpose) threads series are given.

Recessed Heads: Two styles of cross-recesses are available on all screws except hexagon head.

Nominal Size & Thd Pitch	Max. Dia. D mm	Flat Heads & Oval Head		Pan Heads			Hex Head		Slot Width
		C	E	P	Q	S	T	U	J
M2 × M	2.0	3.5	1.2	4.0	1.3	1.6	3.2	1.6	0.7
M2.5 × 0.45	2.5	4.4	1.5	5.0	1.5	2.1	4.0	2.1	0.8
M3 × 0.5	3.0	5.2	1.7	5.6	1.8	2.4	5.0	2.3	1.0
M3.5 × 0.6	3.5	6.9	2.3	7.0	2.1	2.6	5.5	2.6	1.2
M4 × 0.7	4.0	8.0	2.7	8.0	2.4	3.1	7.0	3.0	1.5
M5 × 0.8	5.0	8.9	2.7	9.5	3.0	3.7	8.0	3.8	1.5
M6 × 1	6.0	10.9	3.3	12.0	3.6	4.6	10.0	4.7	1.9
M8 × 1.25	8.0	15.14	4.6	16.0	4.8	6.0	13.0	6.0	2.3
M10 × 1.5	10.0	17.8	5.0	20.0	6.0	7.5	15.0	7.5	2.8
M12 × 1.75	12.0	...	...	...	...	...	18.0	9.0	...

Nominal Size	Metric Machine Screw Lengths—L[b]																				
	2.5	3	4	5	6	8	10	13	16	20	25	30	35	40	45	50	55	60	65	70	80	90
M2 × 0.4	PH	A	A	A	A	A	A	A	A	A												
M2.5 × 0.45		PH	A	A	A	A	A	A	A	A	A	Min. Thd Length—28 mm										
M3 × 0.5			PH	A	A	A	A	A	A	A	A	A										
M3.5 × 0.6				PH	A	A	A	A	A	A	A	A	A	Min. Thd Length—38 mm								
M4 × 0.7				PH	A	A	A	A	A	A	A	A	A									
M5 × 0.8					PH	A	A	A	A	A	A	A	A	A	A	A						
M6 × 1						A	A	A	A	A	A	A	A	A	A	A	A					
M8 × 1.25						A	A	A	A	A	A	A	A	A	A	A	A	A	A	A		
M10 × 1.5							A	A	A	A	A	A	A	A	A	A	A	A	A	A	A	
M12 × 1.75							A	A	A	A	A	A	A	A	A	A	A	A	A	A	A	A

[a]Metric Fasteners Standard. IFI-513(1982).
[b]PH = recommended lengths for only pan and hex head metric screws. A = recommended lengths for all metric screw head styles.

20 KEYS—SQUARE, FLAT, PLAIN TAPER,[a] AND GIB HEAD

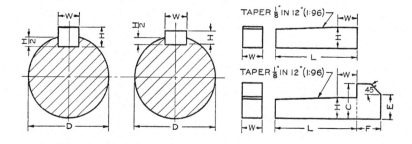

Shaft Diameters	Square Stock Key	Flat Stock Key	Gib Head Taper Stock Key					
			Square			Flat		
			Height	Length	Height to Chamfer	Height	Length	Height to Chamfer
D	$W = H$	$W \times H$	C	F	E	C	F	E
$\frac{1}{2}$ to $\frac{9}{16}$	$\frac{1}{8}$	$\frac{1}{8} \times \frac{3}{32}$	$\frac{1}{4}$	$\frac{7}{32}$	$\frac{5}{32}$	$\frac{3}{16}$	$\frac{1}{8}$	$\frac{1}{8}$
$\frac{5}{8}$ to $\frac{7}{8}$	$\frac{3}{16}$	$\frac{3}{16} \times \frac{1}{8}$	$\frac{5}{16}$	$\frac{9}{32}$	$\frac{7}{32}$	$\frac{1}{4}$	$\frac{3}{16}$	$\frac{5}{32}$
$\frac{15}{16}$ to $1\frac{1}{4}$	$\frac{1}{4}$	$\frac{1}{4} \times \frac{3}{16}$	$\frac{7}{16}$	$\frac{11}{32}$	$\frac{11}{32}$	$\frac{5}{16}$	$\frac{1}{4}$	$\frac{3}{16}$
$1\frac{5}{16}$ to $1\frac{3}{8}$	$\frac{5}{16}$	$\frac{5}{16} \times \frac{1}{4}$	$\frac{9}{16}$	$\frac{13}{32}$	$\frac{13}{32}$	$\frac{3}{8}$	$\frac{5}{16}$	$\frac{1}{4}$
$1\frac{7}{16}$ to $1\frac{3}{4}$	$\frac{3}{8}$	$\frac{3}{8} \times \frac{1}{4}$	$\frac{11}{16}$	$\frac{15}{32}$	$\frac{15}{32}$	$\frac{7}{16}$	$\frac{3}{8}$	$\frac{5}{16}$
$1\frac{13}{16}$ to $2\frac{1}{4}$	$\frac{1}{2}$	$\frac{1}{2} \times \frac{3}{8}$	$\frac{7}{8}$	$\frac{19}{32}$	$\frac{5}{8}$	$\frac{5}{8}$	$\frac{1}{2}$	$\frac{7}{16}$
$2\frac{5}{16}$ to $2\frac{3}{4}$	$\frac{5}{8}$	$\frac{5}{8} \times \frac{7}{16}$	$1\frac{1}{16}$	$\frac{23}{32}$	$\frac{3}{4}$	$\frac{3}{4}$	$\frac{5}{8}$	$\frac{1}{2}$
$2\frac{7}{8}$ to $3\frac{1}{4}$	$\frac{3}{4}$	$\frac{3}{4} \times \frac{1}{2}$	$1\frac{1}{4}$	$\frac{7}{8}$	$\frac{7}{8}$	$\frac{7}{8}$	$\frac{3}{4}$	$\frac{5}{8}$
$3\frac{3}{8}$ to $3\frac{3}{4}$	$\frac{7}{8}$	$\frac{7}{8} \times \frac{5}{8}$	$1\frac{1}{2}$	1	1	$1\frac{1}{16}$	$\frac{7}{8}$	$\frac{3}{4}$
$3\frac{7}{8}$ to $4\frac{1}{2}$	1	$1 \times \frac{3}{4}$	$1\frac{3}{4}$	$1\frac{3}{16}$	$1\frac{3}{16}$	$1\frac{1}{4}$	1	$1\frac{13}{16}$
$4\frac{3}{4}$ to $5\frac{1}{2}$	$1\frac{1}{4}$	$1\frac{1}{4} \times \frac{7}{8}$	2	$1\frac{7}{16}$	$1\frac{7}{16}$	$1\frac{1}{2}$	$1\frac{1}{4}$	1
$5\frac{3}{4}$ to 6	$1\frac{1}{2}$	$1\frac{1}{2} \times 1$	$2\frac{1}{2}$	$1\frac{3}{4}$	$1\frac{3}{4}$	$1\frac{3}{4}$	$1\frac{1}{2}$	1

[a]Plain taper square and flat keys have the same dimensions as the plain parallel stock keys, with the addition of the taper on top. Gib head taper square and flat keys have the same dimensions as the plain taper keys, with the addition of the gib head. *Stock lengths for plain taper and gib head taper keys:* The minimum stock length equals 4W, and the maximum equals 16W. The increments of increase of length equal 2W.

21 SCREW THREADS,[a] SQUARE AND ACME

Size	Threads per Inch	Size	Threads per Inch	Size	Threads per Inch	Size	Threads per Inch
$\frac{3}{8}$	12	$\frac{7}{8}$	5	2	$2\frac{1}{2}$	$3\frac{1}{2}$	$1\frac{1}{3}$
$\frac{7}{16}$	10	1	5	$2\frac{1}{4}$	2	$3\frac{3}{4}$	$1\frac{1}{3}$
$\frac{1}{2}$	10	$1\frac{1}{8}$	4	$2\frac{1}{2}$	2	4	$1\frac{1}{3}$
$\frac{9}{16}$	8	$1\frac{1}{4}$	4	$2\frac{3}{4}$	2	$4\frac{1}{4}$	$1\frac{1}{3}$
$\frac{5}{8}$	8	$1\frac{1}{2}$	3	3	$1\frac{1}{2}$	$4\frac{1}{2}$	1
$\frac{3}{4}$	6	$1\frac{3}{4}$	$2\frac{1}{2}$	$3\frac{1}{4}$	$1\frac{1}{2}$	over $4\frac{1}{2}$	1

[a]See Appendix 14 for general-purpose acme threads.

22 WOODRUFF KEYS[a]—AMERICAN NATIONAL STANDARD

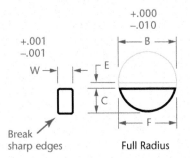

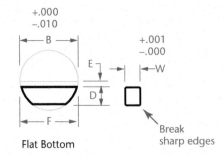

Break sharp edges   Full Radius   Flat Bottom   Break sharp edges

23 WOODRUFF KEY SIZES FOR DIFFERENT SHAFT DIAMETERS[a]

Key No.[b]	Nominal Size $W \times B$	Length F +.000 −.010	Height C Max.	C Min.	D Max.	D Min.	E
202	1/16 × 1/4	0.248	0.109	0.104	0.109	0.104	1/64
202.5	1/16 × 5/16	0.311	0.140	0.135	0.140	0.135	1/64
302.5	3/32 × 5/16	0.311	0.140	0.135	0.140	0.135	1/64
203	1/16 × 3/8	0.374	0.172	0.167	0.172	0.167	1/64
303	3/32 × 3/8	0.374	0.172	0.167	0.172	0.167	1/64
403	1/8 × 3/8	0.374	0.172	0.167	0.172	0.167	1/64
204	1/16 × 1/2	0.491	0.203	0.198	0.194	0.188	3/64
304	3/32 × 1/2	0.491	0.203	0.198	0.194	0.188	3/64
404	1/8 × 1/2	0.491	0.203	0.198	0.194	0.188	3/64
305	3/32 × 5/8	0.612	0.250	0.245	0.240	0.234	1/16
405	1/8 × 5/8	0.612	0.250	0.245	0.240	0.234	1/16
505	5/32 × 5/8	0.612	0.250	0.245	0.240	0.234	1/16
605	3/16 × 5/8	0.612	0.250	0.245	0.240	0.234	1/16
406	1/8 × 3/4	0.740	0.313	0.308	0.303	0.297	1/16
506	5/32 × 3/4	0.740	0.313	0.308	0.303	0.297	1/16
606	3/16 × 3/4	0.740	0.313	0.308	0.303	0.297	1/16
806	1/4 × 3/4	0.740	0.313	0.308	0.303	0.297	1/16
507	5/32 × 7/8	0.866	0.375	0.370	0.365	0.359	1/16
607	3/16 × 7/8	0.866	0.375	0.370	0.365	0.359	1/16
707	7/32 × 7/8	0.866	0.375	0.370	0.365	0.359	1/16
807	1/4 × 7/8	0.866	0.375	0.370	0.365	0.359	1/16
608	3/16 × 1	0.992	0.438	0.433	0.428	0.422	1/16
708	7/32 × 1	0.992	0.438	0.433	0.428	0.422	1/16
808	1/4 × 1	0.992	0.438	0.433	0.428	0.422	1/16
1008	5/16 × 1	0.992	0.438	0.433	0.428	0.422	1/16
1208	3/8 × 1	0.992	0.438	0.433	0.428	0.422	1/16
609	3/16 × 11/8	1.114	0.484	0.479	0.475	0.469	5/64
709	7/32 × 11/8	1.114	0.484	0.479	0.475	0.469	5/64
809	1/4 × 11/8	1.114	0.484	0.479	0.475	0.469	5/64
1009	5/16 × 11/8	1.114	0.484	0.479	0.475	0.469	5/64
610	3/16 × 11/4	1.240	0.547	0.542	0.537	0.531	5/64
710	7/32 × 11/4	1.240	0.547	0.542	0.537	0.531	5/64
810	1/4 × 11/4	1.240	0.547	0.542	0.537	0.531	5/64
1010	5/16 × 11/4	1.240	0.547	0.542	0.537	0.531	5/64
1210	3/8 × 11/4	1.240	0.547	0.542	0.537	0.531	5/64
811	1/4 × 13/8	1.362	0.594	0.589	0.584	0.578	3/32
1011	5/16 × 13/8	1.362	0.594	0.589	0.584	0.578	3/32
1211	3/8 × 13/8	1.362	0.594	0.589	0.584	0.578	3/32
812	1/4 × 11/2	1.484	0.641	0.636	0.631	0.625	7/64
1012	5/16 × 11/2	1.484	0.641	0.636	0.631	0.625	7/64
1212	3/8 × 11/2	1.484	0.641	0.636	0.631	0.625	7/64
...	...	...	...	...	...	...	...

Shaft Diameter	Key No.
5/16 to 3/8	204
7/16 to 1/2	304, 305
9/16 to 3/4	404, 405, 406
13/16 to 15/16	505, 506, 507
1 to 1 3/16	606, 607, 608, 609
1 1/4 to 1 7/16	807, 808, 809
1 1/2 to 1 3/4	810, 811, 812
1 13/16 to 2 1/8	1011, 1012
2 3/16 to 2 1/2	1211, 1212

[a]Suggested sizes; not standard.

[a]ANSI B17.2-1967 (reaffirmed 2013)

[b]Key numbers indicate the nominal dimensions. The last two digits give the nominal diameter B in eighths of an inch, and the digits preceding the last two give the nominal width W in thirty-seconds of an inch.

24 PRATT AND WHITNEY ROUND-END KEYS

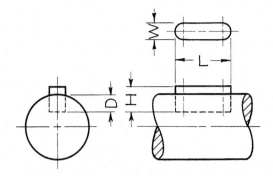

KEYS MADE WITH ROUND
ENDS AND KEYWAYS CUT
IN SPLINE MILLER

Maximum length of slot is 4" + W. Note that key is sunk two-thirds into shaft in all cases.

Key No.	L^a	W or D	H	Key No.	L^a	W or D	H
1	$\frac{1}{2}$	$\frac{1}{16}$	$\frac{3}{32}$	22	$1\frac{3}{8}$	$\frac{1}{4}$	$\frac{3}{8}$
2	$\frac{1}{2}$	$\frac{3}{32}$	$\frac{9}{64}$	23	$1\frac{1}{38}$	$\frac{5}{16}$	$\frac{15}{32}$
3	$\frac{1}{2}$	$\frac{1}{8}$	$\frac{3}{16}$	F	$1\frac{3}{8}$	$\frac{3}{8}$	$\frac{9}{16}$
4	$\frac{5}{8}$	$\frac{3}{32}$	$\frac{9}{64}$	24	$1\frac{1}{2}$	$\frac{1}{4}$	$\frac{3}{8}$
5	$\frac{5}{8}$	$\frac{1}{8}$	$\frac{3}{16}$	25	$1\frac{1}{2}$	$\frac{5}{16}$	$\frac{15}{32}$
6	$\frac{5}{8}$	$\frac{5}{32}$	$\frac{15}{64}$	G	$1\frac{1}{2}$	$\frac{3}{8}$	$\frac{9}{16}$
7	$\frac{3}{4}$	$\frac{1}{8}$	$\frac{3}{16}$	51	$1\frac{3}{4}$	$\frac{1}{4}$	$\frac{3}{8}$
8	$\frac{3}{4}$	$\frac{5}{32}$	$\frac{15}{64}$	52	$1\frac{3}{4}$	$\frac{5}{16}$	$\frac{15}{32}$
9	$\frac{3}{4}$	$\frac{3}{16}$	$\frac{9}{32}$	53	$1\frac{3}{4}$	$\frac{3}{8}$	$\frac{9}{16}$
10	$\frac{7}{8}$	$\frac{5}{32}$	$\frac{15}{64}$	26	2	$\frac{3}{16}$	$\frac{9}{32}$
11	$\frac{7}{8}$	$\frac{3}{16}$	$\frac{9}{32}$	27	2	$\frac{1}{4}$	$\frac{3}{8}$
12	$\frac{7}{8}$	$\frac{7}{32}$	$\frac{21}{64}$	28	2	$\frac{5}{16}$	$\frac{15}{32}$
A	$\frac{7}{8}$	$\frac{1}{4}$	$\frac{3}{8}$	29	2	$\frac{3}{8}$	$\frac{9}{16}$
13	1	$\frac{3}{16}$	$\frac{9}{32}$	54	$2\frac{1}{4}$	$\frac{1}{4}$	$\frac{3}{8}$
14	1	$\frac{7}{32}$	$\frac{21}{64}$	55	$2\frac{1}{4}$	$\frac{5}{16}$	$\frac{15}{32}$
15	1	$\frac{1}{4}$	$\frac{3}{8}$	56	$2\frac{1}{4}$	$\frac{3}{8}$	$\frac{9}{16}$
B	1	$\frac{5}{16}$	$\frac{15}{32}$	57	$2\frac{1}{4}$	$\frac{7}{16}$	$\frac{21}{32}$
16	$1\frac{1}{8}$	$\frac{3}{16}$	$\frac{9}{32}$	58	$2\frac{1}{2}$	$\frac{5}{16}$	$\frac{15}{32}$
17	$1\frac{1}{8}$	$\frac{7}{32}$	$\frac{21}{64}$	59	$2\frac{1}{2}$	$\frac{3}{8}$	$\frac{9}{16}$
18	$1\frac{1}{8}$	$\frac{1}{4}$	$\frac{3}{8}$	60	$2\frac{1}{2}$	$\frac{7}{16}$	$\frac{21}{32}$
C	$1\frac{1}{8}$	$\frac{5}{16}$	$\frac{15}{32}$	61	$2\frac{1}{2}$	$\frac{1}{2}$	$\frac{3}{4}$
19	$1\frac{1}{4}$	$\frac{3}{16}$	$\frac{9}{32}$	30	3	$\frac{3}{8}$	$\frac{9}{16}$
20	$1\frac{1}{4}$	$\frac{7}{32}$	$\frac{21}{64}$	31	3	$\frac{7}{16}$	$\frac{21}{32}$
21	$1\frac{1}{4}$	$\frac{1}{4}$	$\frac{3}{8}$	32	3	$\frac{1}{2}$	$\frac{3}{4}$
D	$1\frac{1}{4}$	$\frac{5}{16}$	$\frac{15}{32}$	33	3	$\frac{9}{16}$	$\frac{27}{32}$
E	$1\frac{1}{4}$	$\frac{3}{8}$	$\frac{9}{16}$	34	3	$\frac{5}{8}$	$\frac{15}{16}$

[a]The length L may vary from the table, but equals at least $2W$.

25 WASHERS,ª PLAIN—AMERICAN NATIONAL STANDARD

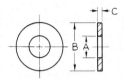

For parts lists, etc., give inside diameter, outside diameter, and the thickness; for example, .344 × .688 × .065 Type A Plain Washer. Preferred Sizes of Type A Plain Washers.ᵇ

Nominal Washer Sizeᶜ			Inside Diameter A	Outside Diameter B	Nominal Thickness C
...	...		0.078	0.188	0.020
...	...		0.094	0.250	0.020
...	...		0.125	0.312	0.032
No. 6	0.138		0.156	0.375	0.049
No. 8	0.164		0.188	0.438	0.049
No. 10	0.190		0.219	0.500	0.049
3/16	0.188		0.250	0.562	0.049
No. 12	0.216		0.250	0.562	0.065
1/4	0.250	N	0.281	0.625	0.065
1/4	0.250	W	0.312	0.734	0.065
5/16	0.312	N	0.344	0.688	0.065
5/16	0.312	W	0.375	0.875	0.083
3/8	0.375	N	0.406	0.812	0.065
3/8	0.375	W	0.438	1.000	0.083
7/16	0.438	N	0.469	0.922	0.065
7/16	0.438	W	0.500	1.250	0.083
1/2	0.500	N	0.531	1.062	0.095
1/2	0.500	W	0.562	1.375	0.109
9/16	0.562	N	0.594	1.156	0.095
9/16	0.562	W	0.625	1.469	0.109
5/8	0.625	N	0.656	1.312	0.095
5/8	0.625	W	0.688	1.750	0.134
3/4	0.750	N	0.812	1.469	0.134
3/4	0.750	W	0.812	2.000	0.148
7/8	0.875	N	0.938	1.750	0.134
7/8	0.875	W	0.938	2.250	0.165
1	1.000	N	1.062	2.000	0.134
1	1.000	W	1.062	2.500	0.165
1 1/8	1.125	N	1.250	2.250	0.134
1 1/8	1.125	W	1.250	2.750	0.165
1 1/4	1.250	N	1.375	2.500	0.165
1 1/4	1.250	W	1.375	3.000	0.165
1 3/8	1.375	N	1.500	2.750	0.165
1 3/8	1.375	W	1.500	3.250	0.180
1 1/2	1.500	N	1.625	3.000	0.165
1 1/2	1.500	W	1.625	3.500	0.180
1 5/8	1.625		1.750	3.750	0.180
1 3/4	1.750		1.875	4.000	0.180
1 7/8	1.875		2.000	4.250	0.180
2	2.000		2.125	4.500	0.180
2 1/4	2.250		2.375	4.750	0.220
2 1/2	2.500		2.625	5.000	0.238
2 3/4	2.750		2.875	5.250	0.259
3	3.000		3.125	5.500	0.284

ªFrom ANSI B18.22.1-1965 (R1981). For complete listings, see the standard.
ᵇPreferred sizes are for the most part from series previously designated "Standard Plate" and "SAE." Where common sizes existed in the two series, the SAE size is designated "N" (narrow) and the Standard Plate "W" (wide).
ᶜNominal washer sizes are intended for use with comparable nominal screw or bolt sizes.

26 WASHERS,ᵃ LOCK—AMERICAN NATIONAL STANDARD

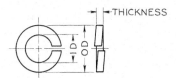

For parts lists, etc., give nominal size and series; for example, $\frac{1}{4}$ regular lock washer (preferred series).

Nominal Washer Sizeᵇ		Inside Diameter, Min.	Regular		Extra Duty		Hi-Collar	
			Outside Diameter, Max.	Thickness, Min.	Outside Diameter, Max.	Thickness, Min.	Outside Diameter, Max.	Thickness, Min.
No. 2	0.086	0.088	0.172	0.020	0.208	0.027	. . .	. . .
No. 3	0.099	0.101	0.195	0.025	0.239	0.034	. . .	. . .
No. 4	0.112	0.115	0.209	0.025	0.253	0.034	0.173	0.022
No. 5	0.125	0.128	0.236	0.031	0.300	0.045	0.202	0.030
No. 6	0.138	0.141	0.250	0.031	0.314	0.045	0.216	0.030
No. 8	0.164	0.168	0.293	0.040	0.375	0.057	0.267	0.047
No. 10	0.190	0.194	0.334	0.047	0.434	0.068	0.294	0.047
No. 12	0.216	0.221	0.377	0.056	0.497	0.080	. . .	. . .
$\frac{1}{4}$	0.250	0.255	0.489	0.062	0.535	0.084	0.365	0.078
$\frac{5}{16}$	0.312	0.318	0.586	0.078	0.622	0.108	0.460	0.093
$\frac{3}{8}$	0.375	0.382	0.683	0.094	0.741	0.123	0.553	0.125
$\frac{7}{16}$	0.438	0.446	0.779	0.109	0.839	0.143	0.647	0.140
$\frac{1}{2}$	0.500	0.509	0.873	0.125	0.939	0.162	0.737	0.172
$\frac{9}{16}$	0.562	0.572	0.971	0.141	1.041	0.182	. . .	. . .
$\frac{5}{8}$	0.625	0.636	1.079	0.156	1.157	0.202	0.923	0.203
$\frac{11}{16}$	0.688	0.700	1.176	0.172	1.258	0.221	. . .	. . .
$\frac{3}{4}$	0.750	0.763	1.271	0.188	1.361	0.241	1.111	0.218
$\frac{13}{16}$	0.812	0.826	1.367	0.203	1.463	0.261	. . .	. . .
$\frac{7}{8}$	0.875	0.890	1.464	0.219	1.576	0.285	1.296	0.234
$\frac{15}{16}$	0.938	0.954	1.560	0.234	1.688	0.308	. . .	. . .
1	1.000	1.017	1.661	0.250	1.799	0.330	1.483	0.250
$1\frac{1}{16}$	1.062	1.080	1.756	0.266	1.910	0.352	. . .	. . .
$1\frac{1}{8}$	1.125	1.144	1.853	0.281	2.019	0.375	1.669	0.313
$1\frac{3}{16}$	1.188	1.208	1.950	0.297	2.124	0.396	. . .	. . .
$1\frac{1}{4}$	1.250	1.271	2.045	0.312	2.231	0.417	1.799	0.313
$1\frac{5}{16}$	1.312	1.334	2.141	0.328	2.335	0.438	. . .	. . .
$1\frac{3}{8}$	1.375	1.398	2.239	0.344	2.439	0.458	2.041	0.375
$1\frac{7}{16}$	1.438	1.462	2.334	0.359	2.540	0.478	. . .	. . .
$1\frac{1}{2}$	1.500	1.525	2.430	0.375	2.638	0.496	2.170	0.375

ᵃFrom ANSI/ASME B18.21.1-1994. For complete listing, see the standard.
ᵇNominal washer sizes are intended for use with comparable nominal screw or bolt sizes.

27 WIRE GAGE STANDARDS[a]

Dimensions of sizes in decimal parts of an inch.[b]

No. of Wire	American or Brown & Sharpe for Non-ferrous Metals	Birming-ham, or Stubs' Iron Wire[c]	American S. & W. Co.'s (Washburn & Moen) Std. Steel Wire	American S. & W. Co.'s Music Wire	Imperial Wire	Stubs' Steel Wire[c]	Steel Manu-facturers' Sheet Gage[b]	No. of Wire
7-0's	.651354	...	.4900	...	.500	...	...	7-0's
6-0's	.580049	...	.4615	.004	.464	...	...	6-0's
5-0's	.516549	.500	.4305	.005	.432	...	...	5-0's
4-0's	.460	.454	.3938	.006	.400	...	...	4-0's
000	.40964	.425	.3625	.007	.372	...	...	000
00	.3648	.380	.3310	.008	.348	...	...	00
0	.32486	.340	.3065	.009	.324	...	...	0
1	.2893	.300	.2830	.010	.300	.227	...	1
2	.25763	.284	.2625	.011	.276	.219	...	2
3	.22942	.259	.2437	.012	.252	.212	.2391	3
4	.20431	.238	.2253	.013	.232	.207	.2242	4
6	.16202	.203	.1920	.016	.192	.201	.1943	6
7	.14428	.180	.1770	.018	.176	.199	.1793	7
8	.12849	.165	.1620	.020	.160	.197	.1644	8
9	.11443	.148	.1483	.022	.144	.194	.1495	9
10	.10189	.134	.1350	.024	.128	.191	.1345	10
11	.090742	.120	.1205	.026	.116	.188	.1196	11
12	.080808	.109	.1055	.029	.104	.185	.1046	12
13	.071961	.095	.0915	.031	.092	.182	.0897	13
14	.064084	.083	.0800	.033	.080	.180	.0747	14
15	.057068	.072	.0720	.035	.072	.178	.0763	15
16	.05082	.065	.0625	.037	.064	.175	.0598	16
17	.045257	.058	.0540	.039	.056	.172	.0538	17
18	.040303	.049	.0475	.041	.048	.168	.0478	18
19	.03589	.042	.0410	.043	.040	.164	.0418	19
20	.031961	.035	.0348	.045	.036	.161	.0359	20
21	.028462	.032	.0317	.047	.032	.157	.0329	21
22	.025347	.028	.0286	.049	.028	.155	.0299	22
23	.022571	.025	.0258	.051	.024	.153	.0269	23
24	.0201	.022	.0230	.055	.022	.151	.0239	24
25	.0179	.020	.0204	.059	.020	.148	.0209	25
26	.01594	.018	.0181	.063	.018	.146	.0179	26
27	.014195	.016	.0173	.067	.0164	.143	.0164	27
28	.012641	.014	.0162	.071	.0149	.139	.0149	28
29	.011257	.013	.0150	.075	.0136	.134	.0135	29
30	.010025	.012	.0140	.080	.0124	.127	.0120	30
31	.008928	.010	.0132	.085	.0116	.120	.0105	31
32	.00795	.009	.0128	.090	.0108	.115	.0097	32
33	.00708	.008	.0118	.095	.0100	.112	.0090	33
34	.006304	.007	.0104	...	.0092	.110	.0082	34
35	.005614	.005	.0095	...	.0084	.108	.0075	35
36	.005	.004	.0090	...	.0076	.106	.0067	36
37	.004453	...	.0085	...	.0068	.103	.0064	37
38	.003965	...	.0080	...	.0060	.101	.0060	38
39	.003531	...	.0075	...	.0052	.099	...	39
40	.003144	...	.0070	...	.0048	.097	...	40

[a]Courtesy Brown & Sharpe Mfg. Co.

[b]Now used by steel manufacturers in place of old U.S. Standard Gage.

[c]The difference between the Stubs' Iron Wire Gage and the Stubs' Steel Wire Gage should be noted, the first being commonly known as the English Standard Wire, or Birmingham Gage, which designates the Stubs' soft wire sizes and the second being used in measuring drawn steel wire or drill rods of Stubs' make.

28 TAPER PINS[a]—AMERICAN NATIONAL STANDARD

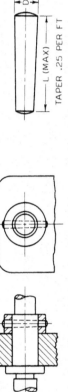

L (MAX) — TAPER .25 PER FT

To find small diameter of pin, multiply the length by .02083 and subtract the result from the larger diameter. All dimensions are given in inches. Standard reamers are available for pins given above the heavy line.

Number	7/0	6/0	5/0	4/0	3/0	2/0	0	1	2	3	4	5	6	7	8
Size (Large End)	.0625	.0780	.0940	.1090	.1250	.1410	.1560	.1720	.1930	.2190	.2500	.2890	.3410	.4090	.4920
Shaft Diameter (Approx)[b]		$\frac{7}{32}$	$\frac{1}{4}$	$\frac{5}{16}$	$\frac{3}{8}$	$\frac{7}{16}$	$\frac{1}{2}$	$\frac{9}{16}$	$\frac{5}{8}$	$\frac{3}{4}$	$\frac{13}{16}$	$\frac{7}{8}$	1	$1\frac{1}{4}$	$1\frac{1}{2}$
Drill Size (Before Reamer)[b]	.0312	.0312	.0625	.0625	.0781	.0938	.0938	.1094	.1250	.1250	.1562	.1562	.2188	.2344	.3125
Length L															
.250	X	X	X	X	X		X								
.375	X	X	X	X	X	X									
.500	X	X	X	X	X	X	X								
.625	X	X	X	X	X	X	X	X	X						
.750	X	X	X	X	X	X	X	X	X	X					
.875	X	X	⋮	⋮	X	X	X	X	X	X	X				
1.000	X	X	⋮	X	X	X	X	X	X	X	X	X			
1.250	⋮	X	⋮	X	X	X	X	X	X	X	X	X	X	X	X
1.500	⋮	X	⋮	X	X	X	X	X	X	X	X	X	X	X	X
1.750			⋮	⋮	⋮	X	X	X	X	X	X	X	X	X	X
2.000				⋮	⋮	X	X	X	X	X	X	X	X	X	X
2.250					⋮	X	X	X	X	X	X	X	X	X	X
2.500					⋮	⋮	X	X	X	X	X	X	X	X	X
2.750						⋮	⋮	X	X	X	X	X	X	X	X
3.000						⋮	⋮	X	X	X	X	X	X	X	X
3.250							⋮	⋮	⋮	X	X	X	X	X	X
3.500							⋮	⋮	⋮	X	X	X	X	X	X
3.750							⋮	⋮	⋮	X	X	X	X	X	X
4.000								⋮	⋮	⋮	X	X	X	X	X
4.250								⋮	⋮	⋮	X	X	X	X	X
4.500								⋮	⋮	⋮	X	X	X	X	X

[a] ANSI/ASME B18.8.2-1994. For Nos. 9 and 10, see the standard. Pins Nos. 11 (size .8600), 12 (size 1.032), 13 (size 1.241), and 14 (size 1.523) are special sizes; hence their lengths are special.

[b] Suggested sizes; not American National Standard.

29 COTTER PINS[a]—AMERICAN NATIONAL STANDARD

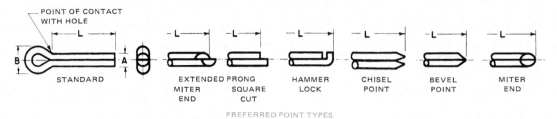

PREFERRED POINT TYPES

All dimensions are given in inches.

Nominal Size or Pin Diameter		Diameter A		Outside Eye Diameter B Min.	Extended Prong Length Min.	Hole Sizes Recommended
		Max.	Min.			
$\frac{1}{32}$	.031	.032	.028	.06	.01	.047
$\frac{3}{64}$	.047	.048	.044	.09	.02	.062
$\frac{1}{16}$	.062	.060	.056	.12	.03	.078
$\frac{5}{64}$	.078	.076	.072	.16	.04	.094
$\frac{3}{32}$	.094	.090	.086	.19	.04	.109
$\frac{7}{64}$	.109	.104	.100	.22	.05	.125
$\frac{1}{8}$	.125	.120	.116	.25	.06	.141
$\frac{9}{64}$	.141	.134	.130	.28	.06	.156
$\frac{5}{32}$	.156	.150	.146	.31	.07	.172
$\frac{3}{16}$	.188	.176	.172	.38	.09	.203
$\frac{7}{32}$	.219	.207	.202	.44	.10	.234
$\frac{1}{4}$	.250	.225	.220	.50	.11	.266
$\frac{5}{16}$	.312	.280	.275	.62	.14	.312
$\frac{3}{8}$	.375	.335	.329	.75	.16	.375
$\frac{7}{16}$	.438	.406	.400	.88	.20	.438
$\frac{1}{2}$	.500	.473	.467	1.00	.23	.500
$\frac{5}{8}$	.625	.598	.590	1.25	.30	.625
$\frac{3}{4}$	.750	.723	.715	1.50	.36	.750

[a]ANSI/ASME B18.8.1-1994.

30 METRIC EQUIVALENTS

U.S. to Metric	Metric to U.S.
Length	
1 inch = 2.540 centimeters 1 foot = .305 meter 1 yard = .9l4 meter 1 mile = 1.609 kilometers	1 millimeter = .039 inch 1 centimeter = .394 inch 1 meter = 3.281 feet or 1.094 yards 1 kilometer = .621 mile
Area	
1 inch^2 = 6.451 centimeter^2 1 foot^2 = .093 meter^2 1 yard^2 = .836 meter^2 1 acre^2 = 4,046.873 meter^2	1 millimeter^2 = .00155 inch^2 1 centimeter^2 = .155 inch^2 1 meter^2 = 10.764 foot^2 or 1.196 yard^2 1 kilometer^2 = .386 mile^2 or 247.04 acre^2
Volume	
1 inch^3 = 16.387 centimeter^3 1 foot^3 = .028 meter^3 1 yard^3 = .764 meter^3 1 quart = 0.946 liter 1 gallon = .003785 meter^3	1 centimeter^3 = .061 inch^3 1 meter^3 = 35.314 foot^3 or 1.308 yard^3 1 liter = .2642 gallons 1 liter = 1.057 quarts 1 meter^3 = 264.02 gallons
Weight	
1 ounce = 28.349 grams 1 pound = .454 kilogram 1 ton = .907 metric ton	1 gram = .035 ounce 1 kilogram = 2.205 pounds 1 metric ton = 1.102 tons
Velocity	
1 foot/second = .305 meter/second 1 mile/hour = .447 meter/second	1 meter/second = 3.281 feet/second 1 kilometer/hour = .621 mile/second
Acceleration	
1 inch/second^2 = .0254 meter/second^2 1 foot/second^2 = .305 meter/second^2	1 meter/second^2 = 3.278 feet/second^2
Force	
N (newton) = basic unit of force, kg-m/s^2. A mass of one kilogram (1 kg) exerts a gravitational force of 9.8 N (theoretically 9.80665 N) at mean sea level.	

31 WELDING SYMBOLS AND PROCESSES—AMERICAN WELDING SOCIETY STANDARD[a]

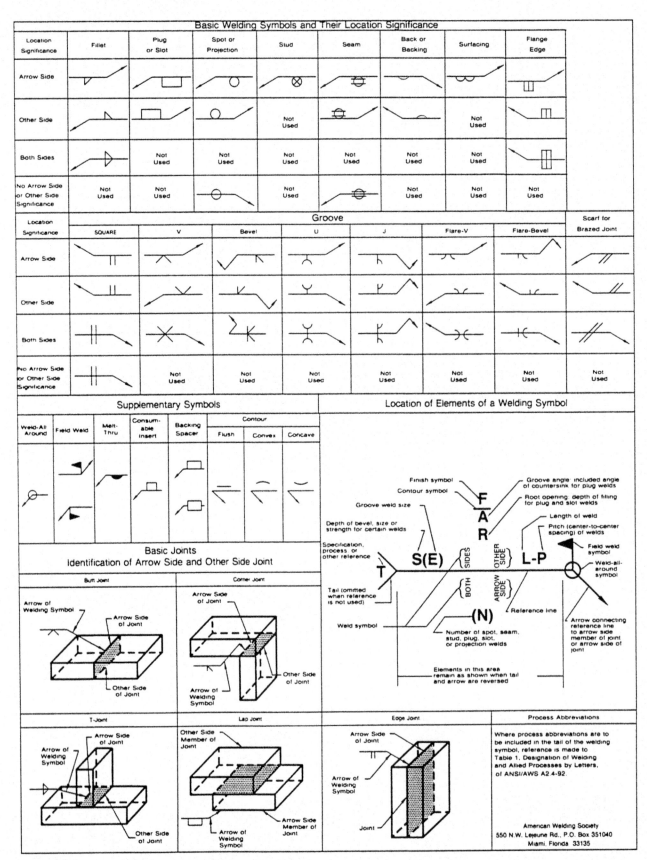

31 WELDING SYMBOLS AND PROCESSES—AMERICAN WELDING SOCIETY STANDARD[a] (continued)

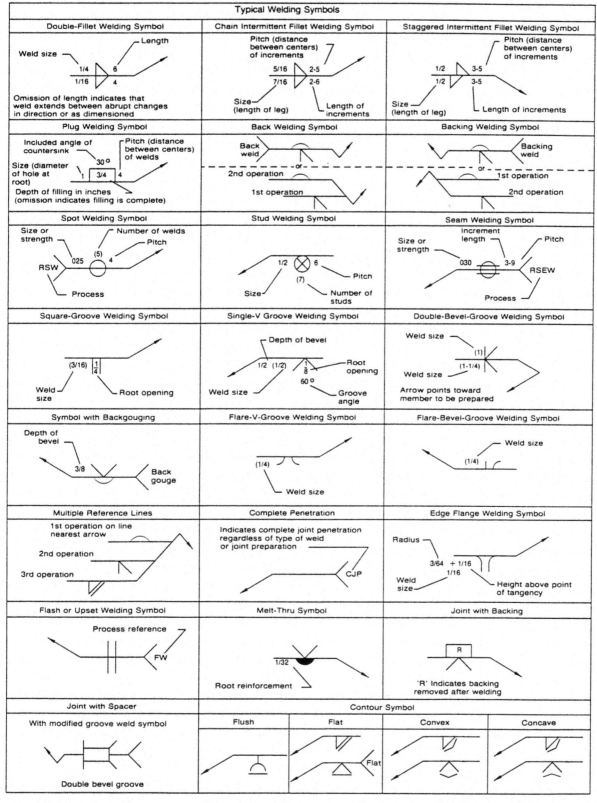

Typical Welding Symbols

[a]ANSI/AWS A2.4-2007

31 WELDING SYMBOLS AND PROCESSES—AMERICAN WELDING SOCIETY STANDARD[a] (continued)

MASTER CHART OF WELDING AND ALLIED PROCESSES

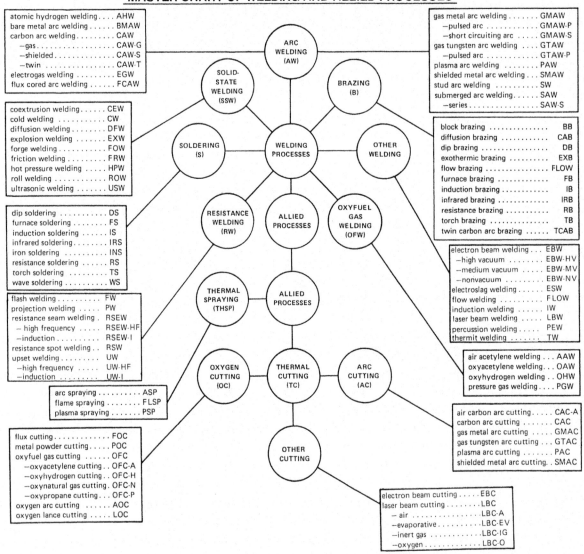

atomic hydrogen welding.... AHW
bare metal arc welding...... BMAW
carbon arc welding.......... CAW
— gas.................... CAW-G
—shielded............... CAW-S
—twin .... CAW-T
electrogas welding .... EGW
flux cored arc welding ...... FCAW

coextrusion welding...... CEW
cold welding .... CW
diffusion welding........ DFW
explosion welding .... EXW
forge welding........... FOW
friction welding......... FRW
hot pressure welding ..... HPW
roll welding .... ROW
ultrasonic welding .... USW

dip soldering .... DS
furnace soldering .... FS
induction soldering ...... IS
infrared soldering........ IRS
iron soldering .... INS
resistance soldering ...... RS
torch soldering .... TS
wave soldering .... WS

flash welding .... FW
projection welding ..... PW
resistance seam welding . RSEW
— high frequency ...... RSEW-HF
—induction .... RSEW-I
resistance spot welding .. RSW
upset welding .... UW
—high frequency ..... UW-HF
—induction .... UW-I

arc spraying .... ASP
flame spraying .... FLSP
plasma spraying .... PSP

flux cutting............ FOC
metal powder cutting..... POC
oxyfuel gas cutting ...... OFC
—oxyacetylene cutting.. OFC-A
—oxyhydrogen cutting.. OFC-H
—oxynatural gas cutting. OFC-N
—oxypropane cutting... OFC-P
oxygen arc cutting ...... AOC
oxygen lance cutting ..... LOC

gas metal arc welding....... GMAW
—pulsed arc .... GMAW-P
—short circuiting arc ..... GMAW-S
gas tungsten arc welding .... GTAW
—pulsed arc .... GTAW-P
plasma arc welding .... PAW
shielded metal arc welding ... SMAW
stud arc welding .... SW
submerged arc welding...... SAW
—series .... SAW-S

block brazing .... BB
diffusion brazing .... CAB
dip brazing .... DB
exothermic brazing .... EXB
flow brazing .... FLOW
furnace brazing .... FB
induction brazing .... IB
infrared brazing .... IRB
resistance brazing .... RB
torch brazing .... TB
twin carbon arc brazing ...... TCAB

electron beam welding... EBW
—high vacuum .... EBW-HV
—medium vacuum ..... EBW-MV
—nonvacuum .... EBW-NV
electroslag welding ...... ESW
flow welding .... FLOW
induction welding ...... IW
laser beam welding ..... LBW
percussion welding ..... PEW
thermit welding .... TW

air acetylene welding ... AAW
oxyacetylene welding... OAW
oxyhydrogen welding ... OHW
pressure gas welding.... PGW

air carbon arc cutting..... CAC-A
carbon arc cutting .... CAC
gas metal arc cutting ..... GMAC
gas tungsten arc cutting ... GTAC
plasma arc cutting .... PAC
shielded metal arc cutting.. SMAC

electron beam cutting..... EBC
laser beam cutting........ LBC
— air .... LBC-A
—evaporative.......... LBC-EV
—inert gas .... LBC-IG
—oxygen .... LBC-O

[a]ANSI/ANS A3.0-94

32 TOPOGRAPHIC SYMBOLS

Highway	National or State Line
Railroad	County Line
Highway Bridge	Township or District Line
Railroad Bridge	City or Village Line
Drawbridges	Triangulation Station
Suspension Bridge	Bench Mark and Elevation
Dam	Any Location Station (WITH EXPLANATORY NOTE)
Telegraph or Telephone Line	Streams in General
Power-Transmission Line	Lake or Pond
Buildings in General	Falls and Rapids
Capital	Contours
County Seat	Hachures
Other Towns	Sand and Sand Dunes
Barbed Wire Fence	Marsh
Smooth Wire Fence	Woodland of Any Kind
Hedge	Orchard
Oil or Gas Wells	Grassland in General
Windmill	Cultivated Fields
Tanks	Commercial or Municipal Field
Canal or Ditch	Airplane Landing Field Marked or Emergency
Canal Lock	Mooring Mast
Canal Lock (POINT UPSTREAM)	Airway Light Beacon (ARROWS INDICATE COURSE LIGHTS)
Aqueduct or Water Pipe	Auxiliary Airway Light Beacon, Flashing

33 PIPING SYMBOLS—AMERICAN NATIONAL STANDARD

	FLANGED	SCREWED	BELL & SPIGOT	WELDED	SOLDERED
1. Joint					
2. Elbow—90°					
3. Elbow—45°					
4. Elbow—Turned Up					
5. Elbow—Turned Down					
6. Elbow—Long Radius					
7. Reducing Elbow					
8. Tee					
9. Tee—Outlet Up					
10. Tee—Outlet Down					
11. Side Outlet Tee—Outlet Up					
12. Cross					
13. Reducer—Concentric					
14. Reducer—Eccentric					
15. Lateral					
16. Gate Valve—Elev.					
17. Globe Valve—Elev.					
18. Check Valve					
19. Stop Cock					
20. Safety Valve					
21. Expansion Joint					
22. Union					
23. Sleeve					
24. Bushing					

[a]ANSI/ASME Y32.2.3-1949 (R1994)

34 HEATING, VENTILATING, AND DUCTWORK SYMBOLS[a]—AMERICAN NATIONAL STANDARD

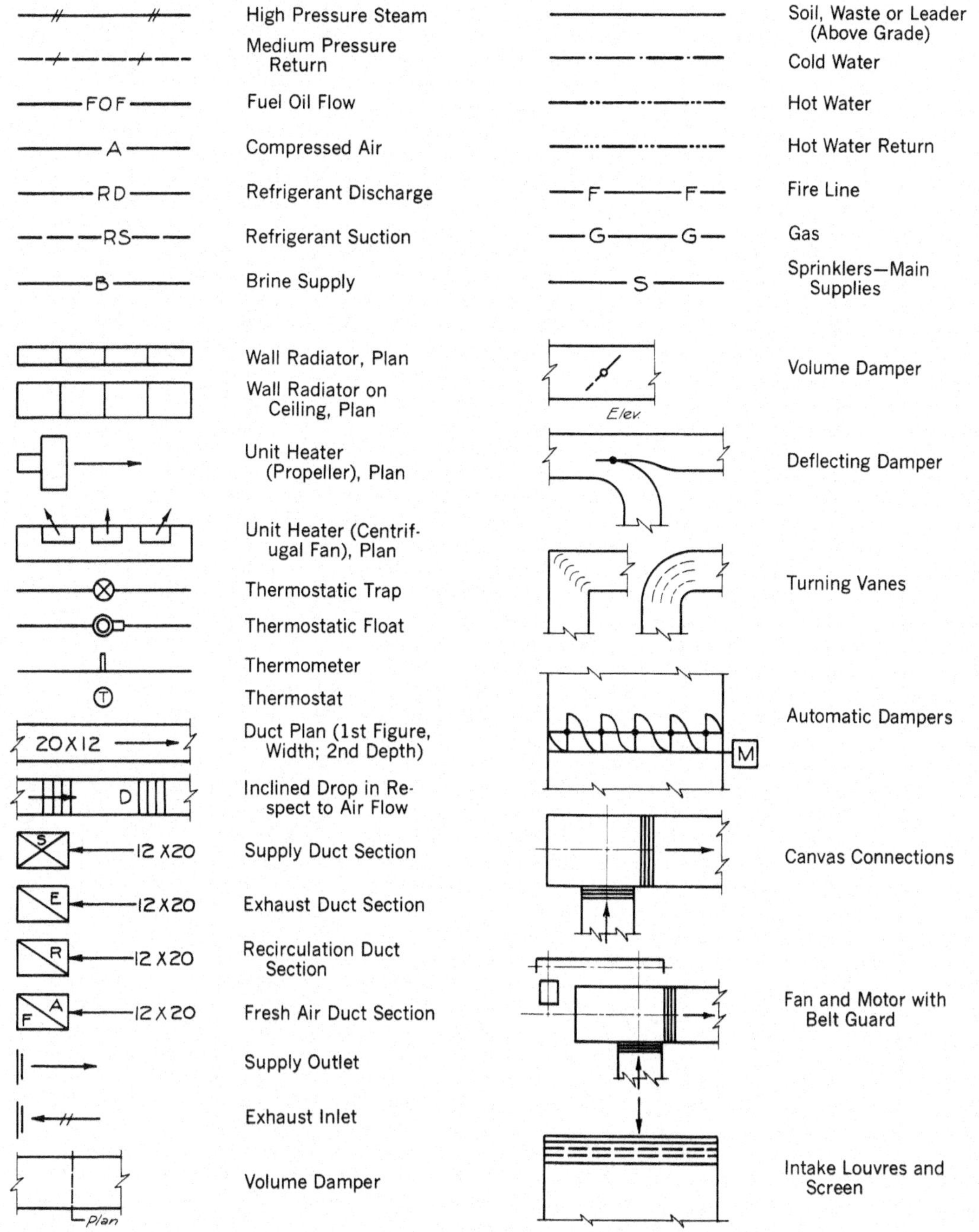

High Pressure Steam
Medium Pressure Return
FOF
Fuel Oil Flow
A
Compressed Air
RD
Refrigerant Discharge
RS
Refrigerant Suction
B
Brine Supply
Wall Radiator, Plan
Wall Radiator on Ceiling, Plan
Unit Heater (Propeller), Plan
Unit Heater (Centrifugal Fan), Plan
Thermostatic Trap
Thermostatic Float
Thermometer
T
Thermostat
20X12
Duct Plan (1st Figure, Width; 2nd Depth)
D
Inclined Drop in Respect to Air Flow
S
12 X20
Supply Duct Section
E
12X20
Exhaust Duct Section
R
12 X20
Recirculation Duct Section
F
A
12X20
Fresh Air Duct Section
Supply Outlet
Exhaust Inlet
Plan
Volume Damper
Soil, Waste or Leader (Above Grade)
Cold Water
Hot Water
Hot Water Return
F
F
Fire Line
G
G
Gas
S
Sprinklers—Main Supplies
Elev.
Volume Damper
Deflecting Damper
Turning Vanes
M
Automatic Dampers
Canvas Connections
Fan and Motor with Belt Guard
Intake Louvres and Screen

[a]ANSI/ASME Y32.2.3-1949 (R1994) and ANSI Y32.2.4-1949 (R1993).

35 AMER. NAT'L STD. GRAPHICAL SYMBOLS FOR ELECTRONIC DIAGRAMS

Common Schematic Symbols Used in Circuit Diagrams

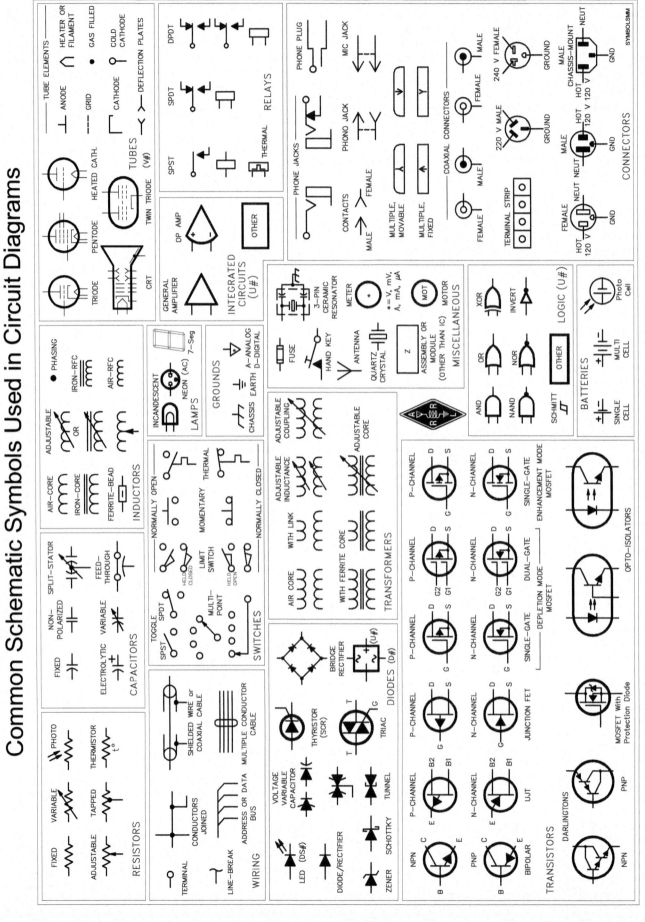

36 FORM AND PROPORTION OF DATUM SYMBOLS[a]

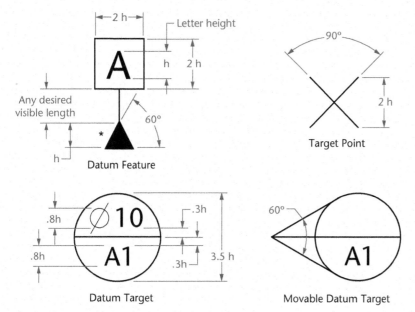

*May be filled or not filled

[a]Reprinted from ASME Y14.5-2009, by permission of The American Society of Mechanical Engineers. All rights reserved.

37 FORM AND PROPORTION OF GEOMETRIC CHARACTERISTIC SYMBOLS[a]

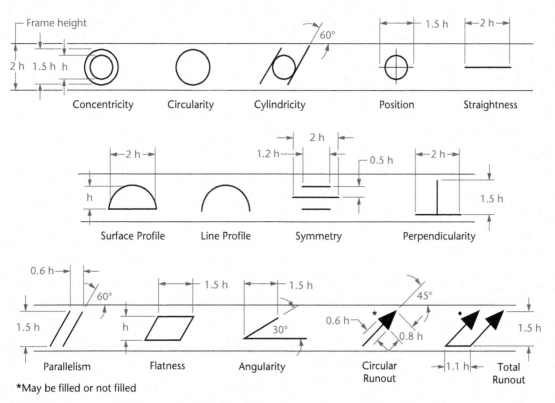

*May be filled or not filled

[aa]Reprinted from ASME Y14.5-2009, by permission of The American Society of Mechanical Engineers. All rights reserved.

38 FORM AND PROPORTION OF GEOMETRIC DIMENSIONING SYMBOLS[a]

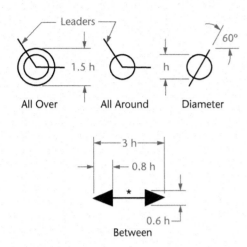

All Over   All Around   Diameter

Between

*May be filled or not filled

39 FORM AND PROPORTION OF MODIFYING SYMBOLS[a]

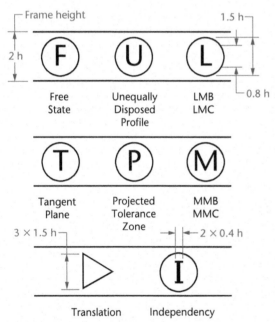

Free State	Unequally Disposed Profile	LMB LMC
Tangent Plane	Projected Tolerance Zone	MMB MMC
Translation	Independency

40 FORM AND PROPORTION OF DIMENSIONING SYMBOLS AND LETTERS[a]

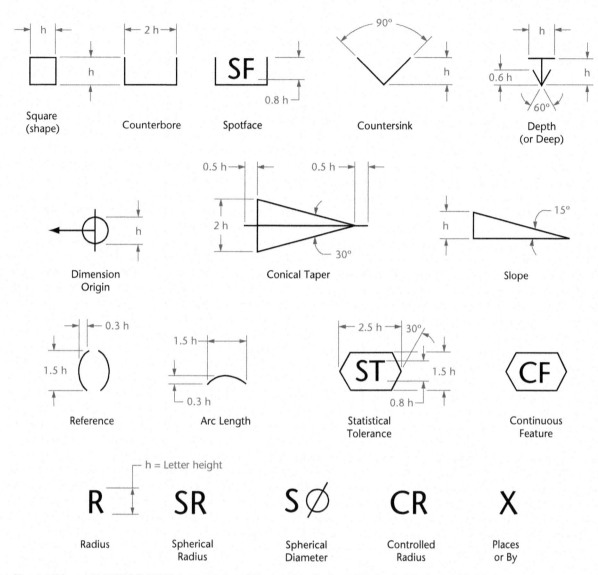

41 COMPARISON OF SYMBOLS[a]

SYMBOL FOR:	ASME Y14.5	ISO
STRAIGHTNESS	—	—
FLATNESS	▱	▱
CIRCULARITY	○	○
CYLINDRICITY	//	//
PROFILE OF A LINE	⌒	⌒
PROFILE OF A SURFACE	⌓	⌓
ALL AROUND	⟳	⟳
ALL OVER	⟳	⟳ (proposed)
ANGULARITY	∠	∠
PERPENDICULARITY	⊥	⊥
PARALLELISM	//	//
POSITION	⊕	⊕
CONCENTRICITY (Concentricity and Coaxiality in ISO)	◎	◎
SYMMETRY	≡	≡
CIRCULAR RUNOUT	*↗	*↗
TOTAL RUNOUT	*↗↗	*↗↗
AT MAXIMUM MATERIAL CONDITION	Ⓜ	Ⓜ
AT MAXIMUM MATERIAL BOUNDARY	Ⓜ	NONE
AT LEAST MATERIAL CONDITION	Ⓛ	Ⓛ
AT LEAST MATERIAL BOUNDARY	Ⓛ	NONE
PROJECTED TOLERANCE ZONE	Ⓟ	Ⓟ
TANGENT PLANE	Ⓣ	NONE
FREE STATE	Ⓕ	Ⓕ
UNEQUALLY DISPOSED PROFILE	Ⓤ	UZ (proposed)
TRANSLATION	▷	NONE
DIAMETER	⌀	⌀
BASIC DIMENSION (Theoretically Exact, Dimension in ISO)	50	50
REFERENCE (Auxiliary in ISO)	(50)	(50)
DATUM FEATURE	*⊣▲ A	*⊣▲ or *⊣▲ A
	★ May be filled or not filled	

42 WROUGHT STEEL PIPE[a] AND TAPER PIPE THREADS[b]— AMERICAN NATIONAL STANDARD

All dimensions are in inches except those in last two columns.

Nominal Pipe Size	D Outside Diameter of Pipe	Threads per Inch	L₁ Normal Engagement by Hand Between External and Internal Threads	L₂ Length of Effective Thread	Sched. 10	Sched. 20[c]	Sched. 30[c]	Sched. 40[c]	Sched. 60[d]	Sched. 80[d]	Sched. 100	Sched. 120	Sched. 140	Sched. 160	Length of Pipe, Feet, per Square Foot External Surface[e]	Length of Standard Weight Pipe, Feet, Containing 1 cu. ft.[e]
1/8	.405	27	.1615	.2639	...	...	...	**.068**	...	**.095**	...	...	...	...	9.431	2,533.8
1/4	.540	18	.2278	.4018	...	...	...	**.088**	...	**.119**	...	...	...	...	7.073	1,383.8
3/8	.675	18	.240	.4078	...	...	...	**.091**	...	**.126**	...	...	...	...	5.658	754.36
1/2	.840	14	.320	.5337	...	...	...	**.109**	...	**.147**	...	...	...	.188	4.547	473.91
3/4	1.050	14	.339	.5457	...	...	...	**.113**	...	**.154**	...	...	...	.219	3.637	270.03
1	1.315	11.5	.400	.6828	...	...	...	**.133**	...	**.179**	...	...	...	.250	2.904	166.62
1¼	1.660	11.5	.420	.7068	...	...	...	**.140**	...	**.191**	...	...	...	.250	2.301	96.275
1½	1.900	11.5	.420	.7235	...	...	...	**.145**	...	**.200**	...	...	...	.281	2.010	70.733
2	2.375	11.5	.436	.7565	...	...	...	**.154**	...	**.218**	...	...	...	.344	1.608	42.913
2½	2.875	8	.682	1.1375	...	...	...	**.203**	...	**.276**	...	...	...	.375	1.328	30.077
3	3.500	8	.766	1.2000	...	...	...	**.216**	...	**.300**	...	...	...	.438	1.091	19.479
3½	4.000	8	.821	1.2500	...	...	...	**.226**	...	**.318**	...	...	...	...	.954	14.565
4	4.500	8	.844	1.3000	...	...	...	**.237**	...	**.337**	...	.438	...	.531	.848	11.312
5	5.563	8	.937	1.4063	...	...	...	**.258**	...	**.375**	...	.500	...	.625	.686	7.199
6	6.625	8	.958	1.5125	...	...	...	**.280**	...	**.432**	...	.562	...	.719	.576	4.984
8	8.625	8	1.063	1.7125	...	.250	.277	**.322**	.406	.500	.594	.719	.812	.906	.443	2.878
10	10.750	8	1.210	1.9250	...	.250	.307	**.365**	**.500**	.594	.719	.844	1.000	1.125	.355	1.826
12	12.750	8	1.360	2.1250	...	.250	.330	.406	**.562**	.688	.844	1.000	1.125	1.312	.299	1.273
14 OD	14.000	8	1.562	2.2500	.250	.312	**.375**	.438	.594	.750	.938	1.094	1.250	1.406	.273	1.065
16 OD	16.000	8	1.812	2.4500	.250	.312	**.375**	**.500**	.656	.844	1.031	1.219	1.438	1.594	.239	.815
18 OD	18.000	8	2.000	2.6500	.250	.312	.438	.562	.750	.938	1.156	1.375	1.562	1.781	.212	.644
20 OD	20.000	8	2.125	2.8500	.250	**.375**	.500	.594	.812	1.031	1.281	1.500	1.750	1.969	.191	.518
24 OD	24.000	8	2.375	3.2500	.250	**.375**	.562	.688	.969	1.219	1.531	1.812	2.062	2.344	.159	.358

[a]ANSI/ASME B36.10M-1995.
[b]ANSI/ASME B1.20.1-1983 (R1992).
[c]Boldface figures correspond to "standard" pipe.
[d]Boldface figures correspond to "extra strong" pipe.
[e]Calculated values for Schedule 40 pipe.

43 CAST IRON PIPE, THICKNESSES AND WEIGHTS—AMERICAN NATIONAL STANDARD

Size, Inches	Thickness, Inches	Outside Diameter, Inches	16 ft Laying Length Avg. per Foot[a] Weight (lb) Based on	Per Length Weight (lb) Based on
Class 50: 50 psi Pressure—115 ft Head					
3	.32	3.96	12.4	195
4	.35	4.80	16.5	265
6	.38	6.90	25.9	415
8	.41	9.05	37.0	590
10	.44	11.10	49.1	785
12	.48	13.20	63.7	1,020
14	.48	15.30	74.6	1,195
16	.54	17.40	95.2	1,525
18	.54	19.50	107.6	1,720
20	.57	21.60	125.9	2,015
24	.63	25.80	166.0	2,655
30	.79	32.00	257.6	4,120
36	.87	38.30	340.9	5,455
42	.97	44.50	442.0	7,070
48	1.06	50.80	551.6	8,825
Class 100: 100 psi Pressure—231 ft Head					
3	.32	3.96	12.4	195
4	.35	4.80	16.5	265
6	.38	6.90	25.9	415
8	.41	9.05	37.0	590
10	.44	11.10	49.1	785
12	.48	13.20	63.7	1,020
14	.51	15.30	78.8	1,260
16	.54	17.40	95.2	1,525
18	.58	19.50	114.8	1,835
20	.62	21.60	135.9	2,175
24	.68	25.80	178.1	2,850
30	.79	32.00	257.6	4,120
36	.87	38.30	340.9	5,455
42	.97	44.50	442.0	7,070
48	1.06	50.80	551.6	8,825
Class 150: 150 psi Pressure—346 ft Head					
3	.32	3.96	12.4	195
4	.35	4.80	16.5	265
6	.38	6.90	25.9	415
8	.41	9.05	37.0	590
10	.44	11.10	49.1	785
12	.48	13.20	63.7	1,020
14	.51	15.30	78.8	1,260
16	.54	17.40	95.2	1,525
18	.58	19.50	114.8	1,835
20	.62	21.60	135.9	2,175
24	.73	25.80	190.1	3,040
30	.85	32.00	275.4	4,405
36	.94	38.30	365.9	5,855
42	1.05	44.50	475.3	7,605
48	1.14	50.80	589.6	9,435
Class 200: 200 psi Pressure—462 ft Head					
3	.32	3.96	12.4	195
4	.35	4.80	16.5	265
6	.38	6.90	25.9	415

Size, Inches	Thickness, Inches	Outside Diameter, Inches	16 ft Laying Length Avg. per Foot[a] Weight (lb) Based on	Per Length Weight (lb) Based on
Class 200: 200 psi Pressure—462 ft Head					
8	.41	9.05	37.0	590
10	.44	11.10	49.1	785
12	.48	13.20	63.7	1,020
14	.55	15.30	84.4	1,350
16	.58	17.40	101.6	1,625
18	.63	19.50	123.7	1,980
20	.67	21.60	145.9	2,335
24	.79	25.80	205.6	3,290
30	.92	32.00	297.8	4,765
36	1.02	38.30	397.1	6,355
42	1.13	44.50	512.3	8,195
48	1.23	50.80	637.2	10,195
Class 250: 250 psi Pressure—577 ft Head					
3	.32	3.96	12.4	195
4	.35	4.80	16.5	265
6	.38	6.90	25.9	415
8	.41	9.05	37.0	590
10	.44	11.10	49.1	785
12	.52	13.20	68.5	1,095
14	.59	15.30	90.6	1,450
16	.63	17.40	110.4	1,765
18	.68	19.50	133.4	2,135
20	.72	21.60	156.7	2,505
24	.79	25.80	205.6	3,290
30	.99	32.00	318.4	5,095
36	1.10	38.30	425.5	6,810
42	1.22	44.50	549.5	8,790
48	1.33	50.80	684.5	10,950
Class 300: 300 psi Pressure—693 ft Head					
3	.32	3.96	12.4	195
4	.35	4.80	16.5	265
6	.38	6.90	25.9	415
8	.41	9.05	37.0	590
10	.48	11.10	53.1	850
12	.52	13.20	68.5	1,095
14	.59	15.30	90.6	1,450
16	.68	17.40	118.2	1,890
18	.73	19.50	142.3	2,275
20	.78	21.60	168.5	2,695
24	.85	25.80	219.8	3,515
Class 350: 350 psi Pressure—808 ft Head					
3	.32	3.96	12.4	195
4	.35	4.80	16.5	265
6	.38	6.90	25.9	415
8	.41	9.05	37.0	590
10	.52	11.10	57.4	920
12	.56	13.20	73.8	1,180
14	.64	15.30	97.5	1,605
16	.68	17.40	118.2	1,945
18	.79	19.50	152.9	2,520
20	.84	21.60	180.2	2,970
24	.92	25.80	236.3	3,895

[a]Average weight per foot based on calculated weight of pipe before rounding.

44 CAST IRON PIPE SCREWED FITTINGS,[a] 125 LB—AMERICAN NATIONAL STANDARD

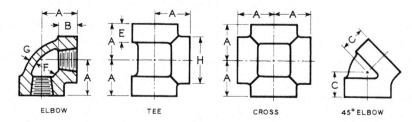

ELBOW   TEE   CROSS   45° ELBOW

Dimensions of 90° and 45° elbows, tees, and crosses (straight sizes). **All dimensions given in inches.** Fittings having right- and left-hand threads shall have four or more ribs or the letter "L" cast on the band at end with left-hand thread.

Nominal Pipe Size	Center to End, Elbows, Tees, and Crosses A	Center to End, 45° Elbows C	Length of Thread, Min. B	Width of Band, Min. E	Inside Diameter of Fitting F		Metal Thickness G	Diameter of Band, Min. H
					Max.	Min.		
$\frac{1}{4}$	.81	.73	.32	.38	.58	.54	.11	.93
$\frac{3}{8}$	.95	.80	.36	.44	.72	.67	.12	1.12
$\frac{1}{2}$	1.12	.88	.43	.50	.90	.84	.13	1.34
$\frac{3}{4}$	1.31	.98	.50	.56	1.11	1.05	.15	1.63
1	1.50	1.12	.58	.62	1.38	1.31	.17	1.95
$1\frac{1}{4}$	1.75	1.29	.67	.69	1.73	1.66	.18	2.39
$1\frac{1}{2}$	1.94	1.43	.70	.75	1.97	1.90	.20	2.68
2	2.25	1.68	.75	.84	2.44	2.37	.22	3.28
$2\frac{1}{2}$	2.70	1.95	.92	.94	2.97	2.87	.24	3.86
3	3.08	2.17	.98	1.00	3.60	3.50	.26	4.62
$3\frac{1}{2}$	3.42	2.39	1.03	1.06	4.10	4.00	.28	5.20
4	3.79	2.61	1.08	1.12	4.60	4.50	.31	5.79
5	4.50	3.05	1.18	1.18	5.66	5.56	.38	7.05
6	5.13	3.46	1.28	1.28	6.72	6.62	.43	8.28
8	6.56	4.28	1.47	1.47	8.72	8.62	.55	10.63
10	8.08[b]	5.16	1.68	1.68	10.85	10.75	.69	13.12
12	9.50[b]	5.97	1.88	1.88	12.85	12.75	.80	15.47

[a]From ANSI/ASME B16.4-1992.
[b]This applies to elbows and tees only.

45 CAST IRON PIPE SCREWED FITTINGS,ª 250 LB— AMERICAN NATIONAL STANDARD

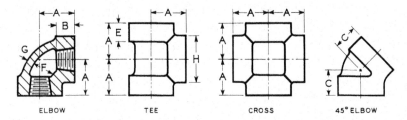

ELBOW   TEE   CROSS   45° ELBOW

Dimensions of 90° and 45° elbows, tees, and crosses (straight sizes). **All dimensions given in inches.** The 250-lb standard for screwed fittings covers only the straight sizes of 90° and 45° elbows, tees, and crosses.

Nominal Pipe Size	Center to End, Elbows, Tees, and Crosses A	Center to End, 45° Elbows C	Length of Thread, Min. B	Width of Band, Min. E	Inside Diameter of Fitting F		Metal Thickness G	Diameter of Band, Min. H
					Max.	Min.		
$\frac{1}{4}$	.94	.81	.43	.49	.58	.54	.18	1.17
$\frac{3}{8}$	1.06	.88	.47	.55	.72	.67	.18	1.36
$\frac{1}{2}$	1.25	1.00	.57	.60	.90	.84	.20	1.59
$\frac{3}{4}$	1.44	1.13	.64	.68	1.11	1.05	.23	1.88
1	1.63	1.31	.75	.76	1.38	1.31	.28	2.24
$1\frac{1}{4}$	1.94	1.50	.84	.88	1.73	1.66	.33	2.73
$1\frac{1}{2}$	2.13	1.69	.87	.97	1.97	1.90	.35	3.07
2	2.50	2.00	1.00	1.12	2.44	2.37	.39	3.74
$2\frac{1}{2}$	2.94	2.25	1.17	1.30	2.97	2.87	.43	4.60
3	3.38	2.50	1.23	1.40	3.60	3.50	.48	5.36
$3\frac{1}{2}$	3.75	2.63	1.28	1.49	4.10	4.00	.52	5.98
4	4.13	2.81	1.33	1.57	4.60	4.50	.56	6.61
5	4.88	3.19	1.43	1.74	5.66	5.56	.66	7.92
6	5.63	3.50	1.53	1.91	6.72	6.62	.74	9.24
8	7.00	4.31	1.72	2.24	8.72	8.62	.90	11.73
10	8.63	5.19	1.93	2.58	10.85	10.75	1.08	14.37
12	10.00	6.00	2.13	2.91	12.85	12.75	1.24	16.84

ªFrom ANSI/ASME B16.4-1992.

46 CAST IRON PIPE FLANGES AND FITTINGS,[a] 125 LB— AMERICAN NATIONAL STANDARD

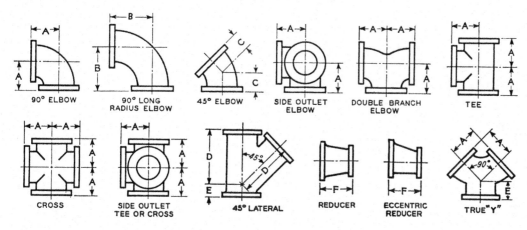

Dimensions of elbows, double branch elbows, tees, crosses, laterals, true Y's (straight sizes), and reducers. **All dimensions in inches.**

Nominal Pipe Size	Inside Diameter of Fittings	Center to Face 90° Elbow, Tees, Crosses True "Y" and Double Branch Elbow A	Center to Face, 90° Long Radius Elbow B	Center to Face 45° Elbow C	Center to Face Lateral D	Short Center to Face True "Y" and Lateral E	Face to Face Reducer F	Diameter of Flange	Thickness of Flange, Min.	Wall Thickness
1	1.00	3.50	5.00	1.75	5.75	1.75	...	4.25	.44	.31
1¼	1.25	3.75	5.50	2.00	6.25	1.75	...	4.62	.50	.31
1½	1.50	4.00	6.00	2.25	7.00	2.00	...	5.00	.56	.31
2	2.00	4.50	6.50	2.50	8.00	2.50	5.0	6.00	.62	.31
2½	2.50	5.00	7.00	3.00	9.50	2.50	5.5	7.00	.69	.31
3	3.00	5.50	7.75	3.00	10.00	3.00	6.0	7.50	.75	.38
3½	3.50	6.00	8.50	3.50	11.50	3.00	6.5	8.50	.81	.44
4	4.00	6.50	9.00	4.00	12.00	3.00	7.0	9.00	.94	.50
5	5.00	7.50	10.25	4.50	13.50	3.50	8.0	10.00	.94	.50
6	6.00	8.00	11.50	5.00	14.50	3.50	9.0	11.00	1.00	.56
8	8.00	9.00	14.00	5.50	17.50	4.50	11.0	13.50	1.12	.62
10	10.00	11.00	16.50	6.50	20.50	5.00	12.0	16.00	1.19	.75
12	12.00	12.00	19.00	7.50	24.50	5.50	14.0	19.00	1.25	.81
14 OD	14.00	14.00	21.50	7.50	27.00	6.00	16.0	21.00	1.38	.88
16 OD	16.00	15.00	24.00	8.00	30.00	6.50	18.0	23.50	1.44	1.00
18 OD	18.00	16.50	26.50	8.50	32.00	7.00	19.0	25.00	1.56	1.06
20 OD	20.00	18.00	29.00	9.50	35.00	8.00	20.0	27.50	1.69	1.12
24 OD	24.00	22.00	34.00	11.00	40.50	9.00	24.0	32.00	1.88	1.25
30 OD	30.00	25.00	41.50	15.00	49.00	10.00	30.0	38.75	2.12	1.44
36 OD	36.00	28.00	49.00	18.00	...	...	36.0	46.00	2.38	1.62
42 OD	42.00	31.00	56.50	21.00	...	...	42.0	53.00	2.62	1.81
48 OD	48.00	34.00	64.00	24.00	...	...	48.0	59.50	2.75	2.00

[a]ANSI/ASME B16.1-1989.

47 CAST IRON PIPE FLANGES, DRILLING FOR BOLTS AND THEIR LENGTHS,[a] 125 LB—AMERICAN NATIONAL STANDARD

Nominal Pipe Size	Diameter of Flange	Thickness of Flange, Min.	Diameter of Bolt Circle	Number of Bolts	Diameter of Bolts	Diameter of Bolt Holes	Length of Bolts
1	4.25	.44	3.12	4	.50	.62	1.75
$1\frac{1}{4}$	4.62	.50	3.50	4	.50	.62	2.00
$1\frac{1}{2}$	5.00	.56	3.88	4	.50	.62	2.00
2	6.00	.62	4.75	4	.62	.75	2.25
$2\frac{1}{2}$	7.00	.69	5.50	4	.62	.75	2.50
3	7.50	.75	6.00	4	.62	.75	2.50
$3\frac{1}{2}$	8.50	.81	7.00	8	.62	.75	2.75
4	9.00	.94	7.50	8	.62	.75	3.00
5	10.00	.94	8.50	8	.75	.88	3.00
6	11.00	1.00	9.50	8	.75	.88	3.25
8	13.50	1.12	11.75	8	.75	.88	3.50
10	16.00	1.19	14.25	12	.88	1.00	3.75
12	19.00	1.25	17.00	12	.88	1.00	3.75
14 OD	21.00	1.38	18.75	12	1.00	1.12	4.25
16 OD	23.50	1.44	21.25	16	1.00	1.12	4.50
18 OD	25.00	1.56	22.75	16	1.12	1.25	4.75
20 OD	27.50	1.69	25.00	20	1.12	1.25	5.00
24 OD	32.00	1.88	29.50	20	1.25	1.38	5.50
30 OD	38.75	2.12	36.00	28	1.25	1.38	6.25
36 OD	46.00	2.38	42.75	32	1.50	1.62	7.00
42 OD	53.00	2.62	49.50	36	1.50	1.62	7.50
48 OD	59.50	2.75	56.00	44	1.50	1.62	7.75

[a]ANSI B16.1-1989.

48 SHAFT CENTER SIZES

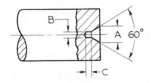

Shaft Diameter D	A	B	C	Shaft Diameter D	A	B	C
$\frac{3}{16}$ to $\frac{7}{32}$	$\frac{5}{64}$	$\frac{3}{64}$	$\frac{1}{16}$	$1\frac{1}{8}$ to $1\frac{15}{32}$	$\frac{5}{16}$	$\frac{5}{32}$	$\frac{5}{32}$
$\frac{1}{4}$ to $\frac{11}{32}$	$\frac{3}{32}$	$\frac{3}{64}$	$\frac{1}{16}$	$1\frac{1}{2}$ to $1\frac{31}{32}$	$\frac{3}{8}$	$\frac{3}{32}$	$\frac{5}{32}$
$\frac{3}{8}$ to $\frac{17}{32}$	$\frac{1}{8}$	$\frac{1}{16}$	$\frac{5}{64}$	2 to $2\frac{31}{32}$	$\frac{7}{16}$	$\frac{7}{32}$	$\frac{3}{16}$
$\frac{9}{16}$ to $\frac{25}{32}$	$\frac{3}{16}$	$\frac{5}{64}$	$\frac{3}{32}$	3 to $3\frac{31}{32}$	$\frac{1}{2}$	$\frac{7}{32}$	$\frac{7}{32}$
$\frac{13}{16}$ to $1\frac{3}{32}$	$\frac{1}{4}$	$\frac{3}{32}$	$\frac{3}{32}$	4 and over	$\frac{9}{16}$	$\frac{7}{32}$	$\frac{7}{32}$

49 CAST IRON PIPE FLANGES AND FITTINGS,[a] 250 LB— AMERICAN NATIONAL STANDARD

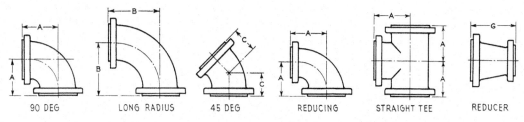

90 DEG   LONG RADIUS   45 DEG   REDUCING   STRAIGHT TEE   REDUCER

Dimensions of elbows, tees, and reducers. **All dimensions are given in inches.**

Nominal Pipe Size	Inside Diameter of Fitting, Min.	Wall Thickness of Body	Diameter of Flange	Thickness of Flange, Min.	Diameter of Raised Face	Center-to-Face Elbow and Tee A	Center-to-Face Long Radius Elbow B	Center-to-Face 45° Elbow C	Face-to-Face Reducer G
1	1.00	.44	4.88	.69	2.69	4.00	5.00	2.00	. . .
1¼	1.25	.44	5.25	.75	3.06	4.25	5.50	2.50	. . .
1½	1.50	.44	6.12	.81	3.56	4.50	6.00	2.75	. . .
2	2.00	.44	6.50	.88	4.19	5.00	6.50	3.00	5.00
2½	2.50	.50	7.50	1.00	4.94	5.50	7.00	3.50	5.50
3	3.00	.56	8.25	1.12	5.69	6.00	7.75	3.50	6.00
3½	3.50	.56	9.00	1.19	6.31	6.50	8.50	4.00	6.50
4	4.00	.62	10.00	1.25	6.94	7.00	9.00	4.50	7.00
5	5.00	.69	11.00	1.38	8.31	8.00	10.25	5.00	8.00
6	6.00	.75	12.50	1.44	9.69	8.50	11.50	5.50	9.00
8	8.00	.81	15.00	1.62	11.94	10.00	14.00	6.00	11.00
10	10.00	.94	17.50	1.88	14.06	11.50	16.50	7.00	12.00
12	12.00	1.00	20.50	2.00	16.44	13.00	19.00	8.00	14.00
14 OD	13.25	1.12	23.00	2.12	18.94	15.00	21.50	8.50	16.00
16 OD	15.25	1.25	25.50	2.25	21.06	16.50	24.00	9.50	18.00
18 OD	17.00	1.38	28.00	2.38	23.31	18.00	26.50	10.00	19.00
20 OD	19.00	1.50	30.50	2.50	25.56	19.50	29.00	10.50	20.00
24 OD	23.00	1.62	36.00	2.75	30.31	22.50	34.00	12.00	24.00
30 OD	29.00	2.00	43.00	3.00	37.19	27.50	41.50	15.00	30.00

[a]ANSI B16.1-1989.

50 CAST IRON PIPE FLANGES, DRILLING FOR BOLTS AND THEIR LENGTHS,[a] 250 LB—AMERICAN NATIONAL STANDARD

Nominal Pipe Size	Diameter of Flange	Thickness of Flange, Min.	Diameter of Raised Face	Diameter of Bolt Circle	Diameter of Bolt Holes	Number of Bolts	Size of Bolts	Length of Bolts	Length of Bolt Studs with Two Nuts
1	4.88	.69	2.69	3.50	.75	4	.62	2.50	...
1¼	5.25	.75	3.06	3.88	.75	4	.62	2.50	...
1½	6.12	.81	3.56	4.50	.88	4	.75	2.75	...
2	6.50	.88	4.19	5.00	.75	8	.62	2.75	...
2½	7.50	1.00	4.94	5.88	.88	8	.75	3.25	...
3	8.25	1.12	6.69	6.62	.88	8	.75	3.50	...
3½	9.00	1.19	6.31	7.25	.88	8	.75	3.50	...
4	10.00	1.25	6.94	7.88	.88	8	.75	3.75	...
5	11.00	1.38	8.31	9.25	.88	8	.75	4.00	...
6	12.50	1.44	9.69	10.62	.88	12	.75	4.00	...
8	15.00	1.62	11.94	13.00	1.00	12	.88	4.50	...
10	17.50	1.88	14.06	15.25	1.12	16	1.00	5.25	...
12	20.50	2.00	16.44	17.75	1.25	16	1.12	5.50	...
14 OD	23.00	2.12	18.94	20.25	1.25	20	1.12	6.00	...
16 OD	25.50	2.25	21.06	22.50	1.38	20	1.25	6.25	...
18 OD	28.00	2.38	23.31	24.75	1.38	24	1.25	6.50	...
20 OD	30.50	2.50	25.56	27.00	1.38	24	1.25	6.75	...
24 OD	36.00	2.75	30.31	32.00	1.62	24	1.50	7.50	9.50
30 OD	43.00	3.00	37.19	39.25	2.00	28	1.75	8.50	10.50

[a]ANSI B16.1-1989.

51 TYPES OF SCALES

Scales are measuring tools used to quickly enlarge or reduce drawing measurements. Figure A51.1 shows a number of scales, including (a) metric, (b) engineers', (c) decimal, (d) mechanical engineers', and (e) architects' scales. On a full-divided scale, the basic units are subdivided throughout the length of the scale. On open-divided scales, such as the architects' scale, only the end unit is subdivided.

Scales are usually made of plastic or boxwood. The better wood scales have white plastic edges. Scales can be either triangular or flat. The triangular scales combine several scales on one stick by using each of the triangle's three sides. A scale guard, shown in Figure A51.1f, can save time and prevent errors by indicating the side of the scale currently in use.

Several scales that are based on the inch-foot system of measurement continue in domestic use today, along with the metric system of measurement, which is accepted worldwide for science, technology, and international trade.

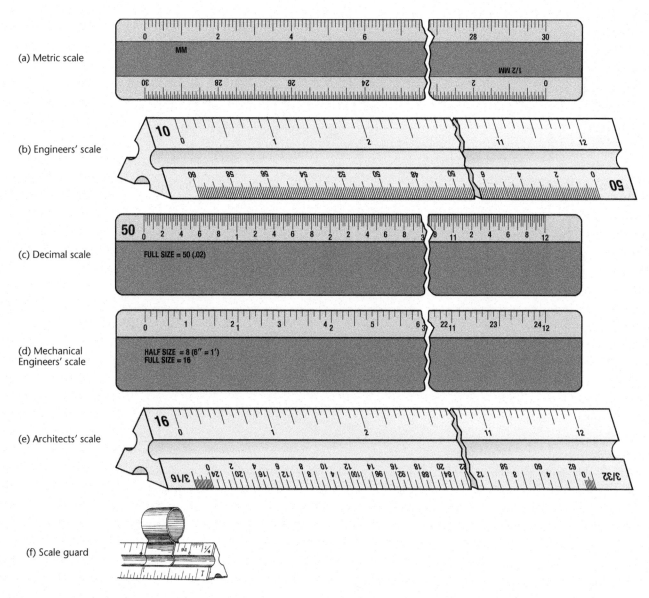

A51.1 Types of Scales

Metric Scales

Metric scales are available in flat and triangular styles with a variety of scale graduations. The triangular scale illustrated (Figure A51.2) has one full-size scale and five reduced-size scales, all fully divided. With these scales, a drawing can be made full size, enlarged sized, or reduced sized.

Full Size The 1:1 scale (Figure A51.2a, top) is full size, and each division is actually 1 mm in width with the calibrations numbered at 10-mm intervals. The same scale is also convenient for ratios of 1:10, 1:100, 1:1000, and so on.

Half Size The 1:2 scale (Figure A51.2a, bottom) is half size, and each division equals 2 mm with the calibration numbering at 20-unit intervals. This scale is also convenient for ratios of 1:20, 1:200, 1:2000, and so on.

The remaining four scales on this triangular metric scale include the typical scale ratios of 1:5, 1:25, and 1:75 (Figures A51.2b and c). These ratios may also be enlarged or reduced by multiplying or dividing by a factor of 10. Metric scales are also available with other scale ratios for specific drawing purposes.

Metric scales are also used in map drawing and in drawing force diagrams or other graphical constructions that involve such scales as 1 mm = 1 kg and 1 mm = 500 kg.

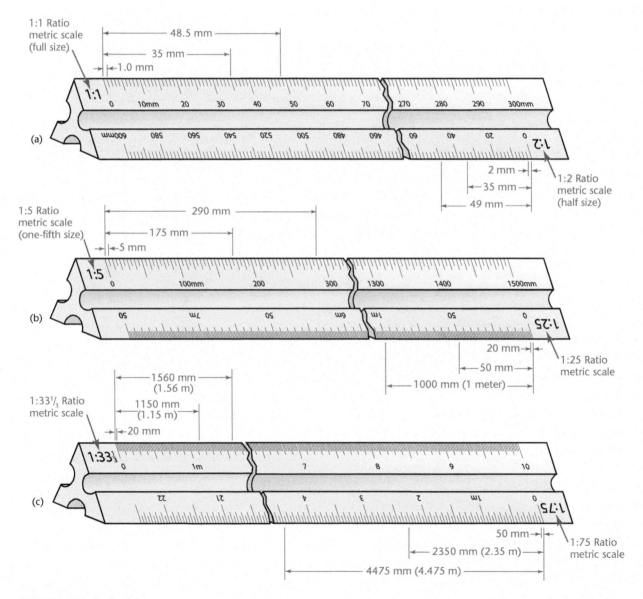

A51.2   Metric Scales

Engineers' Scales

An *engineers' scale* is a decimal scale graduated in units of 1 inch divided into 10, 20, 30, 40, 50, and 60 parts. These scales are also frequently called civil engineers' scales because they were originally used in civil engineering to draw large-scale structures or maps. Sometimes the engineers' scale is referred to as a *chain scale,* because it derived from a chain of 100 links that surveyors used for land measurements.

Because the engineers' scale divides inches into decimal units, it is convenient in machine drawing to set off inch dimensions expressed in decimals. For example, to set off 1.650″ full size, use the 10 scale and simply set off one main division plus 6-1/2 subdivisions (Figure A51.3). To set off the same dimension half size, use the 20 scale, since the 20 scale is exactly half the size of the 10 scale. Similarly, to set off the dimension quarter size, use the 40 scale.

An engineers' scale is also used in drawing stress diagrams or other graphical constructions to such scales as 1″ = 20 lb and 1″ = 4000 lb.

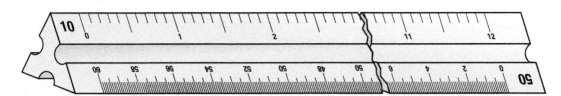

A51.3   Engineers' Scale

Decimal-Inch Scales

The widespread use of *decimal-inch* dimensions brought about a scale specifically for that use. On its full-size scale, each inch is divided into fiftieths of an inch, or .02″. On half- and quarter-size decimal scales, the inches are compressed to half size or quarter size and then are divided into 10 parts, so that each subdivision stands for .1″ (Figure A51.4).

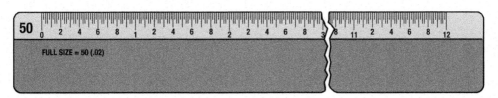

A51.4   Decimal-Inch Scale

Mechanical Engineers' Scales

The objects represented in machine drawing vary in size from small parts that measure only fractions of an inch to parts of large dimensions. For this reason, *mechanical engineers' scales* are divided into units representing inches to full size, half size, quarter size, or eighth size (Figure A51.5). To draw an object to a scale of half size, for example, use the mechanical engineers' scale marked half size, which is graduated so that every 1/2″ represents 1″. In other words, the half-size scale is simply a full-size scale compressed to half size.

These scales are useful in dividing dimensions. For example, to draw a 3.6″-diameter circle full size, it is necessary to use half of 3.6″ as the radius. Instead of using math to find half of 3.6″, it is easier to set off 3.6″ on the half-size scale.

TIP

Triangular combination scales are available that include full- and half-size mechanical engineers' scales, several architects' scales, and an engineers' scale all on one stick.

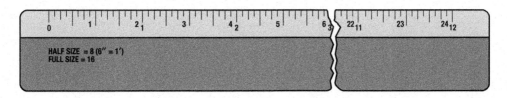

A51.5   Mechanical Engineers' Scale

52 ADDITIONAL GEOMETRIC CONSTRUCTIONS

Drawing an Approximate Ellipse

For many purposes, particularly where a small ellipse is required, use the approximate circular arc method (Figure A52.1). Such an ellipse is sure to be symmetrical and is quick to draw.

Given axes AB and CD,

Step 1.   Draw line AC. With O as center and OA as radius, draw the arc AE. With C as center and CE as radius, draw the arc EF.

Step 2.   Draw perpendicular bisector GH of the line AF; the points K and J, where they intersect the axes, are centers of the required arcs.

Step 3.   Find centers M and L by setting off OL = OK and OM = OJ. Using centers K, L, M, and J, draw circular arcs as shown. The points of tangency T are at the junctures of the arcs on the lines joining the centers.

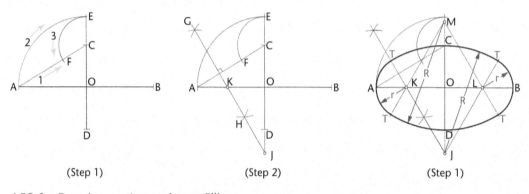

(Step 1)   (Step 2)   (Step 1)

A52.1   Drawing an Approximate Ellipse

TIP

An ordinary piece of solder wire can be used very successfully by bending the wire to the desired curve.

First, lightly sketch a curve through the points you have determined. Then, match the irregular curve along your lightly sketched pencil line for some distance beyond the segment to be drawn. This aids in creating curve portions that blend smoothly together at their tangencies. Try to avoid drawing below the curve.

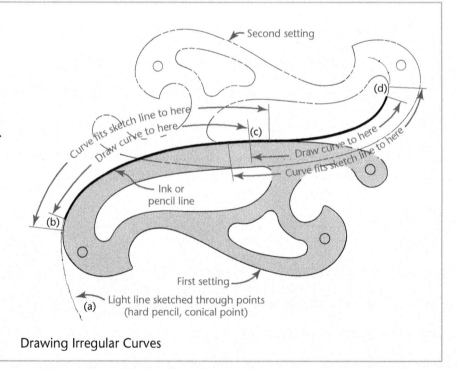

Drawing Irregular Curves

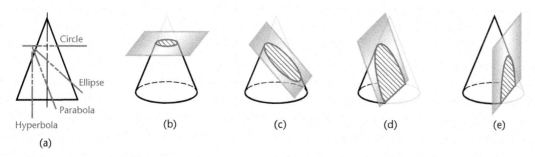

A52.2   Conic Sections

Drawing a Parabola

The curve of intersection between a right circular cone and a plane parallel to one of its elements is a *parabola* (see Figure A52.2d). The parabola is used to reflect surfaces for light and sound, for vertical curves in highways, for forms of arches, and approximately for forms of the curves of cables for suspension bridges. It is also used to show the bending moment at any point on a uniformly loaded beam or girder.

A parabola is generated by a point moving so that its distances from a fixed point, the *focus*, and from a fixed line, the *directrix*, remain equal.

Focus F and directrix AB are given. A parabola may be generated by a pencil guided by a string (Figure A52.3a). Fasten the string at F and C; its length is GC. The point C is selected at random; its distance from G depends on the desired extent of the curve. Keep the string taut and the pencil against the T-square, as shown.

Given focus F and directrix AB, draw a line DE parallel to the directrix and at any distance CZ from it (Figure A52.3b). With center at F and radius CZ, draw arcs to intersect line DE at the points Q and R, which are points on the parabola. Determine as many additional points as are necessary to draw the parabola accurately, by drawing additional lines parallel to line AB and proceeding in the same manner.

A tangent to the parabola at any point G bisects the angle formed by the focal line FG and the line SG perpendicular to the directrix.

Given the rise and span of the parabola (Figure A52.3c), divide AO into any number of equal parts, and divide AD into a number of equal parts amounting to the square of that number. From line AB, each point on the parabola is offset by a number of units equal to the square of the number of units from point O. For example, point 3 projects 9 units (the square of 3). This method is generally used for drawing parabolic arches.

To find the focus, F, given points P, R, and V of a parabola (Figure A52.3d), draw a tangent at P, making a = b. Draw the perpendicular bisector of AP, which intersects the axis at F, the focus of the parabola.

Draw a parabola given rectangle or parallelogram ABCD (Figure A52.4a and b). Divide BC into any even number of equal parts, divide the sides AB and DC each into half as many parts, and draw lines as shown. The intersections of like-numbered lines are points on the parabola.

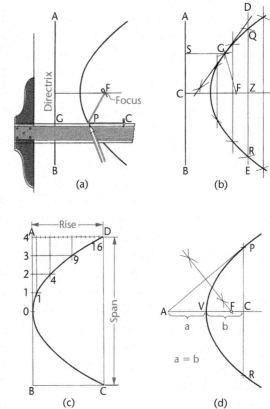

A52.3   Drawing a Parabola

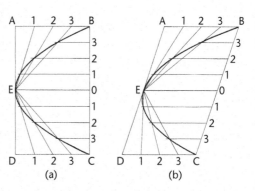

A52.4   Drawing a Parabola

Joining Two Points by a Parabolic Curve

Let X and Y be the given points (Figure A52.5). Assume any point O, and draw tangents XO and YO. Divide XO and YO into the same number of equal parts, number the division points as shown, and connect corresponding points. These lines are tangents of the required parabola and form its envelope. Sketch a light smooth curve, and then darken the curve with the aid of an irregular curve.

These parabolic curves are more pleasing in appearance than circular arcs and are useful in machine design. If the tangents OX and OY are equal, the axis of the parabola will bisect the angle between them.

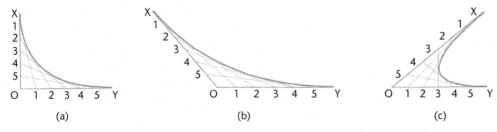

(a)   (b)   (c)

A52.5 Parabolic Curves

TIP

Irregular Curves

The curves are largely successive segments of geometric curves, such as the ellipse, parabola, hyperbola, and involute. Among the many special types of curves available are hyperbolas, parabolas, ellipses, logarithmic spirals, ship curves, and railroad curves. Adjustable curves consist of a core of lead, enclosed by a coil spring attached to a flexible strip. The figure shows a spline to which "ducks" (weights) are attached. The spline can be bent to form any desired curve, limited by the elasticity of the material.

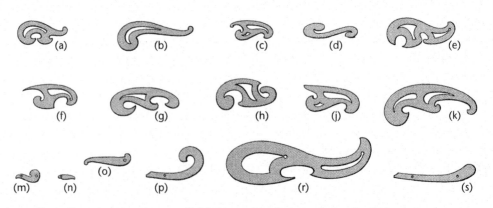

Irregular or French curves are available in a wide variety of sizes and shapes

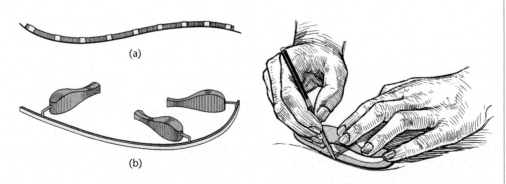

Adjustable Curves   Using the Irregular Curves

Drawing a Hyperbola

The curve of intersection between a right circular cone and a plane making an angle with the axis smaller than that made by the elements is a *hyperbola* (see Figure A52.2e). A hyperbola is generated by a point moving so that the difference of its distances from two fixed points, the foci, is constant and equal to the transverse axis of the hyperbola.

Let F and F′ be the foci and AB the transverse axis (Figure A52.6a). The curve may be generated by a pencil guided by a string, as shown. Fasten a string at F′ and C; its length is FC minus AB. The point C is chosen at random; its distance from F depends on the desired extent of the curve.

Fasten the straightedge at F. If it is revolved about F, with the pencil point moving against it and with the string taut, the hyperbola may be drawn as shown.

To construct the curve geometrically, select any point X on the transverse axis produced (Figure A52.6b). With centers at F and F′ and BX as radius, draw the arcs DE. With the same centers, F and F′, and AX as radius, draw arcs to intersect the arcs first drawn through the points Q, R, S, and T, which are points of the required hyperbola. Find as many additional points as are necessary to draw the curves accurately by selecting other points similar to point X along the transverse axis and proceeding as described for point X.

To draw the tangent to a hyperbola at a given point P, bisect the angle between the focal radii FP and F′P. The bisector is the required tangent.

To draw the asymptotes HCH of the hyperbola, draw a circle with the diameter FF′ and draw perpendiculars to the transverse axis at points A and B to intersect the circle at points H. The lines HCH are the required asymptotes.

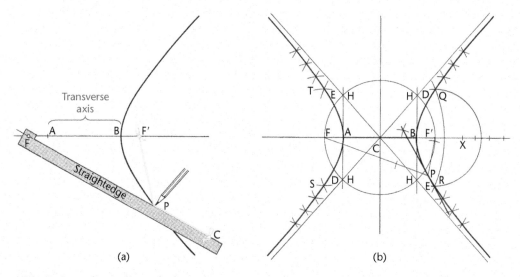

(a)   (b)

A52.6   Drawing a Hyperbola

Drawing an Equilateral Hyperbola

Asymptotes OB and OA, at right angles to each other, and point P on the curve are given (Figure A52.7).

In an equilateral hyperbola, the asymptotes, which are at right angles to each other, may be used as the axes to which the curve is referred. If a chord of the hyperbola is extended to intersect the axes, the intercepts between the curve and the axes are equal (Figure A52.7a). For example, a chord through given point P intersects the axes at points 1 and 2, intercepts P–1 and 2–3 are equal, and point 3 is a point on the hyperbola. Likewise, another chord through P provides equal intercepts P–1' and 3'–2', and point 3' is a point on the curve. Not all chords need be drawn through given point P, but as new points are established on the curve, chords may be drawn through them to obtain more points. After finding enough points to ensure an accurate curve, draw the hyperbola with the aid of an irregular curve.

In an equilateral hyperbola, the coordinates are related, so their products remain constant. Through given point P, draw lines 1–P–Y and 2–P–Z parallel, respectively, to the axes (Figure A52.7b). From coordinate O, draw any diagonal intersecting these two lines at points 3 and X. At these points draw lines parallel to the axes, intersecting at point 4, a point on the curve. Likewise, another diagonal from O intersects the two lines through P at points 8 and Y, and lines through these points parallel to the axes intersect at point 9, another point on the curve. A third diagonal similarly produces point 10 on the curve, and so on. Find as many points as necessary for a smooth curve, and draw the hyperbola with the aid of an irregular curve. From the similar triangles O–X–5 and O–3–2, it is evident that lines P–1 × P–2 = 4–5 × 4–6.

The equilateral hyperbola can be used to represent varying pressure of a gas as the volume varies, because the pressure varies inversely with the volume; that is, pressure × volume is constant.

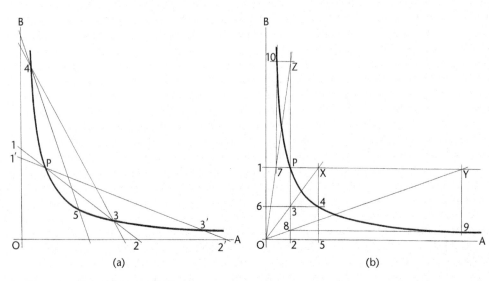

(a)   (b)

A52.7   Equilateral Hyperbola

Drawing a Spiral of Archimedes

To find points on the curve, draw lines through the pole C, making equal angles with each other, such as 30° angles (Figure A52.8). Beginning with any one line, set off any distance, such as 2 mm or 1/16″, set off twice that distance on the next line, three times on the third, and so on. Use an irregular curve to draw a smooth curve.

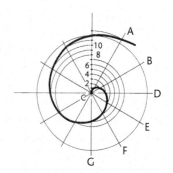

A52.8   Spiral of Archimedes

Drawing a Helix

A *helix* is generated by a point moving around and along the surface of a cylinder or cone with a uniform angular velocity and a uniform linear velocity about the axis, and with a uniform velocity in the direction of the axis (Figure A52.9). A cylindrical helix is simply known as a helix. The distance measured parallel to the axis traversed by the point in one revolution is called the *lead*.

If the cylindrical surface on which a helix is generated is rolled out onto a plane, the helix becomes a straight line (Figure A52.9a). The portion below the helix becomes a right triangle, the altitude of which is equal to the lead of the helix; the length of the base is equal to the circumference of the cylinder. Such a helix can be defined as the shortest line that can be drawn on the surface of a cylinder connecting two points not on the same element.

To draw the helix, draw two views of the cylinder on which the helix is generated (Figure A52.9b). Divide the circle of the base into any number of equal parts. On the rectangular view of the cylinder, set off the lead and divide it into the same number of equal parts as the base. Number the divisions as shown (in this case 16). When the generating point has moved one sixteenth of the distance around the cylinder, it will have risen one sixteenth of the lead; when it has moved halfway around the cylinder, it will have risen half the lead; and so on. Points on the helix are found by projecting up from point 1 in the circular view to line 1 in the rectangular view, from point 2 in the circular view to line 2 in the rectangular view, and so on.

Figure A52.9b is a right-handed helix. In a left-handed helix (Figure A52.9c), the visible portions of the curve are inclined in the opposite direction—that is, downward to the right. The helix shown in Figure A52.9b can be converted into a left-handed helix by interchanging the visible and hidden lines.

The helix is used in industry, as in screw threads, worm gears, conveyors, spiral stairways, and so on. The stripes of a barber pole are helical in form.

The construction for a right-handed conical helix is shown in Figure A52.9d.

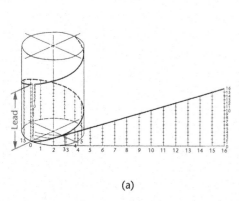

(a)

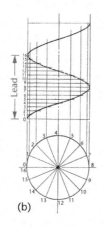

(b)

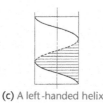

(c) A left-handed helix

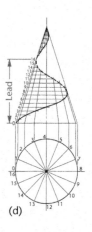

(d)

A52.9   Helix

Drawing an Involute

An *involute* is the path of a point on a string as the string unwinds from a line, polygon, or circle.

To Draw an Involute of a Line Let AB be the given line. With AB as radius and B as center, draw the semicircle AC (Figure A52.10a). With AC as radius and A as center, draw the semicircle CD. With BD as radius and B as center, draw the semicircle DE. Continue similarly, alternating centers between A and B, until the figure is completed.

To Draw an Involute of a Triangle Let ABC be the given triangle. With CA as radius and C as center, draw arc AD (Figure A52.10b). With BD as radius and B as center, draw arc DE. With AE as radius and A as center, draw arc EF. Continue similarly until the figure is completed.

To Draw an Involute of a Square Let ABCD be the given square. With DA as radius and D as center, draw the 90° arc AE (Figure A52.10c). Proceed as for the involute of a triangle until the figure is completed.

To Draw an Involute of a Circle A circle may be considered a polygon with an infinite number of sides (Figure A52.10d). The involute is constructed by dividing the circumference into a number of equal parts, drawing a tangent at each division point, setting off along each tangent the length of the corresponding circular arc (Figure A52.10c), and drawing the required curve through the points set off on the several tangents.

An involute can be generated by a point on a straight line that is rolled on a fixed circle (Figure A52.10e). Points on the required curve may be determined by setting off equal distances 0–1, 1–2, 2–3, and so on, along the circumference, drawing a tangent at each division point, and proceeding as explained for Figure A52.10d.

The involute of a circle is used in the construction of involute gear teeth. In this system, the involute forms the face and a part of the flank of the teeth of gear wheels; the outlines of the teeth of racks are straight lines.

(a)

(b)

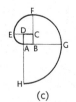
(c)

(d)

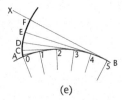
(e)

A52.10 Involutes

Drawing a Cycloid

A *cycloid* is generated by a point P on the circumference of a circle that rolls along a straight line (Figure A52.11).

Given the generating circle and the straight line AB tangent to it, make both distances CA and CB equal to the semicircumference of the circle (see Figure A52.11). Divide these distances and the semicircumference into the same number of equal parts (six, for instance) and number them consecutively, as shown. Suppose the circle rolls to the left; when point 1 of the circle reaches point 1' of the line, the center of the circle will be at D, point 7 will be the highest point of the circle, and the generating point 6 will be at the same distance from line AB as point 5 is when the circle is in its central position. To find point P', draw a line through point 5 parallel to AB and intersect it with an arc drawn from the center D with a radius equal to that of the circle. To find point P", draw a line through point 4 parallel to AB, and intersect it with an arc drawn from the center E, with a radius equal to that of the circle. Points J, K, and L are found in a similar way.

Another method is shown in the right half of Figure A52.11. With the center at 11' and the chord 11–6 as radius, draw an arc. With 10' as center and the chord 10–6 as radius, draw an arc. Continue similarly with centers 9', 8', and 7'. Draw the required cycloid tangent to these arcs.

Either method may be used; however, the second is shorter. The line joining the generating point and the point of contact for the generating circle is a normal of the cycloid. The lines 1'–P' and 2'–P", for instance, are normals; this property makes the cycloid suitable for the outlines of gear teeth.

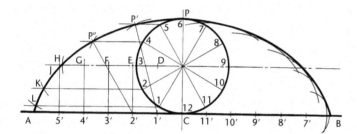

A52.11   Cycloid

Drawing an Epicycloid or a Hypocycloid

If the generating point P is on the circumference of a circle that rolls along the convex side of a larger circle, the curve generated is an epicycloid (Figure A52.12a). If the circle rolls along the concave side of a larger circle, the curve generated is a hypocycloid (Figure A52.12b). These curves are drawn in much the same way as the cycloid (Figure A52.11). Like cycloids, these curves are used to form the outlines of certain gear teeth and are therefore of practical importance in machine design.

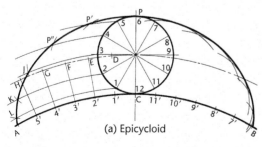

(a) Epicycloid

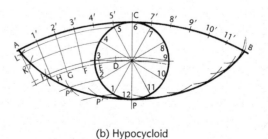

(b) Hypocycloid

A52.12   Epicycloid and Hypocycloid

INDEX

CREDITS

The following figures are reprinted with permission from *Engineering Design Communication*, 2e, by Lockhart and Johnson, © 2012, Pearson Education, Inc.

CHAPTER ONE

(pages 23–27) Reverse Engineering Project 1.

CHAPTER THREE

Figures 3.11, Tip (page 67), 3.15, 3.16, 3.30, 3.66, 3.67.

CHAPTER FOUR

Figures 4.1, 4.2, 4.3, 4.4, 4.8, 4.9, 4.10, 4.11ab, 4.13, 4.14, 4.15abcd, 4.16, Spotlight (page 132), 4.19, 4.20, 4.38, 4.39, Spotlight (page 141), Spotlight (page 141), 4.41, 4.42, 4.43, 4.44, 4.45, 4.48, 4.49, 4.50, 4.51, 4.52ab, 4.53, 4.54, 4.55, 4.56, 4.57, 4.58, 4.59 (phone illustration), Table 4.1, 4.60, 4.61, 4.62, 4.63, 4.64, 4.65, 4.66, 4.67, 4.70, 4.71, Spotlight (page 151), 4.72, 4.73, 4.74, 4.75, 4.76, 4.77, 4.78, 4.79, 4.80, 4.81abcde, 4.82abcd, 4.83abcdef, Review Question 4.11a–d, Exercise 4.45a–e, Exercise 4.46a–f, Exercise 4.47a–d, Exercise 4.48a–d, Exercise 4.49a–d, Exercise 4.50, Exercise 4.51, Exercise 4.52.

CHAPTER FIVE

Figures 5.1, Tip (page 177), 5.14, 5.15, 5.16, 5.17, 5.19ab, 5.20abc, 5.21, 5.25, 5.27, 5.28, 5.30, 5.31, 5.34, 5.35, 5.36ab, 5.37, 5.38, 5.39, 5.40, 5.41, Spotlight (page 200), Table 5.3, 5.43, 5.44, 5.45ab, 5.46ab, 5.47, 5.48, 5.49, 5.50, 5.54, 5.59, 5.60abc, 5.61, Table 5.4, 5.63, Spotlight (page 214), 5.64, 5.65.

CHAPTER SIX

Figures 6.38, 6.39, 6.40, Exercise 6.18a–f, Exercise 6.19, Exercise 6.20, Exercise 6.21, Exercise 6.22, Exercise 6.23, Exercise 6.24, Exercise 6.25, Exercise 6.26a–d, Exercise 6.27.

CHAPTER SEVEN

Figures 7.1, Table 7.1, 7.2ab, 7.3ab, Exercise 7.60, Exercise 7.61, Exercise 7.62, Exercise 7.63, Exercise 7.64, Exercise 7.65.

CHAPTER TEN

Figures 10.3, Table 10.1, 10.11ab, 10.25, 10.35, 10.36, 10.37, 10.50, 10.51, 10.52, 10.53, 10.55, 10.56abcd, 10.57, 10.58abc, 10.59, 10.60ab, 10.61, 10.62, 10.63ab, 10.67, 10.68, 10.69, 10.70, 10.71, 10.72, 10.73, 10.74, 10.75, 10.84, 10.85, 10.86abcd, Review Question 10.9ab, Review Question 10.4, Exercise 10.1a–d, Exercise 10.4, Exercise 10.3, Exercise 10.5, Exercise 10.6, Exercise 10.7, Exercise 10.8, Exercise 10.9, Exercise 10.10, Exercise 10.11, Exercise 10.12, Exercise 10.13a–d, Exercise 10.14, Exercise 10.15.

CHAPTER TWELVE

Figures 12.19, 12.21.

CHAPTER THIRTEEN

Bracket photo (page 598), Step-byStep (page 603), Spotlight (page 610), Figure 13.59.

CHAPTER FIFTEEN

Figures 15.1, 15.4, 15.7, 15.8, 15.11, Exercise 15.6, Exercise 15.7.

APPENDICES

Appendix 3.